D1784659

European Directory of
Migrant and Ethnic Minority Organisations
1996

Joint Council for the Welfare of Immigrants

♦

European Research Centre on Migration and Ethnic Relations

European Directory of
Migrant and Ethnic Minority Organisations

1996

compiled and edited by Ciarán Ó Maoláin

published for

Joint Council for the Welfare of Immigrants

by

European Research Centre on Migration and Ethnic Relations

This publication has been supported by
a grant from the European Commission

© 1996 Joint Council for the Welfare of Immigrants

ISBN 90 75719 03 5

compiled and edited by

Ciarán Ó Maoláin, Armagh, Ireland
telephone/fax [+44] (01861) 526881
e-mail ciaran@mcr1.poptel.org.uk

for

Joint Council for the Welfare of Immigrants (JCWI)
115 Old Street
London EC1V 9JR
United Kingdom
telephone [+44] (0171) 251 8708 (administration), 251 8786 (advice)
fax [+44] (0171) 251 8707
e-mail jcwi@mcr1.poptel.org.uk

with the financial support of

Joseph Rowntree Charitable Trust, York
European Commission, Brussels

cover design by

Pat Kahn, London
telephone [+44] (0171) 622 8530

published by

European Research Centre on Migration and Ethnic Relations (ERCOMER)
Universiteit Utrecht
Heidelberglaan 2
3584 CS Utrecht
Netherlands
telephone [+31] (030) 253 9220
fax [+31] (030) 253 9280
e-mail ercomer@fsw.ruu.nl

The information in this directory and the associated database has been compiled for and is the property of the Joint Council for the Welfare of Immigrants, London, which asserts all authorial rights. The directory is published for JCWI by the European Research Centre on Migration and Ethnic Relations, an interdisciplinary research unit at Utrecht University, Holland. Copyright resides with JCWI but a limited-use licence is given in the introductory text; you must contact JCWI if you want to use the data in any way not explicitly covered by that licence.

We (the compiler, JCWI and ERCOMER) have tried to ensure that the information given is accurate as of 1995 (or earlier where specified in particular entries), but we cannot accept liability for errors or omissions. In a publication of this nature and size, there will inevitably be many such mistakes, and we apologise for these. Any information which helps to improve the accuracy of the data will be appreciated, and should be posted, faxed or e-mailed to JCWI. Inclusion in the Directory does not mean that we approve of or recommend any organisation, nor does omission imply disapproval.

Additional copies of this directory are available from three sources, at similar prices:

— *direct from JCWI:* for purchasers anywhere, orders to the London address above (payment by UK cheque, postal order, bank transfer, Eurocheque or other instrument payable to JCWI in sterling);

— *direct from ERCOMER:* only for purchasers in the Netherlands, orders to the Utrecht address (payment by Dutch cheque, bank transfer, Eurocheque or other instrument payable to Universiteit Utrecht in Dutch guilders);

— *from ERCOMER's distributors:* for purchasers in or outside the Netherlands, orders to Lavis Marketing, 73 Lime Walk, Headington, Oxford OX3 7AD, England, *tel. [+44]* (01865) 67575, *fax [+44]* (01865) 750079 (payment by credit card or by sterling cheque to Lavis Marketing).

Please enquire about current prices, discounts and postage charges before ordering. Both JCWI and ERCOMER publish extensively on migration-related topics; when you order the book your name will be added to mailing lists for information about new editions of the Directory and other JCWI and ERCOMER publications, unless you state that you do not want to receive such mailings.

CONTENTS

Introduction || How to use the Directory vii
  How the entries are grouped vii
  The structure of entries viii
  About the indexes ix
  Notes on spelling, alphabetical order and abbreviations ix

Copyright and licensing information x

Background information xi
  About this Directory xi
  About JCWI xii
  About ERCOMER xii

Acknowledgements xiii

1 || **COMMUNITY AND SOLIDARITY ORGANISATIONS** 1
  arranged alphabetically, by ethnic or national origin and then by country

2 || **SUPPORT AND SERVICE ORGANISATIONS** 129
  arranged by country

3 || **ANTI-RACISM, ANTI-FASCISM, MULTICULTURALISM, INTERNATIONALISM AND DEVELOPMENT EDUCATION** 159
  arranged by country

4 || **AGENCIES AND AUTHORITIES** 187
  arranged by country

5 || **RESEARCH AND DOCUMENTATION CENTRES** 231
  arranged by country

Indexes || Organisations and publications 249
  Acronyms 283

Appendix || Amendments and corrections form 287

How to use the Directory

The primary purpose of the Directory is to make it easier for organisations which represent migrants, refugees and ethnic minorities to get in touch with each other, with a view to building the kind of national and international links which are needed to ensure an effective and efficient representation of their interests in what is often a hostile social, political and legal environment. The Directory is also aimed at bodies — in the voluntary and public sectors — which work with or for migrants, refugees and minorities. Our aim is not to give very detailed information on every group mentioned, but to give a general idea of what each group does, and how to make contact with it.

The Directory consists of around 9,100 entries, most of which describe a single organisation, federation or agency. Other entries cover two or more related groups at the same address, or give cross-references, for example from one organisation to another, or between related terms. The Directory was compiled using relational database software, which allows us to sort the data in any number of ways (for example, listing organisations alphabetically by country). For this publication, we have decided to arrange the listings in five sections, described in detail below. We would be glad to have your suggestions about other ways of presenting the data in future editions.

The JCWI database is constantly being updated. At the time of going to press, in January 1996, over half the entries were reasonably up-to-date (meaning 1991-96, but mainly 1994-95) and the rest were older (mainly 1989-90). We could have left out the older entries but in most cases we think that the organisations are still active, but not necessarily at the addresses or telephone numbers we hold for them. We are trying hard to check all the older entries and will update or delete or records of them as soon as possible. If you can help with information or funding for this time-consuming work, please let us know.

How the entries are grouped

The five main parts of the book are as follows:

PART ONE: Community and Solidarity Organisations: this lists organisations which are mainly for people of a single nationality or ethnic group. There are headings for each nationality or ethnicity, from Afghan to Zimbabwean, and under each heading the organisations are listed country by country in alphabetical order. (International dialling codes are shown after the country name.) When more than one ethnic term could be used of a particular organisation, we have tried to follow the usage and preference of the group itself. So, while most headings refer to nationalities, we also use terms for national minorities and for ethnic groups based in more than one state (for example Kurdish, Tigray, Palestinian, Armenian); for regional groupings (African, Arab, Eastern European, Central American, Maghrebi); for some religions (Hindu, Islamic, Sikh); for some languages (Bengali, Urdu); and for the term "Black". Some ethnic groups use more than one term to describe themselves, so we have given them more than one heading (African Caribbean, Afro-Caribbean, Caribbean, West Indian; Gypsy, Romany, Traveller). With a few exceptions, we have excluded linguistic or ethnic minorities which are usually regarded as indigenous citizens of a European state (Basques in Spain, Irish-speakers in Ireland, Greenlanders in Denmark), since their status and experience is different from that of migrant-origin minorities. On this, and other points, we are open to persuasion: groups which do not like their classification should tell us.

PART TWO: Support and Service Organisations: this lists organisations which provide specialist services such as immigration advice, refugee housing, training for migrant workers, or help with nationality problems, or which campaign for the rights of migrants, refugees or minorities. It includes multi-ethnic umbrella groups, and a few groups for which we are unsure of the ethnic category. They are listed country by country, in alphabetical order, as are groups in Parts Three to Five (with dialling codes after the country name).

PART THREE: Anti-racism, Anti-fascism, Multiculturalism, Internationalism and Development Education: this section covers groups which campaign against racism, fascism, intolerance and discrimination, which provide support to victims of racism, which promote equal opportunities, or which promote inter-ethnic and cross-cultural contact and understanding, awareness of minority issues, and global development or Third World concerns.

PART FOUR: Agencies and Authorities: this covers voluntary groups, government offices and other agencies and organisations which are concerned with migrant, refugee and minority issues *either* in the context of broader issues, e.g. human rights in general, *or* in the context of governmental or inter-governmental policy towards migrants, refugees or minorities. It includes, for example, international humanitarian aid agencies which sometimes work with refugees, consumer legal advice centres which also offer immigration advice, government immigration and nationality departments, and airport social services.

PART FIVE: Research and Documentation Centres: the last section covers university research and teaching departments, independent research units, libraries, documentation centres and other places which collect or publish information about migrants, minorities and refugees. It does not include centres specific to one ethnic or national group, which are listed under that ethnic or national heading in Part One. Of course many organisations listed in the other sections also collect or publish information; we have listed each organisation only once, under whichever of our five categories seemed to suit it best.

The structure of entries

Each entry for an organisation consists of a number of items.

The name of the organisation is given in **bold type,** in the language by which it is normally known, preceded by one of these symbols:

☆ for a local or minor regional organisation;

● for a major regional or minor national organisation;

♦ for a major national organisation, or branch of an international body;

█ for the headquarters of an international organisation.

Our use of one or other of these symbols should not be taken as a definitive statement of the status or scope of a particular group; in most cases our knowledge of the group is quite limited. "Major" and "minor" is used in terms of the importance of the group to migrant communities and minority issues. Where the symbol ≡ appears, this means that the name of the organisation is the same as that of the group just before it (the bold-type part only): note that groups with the same name are not always related to each other.

This is followed by the group's initials or acronym, and often by an English translation of the name (and/or alternative-language versions of the name). Unofficial translations are given in italics *(like this)* for information only, not to be used in correspondence; translations not in italics are usually official versions used by the groups concerned. Translations are not given where the meaning of the name should be clear to anyone who reads English: we would not give a translation for *Association Culturelle Islamique*. There is sometimes a cross-reference or other information such as the name of a parent organisation, or whether this is a head office or a local one. Associated organisations at the same address are then listed.

Next comes the name and job title of a contact person (if known); personnel often change so it is best to use the form "Mary Smith (or Secretary)" when writing to an organisation for the first time, especially if our information is more than a year old.

Then we give the postal address, in the language and style of the country concerned; if the street address is different that is given separately. In countries where addresses can be given in more than one language, we use the version which we think the organisation prefers. Some addresses, for example of women's refuges or of politically persecuted groups, are confidential and JCWI does not record these on its database or disclose them. We have included many listings where addresses are unknown or uncertain, firstly because users who have at least the name of an organisation may be able to find it independently, and secondly, because we want to encourage readers to send us corrections.

Next we give the telephone number, or numbers (preceded by *t*) and fax number (*f*); and in a few cases telex (*Tx*), telegraphic (*Tg*) or e-mail (*e*) address. For international dialling, remember the country code is given in the sub-heading. When dialling one country from another, you should generally leave out the first 0 or 9 of the area code (if there is one).

For organisations whose nature or activity are not clear from the name, we have tried to give a brief description. Publications are listed with their frequency (52/yr means weekly, 12/yr monthly and so on). Finally there is a code (»93, »94, »95) to show when our information for this group was last updated. This does not mean that everything in the entry was definitely correct in the year indicated: only that the most recent information available to the compiler dated from that year. (Here and throughout we give years in the Common Era format, CE, same as the Christian AD.) Information dated 1992-96 usually came from the organisation concerned, from its publications, or from groups to which it was affiliated; earlier dates mean that the information is carried forward from the 1991 JCWI Directory, or from some secondary source, and it is less reliable. We have tried to ensure that our information is first-hand, up-to-date and accurate, but with limited time and resources this has not always been possible. We hope to make more use of questionnaire mailings for future editions.

About the indexes

For this edition we have provided two indexes. The first (p249) gives country and page references for the original names and official translations of the names of organisations, and for publication titles, in the English-language order of each significant whole word (see the note on alphabetical order below). Unofficial translations are not indexed. The second index (p283) gives country and page references for acronyms (initials and abbreviations). Let us know if you would find other indexes useful, for example by city or by activity.

Notes on spelling, alphabetical order and abbreviations

In compiling, with limited time, skill and resources, a directory containing thousands of names and addresses in over 30 languages, and words transliterated from many other languages using non-Roman scripts, it is inevitable that there will be many errors of spelling. Please bring these to our attention. We are sorry that our production systems cannot, at present, record or reproduce non-Roman scripts, nor can they cope properly with the Danish character for which we have used *ф* as both upper and lower case, nor with several Turkish, Irish and Polish characters for which we have used near equivalents, just as we have used *ss* or beta (*ß*) for the German double-s character. In general we have not accented upper-case letters if the everyday practice in that language does not insist on it.

In all listings and indexes, the alphabetical order ignores accents, diacritical marks and case, and breaks compound letters (so for example *á, â, ä, Ä* and *à* are all treated as A; *n, N, ñ* and *Ñ* are all treated as N; the Spanish *ch* and *ll* and the German *ß* are treated as two letters each, rather than single letters; and so on). However the Scandinavian and Danish *Å/å* is treated as AA, and *Æ/æ* is treated as AE; these are accordingly listed under A, and *ф* with the Os, although in Denmark they would come at the end of the alphabet. The sorting order takes account only of significant whole words, ignoring words like *the, and, of, in, at, with, for, to*, and so on (in all the major European languages, but not in Arabic, Urdu and some other languages). This means that, for example, a newspaper called *The Voice* would appear under V; and *Association of Algerian Students* would appear before *Association* <u>for</u> *Algerian Studies* or *Association* <u>des</u> *étudiants algériens*. Where personal names form part of the names of organisations, our sorting ignores the forename; for example *Circolo Alcide de*

Gasperi would be spelt out in full, but placed as if it were *Circolo Gasperi*. There are a few exceptions such as the Anne Frank Stichting, under A. We hope that this is not confusing.

We have generally avoided abbreviations, even in postal addresses, to help those who are unfamiliar with the languages concerned. However in a few places, where they save a useful amount of space, the following abbreviations are used: *Ave.* Avenue, *bvd* boulevard, *Dve* Drive, *Gdns* Gardens, *Hse* House, *Pl.* Place, *pza* plaza (Spain) or piazza (Italy), *Rd* Road, *Sq.* Square, *St* Street or Saint, *str.* straat (in Dutch) or Straße (German), and *Tce.* Terrace. Some standard abbreviations of county or region names are also used where the counties or regions are optional for postal use. Other standard address abbreviations are used, in various languages, for terms like apartment number, care of, Post Office Box and so on.

Copyright and licensing information

The data is copyright and except for the use described in the Restricted Use Licence below no part of it may be reproduced in any form, including electronic storage or printing, without the prior written permission of JCWI. Such permission will not be unreasonably withheld in the case of non-commercial organisations working in the interests of migrants, minorities and refugees. If you want to use the data outside the terms of the Licence, **ask JCWI first**. For any large-scale use of the data you will probably find it more convenient to use electronic versions, which we can supply on floppy disk or through an on-line database (currently in test phase); it should be possible in future to develop CD-ROM versions. For information about electronic versions, contact JCWI.

RESTRICTED USE LICENCE

While reserving copyright, JCWI wishes to encourage the widest possible use of this data to build national, international and inter-ethnic contacts among migrant and minority organisations and those who work with or for them. JCWI therefore grants purchasers of the book, or authorised users of electronic versions of the Directory, the right to record, reproduce, circulate, publish and otherwise use elements of the data strictly subject to the conditions set out below.

Users of the on-line database may, subject to payment of the normal access charges or JCWI affiliation fee, download and keep for their private reference and use any of the data in the database, provided that it is not copied, sold or distributed to any person or organisation other than the person or organisation paying the on-line access charges or affiliation fee, that it is not used for marketing purposes by commercial organisations, that it is held and protected in accordance with the relevant data protection legislation, and that it is not used in the preparation of a list or directory-style publication, whether a printed or photocopied book or booklet, a computer disk, an on-line data set, or in any other form.

This licence permits, for example, the use of the data for compiling printed-out or electronic address lists or mailing lists for use ONLY by the person or organisation paying the access charges or JCWI affiliation fee. It does not permit, for example, the use of the data in mailshots to sell publications or services, or in compiling commercially-distributed mailing lists, or specialist directories. If you want to use the data in any way which you think may be outside the terms of this licence, you MUST first write to JCWI, which is willing to consider licensing any proposed use in the light of its policies and objectives.

The user accepts that the data is subject to JCWI copyright; accepts the terms of this licence; and accepts the disclaimers above. **(Note: you may only consult, download or use the data if you agree to these terms.)**

Purchasers of disk versions or of this printed version of the Directory are granted broadly similar permissions covering the use of the data: for manually compiling mailing lists or label runs for non-commercial purposes; for private use by migrant, minority and voluntary organisations; for academic, journalistic or other non-commercial, non-governmental research or review purposes. Up to 25 pages of the book may be photocopied or scanned for these purposes without reference to JCWI. You may not copy or reproduce the text or parts of it for the production of any for-sale publication in any paper or electronic format.

If in doubt as to whether any intended use of the data falls within the permitted categories; if you want to obtain the data in a different format, for example on disk; or if you want to use it in a way not covered by the licence, please contact JCWI by fax, mail or e-mail. If the proposed use seems to us to be in the best interests of migrants and minorities we are more than likely to give the necessary permission.

Background information

About this Directory

This Directory is partly based on a book (*Ethnic Minority and Migrant Organisations: European Directory 1991*) published by JCWI in 1991. It had around 4,800 substantive listings and extensive cross-references and indexing. The publication rapidly became an essential resource not only for the migrant voluntary sector which was its primary market, but for academics and practitioners in many countries. The Joseph Rowntree Charitable Trust, JRCT, which funded the 1991 project, agreed to fund an updated version. Work was under way when the European Research Centre on Migration and Ethnic Relations, in Utrecht, agreed to publish the new Directory on generous terms which permitted a substantial extension of the research exercise. The resulting Directory has about twice as many entries (around 9,300), the majority either added or updated since the 1991 publication.

JCWI's ongoing work in this area arose from the growing awareness of the implications of European legal and political harmonisation for national migration, asylum, minority rights and race relations policies, and thus of the need for organisations serving migrants, refugees and minority populations to make contact and form alliances with their counterparts across Europe. The Maastricht Treaty on European Union and the Inter-governmental Conference which follows it mean that there is a real chance to influence developments in many European countries. Working together is important and the Directory is intended to be of use for this. It will be widely used by migrant and community groups as well as being a valuable source of reference for research and academic institutions and libraries. Its primary purpose is as a tool for active use, to work towards an anti-racist and changed Europe. If traditionally marginalised groups are to influence future European policy, they must develop frequent and effective contacts and information exchanges across national borders. In recent years there has been increasing bilateral and multinational co-operation among migrant and minority groups, helped by major initiatives sponsored by the European Union and the Council of Europe, but most of the relevant community groups still work only at local, regional or national level. It is the firm view of JCWI and its partners in this work that as many organisations and agencies as possible should join pan-European networks, able to identify issues and opportunities, to exchange information, to develop common perspectives and priorities, and to carry out joint and effective campaigns.

We hope that this publication, by making basic information widely available at low cost and in what we hope is an accessible format, will encourage groups to seek out their own European friends, allies and partners. Although the period since the 1991 Directory has seen the enlargement of what is now the European Union, with the accession of Austria, Sweden and Finland, we do not insist on defining Europe in terms of the EU: the data here covers more than forty states, although coverage is significantly better for the EU states. (For a full list of countries covered, see the country index.)

It is to be hoped that the co-operation of ERCOMER and JCWI in this venture will encourage migrant and refugee community groups, migration rights activists, community-based research, information and advice services, and other concerned professionals and voluntary bodies to form mutually beneficial partnerships with the academic community; and that they will find academic centres able and willing to respond to their need for timely and effective support in relation to information resources, networking and informed analysis.

About JCWI

Since its establishment in 1967, the Joint Council for the Welfare of Immigrants has been the only independent national voluntary organisation working solely in the area of British immigration, nationality and asylum law and practice. Every year JCWI provides legal representation for around 900 people with problems caused by these laws; campaigns and lobbies to change the laws; gives specialist advice to about 8,000 individuals, families and ethnic minority community groups; runs training courses for immigration advisers and community groups; provides expert information by telephone for immigration law practitioners; and publishes the quarterly *JCWI Bulletin* and a range of booklets and leaflets, including an immigration and nationality law handbook.

JCWI is a membership organisation, and in addition to the other benefits of membership, payment of the annual fee allows you to use the electronic version of this directory free of the normal access charges. (So if you intend to use the database frequently, or for long periods on-line, it will probably be much cheaper for you to affiliate to JCWI.) Its hundreds of affiliates include individuals affected by or interested in immigration and nationality issues, advice agencies, solicitors, student unions, community groups, churches, trade unions, law centres, Members of Parliament and journalists. For details of current subscription rates, or for more information on our work and publications, please write, fax or e-mail us.

About ERCOMER

The European Research Centre on Migration and Ethnic Relations, ERCOMER, was established in 1993 as a multi-disciplinary social science research organisation to promote and undertake comparative European research on migration, racism, ethnic relations and related topics, to engage in advanced training and to disseminate information and research-based material in this field. ERCOMER operates wherever possible with partner organisations in networks and publishes a newsletter, *Merger*, three times a year.

The research programmes at ERCOMER are divided into a number of themes covering the study of xenophobia, nationalism and ethnic conflict in Western, Central and Eastern Europe, new patterns of migration (including refugees and asylum seekers), migrants and ethnic minorities in European cities, and comparative studies of education, health care and political integration. This research is funded by the European Commission, the European Science Foundation and national organisations.

ERCOMER is recognised by the European Commission as a centre for advanced training. It receives fellowships under the Human Capital and Mobility Programme and welcomes selected researchers under the Training and Mobility in Research Programme or other fellowship schemes. The Centre is also involved in supervising doctoral students on behalf of the Dutch government and the national research council.

ERCOMER publishes an academic journal, *New Community*, and a book series entitled *Comparative Studies in Migration and Ethnic Relations*. ERCOMER also supports the European Documentation Centre and Observatory on Migration and Ethnic Relations, EDCOMER, which monitors migration processes and relevant policy developments and also contains files of surveys and statistical data. EDCOMER also received financial support from the European Commission. This Directory, although published under the ERCOMER imprint, may be seen as the first in an occasional series of information documents to be produced by EDCOMER.

Further information on all of ERCOMER's activities including publications, the text of *Merger*, conferences, current staff and other activities are contained on the World Wide Web at http://www.ruu.nl/ercomer/index.html.

Acknowledgements

This Directory, and the earlier version published in 1991, could not have been produced by JCWI without the support and practical assistance offered by several bodies.
— The Joseph Rowntree Charitable Trust, one of Britain's leading philanthropic organisations with a long and distinguished record in the field of social research, funded the compilation of the 1991 version, and provided a further grant for updating work in 1994. We are most grateful for their continued support for and belief in the project.
— Additional financial support from our publisher, the European Research Centre on Migration and Ethnic Relations, in Utrecht, allowed us to extend both the research period and the geographical coverage of our data.
— The Paris-based Centre d'Information et d'Etudes sur les Migrations Internationales, CIEMI, which had been working independently on a similar directory project, agreed in 1990 to share information with JCWI, and although both its 1991 directory and an updated version published in 1994 were rather different from ours in design and scope, there was a considerable overlap and we were and are extremely grateful for their co-operation.
— The Centre for Research in Ethnic Relations, based at the University of Warwick, helped JCWI to develop and refine the original proposal, and hosted the project in 1990-91.
— Finally, the European Commission, specifically the Division of its fifth Directorate-General responsible for migration policy, freedom of movement and migrant social security, funded the printing of the 1991 Directory and gave similar support for this edition.
The individuals most directly involved with the preparation of the database, and the 1995 print version, were as follows: Ciarán Ó Maoláin, a freelance journalist based in Armagh, Ireland, who researched and compiled the database and produced and edited the Directory, travelling throughout Europe and working in many languages; Don Flynn, European Projects Worker of JCWI in London who oversaw and co-ordinated the work; Milan Shah, our computer consultant in his capacity as a volunteer with the Manchester Citizens Advice Bureau; and representing our institutional supporters, Malcolm Cross, Director of ERCOMER, Stephen Pittam, Assistant Secretary of the JRCT, and Claude Moraes, Director of JCWI. Sue Shutter of JCWI, the London-based designer Pat Kahn, and Jette Johst and others in Utrecht were very helpful with proofreading and design matters. Moira Simpson assisted with the inputting of data, the preparation for print of the output, and the tedious re-keying of a massive amount of material wiped out in one of those computer disasters that you convince yourself can only happen to other people. (Back up your data now!)
The other individuals and organisations who helped with the compilation and production of the database are unfortunately too many to list here — literally hundreds — including all those who were kind enough to reply to our written or telephone enquiries, and a number of organisations and centres which provided us with lists of addresses for their countries or fields of activity. We would like to thank all of them, and hope that they will excuse our inability to record our gratitude more specifically; that they will find the Directory useful; and that they will continue to provide us with additions and corrections to the information.
Neither JCWI nor the organisations or individuals mentioned above can accept liability for errors of fact in nor for omissions from this Directory. In the certainty that such mistakes will have occurred in a work of this size and nature, we offer sincere apologies. We will try to correct mistakes as soon as we are notified of them.

Part One

Community and Solidarity Organisations

More than half of the entries cover Community and Solidarity Organisations. These are associations, federations, committees, publications or clubs with a specific ethnic or national focus, for example serving refugees or immigrants from one country, or promoting aid to or solidarity with a particular country. We list these according to the appropriate ethnic or other term, and then alphabetically by the European country in which they are based. Mostly these terms (Afghan, Albanian, Bangladeshi, Bulgarian and so on) refer to the nation-state of origin, but we also use terms for 'stateless nations' or national minorities (such as Kurdish, Tigray, Palestinian, Armenian); for regions of the world (e.g. African, Arab, Eastern European, Central American, Maghrebi); for some religions especially associated with migrants in Europe (Hindu, Islamic, Sikh); and for some languages (Bengali, Urdu); and we use the mainly-British term 'Black', which usually refers to all 'visible minorities'.

Many of the ethnic terms overlap with or have more or less the same meaning as other terms, so it is important to read the cross-reference entries for each term. We have not tried to merge headings if this would list groups under terms which they might not want to use. (For example, we have separate headings for African Caribbean, Afro-Caribbean, Caribbean, West Indian; and for Gypsy, Romany, Traveller.) The cross-reference entries link these similar terms, as well as referring from narrow terms to broader ones (e.g. from Moroccan to North African) and from broad terms to narrower ones (e.g. from Asian to Pakistani).

AFGHAN

see also Asian, Islamic

◎ AUSTRIA 43

● Österreichisches Hilfskomitee für Afghanistan (Austrian Aid Committee for Afghanistan)
Dr A. Janata: Salztorgasse 6/7, 1010 Wien; t (01) 535 8305
Assistance to Afghan refugees in Peshawar (Pakistan) and rural development aid in Afghanistan. »93

◎ DENMARK 45

● Danish Committee for Aid to Afghan Refugees, DACAAR
Postboks 53, Borgergade 10/3 sal., 1002 København K;
t 3391 2700, f 3332 8448
A specialist section, established 1984, of the Danish Refugee Council (p146); refugee welfare, assistance in returning. »93

◎ FRANCE 33

● Amitié Franco-Afghane, AFRANE
BP 254, 75524 Paris Cedex 11 »93
● Bureau International Afghanistan, BIA
24 rue Chaligny, 75012 Paris; t (1) 4307 1567, 4341 5560
Activities include agricultural development aid. »90

◎ GERMANY 49

● Verein für Afghanische Flüchtlingshilfe e.V. (Union for Aid to Afghan Refugees)
Kaiserplatz 3, 5300 Bonn; t (0228) 225563
Aid to Afghan refugees. »90

◎ NETHERLANDS 31

✿ Afghanistan Vereniging (Afghanistan Union)
Postbus 5168, 2701 GD Zoetermeer »95

✿ Gulistan
Postbus 6167, 5600 HD Eindhoven »95

◎ NORWAY 47

● Den Norske Afghanistanhjelpen (Norwegian Aid to Afghanistan)
Urtegt. 50, 0187 Oslo 1 »93

◎ SWEDEN 46

● Svenska Afghanistankommitten, SAK
Essingeringen 90, 11264 Stockholm; t (08) 133000, f 13011
Medical, educational and development aid to returned refugees and rural communities in Afghanistan. »93

◎ UNITED KINGDOM 44

● Afghan National Credit and Finance Ltd
The Secretary: New Roman House, 10b East Road, London
N1 6AD; t (0171) 251 4100 »95
● Afghan Society
98 Grinthorpe House, Percival Street, London EC1 »88
● Afghanaid
Marina Afzal/Donna Copnall: 292 Pentonville Road, London N1
9NR; t (0171) 278 2832, f 837 8155
Charity formed 1983; humanitarian assistance, agricultural and development aid in Afghanistan and among refugees, mainly in Peshawar, Pakistan; 12 staff in UK, about 180 abroad. »96
● Islamic Alliance of Afghan Mujahideen in the UK
250 Chapter Road, Dollis Hill, London NW2; t (0181) 451 3032
Supports Islamist movement in Afghanistan. »90
● Society of Afghan Residents in the United Kingdom, SAR
K. Ahmad: West Acton Community Centre, Churchill Gardens, Acton, London W3 0JN; t (0181) 993 8168, 993 6598, f 993 2129
Community group; visa, refugee status, nationality advice. »94

AFRICAN

see also African Caribbean, Afro-Caribbean, Algerian, Angolan, Arab, Beninese, Black, Burkinabe, Cameroon, Cape Verdean, Central African, Comoros, Congolese, East African, Egyptian, Equatorial Guinean, Eritrean, Ethiopian, Gabonese, Gambian, Ghanaian, Guinea Bissau, Guinean, Islamic, Ivorian, Liberian, Libyan, Madagascan, Maghrebi, Malian, Mauritanian, Mauritian, Middle Eastern, Moroccan, Mozambican, Namibian, Nigerian, North African, Oromo, Réunion, Rwandese, Saharan, São Tomé, Senegalese, Seychellois, Sierra Leonean, Somali, South African, Southern African, Sudanese, Tanzanian, Tigray, Togolese, Tunisian, Ugandan, West African, Zairean, Zimbabwean

◎ BELGIUM *32*

✧ **Centre Social et Culturel Africain**
Rue Dupont 12, 1210 Bruxelles; *t* (02) 219 5522   »90

● **Conseil des Communautés Africaines en Europe: Belgique,
CCAE** *(Council of African Communities in Europe: Belgium)*
S. Monkasa: Rue Royale 171, Boite 5, 1210 Bruxelles;
t (02) 539 2620, *f* 539 1343
Information, advice, cultural activities. See also CCAE in
France and Italy, p3.   »94

● **Conseil des Femmes Francophones de Belgique** *(Council
of Women in Belgium from French-Speaking Countries)*
Square de Meeus 28, 1040 Bruxelles
Information and advice.   »94

◎ DENMARK *45*

✧ **African Cultural Association**
Grønningen 3, 8000 Århus C; *t* 8613 1014   »89

✧ **All-African Council**
[address uncertain] MS-Huset, Mejlgade 49, 8000 Århus C
Also listed (1990) as Klostergade 37. Immigrant welfare. »94

◎ FRANCE *33*

✧ **A comme Afrique: Regards Croisés—Dialogue des Cultures**
(A as in Africa: Sideways Glances—Cultural Dialogue)
Yvon Dupré: 17 lotissement de la Chartreuse, 56400 Auray;
t 9756 3332
Cultural exchange, education, information.   »94

● **Africatrack**
10 rue Jacquemont, 75017 Paris; *t* (1) 4229 3651
Development issues.   »90

✧ **Afrique espoir** *(Africa Hope)*
Institut National des Télécommunications, 5 rue Charles-
Fourier, 91011 Evry   »89

✧ **Amicale Africaine** *(African Friends Society)*
David Mayinbila: 3c rue Théodule Ribot, 70000 Vesoul;
t 8475 8304, *f* 8476 6921
Aid to refugees and migrants, inter-cultural contact.   »94

● **Association pour l'aide social aux travailleurs africains,
ASSOTRAF** *(Society for Welfare Aid to African Workers)*
Francis Bleher: 11 bis passage Dartois-Bidot, 94100 Saint
Maur-des-Fossés; *t* (1) 4283 0303, *f* 4283 1728
Housing and advice services.   »94

✧ **Association de l'amitié française et africaine** *(French-African
Friendship Association)*
52 rue du Maréchal-Foch, 66000 Perpignan   »89

✧ **Association des artistes et créateurs africains** *(Association
of African Artists and Craftspeople)*
188 boulevard Victor-Hugo, 59000 Lille   »89

✧ **Association champenoise de coopération inter-régionale,
ACCIR** *(Champagne Inter-Regional Co-operation Association)*
6 rue Eustache Deschamps, 51000 Châlons-sur-Marne;
t 2664 2858
Development education, rural development in Africa; reception,
integration, return assistance to refugees and migrants.   »93

✧ **Association culturelle de la communauté africaine d'Orléans,
ASCAO** *(African Community Cultural Society of Orleans)*
Lamine Dieye: 11 rue des Frères-Chappe, 45100 Orléans »90

✧ **Association Culturelle et d'Intégration des Etudiants
Africains, ACIEAM**
BP 81, 8 rue St-Claude, 34000 Montpellier; *t* 6758 9758 »94

✧ **Association culturelle La musique et l'Afrique**
13 chemin de la Ferme, 69120 Vaulx-en-Velin   »89

● **Association pour la défense des droits de l'homme en
Afrique, ADDHA** *(Association for Human Rights in Africa)*
BP 8375, 95805 Cergy Pontoise Cedex; *t* (1) 3030 4034,
f 3424 9264
Human rights in Africa; advice service for African migrants.
Development aid and relief of refugees in Africa.   »93

✧ **Association d'entraide des femmes africaines** *(Mutual Aid
Association of African Women)*
83 rue de la Parabole, 95800 Cergy-Saint-Christophe
Social welfare.   »89

✧ **Association des Etudiants Africains de la Sarthe, ASSEAS**
(Sarthe Association of African Students)
cité universitaire, route de Laval, 72040 Le Mans
Educational welfare, interests of students.   »90

✧ **Association des Etudiants Africains du térritoire de Belfort**
(Belfort Association of African Students) and Association des
Etudiants d'Afrique Centrale et de l'Ouest
M. Fotso: 28 rue de Bruxelles, 90000 Belfort   »90

✧ **Association des Etudiants d'Afrique Noire de Tours** *(Tours
Association of Black African Students)*
résid. universitaire, parc Grandmont A 20B, 37200 Tours »90

✧ **Association euro-africaine**
10 rue de Gens-d'Armes, 14000 Caen
Inter-cultural understanding, interests of migrants.   »90

✧ **Association euro-africaine d'entraide** *(Euro-African Mutual
Aid Association)*
14 rue Robespierre, 77340 Pontault-Combault
Formerly Association de l'union africaine d'entraide des
immigrés de l'Afrique Noire pour l'Europe en France.   »90

✧ **Association femmes inter cultures, AFIC** *(Women's Inter-
Cultural Association)*
espace des fetes, 10 rue Augustin-Thierry, 75019 Paris
Welfare of African women in France.   »90

✧ **Association des femmes du Sud-Sahara—Afrique Yakhareu**
(Yakhareu Association of Sub-Saharan African Women)
1 rue des Montagnes-Bleues, 77181 Emerainville   »90

✧ **Association pour la formation et la réinsertion des africains
migrants, AFRAM** *(Society for the Training and Resettlement
of African Migrants)*
1678 allée du Vieux Pont de Sèvres, 92100 Boulogne-
Billancourt   »93

✧ **Association Française d'Amitié et de Solidarité avec les
Peuples d'Afrique, AFASPA** *(French Association for Friendship
and Solidarity with the Peoples of Africa)*
Claude Gatignon/François Lancon: 21 rue Marceau, 93100
Montreuil; *t* (1) 4858 7120, *f* 4870 9126
Advice and assistance to African migrants in France; solidarity
and development aid in Francophone Africa. *Aujourd'hui
l'Afrique* (4/yr).   »94

● **Association Française des Volontaires du Progrès, AFVP**
(French Association of Volunteers for Progress)
BP 207, 91311 Montlhéry Cedex; *t* (1) 6901 1095,
f 6980 7534
Volunteer programmes for young French people in 30 African
countries, including refugee housing and health aid.   »93

✧ **Association Générale pour l'Enseignement et la Culture Peul
Langue Poular, KAWTAL**
1 rue des Emeraudes, 45140 Saint Jean de la Ruelle;
t 3872 0126
Research, education, cross-cultural contact.   »94

● **Association pour la médecine et la recherche en Afrique**
(Association for Medicine and Research in Africa)
66 bis rue St Didier, 75016 Paris; *t* (1) 4553 2729
Development of African health care.   »90

✧ **Association noire africaine d'Elancourt** *(Black African
Association of Elancourt)*
allée des Cordeliers, 78990 Elancourt
Cultural, social and welfare.   »90

✧ **Association pour la Promotion de la Langue et de la Culture
du Soninké, APS** *(Association for Soninké Language and
Culture)* formerly Association pour la promotion du Soninké
Diadié Soumaré: 5 rue Victor Letalle, 75020 Paris;
t (1) 4349 5131   »94

✧ **Association socioculturelle africaine Drome-Ardèche**
Maison de quartier Fontbarletts, 26000 Valence   »90

✧ **Association de solidarité africaine**
Tujac, batiment Glycine 12, 19100 Brive   »89

● **Association de Solidarité des Africains en France, ASAF**
32 rue Traversière, 75012 Paris; *t* (1) 4341 5080
Welfare, advice service.   »90

✧ **Association pour la solidarité et l'insertion des femmes
africaines du Havre, ASIFAH** *(Association for Solidarity
and Integration of African Women of Le Havre)*
27 rue Gustave-Brindeau, 76600 Le Havre   »89

✧ **Association Sportive et Culturelle des Etudiants Africains
d'Angers** *(Angers African Students' Sports & Cultural Society)*
Dossou Ayao: 95 avenue Patton, 49000 Angers   »90

✧ **Association des Travailleurs Africains de la Somme** *(African
Workers' Association of the Somme)*
4 rue Stendhal, 80080 Amiens; *t* 2252 1690
Labour rights, social solidarity.   »94

✿ **Association Tsholo Nkese**
5e groupe Voltaire-Mermoz, 10600 La Chapelle-Saint-Luc
Music. »89
● **ATLIK**
[address unknown] 06390 Coaraze; *t* 9379 3343, 9379
3508, *f* 9379 3754
Solidarity with the Tuaregs of Mali; emergency aid and longer-
term assistance to refugees in Mali; other aid projects in
Mauritania, Niger, Mali and Algeria. *ATLIK* (4/yr). »93
✿ **Aubergenville Intégration Fraternité Africaine**
54 rue Marcel-Pagnol, 78410 Aubergenville »90
✿ **Centre culturel africain**
[address unknown] Paris »90
✿ **Cercle africain des entrepreneurs de France**, CADEF
(African Enterprise Circle of France)
5 rue Montebello, 69003 Lyon »89
✿ **Club Afrique-France**, CAF
faculté de droit et des sciences sociales, avenue Léon-Duguit,
33604 Pessac
African exchanges with Université de Bordeaux. »89
✿ **Collectif Africain de Solidarité**, CAS
BP 143, 17 rue Pierre Corneille, 14009 Caen Cedex; *t* 3186
2713, 3193 3667
Cultural and social group. »94
✿ **Comité de coordination africaine pour la démocratie**
(African Co-ordinating Committee for Democracy)
57 bis rue du Réveil-Matin, 78800 Houilles
Democracy, return migration, economic development. »90
✿ **Conseil des Communautés Africaines en Europe—Ile de
France**, CCAE-IDF: African Communities Council in Europe,
ACCE—Paris region
Emmanuel Manyo: CIEMI, 46 rue de Montreuil, 75011 Paris
See also CCAE in Belgium, p2, and Italy, below. »94
✿ **Coup de Pilon**, CP
Moma Talla N'Diaye: 6 rue Sainte-Marie-des-Terreaux, 69001
Lyon; *t* 7827 7758
Cultural and educational concerns. »94
✿ **Fédération des Associations Africaines d'Echanges et de
Développement** *(Federation of African Exchange and
Development Associations)*
Makan Sidibe: 42 bis avenue Edouard Vaillant, 93500 Pantin;
t (1) 4915 4000 »94
● **Fédération des Travailleurs de l'Afrique Noire**, FETAF *(Black
African Workers' Federation)*
Joseph Kouamba Kitiki: Bourse du Travail, Esplanade B.
Frachon, 93100 Montreuil-sous-Bois; *t* (1) 4859 5784-87
Migrant labour rights. »94
◆ **Fédération des Travailleurs d'Afrique Noire Immigrés**,
FETRANI *(Black African Immigrant Workers' Federation)*
Tom Taylor: 5 rue Regnault, 93500 Pantin; *t* (1) 4891 2669,
4891 2682, *f* 4891 0217
Migrant labour rights; represented in EU Migrants Forum,
p131. See also UTAF, below, and CAIF and CAIE, p136. »94
✿ ≡ Adolphe Memevigni: 13 place des Fédérés, 93160
Noisy-le-Grand »90
✿ **Interafricaine de Goussainville**
46 avenue des Marronniers, 95190 Goussainville »90
● **Organisation Pan Africaine de Lutte contre le Sida**, OPALS
(Pan-African Organisation for Combatting AIDS)
55 bis rue Lyon, 75012 Paris; *t* (1) 4307 3673
Health education and research. »90
✿ **Soutien Dignité Aide Travailleurs Africains**, SOUNDIATA
(African Workers Support, Dignity, Assistance)
15 rue de Maubeuge, 75009 Paris; *t* (1) 4285 2700
Housing and welfare aid. »94
✿ **Union Africaine pour le Service, la Solidarité et l'Entraide**,
UNASSE
2 rue Lavoisier, 02000 Laon; *t* 2323 1123 »94
✿ **Union des Communautés Africaine et Malgache**, UCAM
(Union of the African and Malagasy Communities)
rue Brossolette, 80000 Amiens
Welfare of migrants from the continent and Madagascar. »94
● **Union des Travailleurs Africains en France**, UTAF *(Union of
African Workers in France)*
Thomas Omores: 5 rue Régnault, 93500 Pantin; *t* (1) 4844
6487, *f* 4844 6551
Employment, training, welfare; see also FETRANI, above. »94
✿ **Union des Travailleurs d'Afrique Noire de l'Oise**, UTANO
15 rue Denis Papin, 60870 Villiers-St-Paul; *t* 4471 9363 »94

◉ **GERMANY** *49*

● **Stiftung Kinder in Afrika** *(Children of Africa Foundation)*
Holsteiner Straße 12c, 2057 Reinbek; *t/f* (040) 722 1105
Refugee, educational and other relief activities in Africa. »93

◉ **IRELAND** *353*

● **Africa Society**
16-18 Lower Ormond Quay, Dublin 1; *t* (01) 872 3500,
f 872 3348 »94

◉ **ITALY** *39*

● **Africa Insieme** *(Africa Together)* also known as Associazione
Africa Insieme, or Circolo Culturale Africa Insieme
Justin Mvondo, President: [address uncertain] presso ARCI,
via F. Carrara 24, 00196 Roma; *t* (06) 361 0800, 360 1541
Also listed (1990) as via dei Monti de Pietralta 16, 00157
Roma; or presso Circolo ARCI, via Val Tromria 108/1, 00141
Roma, which is also the address given for its student wing,
Studenti Insieme. Advice work, culture, education, youth
integration; services to students, migrants and refugees from
Africa. »94
✿ ≡ piazza della Vittoria 2, 50067 Firenze »90
✿ ≡ CP 114, 74024 Mandica; *t* (099) 679 8102 »90
✿ ≡ Fallu Kebe: via Domenico Cavalla 58, 56100 Pisa;
t (050) 21536 »90
✿ **Associazione Africa Oggi** *(Africa Today Association)*
Adriano Zanini: via Metauro 16, 20146 Milano
African solidarity, migrant welfare. *Africa Oggi* (12/yr). »94
✿ **Associazione degli Africani in Piemonte**, AAP *(Association
of Africans in Piedmont)*
Thomas Deza/Mambu Bomapi: via A. Massena 31, 10128
Torino; *t* (011) 765376
Welfare, immigration and other rights advice, employment and
training issues. »90
✿ **Associazione Baobab per la Promozione Culturale**
Godwin Chuckhwu: [address uncertain] Carlo Baravalle 49,
00139 Roma; *t* (06) 612 2000
Also listed (1990) at via Val Tromria 108, 00141 Roma,
suggesting a link with Africa Insieme. »90
✿ **Associazione Culturale Africana Samory Touré**
via Plinio 20, 20129 Milano »90
✿ **Associazione Culturale di Studenti Africani a Bari**, ACSAB
via Trevisani 161, 70122 Bari »90
✿ **Associazione Donne Africane** *(African Women's Society)*
via Domodossola 74, 10145 Torino; *t* (011) 744026
Social, cultural and welfare activities. »90
● **Associazione Donne Immigrate Africane**, ADIA *(Society
of African Immigrant Women)*
Bove Khadigia: via Arcione 114, 00187 Roma; *t* (06) 679
4125
Women's welfare, information, advice. »94
✿ **Associazione Panafricana**
via G. Rossi 13, 40138 Bologna »90
✿ ≡ CIERC, via S. Anna dei Lombardi 16, Napoli »90
✿ **Associazione di Studenti Africani di Firenze e Province**,
ASAFP
Anthony Adekoge Aladesanmi, President: presso Centro
Internazionale per gli Studenti, via Pescione 3, 50125 Firenze;
t (055) 877 7041
Culture, educational welfare. »90
✿ **Associazione di Studenti Africani a Roma**, ASAR
Gabriele Meldini, President: via del Conservatorio 1, 00186
Roma; *t* (06) 6880 2568, 686 1019
Educational welfare, cultural activities. »94
✿ **Baobab**
viale Vasco de Gama 191, 00121 Lido di Ostia
See also Associazione Baobab, above. »90
✿ **Centro Culturale Nelson Mandela**
via Genova 12, 39100 Bolzano »90
✿ **Comunità Cristiana Afro-Araba in Lombardia**
via Anfiteatro 14, 20121 Milano; *t* (02) 869 3194
Third World Christian fellowship. »90
◆ **Consiglio delle Comunità Africane in Europa**, CCAE: African
Communities Council in Europe, ACCE
c/o ARCI, via Francesco Carrara 24, 00196 Roma; *t* (06) 361
0731
See also CCAE in Belgium, p2, and France, above. »94
✿ **Cooperativa di Solidarietà Africana**
Fall Alioune, President: via Pucci 34, 55049 Viareggio;
t (0584) 463 8585
Interests of West African and other migrant workers and
students. »90
✿ **Coordinamento della Baia Domizia**
Isidoro Longo Yegi Mobey: via Roma 67, 81190 Vila Literno
Caserta
Social conditions, rights, problems of North and West African
migrants. »90
● **Euro African Foundation**, EAF
via XX Settembre 26, 00187 Roma; *t* (06) 494 0583 »90

✧ **Gruppo Africano Cultura e Sport**
Dr John Amantchi: via Alpignano 14, 10143 Torino;
t (011) 771 3354   »90
● **Istituto Italo-Africano, IIA**
Tullia Carettoni: via U. Aldrovandi 16, 00197 Roma;
t (06) 872246, 321 6712, 321 6949, *f* 322 5348
Research, promotion of African culture. *Africa* (4/yr).   »94
✧ **Maboko Na Maboko, MNM**
Cristina Loreti: presso ACLI, via Giuseppe Marcora 18-20,
00153 Roma; *t* (06) 584 0459, *f* 584 0436   »94
✧ **Maisha—Centro di Cultura Africana** *(African Culture Centre)*
Okondo Ongonda Yombo-D'jema, President: via dei Magazzini
Generali 8, 00154 Roma; *t* (06) 574 5761, 574 1609
Youth, educational and cultural issues.   »94
✧ **Mediazione—Cooperativa Sociale**
Lukenge Lunanga: via delle Orfane 3 A, 10122 Torino;
t (011) 436 3298, 669 3680   »94
✧ **Organizzazione di Studenti Africani a Genova, OSAG**
(Organisation of African Students in Genoa)
c/o Caritas, via Milano, 16126 Genova
Educational welfare.   »90
✧ **Sardegna Africa** *(Sardinia Africa)*
Bacary Dieme/Pierre Ble: c/o CGIL, via del Piave 46, 07026
Olbia; *t* 25050
Organisation and representation of West African and other
migrants.   »90
✧ **Voce degli Afro-Italiani** *(Voice of the Afro-Italians)*
via Carducci 32, 70010 Valenzano, BA
Minority rights.   »94

◉ NETHERLANDS *31*

● **African-European Institute**
[address unknown] Den Haag
Linked with the anti-apartheid movement.   »90

◉ PORTUGAL *351*

● *Africa*
Leston Bandeira, Editor: Rua Possidónio da Silva 105-1°, 1300
Lisboa; *t* (01) 675182-83, *f* 396 9752, *Tx* 64923 Tribo P
Newspaper (52/yr), founded 1985, covering African,
Portuguese and international current affairs.   »90
✧ **Associação Africa Solidariedade**
Rua Aníbal Cunha 193, 4000 Porto; *t* (02) 208 6926   »94
✧ **Associação Africana** *(African Association)*
Augusta Ferreira: Rua Miguel Bombarda 66A, 2830 Barreiro;
t (01) 204 2038, 215 2925
Cultural and welfare group.   »94
✧ **Associação Estrela d'Africa** *(Star of Africa Association)*
Bairro Estrela d'Africa, 2700 Amadora
Neighbourhood association.   »94
● **Associação Luso-Africana de Solidariedade** *(Luso-African Solidarity Association)*
Maria Lisette Silva: Rua da Madalena 125-3°, 1100 Lisboa
African culture, international solidarity, development.   »94
✧ **Associação Moinho da Juventude** *(The Mill Youth Association)*
Eduardo Pontes: Rua Pinheiro Chagas 77-2 esq., 1000 Lisboa;
t (01) 574718
Formed 1985; solidarity among African and Portuguese youth.
Same as Associação Cultural Moinho da Juventude, p148?»90
✧ **Casa Africana** *(House of Africa)*
Sapateiros 112-3°, 1100 Lisboa; *t* (01) 347 6210   »95
✧ ≡ Augusta 161/71, 1100 Lisboa; *t* (01) 347 6464   »95
✧ **Clube Marítimo Africano de Lisboa, CMAL**
Mário Van Dunem: Rua do Paraíso 47-1°, 1100 Lisboa;
t (01) 886 9285
Cultural, social and leisure activities.   »94
✧ **Liga dos Africanos e Amigos de Africa, LIAFRICA** *(League of Africans and Friends of Africa)*
Rua Forno do Tijolo 46-2°D, 1100 Lisboa; *t* (01) 814 5394
Cultural and welfare group. Name suggests a link with
LIANGOLA, p9.   »94
● **Liga de Imigrantes Africanos de Expressão Portuguêsa,**
LIAEP *(Portuguese-Speaking Africa Immigrants' League)*
F.A. Carlos: Apartado 2492, 1112 Lisboa Codex   »93

◉ SPAIN *34*

✧ **Africans de Lleida**
La Palma 33, 25002 Lleida, Catalunya; *t* (973) 266590 »94
✧ **Asociación de Africanos**
Tápia 33, 17600 Figueres, Girona, Catalunya   »94
✧ **Asociación de Africanos de Girona**
a/c Oficina de Inmigración de la UGT, Carretera de Barcelona
71-73, 17000 Girona, Catalunya   »94

✧ **Asociación Afro-Catalana**
Hotel d'Entitats, Empordá 33, La Pau, 08020 Barcelona,
Catalunya; *t* (93) 278 0294   »94
✧ **Asociación Afro-Hispana para la Integración del Marginado y Freno a la Emigración Clandestina, AAHIMAFE** *(Afro-Hispanic Society for Integrating the Marginalised and Halting Secret Emigration)*
Basile Nkoenke: plaza de las Meninas 4, 28025 Madrid;
t (91) 469 0146
Welfare of African migrants; social activities.   »94
● **Asociación Afro-Vasca** *(Basque-African Association)*
Ondarroa kalea 10, Txurdinaga, 48004 Bilbo, Bizkaia, Euskadi
Migrant and refugee welfare association; advice, cultural
events, sports, languages classes; supported by Cáritas. »95
✧ **Asociación Amigos de Africa** *(Friends of Africa Society)*
Torres y Bages 11, 08400 Granollers, Barcelona   »94
● **Asociación Española de Africanistas**
Colegio Mayor N.S. de Africa, Obispo Trejo 1, 28040 Madrid
Promotes African studies; see also ACUGE, p33.   »90
✧ **Asociación Familiar Mixta de Africanos de Catalunya,**
AFMAC *(Mixed Family Association of Africans in Catalonia)*
carrer Gravina 27, 08001 Barcelona; *t* (93) 790 4066   »94
● **Asociación de Intelectuales Africanos en España** *(Society of African Intellectuals in Spain)*
Inongo vi Makome: Galileo 286-5° 1ª, 08028 Barcelona,
Catalunya; *t* (93) 490 5890, 357 6840
Cultural and social group.   »94
✧ **Asociación Karibu para Refugiados Africanos** *(Caribou Society of African Refugees)*
calle Santa Engracia 140, 28003 Madrid; *t* (91) 553 1873
Also listed (1994) at calle Silva 21, Madrid, *t* 547 7126. »94
● **Asociación Mediadora de los Problemas Africanos en España,**
AMPAE *(Society for Mediation of African Problems in Spain)*
Hortaleza 70-2° D, of. 5, 28005 Madrid; *t* (91) 521 0958»90
✧ **Asociación de Trabajadores Africanos de Lleida** *(Lérida African Workers' Association)*
Djibril Traore: Blondel 35, 25002 Lleida
Information, advice, cultural activities.   »94
✧ **Casa de la Palabra, Centro de Africanos** *(House of the Word, African Centre)*
calle Cava Alta 25-1°, 28005 Madrid; *t* (91) 364 1266
Catholic welfare body; also listed (1990) at Bocángel 45,
28008 Madrid, *t* 246 7139.   »94
✧ **Centre d'Acol.liment per Africans Sant Pau** *(St Paul African Reception Centre)*
Ignasi Márques Rodríguez: carrer Madern i Clariana 8, 08304
Mataró, Barcelona, Catalunya; *t* (93) 790 1329
Welfare of immigrants, anti-racism, health promotion.   »94
● **Centre d'Estudis Africans, CEA** *(Centre for African Studies)*
Centro de Estudios Africanos
Travessa de Gracia 100 pral 1, 08012 Barcelona, Catalunya;
t (93) 415 3192   »94
✧ **Centro Cultural Africano Mabana**
carrer Hospital 107 bis, 2ª pta, 08001 Barcelona, Catalunya;
t (93) 441 7188
Also listed (1994) at Riera Baixa 12. Social contact, cultural
activities.   »94
✧ **Centro de Información y Documentación Africanas, CIDAF**
(African Information and Documentation Centre) and
Asociación Africana
José María Sarasola: calle Gatzambide 31, 28015 Madrid;
t (91) 574 0400, 574 0409, *f* 504 2717
Resource centre on African affairs. *Cuadernos del CIDAF*
(6/yr), *Boletín* (12/yr).   »94
✧ **Centro Interafricano de Iniciativas Culturales, CIIC**
Alloza 18-1° 3ª, 08016 Barcelona; *t* (93) 351 2293   »94
✧ **Cultura Africana**
Torrecilla del Leal 4, 28012 Madrid; *t* (91) 539 3263   »94
✧ **Darek Nyuma**
calle Alcalá 41-3°, 28014 Madrid; *t* (91) 532 6250   »94
✧ **Equip de Treball Africa Negra a l'Ensenyament, ETANE**
(Education for Black Africa Working Group)
Edmundo Sepa Bonaba: Hotel d'Entitats, Edif. Piramidón 6ª,
Empordá 33, 08020 Barcelona; *t* (93) 278 0294, 278 0174
See also Centre Avaroes, p90.   »94
● **España Africans' Social Unity, EASU**
Ivonne David: a/c Virgen del Pilar 60, loc. izq., 08330 Premiá
de Mar, Barcelona; *t* (93) 752 2978-75, *f* 751 6811
Also listed (1994) at Unión 65. Represented in EU Migrants'
Forum, p131; employment, legal advice.   »94
✧ **Foro Africano** *(African Forum)*
carrer Gacela 2-6, 5° 4ª, Barcelona, Catalunya   »94
✧ **Liga Africana de Defensa de los Derechos Humanos**
(African League for Human Rights)
Font del Remei 15-2° 2ª, 08023 Barcelona, Catalunya   »94

• **Mundo Negro** *(Black World)*
calle Arturo Soria, Madrid; *t* (91) 415 2412, 415 8000
Mainly Catholic priests working in Africa. »90

◎ **SWEDEN** *46*

• **Scandinavian Institute of African Studies**
PO Box 1703, 75147 Uppsala »93

◎ **SWITZERLAND** *41*

▌ **Comité Inter-Africain sur les pratiques traditionelles ayant effet sur la santé des femmes et des enfants** *(Inter-African Committee on Traditional Practices affecting the Health of Women and Children)*
rue de Lausanne 147, 1202 Genève; *t* (022) 731 2420,
738 0821, *f* 738 1823
Works for eradication of female genital mutilation and other injurious practices in Africa, and develops health education around that and other themes for African women, both in Africa and in Europe. »93

◎ **UNITED KINGDOM** *44*

• **africa 95**
Helen Denniston/Clementine Deliss: Richard House, 30-32 Mortimer Street, London W1N 7RA; *t* (0171) 637 4388,
636 5950, *f* 637 4580
A season of African cultural promotion events involving galleries, theatres, cinemas, arts centres and the media in Britain, with several international workshops in African countries. »95

• **Africa Analysis**
Richard Hall: 6th Floor, 107 Fleet Street, London EC
Journalism on contemporary African affairs. »95

• **The Africa Centre** and Africa Book Centre Ltd
Adotey Bing, Director: 38 King Street, Covent Garden, London WC2E 8JT; *t* (0171) 836 1973
Founded 1963; public education on Africa, social centre for Africans in Britain, cultural activities. Promotes awareness of Africa and its arts and culture. Brian Eccles, Wanjiru Kihoro, Susan Odamtten. Book Centre retails and markets books on Africa and the wider world. *Centrepoint* (12/yr). »94

• *Africa Confidential*
Patrick Smith, Editor: Miramoor Publications, 73 Farringdon Road, London EC1M 3JB; *t* (0171) 831 3511, *f* 831 6778
African politics, economics and current affairs magazine (26/yr) founded 1960. »95

• **Africa Educational Trust**, AET
38 King Street, Covent Garden, London WC2E 8JT; *t* (0171) 836 5075, *f* 379 0090
Educational counselling and scholarships for refugees. »95

• **Africa Evangelical Fellowship**
17 Westcote Rd, Reading, Berkshire; *t* (01734) 583848 »90

• **Africa Now**
S. Kaussari: Bovis House, Townmead Rd, London SW6 2QD
International charity founded 1981, involved in community-based sustainable development projects. »95

• **Africa Research and Information Bureau**
Napoleon Abdulai: Room 202, 5 Westminster Bridge Road, London SE1 7XW; *t* (0171) 620 1430, *f* 620 1431
Also listed (1994) at 18 Pilgrimage Street, London SE1 4LJ.
Research and publishing. *Africa World Review* (4/yr). »96

• **African Churches Council on Immigration and Social Justice**, ACCIS
Dr Wellington Chirwa, Chairman: Unit 6-7, 321 Essex Road, London N1 3PS; *t* (0171) 704 2331
Liaison group on family reunification, refugees, other migration issues affecting African and other Black people in Britain. »95

✧ **African Community of Greater Manchester**
F. Zubairu/D. Aisuemi: 49 Crofton Street, Moss Side, Manchester M14 7WD; *t* (0161) 257 3615, 445 0136
Drop-in centre; immigration and welfare advice, prison visiting, health/social work with elderly, women, mentally ill. »93

✧ **African Cultural Society**
Chris Olaniyan: 83 Shirley Road, Cheetham Hill, Manchester M8 7WD; *t* (0161) 795 1894
Promotion of African music, literature, drama, dance, crafts and culture; exhibitions, workshops. »93

• **African Family Advisory Service**
49 Goldhawk Road, London W12 8QP; *t* (0181) 749 7324»90

• **African Human Rights Centre**
76 Mayhall Road, Herne Hill, London SE24 0PJ; *t* (0171) 733 9724
Information and pressure group on human rights issues. »94
African People's Historical Monument Association: see The Black Cultural Archives, p243

✧ **African Refugee Housing Action Group**, ARHAG, and African Refugee Women's Group
Ronnie Moodley, Director: 2nd floor, St Margaret's, 25 Leighton Road, London NW5 2QD; *t* (0171) 482 3829
Housing, employment advice, welfare services, community development for African refugees. »94

• **African Refugees and Migrants Monitoring Project**
[address unknown] London »96

• **African Reparations Movement**, ARM
c/o Bernie Grant MP: House of Commons, Westminster, London SW1A 0AA
Proposes compensation for exploitation of Africans. »94

• **African Rights**
Rebecca Hallam/Shaki Sanussi: Docklands Enterprise Centre, 11 Marshalsea Road, London SE1 1EP; *t* (0171) 717 1224,
403 3383, *f* 403 4023
Rakiya Omaar, Yoanes Ajawin. Documentation and campaigns on human rights of people in and from Africa, including rights of migrants, refugees and national minorities. »95

✧ **African Society**
Daphne Obang: 4 Hillyfield, Lewes BN7 1LA; *t* (01273) 477595 »94

• **African Studies Association of the UK**, ASAUK
Dr N. Nelson, Honorary Secretary: 18 Northumberland Ave., London WC2N 5BJ; *t* (0171) 930 1662
Founded 1963. See also Royal African Society, p6. »90

✧ **African Welfare and Advice Centre**
91-97 Tooting High Street, London SW17 0SA; *t* (0181) 767 3445 »94

✧ **African Women's Association**
135 Clarence Road, London E5 8EE; *t* (0181) 985 0147
Social, welfare; women's rights; anti-racism. »94

✧ **African Women's Welfare Association**
Unit 14, 321 Essex Road, London N1 3PS; *t* (0171) 226 3899 ext. 4855 »95

✧ **African Women's Welfare Group**, AWWG
Annexe C, Tottenham Town Hall, Town Hall Approach Road, London N15 4RY; *t* (0181) 885 5822
Refugee and immigrant welfare, advice, employment, English classes. »95

▌ **Agency for Co-operation and Research in Development**, ACORD
Francis House, Francis Street, London SW1P 1DQ; *t* (0171) 827 7611, *f* 976 6113
A consortium of development NGOs working in 16 countries to promote, and help people cope with, change in Africa. »96

✧ **Akina Mama wa Afrika** *(African Women's Association)*
Bisi Adeleye-Fayemi: c/o London Women's Centre, Wesley House, 4 Wild Court, London WC2B 5AU; *t* (0171) 405 0678
Community development; training in HIV prevention; rights of African women in Europe. »95

✧ **Amakhosikazi e Afrika** *(African Women's Association)*
F. Zubairu: 9 Hadley Avenue, Longsight, Manchester M13 0UU; *t* (0161) 257 3615, 445 0136
Awareness raising among women of African descent; training, child care, immigration/welfare advice, counselling. »93

✧ **Broad African Representative Council**, BARC
A.E. Chaba: 34 Anson Road, Rusholme, Manchester M14 5BQ; *t* (0161) 257 3050
Employment, housing, immigration, nationality, education, health, welfare advice; child care; community advocacy. »93

• **Confederation of African Nationals and Descendants**, CAND
Osakne Osifo: 25 Elaine Grove, Gospel Oak, London NW5 4QH; *t* (0171) 482 1153, *f* 267 6375
Social, cultural, welfare activities. »94

• **Food and Agricultural Research Management Ltd**, FARM: usually known as FARM-Africa
David Campbell, Executive Director: 9-10 Southampton Place, London WC1A 2EA; *t* (0171) 430 0440
Development charity; Canadian- and UK-funded agricultural projects in Ethiopia, Kenya, Tanzania and South Africa. »95

• **Foundation for African Arts**
Old George Orwell Building, Holland Park, London N19 3EU; *t* (0171) 263 8141 »94

✧ **Horn of Africa Community Group**
51 Hammersmith Bridge Road, London W6; *t* (0181) 748 2950, *f* 846 9579 »95

• **Institute for African Alternatives**
W. Lune/Mohamed Suleiman: 23 Bevenden St, London N1 6BH
Research/documentation on contemporary African affairs.»94

• **International Society of African Lawyers**
9 Stone Buildings, Lincoln's Inn, London WC2; *t* (0171) 405 1951 »95

✧ **Islington African Project**
7 Elthorne Rd, London N19 4AE; *t* (0171) 272 8960-61 »95

● **Link Africa**
Sally Bourne: 11-12 Trumpington Street, Cambridge
CB2 1QA; *t* (01223) 322983
Solidarity, development aid; educational training projects in
partnership with local organisations in Southern Africa.   »95
✵ **MDN Ltd**
[address unknown] Liverpool; *t* (0151) 236 1548
Among other activities, manages a project helping adult
Africans with learning difficulties to live independently.   »94
● *New African*
IC Publications, 7 Coldbath Square, London EC1R 4LQ;
t (0171) 713 7711
News magazine (12/yr). Also *African Business* (12/yr), *New
African Yearbook* and travel guides.   »95
✵ **Pan African Legal Advisory Services**
Samuel Yaw Bekoe: 31 Bartholemew St, London SE1 4AL;
t/f (0171) 403 9991
Legal practice specialising in immigration matters.   »95
✵ **Pan African Organization**
2nd Floor, 7 Taplow Block, Aylesbury Estate, Merrow Street,
London SE17; *t* (0171) 701 3320, 703 0777
Pressure group, advice centre.   »95
✵ **Pan African Refugee Housing Co-op**
Tony Fernandes: 49 St Pancras Way, London NW1 0DQ;
t (0171) 388 1301, *f* 388 0759
Presumably related to the Pan-African Housing Co-operative
listed (1988) at 53 Crowndale Road, NW1.   »95
● *Review of African Political Economy*, ROAPE
ROAPE Publications Ltd, Regency House, 75-77 St Mary's
Road, Sheffield S2 4AN; *t* (0114) 275 2671
Academic and general review (3/yr); book publishers.   »90
● **Royal African Society**
18 Northumberland Avenue, London WC2N 5BJ; *t* (0171)
930 1662
See also ASAUK, p5. *African Affairs* (4/yr).   »90
✵ **Southwark African Organisation**, SAO
226 Camberwell Road, London SE5 0ED; *t* (0171) 703 5811
The SAO may be a successor to the African People's
Movement listed (1988) at same address (*t* 701 7121).   »91
● **Village Aid**
Riverside Works, Buxton Road, Bakewell DE45 1GJ; *t* (01629)
814434
Solidarity, fundraising, sustainable development projects.   »95
✵ **Yaa Asantewaa Arts Centre**
1 Chippenham Mews, London W9 2AN; *t* (0171) 286 1656
Promotion of, education on African and Caribbean arts.   »96

🔲 **NORTHERN IRELAND** *44*

✵ **Northern Ireland African Cultural Centre**
c/o NICEM, 17 Eblana Street, Belfast BT7 1LD   »96

AFRICAN CARIBBEAN

*see also African, Afro-Caribbean, Anglo-Caribbean, Antillean,
Barbadian, Black, Caribbean, Cuban, Dominican, Dominican
Republic, French: DOM/TOM, Grenadian, Guadeloupean,
Guyanese, Haitian, Jamaican, Kittitian, Montserrat, Puerto
Rican, Rastafarian, Trinidadian and Tobagan, Vincentian, West
Indian*

🔲 **UNITED KINGDOM** *44*

✵ **African Caribbean Business Association**, ACBA
Manny Kawooya/Dr Kennedy Akabogu: c/o Business Link, 646
Foleshill Rd, Coventry CV6 5HR; *t* (01203) 637575, 831283
Voluntary organisation which seeks to foster business growth
within the local African-Caribbean community.   »92
✵ **African Caribbean Community Development Unit**, ACCDU:
London Voluntary Service Council, LVSC
London Voluntary Sector Resource Centre, 356 Holloway
Road, London N7 6PA; *t* (0171) 700 8114
Specialist advocacy, networking and support services to Black
community organisations.   »95
● **African-Caribbean Development Network**
Clyde Williams: c/o Birmingham Training and Enterprise
Council, Chaplin Court, 80 Hurst Street, Birmingham B5
Partnership between public and private sectors and the city's
African-Caribbean community; aims to increase the number of
African-Caribbean professionals by promoting strategic action
plans in education, training, enterprise and employment.   »94
✵ **African Caribbean Family Mediation Service**
[address unknown] London; *t* (0171) 737 2366
Voluntary mediation service for black couples going through
divorce.   »95

● **African and Caribbean Finance Forum**, ACFF
Mervin Archer: [address unknown] London
Founded 1990 as a forum for black professionals and
employers in the banking and finance industries.   »94
✵ **African Caribbean Leadership Council**, ACLC, formerly
West Indian Leadership Council
Jessie M.F. Stephens: West Indian Cultural Centre, 9
Clarendon Road, London N8 0DJ; *t* (0181) 881 5881-84,
888 0475, *f* 888 5037
Arthur Lawrence, secretary; G.F. Gederon; umbrella group for
local advice, information, cultural organisations.   »95
● **African Caribbean National Artistic Centre**, ACNA
G. Leigh, Manager: [address unknown] St Ann's, Nottingham
NG3; *t* (0115) 969 1364
Artistic, cultural and leisure centre, with youth activities.   »94
✵ **Arawak Housing Association**
B. Quarless: Unit 45, 2 Hellidon Close, Cariocca Enterprise
Park, Manchester M12 4AH; *t* (0161) 272 6094
Promotes social housing for black and ethnic minority tenants,
and use of black and ethnic minority building contractors.   »93
✵ **Black Businesses in Birmingham**, BBB
5 The Square, Broad St, Birmingham B15; *t* (0121) 631 2860
Forum for black entrepreneurs, which seeks to challenge
stereotypes, change attitudes and boost confidence.   »95
✵ **Bolton West Indian Association**
Johnson Street, Bolton BL1 1NX; *t* (01204) 394944
Community development; promotes volunteering, training,
leisure and care based projects.   »94
✵ **Greenwich Mind Networks**
38 Floyd Road, Charlton, London SE7 8AN; *t* (0181) 305
2388, 853 1473
African and African-Caribbean mental health project.   »94
✵ **Hounslow Afro-Caribbean Association**, HACA
12 School Road, Hounslow TW3 1QZ; *t* (0181) 577 3226
Advice, support and service provision in housing, community
care, welfare benefits, services for elderly, other matters.   »94
✵ **Imani Ujima Centre**, formerly Highfields Workshops
Carlton Howson, Chair: Maidstone Road, Highfields,
Leicester LE2 0UA; *t* (0116) 262 2815
Resources, community arts activities, entertainment.   »95
✵ **Leeward Islands People's Association**
A.G. Jones: 52 Athol Road, Whalley Range, Manchester
M16 8QN; *t* (0161) 881 7046
Social events; services to elderly from Dominica, St Kitts-
Nevis, Antigua and other Leeward Islands.   »93
✵ **Mangrove First Base**
3 All Saints Road, London W11 1HH
Hostel/counselling/support service for female ex-offenders.»95
✵ **Merton African Caribbean Organisation**
J. Senior: The Vestry Hall, London Road, Mitcham CR4 3UD;
t (0181) 648 9889   »95
✵ **Newham African Caribbean Centre**
Alex Imu: [address unknown] Newham, London E6; *t* (0181)
472 0528
Activities include enterprise and vocational training.   »95
✵ **One Love Training Centre**
Herby Boudier: [address unknown] Newham, London E6;
t (0181) 472 1056
Activities for under-14s; training for unemployed youth.   »95
● **Organisation of Blind African Caribbeans**, OBAC
Chigor Chike: [address unknown] London; *t* (0171) 703 3688
Advice and information service.   »95
✵ **Sandwell African Caribbean Development Agency**, SACDA
Chairman: c/o 25-27 Bull Street, Ringway, West Bromwich
B70 6EU
Business advice, training and support.   »94
✵ **Sheffield African Caribbean Mental Health Association**,
SACMHA
David Bussue: 10 Breinburg Court, 263 Pitsmoor Road,
Sheffield S3 9AQ; *t* (0114) 272 6393
Works to improve services.   »94
✵ **Sheffield and District Afro Caribbean Community Association
Ltd**, SADACCA
Isadora Aiken, General Manager: 48 Wicker, Sheffield
S3 8JB; *t* (0114) 275 3915, 275 3479
Charity addressing employment, welfare and social needs of
African Caribbean people in Sheffield. Services include day
care centre for senior citizens.   »95
✵ *The Voice*
Winsome-Grace Cornish, Editor: Nu Vox House, 370
Coldharbour Lane, London SW9 8PL; *t* (0171) 737 7377,
f 274 8994, *e* veeteeay@gn.apc.org
Val McCalla proprietor, Isabel Appio editor-in-chief, Annie
Stewart deputy editor. Biggest-selling newspaper (52/yr) for
the black community. See also *The Weekly Journal*, p23.»96

✧ **Whalley Range Afro Care Group**
I. Thomas: 46 Park Drive, Whalley Range, Manchester
M16 0AH; *t* (0161) 882 0312
Community services; luncheon club; classes in English,
keyboard skills, sewing, knitting. »93

AFRO-ASIAN

*see African, African Caribbean, Anglo-Caribbean, Antillean,
Asian, Black, Caribbean, West Indian; and related terms*

AFRO-CARIBBEAN

*see also African, African Caribbean, Anglo-Caribbean,
Antillean, Barbadian, Black, Caribbean, Cuban, Dominican,
Dominican Republic, French: DOM/TOM, Grenadian,
Guadeloupean, Guyanese, Haitian, Jamaican, Kittitian,
Montserrat, Puerto Rican, Rastafarian, Trinidadian and
Tobagan, Vincentian, West Indian*

◉ **UNITED KINGDOM** *44*

✧ **Afro-Caribbean Association**
44b Princes Street, Oxford OX4 1DD; *t* (01865) 251939
Social and cultural. »90

✧ **Afro-Caribbean Care Group**
Ben Abiodun/Evelyn Aitken: Woodville Resource Centre,
Shirley Road, Cheetham, Manchester M8 7NE; *t* (0161)
740 3140 »93

✧ **Afro-Caribbean Co-operative Society**
24 Porchester Drive, Newtown, Birmingham B19 2LU »90

✧ **Afro-Caribbean Co-ordinating Council**
212 Winson Green Road, Birmingham B18 4BA
Liaison among community groups. May be successor to
West Indian Federation listed (1990) at same address. »90

✧ **Afro-Caribbean Cultural Centre**
D.O. Brown, Co-ordinator: 2 Clarence Road, Wolverhampton
WV1 4JH; *t* (01902) 24005, 20109 (?)
Social and cultural centre; information. »94

✧ **Afro-Caribbean Development Unit**
Adelaide Street, Coventry, Warwickshire; *t* (01203) 553214
Community development. »90

● **Afro-Caribbean Focus**
[address unknown] »88

● **Afro-Caribbean Mental Health Association, ACMHA**
Audrey Morgan: 35-37 Electric Avenue, Brixton, London
SW9 8JP; *t* (0171) 737 3603
Charity providing long-term support, including residential
care, to black people with mental health problems. »94

✧ **Afro-Caribbean Mental Health Project**
Dawn Bryan, Administrative Officer: Zion Community Health
and Resource Centre, Zion Crescent, Hulme, Manchester M15
5BY; *t* (0161) 226 9562
C.D. Moore manager. Community-based self-help, advocacy,
training, consultancy, counselling service. Liaises with
relatives, carers, black communities and service providers to
identify needs and develop good practice. »95

✧ **Afro-Caribbean Organisation**
422 Seven Sisters Rd, London N4 2LX; *t* (0181) 800 9836
Training, employment, rights information; anti-racism. »95
✧ ≡ 335 Gray's Inn Rd, London WC1; *t* (0171) 837 0396 »90

✧ **Afro-Caribbean Resource Centre**
Steve Batchelor: 337-339 Dudley Road, Winson Green,
Birmingham B18 4HB; *t* (0121) 455 6382
Community development, information on Black issues and
Afro-Caribbean heritage; immigration/welfare advice; day care,
other projects for senior citizens; community radio training
project; meetings, social/cultural/educational events. »94

✧ **Afro-Caribbean Self-Help Organization**
104 Heathfield Road, Birmingham B19
Community development. »90

● **Afro-Caribbean Social Workers' Association**
c/o OSCAR, 12 Bell Barn Shopping Centre, Cregoe Street,
Lee Bank, Birmingham B15 2DZ
Development of social work theory and practice in relation
to black community; interests of black social workers. »90

✧ **Afro-Caribbean Society**
Trevor Grant/Augustina Telsole: Top Floor Flat, 45 Osmond
Road, Hove BN3 1TF; *t* (01273) 600958, 288511 »94

● **Afro-Caribbean Teachers' Association**
[address unknown] Birmingham
Discussion group on issues affecting Black teachers and
students. See also Caribbean Teachers' Association, p27.»91

✧ **Afro-Caribbean Youth Council**
D. Richardson: 36 Wolverhampton Rd, Walsall WS2 8PR »90
● **Afro-West Indian United Council of Churches**
Rev. Eric Brown, General Secretary: New Testament Church
of God, Main House, Overstone, Northampton NN6 0AD;
t (01604) 43311
12 Afro-Caribbean churches; spiritual and social welfare. »88
✧ **Barnet African-Caribbean Association**
71 Park Road, London NW4 3UG; *t* (0181) 202 4233
Local social, cultural and welfare group. »90
✧ **Bedford Afro-Caribbean Self-Help Association**
Fay Christian: Lower Ground Floor, 43 Ashburnham Road,
Bedford MK40 1BX; *t* (01234) 272852 »90
✧ **Foundation Housing Association, FHA**
1 Lonsdale Street, Highfields, Leicester LE2 1BP; *t* (0116)
254 4230
Developing social housing provision in Leicester. »91
✧ **Hackney Afro-Caribbean Mental Health Programme,
HACMHP**
[address unknown] Hackney, London E; *t* (0171) 923 3546
Culturally sensitive counselling services for black people
experiencing mental health difficulties. »95
✧ **Huddersfield Caribbean Association**
Elwyn Bailor, Co-ordinator: [address unknown] Huddersfield,
Yorkshire; *t* (01484) 539552
Support and service to local Afro-Caribbean community;
initiatives include Afro-Caribbean Mental Health Project in
partnership with Kirklees Social Services. »93
✧ **Kings Heath Afro-Caribbean Club**
8 Heathfield Rd, Birmingham B14; *t* (0121) 443 1047 »95
✧ **Moss Side Afro-Caribbean Luncheon Club**
Raphael Phipps: The Birley Community Education Centre,
Chichester Road, Hulme, Manchester M15 5FU; *t* (0161)
226 1416 ext. 170
Elderly day care, luncheon club, social activities, crafts. »93
✧ **Pepper Pot Club**
David Idiabana, Co-ordinator: 2nd Floor, 39-41 Acklam Road,
London W10 5YU; *t* (0181) 968 6940
Club for Afro-Caribbean elderly in North Kensington. »95
✧ **Roots of Culture Foundation**
Sam Lee, Co-ordinator: St Michael and All Angels Church,
96 Lavender Grove, Hackney, London E8 3LR; *t* (0171) 241
5054, *f* 275 7475
A. McAllister chair. Afro-Caribbean culture and interests;
publications, meetings. *Roots* (4/yr). »94
● **Sickle Cell Society**
54 Station Road, Harlesden, London NW10 4UA; *t* (0181)
961 4006
Voluntary group raising awareness among professionals,
sufferers, the media and the public about an anaemia
affecting some 6,000 Afro-Caribbeans in the UK. »95
✧ **Sojourners House**
c/o Women's Aid Centre, PO Box 156, Newton Street,
Manchester M60 2DB; *t* (0161) 839 8574
Refuge for Afro-Caribbean and other women and children
facing domestic violence. »93
✧ **Unity of Afro-Caribbean People**
29 Featherstone Road, Southall UB2, Middlesex »90
✧ **Waltham Forest Afro-Caribbean Senior Citizens Club**
I.P. City Mission Church Inc., Gainsborough Bridge, Fillebrook
and Colworth Road, London E11
Charity which aims to improve the quality of life of local
African-Caribbean elders and their carers. »94
✧ **West Bromwich Afro-Caribbean Resource Centre**
Thomas Street, West Bromwich B70 6LY
Information, social and cultural activities. »95
✧ **Wolverhampton Afro-Caribbean Development Agency,
WACDA**
Naomi Diamond/Llewellyn Graham: [address uncertain] 52-54
Worcester St, Wolverhampton WV2 4II; *t* (01902) 24005
Also listed (1991) at Unit 20, Business Development Centre,
21 Temple Street, Wolverhampton. Community development,
welfare, research into social provision. »91

AHMADIYYA

*see Islamic, Pakistani, West African (Note: the Ahmadiyya
define themselves as Muslim, although most Muslims do not
recognise them as such. By listing their groups as Islamic we
are not stating any view on that issue. It just reflects our
policies of using groups' self-definitions; avoiding sectarian
subdivisions in religion listings; and merging categories with
very few entries into broader categories.)*

ALBANIAN

see also East European, European, South-East European

◎ **BELGIUM** *32*

✿ **Centre Culturel et Sportif Albanais** *(Albanian Cultural and Sports Centre)*
Rue J.B. Brabant 47, 5000 Namur; *t* (081) 230473 »94

◎ **PORTUGAL** *351*

● **Associação de Amizade Portugal-Albania** *(Portugal-Albania Friendship Association)*
Rua Rodrigo Faria 105 r/c D, Lisboa; *t* (01) 648950 »90

◎ **UNITED KINGDOM** *44*

● **Albanian Society**
William Bland, Honorary Secretary: 26 Cambridge Road, Ilford IG3 8LU; *t* (0181) 590 9977
Formed 1957; friendship, culture. *Albanian Life* (3/yr). »90
● **Anglo-Albanian Association**
Denys Salt, Secretary: Flat 6, 38 Holland Park, London NW11 3RP; *t* (0171) 727 0287
Founded 1922; refugee welfare. »94

ALGERIAN

see also Arab/Arabic, African, Beur, Islamic, Jewish, Maghrebi, Middle Eastern, North African

◎ **BELGIUM** *32*

● **Amicale des Algériens en Belgique** *(Society of Algerians in Belgium)*
Rue Rogier 75, 1030 Bruxelles; *t* (02) 245 2145, 215 0902
Culture, information, education. *Actualités de l'Emigration*.»94
● **Front islamique du salut, FIS** *(Islamic Salvation Front)* al-Jabha al-Islamiya li-Inqadh
Abdelkrim Ouled Adda: [address unknown] Bruxelles
Radical Islamist political movement, founded in 1989 and by 1992 representing majority opinion in Algeria. It was then outlawed and many of its members live in exile. »94

◎ **FRANCE** *33*

✿ **AMEL-Espoir, Association des Algériens de Provence** *(Provence Algerian Association)*
chez Mme Rachida Bouazza: batiment Les Tritons no. 3, ZAC, 13090 Aix-en-Provence
Interests of Algerian community; anti-racism. »90
▌**Amicale des Algériens en Europe, AAE** *(Association of Algerians in Europe)* Head Office
Ahmed Nadir: 40 rue Boileau, 75016 Paris; *t* (1) 4651 7777, *f* 4651 3385
Training, employment, welfare. Represented in EU Migrants Forum. *Actualités de l'Emigration*. »94
✿ ≡ 41 bvd Strasbourg, 75010 Paris; *t* (1) 4770 0304 »90
✿ ≡ 65 bvd Belleville, 75011 Paris; *t* (1) 4355 3770 »90
✿ ≡ 134 rue Charenton, 75012 Paris; *t* (1) 4340 0620 »90
✿ ≡ 37 rue Juge, 75015 Paris; *t* (1) 4577 9013 »90
✿ ≡ 5 rue Affre, 75018 Paris; *t* (1) 4259 8648 »90
✿ ≡ 30 rue Partants, 75020 Paris; *t* (1) 4366 9040 »90
● **Association algérienne pour le décès** *(Algerian Society for Bereavement)*
34 rue Garibaldi, 13330 Pélisanne
Funeral rites, repatriation of bodies. »90
✿ **Association algérienne pour la promotion de la culture et de la langue arabe** *(Algerian Society for Promotion of Arabic Language and Culture)*
Centre Socioculturel, 19 rue du Docteur Schweitzer, Les Coudreaux, 77490 Chelles
Cultural, leisure and educational activities among Arab community; inter-cultural contacts. »90
✿ ≡ 71 rue de la Loge, 91000 Evry »90
✿ ≡ 30 allée des Cèdres, 77400 Lagny-sur-Marne »90
✿ ≡ 3 rue Paul-Verlaine, 92240 Malakoff »90
✿ ≡ 8 rue du Jura, Les Merisiers, 78200 Mantes-la-Jolie »90
✿ ≡ 9 rue Gambetta, 77330 Oizir-la-Ferrière »90
✿ **Association des Algériens en Savoie**
520 rue du Pré-de-l'Ane, centre commercial des Combes, 73000 Chambéry
Assistance in settlement, integration and old age. »90
✿ **Association de la communauté algérienne de la Sarthe**
[address unknown] »90

✿ **Association culturelle des Algériens du Doubs**
3 rue de l'Industrie, 25000 Besançon
Cultural and leisure activities promoting friendship among Maghrebi, French and other groups; Arabic lessons, arts. »90
✿ **Association culturelle des Algériens de la Haute-Savoie**
chez M Ferhat Arhab: 7 allée du Déjeuner-sur-l'Herbe, 74000 Cran-Gevrier »90
✿ **Association culturelle des Algériens des Vosges**
20 rue du Bouton-d'Or, 88000 Epinal »90
✿ **Association culturelle de la communauté algérienne de l'Indre**
8/962 avenue Bernard-Louvet, 36000 Châteauroux
Mutual aid, solidarity, friendship, culture. »90
✿ **Association décès familiale algérienne** *(Algerian Family Bereavement Association)*
79 boulevard du Roi-René, 13300 Salon-de-Provence
Funeral rites, repatriation of bodies. »90
✿ **Association entraide et promotion des travailleurs algériens** *(Algerian Workers' Mutual Aid and Advancement Society)*
55 rue Jean-Jaurès, 60100 Creil
Social activities, cultural and youth work; improvement of living and working conditions. »89
✿ **Association des Etudiants Algériens d'Europe, ASDEALE** *(Association of Algerian Students in Europe)*
24 bis rue Venel, 13100 Aix-en-Provence
Interests of students, mediation with authorities. »90
✿ ≡ 31 rue Père-Chevrier, 69007 Lyon »90
✿ ≡ Atrami, 17 boulevard de la Paix, 51100 Reims »90
✿ ≡ USI-EALE, 9 pont Guilhemery, 31000 Toulouse »90
● **Association des Etudiants issus de l'Immigration Algérienne en France, ASSETIMA** *(Student Association of the Algerian Immigrant Community)*
Mourad Tagzout, President: BP 106, 75223 Paris Cedex; *t* (1) 4634 5305
Location: 115 boulevard St-Michel. Abdelaziz Tabouri, secretary; student welfare, anti-racism. *El Fac-isard*. »94
✿ **Association pour la formation contre le racisme et pour l'identité culturelle algérienne, AFRICA** *(Association for Anti-Racist Training and Algerian Cultural Identity)*
Fissa Tekkoue/Aissa Zekkour: 1 place Georges Bracque, 93120 La Courneille; *t* (1) 4836 9574 »94
✿ **Association Générale des Etudiants Algériens d'Aix-Marseille, AGEAM** *(Aix-Marseilles Algerian Student Society)*
[address unknown] »90
● **Association générale des femmes algériennes en Europe, AGEFALE** *(General Association of Algerian Women in Europe)*
67 rue d'Aboukir, 75002 Paris
Solidarity, self-expression, cultural, social and economic advancement of Maghrebi women in Europe. »90
✿ **Association locale des femmes algériennes, ALFA**
F4, Le Gallieni, La Gabelle, 83600 Fréjus
Solidarity among Algerian, Maghrebi and French women and girls; justice, health, economic and social promotion. »90
✿ ≡ 10 allée des Ramiers, 13800 Istres »90
✿ ≡ 11 rue Pruiquiau, 44100 Nantes »90
✿ ≡ 41 boulevard de Strasbourg, 75010 Paris »90
✿ ≡ 3 rue de Louvain, batiment Les Mouettes, 54500 Vandoeuvre-les-Nancy »90
✿ **Association loisirs, entraide de la communauté algérienne de Pompey, ALECA** *(Leisure and Mutual Aid Society of the Pompey Algerian Community)*
128 rue du Général-de-Gaulle, 54340 Pompey »90
✿ **Association pour la promotion et l'insertion de la communauté algérienne, APICA** *(Algerian Community Advancement and Integration Association)*
bât. Suffren, entrée 3, 3 rue Lorient, 54250 Champigneulles
Cultural and social development of Algerian community, joint anti-racist work with Maghrebi and French communities. »90
✿ **Association de solidarité de l'immigration algérienne** *(Algerian Immigrants' Solidarity Association)*
12 rue Louis-Braud, 31100 Toulouse
Solidarity in Algerian community, inter-cultural dialogue and integration, fights racial and sexual discrimination. »90
✿ **Association de solidarité des travailleurs algériens, ASTA** *(Algerian Workers' Solidarity Association)*
8 avenue de Bourgogne, 60000 Beauvais
Social work, settlement help, anti-racism. »89
● **Association des travailleurs algériens en France** *(Algerian Workers' Association of France)*
[address unknown] Paris »91
✿ **Association des travailleurs et familles algériennes du Sud de la France, ATFA** *(Algerian Workers and Families Association of the South of France)*
71 rue Saint-Jacques, 13006 Marseille »89
✿ ≡ 15 bis rue Adam-de-Crapone, 34000 Montpellier »89
✿ ≡ 11 place Fontaine-Neuve, 66000 Perpignan »89

• **Comité international de soutien aux intellectuels algériens,** CISIA *(International Support Committee for Algerian Intellectuals)*
Hugo Colonna: [address unknown] Paris
Established 1993 to express solidarity with Algerian intellectuals victimised by radical Islamic activists.　　»94

✿ **Comité des travailleurs algériens, CTA** *(Algerian Workers' Committee)*
37 bis bvd de la Chapelle, 75010 Paris; *t* (1) 4803 3404　»90

• **France Algérie**
16 avenue de l'Opéra, 75001 Paris; *t* (1) 4261 0874
Relations between French and Algerian peoples.　　　»90

• **Fraternité Algérienne en France, FAF**
Moussa Kraouche: [address unknown]
Close to the Islamic radical movement, FIS, in Algeria.　»95

✿ **Jeunesse sportive culturelle algérienne et de loisirs de Givors** *(Givors Algerian Youth for Sport, Culture and Leisure)*
1 quai Rosenberg, 69700 Givors　　　　　　　　　»89

• **Rassemblement des Etudiants Algériens en Europe, REALE** *(Union of Algerian Students in Europe)*
161 bis rue Saint-Jacques, 75005 Paris
Advocacy on student issues. See Reperes, p137.　　»89

• **Solidarité-Femmes-Algérie, SOFA** *(Algeria Women's Solidarity)*
34 rue Pouchet, 75017 Paris
Self-expression for Algerian women.　　　　　　　»90

✿ **Union des Etudiants Algériens de Nantes**
33 rue de la Branchoire, 44800 Saint-Herblan　　　»89

◉ **GERMANY** *49*

• **Front islamique du salut, FIS** *(Islamic Salvation Front)* al-Jabha al-Islamiya li-Inqadh
Rabah Kebir, spokesman: [address unknown]
Radical Islamist opposition group, outlawed in Algeria. Many of its leaders live in exile, including some in Germany.　»94

◉ **ITALY** *39*

✿ **Associazione Algerina** *(Algerian Association)* also known as Associazione Cittadini Algerini
Hamidi Arezki: via Rigola 25, 40133 Bologna; *t* (051) 619 1401
Social and cultural activities.　　　　　　　　　»94

• **Associazione Italia-Algeria**
viale Carso 67, 00195 Roma; *t* (06) 359 9787
International friendship, aid to immigrants.　　　　»90

◉ **UNITED KINGDOM** *44*

• **Algerian Community Association**
c/o Union Chapel, The Vestry, Compton Avenue, London N1 2XD; *t* (0956) 453903　　　　　　　　　　　»96

• **Algerian Refugee Council**
Dr Mohammed Sekkoum: Twelve Acres Reception Centre, 393 Highbury Quadrant, London N5; *t* (0956) 911883
Welfare of refugees; advice, representation.　　　»96

• **Front islamique du salut, FIS** *(Islamic Salvation Front)* al-Jabha al-Islamiya li-Inqadh
Mohammed Dnini/Jaafer al Hawari: [address unknown] Southall, London
Islamist movement, founded in 1989 and later banned; many leading members live in exile, including Dnini, who edited its weekly newspaper. Bulletin, *The Enlightenment*.　　»95

AMERICAN

see Canadian, Caribbean, Central American, Latin American, Puerto Rican, Québécois, United States

ANGLO-CARIBBEAN

see also African Caribbean, Afro-Caribbean, Barbadian, Black, Caribbean, Dominican, Jamaican, Kittitian, Montserrat, Trinidadian and Tobagan, Vincentian, West Indian

◉ **UNITED KINGDOM** *44*

• **Joint Council for Anglo-Caribbean Churches**
Rev. Esme Beswick: 6 Leasowes Road, Leyton, London E10 7BE; *t* (0181) 539 3828　　　　　　　　　»90

• **United Anglo-Caribbean Society**
N.G. Doyley: Berrymede Middle School Annexe, Osborne Road, London W3 8SJ　　　　　　　　　　　»92

ANGOLAN

see also African, Central African, Portuguese

◉ **BELGIUM** *32*

• **Association Socio-Culturelle des Angolais, ASCA** *(Angolan Social and Cultural Association)*
R. Nsumbu Mbala: Rue de l'Alliance 30, 1030 Bruxelles; *t* (02) 217 8438
Cultural and social.　　　　　　　　　　　　　»94

◉ **PORTUGAL** *351*

• **Associação Amigos da Mulher Angolana, AAMA** *(Society of Friends of Angolan Women)*
Aurora Antónia Martins Verdades: Rua General Ferreira Martins Algés, 1495 Lisboa; *t* (01) 410 4778, 410 0098
Social and cultural activities for Angolan migrant women. *Respontar de Angola* (4/yr).　　　　　　　　»94

• **Associação de Amizade Portugal-Angola** *(Portugal-Angola Friendship Association)*
Rua Portas de Santo Antão 117-2°, 1100 Lisboa　　»93

• **Associação de Coordenação e Integracão dos Migrantes Angolanos, ACIMA** *(Association for the Co-ordination and Integration of Angolan Migrants)*
Januario Domingos: Sapateiros 123-2°, 1100 Lisboa　»94

• **Associação Cultural e Recreativa Angolana, ACRA** *(Angolan Cultural and Leisure Association)*
João Cordeiro: Lote 250, 3°B, Rua Adães Bermudes, 1900 Lisboa; *t* (01) 859 3627
Jorge Emanuel Gomes Da Silva. Cultural, recreational and social activities, youth work.　　　　　　　　　»94

✿ ≡ António José Soares Saraíva: Póvoa de Santo Adrião, Praceta João Vilarett 5 2-E, 2675 Odivelas　　　»94

• **Associação de Espoliados de Angola** *(Association of Dispossessed of Angola)*
Calçada Palma Baixo 25 r/c E, Lisboa; *t* (01) 726 1183　»90

✿ **Associação de Estudantes Angolanos** *(Angolan Student Association)*
Sá Bandeira 538-1°, 4000 Porto; *t* (02) 200 6910　　»94

✿ **Casa de Angola do Algarve** *(Algarve Angolan Centre)*
Silva Carvalho: Rua da Trinidade 12-1° E, 8000 Faro
Migrant welfare, housing, cultural interests.　　　　»94

✿ **Grupo Desportivo Assomada**
Rolando Helder Sequeira Miranda: Alto de Santa Catarina, Rua Dois 124, 1495 Lisboa; *t* (01) 415 1456
Sports and social club.　　　　　　　　　　　»94

• **Liga dos Angolanos e Amigos de Angola, LIANGOLA** *(League of Angolans and Friends of Angola)*
Rua Victor Cordon 45b, 1200 Lisboa; *t* (01) 901221
See also LIAFRICA, p4.　　　　　　　　　　　»94

◉ **UNITED KINGDOM** *44*

Angola Emergency Campaign, AEC: see Mozambique Angola Committee, p91

• **Angolan Action and Fraternity Group**
171 Dumbarton Court, Brixton Hill, London SW2　　»88

ANGUILLAN

see African Caribbean, Afro-Caribbean, Anglo-Caribbean, Caribbean, Kittitian, West Indian

ANTILLEAN

here meaning the Netherlands Antilles and Aruba; see also African Caribbean, Afro-Caribbean, Anglo-Caribbean, Caribbean, Cuban, Dominican Republic, Dutch, French: DOM/TOM, Guadeloupean, Latin American, Puerto Rican, West Indian

◉ **NETHERLANDS** *31*

Fundashon pa Organisashonnan Regional y Sentral Antiano y Arubano, FORSA; landelijk steunpunt Antillianen en Arubanen Nederland (Foundation for Regional and Central Antillean and Aruban Groups): until 1995 this body was the major umbrella group for migrants from the Dutch-speaking Caribbean, but in that year it and eight other groups merged to create what is now FORUM—Instituut voor Multiculturele Ontwikkeling; see p146.

✧ **Internationaal Vrouwen Centrum Antillianen** *(International Antillean Women's Centre)*
E.L. Adriaan: Burchstraat 49, 6511 RG Nijmegen »90
● **Stichting Landelijke Inspraakorgaan Antillianen en Arubanen**, LIA *(National Antillean & Aruban Representation Foundation)*
R.A.M. Pieters/Carine H.G. Aben: Huygensstraat 5, 2515 BC Den Haag; *t* (070) 380 3301, *f* 388 9976
Umbrella group for organisations of the Dutch Caribbean communities; represented in the LAO forum, p146. »95
● **Plataforma di Organisaschonnan Antiano e Arubano**, POA *(Platform of Antillean and Aruban Organisations)*
Richard Son, President: Voorstraat 36-38, 3512 AP Utrecht; *t* (030) 231 7734
Umbrella group representing Antillean-born, Papiamento-speaking minority; employment, welfare issues. »90

ARAB; ARABIC

see also African, Algerian, Beur, Egyptian, Iraqi, Islamic, Israeli, Jordanian, Kuwaiti, Lebanese, Libyan, Maghrebi, Middle Eastern, Moroccan, North African, Palestinian, Saudi Arabian, Saharan/Sahrawi, Sudanese, Syrian, Tunisian, Yemeni

◎ AUSTRIA 43

▌**European Union of Arabic and Islamic Scholars**: Institut für Orientalistik
Dr Arne Ambros, Secretary: Liebiggasse 6, 1010 Wien; *t* (01) 40103 2593
Learned society founded 1964; 220 members; congresses, promotion of research. »93

◎ BELGIUM 32

✧ **Centre Arabe d'Accueil et d'Information** *(Arab Reception and Information Centre)*
Rue Haute 135, 1000 Bruxelles; *t* (02) 513 0014
Advice, counselling, education, training, employment; settlement assistance. »94
● **Centre Arabe de l'Art et de la Littérature**, CAAL
Hawa Djabali: Rue du Méridien 20, 1030 Bruxelles; *t* (02) 218 6474
Cultural activities, research and documentation. »94
✧ **Centre de Service de la Docherie** also known as Maison Arabe de Culture Ouvrière
Hamid Bidou: Rue Léon Dubois 201, 6030 Charleroi; *t* (071) 323760
Culture, sport, youth integration. »94
✧ *El Kalima*
Marianne Goffoel: Rue du Midi 69, 1000 Bruxelles; *t* (02) 511 8217
Magazine. »94

◎ FRANCE 33

✧ *al-Watan al-Arabi*
[address unknown] Paris
Newspaper. »94
● **Association arabe des droits de l'homme**, ASADH *(Arab Association for Human Rights)*
[address unknown] »90
✧ **Association culturelle franco-arabe Roanne** *(Franco-Arab Cultural Association of Roanne)*
M. Grisot: 2 rue Villa-Commellis, 42120 Commelle-Vernay »89
✧ **Association culturelle et de promotion de la langue arabe** *(Cultural Association for the Promotion of Arabic)*
36 rue Michel-de-l'Hospital, 78300 Poissy
Youth activities; Arabic lessons; inter-cultural friendship. »89
● **Association de défense des droits de l'homme et des libertés démocratiques dans le monde arabe**, ADHMA *(Society for Human Rights and Democratic Freedoms in the Arab World)*
[address unknown] Paris
Campaigns on human rights issues in Arab countries, and rights of Arab migrants in France. »91
✧ **Association Educative et Culturelle de la Langue Arabe**, AECLA *(Arabic Language Educational and Cultural Society)*
6 rue Jules-Vallès, n° 4, 76800 St-Etienne-du-Rouvray »89
● **Association Euro-Arabe pour le Travail et l'Echange**, AETE *(Euro-Arab Association for Work and Exchange)*
[address unknown] »90
✧ **Association musulmane culturelle d'enseignement de langue arabe de La Duchère** *(La Duchère Muslim Cultural Society for Teaching Arabic)*
548 La Sauvegarde, La Duchère, 69009 Lyon
Arabic teaching, Koranic education, religious activities. »90

● **Association pour la promotion de l'enseignement de la langue arabe en France**, APPELAF
149 rue Ordener, 75018 Paris »90
✧ **Association des Travailleurs Arabes du Mans et de la Sarthe**, ATAMS *(Arab Workers' Association of Le Mans & the Sarthe)*
Driss Nabi: Centre Social, boulevard des Glonnières, 72100 Le Mans; *t* (1) 4386 1367
Advice, cultural promotion, anti-racism. *ATAM info*. »94
✧ **Centre de Culture et d'Information sur le Monde Arabe**
38 boulevard de Strasbourg, 13003 Marseille; *t* 9150 4494, 9148 4361 »94
✧ **Comité des Femmes Arabes Immigrées** *(Committee of Immigrant Arab Women)*
21 place des Chanons, 57000 Metz »90
✧ **El Hawakati Le Conteur** *(The Storyteller Cultural Centre)*
151 avenue Jean-Jaurès, 75019 Paris
Cinema, theatre, arts, encounters between Palestinian and Arab artists and those of the West. »89
● **Institut du Monde Arabe**, IMA *(Arab World Institute)*
Edgard Pisani: 1 rue Fossés-St-Bernard, 75005 Paris; *t* (1) 4051 3838, *f* 4354 7645
Research on Arab culture, societies and history. *Bulletin IMA*, *Répertoire sur le monde arabe*. »94
✧ **Jeunes Arabes de Lyon et Banlieue**, JALB *(Arab Youth of Lyons and District)* also known as Association d'Expression des Jeunes Immigrés
Mona Kabounny: 254 rue Du Guesclin, 69003 Lyon Cedex 03; *t* 7860 3462, *f* 7895 0167
Youth welfare, integration; legal advice, anti-racist activity. »94

◎ IRELAND 353

● **Irish Arab Society**
PO Box 2052, 79 Merrion Square, Dublin 2; *t* (01) 676 2959
Friendship, solidarity. »90

◎ ITALY 39

✧ **Associazione Donne Arabe e Straniere in Emilia Romagna**, ADASER *(Emilia Romagna Society of Arab & Foreign Women)*
Dr Zeinab El Saddany: via Ripa Inferiore 14, 41013 Castelfranco Emilia, MO; *t* (059) 209446
Anti-racism; cultural/social activities for migrant women. »94
✧ **Associazione Immigrati Arabi**
c/o C. Club, via Galeno 6, 20126 Milano; *t* (02) 809100 »90
● **Associazione Nazionale di Amicizia e di Cooperazione Italo-Araba** *(Society for Italo-Arab Friendship and Co-operation)*
Emo Egoli: via Di Parione 44, 00186 Roma; *t* (06) 687 7326, 686 1060, *f* 689 3252
International friendship, aid to immigrants and refugees. »94
✧ **Centro Comunità Araba**, CCA *(Arab Community Centre)*
Kamil Elmahdi: via Lorenzo il Magnifico 68, 50100 Firenze; *t* (055) 489853
Social and cultural centre, advice, representation; anti-discrimination campaigns. »94
✧ **Centro Culturale Italo-Arabo** *(Italo-Arab Cultural Centre)*
c/o Cambridge Institute, corso Vittorio Emanuele 108, 10121 Torino; *t* (011) 539171
Language, culture. »90
✧ **Centro per le Relazioni Italo-Arabe**
Francesco Mezzalama: via Alberto Caroncini 19, 00197 Roma; *t* (06) 807 7291, 807 8029
Promotion/study of Italo-Arab cultural and political relations. See Istituto per l'Oriente C.A. Nallio, p239. *Levante* (4/yr). »94

◎ NETHERLANDS 31

● **Landelijke Vereniging van Alleenstaande Arabische Vrouwen**, LVAAV *(National Union of Independent Arab Women)*
Bredestraat 168, 6543 ZZ Nijmegen; *t* (024) 373 2256 (?)
Counselling, legal advice, personal development; research and information. »95

◎ SPAIN 34

✧ **Asociación de Amistad Hispano-Arabe** *(Spanish-Arab Friendship Association)*
calle Príncipe de Vergara 57, Madrid »94
✧ **Asociación Española de Amistad con los Pueblos Arabes Bayt Al-Thaqafa**, AEAPA *(Spanish-Arab Friendship Society)*
Teresa Losada Campos: carrer Princesa 14-1° 2ª, 08003 Barcelona, Catalunya; *t* (93) 319 8869
International/inter-cultural friendship, welfare of Arabs. »94
✧ **Asociación de Estudio del Mundo Arabe Contemporáneo y la Cooperación**, AEMACC *(Association for Contemporary Arab Studies and Co-operation)*
plaça de Sant Toc 17, 46900 Torrent, País Valencia »94

✿ Asociación Socio-Cultural Arabe
Pintorería 33 b., 01001 Vitoria/Gasteiz; *t* (945) 241867   »94
✿ Escuela de Estudios Arabes *(School of Arab Studies)*
Luis Molina Martínez: Cuesta del Chapiz 22, 18010 Granada;
t (958) 222290, 223459, *f* 224754   »94
● Instituto Hispano-Arabe de Cultura *(Spanish-Arab Cultural
Institute)* and Instituto de Cooperación con el Mundo Arabe
Miguel Angel Moratinos: paseo de Juan XXIII 5, 28040
Madrid; *t* (91) 583 8100, 234 3462
Funded through official Agencia Española de Cooperación
Internacional, p212; cultural exchanges with Arab countries,
research, documentation. *Awraq* (1/yr); *Arabismo* (3/yr). »94

◎ **UNITED KINGDOM** 44

● Anglo-Arab Association
D.R. Collard, Chief Executive: 21 Collingham Road, London
SW5 0NU; *t* (0171) 373 8414
Founded 1946.   »90
✿ Arab Advice and Information Bureau and Arab Line
Aboud Tuma: 3 James Cameron House, Castlehaven Road,
London NW1 8QW; *t* (0171) 436 1375
Advice, casework with refugees and immigrants. Arab Line
telephone counselling service.   »92
● Arab Studies Society London Office
29 Enford Street, London W1 1DG; *t* (0171) 724 7201   »90
● Arab Women's Association
London House, Kensington High Street, London W8; *t* (0171)
376 0951   »90
● Arab Women's Group
4 Springvale Terrace, London W14 0AE; *t* (0171) 371 6833
Arab feminism; information, welfare of migrant women. »94
● Arab Workers' Union
Mount Pleasant Centre, Balsall Heath, Birmingham B12   »90
✿ Arabic Mosque
275 Staniforth Road, Sheffield S9; *t* (0114) 244 6179
Mosque for Yemeni and other Arabic-speaking Muslims.   »94
✿ Arabic Speaking Community
Dr Najla al-Wahabi: 11 Denmark Road, Portslade, Brighton
BN4 1GJ; *t* (01273) 422997   »94
● Centre for Arab Gulf Studies
University of Exeter, Exeter EX4 4QJ   »95
● Council for the Advancement of Arab-British Understanding,
CAABU
Chris Doyle: 21 Collingham Road, London SW5 0NU   »95
● Middle East Broadcasting Centre, MBC
80 Silverthorne Road, Battersea, London SW8 3XA
Satellite television company.   »95
✿ Oxford Arab Group
[address unknown] Oxford   »90
● *Voice of the Arab World*
Ann Morris, Editor: 15a Lowndes Street, London SW1   »94
✿ West Sussex Arabic Community
Majeed Tawil: 52 South Farm Road, Worthing BN14 7AE;
t (01903) 202981   »94

ARGENTINIAN

see also Falkland Islands (Islas Malvinas), Latin American

◎ **ITALY** 39

✿ Argentina Democrática
José Luis Tagliaferro: via Bagutta 12, 20121 Milano;
t (02) 780801
Training, employment, cultural interests of Argentinians. »94
✿ Associazione Argentini in Campania
via Lucullo 104, 80070 Baia   »90
✿ Associazione Italia-Argentina, ASSIA
M. Arias: [address uncertain] via Greve 105, 00146 Roma;
t (06) 550 2347, *f* 718 0709
Welfare of immigrants and Italian emigrants. Also listed
(1990) at via Elio Andrisco 34, 00178 Roma, *t* 677 9908.»94
✿ Associazione Residenti Argentini
Emilia Romagna: via Saffi 72, 40059 Milano   »90
✿ ≡ via Bruno Buozzi 83, 20099 Sesto San Giovanni   »90
✿ Comunità Argentina
via Montenero 2a, 01100 Viterbo   »90
● Comunità Italo-Argentina *(Italo-Argentinian Community)*
CSER, via Calandrelli 11, 00153 Roma   »90

◎ **SPAIN** 34

● Asociación Argentina de Derechos Humanos *(Argentinian
Human Rights Association)*
Hortaleza 19-1° dcha, 28004 Madrid; *t* (91) 435 6550   »94

● Asociación Cultural Club Argentino
Apd° de Correos 14709, 28000 Madrid; *t* (91) 455 1125 »87
✿ Casa Retruco Solidaridad con Argentina *(Answer Back
House—Solidarity with Argentina)*
Gregoria Marín: Iglesia 23, 08860 Castel de Fels; *t* (93)
636 2660, *f* 665 4432
Also at carrer Contesa de Sobradiel 1, ent. 2, 08200
Barcelona, *t* 301 7476. *Boletín*.   »94
✿ Centro Argentino de Asturias *(Asturias Argentine Centre)*
calle Juan Alvargonzález 85, Gijón, Asturias   »87
✿ Centro de Intercambio Cultural Argentino-Catalán
(Argentine-Catalan Cultural Exchange Centre)
carrer Valencia 302, 08009 Barcelona; *t* (93) 232 9312   »87

◎ **UNITED KINGDOM** 44

● Anglo-Argentine Society
J.B. Lee, Honorary Secretary: 2 Belgrave Square, London
SW1X 8PJ; *t* (0171) 235 9505
Culture, international friendship; founded 1948.   »95

ARMENIAN

see also Asian, Assyrian, Turkish

◎ **BELGIUM** 32

✿ Eglise Arménienne Apostolique *(Armenian Apostolic Church)*
Rue Kindermans 1a, 1050 Bruxelles   »90

◎ **DENMARK** 45

✿ Armensk Kulturforening *(Armenian Culture Society)*
[address uncertain] Valby Langgade 122, 2500 Valby   »90
✿ Assurisk-Armensk Forening i Horsens *(Horsens Armenian-
Assyrian Society)*
Verej Nazarian: Bakkesvinget 28-1, 8700 Horsens
Armenian and Assyrian-rite Christians; culture, employment,
training, information.   »94

◎ **FRANCE** 33

✿ Association arménienne d'aide sociale
77 rue La Fayette, 75009 Paris; *t* (1) 4878 0299, 4281
1780, *f* 4280 6145
Welfare of Armenian exiles.   »90
● La Croix Bleu des Arméniens de France *(French Armenian
Blue Cross)*
17 rue Bleue, 75009 Paris; *t* (1) 4824 4657
Refugee welfare.   »90
✿ Maison de la culture arménienne *(House of Armenian Culture)*
17 rue Bleue, 75009 Paris; *t* (1) 4824 6389
Armenian art, literature, music. See also Croix Bleue des
Arméniens en France, above.   »90
● Solidarité franco arménienne *(French Armenian Solidarity)*
6 rue de Trétaigne, 75018 Paris; *t* (1) 4606 1590
National liberation, refugee assistance.   »90
● Union Culturelle Française des Arméniens de France,
UCFAF *(Cultural Union of Armenians in France)*
6 cité Wauxhall, 75010 Paris; *t* (1) 4208 7649
Social and cultural activities.   »90

◎ **GERMANY** 49

● Verband Armenischer Vereinigungen in der Bundesrepublik
Deutschland, VAVBD *(League of Armenian Societies in the
Federal Republic of Germany)*
V.M. Hakobians: Donnerschweerstraße 8, 26123 Oldenburg;
t (0441) 83181, *f* 885 9250   »94

◎ **GREECE** 30

● Armenian Popular Movement, APM
Kristina Bacharian: Meltiou Vassiliou 26, Neos Kosmos,
11744 Athinai; *t* (01) 901 2312
Formed 1982; defence of Armenian national identity, social
and cultural activities for Armenian migrants.   »94

◎ **UNITED KINGDOM** 44

● Armenian Aid
25 Cheniston Gardens, London W8; *t* (0171) 937 9452
Solidarity with Armenia.   »90
● Armenian Relief Society of Great Britain
Silva Dadourian, Chairwoman: West End Road, Northolt,
Middlesex; *t* (0181) 998 1545
Seeks self-determination for the Armenian people; solidarity
with Armenians in Nagorno-Karabakh.   »92

- Centre for Armenian Information and Advice, CAIA
Misak Ohanian: [address uncertain] Room 4, Capital House, Market Place, London W3 6QS; t (0181) 992 4621, 993 8953, f 993 8953
Address also listed (1994) as 105a Mill Hill Road, London W3 8JF. Advice, casework with refugees; information on Armenia. *Armenian Voice* (4/yr).   »94
- Popular Movement for the Liberation of Armenia
137a High Street, London W3   »90

ARYA SAMAJ

see Hindu

ASIAN

see also Afghan, Armenian, Australian, Bangladeshi, Bengali, Black, Burmese, Cambodian, Chinese, Comoros, East African, Filipino, Goan, Gujarati, Hindi, Hindu, Hmong, Indian, Indonesian, Iranian, Iraqi, Islamic, Jain, Japanese, Kashmiri, Khmer, Korean, Laotian, Malaysian, Mauritian, Middle Eastern, Moluccan, Mongolian, Nepalese, New Zealand, Pacific, Pakistani, Punjabi, Seychellois, Sikh, South-East Asian, Sri Lankan, Tamil, Thai, Tibetan, Turkish, Urdu, Vietnamese

⊙ FRANCE *33*

✧ Amitiés France-Asie *(France-Asia Friendship)*
1047 rue de Viviers, 34830 Clapiers
French-Asian humanitarian, social and cultural contact.   »89
- Association des amitiés asiatiques, AAA *(Asian Friendships)*
24 rue de 4-Septembre, 75002 Paris
Conditions for Asians in France, including refugees.   »89
✧ Association culturelle et artistique des Asiates de France
5 rue du 8-Mai-1945, 93260 Les Lilas
Social, cultural, artistic activities; French classes.   »89
- Association Eurasia
16 rue Elzévir, 75003 Paris; t (1) 4277 1356
Cultural interaction.   »90
- Association Euro-Asie d'Education et des Echanges Culturels *(Euro-Asian Education and Cultural Exchange Society)*
13 rue Rampal, 75019 Paris   »89
✧ Centre France Asie, CFA or CEFRA *(France-Asia Centre)*
Joseph Parais: 16 rue Royer Collard, 75005 Paris; t (1) 4325 7764
Cultural and social activities for migrants and refugees, international issues.   »94
✧ Foyer d'Etudiants Asiatiques *(Asian Students' House)*
Jean Hirigoyen: 28 rue de Babylone, 75007 Paris; t (1) 4549 2130   »94

⊙ GERMANY *49*

✧ South Asia Bureau
Kiefernstraße 45, 5600 Wuppertal 2   »93

⊙ ITALY *39*

✧ United Asian Workers' Association
[address uncertain] via Federico Mastrigli 15, Roma
Also listed (1990) as via Rocca Romana 5, or via Montebello 22, 00100 Roma. Mainly Indian membership.   »90

⊙ UNITED KINGDOM *44*

- ADiTi: The National Organisation of South Asian Dance
Sue Hayton, Acting Director: Willowfield Street, Bradford BD7 2AH; t (01274) 522059
Communicates, lobbies and advocates on behalf of South Asian dance.   »95
- All-Asia Christian Consultative Group
Charles Ambrose Watson, Secretary: 33 Mitcham Road, Ilford IG3 8QW; t (0181) 472 8947
Meetings, conferences.   »90
- Alliance of Asian Christians, AAC
Raj Patel/Pradip Sudra: 194 London Road, Leicester LE2 1ND; t (0116) 254 0870
Founded 1990; religious fellowship, social meetings.   »90
✧ Anglo-Asian Women's Association, AAWA, and Anglo-Asian Cultural Association, AACA
25 Evershot Road, Finsbury Park, London N4 3DG; t (0171) 272 7031
The AAWA represents the interests of Asian, Turkish and African women in Islington. See also Bazmi-i-Tafreeh and Islamic Educational Welfare Association, both p56.   »94

✧ Anjuman-e-Khawateen Centre; Cheetham Asian Women's Association; Cheetham Asian Girls Project
Masarat Shafi: Temple School Nursery Annexe, Smedley St, Cheetham, Manchester M8 8UN; t (0161) 205 9124
Educational and leisure activities, social support for Asian (mainly Pakistani Muslim) women and girls.   »93
✧ Ankur Brent Asian Youth Service
c/o HAC, 2 Tavistock Road, Harlesden, London NW10 4ND; t (0181) 961 3230   »90
✧ Apna Ghar
Sudarshan Bhuhi: Community Links, Canning Town Public Hall, 105 Barking Road, London E16 4HQ
Domestic violence advice, other services to women.   »96
✧ Apna Ghar Day Care Centre
John Knight, Support Services Manager: Age Concern, 4 King Street, Blackburn BB2 2DN; t (01254) 672592   »95
✧ ASHA Asian Women's Aid
ASHA Resource Centre, 27 Santley Street, London SW4 7QF; t (0171) 737 5901, 274 8854
Refuge and support for women facing domestic violence. »94
✧ Ashiana Housing Association, formerly Asian Special Housing Initiative Agency
104-06 Drake St, Rochdale OL16 1PQ; t (01706) 712252
Social housing association, 300 properties in North-West. »95
✧ Ashiana Project
Greater London House, 547-551 High Road, Leytonstone, London E11 4BT; t c/o (0181) 556 6065
Provides temporary supportive safe housing for young south Asian women who have experienced domestic violence.   »96
✧ ASIAN Ltd, formerly Newham Advice Service
Shenaz Bhatti: 115 Wakefield Street, East Ham, London E6 1LG; t (0181) 503 5088, f 471 8303
General advice centre, largely ethnic minority clientele.   »95
✧ Asian Action Group
115-117 Ealing Rd, Wembley HA0 4BP; t (0181) 900 0478
Education, youth integration, culture.   »94
✧ ≡ Philip Matthews: 30 Willoughby Road, London N8 0JG »96
✧ Asian Arts Group
Ali Zaidi: 130 Plashet Road, Upton Park, London E13 0QS; t (0181) 471 8404   »91
✧ Asian Association
842 Coventry Road, Small Heath, Birmingham B10   »90
✧ Asian Bookshop
45 Grafton Way, London W1   »91
✧ Asian Centre
8 Caxton Road, Haringey, London N22; t (0181) 889 6938, 889 8981   »95
✧ Asian Chaplaincy
Fr Anthony Furtado: 48 Great Peter Street, London SW1; t (0171) 222 2895
Church service founded 1981; serves Indian, Pakistani, Filipino, Chinese, Sri Lankan and other Asian Catholics.   »91
- *Asian Chronicle*
Anwar Khalid, Editor: 30 Featherstone Road, Southall UB2 5AB; t (0181) 574 1414
Newspaper (52/yr). See also *Punjab Times*, p102.   »88
✧ Asian Community Action Group
Ram Mittal, Secretary: 322a Brixton Rd, London SW9 7AA; t (0171) 733 7494, 733 7495
Founded 1978; welfare rights, housing, immigration advice; casework; elderly group, women and youth activities, general community development work, anti-racism.   »94
- Asian Congress on Local Affairs
[address unknown] London   »96
✧ Asian Dance Group
Derval Singh: 390 Rotton Park Road, Birmingham B16   »90
- Asian Dub Foundation
Aniruddha Das: [address unknown]
Anti-racism; see Community Music Education Project, p244.»95
✧ Asian Elderly Group of Merton, AEGM
28 St George's Road, Wimbledon, London SW19 4DP
Caring service, liaison with statutory and other bodies.   »94
- *Asian Express*
M.V. Kaviraj, Editor: Suite 411, International Press Centre, 76 Shoe Lane, London EC4A 3JB; t (0171) 353 0186
Magazine (12/yr).   »88
- Asian Family Counselling Service
Kulbir Randhawa: [address unknown] London   »95
- ≡ and National Asian Marriage Guidance Council: 2nd floor, Rooms 4/5, Equity Chambers, 40 Piccadilly, Bradford BD1 3NN; t (01274) 720486
Counselling, conciliation, training; focus on issues of special concern to Asian families, including arranged marriage.   »90
- The Asian Forum: Confederation of Asian Organisations
63 Montpelier Rd, London SE15 2HD; t (0171) 639 5168 »94

✿ Asian Girls' Club
Stanway Centre, Stanmore Road, Birmingham B16   »90
✿ Asian Girls' Project
8 Manor Gdns, London N7; t (0171) 263 6270, 272 4231»94
✿ Asian Health Awareness Project
229 Long Elmes, Harrow HA3 6LE; t (0181) 421 4233,
f 861 1473
Health promotion in the local Asian community; liaison with
local health and social services providers. See WHIA, p44.»94
✿ Asian Health Group
Sohail Elahi/Shirley Jones: [address unknown] Bristol;
t (0117) 955 6098, 954 8621
Voluntary organisation; developing elder day care centre. »94
• Asian Herald and Jagaran News; Nutan Din
Dr M. Taludkar, Editor: Wickham House, 10 Cleveland Way,
London E1 4TR; t (0171) 790 2424 ext 12
Asian community newspaper (52/yr) and magazines.   »90
• Asian Herald
S. Mazumdar, Editor: 20 Orchard Avenue, London N14 4ND;
t (0181) 886 4231
Periodical (4/yr) for Bengali and other Asian communities.
See also Probashi Samachar, p19.   »88
✿ Asian House Cultural Association
21 Yonge Road, Finsbury Park, London N4   »94
✿ Asian Mental Health Team
Mental Health Resource Centre, 19 Paradise Street, Oxford
OX1 1LD; t (01865) 728981
Works on mental health issues with Asian communities and
voluntary groups; training, translation of information. »94
✿ Asian Music Circuit
Ground Floor Unit F, 33-34 Warple Way, London W3 0RG
Charity promoting Asian music throughout the UK.   »94
• Asian Observer
J.S. Sachar, Editor: 47 Beatyville Gardens, Barkingside, Ilford
IG6 1JW; t (0181) 550 3745
Magazine (12/yr).   »88
• Asian People with Disabilities Alliance, APDA
Ground Floor, Willesden Hospital, Harlesden Road, London
NW10 3RY; t (0181) 459 5793
Advice, casework, advocacy, tribunal representation for
disabled people and their carers and families.   »93
• Asian People's National Association, APNA
Dr Tariq Madood, Chairman: [address unknown] Oxford   »90
✿ Asian Resource Centre, ARC
Harmesh Lakha/Muhammed Idrish: 101 Villa Road,
Handsworth, Birmingham B19 1NH; t (0121) 551 4518,
523 0580, f 554 4553
Community-based social welfare agency. Includes women's
hostel; sheltered housing, services to elders; immigration
advice, counselling, information and support services. »94
✿ ≡ 229 Seven Sisters Road, London N4 2DA; t (0171)
263 3182   »93
✿ ≡ Jarnail Flora: MacBean Centre, LEB Building, MacBean
Street, London SE18 6LW; t (0181) 854 1188
Information, advice, welfare work on immigration and other
matters, covering Eltham and Woolwich.   »94
✿ Asian Resource Project
Khela: 58-60 Waterloo Road, Smethwick, Sandwell, West
Midlands; t (0121) 558 5648
Information, documentation, welfare advice.   »94
✿ Asian Sheltered Residential Accommodation, ASRA
Unit 15, Arches Industrial Estate, Spon End, Coventry,
Warwickshire; t (01203) 715221   »90
✿ ≡ Parpinder Dhatt: [address unknown] Smethwick, W. Mids.
Includes Asian Women's Health Initiative. See also ASRA in
London and Leicester, right.   »96
✿ Asian Sound Radio
Shujat Ali: PO Box 63, North District Office, Manchester
M8 7EN; t (0161) 740 2242
Programmes in Bengali, English, Gujerati, Hindi, Punjabi and
Urdu.   »93
• Asian Students Christian Trust
228 Jessop Road, Pin Green, Stevenage SG1; t (01438)
364044   »90
• Asian Teachers' Association
180 Plants Brooke Road, Sutton Coldfield, West Midlands
Multi-cultural educational practice, career development. »90
• Asian Times: Hansib Publishing Ltd
Prakash Singh, Editor: Tower House, 139-149 Fonthill Road,
London N4 3HF; t (0171) 281 1191, f 263 9656
Arif Ali publisher. General Asian newspaper (52/yr) founded
1983. See also Caribbean Times, p27.   »95
• The Asian Weekly
1a The Tower, Merrick Road, Southall UB2 4AU; t (0181)
569 6440   »93

✿ Asian Welfare Association
90 Whitebarn Lane, Dagenham RM10 9LP; t (0181) 592 3878
Social welfare, employment issues, anti-racism.   »94
✿ Asian Women and Girls Cultural Project
Raksha Vashi: 422 Stockport Road, Longsight, Manchester
M13; t (0161) 234 3305
Educational, social and leisure facility; counselling,
playschemes, Urdu classes.   »93
• Asian Women Writers' Collective
76 Hindle House, Arcola Street, London E8 2DX; t (0171)
241 4205
Formed 1984; holds workshops in London, Manchester,
Sheffield, Luton and Birmingham.   »91
✿ Asian Women's Adhikar Association, AWAAZ: also known
as AWAAZ Asian Women's Advice Centre
[address unknown] Wolverhampton; t (01902) 29414
Advice, counselling and support for Asian women.   »95
• Asian Women's Advisory Service and Asian Women's
Support Group
31b Chatsworth Road, London E5 0LH; t (0181) 986 4804
Counselling, advice, health and welfare. Based in Asian
Women's Centre: see Asian Women's Association, below.»95
✿ Asian Women's Association, AWA
C. Bhatia: 40 Argyle Road, Ilford IG1 3SN
Aims to empower Asian women by providing them with
information, support and advocacy.   »94
✿ ≡ and Asian Women's Centre: 31b Chatsworth Road,
London E5 0LH; t (0181) 986 4804   »95
✿ ≡ Jyotsna Pala: 72 High Street, Nuneaton CV11 5DA;
t (01203) 375639
Community organisation, immigration advice work on visa
rules, family reunification, primary purpose.   »93
✿ Asian Women's Health Group
Rukiya Kassim: Cheetham Community School, Haliwell Lane,
Manchester M13; t (0161) 740 1491 ext. 327
Health education, exercise and relaxation classes, liaison
with health services.   »93
Asian Women's Mental Health Service: see Creative Support
Ltd, p222
✿ Asian Women's Refuge
[address confidential] Hounslow TW3, Middlesex; t (0181)
572 8693, 893 4206
Refuge, counselling, educational and resettlement support for
women and children fleeing domestic violence.   »95
✿ Asian Women's Resource Centre
Brixton Enterprise Centre, Room 315, 442-444 Brixton Road,
London SW9 8EJ; t (0171) 274 4000
Research, information on issues affecting Asians in UK. »95
✿ ≡ and Asian Girls Project: 134 Minet Avenue, Harlesden,
London NW10 8AP; t (0181) 961 6549, 961 5701
Collective offering advice on immigration and citizenship,
women's rights, health issues including diabetes, HIV and
sexual health; advice and education, outreach work. »96
✿ Asian Women's Welfare Group
Ravat Amin: 40 Brentbridge Road, Fallowfield, Manchester
M14; t (0161) 434 3833, 881 2710
Health, welfare, educational and leisure activities from
Pakistani and other Asian women.   »93
✿ Asian Youth Movement
[address unknown]
Several groups of this name.   »90
✿ Asian Youth Project
[address unknown] Belgrave, Leicester
Youth centre serving Asian, Afro-Caribbean and white young
people in the Belgrave area.   »94
✿ ASRA Greater London Housing Association
Liv Singh: 239-241 Kennington Lane, London SE11 5QU;
t (0171) 793 8294
Specialist social housing organisation for Asian and other
people, with about 1,200 units in London and the home
counties; residential care, social and cultural support; runs
Asian Frail Elderly Scheme in south London.   »95
✿ ASRA Housing Association Ltd
The Director: 58 Earl Howe Street, Leicester LE2 0DI;
t (0116) 255 8121, f 255 7337
Social housing organisation for Asian elderly, families and
people with special needs.   »92
• Association of Blind Asians
322 Upper Street, Islington, London N1 2QX; t (0171)
226 1950   »95
✿ Association for East African Asians
480 Stockport Road, Longsight, Manchester M12; t (0161)
248 7112
Social and welfare activities, immigration advice, services to
elderly.   »93

✿ **Avon and Bristol Asian Women's Network**
c/o BBVS DU, The Inkworks, 20-22 Hepburn Road, St Pauls,
Bristol BS2 8UD; *t* (0117) 942 3960   »96
✿ **Awaaz**
PO Box 316, Sheffield S1 3EX; *t* (0114) 275 6951
National women's training project on issues of violence and
oppression as they affect Asian women living in Britain. See
also Asian Women's Adhikar Association, p13.   »90
✿ **Barnardo's Greater Manchester Asian Women's Project**
Sue Tracy: Barnardo's North West Division, 7 Lineside Close,
Liverpool L25 2UD; *t* (0151) 487 3857
Project founded 1995 to provide support and emergency
accommodation for Asian women and their dependent children
who are escaping violence in their homes.   »95
✿ **Barnet Asian Women's Association**
c/o Barnet REC, 1 Friern Park, North Finchley, London
N12 9DE; *t* (0181) 446 9897   »94
✿ **Basera Asian Women's Aid**
PO Box 1558, London N16 5JJ; *t* (0181) 800 7263
Provides refuge, counselling and other support services for
women and children threatened by domestic violence.   »95
✿ **Bassera Women's Project**
Sheena Hannon: PO Box 99a, Municipal Buildings,
Middlesbrough TS1 2QQ; *t* (01642) 246896, 263520
Accommodation, support and a telephone advice line for ethnic
minority women suffering violence or mental cruelty.   »95
✿ **Bazm-e-Adab Manchester** *(Manchester Literary Society)*
A.R. Ansari: 51 Birch Lane, Manchester M13 0WW;
t (0161) 224 2816
Promotion of Pakistani and other Asian poetry and literature;
organises an annual *musharia* (classical poetry convention).
Sajad (4/yr).   »93
✿ **Belgrave Baheno** including the Manushi Project
Rita Patel: 14 Melrose Street, Leicester LE4 6FA; *t* (0116)
266 7673
Voluntary organisation: holistic approach to Asian women's
needs; advice, research, domestic violence casework. The
Manushi Project supports women and children facing domestic
violence. Works mainly with Gujerati speakers.   »94
✿ **Bethnal Green Asian Children and Women's Association**
1 Hume House, Turin St, London E2; *t* (0171) 739 3498
Family welfare, women's rights.   »90
✿ **Bhavan**
[address confidential] London SW; *t* c/o (0181) 640 7652
(Sutton REC)
Refuge and support service for Asian women and their
dependent children who are escaping domestic violence.   »95
✿ **Brighton Asian Circle**
Chandrakant Mehta: 92 Osborne Road, Brighton BN1 6LW;
t (01273) 321716   »94
✿ **Bromley Asian Community Organisation** and Bromley
Muslim Council
Khalid Sharif, Chairman: 11 High Street, Penge, London SE20
7HJ; *t* (0181) 659 0640
Umbrella group for Asian voluntary organisations. Muslim
Council represents local mosques, organises religious and
cultural events and takes part in interfaith activities.   »94
✿ **Camden United Asian Youth**
[address unknown] Camden, London NW1   »88
✿ **Centre for Asian Women**
39 Leswin Road, London N16; *t* (0171) 249 7597   »95
● **Department of East Asian Studies**
Prof. Don Rimmington/Dr Penny Francks: University of Leeds,
Leeds LS2 9JT; *t* (0113) 233 3470, 233 3464
Research, teaching on Japanese and East Asian affairs.   »95
✿ **Detached Asian Girls Project**
Farida Rawat/Janet Pahal: The Lodge, Daisy Bank Adult
Education Centre, Daisy Bank Rd, Victoria Park, Manchester
M14 5SL; *t* (0161) 224 6257
Welfare rights information, counselling service for Asian
women aged 14-25.   »93
● **Disabled Asian Women's Network, DAWN**
Rita Chadha: PO Box 658, Ilford IG1 3UE; *t* (0181) 518 4658
Volunteer support for mainly Gujerati, Hindi and Urdu-speaking
women with disabilities.   »95
✿ **Diwa Asian Women's Network, DAWN: and Yakeen Asian**
Women's Counselling Project *(Yakeen = trust)*
Krishna/Bhagya: 1 St Kilda's Road, Harrow HA1 1QD
Among other community development activities, DAWN has
established (1995) a counselling service.   »96
✿ **Dostiyo Asian Women and Girls Organisation**
Kalpana Desai: 26 Cloutsham Street, Northampton NN1 3LN;
t (01604) 601097
Health and social care support for Asian women, especially
those experiencing domestic crisis.   »95

✿ **Drummond Street Four Campaign**
c/o 1 Robert Street, London N1
Group formed to support young Asians who faced criminal
charges in 1994 after responding to a racial attack.   »94
● *Eastern Digest*
Paul Murphy: PO Box 1491, Moseley, Birmingham B14 7HA
Magazine.   »90
● *Eastern Eye*: Eastern Eye Publications Ltd
Sarwar Ahmed: 138-148 Cambridge Heath Road, London E1
5QJ; *t* (0171) 702 8012, *f* 702 9737
Youth-oriented news magazine (52/yr) founded 1989.   »95
✿ **Eastwards Trust (Hostels) Ltd**
[address unknown] Newham, London; *t* (0181) 514 7730
Sheltered housing for Asian elders in the London Borough of
Newham.   »94
✿ **Elderly Asian Development Group**
16 Blair Road, Whalley Range, Manchester M16 8NS
Health education, advice, social activities for over-50s.   »93
✿ **Enfield Saheli Asian Women's Centre**
The Co-ordinator: Edmonton Portacabin, Knights Lane,
Edmonton, London N9 0PD; *t* (0181) 986 4804
Seeks to empower Asian women of all ages by providing them
with information, guidance, support and access to equal
opportunities.   »95
● **Federation of Pathidar Associations**
26 Castlebar Park, Ealing, London W5 1BX; *t* (0181) 991
2199
Community group.   »89
✿ **Foleshill Asian Group**
Broad Heath Primary Community School, Broad Street,
Coventry CV6, Warwickshire; *t* (01203) 681230
Local community issues.   »90
✿ **Gosford Asian Group**
27 Wren Street, Coventry, Warwickshire; *t* (01203) 555497
Community welfare.   »90
✿ **Greenwich Asian Women's Refuge**
c/o London Borough of Greenwich Women's Unit, 45 Hare
Street, London SE18 6NE; *t* c/o (0181) 316 5964
Support and accommodation for Asian women and children
seeking refuge from domestic violence.   »92
✿ **Greenwich Asian Women's Resource Centre**
307 Plumstead High Street, Plumstead, London SE18 1JX;
t (0181) 311 6200
Welfare rights, housing, matrimonial law, Asian women's
issues; refuge for women at risk from domestic violence.   »94
✿ **Havan Project**
Manager: [address uncertain] PO Box 161, Leicester;
t (0116) 270 8938
Address from 1991. A charity providing temporary refuge,
counselling and after-care for young Asian women
experiencing domestic violence or family conflict.   »94
✿ **Hounslow Asian Women's Community Centre**
Mrs Trehan: [address unknown] Hounslow TW3, Middlesex;
t (0181) 572 2484, 572 0336
Social, cultural, welfare.   »92
✿ **Jagonari Asian Women's Educational Resource Centre**
183-185 Whitechapel Road, London E1; *t* (0171) 375 0520,
375 0615
Development of education for Asian women.   »90
✿ **Kala Sangam Academy of South Asian Performing Arts**
Dr S. Uphadhyaya: 29 Deighton Avenue, Snerburn in Elmet,
Leeds LS25 6BR
Teaching of Indian and South Asian music and dance.   »94
✿ **Kali Theatre Company**
59 Helix Road, London SW2; *t* (0181) 671 3559
Asian women's thatre company; runs workshops on writing,
drama skills and stage management.   »94
✿ **Kinara Asian Women's Refuge**
c/o Stonham Housing Association, 2nd Floor, High Point,
Thomas Street, Taunton, Somerset; *t* c/o (01823) 327388
A residential project established in 1994-95 to provide safe
and secure environment for Asian women and their children
escaping from domestic violence.   »95
✿ **Kiran Asian Women' Aid**
N. Mumtaz, Co-ordinator: PO Box 899, London E11 1AA
Refuge for Asian women and children experiencing domestic
violence.   »94
✿ **Kirklees Asian Women's Welfare Association**
[address confidential] West Yorkshire; *t* (01484) 426390
Provides emergency accommodation to Asian women and
children fleeing violence and abuse.   »94
✿ **Lohana Community North London**
Rasikbhai Thakrar, Honorary Treasurer: 13 Grange Avenue,
Stanmore HA7 2LG; *t* (0181) 907 2636, *f* 900 1134
Gunvantbhai Thacker, M. Raichura. Equal rights.   »94

✪ **Longsight and Moss Side Community Women's Project**
Mohina Puri: Church Buildings, 4a Anson Road, Longsight,
Manchester M13; *t* (0161) 225 8583
Counselling, training, social activities, information service.»93

✪ **Luton Women's Aid Asian Refuge**
Jenny Moody: c/o 144 Wardown Crescent, Luton LU2 7JU
Refuge for women and children fleeing domestic violence.»95

✪ **Midlands Asian Sports Forum**
Raj Patel/Jas Bains, Project Directors: c/o Salle Westwood,
Senior Lecturer, University of Leicester, Leicester
A research project addressing under-representation of Asian
youth in British soccer at higher levels. »94

● **National Association of Asian Youth**
[address unknown] Southall, Middlesex »90

✪ **Neesa Well Women Drop-in Project**
Farah Akhtar: Woodville Resource Centre, Shirley Road,
Cheetham, Manchester M8 7NE; *t* (0161) 740 2995
Health education, advice, counselling and advocacy. »93

● *New Life* and *Asian Business*; *Gujarat Samachar*
C.B. Patel, Editor: 8-16 Coronet Street, London N1 6HD;
t (0171) 729 5453
Newspaper (52/yr), founded 1977; business review (26/yr);
Gujarati magazine. »90

● *New Voice*
K. Amiruzzaman, Editor: 370-372 High Street North, Manor
Park, London E12 6PH; *t* (0181) 552 8791
Newspaper (52/yr). »88

✪ **Newham Asian Women's Project**, NAWP
PO Box 225, London E7 9AA; *t* (0181) 472 0528
Refuge for Asian women and children experiencing domestic
violence; outreach work, campaigns. Resource centre, second-
stage hostel; researching mental health care provision. »96

● **One Nation Forum**
[address unknown] London
Conservative Party support group. »95

✪ **Peshkar**
Aziz Zeria, Asian Arts Officer: [address unknown] Oldham
Council, Oldham, Lancashire; *t* (0161) 911 4084
A multicultural Asian community theatre company. »95

✪ **Pragati Asian Women's Association** Haringey
Indira Thakrar, Chair: [address unknown] London N8 »95

✪ **Project Pehchan**
c/o Leisure Services: Nottingham County Council, Trent Bridge
House, Fox Road, West Bridgford NG2 6BJ
Detached youth project, working with young people and
voluntary groups from the (mainly Pakistani) community in
Sneinton, Nottingham. »94

✪ **The Qalb Centre**
[address unknown] Waltham Forest, London E17; *t* (0181)
558 6241
An Asian mental health project providing holistic forms of
counselling and therapy. »94

✪ **Roshni Asian Women's Resource Centre** and Aman Project
Abda Sadiq: 444 London Road, Sheffield S2 4HP; *t* (0114)
250 8898, 273 8459
Training, information and resources; community development
work aimed at enabling and empowering Asian women to
make informed choices about their lives. Aman Project
provides transcultural counselling/therapy service for Asian
women, in conjunction with local health trust. »95

✪ **Roshni (Nottingham Asian Women's Aid) Ltd**
PO Box 209, Nottingham; *t* (0115) 924 2864, 948 3450
Development of services for Asian women and children who
are subject to domestic violence. »96

✪ **Sahara Asian Women's Project**
Alpa Kapasi/B. Randhawa: c/o The Women's Information
Centre, PO Box 324, Reading RG1 6AW; *t* (01734) 311939
Emergency accommodation, emotional/practical support for
Asian women and children at risk from domestic abuse. »95

✪ **Saheli**
PO Box 25, SWDO, Manchester M16 5FX
Provides a refuge for women and children who have had to
leave home because of marital and family violence. »94

✪ **Sangam Association of Asian Women**
Jyoti Kamath: Advice Centre, Library, 235-237 West Hendon
Broadway, London NW9 7DM; *t* (0181) 202 4629 »90

✪ **Sandwell Asian Mental Health Service**
Julie Wilson: Friendship Care Choices [address unknown] West
Midlands; *t* (0121) 506 2822, *f* 766 8091
Culturally appropriate community/home-based services. »96

✪ **SATHI Project**, West London Asian Health Agency
5th Floor, Holdsworth House, 65-73 Staines Road, Hounslow
TW3 3HW
Promotes awareness of, and access to, services for Asian
children with disabilities. Information, advice, advocacy. »95

● **School of East Asian Studies**, University of Sheffield
Western Bank, Sheffield S10 2TN; *t* (0114) 276 8555
Postgraduate research on East Asian countries and peoples.
See also Centres for Japanese/Korean Studies, pp78/82. »95

● **Scottish Asian Action Committee**
S.S. Sokhi: 4 La Belle Place, Glasgow G3 7LH, Scotland;
t (0141) 331 1069, *f* 226 5308
Janice Fawkes, Neelam Bakshi; umbrella group of about 20
Indian, Pakistani, other community groups; casework. »94

● *Scottish Asian Voice*
[address unknown]
Community newspaper. »95

✪ *Shakti*
Sadhana Ghosh, Editor: 46 High Street, Southall UB1 3DB;
t (0181) 843 1689
Magazine. »88

● **Shakti (South Asian Lesbian and Gay Network)**
[address unknown] London »90

✪ **Shanti Asian Women's Refuge**: Battersea Churches and
Chelsea Housing Trust, BCHT
c/o BCHT, Estra House, Station Approach, Streatham, London
SW16 6EJ; *t* c/o (0181) 664 4006
Refuge for Asian women and children fleeing domestic
violence. Based at a confidential address in Wandsworth.»95

● **Society of Asian Lawyers**
[address unknown] London
Concerns include immigration and asylum rights. »96

● **South Asia Solidarity Group**
c/o LONDEC, Instrument House, 205-217 King's Cross Road,
London WC1X 9DB »95

✪ **Southwark Asian Women's Refuge Group**
c/o Hexagon, 235 Queen's Rd, Peckham, London SE15 2NG
Works with South Asian, Chinese, Vietnamese women and
children escaping violence or the threat of violence. »90

✪ **Stonebridge Asian Elders Social Group**
130 Barry Road, Stonebridge, London NW10 8DH; *t* (0181)
965 5343 »91

✪ **Subah**
PO Box 30, SEDO, Manchester M12 4LL; *t* (0161) 839 8574
Women's organisation providing hostel-based refuge/support
service to young women experiencing domestic crises. »94

✪ **Subco Elders Day Centre**
[address unknown] Newham, London; *t* (0181) 548 0070
Voluntary day care for Asian elders; crisis intervention and
befriending schemes. »95

✪ **Suman**
Ramesh Bhargava: [address unknown] Southall, Middlesex
One of around 80 marriage bureaux serving the Asian
community in Britain. »95

✪ **Support Project for Asian Women and Families with a Child
with a Disability**
Sarwar Khan: c/o Voluntary Action Sheffield, 69 Division
Street, Sheffield S1 4GE; *t* (0114) 275 5138
Improvement and development of community care services for
Asian children with disabilities; advice, community work
(mainly with Pakistani families) in Urdu and Punjabi. Project
based in Pakistan Moslem Centre. »94

✪ **TV Asia**
Anita Anand: [address unknown] London; *t* (0181) 841 5112
Programme making. »93

✪ **United Asian Organization**
Omprakash Sharma, President: [address unknown] Leeds,
Yorkshire »88

● **United Kingdom Asian Women's Association**
1 Stanford Road, Lozells, Birmingham B19
Women's issues, social and cultural. »90

● **United Kingdom Asian Women's Conference** also known as
Asian Women's Conference UK
H. M. Patel: Vaughan Centre, Wilson Gardens, West Harrow
HA1 4EA
Indian, Pakistani, other Asian women; advice, support, primary
purpose and other immigration rules. »94

✪ **Waltham Forest Asian Centre**
Orford Road, Walthamstow, London E17 9LN; *t* (0181) 520
4511
Serves the needs of Asian communities and organisations in
the borough. »94

✪ **West London Asian Health Agency**, WLAHA: and Asian
Community Care Resource Centre
8 Pownall Gardens, Hounslow TW3 1YW; *t* (0181) 814
0838, 748 5769
Independent agency providing elderly day care, health
promotion, lunch club and other services; Resource Centre in
Hammersmith; with Hounslow Monitoring Project, p179, runs
women's counselling service. See SATHI Project, left. »95

✿ **Women's Roof (Leicester) Ltd** also known as Roof Group
PO Box 142, Leicester; *t* (0116) 273 4050
Hostel and after care support for women and children who
have suffered domestic violence or harassment.   »95
✿ **XYZ Women's Group**
G. Evans: c/o 42nd Street, Ground Floor, 22 Lloyd Street (off
Albert Sq.), Manchester M2; *t* (0161) 830 0170, 224 6257
Counselling and support group for young Asian women.   »93
✿ **Zara Elderly Asian Group**
Nunhead Community Education Centre, Whorlton Road,
London SE15; *t* (0171) 635 7011   »95
✿ **Zawiya Centre**
126 Pershore Rd, Birmingham B5 7NY; *t* (0121) 440 1347»95

◉ **NORTHERN IRELAND** *44*

✿ **Craigavon Asian Women's Centre**
c/o NICEM, 17 Eblana Street, Belfast BT7 1LD   »96

ASSYRIAN

see also Arab/Arabic, Armenian, Egyptian, Middle Eastern

◉ **BELGIUM** *32*

✿ **Centre Culturel Assyro-Chaldéen**
Rue des Eburons 44, 1040 Bruxelles
Assyrian and Chaldean-rite Christians.   »90

◉ **GERMANY** *49*

✿ **Mesopotamien Assyrischer Verein e.V.** *(Mesopotamian-Assyrian Union)*
Klein Langaße 7, 6200 Wiesbaden
Religious, social and welfare interests of Assyrian and
Chaldean-rite Christians.   »90
♦ **Zentralverband der Assyrischen Vereinigungen in
Deutschland und Europäische Sektionen e.V.**, ZAVD
*(Federation of Assyrian Societies, German and European
Branches)*
Melek Simsek, President: Postfach 112305, Mendelssohn-
straße 21, 86154 Augsburg; *t* (0821) 155195, 418405,
(030) 781 6864, *f* (030) 781 7021
Aziz Saïd. Cultural, educational and welfare concerns. »94

◉ **UNITED KINGDOM** *44*

● **Assyrian Culture and Advice Centre**
PO Box 1314, London W5 5QH; *t* (0181) 579 0192
Albert Yelda. Location: 18 The Green, London W5 5DA. »95
● **Assyrian Refugees Relief Foundation**, ARRF
PO Box 2148, Ealing, London W13 0XT
Advice services to Assyrian refugees, including immigration,
asylum and welfare benefit matters. Funded by London
Boroughs.   »94
● **Assyrian Society of Great Britain**
1 Temple Road, London W5 4SN; *t* (0181) 567 3768   »95

AUSTRALIAN

see also Asian, Pacific

◉ **UNITED KINGDOM** *44*

*Australia and New Zealand Emigrants and Families Association:
believed defunct (1992)*
● **Britain-Australia Society**
Stephen Stuart, Director-General: Borax House, Carlisle Place,
London SW1P 1HT; *t* (0171) 976 5611, *f* 976 5603
Founded 1937; friendship.   »90
● **Sir Robert Menzies Centre for Australian Studies**
Dr Richard Nile, Acting Head: University of London, 28 Russell
Square, London WC1B 5DS; *e* k.mcintyre@sas.ac.uk
Postgraduate study and research centre within Institute of
Commonwealth Studies; administers academic exchanges.»96

AUSTRIAN

see also European, German

◉ **FRANCE** *33*

● **Institut Autrichien** *(Austrian Institute)*
30 boulevard des Invalides, 75007 Paris; *t* (1) 4705 2710
Culture, education.   »90

◉ **UNITED KINGDOM** *44*

● **Anglo-Austrian Society**
W.J. Foster, Secretary: 46 Queen Anne's Gate, London SW1H
9AU; *t* (0171) 222 0366
International friendship, exchanges; founded 1944; Lord Clark
of Kempston, chairman; Lord Campbell of Croy, president.»94
✿ **Austrian Catholic Centre**
29 Brook Green, London W6; *t* (0171) 603 2697
Religious community centre.   »90

AZERI

see also Asian, East European, Russian

◉ **ITALY** *39*

✿ **Comunità Azerbagiana in Italia** *(Azeri Community in Italy)*
Ataman Cling: via Conteverde 58, 00185 Roma; *t* (06) 446
7676, *f* 678 1182
Welfare of Azeri refugees and immigrants.   »94

BAHA'I

selective listing only; see also Indian, Iranian

◉ **IRELAND** *353*

● **National Spiritual Assembly of the Baha'is of the Republic of
Ireland**
Elizabeth Omidvaran, Secretary: 24 Burlington Road, Dublin 4;
t (01) 668 3150, *f* 668 9632   »94

◉ **SWITZERLAND** *41*

▮ **Baha'i International Community**
route des Morillons 15, Grand-Saconnex, 1218 Genève;
t (022) 798 5400, *f* 798 6577
Represents the worldwide Baha'i community and 165 Baha'i
organisations to the United Nations and its organs; special
interests include human rights, protection of minorities,
refugee welfare.   »93

◉ **UNITED KINGDOM** *44*

● **Baha'i National Centre**
27 Rutland Gate, London SW7 1PD; *t* (0171) 584 2566 »95

BALTIC

see also East European, Estonian, Latvian, Lithuanian, Russian

◉ **UNITED KINGDOM** *44*

● **Baltic Association of Great Britain**, BAGB
Chris Last, Chairman: Lithuanian House, 2 Ladbroke Gardens,
London W11 2PT
Founded 1985; information, support for emigré communities,
cultural and social activities.   »90
● **Baltic Council**
[address unknown]
Umbrella group of Baltic organisations.   »90
● **Baltic Research Unit** University of Bradford
Prof. John Hilden/Thomas Lane: Department of European
Studies, Richmond Road, Bradford BD7 1DP; *t* (01274)
733466 exts. 3809, 3814, *f* 305340
Research into the history, politics and economics of Latvia,
Estonia and Lithuania and the wider Baltic region, including
Poland; fostering of trade links with Britain.   »91

BALUCH

see Afghan, Iranian, Islamic, Pakistani

BANGLADESHI

see also Asian, Bengali, Islamic

◉ **DENMARK** *45*

● **Dansk Kontaktkreds for Bangladesh International Action
Group**
c/o Dansk Ungdoms Fællesråd, Knabrostræde 3, 1210
København K   »93

ITALY *39*

✿ **Associazione Bangladesh** *(Bangladesh Association)*
via Levi 24, 00133 Roma; *t* (06) 736948 office, 733561 albergo
Migrant workers: culture, training, employment, hostel accommodation. »94
✿ ≡ c/o CeLSI-CGIL, via Adua 22, 00199 Roma; *t* (06) 683 4460, 683 6630 (?) »90
✿ ≡ via del Frassini 24, Roma »90
✿ ≡ via Taranto 130, 00100 Roma »90
✿ ≡ via Giacomo Zanella 71, 00137 Roma »90
✿ ≡ [address uncertain] via Valfurva 9, 00141 Roma
Also listed (1990) as via Quinta Ortensio 28. »90
✿ ≡ via Filippo Turati 62, 00185 Roma »90
✿ ≡ viale G. Cesare 78, 00192 Roma »90
● **Bangladesh Association in Italy, BAI**
Lutfar Rohman Khan: via Silvi Benco 51-5, 00177 Roma; *t* (06) 271 2618
Advisory service, founded 1989. »90

NETHERLANDS *31*

✿ **Bangladesh People's Solidarity Centre, BPSC**
Postbus 11347, 1001 GH Amsterdam; *t* (020) 693 7681 (?)
For left unity, and peasant and labour mobilisation in Bangladesh. *Samachar* (6/yr). »90

UNITED KINGDOM *44*

✿ **Al Jamat-ul-Muslimin of Bangladesh**
G.A. Choudhury, Chairperson: 8 St George's Street, Regent Square, Northampton NN1 2TR; *t* (01604) 24930, 34151
Community centre and place of worship, founded 1967. »94
✿ **Al Muttaqiin**
Barik Chowdhury, Secretary: 62 West Avenue, Wallington, Sutton SM6 8PH; *t* (0181) 686 1637
Islamic youth welfare and recreational activities. »94
✿ **Asha Women's Group**
11B Fieldgate Mansions, Myrdle Street, London E1 1HA; *t* (0171) 375 2404 »94
✿ **Bangla Educational and Cultural Centre**
91 Highbury Hill, London N5 1SX; *t* (0171) 354 0550
Language, arts, culture. »90
✿ **Bangladesh Allaya Mosque and Islamic Centre**
16-18 Swarcliffe Rd, Sheffield S9 3FA; *t* (0114) 243 0102
Mosque also listed (1993) at Roundle Street, S9 3LE. »94
✿ **Bangladesh Association**
3 The Coombes, Highgate Park, Fulwood, Preston PR2 4LH »90
✿ **Bangladesh Caterers' Association**
6 Bristol Street, Birmingham B14 »90
✿ **Bangladesh Centre**
97 Walford Road, Sparkhill, Birmingham B11 1NP
Social and cultural centre. »90
✿ ≡ Khalil R. Kazi: 24 Pembridge Gardens, Notting Hill Gate, London W10 4DX; *t* (0171) 229 9404, *f* 229 5197
Social and cultural centre; affiliate of EU Migrants Forum. »94
✿ ≡ 29 Chetwynd Road, Blakenhall, Wolverhampton »90
✿ **Bangladesh Centre Association**
30 Red House Road, Tettenhall, Wolverhampton WV6 »90
✿ **Bangladesh Cultural Society (Midlands)**
[address uncertain] 112 Reginald Road, Saltley, Birmingham B8 1LU
Also listed (1990) at 1st Floor, Abbey House, 284 Witton Road, Aston, B6 6NX; and 420a Old Walsall Road, Great Barr, B42 1HU. These may be separate branches. »90
✿ **Bangladesh Eshat-Ul-Islam (UK)**
M. Younus: 99 Edward Street, West Bromwich B70 8NT; *t* (0121) 553 4567, 558 7581
See also Young Muslims Organisation (Smethwick), p73. »94
✿ **Bangladesh International Women's Association**
49 Armitage Road, London NW11 8QT; *t* (0181) 455 4009
Interests of Bangladeshi women in UK and Bangladesh. »90
✿ **Bangladesh Islamic Association**
Toymus Ali: 20 Clarendon Street, Keighley BD21 »94
✿ ≡ Hiron Miah: 10-11 Lewisham Road, Smethwick, Warley B66 2BP; *t* (0121) 561 2055, 558 8204
Worship, Islamic education, Bengali classes; welfare, advice and information service on health, housing, immigration and other matters. See also Blackheath Bangladesh Association, p18; Bengali Muslim Mosque and Community Centre, p19. »94
✿ **Bangladesh Islamic Centre**
A. Jalil, Secretary: 67 Dartmouth St, West Bromwich B70 8BZ; *t* (0121) 553 5598 »94
✿ ≡ & Mosque: 296 Burbury St, Lozells, Birmingham B19 »94
Bangladesh Islamic Consultative Committee; Bangladesh Islamic Organisation: see Jamia Masjid & Islamic Centre (B'ham), p62

✿ **Bangladesh Islamic Cultural Association**
Jayfar Ali: 9 Mount Street, Walsall WS1, West Midlands »94
✿ ≡ and Mosque: Kaisor Ali, Secretary: 74 Wednesbury Rd, Walsall WS1 3RR; *t* (01922) 20051, 20618, 641073
New mosque, with range of community welfare activities. »94
✿ **Bangladesh Islamic Organisation** and Shahjalal Mosque
Mohammed Tahir: Temple Row, Keighley BD21 2AH; *t* (01535) 603444
Possibly same as the Shahjalal Mosque and Madrassa listed (1993) at Sefton Place, Keighley (Jahir Ali secretary). »94
✿ **Bangladesh Islamic Society**
Ramzan Ali Choudhury: 134 Franchise Street, Darlaston WS10, West Midlands; *t* (0121) 526 5750 »94
✿ ≡ 24 Birchwood Avenue, Leeds LS17 8PL »94
✿ ≡ and Mosque: 48 Cook Street, Darlaston WS10, West Midlands; *t* (0121) 526 4443 »94
✿ **Bangladesh Jubok Somity**
151 St Paul's Road, Balsall Heath, Birmingham B12
Cultural and religious. »90
● **Bangladesh Medical Association (UK)**
Dr A. Hossain, President: 164 Lee High Rd, London SE13 5PL
Possibly same as Bangladeshi Medical Association. »90
✿ **Bangladesh Muslim Association**
13 Miskin Street, Cathays, Cardiff CF2 4AQ, Wales »94
✿ ≡ and Mosque: Siddat Ali: 117 Gibbet Street, Halifax HX1, West Yorkshire; *t* (01422) 355218 »94
✿ **Bangladesh Muslim Organisation**
90 Sydney Road, London N8 »94
✿ **Bangladesh People's Association**
9 Cornwall Terrace, Bradford BD8 7JS »90
✿ **Bangladesh Residents' Welfare Association**
208 Osborn Road, Sparkbrook, Birmingham B11
Family reunion, immigration, welfare. »90
✿ **Bangladesh Shomity**
M. Ali: 52 Upton Park Road, Forest Gate, London E7 8LD; *t* (0181) 471 0800
Advice, language teaching. »94
✿ **Bangladesh United Muslim Society**
A. Noor: 56 Fox Street, Scunthorpe DN15, South Humberside; *t* (01724) 853694 »94
✿ **Bangladesh Welfare Association**
39 Fournier St, Spitalfields, London E1; *t* (0171) 247 2105
Campaigning, advice, referrals, translation; mosque. »94
✿ ≡ 19 St Joseph's Road, Ward End, Birmingham B8 2JX »90
✿ ≡ 14 Albert Grove, Southsea, Portsmouth PO1 »90
✿ ≡ H.J. Kabir: 32 Mollison Dve, Wallington, Sutton SM6 9BY
Islamic education group for young women. »94
✿ ≡ and Mosque: A. Rahman: 19-21 Alum Rock Rd, Saltley, Birmingham B8 1LL; *t* (0121) 328 4746, 328 4682
Community association and Sunni mosque. »94
✿ ≡ also Shah Jalal Mosque, Madrassa: N. Miah, Secretary: 66 Belford Street, Burnley BB12 0DF; *t/f* (01282) 450269
Welfare, legal advice; religious, educational activities. »94
✿ **Bangladesh Welfare Organization**
161 Walford Road, Sparkbrook, Birmingham B11 »90
✿ ≡ 208 Lozells Road, Birmingham B19 1NP »90
✿ **Bangladesh Women's Association**
Badrun Pasha, Chair: 5 Birch Close, Bourneville, Birmingham B30 1NA; *t* (0121) 459 6754 »93
✿ ≡ 58 Hanley Rd, London N4 3DR; *t* (0171) 263 7005 »92
● **Bangladesh Women's Association in Great Britain**
Sophia Rahman: Bangla Educational and Cultural Centre, 91 Highbury Hill, London N5 1SX; *t* (0171) 359 5836 »94
✿ **Bangladesh Workers Association**
97 Walford Road, Sparkbrook, Birmingham B11 1NP »90
✿ ≡ 26 Painswick Rd, Hall Green, Birmingham B28 0HF »90
✿ **Bangladesh Youth and Cultural Shamiti**
[address uncertain] 30-32 Oldulph Street, Leicester LE2 1BF; *t* (0116) 254 3504
Founded 1974. »90
✿ **Bangladesh Youth League**
175 Broad Street, Birmingham B15 1DX
Anti-racism, second generation, integration, education. »90
✿ **Bangladeshi Advice Centre**
104 Wills Street, Lozells, Birmingham B19 2AZ
Advice, counselling, advocacy. »90
✿ **Bangladeshi Islamic Education Centre** and Mosque
L. Rahman, Assistant Secretary: 57 Cowley Road, Oxford OX4 1HR; *t* (01865) 793118
Small mosque with voluntary Islamic education service. »94
● **Bangladeshi Medical Association**
18 Crofton Drive, Tettenhall, Wolverhampton WV6 8NR
Possibly same as Bangladesh Medical Association (UK). »90
✿ **Bangladeshi Mosque**
29 Gilliatt Street, Scunthorpe DN15, South Humberside »94

✿ **Bangladeshi Muslim Association**
13 St Thomas Road, Lockwood, Huddersfield HD2 »94
✿ ≡ Gous Ahmed: 93 Vicarage Road, Wednesbury, West
Midlands; *t* (0121) 556 0491, 556 2047, 502 2137 »94
✿ **Bangladeshi Workers Association**
Nur ul-Haq, Chair: 2 Alum Rock Road, Saltley, Birmingham
B8 1JB »95
✿ **Blackheath Bangladesh Association**
Hiron Miah: 34 Beeches Road, Rowley Regis, Warley B65
0BT; *t* (0121) 561 2055
See also Bangladesh Islamic Association, p17; Bengali Muslim
Mosque and Community Centre, p19. »94
✿ **Bolton Bangladesh Association**
Dr F.R. Bhuiyan: 8 Bury/Bolton Road, Radcliffe M26 0LD »94
✿ **Bradford Bangladeshi Parishad** or Bangladesh Porishad
31 Cornwall Road, Bradford BD8 7JN; *t* (01274) 722069
Community service, advice on immigration and welfare. »95
● **Committee for Bangladeshi Rights in the United Kingdom**
Mohammed Haque, Chairman: [address unknown] London
Campaigns on a range of issues including racial violence. »95
● **Confederation of Bangladeshi Organisations**
[address unknown]
Community development; outreach work in conjunction with
local Bangladeshi groups. »94
✿ **Ethnic Community Service**, ECS
Ali Reza Khan: 72 Brick Lane, London E1 6RL; *t* (0171) 247
9825 »94
✿ **Federation of Bangladeshi Associations**
[address uncertain] 275 Alton Boulevard West, Tyseley,
Birmingham B11 3HY
Umbrella group. »90
✿ ≡ [address uncertain] 230 Witton Road, Birmingham B6 »90
● ≡ and Federation of Bangladeshi Women's Associations:
[address uncertain] 52 Ashmead Road, London SE8 »90
● **Federation of Bangladeshi Youth Organisations**
Montefiore Centre, Deal Street, London E1 5JB; *t* (0171)
247 8818
Umbrella group for youth movements and services. »94
✿ **Friends of Bangladesh**
39b High Street, Harrow-on-the-Hill HA1 3HT
International and inter-cultural understanding/co-operation.»90
✿ **Glodwick Bangladesh Mosque Committee** and Jalalabad
Mosque
Abdul Rahman, Chair: 52 Orme Street, Oldham OL4 1RZ;
t (0161) 626 0132, 624 4565
Worship, religious education. Also listed (1993) c/o Janab
Ali, 231 Park Rd, Oldham OL4 1RW, *t* 633 9865. »94
✿ **Greater London Bangladeshi Catering Association**
Rashid Ali, General Secretary: c/o Dewaniam Restaurant,
Forest Hill Road, London SE22 »94
✿ **Greater Manchester Bangladeshi Association**, GMBA: and
Bangladeshi Youth Association
M.A. Choudhury: 19a Birch Lane, Longsight, Manchester
M13 0NW; *t* (0161) 225 4012, *f* 257 2071
Jabir Ahmed JP, Ian Dempsey. Community centre, welfare
advice, employment training, health education, economic
development, anti-racism; founded 1972. »94
✿ **Gwent Bangladeshi Association**
Tahir Ullah: 12 Cedar Road, Mainsee, Newport NP9 0BA,
Wales; *t* (01633) 212254, 263847
Islamic religious and welfare society. »94
✿ **Hopscotch Asian Women's Centre**
St Richard's House, Eversholt Street, Somers Town, London
NW1; *t* (0171) 388 1231
Also at 22 Phoenix Road, NW1. Counselling and support on
social, health and educational issues to Bangladeshi families;
research, liaison with public services. »95
✿ **Hyde Bangladesh Welfare Association**
19 Chapel Street, Hyde SK14, Cheshire; *t* (0161) 368 1349
Advice and welfare. »95
✿ **Jalalabad Association**
M.A. Islam: 12 Pugh Road, Birmingham B6 5LL »94
● **Jalalabad Overseas Organization**
126 St Julian's Farm Road, London SE27
Formed to represent southern Bangladeshi immigrants. »90
● ≡ 209 Deptford High Street, London SE8 3NT »90
✿ **Manchester Bangladeshi Women's Project**
Yasmin Begum: Slade Lane Neighbourhood Centre, 642
Stockport Road, Manchester M13 0RZ; *t* (0161) 257 3867
Anita Baishnab, Shahara Mia. Advice, language classes,
health education, child care, cultural/social events. »93
✿ **Masjid Shah Jalal** and Bangladesh Islamic Society
27 Ellers Road, off Markham Avenue, Leeds LS8 4JH;
t (0113) 240 6558, 248 1860
Mosque and Islamic society. »94

✿ **Mitalee Women's Employment and Training**
Rowshan Islam: BWA (Haringey) Ltd, Stanley Road, London
N15 3HB; *t* (0181) 365 7498
Women's training services; child care centre. Offshoot of
Bangladeshi Workers/Women's Association? »94
● **National Council of Bangladeshi Organizations in the United
Kingdom**
39 Park Avenue, Mitcham CR4 2ER; *t* (0181) 648 1684 »90
✿ **Newham Bengali Community Trust**
2 Wyndham Road, East Ham, London E6 1AU
Voluntary welfare organisation; activities include advice and
advocacy for chronically ill/disabled people and carers. »94
✿ **North Lambeth Bangladesh Welfare Association** and Mosque
251 Pentonville Road, London N1; *t* (0171) 278 0877 »95
✿ **Nottingham Bangladeshis' Association**
71-73 Alfreton Road, Nottingham NG7
Local community group. »90
✿ **Popda Muslim Welfare Association** and Darlaston
Bangladeshi Muslim Organisation, DBMO
Ismail Adam Mohammed, Secretary: 197 Walsall Road,
Darlaston WS10, West Midlands; *t* (0121) 526 5830
Gujarati association; activities include development aid to
Sarikhurad, India. DBMO secretary is Abrus Miah. »94
✿ **Sandwell Confederation of Bangladeshi Muslim
Organisations**, SCOMBO
Z.S. Chowdhury, Development Officer: [address uncertain]
143 High St, West Bromwich B70 6NY; *t* (0121) 500 5441
Also listed (1994) at Bond Wolf House, 312-314 High Street,
B70 8EN. Umbrella organisation for Bangladeshi groups in
Sandwell; representation, liaison, information and advice. »94
✿ **Smethwick Bangladeshi Muslim Welfare Association**
Assad Uddin, Secretary: 253 Halfords Lane, Smethwick,
Warley B66, West Midlands; *t* (0121) 558 9449
Religious and welfare activities. »94
✿ **South Tyneside Bangladesh Muslim Cultural Association**
and Mosque
Syed F. Hussain, Chair: 3-5 Baring Street, off Ocean Road,
South Shields, Tyne and Wear; *t* (0191) 454 2501
Religious, educational and community welfare group. »94
✿ **Sussex Bangladeshi Association**
Faruque Ahmed, President: 7 Kings Parade, Ditchling Road,
Brighton BN1 6JT; *t* (01273) 321636, 734738
Dr Manzur ul-Haq secretary. »95
✿ **Training and Development Consortium**, TADCO
c/o Crispin Jones, CME, Institute of Education, 20 Bedford
Way, London WC1H 0AL; *t* c/o (0171) 612 6722
Training and employment creation projects for unemployed
Bangladeshis in Tower Hamlets. »95
✿ **Wednesbury Bangladesh Muslim Welfare Association**
Arju Miah: 9 Brunswick Park Road, Wednesbury, West
Midlands; *t* (0121) 502 0521 »94
✿ **West Sussex Bangladeshi Association**
Angur Miah, Secretary: c/o Anurag, 98 Canterbury Road,
Worthing BN13 1AN; *t* (01903) 266384
Sirajul Muslim community. »94

BARBADIAN

*see also African Caribbean, Afro-Caribbean, Anglo-Caribbean,
Caribbean, West Indian*

🅾 **UNITED KINGDOM** *44*

✿ **Barbados Association**
H.L. Jordan: 83 Cannon Hill Road, Balsall Heath, Birmingham
B12 9NJ
Social activities, welfare, choir. »90
✿ **Barbados Overseas Association**
G. Browne: West Indian Centre, Carmoor Road, Charlton-on-
Medlock, Manchester M13 0FB; *t* (0161) 257 2092
Dances and other social events. »93

BASQUE

see also European, French, Spanish

🅾 **FRANCE** *33*

● **Comité pour la Défense des Droits de l'Homme en Pays-
Basque**, CDDHPB *(Committee for Human Rights in Euskadi)*
Camille Frossard: MJC Polo Beyris, 64100 Bayonne
Refugee welfare; policing, extradition, civil rights, self-
determination for Basques in the Spanish state and in Iparralde,
the French Basque region. *Jakilea* (4/yr). »94

- **Inxauseta**
[address unknown] Paris
Cultural association. »94

BELGIAN

see also European

◎ **GREECE** *30*

- **Amicale Belgo-Héllénique** *(Belgian-Greek Friendship)*
Odos Gounari 27, Agia Paraskevi, 15343 Athinai; *t* (01)
639 6938
Belgians in Greece, mixed families, international friendship,
links with Greeks in Belgium. »94

◎ **UNITED KINGDOM** *44*

- **Anglo-Belgian Society**, ABS
S. Ault, Honorary Secretary: 46 Belgrave Manor, Brooklyn
Road, Woking GU22 7TW
Founded 1918; friendship, cultural exchanges. »90

BENGALI

see also Asian, Bangladeshi, Indian, Islamic

◎ **UNITED KINGDOM** *44*

- ✤ *Angikar*
Prachee, 1 Avondale Avenue, Esher KT10 0DB
Magazine (4/yr). See also Islamic Marriages Introductory
Service and Counselling, p61. »88
- ✤ **Bengali Association of the West Midlands**
120 Yewtree Road, Witton, Birmingham B6 6RU »90
- ✤ **Bengali Community Education Project**
1 St Stephen's Road, Leicester LE2 1DR; *t* (0116) 254 5939,
f 255 9439 »95
- ✤ **Bengali Muslim Mosque and Community Centre**
Hiron Miah, Chair: 149-150 New John Street, Halesowen
B62 8HT
Worship, Islamic education, Bengali classes. »94
- ✤ **Bengali Women's Group**
Orkney House, 199 Caledonian Road, London N1 0SQ;
t (0171) 278 9500 »95
- ✤ **Bengali Workers' Association Ltd** and Bengali Workers'
Action Group; Surma Community Centre
1 Robert Street, London NW1 3JU; *t* (0171) 388 7313,
f 387 8731
Progressive community organisation established 1976 to
address socio-economic disadvantage of Bengali people in
Camden through community development and self-help. The
BWAG was involved in the Camden Monitoring Project,
campaigning against racial harassment in north London, in
1994. »95
- **British Bangla Alliance**
[address unknown] »90
- *Desh Barta Newsweekly*
G.H. Khan, Editor: 170 Brick Lane, London E1 6RU; *t* (0171)
377 1584, (0181) 889 0763
Newspaper (52/yr). »90
- *Jagoran*
Dr M. Talukdar, Editor: 44 Torrington Gardens, Perivale,
Middlesex; *t* (0181) 998 3876, (0171) 609 2364
Newspaper (52/yr). »88
- *Janomot Newsweekly*
A.T.M. Walie-Ashraf, Editor: 80 Hearnville Road, London
SW12 8RR; *t* (0181) 673 2136, 2137
Newspaper (52/yr). »90
- *Probashi Samachar*
S. Mazumdar, Editor: 20 Orchard Avenue, London N14 4ND;
t (0181) 886 4231
See also *Asian Herald*, p13. Review (4/yr). »88
- *Sagar*
H. Bhattacharya, Editor: 5 Avondale Crescent, Redbridge,
Essex; *t* (0181) 550 4697
Review (6/yr). »88
- *Sanglap*
107 Warren Road, Kingstanding, Birmingham B44 8QN
Journal (12/yr). »88
- *Surma Newsweekly*
A. Ahmed, Editor: 40 Wessex Street, London E2 0LB
Magazine (52/yr). »90

BENINESE

see also African, West African

◎ **FRANCE** *33*

- **Démocratie et progrès (pour le Bénin)**
30 rue Gramme, 75015 Paris
Solidarity group for emigrants and friends of Benin; economic
and social development, culture. »89
Espoir Togo-Bénin Organisation Amitié: see p116
- **Jeunes Juristes Béninois pour un Etat de Droit**, JJBED *(Young
Beninese Lawyers for Legal Rights)*
43 rue Gabrielle, 94220 Charenton-le-Pont; *t* (1) 4368 9048,
f 4570 9123
Humanitarian aid in Benin and Togo; promotion of democracy
and civil rights; aid to migrants and refugees in France. »93

BERBER

*see African, Algerian, Arab, Islamic, Libyan, Moroccan, North
African, Tunisian*

BEUR

see also Algerian, French, Maghrebi

◎ **FRANCE** *33*

- ✤ **Association Les Nanas Beurs** *(Beur Babes Association)*
Souad Bennani: 70 rue Casteéja, 92100 Boulogne; *t* (1) 4621
0729, *f* 4621 7672
Beur women's cultural and social organisation. »94
- **Génération Beur**
Nordine Cherif: BP 46, 93202 Saint-Denis Cedex 1; *t* (1)
4243 0210
Location: 30 rue de Strasbourg. Youth group. »94
- ✤ **Radio Beur**
8 rue de la Madeleine, 93400 St-Ouen; *t* (1) 4012 7676
Youth-oriented broadcasting organisation. »90

BLACK

*see also African, African Caribbean, Afro-Caribbean, Anglo-
Caribbean, Asian, Caribbean, West Indian, and the national and
ethnic terms encompassed by those. This term is not widely
used outside Britain, and is used in Britain in two senses: to
mean all who experience discrimination on the grounds of race,
colour or nationality; or in a more restricted way, to mean
those of African Caribbean, African and Asian origin*

◎ **FRANCE** *33*

- ✤ **Association des Travailleurs Noirs de la Région Toulonnaise**,
ATNRT *(Toulon Regional Black Workers' Association)*
Louis Mendy/Ahmala Diatta: BP 41, 83500 La Seyne-sur-Mer;
t 9494 2211, 9463 1278
Location: 10 rue d'Alsace. Cultural and welfare society. »94
- ✤ **Rencontre Internationale des Femmes Noires**, RIFEN
(International Black Women's Group)
Eliane Aissi: 16 rue d'Amaillé, 75017 Paris; *t/f* (1) 4572 5039
Anti-racism, women's welfare. See also IFCOD, p198. »94

◎ **GERMANY** *49*

- ✤ **Afro-German Women**
Flois Knolle Hicks: Niedenau 43, 6000 Frankfurt am Main 1;
t (069) 729690 »90
- **Black German Women**
Helga Emde: Baumweg 25, 6000 Frankfurt am Main 1;
t (069) 439100 »90
- ♦ **Initiative Schwarze Deutsche—Koordinationsekretariat BRD**,
ISD *(Black German Initiative Federal Secretariat)*
SHZ, Bayerstr. 77a, 80335 München; *t* (089) 5329 5613 »94

◎ **NETHERLANDS** *31*

- **Institute of Black Economic Empowerment**
Dr Th.M.J. Leeuw: [address uncertain] A.J. Ernststraat 102,
1082 LP Amsterdam »90
- ✤ **Workgroup Black Feminist**
Bukelwa Kalipa-Alam: [address uncertain] Silene 126, 8265
HK Kampen; *t* (038) 331 7058 (?) »90

◎ **UNITED KINGDOM** *44*

✿ **Abasindi Co-operative**
Abina Likoya: Moss Side People's Centre, St Mary's St, Moss Side, Manchester M15 5NA; *t* (0161) 226 6837, 226 0904
Kath Locke, Paula Asgill. Training, workshops, performance in African and Caribbean percussion for black women.   »93

● **African and Caribbean Music Circuit** also known as The A & C Music Circuit, or ACMC
Charles Easmon: The Granville Centre, 80 Granville Road, London NW6 2BX; *t* (0171) 372 4591
Music tour management, promotion; educational work.   »96

✿ **Afro-Caribbean and Asian Forum**
Gulza Khan: Unit 4, 35 Ebury Road, Sherwood Rise, Nottingham NG5 1BB; *t* (0115) 969 1224
Umbrella body for black organisations; represented in EU Migrants Forum, p131. Anti-racism, information.   »94

✿ **Ajani Centre**
Patricia Powell: 3 Mill Hill Lane, Highfields, Leicester; *t* (0116) 255 6796
Afrikan/Caribbean women-only centre, founded 1983. Activities include counselling, information, outreach and development work, liaison with other agencies.   »91

✿ **The Angelou Centre**
2 Brighton Grove, Fenham, Newcastle NE4 5NR
Training, employment, enterprise centre for Black women. »95

✿ **Asante Sana Ltd**
PO Box 226, Nottingham NG1 5LJ; *t* (0115) 958 0873
Manages supported housing for African-Caribbean and Asian women, including short-stay project for young homeless. »95

✿ **Association of Black Churches**
John Samuels: 102 Mersey Bank Avenue, Chorlton-cum-Hardy, Manchester M21 2WW; *t* (0161) 445 2904
Ecumenical relations, liaison with public bodies.   »93

● **Association of Black Clergy**
Clarry Hendricks: [address uncertain] Christ Church Vicarage, Sedgemoor Road, Norris Green, Liverpool L11 3BR   »90

● **Association of Black Counsellors**
4 Alexandra Ave., Sutton SN1 2NZ; *t* (0181) 644 5479   »90

● **Association of Black Probation Officers**, ABPO
David Reardon, Chair: Inner London Probation Service, 75 Marsham Street, London SW1P 3DX; *t* (0171) 222 0331
Support of probation staff, provision of appropriate services to Black offenders. Specific concerns include development of practice, professional issues, race and criminal justice.   »91

● **Association of Black Social Workers and Allied Professions**
403-405 Brixton Rd, London SW9 7AW; *t* (0171) 733 1263
Forum on social work issues affecting black people, and on position of black people in social services.   »90

● **Autograph—Association of Black Photographers**
Mark Sealy: [address unknown]   »95

✿ **BAWSO**
PO Box 270, Cardiff CF1 8YJ, Wales
Charity operating black women's refuge; advice, counselling service, empowerment.   »94

✿ **Steve Biko Housing Association**
1 Lesseps Road, Liverpool L8 0RD   »91

✿ **Birmingham Black Oral History Project**
[address uncertain] 70 Villa Road, Handsworth, Birmingham B21
Also listed (1990) as c/o 34 Farnham Road, Handsworth, B21 8EG. Collects oral histories from black immigrants who came to Birmingham in the 1940s-'60s; plans development and publication of educational and information materials.   »91

● **Black Action**
[address unknown] London
Socialist group.   »95

● **Black Advice Workers Forum**
c/o FIAC, 13 Stockwell Road, London SW9 9AV; *t* (0171) 274 1839
Professional development group for counsellors and advice service workers.   »90

✿ **Black Arts Alliance**
Su Andi: c/o 111 Burton Road, Withington, Manchester M20 8HZ; *t* (0161) 445 4168, 796 0378
Promotion of black art and cultural expression. Education, performances, exhibitions, networking.   »93

✿ **Black Arts Network**
28-30 Mosley Street, Newcastle-upon-Tyne NE1
Concerns include funding and venues for black artists in the North of England.   »93

✿ **Black and Asian Police Association**
Ch.Insp. Ron Hope, Chairman: [address unknown] London
Established 1994 to represent the 700 ethnic minority officers, and many civilian staff, in the Metropolitan Police.   »94

● **Black Beauty and Hair**
Irene Shelley: Hawker Publications Ltd, 13 Park House, 140 Battersea Park Road, London SW11 4NB; *t* (0171) 720 2108, *f* 498 3023
Black women's magazine (4/yr), founded 1982.   »95

✿ **Black Business Development Association**
Randolph Beresford Centre, 51 Hugon Road, London SW6 3ER; *t* (0171) 731 7399
Fosters business skills and enterprise in black community. »94

✿ **Black Children Counselling Project**
Robert Jones: Black Resource Centre, Old Library, Cheetham Hill Road, Manchester M8 7NJ; *t* (0161) 740 7575   »93

✿ **Black Community Forum**
c/o Diane Mitchell, Sheffield TEC, 55 St Mary's Road, Sheffield S2 4AQ
Represents ethnic minority communities and organisations in matters including regional economic development plans.   »95

✿ **Black Community Safety Project**
Depak Patel: c/o 108 Narborough Road, Leicester LE3 0BS; *t* (0116) 254 2633
Three staff; aims to reduce the level and fear of crime and racism in inner Leicester's ethnic minority communities.   »95

✿ **Black Direct Action for Equal Rights and Justice**
Paul Auber: [address unknown] Chapeltown, Leeds LS7
Anti-racist campaigns.   »95

✿ **Black Elderly Group Southwark**
Elim House, 86 Bellenden Road, Peckham, London SE15 4RQ
Operates a day centre for black and ethnic minority elderly. »94

♦ **Black Employment Institute**, BEI
Director: PO Box 33, North PDO, Nottingham NG5 1LD
New national organisation (relocating to London) to improve employment and training opportunities for Black people. Research on labour market, information, campaigning.   »94

● **Black Environment Network**
Jakesh Mahey, Administrator: c/o NCVO, Regents Wharf, All Saints Street, London N1 9RL
Encourages young blacks from inner cities to visit the countryside and take part in rural activities.   »94

● **Black Europe Concern**
Roddy Crozier: [address unknown] London E17 3JE
Pressure group defending rights of black people in the EU.»95

✿ **Black European Media Project**
86 Dumbryden Gardens, Edinburgh EH14 2NZ, Scotland; *t* (0131) 453 1538, *f* 458 3946
Research on treatment of racism and migrant, minority and refugee issues in European media.   »94

✿ **Black Family Coalition**
Bill Dufus: [address unknown] Erdington, Birmingham B23
Welfare of local black community; monitors racial attacks.»95

✿ **Black HIV/AIDS Forum (Manchester)**, BHAF
Evelyn Asante-Mensah, Project Manager: Zion Community Health & Resource Centre, Zion Crescent, Hulme, Manchester M15 5BY; *t* (0161) 226 9145
Registered charity developing counselling, advice, education and other services for African, Caribbean, Asian, Chinese and Vietnamese communities around sexual health and HIV.   »96

✿ **Black HIV/AIDS Forum—West Midlands**, BHAF-WM
c/o AWM, 4th Floor, Smithfield House, Digbeth, Birmingham B5 6BS
A network of Black workers and communities from voluntary and statutory sectors, established 1990 to improve services for Black people affected by HIV or AIDS.   »92

● **Black HIV/AIDS Network**, BHAN
The Administrator: 1st Floor, St Stephens House, 41 Uxbridge Road, London W12 8LH; *t* (0181) 749 2828
Involved in HIV and sexual health promotion outreach initiatives, community care and support services for African, Asian and Caribbean people mainly in Brent and Harrow.   »95

✿ **Black HIV AIDS South East London**, BHASEL
PO Box 7953, London SE4 1ZA; *t* (0181) 694 6639
Works with minority ethnic communities providing support to pepople affected by HIV, and information on HIV prevention and awareness. Drop-in service mainly for African men.   »95

● **Black-Led Churches Liaison**
Rev. Corbett: 29 Trinity Road, Aston, Birmingham B6 6AJ; *t* (0121) 551 1207
Community development, co-ordination of black churches; see United Evangelical Project Legal Centre, p228.   »94

✿ **Black Lesbian and Gay Centre**
Arch 196, Bellenden Road, London SE15 4RF; *t* (0171) 732 3885   »95

✿ **Black Lesbian and Gay Group**
Shaky Shergill: c/o Manchester Gay Centre, Manchester M60 1LP; *t* (0161) 274 3814 (inc. minicom)
Support and social group.   »93

✿ **Black Mental Health Resource Centre**
Jamaica House, 277 Chapeltown Road, Leeds LS7 3HA;
t (0113) 237 4229
Counselling and therapy for Black people with mental health
problems; established 1992 by Leeds Black Health Forum.»92

▌ **Black Migrant and Refugee Women's European Network**
c/o Islington Women's Equality Unit, Town Hall, Upper Street,
London N1 2UD; *t* (0171) 477 3133-34   »94

✿ **Black Music Association (UK) Ltd**
[address unknown]   »90

✿ **Black People's Entertainment**
[address uncertain] Flat 9, 216 Finchley Road, London
NW3; *t* (0171) 328 5362   »90

✿ **Black Perspectives in Volunteering Group**
[address unknown]
Supports anti-racist recruitment, training and deployment
practices in NGOs.   »90

✿ **Black Research Workers Network**
c/o 46 High Street, Southall UB1 3BD   »90

✿ **Black Roof Housing Co-op Ltd**
17b Groveway, London SW9 0AH; *t* (0171) 582 4436
Provides housing for black and ethnic minority people. See
also Mbaaku Black Roof Women's Group, p22.   »90

● **Black Socialist Society**
Faz Hakim: John Smith House, 150 Walworth Road, London
SE17 1JL; *t* (0171) 701 1234
Labour Party support group, established in 1990 in response
to agitation for the formation of black sections.   »95

✿ **Black Star Housing Association Ltd**
Sharon Annakie, Chief Executive: 4 Park Avenue, Hockley,
Birmingham; *t* (0121) 523 4421
Social housing in the West Midlands region.   »96

✿ **Black Theatre Co-operative**, BTC
8 Bradbury Street, London N16 8JN   »95

● **Black Training and Enterprise Group**, BTEG
c/o National Council of Voluntary Organisations, Regents
Wharf, All Saints Street, London N1 9RL; *t* (0171) 713 6161
National pressure group, supported by Project Fullemploy and
the NCVO, which monitors and reports on the equal
opportunity plans of local Training and Enterprise Councils.»95

▌ **Black Women and Europe Network**
PO Box 3073, London N15 5DO; *t* (0181) 802 0911, *f* 809
7078
International forum of minority ethnic women, focussing on
discrimination and disadvantage in the European Union.   »94

✿ **Black Women and Mental Health Group**
St Giles Parish Hall, Benhill Road, London SE5; *t* (0171) 701
2651
Psychiatric problems of and provision for black women.   »90

✿ **Black Women for Wages for Housework**
Cristel Amiss: [address uncertain] 30 Coburg Road,
Montpellier, Bristol BS6 5HX; *t* (0117) 955 6988
Radical feminist group.   »90

✿ **Black Women's Action Group**
Elstead Street, London SE17; *t* (0171) 708 1643
Radical feminist group.   »94

✿ ≡ Surinder Kaur/Rhonda Finlayson: Black Resource Centre,
The Old Library, Cheetham Hill Road, Manchester M8 7NJ;
t (0161) 740 7575, 225 7402
European race equality issues; feminist discussion group. »93

✿ **Black Women's Co-operative**
10 Wiltshire Court, Tugford Gardens, Birmingham B18   »90

✿ **Black Women's Creativity Project**
Wedge Tape and Drama Centre, Princeton Project, London
WC1; *t* (0171) 242 6807   »90

✿ **Black Women's Editorial and Consultancy Collective**
[address unknown]   »90

✿ **Black Women's Family Support Group**
7c Station Road, Cambridge; *t* (01223) 69753   »90

✿ **Black Women's Group**
Judy Richards/Amarjeet Mandan: Women's Centre, Lettice
House, 10 St George Mews, Brighton BN1 4EH; *t* (01273)
600935, 749374   »94

✿ **Black Women's Support Group**
Paulette Hanley: Moss Side Probation Office, 87 Moss Side
West, Moss Side, Manchester M15 5PE; *t* (0161) 226 3515
Support/rehabilitation of black women offenders; human rights,
equity of treatment, court translation, deportation issues. »93

✿ **Black Workers' Association**
A.M. Burnett: 5 Oak Drive, Erdington, Birmingham B23 5DQ
Black Voices.   »90

✿ **Black Workers' Group**
c/o 4 Livingstone Drive, Liverpool L15   »91

✿ **Black Youth and Community Workers Association**
[address unknown]   »90

✿ **Black Youth Movement**, BYM
262 Westgate Road, Newcastle-upon-Tyne NE4 6AQ;
t (0191) 230 5805
Charity promoting interests of local minority ethnic youth. »94

✿ **Blackliners**
[address unknown] London; *t* (0171) 738 7468
Information, counselling, emotional support, advice and
housing for black people affected by HIV and AIDS.   »95

✿ **The Bridges Project**
109 Pilgrim Street, Newcastle-upon-Tyne NE1 6QF
HIV prevention/sexual health work with Black communities.»95

✿ **Bristol Black Business**
L. McDonald: 8 Lower Ashley Street, St Paul's, Bristol BS2;
t (0117) 955 0935
Enterprise agency.   »94

✿ **Bristol Black Voluntary Sector Development Unit**, BBVS
Berrenga Bandele: Unit 6, Kuumba Project, 20-22 Hepburn
Road, St Pauls, Bristol BS2 8UD; *t* (0117) 942 3960
Local government-funded unit developing community
organisations. Other groups at this address include Bristol
Black Parents and Governors Support Group.   »96

✿ **Brixton Black Women's Centre**
41a Stockwell Green, London SW9; *t* (0171) 274 9220   »90

✿ **Camden Black Parents and Teachers Group**
25 Bayham Street, London NW1; *t* (0171) 388 0145   »90

✿ **Camden Black Sisters**
2c Falkland Road, London NW5 2PT; *t* (0171) 284 3336   »94

✿ **Cheetham Electronic Village**
Sello Rasatheba: Black Resource Centre, The Old Library,
Cheetham Hill Rd, Manchester M8 7NJ; *t* (0161) 740 7575
Information technology education and training.   »93

● **Committee for Black Affairs**
Rev. Rajinder Daniel: 133 Church Lane, Handsworth Wood,
Birmingham B20 2HJ; *t* (0121) 551 5445   »90

● **Council of African and Afro-Caribbean Churches**
Most Rev. Fr Oluwole A. Abiola: 31 Norton House, Sidney
Road, London SW9 0UJ; *t* (0171) 274 5589
Represents 18 Black-led churches; ecumenical work.   »94

✿ **Coventry Black Mental Health Association**, CBMHA
D. Richardson/J. Burchell: 35 Vine Street, Hillfields, Coventry
CV1, Warwickshire; *t* (01203) 227712, 225512
Charity founded 1989; empowerment of Black people with
mental health difficulties and their families; links with other
agencies; developing telephone helplines.   »96

✿ **Cultureword Publishers and Identity Writing Group** also
known as Commonword
Pete Kalu: Cheetwood House, 21 Newton Street, Piccadilly,
Manchester M1 1FZ; *t* (0161) 236 2773
Network of black writers and publishers; workshops,
performance, dissemination of black writing.   »93

✿ **East London Black Women's Organisation**, ELBWO
Clinton Rd, Forest Gate, London E7 0HD; *t* (0181) 534 7545
Resource centre; advice, education, training, childcare. »96

✿ **Ebony Sistren Housing Association**, ESHA
Project Enterprise, 16 Askew Crescent, Shepherd's Bush,
London W12 9DP; *t* (0181) 740 7271
Social housing for black and ethnic minority women; several
units in West London; women's refuge opened 1994.   »94

● **Federation of Black Housing Organisations**, FBHO
Jheni Williams, Director: 374 Gray's Inn Road, London
WC1X 8BB; *t* (0171) 837 8288, *f* 278 6571
Louis Julienne, Bina Patel. Founded 1983; forum for housing
associations run by or for black and ethnic minority people;
training and advice for housing workers; research on black
housing association financing. *Black Housing* (12/yr). »95

✿ ≡ 36 Princes Road, Liverpool L8   »91

✿ **The Forward Project**
Kofi Sunu: 15 Coverdale Road, Shepherd's Bush, London
W12 8JJ; *t* (0181) 749 8747, (0171) 403 2695
Mental health resource centre, short-stay accommodation,
community psychotherapy, support to young adults.   »95

● **Foundation for Black Bereaved Families**
Larreene Hunt: 11 Kingston Square, Salters Hill, London
SE19 1JE; *t* (0171) 761 7288   »90

✿ **Frontline**
Sheron Carter: [address unknown] London
Black housing advice centre.   »94

✿ **Harambee Housing Association**
27-29 Grove Lane, Handsworth, Birmingham B21 9ES
Black community housing action group.   »90

✿ **The Inkworks Project**
Alfredo Vásquez, Director: 20-22 Hepburn Road, St Paul's,
Bristol BS2 8UD; *t* (0117) 942 1870, *f* 944 1478
Promotes arts and culture of the African and Caribbean people
of Bristol region. See BBVS Development Unit, above.   »93

✧ **Inquilab Housing Association**
S. De Coteau [address unknown] Southall; *t* (0181) 843 1263
Social housing for black communities in West London.   »95
✧ **IRIE! Dance Theatre**
The Albany Centre, Douglas Way, Deptford, London SE8
4AG; *t* (0181) 691 6099
Dance company; dance education, promotion of Black art.»95
✧ **Claudia Jones Organization**
103 Stoke Newington Road, London N16 8BX; *t* (0171) 241
1646   »95
✧ **Justice Alliance Campaign**
[address unknown] Birmingham
Campaigns against racist attacks; founded 1993.   »95
✧ **Kemet**
Unit 29.1, Lynwood Business Development Centre, Lynwood
Terrace, Newcastle-upon-Tyne NE4 6UL
Practice learning for social workers in Black-led agencies;
focus on anti-discriminatory/anti-oppressive issues.   »94
✧ **Kirklees Black Workers' Group**
Atma Singh: c/o Kirklees REC, 24 Westgate, Huddersfield
HD1 1NU; *t* (01484) 540225   »88
● **Labour Party Black Section**
Palma Black, Secretary: 57 Birnam Road, London N4 3LT
Pressure group, not officially recognised, which seeks to
increase black participation in the British Labour Party.   »95
✧ **Leeds Black Health Forum**, LBHF
Black Mental Health Resource Centre, Jamaica House, 277
Chapeltown Road, Leeds LS7 3HA; *t* (0113) 237 4229
Development of community health services in Leeds.   »92
● **Lesbian and Gay Black Group**
BM Box 4390, London WC1N 3XX   »90
✧ **London Black Women Health Action Project**, LBWHAP
1 Cornwall Avenue, London E2 0HW; *t* (0181) 980 3503
Health education/promotion among black women; includes
African Young People's HIV/AIDS Education Project, working
mainly with Somali and Horn of Africa young people.   »94
✧ **Lothian Black Forum**
c/o 12 Picardy Place, Edinburgh EH1 3JT, Scotland
Discussion and representative group for black Scots.   »90
✧ **Malcolm X Centre**
c/o BBVS DU, The Inkworks, 20-22 Hepburn Road, St Pauls,
Bristol BS2 8UD; *t* (0117) 942 3960   »96
✧ **Manchester Black Environment Network**
Nitin Thakrar: 24 Seymour Grove, Manchester
Environmentalist concerns; possibly linked with Black
Environment Network, p20?   »94
✧ **Manchester Black Lesbian Support Group**
Quibilah Montsho: PO Box 26, 1 Newton Street, Piccadilly,
Manchester M1 1HW; *t* (0161) 226 0787
Information, mutual support. Manchester Black Lesbian
Writing Group runs workshops, performances.   »93
✧ **Manchester Black Resource Centre**
Nusreth Ahmed/Robert Jones: The Old Library, Cheetham Hill
Road, Cheetham, Manchester M8 7JN; *t* (0161) 740 7575
Resource centre for community projects including Black Heath
Forum, Black Children Counselling Project; Book and Craft
Shop.   »93
✧ **Mbaaku Black Roof Women's Group**
21a Groveway, London SW9 0AH
See also Black Roof Housing Co-op, p21.   »94
✧ **Moss Side and Hulme Black Women One Parent Family
Group**
Lucille Jamieson: c/o Flat 3, Wheale House, 36-38 Upper
Chorlton Road, Manchester   »93
✧ **Moss Side Netball and Gospel Women's Group**
Rosemary Knox/Andrea Reid: 140 Raby Street, Moss Side,
Manchester M14 4SQ
Religious and leisure activities, visits to other groups.   »93
✧ **Nailah—Black Women's Writing Performance Group**
c/o Pauline Omoboye: 9 Ulverston Avenue, Withington,
Manchester M20 8DU; *t* (0161) 226 5000
Workshops, performances, support for writers. *Nailah*.   »93
♦ **National Black Alliance**
Lee Jasper/Atma Singh: c/o 22 Hanbury Street, London E1
Formerly linked with the Anti-Racist Alliance, p176, now with
National Assembly against Racism, p181.   »96
● **National Black Business Association**
[address unknown]   »90
♦ **National Black Caucus**
Murray Hatcher: [address unknown] London; *t* (0171)
717 1585
Umbrella group of community-based anti-racist organisations.
Formerly (?) affiliated to the Anti-Racist Alliance, p176.   »96
● **National Convention of Black Mental Health**
[address unknown]   »90

● **National Convention of Black Teachers**
[address unknown]   »90
✧ **Newham African, Caribbean and Asian Advocacy Project,
NACAAP**
[address unknown] Newham, London; *t* (0181) 519 8311
Founded 1995; group of black women who represent and
support black women subject to child care investigations. »95
✧ **The Nia Centre**
Jasmine Hendry/Jennifer Laing: Chichester Road, Hulme,
Manchester M15 5EU; *t* (0161) 227 9268, 266 6461
A 1,000-seat multipurpose performing arts venue, founded
1991 to promote positive image, enjoyment and awareness
of African and Caribbean arts and culture.   »96
✧ **North East Black Housing Development Project**, NEBHDP
Development Worker: c/o Newcastle Tenants Federation,
1st Floor, 1 Pink Lane, Newcastle-upon-Tyne NE1 5DW
Established 1993 to identify housing needs of Black and
minority ethnic communities in the North East, develop Black
housing initiatives, and liaise with housing providers.   »94
✧ **North Manchester Black Health Forum**
Nusret Ahmed/Maqbool Ahmed: Black Resource Centre, The
Old Library, Cheetham Hill, Manchester M8 7JN; *t* (0161)
740 7575
Training, conferences, seminars on black health issues; mental
health counselling and support services, drop-in centre.   »93
✧ **Nottingham Black Initiative**, NBI
J. Wint: 73 Raleigh Street, Radford, Nottingham NG7 2DL;
t (0115) 979 2123
Services, training and consultancy, including Black Access
Initiative (for aspiring entrants to social work, probation, youth
service, community work) and Black Drugs Initiative
(researching need for and takeup of drug-related services).»93
● **Organisation for Black Arts Advancement and Learning
Activities**, Obaala
Obaala House, 225 Seven Sisters Road, London N4 2DA;
t (0171) 263 1918   »94
● **Organisation Development Unit**, ODU
Rifat Wahhab: NCVO, 26 Bedford Square, London WC1B
3HU; *t* (0171) 636 4066
Promotes Black voluntary sector. *PrODUct for Action*.   »90
● **Organisation for Sickle Cell Anaemia Research**, OSCAR
12 Bell Barn Shopping Centre, Cregoe Street, Lee Bank,
Birmingham B15 2DZ
Funds research into an anaemia affecting black people.   »90
✧ **Panah**
c/o Shamshad Iqbal: Mind, 52 Clifton Road, Elswick,
Newcastle-upon-Tyne NE4
A refuge from domestic violence; outreach work to heighten
awareness of violence against women in Black communities,
and to support women living independently.   »94
● **Panther UK**
[address unknown]
Anti-racism, policing issues; Black self-organisation.   »95
● **Parliamentary Black Caucus** (possibly defunct)
Bernie Grant MP: House of Commons, Westminster, London
SW1A 0AA
Forum of black members of Parliament; dissolved 1994? »94
✧ **Peckham Black Women's Centre**
69 Bellenden Road, London SE15 5BH; *t* (0171) 358 1486
Advice bureau.   »91
✧ **Rafiki**
Aitha Mohamed: c/o The Pankhurst Centre, 60-62 Nelson
Street, Manchester M13 9WP
Social, cultural and educational activities for all black and
ethnic minority women; health promotion.   »93
● **Resource Unit to Promote Black Volunteering**, RUBV, formerly
National Coalition for Black Volunteering, NCBV
David E.R. Obaze: Brixton Enterprise Centre, 442-444 Brixton
Road, London SW9 8EJ; *t* c/o (0171) 274 4000
Resource centre and information work to increase black
participation in the voluntary sector.   »95
✧ **Aled Richards Trust Black Communities Project**
Di Robinson, Administrator: 8-10 West Street, Old Market,
Bristol BS2 0BH
One of several HIV prevention and health promotion projects
run by the Trust, a voluntary agency providing counselling and
other services to people affected by HIV in the Bristol area.»94
✧ **SADAA Housing Association**, SADAA
Gurmit Bains: 1 Causeway, Blackheath, Halesowen B65
0DR; *t* (0121) 559 0010
A small Black and minority-ethnic association working in the
Black Country to provide housing to meet local needs.   »94
✧ **Saheli**
4a Callerton Place, Fenham, Newcastle-upon-Tyne NE4 0NQ
Black women's organisation in West End of Newcastle.   »94

✿ **Salongo Afrikan and Caribbean Dance and Music Resource Project**, formerly Bristol and Avon Black Dance Project
The Inkworks, 20-22 Hepburn Road, St Paul's, Bristol BS2 8UD; t (0117) 942 1870, 944 5579, f 944 1478
Founded 1991; events management, fundraising and liaison work to promote Afrikan and Caribbean dance and music. »95
● **Society of Black Lawyers**
Peter Herbert/Joy Osobia: Unit 149, Brixton Enterprise Centre, 442-444 Brixton Road, London SW9 8EJ; t (0171) 274 4000
Campaigns for equitable black participation in legal professions, and against racism.   »96
✿ **Southall Black Sisters**
52 Norwood Road, Southall UB2 4DW; t (0181) 571 9595, f 574 6781
Support group for (mainly Asian) women; in 1995 assisted some 1,500 women faced with domestic violence.   »96
✿ **Southall Black Women's Centre**
86 Northcote Ave., Southall UB1 2AZ; t (0181) 843 0578 »90
✿ **Southwark Black Workers Group**
Errol Reid: 352-354 Camberwell New Road, Camberwell Green, London SE5 0RW   »90
● **Talawa Theatre Company**
3rd Floor, 23-25 Great Sutton Street, London EC1V 0DN; t (0171) 251 6644
London/touring productions, education, writers' projects. »95
✿ **Unity Centre of South London**
2-4 Ravenstone Street, Balham, London SW12 9SS
Social care and rehabilitation, and housing (in 10-bed hostel, Trinity Road, Tooting, SW7) for African and Caribbean people with mental health problems. See Unity Helpline, p158. »94
✿ **Waltham Forest Young People's Housing Project Ltd,** WFYPHP
[address unknown] London E17; t (0181) 556 6065
Provides managed housing for Asian and Black young people. Sponsor of Ashiana Project, p12.   »91
● *The Weekly Journal* and *Pride*
Andrew Verity: NuVox House, 370 Coldharbour Lane, London SW9 8PL; t (0171) 737 7377, f 274 8994
The *Journal* (52/yr) is a black community newspaper; *Pride* (26/yr, editor Deirdre Forbes) is a women's magazine launched 1994. See also *The Voice*, p6.   »95
✿ **Wolverhampton Black Community Action Group**
Gamba Badele: [address unknown] Wolverhampton   »88

BOLIVIAN

see also Latin American

◙ **FRANCE** *33*

● **Wara Wara—Association des Aymaras de la Bolivie** *(Association of Bolivian Aymaras)*
Eduardo Conde Quispe: [address uncertain] 18 boulevard Barbès, 75018 Paris; t (1) 4262 3756   »90

◙ **ITALY** *39*

● **Associazione Bolivia Italia** *(Bolivia-Italy Association)*
c/o Parrochia S.M. Goretti, via V. Actis 20, 10146 Torino; t (011) 794827   »90
✿ **Associazione Boliviana della Liguria** *(Bolivian Association of Liguria)*
Fernando Torres: via Bruzza 8-2a, 16125 Genova; t (010) 303588
Formed 1988; migrant rights.   »90
✿ **Gruppo Boliviani** *(Bolivians' Group)*
via Carisio 11, 10143 Torino; t (011) 798667   »90

◙ **UNITED KINGDOM** *44*

● **Asociación de Residentes Bolivianos en Inglaterra** *(Association of Bolivian Residents in England)*
112 Camden High Street, London NW1 0LU; t (0171) 482 5243   »88

BOSNIAN

including Hercegovin; see also Croatian, East European, Islamic, Serbian, (Ex-)Yugoslav

◙ **IRELAND** *353*

✿ **Cork Action for Bosnia-Hercegovina**
Gerard Neff: Spur Hill, Cork
Solidarity with people of Bosnia-Hercegovina.   »94

◙ **ITALY** *39*

● **Associazione dei Cittadini di Solidarietà con la Bosnia Erzegovina,** CBH *(Citizens' Society for Solidarity with Bosnia Hercegovina)*
Adnan Kemura: via Rapolano 30, 00138 Roma; t (06) 880 4804, f 678 1182
Welfare of Bosnian refugees; international solidarity.   »94

◙ **NETHERLANDS** *31*

● **hCa Balkan Project** and hCa Tuzla
Mary Kaldor/Mient Jan Faber: Postbus 85893, 2508 CN Den Haag
Promotes peaceful resolution of the Balkan conflict, protection of human rights; denounces Serbian aggression in Bosnia-Hercegovina.   »95

◙ **UNITED KINGDOM** *44*

● **Alliance to Defend Bosnia-Herzegovina**
Prof. Adrian Hastings: 12 Flitcroft Street, London WC2H 8DJ
Solidarity with the people of Bosnia-Hercegovina; opposes Serbian and Croatian aggression.   »95
● **The Bosnia and Herzegovina Fund of Britain**
Jasmina Ljubar, Secretary: [address unknown] London
Charity providing humanitarian relief in Bosnia.   »92
● **Bosnia Project**
Nick Scott-Flynn: c/o Refugee Council, 3-9 Bondway, London SW8 1SJ; t (0171) 582 6922
Established by the Home Office in 1992 to receive 4,000 refugees from Bosnia. Funding, mainly used for 11 reception hostels, withdrawn 1995-96 after 2,000 arrivals.   »95
● **Bosnia Solidarity Campaign**
Alyoscia D'Onofrio: c/o 12 Flitcroft St, London WC2H 8DJ
Solidarity with the people of Bosnia against Serbian and Croatian aggression.   »95
✿ **Bosnian Advisory Centre**
Indira Arnautovic: 5 Canalside House, 383 Ladbroke Grove, London W10 5AA
Advice, housing and welfare assistance and community development service for Bosnian refugees.   »95
● **Bosnian Students Appeal**
Celia Hawkesworth: School of Slavonic and East European Studies, University of London, London WC1E 7HU
Solidarity with Bosnia; fundraising, other support to students in and from Bosnia.   »94
● **British Red Cross Bosnian Refugee Programme,** BRC
Bosnian Refugee Manager: Tyntersfield School Accommodation Block, Overslade Lane, Rugby CV22 6DY
Reception centres in Cambridge, Rugby and Oxford, and a resettlement service based in Birmingham, for evacuees from the conflict in Bosnia. Liaises with statutory and voluntary agencies on educational, social, other needs of refugees. »94
✿ **Convoy of Mercy**
A. Khan, Trustee: [address unknown] London N15
Humanitarian aid organisation providing relief supplies to Bosnia-Hercegovina since 1991.   »94
✿ **Edinburgh Direct Aid to Bosnia-Herzegovina and Croatia**
Denis Rutovitz, Chairman: 29 Starbank Road, Edinburgh, Scotland
Solidarity with, and practical assistance to, the peoples of Bosnia-Hercegovina and Croatia.   »94

BRAZILIAN

see also Latin American, Portuguese

◙ **DENMARK** *45*

● **Dansk-Brasiliansk Selskab**
Bredeshave Strand 1, 4733 Tappernøje; t 5376 5421   »95

◙ **GERMANY** *49*

✿ **Brasilieninitiative Freiburg** *(Freiburg Brazil Initiative)*
In den Weihermatten 27, 7800 Freiburg   »90

◙ **ITALY** *39*

✿ **Comunità Brasiliana in Italia**
José Patrício Djalma: via Conteverde 58, 00185 Roma; t (06) 446 7676, f 678 1182   »94
✿ **Comunità Brasiliana di Roma** *(Brazilian Community of Rome)*
CSER, via Calendrelli 11, 00153 Roma   »90
● **Forum Comunità Brasiliana** *(Brazilian Community Forum)*
via Santa Eufemia 19, 00187 Roma   »90

◎ **PORTUGAL** *351*

✿ **Associação dos Brasileiros** *(Association of Brazilians)*
Diva Ferreira: Sampaio Pina 26, 1200 Lisboa; *t* (01) 682071
Founded 1988. Cultural events, advice, information.   »94
✿ **Casa do Brasil de Lisboa** *(Lisbon Brazilian House)*
Virgínia Freitas: Rua S. Pedro de Alcântara 63-1° D, 1250
Lisboa; *t/f* (01) 347 1580   »95
✿ **Centro Cultural Brasileiro**
Largo Dr A.S. Macedo 5, Lisboa 1200; *t* (01) 608760   »95
✿ **Clube de Empresários do Brasil** *(Brazilian Business Club)*
São Marçal 77, 1200 Lisboa; *t* (01) 342 4423, *f* 342 4388 »95

◎ **SPAIN** *34*

● **Asociación Amigos do Brasil** *(Friends of Brazil Association)*
carrer Matanzas 17, 08027 Barcelona; *t* (93) 349 1434   »87

◎ **UNITED KINGDOM** *44*

● **Anglo-Brazilian Society**
32 Green Street, London W1Y 3FD; *t* (0171) 493 8493
Friendship, cultural exchanges; founded 1943.   »95
✿ **Brazilian Arts and Community Centre**
Gilson Antonio Maximo: 1 Elgin Avenue, London W9 3PR;
t (0171) 266 1270   »94
✿ **Brazilian Support Centre**
207-215 King's Cross Road, London WC1X 9DB; *t* (0171)
837 1391   »94

BRITISH

see also European, Irish; includes English-speaking groups

◎ **BELGIUM** *32*

✿ **Anglican Church of the Holy Trinity**
Rue Crespel 29, 1150 Bruxelles   »90
✿ **British School of Brussels**
[address unknown] Bruxelles
Secondary school mainly for children of British migrants. »91
✿ *The Bulletin*
Brigid Grauman: Ackroyd Publications SA, 329 Avenue
Molière, 1060 Bruxelles; *t* (02) 343 9909, *f* 343 9822
English-language newspaper (52/yr) mainly serving the
expatriate community and tourists; founded 1962.   »95
✿ **St Andrew's Church of Scotland**
Vleurgatsesteenweg 181, 1050 Brussel   »90

◎ **CZECH REPUBLIC** *42*

● *The Prague Post*
Martin Huckerby, Editor: [address unknown] Praha; *f* (02)
2487 5050
English-language business and politics newspaper (52/yr).»95

◎ **DENMARK** *45*

✿ **British Workers' Association**
M. Hafiz: Kanalens Kvarter 76-2, 2620 Albertslund   »90
✿ **British Workers' Union**
Glentevej 37, 2600 Glostrup, København   »90

◎ **FRANCE** *33*

● **Association Franco-Britannique** *(Franco-British Association)*
16 place Havre, 75009 Paris; *t* (1) 4285 1636   »90
✿ **British Institute in Paris**: Institut Britannique de Paris
9-11 rue Constantine, 75007 Paris; *t* (1) 4555 7199
Educational, cultural; associated with University of London.»90

◎ **IRELAND** *353*

● **Anglo-Irish Encounter**
57-61 Lansdowne Road, Dublin 4; *t* (01) 668 6233
Promotes international friendship, peace and mutual
understanding through exchanges, meetings, seminars.   »93
● **The British Council**
Ken Churchill, Director: [address unknown] Dublin
Part-funding of cultural exchanges and of British culture in
Ireland. Office opened 1989.   »92

◎ **ITALY** *39*

✿ **Chiesa Inglese** *(English Church)*
Parrochia S. Carlo al Corso, piazza S. Fedele, 20121 Milano;
t (02) 804441
English-speaking Roman Catholic church.   »90
✿ ≡ piazza S. Silvestro, 00187 Roma; *t* (06) 679 7775   »90

◎ **LUXEMBOURG** *352*

● **Association for the Rights of Britons Abroad, ARBA**
Emma Wagner: 92 rue Principale, 6990 Rammeldange;
t 348369   »94
✿ **British Ladies Club of Luxembourg**
Jill Cresswell: 5 rue des Aubépines, 8053 Bertrange
Mainly expatriate workers and families. *Newsletter*.   »94
✿ **Luxembourg Scottish Country Club**
S. Robertson: 34 rue Jean l'Aveugle, 1148 Luxembourg;
t 20479   »90

◎ **PORTUGAL** *351*

● **British Historical Society of Portugal**
Rua Arriaga 13 r/c, 1200 Lisboa; *t* (01) 397 8603   »95
● **Instituto Británico em Portugal**
São Marçal 174, 1200 Lisboa; *t* (01) 315 6141
Cultural and language teaching centre.   »95

◎ **SPAIN** *34*

✿ **Capilla Británica** *(British Catholic Chapel)*
calle Núñez de Balboa 43, Madrid; *t* (91) 576 5109   »90
✿ **Club Británico**
Gran Vía 1, Madrid   »90
✿ ≡ Camino Viejo de Leganés 100, Madrid   »90
✿ **Iglesia Británica de San Jorge** *(British Church of St George)*
calle Maiquéz 18, Madrid   »90
✿ **Parroquia y Capilla de Nuestra Señora de la Merced** *(Parish
and Chapel of Our Lady of Mercy)*
avenida Alfonso XIII 165, Madrid; *t* (91) 533 2032   »90

BUDDHIST

*see also Burmese, Cambodian, Chinese, Indian, Indonesian,
Japanese, Khmer, Korean, South-East Asian, Sri Lankan, Thai,
Tibetan, Vietnamese*

◎ **UNITED KINGDOM** *44*

✿ **Western Buddhist Order Padmaloka Madhyamaloka, WBO**
J. Hunter: Lesingham House, Surlingham, Norwich NR14 7AL;
t (01508) 538310, *f* 538076
The Western Buddhist Order is one of the largest Buddhist
organisations in Europe.   »94

BULGARIAN

see also East European, South-East European

◎ **DENMARK** *45*

● **Dansk-Bulgarsk Selskab**
Hvidtjørnen 35, København; *t* 3253 0846   »95

◎ **ITALY** *39*

✿ **Chiesa Bulgara** *(Bulgarian Church)*
via del Serafico 1, 00142 Roma; *t* (06) 698 4605   »90
● **Lega Bulgara per i Diritti del'Uomo** *(Bulgarian League for
Human Rights)*
Dimko Stateff: via del Giordano 36, 00144 Roma; *t* (06)
592 5668, 701 6935
Civil rights in Bulgaria, and for Bulgarian migrants.   »94

◎ **PORTUGAL** *351*

● **Associação Portugal Bulgaria** *(Portugal-Bulgaria Association)*
Rua São Nicolau 119-2° D, Lisboa; *t* (01) 323963   »90

◎ **UNITED KINGDOM** *44*

● **British Bulgarian Friendship Society, BBFS**
Ita Purton, General Secretary: Finsbury Library, 245 St John
Street, London EC1V 4NB; *t* (0171) 837 2304
Founded 1952; culture, international friendship.   »95

BURKINABE

see also African, West African

◎ **FRANCE** *33*

✿ **4 L Tiers Monde**
Greta Sud-Vendée, 45 rue Rabelais, 85200 Fontenay-le-Comte
Development aid, educational and cultural exchanges.   »89

BURMESE

see also Asian, South-East Asian

⊙ SWEDEN *46*
● All Burma Students' Democratic Front
Box 4034, 18104 Stockholm   »93

⊙ UNITED KINGDOM *44*
● Burma Action Group UK, BAG UK
1a Bonny St, Camden, London NW1 9PE; *t* (0171) 267 9660
Solidarity with the Burmese people; campaign for democracy
and for release of political prisoners.   »91

BURUNDI

see African, Central African, Rwandese, Southern African

CAMBODIAN

see also Asian, Khmer, South-East Asian

⊙ BELGIUM *32*
● Amitiés Belgo-Cambodgiennes, ABC *(Belgian-Cambodian
Friendship Association)*
Avenue Maréchal Foch 86, 1030 Bruxelles   »93

⊙ FRANCE *33*
✿ Accueil Cambodgien *(Cambodian Welcome)*
Bernard Jean Berger: 10 rue de l'Orme, 75019 Paris;
t (1) 4240 5686, 4240 5048, *f* 4208 7862
Education, information, research and documentation.   »94
✿ Association des jeunes cambodgiens de l'Ile-de-France
(Young Cambodians' Association of the Ile-de-France)
9 rue Henri-Guillaumet, 77400 Lagny-sur-Marne
Asian culture, sport, support for orphans in Cambodia.   »89
✿ Association des réfugiés cambodgiens de l'Aube *(Society
of Cambodian Refugees of the Aube)*
2 rue Franklin, 10600 La Chapelle-Saint-Luc   »90
✿ Association de solidarité franco-cambodgienne, ASFC
(French-Cambodian Solidarity Association)
4 résidence Château-Double, rue Alexander-Fleming, 13090
Aix-en-Provence   »90
● Comité International d'Entraide Humanitaire pour la
Population Khmère, CIEHPK *(International Committee for
Humanitarian Aid to the Cambodian People)*
Héng Moeun: 22 bis rue de Provence, 68100 Mulhouse;
t 8965 0121   »94
✿ Espace Cambodge
François Ponchaud: 98 rue d'Aubervilliers, 75019 Paris;
t (1) 4035 5740, *f* 4037 5617   »94

⊙ UNITED KINGDOM *44*
● The Cambodia Trust
21 Union Street, Woodstock, Oxfordshire
Medical relief in Cambodia, rehabilitation of mine victims. »94

CAMEROON

see also African, Central African, Islamic

⊙ FRANCE *33*
✿ Amicale des camerounais de Bordeaux *(Cameroon Society
of Bordeaux)*
4 rue de l'Armistice, 33150 Cenon   »89
✿ Association Culturelle des Elèves et Etudiants Camerounais
d'Amiens *(Cultural Association of Cameroon Pupils and
Students)*
9 rue Picasso, appt 69, 80080 Amiens   »89
✿ Association des Stagiaires et Etudiants Camerounais de
Bordeaux, ASECB *(Association of Cameroon Trainees and
Students in Bordeaux)*
résidence Les Aubiers, appt 47, 47 rue Charles-Tournemire,
33300 Bordeaux
Welfare of students, representation, mediation.   »90
● Communauté Camerounaise de France, CCDF
8 rue du Sergent-Maginot, 75016 Paris
Social, educational, cultural, welfare issues.   »90

✿ Livres sans frontières *(Books Without Frontiers)*
2 rue Maréchal-de-Lattre-de-Tassigny, 76960 Notre-Dame-de-
Bondeville
Cultural emancipation of Cameroon villagers by reading.   »90

⊙ ITALY *39*
✿ Associazione Camerunesi in Italia, ACAI *(Cameroon
Nationals' Association of Italy)*
Antagana Jeanve: via Sangallo 29, 20133 Milano
Migrant rights, campaigns against discrimination, training and
employment issues.   »94
✿ Associazione degli Studenti Camerunesi a Firenze
(Association of Cameroon Students in Florence)
Clotilda Assako: piazza Vittoria 2, 50067 Firenze Rignano;
t (055) 834 8632
Founded 1979; advice and representation.   »90
● Associazione degli Studenti Camerunesi in Italia *(Association
of Cameroon Students in Italy)*
Teodoro Ndgock Ngana: via dei Monti di Pietralta 16, 00186
Roma; *t* (06) 412 9535
Founded 1987; advice and representation.   »94
✿ Gruppo Camerunesi
corso Emilia 5, 10152 Torino; *t* (011) 839 6909   »90

⊙ SPAIN *34*
✿ Rassemblement des Camerounais Résidents à Barcelone,
RACAMERS *(Union of Cameroon Residents of Barcelona)*
Rambla de Catalunya 11-2° 1ª, 08007 Barcelona   »94

CANADIAN

see also Québécois

⊙ DENMARK *45*
● Dansk Canadisk Selskab
Søvej 26, 3500 Værløse; *t* 4248 2851   »95

⊙ FRANCE *33*
● Association France-Canada
5 rue Constantine, 75007 Paris; *t* (1) 4555 8365   »90

⊙ UNITED KINGDOM *44*
● British Association for Canadian Studies, BACS
21 George Square, Edinburgh EH8 9LD, Scotland
Promotion of academic study of Canada in Great Britain,
Canadian-British cultural relations.   »95
● Canadian-American Overseas Association
N. Staley: 83 Rownheath Road, Birmingham   »90
● Canadian Women's Club
Alberta House, 1 Mount Street, London W1; *t* (0171) 408
2459   »95

CAPE VERDEAN

see also African, Portuguese, West African

⊙ FRANCE *33*
✿ Mouvement de Solidarité pour les Iles du Cap-Vert
Luis Pedro da Silva: [address unknown] 95200 Sarcelles »90

⊙ ITALY *39*
✿ Associação das Mulheres Caboverdeanas em Palermo
(Association of Cape Verdean Women in Palermo)
Balbina Francisca Dias: via Salvatore Minutila 13-23, 90100
Palermo, Sicilia; *t* (0916) 713322
Associazione delle Donne Capoverdiane a Palermo. Founded
1989; migrant women's rights.   »90
✿ Associazione Capoverdiana
Maria de Lourdes Jesus: via Peccoli 56, 00159 Roma;
t (06) 811 0722
M. de Lourdes Jesus is Italy's rapporteur for MAINE, p146.»90
✿ Associazione Capoverdiana a Firenze e Provincie, ACVFP
(Cape Verdean Association of Florence and Province)
Hipolito Daniel Soares, President: via Chiantigiana 143,
50126 Firenze; *t* (055) 641103
Culture, education, youth welfare.   »94
✿ Associazione Italo-Capoverdiana a Napoli
Sergio Dias Gomes, President: [address uncertain] via
Nardone 109 (101?), 80132 Napoli; *t* (081) 414684
Social and cultural group; administrative advice.   »90

✿ **Associazione Popolo di Capo Verde** *(Cape Verdean People's Association)*
José Antonio Gomes Lima: via Ventaglieri 76 A, 80135 Napoli; *t/f* (081) 544 2105   »94

✿ **Centro Assistenza Capoverdiani** *(Cape Verdean Welfare Centre)*
via Conservatorio 2, 20122 Milano; *t* (02) 700987   »90

✿ **Chiesa Portoghese e Capoverdiana** *(Portuguese and Cape Verdean Church)*
via Nicolo V, 3, 00165 Roma; *t* (06) 638 1609
Portuguese-speaking Catholic Church.   »90

✿ **Comunità Isola Capo Verde, CICV** *(Cape Verde Island Community)*
presso via Curti 12, Bagno, 42100 Reggio Emilia; *t* (0522) 343409   »94

✿ **Comunità Lavoratrici di Capoverde in Piemonte** *(Cape Verdean Women Workers' Community of Piedmont)*
[address unknown] Torino   »90

● **Organização das Mulheres Caboverdeanas na Itália, OMCVI** *(Organisation of Cape Verdean Women in Italy)*
Organizzazione delle Donne Capoverdiane in Italia
via del Velabro 5, 00186 Roma; *t* (06) 678 2596, 669 0569
Founded 1988; employment, education, training, immigration advice.   »94
✿ ≡ Florence: Organização das Mulheres Caboverdeanas em Firenze e Província, OMCVFP: Maria Filomena Rosario Almeida: piazza d'Azeglio 24, 50120 Firenze; *t* (055) 241285   »94

◎ **LUXEMBOURG** *352*

● **Associação Luso-Caboverdeana** *(Portuguese-Cape Verdean Association)*
Pedro Dos Santos: 26a rue Pierre Krier, 1880 Luxembourg
Migrants and refugees from Portugal and Cape Verde.   »94

● **Association d'Amitié Luxembourg-Cap Vert** *(Luxembourg-Cape Verde Friendship Association)* also known as Association d'Amitié avec le Peuple Capverdien
Carlo Back: 10 rue M. Hengels, 1465 Luxembourg
Founded 1987; international friendship, understanding. »94

✿ **Association des Cap-Verdiens d'Esch**
75 rue du Canal, 4051 Esch-sur-Alzette
Cultural and leisure activities.   »94

● **Association des Cap-Verdiens du Luxembourg** *(Luxembourg Association of Cape Verdeans)*
José da Luz: 19 rue M. Welter, 2730 Luxembourg; *t* 495515
Cultural and social activities.   »94

✿ **Association des Cap-Verdiens du Nord** *(Northern Cape Verdean Association)*
José Antônio da Cruz: 3 route de Bastogne, 9177 Niederfulen
Social, cultural and welfare group.   »94

✿ **Union Familiale Cap-Verdienne**
Armand Geisbusch: 7 rue Rumelange, 4309 Esch-sur-Alzette; *t* 544444   »94

◎ **NETHERLANDS** *31*

● **Kaapverdianse Arbeidersvereniging in Nederland, KVAVN** *(Cape Verdean Workers' Society of the Netherlands)*
Mauritsweg 20, 3012 JR Rotterdam; *t* (010) 413 1886 »94

◎ **PORTUGAL** *351*

● **Associação de Amizade Portugal-Cabo Verde** *(Portugal-Cape Verde Friendship Association)*
Dr Sergio Ribeiro: Rua das Portas de Santo Antão 117-2°, 1100 Lisboa; *t* (01) 346 9777
Formed 1978. See also Associação de Amizade Portugal-Angola, p9.   »90

✿ **Associação dos Antigos Alunos do Ensino Secundário de Cabo Verde** *(Association of Cape Verdean High School Graduates)* and Associação dos Antigos Alunos do Liceu Gil Eanes, other old-school groups
Manuela Porto 12 a/b, Carnide, 1500 Lisboa; *t* (01) 715 2991
Founded 1985; migrant welfare, cultural/social events. »95

✿ **Associação Caboverdeana de Lisboa** *(Lisbon Cape Verdean Association)*
Arnaldo Andrade: Rua Duque de Palmela 2-8° E, 1250 Lisboa; *t* (01) 353 1932
Social and cultural group founded 1971; represented in EU Migrants Forum, p131.   »95

✿ **Associação Caboverdeana de Sines, ACVS**
Rua da Floresta, Pinhal CNP, 7520 Sines; *t* (069) 635267
Cultural and social concerns.   »94

✿ **Associação 5 de Julho** *(5 July Association)*
Rua de Cabo Verde, Alto da Cova da Moura, 2700 Amadora; *t* (01) 490 4706, 410 6695
Cultural and welfare activities.   »94

✿ **Associação Cultural e Desportiva da Pedreira dos Húngaros** *(Pedreira Cultural and Sporting Association)*
E. Monteiro: Rua Vitor Duarte Pedroso A/Q, 2975 Linda-a-Velha; *t* (01) 410 8727, 410 8670
Youth activities, sport, leisure.   »94

✿ **Associação Bento Gonçalves**
Rua Principal 76B, Pedreira dos Húngaros, 2795 Linda-a-Velha
Cultural and social group.   »94

● **Associaçãos Unidas de Caboverde, AUCV** *(United Cape Verdean Associations)*
Andres Horta Semedo: Rua das Fontainhas 119, Venda Nova, 2700 Amadora
Founded 1982. Training, employment and welfare issues.»94

✿ **Comissão Caboverdiana de Setubal**
Tomé Tavares Lopes: Prof. Egas Moniz 18, 2900 Setubal »94

✿ **Comissão Pró-Associação Caboverdiana do Algarve** *(Algarve Cape Verdean Association Steering Committee)*
Rua dos Pescadores 71B, 8125 Quarteira   »94

✿ **Comissão Pró-Associação Caboverdiana do Porto**
Avenida dos Aliados 151-3°, sala 4, 4000 Porto   »94

✿ **Comissão Pró-Associação Caboverdiana do Seixal**
Quinta da Vinha, Lote 8-2° D, 2840 Seixal   »94

✿ **Comunidade Católica Caboverdeana**
Pe. Afonso Cunha, Administrator: Rua de Santo Amaro à Estrela 51, 1200 Lisboa; *t* (01) 661424
Three priests, 13 nuns and a lay worker serve the Cape Verdean communities in Lisbon, Amadora and Cascais. »90

● **Federação das Associações de Cabo Verde em Portugal**
Prolong. da Avenida Gen. Delgado s/n, Apartado 69, 2700 Amadora; *t* (01) 492 1571   »94

✿ **Organização dos Médicos Caboverdianos** *(Cape Verdean Doctors' Organisation)*
Helena Lopes Da Silva: Rua Arneiros 58-3°, 1800 Lisboa »94

✿ **Organização de Quadros Técnicos Caboverdianos** *(Organisation of Cape Verdean Technical Staff)*
Orlando Barbosa: Rua José Falcão 8-2°, 1100 Lisboa; *t* (01) 815 0015   »94

♦ **Secretariado Coordenador das Associações para a Legalização, SCAL** *(Liaison Centre for Legalisation Societies)*
Campo Mártires da Pátria 43, 1100 Lisboa
Links campaigning groups working for migrant rights. »94

CARIBBEAN

see also African, African Caribbean, Afro-Caribbean, Anglo-Caribbean, Antillean, Barbadian, Black, Cuban, Dominican, Dominican Republic, French: DOM/TOM, Grenadian, Guadeloupean, Guyanese, Islamic, Jamaican, Kittitian, Latin American, Montserrat, Puerto Rican, Rastafarian, Trinidadian and Tobagan, Vincentian, West Indian

◎ **DENMARK** *45*

● **Caribbean Scandinavian Association, CSA**
Ansel Henry Hollis: Gogervang 10, 2790 Hørsholm; *t* 4286 1414, 4286 2191, *f* 4576 5999
Afro-Caribbean culture; social and welfare activities. »94

◎ **FRANCE** *33*

● **Communauté antillo guyanaise de France** *(Caribbean and Guyanese Community in France)*
51 rue Riquet, 75019 Paris; *t* (1) 4035 7350   »90
✿ **Espace Culturelle Caraïbéen** *(Caribbean Cultural Workshop)*
9 rue Grands Augustins, 75006 Paris; *t* (1) 4325 8537 »90

◎ **UNITED KINGDOM** *44*

● **Association of Caribbean Nationals**
Alperton Youth and Community Centre, Ealing Road, Wembley HA0 4QL; *t* (0181) 902 7509   »90
● **Cardinal Hume's Committee for the Caribbean**
Leela Ramdeen: [address unknown] London
Catholic Church consultative body on Caribbean affairs. »96
✿ **Caribbean Centre**
1 Amberley Street, Liverpool L8   »91
● **Caribbean Communication Project**
285 Edgware Road, London W2 1BB; *t* (0171) 262 7515 »90
✿ **Caribbean Community Centre**
Rev. John Robson: 416 Seven Sisters Road, London N4 2LX; *t* (0171) 802 0550   »94
▌ **Caribbean Council for Europe**
Nelson House, 819 Northumberland Street, London WC2N 5RA; *t* (0171) 976 1493, *f* 976 1541
Private-sector group founded 1992; concerns include trading links between Caribbean countries and the EU. »93

✿ **Caribbean Crafts Circle**
7 Gayford Street, London W12 9BY; *t* (0181) 749 0050 »91
✿ **Caribbean Cricket Club**
Scott Hall Road, Leeds, Yorkshire; *t* (0113) 262 6543 »90
✿ **Caribbean Cultural International**
300 Westbourne Park Road, London W11 1EH; *t* (0171)
229 3086 »94
● **Caribbean Development Project Foundation**
8 Penpoll Rd, Hackney, London E8 1EX; *t* (0181) 986 5634
May be same as Caribbean Development Foundation listed
(1990) at 4-8 Arcola Street, E8. Cultural exchanges, advice
service, training courses, exhibitions. »94
✿ **Caribbean Golden Age Club**
161 Cromwell Rd, Peterborough PE1; *t* (01773) 896313 »95
● **Caribbean Heritage Group**
Tara MacArthur: Lee Community Education Centre, 1 Aislibie
Road, London SE12 8QH; *t* (0181) 852 4700 »90
✿ *Caribbean Insight* also known as *Insight*
Nelson House, 8 Northumberland St, London WC2N 5RA »93
● **Caribbean Labour Solidarity**
Frank Archer: [address unknown]
Supports socialist movements in Caribbean countries. »94
● **Caribbean Links Organisation**
[address unknown] »96
✿ **Caribbean Pensioners and Friends**
91 Tollington Way, London N7; *t* (0171) 263 3501 »95
✿ **Caribbean Peoples Association**
Newlands Club, Octagon Parade, High Wycombe HP11,
Buckinghamshire; *t* (01494) 20335 »90
✿ **Caribbean Senior Citizens Centre**
Chesnut Road, London N17; *t* (0181) 365 1593 »95
✿ **Caribbean Sunrise Social Club**
Paradise Square, Oxford; *t* (01865) 722956 »90
● **Caribbean Teachers Association, CTA**
Cecily Haynes-Hart: 8 Camberwell Green, London SE5;
t (0171) 708 1293
Founded 1975; professional development, educational
resources, anti-racism and multi-culturalism. *CTA News*. »91
● *Caribbean Times*: Hansib Publishing Ltd
Dan Marriot, Editor: Tower House, 3rd floor, 139-149 Fonthill
Road, London N4 3HF; *t* (0171) 281 1191, *f* 263 9656
Newspaper (52/yr) founded 1981; see *Asian Times*, p13. »95
✿ **Caribbean Women's Association**
c/o OSCAR, 12 Bell Barn Shopping Centre, Cregoe St, Lee
Bank, Birmingham B15 2DZ »90
✿ **Hibiscus Caribbean Elderly Group**
The Chatsworth Community Centre, Buckingham Road,
Stratford, London E15; *t* (0181) 519 6159
Development and promotion of community services for
Caribbean elders; seeks to reduce loneliness and isolation.»92
✿ **Ipswich Caribbean Association, ICA**
Brenda Shelley: [address unknown] Ipswich, Suffolk
Anti-racism; social and cultural activities. »94
✿ **United Caribbean Association, UCA**
UCA House, 12 Hall Lane, Leeds; *t* (0113) 262 6537 »90
✿ **West Midlands Caribbean Parents and Friends Association**
372 Newhampton Road West, Whitmore Reans,
Wolverhampton WV6 0RX; *t* (01902) 21783 »96

CATALAN

see also *European, French, Spanish*

◎ **LUXEMBOURG** *352*
● **Centre Català de Luxembourg, CCL**
c/o Antoni Montserrat i Moliner: 24 avenue Victor Hugo,
3ème, 1750 Luxembourg; *t* 220678, 4301 3249
Resum d'Activitats (4/yr). »94

CENTRAL AFRICAN

see also *African, Angolan, Cameroon, Congolese, Gabonese,
Rwandese, Zairean*

◎ **FRANCE** *33*
✿ **Amicale des ressortissants centrafricains, ARCA** *(Society
of Central African Nationals)*
152 rue Baraban, 69003 Lyon »90
✿ **Association génération future**
12 rue du Château, 77000 Melun
Communication/encounters between immigrants and French,
cultural and artistic events, trips to Central Africa. »90

● **Union des ressortissants d'Afrique Central et d'Angola**
(Union of Nationals of Central Africa and Angola)
[address unknown] Paris »90

◎ **SPAIN** *34*
✿ **Asociación Jama Kafo**
Sheriffo Jarju: José Monserrat i Cuadrada 39, 08303
Mataró, Barcelona, Catalunya; *t* (93) 799 6175
Social and cultural club. »94

CENTRAL AMERICAN

see also *Guatemalan, Honduran, Latin American, Nicaraguan,
Salvadorean; and see Mexican*

◎ **BELGIUM** *32*
● **Agencia Centroamericana de Noticias** *(Central American
News Agency)*
[address unknown] Bruxelles
Enfoprensa magazine. »90
● **Service euro-centroaméricain pour la coopération
démocratique, Seucode** *(European-Central American
Democratic Co-operation)*
[address unknown] Bruxelles »88

◎ **SPAIN** *34*
● **Asociación Las Segovias para la Cooperación con
Centroamérica**
carrer Valencia 366-2° 3ª, 08009 Barcelona, Catalunya;
t (93) 207 7443, 459 1662, *f* 459 2510
Human rights and development aid; refugee reintegration in
Nicaragua and El Salvador. *Las Segovias* (4/yr). »93

◎ **SWITZERLAND** *41*
▌ **Secretariado Europeo Oscar Romero de Solidaridad con los
Pueblos Centroamericanos** *(European Romero Centre for
Solidarity with Central America)*
Karl Heuberger: Witikonstrasse 36, 8037 Zürich »93

◎ **UNITED KINGDOM** *44*
✿ **Aylesbury Central America Group**
Eve Howes: [address unknown] Aylesbury HP20, Bucks.
Solidarity with Central America and the Caribbean. »94
● **Central America Human Rights Committee, CAHRC,**
formerly Central America Human Rights Co-ordination
General Secretary: 83 Margaret Street, London W1N 7HB;
t (0171) 631 4200, *f* 436 1129
Andy McEntee. Promotes human rights and social justice in
Central America. See also El Salvador, Guatemala and
Honduras Committees for Human Rights, pp104, 39, 43.
Central America Report; Human Rights Bulletin. »94
● **Central America Week**
82 Margaret Street, London W1N 8LH; *t* (0171) 631 5173
Coalition of 21 NGOs; organises week of Central American
public education activities. »90
● **Central America Women's Network**
[address unknown] London
Solidarity with women in Central America; networking with
Central American women in Britain. »92
✿ **Telford Central America Group**
[address unknown] Telford, Shropshire »92
✿ **West Scotland Central America Network**
[address unknown] Scotland »92

CENTRAL EUROPEAN

see *East European*; see also *Albanian, Austrian, Bosnian,
Bulgarian, Croatian, Czech, Estonian, Hungarian, Latvian,
Lithuanian, Polish, Romanian, Serbian, Slav, Slovene,
Ukrainian, (Ex-)Yugoslav*

CHADIAN

see also *African, Central African*

◎ **FRANCE** *33*
✿ **Solidarité et Développement Tchad-France**
Sou Ngadoy: 39 avenue du Président Wilson, 91300
Montreuil; *t* (1) 4859 5782 »94

Ⓞ **ITALY** *39*

✤ **Associazione Sao del Ciad,** Sao
Mahamat Taher: c/o ARCI Nova, Strada Massetana, Ito 3,
53100 Siena; *t* (0577) 364526, 271567, *f* 271538   »94

CHILEAN

see also Latin American

Ⓞ **BELGIUM** *32*

✤ **Casa Chile** *(Chile House)*
Lange Beeldekenstr. 35, 2060 Antwerpen; *t* (03) 231 4352
Refugee education and training, women's interests. *Casa
Chile Info.*   »94
✤ **Collectif d'Accueil aux Réfugiés du Chili,** COLARCH
(Chilean Refugee Reception Committee) Kollektief voor het
Onthaal van Chileense Vluchtelingen, KolOCh
Rue Traversière 4, 1030 Bruxelles; *t* (02) 218 1094
Coalition of NGOs working with Latin American refugees. »94

Ⓞ **DENMARK** *45*

● **Chilensk-Dansk Solidaritetsforening** *(Danish Chile Solidarity
Association)*
Klostergade 37, 8000 Århus C   »89

Ⓞ **FRANCE** *33*

● **Coordination des Comités Chili**
49 rue de Vaugirard, 75006 Paris
Solidarity committees.   »90

Ⓞ **IRELAND** *353*

● **Ireland-Chile Solidarity Group**
37 Kilcarrig Crescent, Fettercairn, Tallaght, Dublin 24;
t (01) 512034 (?)   »90

Ⓞ **ITALY** *39*

✤ **Associazione Cile Lombardia,** ACL
Lucy Resischel Rojas: via Bagutta 12, 20121 Milano;
t (02) 614 0552, 669 7723
Refugee welfare, cultural activities. Also listed (1990) at via
Salvador Allende 11, 20091 Bresso, MI, *t* (02) 730811.   »94
✤ **Associazione Donne Cilene Esuli Emilia Romagna** *(Emilia
Romagna Association of Chilean Exile Women)*
via Moro 16, 40100 Bologna   »90
✤ **Chiesa Cilena** *(Chilean Catholic Church)*
piazza Ateneo Salesiano 1, 00139 Roma; *t* (06) 813 2041»90
✤ **Comitato Cile** *(Chile Committee)*
via Castelfidardo 50, 00185 Roma; *t* (06) 495 8626   »90
✤ **Comunità Cilena:** Emilio Romagna
via IV Giornate di Napoli 4, 42100 Reggio Emilia   »90
✤ **Comunità Cilena di Roma**
Mario González: via dei Mille 23, 00185 Roma; *t* (06) 497801
Refugee association formed 1974, now involved in return
migration assistance. May be same as the group of this name
listed (1990) at viale Appio Claudio 314, 00174 Roma.   »94

Ⓞ **LUXEMBOURG** *352*

✤ **Association Culturelle du Chili** *(Chile Cultural Association)*
Teddy Contreras: c/o 10 rue des Jardins, 7232 Bereldange;
t 331093   »94
✤ **Frente Patriótico Manuel Rodríguez** *(Rodríguez Patriotic Front)*
BP 1773, 1017 Luxembourg
Marxist movement.   »90

Ⓞ **SPAIN** *34*

✤ **Agrupación Chile Democrático** *(Democratic Chile Grouping)*
Ronda de San Pedro 20-21, 08010 Barcelona; *t* (93) 245 8000
Umbrella group of Pinochet-era exiles.   »87
● **Asociación Chilena de Derechos Humanos** *(Chilean
Association for Human Rights)*
pza Tirso de Molina 3-1°, 28012 Madrid; *t* (91) 369 1652»94
✤ **Asociación de Mujeres Chilenas** TRALUN
Martín de los Heros 23-4° BD, 28008 Madrid; *t* (91) 247 2981
Women's group.   »87
✤ **Asociación Pablo Neruda**
2 de Mayo 18-1° dcha, 48003 Bilbo, Bizkaia, Euskadi
Information on Chile, social and cultural support for Latin
Americans; charitable activities in Chile. *Elcahuih.*   »94
✤ **Centro de Estudios Salvador Allende** *(Allende Study Centre)*
calle Preciados 35-2° izq., 28013 Madrid; *t* (91) 247 5478
Chilean studies.   »90

Ⓞ **UNITED KINGDOM** *44*

● **Anglo-Chilean Society**
Michael Cannon, Secretary: 12 Devonshire Street, London
W1N 2DS; *t* (0171) 580 1271
Friendship, cultural exchanges; founded 1944.   »90
● **Chile Democrático** *(Democratic Chile)*
Julio Concha Contreras: [address uncertain] 15 Wilkin Street,
London NW5 3NL
Organisation of political refugees from 1970s-80s.   »96
✤ **Chilean Society**
Jorge Okrego: 4 Adamson Walk, Rusholme, Manchester M14
5WW; *t* (0161) 225 7834
Immigration/welfare advice; sporting, social and cultural
events; adult education; care of elderly and disabled.   »93
● **Comité Exterior Mapuche** *(Mapuche Committee in Exile)*
Vicente Mariqueo: 6 Lodge Street, Bristol BS1 5LR;
t/f (0117) 927 9391
Support for Mapuche communities in Chile and Argentina, and
welfare of Mapuches who came to UK as refugees.   »93

CHINESE

*including Taiwanese and Hong Kong; see also Asian,
Mongolian, Tibetan, Vietnamese*

Ⓞ **BELGIUM** *32*

● **Centre Culturel Belgique Chine asbl**
Rue Edith Cavell 88, 1180 Bruxelles; *t* (02) 343 1199   »90

Ⓞ **DENMARK** *45*

● **Venskabsforening Danmark-Kina**
Klareboderne 12, København; *t* 3391 2303   »95

Ⓞ **FRANCE** *33*

✤ **Amicale Chinoise Côte-d'Azur** *(Chinese Friends Society of
the Côte d'Azur)*
Philippe Chau: 7 rue de la Russie, 06000 Nice; *t* 9387 9511,
f 9387 5989
Culture, social activities.   »94
● **Amitiés franco-chinoises** *(Franco-Chinese Friendship)* Head
Office and travel service
51 rue Rivoli, 75001 Paris; *t* (1) 4236 4430   »90
✤ ≡ Comité de Paris: 5 avenue Maine, 75015 Paris   »90
● **Association des Chinois résidents en France**
43 rue Temple, 75004 Paris; *t* (1) 4277 1360   »90
✤ **Association Régionale Provence des Amitiés Franco-
Chinoises,** ARPAFC *(Provence Region Franco-Chinese
Friendship Association)*
Claudette Castan: 3a rue St Dominique, 13211 Marseille;
t 9191 6329   »94
✤ **Association des résidents d'origine chinoise**
37 rue Disque, 75013 Paris; *t* (1) 4586 8099   »90
✤ **Centre Culturel Chinois**
78 rue Dunois, 75013 Paris; *t* (1) 4582 9678   »90
✤ **Centre culturel franco-chinois, Alpes-Maritimes**
37 avenue de Cannes, 06160 Juan-les-Pins
Non-political cultural exchanges, promotion of traditional
Chinese culture, international friendship.   »90
● **Minzhuzhongguo Zhen Xian:** Federation for a Democratic
China
10 rue Faraday, 75017 Paris; *t* (1) 4440 0574, *f* 4763 2917
Emigré organisation campaigning for human rights.   »93

Ⓞ **IRELAND** *353*

● **Irish Chinese Cultural Society**
Norman O'Galligan, Honorary Secretary: 5 Claremont Road,
Sandymount, Dublin 4; *t* (01) 668 4721
Promotes Chinese arts and culture. Also c/o Chester Beatty
Library, Shrewsbury Road, Dublin 4, *t* 668 3026, which has
important Oriental holdings. Newsletter, magazine.   »95

Ⓞ **ITALY** *39*

✤ **Associazione dei Cinesi a Milano**
Hu San Cun: via Paolo Sarpi 19, 20154 Milano
Employment, training, culture.   »94
✤ **Comunità Cinese**
c/o China Trading, via G. Bruno 14, 20154 Milano; *t* (02) 318
2050   »90
✤ ≡ corso Vittorio Emanuele 66, 10121 Torino   »90
✤ **Istituto Italo Cinese** *(Italian Chinese Institute)*
Lungo Po A. Antonelli 177, 10153 Torino; *t* (011) 890406»90

◎ **LUXEMBOURG** *352*

● **Association Luxembourg-Chine**
4 boulevard Pierre Dupont, 1430 Luxembourg; *t* 448865 »95

◎ **NETHERLANDS** *31*

● **The Federation for a Democratic China**
Topaas 15, 6922 NK Duiven; *t* (010) 419 2799 »95
● **International Committe for Human Rights in Taiwan**
Postbus 91542, 2509 EC Den Haag; *t/f* (070) 385 8589 »93
● **Sinologisch Instituut** *(Chinese Studies Institute)*
F.N. Pieke: Rijksuniversiteit, Postbus 9555, 2300 AB Leiden
Includes Documentatiecentrum voor het huidige China. »89

◎ **SPAIN** *34*

● **Asociación de Amigos de China** *(Friends of China Society)*
calle Fracisco Zea 2, Madrid; *t* (91) 361 4573 »95
✿ **Centro Sun Yat Sen** *(Sun Yat-sen Centre)*
paseo de la Habana 12, Madrid; *t* (91) 411 3463 »90

◎ **UNITED KINGDOM** *44*

● **Alliance for a Better China**
Dr A. Chan: [address unknown] »90
✿ **Birmingham Chinese Society**
138 Digbeth, Birmingham B5 6DR; *t* (0121) 643 4343
Social and cultural activities; employment and training. »94
✿ **Birmingham Chinese Youth Association**
133 High Street, Kings Heath, Birmingham B14 »90
✿ **Birmingham Chinese Youth Project, BCYP**
James Li, Co-ordinator: 156 Bleakhouse Rd, Oldbury, Warley
B68 0LU; *t* (0121) 693 7007, 622 4292, *f* 693 7008
Support, training, health and HIV prevention advice. »95
● **Bishop Ho Ming Wah Association**
Sandie Chung: Bishop R.O. Hall Chinese Centre, 5 St Martin's
Place, London WC2N 4JT; *t* (0171) 839 5581, 825 0755
Culture, education, youth welfare. »94
✿ **Brent Chinese Centre**
31 First Avenue, Wembley HA9 3QG; *t* (0181) 904 9467 »94
✿ **Bristol and Avon Chinese Women's Group**
c/o BBVS DU, The Inkworks, 20-22 Hepburn Road, St Pauls,
Bristol BS2 8UD; *t* (0117) 942 3960 »96
● **British Association for Chinese Studies**
Anna Johnston, Secretary: Great Britain-China Centre, 15
Belgrave Square, London SW1X 8PG; *t* (0171) 235 9216
Promotes academic study of China; founded 1976. »90
● **British Chinese Artists' Association**
Andy Gunn: [address unknown] London; *t* (0171) 267 6133 »96
✿ **Camden Chinese Community Centre, CCCC**
173 Arlington Road, London NW1 7EY; *t* (0171) 267 3019
Grace Tan: community centre; elderly group, women's group;
Chinese/Vietnamese immigration and welfare work. »95
● **China Appeal**
Lua Bing Sum: 152 Camden High St, London NW1 0NE »91
● **China Cultural Funds**
18 Essex Road, London N1; *t* (0171) 704 8169 »95
● *The China Quarterly*
Dr David Shambaugh: School of Oriental & African Studies,
Thornhaugh Street, Russell Square, London WC1H 0XG;
t (0171) 323 6129, *f* 580 6836 »95
● **China Society**
Sir John Grey, Secretary: 31b Torrington Square, London
WC1E 7JL; *t* (0171) 636 7985
Founded 1906; study of culture, history, language. »90
✿ **Chinese Arts Centre**
Joanna Tong: 1st floor, Fraser House, 36 Charlotte Street,
Manchester M1 4FD; *t* (0161) 236 9251
Art exhibitions, educational and community activities. »95
✿ **Chinese Arts For All**
342 S Lambeth Rd, London SW8 1UQ; *t* (0171) 498 0313 »94
✿ **Chinese Association**
M.C. Lui, Centre Manager: 77 Preston Street, Brighton BN1
2HG; *t* (01273) 327698
Kwai Cheung chair, Arlene Lui. Social and welfare centre. »94
✿ **Chinese Christian Fellowship**
29 Portland Road, Birmingham B16 »90
✿ **Chinese Community Association**
A. Hung: 146 Stratford Road, Birmingham B11 1AG »90
✿ **Chinese Community Centre**
Stanley Hui: Unit B206, Cathay Street, Arcadian Centre,
Pershore Street, Birmingham B5 4TD; *t* (0121) 622 3003 »94
✿ ≡ and Chinese Advisers Forum: 2nd floor, 44 Gerrard Street,
Soho, London W1V 7LP; *t* (0171) 439 3822, 734 3572
Gill Tan, Suk Man Hui. Voluntary centre, founded 1980.
Welfare advice, arts and cultural promotion, visits elderly. »94

✿ *Chinese Community Newsletter*
Kwai Sum Lee: 319 Slade Lane, Levenshulme, Manchester
M19; *t* (0161) 224 1033 »93
✿ **Chinese Cultural Centre**
27 Old Gloucester Street, London WC1N 3XX; *t* (0171)
633 9878 »94
✿ **Chinese Cultural Development Centre**
Tony Wang/Joyce Patterson: 6 Headland Park, North Hill,
Plymouth PL4 8HT; *t* (01752) 266866, *f* 253097
Advice centre serving Chinese of Devon and Cornwall. »94
✿ **Chinese Education, Culture and Community Centre**
Loret Lee: Ground Floor, 61 Dickenson Street, Manchester
M1 4LF; *t* (0161) 228 3926
Language classes, cultural/welfare activities, interpreting. »93
✿ **Chinese Health Information Centre**
Mary Kam Ha Ramscar: 39 George Street, Manchester M1;
t (0161) 228 0138
Primary care, interpreting, liaison with other agencies. »93
✿ **Chinese Information and Advice Centre, CIAC**
Maria Lin Wong/Katie Ku: 68 Shaftesbury Avenue, London
W1V 7DF; *t* (0171) 494 3273, 836 8291
Founded 1983; equal opportunities, welfare, immigration,
housing, domestic violence, employment advice. »95
● **Chinese Information Centre Co-op Ltd**
Simon Jones/Li Yan: 4th floor, 16 Nicholas St, Manchester
M1 4EJ; *t* (0161) 228 0420
Information on and for the Chinese community; translation,
interpreting. *Si Yu Chinese Times* (12/yr). »95
✿ **Chinese Mental Health Association**
Oxford House, Derbyshire Street, London E2 6HG; *t* (0171)
613 1008
Development of housing and support services in London. »96
✿ **Chinese Professional Association (North-West)**
Peter Chui: c/o C.K. Chui & Co., Accountants, 1st Floor,
2 Waterloo St, Manchester M1 6HY; *t* (0161) 236 3557
Community advice, information, translation service. »93
● **Chinese Solidarity Campaign**
Cheung Siu Ming: [address unknown] »90
● **Chinese Women's Domestic Violence Helpline**
[address confidential] London; *t* (0171) 494 3861 »91
✿ **Chinese Women's Group**
Kwai Sum Lee: 308 Slade Lane, Levenshulme, Manchester
M19 2BY; *t* (0161) 224 1033
Social, economic and health issues. »93
✿ **Chinese Women's Refuge Group, CWRG**
Instrument House, 207-215 King's Cross Road, London
WC1X 9DB; *t* (0171) 837 7297
Refuge, support services for Chinese women and children
experiencing domestic violence throughout Britain. »96
✿ **Chinese Women's Research and Health Project**
C. Mei-Sheung Chan: 13 Biaston Avenue, Fallowfield,
Manchester M14 7BR; *t* (0161) 256 3763, 275 5218 »93
✿ **East London Chinese Association of Tower Hamlets**
880 (680?) Commercial Road, Sailors Place, London E14
7HA; *t* (0171) 515 5598, 538 2546 »94
● **Federation for a Democratic China, UK Branch**
Siyun Wang: St Anthony's College, Oxford »91
✿ **Gloucester Chinese Community Group**
66 Star Youth & Community Centre, Wesley Hall, Seymour
Road, Gloucester GL1 5GN »94
● **Great Britain-China Centre**
The Director: 15 Belgrave Square, London SW1X 8PS;
t (0171) 235 6696
Public body promoting non-governmental relations between
Britain and China; bilateral exchanges, information on China,
advice and help to other organisations, individual membership
in UK. See British Association for Chinese Studies, left. »95
✿ **Greenwich Chinese Association** and Greenwich Chinese
Community School
Josephine Chan, Organiser: West Greenwich House, 111
Greenwich High Road, London SE10; *t* (0181) 858 2410 »94
✿ **Hackney Chinese Community Services**
Mr Hau: 28-32 Ellingfort Road, Hackney, London E8 3PA;
t (0181) 986 6171, *f* 533 5066
Community welfare, mental health work, advice services. »96
✿ **Haringey Chinese Centre** and Haringey Chinese Community
School
Sui Lau, Administrator: 211 Langham Road, London N15
3TL; *t* (0181) 881 8649 »95
✿ **Hounslow Chinese Community Centre**
Hounslow United Reformed Church Hall, 114 Hanworth
Road, Hounslow TW3 1UF; *t* (0181) 577 2034 »94
✿ **Islington Chinese Association, ICA**
33 Giesbach Road, London N19 3DA; *t* (0171) 263 5986
Community development, cultural and social activities. »94

- **June 4 China Support Group**
Philip Baker: 152 Camden High Street, London NW1 0NE;
t (0171) 482 4292   »91
✿ **King's Cross Chinese Women's Group**
c/o King's Cross Neighbourhood Centre, 51 Argyle Street,
London WC1H 8EF; *t* (0171) 837 4025   »94
✿ **Lambeth Chinese Community Association, LCCA**
Elsa Lin: Chinese Community Centre, 69 Stockwell Road,
London SW9 9BY; *t* (0171) 733 4377, 738 4589, 733 5045
Community development, services to Chinese women and
elderly, advice on welfare rights; six staff.   »95
✿ **London Chinese Health Resource Centre, LCHRC**
Queen's House, 1 Leicester Place, Leicester Square, London
WC2H 7BP; *t* (0171) 287 0904, 434 2000, *f* 287 3227
Addresses language and cultural barriers to access to health
services. Health promotion, survey on Chinese/Vietnamese
menta health needs, Chinese Carers' Project.   »96
✿ **London Federation of Chinese Women, LFCW**
c/o CIAC, 68 Shaftesbury Avenue, London W1V 7DF;
t (0171) 748 3020 ext. 2187
Community work, refugee concerns.   »90
✿ **Manchester Alliance for a Democratic China**
Chi Hong Wong: PO Box 545, Manchester M60 1HA   »91
✿ **Manchester Chinese Christian Church; Manchester Chinese
Youth Group; Manchester Chinese Elderly People's Group**
Rev. D. Jacob Tsang: 100 Yarburgh Street, Whalley Range,
Manchester M16 7EH; *t* (0161) 225 0265, 862 9553
Church; Chinese language classes, cultural and social activities
for young people; social and welfare activities for elders. »93
✿ ≡ **Gospel Centre:** George Chung: 39 George Street,
Manchester; *t* (0161) 237 9198   »93
✿ **Manchester Federation of Chinese Associations**
Loret Lee: 61 Dickenson Street, Manchester M1 4LF;
t (0161) 228 3926, 228 7506
Umbrella body for Chinese community groups.   »93
✿ **Manchester Wai Yin Chinese Women Centre:** also known
as Wai Yin Chinese Women Society, or Wai Yin Centre
Dora Chu: 1st floor, Rother House, 11-13 Spear Street,
Manchester M1 1JU; *t* (0161) 228 3096, 237 5908
Adult education and training; other services and activities.»96
✿ **Merseyside Chinese Community Services**
The Pagoda, Henry Street, Liverpool L1   »91
✿ **Merton Chinese Community Association**
J. Chang, Chair: The Vestry Hall, London Road, Mitcham
CR4 3UD; *t* (0181) 648 9889   »94
✿ **Midlands Chinese Association**
Senna Smith: [address unknown] Birmingham   »90
✿ **Newham Chinese Association**
The Co-ordinator: Room 3, Park House, 64 West Ham Lane,
Stratford, London E15 4PT; *t* (0181) 519 6488
Small voluntary group, seeking to provide advisory and other
community services to Newham Chinese community.   »95
✿ **Ng Yip Chinese Association**
Charles Chan JP: 3rd Floor, 16 Nicholas Street, Manchester;
t (0161) 228 7871, 881 9713
Social group for people from five Chinese counties.   »93
✿ **North West Chinese Sunday School**
Raymond Chui: Shena Simon Sixth Form College, 1
Whitworth Street, Manchester; *t* (0161) 864 3825
Chinese language classes for children, English for adults. »93
- **Overseas Chinese Association**
108 Bromsgrove Street, Birmingham B5 6QS   »90
✿ **Oxfordshire Chinese Community & Advice Centre, OCCAC**
44b Princes Street, Oxford OX4 1DD; *t* (01865) 204188
Advice on benefits, immigration, nationality, other matters;
social and cultural activities.   »94
✿ **Project Kiu Wah**
Social Services Department, City of Westminster Council,
London SW1
Project to identify and meet the social work and community
care needs of local Chinese; counselling, information, liaison
with voluntary sector and public services; seven staff.   »95
✿ **Qing Hua Chinese School**
Ching Yun Yang: 5 Hamilton Road, Harrow HA1 1SU;
t (0181) 861 4983   »94
- *Sing Tao*
Kenneth Yau, Editor: 46 Dean Street, London W1Y 5AP;
t (0171) 734 0826, 0828
Daily newspaper.   »88
- **Society for Anglo-Chinese Understanding, SACU**
109 Promenade, Cheltenham GL50 1NW
International friendship, culture. *China Magazine*.   »90
- **Trade Union China Campaign**
Bobby Chan: [address uncertain] 85b Glengall Road, London
NW6   »90

✿ **Tung Sing (Orient) Housing Association Ltd**
Janis Wong: 1st Floor, Richmond House, 15 Bloom Street,
Manchester M1 3HZ; *t* (0161) 236 5294
Social housing provision, advice to Chinese and others.   »93
- *Wen Wei Po*
K.K. Cheung, Editor: 11 Little Newport Street, London WC2;
t (0171) 734 2144
Daily newspaper.   »88
- **Workers' Autonomous Federation of China, WAFC**
Li Chang Long: 47-49 Charing Cross Rd, London WC2H 0AN
Campaigns for independent trade unions in China.   »95

⊙ **CHANNEL ISLANDS** *44*

✿ **Jersey Chinese Association**
3 Union Court, Union Street, St Helier, Jersey JE2 3RH;
t (01534) 880814   »95

⊙ **NORTHERN IRELAND** *44*

✿ **Barnardo's Chinese Lay Health Project**
c/o NICEM, 17 Eblana Street, Belfast BT7 1LD   »96
- **Chinese Welfare Association**
Patrick Yu/Eleanor McKnight: 17 Eblana Street, Belfast BT7;
t (01232) 238220
Cultural activities, interpreting, hospital visiting, advice, youth
groups, resource centre, campaigning against racism.   »95

COLOMBIAN

see also Latin American

⊙ **BELGIUM** *32*

- **Amitiés Belgo-Colombiennes** *(Belgian-Colombian Friendship)*
Jean-Jacques Leduc: Rue d'Oultremont 52, 1040 Bruxelles;
t (02) 732 1575
Cultural links, solidarity, information. *Macondo*.   »94

⊙ **FRANCE** *33*

- **Comité France-Colombie pour les Droits de l'Homme** *(France-
Colombia Committee for Human Rights)*
[address unknown] Paris   »90

⊙ **IRELAND** *353*

- **Irish Colombian Support Group**
11 Ashdale Park, Terenure, Dublin
Solidarity with the people of Colombia and with refugees.»94

⊙ **ITALY** *39*

- **Associazione Italia Colombia**
J.M. Guerra: c/o Collegium Clarentianum Studenti, Largo
Lorenzo Mossa, 00165 Roma; *t* (06) 623 6924
Founded 1988; migrants'rights.   »90

⊙ **SPAIN** *34*

✿ **Centro de Información Cultural de Colombia**
carrer San Juan 3, Sitges, Barcelona, Catalunya   »87
- **Comité Pro Derechos Humanos de Colombia, CPDHC**
(Colombia Committee for Human Rights)
Ortega y Gasset 77-2° A, 28006 Madrid; *t* (91) 402 2321»94

⊙ **UNITED KINGDOM** *44*

- **Colombia Committee for Human Rights**
[address unknown] London
Campaigns on human rights in Colombia; refugee rights. »92
- **Colombia Solidarity Committee**
Latin American House, Kingsgate Place, London NW6 4TA;
t (0171) 372 6662
International solidarity; support for progressive forces in
Colombia, and for refugees from violence in Colombia.   »94
- **Colombian Refugee Association, CORAS**
12-14 Thornton Street, London SW9 0BL
Educational, employment, housing, welfare advice.   »93

COMOROS

see also African, Asian, Islamic, Southern African

⊙ **FRANCE** *33*

*Association pluriculturelle de contact avec les Comores: see
Association pluriculturelle pour la coopération (etc.), p162*

Fédération des associations islamiques d'Afrique, des Comores et Antilles, FAIACA: see Islamic listing, p53

CONGOLESE

see also African, Central African

◎ FRANCE 33

✿ **Association congolaise Temo**, ACT
44 avenue Boileau, 94500 Champigny-sur-Marne »89
✿ **Association Jeunesse congolaise en France**, JCEF
(Congolese Youth Association in France)
chez M. Kimbally: 1 rue du Capitaine-Bossard, 92600 Asnières-sur-Seine
Solidarity and mutual assistance, documentation. »89

◎ ITALY 39

● **Associazione Studenti del Congo/Unione dei Giovani Socialisti Congolesi**, AEC/UGSC: Congo Students Association/ Union of Congolese Socialist Youth
Firmin Bonzangabato: via Modena 50, 00184 Roma; *t* (06) 339 8027
Formed 1983; advice and mediation service. »94

COTE D'IVOIRE

see African, Ivorian, West African

CROATIAN

see also Bosnian, East European, European, Islamic, South-East European, (Ex-)Yugoslav

◎ FRANCE 33

✿ **Amitié franco-croate Lyon**, AFCL *(Lyons Franco-Croatian Friendship Group)*
Marie-Hélène Angely: BP 5022, 69245 Lyon Cedex 05; *t* 7859 5723, *f* 7837 1953
Solidarity and friendship with Croatia, welfare of refugees, cultural activities. »94
✿ **Conseil Représentatif des Instituts et Communautés Croates de France**, CRICF *(Board of Deputies of Croatians in France)*
36 avenue Georges Mandel, 75116 Paris
Umbrella group of cultural and political societies. »94

◎ ITALY 39

✿ **Chiesa Croata** *(Croatian Catholic Church)*
piazza S. Ufficio 11, 00193 Roma; *t* (06) 698 3807 »90

CUBAN

see also African Caribbean, Afro-Caribbean, Caribbean, Latin American

◎ DENMARK 45

● **Dansk-Kubansk Forening**
Kulturhuset Cikaden, Griffenfeldsgade 35, 2200 København N; *t* 3537 1430, *f* 3537 1980 »95

◎ IRELAND 353

● **Cuba Support Group**
Declan McKenna: [address unknown] »95
● **Ireland Cuba Solidarity Campaign**
Bernie Dwyer: 20 Seaview Terrace, Howth, Co. Dublin; *t* (01) 832 4169, *f* 706 1195
Solidarity with the people of Cuba; organisation of voluntary work brigades. *Cuba Sí.* »95

◎ PORTUGAL 351

● **Associação de Amizade Portugal-Cuba** *(Portugal-Cuba Friendship Association)*
Rodrigo Fonseca 107 r/c E, 1070 Lisboa; *t* (01) 385 7305»95

◎ SPAIN 34

● **Asociación de Amistad Hispano-Cubana Bartolomé de las Casas** *(Spanish-Cuban Friendship Society)*
calle San Marcos 37, Madrid; *t* (91) 522 2025 »95

✿ **Asociación de Cubanos** *(Cuban Association)*
Raúl Alvarez: calle Sevilla 4-2° izq., 39001 Santander, Cantabria; *t* (942) 210646, 210302 »87
✿ **Asociación de Cubanos La Palmera** *(Palm Tree Cuban Association)*
Simón Bolívar 19-7°, 48010 Bilbao; *t* (94) 432 7852 »87
✿ **Centro de Acogida Santa Luisa de Marillac** *(St Louise Reception Centre)*
[address uncertain] Ponzano 28-1° dcha., 28003 Madrid; *t* (91) 442 6704
Also listed (1987) at calle General Martínez Campo 18, 28010 Madrid, *t* 445 7412. »87
● **Centro Cubano de España**
calle Claudio Coello 41-1°, 28001 Madrid; *t* (91) 576 4735
Social centre, restaurant. »90
✿ **Centro de Encuentro y Acogida El Cobre** *(El Cobre Reception and Social Centre)*
Francisco Carrera: calle Noviciado 14, 28015 Madrid; *t* (91) 231 9167, 415 2412 »91
● **Comité pro Derechos Humanos en Cuba** *(Committee for Human Rights in Cuba)*
calle General Pardiñas 29, Madrid; *t* (91) 575 9095 »90
✿ **Unión de Cubanos de Tenerife**
Serrano 21, Apd° 538, 38004 Santa Cruz; *t* (922) 267127»87
● **Unión Liberal Cubana** and Fundación Liberal José Martí
Carlos Alberto Montaner, President: Santa Clara 4, 28013 Madrid; *t* (91) 541 2804, *f* 541 0368
Antonio Guedes general secretary, Humberto López director. Opposition party in exile; member of Liberal International since 1992; 2,000 members in USA/Spain. *Unión Próxima.* »95

◎ UNITED KINGDOM 44

● **Britain Cuba Resource Centre**, BCRC
[address unknown] London
Solidarity with the people of Cuba. »92
● *CubaSí*
Steve Wilkinson, Editor: 21 Knights House, South Lambeth Road, London SW8 1UU
Solidarity with Cuba. »95
● **Cuba Solidarity Campaign**, CSC
129 Seven Sisters Road, London N7 7QG
Supports Cuba's right to sovereignty, opposes US blockade; campaigns, publications, videos; local branches. »94
● **Scottish Cuba Defence Campaign**
[address unknown]
Solidarity with Cuba, support for national sovereignty. »94
● **United Kingdom-Cuba Friendship Society**
John McCallion MP, Chair: House of Commons, Westminster, London SW1A 0AA
Harry Kay, president. International friendship, solidarity, support for Cuban sovereignty, opposes US policy. »94

CYPRIOT

see also European, Greek, Islamic, South-East European, Turkish

◎ GREECE 30

● **Federation of Cypriot Organisations in Greece**
Andreas Procopiou, President: Odos Kekropos 3, Plaka, 10558 Athinai; *t* (01) 323 1339, *f* 322 0520
H. Kalotaridou, Panayotis Ifestos. In EU Migrants Forum. »95

◎ UNITED KINGDOM 44

● **Anglo-Akanthou Aid Association**
7 Elthorne Rd, Archway, London N19; *t* (0171) 272 4434»94
✿ **Arachne Greek-Cypriot Women's Group**
[address uncertain] 3rd Floor, 67-83 Seven Sisters Road, London N7 6AE
Also listed (1994) at 53 Corker Walk, Andover Estate, N7, *t* (0171) 263 6261. »95
● **Camden Cypriot Women's Group**
94 Camden Road, London NW1; *t* (0171) 267 7194 »95
✿ **Cypriot Advisory Service**
26 Crowndale Road, London NW1; *t* (0171) 388 7971 »90
● **Cypriot Women's League**
Fairfax Road, London N15 3ST; *t* (0181) 800 8398 »95
● **Federation of Educational Societies of Greek Cypriots** and Cypriot Community Centre
Earlham Grove, London N22 5HJ; *t* (0181) 881 2329 »95
✿ **Greek Cypriot Association**
Beba Bootan: 18 Roman Crescent, Southwick, Brighton BN42 1LA; *t* (01273) 595839 »94

✿ **Hackney Cypriot Association**
5 Balls Pond Rd, London N1; *t* (0171) 249 4494, 254 8605»90
✿ **National Federation of Cypriots in Great Britain**
4 Porchester Terrace, London W2 3TL; *t* (0171) 402 8904
Umbrella group for cultural and social organisations.   »95
● **Northern Cyprus Group**
John Taylor MP: House of Commons, Westminster, London SW1A 0AA
All-party group of MPs and peers with financial or other interests in the Turkish-occupied area of Cyprus.   »95
✿ **Overseas Paphos Association in England, SAPA**
Pviolaris H. Glafkis: 29 Gisburn Road, London N8 7BS;
t (0181) 348 4700, (0171) 703 4230   »94
✿ **Southwark Cypriot Community Group**
33 Peckham High St, London SE15; *t* (0171) 703 8704   »90
✿ **Theatro Technis**
26 Crowndale Road, London NW1; *t* (0171) 388 7971   »95
✿ **Turkish Cypriot Community Association**
Niyazi Enver: 117 Green Lanes, London N16 9DA; *t* (0181) 359 5231, *f* 354 0313
Advice work.   »95
● **Turkish Cypriot Research Group**
18 Ashwin Street, London; *t* (0171) 241 3645   »95

CZECH

see also East European, German 'National', Jewish, Slovak

◎ **FRANCE** *33*

● **Association France Tchécoslovaquie**
24 rue Yves Toudic, 75010 Paris; *t* (1) 4208 4010   »90

◎ **ITALY** *39*

● **Assistenza Religiosa ai Cecoslovachi** *(Czechoslovakian Chaplaincy)*
via Liberiana 27, 00185 Roma; *t* (06) 475 8710   »90

◎ **UNITED KINGDOM** *44*

● **Anglo-Czechoslovak Welfare Association**
22 Ladbroke Square, London W11 3NA   »88

DANISH

see also European, and—though not strictly applicable to Danes—Scandinavian

◎ **LUXEMBOURG** *352*

● **Association des Danois au Luxembourg**
Vibeke Gottlieb: 26 rue des Vignes, 5431 Luxembourg Posten.   »94

◎ **UNITED KINGDOM** *44*

● **Anglo-Danish Society**
4 Daleside, Gerrards Cross SL9 7LF; *t* (01753) 884846
Friendship, cultural exchanges; founded 1924.   »90

DOMINICAN

see also African Caribbean, Afro-Caribbean, Anglo-Caribbean, Caribbean, Dominican Republic, West Indian

◎ **UNITED KINGDOM** *44*

● **Dominica Overseas Nationals Association, DONA**
260 Mansel Road, Small Heath, Birmingham B10   »90
● **Dominica UK Association**
[address unknown]   »88

DOMINICAN REPUBLIC

see also African Caribbean, Afro-Caribbean, Caribbean, Dominican, Latin American

◎ **SPAIN** *34*

● **Asociación de Mujeres Dominicanas en España, AMDE**
(Association of Dominican Republic Women in Spain)
María Paredes: Casa de la Mujer, calle Almagro 28, 28010 Madrid; *t* (91) 319 0345, 361 4980, *f* 408 7047
Welfare activities, anti-racism, intercultural contact.   »95

✿ **Centro de Acogida Quisqueya** *(Quisqueya Reception Centre)* also known as Centro Santa Isabel
Hortaleza 77, 28004 Madrid; *t* (91) 410 1713, 410 2510
Refugee and migrant welfare.   »94
✿ **Unión de Inmigrantes Dominicanos en España, UIDE**
calle Arturo Soria 187, 28034 Madrid; *t* (91) 413 6577   »94
✿ **Voluntariado de Madres Dominicanas, VOMADO**
(Dominican Mothers' Voluntary Group)
Bernarda Jiménez: calle Leganitos 35-1° D, 28013 Madrid; *t* (91) 559 2056, *f* 314 6464
Social and welfare group; information, anti-racism.   »94

DUTCH

see also Antillean, European, Moluccan, Surinamese

◎ **DENMARK** *45*

● **Dansk Hollandsk Selskab**
Åbenrå 18, København; *t* 3312 1078   »95

◎ **FRANCE** *33*

● **Institut Néerlandais** *(Dutch Institute)*
121 rue Lille, 75007 Paris; *t* (1) 4705 8599   »90
● **Union néerlandaise en France** *(Dutch Union of France)*
5 rue Saulnier, 75009 Paris; *t* (1) 4770 8654   »90

◎ **GREECE** *30*

● **Dutch Association of Greece**
PO Box 52820, Nea Erythrea, 14610 Athinai; *t* (01) 801 2819
Social, cultural and sporting association; youth welfare.   »94

◎ **UNITED KINGDOM** *44*

● **Anglo-Netherlands Society**
PO Box 68, Unilever House, Blackfriars Embankment, London EC4P 4BQ; *t* (0171) 353 5729
Friendship, cultural exchange; founded 1920.   »95

EAST AFRICAN

see also African, Asian, Eritrean, Ethiopian, Indian, Islamic, Oromo, Sudanese, Tanzanian, Tigray, Ugandan

◎ **DENMARK** *45*

✿ **Den østafrikanske Forening** *(East African Society)*
Ismail Abdullahi: Farum Hovedgade 10 E, 3520 Farum   »90

◎ **UNITED KINGDOM** *44*

✿ **East Africa Association**
Sir John Lyon House, High Timber St, London EC4V 3DP;
t (0171) 248 5721   »94
✿ **East African Association**
Mount Pleasant Centre, Birmingham B12   »90
✿ ≡ 120 Squires Lane, London N3; *t* (0181) 349 1412
Community welfare, anti-racism.   »91
✿ **East African Muslim Association**
Wali Din: 55 Stowell Green Lane, Sparkhill, Birmingham B11; *t* (0121) 771 4511
Also (1990) at 265 Golden Hillock Rd, Small Heath, B10. »94
✿ **East African Sunni Muslim Jama'at**
77 Hertford Road, East Finchley, London N2   »94

EAST EUROPEAN

see also Albanian, Armenian, Baltic, Bosnian, Bulgarian, Croatian, Czech, Estonian, European, German 'National', Hungarian, Jewish, Latvian, Lithuanian, Macedonian, Polish, Romanian, Russian, Serbian, Slav, Slovene, Transylvanian, Ukrainian, (Ex-)Yugoslav

◎ **BELGIUM** *32*

● **Fondation Tolstoï: Tolstoy Foundation**
Rue de la Paix 20, 1050 Bruxelles; *t* (02) 512 4258
National office of international agency providing aid mainly to East European refugees.   »95

◎ **DENMARK** *45*

✿ **Maziar**
Postbox 101, 3050 Humlebaek   »90

◎ **FRANCE** *33*

● **Fondation Tolstoï:** Tolstoy Foundation
24 rue St-Martin, 75008 Paris; *t* (1) 4261 6354
National section of German-based foundation assisting
refugees, mainly from the former Soviet bloc. »83

◎ **GERMANY** *49*

▮ **Tolstoy Foundation:** Overseas Headquarters
Thierschstraße 11/v, 8002 München 22; *t* (089) 982664
Emergency assistance and resettlement help, for emigrants
mainly from the former Soviet Union. »93

◎ **GREECE** *30*

● **Tolstoy Foundation**
Odos Dodekanissou 6, Agios Panteleimon, Ana Kalamaki,
17456 Athinai; *t* (01) 991 9040 »83

◎ **ITALY** *39*

● **Fondazione Tolstoï:** Tolstoy Foundation
via Capodistria 10, 00198 Roma; *t* (06) 844 8137
National section of German-based foundation resettling
migrants mainly from the former Soviet Union. »90

◎ **UNITED KINGDOM** *44*

● **British Association for Central and Eastern Europe,** BACEE
The Director: 50 Hans Crescent, 4 Floor, London SW1X
0NB; *t* (0171) 524 0766
State-funded NGO promoting democratic renewal in former
communist bloc. Concerns include parliamentary practice,
justice, media law; 350 members. *BACEE Journal.* »95
● **Central European University,** CEU
24 Tantallon Rd, London SW12 8DG; *t/f* (0171) 673 1607
Institution associated with the US-based Soros Foundation;
postgraduate campuses in Central and Eastern Europe. »94
✧ **East European Advice Centre**
The Administrator: POSK, Room 12c, 238 King Street,
London W6 0RF; *t* (0181) 748 3085
Advice and information, some casework. »94
● **Enterprise Europe**
Pippa Markus, Director: ZLR Studios, West Heath Yard,
174 Mill Lane, London NW6 1TB; *t* (0171) 431 4134
Charity established 1990 to offer business placements to
young East Europeans. »94

◎ **NORTHERN IRELAND** *44*

✧ **Eastern European Aid**
[address unknown] Belfast
Charity sending humanitarian aid to Romania. »95

EAST TIMOR

see Asian, Portuguese, South-East Asian, Timorese

EGYPTIAN

*see also African, Arab/Arabic, Islamic, Middle Eastern, North
African*

◎ **DENMARK** *45*

● **Ægyptisk Forbund i Danmark**
Mohamed Abaza: Rendsagervej 27, 2625 Vallensbæk »89

◎ **FRANCE** *33*

● **Les Amis de la Haute Egypte:** Association of Upper Egypt
Mme Claudine Pezerat, Secretary General: 74 rue du Faubourg
St-Honoré, 75008 Paris; *t* (1) 4256 6749, *f* 4736 4140
Supports Association of Upper Egypt, a Cairo-based Christian
welfare and educational charity. »94
✧ **Centre Culturel Egyptien**
111 boulevard St Michel, 75005 Paris; *t* (1) 4633 7567 »90

◎ **GREECE** *30*

● **Egyptian Community in Greece,** ECG
Magdy Helmy: [address uncertain] Pendelles 14, Vrelissa,
15235 Athinai; *t* (01) 685 2522, *f* 685 2521
Also listed (1994) at 51 Agiou Konstantinou Street, *t* 777
1226 or 771 1213, *f* 364 7769. Culture, information, social,
welfare activities; represented in EU Migrants Forum, p131.»94

◎ **ITALY** *39*

✧ **Ahram—Associazione Egiziana in Piemonte,** AHAEP
(Egyptian Association of Piedmont) formerly Associazione
Italo Egiziana in Piemonte, AIEP
Abdel Aziz Magdy: c/o FILEF, via S. Massimo 14, 10123
Torino; *t* (011) 839 8614
Social and cultural group founded 1982; employment,
educational, welfare advice. »94
✧ **Associazione Comunità Egiziana** *(Egyptian Community
Association)*
via dei Bichi 27, int. 2, 00164 Roma; *t* (06) 6616 0573 »94
✧ **Associazione Egiziana** *(Egyptian Association)* Lazio
corso Matteotti 61, 04100 Latina »90
✧ ≡ Ahmed Omar: via Arezzo 34, 41100 Modena; *t* (059)
003959 (?), *f* 442342
International solidarity, migrant welfare. »94
✧ ≡ M. Mohamed: via Luigi Pigorine 16 R, 00162 Roma;
t (06) 424 2803
Founded 1987; immigration and integration advice. »90
✧ ≡ also known as Associazione Cittadini Egiziani: Mohamed
Hassan Salama: [address uncertain] via Spani 12, 42100
Reggio Emilia; *t* (0522) 5813 (?)
Also listed (1990) as via F. de Sanctis 8, *t* 582113. Social
and cultural interests. »94
● **Associazione Lavoratori Egiziana** *(Egyptian Workers'
Association)*
presso Comunità San Egidio, via della Paglia 14c, 00153
Roma; *t* (06) 589 5945, 585530 »94
✧ **Comunità Egitto**
via di Scandicci 140, 50143 Firenze; *t* (055) 717758 »90
✧ **Comunità Egiziana**
via da Palestrina 31, 40100 Bologna »90
✧ ≡ Salem Salem, President: via Guicciardini 10, 20100 Milano
Employment and welfare advice. »94

EL SALVADOR

see Central American, Latin American, Salvadorean

EQUATORIAL GUINEAN

see also African, Central African, Guinean, West African

◎ **SPAIN** *34*

✧ **Asociación de Amigos de los Pueblos de Guinea Ecuatorial,**
AAPGE *(Friends of the Peoples of Equatorial Guinea)*
Jesús Racale Nuse-Angono: calle Santa Orosía 3-5° C,
50010 Zaragoza; *t* (976) 342402
Culture, solidarity. »94
✧ **Asociación Cultural Bubi**
[address unknown] Madrid »87
✧ **Asociación Cultural Maleva**
Los Urquiza 34-1° C, 28027 Madrid; *t* (91) 408 3888 »87
✧ **Asociación Cultural Rhombe**
Evaristo Oko Kongwe: carrer Urgel 251-6° 1ª, Barcelona,
Catalunya; *t* (93) 749 2066, 780 0684, 430 7579
Information, Ndowe culture. »94
✧ **Asociación Cultural Riebapua**
carrer Mila i Fontanals 60-62, 08012 Barcelona, Catalunya;
t (93) 210 1683, 245 0668 »94
✧ **Asociación Cultural de Universitarios de Guinea Ecuatorial,**
ACUGE *(Equatorial Guinean University Students Cultural
Association)*
calle Obispo Trejo 1, 28040 Madrid
Based at Colegio Mayor Nuestra Señora de Africa. »94
✧ **Asociación Cultural Viyil**
carrer Sant Climent 5-4° 4ª, 08001 Barcelona, Catalunya »94
✧ **Asociación de Estudiantes Ecuatoguineanos**
calle Ramiro de Maetzu s/n, 28024 Madrid; *t* (91) 554
0576, 554 2400 »94
● **Asociación para el Progreso de Guinea Ecuatorial,** APGE
[address unknown] Madrid »87
✧ **Centro Cultural de Guinea Ecuatorial**
plaza de la Constitución 10-9° 3ª, 08191 Rubi, Catalunya;
t (93) 300 9525, 699 2217 »94
✧ **Organización de Técnicos y Profesionales Guineanos en
España,** OTEPGE: Organisation of Guinean Professionals and
Technicians in Spain
Augusto Iyanga Pendi: Profesor Blanco 22, 46014 Valencia;
t (96) 357 6840
Cultural and social group. »94

ERITREAN

see also African, East African, Ethiopian

◎ **DENMARK** *45*

• **Den Eretrianske Forening i Danmark** *(Eritrean Society of Denmark)*
Postobox 605, 8100 Århus C   »90
• **Den Eritreanske Hjælpeorganisation i Danmark:** Eritrean Relief Association, ERA
Kulturhuset Cikaden, Griffenfeldsgade 35, 2200 København N; *t* 3537 1430, *f* 3537 1980
Also listed (1993) as PO Box 2072, 1013 København K. »95

◎ **GERMANY** *49*

✿ **Eritreische Vereinigung zur Gegenseitigen Unterstützung** *(Eritrean Mutual Aid Society)*
Gherima Meskel: Strohbergstraße 17, 70180 Stuttgart; *t* (0711) 605628
Refugees and immigrants; legal aid, settlement help.   »94

◎ **GREECE** *30*

• **Union of Eritreans**
Lambros Kiriakakos: Odos Gladstonos 8, 10677 Athinai; *t* (01) 362 8325
Founded 1983; refugee welfare, advice, cultural activities. »94

◎ **ITALY** *39*

✿ **Associazione Eritrei** *(Association of Eritreans)* also known as Comunità Eritrea a Genova
M. Elsa: Vico della Casana 6, 16123 Genova; *t* (010) 247 0198
Improvement of living conditions of refugees.   »94
✿ **Associazione Lavoratori, Donne e Studenti Eritrei a Torino,** LADOSEI *(Society of Eritrean Workers, Women and Students in Turin)*
Joseph Taque: corso Orbassano 216, 10137 Torino; *t* (011) 353760
Founded 1987; advice and welfare agency.   »90
✿ **Associazione Lavoratori Eritrea** *(Eritrean Workers' Society)*
Ghebremedhin Mekonen: via Sergente Maggiore 14, 80132 Napoli; *t* (0181) 404115   »94
✿ **Comunità Eritrea** *(Eritrean Community)*
Deres Haraia: via Reginaldo Giuliani 202, 50141 Firenze; *t* (055) 433335
Rights advice, representation to authorities, general welfare issues; formed 1986.   »94
✿ ≡ Dr Seghid Hurui, President: via Friuli 26, 20100 Milano; *t* (02) 546 2853, 53414   »94
✿ ≡ via di Padule 22, 56100 Pisa; *t* (050) 578592   »90
• **Fronte Popolare di Liberazione della Eritrea,** FPLE: Eritrean People's Liberation Front, EPLF
Solomon Keflay, General Secretary: [address uncertain] via Napoleone III 99, 00185 Roma; *t* (06) 732636
Also listed (1990) as via Ferruccio 44, int. 2, 00185 Roma. Interests, welfare of Eritrean refugees. See also Unione Nazionale Lavoratori Eritrei, below.   »90
• **Unione Generale Lavoratori Eritrei,** UGLE: General Union of Eritrean Workers, GUEW
Ali Moussa/Zazeggai Kashai: via Palestro 49, int. 24, 00185 Roma; *t* (06) 446 9820, 446 7676, *f* 678 1182
See also the Unione Nazionale, below.   »94
• **Unione Nazionale Donne Eritree in Italia:** National Union of Eritrean Women, NUEW
Aimon Marikos: via Tallonce 7, 20100 Milano; *t* (02) 738 6959
Founded 1978; rights and welfare of Eritrean women.   »94
• **Unione Nazionale Lavoratori Eritrei:** National Union of Eritrean Workers, NUEW
via Ferruccio 44, 00185 Roma; *t* (06) 736671, 732636
See also FPLE and UGLE, above.   »94

◎ **UNITED KINGDOM** *44*

✿ **Eritrean Community in Haringey**
Selby Centre, Selby Road, White Hart Lane, London N17 8JN; *t* (0181) 365 0819   »94
• **Eritrean Community in the United Kingdom,** ECUK
266-268 Holloway Rd, London N7 6NE; *t* (0171) 700 7995
Education, training, employment and welfare advice.   »94
• **Eritrean Relief Association,** ERA
96 White Lion St, London N1 9PF; *t* (0171) 837 9236   »95

ESTONIAN

see also Baltic, East European, European

◎ **UNITED KINGDOM** *44*

• **Association of Estonians in Great Britain**
[address unknown]   »90

ETHIOPIAN

see also African, East African, Eritrean, Oromo, Tigray

◎ **GREECE** *30*

• **Ethiopian Evangelical Christian Fellowship**
M. Kuluberehan: Odos Mikina 130, Zografou, 15770 Athinai; *t* (01) 771 3756
Refugee religious and welfare group formed 1986.   »94

◎ **ITALY** *39*

• **Associazione delle Comunità Etiopi in Italia,** ACEI, and Associazione Rifugiati Politici Etiopi in Italia, ARPEI
Aster Carpanelli: via Pesaro 6, 00176 Roma; *t* (06) 701 0543
Refugee welfare, information, social centre. *Ethiopia Information* (12/yr), *Free Ethiopia* (6/yr).   »94
✿ **Associazione Hararki Etiopia** *(Association of Ethiopians from Harar)*
presso Comunità San Egidio, via della Paglia 14c, 00153 Roma; *t* (06) 589 5945, 585530   »90
✿ **Associazione Rifugiati Etiopici per l'Autoassistenza** *(Self-Help Association of Ethiopian Refugees)*
presso Convento S. Maria de Jesu, Artena, Roma; *t* (06) 953 0291   »90
✿ **Capellania della Comunità Etiope-Eritrea** *(Ethiopian and Eritrean Chaplaincy)*
Haile Teklemariam: viale Piave 2, 20129 Milano; *t* (02) 7600 1081, 799141, *f* 7601 2875
Religious and community services. Church (Chiesa Etiope) is at via A. Kramer 5.   »94
✿ **Chiesa Etiope**
via di Parione 33, 00186 Roma; *t* (06) 656 9540
Catholic church.   »90
✿ **Comunità San Egidio—Associazioni Immigrati Etiopia, Eggito, Oromo** *(St Egidio Community—Ethiopian, Egyptian and Oromo Immigrant Associations)*
via della Paglia 14c, 00153 Roma; *t* (06) 585530
See Associazione Culturale di Assistenza Popolare, p168. »90

◎ **UNITED KINGDOM** *44*

✿ **All Amhara People's Organization**
PO Box 14PB, London W2 7AS; *t* (0171) 267 1448   »96
• **Ethiopian Community in Great Britian**
Tadesse Tatesse: 66 Hampstead Road, London NW1 2NT; *t* (0171) 388 4944, 388 3984
Zena (4/yr).   »95

EUROPEAN

see also Albanian, Austrian, Baltic, Basque, Belgian, Bosnian, British, Bulgarian, Catalan, Croatian, Cypriot, Czech, Danish, Dutch, East European, Estonian, Finnish, French, German, German 'National', Greek, Gypsy, Hungarian, Icelandic, Irish, Italian, Latvian, Lithuanian, Macedonian, Norwegian, Polish, Portuguese, Romanian, Romany, Russian, Scandinavian, Serbian, Slav, Slovene, South-East European, Spanish, Swedish, Swiss, Transylvanian, Traveller, Tsigane, Turkish, Ukrainian, (Ex-)Yugoslav

◎ **ITALY** *39*

• **Comunità Europea Giornalisti**
via XX Settembre 26, 00187 Roma; *t* (06) 494 0583
Supports refugee groups.   »90

◎ **NETHERLANDS** *31*

✿ **Landelijk Inspraakorgaan Zuideuropeanen,** LIZE
Mgr. van de Weteringstraat 136, 3581 EN Utrecht; *t* (030) 332100, *f* 322571
A.S. Punter y Acoyent, B.S. Andreev, Manuel Espadz.
Umbrella body for Southern European immigrant groups; affiliate of national LAO forum, p146.   »95

EX-YUGOSLAV

see under Yugoslav; see also Bosnian, Croatian, Macedonian, Serbian

FALKLAND ISLANDS

(Islas Malvinas)

ⓞ UNITED KINGDOM 44

● **Falkland Islands Association**
2 Greycoat Place, London SW1; *t* (0171) 222 3445   »95

FILIPINO

see also Asian, South-East Asian

ⓞ BELGIUM 32

● **Philippine International Center for Human Rights**, PICHR
Maria L. Van der Meer Altamirano, Director: Vlasfabriekstr.
II, 1060 Brussel; *t* (02) 539 2620, *f* 539 1343, *Tx* 61771
DEVCO B
Campaigns on human rights issues affecting the Philippines
and South East Asia. *Journal* (4/yr).   »94

ⓞ DENMARK 45

● **Dansk Filippinsk Kvindegruppe** *(Danish Filipino Women's Group)*
c/o Nina Ellinger: Grøndalsvænge Alle 7, 2400 København
NV; *t* 3119 6264   »89

ⓞ GERMANY 49

● **Philippine Women's Network in Europe Babaylan**
Postfach 2136, 28868 Ottersberg   »94
✿ **Sozialdienst für Philippinos** *(Social Service for Filipinos)*
Georgstraße 7, 50676 Köln; *t* (0221) 201 0124   »94

ⓞ GREECE 30

✿ **Catholic Union of Filipinos in Athens**, CUFA
Juanita Ilagan: St Llenis Catholic Cathedral, Odos Omirou-
Panipistimiou, Athinai; *t* (01) 683 4003
Social and welfare group.   »94
● **Filipino Christian Fellowship**, FCF
Rev. Dave Pederson/Bella Sanchez: Odos Papanikoli 3,
Papagou, 15669 Athinai   »90
● **Filipino Seamen's Organization**
Georgios Skianis: Odos Ippokratous 106, 10680 Athinai   »94
● **Greek-Filipino Friendship Association**
163 3rd September Street, Athinai   »90
● **Kaisahan Samahan ng Migranteng Pilipino sa Gresya**,
KASAPI, formerly Kaisahan at Samahan ng Mangagawan
Pilipino *(Filipino Pastoral Group/Union of Filipino Workers)*
Deborah Carlos-Valencia: PO Box 4035, 10210 Athinai;
t (01) 361 4921, 883 6917, *f* 361 4917
Rosa C. Datul, Eduardo Bonsanto. Also listed (1990) at
Methonis 54-56, Exarchia, 10681 Athinai. Formed 1985;
member of EU Migrants Forum, p131; Carlos-Valencia has
been the Greek national rapporteur for the MAINE network,
p146. *Newsletter* (6/yr), *Migrant Women* (6/yr).   »94

ⓞ IRELAND 353

● **Filipino Irish Group**
Muireann Ó Briáin: 17 Charleville Road, Rathmines, Dublin
6; *t* (01) 496 0495
Cultural and welfare group.   »94
● **Filipino Trade Union Society**
Liberty Hall, Dublin 1
Trade union body for Filipino workers, founded by the Irish
Transport and General Workers' Union.   »94

ⓞ ITALY 39

✿ **Associazione Filippina** *(Filipino Association)*
Natividad M. Cuchapin: c/o San Germano, corso Galileo
Ferraris 71c, 10128 Torino; *t* (011) 597700   »94
● **Commission for Filipino Migrant Workers**, CFMW
Fr Benitius Egberink, Chairman: via Capo d'Africa 37 int. 2,
00134 Roma; *t* (06) 731 5703
Founded 1980; pastoral work and research on emigration.
Kabisag (6/yr).   »86

✿ **Comunità Cristiana Filippine di Bologna**, FCCB *(Filipino Christian Community of Bologna)*
Thelma Reyes Ayco: via Scipione del Ferro 4, 40100
Bologna; *t* (051) 345834, 321422   »94
✿ **Comunità Filippina** *(Filipino Community)*
presso Parrocchia, piazza del Carmine 2, 20121 Milano;
t (02) 805 9730
Also listed (1990) at piazza S. Fedele, *t* 469 2996.   »94
✿ ≡ CP 27, 31100 Treviso   »90
● **Kaisajan Nan Mga Mangagawan Pilipino sa Italia**, KAMPI:
Associazione dei Lavoratori Filippini in Italia *(Association of Filipino Workers in Italy)*
Salita S. Onofrio 7A, 00165 Roma; *t* (06) 686 9272
Also listed (1990) c/o FILEF, via IV Novembre 114, 00187
Roma, *t* 623 2000.   »94
✿ ≡ c/o SEMERE, via Salvini 4, 20122 Milano   »90
✿ ≡ via Firenze 54, 80142 Napoli; *t* (081) 554 3224   »90
✿ ≡ Piedmont: Efren Perea: via Saffi 15B, 10100 Torino;
t (011) 362030   »94
● **Lega Italo-Filippina di Emigrati**, LIFE *(Filipino-Italian Emigrants' League)*
Corazon C. Sim: via dei Mille 7B, int. 3, 00185 Roma;
t (06) 445 7723, 446 0394-95, *f* 445 7622
Welfare of Filipino women and men working in Italy. Member
of EU Migrants Forum, p131.   »94
● **Movimento Filippine**
via della Camilluccia 591, 00136 Roma; *t* (06) 324220   »90

ⓞ NETHERLANDS 31

● **Commission for Filipino Migrant Workers**, CFMW
Ledesma Maitet/N. Hacbang: Haarlemmerdijk 173, 1013 KH
Amsterdam; *t* (020) 625 4829
Advice, information, welfare of Filipino migrant workers.
Kababayan (6/yr).   »95
● **Filipijnengroep Nederland** *(Netherlands Filipino Group)*
Korte Jansstraat 2a, 3512 CN Utrecht; *t* (030) 231 9323,
f 232 1379   »95
✿ **National Democratic Front of the Philippines**
Postbus 19195, 3501 DD Utrecht
Revolutionary left group. *Balita ng Malayang Pilipinas* (BMP,
Free Philippines News Service).   »90

ⓞ SPAIN 34

● **Asociación Amistad de las Mujeres Filipinas**, AAMF
(Friendship Association of Filipina Women) and Asociación
de Inmigrantes Filipinos, AIF
Nicarita Amaqui: Apartad de Correus 1243, 08080 Barcelona,
Catalunya; *t* (93) 750 8645, 329 0702
Social and leisure activities. Location: Riera Baixa 4-6, 1°,
08001 Barcelona.   »94
✿ **Asociación Laboral Luzvim** *(Luzvim Workers' Association)*
[address uncertain] avda de Bethancourt 53-6°B, 35003 Las
Palmas, Gran Canaria; *t* (928) 365820   »90
✿ **Asociación de Trabajadores Filipinos**, OWWA *(Filipino Workers' Association)*
calle Arenal 20-3° A, 28013 Madrid; *t* (91) 429 4170   »94
✿ **Tahanan—Centro de Filipinos** *(Tahanan Filipino Centre)*
Erasio Flores: Cristo de la Victoria, calle Blas Garay 33,
28015 Madrid; *t* (91) 416 3447, 543 7657
This may be the same as the Centro de Acogida Tahanan,
listed (1990) at plaza Madre Molas 1, 28036, *t* 234 9727, or
Marqués de Urquijo 18, 28008; or the Centro de Filipinos
Tahanan, listed (1990) at Fernando el Católico 46, 28015, *t*
243 2051; or the Centro de Encuentro Tipanan, listed (1987)
at Villalar 5-4° izq., 28001 Madrid. *Sandiwan* (4/yr).   »94

ⓞ SWEDEN 46

● **Svensk Filippinska Foreningen**, SFF: Swedish Filipino
Association
Barnängsgatan 23 3 tr, 11641 Stockholm; *t* (08) 642 9726,
f 641 1135
Solidarity with the Filipino people, support for human rights
and democracy; aid to development projects. See also
Internationella Arbetslag, p152.   »93

ⓞ UNITED KINGDOM 44

● **Anglo-Philippine Association for Real Togetherness**, APART
Ken Strudwick: 46 Hayley Road, Lancing, West Sussex
Also listed (1994) c/o T. McGowan (chair), 33 Augustus Road,
Stony Stratford, Milton Keynes MK11 1HJ; or c/o J. Smith, 5
Sunrise Avenue, Surprise View, Bestwood, Nottingham NG6
8UJ. Welfare of domestic and other migrant workers, divided
families.   »95

✧ **Bahay Kubo Housing Association**
[address unknown] London
Founded 1989. Name derives from the Tagalog expression
for the traditional Filipino home.   »90
● **Commission for Filipino Migrant Workers**, CFMW
Aida Dunlea: St Francis of Assisi Centre, Pottery Lane,
London W11 6NG; *t* (0171) 221 0356
Also listed (1995) at 57 Chalton St, NW1, *t* 388 5845.   »95
✧ **Filipino Chaplaincy**
18 Gunnersbury Crescent, London W3 9AH; *t* (0181) 992
9347   »91
✧ **Filipino Women's Association Manchester**
Leth Packham/Sue Wood: 2 Barway Road, Chorlton-cum-
Hardy, Manchester M21; *t* (0161) 881 6950, 600 3149
Cultural, social and welfare activities, for Filipino and other
ethnic minority women.   »93
◆ **Kalayaan—Justice for Overseas Domestic Workers**
Margaret Healy: St Francis of Assisi Centre, Pottery Lane,
London W11 4NQ; *t* (0171) 243 2942-43, *f* 792 3060
Defends rights of resident domestic workers, mainly but not
exclusively of Filipino origin.   »95
● **Philippine British Residents League**
5 Monmouth Place, London W2 5SA; *t* (0171) 727 3519 »90
✧ **Philippine Centre**
c/o 17 Bakers Row, London E15 3NF; *t* (0181) 555 6690 »94
✧ **Philippines Resource Centre**
23 Bevenden Street, London EC1; *f* (0171) 251 5914   »95

◎ **NORTHERN IRELAND** *44*

✧ **Filipino Association**
c/o NICEM, 17 Eblana Street, Belfast BT7 1LD   »96

FINNISH

see also European, Scandinavian

◎ **DENMARK** *45*

● **Københavns Finske Forening** *(Copenhagen Finnish Society)*
[address uncertain] Nørrebrogade 106A, 2200 København »90

◎ **IRELAND** *353*

● **Irish Finnish Society**
69 St Stephen's Green, Dublin 2; *t* (01) 475 8291   »94

◎ **UNITED KINGDOM** *44*

✧ **Finnish Church Guild**
33 Albion St, London W2; *t* (0171) 237 7736, 252 3790 »90
● **Finnish Institute**
Pirkko Haavisto, Chair: [address unknown] London
Prof. David Arter, deputy chair, *t* (0224) 272003. Promotes
UK-Finland academic, cultural and economic links.   »95

FRENCH

*see also Basque, European, French: DOM/TOM, Guadeloupean,
Réunion, Tahitian; and other Francophone nationalities*

◎ **BELGIUM** *32*

✧ **Commission Française de la Culture de l'Agglomération
Bruxelloise** *(French Cultural Committee of Greater Brussels)*
[address unknown] Bruxelles   »90
✧ **Lycée Français de Belgique Jean Monnet** *(Jean Monnet
French Lyceum, Belgium)*
[address unknown]
Secondary school mainly for children of French migrants. »91

◎ **GERMANY** *49*

● **Deutsch-Französisches Jugendwerk**, DFJW *(German-French
Youth Agency)*
Rhöndorferstraße 23, 53604 Bad Honnef; *t* (02224) 18080,
f 180852
Foundation promoting Franco-German youth exchanges and
mutual understanding.   »94

◎ **GREECE** *30*

● **Amicale Française des Ingénieurs et Cadres** *(French
Engineers and Managers Society)*
Odos Thassou-Kritis 7, Nea Erythrea, 14671 Athinai;
t (01) 807 3409
Information, cultural and social activities.   »94

● **Amicale des Institutrices et Gouvernantes Françaises en
Grèce** *(Society of French Primary Teachers and Governesses)*
Odos Efpolidou 43, Ilioupoli, 43100 Athinai; *t* (01) 992 2717
Welfare, social activities for young migrant workers. »94
● **Association de Bienfaisance** *(Benevolent Association)*
Consulat français: Vas. Konstantinou Avenue 5-7, Athinai;
t (01) 729 0151   »90

◎ **IRELAND** *353*

● **Alliance Française**
Kildare Street, Dublin
Located in same building as Service Culturelle of French
Embassy. Promotes French culture, primarily through French
language classes.   »92

◎ **ITALY** *39*

✧ **Association Démocratique des Français à l'Etranger**, ADFE:
Associazione Democratica Francese all'Estero *(Democratic
Association of French Abroad)*
via Fratelli Canale 28, 16132 Genova; *t* (010) 385653 »90
✧ **Chiesa Francese**
via S. Tommaso 2, 20121 Milano; *t* (02) 863476
Catholic church.   »90
✧ ≡ corso Europa 84, 80127 Napoli; *t* (081) 650012   »90
✧ ≡ Istituto Salesiano Valsalice, viale Enrico Thovez 37,
10131 Torino   »90
✧ **Ecole française de Rome** *(French School of Rome)*
[address unknown] Roma   »89

◎ **LUXEMBOURG** *352*

● **Association Démocratique des Français à l'Etranger**
(Democratic Association of French Abroad)
Jacques Danis: BP 1526, 1015 Luxembourg; *t* 310050
Location: 13 rue Raoul Follereau, 8027 Strassen. *Bulletin
mensuel* (12/yr).   »95

◎ **PORTUGAL** *351*

✧ **Associação dos Franceses do Norte de Portugal** *(French
Association of Northern Portugal)*
717-5° Heróis França-Matosin, Porto; *t* (02) 938 2114 »94
✧ **Communauté Catholique Française** *(French Catholic
Community)*
Père Denis-Marie Bouchard: Igreja de S. Luís dos Franceses,
Rua Portas de S. Antão, 1100 Lisboa; *t* (01) 325821 »90
✧ **Institut Franco-Portugais de Lisbonne**
Avenida Luís Bilar 91, 1050 Lisboa; *t* (01) 311 1400, *f* 311
1463   »95
✧ **Interacção França-Portugal**
Largo da Amoreira 2, Lavacolhos, 6230 Fundão; *t* (075)
58328   »94

◎ **SPAIN** *34*

✧ **Centro Cultural Hispano-Francés**
calle Dr Castelo 32, Madrid; *t* (91) 574 3713   »90
✧ **Parroquia San Luis de los Franceses** *(Parish of St Louis of
France)*
calle Lagasca 89, Madrid; *t* (91) 435 5160   »90

◎ **UNITED KINGDOM** *44*

● **Franco-British Council** British Section
Ann Kenrick: 11 Tufton Street, London SW1P 3QB
Established 1972, offices in Paris and London; promotes
Franco-British understanding. Conferences, research. Shares
address with the European Movement, p223.   »95
● **Franco-British Society**
Room 636, Linen Hall, 162-168 Regent Street, London W1;
t (0171) 734 0815   »95
● **Franco-Scottish Society**: Association franco-écossaise
[address unknown] Scotland
Friendship, cultural exchanges.   »90

FRENCH: Départements d'Outre-mer et Territoires d'Outre-mer (DOM/TOM)

*i.e. Overseas Departments and Overseas Territories; see also
Caribbean, French, Guadeloupean, Guyanese, Latin American,
Pacific, Réunion, Tahitian*

◎ **FRANCE** *33*

● **Centre d'information Guadeloupe, Guyane, Martinique**
14 rue de Nanteuil, 75015 Paris   »90

Fédération des associations islamiques d'Afrique, des Comores et Antilles, FAIACA: see Islamic listing, p53
- **Mouvement Kanaky-Solidarité**
[address unknown] Paris
Supports the FLNKS liberation movement, New Caledonia.»94

GABONESE

see also African, Central African

◉ **FRANCE** *33*

- **Association France Gabon**
11 rue Lincoln, 75008 Paris; *t* (1) 4256 2012, 4562 6865»90

GAMBIAN

see also African, West African

◉ **DENMARK** *45*

- **Den Gambianske Forening i Danmark** *(Gambian Society)*
Box 23, Vesterbrogade 208, 1800 Frederiksberg C »89

◉ **UNITED KINGDOM** *44*

✿ **Gambia Association of Great Britain**
Alhaji M.M. Kinteh: c/o 7 Hulton Drive, Alexandra Park, Manchester M16 7AA; *t* (0161) 257 3050 »93

GERMAN

see also European, German 'National', Jewish, Romanian

◉ **ALBANIA** *355*

- **Albanian-German Humanist Association**
Bulevardi Deshmoret e Kombit—Zeri i Popullit, Tirana; *t* (042) 26497, *f* 28323 »94

◉ **BELGIUM** *32*

✿ **Deutsche Schule Brussel** *(German School of Brussels)*
[address unknown] Brussel
Secondary school mainly for children of German migrants.»91

◉ **FRANCE** *33*

- **Association Culturelle Franco Allemande**
32 rue Rasselins, 75020 Paris; *t* (1) 4356 2205 »90
- **Cercle franco allemand** *(Franco-German Circle)*
50 rue Laborde, 75008 Paris; *t* (1) 4294 1245 »90

◉ **GREECE** *30*

- **Deutsches Kontakt Informationszentrum** *(German Contact and Information Centre)*
Vera Dimopoulos-Vosikis: Odos Massalias 24, 10680 Athinai; *t* (01) 361 2288 »94

◉ **IRELAND** *353*

- **Evangelisch-Lutherische Kirche:** Lutheran Church in Ireland
Rev. Paul Fritz, pastor: Gemeindehaus St Finian's, 24 Adelaide Road, Dublin; *t* (01) 669 2529
Weekly religious services in German, in Dublin; services also provided in Cork, Galway and Killarney. »94
- **Goethe-Institut**
Dr Inge Rott, Director: Merrion Square, Dublin
German culture, exchanges; library; language classes. »92

◉ **ITALY** *39*

✿ **Chiesa Nazionale Germanica** *(German National Church)*
P. Paul Knopp: Sta. Maria dell'Anima, via della Pace 20, 00186 Roma; *t* (06) 686 4160, 683 3729. »90
✿ **Chiesa Tedesca** *(German Catholic Church)*
via Pasubio 7, 21020 Brebbia, VE; *t* (0332) 772084 »90
✿ ≡ Salita Fieschine 9, 16122 Genova; *t* (010) 892430 »90
✿ ≡ via Rossellini 2, 20124 Milano; *t* (02) 688 2215 »90
✿ ≡ P. Dietrich Esser: Katholische Gemeinde, Parco Margherita 26, 80121 Napoli; *t* (081) 415192 »90

◉ **PORTUGAL** *351*

✿ **Igreja dos Católicos da lingua Alemã**
Pater Hermann Hungerbühler: Rua do Patrocínio 8, 1350 Lisboa; *t* (01) 396 4114 »95

✿ **Igreja Evangélica Alemã** *(German Protestant Church)*
Avenida Columbano B. Pinheiro 48, 1070 Lisboa; *t* (01) 726 0976, 727 5176 »95
✿ **Instituto Alemão** *(German Institute)*
Campo dos Mártires da Pátria 36/7, 1150 Lisboa; *t* (01) 885 0549 »95
✿ **Katholische Gemeinde Deutscher Sprache** *(German-Speaking Catholic Community)*
Rua Boavista 754-2° d, 4000 Porto; *t* (02) 609 2663 »94

◉ **SPAIN** *34*

✿ **Asociación Alemana de Beneficiencia de Madrid** *(German Benevolent Association of Madrid)* and Asociación Hispano Alemana de Enseñanzas Técnicas
avenida Burgos 12, Madrid; *t* (91) 766 2609, 766 8454
International friendship and co-operation. »95
✿ **Asociación del Colegio Alemán** *(German College Society)*
Colegio Alemán, avenida Concha Espina 32, Madrid; *t* (91) 563 8177
Catholic religious and social centre. »95
✿ **Deutschsprachige Evangelische Gemeinde** *(German-Speaking Protestant Congregation)*
paseo de la Castellana 6, Madrid; *t* (91) 435 4781 »90

◉ **UNITED KINGDOM** *44*

- **Anglo-German Association;** also Anglo-German Foundation for the Study of Industrial Society; German Academic Exchange Service
A. Scales, Secretary: 17 Bloomsbury Square, London WC1A 2LP; *t* (0171) 404 4065, 404 3137, 831 8696
Friendship, cultural and academic exchanges; Association founded in 1951. The Foundation (Christine Untereiner/ Caroline Earle) funds research and conferences on UK and German economic, environmental and social policy issues. Exchange Service is the London office of the DAAD based in Germany. *Anglo-German Review* (4/yr). »95
✿ **German Lutheran Church**
Carrs Lane, Birmingham B4 »90
- **German Welfare Council**
59 Birkenhead St, London WC1H 8BB; *t* (0171) 278 6955
Voluntary social work agency; advice on German welfare system, crisis intervention for persons of German origin. »95
- **Goethe-Institut**
50 Princes Gate, Exhibition Road, London SW7 2PH
Munich-based foundation promoting German language/culture, cultural and educational co-operation and exchanges. Hosted seminar comparing UK and German migration policy. »94
- **Institute for German Studies**
Jane Parker: University of Birmingham, Edgbaston, Birmingham B15 2TT; *t* (0121) 414 7182, *f* 414 7329
Funded by the University and the German Academic Exchange Service, DAAD; research/teaching/library on German society, economics, politics, law, culture; conferences, seminars. »95

GERMAN 'NATIONAL'

i.e. ethnic Germans from other countries, accorded nationality under German law; see also Czech, East European, Romanian

◉ **GERMANY** *49*

- **League of Sudeten German Expellees**
Konrad Badenheuer: [address unknown] München
Represents families of 3 million Germans expelled from the Sudetenland (now the NW of the Czech Republic) in 1945-46. Campaigns for reparations, dual citizenship, right of return.»95
- **Silesian People's Association**
Herbert Hupka: [address unknown]
Represents ethnic Germans expelled from Silesia (in German Schlesien, in Polish Slask) in 1945-46. »88
- **West German Federation of Expellees**
Hartmut Koschyk, General Secretary: [address unknown]
Represents ethnic Germans expelled from Central Europe. »88

GHANAIAN

see also African, West African

◉ **DENMARK** *45*

✿ **Ghana Union:** Den Ghanesiske Forening
Hornemanns Vænge 45 3 th., 2500 Valby »90

◎ **FRANCE** *33*

✿ **Association franco-ghanéenne**
3 rue Couperin, appt 387, 80000 Amiens   »89

◎ **GERMANY** *49*

✿ **Ghana Community München e.V.**
Albert Osei-Wusu: Quidde Straße 52, 8000 München 83;
t (089) 637 7200   »93
● **National Association of Ghanaian Communities in Germany e.V.**, NAGG
Postfach 110 266, 3400 Göttingen
Umbrella group of local societies.   »93

◎ **ITALY** *39*

✿ **Association of Ghanaian Immigrants in Naples**, AGIN
Benedictus Agleb: via Firenze 54, 80100 Napoli; *t* (081) 281511, *f* 741 6518
Social, cultural and welfare group.   »94
✿ **Comunità Ghanese** *(Ghanaian Community)*
Casa di Riposo, Villa Ospizio, via Emilia Ospizio, 42100 Reggio Emilia   »90
✿ **Social Community of Ghanaians in Lombardy**, SCOGIL
Frank Obena: viale Romagna 29 c, 20092 Cinisello Balsamo, MI; *t* (02) 612 2655
Social and welfare assistance.   »94

◎ **UNITED KINGDOM** *44*

● **Ghana Human Rights Committee**
PO Box 848, London SE1 7YE; *t* (0171) 620 1430   »96
● **Ghana Kwambo Refugees and Migrants Community Action Group**
[address unknown] London
Involved in asylum rights campagns.   »96
● **Ghana Muslim Union**
Ahmed Jimbah: 15 Exton Crescent, Stonebridge, London NW10 8DA   »95
✿ **Ghana Refugee Welfare Group**
5 Westminster Bridge Road, London SE1 7XW; *t* (0171) 620 1430, *f* 620 1431   »96
● **Ghana Union**
431 Caledonian Road, London N7 2LT; *t* (0171) 700 5634
Community welfare, social, cultural activities; immigration, policing issues.   »95
✿ ≡ Mr Kofi: 4a South Road, Hockley, Birmingham B18   »90
✿ ≡ E. Alex Djang: 127 Leicester Road, Broughton Park, Manchester M7 0HJ; *t* (0161) 627 8336, 720 7448   »93
✿ ≡ Ladies Group: Rose Larbi: 13 Kelstern Square, Longsight, Manchester M13 0XW; *t* (0161) 248 5200, 231 1133
Accommodation help for students; cultural and social events and services for children, elderly, disabled and women.   »93

GIPSY; GITANO

see Gypsy, Romany, Traveller

GOAN

see also Asian, Indian, Portuguese

◎ **PORTUGAL** *351*

✿ **Casa de Goa** *(Goa House)*
Rua Voz do Operário 23, 1100 Lisboa; *t* (01) 888 2752
Welfare of Goan immigrants; housing, cultural issues.   »95

◎ **UNITED KINGDOM** *44*

✿ **Goan Welfare Association**
Eddie D'Sa: 6f South Park Road, London SW19 8ST   »94

GREEK

see also Cypriot, European, Macedonian, South-East European

◎ **BELGIUM** *32*

✿ **Association des Etudiants Grecs de Limbourg** *(Greek Students' Association of Limburg)*
Wilderozentuin 15, 3600 Genk   »94
✿ **Centre Culturel Grec** *(Greek Cultural Centre)*
Penelope Yannouli: Rue Destouvelles 2, 1210 Bruxelles;
t (02) 235 8271   »94

✿ **Centre Hellénique de Culture et de Formation—Ecole Ouvrière Grècque**, CHCF *(Greek Culture and Training Centre— Greek Workers' College)*
Sakis Dimitrakopoulos: Rue de Suède 37, 1060 Bruxelles;
t (02) 538 6212, 237 3469
Training, legal advice, social support. *Protoporos* (6/yr).   »94
✿ **Chapelle Orthodoxe Grècque de la Ste-Trinité et St-Côme et Damien**: Kerk v.d. Heilige Drievuldigheid en SS Cosmos en Damiaan *(Greek Orthodox Chapel of the Holy Trinity and Saints Cosmo and Damien)*
Rue Crespel 19, 1050 Bruxelles   »90
✿ **Communauté Hellénique de Liège** *(Liège Greek Community)*
Georges Mitsocapas: Rue St Léonard 33, 4000 Liège;
t (041) 270102
Social, cultural, information centre. *Nicandros* (4/yr).   »94
✿ **Eglise Orthodoxe Grècque des Archanges St-Michel et St-Gabriel**: Kerk v.d. Aartsengelen Michaël en Gabriël *(Greek Orthodox Church of the Archangels Michael and Gabriel)*
Avenue de Stalingrad 34, 1000 Bruxelles   »90
✿ ≡ Rue de Stassart 92, 1050 Bruxelles   »90
✿ **Eglise Orthodoxe Grècque de St-Jean Baptiste**: St Jan-Baptistkerk—Griekse Orthodoxe
Parvis St-Jean-Baptiste, 1080 Bruxelles   »90
✿ **Evrou Thrakis—Griekse Cultuur en Dansvereniging** *(Thracian Society—Greek Cultural and Dance Society)*
Anijsstraat 9/Socialestraat 28, 3600 Genk
Culture, music and dance.   »94
● **Fédération des Communautés Helléniques de Belgique**
Communauté Hellenique de Bruxelles, Rue de Suède 37, 1060 Bruxelles; *t* (02) 538 3947   »90
✿ **Grieks Cultureel Centrum Hellas**
Watersportlaan 19, 3580 Beringen
Cultural and social activities.   »94
✿ **Griekse Gemeenschap Genk** *(Genk Greek Community)*
Halenstraat 57, 3600 Genk; *t* (089) 384375   »94
✿ **Oratoire St-Jean-l'Evangeliste—Orthodoxe Grècque**:
Oratorium St Jan v.h. Evangelie—Griekse Orthodoxe *(Greek Orthodox Oratory of St John the Evangelist)*
Avenue de la Renaissance 40, 1040 Bruxelles   »90

◎ **DENMARK** *45*

● **Den Græske Forening i Danmark**, GFD *(Greek Association)*
Vesterbrogade 107E, 4 sal., 1620 København V; *t* 3121 9449
Culture, friendship, festivals, mutual aid; formed 1975.   »90

◎ **FRANCE** *33*

✿ **Centre Culturel et Artistique France-Grèce**
113 bvd Beaumarchais, 75003 Paris; *t* (1) 4804 0153   »90
✿ **Institut d'Etudes Néohelléniques de Paris** *(Contemporary Greek Studies Institute of Paris)*
19 bis rue Fontaine, 75009 Paris; *t* (1) 4874 0956   »90

◎ **GERMANY** *49*

✿ **Arbeitskreis von Sozialberatern für Fragen der Reintegration griechischer Arbeitnehmer und ihrer Familien in Griechenland** *(Social Work Group on Issues in the Return Migration of Greek Workers and their Families)*
Lenaustraße 41, 4000 Düsseldorf 30; *t* (0211) 639 8254, 639828 (?)   »90
▌**Co-ordination of Greek Immigrants in Europe**, CAGE:
Verein Griechischen Bürger in Europa
BAGIV, Poppelsdorfer Allee 19, 53115 Bonn   »94
✿ ≡ c/o BAGIV, Lichenstraße 31, 4000 Düsseldorf   »90
✿ **Griechische Gemeinde** *(Greek Community)*
Karl-Marx-Straße 21, 1000 Berlin; *t* (030) 623 8965   »90
✿ ≡ Hemshofstraße 69, 67059 Ludwigshafen; *t* (0621) 621142   »90
✿ ≡ Atanasia Siskou: Hüttenstraße 87, 40215 Düsseldorf;
t (0211) 379742   »94
✿ ≡ Alleeweg 7, 30449 Hannover; *t* (0511) 456808   »94
✿ ≡ Aberlestraße 1, 81371 München; *t* (089) 725 5324   »94
✿ ≡ Hegelstraße, 70174 Stuttgart; *t* (0711) 297974   »94
✿ **Sozialdienst für Griechen** *(Social Service for Greeks)*
Meister-Gerhard-Straße 10-14, 50674 Köln; *t* (0221) 201 9263   »94
● **Zentralverband der Griechischen Gemeinden in der BRD**, OEK *(Confederation of Greek Communities in the FRG)*
Kostas Poppas: BAGIV, Poppelsdorfer Allee 19, 53115 Bonn»94

◎ **ITALY** *39*

● **Federazione di Studenti Grecchi**
c/o Comitato di Quartiere S. Lorenzo, via dei Salentini 3, 00185 Roma   »90

◎ LUXEMBOURG *352*

● **Association des Grecs** *(Greek Association)*
3 rue Pivermuhl, BP 2316, 2356 Luxembourg »90
✿ **Club de Culture et Danse Hélléniques, CCDH** *(Greek Culture and Folk Dance Club)*
Helène Kavvadia: c/o Banque Européenne de l'Investissement, 100 boulevard Konrad Adenauer, 1020 Luxembourg;
t 4379 3255, 447127, *f* 437709 »94

◎ NETHERLANDS *31*

● **Federatie van Griekse Verenigingen** *(Federation of Greek Societies)*
p/a Platform Rijmond, Postbus 394, 4200 AJ Gorinchem »90
● **Griekse Federatie voor Gemeenschappen** *(Greek Communities Federation)*
E. Adam: Hendrikstraat 74, 3314 ZM Dordrecht; *t* (078) 614 4380 »95
✿ **Griekse Gemeenschap Gorinchem Archemidis** *(Archimedes Greek Society of Gorinchem)*
Nikos Kapinos: Postbus 693, 3500 AR Utrecht »90
✿ **Griekse Ortodoxe Kerk** *(Greek Orthodox Church)*
Springweg 89 bis, Utrecht; *t* (030) 233 1489 »95
✿ **Griekse Vereniging Anagennisi** *(Annagenisi Greek Society)*
Weerdsingel wz 20/22, Utrecht; *t* (030) 231 8806, 234 1039 »95
● **Union of Greeks in the Netherlands**
Van Vollenhovest 18, 3016 BH Rotterdam »90

◎ SPAIN *34*

✿ **Iglesia Ortodoxa Griega** *(Greek Orthodox Church)*
calle Nicaragua 12, Madrid; *t* (91) 457 4085 »90

◎ TURKEY *90*

● **Greek Orthodox Church**
H.A.H. Patriarch Bartholemew: [address unknown] Istanbul
The Greek Orthodox community in Turkey consists at present of some 4,000 people. Bartholemew, as the Ecumenical Patriarch, is usually acknowledged as spiritual leader of the 150 million Orthodox Christians, although he has no direct authority over the patriarchs of non-Greek (e.g. Syrian, Coptic and Armenian) Orthodoxy. »95

◎ UNITED KINGDOM *44*

✿ **Anglo-Hellenic Association**
Highgate Hill Annexe, 16 Highgate Hill, Archway, London N19 5NS; *t* (0171) 263 6445
Interests of Greeks and Cypriots, primarily in Islington. »94
● **Anglo-Hellenic League**
N. White-Gaze, Secretary: Room 1B, Chelsea College, Manresa Road, London SW3 6LX; *t* (0171) 351 6913
Friendship, cultural exchanges; founded 1913. »90
✿ **Greek Orthodox Church**
Summer Hill Terrace, Birmingham B1 »90
✿ **Greek Orthodox Church of the Holy Transfiguration**
Westwood Heath Road, Coventry; *t* (01203) 464286 »90
✿ **Greek Orthodox Community Church**
The Chairperson: Bury New Road, Salford M7 0EA;
t (0161) 792 2694
Greek Orthodox religion; community welfare; women's and youth activities. »93
✿ **Hellenic Centre**
16-18 Paddington St, London W1; *t* (0171) 487 5060 »95
● *Parikiaki*
K. Tsioupras, Editor: Cosmart House, 534a Holloway Road, London N7 6JP; *t* (0171) 272 6777, 6779
Periodical. »88
● *Ta Nea*
[address unknown] London
Newspaper. »94

GRENADIAN

see also African Caribbean, Afro-Caribbean, Anglo-Caribbean, Caribbean, West Indian

◎ UNITED KINGDOM *44*

● **Maurice Bishop Patriotic Movement**
[address unknown]
Left-wing political party. »88
● **New Jewel Movement Support Group**
[address unknown] »88

GUADELOUPEAN

see also Caribbean, French: DOM/TOM

◎ FRANCE *33*

● **Association des Etudiants Guadeloupéens** *(Association of Guadeloupean Students)*
85 rue Beaubourg, 75004 Paris »90

GUATEMALAN

see also Central American, Latin American

◎ ITALY *39*

● **Quetzal—Associazione Culturale Italo-Guatemalteca** *(Quetzal Italian-Guatemalan Cultural Association)*
Debora Leiva: via Galilei 55, 00185 Roma; *t* (06) 734915, *f* 7049 5275
This association (named after the winged serpent of Guatemalan mythology) works in solidarity with the people of Guatemala, and with refugees and migrants from Guatemala. See also Cooperativa di Servizio, p143. »94

◎ SPAIN *34*

● **Comisión de Derechos Humanos de Guatemala, CDHG** *(Guatemala Commission for Human Rights)*
Embajadores 216-3° D, 28045 Madrid; *t* (91) 530 7705 »94

◎ UNITED KINGDOM *44*

● **Guatemala Committee for Human Rights**
83 Margaret Street, London W1N 7HB; *t* (0171) 631 4200, 631 4203 »90

GUINEA BISSAU

see also African, Guinean, Portuguese, West African

◎ FRANCE *33*

✿ **Union des femmes immigrées originaires de la Guinée-Bissau** *(Union of Immigrant Guinea-Bissau Women)*
112 rue de la Liberté, 76410 Cléon
Mutual aid, culture. »89

◎ PORTUGAL *351*

◆ **Associação Guineense de Solidariedade Social** *(Guinean Association for Social Solidarity)*
Fernando Gomes Ka: Avenida João Paulo II, lt. 528-2° A, Zona J. Chelas, 1900 Lisboa; *t* (01) 837 0436, 837 0597, *f* 837 0287
Welfare, training and employment issues. »95
✿ **Associação de Guineenses** *(Guinean Association)*
Rua São João de Praça 83-2° D, Casa de Guiné Bissau, 1100 Lisboa; *t* (01) 865285 »90

◎ SPAIN *34*

✿ **Asociación Cultural Amilcar Cabral** *(Amilcar Cabral Cultural Association)*
calle Lope de Vega s/n, 24300 Bembibre, León; *t* (987) 510920
Based at the local CITE, trade union migrant centre, p150. »87

GUINEAN

see also African, Equatorial Guinean, Guinea Bissau, West African

◎ DENMARK *45*

● **Foreningen af Guinea i Danmark, GuiDanAss** *(Guinea Denmark Association)*
Rode Mellemvej 94D-109, 2300 København S
Employment and welfare of Guinean migrants. »94

◎ FRANCE *33*

✿ **Association des ressortissants guinéens de Toulouse-Midi-Pyrénées** *(Toulouse-Midi-Pyrenees Guinean Nationals Society)*
34 rue de la Providence, 31500 Toulouse »89

GUJARATI

or Gujerati; see also Asian, Hindu, Indian, Islamic

◎ **UNITED KINGDOM** *44*

✿ **Anjuman-e-Gujerati Mosque**
Yusuf Ismail Badat, President: 260-261 Stoney Stanton Rd,
Foleshill, Coventry CV1 4FR; *t* (01203) 22774, 550322
May be linked with Ajuman-e-Gujerati Muslim Association,
listed (1994) at 115 Leicester Causeway, CV1 4HL.   »94

● *Asian Trader* and *Garavi Gujrat*
Kalpesh R. Solanki, Editor: 1-2 Silex Street, Southwark,
London SE1 0DW; *t* (0171) 928 1234
Bilingual business magazine (26/yr); newspaper (52/yr).   »95

● **Bohra Jamaat (UK)** *(Vohora (Trader) Association)*
Dr Idris Zainuddin, President: [address unknown]
An Isma'ili Shi'ite society, of the Must'ali sect.   »94

✿ **Greenwich Gujarati Samaj**
Kanta Patel, Co-ordinator: 78a Sandy Hill Road, Woolwich,
London SE18 7AZ; *t* (0171) 316 2065
Information, advice, community welfare work.   »95

✿ **Gujarat Muslim Association**
Amanullah Khan Pathan: [address unknown] Leicester   »94

✿ **Gujarat Muslim Society**
Salim M. Patel: [address unknown] Blackburn, Lancashire »94

● *Gujarat Samachar; Vishwadharma, New Life, Asian Business*
8-16 Coronet Street, London N1 6HD; *t* (0171) 729 5453,
f (0181) 739 0388
Newspaper, magazines.   »95

✿ **Gujarat Sunni Muslim Community Centre**
G.H. Mulla: 15 Eldon St, Preston PR1; *t* (01772) 825658 »94

✿ **Gujarati Muslim Al-Madina**
Hafiz Mohammed Hanif Munshi: 21c Bedford Place, Brighton
BN1 2PT; *t* (01273) 737721   »94

✿ **Gujarati Sunni Muslim Society**; also Masjid-e-Noor;
Madrassa Noor-ul-Islam
Noor Hall, Noor St, Preston PR1; *t* (01772) 881786, 827531
Mosque also listed (1993) at 29 Stansfield Rd, PR1 1QL. »94

✿ **Gujerati Cultural Association**
Dr Amrat Shah/Bipin Patel: 51 Woodland Drive, Hove BN3
6DH; *t* (01273) 559921, 563579   »95

● *New Britain*
Vanoo Jiv Raj, Editor: 116 Brium Street, Leicester LE4 5AY
Magazine (12/yr), possibly defunct.   »88

✿ **Preston Gujarati Muslim Society** and Medina Mosque
Musa Roked, Secretary: 26-28 Fishwick Parade, Preston
PR1 4XQ; *t* (01772) 798847
Sunni congregation.   »94

GUYANESE

see also African Caribbean, Afro-Caribbean, Anglo-Caribbean, Caribbean, French: DOM/TOM, Latin American, West Indian

◎ **UNITED KINGDOM** *44*

● **Association of Guyanese Nationals**
[address unknown]   »88
● **Guyana Berbice Association**
[address unknown]   »96
● **Guyana Friends Association**
[address unknown]   »96
● **Guyana United Sad'r Islamic Anjuman**
Haji Abdool Hafiz Rahaman, Vice President: 8 Hazeldene Rd,
Craven Rd, London NW10; *t* (0181) 961 3814, *f* 961 3814
Branch of a Guyanese Sunni movement founded 1936.   »95
● **People's Progressive Party**, PPP
[address unknown]
Expatriate British branch of the Guyanese political party. »90
● **Working Peoples Alliance Support Group**
[address unknown]   »88

GYPSY

see also Romany, Traveller; and see Hungarian, Irish, Romanian, Spanish

◎ **CZECH REPUBLIC** *42*

♦ **Foundation for Improvement of Status of Gypsies**, FISOG
Helénská Street 4, 12000 Praha 2; *t* (02) 2195 3404,
f 204267.   »94

◎ **FRANCE** *33*

✿ **Association gitane Saint-Jacquoise et du Roussillon** *(St-Jacques and Roussillon Gypsy Association)*
16 rue du Sentier, 66000 Perpignan
Sports, culture. May succeed Association des gens du voyage
nomades et sédentaires, at same address, p117.   »90
✿ **Association des Gitans d'origine espagnole en France**
(Association of Gypsies of Spanish Descent in France)
chez M Joseph Moreno: 110 rue de Liège, La Paillade,
34100 Montpellier
Defends identity/interests of travelling or settled Gypsies. »90
✿ **Association des Gitans sédentaires d'Aix-en-Provence et de la région** *(Association of Settled Gypsies of Aix and District)*
mairie annexe, Jas-de-Bouffan, 13090 Aix-en-Provence   »89
● **Centre de Recherches Tsiganes** *(Tsigane Research Centre)*
106 quai de Clichy, 92110 Clichy; *f* (1) 4731 2923
Documents Tsigane life, culture, migration; human rights. »94
● *Les Etudes Tsiganes* (Gypsy Studies)
Jacqueline Charlemagne: 2 rue d'Hautpoul, 75019 Paris;
t (1) 4040 0905
Review (2/yr) of Gypsy historical and cultural studies.   »94
● **Tzigane International**
5 rue de Douai, 75009 Paris
Tzigane cultures world-wide, inter-cultural exchanges.   »89

◎ **GERMANY** *49*

● **Kölner Appell** *(Cologne Appeal)*
Kurt Holl: Wahlenstraße 1, 50823 Köln; *t* (0221) 528390,
f 511343
Solidarity, anti-racism. Campaigns for implementation of
human rights for Gypsies (Sinti and Roma).   »94

◎ **HUNGARY** *36*

● **Cigány Ház** *(Gypsy House)*
Enekes útca 10-b, 1151 Budapest
Campaigns for the civil rights of Hungary's 500,000-strong
Gypsy minority; promotion of Gypsy culture, anti-racism. »95
✿ **Gandhi School**
Janos Bogdan, Director: [address unknown] Pecs
School founded 1993 with state and Soros Foundation
funding, to provide specialist education to the Gypsy
population in the southern region: only 1 in 200 finish
secondary school. Aims to help Gypsies enter professional life
while retaining their culture and traditions.   »95

◎ **ITALY** *39*

● **Centro Studi Zingari Romano Sicharimesko Than** *(Centre for Romany Gypsy Studies)*
Mirella Karpati, President: via dei Barbieri 22, 00186 Roma;
t (06) 687 2824
Don Bruno Nicolini; founded 1965 by Opera Nomadi; linguistic,
educational, sociological research, resource centre; occasional
papers. *Lacio Drom* (6/yr), *Romano Lil* (12/yr).   »94
● **Opera Nomadi, Associazione de Promozione della Cultura Nomade** *(Travellers Service, Society for Traveller Culture)*
Dr Secondo Massano: via Arco del Monte 99, 00186 Roma;
t (06) 687 2824, 1172 1308, *f* 687 8498
Pastoral care service; see research/publishing arm, above. »94
✿ ≡ via San Luca 14/4, 16124 Genova; *t* (010) 208712 »90

◎ **NETHERLANDS** *31*

Stichting Landelijk Platform Woonwagenbewoners en Zigeuners,
LPWZ (National Coalition of Caravan Dwellers and Gypsies):
an umbrella group, based in Amersfoort, representing ethnic
Gypsies and other travelling peoples, which was one of the
nine groups which merged to create the major national body
relaunched in Utrecht in January 1996 as FORUM—Instituut
voor Multiculturele Ontwikkeling, see p146.
● **Landelijke Sinti Organisatie** *(National Sinti Organisation)*
Terraweg 28, 5681 RD Best; *t* (0499) 371212, *f* 372915 »95

◎ **PORTUGAL** *351*

● **Obra Nacional de Pastoral e Promoção dos Ciganos,**
ONPPC *(National Gypsy Pastoral and Development Service)*
Irma Zulmira da Conceiçao Cunha, Director: Avenida Dr
Alfonso Bensaúde, 1100 Lisboa; *t* (01) 335048
An agency of the Catholic Church's Comissão Episcopal Sócio-
Caritativa, responsible for the pastoral care of Gypsies and
promoting their socio-economic advancement. *A Caravana*
(6/yr).   »94
✿ ≡ Lisbon Diocesan secretariat: Fernanda Reis: Rua Cidade de
Lisboa 5, 2° E, 1800 Lisboa; *t* (01) 851 6938   »94

SPAIN *34*

- **Asociación de Desarrollo Gitano** *(Gypsy Development Association)* and Asociación de Enseñantes con Gitanos
calle Lelé del Pozo 20, Madrid; *t* (91) 785 1028
Community development, improved educational provision. »95
- **Asociación Española de Integración Gitana**, AEIG *(Spanish Association for Gypsy Integration)*
calle Cabestreros 12 bajo, 28012 Madrid; *t* (91) 468 1676, 468 6061, training college 785 7866
Founded 1978; education, welfare, anti-racism. »95
- **Asociación Juvenil de Expresión Gitana** *(Youth Association for Gypsy Culture)*
calle Cabestreros 12 bajo, 28012 Madrid; *t* (91) 468 6061, *f* 468 1676
Founded 1986 by AEIG; anti-racism, youth welfare. »94
- **Asociación de Mujeres Españolas Gitanas** *(Spanish Gypsy Women's Association)*
calle Moratines 30, Madrid; *t* (91) 517 5652 »95
- **Asociación de Mujeres Españolas Gitanas Romi Serseni**
calle Valencia 20-1° C, 28017 Madrid; *t* (91) 530 0718
Founded 1991. »94
- **Asociación Nacional Presencia Gitana** *(Gypsy Presence National Association)* also known as Presencia Gitana
Manuel Martín Ramírez: Valderrodrigo 76-78 bajos A, 28039 Madrid; *t* (91) 373 6207, college 373 8282, *f* 373 4462
Gypsy culture, civil rights; combats racism, intolerance. »95
- **Asociación Romapall**
calle Pico Balaitus 13 bajo, 28035 Madrid; *t* (91) 739 2178
Founded 1984. »94
- **Asociación del Secretariado General Gitano** *(Gypsy General Secretariat Association)*
calle Fuencarral 129-5° A, 28010 Madrid; *t* (91) 448 1098, 448 1202
Founded 1983 as national representative body. »95
- ◆ **Coordinadora de Asociaciones Gitanas** *(Gypsy Associations Liaison Committee)*
[address unknown]
Boletín de las Asociaciones Gitanas. »91
- ✿ **Fundación Santa Lucía**
Andrés Domínguez Iglesias: Carlos III 14-1° izq., 31002 Pamplona, Nafarroa; *t* (948) 112248, *f* 213244
Education and welfare of Gypsies. »94
- ✿ **Gao Lacho Drom**
Paula Montal 26 bajo, 01010 Vitoria/Gasteiz; *t* (945) 225039
Rights of Gypsies and other ethnic minorities; educational welfare, training, employment initiatives; founded 1984. »94
- ✿ **Iniciativa Gitana** *(Gypsy Initiative)*
Julián Gayarre 57 bajo, 48004 Bilbao; *t* (94) 412 9730
Housing and educational welfare issues. »95
- **Instituto Hispánico de Estudios Gitanos** *(Hispanic Institute of Gypsy Studies)*
La Cenia 10, 46001 Valencia; *t* (96) 391 8604-05
Research and study centre founded 1986. »94

SWEDEN *46*

- **Nordiska Zigenarrådet** *(Nordic Gypsy Council)*
Sockengatan 83, 25251 Helsingborg
Gypsy civil rights, anti-racism, supports Gypsy refugees. »94

UNITED KINGDOM *44*

- **Advisory Council on the Education of Romany and other Travellers**, ACERT
Bill Forrester: Moot House, The Stow, Harlow CM20 3AG, Essex; *t* (01279) 418666, c/o (01622) 844482
Also listed (1990) at Mary Ward Centre, 42 Queen Street, London WC1N 3AS. Founded 1972; charity, partly state-funded; welfare of Gypsies, sensible site planning. »95
- **Association of Gypsy Organisations**, AGO
Dr Donald Kenrick, Secretary: 61 Blenheim Crescent, London W11 2EG; *t* (0171) 727 2916
Founded 1970, 12 member groups; affiliated to World Romany Congress, p103. »90
- ✿ **Gypsy Council for Education, Culture, Welfare and Civil Rights**
Peter Mercer, President: 3 The Travellers Site, Oxney Road, Peterborough PE1 5NX; *f* (01733) 893418 »95
- **Life and Light**
David Jones, Chairman: [address unknown] Birmingham
French-based evangelical Christian movement, claims support of 8,000 of Britain's 30,000 Gypsies; annual gatherings. »95
- **National Gypsy Council**
Hughie Smith, President: Caravan Site, Greengate, Oldham, Lancashire; *t* (0161) 665 1924
Research and action on education, discrimination, rights. »90

- **National Gypsy Education Council**
32 Marshall Close, Feering, Colchester CO5 9IQ
Promotes education of Traveller children in mainstream schools. »90

HAITIAN

see also African Caribbean, Afro-Caribbean, Caribbean

FRANCE *33*

- **Aide et Soutien aux Haïtiens de France**, AISOHAF *(Assistance and Support for Haitians in France)*
Gabriel Frederik: c/o GISTI, 30 rue des Petites Ecuries, 75010 Paris; *t* (1) 4345 5040, *f* 4345 0394
Information and advice for migrants and refugees. »94
- ✿ **Collectif Haïti de France**, CHF
Jean Claude Pattacini: 31 rue de Reuilly, 75012 Paris; *f* (1) 4370 4314
International solidarity, human rights. See also AEC, p196.
Une semaine en Haïti (52/yr). »94

UNITED KINGDOM *44*

- **Haiti Support Campaign** also known as Haiti Support Group
Christian Wisskirchen: Trinity Church, Hodford Road, London NW11
Solidarity with the people of Haiti and with refugees from Haiti; opposition to military rule and human rights abuses. »94

HERCEGOVIN

see Bosnian, (Ex-)Yugoslav

HINDI

see also Asian, Hindu, Indian

UNITED KINGDOM *44*

- ✿ *Amar Deep*
J.M. Kaushal, Editor: 2 Chepstow Road, London W7; *t* (0181) 840 3534, 579 2848
Magazine (52/yr). »88
- *Hind Samachar*
A.S. Bedi, Editor: 478 Lady Margaret Road, Southall UB1 2NW; *t* (0181) 575 8694
Magazine (52/yr). »88
- **Hindi International Development Instigator**
37 Stowe Crescent, Ruislip HA4 7SR »90
- *Navin Weekly*
Ramesh Kumar, Editor: 307a North End Road, London W14 9NS; *t* (0171) 385 8966
See also Urdu journal *Milap*, p123. »88
- ✿ **Sussex Hindu Union**
Dr Bhanu Patel: 136 Phyllis Avenue, Peacehaven BN10 7SN; *t* (01273) 585560 »94
- **United Kingdom Hindi Samiti** *(Hindi Working Party)*
c/o Satish Agrawal: [address unknown] London; *t* (0181) 472 4589
Promotion of Hindi language in London. »90

HINDU

see also Asian, Gujarati, Hindi, Indian, Jain, Mauritian, Nepalese, Sri Lankan, Surinamese. Most temples (Mandirs, Mandals etc.) are run by local temple societies, and include cultural or community centres. Some Hindu bodies, notably the ISKCON, have a significant non-immigrant following; no judgement is made here on the status within Hinduism of that or other 'new religious movements' such as the Sai Baba sect.

DENMARK *45*

- **Vishwa Hindu Parishad**, VHP
Nørrebrogade 59, 2200 København N
Danish section of India-based Hindu political party. »90

IRELAND *353*

- **International Society for Krishna Consciousness**, ISKCON
Hare Krishna Cultural Centre, 56 Dame Street, Dublin 2; *t* (01) 679 1306 »88

◉ **PORTUGAL** *351*

✿ **Comunidade Hindú** *(Hindu Community)*
Kantilal Jamnadas: Cave e Galeria da Torre 1, Rua Frei
Manuel do Cenáculo, 1170 Alto do Eira, Sapadores, Lisboa;
t (01) 812 1734   »95
● **Comunidade Hindú de Portugal**
Alameda Mahatma Gandhi, 1600 Lisboa; *t* (01) 757 6524»95

◉ **UNITED KINGDOM** *44*

✿ **Arya Pratinidhi Sabha (UK)**
Prof. S.N. Bhardwaj, President: 69a Argyle Rd, West Ealing,
London W13; *t* (0181) 997 9573 office, 991 1732 Mandir
Six affiliated Arya Samaj Mandirs, including one here and
others in Birmingham, Coventry, Ealing and Milton Keynes,
promoting the Vedic Dharma. Newsletter, yearbook.   »90
✿ **Arya Samaj Birmingham**
167 Holly Road, Handsworth, Birmingham B20 2BZ   »90
✿ **Brahma Kumaris Centre**
Shoba Patel: 62 Preston Street, Brighton BN1 2HE;
t (01273) 329545
Mainly women-led movement founded 1937; educational and
philanthropic activities, Global Vision peace project; 800 UK
members, 250,000 worldwide; see Raj Yoga Centre, right.»94
✿ **Central Valmik Sabha Ashram**
54 Leyton Road, Handsworth, Birmingham B21   »90
✿ **Geeta Bhavan** also known as Gita Bhavan
9 Newton Close, Loughborough LE11; *t* (01509) 214502 »88
✿ **Hindu Association of Leamington Spa**
18 Gainsborough Drive, Sydenham, Leamington Spa CV32,
Warwickshire; *t* (01926) 313108, 313745   »88
✿ **Hindu Centre**
81 London Rd, Gloucester GL1 3HH; *t* (01452) 653314 »88
✿ ≡ K.K. Singh: 39 Grafton Terrace, London NW5; *t* (0171)
485 8200   »90
✿ **Hindu College**
Dr J.C. Sharma: [address unknown] London   »90
✿ **Hindu Community Centre**
64 Swindon Road, Cheltenham GL50; *t* (01242) 584250 »88
✿ **Hindu Cultural Centre**
South Meadow Lane, off Fishergate Hill, Preston PR1,
Lancashire; *t* (01772) 253901   »88
✿ **Hindu Cultural Society of Slough**
Hindu Temple, Keel Drive, Slough; *t* (01753) 30686 (?) »90
✿ **Hindu Religious and Cultural Society**
6 Brancaster Close, Leicester; *t* (0116) 235 0667   »88
✿ **Hindu Swayam Sevada Sang**
Court Road, Sparkhill, Birmingham B11   »90
✿ **Hindu Temple**
36 Alexandra Road, Leeds, Yorkshire; *t* (0113) 275 7024 »90
✿ ≡ 172 West Rd, Newcastle-upon-Tyne; *t* (01632) 850774 »88
✿ ≡ 215 Carlton Road, Nottingham; *t* (0115) 959 8284   »88
✿ ≡ King Street, Southall UB2; *t* (0181) 574 5276   »88
✿ ≡ 133 Highfield Rd, Wellingborough; *t* (01933) 222250 »88
✿ **Hindu Women's Group**
Nalini Patel: 259 Preston Drove, Brighton BN1 6FL;
t (01273) 552004   »94
✿ **Hove Hindu Community**
Jayant Lal Pandit: 59 Addison Road, Hove BN3 1TQ;
t (01273) 736446   »94
✿ **Hove Hindu Group**
R.N. Patel: 68 Westbourne Gardens, Hove BN3 5PQ;
t (01273) 729398   »94
✿ **Ilford Hindu Centre**
[address unknown] Ilford IG1, Essex   »88
▌ **International Society for Krishna Consciousness**, ISKCON
(informally known as the Hare Krishna movement)
Bhaktivedanta Manor, Letchmore Heath, Watford, Herts.;
t (019276) 6269, 7245
Often seen as a new religious movement, ISKCON, founded
1966, derives from the Bengali Gaudiya-sampradaya cult of
the 16th century CE. Other centres are not listed as most
members are not migrants or ethnic minority members.   »94
✿ **Jalaram Prathna Mandal**
85 Narborough Rd, Leicester LE3 0LF; *t* (0116) 254 0117»88
✿ **Krishna Yoga Mandir**
57 Balham Road, Edmonton, London N9   »88
✿ **Maharashtra Mandal London**
30 Penney Close, Dartford DA1 2NE   »87
✿ **Manchester Hindu Cultural Society** and Gita Bhavan Hindu
Temple
R. Kaushal: 517 Wilbraham Road, Chorlton-cum-Hardy,
Manchester M21 1UT; *t* (0161) 861 9083
Hindu religion; classes in Hindi language, Indian classical
music and dance, sporting and cultural events.   »93

● **National Association of Vanik Associations**
4 The Spinney, Cheadle Hulme, Cheadle SK8 1JA; *t* (0161)
428 7349, 205 6673
Gujarati Vaniks; interest in immigration issues.   »91
● **National Council of Hindu Temples**
T.K. Shingdia, Secretary: 559 St Albans Road, Watford
WD2 6JH; *t* (01923) 674168
The main body co-ordinating, promoting and representing
temples in Britain; organises festivals and events.   »93
● **National Hindu Student Forum**
[address unknown]   »95
✿ **Radha Krishna Temple**
5 Cedars Road, London E15; *t* (0181) 534 8879   »88
✿ ≡ 10 Soho Street, London W1V 5DA   »88
✿ **Raj Yoga Centre**
Linda Lee: 23 Picton Street, Brighton BN2 EAP; *t* (01273)
688959
Teaches a form of yoga associated with the Brahma Kumaris
movement, a 20th-century offshoot of the Hindu tradition.»94
✿ **Satya Sai Baba Satsang** *(Sai Baba Centre)*
Amarjit Mandan/David Bryant: 44 Coniston Court, Holland
Road, Hove BN3 3WB; *t* (01273) 749370, 725143
An Indian-based new religious movement within the Hindu
tradition, claiming 10,000 followers in Britain.   »94
✿ **Shree Ganapathy Temple**
Rat Nasinghaam: 125-133 Effra Road, Wimbledon, London
SW19; *t* (0181) 542 7482   »95
✿ **Shree Gita Bhavan Mandir**, SGB
S.S. Sharma: 107-115 Heathfield Road, Handsworth,
Birmingham B19 1HL; *t* (0121) 523 7797, 554 4120
Temple with associated cultural and social activities. »94
✿ **Shree Hindu Community Centre**
56 Grantham Road, Sparkbrook, Birmingham B11 1LX   »90
✿ ≡ [address uncertain] 541a Warwick Road, Tyseley,
Birmingham B11 5JF; *t* (0121) 558 0087, 707 3154   »88
✿ **Shree Hindu Gujarati Samaj**
366a Higham Lane, Weddington, Nuneaton CV11   »88
✿ **Shree Hindu Mandir**
90 Milton Street, Pleck, Walsall WS1, West Midlands;
t (01922) 664640, 647428, 648321   »88
✿ **Shree Hindu Samaj Mandal**
18 Salisbury Road, off Walsall Road, Darlaston WS10,
Staffordshire; *t* (0121) 526 4769, 526 6618   »88
✿ **Shree Hindu Temple**
47 Cromford Street, Leicester LE2 0FW   »88
✿ **Shree Hindu Temple Geeta Bhawan**
312 Normanton Road, Derby; *t* (01332) 380407   »88
✿ **Shree Hindu Temple Society**
274 Stoney Stanton Road, Foleshill, Coventry CV1,
Warwickshire; *t* (01203) 685898   »88
✿ **Shree Kadwa Patidas Samaj UK**
G.S. Patel: 55 Crummock Gardens, London NW9 0DE;
t (0181) 200 5800   »94
✿ **Shree Kalyan Mandal**
4 Kimberley Road, Rugby CV21; *t* (01788) 565105   »90
✿ **Shree Krishna Mandir**
92a Stoney Stanton Road, Foleshill, Coventry CV1,
Warwickshire; *t* (01203) 223633
Temple.   »90
✿ **Shree Ram Krishna Centre**
Alfred Street, Loughborough LE11; *t* (01509) 32401   »88
✿ **Shree Sanatan Deevya Mandal**
163b Church Rd, Bristol BS5 9LA; *t* (0117) 955 9222   »88
✿ **Shree Sanatan Dharma Mandal**
84 Northcote Rd, Southall, Middlesex; *t* (0181) 574 2981»88
✿ **Shree Sanatan Mandir**
Weymouth Street, off Catherine Street, Leicester LE4 6FP;
t (0116) 266 1402, 266 2801   »88
✿ **Shree Sanatan Seva Samaj**
Community Centre, Lewsey Farm, Hereford Road, Luton
LU4 0PS; *t* (01582) 663414   »90
✿ **Shree Swaminarayan Hindu Temple**
847 Finchley Road, Golders Green, London NW11; *t* (0171)
267 6218, 458 5356
Gujarat-based puritan movement devoted to the 19th-century
ascetic Sahajanand, given the title Swami Narayan.   »91
✿ **Shri Krishna Mandir Sabha**
18 Hinley Road, Goldthorn Park, Wolverhampton, West
Midlands; *t* (01902) 340324   »88
✿ **Shri Narthi Sanatan Hindu Mandir**
159-161 Whipps Cross Road, Leytonstone, London E11;
t (0181) 995 2335   »88
✿ **Shri Swaminarayan Sanatan Hindu Mandir**
54-62 Meadow Garth, London NW10 8HD; *t* (0181) 965
2651, *f* 965 6313   »95

✿ **Swaminarayan Hindu Mission**
80 Castleford Road, Sparkhill, Birmingham B11   »90
✿ ≡ Dr R.B. Shah: 14 Michelham Down, Woodside Park,
London N12 7JN; *t* (0171) 521 2221, 521 2222   »88
● **Vedic Society**
65-179 Radcliffe Road, off Northam, Southampton,
Hampshire; *t* (01703) 32275, 553326   »88
✿ **Vishwa Hindu Parishad, VHP**
Lal Chand Pounj, National President: 208 Mansel Road, Small
Heath, Birmingham B10
Support group for Hindu party in India; Hindu unity, charity,
educational and religious activities. *Hindu Vishwa* (4/yr). »90
✿ ≡ 5 Rosemary Drive, Redbridge, Ilford IG4 5JD; *t* (0181)
550 6096   »88
✿ **Vishwa Hindu Temple**
2 Lady Margaret Road, Southall UB1; *t* (0181) 574 3874 »88
✿ **Visva Adhyatmik Sansthan (Charitable Trust)**
48 Sutton Lane, Hounslow TW3 3RD   »90
● **World Council of Hindus**
Hasmukh Shah: [address unknown] Bradford   »96
✿ **Young Hindu Progressive Mandal**
3 Parkside Road, Handsworth Wood, Birmingham B21   »90

◉ **NORTHERN IRELAND** 44

✿ **Krishna Temple** and Iskcon NI Ltd
Inis Rath, Lisnaskea, Co. Fermanagh; *t* (013657) 21512
A base of the Hare Krishna sect, the International Society for
Krishna Consciousness.   »94
✿ **Radha Krishna Temple**
49 Malone Road, Belfast BT9 6RY   »88

HMONG

see Asian, Laotian, South-East Asian

HONDURAN

see also Central American, Latin American

◉ **UNITED KINGDOM** 44

● **Honduras Committee for Human Rights**, also known as
Committee for Human Rights in Honduras
83 Margaret St, London W1N 7HB; *t* (0171) 323 2151   »92

HONG KONG

see Chinese, Vietnamese

HUNGARIAN

see also East European, European, Gypsy, Tsigane

◉ **ITALY** 39

✿ **Chiesa Ungherese** *(Hungarian Catholic Church)*
via Vittorio Veneto 27, 00187 Roma; *t* (06) 462850   »90
✿ ≡ via Conciliazione 14, 00193 Roma; *t* (06) 656 1368   »90

◉ **ROMANIA** 40

● **Hungarian Democratic Union of Romania**
[address unknown]
Political party promoting interests of the Magyar minority. »95
♦ **Union of Hungarian Youth Organisations of Romania,
MISZSZ**
St. Kossuth Lajos 20, 4150 Ordorheui-Secuiesc; *t/f* (066)
213371
Represents youth groups of Magyar minority population.   »94

◉ **UNITED KINGDOM** 44

● **British Hungarian Friendship Society**
[address unknown]   »88
● **Federation of Hungarian Jews in Great Britain**
R. Adler, Secretary: 143-145 Brondesbury Park, London
NW2 5JL; *t* (0181) 451 0674
Founded 1953 to help resettlement of emigrés.   »89
✿ **Hungarian Catholic Chaplaincy**
St Dunstan Hse, 141 Gunnersbury Ave., London W3 8LG »88
● **Hungarian Society**
[address unknown]   »88

ICELANDIC

see also European, Scandinavian

◉ **DENMARK** 45

● **Dansk-Islandsk Samfund**
Nybrovej 116, 2800 Lyngby; *t* 4527 7200   »95

INDIAN

*see also Asian, Baha'i, Bengali, Black, East African, Goan,
Gujarati, Hindi, Hindu, Islamic, Jain, Kashmiri, Punjabi, Sikh,
Tamil, Urdu*

◉ **DENMARK** 45

✿ **Indian Cultural Association, ICA**
Kartar Singh Grewal: Ingstrup Alle 25B, 2770 Kastrup;
t 3252 4323   »94
● **Indian Welfare Association in Denmark**
Inderjit S. Suri: Pinjevej 10, 3000 Helsingør; *t* 4222 2705»89

◉ **FRANCE** 33

✿ **Centre Culturel Indo-Français**
12 rue N.D. de Nazareth, 75003 Paris; *t* (1) 4278 8053   »90

◉ **IRELAND** 353

● **Irish Indian Cultural Society**, also known as Ireland India
Cultural Society
c/o Breandán Ó Tíghearnaigh: [address uncertain] 66
Redesdale Rd, Mount Merrion, Dublin; *t* (01) 288 0875
Also listed (1993) c/o Mrs K. Thakore, 21 Aranleigh Court,
Rathfarnham, Dublin 14; or Jacob Rajan, 78 Mount Anville
Park, Dublin 14, *t* (01) 288 1490. Member of EU Migrants
Forum, p131. Cultural and social activities.   »94

◉ **ITALY** 39

✿ **Rappresentanti Indiani** *(Indian Representatives)*
c/o Consulta Cittadini dell'Immigrazione, via Merulana 123,
00185 Roma   »90

◉ **NETHERLANDS** 31

● **Landelijk India Werkgroep**
Oudegracht 36, Utrecht; *t* (030) 232 1340   »95

◉ **PORTUGAL** 351

● **Instituto Indo-Português** *(Indo-Portuguese Institute)*
Rua Custódio Vieira 3-2° D, 1250 Lisboa; *t* (01) 388 3774»95

◉ **UNITED KINGDOM** 44

✿ **The Academy of Indian Dance**
The Place, 17 Dukes Road, London WC1H 9AT; *t* (0171)
387 0980
Promotion of, and education in, South Asian dance.   »95
✿ **Bharat Sevaf Samaj**
Edward Street, Rugby CV21, Warwickshire
Hindu temple?   »90
● **Bharatiya Vidya Bhavan** *(Institute of Indian Arts and Cultures)*
Mathoor Krishnamurti, Director: Old Church Building, 4a
Castletown Road, London W14 9HE; *t* (0171) 381 3086
Multi-cultural, multi-faith educational resource centre.   »94
✿ ≡ Dr H.V.S. Sastry: Flat 1, 241 Dickenson Road, Longsight,
Manchester M13; *t* (0161) 248 5073
Promotion of Indian philosophy, Hindu religion, music, dance
and culture; celebration of Indian festivals.   »93
● **Books from India**
45 Museum St, London WC1A 1LR; *t* (0171) 405 7226
Specialist bookshop.   »91
✿ **Brent Indian Association and Community Centre, BIA**
A.G. Desai: 116 Ealing Road, Wembley HA0 4TH; *t* (0181)
903 3019
Counselling, advice, casework; community development;
interpreting, training, leisure, multi-faith/cultural activities. »95
● **British Indian Councillors Association**
Peter Pendsay: [address unknown]
Forum for Indian members of local authorities.   »95
● **Centre for Indian Studies** University of Hull
Hull HU6 7RX; *t* (01482) 465277, *f* 466570
Postgraduate study and research on Indian politics and history.
There is an associated CR Parekh Chair of Indian Politics in the
Department of Politics.   »95

♦ **Confederation of Indian Organisations, CIO**
Kanti Nagda, Secretary: 5 Westminster Bridge Road, London
SE1 7XW; *t* (0171) 928 9889, *f* (0171) 620 4025
Tanzeem Ahmed, Tara Kumar Mukherjee; umbrella body for
community groups; member EU Migrants Forum, p131.　»96

✿ **Federation of Indian Organisations**
213 Worlds End Lane, Birmingham B32　»90
✿ ≡ 267-271 High Street, Smethwick, Warley B66　»90

✿ **Friends of India Society**
30 Fernley Road, Birmingham B11　»90

● **India Society**
Dr B.N. Bhargava: 37 Stowe Crescent, Ruislip HA4　»90

● *India Weekly*
97 London Fruit Exchange, Brushfield Street, London E1;
t (0171) 377 9969　»88

● *Indiamail*
Tanya Datta, Women's Editor: 150a Ealing Road, Wembley
HA0 4PV; *t* (0181) 900 1781, *f* 903 2156
Newspaper.　»95

● **Indian Arts Council in the UK**
Sashi Deo: Horizon Gallery, 70 Marchmont Street, London
WC1N 1AB; *t* (0171) 837 1431　»90

✿ **Indian Association**
A. Raman: 18 Eildon Street, Edinburgh EH3 5JU, Scotland;
t (0131) 556 5286　»94
✿ ≡ M.K. Himavat: 57-59 Fern Street, Oldham OL8 1SH;
t (0161) 633 0043
Religious, community and advice centre; immigration advice;
Indian clientele with some Pakistanis, Bangladeshis.　»94
✿ ≡ 145 High Street, West Bromwich B70, West Midlands»90

✿ **Indian Association of Manchester** and Indian Senior
Citizens' Centre
Dr B.C. Das: Gandhi Hall, Brunswick Road, Withington,
Manchester M20 9QB; *t* (0161) 445 1134
Women's and youth activities, leisure and cultural events,
language classes. Care of elderly, entertainment, health
education, welfare advice and interpreting.　»93

✿ **Indian Business Forum**
Umarji Musa Patel: [address unknown] Preston, Lancs.　»94

✿ **Indian Centre**
360 Soho Road, Handsworth, Birmingham B21　»90

✿ **Indian Community Centre**
Randon Street, Derby; *t* (01332) 42892　»90
✿ ≡ 2 Norris Road, Reading RG6 1NG; *t* (01734) 667262 »90
✿ ≡ and Indian Community Centre Association: J.S. Bassi:
Rawson Street, New Basford, Nottingham NG7 7FR;
t (0115) 978 5985, 970 3374
Represented in EU Migrants Forum, p131. Meeting place for
many groups; base for arts and community projects.　»94

✿ **Indian Cultural and Educational Forum**
143 Soho Road, Handsworth, Birmingham B21　»90

✿ **Indian Muslim Association**
Abdulkarim Gheewala/Mohammed Sabat: [address unknown]
Leicester　»94
✿ ≡ A.B. Abdulla Kamani: [address unknown] Manchester »94

● **Indian Muslim Federation (UK)**
Ismail Yusuf Shaikh, Chairman: Indian Muslim Hall, Trinity
Close, London E11 4RP; *t* (0181) 558 6399
Also branch in Blackburn, Lancashire (Adam Patel).　»94
✿ ≡ 70 Turner Road, Edgware HA8, Middlesex　»94

✿ **Indian Muslim Professionals Group**
Mahmud Hosain: 66 Nevill Avenue, Hove BN3 7NA;
t (01273) 739857　»94

✿ **Indian Muslim Welfare Society, IMWS**
A.Y. Lunat, President: Community Centre, Taylor Street,
Batley WF17 5BA; *t* (01924) 474358, *f* 420890　»94

● **Indian Muslims Relief Committee**
PO Box 415, London NW1 2LD; *t* (0171) 338 3678　»94

✿ **Indian Overseas Congress (UK)**
151-153 Soho Road, Handsworth, Birmingham B21　»90
✿ ≡ 94-95 Shireland Road, Smethwick, Warley B66　»90

✿ **Indian Overseas Youth Congress UK**
Amarjeet Singh Bhamra: PO Box 1551, Windsor SL4 1TZ »93

✿ **Indian Parents' Association, IPA**
A. Daji: 45 Warwick Rd, Batley WF17 6AP; *t* (01924) 444110
May be same as Asian Parents, listed (1990) at same address,
formed 1984 in response to racist attacks on children.　»94

✿ **Indian Parents' Association** and Indian Ladies Club
48 Vernon Road, Handsworth Wood, Birmingham B20　»90

● **Indian Volunteers for Community Service, IVCS:** and
International Task Force for the Rural Poor, INTAF
12 Eastleigh Avenue, South Harrow HA2 0UF; *t* (0181)
864 4740
Volunteer work and funding for rural development schemes
in India, and for Indian communities in UK.　»93

✿ **Indian Welfare Society**
11 Middle Row, London W10 5AT; *t* (0181) 969 9493　»90

✿ **Indian Women's Association**
Dr Lata Patsak: Gandhi Hall, Brunswick Road, Withington,
Manchester M20 9QB; *t* (0161) 224 2452, 969 0972
Cultural, welfare, leisure activities; advice, information.　»93

✿ **Indian Workers' Association, IWA**
Ibrahim Master: [address unknown] Blackburn, Lancashire»94
✿ ≡ Mohinder S. Chatrick: 52 Old South Street, Springwood,
Huddersfield HD1 4BU; *t* (01484) 514275, *f* 514276　»94
✿ ≡ 2 Wilkes Street, Willenhall WV13 2BS; *t* (01902) 632854
Community welfare project affiliated to the IWA(GB).　»91

● **Indian Workers' Association, Great Britain, IWA(GB)**
Avtar Sadiq, General Secretary: 13 Greenford Avenue, Southall
UB2, Middlesex; *t* (0181) 574 8838, 870 0122 (?)
Harpal Brar, president; Teja S. Sahota. A major community
group, split by early 1990s into two main factions: a Maoist/
Naxalite West Midlands group, led by Avtar Jouhal, and a
more pragmatic group in London. Other IWA(GB) groups were
in Derby (led by Prem Singh) and Huddersfield. The current
situation was not known as we went to press; it is thought
that the main tendencies had reunited as the IWA(GB) but with
some IWA groups remaining independent. See also Migrant
Advisory Service, p156. Journal *Lalkar* (in Punjabi).　»92

✿ **Indian Workers' Association Shaheed Udham Singh, IWA**
Welfare Centre, 346 Soho Road, Handsworth, Birmingham
B20; *t* (0121) 551 4679　»95

● **Indian Workers' Association (Southall), IWA(S)**
Piara Singh Khabra MP, Chairman: Voluntary Action Centre,
51 Grove Road, Hounslow TW3 3PR; *t* (0181) 574 6019
Local community group, independent of other IWAs.　»95

✿ **The Karuna Trust**
186 Cowley Road, Oxford OX4 1UE; *t* (01865) 728794,
f 792941
Relief work in India: rights of so-called untouchables, rural
development, urban poor, Tibetan refugees.　»93

● *The Overseas Indian*
Jaswant Singh, Editor: 4 Station Road, Manor Park, London
E12 5BT; *t* (0181) 514 3713
Magazine (6/yr).　»88

✿ **Shobana Jeyasingh Dance Company**
[address unknown] London; *t* (0171) 383 3252
Bharatha Natyam and other traditional and contemporary
Indian dance; dance education.　»95

● **South Indian Muslim Association (UK)**
A.K. Salim: 123 Burgess Road, East Ham, London E6 2BL;
t (0181) 471 9394　»94

● *Telugu Talli*
17 Gleneagles Close, Orpington BR6 8DM; *t* (01689) 31528
Newsletter.　»88

✿ **Wembley and Harrow Indian Association, WHIA**
K. Nagda: 229 Long Elmes, Harrow HA3 6LE; *t* (0181) 421
4233, 863 9089, *f* 861 1473
Welfare work; see Asian Health Awareness Project, p13. »94

West Midlands Consortium Project on Indian Teacher Training:
see Indian Teacher Training and Ethnic Minorities Recruitment
and Retention Project, p245

✿ **Young Indian Forward Block**
119 Thornhill Road, Handsworth, Birmingham B21　»90

◎ **NORTHERN IRELAND** 44

✿ **Indian Chamber of Commerce in Northern Ireland**
Diljit Rana: Plaza Hotel, 15 Brunswick Street, Belfast BT2
7GE; *t* (01232) 333555, *f* 232999
Represents Indian business community; integration, cultural
awareness; celebrates major Indian festivals.　»95

✿ **Indian Community Centre**
86 Clifton Street, Belfast BT13; *t* (01232) 249746　»95

INDO-CHINESE

*see Asian, Cambodian, Khmer, Laotian, South-East Asian,
Vietnamese*

INDONESIAN

see also Asian, Moluccan, South-East Asian, Timorese

◎ **GERMANY** 49

● **Initiative für Menschenrechte in Indonesien** *(Initiative for
Human Rights in Indonesia)*
[address unknown] Berlin　»90

NETHERLANDS *31*

NETHERLANDS *31*

● **Indonesisch Documentatie en Informatie Centrum, INDOC**
M. Meijer, Co-ordinator: Postbus 11250, 2301 EG Leiden;
t (071) 512 4739
Information on human rights issues in Indonesia.   »95

UNITED KINGDOM *44*

● **TAPOL, The Indonesia Human Rights Campaign**
Carmel Budiardjo, Secretary: 111 Northwood Road, Thornton
Heath CR7 8HW; *t* (0181) 771 2904, *f* 653 0322   »96

IRANIAN

see also Baha'i, Islamic, Kurdish, Middle Eastern

DENMARK *45*

✿ **Cultural Iranian Union Club Roubek Khoudy-Barbaroudy**
Daniel Shadmuni: Blågårdsgade 4, 2200 København N;
t 3139 7212, *f* 4995 5192
Refugee welfare, information, cultural activities.   »94
✿ **Iransk-Danske Kulturel of Social Forening** *(Iranian-Danish Social and Cultural Society)*
Inspektørboligen, Stolpedalsvej 4, 9000 Aalborg; *t* 9810 3159   »89
✿ **Den Iransk-Danske Kulturforening**
Bentesvej 41 kld., 8220 Brabrand   »94
● **Iransk-Danske Solidaritetsforening** *(Iranian-Danish Solidarity Association)*
Klostergade 37, 8000 Århus C   »89
● **Den Iranske Forening i Danmark**
Amin Bahur/Rauf Hasanzadeh: c/o IND-sam, Blegdamsvej 35 st., 2200 København N; *t* 3332 7181
Location: Frederiksborggade 35, st., 1360 København K.
Represented in EU Migrants Forum, p131.   »90

GERMANY *49*

✿ **Autonome Iranische Frauenbewegung im Ausland e.V.** *(Independent Movement of Iranian Women Abroad)*
Kasselerstraße 1A, 60486 Frankfurt am Main; *t* (069) 772050, *f* 772059
Information/welfare work for refugees; see AGISRA, p166.»94
✿ **Verein Iranischer Flüchtlinge in Berlin e.V.,** VIFB *(Union of Iranian Refugees in Berlin)*
Hamid Nowzari: Tegeler Weg 25, 10589 Berlin; *t* (030) 344 7729   »94

ITALY *39*

✿ **Associazione Iraniani in Liguria** *(Liguria Iranian Association)*
M. Milad: c/o Coordinamento Immigrati Extracomunitari, Salita S. Francesco 4, 16122 Genova; *t* (010) 887225   »94
✿ **Centro Culturale Italia-Iran**
Chagiz Sanii: via delle Porte Nuove 17 R, 50144 Firenze;
t (055) 368019   »94
✿ **Comunità Iraniana in Italia** *(Iranian Community in Italy)*
c/o Provincia di Roma, Ufficio Immigrazione, via Santa Eufemia 19, 00187 Roma; *t* (06) 787926   »90
✿ ≡ c/o Ufficio Emigrazione Provinciale: Palazzo Valentino, piazza Venezia 119, 00187 Roma; *t* (06) 275 3106 (ab.)   »90
● **Coordinamento dei Lavoratori, Studenti e Rifugiati Iraniani in Italia, CLSRI** *(Iranian Workers, Students & Refugees Liaison)*
Kurosh Danesh: c/o CeLSI-CGIL, via Adua 22, 00199 Roma; *t* (06) 686 8328   »94
✿ **Iraniani Democratici** *(Democratic Iranians)*
via Pernigotti 37, 15057 Tortona; *t* (0131) 800267   »90
● **Lega per i Diritti dei Lavoratori Iraniani** *(League for Iranian Workers' Rights)*
[address unknown]   »90
● **Lega Internazionale per la Difesa dei Diritti Civili e Democratici in Iran** *(International League for the Defence of Civil and Democratic Rights in Iran)*
Rahmat Khosrovi: via Calalzo 51, 00135 Roma; *t* (06) 303 8022
Welfare of Iranian refugees; defence of human rights in Iran.
May be same as Lega per la Difesa dei Diritti in Iran listed (1990) at via della Dogana Vecchia 4, 00186 Roma.   »94
● **Unione Artisti Iraniani in Italia**
[address uncertain] via S. Giovanna Elisabetta 46a, 00138 Roma; *t* (06) 892 7623 (?)   »90

NETHERLANDS *31*

● **Iraanse Studenten Associatie**
Postbus 84021, 3009 CA Rotterdam   »95

● **Iraanse Vluchtelingen-Zelforganisatie,** IVZO *(Independent Organisation of Iranian Refugees)*
Weena 745, 3013 AL Rotterdam; *t* (010) 433 1390
Based at VluchtelingenWerk Rijnmond, p147.   »95
● **Vereniging van Iraanse Vluchtelingen in Nederland,** VIVN *(Union of Iranian Refugees in Holland)*
Hogevecht 229, 1102 HM Amsterdam; *t* (020) 697 8967
Also contactable through the VON office in Utrecht, p146.»95

SPAIN *34*

✿ **Centro de Defensa de los Refugiados Iraníes,** CEDRI *(Iranian Refugees Defence Centre)*
Club de la Unesco de Madrid, plaza Tirso de Molina 8-1°, 28012 Madrid; *t* (91) 227 0557-58
Support group for all Iranian opposition refugees.   »94

SWEDEN *46*

● **Swedish Iran Committee**
Gunnarbovägen 2B, 17165 Solna   »93

UNITED KINGDOM *44*

● **British Institute of Persian Studies,** BIPS
13 Cambrian Rd, Richmond TW10 6JQ; *t* (0181) 940 0647
Culture, history, education. *Iran Yearbook*.   »90
Committee for the Welfare of Iranian Jews in Great Britain: see Jewish listing, p80
● **Friends of Iran Campaign for Democracy and Human Rights**
B. Massoudi: [address unknown] Putney, London SW15   »90
● **Iranian Association**
Palingswick House, 241 King Street, London W6 9LP;
t (0181) 748 6682
Refugee and immigrant welfare and advice.   »91
✿ **Iranian Community Centre**
Anahita Amin: 266-268 Holloway Road, London N7 6NE;
t (0171) 700 0341, 700 0477
Support services include joint project with Refugee Housing, p157; also has a Women's Section.   »95
✿ **Iranian Counselling and Advice Society,** ICAS
Abbas Reyahi: 221 Beechwood Road, Luton LU4 9RZ;
t (01582) 595126, 452147, *f* 450573   »94
✿ **Iranian Welfare Association**
Pari Shariati Panobi, Chair: PO Box 913, Brighton BN1 8GB;
t (01273) 735867, 323382   »94
✿ ≡ PO Box 418, Hove BN3 2EZ   »94
✿ **North London Zoroastrian Association**
c/o Faridoon Madon: 1 Salisbury Mansions, St Ann's Road, London N15 3JP
Community group; counselling, some primary purpose and divided families immigration casework.   »90
● **Union of the Iranian Community in Leeds,** UICL
E.A. Abdulahzadeh: 229 Woodhouse Lane, Leeds LS2 9LF;
t (0113) 244 8921   »90
✿ **Zoroastrian Community**
Parveen Durrawala: 73 Shaftesbury Road, Brighton BN1 4NG; *t* (01273) 670249   »94

IRAQI

see also Arab/Arabic, Islamic, Kurdish, Middle Eastern

DENMARK *45*

● **Den Iraqiske-Turkmenske Forening i Danmark** *(Iraqi and Turkmenistani Society in Denmark)*
[address uncertain] Peter Fabersgade 18, kld., 2200 København N   »90

ITALY *39*

● **Lega Artisti Scrittori Giornalisti Iracheni in Italia** *(League of Iraqi Artists, Writers and Journalists in Italy)*
c/o Consulta Cittadina dell'Immigrazione, via Merulana 123, 00185 Roma   »90

NETHERLANDS *31*

✿ **Iraaks Culturele Vereniging**
Berkstraat 7, 4621 EA Bergen op Zoom   »95
✿ **Iraaks Democratisch Centrum**
Weena 745, 3013 AL Rotterdam; *t* (010) 433 0099
Based at VluchtelingenWerk Rijnmond, see p147.   »95
● **Organisatie van Mensenrechten in Irak,** OMRI *(Organisation for Human Rights in Iraq)*
Postbus 26, 2150 AA Nieuw Vennep; *t* (050) 265739 (?)»95

◎ SPAIN *34*

• **Asociación de Amigos Hispano-Iraquíes** *(Spanish-Iraqi Friendship Association)*
M. Abdul R. Bushra: calle Amaniel 5-2° 4, 28015 Madrid; *t* (91) 547 6165, bar 429 1601
Refugee welfare; represented in EU Migrants Forum, p131.»95

◎ SWEDEN *46*

• **International Organisation for Human Rights in Iraq**
PO Box 7145, 10387 Stockholm   »93

◎ UNITED KINGDOM *44*

• **Campaign Against Repression and for Democratic Rights in Iraq**
Ann Clwyd MP, Chair: House of Commons, Westminster, London SW1A 0AA
Human rights in Iraq; opposition to Saddam regime.   »96
• **Campaign for Democratic Opposition in Iraq**
Clive Furness, Secretary: [address unknown] London
Supports anti-Saddam groups in Iraq, and campaigns on issues including human rights and Kurdish self-determination.   »95
• **Free Iraqi Council**
Saad Salih Gahi: [address unknown] Kensington, London W
One of the main opposition groups among Iraqi emigrés in London; seeks isolation and overthrow of government.   »95
✿ **Iraqi Community Association, ICA**
Talal Ahmed: Iraqi Community Centre, 5 Bradbury Street, London N16 8JN; *t* (0171) 249 3788
Charity; welfare of Iraqis in Britain.   »94
✿ ≡ c/o 123 Manchester Road, Chorlton-cum-Hardy, Manchester M21 1PG; *t* (0161) 861 9335
Refugee welfare, social/cultural events, language classes.»93
• **Iraqi National Congress, INC**
Dr Ahmed Chalabi: [address unknown] London
CIA-backed Kurdish/Iraqi opposition coalition formed 1992.»95
• **Organisation of Human Rights in Iraq**
72 Tooting Bec Rd, London SW17 8BE; *t* (0181) 672 1494»90
• **Supreme Council for the Islamic Resistance in Iraq**, SCIRI
Hamid al-Bayati: [address unknown] Bloomsbury, London WC1
Iranian-backed opposition movement to the Saddam Hussein government. Media/lobbying campaigns on human rights.»95

IRISH

see also British, European, Gypsy, Traveller

◎ BELGIUM *32*

✿ **De Ierse Vriendenkring** *(Circle of Friends of Ireland)*
c/o Dr Jur. L. Roppe: Eidenkreef 13, 3500 Hasselt   »90
• **Irish Chaplains in Europe—Belgian Chaplaincy**
Rev. Vincent Gallogly OFM Cap.: Avenue des Anciens Combattants 23-25, 1950 Kraainem; *t* (02) 720 1970
Catholic Chaplaincy to Irish migrant workers and families; liaises with Irish Episcopal Commission for Emigrants, p141.»95
• **Irish Club of Belgium**
Paul Ronayne, President: Ave. Coloniale 31, 1170 Bruxelles»90
• **Irish Institute for European Affairs**: Foras Eireannach Gnóthaí Eorpacha
Malachy Vallely, Director: Broekstraat 1, 3000 Leuven; *t* (016) 220261, *f* 205634
AnneMie de Laounoit manager, Dr T.P. Hardiman chairman. Founded 1984; cultural centre in former seminary. Events/ courses with University of Louvain or Irish institutions. Funded by Louvain Development Trust. *Leuven/Louvain* bulletin.   »91

◎ DENMARK *45*

• **Danish-Irish Society**
Postbox 353, 1504 København V   »90
• **Irish Chaplains in Europe—Danish Chaplaincy**
Fr Patrick Shiels CSsR: Skt Annæ Kirke, 2 Hans Bogbinders Alle, 2300 København S; *t* 3158 2102
Service of Irish Episcopal Commission for Emigrants, p141.»94

◎ FRANCE *33*

✿ **Anamchara na nGael i bPáras**: Aumonier des Irlandais de Paris: Irish Chaplaincy in Paris
Fr Desmond Knowles: 5 rue des Irlandais, 75005 Paris; *t* (1) 4331 3265, 4535 5979; 4707 3313 (?)   »94
✿ ≡ Fr Paul Francis Spencer CP: St Joseph's Church, 50 avenue Hoche, 75008 Paris; *t* (1) 4227 2856
Fr Anthony Behan, Fr Brendan McKeever. Pastoral service associated with the Irish Episcopal Commission, p141.   »94

✿ **Association irlandaise** *(Irish Association)*
Eoin Doogan: 6 rue de Belfort, 75011 Paris
Young migrant workers' group; language classes, dances.»90
✿ **Collège des Irlandais—Centre Culturel Irlandais**: Coláiste na nGael—Cultúrlann Eireannach: Irish College—Irish Cultural Centre
The Administrator: 5 rue des Irlandais, 75005 Paris; *t* (1) 4535 5979, 4707 3133, *f* 4535 7209
Former Irish seminary, now social and cultural centre providing accommodation for Irish students and workers.   »94
• **Comité France-Irlande** *(France-Ireland Committee)*
1 rue Auguste Vacquerie, 75016 Paris; *t* (1) 4720 9390
Literary and historical interests.   »90
✿ **Foyer Notre Dame** *(Our Lady House)*
Sr Elizabeth Whyte: 26 bis rue de Lubeck, 75016 Paris; *t* (1) 4727 4915
Pastoral care/advice/accommodation for young women.   »90
• **Société Française d'Etudes Irlandaises** *(French Society for Irish Studies)*
Paul Brennan: Université de Paris III, Paris; *t* (1) 4326 7489
Cultural and historical studies; members in Paris, Lyon, Rennes, Lille universities.   »90

◎ GERMANY *49*

✿ **Deutsch-Irische Gesellschaft** *(German-Irish Society)*
Dr Eugene O'Neill, President: [address uncertain] Friedrichlausstraße 26, 4000 Düsseldorf 30   »90
✿ ≡ Frau Sperath, President: [address uncertain] Bilenbarg, 2000 Hamburg 65   »90
✿ ≡ Dr Donal Thaler: Elisabethstraße 16, 8000 München 40»90
• **Irish Chaplains in Europe—German Chaplaincy**: Irische Pfarrkommission
Fr Tom Healy/Hugh Jones: St Kilian's Pastoral Centre, Senerfelderstrasse 14, 8000 München 2; *t* (089) 557422
Pastoral service associated with the Irish Episcopal Commission for Emigrants, p141.   »94
• **Irland Verein e.V.** *(Ireland Union)*
Irish Club, Oktaviostraße 15, 2000 Hamburg 70   »90

◎ GREECE *30*

• **Greek Irish Society**
Odos Amarilidos 16, Agia Paraskevi, 15301 Athinai; *t* (01) 657 0418   »94

◎ ITALY *39*

• **Irish Chaplains in Europe—Italian Chaplaincy**
Very Rev. Thomas A. Hunt OSA: St Patrick's Church, via Piemonte 60, 00187 Roma; *t* (06) 465716
Fr Brian O'Sullivan, Fr Martin Nolan. Pastoral service in association with the Dublin-based IECE, p141.   »94

◎ LUXEMBOURG *352*

✿ **Comhaltas Ceoltóirí Eireann, CCE** *(Irish Musicians' Society)*
Martin Joyce, Chair, CCE Luxembourg: 50 rue de la Toison d'Or, 2265 Luxembourg
Branch of Dublin-based Irish folk music society.   »90
✿ **Craobh Naomh Fiachra** *(St Fiacre's Branch)*
Philomena Lane: 27 rue M. Georgen, 8028 Strassen; *t* 318512
Social group named after early Irish missionary to Europe. »94
• **Cumann Lúthchleas Gael, CLCG**: Gaelic Athletic Association, GAA
Clíodhna Dempsey: c/o Parlement Européen, Centre Européen, Plateau de Kirchberg, Luxembourg
Irish-based body governing national sports including hurling, camogie, handball and Gaelic football.   »90
• **Irish Chaplains in Europe—Luxembourg Chaplaincy**
Rev. Pat O'Connor CSsR: European Parish, 34 rue des Capuchins, BP 175, Luxembourg; *t* 470039
Catholic pastoral service associated with the Irish Episcopal Commission for Emigrants, p141.   »94

◎ NETHERLANDS *31*

• **Irish Chaplains in Europe—Netherlands Chaplaincy**
Fr C.J.T. Talar/Fr Finlay: Parish of Our Saviour, Ruycrochlaan 126, 2957 ES Den Haag; *t* (070) 328 0816 (?)
Service of Irish Episcopal Commission for Emigrants, p141.»94
• **Netherlands Irish Society**
Nassau Zuilensteinstraat 9, 2596 CA Den Haag   »90

◎ PORTUGAL *351*

✿ **Comunidade Católica Irlandesa e Inglesa**
Fr Patrick Joseph McLaughlin: Igreja do Corpo Santo, Largo do Corpo Santo, 1200 Lisboa; *t* (01) 323208   »90

● **Irish Chaplains in Europe—Portuguese Chaplaincy**
Fr Humbert O'Brien OP: St Mary's, Rua do Murtal 368, San
Pedro do Estoril, 2765 Estoril; *t* (046) 73771, 81676
Service of the Episcopal Commission for Emigrants, p141.»94

◉ **SPAIN** *34*

● **Irish Hispanic Society**
calle Narvaez 32, Madrid; *t* (91) 577 4524   »95

◉ **UNITED KINGDOM** *44*

✿ **Abbeyfeale Society**
P. Byrne: [address unknown] London; *t* (0181) 878 9161
Social group based on origins in County Limerick.   »89

● **Action Group for Irish Youth**, AGIY
Lisa Murphy, Director: London Voluntary Sector Resource
Centre, 356 Holloway Road, London N7 6PA; *t* (0171) 700
8137, *f* 700 0099
Séamus Taylor chair, Brian McCarthy co-ordinator. Formed
1984. Research, advice leaflets, handbooks; liaison with other
agencies in UK and pre-emigration services in Ireland. Runs
London Irish Youth Forum, p51; promotes inclusion of Irish in
ethnic monitoring. *AGIY-Info* (9/yr).   »95

✿ **An Teach Irish Housing Association**
Mike Farrell: c/o Haringey Irish Centre, Pretoria Road,
Tottenham, London N17; *t* (0181) 365 1751
Short-life housing for young Irish in London; *An Teach* in Irish
means house or home. Funders include Irish government.»94

✿ **Ardagh and Clonmacnois Society**
[address unknown] London; *t* (0181) 697 0173
Social group based on Irish district of origin.   »89

✿ **Athenry Society**
[address unknown] London; *t* (0181) 598 8153
Social group based on County Galway town of origin.   »89

✿ **Aughagower and Cushlaigh Society**
N. Heneghan: [address unknown] London; *t* (0181) 904 2241
Social group based on origin in district of County Mayo. »89

✿ **Austin House Hostels**, an Irish Welfare Bureau service
72-76 Hammersmith Grove, Hammersmith, London W6 7HA;
t (0181) 741 0466, 748 1066, 741 3712
Supportive housing for 17-25 year old Irish migrant workers
and trainees; linked with Irish Support and Advice Service,
p50, through the Irish Welfare Bureau.   »95

✿ **Aylesbury and District Irish Society**
Martin O'Gorman, Secretary: 16 Dalesford Road, Acorns,
Aylesbury HP21 9XD; *t* (01296) 86444
Jim O'Connor chair. Social and cultural group.   »93

✿ **Ballycroy Society**
[address unknown] London; *t* (0181) 883 0329
Social group based on origin in district of County Mayo.   »89

✿ **Basildon Irish Club**
James Muldoon, Secretary: Basildon Road, Basildon SS13,
Essex; *t* (01268) 545456, 280610
J. Naughton chair. Social club.   »94

✿ **Basingstoke Irish Society**
Andy McFadden, Secretary: Basingstoke Irish Centre, Council
Road, Basingstoke RG21; *t* (01256) 53143, 461949
Paddy Hurl chairman. Social and cultural society.   »94

✿ **Battersea and Wandsworth Irish Group** (possibly defunct)
John Tuohy: [address unknown] London SW   »90

✿ **Beara Society**
[address unknown] London; *t* (0181) 997 5041
Social group based on town of origin in County Cork.   »89

✿ **Benburb Base**
371 Camden Road, London N7; *t* (0171) 607 7968
Short-stay hostel for 12 vulnerable single Irish people; acquired
from a religious order by Cara Irish Housing Association. »95

✿ **Birmingham Irish Welfare and Information Centre** and
Birmingham Irish Forum
Fr Joe Taaffe OMI, Treasurer: Plunkett House, 72 Digbeth,
Birmingham B5 6DH; *t* (0121) 604 6111, (01831) 847279
Helen Conboy secretary. Community and youth work, advice
on welfare, housing, rights. Forum links local voluntary
groups; works with Cara Irish Housing Association, right, on
sheltered flats for elderly. Centre is linked with the Irish
(Catholic) Chaplaincy in Britain, p49, but open to all.   »95

✿ **Blackburn Irish Society**
P. Keighes: [address unknown] Blackburn, Lancashire;
t (01254) 668215   »89

✿ **Blackpool Irish Society**
J. Hardy: [address unknown] Blackpool; *t* (01253) 47071 »89

✿ **Bolton Irish Community Association**
Patricia Coan, Secretary: 34 Woodfield Street, Great Lever,
Bolton BL3 2HD; *t* (01204) 361893
Kevin Gargan chair. Social and cultural society.   »94

✿ **Bournemouth and Poole Irish Society**
Pat Flanagan, Secretary: 52 Southwick Road, Boscombe
East, Bournemouth BH6 5PT; *t* (01202) 420942
Jim Graven chair. Social and cultural society.   »94

✿ **Brent Irish Cultural and Community Centre**, Brent Irish
Advisory Service, BIAS, and Brent Irish Mental Health Group,
BIMHG
Brendan Mulkere, Company Secretary: Aras na nGael, 76-82
Salusbury Road, London NW6 6NY; *t* (0171) 625 9585
The Centre, the management of which has attracted some
controversy, provides a range of social and cultural activities.
BIAS (Catherine Mulvenna, Jonathan Moore), founded 1978;
also listed (1995) at 99 Villiers Road, NW2 5QB; *t* (0181) 830
3232; and (1994) at 296 Willesden Lane, NW2, *t* 459 6286.
Information, welfare, cultural activities, migration research,
advice and training; publishes *Irish in Britain Directory*. The
BIMHG researches, campaigns, advises on health issues. »96

✿ **Brent Irish Society**
Sheila Casey, Secretary: 20 Quainton Street, Neasden, London
NW12; *t* (0181) 208 0232
Eileen Wagstaff chair. Social and cultural society; youth,
community care activities.   »94

✿ **Brent Irish Women's Group**
232 High Rd, Willesden, London NW10; *t* (0181) 459 7660»90

✿ **Brighton Irish Society**
Nollag Grealish, Secretary: 169-170 Kings Road Arches, Kings
Road, Brighton BN1 1NP; *t* (01273) 323624
Margaret Parsons chair. Social club.   »95

✿ **Bristol Irish Society**
Kathy Nash, Secretary: PO Box 1087, Bristol BS99 1TZ;
t (0117) 955 3931
Amelia Dunford chair. Social and cultural society.   »93

✿ **Bristol Roscommon Association**
B. Lynch: c/o 450 Fishponds Road, Bristol BS16   »89

● **British Association for Irish Studies**, BAIS
Tom Dooley: 142 Rydal Crescent, Perivale UB6 8EQ
Scholarly association; 300 members, promotes research and
teaching on Irish history and culture. It is associated with the
Irish Studies Review, p50. Newsletter (2/yr).   »94

● **British Irish Association**
9 Poland Street, London W1V; *t* (0171) 437 4185   »90

● **British Irish Rights Watch**
Jane Winter, Director: 20-21 Took's Court, Cursitor Street,
London EC4A 1BL; *t* (0171) 405 6415, *f* 405 6417
Monitors and campaigns on human rights issues, mainly
related to the Northern Ireland conflict.   »95

✿ **Bruff and District Society**
O. Flaherty: [address unknown] London; *t* (0181) 903 0533
Social group based on origins in County Limerick.   »89

✿ **Cairde** *(Friends)*
c/o London Friend, 86 Caledonian Road, London N1 9DN;
t (0171) 837 2782
Lesbian social and discussion group, fortnightly meetings. »95

✿ **Cairde na nGael**: Newham and District Friends of Ireland
Durning Hall, Earlham Grove, Forest Gate, London E7 9AB;
t (0181) 519 5089
Information, welfare/employment advice, social activities. »94

✿ **Cara Irish Housing Association Ltd**, Cara
John Brennan, Director: 339 Seven Sisters Road, London
N15 6RD; *t* (0181) 800 2744, 800 2886, *f* 802 4910
Gearoid Ó Meachair chair, Sr Joan Kane secretary, Siobhán
Peoples, Patrick Walsh. Founded 1984; support/housing for
homeless, 225 units in London. Research; combats anti-Irish
racism and discrimination. Works with other groups; some
projects outside London. Cara Welfare Fund provides grants
to residents. *Annual Report*; *Cara Newsletter* (4/yr).   »96

✿ **Roger Casement Irish Centre**
Gerry McLoughlin, Co-ordinator: Eastgate Building, 131 St
John's Way, Islington, London N19 3RQ; *t* (0171) 281 4973
Social/cultural activities; see Irish in Islington Project, p49.»95

✿ **Cavan Association**
[address unknown] Birmingham; *t* (0121) 777 4609   »89
✿ ≡ [address unknown] Manchester; *t* (0161) 431 3794   »89

● **Celtic League**
58 Flordd Eryri, Parc Hendre, Caernarfon LL55 2UR, Cymru
Campaigns around languages, cultures, demilitarisation and
self-determination of the six Celtic countries. *Carn* (4/yr).»93

✿ **Charlestown and District Society**
[address unknown] London; *t* (0181) 995 1234
Social group based on origin in district of County Mayo.   »89

● **Clann na hEireann** *(Family of Ireland, literally)*
30 Camden Road, London NW1
Support group for the Workers' Party, an Irish socialist group;
also branches in Leeds and Glasgow.   »90
✿ ≡ 173-175 Lozells Road, Lozells, Birmingham B19   »90

⋄ **Clare Association**
P. Mooney: [address unknown] Manchester; *t* (0161) 442 6306
Social group based on Irish county of origin.   »89

⋄ **Clonfert Society**
[address unknown] London; *t* (0181) 348 4096
Social group based on County Galway town of origin.   »89

⋄ **Club Cheoil** *(Music Club)*
Lynn Percival, Events Organiser: 20 Alderfield Road, Chorlton, Manchester M21; *t* (0161) 861 8787
Promotion of Irish traditional music.   »94

● **Comhaltas Ceoltóirí Eireann, CCE** *(Musicians' Association of Ireland)* Provincial Council of Britain
Pat Sweeney, Chair: 5 Delaine Road, Withington, Manchester M20 9QP; *t* (0161) 445 9615, 434 5108
Mary McAndrew secretary, *t* (0151) 922 3503. Teaching, promotion of Irish music, dance and culture.   »94

● **Connolly Association:** Head Office
244-246 Gray's Inn Road, London WC1X 8JR; *t* (0171) 833 3022
Stands for socialism, Irish self-determination; associated with the Communist Party of Ireland. *Irish Democrat* (12/yr).   »95
⋄ ≡ 5 Woodland Avenue, Northampton NN3 2BY; *t* (01604) 715793   »90

● **Co-operation Ireland**
[address unknown] London
Fundraising arm of Co-operation North, promoting co-operation between groups in Northern Ireland and the Republic.   »95

⋄ **Corby Irish Centre**
Seán Hogan, Secretary: Patrick Road, Corby NN18 9NT; *t* (01536) 743064
Seán Farrell chair. Social club.   »94

⋄ **Council of Irish Associations**
Frances Lawrence, Secretary: 118 Heys Road, Prestwich, Manchester M25 5LA; *t* (0161) 773 8265, 428 2949
Seán Mitchell chair. Represents Irish county associations in Manchester. Cultural events, youth work.   »94

● **Council of Irish County Associations**
John Connolly, Secretary: 52 Camden Square, London NW1 9XB; *t* (0171) 916 2222, (0181) 452 6077
Mary Allen chair. Umbrella group of Irish county and district clubs; annual festival, co-ordinates welfare work. »94

⋄ **Cumann Lúthchleas Gael, CLCG:** Gaelic Athletic Association, GAA
c/o Pat Griffin: 114 Burnley Road, London NW10; *t* (0181) 450 2772
Irish-based body governing national sports including hurling, camogie, handball and Gaelic football.   »90

● **Democracy Now**
James Winston, Secretary: 35c Leigh Road, London N5 1AH
Campaigns largely within the Labour Party for a settlement of the Northern Ireland conflict, and for extension of British parties to the region; membership includes 37 MPs.   »95

⋄ **Derby Irish Association**
Angela Grogan, Secretary: Becket Street, Derby DE; *t* (01332) 32842, 771413
Philip McHugh chair. Social club.   »94

⋄ **Dewsbury Irish National League Club**
Park Parade, Westtown, Dewsbury WF12, West Yorkshire; *t* (01924) 462615, 469509   »90

♦ **Dion** *(Shelter, literally; only Irish name is used)* formally Advisory Committee on Emigrant Welfare Services
Melanie Pine, Chairperson: Ambasáid na hEireann, 17 Grosvenor Place, London SW1X 7HR; *t* (0171) 235 2171, *f* 245 6961, *Tx* 916104
This body (often referred to as the Dion Committee) allocates Irish government funds to emigrant groups in Britain. Founded 1984; includes Irish state and voluntary agencies.   »95

⋄ **Donegal Association**
P. McElhinney: [address unknown] Manchester; *t* (0161) 431 8997   »89

⋄ **Terry Downing Centre**
Vin Granger: Wythenshawe Social Centre, Brownley Road, Wythenshawe, Manchester M22; *t* (0161) 976 4485   »93

⋄ **Dublin Association**
John A. McGuiness: 98 Greenhill Road, Crumpsall, Manchester M8 7WG; *t* (0161) 740 6193   »93

⋄ **Eastleigh and District Irish Society**
Seán McManus, Secretary: 8-10 Station Hill, Eastleigh, Hampshire; *t* (01703) 613835-37
Nicky Ingram chair. Social club, welfare activities.   »94

⋄ **Emerald Social Club**
John McEntee, Secretary: Cross Street North, Wolverhampton WV1 1PP; *t* (01902) 35149, 781408
Tom Collis chair. Social and cultural society.   »93

⋄ **Epsom and District Irish Society**
Mary Finn, Secretary: 4 Melton Place, Epsom KT19 9EE; *t* (013727) 27731   »94

● **Federation of Irish Societies, FIS**
Maria O'Sullivan: The Irish Centre, 52 Camden Square, London NW1 9XB; *t* (0171) 916 2725, 916 2733, *f* 916 2753
Liam McNally chair, Paul Murphy secretary *t* (0181) 741 0466, Joan Kane community care officer, Seán Hutton co-ordinator, Michael Canning PR officer *t* (01923) 819923. Founded 1973 as umbrella group for community centres, social and sports clubs, now has 100 affiliates with some 70,000 members in all; community care, welfare role including co-ordination of housing advice; educational, youth work, cultural sections.»95

⋄ **Fethard and Killusty Society**
P. Shine: [address unknown]; *t* (01992) 760016
Social group based on place of origin in Tipperary.   »89

⋄ **Fulham Irish Society**
Sarah Quinn, Secretary: 11 Halford House, Chartfield Avenue, Putney, London SW15 6DE; *t* (0181) 789 2795
Thomas Nolan chair. Social and cultural society.   »94

⋄ **Gagile Theatre Company**
Maria O'Sullivan, Administrator: 113 Little Ealing Lane, London W5 4EJ; *t* (0181) 567 3994
Paddy O'Connor artistic director. Irish drama society.   »94

⋄ **Galway Association** Bedfordshire and Hertfordshire
[address unknown] St Albans, Herts.; *t* (01727) 65634
Social group based on Irish county of origin.   »89

⋄ **Glasgow Irish Society**
[address unknown] Glasgow, Scotland; *t* (0141) 424 1443
Social and cultural society.   »89

⋄ **Glenamaddy Society**
[address unknown] Manchester; *t* (0161) 434 1378
Social group based on County Galway town of origin.   »89

⋄ **Glenbeigh and District Society**
B. Sweeney: [address unknown] London; *t* (0181) 568 4552
Social group based in County Kerry.   »89

● **Glór an Deorí** *(Voice of the Emigrant; only Irish name is used)*
Dave Reynolds: [address unknown] London
Campaigns for emigrants' right to vote in Irish elections. Founded 1983; sister organisations in USA, Australia.   »95

⋄ **Gloucester and District Irish Club**
J. Searls: Horton Road, Gloucester; *t* (01452) 25728   »89

⋄ **Gneeveguilla Society**
J. Crawley: [address unknown] London; *t* (0181) 450 1709
Social group based on origin in County Kerry.   »89

⋄ **Graiguenamanagh and District Society**
[address unknown] London; *t* (0181) 764 9016   »89

⋄ **Green Ink Writers' Co-operative**
Green Ink Books, 8 Archway Mall, London N19; *t* (0171) 263 4748
Irish writers' group and bookshop.   »90

⋄ **Hackney Irish Association**
[address unknown] London; *t* (0171) 886 7126   »90

⋄ **Haringey Irish Association**
B. Aulsberry: c/o 2a Brabant Road, Wood Green, London N22; *t* (0181) 886 7126, 081 889 6579
Social and cultural society.   »90

⋄ **Haringey Irish Community Care Centre Ltd,** HICCC
Donal Kennedy, Secretary: 72 Stroud Green Road, London N4 3ER; *t* (0171) 272 9230, 272 7594, 263 4194, *f* 263 6641
Advice, information, emergency help, referral, resettlement; elderly day care, alcohol counselling. Chaplaincy/welfare worker (Sr Joan Kane). Ran The Irish Community Census Campaign, TICC, urging Irish people to assert that identity in 1991 census, to win recognition as an ethnic minority.   »96

⋄ **Haringey Irish Cultural and Community Centre** and Haringey Advice and Information Service
Karen O'Dea, Secretary: Pretoria Road, Tottenham, London N17 8DX; *t* (0181) 885 3490, 365 1125
Advice on employment, housing, social welfare; social, leisure and cultural activities.   »94

⋄ **Harlow Irish Association**
B. Gibson: [address uncertain] Four Provinces Club, Parloe Road, Harlow, Essex; *t* (01279) 417271   »89

⋄ **Hemel Hempstead Irish Society**
D. O'Sullivan: c/o 41 Long Arrotts, Gladesbridge, Hemel Hempstead, Hertfordshire   »89

⋄ **High Wycombe Irish Association**
Jack Sealy, Correspondence Secretary: 1 Station Road, High Wycombe HP11; *t* (01494) 521948, 445947
S. Mulry secretary, Joe Houston chair. Social club.   »94

⋄ **Hillingdon Borough Irish Association**
Finbarr Myers, Secretary: Unit 3, Royal Lane, Hillingdon, Middlesex; *t* (01895) 446515, (0181) 845 5358
J. Kiely chair. Social, cultural and welfare society.   »94

✿ **Huddersfield Irish Society**
Brian McCarthy, Secretary: St Patrick's Presbytery, 34 New
North Road, Huddersfield HD2; *t* (01484) 531483, 537924
Michael Gallagher president. Social and cultural society. »94

✿ **Hull Irish Society**
Margaret Stockford, Secretary: Chamberlain Road, Hull, North
Humberside; *t* (01482) 27667, 705705
J. Pay chair. Social and cultural society; youth activities. »94

● **Information on Ireland**
Liz Curtis: PO Box 958, London W14 0JF; *t* (0171) 602 4195
Research and information on the Irish conflict, the British
presence in Ireland, civil rights, policing, media issues. »94

✿ **Innisfree Housing Association**
Clare Winstanley: [address uncertain] 3 The Avenue, Kilburn,
London NW6 7YG; *t* (0171) 625 1818
Housing association managing over 200 homes in 11 London
Boroughs. Shared housing, short-life housing and permanent
units; welfare, employment, training and education work. »95

● **Institute of Irish Studies** University of Liverpool
Prof. Patrick Buckland, Director: PO Box 147, Liverpool L69
3BX; *t* (0151) 794 3831, 794 2901
National centre for the development of the study of Ireland;
developing Irish studies elements for school curriculum. »95

✿ **Ipswich and District Irish Society**
John O'Donohue, Secretary: 186 Fonnereau Road, Ipswich
Social and cultural society. »94

● **Irish Artists in Britain**
St Claire Allen, Cultural Co-ordinator: 50 Queensdale Road,
London W11 4SA; *t* (0171) 602 1563, secretary 289 1198
Máire Gartland chair; Mary McGowan secretary. »94

✿ **Irish in Britain History Centre**
76-82 Salusbury Road, London NW6 6NY; *t* (0171) 624 7438
Migration history, economics, sociology of Irish in Britain. »90

● **Irish in Britain Representation Group**, IBRG: Head Office and
Lambeth branch
Pat Reynolds: 245 Coldharbour Lane, London SW9 8RR;
t (0171) 326 4740
Founded 1981; civil rights, welfare and other interests of Irish
people in Britain; Irish self-determination, voting rights for
emigrants, recognition of the ethnic minority status of the
Irish; campaigns on anti-Irish racism, oppressive policing; seen
as representing younger, more radical emigrants. »95
✿ ≡ PO Box 540, Sparkhill, Birmingham B11 »89
✿ ≡ Islington: Eastgate Building, 131 St John's Way, London
N19 3RQ; *t* (0171) 281 3225 »91
✿ ≡ c/o Hornsey Library, Haringey Park, Crouch End, London
N8; *t* (0181) 348 3351 ext. 1432 »91
✿ ≡ Frontline Books, Box 9, 1 Newton Street, Piccadilly,
Manchester M1 1DH; *t* (0161) 236 1101 »93

✿ **Irish Centre**
Charles Lysaght, Secretary: York Road, Leeds LS9, Yorkshire;
t (0113) 248 0613, 248 0887
Social club; cultural and youth activities. »93

✿ **Irish Centre Birmingham**, formerly Irish Development Centre
Patrick McGrath, Secretary: 14-20 High Street, Deritend,
Birmingham B12 0LN; *t* (0121) 622 2332
Patrick McCourt chair. Social club with youth and welfare
activities, the latter in association with Birmingham Irish
Welfare and Information Centre, p47. »94

✿ **Irish Centre Housing Ltd**, ICH, formerly Irish Centre Hostels
Fr Pat Carolan, Director: 20-22 Quex Road, London NW6
4PS; *t* (0171) 372 6633, *f* 624 2918
Housing for migrants in London (900 tenants, 40 per cent
Irish); male Conway House hostel, Aidan O'Kane manager;
130-bed female St Louise Project, Sr Rosalie Hayes manager,
at 33 Medway Street, SW1P 2BE (*t* 222 2071); Hackett
House for 10 men with alcohol problems, and An Caisleán
home for elderly; five other units. Employment and training
advice, Job Powerhouse at the London Irish Centre, p50. »96

● **Irish Chaplaincy in Britain**: Head Office
Fr Bobby Gilmour/Br M. J. Curran: St Mellitus' Church,
Tollington Park, London N4 3AG; *t* (0171) 263 1477, 392
3011, *f* 281 7511
Fr Colm Ó Gallchoir assistant director; 40 priests, lay and
religious staff; founded 1950s. Catholic service providing
help, advice and counselling to immigrants; includes specialist
Apostolates, all contactable at above address: to Homeless (Sr
H. Mellett (0171) 791 0301; Br Barry Butler (0181) 340 9952,
203 0236; Sr Bridie Dowd (0171) 828 4183, 821 6980; Br
Ignatius Galvin), to People with AIDS (Fr Tim O'Keeffe), to
Prisoners (see Irish Commission for Prisoners Overseas, right);
Counselling Service (Sr Eileen O'Sullivan, Rev. Dermot Dunne),
Outreach to Immigrants (Rev. Ian Tonge (0171) 287 9067),
Hospital Chaplaincy (Rev. Bernard Costello, Sr Veronica
Gannon (0181) 969 2488), Hotel Chaplaincy (Fr Noel Clarke

(0171) 437 2010), Student Outreach (Br Michael Curran).
Local chaplaincies are in London W4 (Rev. Billy O'Donovan,
(0181) 994 2877); N19 (Rev. John Beatty (0171) 272 8195);
SE6 (Rev. John Mulligan (0181) 698 3672); SE13 (Rev. Billy
Murphy (0181) 672 2179); SW17 (Rev. Noel Naughton (0181)
672 2179); Luton (Rev. Hugh Kavanagh (01582) 28849, and
see Luton Irish Advice Bureau, p51); Northampton (Rev.
Michael O'Donnell (01604) 768483).
See also Haringey Irish Community Care Centre, Irish Support
and Advice Centre, London Irish Centre, South London Irish
Welfare Association; Birmingham Irish Welfare and Information
Centre, Liverpool Irish Centre, Irish Community Care. »95

✿ **Irish Club**
82 Eaton Square, London SW1; *t* (0171) 235 4164 »95

● **Irish Commission on Culture and Education**
76 Salusbury Road, London NW6 6NY; *t* (0171) 624 3158,
624 9990
Irish language, dancing and other cultural courses. »95

● **Irish Commission for Prisoners Overseas**, ICPO
Fr Gerry McFlynn: St Mellitus' Church, Tollington Park, London
N4 3AG; *t* (0171) 263 1477, *f* 281 7511
Dublin-based agency, see p141; welfare of 1,000 prisoners in
Britain, and their families; Catholic agency, but serves all. »95

✿ **Irish Community Alcohol Service—Brent**
Arlington Housing Association, 33-55 Jamestown Road,
London NW1 7DB; *t* (0171) 267 5534
Culturally sensitive counselling and support services to Irish
men and women with alcohol related problems. »96

✿ **Irish Community Care**
Sr Elizabeth Cahill, Care Worker: 289 Cheetham Hill Road,
Manchester M8 7SN; *t* (0161) 205 9105, 773 8220
Advice and information, social activities, welfare and
emergency aid; associated with Irish Catholic chaplaincy. »94

✿ **Irish Democratic League Club**
15 High Street, Birstall, Batley WF17; *t* (01924) 472869 »90
✿ ≡ Churchfield Street, Batley WF17; *t* (01924) 472852 »90

✿ **Irish Drama and Folk Dance Company**, formerly Irish Drama
and Folk Ballet Group
Rosemary Kennedy, Administrator: St Joseph's Community
Centre, Highgate, London N6; *t* (0181) 361 0678 »94

● *The Irish Echo*
Hadfield House, Lancashire Hill, Stockport SK4, Lancs.;
t (0161) 476 2203
Community newspaper. »95

● **Irish Freedom Movement**
[address unknown] London
Campaigns for British disengagement from Ireland. »93

✿ **Irish Gay Helpline**
[address confidential] London; *t* (0181) 983 4111
Information and counselling service, evenings only. »95

✿ **Irish Gay Men's Network**
c/o Lesbian and Gay Centre, Cowcross Street, London EC1;
t (0171) 249 4191 »90

✿ **Irish in Greenwich Project**
Clare Keeley, Administrator: 144 Greenwich High Road,
London SE10 8NN; *t* (0181) 317 1435, 305 2545
Tom Lynam chair. Advice, information, social and cultural
events. Co-operates with Lewisham Irish Centre, p50, in
providing advice service to the community in south London.»95

✿ **Irish Heritage**
Orla Byrne, Honorary Secretary: 32 The Grove, Finchley,
London N3 1QJ; *t* (0181) 346 2726
Niall Gallagher chair. Cultural society. »94

● **Irish Housing Forum**
c/o Action Group for Irish Youth, LVSRC, 356 Holloway Road,
London N7 6PA; *t* (0171) 700 8137
Campaign group of six Irish community organisations. »95

✿ **Irish in Islington Project**, at Roger Casement Irish Centre
Eastgate Building, 131 St John's Way, Islington, London N19
3RQ; *t* (0171) 281 3225
Advice, information, campaigns on housing, social security;
community work, women's health and welfare. »90

✿ **Irish Legion**
Con J. Harnett, Secretary: 120 Heybarnes Road, Small Heath,
Birmingham B10 0JE; *t* (0121) 772 0614 »94

✿ **Irish Mental Health Group**
Phil Mac Giolla Bhain: PO Box 3609, London NW9 7EN
Committee formed 1994 following Dochas conference on
mental health issues among Irish in Britain. »95

● **Irish National Council**
[address unknown] »88

● **Irish Peace Initiative**
Box 3, Roger Casement Centre, Eastgate Building, 131 St
John's Way, London N19 3RQ; *t* (0171) 609 1743
Campaign for all-party talks and self-determination. »95

- *The Irish Post*
[address unknown] London
Emigrant community newspaper (52/yr).   »95
- Irish in Scotland Forum
Anne Curran, Secretary: PO Box 346, Govanhill, Glasgow
G42 8JL, Scotland
Michael Moran chair. Umbrella group for Irish community
organisations.   »94
✿ Irish Society of Harrow
Mary Brennan, Secretary: 10 Swift Close, South Harrow HA2
0TH; *t* (0181) 864 6293, 427 3166
Michael Thornton chair. Social and cultural society.   »94
✿ Irish Student Network and Irish Chaplaincy Student Outreach
Br Michael Curran CFC: St Mellitus' Church, Tollington Park,
London N4 3AG; *t* (0171) 272 9843, *f* 281 7511   »95
- *Irish Studies in Britain*
c/o 14 Tremayne Close, Brockley, London SE4 1YF
Academic journal.   »91
- Irish Studies Centre University of North London
Jackie Harnett/Dr Mary Hickman: UNL, 1 Prince of Wales
Road, London NW5; *t* (0171) 753 5018, *f* 753 7069
Academic research, teaching, conferences on Irish affairs
and the Irish minority in Britain.   »95
- *Irish Studies Review*
Neil Sammells/Paul Hyland, Editors: Bath College of Higher
Education, Newton Park, Bath BA2 9BN; *t* (01225) 873701,
f 874082
Journal (4/yr) on cultural/social/historical issues, published in
association with British Association for Irish Studies, p47.»94
✿ Irish Support and Advice Service, Hammersmith & Fulham
Irish Centre: and Irish Chaplaincy in Britain (Hammersmith &
Fulham)
Caroline Judge, Secretary: Blacks Rd, Hammersmith, London
W6 9DT; *t* (0181) 741 0466-67, 741 3712, 748 1066
Registered charity (as Irish Welfare Bureau). Advice, help to
newly arrived and settled and others: welfare rights,
employment advice, counselling, housing assistance, training
issues; social work, Catholic chaplaincy (Fr Jim Kiely).   »95
✿ Irish Women Artists Group
Ann Tallemtire: 12 Hornsey Road, London N7; *t* (0171) 609
8916   »90
✿ Irish Women in Greenwich
115-118 Powis Street, Woolwich, London SE18; *t* (0181)
317 1435
Women's support group, social activities.   »90
✿ Irish Women in Islington
12 Hornsey Road, London N7; *t* (0171) 609 8916   »90
✿ Irish Women in Wandsworth
Jeanne Rathbone: [address unknown] Wandsworth, London
SW18; *t* (0171) 228 2327   »90
- Irish Women's Abortion Support Group, IWASG (possibly
defunct)
[address unknown] London
Established 1981 to help some of the 6,000 or more Irish
women per year who travel to London for abortions.   »90
*Irish Women's Housing Action Group/Video Production Group/
Writing Group: see London Irish Women's Centre, p51*
- *Irish World*
307a High Road, London NW10; *t* (0181) 451 5014
Emigrant community newspaper (52/yr).   »91
✿ Irish World Heritage Centre
Dermot Maguire, Secretary: 10 Queens Road, Cheetham Hill,
Manchester M8 8UR; *t* (0161) 205 4007, 273 4511, *f* 205
9285
Social club; educational, cultural and artistic events; resource
centre for community groups.   »94
✿ Isle of Wight Irish Society
Angela Taylor, Secretary: 16 Shippards Road, Brightstone,
Isle of Wight, Hampshire; *t* (01983) 740678
Malcolm Shaw treasurer. Social and cultural society.   »94
✿ Kerry Association
[address unknown] Birmingham; *t* (0121) 449 6880
Social group based on origin in County Kerry.   »89
✿ Kilburn Irish Pensioners Group
Marie Sargent, Chair: 14 Kenilworth Road, Kilburn, London
NW6 7JH; *t* (0171) 624 8772   »94
✿ Kilburn Irish Young Women's Group
c/o Camden Youth Unemployment Project, 2-6 Camden High
Street, London NW1 0JH; *t* (0171) 388 4343
Women's advice, information, discussion group, social and
cultural activities, mother-and-baby group.   »90
✿ Kilburn Irish Youth Action Group, KIYAG
Abbey Community Centre, 222c Belsize Road, London NW6
4DJ; *t* (0171) 624 8378
Social events, sport, advice, discussion groups.   »90

✿ Kilburn Irish Youth Project and Saoirse; Trasna; Young Irish
Men's Group
Eugene Scanlan, Co-ordinator: Kingsgate Community Centre,
107 Kingsgate Road, London NW6 2JH; *t* (0171) 372 1764
The Project may have superseded KIYAG (below, left).
Counselling and advice, cultural and social support for young
Irish; staff include Youth Officers of the Local Education
Authority. Trasna (Susan Russell, *t* 328 9701) is a mothers-
and-children project; Saoirse group is for young Irish women,
run with London Irish Women's Centre. These may have
superseded Kilburn Irish Young Women's Group (also below,
left). The Men's Group works with homeless and hostel-based
young men.   »95
✿ Kildare Association, Bedfordshire and Hertfordshire
[address unknown] Letchworth; *t* (01462) 677504   »89
✿ Kilkenny Association, Bedfordshire and Hertfordshire
[address unknown] Luton, Bedfordshire   »89
✿ Kilrush Society
C. Enright: [address unknown] London; *t* (0171) 609 3837
Social group based on County Clare town of origin.   »89
✿ Kiltane Society
[address unknown] London; *t* (0181) 693 7328
Social group based on origin in district of County Mayo. »89
✿ Kilteely and Dromkeen Society
[address unknown] London; *t* (0181) 743 7577
Social group based on origins in County Leitrim.   »89
✿ Kinsale Society
c/o 52 Camden Square, London NW1 9XB; *t* (0171) 485 0051
Social group based on town of origin in County Cork.   »89
- Labour Committee on Ireland
[address uncertain] BM Box 5355, London WC1N 3XX
Campaigns within the British labour movement for Irish self-
determination and unity and British disengagement; includes
Labour Women for Ireland, and Time to Go campaign.   »95
- Labour Party Irish Society
[address unknown] London   »95
✿ Lambeth Irish Women's Group
Women's Centre, 55 Acre Lane, London SW9; *t* c/o (0171)
326 4740   »90
✿ Langley Irish Society
c/o Tara, Rowley Lane, Wexham, Berkshire; *t* (012816) 2552 »89
✿ Laois Association
P. Keogh: [address unknown] Manchester; *t* (0161) 654 8385
Social group based on county of origin.   »89
✿ Leamington Irish Club
Martin Deasy, Secretary: 34 Hamilton Terrace, Holly Walk,
Leamington Spa CV32; *t* (01926) 425795, 451196   »93
✿ Leicester Irish Society
Paul Murphy, President: 31 New Forest Close, Wigston,
Leicester LE8 2RW; *t* (0116) 288 8002, 260 7983
Social group, youth activities.   »93
✿ Leitrim Association
S. Mitchell: [address unknown] Manchester; *t* (0161) 428
2949   »89
✿ ≡ Hertfordshire and Bedfordshire: K. Barry: [address
unknown] St Albans, Hertfordshire; *t* (01727) 52680   »89
✿ Lewisham Irish Community Centre, also known as
Lewisham Irish Centre
2a Davenport Road, London SE6 2AZ; *t* (0181) 695 6264
Advice service with Irish in Greenwich Project, p49.   »95
✿ Liverpool Irish Centre and Irish Community Care Merseyside
Tommy Walsh/Sheila Loughran: 127 Mount Pleasant,
Liverpool L3 5TF; *t* (0151) 707 1532, 709 4120
Rights advice, information on accommodation, employment;
social activities, community groups, Catholic chaplaincy.
The Centre includes a commercially-run bar.   »94
✿ London Camogie Board
Mary Noonan, Secretary: [address unknown] London;
t (0181) 688 4941
Irish women's sports.   »90
✿ London Irish Centre (also known as Camden Irish Centre)
and Irish Centre Drama Group
Mary Allen, Secretary: 50-52 Camden Square, London NW1
9XB; *t* (0171) 916 2222, 916 2638
Charity founded by the Catholic Church, one of the largest
Irish centres in Britain; advice and information, social and
cultural activities; Drama Group, contact Doris Daly; Irish
Chaplaincy (Rev. Denis Corcoran OMI, director).   »96
✿ London Irish Network
Michael Cronin, Secretary: 35 Jeddo Road, London W12;
t (0181) 740 6765, (0171) 737 6003
Patrick Conlon chair.   »93
✿ *London Irish News*
[address unknown] London
Community newspaper (52/yr).   »90

✧ **London Irish Pensioners Action Group**
Paudey Lynch, Chair: 58 Torbay Road, Kilburn, London NW6 7DZ; *t* (0171) 624 0641
Chris Conroy vice-chair, *t* 251 0761. »93

✧ **London Irish Rugby Football Club**
[address unknown] London
Sporting and social club. »94

✧ **London Irish Women's Centre**
Angie Birtell: 59 Stoke Newington Church Street, London N16 0AR; *t* (0171) 249 7318
Advice and information on housing, health, welfare; cultural events, campaigns, conferences; base for Irish Women's Video Production Group, Irish Women's Writing Group, Irish Lesbian Network and Irish Women's Housing Action Group, IWHAG.»95

✧ **London Irish Youth Forum, LIYF**
c/o AGIY, 356 Holloway Road, London N7 6PA
Co-ordination and discussion group founded 1987 for youth workers from voluntary and statutory sectors. Six meetings per year, with representation from 50 agencies. »95

✧ **London Ladies' Football Board**
Anne Marie Kirwan, PR Officer: [address unknown] London; *t* (0171) 724 2824
Gaelic football. »90

✧ **Longford Association**
E. Flanagan: [address unknown] Birmingham; *t* (0121) 743 8509 »89
✧ ≡ K. Farrell: [address unknown] Manchester; *t* (0161) 224 5483 »89

✧ **Loughborough Irish Association**
Tom Harkin, Secretary: c/o Catholic Club, 20 Fennel Street, Loughborough LE11, Leicestershire; *t* (01509) 216383
Address uncertain (1989); secretary's address (1993) is 23 Meadow Avenue, Loughborough LE11 1JS. Social club. »93

✧ **Louisburg and District Society**
J. Ferins: [address unknown] London; *t* (0181) 208 0998
Social group based on origin in district of Mayo. »89

✧ **Luton and Dunstable Irish Care and Advice Association**
203 Dunstable Road, Luton, Bedfordshire; *t* (01582) 404899
Social and welfare society; see also Advice Bureau. »90

✧ **Luton Irish Advice Bureau** and Irish Chaplaincy
Jim Harte, Secretary: Luton Day Centre, 141 Park Street, Luton LU1 3HS; *t* (01582) 28416, 598971
Welfare advice, social activities; includes one of two Luton offices of the Irish Chaplaincy in Britain (Sr Eileen O'Mahony, Sr Antoinette McGrath). »94

✧ **Manchester Celtic Cultural Society**
B. Lofthouse: c/o 16 Dudley Park, Didsbury, Manchester M20
Social and cultural society. »89

✧ **Manchester Irish Education Group**
Joe Flynn: Irish World Heritage Centre, 10 Queens Road, Cheetham Hill, Manchester M8 9UR; *t* (0161) 273 4232
Promotion of Irish language and culture, and of interest in Irish history and heritage. *Irish Heritage* magazine. »93

✧ **Mayo Youth Association**
Seán McGuire: Irish World Heritage Centre, 10 Queen's Road, Cheetham Hill, Manchester M8 8UQ; *t* (0161) 205 4007
Social group. May be linked with Mayo Association, *t* (1989) (0161) 881 8560. »93

✧ **Midleton Society**
K. Gavin: [address unknown] London; *t* (0181) 568 8059
Social group based on town of origin in County Cork. »89

✧ **Milton Keynes Irish Society**
Ann Scott: Denbigh Sports Grounds, Mountfarm, Saxon Street, Bletchley, Milton Keynes MK2; *t* (01908) 375978 »94

✧ **John Mitchel's 32-County Social Club**
486 Stratford Road, Sparkhill, Birmingham B11; *t* (0121) 774 4555 »95

✧ **Mitchelstown and District Society**
J. Flynn: [address unknown] London; *t* (0181) 202 4672
Social group based on town of origin in County Cork. »89

● **New Consensus**
Gary Kent, Chairperson, GB: c/o Harry Barnes MP, House of Commons, London SW1A 0AA
British section of a cross-party campaign group committed to political progress in Ireland; opposes use of violence in pursuit of political aims; joint president Peter Bottomley MP. »94

✧ **Newham Irish Society**
Jim Forsyth: 47 St Anthony's Road, Forest Gate, London E7 9EJ; *t* (0181) 552 7502 »94

✧ **Newmarket Society**
N. O'Donnell: c/o BIAS, Electric House, 296 Willesden Lane, London NW2; *t* (0181) 459 6286 »89

✧ **Newport and Burrishroole Society**
[address unknown] London; *t* (0181) 427 2675
Social group based on origin in district of Mayo. »89

✧ **North Hertfordshire Irish Association**
M. Reade, Secretary: 20 Northfields, Letchworth SG6 4RD; *t* (01462) 480391 »93

✧ **Northampton Irish Centre**
Paul Murray, Chair: 32-34 Abingdon Square, Northampton; *t* (01604) 32375, 22455 »93

✧ **Nottingham and East Midlands Irish Social Centre**
Ronan Dirrane: 2-4 Wilford Street, Nottingham NG2 1AA; *t* (0115) 947 5659, 947 3424
Frances Harrison secretary. Social club. »93

✧ **Portsmouth Irish Society**
John Cunningham, Secretary: 77 Elm Grove, Southsea, Portsmouth PO5 1JF; *t* (01705) 825152
Social club, sporting and cultural activities. »94

● **Positively Irish Action on AIDS, PIAA**
Gwyneth Hughes/Siobhán Riordan/Oonagh O'Brien: 21 Old Ford Road, London E2 9PL; *t* (0181) 983 0192, 983 4293
Community-based charity providing information, advice and support to Irish migrants affected by HIV, ARC and AIDS. »96

● **PTA Research and Welfare Association**
PO Box 817, Camp Hill, Birmingham B11 4AF; *t* (0121) 773 7362 (24 hours)
Research, advice and information on the use of the Prevention of Terrorism Act in the policing of the Irish community. »90

✧ **Radlett Irish Society**
[address unknown] Radlett, Herts.; *t* (01927) 63283 »89

✧ **Reading and District Irish Association**
Maureen Henwood, Secretary: 96-104 Chatham Street, Reading RG1 7RD; *t* (01734) 393096
Patrick Power chair. Social and cultural society. »94

✧ **Richmond and District Irish Society**
[address unknown] Richmond, Surrey; *t* (0181) 940 5410»89

✧ **Roscommon Association**
[address unknown] Bristol; *t* (0117) 965 7058 »89
✧ ≡ A. Smith: [address unknown] Manchester; *t* (0161) 998 3503 »89

✧ **Rugby Irish Association**
Gas Street, Rugby CV21; *t* (01788) 565696 »90

✧ **Safestart Foundation**
Seamus McGarry/Joe McKenna: 71 Cricklewood Broadway, London NW2 3JR; *t* (0181) 452 0181-83, 208 1058, *f* 208 1059
Settlement and employment assistance and advice to young Irish people; mainly privately funded, Catholic ethos but non-discriminatory in services. Employment training (Ruth McKeeman co-ordinator; 189 The Broadway, West Hendon, London NW9 7DD, *t* (0181) 203 7788, *f* 203 8731). »94

✧ **St Albans Irish Association**
Brian Lynch, Secretary: Cotlandswick, North Orbital Road, London Colney AL3 5TR; *t* (01727) 822251 »93

✧ **St Brendan's**
4 Craven Park, London NW10; *t* (0181) 965 9089
Short-stay hostel for men. »90

✧ **St Brendan's Irish Centre**
Liam Bradshaw: City Road, Old Trafford, Manchester M15 4DE; *t* (0161) 872 1979
Social club; cultural events, entertainment. »93

✧ **St Finbarr's Social Club**
Stoney Stanton Road, Foleshill, Coventry CV1, Warwickshire; *t* (01203) 687635 »90

✧ **St Patrick's Club**
Brian Thurlow, Secretary: Adelaide Road, Leamington Spa CV32, Warwickshire; *t* (01926) 420265
Tom Kennedy chair. Social and cultural society. »93

✧ **Scarborough Irish Society**
Pat O'Rourke, Chair: 34 Highfield Avenue, Driffield, North Humberside; *t* (01377) 46407 »93

✧ **Scunthorpe Irish Society**
M. McInerney: [address unknown] Scunthorpe DN15, Lincolnshire; *t* (01724) 864887 »89

✧ **Sheffield Irish Social Centre**
Kevin Hegarty, Secretary: 151 Brunswick Road, Sheffield S3 9LQ, Yorkshire; *t* (0114) 273 1578 »93

✧ **Skibbereen and District Society**
C. Malone: [address unknown] London; *t* (0181) 204 4124
Social group based on town of origin in County Cork. »89

✧ **Slough Irish Society Club**
Grace Bennett, Secretary: Sheehy Way, Slough SL2 5SS; *t* (01753) 528600, 573549 »93

✧ **Sólás Anois** *(Refuge Now, literally; only Irish form is used)*
Siobhán Peoples/Kathleen Egan: 27b Cantelowes Road, London NW1; *t* (0181) 291 4452, 800 2744
Irish women's domestic violence project established 1993; 20-bed refuge opened 1994, child care, advice and support, outreach and resettlement services. »96

✧ **South East London Irish Society**
S. Vida Egan: 88b Crofton Road, London SE5; *t* (0171) 701
9882   »94
✧ **South London Irish Association** also known as South London
Irish Welfare Association
Sr Carmel Keegan IISC, Care Officer: 138-140 Hartfield Road,
Wimbledon, London SW19 3TG; *t* (0181) 543 0608 centre,
540 0759 advice
Doris Waters secretary. Advice and information, social club,
cultural activities, housing aid; it is associated with the
(Catholic) Irish Chaplaincy in Britain, p49, but its services are
available to anyone in need.   »94
✧ **Southend Irish Association**
Richard Ryan, Secretary: 232 Woodgrange Drive,
Southend-on-Sea SS1 2SH; *t* (01702) 614061   »94
✧ **Stafford Irish Society**
T. Heffernan, Secretary: Stafford Irish Centre, Fancy Walk,
Stafford; *t* (01785) 42752
Social club, welfare service.   »93
✧ **Stevenage and District Irish Association**
Anne Rowland: 38 Cuttys Lane, Stevenage SG1 1UW;
t (01438) 312719   »93
✧ **Stratford Irish Community Association** also known as
Stratford Irish Society
G. Conway: 128 Blythsword Road, Seven Kings, Ilford IG3
8SG; *t* (0181) 590 6996, 534 7698   »93
✧ **Surbiton Irish Society**
[address unknown] Surbiton, Surrey; *t* (0181) 399 1574 »89
✧ **Swinford Society**
J. Scully: [address unknown] London; *t* (0181) 450 4092
Social group based on origin in district of Mayo.   »89
✧ **Templemore Society**
[address unknown] London; *t* (0181) 422 0596
Social group based on place of origin in Tipperary.   »89
✧ **Thames Valley Irish Society**
Cathy Howard, Secretary: 193 Jersey Road, Isleworth
TW7 4QJ; *t* (0181) 568 7621   »93
✧ **Thurles, Moycarkey and Borris Society**
B. Stapleton: [address unknown] London; *t* (0181) 560 3737
Social group based on place of origin in Tipperary.   »89
✧ **Thurrock and Tilbury Irish Association**
152 Dock Road, Tilbury; *t* (01375) 25032, 24863   »90
● **Wolfe Tone Society**
[address unknown] London
Republican group.   »95
✧ **Tooting Irish Society**
B. Mannion: [address unknown] Tooting, London SW17;
t (0181) 767 2714   »89
✧ **Tottenham Irish Women's Group**
Selby Centre, Selby Rd, White Hart Lane, London N17 8JN »90
✧ **Tralee Society**
[address unknown] London; *t* (0181) 969 8330
Social group based on origin in Kerry.   »89
● **Troops Out Movement, TOM**
[address unknown] London
Campaigns for British military withdrawal from Ireland, and
against oppression of the Irish community in Britain.   »95
✧ **Tyneside Irish Centre**
Terry McDermott, Chairperson: 43 Gallogate, Newcastle-upon-
Tyne NE1 4SG; *t* (0191) 261 0384, 536 3859
Fr Joseph Travers secretary. Social and welfare society.   »93
✧ **Tyrone Association**
[address unknown] Manchester; *t* (0161) 225 6198   »89
♦ **United Kingdom-Ireland Trans-Frontier Committee, TFC**
Margaret Toale, FAS UK Officer: Employment Service South
East Region, Room 503, 236 Grays Inn Road, London WC1X
8HL; *t* (0171) 211 4320, *f* 211 4995
Founded 1991 to facilitate entry to UK and Irish training and
job markets by arriving or returning migrants from either state.
Government and voluntary sector liaison. Initiatives include
orientation programme for newcomers to London, and London
presence for FAS, the Irish employment agency, p204.   »95
✧ **Waltham Forest Irish Association**
Margaretta Rooney, Secretary: 172 Essex Road, Leyton,
London E10 6BT; *t* (0181) 539 9694   »93
✧ **Waltham Forest Irish Project**
[address unknown] London; *t* (0181) 558 4577   »90
✧ **Waterford Association**
M. Doyle: [address unknown] Birmingham; *t* (0121) 472 2656
Social group based on Irish county of origin.   »89
✧ **Watford and District Irish Association**
Mary Woodruff, Secretary: Watford Irish Centre, Oxhey Park,
Wiggenhall Road, Watford, Herts.; *t* (01923) 212354   »93
✧ **Wellingborough Irish Association**
Irish Centre, Market Square, Wellingborough, Northants.   »89

✧ **West London Irish Society**
Noel Gargan, Secretary: 20 Spencer Road, Isleworth TW7
4BH; *t* (0181) 579 3980, 998 3628   »93
✧ **Wexford Association** Bedfordshire, Buckinghamshire and
Hertfordshire
J. Doyle: [address unknown] Luton, Bedfordshire; *t* (01582)
592981
Social group based on Irish county of origin.   »89
✧ ≡ B. Corbett: [address unknown] Manchester; *t* (0161)
339 4059   »89
✧ **Witham and District Irish Association**
Tessa Carradine, Secretary: 6 Janmead, Witham, Essex;
t (01376) 517768   »93
✧ **Woking and District Irish Society**
Margaret McCloskey, Secretary: 19 Thornash Close, Horsell,
Woking GU21 4UP; *t* (01483) 767952, 797747   »93
● **Women and Ireland Network**
[address unknown] London   »95
✧ **Wythenshawe Irish Society**
Vincent Grainger, Chair: 101 Calvecroft Road, Peel Hall,
Manchester M22; *t* (0161) 437 0450   »93

◎ **CHANNEL ISLANDS** *44*

✧ **Jersey Irish Society**
Marie Brown, Secretary: Clubroom, La Motte Street, St Helier,
Jersey JE2 4SY; *t* (01534) 33499
Social and cultural centre.   »95

◎ **ISLE OF MAN** *44*

✧ **Isle of Man Irish Society**
Sharon Knight, Secretary: King Orry House, Ramsey Road,
Laxey, Isle of Man; *t* (01624) 862495
Social and cultural society.   »94

ISLAMIC

*Mosques, madrassas and other Islamic centres, bodies or
organisations which are closely identified with one ethnic
group are listed under the relevant ethnic heading, but where
ethnic and religious identity overlap (e.g. Khoja Shi'a Ishna
Atheris), or if an 'ethnic' mosque is attended by other ethnic
groups, we use this Islamic heading: so see also Afghan,
African, Algerian, Arab/Arabic, Asian, Bangladeshi, Bengali,
Bosnian, Cameroon, Comoros, Cypriot, East African, Egyptian,
Filipino, Ghanaian, Gujarati, Indian, Indonesian, Iranian, Iraqi,
Ivorian, Jordanian, Kashmiri, Kuwaiti, Lebanese, Libyan,
Maghrebi, Malaysian, Mauritian, Middle Eastern, Moroccan,
Nigerian, North African, Pakistani, Palestinian, Saharan,
Senegalese, Sierra Leonean, Somali, Sri Lankan, Sudanese,
Surinamese, Syrian, Tunisian, Turkish, Urdu, Yemeni. We do
not give separate listings for Shia, Sunni and other traditions,
but when possible we mention such allegiances: a number of
Ahmadiyya groups are also listed here since they assert an
Islamic identity, but we know that this is contested by most
Muslims. Most mosques are managed by a Committee,
Jama'at or Society which can function as a welfare and
representative body for the local community; these are not
listed separately from the mosques unless they have very
different names, or activities beyond the usual range. Finally,
note that we have not imposed uniformity in transliterations
such as Jamiat/Jamaat, Madrassa/Madressa, Kokni/Kokani,
and so on, in the names of organisations.*

◎ **BELGIUM** *32*

✧ **Association de la Culture Islamique de la Région du Centre**
(Central Region Islamic Culture Association)
Rue A. France 2, 7100 La Louvière; *t* (064) 263006   »94
✧ **Association de Foi et Pratique de la Religion Islamique**
(Association for the Faith and Practice of Islam)
Rue Pige Croly 67, 6000 Charleroi; *t* (071) 310582
Religious and cultural.   »94
✧ **Association Mira Femmes Musulmanes** *(Mira Association of
Muslim Women)*
Rue Français 19, 6020 Dampremy; *t* (071) 310203   »94
✧ **Centre Islamique** *(Islamic Centre)*
Erol Gürsever: Rue de l'Etoile 15, 5000 Namur
Religious and cultural activities.   »94
● **Centre de Sociologie de l'Islam**
Avenue F.D. Roosevelt 17, 1050 Bruxelles; *t* (02) 642 3359
Research centre in Université Libre de Bruxelles.   »94
✧ **Mosquée de Bruxelles** *(Brussels Mosque)* Moskee van Brussel
Parc du Cinquantenaire 14, 1040 Bruxelles   »90

◉ **DENMARK** *45*

● **World Islamic Forum**
Mohammed Farooq Sultan: [address unknown] København»94

◉ **FRANCE** *33*

✧ **Arche Essalem**
51 rue Bernard-Dubois, 13001 Marseille
Islam, inter-faith contact, culture, science.   »90
✧ **Association de la boucherie islamique** *(Islamic Butchery Association)*
4 rue Saint-Laurent, 63000 Clermont Ferrand
Halal butchery, animal trade, pressure group.   »90
✧ **Association pour la connaisance de l'Islam** *(Association for the Understanding of Islam)*
3 rue Emile-Zola, 69170 Tarare   »90
✧ **Association de culture islamique et arabe**
20 rue de Lannoy, 59800 Lille
Religion, Arabic teaching.   »89
✧ **Association culturelle arabo-islamique**
6 rue Henri-Dunant, La Guérinière, 1400 Caen   »90
✧ **Association culturelle islamique, récréative et sportive**
26 bvd des Provinces, Le Grand-Pont, 42800 Rive-de-Gier
Islam, Arabic language, culture; non-political.   »89
✧ **Association culturelle et islamique de Vernon**
3 rue E.-Blanchet, appt 304, les Boutardes, 27200 Vernon
Inter-faith understanding, diffusion of Islamic culture. »89
✧ **Association culturelle musulmane** *(Muslim Cultural Society)*
4-6 rue Louise-Michel, 93440 Dugny   »89
✧ ≡ 23 rue Léon, 75018 Paris; *t* (1) 4254 8926   »90
✧ **Association de l'éducation et l'enseignement des enfants islamiques en France, AEEEIF** *(Association for the Education and Teaching of Muslim Children in France)*
batiment B4, appt 146, Frais-Vallon, 13013 Marseille   »89
✧ **Association des Etudiants islamiques, section Lyon**
1 rue Claude-Debussy, 69200 Vénissieux   »89
✧ **Association des français islamiques de La Rocque-d'Anthéron** *(Association of French Muslims)*
La Jacourelette, 13640 La Rocque-d'Anthéron
Cultural, educational, social, religious.   »89
✧ **Association Islah**
22 rue de Turenne, 59200 Tourcoing
Introduction to Arabic-Islamic culture.   »89
✧ **Association islamique**
8 rue Pierre-Loti, 42100 Saint-Etienne
Religious concerns including funeral arrangements.   »89
✧ **Association islamique culturelle sunnite des français musulmans rapatriés** *(Sunni Islamic Cultural Association of Repatriated French Muslims)*
chemin de l'Ausselon, 30600 Vauvert   »89
✧ **Association islamique des jeunes musulmans de la Charente** *(Charente Islamic Association of Young Muslims)*
chez Gueye-M'Baye, cité Grand-Poirier, lotissement 13, 16000 Angoulême
Religious, moral and social welfare.   »90
✧ **Association islamique pour le progrès des femmes** *(Islamic Association for the Advancement of Women)*
32 avenue de Stalingrad, 94120 Fontenay-sous-Bois
Promotes progressive discourse on women's issues.   »90
✧ **Association islamique de Rieux-Minervois**
rue du Barry, 11160 Rieux-Minervois
Religion, culture, solidarity.   »90
✧ **Association des jeunes Français musulmans de Joué-lès-Tours** *(Joué-lès-Tours Association of Muslim French Youth)*
3 rue Pierre-Lescot, appt 10, 37300 Joué-lès-Tours
Full social integration of second-generation youth.   »89
✧ **Association des jeunes musulmans français** *(Association of Young French Muslims)*
13 rue Léon-Trulin, 59170 Croix   »89
✧ **Association musulmane d'Albi**
4 rue du Maréchal-Augereau, appt 4156, Cantepau, 81000 Albi
Religion, friendship, culture, national/international links. »90
✧ **Association musulmane culturelle de la paix** *(Muslim Cultural Association for Peace)*
batiment BB, escalier A n° 7, 16 rue Marcel-Proust, 28200 Châteaudun
Leadership in Muslim community affairs.   »90
✧ **Association des musulmans de Montluçon**
1 avenue Jules-Guesde, 03100 Montluçon   »89
✧ **Association socio-éducative et culturelle franco-musulmane Rabita** *(Franco-Islamic Social, Educational & Cultural Societ*
21 rue Paul-Bert, 69003 Lyon   »89
● **Association de l'Union Islamique en France**
64 rue Faubourg St Denis, 75010 Paris; *t* (1) 4523 5512 »90

✧ **Comité des jeunes de Vénissieux** *(Vénissieux Youth Committee)*
18 avenue Jean-Gagne, Minguettes, 69200 Vénissieux
Youth/anti-drugs work, Islamic funerals *(El Djanaïz)*.   »90
♦ **Conseil National des Français Musulmans** *(National Council of French Muslims)*
211 avenue Gambetta, 75020 Paris; *t* (1) 4031 7617, *f* 4031 7621   »94
● ≡ BP 100, 39108 Dole Cedex; *t* 8482 9701, *f* 8482 9745»94
✧ **Défense des droits des français musulmans de Romans et ses environs** *(Defence of the Rights of French Muslims)*
les IFS A1 n° 22, La Monnaie, 26100 Romans   »89
● **Fédération des associations islamiques d'Afrique, des Comores et Antilles, FAIACA** *(Federation of Islamic Societies of Africa, the Comoros and the Caribbean)*
M Cherif Ndiaye: 33 rue Desnouettes, 75015 Paris
Cultural, social and moral leadership.   »89
✧ **Fédération Nationale des Musulmans de France, FNMF**
Daniel Youssof Leclerc: 450/4 rue Paul Eluard, 93000 Bobigny; *t* (1) 4832 7985   »94
✧ **Fédération régionale des associations musulmanes du Sud-est de France** *(South-East France Regional Federation of Muslim Societies)*
21 rue Paul-Bert, 69003 Lyon
Religious, non-political; for social integration of Muslims. »89
✧ **Femmes sous lois musulmanes** *(Women under Islamic Law)*
BP 23, 34790 Grabels, Montpellier
Pressure group on status of women within Sharia law. »93
✧ **Groupement des français musulmans pour la jeunesse et l'entraide** *(French Muslims' Group for Youth and Mutual Aid)*
Bottet, Cogelore, 4 avenue de l'Europe, 69140 Rillieux
Religious, social, cultural, charitable.   »89
✧ **Islam et jeunesse** *(Islam and Youth)*
205 rue de Champagne, 73000 Chambéry
Moral, religious and cultural youth work.   »89
✧ **Mosquée de Paris** *(Paris Mosque)*
place du Puits de l'Ermite, 75005 Paris; *t* (1) 4535 9733
Main Paris mosque and Islamic centre.   »90
● **Société-Bureau Organisation Ligue Islamique Mondiale** *(Organising Office of the World Islamic League)*
22 rue François Bonvin, 75015 Paris; *t* (1) 4273 0548   »90
● **Tabligh**
[address unknown] St-Denis, Paris
Clandestine Islamic radical grouping, alleged to have 2,000 supporters in the Paris region and to be involved in guerrilla training in Pakistan and Afghanistan.   »94
✧ **Tendance nationale union islamique en France, Section Bourgoin-Jallieu** *(National Tendency of the Islamic Union)*
212 bis rue de la Libération, 38300 Bourgoin-Jallieu
Cultural, spiritual, social and economic welfare of Muslims living in France.   »89
✧ **Union islamique d'enseignement et de recherche** *(Islamic Teaching and Research Union)*
6 allée du Professeur-Debré, 77330 Ozoir-la-Ferrière
Koranic teaching and research, French language and culture classes, mutual aid, leisure.   »90
✧ **Union Islamique des Etudiants en France** *(Islamic Students' Union of France)*
Abdeslem Hafidy: 3 rue Marcel-Madoumier, 87100 Limoges
Material and moral interests of students; leisure, culture. »90
✧ ≡ résidence-château Raba, appt 1616, 33400 Talence   »90
✧ **Union des Rapatriés Musulmans** *(Union of Repatriated Muslims)*
6 rue de la 2ème DB, 75150 Chagny
Mainly ex-Algerian *harkis*.   »90

◉ **GERMANY** *49*

✧ **Al Aqsa**
M. Amr: Schurzetterstraße 567, 52074 Aachen; *t* (0241) 872478, *f* 872334
Religious and cultural.   »94
♦ **Islam-Rat für die Bundesrepublik Deutschland** *(Islamic Council for the Federal Republic of Germany)*
Am Kuhfuss 8, 59475 Soest   »94
● **Verband der Islamischen Kulturzentren, VIKZ** *(League of Islamic Cultural Centres)*
Tahsin Safak: Vogelsanger Straße 290, 50825 Köln; *t* (0221) 954 4100, *f* 542616
Federation of (mainly Turkish) local cultural centres. »94

◉ **IRELAND** *353*

✧ **Ballyhaunis Mosque**
[address unknown] Ballyhaunis
Founded for Pakistani employees of local halal meat plant.»94

♦ **Islamic Foundation of Ireland** and Dublin Islamic Society;
Islamic Relief Agency, ISRA
163 South Circular Road, Dublin 8; *t* (01) 453 3242, shop
453 8338
Prayers, library, study circles; serves Malaysian students and
other Muslims; ISRA sends aid to Bosnia.   »95

◎ ITALY *39*

✿ **Casa della Cultura Islamica di Milano** *(Milan Islamic
Cultural Centre)*
Anwar Jolani: via Padova 38, 20127 Milano; *t* (02) 288
20425, *f* 289 2912
Religion, education, youth welfare. *Al-Giamia* (12/yr).   »94
✿ **Centro Culturale Islamico in Italia**
Zine el Abidine Sebti, President: [address unknown] Roma
Established Europe's largest mosque, which opened in Rome
in June 1995 (Dr Mahmoud Hammad Sheweita, imam).   »95
✿ **Centro Islamico** *(Islamic Centre)*
via Venezia 10/10A, 16126 Genova; *t* (010) 261726   »90
✿ ≡ Dr Ali abu Shwaima: via Anacreonte 7, 20132 Milano;
t (02) 289 5606
Il Messaggero del Islam.   »90
✿ ≡ via A. Bertolini 22, 00197 Roma; *t* (06) 802258   »90
✿ **Centro Islamico Torino** *(Islamic Centre of Turin)*
corso San Martino 2, 10122 Torino; *t* (011) 515993
See also Associazione di Amicizia Italo-Marocchina, p89. »90
✿ **Comunità Islamica di Brescia**
Vico delle Sguizzette 7/A, 25121 Brescia; *t* (030) 230
4731   »90
✿ **Comunità Islamica in Italia** *(Islamic Community of Italy)*
[address unknown] Catania, Sicilia   »90
✿ **Comunità Islamica e Moschea di Napoli** *(Naples Muslim
Community and Mosque)*
A. Abdullah: via Parma 54, 80143 Napoli; *t/f* (081) 554
0149   »94
✿ **Comunità Islamica del Trentino Alto Adige**, CITAA
Aboulkheir Bregheche: via Tommaso Gar 8, 38100 Trento;
t/f (0461) 605577   »94
✿ **Comunità dei Musulmani in Piemonte**
via C.L. Berthollet 24, 10125 Torino; *t* (011) 669 8999   »90
♦ **Unione delle Comunità ed Organizzazioni Islamiche in Italia**,
UCOII *(Union of Islamic Communities and Groups in Italy)*
Boubaker Gueddouda/Anwar Jolani: via Padova 38, 20127
Milano; *t* (02) 2882 0425, *f* 289 2912
Il Musulmano (12/yr).   »94
✿ **Unione Studenti Musulmani** *(Union of Muslim Students)*
piazza G. Grandi 18, 20135 Milano; *t* (02) 735165   »90
✿ **Unione Studenti Musulmani in Italia**, USMI
Bov Konate: via Ireneo della Croce 3, 34100 Trieste;
t (040) 567808   »94

◎ LUXEMBOURG *352*

● **Centre Culturel Islamique**
2 route d'Arlon, 8210 Mamer; *t* 311695, 310060   »95

◎ NETHERLANDS *31*

● **Department of Islamic Languages and Culture**, Universiteit
Utrecht
Fulya Atacan: Drift 15, 3512 BR Utrecht   »90
✿ **Moskee Al-Kabir**
Postbus 4424, 1009 AK Amsterdam   »94
● **Nederlandse Moslimraad**, NMR *(Islamic Council of the
Netherlands)*
Postbus 84204, 3009 CE Rotterdam; *t/f* (010) 456 9117 »95
● **Stichting Nederlandse Moslimvrouwen Al-Nisa** *(Al-Nisa
Dutch Muslim Women's Foundation)*
Sajidah Abdus Sattar: [address unknown] Almere   »90
✿ **Stichting Promotie door Turkse en Arabische Vrouwen**
(Promotion Foundation for Turkish and Arab Women)
Postbus 404, 5900 AK Venlo; *t* (077) 522235, *f* 517794
Location: Reigerstraat 2. Promotes the status of Muslim
women and their integration in society.   »95

◎ PORTUGAL *351*

✿ **Centro Cultural Ismaelita** *(Isma'ili Cultural Centre)*
Rua Agosto Lowq 22 C, 1000 Lisboa; *t* (01) 848 1181
Shi'a sect; followers of Aga Khan.   »95
✿ **Comunidade Islâmica** *(Islamic Community)* and Mesquita
de Lisboa
M. Asfaque Tayob: Avenida José Malhoa à Praça de Espanha,
1000 Lisboa; *t* (01) 387 4142, 387 2220
Abdul Magid A.K. Vakil. Mosque, community centre; member
of EU Migrants Forum, p131.   »95

✿ **Comunidade Islâmica de Oeiras**
Praçeta António Ferro 16-11°, 2780 Oeiras; *t* 556030   »90
● **Fundação Aga-Khan e da Comunidade Ismaelita** *(Aga Khan
and Isma'ili Community Foundation)*
Rua das Amoreiras 80-6° D, 1200 Lisboa; *t* (01) 657632 »95
✿ ≡ Francisco Andrade 12, 1700 Lisboa; *t* (01) 805742   »95

◎ RUSSIA *7*

♦ **Islamic Cultural Centre**
Abdul-Vakhed Niyazov: [address unknown] Moscow
Cultural institution serving the million Muslim Muscovites,
mainly migrants from the Caucasus.   »94

◎ SPAIN *34*

✿ **Agrupación de la Comunidad Musulmana** *(Muslim
Community Group)*
M.A. Moli: Apartado de Correos 458, 29802 Melilla;
t (952) 687037   »87
✿ **Asociación Musulmana** *(Muslim Society)*
Mohamed Ali: [address unknown] Ceuta   »87
● **Asociación Musulmana en España** *(Muslim Society of Spain)*
Anastasio Herrera 5-7, Madrid; *t* (91) 579 1355, 570 8889»95
✿ **Centro Islámico**
Meridiana 326-1° 6ª, 08027 Barcelona; *t* (93) 351 4901 »87
● **Centro Islámico para España** *(Islamic Centre of Spain)*
calle Alfonso Cano 3, Madrid; *t* (91) 448 0554   »90
✿ **Comunidad Musulmana** *(Muslim Community)*
Ahmed M. Subeire: [address unknown] Ceuta
Located in Spanish North African enclave.   »87
● **Instituto de Estudios Islámicos** *(Institute of Islamic Studies)*
Francisco de Asis: calle Méndez Casariego 1, Madrid;
t (91) 563 9468   »90
✿ **Mezquita** *(Mosque)*
[address unknown] Córdoba, Andalucía
In addition to the famous Mezquita-Catedral, part of which is
preserved as a mosque, the city has a modern mosque.   »94
✿ ≡ [address unknown] 41004 Sevilla, Andalucía
A small modern mosque in the city centre.   »94

◎ SWEDEN *46*

● *al-Ansar* (The Patriot)
[address unknown] Stockholm
Radical Islamist newsletter, close to the Algerian Front
islamique du salut, see pp8-9.   »95
● **Human Concern International**
[address unknown] Stockholm
Funds relief projects in Islamic countries.   »95
● **Svenska Muslimska Ungdomsförbund** *(Swedish Muslim
Youth League)*
Box 175, 10123 Stockholm; *t* (08) 642 1653, *f* 642 3420»94

◎ SWITZERLAND *41*

▌ **Jamiat al Da'wa**: World Islamic Call Society, and Motamar
al-Alam al-Islami: World Muslim Congress
Case postale 82, rue de Lyon 81, 1203 Genève; *t* (022) 344
2268, *f* 344 3613, *Tx* 415877
The Jamiat is a Libyan-based aid organisation active mainly in
Africa, Asia, the Middle East and Bosnia; builds mosques and
schools, provides practical help to refugees and displaced
persons, propagates Islam. The Motamar is a Pakistan-based
agency engaged in similar activities.   »93
▌ **World Muslim League**
Case postale 212, chemin Colladon 34, 1211 Genève 19 »93

◎ UNITED KINGDOM *44*

✿ **1924 Committee**
Burhan Hanif, President: School of Oriental and African
Studies Student Union, 7 Malet Street, London WC1
Student Islamic organisation, named for the year when the
Islamic Ottoman state was dismantled.   »94
✿ **Abrat Islamic Foundation**
3-5 Dorset Square, London NW1 6PU; *t* (0171) 724 7939
Developing religious, cultural and social centre.   »94
✿ **Abu-Bakar Mosque**
479 Leeds Road, Bradford BD3; *t* (01274) 668343
Was listed (1993) as 16-18 Lapage St, Leeds Rd, BD3.   »94
✿ **Abu Bakr Mosque**
Abu-Ammar Zahid-ur-Rashdi: 30 Villiers Road, Southall
UB1 3BS; *t* (0181) 571 6839, *f* 813 9122
Associated with Pakistan-based World Islamic Forum.   »94
✿ **Acton Mosque**
40 Churchfield Road, London W3
Same as Mosque listed (1994) at 26 Churchfield Road?   »94

✿ **H.H. Aga Khan Ismaili Mosque**
113 Blegborough Road, Streatham, London SW16
Centre for Ismaili Shi'ites, who recognise His Highness
Prince Karim Aga Khan as the 49th Imam.   »94

✿ **H.H. Prince Aga Khan Shia Imami Ismaili Jamat Khana**
A.F. Sayani: 2 Westcote Drive, Leicester LE3 0QR; *t* (0116)
254 6006, 266 0620   »94

● **Ahmadiyya Muslim Association** and The London Mosque
Rashid Chaudhry, Press Secretary: 16 Cressenhall Road,
Putney, London SW18 5QL; *t* (0181) 870 8517, 874 6298
The Ahmadiyya movement emerged in India in the 19th
century CE; 40 centres in UK include a community in Woking
and the Islamabad missionary centre near Tilford.   »95

✿ **Ahmadiyya Muslim Association Darul-Amaan** also known
as Darul-Amaan Association
A.B. Rajpot: 4 Greenheys Lane, Hulme, Manchester M15
6NQ; *t* (0161) 226 9918
Religious, youth welfare, education, charitable activities. See
Khuddan-ul-Ahmadiyya and Lajna Ama-u-Lah, both p64. »93

✿ **Ahmadiyya Muslim Community Centre**
M.U. Dard: 50 The Broadway, Birmingham B20 3EA   »90

✿ **Al Falah Islamic Youth Mission**
Richmond Road, Bradford BD7 1DR   »94

✿ **Al-Furqan Islamic Heritage Foundation**
Eagle House, High Street, Wimbledon, London SW19 5EF
Research and study of Islamic manuscripts. May be related to
the Al-Furqan Trust listed (1994) at 1 Wynne Road, SW9 0BB,
t (0171) 737 7266; see also Ta Ha Publishers, p71.   »94

✿ **Al Hijra School**
Abdul Karim Saqib: Midland House, 71 Hobmoor Rd, Small
Heath, Birmingham B10 9AZ; *t* (0121) 766 5454, *f* 766 7706
Fee-paying primary and secondary school, opened 1988. »95

✿ **Al Hilal Masjid**
Dr Sayed Almohmoud Deewan: 24 Brailsford Road, Tulse Hill,
London SW2 2TB; *t/f* (0181) 671 5574
Mosque and cultural society.   »94

✿ **Al-Huda Bookshop** also known as Al-Hoda Booksellers
76-78 Charing Cross Road, London WC2H 0BB; *t* (0171)
240 8381   »94

✿ **Al-Huda Islamic Centre**
Maulana Naqui, Imam: 65 Albert Road, Glasgow G42,
Scotland; *t* (0141) 423 7003
Twelver Shi'ite mosque, mostly ex-East African Indian (Khoja
Ithna 'Ashari) membership.   »94

✿ **Al-Isra Islamic College**
Heathland, Upper Welland Road, Malvern WR14 4HN;
t (01684) 892300, *f* 892757   »94

✿ **Al-Kashkool Bookshop**
Riad El-Rayyes Booksellers Ltd, 56 Knightsbridge, London
SW1 7NJ; *t* (0171) 235 4240   »94

✿ **Al Khoei Foundation** also known as Khoei Foundation
Syed Nadeem Kazmi: Stone Hall, Chevening Road, London
NW6 6TN
One of London's main Shia organisations; Shias form 15 per
cent of UK Muslims. See World Ahl Ul Bayt League, p72.»95

✿ **Al Medina Muslim Association**
20 Middle Street, Worcester; *t* (01905) 295382   »94

✿ **Al-Medina Trust**
161 South Park Road, Wimbledon, London SW19; *t* (0181)
542 6269
Mosque society.   »94

✿ **Al-Muntada Al-Islami School** and bookshop
7 Bridges Place, off Parsons Green Lane, London SW6 4HR;
t (0171) 736 9060, 371 7308, 731 8203, *f* 736 4255
Fee-paying co-educational primary school, opened 1989. »95

✿ **Al-Noor Bookshop**
54 Park Road, London NW1 4SH; *t* (0171) 723 5414   »94

✿ **Al-Noor Mosque**
A.R. Mujahid: 23a Harrow Road, Newport, Gwent, Wales;
t (01633) 244395, 212945   »94

✿ **Al-Rahmah Mosque** and Liverpool Muslim Society; Islamic
Book Centre
M.A. Ali: 29-37 Heatherley Street, off Mulgrave Street,
Liverpool L8 2TJ; *t* (0151) 709 7504, 709 2560   »94

✿ **Al-Rahman Mosque**
F. Nasser: 26 Ruperra Street, Newport, Gwent, Wales;
t (01633) 255150   »94

✿ **Al-Saqi Bookshop**
26 Westbourne Grove, London W2 5RH; *t* (0171) 229
8543   »94

✿ **Alamadina Jamia Mosque** and Leeds Muslim Council
33 Brundell Grove, Leeds LS6 1HR; *t* (0113) 275 8615,
275 2535   »94

✿ **Alazhar Mosque**
Laygate Lane, South Shields NE33; *t* (0191) 454 0738   »94

✿ **Alexandra Road Mosque**
M. Mahmoud: 20 Alexandra Road, Newport, Gwent, Wales;
t (01633) 257781   »94

● **All Muslim Funeral Society**
Abdul Shakur, General Secretary: 127 Kingsway, Luton LU1
1TS; *t* (01582) 451853   »94

✿ **All-Muslim Welfare Association**
91 Soho Road, Birmingham B21 9SP   »94

✿ **Alliance of Newham Muslim Associations**
M. Farhat: 159 Plashet Road, Upton Park, London E13 0QZ;
t (0181) 470 5233
Umbrella group for mosque societies and other groups.   »94

✿ **Amana**, also known as Amaana Trust
Umar Hegedus, Director: PO Box 2842, London W6 9ZH;
t (0181) 748 2424
Khadijah Knight. Islamic educational trust, addressing both
Muslims and non-Muslims and focussing on issues in the UK
and Europe such as the schooling of Muslim children.   »95

✿ **Amir-e-Millat Mosque and Islamic Centre**
144 Stoney Lane, Sparkhill, Birmingham B11; *t* (0121) 449
5695, 449 6001
Sunni mosque and community centre.   »94

✿ **An-Nisa Society**
Khalida Khan, Co-ordinator: 110 Thurlby Road, Wembley
HA0 4RS; *t* (0181) 900 0605
Women's counselling group: faith and family welfare.   »95

✿ **Anjuman Ahle Sunnat Wal Jamaat** *(Islamic Centre)*
2 South Street, Rochdale OL11; *t* (01706) 45095
Sunni mosque and Islamic community centre.   »94

✿ **Anjuman-e-Eshaate Islam**, also known as Anjuman-I-Ishat
e Islam
102-104 Wednesbury Rd, Walsall WS1; *t* (01922) 22936
Mosque. Possibly the same as Anjuman Isha'at Islam listed
(1994) at 110 Prince Street, Walsall (A. Hussain).   »94

✿ **Anjuman-e-Haideria**
Syed Shamsher Kazmi, General Secretary: 47-48 Southfield
Square, Bradford BD8 7SL; *t* (01274) 391667
Shi'ite religious and educational centre.   »94

✿ **Anjuman-e-Hamidiyak**
10 Tollgate Close, Longsight, Manchester M13 0LG
Sufi society.   »94

✿ **Anjuman-e-Islahul-Muslimeen Mosque** and Dewsbury
Muslim Association
M.M. Artez: Markazi Mosque, 25 South Street, Savile Town,
Dewsbury WF12; *t* (01924) 460760, 454178
Association formed 1978.   »94

✿ **Anjuman-e-Islamia (Newham)**
266-268 High Street North, Manor Park, London E12 6SB;
t (0181) 472 5663
Religious and cultural centre.   »94

✿ **Anjuman-e-Jaarania**
Syed Munawar Shah: 74 Kensington Avenue, Watford WD1
7RY; *t* (01923) 47362 (?)   »94

✿ **Anjuman-e-Khwateen**
Ahsan Shah: 28 Lansdowne Road, Hounslow TW3 1LQ;
t (0181) 570 1394   »94

✿ **Anjuman-e-Muhibban-e-Ahl-e-Bait Hussainia Mosque**
37 Grey Street, Burnley BB10 1BA; *t* (01282) 427170
Mosque; welfare and educational activities.   »94

♦ **Anjuman e Naqibul Islam Mosque**
82 Washwood Heath Road, Birmingham B8 1RD; *t* (0121)
328 4930   »94

✿ **Anjuman-e-Saifee**
S.H. Jaffer/A. Kapasi: 3-5 Wellington Street, Leicester LE1
6HH; *t* (0116) 247 0446
Indian Bohra (Daudi, i.e. Musta'li Ismaili) Shi'ite mosque and
community centre; worship, cultural and social activities. »94

✿ **Anjuman-e-Taraqqi-Urdu**
55 Langley Road, Olton, Birmingham   »94

✿ **Anjuman-e-Zinatul-Islam**
78 Taylor Street, Batley WF17; *t* (01924) 472216
Mosque.   »94

✿ **Anjuman Faiz-ul-Quran**
188 Somerville Road, Small Heath, Birmingham B10;
t (0121) 772 1059
Sunni mosque society.   »94

✿ **Anjuman Ghulaman-e-Rasool**
A.Q. Butt: 46 Palmer Park Avenue, Reading RG6 1DN;
t (01734) 265132, *f* 352364
Social welfare.   »94

✿ **Anjuman-i-Tareej Taraqqi-i-Urdu** and Jamiate-Nizam-e-Islam
Malik Fazal Hussain, Director: 64 Somerville Road, Small
Heath, Birmingham B10 9EL; *t* (0121) 328 8466
Pakistani organisation promoting Dawah (mission), Islamic
unity and knowledge of Muslim Ummah.   »94

✧ **Anjuman Islah-ul-Muslemeen**
Dr R. Chaudhry: 18 Rothwell Rd, Halifax; *t* (01422) 380934
Religious and language education for Muslim children.   »94

✧ **Anjuman Islahul Muslimin**
Rana Farooq Alam Khan: 7 Parrock Street, Nelson BB9,
Lancashire; *t* (01282) 696987   »94

✧ **Anjuman Khuddam-ud-Din** and Mosque
11-15 Woodstock Road, Moseley, Birmingham B13 9BB;
t (0121) 429 1193
See also Council of Mosques, Birmingham, p57.   »94

✧ **Anjuman Muhibban-e-Rasool**
J.M. Banaras: 15 Bulmershe Road, Reading RG1 5RM;
t (01734) 597977   »94

✧ **Anjuman Noor-ul-Islam** and Mosque
33 Yewtree Road, Witton, Birmingham B6 6RT; *t* (0121)
328 1297
Religious, educational and cultural activities.   »94

✧ **Ansaru Allah Community** *(Helpers of God)*
70 Fitzgerald House, Stockwell Park Rd, London SW9 0UQ
No information available; linked with Sudanese Ansar
movement? See also Majlis Ansarullah, p65.   »94

✧ **Anwar-e-Mohammedia Mosque**
51 Cobden Street, Fallingheath, Darlaston WS10, West
Midlands; *t* (0121) 526 4307, 526 2988
Sunni mosque.   »94

✧ **Arabic Language and Islamic Culture**
Dr Hussain Al Shamari: PO Box 408, London WC1H 0XP »95

✧ **Arafat Book Service**
521 Coventry Road, Small Heath, Birmingham B10 0JF;
t (0121) 771 3798
Bookshop; may be linked with Jamia Masjid and Islamic
Centre, p62, or Darul Uloom Islamic High School, p58.   »94

✧ **Asian Muslim Welfare Association**
Shamim Akhtar Khan: 196 Waterloo Street, Glodwick,
Oldham OL4 1ES   »94

✧ **Asna Ashriyya Shia Mosque**
19 Ashley St, Glasgow G3, Scotland; *t* (0141) 332 9639
Khoja Twelver mosque.   »94

● **Association of Muslim Lawyers**
[address unknown]   »96

● **Association of Muslim Researchers**
Sabina Haulkhory/Dr Ihab El Saie: 52 Westmoor Road,
Enfield EN3 7LF   »95

● **Association of Muslim Scholars in Britain**
M. Ismail, Secretary: 54 Sheldon Road, Nether Edge,
Sheffield S7 1GW; *t* (0114) 255 0318   »95

● **Association of Muslim Youth and Community Workers**
Shams-uddeen Hassan, Chair: 81 Melbourne Road, Spinney
Hill North, Leicester LE2 0GW; *t* (0116) 251 5296
Promotes liaison among Muslim, non-Muslim and public-sector
youth and community workers. Seminars, conferences. »95

● **Association of Sunni Muslims**
[address unknown]
Reported to have 800,000 members in UK.   »90

✧ **Azeemia Foundation (UK)**
A. Azeemi: Azeemia House, 92b Hampton Road, Forest
Gate, London E7 0NU; *t* (0181) 555 4577
Meditation, spiritual healing.   »94

✧ **Balham Mosque**
Farooq Valimahomed, Secretary: 47-51 Balham High Road,
Balham, London SW12 9AW; *t* (0181) 675 7912
Large Sunni religious, social, educational, welfare centre. »94

✧ **Banbury Mosque**
18 The Bye Way, Banbury OX16 7HW; *t* (01295) 267432,
276662
Sunni mosque.   »94

✧ **Barking Muslim Social and Cultural Society**
1 Monteagle Ave., Barking IG11 8RA; *t* (0181) 591 1831 »94

✧ **Basildon Muslim Association**
Sarfraz Sarwar: 36 Gordons, Basildon SS13 3DZ;
t (01268) 554235
Small welfare association and house mosque.   »94

✧ **Bath Islamic Centre and Mosque**
8 Pierrepoint Street, Bath BA1 1LA; *t* (01225) 60922   »94

✧ **Bath Sufi Healing Order**
Peggie Phillips: 29 Grosvenor Place, London Road, Bath
BA1 6BA; *t* (01225) 312694   »94

✧ **Bazmi-i-Tafreeh** and Islamic Educational Welfare Association
Abdul Aleem Siddiqui: 25 Evershot Road, London N4 3DG;
t (0171) 272 7031
Welfare advice and assistance; works for culturally appropriate
educational and health services.   »94

✧ **Beaumont Leys Muslim Association**
Yusuf Subedar, Chairperson: 47 Calder Road, Leicester LE4
0RF; *t* (0116) 235 3694   »94

✧ **Bedford Study Centre**
15 Goldington Road, Bedford MK42; *t* (01234) 264161   »94

✧ **Birmingham Anjumane Islam Mosque Trust**
23 Arden Road, Birmingham B6 6AP; *t* (0121) 554 9157
Also at President Saddam Hussein Mosque, Trinity Road,
Aston B6 6AG. Worship, Islamic education, welfare work,
immigration and rights advice.   »94

✧ **Birmingham Mosque Trust Ltd** (Birmingham Central Mosque)
Khurram Bashir/Dr M. Nasim: 180 Belgrave Middleway, Balsall
Heath, Birmingham B12 0XS; *t* (0121) 440 6150
Large mosque and community centre; listed (1993) as address
of Muslim Liaison Committee (M.Y. Qamar), *t* 440 5355, and
Islamic Book Service, *t* 446 4157.   »95

✧ **Blackburn Council of Mosques**
Ibrahim Chopdat, Secretary: 3 Wareham Street, Blackburn
BB1 5PH; *t* (01254) 691212   »94

✧ **Blackheath Islamic Community Centre** and UK Islamic
Mission, Blackheath
314-318 Long Lane, Halesowen B26 9LQ; *t* (0121) 559
7314   »95

✧ **Blackheath Jamia Mosque**
Abdul Razzaq, Secretary: 143-150 Malt Mill Lane, Halesowen
B62 8JA; *t* (0121) 559 3478
Sunni mosque; organising society is Blackheath Jamia Mosque
Trust, listed (1994) at 21 Vicarage Road, Halesowen.   »94

✧ **Blackpool Islamic Community**
Dr Abdul Rahim Khan: 59 Headroomgate Road, Lytham St
Annes   »95

✧ **Bolton Muslim Community Association**
M. Atcha: 392 Derby Street, Bolton, Lancashire   »94

✧ **Bolton Surti Sunni Vohra Muslim Association**
K. Motala, Manager: 98 High Street, Bolton BL3 6SZ;
t (01204) 26489
A society of the small, traditionally agrarian, Sunni sect of
Bohoras, arising from a 15th-century CE schism from what is
now the Isma'ili majority.   »94

✧ **Bordesley Green Mosque and Islamic Centre**
122 Bordesley Green Road, Birmingham B9 4TS; *t* (0121)
776 6371
Mainly Bengali mosque; close to the Jama'at-i Islami.   »95

✧ **Bournemouth Islamic Centre**
170 Old Christchurch Road, Bournemouth BH1 1NU;
t (01202) 21022   »94

✧ **Bradford Council of Mosques**
Sher Azam, President: 75 Farnham Road, Bradford BD7 3JE;
t (01274) 732479
Also listed (1994) at 6 Claremont, Bradford BD7 1BQ. Khadim
Hussain general secretary, Liaqat Hussein, Ishtiaq Ahmed;
represents 75,000 Muslims in Bradford area.   »96

✧ **Bradford Khalifa Muslim Society**
Abdul Hamid Ismail, Chair: 32 Bertram Rd, Bradford BD8 7LN
Religious/educational/youth/community welfare activities. »94

✧ **Bradford Muslim Welfare Society and Mosque**
A.H. Pandor, Secretary: 62 St Margaret's Road, Bradford
BD7 3AE; *t* (01274) 575919   »94

✧ **Brent Islamic Bureau**
[address unknown] Brent, London N
Radical Islamist group.   »95

✧ **Brighton Islamic Mission**
Imam Dr Abduljalil Sajid, Trustee: PO Box 234, Brighton
BN1 3QD; *t* (01273) 722438, *f* 540058
Location: 8 Caburn Road, Hove BN3 6EF. Founded 1980;
religious/educational/welfare body, linked with Sussex Muslim
Society, p71, and Brighton Muslim Community Centre.   »94

✧ **Bristol and Avon Muslim Association**
I. Shaheen: 10 The Old Co-Op, 42 Chelsea Road, Easton,
Bristol BS5 6AF; *t* (0117) 955 2686   »94

✧ **Bristol Mosque Committee** and Jamia Masjid
Saeed Abu Rahman, Secretary: Green Street, Totterdown,
Bristol BS3 4UB; *t* (0117) 977 0944
Worship, social and educational activities.   »94

✧ **British Islamic Academy**
Dr Mannan: 40 Park Lane, Wallington, Sutton SM6 0TN;
t (0181) 647 1748   »94

● **British Muslim Action Front**
Muenuddin Chowdray, spokesman: [address unknown]
Conducted legal campaign against Rushdie novel.   »90

✧ **British Muslim Association**
M.A. Shah Siddique, Secretary: 45 Springfield Drive,
Barkingside, Ilford IG2 6PT; *t* (0181) 518 2469
Religious, social and educational concerns; advice service on
welfare rights and immigration.   »94
✧ ≡ M.A. Siddiqi: 56 Harold Road, Plaistow, London E13
0SQ; *t* (0181) 471 2107   »94
✧ ≡ Dr Rashid Skinner: 53 Barncliffe Rd, Sheffield S10 4DG»95

✪ **British Muslim Council**
22 Lynmouth Road, London N16 6XL »94
● **British Muslim Engineers and Scientists Association**
Islamic Centre, 523-525 Coventry Road, Small Heath,
Birmingham B10 0LL »94
● **British Muslim Forum**
Tariq Azim-Khan, Chairman: [address unknown] »94
✪ **British Muslim Solidarity** and Islamic Socialist Movement
155 Halifax Old Road, Birkby, Huddersfield HD2 »94
● **British Shia Muslim Action Committee** and Ahl Ul-Bayt
Islamic Centre
Kazmi Al Mashadi: 11-13 Edgeley Road, London SW4 6EH;
t (0181) 627 2230 »95
✪ **Brixton Mosque**
Sheikh Salah: 1 Gresham Road, London SW9 3QG;
t (0171) 274 1757
Also listed (1988) at 30 Bellfield Road, SW9, t 274 1757.»95
✪ **Broadfield Mosque**
20 Selsey Road, Crawley RH11 9HP; t (01293) 512555 »94
✪ **Burhani Community Centre**
Idris Zainuddin, Chairperson: 354 Lillie Road, London SW6;
t (0171) 229 6404 »94
✪ **Burnley Council of Mosques**
Mohamed Shareef Quadri, Secretary: 3 Elm Street, Burnley
BB10 1AJ; t (01282) 412107 »94
✪ **Bury Park Masjid**
28 (25?) Bury Park Road, Luton, Beds.; t (01582) 25412 »94
● **Calamus Foundation**
Saba Risaluddin: [address unknown] London SW1W 9DD
Seeks to improve relations between Muslims, Christians and
Jews, and to promote public understanding of Islam. »95
✪ **Cambridge Muslim Welfare Society and Mosque**
1 Mawson Road, Cambridge CB1 2DZ; t (01223) 240354,
351034 »94
✪ **Canning Town Islamic Centre**
M.Y. Iqbal, Secretary: 5 Market Place, Ordinance Road,
London E16; t (0181) 474 3674 »94
✪ **Canning Town Mosque and Welfare Association**
S. Ali, Secretary: Muslim Community Centre, 269 Barking
Road, Plaistow, London E13 8EQ; t (0181) 472 5096 »94
✪ **Canterbury Islamic Centre**
PO Box 98, Canterbury CT2 2XB »94
✪ **Central Ahl-e-Sunnat wa Jamat**
Altaf Hussain: 31 Sackville Street, Ravensthorpe, Dewsbury
WF13 3BX
Local mosque society of the South Asian Barelvi 'true Sunni'
movement, one of the largest Muslim sects in Britain. »94
✪ **Central Jamia Masjid**
G. Syed, Chair: 12 Montague Way, off King Street, Southall
UB2 5NZ; t (0181) 574 5115
Worship, education and welfare centre; Muslim Women's
Association (N. Haq, t 574 5380). »94
✪ **Central Mosque of Brent**
Raja M. Riaz, Chair: Marley Walk, off Station Parade, London
NW2; t (0181) 450 9428
May be linked with the Mosque and Islamic Centre of Brent
listed (1993) at 26a Chichele Rd, NW2 3DA, t 450 7403.»94
● **Centre for Islamic Studies**
Dr Ahmed Beloufi: [address unknown] Birmingham
Possibly same as Islamic Study Centre. »94
● **Centre for the Study of Islam and Christian-Muslim
Relations**, CSIC
Dr Jorgen Nielsen, Director: Selly Oak Colleges, Bristol Road,
Birmingham B29 6LQ; t (0121) 472 4231
Dr Bert Breiner. Academic centre researching Islam in Europe,
Christian-Muslim relations in Africa; newsletter, papers. »92
✪ **Charlton Mosque**
Asghar Hamid, Chair: 30 Ransome Road, Charlton, London
SE7 8SR; t (0181) 858 4479, 858 0209
Worship, community welfare, advice on immigration and social
security, interfaith relations. Mainly Pakistani. »94
✪ **Chashma-e-Rahmat Mosque**
Oldbury Road, Smethwick, Warley B66, West Midlands;
t (0121) 552 8729
Sunni mosque. »94
✪ **Chesterfield Muslim Association** and Azad Youth Club;
Chesterfield Muslim Women Welfare Group
Aftab Saddiq: 12a Saltergate, Chesterfield S40 1UT;
t/f (01246) 277284
Founded 1987; translation, educational, advice services, youth
and women's groups, Chakswari Cricket Club. Kashmiri? »94
✪ **Confederation of Sunni Mosques—Midlands**
M. Saleem Akhtar: 107 Golden Hillock Road, Small Heath,
Birmingham B10 0DP; t (0121) 328 0837, 771 4533
Umbrella group for mosques and Islamic societies. »95

▌**Council of European Jamaats**
4 Burton Street, Peterborough PE2 5HD; t (01773) 340261
Presumably Shia Itha Asheri federation; mosque next door.»95
✪ **Council for Islamic Affairs**
2 Marchwood Road, Sheffield S6 5LD
Also listed (1994) at 71 Broad Oaks, S6. »94
✪ **Council of Mosques**
c/o Khuddam-ud-Din Mosque, 15 Woodstock Road, Moseley,
Birmingham B13 9BB; t (0121) 429 1193 »94
✪ **Council of Mosques and Islamic Organisations in Sheffield**
C.M. Walayat, Secretary: 226 Darnell Road, Sheffield S9 »94
♦ **Council of Mosques (UK and Eire)**
Nazr Ul-Islam Bose, Vice-President: 46 Goodge Street,
London W1P 1FJ; t (0171) 580 4504
Open to mosques and Islamic bodies; maintenance of mosques
and of Islamic identity; relations with other faiths (through the
Inter Faith Network, p180). See also Institute of Muslim
Minority Affairs, p60; Darul Ifta UK, p58; Islamic Council on
Palestine, p95; World Muslim League, p72. »94
✪ **Council for the Preservation of the Holy Places of Islam**
34 Francis Road, Leyton, London E10; t (0181) 558 0581
See also Madrasa al-Tawhid and Ahle Hadith Mosque, p65. »94
✪ **Cradley Heath Mosque and Muslim Association**
Basharat Ali: 43 Highgate St, Old Hill, Cradley Heath, Warley
B64 5RX; t (01384) 66203, 62049; (0121) 559 6813
Sunni society; mosque at Canal Street, Oldbury, Warley. »94
✪ **Crawley Islamic Centre and Mosque**
Mohammed Hussain, Secretary: 157 London Road, Crawley
RH10 2TA; t (01293) 528488
Imam Inamul Haque. Religious/advisory/welfare services. »94
✪ **Cultural and Islamic Society of Harrow**
Mohammed Ajaz-Haque, Secretary: 17 Ferncroft Avenue,
Eastcote, Harrow HA4 9JE; t (0181) 868 6514
Social, cultural, educational and religious activities. »94
✪ **Dalston Mosque**
160 Dalston Lane, London E8; t (0171) 254 3266 »94
✪ **Dar Al-Dawa**
32 Hereford Road, off Westbourne Grove, London W2 4AJ;
t (0171) 221 6256
Islamic mission centre and bookshop. »94
✪ **Dar al Da'wa al Islamiya** *(Islamic Propagation Centre)*
Haji Mohammed Sadiq Chowdhry, Chairperson: 69 Victoria
Street, Blackburn BB1 6DN; t (01254) 675528
Religious and community welfare; advice service. »94
✪ **Dar Al-Taqwa**
7a Melcombe Street, off Baker Street, London NW1 6AE;
t (0171) 935 6385
Islamic bookshop. »94
✪ **Dar ul Aloom Siddiqia Mosque**
24 Burngreave Rd, Sheffield S3 9DD; t (0114) 270 1034 »94
♦ **Dar-ul-Ehsan Publications**, also known as Darul Ahsan
Dr Muhammad Iqbal, Secretary: 252 Almondbury Bank,
Huddersfield HD5 8EL; t (01484) 541304
International religious charity distributing free literature. »95
✪ **Dar-ul-Uloom Islamia Education and Cultural Society** and
Young Muslim Organisation
M. Bashir/Zahir Ahmad: 81 Stamford Road, Longsight,
Manchester M13 0SJ; t (0161) 225 7897, 256 2812
Mainly Pakistani membership. Mosque, educational centre;
Arabic, Urdu and Koran classes for children; social events.
Also listed (1994) at 1 Hawkhurst Road, t 256 2812. »94
✪ **Dar-ul-Uloom Islamia and Mosque**
Saleem Akhtar: 107-113 Golden Hillock Road, Small Heath,
Birmingham B10 0DP; t (0121) 771 4534
Religious and educational centre; see also Confederation of
Sunni Mosques, left. »94
✪ **Dar-ul-Uloom Jamia Chashtiah** *(Chishtiya Society Teaching
Centre)*
A.H. Chishti, General Secretary: 49-53a Milkstone Road,
Rochdale OL11 1EB; t (01706) 50487
Worship and educational centre of the South Asian Chishtiya
Sufi order. Founded 1986. »94
✪ **Dar-Uloom Qadiria Jilania**
Muhammed Zafar Iqbal Qazi, Secretary: 95 Burlington St,
Ashton-under-Lyne OL6 6HQ; t (0161) 344 1006
Religious and community centre named for the Sufi saint
'Abd al-Qadir al-Jilani; welfare and immigration rights advice,
interpreting, educational services. »94
✪ **Dar-us-Salam Mosque**
C.M. Haque, Chairman: 55-57 Upper Tichbourne St, Leicester
LE2 0QN; t (0116) 254 3887, 254 0592, 254 3257 »94
✪ **Darul Aman Trust**
Dr A.K. Kabir: 54 High Street, Colliers Wood, London SW19
2JF; t (0181) 543 5687
Mosque and community centre. »94

✷ **Darul Ifta UK**, also known as Dar Al-Ifta
Dr Saud Al-Guzyan, Director: 46 Goodge Street, London
W1P 1FJ; *t* (0171) 636 2080
See also World Muslim League, p72, and Council of Mosques
(UK and Eire), p57.   »94

✷ **Darul Muslimat**
3 Dunraven St, London W1Y 3FG; *t* (0171) 499 4741   »94

✷ **Darul Uloom**
141 Leyland Road, Burnley BB11 3DN
Islamic educational centre.   »94

✷ **Darul Uloom Al Arabiya Al Islamiya**
Yusuf Motala/Mufti Shabbir Ahmed: Holcombe Hall,
Holcombe Brook, Ramsbottom, North Bury BL8 4NG;
t (01706) 825160, 826106-08
Fee-paying school for 300 boys, opened 1979; mosque. »95

✷ **Darul Uloom Islamic High School**
521 Coventry Road, Small Heath, Birmingham B10 0LL;
t (0121) 772 6408, 773 7706, *f* 773 4340
Fee-paying school. See also Arafat Book Service, p56.   »94

✷ **Darwen Mosque and Madressa**
Hamid Khan, President: 21-23 Victoria Street, Darwen,
Blackburn BB3 3HB; *t* (01254) 774508   »94

✷ **Daubhill Muslim Society** and Masjid al-Rahman
The President: 2-14 Randal Street, Daubhill, Bolton BL3
4AQ; *t* (01204) 660177   »94

✷ **Dawat Ul Islam Mosque**
142 Lyons Lane, Chorley PR6 0PJ; *t* (01257) 268644   »94

● **Dawatul Islam** *(Call of Islam)*
Dr Z.U. Rahman: 31 Oakfield Avenue, Glasgow G12 8LL,
Scotland; *t* (0141) 334 5559
Mosque. A branch of the Shi'ite Al-Dawa movement?   »95

✷ **Dawatul Islam Central Co-ordinating Committee**, DICCC,
and Tottenham Mosque
Chowdhury Mueenudeen/Nur Ahmed: 115 Clyde Road, London
N15 4JS; *t* (0181) 809 2137
Mainly South Asian Islamic renewal movement mosque and
community centre.   »95

✷ **Dawatul Islam Coventry Cross Mosque and Islamic Centre**
6 Broxbourne House, Devas Street, London E3 3LS;
t (0171) 515 6714, 987 2133   »94

● **Dawatul Islam Youth Group** and Islamic Book Service
K.M. Abu Taher Chowdhury, Youth Secretary: 52 Fieldgate
Street, London E1 1DL; *t* (0171) 247 0689, 247 6851,
f 247 3832
Youth section of Dawatul Islam; youth welfare, leisure
activities, study, promotion of positive Islamic lifestyle.   »95

✷ **Dawoodi Bohra Welfare Society**
D. Kapasi, Secretary: 106 Jean Drive, Leicester LE4 0GF;
t (0116) 283 2600
Religious and community association of the Indian Daudi
Isma'ili sect, prominent in Gujarat and East Africa, which
follows the Dai-al-Mutlaq (or Mulla-ji) of Bombay.   »94

✷ **Dearne Muslim Society** and Ashrafia Mosque
G.H.M. Kotwal, Secretary: Cannon Street North, Bolton
BL3 5JT; *t* (01204) 27310, 384713
Mosque at 41 Park Road, Bolton BL1 4RX.   »94

✷ **Dhar ul Ehsan Centre**
Imdad Ali Poswal: 564 Eighth Avenue, Bristol BS7 0QS;
t (0117) 969 5581   »94

✷ **Didsbury Mosque and Islamic Centre**
271 Burton Road, off Barlow Moor Road, West Didsbury,
Manchester M20 8WA; *t* (0161) 434 2254   »94

✷ **Doncaster Mosque Trust**
M.M. Mufti, Secretary: Bentinck Close, St James Street,
Doncaster DN1 3ST; *t* (01302) 368336, 326350
Worship, youth activities.   »94

✷ **Dudley Mosque**
M. Hanif, General Secretary: Birmingham Street, Castle Hill,
Dudley DY1, West Midlands; *t* (01384) 233081, 53951
Sunni mosque; community welfare, educational concerns.»94

✷ **East London Mosque Trust** and Whitechapel Mosque
Abdul Awwal: 92 Whitechapel Road, London E1 1JE;
t (0171) 247 1357, 247 2625, *f* 377 9879
Mosque and bookshop at 45 Fieldgate Street, off
Whitechapel Road.   »95

✷ **East Sussex Islamic Association**
Magdi Osman: 46 Essenden Road, St-Leonards-on-Sea,
Hastings TN38, Sussex; *t* (01424) 444086
Also listed (1994) at 73 Parkstone Road, Hastings TN34
2NT, *t* (01424) 431837.   »94

✷ ≡ and Masjid al Haque: Shukri Tumi, Amir: Mercatoria, St-
Leonards-on-Sea, Hastings TN38 0EB; *t* (01424) 426232,
442075
Bakhtyar Ali Khan, mosque secretary. Worship, education,
welfare, women's and youth activities.   »94

✷ **Eastbourne Islamic Project**
Dr Ilias Baig: 2 Barn Close, Stone Cross, Pevensey BN24
5EN; *t* (01323) 766988   »94

✷ **Eastbourne Islamic Society**
Azizul Islam: 18 Furness Road, Eastbourne BN21 4EY;
t (01323) 27381   »94

✷ **Eastbourne Mosque**
Al-Islam Restaurant, 6 South Street, Eastbourne BN21,
Sussex; *t* (01323) 26882, 38288   »94

✷ **Easton Masjid**
St Mark's Rd, Easton, Bristol BS5 6JH; *t* (0117) 951 0317»94

✷ **Eccles and Salford Islamic Society**
Sheikh Awadalla Youssef, Imam: 5 Liverpool Road, Eccles,
Manchester M30 0WB; *t* (0161) 789 2609
Worship, religious education, information/welfare service. »94

✷ **Edara Talimul Islam**
Mohd Anwar, Chairman: 43 William Street, Rochdale OL11
1HW; *t* (01706) 45135, *f* 42517
Mosque.   »94

● **Edhi International Foundation UK**
Haroon Dada: 7 Shakespeare Road, Finchley Central, London
N3 1XE
Support group for major Muslim philanthropic organisation,
with 5,000 staff and 40,000 volunteers in Pakistan.   »95

✷ **Elahi Mosque and Islamic Cultural Centre**
305 Staniforth Road, Darnall, Sheffield S9, Yorkshire;
t (0114) 243 1270   »94

✷ **Esha'atul Islam Mosque**
Mr Thohuruddin, President: 16 Ford Square, off Commercial
Road, Aldgate East, London E1 2HS; *t* (0171) 790 0693
Mainly Bangladeshi religious and welfare group, founded
1983. Madrassa with 250 pupils.   »94

✷ **Essex Islamic Education Trust**
K.A. Siddiqui: 67 Essex Road, Romford SS0 7HT; *t* (01708)
726901   »94

✷ **Evington Muslim Centre** and Masjid Tabuk
Mohamed Seedat: 59 Stoughton Drive North, Leicester LE5
5UD; *t* (0116) 273 5529, 273 7183, *f* 246 1611
Mosque and educational centre.   »94

✷ **Faiz-ul-Quran Madrassa**
298 Dudley Road, Winson Green, Birmingham B18 4EL;
t (0121) 455 6581   »94

✷ **Federation of Mosques**
Mr Raja, Director: 53 Mulgrave Street, Hanley, Stoke-on-
Trent ST1 5EP; *t* (01782) 46765   »94

✷ **Federation of Muslim Organisations of Leicestershire**
Ebrahim Bayat/S.M. Hassan: [address uncertain] 65 Berner
Street, Leicester LE2 0FU; *t* c/o (0116) 262 3518
Also listed (1994) c/o Mahboob Ismail Khantharia, 26 Roundhill
Road, LE5 5RJ; or c/o Tarik Iqbal, 88 Sparkenhoe Street, LE2
0TA. Founded 1983; 42 affiliated bodies; welfare activities,
interfaith relations, representation of Islamic community. »95

● **Federation of Student Islamic Societies**, FOSIS, and
Muslim Book Service
Riadh Ar Rawi/T. Othman: 38 Mapesbury Road, London
NW2 4JD; *t* (0181) 452 4493, 452 9340, *f* 208 4161
Founded 1962. Promotes da'wah (missionary) work. Close to
the Islamic Brotherhood; see also Islamic Relief, p61.   »95

✷ **Gamkol Sharif Mosque**
Sufi Abdullah Khan: 38 Warwick Road, Sparkhill,
Birmingham B11 4QR; *t* (0121) 773 (772?) 8120
A Sunni Sufi mosque of the Naqshabandiya order.   »94

✷ **Ghamkol Mosque**
126 Durham Road, Sparkbrook, Birmingham B11 4LJ   »94

● **Gathering of Muslim Parents**
[address unknown]   »96

✷ **Ghosia Mosque** and Madrassa
S. Akuji, President: 81 Anburn Street, Bolton BL3 6TQ;
t (01204) 64085   »94

✷ **Ghousia Jamia Masjid**
66 Colne Road, Burnley BB10 1LG; *t* (0116) 262 3518 (?)
Mosque and religious society.   »94

✷ **Ghousia Jamia Mosque**
1-5 Cross Street, Nelson BB9; *t* (01282) 694471
See also Pendle Council of Mosques, p69.   »88

✷ **Ghousia Mosque**
M. Ashraf, Secretary: 1 Park Street, Great Harwood,
Blackburn BB6 7BP
Religious and educational activities.   »94

✷ ≡ Owler Lane, Sheffield S4; *t* (0114) 238 7966   »94

✷ ≡ and Community Centre: M. Azim, President: 237 Albert
Rd, Aston, Birmingham B6 5LX; *t* (0121) 328 1108, 327 1123
Sunni mosque.   »94

✷ ≡ and Community Centre: Birchills Street, Walsall WS2,
West Midlands; *t* (01922) 640787   »94

✿ **Ghousia Mosque Trust**
232 Slade Road, Erdington, Birmingham B23; *t* (0121) 328 4627, 328 1190
Sunni society; mosque at 50 Tyburn Rd, Erdington, B24. »94

✿ **Ghousia Qasmia Mosque and Darul Uloom**
34-35 Mount Street, Walsall WS1; *t* (01922) 34862
Sunni mosque and teaching centre, presumably managed by the Ghausia Qasmia Trust listed (1994) at 28 Little London, Walsall (M. Yasin). See also Shah Jalal Mosque, p70. »94

✿ **Ghousia Razvia Jamiah Mosque and Islamic Centre**
M. Iqbal: Higher Antley Street, Accrington BB5 0QH;
t (01254) 397398, 389972

✿ **Gilani Noor Mosque**
K. Hussain: 2 Chaplin Road, Longton, Stoke-on-Trent ST3 4QS; *t* (01782) 335606 »94

✿ **Girlington Muslim Welfare Association** and Madrassa Talim-ul-Islam; Mosque
182a Durham Road, Bradford BD8; *t* (01274) 480055 »94

✿ **Glasgow Central Mosque and Islamic Centre**
Mufti Maqbool/Abu Zar Choudhury: 1 Mosque Ave., Glasgow G5 9TX, Scotland; *t* (0141) 429 3132, *f* 429 7171
Worship, community welfare services, religious education, cultural resource centre. »95

✿ **Gloucester Islamic Trust** and Jamia Masjid
Mahmood E. Moolla: All Saints Road, Gloucester GL1 4EE;
t (01452) 506870
Mosque society; welfare/social/youth activities. »95

✿ **Golden Mosque**
Lower Sheriff St, Rochdale OL12 6TG; *t* (01706) 48681 »88

✿ **Gravesend and Dartford Muslim Association**
M.E. Aslam, Secretary: 14 Brandon Street, Gravesend DA11 0PL; *t* (01474) 351336
Founded 1972. »94

✿ **Greenwich Mosque and Islamic Centre**
40 Woolwich New Road, London SE18 6HD »88

✿ **Hackney Muslim Council** and Union of Muslims in Hackney
14 Warneford St, London E9 7NG; *t* (0181) 985 3258 »94

✿ **Hackney Muslim Women's Council**
101 Clapton Common, London E5; *t* (0181) 809 0993 »94

✿ **Handsworth Mosque**
10 Holly Road, Birmingham B20 2DB; *t* (0121) 523 7529 »94
✿ ≡ and Islamic Centre: Alhaj Fazlur Rahman, Secretary: 23 Booth Street, Birmingham B21 0NG; *t* (0121) 551 3049
Mosque, evening school. »94

✿ **Hanfi Sunni Muslim Association** and Jamia Masjid e Raza
Malik Khadam Hussain: 33a Randall Street, Blackburn BB1 7LG; *t* (01254) 52170
Community group, mosque committee of the Hanafi rite. »94

✿ **Hanifa Masjid**
Allama Mehmood Nishtar: Carlisle Road, Bradford BD8
Sunni (Hanafi rite) mosque. »95

✿ **Haroonia Islamic Centre**
74 College Road, Alum Rock, Birmingham B8; *t* (0121) 327 5180
Sunni religious centre. »94

✿ **Harrow Muslim Education Society**
417 Pinner Road, North Harrow HA2; *t* (0181) 427 1481 »94

✿ **Hartlepool Muslim Welfare Association**
Karem Elahi: 94 Milton Road, Hartlepool TS26 8DS »94

✿ **Hathanuri Islamic Book Centre**
Kassim Pandor: 70 Alexandra Terrace, Dewsbury WF13 4HD; *t* (01924) 452042 »94

✿ **Hazrat Dewan Hazoori Centre**, also known as Dar-ul-Uloom Ahl-e-Sunnat
29a Churchill Avenue, Foleshill, Coventry CV6 5JJ;
t (01203) 637317
Sunni mosque (possibly of the Indian Barelvi movement, Ahl-e Sunnat wa Jama'at?). »94

✿ **Heaton Mosque**
The Secretary: 1 Rothbury Terrace, Heaton, Newcastle-upon-Tyne NE6 5XH; *t* (0191) 265 4083 »94

✿ **Hendon Islamic Centre and Mosque**
Sayed M. Kadri: 135 The Broadway, West Hendon, London NW9 7DY; *t* (0181) 202 3236
Mosque, community cultural and educational centre. »94

✿ **Heraa Islamic Centre**
135 Ford End Rd, Bedford MK40 4LA; *t* (01234) 46265 »94

✿ **Hidayatul Muslim Society** and Masjid-e-Hidayah (also known as Hijra Mosque)
M.H. Hafeji: 63 Humphrey Road, Old Trafford, Manchester M16 9DE
Mainly Pakistani mosque society. Masjid-e-Hidayah also listed (1994) at 2 Seymour Place, off Humphrey Road. »94

✿ **Hijra School**
Dr A.M. Mangood: 28 Hall Lane, Manchester M23 8AQ »94

✿ **Hillfields Mosque and Muslim Association**
Mr Usmani, Secretary: 1-3 Berry Street, Hillfields, Coventry CV1 5JT; *t* (01203) 251184, 555497
Mainly Gujarati mosque and welfare society, with voluntary educational service. »94

✿ **Hinckley Muslim Association**
Manzoor Moghal, President: 1 Manor Close, Burbage, Hinckley LE10 2NL; *t* (01445) 611480
Social, cultural and religious activities. »95

✿ **Hitchin Mosque**
28 Florence Street, Hitchin SG5 1QZ; *t* (01462) 52067 »94

✿ **Hizb ul Ulama** and Masjid e Aneesul Islam
Moulana Yaqub Miftahi/A. Patel: 7 Troy Street, off Whalley Range, Blackburn BB1 6NY; *t* (01254) 583245
Mosque and religious society. »95

♦ **Hizb ut-Tahrir** *(Party of Liberation)*
Farid Qassem: PO Box 349, Edmonton, London N9 7RR;
t (0181) 880 4197
Pan-Islamic organisation seeking establishment of Khilafah, global Islamic rule; founded in Haifa in the 1950s; banned in some Islamic states. Influential in Muslim Unity Organisation, p68, and in universities; accused of anti-gay and antisemitic statements. Split in 1996: see Muhajiroun, p67. »95

✿ **Holborn Islamic and Welfare Centre**
Fazlul Karim Chowdhury, Chair: 4th Floor, 1a Rosebery Avenue, London EC1 4RT; *t* (0171) 278 3393 ext. 127
Religious, educational and welfare activities. »94

✿ **Holy Party**
S.B. Khawaja: 62 St Stephen's Avenue, Shepherd's Bush, London W12; *t* (0181) 743 9699 »94

✿ **Hounslow Jamia Masjid and Islamic Centre**
A.K. Qureshi, Secretary: 235 Staines Road, Hounslow TW3 3JJ; *t* (0181) 570 0938, 577 1858
Mosque, welfare and educational centre. »94

✿ **Huddersfield Council of Islamic Affairs**
B. Ahmad, Chairperson: Muslim Community Centre, Clare Hill, off St Johns Rd, Huddersfield HD1 5BS; *t* (01484) 435839
Umbrella organisation for mosques in South Kirklees. »94

✿ **Huddersfield Muslim Burial Council**
M. Tariq, Secretary: 2 Hall Avenue, Thornton Lodge, Huddersfield HD1 3NL; *t* (01484) 516544
Assistance with the provision of cemetery space and funeral services for Muslim communities throughout the area. »94

✿ **Hull Mosque and Islamic Centre** and UK Islamic Mission
Dr Ayyub: Berkeley St, Hull HU3 1PR; *t* (01482) 24833 »95

✿ **Hussaini Islamic Mission**
38 Great South West Street, Hounslow West TW4 7NF;
t (0181) 570 3438
Twelver Shi'ite society. »94
✿ ≡ Hojjatol Islam S.M.S. Razavi, Alim: 19 Thornbury Road, Isleworth TW7, Middlesex; *t/f* (0181) 570 3438
Shi'a Ithna Ashari religious and community centre. »94

✿ **Hussania Islamic Mission**
405 Park Road, Glodwick, Oldham OL4 1SQ; *t* (0161) 620 6952 »94

✿ **Hyndburn Council of Mosques**
Mirza Yousuf: 36 Washington St, Accrington BB5 6TF »94

✿ **Idara Isha'at al Islam**
E.Y. Bawa, Trustee: 15 Stratton Road, Gloucester GL1 4HD
Founded 1974; religious publishing in English and Urdu. »95

✿ **Idara Minhaj ul Quran**
19 St Thomas Gdns, Ilford IG1 2PQ; *t* (0181) 553 0498 »94

✿ **Idra-il-Jaaferiya Mosque**
Asad Baig: 18a Church Lane, Tooting, London SW17;
t (0181) 672 5373
Jafari rite (Twelver Shi'ite) mosque. »94

✿ **Ilford Islamic Centre and Mosque**
52-56 Albert Road, Ilford IG1 1HW; *t* (0181) 478 3115
Religious and welfare society founded 1964. »94

✿ **Ilford Muslim Society** and Mosque
112 Balfour Road, Ilford IG1, Essex; *t* (0181) 478 0347 »94

✿ **Ilm-o-Adab Mission**
A. Salimee: 13 Giles Street, Nelson BB9 9UD; *t* (01282) 603296
Publishes Islamic literature in English and Urdu. »94

✿ **Imamia Mission**
Ali Naqui: 519 Romford Road, Forest Gate, London E7 8AD; *t* (0181) 472 3588
Probably a Twelver Shi'ite centre. »94

● **Imams and Mosques Council (UK)**
Mohammad Shahid Raza: [address uncertain] 20-22 Creffield Road, London W5 3RP; *t* (0181) 992 6636, *f* 993 3946
Also listed (1994) at 46 Basing Hill, Wembley Park, Middlesex HA9 9QP. Sheikh Dr Zaki Badawi, chairman; 350 mosques; moral/practical support to mosques, information work. »94

✿ **Imanbarra Mosque**
3 Woodview Drive, Birmingham B15; *t* (0121) 440 4124 »94

✿ **Institute of Islamic Education**
South Street, Dewsbury WF12 9NG; *t* (01924) 455762 »94

✿ **Institute of Islamic Studies**
Khalid Alawi: 34 Kinver Croft, Birmingham B12 9HE »95
✿ ≡ and Islamic Union: Norpak House, Harold Street,
Northampton NN1 »94

• **Institute of Ismaili Studies**
14-15 Great James St, London WC1; *t* (0171) 405 5328
Promotion of Isma'ili Sunni Islam. »95

• **Institute of Muslim Minority Affairs, IMMA**
46 Goodge Street, London W1P 1FJ; *t* (0171) 636 6740
See also Council of Mosques (UK and Eire), p57. »94

• **International Centre for Islamic Studies, ICIS**
Muazzam Ali: 144-146 Kings Cross Rd, London WC1X 9DH
See Islamic Defence Council, p61, and Islamic Arts Centre.»95

✿ **International Islamic Mission** and Madni Jamia Masjid
Safder Hussain: 122-124 Gibbet Street, Halifax, Yorkshire;
t (01422) 55218 »94

• **IQRA Trust**
24 Culcross Street, London W1Y 3HE; *t* (0171) 491 1572,
f 493 7899
Training courses for professionals working with Muslim
children/communities; produces educational resources. »95

✿ **Islami Darasgah**
H.N.K. Khattak, Secretary: 68 Connaught Road, off Albany
Road, Roath, Cardiff CF2 3PX, Wales; *t* (01222) 488454
Mosque and Islamic education centre. »94
✿ ≡ The Secretary: 109 Lower Cheltenham Place, Montpellier,
Bristol BS6 3LA; *t* (0117) 941 4301
Worship, religious studies and language classes. »94

✿ **Islamia Girls' High School**
42 Banks Road, Golcar, Huddersfield HD7 4RE; *t* (01484)
658887
Small fee-paying school, opened 1983. »94

✿ **Islamia Girls' School**
184 Walm Lane, London NW2; *t* (0181) 208 3531
Small fee-paying secondary school, opened 1989. »94

✿ **Islamia Ibadat Khan Association**
62 Osbourne Road, Sparkhill, Birmingham B11 »94

✿ **Islamia Madrassa**
221 Alexandra Road, Acocks Green, Birmingham B27
Sunni educational society. »94

✿ **Islamia Primary School**
Yusuf Islam, Chairman of Governors: 129 Salusbury Road,
Brent, London NW6; *t* (0171) 372 2532
Private school with about 200 pupils, founded 1983 and
owned by Islamic Circle Organisation; seeking funding as the
UK's first voluntary-aided Islamic school. Also listed (1992)
at 8 Brondesbury Park, NW6 7BT, *t* (0181) 451 4547. »95

• **Islamia Schools Trust** and Association of Muslim Schools
2 Digswell Street, London N7 8JX; *t/f* (0171) 607 4943
Trust channels funding for the development of Islamic
education in Britain and Ireland. Association represents full-
time and supplementary Islamic educational centres. »95

✿ **Islamic Academy**
Prof. Syed Ali Ashraf, Director: 23 Metcalfe Road, Cambridge
CB4 2BD; *t/f* (01223) 350976
Founded 1983; curriculum research and development, teacher
education, publishing. *Muslim Education Quarterly* (4/yr).»95

✿ **Islamic Academy of Manchester**
M.A. Mirza, Secretary: 19 Chorlton Terrace, off Upper Brook
Street, Brunswick, Manchester M13 0PP; *t* (0161) 273
1145, 256 3472
Dr Khalid Mahmood. Islamic education, publishing, advice;
mosque founded 1975. *Al Hilal* (13/yr). »95

✿ **Islamic Arts Centre**
Jalaluddin Ahmed: ICIS House, 144-146 Kings Cross Road,
London WC1X 9DH
See also International Centre for Islamic Studies, above. »95

✿ **Islamic Association**
I. Jamal, Secretary: 18 Park Place, Dundee DD1 4HW,
Scotland; *t* (01382) 69950 »94

✿ **Islamic Association of Aberdeen** and Mosque
Dr Ruhul Amin, Chairman: 164 Spital, Aberdeen AB2 3JD,
Scotland; *t* (01224) 493764 »94

✿ **Islamic Association of East Ham** and Medina Mosque;
Muslim Cultural Centre
L. Hussain, Secretary: 225 High Street North, East Ham,
London E6 1JG; *t* (0181) 472 3069
Mosque society; religious education, assistance with Hajj,
welfare and immigration advice. »94

✿ **Islamic Association of South Humberside**
Dr Khalid Khan: 66 Victoria Street, Grimsby DN31 1BP »95

• **Islamic Book Centre**
120 Drummond St, London NW1 2HL; *t* (0171) 388 0710
Publications outlet of the UK Islamic Mission, pp71-72. »95

✿ **Islamic Brotherhood**
M. Ayoub: 57 Leicester Causeway, Coventry CV1 4HL »94
✿ ≡ and Jamia Mosque: M. Ali, Secretary: Eagle Street,
Foleshill, Coventry CV1 4GY; *t* (01203) 222169, 419514
Sunni society and mosque. »94

✿ **Islamic Centre**
Weston Hill, Barry, Glamorgan, Wales; *t* (014462) 79815 »90
✿ ≡ Liaqat Ali: Church St, Bury BL9 6AZ; *t* (0161) 764 7306
Mosque, religious education centre. »94
✿ ≡ 112-114 Hill Town, Dundee, Scotland; *t* (01382) 28374
Also listed (1988): a mosque at 120 Hill Town. »94
✿ ≡ T.H. Shah: 32 Shanklin Drive, Stapleford, Nottingham
NG9 8EZ; *t* (01602) 390254
Community welfare, advice; information on Islam. »94
✿ ≡ 48 Bridgefield St, Radcliffe M26; *t* (0161) 724 5465 »94
✿ ≡ Rana Muhammad Tufail, Director: Bedford Road,
Shelton, Stoke-on-Trent ST1 4PJ; *t* (01782) 280364
Religious, cultural and social centre. »94
✿ ≡ and Library: Fazlur Rehman, Organiser: 273 Montague
Road, Smethwick, Warley B66 4PS; *t* (0121) 565 3782 »94
✿ ≡ and Mosque: Talib H. Shah, Secretary: Sachaveral St,
Derby DE1 2JR; *t* (01332) 292021
Sunni community centre, educational/welfare work. »94
✿ ≡ and Mosque: 3 Curzon Street, St Ann's Well Road,
Nottingham NG3 6DG; *t* (0115) 970 1506, 958 0754
Sunni religious and community centre. »94
✿ ≡ and UK Islamic Mission: 30 Anderton Road, Sparkbrook,
Birmingham B11 1NQ »94

✿ **Islamic Centre of Brent** and Jamia Masjid
33a Howard Road, Cricklewood, London NW2; *t* (0181)
450 1986
Also listed (1993) c/o Jajji Abdul, 26a Chichele Road, NW2
3DA, *t* 450 7403. »94

✿ **Islamic Centre Edgware**
63 North Way, London NW9 0RA; *t* (0181) 204 2461 »94

✿ **Islamic Centre (South Wales)**
Sheikh Said Hassan Ismail, Secretary: 1 Alice Street,
Butetown, Cardiff CF1, Wales; *t* (01222) 460243
Purpose-built mosque; educational/community activities. »94

✿ **Islamic Centre of West Bromwich**
Haji Mohammed Khalid: 19a Victoria Street, West Bromwich
B70 8ET; *t* (0121) 553 5407, 525 1742
Sunni mosque; religious education, language classes. »94

• **Islamic Circle Organisation**
Yusuf Islam: [address unknown] Kilburn, London NW6
Charity which established Islamia School, first Muslim primary
school in UK; campaigns on funding of such schools. »92

✿ **Islamic College**
Moulana Abu Saeed: 16 Settles Street, London E1 1JP;
t (0171) 377 1595
Fee-paying secondary school for boys, opened 1985. »95

✿ **Islamic Community Centre** and Mosque
Limborough House, Wallwood Street, Burdett Estate,
London E14 7AW »94

✿ **Islamic Community Centre and Mosque Bina Mahal**
100 Rigby Road, Blackpool »94

✿ **Islamic Computing Centre**
Mufti Barkatullah: 73 St Thomas' Road, Finsbury Park,
London N4 2QJ; *t* (0171) 359 6233, *f* 226 2024
Associated with World Islamic Forum, p72. »94

▌**Islamic Council of Europe**
Salem Azzam: 16 Grosvenor Crescent, London SW1X 7EP;
t (0171) 235 9832
Founded with Saudi backing 1973, co-ordinates national and
local Muslim groups across Europe; conferences, research,
publishing; promotes interfaith understanding. »95

♦ **Islamic Council of Scotland**
30 Clyde Place, Glasgow G8, Scotland »95

✿ **Islamic Cultural Association**
M.M. Ali, Chair: 108 Walmersley Road, Bury BL9 6DX;
t (0161) 797 7942
Religious education, welfare work, representation of Islamic
community in Bury and Radcliffe and nationally. »94
✿ ≡ B. Rahman: 15 Merton Road, Highfield, Southampton »94
✿ ≡ and Islamic Study Centre: Sheikh Mahmood Rashid,
Chair: 262 Washwood Heath Road, Saltley, Birmingham B8
1JR; *t* (0121) 326 0966, 328 3478
Naqshabandiya Sufi association. »94

✿ **Islamic Cultural Centre**
Henry Street, Batley Carr, Batley WF17, Yorkshire »94
✿ ≡ [address unknown] Dyson Hall, Birmingham B6 »94
✿ ≡ 6 Bevington Road, Aston, Birmingham B6 »90

✪ **Islamic Cultural Centre**
B.A. Awau: 25 Park Street, Aston, Birmingham B6 5SH;
t (0121) 327 1281 »94
✪ ≡ and Jamia Masjid Hanifa: M. Ramsan: 372 Sheffield Rd,
Tinsley, Sheffield S9 1RQ; *t* (0114) 244 3824
The mosque is presumably of the Sunni Hanafi *madhhab*. »94
✪ ≡ and Mosque: 37 Alexander Road, Bedford MK40; *t*
(01234) 47032 (?) »94
✪ ≡ and Mosque: Dr Mazaki Badawi: 26 Walker Road,
Stevenage SG1, Hertfordshire; *t* (01438) 313103 »94
♦ **Islamic Cultural Centre, Regent's Park** and The London
Central Mosque Trust Ltd
Dr Ali Mughram Al-Ghamdi, Director General: 146 Park Rd,
London NW8 7RG; *t* (0171) 724 3363-67
Imam Solaiman; religious, educational, social needs of Muslim
community, inter-faith relations. Technically a local mosque,
the Centre has a leading role among the Sunni majority of the
UK Muslim population. The Trust is part-funded by Saudi
Arabia; other Muslim countries are represented on the board.
Groups based here include Muslim Teachers Association, p68;
Muslim Women's Association, Islamic Book Service and a
playgroup. *Newsletter* (12/yr), *Islamic Quarterly* (4/yr). »95
✪ **Islamic Cultural and Educational Centre** and Battersea
Mosque
Hafiz Nisaruddin Ahmed: 75 Falcon Road, Battersea, London
SW11 2PE; *t* (0171) 228 4267 »94
✪ **Islamic Cultural Foundation**
521 Commercial Rd, London E1 0HQ; *t* (0171) 790 1713 »94
✪ **Islamic Cultural Society** and Luton Mosque
Akbar Dad Khan, General Secretary: 2 Westbourne Road,
Luton, Bedfordshire; *t* (01582) 34988
Manages Luton's central mosque, mainly used by the local
Pakistani Kashmiri community of about 25,000. In 1994
there was a factional struggle for control of the mosque. »95
✪ **Islamic Dawah Academy**
160 Melbourne Road, Leicester LE2 0DT
Missionary school. »94
✪ **Islamic Defence Council**
Bashir Maan: Flat 6, 8 Riverview Gardens, Glasgow G5 »95
✪ ≡ Mukarram Ali: ICIS House, 144-146 Kings Cross Road,
London WC1X 9DH »95
✪ **Islamic Education Centre**
129 Normandy Road, Perry Barr, Birmingham B20; *t* (0121)
327 4202, 328 0837
Sunni religious society. »94
✪ ≡ A. Sabur Choudhury, Chairperson: 232 Witton Road,
Aston, Birmingham B6 6LB; *t* (0121) 523 4256
Worship, language and religious education; founded 1976. »94
✪ ≡ Mohammed Sabir: 44 Devonport Rd, Blackburn BB2 1HW
Small madrassa. »94
✪ ≡ and Mosque: Sultanat Khan: 51 Gassiot Road, Tooting,
London SW17; *t* (0171) 672 5613
Small madrassa, mosque and cultural centre. »94
✪ **Islamic Education and Cultural Society**
59 Highland Road, Earlsdon, Coventry CV5 6GQ »94
✪ ≡ Zarina Choudry: [address unknown] Hayes, Middlesex »95
✪ **Islamic Education Society** and Masjid-e-Nur-ul-Islam *(Light
of Islam Mosque)*
M. Patel, Vice-President: 108-110 Audley Road, Blackburn
BB1 1TF; *t* (01254) 676989
Mosque and madrassa society. »94
✪ **Islamic Education and Training Centre**
30 Rowfant Rd, London SW17 7AS; *t* (0181) 675 0404 »94
● **Islamic Education Trust** and Masjid Al Falah
Ismail Mullah/Ahmed Haji: 3-11 Keythorpe Street, Leicester
LE2 0AL; *t* (0116) 251 1833
Mosque and religious education society. »95
✪ **Islamic Educational Centre and Mosque Trust**
238 Charles Road, Small Heath, Birmingham B10 9AA;
t (0121) 773 1937 »94
✪ **Islamic Educational and Cultural Centre** and Taiba Mosque
Bostan Qadri, President: 9-11 Serpentine Road, Witton,
Birmingham B6 6SB; *t* (0121) 327 4204, 328 0837
Sunni mosque; youth and welfare centre. »95
✪ **Islamic Educational Institute**
9 Ambler Street, off Carlisle Road, Bradford BD8; *t* (01274)
487549 »94
● **Islamic Environmental Research Centre Ltd**
53 Bedford Square, London WC1B 3DZ »94
✪ **Islamic Fhikka Propieshtan Mosque**
Muktar Ali, Secretary: 37 Plantagenet St, off Tudor Road,
Riverside, Cardiff CF1 8RF, Wales; *t* (01222) 221309 »94
▌**Islamic Forum of Europe**
Habibur Rahman/Dr Abdul Bari: 34 Eton Close, 196 Garratt
Lane, London SW18 4ED »95

● **Islamic Foundation**, also known as Markfield Dawah Centre
Prof. Kurshid Ahmad: Markfield Conference Centre, Ratby
Lane, Markfield, Leicester LE67 9RN; *t* (0116) 224 4944
Dr Manazir Ahsan. Educational research; promotes
understanding of Islam. Resource centre; publications include
Focus on Christian-Muslim Relations (12/yr), *Index of Islamic
Literature*, (presumably renamed) *Soviet Muslims Brief* (6/yr),
The Muslim World Book Review (4/yr); books. Associated
with (Pakistan-based) Jama'at-i Islami, Islamic Society of
Britain and the UK Islamic Mission. »95
✪ **Islamic Guidance Society**
248 Ealing Rd, Wembley HA0 4QL; *t* (0181) 902 0108 »94
✪ **Islamic Information Bureau**
PO Box 914, London SE5 9TW; *t* (0171) 708 4222
Itha Ash'ari (Twelver) Shi'ite information/advice service. »94
✪ **Islamic Information Centre**
[address unknown] Bolton, Lancashire
Represents 26,000 Muslims, nine mosques. »88
✪ **Islamic Information Services Ltd**
Trafalgar House, 11 Waterloo Place, London SW1Y 4AS »94
✪ **Islamic Information Trust**
Dr Tariq Rajbee: 38 Little Ridge Ave., Hastings TN37 7IS;
t (01424) 755355 »95
♦ **Islamic International Front**
[address unknown] »96
✪ **Islamic Lending and Reference Library**
55 Whalley New Road, Blackburn BB1 6JY, Lancashire;
t (01254) 681558 »94
● **Islamic Marriages Introductory Service and Counselling**
1 Avondale Avenue, Esher KT10 0DB; *t* (0181) 398 6020
See also *Angikar* Bengali magazine, p19. »94
✪ **Islamic Outreach**
16 Queens Crescent, Glasgow G4 9BL; *t* (0141) 333 9624
See also Muslim House, p68. »94
● **Islamic Party of Britain**
David M. Pidcock, Leader: PO Box 844, Oldbrook MK6 2YL
Sahib Mustaqim Bleher, general secretary. Pressure group
seeking to represent mainstream Muslim opinion in UK. »95
● **Islamic Propagation Centre International**, IPCI, also known
as Islamic Vision
Shamshad Khan: 481 Coventry Road, Small Heath,
Birmingham B10 0JS; *t* (0121) 773 0137, *f* 766 8577
Information on Islam and the Muslim world; *da'wah*
(preaching of Islam); bookshop. »95
● **Islamic Relief**
151b Park Road, London NW8 7HT; *t* (0171) 722 0039
Also listed (1995) at 38 Mapesbury Road, NW2 4JD; see
FOSIS, p58. Humanitarian relief mainly in Bosnia. »96
✪ ≡ Dr Hani Al Banna/Zahira Master: 19 Rea Street South,
Birmingham B5 6LB »95
✪ **Islamic Religious Centre and Mosque**
Yakoob Fancy, President: 209 Preston New Road, Blackburn
BB2 6BN »94
✪ **Islamic Resource Centre**
Mohammed Attaullah/Y. Yacob: 93 Court Rd, Balsall Heath,
Birmingham B12; *t* (0121) 440 3500, *f* 440 8144
Welfare rights and immigration advice, employment and
educational counselling, community information service. »95
● **Islamic Shariah Council**
Dr Sheikh Syed Darsh: 208 Melrose Ave., London NW2 4JY
Was listed (1994) at 34 Francis Rd, E10, *t* (0181) 558 0581
(Dr Suhaib Abdul Ghaffor). Founded 1980; promotion of
Islamic family law; conciliation and marriage guidance. »95
✪ **Islamic Society**
School of Oriental & African Studies Student Union, 7 Malet
Street, London WC1 »94
● **Islamic Society of Britain**
Faruk Murad: PO Box 2, Markfield Conference Centre, Ratby
Lane, Markfield, Leicester LE67 9RN
Associated with the Islamic Foundation. See also UK Islamic
Mission (Liverpool), p72. »95
✪ ≡ Zaheed Parvez: 19 Albert Road, Wolverhampton
WV6 0AD »95
✪ **Islamic Society of Darlington**
Mohamed Sadiq, Secretary: 41 Westmoreland Street,
Darlington DL3 0NX; *t* (01325) 484880
The county's main Islamic community centre and mosque. »94
✪ **Islamic Society of the Faithful**
Nizar Boga, President: 70 Friern Park, North Finchley,
London N12; *t* (0171) 445 3769
Charity providing advice and counselling, and promoting
Islamic values, community welfare, relief of poverty. »94
✪ **Islamic Society of Gwent**
Mr Ramzan, Secretary: 63 Stow Hill, Newport, Gwent,
Wales; *t* (01633) 259005 »94

• Islamic Society for the Promotion of Religious Tolerance
Hesham el Essawy, Director: 20-22 Creffield Road, London
W5 3RP; t (0171) 935 3330   »94

✿ Islamic Teaching and Community Centre
M. Bashir: 141 Nechells Park Road, Nechells, Birmingham
B7 5PH
Sunni mosque and educational society.   »94

• Islamic Texts Society
Batul Salazar: 5 Green Street, Cambridge CB2 3JU;
t (01223) 314387, Tx 818268
Publishing of Islamic texts in English.   »94

✿ Islamic Trust and Jamia Mosque
35 Montem Lane, Slough SL1 2QW; t (01753) 30562 (?) »94

✿ Islamic Trust (Maidenhead) Ltd and Noor ul Aslam Jamia
al-Masjid
A.R. Malik, Chair: Holmanleaze, Maidenhead SL6 8AW,
Berkshire; t (01628) 29423, 30389
Purpose-built mosque; religious, social, educational centre.»94

✿ Islamic Trust Youth Section
I. Patel: 18 Charles Street, Gloucester   »94

• Islamic Universal Association
Mr Abdullah: 20 Penzance Place, Holland Park Avenue,
London W11 4PG; t (0171) 602 5273-74   »94

✿ Islamic Video and Audio Services Centre
10 Hampden Road, London N8 0HT; t (0181) 348 7958,
f 888 3926   »94

✿ Islamic Voluntary Service Newham
M. Rafiq: 205 Harold Road, Plaistow, London E13 0SE;
t (0181) 470 3674
Community welfare, information and advice.   »94

✿ Islamic Welfare Association
Mohammed Hussain, Secretary: 25 Logwood Street,
Blackburn BB1 9TU; t (01254) 583384   »94

✿ ≡ also known as Worthing Islamic Social and Welfare
Society: Abdulhadi Khabaza, Chair: 194 Heene Road,
Worthing BN11 4NT; t (01903) 215845, f 211763
Worship, religious instruction, Arabic teaching. Also listed
(1994) at 48 Lyndhurst Road, Worthing BN11 2DF (Imam
Anisur Rahman).   »95

✿ ≡ and Mosque: Taj Azfal: 62 Wills Street, Lozells,
Birmingham B19; t (0121) 523 0810
Sunni mosque and community welfare society.   »94

✿ Islamic Welfare Circle
Shamim Choudhary: 127 Manley Road, Whalley Range,
Manchester M16
Mainly Pakistani; community welfare group.   »94

✿ Islamic Youth Movement
M.A. Salam: 66 Woodlands Road, Cheetham, Manchester
M8 7NF; t (0161) 740 3351, 740 1665, 740 0577
Welfare of Pakistani and other youth in North Manchester;
sports, play schemes, outings and other leisure activities. »95

✿ Islington Muslim Association
38 Northdown Street, London N1; t (0171) 837 1771   »94

✿ Ismaili Centre and Aga Khan Foundation (United Kingdom)
Shafik Sachedina: 1 Cromwell Gardens, London SW7 2SL;
t (0171) 581 2071, f 589 3246
Place of worship, social and cultural centre for those Shi'ites
who recognise the Aga Khan as their hereditary Imam. The
Foundation is the UK arm of a development aid agency
working on basic needs projects in Africa and Asia.   »95

✿ Ismaili Community
Nagib Jiwa: 2 Marchmont Street, Edinburgh, Scotland;
t (0131) 229 3344
Shi'ite religious and welfare society.   »94

✿ Ismaili Cultural Centre and Mosque
Shafik Sachedina: 126 Suffolk St, Queensway, Birmingham B1
Shi'a Imami Ismaili group, followers of the Aga Khan.   »94

✿ Ismaili Muslim Group
T.A. Uka: 87 Howard Street, Tredworth, Gloucester   »94

✿ Ismalia Moslem Group
13 Keats House, Bexley Lane, Crayford, Kent
Isma'ili Shi'ite congregation.   »94

✿ Ithaad ul Muslimin (Muslim Union) also known as Unity
Hall Committee
Abdul Hafiz Malik, Secretary: Ithaad Community Hall, 7
Cross Street, Nelson BB9 7EN; t (01282) 694700
Voluntary group (also at 27 Hartington Street, Brierfield,
Nelson); welfare, social, youth and women's activities.   »94

✿ Jalalabad Mosque and Islamic Centre
Hira Miah, Secretary: 24-26 Dartmouth Road, Selly Oak,
Birmingham B29 6EA; t (0121) 471 1556   »94

✿ Jalalia Mosque
66 Trafalgar Street, Rochdale, Lancs.; t (01706) 46822
A mosque of the mainly north Indian Suhrawardiya order of
Sufis. Was listed (1988) at Dudley Street.   »94

✿ Jama Masjid
1 Whitaker Street, Batley WF17; t (01924) 472215   »94

✿ Jama Mosque
15 Chesham Place, Knightsbridge, London SW1   »94

✿ Jama'at e Ahl-i Hadith (Society of People of the Traditions)
and Al-Qur'an Society
Dr Suhaib Hasan: 101 Belmont Road, Tottenham, London
N17 6AT; t/f (0181) 881 3984
South Asian movement close to Saudi Wahhabis, in insisting
on purifying Islam of practices not derived from the Holy
Qur'an and the early Traditions. Al-Qur'an society offers
Islamic education to locals, and by correspondence.   »95

✿ Jamatia Mosque and Islamic Centre
181 Woodland Road, Sparkhill, Birmingham B11 4ER;
t (0121) 778 4478, 778 5157
Sunni mosque.   »94

✿ Jame Masjid Gulshane Baghdad
95 Ford End Road, Queens Park, Bedford MK40, Beds.   »88

✿ Jame Masjid-e-Noor and UK Islamic Mission
Raja Muhammad Sharif Qazi, President: 71 Saunders Rd, off
Preston New Rd, Blackburn BB2 6LS; t (01254) 698609
Mosque, with educational, social and welfare services.   »95

✿ Jame Masjid Trust
M. Hayat Khan: 13 Industry Road, Sheffield S9 5SP;
t (0114) 244 7686, 244 1500
Mosque and welfare society.   »94

✿ Jamea Masjid and Islamic Cultural Centre
Cumberland Street, Blackburn BB1 1JP; t (01254) 57553
Mosque society with educational and social activities.   »94

✿ Jamia Al-Karam
M.I.H. Pirzada, Trustee: 1a Bradwell Road, New Bradwell,
Milton Keynes MK13 0EJ; t (01908) 313804
Religious education, worship; residential centre for teenage
students of Islam and Arabic.   »94

✿ Jamia Hanfia-Taleem-ul-Islam
A. Akbar, Secretary: 26 Western Road, Derby DE3 6SE;
t (01332) 204187
Worship, education, community care.   »94

✿ Jamia Islamia and Islamic Study Centre and International
Muslim Organisation
159 Stoney Stanton Road, Coventry CV1 4FW; t (01203)
229113
Sunni religious, education and research society.   »94

✿ Jamia Islamia Mosque
17-21 Ombersley Road, Balsall Heath, Birmingham B12;
t (0121) 440 4096
Sunni mosque.   »94

✿ ≡ 42 Earl Marshal Rd, Sheffield S4; t (0114) 243 2475 »94

✿ Jamia Masjid
Newton Street, Penny Meadow, Ashton-under-Lyne OL6
6EJ; t (0161) 330 0617   »94

✿ ≡ 233 Bath Rd, Hounslow TW4; t (0181) 570 0938   »88

✿ ≡ 32 Upper George Street, Huddersfield HD1 4AW;
t (01484) 420029   »94

✿ ≡ 46 Alexandra Road, Reading RG1 5PF; t (01734)
661565   »94

✿ ≡ and Islamic Centre: 46-48 Spencer Place, Leeds LS7
4BR; t (0113) 262 1300
Mosque and community centre.   »94

✿ ≡ and Islamic Centre; also known as Upton Park Islamic
Centre: Naeem Khan: 72 Selwyn Road, Upton Park, London
E13 0PY; t (0181) 472 7696, 472 2745
Mosque and cultural centre. May be same as the Upton Park
Islamic Centre listed (1994) at 175-177 Plashet Grove,
Upton Park, E13 1BX, t 472 2957 (V.A. Patel).   »94

✿ ≡ and Islamic Centre; Dar-ul-Uloom; Madrassa-e-Hizful
Qur'an; Ulama Board UK: Dr A.S. Abdur Rahim, President:
521-525 Coventry Road, Small Heath, Birmingham B10 0JF;
t (0121) 772 3014, 772 8408, f 773 4340
Religious centre for local Bangladeshi community; training
and employment initiatives, Islamic education, language
classes. Offices of Bangladesh Islamic Consultative
Committee, Bangladesh Islamic Organisation, Birmingham
Dawatul Islam & Women's Group, British Muslim Engineers
and Scientists Association, Young Muslim Organisation.   »94

✿ ≡ and Islamic School Ahl-e-Hadith: M. Shabir: 29 Queen's
Cross, Dudley DY1 1QU; t (01384) 258479, 239417
Mosque and madrassah promoting a purist interpretation of
Islamic tradition.   »94

✿ Jamia Masjid-e-Farooq-e-Azam
Izat Khan: North Street, off Colne Road, Duke Bar, Burnley
BB10 1LU; t (01282) 422321   »94

✿ Jamia Masjid Islamic Centre
83 Stoke Poges Lane, Slough SL1 3NY; t (01753) 225661
Mosque and community centre.   »94

✿ **Jamia Masjid—King Faisal Mosque**
I. Omarji, Secretary: Atkinson Street, off Ashfordby Street,
Leicester LE5 3QK; *t* (0116) 246 0300 »95
✿ **Jamia Masjid Sultania** *(Sultana Mosque Society)*
Raja Jemroze Khan, President: 3-7 Bridge Street, Brierfield,
Nelson BB9 5PE; *t* (01282) 692764 »94
✿ **Jamia Masjid Tajdare**
Mohamad Sadiq, Secretary: 96 Victoria Street, Dundee DD1
2NR, Scotland; *t* (01382) 24817 »94
✿ **Jamia Mosque**
Rehmat Khan: Madeley Centre, 6 Rosehill Street, Derby DE3
8EX; *t* (01332) 366461, 44838
Sunni mosque, Young Muslims Organisation (Shokat Ali, *t*
47509), community welfare/educational activities, library. »94
✿ ≡ 21 Jackson St, Hyde SK14 1BX; *t* (0161) 368 1551 »95
✿ ≡ 70 Bradford Street, Keighley BD21, West Yorkshire »94
✿ ≡ 75 Emily St, Keighley BD21 3EG; *t* (01535) 607039 »94
✿ ≡ A.R. Mujahid: 183-186 Commercial Road, Newport
NP9 2PF, Wales; *t* (01633) 215420, 244395 »94
✿ ≡ 107 West Street, Scunthorpe DN15 6JD; *t* (01724)
842772 »94
✿ ≡ and UK Islamic Mission, Birmingham North: Quari A.
Wafi, President: 27 Putney Road, Handsworth, Birmingham
B20 3PP; *t* (0121) 551 9012, 772 6408 »95
✿ ≡ and UK Islamic Mission, Birmingham East: Niaz Ahmed:
401-403 Alum Rock Road, Birmingham B8 3DT; *t* (0121)
326 9930, 327 0962 »95
✿ ≡ and Islamic Centre: Manningham Lane, Bradford BD1
3ET; *t* (01274) 729418 »94
✿ ≡ and Islamic Centre: A.F.M. Alauddin, Imam: 73-75
Marmion Road, Southsea PO5 2AX; *t* (01705) 832541
Religious, social and welfare activities. »94
✿ ≡ and Muslim Community Centre: Iltaf Hussain Chowdhry,
Chair: 283 Newhampton Road West, Whitmore Reans,
Wolverhampton WV1 4RA; *t* (01902) 742787, 752190
Sunni mosque; madressas at Dudley Rd and 84 Lime St. »94
✿ **Jamia Mosque Trust** and Wycombe Islamic Mission
M. Hanif, Secretary: 34-36 Jubilee Road, High Wycombe
HP11 2PG; *t* (01494) 520807
Mosque, educational and social centre. »94
✿ **Jamia Naqshbandia Nawabia**
108 Bordesley Green Road, Birmingham B9
Sunni society of the Naqshabandiya order of Sufism. »94
✿ **Jamiah Mosque**
Merry Street, off Audley Range, Blackburn BB1, Lancashire;
t (01254) 51073 »88
✿ ≡ and Community Centre: K.M. Shabbir: 114a College Rd,
Rotherham S60 1JF; *t* (01709) 563631 »94
✿ **Jamiat Ahl-e-Hadith** *(Society of People of the Traditions)*
Mohammed Aslam: 21 Thursby Road, Nelson BB9, Lancs.;
t (01282) 690451
Society of the South Asian Islamic puritan movement. »94
✿ ≡ R.A. Mir, Chairman: 100 Crescent Road, Reading RG1
5SN; *t* (01734) 669247 »94
✿ ≡ and Masjid Adam; Madrasah Salfia; Organisation of
Muslim Women: 53 George Arthur Road, Saltley, Birmingham
B8 1LN; *t* (0121) 327 5168 »94
✿ ≡ and Madrasa Salfia: M.L. Bhatti, Secretary: 7 Hastings
Street, Derby DE3 6QQ; *t* (01332) 766237 »94
✿ ≡ also known as Moorgate Mosque Society: Hafiz Abdul
Ghani/N. Ahmed: Broom Grove, Rotherham S60 2TE;
t (01709) 369715, 360594
Traditionalist society (mosque at Moorgate Street, S60 2EY);
Qur'anic, Urdu and Arabic teaching. »94
✿ **Jamiat Ahle-Hadith** *(Society of the People of the Traditions)*
Centre for Religious Learning and Instruction
M. Ashraf: 125 Beresford Road, Longsight, Manchester M13
0TA; *t* (0161) 257 2491 (Makki Masjid)
Religious movement, close to the Wahhabis, which arose in
India; see Jama'at e Ahl-i Hadith, p61, and other spellings.»94
✿ **Jamiat Ahle Hadith Mosque**
11 Ross St, Werneth, Oldham OL9; *t* (0161) 624 2555
May be connected with the Jamiat Ahle Hadith listed (1993) at
23 Villiers Drive, Oldham OL8 1DY (M.I. Bhatti). »94
● **Jamiat-al-Ulama Britain** *(Society of the Ulama, or clerics)*
69 Princess Road, Birmingham B5 7PZ; *t* (0121) 449 7637»90
● ≡ also Shariat Council; Darul Ifta UK and Europe: Mufti
Mohammed Aslam: 98 Fernham Road, Rotherham S61 1BN;
t (01709) 563677
Pakistani Sunni society. The Shariat Council offers guidance
on Islamic family law and religious questions. »95
✿ **Jamiat e Judullah** and Masjid-e-Farooq-e-Azam
M. Hussain, Secretary: 29 (or 39?) Hartington Road, Stockton-
on-Tees TS18 1HD; *t* (01642) 679943
Religious society, mosque; teaching in Urdu and on Islam. »94

✿ **Jamiat Ihyaa Minhaj Al Sunnah**
Munawwar Ali: 24 Bishops Hill, Ipswich UP3 8EN
Sunni religious society and mosque. »95
✿ **Jamiat Islah-ul-Muslimeen** and Makki Masjid (mosque)
Obydur Rahman/M. Bostan: Plantation Road, off Albert Road,
Heely, Sheffield S7 9IJ; *t* (0114) 258 2348 »94
✿ **Jamiat Tabligh-ul-Islam** *(Islamic Mission Society)*
Mohammed Iqbal: 397 (or 371?) Park Road, Glodwick,
Oldham OL4 1SF
Proselytising, Deobandi-derived reform movement. Tabligh-ul-
Islam Mosque listed (1993) at 87 Greengate St. »94
✿ **Jamiat ul Muslimeen** *(Muslim Association)*
K. Mahmood: 20 Aston Court, Broadfield, Crawley RH11
Also (1994) at 1 Strachey Court, Webb Close, Crawley. »94
● **Jamiat-ul-Muslimin** *(Society of Muslims)* and Islamic Library;
Central Hanafiyah Mosque
Adil al-Farooqi, Imam: 28 Tennyson Road, Small Heath,
Birmingham B10 0HA; *t* (0121) 773 6094
Mosque society of the Hanafi Sunni rite. »94
✿ **Jamiat Ulama Markazi**
Maulana Musa Qasmi: 183 St George's Road, Bolton »95
✿ **Jamiyat-e-Tabligh-e-Islam** *(Islamic Missionary Society)*
Hafiz M. Rafique: Bodmin Street, Sheffield S9 3TA; *t* (0114)
244 5618 »94
✿ **Jamiyat-el-Hadith Mosque**
5 Camden Tce, Bradford BD8 7HX; *t* (01274) 728993 »94
● **Jamiyat Tabligh-ul-Islam** *(Islamic Mission Society)*
Pir Maroof Hussein Shah, Leader: 18 Southfield Square, off
Lumb Lane, Bradford, West Yorkshire; *t* (01274) 575919
A South Asian Islamic reform mosque and missionary society
presumably aligned with the (originally Indian) Tablighi
Jama'at. Several mosques and branches in Bradford, including
(1994): Fairbank Road; Hilton Road; 54 Airville Road; Roxy
Buildings, Barkerend Road, BD3 9AP; 2 Browning Street, BD3
9DX; 87-89 Ryan Street, BD5 7AP; 21 Aberdeen Place, BD7
2HG; 2 Grosvenor Road, BD8; 68-69 Southfield Square, BD8
7SN; 564a Thornton Road, BD8 9NF; St Luke's Church Hall,
Victor Street, BD9; 13 Jesmond Avenue, BD9 5DP; most of
these are c/o Mr Hussain, *t* 493764. »94
✿ ≡ and World Islamic Mission Centre: 28 Shearbridge Road,
Bradford BD7 1NX; *t* (01274) 493764
Centre of the South Asian Tablighi Jama'at reform movement.
See also Madressa Ghosia Tabligh-ul-Islam, p65. »94
✿ **Jamme Masjid** *(Mosque Society)*
A.Q. Khan, President: 45 Chomley Road, Reading, Berkshire;
t (01734) 667767 (?) »94
✿ **Jinnah Community Development Service**
M.R. Malik/Fazal Qayyum Khan: Islamic Central Hall, 4
Brougham Street, Stonyholme, Burnley BB12 0AS;
t (01282) 423296
Advice centre; mainly Pakistanis, Bangladeshis; welfare rights,
immigration/nationality work, liaison with public bodies. »94
● *Journal of Islamic Studies*: Oxford Journals, Oxford
University Press
Dr Farhan Ahmad Nizami, Editor: Pinkhill House, Southfield
Road, Eynsham, Oxford OX8 1JJ; *t* (01865) 56767, *f* 56646
Academic journal (2/yr) on all aspects of Islam and Islamic
countries. See Oxford Centre for Islamic Studies, p69. »94
✿ **Juma Masjid** and Islamic Centre
200 Bradford Road, Batley Carr, Dewsbury WF13 2HD;
t (01924) 461700 »94
✿ **Kanz-ul-Iman Muslim Welfare Association**
M. Arif: 8 Peel Street, Tipton DY4 8RG; *t* (0121) 557 6556
Sunni society. »94
✿ **Kashif-ul-Uloom Mosque**
2 Blake Lane, Bordesley Green, Birmingham B9; *t* (0121)
771 3247 »94
✿ **Kensington Mosque**
170 Old Brompton Rd, London SW5 0BD; *t* (0171) 373 0238
Religious and welfare centre. »94
✿ ≡ Mr Bargach: 76 Golborne Road, off Ladbroke Grove,
London W10; *t* (0181) 998 6646 »94
✿ **Kent Muslim Welfare Association**, KMWA
46a Salisbury Road, Chatham ME4, Kent »94
✿ ≡ and Gillingham Mosque: Syed Ikram Ali, Secretary: 114
Canterbury Street, Gillingham ME7 5UH; *t* (01634) 50878,
251312
Sunni mosque and community centre; Urdu and Arabic
lessons, welfare activities, marriage and funeral services. »95
● **Khaniqahi-Ni'matullahi**
Dr Javad Nurbakush (Nur'Ali Shah), spiritual leader: 41
Chepstow Place, London W2 4TS; *t* (0171) 229 0769
A Shi'ite Sufi order, as distinct from the Sunni majority of
Sufis. This section belongs to the Dhu'l-Riyasatyan branch,
one of three main tendencies of the Ni'matullahia in Iran.»95

✿ **Khawateen Association of Asian Muslim Ladies**
Z. Ghaffar: 6 Basing Hill, Golders Green, London NW11 8TH;
t (0181) 458 4033   »94
✿ **Khizra Mosque**
83-85 Walmersley Road, Bury BL9; *t* (0161) 764 1638
Mosque of same name listed (1994) at 55 Hurst Street.   »94
✿ **Khoja Shia Ithna 'Ashari Muslim Jamaat**
Firoz Moti: 17 Clifton Road, Balsall Heath, Birmingham B12
8SX; *t* (0121) 440 0463, 440 2448
Twelver Shia society (not from the Nizari Isma'ili majority of
Khojas). Was (1990) at 6 Forest Road, Moseley, B13.   »94
✿ **Khoja Shia Ithna Asheri Mosque and Muslim Community of
Metropolitan Leeds**
Noorali Bhamamni, Honorary Secretary: 168 Beeston Road,
Leeds LS11 8BD; *t* (0113) 265 9073
Twelver mosque, social, educational and welfare centre. »94
✿ **Khoja Shia Muslim Community of Gloucester**
B. Najafi, President: Wainsbridge, 69 Bristol Rd, Quedgeley,
Gloucester GL2 6NE; *t* (01452) 524262, 412041, *f* 309755
Indian Shi'ite (Nizari) organisation for worship. May be same
as the Khoja Shia Ithna Ashari Community of Gloucester listed
(1993) at 137 Eastgate, Gloucester (Husseini Imambara). »95
✿ **Khuddam-al-Ahmadiyya Youth Association**
Munir Ahmed: 70 Birkby Hall Road, Huddersfield HD2 2TJ»94
✿ **Khuddam-ul-Ahmadiyya Association**
Naseem Butt: 3 Kidderminster Road, Croydon CR0 2UF;
t (0181) 686 6295
Group associated with the Islamabad centre, near Tilbury.»94
✿ **Khuddan-ul-Ahmadiyya**
Waseem Uddin: Association Darul-Amaan, 4 Greenheys Lane,
Hulme, Manchester M15 6NQ; *t* (0161) 226 9918
Ahmadiyya youth group; sports, Islamic education.   »93
✿ **King Fahd Academy**
Shaikh Hamid Khalifa: Bromyard Avenue, London W3 7HD
Dr Ibtisam Al-Bassam. Islamic education centre.   »95
✿ **Kings Cross Mosque and Islamic Centre**
32 Wharton St, London WC1 1TG; *t* (0171) 833 2368   »94
✿ **Kings Heath Mosque and Madressa Islamia Talimuddin**
Abdus Samad Esakjee: 113 Station Road, Kings Heath,
Birmingham B14 7TA; *t* (0121) 444 5428, 444 8988   »94
✿ **Kingston Mosque**
55-55a East Rd, Kingston-upon-Thames; *t* (0181) 549 5315»94
✿ **Kingston Muslim Association**
Mohammed Anwar Malik: 41 Wyndham Road, Kingston-
upon-Thames, Surrey; *t* (0181) 546 0607   »94
✿ **Kingston Muslim Women's Association**
H. Syed, President: 38 Gainsborough Road, New Malden,
Kingston-upon-Thames, Surrey   »94
✿ **Knightsbridge Mosque**
c/o 76 Hazelbourne Road, London SW12 9NS; *t* (0181) 675
5529   »94
✿ **Kokani Muslims**
Sayed Ali Kadiri, Secretary: 127 Hamilton Road, Golders
Green, London NW11 9EG; *t* (0181) 458 4677
Community and religious group; fraternity and racial equality,
welfare, education, cultural promotion, funeral assistance.»94
✿ **Kokni Muslim Association**
14 Arden Road, Aston, Birmingham B6 5AP   »94
✿ ≡ and Masjid-e-Rizwan (mosque): B. Mullah: Newton Street,
Blackburn BB1 1NE; *t* (01254) 263707   »94
• **Kokni Muslim Cultural and Youth Organisation UK**
83 Sheveshill Court, Colindale, London NW9 6LT   »94
✿ **Ksisli Jamaat Hyderi Islamic Centre**
The Secretary: 26 Estreham Road, Streatham, London
SW16 5PQ; *t* (0181) 769 7553
Shi'ite religious, educational, community welfare centre. »94
✿ **Kyrwicks Lane Mosque**
159 Kyrwicks Lane, Sparkbrook, Birmingham B11 1SS   »90
✿ **Lajana Ama-u-Lah**
M. Chaudhury: 4 Greenheys Lane, Hulme, Manchester M15
6NQ; *t* (0161) 226 9918
Ahmadiyya Muslim Association group; educational, counselling
and voluntary work for young women and girls.   »93
✿ **Lanarkshire Muslim Society** and Jamia Islamia (mosque);
Islamic Teaching Centre
Ghulam Saqlain Siddiqui: Motherwell Road, Carfin, Motherwell
ML1 4XE, Scotland; *t* (01698) 262008, 833493, *f* 834806
Mosque, language and religious education, youth activities,
welfare and social centre for the region.   »94
✿ **Lancashire Council of Mosques**
Yusuf M.I. Bhailok: Oak House, Bank Parade, Preston PR1 3TA
Liaison among 50 mosques and Islamic groups. Interfaith
dialogue, community development, anti-racist activities. »95
✿ ≡ M. Rafique Malik, Secretary: 41-43 Gordon Street, Burnley
BB12 0AX; *t* (01254) 692289   »94

✿ **Lancaster Islamic Society**: and Masjid e Ilahi
I. Patel, Secretary: 1-2 Hawarden Cottages, off Hinde Street,
Albion, Lancaster LA1 3AP; *t* (01524) 64131
Also listed (1994) at 53 Dale Street, Lancaster LA1 3AP. »94
✿ **Lea Bridge Mosque**
439 Lea Bridge Road, London E10; *t* (0181) 539 4282   »88
✿ **League of British Muslims**: and Muslim Community Centre
B. Chaudhry, Chairman: Eton Road, Ilford IG1, Essex;
t (0181) 514 0706, 553 5363
Religious, social, cultural and leisure activities; advice,
counselling, employment training.   »94
✿ **Leicester Islamic Centre**
Mohammed Mahmud Begg: 147 East Park Avenue, Leicester
LE5 5AZ   »95
✿ **Lewisham and Kent Islamic Centre**
Dr S. Saleem: 283 Brownhill Road, Catford, London SE6
1AE; *t* (0181) 698 4316
Worship, welfare, social and cultural activities.   »95
✿ **Lewsey Muslim Cultural Society**
Abdul-Khaleq Vazifdar: 9 Sussex Close, Luton LU4 0UE;
t (01582) 608500   »94
✿ **Leytonstone Islamic Association** and Mosque
Dacre Road, London E11 3AG; *t* (0181) 539 7251
Association also listed (1993) at 170 Church Road, E10,
and 32 Barclay Road, E11.   »94
✿ **Liverpool Muslim Society**
M. Akbar Ali: 292 Greenhill Road, Liverpool L18 9SZ   »95
✿ **London Islamic Cultural Society**
42 Park View Road, Tottenham, London N17 9AT   »94
✿ **London Jame Masjid Trust Ltd**
59 Brick Lane, London E1; *t* (0171) 247 3507, 247 6052»94
✿ **Macca Mosque and Muslim Community Centre**
Zahoor Raja, Secretary: Grecian Crescent, Bolton BL3 6QU;
t (01204) 24200
Religious, welfare, educational and social activities. »94
✿ **Madina Islamic Cultural Studies Centre**   »94
35 Whitworth Road, Rochdale OL12 0RA
✿ **Madina Kashif-ul-Aloom**
239 Alum Rock Road, Birmingham B8
The name may suggest an affiliation with the Kashfiya school
of Twelver Shi'ism, but this is a member of the Confederation
of Sunni Mosques, p57.   »94
✿ **Madina Masjid**
Adderley Road/Ash Road junction, Saltley, Birmingham B8;
t (0121) 327 1123   »94
✿ ≡ and Mount Pleasant Islamic Trust: Dr Abdurehaman J.
Rajpura, Chairman: Purlwell Lane, Batley WF17, Yorkshire;
t (01924) 472378, 478330, *f* 420786   »94
✿ ≡ and UK Islamic Mission: 128-130 Oak Road, Luton LU4
8AD; *t* (01582) 27734
Mission also listed (1993) at 78 Selbourne Road, Luton. »95
✿ ≡ and UK Islamic Mission, Manchester South: S.D. Butt:
2 Barlow Road, off Stockport Road, Levenshulme,
Manchester M19 3DJ; *t* (0161) 224 5143   »95
✿ **Madina Mosque**
7 (17?) Park Avenue, Hockley, Birmingham B18 5ND; *t* (0121)
554 6717
Sunni mosque society.   »94
✿ ≡ 19-23 Oak Street, Blackburn, Lancashire   »94
✿ ≡ Bashir Ahmed, Secretary: 128 St George Road, Bolton
BL1 2BZ; *t* (01204) 21691
Mosque and small madrassa. See also Masjeed-e-Quba, p65,
and Sughra Mosque (Preston), p71.   »94
✿ ≡ 3 Chapel Street, Colne BB8 5AH   »94
✿ ≡ Dean Merchant, Chair: 273 Waterloo Road, Cobridge,
Stoke-on-Trent, Staffordshire; *t* (01782) 261429, 267329»94
✿ **Madina Mosque Trust**
2a Lea Bridge Road, Clapton, London E5; *t* (0181) 985 8204
Manages the Madina (or Medina) Mosque, at 16 Mildenhall
Road, E5 9QP.   »94
✿ **Madni Islamic Community Association** and Mosque
Q.M. Siddique: 22 Wincobank Lane, Sheffield S4 8AA;
t (0114) 244 2998   »94
✿ **Madni Masjid**
Blond St, Lockwood, Huddersfield HD2; *t* (01484) 422444»94
✿ ≡ and Muslim Education Centre: Raza Ul Haq: 289
Gladstone Street, Forest Fields, Nottingham NG5 1BS;
t (01602) 691275, 692566
Mosque and supplementary education service.   »94
✿ **Madni Muslim Girls' High School**
1-3 Thornie Bank, off Scarborough Street, Savile Town,
Dewsbury WF12 9AX; *t* (01924) 468516   »94
✿ **Madras House**
14 Blackstock Road, London N4 2DW; *t* (0171) 359 7596
Muslim bookshop.   »94

✿ **Madrasa al-Arabia al-Islamia**
Dr M. Sarwar, President: 490 Paisley Road West, Glasgow
G51, Scotland; *t* (0141) 427 2152
Madrasa (Islamic education centre) and mosque.   »95

✿ **Madrasa al-Tawhid** and Ahle Hadith Mosque
Mohammed Idrees Sethi, Secretary: 34 Francis Road,
Leyton, London E10; *t* (0181) 558 0581, *f* 471 1894
Traditionalist mosque and educational centre.   »94

✿ **Madrasa Taleem-ul-Islam**
Mohammed Iqbal: 161 Nithsdale Road, Glasgow G41,
Scotland; *t* (0141) 424 0787   »94

✿ **Madrassa Arabia Taleemul Qur'an** and Mosque
Richmond Hill, Katherine Street, Ashton-under-Lyne OL7
0AL; *t* (0161) 330 9837
Islamic education centre; mosque in Wellington Street.   »94

✿ **Madrassa Islamia**
58 Thurgarton Street, Nottingham; *t* (01206) 502520
Sunni educational centre.   »94

✿ **Madrassa Jila-ul-Quloob**
253 Bordesley Green, Birmingham B9 5EX
Sunni educational centre.   »94

✿ **Madrassa Karimia**
141 Berridge Road, Forestfield, Nottingham NE7 6HR
Sunni study centre.   »94

✿ **Madrassa Noor ul Islam**
A.S. Patel: 18 Woodsome Estate, Batley WF17 7EB
Madrassas of same name also listed (1994) at 39 Norfolk St,
WF17 7SA, and Snowden St, WF17 7RS (A. Bulbullia).   »94

✿ **Madrassa Taleem ul Qur'an** *(Koranic Teaching Institution)*
Iftikhar Ahmed Naweed, Secretary: 201 Lees Road, Oldham
OL14 1NW; *t* (0161) 678 0593   »94
✿ ≡ and Mosque: 44 Percival Street, Scunthorpe DN15 6JD;
t (01724) 852491   »94

✿ **Madrassa Zia-ul-Qur'an**
M.A. Khan: Bow St, Middlesbrough; *t* (01642) 230408   »94

✿ **Madresa Islamic Talemuddin**
103 Plashet Road, Upton Park, London E13; *t* (0181) 472
4132
Mosque and community centre.   »88

✿ **Madressa Bhinat**
Mrs Bawahad: 44 Mayfield Road, Birmingham B13   »94

✿ **Madressa e Anjuman-e-Ghousia Ashrafia**
Aziz Thadha, Chairman: 3-5 Evington Street, Leicester;
t (0116) 254 6544   »94

✿ **Madressa Ghosia Tabligh-ul-Islam** and Mosque
1-3 Burnett Place, Marsh Field, Bradford BD5 9LX; *t* (01274)
493764
Religious and educational centre; see also Jamiyat Tabligh-ul-
Islam Missionary College, p63.   »94

✿ **Madressa Islam Talimuddin** and Mosque
Mohammed Cassam Bham, Secretary: Bleinham Road, off
Church Street, Bradford BD8 7PD; *t* (01274) 542027
Mosque, educational and community centre.   »94

✿ **Madressa Islamiya**
44 Greaves Street, Great Harwood, Blackburn BB6 7DY;
t (01254) 877528
Also listed (1994) as Segar Street, Great Harwood.   »94

✿ **Madressa Majlis Itihad e Islam** and Mosque
300 Whalley Range, Blackburn BB1 6NL   »94

✿ **Madressa Talim ul Islam** *(Institution for Teaching of Islam)*
Community Centre, Bangor Street, Blackburn BB1 6NZ
Centre of same name at 86 Stansfield Street, BB2 2NG.   »94

✿ **Madressah Talim-ul-Islam**
M.S. Bhatti, Chair: 50 Fountain Street, Accrington BB5 0QP;
t (01254) 231533
Koranic, Arabic and Urdu education; founded 1981.   »94

✿ **Majlis Ansarullah** *(Assembly of Helpers of God)*
M.M.A. Mehmood: 72 St John's Road, Birkby, Huddersfield
HD1 5EY
Possibly connected with the Ansaru Allah Community, p56.»94

✿ **Majlis-e-Iqbal Islamic Education Society** and Ghousia
Razvia Mosque
H.M. Siddique: 3 (33?) Salisbury Avenue, Barking IG11
9XQ; *t* (0181) 594 6519   »94

✿ **Majlis-e-Muhammadi**
Syed Shabbar: 35 Warren Drive North, Surbiton KT5 9LG
Muslim welfare.   »94

✿ **Makki Mosque**
Nazir Patel, Secretary: back Apple Terrace, off Heliver Road,
Bolton BL1 3HH; *t* (01204) 848909   »94

✿ **Manchester Council of Mosques**
Dr Bashir Ahmed: Mazda House, 40b Raby Street, Manchester
M16 7EB; *t* (0161) 226 6527-28, 643 5499, 224 4119
Liaison and representation group for mosques, madrassas and
Islamic organisations in the city.   »94

✿ **Manchester Muslim Welfare Association**
180 Brook Lane, Levenshulme, Manchester M19; *t* (0161)
225 5960
See also Dar-ul-Aman Housing Association, p93.   »94

✿ **Manor Park Islamic Cultural Centre** and Shah Jalal Mosque
M. Khan, Secretary: 724 Romford Road, Manor Park, London
E12 6BT; *t* (0181) 514 7774, 553 5826   »94

✿ **Markazi Jamia Ghousia Masjid**
M. Aslam: 98 (99?) Chester Street, Blackburn BB1 1DR;
t (01254) 51080   »94

✿ **Markazi Jamia Masjid**
49 Rhodes Street, Halifax, Yorkshire; *t* (01422) 330041   »94

✿ **Markazi Jamia Mosque**
12 Grange Street, Wakefield WF2 8TF; *t* (01924) 71469   »94

✿ **Markazi Jamiat-e Ahlehadith and Community Centre** and
Muslim Community Bookshop
M. Abdul Headi, General Secretary: 20 Green Lane, Small
Heath, Birmingham B9 5DB; *t* (0121) 773 0019   »94

✿ **Markazi Mosque**
9-11 Christian Street, off Commercial Road, London E1
1SE; *t* (0171) 481 1294   »94

✿ **Marlborough Road Mosque** and Islamic Youth Movement;
UK Islamic Mission
17 Marlborough Road, Bradford BD8 7LS; *t* (01274)
493414, 306299   »94

✿ **Maroof-e-Islam**
183 Grove Lane, Handsworth, Birmingham B20 2HD   »94

✿ **Masjeed-e-Quba**
Bashir Ahmed, Secretary: 17 Lex Street, Preston PR1 4XL
Sunni mosque. See also Sughra Mosque, Preston, p71, and
Madina Mosque, Bolton, p64.   »94

✿ **Masjid Al Furqan** and Islamic Book Centre
19 Carrington Street, Glasgow G4 9AJ, Scotland; *t* (0141)
332 2811, 331 1119
Mosque with bookshop. Branch of UK Islamic Mission.   »95

✿ **Masjid Al-Islam**
Abdur Rashid Khamis, Mosque Secretary: Ivy Arch Road,
Worthing BN14 6BX; *t* (01903) 215163, 212672   »94

✿ **Masjid-e-al-Ameen**
21 Leopold Street, Leeds LS7 4DA; *t* (0113) 262 1300, 262
1362   »94

✿ **Masjid-e-Bilal and East London Islamic Centre** and UK
Islamic Mission, London East
295 Barking Road, London E6 1LR; *t* (0181) 471 9355   »95

✿ **Masjid-e-Bilal and Islamic Centre**
Said ul-Rahman: 127 Blackburn Road, Haslingden,
Rossendale BB4 5HN; *t* (01706) 25335
Also listed (1993) at 2-4 Beaconsfield Street, BB4 5TD.   »94

✿ **Masjid-e-Bilal and Muslim Community Centre**
Ghulam Hussain, Secretary: Harehills Place, Harehills Road,
Leeds LS14 3DZ; *t* (0113) 248 0711   »94

✿ **Masjid-e-Falah**
135-137 Kent Street, Preston PR1 1PE
Sunni mosque.   »94

✿ **Masjid-e-Hidaya**, also known as Millham Street Mosque
Imam Patel: 48-50 Millham Street, Blackburn BB1 6EU   »94

✿ **Masjid-e-Noor**
8 Stowell Road, Kingstanding, Birmingham B44 8EA   »94
✿ ≡ 158 (109?) Frederick Road, Aston, Birmingham B6 6DG;
t (0121) 328 0156   »94
✿ ≡ also known as Masjidun-Nur: 79 Forth Street, Glasgow
G41 2TA, Scotland; *t* (0141) 429 3383   »94
✿ ≡ Crosland Rd, Thornton Lodge, Huddersfield HD1 3JS   »94
✿ ≡ and Leicester Muslim Society: Ibrahim Bayat: 148-150
Berners Street, Leicester LE2 0FU; *t* (0116) 251 8108
Mosque of the same name listed at 60 Ashbourne Street.   »94
✿ ≡ 115-117 Stamford Street, Old Trafford, Manchester
M16; *t* (0161) 226 9507
See also Old Trafford Muslim Society, p69.   »94
✿ ≡ Mohammed Akram: 28 Eastmoor Street, Redditch B98
9HA; *t* (01527) 63834   »94

✿ **Masjid-e-Noor-ul-Islam**
61 Lena Street, Bolton BL1 8LU   »94
✿ ≡ Sabir Adam/Yunas Musa: Prospect Street, Halliwell
Road, Bolton BL3 6QP; *t* (01204) 393522
Mosque, Islamic education and social centre; also listed
(1993) at 131 Halliwell Road, Bolton BL1 3NF.   »94

✿ **Masjid-e-Raza** and Hanfi Sunni Muslim Circle
Ghulam A. Kausar: 103-105 St Paul's Road, Preston PR1
1PU; *t* (01772) 203578
Large mosque, purpose-built in 1971.   »94

✿ **Masjid-e-Sajideen** and Madrasah e Islamiah
I.H. Chopdat, General Secretary: Plane Tree Street, Little
Harwood, Blackburn BB1 6LS; *t* (01254) 265494
Mosque, social hall, Koranic education, funeral facilities.   »94

✿ **Masjid-e-Tauheed-ul-Islam** and Tauheed-ul-Islam Girls' High School
E.I. Adam: 29-31 Bicknell Street, Blackburn BB1 7EW; *t* (01254) 54318
Mosque and religious society. Associated Tauheed-ul-Islam girls' fee-paying school (Abdullah Patel, *t* 54021, 677654) provides religious and secular curriculum to 150 pupils.   »94

✿ **Masjid-e-Umar** and Madresa-e-Talimuddin
M.I. Dedat, Secretary: North View, Savile Town, Dewsbury WF12 9LF; *t* (01924) 455064
Mosque and Islamic teaching centre, with social and welfare activities.   »94

✿ **Masjid-i-Khizra**
Mr Russell, President: 69 Albert Road, Glasgow G42, Scotland; *t* (0141) 423 1208
Mosque.   »94

✿ **Masjid-ul-Imam-il-Bukhari** and Muslim Education Centre
Gulam Omarji Makadam, Chair: 159 (195?) Loughborough Road, Leicester LE4 5LR; *t* (0116) 266 5472, 266 5506 »94

✿ **Masjid-ul-Momineen** and Kokni Muslim Welfare Society
Ash Street, Little Harwood, Blackburn BB1 6LX
Mosque with welfare and funeral society.   »94

✿ **Masjide-e Jamia Al Madina**
M.A. Durrani, Secretary: 133a Waterloo Rd, Middlesbrough TS1 3JB; *t* (01642) 245855
Mosque and community centre; women's groups, social work, educational and general welfare activities.   »94

✿ **Medina Islamic Mission** and Islamic Centre Heathrow
K.M. Ahmed, President: 35 Martindale Road, Hounslow TW4 7EW; *t* (0181) 577 0647
Sunni religious, welfare and educational organisation.   »94

✿ **Mehr-ul-Millat Islamic Centre and Mosque**
21 Shakespeare Street, Sparkhill, Birmingham B11; *t* (0121) 773 5966
Sunni centre.   »94

✿ **Memon Jamatt** *(Memon Association UK)*
A.A. Yousuf, Honorary Secretary: 3 Weir Road, Balham, London SW12 8UW; *t* (0181) 740 7070, *f* 749 1442
Sunni religious, educational, charitable and counselling organisation. Also listed (1994) c/o I. Sacranie, 37 Wonter Road, Tooting, SW17.   »94

• **Message of Islam Movement** and Islamic College
14 Lea Road, Greet, Sparkhill, Birmingham B11 3LU; *t* (0121) 771 3680   »94

✿ **Middleton Road Mosque**
[address uncertain] 156 Middleton Road, Oldham OL9 6BG; *t* (0161) 678 6748
Also listed (1993) at 55 Middleton Road, and at 101 Mars Street, OL9 6QF.   »94

✿ **Minaret House**
Riadh El-Droubie: 9 Leslie Park Road, East Croydon CR0 6TN; *t* (0181) 654 8801, *f* 667 1280
Founded 1967; develops resources on Islam for schools.   »94

✿ **Mosque**
Canning Street, Accrington BB5, Lancashire   »90
✿ ≡ 71 Stamford Road, Ashton-under-Lyne OL6, Lancs.   »94
✿ ≡ 79 Warwick Road, Batley WF17, Yorkshire   »94
✿ ≡ 2 The Avenue, Bedford MK40   »90
✿ ≡ M.S. Khan, Chair: 10-12 Iddesleigh Road, Bedford MK40 4JU; *t* (01234) 350395
Daily prayer, Urdu classes; advice service open to all.   »94
✿ ≡ 22 Hugh Road, Small Heath, Birmingham B10   »94
✿ ≡ 32 Woodfield Road, Birmingham B11 8UH   »88
✿ ≡ 15 Minstead Road, Erdington, Birmingham B24 8PS; *t* (0121) 328 4627   »94
✿ ≡ 18 Speedwell Road, Birmingham B5 7PT; *t* (0121) 440 1876   »94
✿ ≡ 44 Fantham Rd, Birmingham 6; *t* (0121) 523 9963   »94
✿ ≡ 6 Witton Street, Birmingham B6   »94
✿ ≡ 115 Daisy St, Blackburn, Lancs.; *t* (01254) 52721   »88
✿ ≡ 24 Edmond St, Great Harwood, Blackburn BB6   »94
✿ ≡ 3 Stafford Rd, off Christchurch Rd, Bournemouth BH1»94
✿ ≡ Brown Street, Bradford BD3, West Yorkshire   »94
✿ ≡ 68 Stanacre Place, Bradford BD3; *t* (01274) 638348   »94
✿ ≡ 75 Ryan Street, West Bowling, Bradford BD5   »94
✿ ≡ 5 Thorncliffe Square, Bradford BD8, West Yorkshire   »94
✿ ≡ 9 Stephens Terrace, Bradford BD8, West Yorkshire   »94
✿ ≡ Imam Hanif: 21a Bedford Place, off Western Road, Brighton BN1 2AA; *t* (01273) 25027
Religious, social and youth activities.   »94
✿ ≡ 56 Goodwind Street, Bristol BS5   »94
✿ ≡ 109 Lower Street, Cheltenham Road, Bristol BS6   »94
✿ ≡ Afzal Quarashi: 134 Princess Street, Burton-on-Trent DE14; *t* (01283) 33368
Sunni mosque.   »94

✿ **Mosque**
118 Byrkley Street, Burton-on-Trent DE14   »88
✿ ≡ 67 Thompson Street, Masley Road, Bury BL9   »94
✿ ≡ 17 Peel Street, Cardiff, Wales; *t* (01222) 37838   »94
✿ ≡ 22B Chatham Hill, Chatham ME4; *t* (01634) 47409   »94
✿ ≡ 59 Waterside, Chesham HP5, Buckinghamshire   »88
✿ ≡ 30 Railway Street, Chorley PR6, Lancashire   »94
✿ ≡ 45 Wellesley Rd, Croydon CR9; *t* (0181) 684 7512   »94
✿ ≡ 59 Walsall Road, Darlaston WS10, Staffordshire   »88
✿ ≡ 54 (59?) Dairyhouse Road, Derby DE3 8HL   »94
✿ ≡ 8 Barber Street, Dewsbury WF12; *t* (01924) 465520 »88
✿ ≡ 23-27 Warren Street, Savile Town, Dewsbury WF13; *t* (01924) 462873   »94
✿ ≡ North Road, Ravensthorpe, Dewsbury WF13; *t* (01924) 461089   »94
✿ ≡ 28 Dearnley Street, Ravensthorpe, Dewsbury WF13   »94
✿ ≡ Mohammad Razaq, Secretary: 1 Stoney Bank Street, Scout Hill, Dewsbury WF13 3RJ; *t* (01924) 451085   »94
✿ ≡ Barlowmoor Road, Burton Road, Didsbury M6; *t* (0161) 434 2254   »88
✿ ≡ 20 Bourne Street, Dudley DY1, West Midlands   »94
✿ ≡ 329 High St, Ponders End, Enfield; *t* (0181) 804 2512»88
✿ ≡ 60-61 Carlton Place, Glasgow, Scotland; *t* c/o (0141) 429 3132 (Central Mosque)   »88
✿ ≡ Langside, Govanhill, Glasgow G53; *t* (0141) 423 4242»94
✿ ≡ 24 Broad Acre, Oakfield, Guildford, Surrey   »94
✿ ≡ Mr Islamadean: 2 Albert Street, Haverfordwest, Pembrokeshire, Wales; *t* (01437) 765791
Small prayer house opened 1989.   »94
✿ ≡ 60 Cressex Road, High Wycombe HP12 4TY; *t* (01494) 443925   »94
✿ ≡ 79 Linneaks Street, Hull; *t* (01482) 18792   »88
✿ ≡ 153 Boulevard, Hull HU3 3EJ; *t* (01482) 28808   »94
✿ ≡ 28 St Thomas Street, Hyde SK14, Cheshire   »94
✿ ≡ 70 Marlborough Street, Keighley, Yorkshire   »88
✿ ≡ 48 Radford Avenue, Kidderminster; *t* (01562) 62011   »94
✿ ≡ Wood House Lane, Leeds, Yorkshire   »88
✿ ≡ 45 St Martin's Gardens, Leeds LS7 3LD   »94
✿ ≡ 145 Spencer Pl., Leeds LS7 4DU; *t* (0113) 262 1989 »94
✿ ≡ 15 James Road, Liverpool   »88
✿ ≡ 39 Beaconsfield Road, Leyton, London E10; *t* (0181) 558 5601   »94
✿ ≡ 1 Colvin Road, London E6; *t* (0181) 472 5663   »88
✿ ≡ 204a North Gower Street, Euston, London NW1; *t* (0171) 387 8346
Presumably linked with UK Islamic Mission next door.   »94
✿ ≡ 42 Beverley Drive, Queensbury, London NW9; *t* (0181) 204 2006   »94
✿ ≡ 24 Newington Causeway, London SE1; *t* (0171) 407 1602   »94
✿ ≡ 57 Chatsworth Road, London SE18   »88
✿ ≡ 15 Lattwood Rd, London SW12; *t* (0181) 673 0445   »88
✿ ≡ 49 Lower Richmond Road, Putney, London SW15; *t* (0181) 788 5554   »94
✿ ≡ 12 Melrose Avenue, Wimbledon Park, London SW19; *t* (0181) 946 4784   »94
✿ ≡ 25 Bellfield Road, London SW9; *t* (0171) 274 1757   »94
✿ ≡ 71 Westbourne Grove, Bayswater, London W2; *t* (0171) 727 0729   »94
✿ ≡ 365 Third Avenue, Trafford Park, Manchester M17; *t* (0161) 872 0698   »94
✿ ≡ 94 Bignor Street, Cheetham Hill, Manchester M8; *t* (0161) 205 1359   »94
✿ ≡ 52 Duncombe Street, Bletchley, Milton Keynes MK2 2LY; *t* (01908) 74380   »94
✿ ≡ 43 Argyle Street, Northampton; *t* (01604) 57230   »94
✿ ≡ N. Pathan, Secretary: 120 Frank Street, Nuneaton CV11 5RA; *t* (01203) 343401   »94
✿ ≡ 116 Manchester Road, Oldham OL9 7AX; *t* (0161) 624 5448   »94
✿ ≡ 7 Fishwick Street, Preston; *t* (01772) 253807   »88
✿ ≡ 8 Redstone Drive, Redhill RH1; *t* (01737) 67626   »95
✿ ≡ Earlswood Road, Redhill RH1 6HE; *t* (01737) 60251   »95
✿ ≡ 46 Milton Road, Eastwood, Rotherham S60, Yorkshire»94
✿ ≡ 5 Gardener Street, Salford M6; *t* (0161) 748 9261   »94
✿ ≡ 62 Shirland Lane, Sheffield S9, Yorkshire   »88
✿ ≡ 103 Townsend Road, Southall, Middlesex; *t* (0181) 574 6014, 740 0463   »94
✿ ≡ 189 Northumberland Road, Southampton, Hampshire; *t* (01703) 35941   »94
✿ ≡ B. Ali: 2a Keel St, Tunstall, Stoke-on-Trent; *t* (01782) 813617, 827677
Sunni mosque.   »94
✿ ≡ Station Road, Stoke-on-Trent, Staffordshire   »88
✿ ≡ 133 Broad St, Swindon, Wilts.; *t* (01793) 523831   »94

✿ **Mosque**
Gulzar Khan, Secretary: Eagle Street, Todmorden, Lancs.
OL14 5HQ »94
✿ ≡ 3 Marsland Street, Wakefield, Yorkshire »94
✿ ≡ and Community Centre; Islamic Education Centre: 73
Alston Drive, Bradwell Abbey, Milton Keynes MK13 9HG;
t (01908) 318663
Mosque, madrassah. Education Centre publishes a Muslim
family magazine, *Al Usra* (12/yr, Huda Khattab, editor; PO
Box 3012, Milton Keynes MK13 9JB). »95
✿ ≡ and Community Centre: 165 Woodborough Road,
Nottingham; t (0115) 941 2462 »94
✿ ≡ and Islamic Centre: M.M. Yousuf, Chairman: 525 London
Road, Croydon CR4 6AR; t (0181) 684 8200
Major mosque and cultural centre with social, welfare, advice
and educational services. »94
✿ ≡ and Islamic Centre: Abdul Rahman Al Matrodi: 50 Potter
Row, Edinburgh EH8 9BT, Scotland; t (0131) 667 0140 »94
✿ ≡ and Islamic Centre: 15 York Road, Exeter EX4 6BA;
t (01392) 50597 »94
✿ ≡ and Islamic Centre; UK Islamic Mission: 27 Arlington
Street, Charing Cross, Glasgow G1 6DT, Scotland; t (0141)
429 3383, 332 2811 »94
✿ ≡ and Islamic Centre: Mohammed Salim: 2a Sutherland
Street, Leicester LE2 1DS; t (0116) 255 3867, 254 0404»94
✿ ≡ and Islamic Centre: A.H. Mirza: 36 Long Lane, Finchley,
London N3 2PU; t (0181) 346 2160 »94
✿ ≡ and Islamic Centre: 131 Plumstead Road, opp. Bus Garage,
London SE18 7DU; t (0181) 854 4846, f 854 0514 »94
✿ ≡ and Islamic Centre: 215 Derby Rd, Lenton, Nottingham
NG7 1QJ; t (01602) 412462 »94
✿ ≡ and Islamic Centre; UK Islamic Mission; Young Muslims
Walsall: Saeed Ur Rahman, Imam: 4 Rutter Street, Caldmore,
Walsall WS1 4HN; t (01922) 20982 »95
✿ ≡ and Islamic Community Centre: 12 Roxburgh Street,
Edinburgh EH8 9TA, Scotland; t (0131) 556 1902 »94
✿ ≡ and Islamic Community Centre: M. Khan, Imam: 14 St
Helens Rd, Swansea SA1 4AW, Wales; t (01792) 54532 »94
✿ ≡ and Madrassa Zia-ul-Quran: 218-220 St Saviours Road,
Alum Rock, Birmingham B8; t (0121) 326 0040, 328 1584
Sunni religious and educational centre. »94
✿ ≡ and Madressa Talimuddin: 38 Florence Street, Walsall,
West Midlands; t (01922) 20982 »94
✿ ≡ and Muslim Community Centre: Tallow Hill, Worcester »94
● **Movement for Islamic Resurgence**
11 Turpin House, Battersea Park Road, London SW11 5HR;
t (0171) 627 0425 »94
● **Muhajiroun** *(The Emigrants)*
Omar Bakri: [address unknown] London
Islamist party; split in 1996 from Hizb ut-Tahrir, p59, which
Bakri led; linked with Association of Muslim Lawyers,
Gathering of Muslim Parents, Islamic International Front. »96
✿ **Muhul Islam Saddiqia Mosque**
12 Victoria Rd, Aston, Birmingham B6; t (0121) 554 8277
Sunni mosque society. »94
✿ **Muridin al Haq**
98 Greenwood Road, London E8 1NE
Sufi group. »94
✿ **Muslim Action Group**
Ayub H.V. Bux: [address unknown] Preston, Lancashire »94
✿ **Muslim Advice Centre**
Union of Muslim Families, 46 Goodge Street, London W1P
1FJ; t (0171) 637 1971 »90
✿ ≡ 10 Greenhill Road, Manchester M13 0YL
See also (Pakistani) Al Hilal Community Project, p93. »94
✿ **Muslim Advisory and Community Welfare Council, MACWC**
M. Salah Ud-Din: 317 Markhouse Rd, Walthamstow, London
E17 8EE; t (0181) 556 5750, 521 8288, 527 6514
Advice and representation. »94
● **Muslim Aid**
2 Digswell Street, London N7; t (0171) 609 4426
See also Islamia Schools Trust, p60. »90
✿ **Muslim Association**
19b Freer Road, Birmingham B6 6NE; t (0121) 551 9171 »94
✿ ≡ and Mosque: 416-418 High St, Cheltenham GL50 3JA»94
✿ ≡ and Masjid-e-Umar: 29 Stratford Street, off Dewsbury
Road, Leeds LS11 6JG; t (0113) 270 9356 »94
✿ ≡ Barking and Dagenham: Haji Mohammed: 43 Cecil Ave.,
Barking IG11 9TD; t (0181) 591 0154 »94
✿ **Muslim Association of Bradford** and Jamia Masjid
Afsar Khan, President: 30 Howard Street, Bradford BD5 0DP;
t (01274) 724819 »94
✿ **Muslim Association of Croydon**
M.H. Rahman, Secretary: 7 Stuart Road, Thornton Heath,
Croydon CR4 8RA; t (0181) 684 5830 »94

✿ **Muslim Association of Manchester**
T.H. Shah/Dr M.A. Junejo: 78 Dickenson Road, Rusholme,
Manchester M14 5HF; t (0161) 248 7006, 257 3096
Cultural, social and welfare activities; mainly Pakistani. »93
✿ **Muslim Bazar Kallayan Somity**
45 Gaddesby Road, Kings Heath, Birmingham B14 7EX »94
✿ **Muslim Brothers Association**
59 King Street East, Rochdale, Lancashire »94
✿ **Muslim Butchers Association**
c/o Raza Brothers, 102 Attercliffe Common, Sheffield S9 »94
✿ **Muslim Centre**
Mutteeullah Dard: "Peace", 4 Goffs Close, Harborne,
California Way, Birmingham B32 3XA; t (0121) 426 5261
Promotes tolerance, world peace and universal harmony. »94
✿ ≡ Conway Road, Leeds, Yorkshire; t (0113) 240 4178 »94
✿ **Muslim College**
Sheikh Dr M.A. Zaki Badawi, Director: 20-22 Creffield Road,
London W5 3RP; t (0181) 992 6636, f 993 3946
Teaches on Islam, Arabic, Sufism, Islamic law; offers diploma
courses; see Islamic Society for... Religious Tolerance, p62.»95
✿ **Muslim Community Centre**, also known as Brighton Islamic
Centre and Mosque
Imam Abusaleh Shibbir Ahmed: 150 Dyke Road, Brighton
BN1 5PA; t (01273) 722438, 505247, f 540058
Mosque and community centre founded 1977. Educational
activities; advice on immigration, housing, social security. »94
✿ **Muslim Community Education Centre** and Jamiat-Ahl-e-
Hadith
Haji Mohammed Sadiq, Chairperson: 7-10 York Street,
Burton-upon-Trent DE15 2XL; t (01283) 512026
Traditionalist religious group; education, welfare. »94
✿ **Muslim Community and Education Centre**
69 Woodsley Road, Leeds LS3 1DU »94
✿ **Muslim Community House**
G.H. Choudhary, Chair: 39 Claughton Road, Dudley DY1
7EA; t (01384) 233081
Advice, information and resource centre. Religious, cultural,
educational and youth activities. »94
● **Muslim Community Studies Institute** and Islamic Rights
Movement; Volcano Press
Asaf Hussain, Chair: PO Box 139, Leicester LE2 2YH;
t (0116) 273 6721, f 270 6714
Research and consultancy centre on Islam; publishing;
promotion of human rights and religious tolerance. »95
✿ **Muslim Community and Welfare Centre** and North London
Central Mosque
I.A. Malik, Co-ordinator: 15 St Thomas' Road, Finsbury Park,
London N4 2QH; t (0171) 359 1181
Mosque/community centre founded in 1960s, welfare services
including rights advice (open to all), education, women's and
youth activities, lunch club for elderly, interfaith work. »94
✿ **Muslim Council**
16 Victoria Way, Charlton Road, London SE7; t (0181) 215
5793, 853 4376 »94
✿ **Muslim Cultural Association**
R.T. Khan: 54 Becher Street, Derby DE3 8NN; t (01332)
367439 »94
✿ **Muslim Cultural Society**
Abdul Malik, General Secretary: [address unknown] Leeds
New mosque, due to open mid-1995. »94
✿ ≡ and Mosque: 64 Lawrence St, Farnworth, Bolton BL4 »94
✿ **Muslim Cultural and Welfare Association**
Lal Hussain, Secretary: 11 Park Hill Road, Wallington, Sutton
SM6 0SD; t (0181) 647 9041 »94
✿ **Muslim Culture and Promotional Group**
F.Y. Khan, Secretary: 4 Abbots Way, Westlands, Newcastle-
under-Lyme ST5 2ET; t (01782) 615978 »94
✿ **Muslim Defence Council**
Habib Ullah Siddiqi: 21 Furnace Road, Longton, Stoke-on-
Trent ST3, Staffordshire; t (01782) 341076 »94
● **Muslim Doctors and Dentists Association**
Dr Jafar Qureshi: 136 Linden Lea, Wolverhampton WV3 8BE »95
● **Muslim Education Co-ordinating Council (UK)**
Nazar Mustafa: 49 Kilmartin Avenue, London SW16 4RA
Was listed (1994) at 7 Paul Gardens, East Croydon CR0
5QL, t (0181) 681 6087. Promotion of religious and
citizenship education for Muslim children. »95
✿ **Muslim Education and Family Welfare Society**
M.A. Fardoqui, Chair: Pennsylvania, 249 Llanederyn, Cardiff
CF1 7LW, Wales; t (01222) 731848 »94
✿ **Muslim Education and Literary Service**
Abdul Wahid Hamid: 61 Alexandra Rd, London NW4 2RX »95
✿ **Muslim Education Trust**
Dr A. Rajput: 55 Portland Road, Edgbaston, Birmingham B16
9HS; t (0121) 454 0671 »94

- **Muslim Educational Trust**
Ghulam Sarwar, Director: 130 Stroud Green Road, London
N4 3RZ; *t* (0171) 272 8502, *f* 281 3457
Founded 1966; campaigns for state funding of Muslim
schools; teaching support and curriculum resources.   »95

✿ **Muslim Funeral Association**
M. Asad: 45 Morley Lane, Milnsbridge, Huddersfield   »94

✿ **Muslim Funeral Society**
K. Uddin, President: 181 Manchester Road, Thornton Lodge,
Huddersfield HD1 3TE; *t* (01484) 548298
Arranges local funerals and the repatriation of bodies; see
also Huddersfield Muslim Burial Council, p59.   »94

✿ ≡ M. Akram: 5 Chatham Street, Shelton, Stoke-on-Trent
ST1 4NY; *t* (01782) 269661   »94

✿ **Muslim Girls Community School**
Ryan Street, Manchester Road, Bradford BD5 7DQ;
t (01274) 734693
Small fee-paying secondary school opened 1984.   »94

✿ **Muslim Girls' High School**
c/o 112 Green Lane Road, Leicester LE5 3TJ; *t* (0116) 253
2737, 273 6376   »94

✿ **Muslim Girls' School**
High St, off Derby St, Bolton BL3 6TA; *t* (01204) 361103»94

✿ ≡ c/o 101 Norman Avenue, Nuneaton CV11 5NY; *t* (01203)
350153   »94

✿ **Muslim Girls' Secondary School**
Unit 1, 36 Deepdale Mill Street, Preston PR1 6QL; *t* (01772)
651906   »94

✿ **Muslim Girls and Young Women's Association**
M. Khan/M. Rawson: 4th Floor, Spire House, New Union
Street, Coventry, Warwickshire; *t* (01203) 832590, 668412
Social centre, advice, educational and training activities.   »90

✿ **Muslim Health Clinic**
Dr Farhat Hussein/Dr Fatima Hussein: 145 Portland Road,
Hove BN3 5QJ; *t* (01273) 734888   »94

✿ **Muslim House**
Hassain Hemsy, President: 16 Queens Crescent, Glasgow
G4 9BL, Scotland; *t* (0141) 332 5223   »94

✿ **Muslim Information Service** and Muslim Welfare House
Kazem Al-Rawi/M.A. Hassan: 233 Seven Sisters Road,
London N4 2DA; *t* (0171) 272 5170, 263 3071, *f* 281 2687
Worship and welfare activities; advice, youth service, cultural
events; bookshop with mail order service, *f* 272 3214.   »95

- **Muslim Institute**
Dr Kalim Siddiqui: 6 Endsleigh Street, London WC1H 0DS;
t (0171) 388 2581
Defence of Muslim rights. The Institute is closely identified
with Iranian Twelver Shi'ism; supported the Rushdie fatwa.
Promoted Muslim Manifesto; see Muslim Parliament, below.»94

- **Muslim Institute for Research and Planning**
Dr Yaqub Zaki: [address unknown] London W6 8JA   »94

✿ **Muslim Kumbar Women's Group**
F. Boliya, President: 544 Uxbridge Road, Hayes UB4,
Middlesex; *t* (0181) 561 5253   »94

✿ **Muslim League**
Yusuf Akhtar: 19 Trafalgar Avenue, London SE15   »95

✿ **Muslim Mother Tongue Association**
Allah Dad: 18 Holly Lane, Smethwick, Warley B66 1QN;
t (0121) 558 6982
Mother-tongue education for Muslim children. Also listed
(1994) c/o S. Akhtar, 290 Tat Bank Road, Oldbury, Warley
B68, *t* 552 7376.   »94

- *The Muslim News*
Ahmed Versi, Editor: PO Box 380, Harrow HA2 6LL
Community newspaper.   »95

✿ **Muslim Parents Association** and Madrassa Talim-ul-Islam
M.A. Salam/A. Rahim: 443 Cheetham Hill Road, Cheetham,
Manchester M8 7PF; *t* (0161) 740 3351, 740 0577
Islamic education for local children, mainly Pakistani. See Al
Hilal Community Project, p93; UK Islamic Mission, p72.   »94

✿ **Muslim Parents Association Madressa**
68 Beaufort Street, Nelson BB9; *t* (01282) 606254   »94

- **The Muslim Parliament of Great Britain**
Dr Kalim Siddiqui: 6 Endsleigh Street, London WC1H 0DS;
t (0171) 388 2581, *f* 383 5006
Jahangir Mohammed deputy head, M. Ghaissudden, Massoud
Shadjareh. Also listed (1994) as PO Box 279, London WC1H
0HZ. Founded 1991; associated with the Muslim Institute,
above, and thus with Iranian Ja'fari Shi'ism, although it aspires
to represent all 2 million UK Muslims. Membership consists
largely of businessmen who fund the organisation.   »95

✿ **Muslim Prayer House and Community Centre**
Abdul Rahman: 1 Willow Crescent, Balsall Heath, Birmingham
B12 9NN; *t* (0121) 440 3502
Sunni religious and community centre.   »94

- **Muslim Rights International**
Yusuf M.I. Bhailok: Oak House, Bank Parade, Preston PR1 3TA
See also Lancashire Council of Mosques, p64.   »95

- **Muslim Schools Trust**
78 Gillespie Road, London N5 1LN; *t* (0171) 359 0280
Produces educational materials, including encyclopedia.   »94

✿ **Muslim Shia Ithna Asheri Jamaat of Essex**
32 Ockelford Avenue, Chelmsford CM1 2AP; *t* (01245)
250059
East African Asian society of Twelver Shi'ites.   »94

✿ **Muslim Society and Mosque**
152 Edward St, Nuneaton CV11 5RA; *t* (01203) 327882 »94

- **Muslim Solidarity Committee**
S.M.T. Wasti, General Secretary: 202 North Gower Street,
London NW1 2LY
Defends rights and values of the Islamic communities.   »95

✿ **Muslim Study Group**
26 Wilton Road, Sparkhill, Birmingham B11 4PX; *t* (0121)
773 2883   »94

- **Muslim Teachers Association**
S. Syed, Secretary: 146 Park Road, London NW8 7RG;
t (0171) 724 3363
Promotes Islamic education, and educational welfare of Muslim
children throughout UK; represents Muslim teachers and
parents; information and advice on educational matters.   »94

- **Muslim Unity Organisation**
[address unknown]
Hosted Wembley Islamic conference August 1994; reportedly
associated with Hizb Ut-Tahrir (Party of Liberation, p59) which
seeks establishment of global Islamic state.   »94

✿ **Muslim Welfare Association**
Qari Tassawar Ul-Haq, Chair: 98 Walford Road, Sparkbrook,
Birmingham B11 1QA; *t* (0121) 772 2396
Worship, education, advice service; represents local Muslim
community. See Washwood Heath Muslim Centre, p72.   »94

✿ ≡ Fazal Rahaman: 1 Lynndale Ave., Birkby, Huddersfield HD1
Association of same name listed (1993) c/o Manzoor Hussain,
39 St Johns Road, Birkby; there are several mosques in the
area so they may be separate groups.   »94

✿ ≡ N. Malik: 64 Beeches Road, West Bromwich B70 6HH;
t (0121) 236 0493   »94

✿ ≡ and Ghousia Mosque: R.G. Khan, President: 2a High
Street, Lye, Stourbridge DY9 8LF; *t* (01384) 893110
Sunni mosque, educational and community group. May be the
Lye Islamic Welfare Association listed (1993) at 92 Brook
Street, Lye, and at 13c Vale Street, Amblecote.   »94

✿ ≡ and Mosque: I.Y. Ginwalla, Secretary: 44-46 Rycroft
Street, Gloucester; *t* (01452) 416830
Founded 1961; religious education, funeral facilities.   »94

✿ ≡ and Jamia Mosque: Mohammed Riaz, Secretary: 52
Shrubhill Road, Worcester; *t* (01905) 396044   »94

✿ **Muslim Welfare Association Plaistow**
40 Newham Way, Canning Town, London E16 4ED; *t* (0181)
474 4936   »94

✿ **Muslim Welfare Centre**
Abdul Khaliq, Chair: 69 Fox Street, Edgley, Stockport SK3,
Lancashire; *t* (0161) 477 6592
Religious education, welfare; development of mosque.   »94

✿ ≡ and Mosque: 2 Nancroft Terrace, Leeds LS12 2DQ   »94

✿ **Muslim Welfare and Community Centre**
M. Dad: 61 Algernon Rd, Edgbaston, Birmingham B16 0HX»94

✿ **Muslim Welfare House**
196 Cheltenham Road, Cotham, Bristol BS6 5QZ   »94

✿ ≡ Mahmoud El-Kurdi, Secretary: 6 North Terrace, Spital,
Tongues, Newcastle-upon-Tyne NE2 4AD; *t* (0191) 232 3055
Islamic educational and social service organisation.   »94

✿ ≡ also Young Muslims Sheffield; Young Muslims Girls
Group: Abdul Razak Bougara, Chair: 10 Severn Road, Sheffield
S10 2SU; *t* (0114) 266 6446
Sunni religious, charitable and educational centre.   »94

✿ **Muslim Welfare Society, Darlaston and Wednesbury** and
Masjid-e-Omar
Mahmood Ebrahim Patel, Honorary Secretary: Bills Street,
Darlaston WS10 8BB; *t* (0121) 526 6596
Sunni mosque and educational society.   »94

✿ **Muslim Welfare Society, Madrassa and Mosque**
24-26 Hope Street, Dewsbury WF13 2BT; *t* (01924) 463529,
463524   »94

✿ **Muslim Welfare Society and Parents Association**
M. Rafique: 35 Selly Park Road, Birmingham B29 7PH
Possibly the same as the Selly Park Muslim Welfare Society,
listed (1994) c/o S.A. Malik, 1014 Pershore Road, Selly
Park, B29 7PX.   »94

- **Muslim Welfare Trust**
M. Hanif Hazi: [address unknown]   »94

✿ **Muslim Women's Association**
Mrs Bajwa: 57 Muirfield Drive, Mickleover, Derby DE3 5SP;
t (01332) 519212
Social, cultural, advisory and religious activities. »95
✿ ≡ Kharam Hasan: 63 Coombe Lane, London SW20 0BD »95
✿ ≡ and Madina House: Khanam Hassan, Chair: 146
Gloucester Place, London NW1 6DT; *t* (0171) 262 5314
Religious, charitable and social activities; children's home
offering temporary residential care. *The Muslim Woman.* »95
✿ **Muslim Women's Association of Croydon**
N. Sami: 61a Windmill Road, West Croydon, Surrey;
t (0181) 684 0599 »94
✿ **Muslim Women's Centre**
52 Mackenzie Road, Moseley, Birmingham B11 4EL »94
✿ **Muslim Women's Counselling Service**
6 Baldovan Place, Leeds LS8, Yorkshire »94
✿ **Muslim Women's Group** and Muslim Youth Organisation
Mrs Siddiqui: 72 Upper Tooting Road, Tooting, London
SW17; *t* (0181) 767 4894 »94
✿ **Muslim Women's Helpline**
Zarina Choudhry/Sarah Sheriff: 1st Floor, Unit 3, GEC Estate,
East Lane, Wembley HA9 7PX »95
✿ **Muslim Women's Welfare Association**
Meher Khan, Co-ordinator: School Annexe, Bickley Road,
Leyton, London E10 7HL; *t* (0181) 539 7478
Welfare, social security and immigration rights advice,
language classes, leisure and social activities. »94
✿ ≡ S. Sarwar: 83 Stopford Road, Plaistow, London E13
0NA; *t* (0181) 471 7648 »94
✿ ≡ Co-ordinator: 18 Trinity Road, Tooting, London SW17
7RE; *t* (0181) 767 6474
Women's advice and welfare service; housing, health, social
security, immigration, interpreting, childcare assistance. »94
● **Muslim Youth Association in the UK**
49 Chearsley Street, Deacon Way, London SE7 1SW »94
✿ **Muslim Youth Centre**
Waseem Siddiqui: 64 Foulser Road, Tooting, London SW17;
t (0181) 767 4894 »94
✿ **Muslim Youth Cultural Society**
M. Yasin: 3 Cranmer Grove, Cranmer Street, Nottingham
NG3 4HE; *t* (01602) 70325, 525177 »94
✿ **Muslim Youth Foundation**
Ali Akbar: c/o Jawaid Hosiery, Clydesdale House, 27 Turner
St, Manchester M4 1DY; *t* (0161) 832 5352, *f* 839 2104
Worship, welfare and recreational activities. »94
✿ **Muslim Youth Movement**
7 Kerry Terrace, Walton Road, Woking, Surrey »94
✿ **Muslimat UK**
Tahera Arju: 64 Tunis House, Harford St, London E1 4RP »95
● *MuslimWise*
Wise Muslim Publications, BM MuslimWise, London WC1N
3XX; *t* (0181) 902 5968, 902 6074
Youth and general interest magazine (12/yr). »90
✿ **Nagina Mosque and Urdu School**
Raja Zafer Iqbal, Secretary: 74 Werneth Hall Road, Coppice,
Oldham OL8 1QZ; *t* (0161) 626 0522
May be Nagina Mosque listed (1993) at 23a Fern St. »94
● **Naqshbandi Order**
175 Warren Road, Washwood Heath, Birmingham B8 2YD;
t (0121) 328 3478
A Sunni Sufi order characterised by an inner journey of faith,
and silent prayer (*dhikr khafi*). See also Jamia Naqshbandia
Nawabia, p63, and Naqshbandia Aslamiyya Spiritual Centre,
below; there is also a group of Naqshabandiya in Oxford. »94
✿ **Naqshbandia Aslamiyya Spiritual Centre**
1-5 Cob Wall, Whalley Old Rd, Blackburn BB1 5JJ »94
● **National Association of Muslim Youth (UK)**, NAMY
Mohammed Dhalech, Development Officer: Markfield
Conference Centre, Ratby Lane, Markfield, Leicester LE67
9RN; *t* (0116) 224 4950, *f* 224 4946
Also listed (1994) at 16 Stratton Road, Gloucester GL1 4HB;
t (01452) 504147, *f* 308739. Youth work and youth group
network. See Young Muslims, p73; CEMYC UK, p154. »94
✿ **Neeli Masjid and Islamic Centre** and Islamic Youth
Movement; UK Islamic Mission, Rochdale
M.S. Baleem: 25 Hare Street, Rochdale OL11 1JL; *t* (01706)
48094
Mosque, educational centre; weddings, funerals. »95
✿ **New Muslim Project**
Noor Camp/Batool Al Toma: Markfield Conference Centre,
Ratby Lane, Markfield, Leicester LE67 9RN »95
✿ **Newham Muslim Citizens Association**
M. Ahmad, Secretary: 81 Katherine Road, East Ham, London
E6; *t* (0181) 472 0018
Advice and information service. »94

✿ **Newham Muslim Council**
Z. Ali: 72 Boleyn Road, Forest Gate, London E7 9QE; *t* (0181)
472 1615 »94
✿ **Newham Muslim Women's Association**
Mrs Modi: 423 Romford Road, Forest Gate, London E7 8AB;
t (0181) 555 3784 »94
✿ **Newham North Islamic Association**
Shahan Hussain, Secretary: 88 Green Street, London E7 8JG;
t (0181) 472 6887
Mosque and community centre. »95
✿ **Noor-ul-Islam Mosque** *(Light of Islam Mosque)*
Raja Ajaib Khan, President: 2-4 Yarwood Street, off Rochdale
Road, Bury BL8, Lancashire; *t* (0161) 705 2891
Jinnah cultural, religious, educational and leisure centre. »94
✿ **Noor-Ul-Uloom Mosque**
M. Sadiq: 85 St Oswald Road, Small Heath, Birmingham B10
9RB; *t* (0121) 773 7036
Sunni mosque society. »94
✿ **North British Muslim Trust**
M. Chishti: 19 Lancaster Place, Blackburn BB2 6GT;
t (01254) 676618 »94
✿ **North London Mosque** and Muslim Community Centre
68-72 Cazenove Road, Stamford Hill, London N16; *t* (0181)
806 6540 mosque, 806 1147 centre »95
✿ **North Manchester Mosque**: Ibadur Rahman Trust
Dr Bashir Ahmed: 3 Woodlands Road, Cheetham Hill,
Manchester M8; *t* (0161) 740 3696, 643 5499
Mosque with largely Pakistani membership. »94
✿ **Norwich Ihsan Mosque**
A. Abdullah: Chapelfield East, Norwich; *t* (01603) 23337 »94
✿ **Nusrat-ul-Islam Mosque**
94-98 Preston Street, Bradford BD7 1JE; *t* (01274) 724488
Also listed (1993) at 10 Great Russell Street, BD7. »94
✿ ≡ 84 Hardy St, Oldham OL4 1DL; *t* (0161) 624 5727 »94
✿ **Obaid ul Rahman Islamic Society**
123 Biscot Road, Luton LU3 1AN; *t* (01582) 455092 »94
✿ **Old Trafford Muslim Society**
A. Chunara: 38 Carlton Street, Old Trafford, Manchester
M16 7EG; *t* (0161) 834 7268
Mainly Indian and Pakistani membership. Meets at and
manages Masjid-e-Noor, Stamford St, p65; runs madrassa.»93
✿ **Oldbury Mosque and Muslim Welfare Association** and
Sandwell Muslims Organisation, SMO
M. Hanif/Ghulam Choudhary: Old Labour Club, Oldbury Road,
Smethwick, Warley B66 1HN; *t* (0121) 565 2666, 565 5062
Worship; Islamic education. SMO provides welfare, housing,
immigration and social security advice, and interpreting. »94
✿ **Oldham Muslim Housing Association Ltd**, OMHA
The Director: 121 Union Street, Oldham OL1 1TE; *t* (0161)
620 2992, *f* 620 3973
Social housing for minority ethnic communities in Oldham,
Tameside, Bury, Manchester; 250 units in 1991. »91
✿ **Omar Mosque and Islamic Society**
85 King St, Loughborough LE11 1SD; *t* (01509) 214500 »94
● **Oxford Centre for Islamic Studies**
Dr Basit Mustafa/Dr F.A. Nizami: St Cross College, Oxford
OX1 3LZ; *t* (01865) 725077
Academic centre in association with the University of Oxford;
research, teaching and publishing on Islam and the Islamic
world. See *Journal of Islamic Studies*, p63. »95
✿ **Oxford Islamic Centre**
Sheikh Ahmed Bullock: 62 Kelburn Rd, Oxford OX4 3FH »95
✿ **Oxford Mosque Society**
Abdul Rashid, Secretary: 10-11 Bath Street, Oxford OX4
1AY; *t* (01865) 245547
Worship, religious education. »94
✿ **Oxford Muslim Welfare House** and Mosque
Aslam Khan: 2 Stanley Road, Cowley, Oxford OX4 1QZ;
t (01865) 243149 »94
✿ **Pan-Islamic Cultural Organization**
45a Barker Street, Lozells, Birmingham B19 »90
✿ **Pargham-e-Islam Trust** and UK Islamic Mission Birmingham
South; Muslim Booksellers
H.M. Idrees: 423 Stratford Road, Sparkhill, Birmingham B11
4LB; *t* (0121) 773 8301
Mosque, madrassa and bookshop. »95
✿ **Peckham Mosque**
1 Peckham High St, London SE15; *t* (0171) 703 5995 »94
✿ **Pendle Council of Mosques** and Medina Masjid and Islamic
Centre; Islamic Book Centre
Ghulam Hussain/Syed Akhtar Shah: 4-8 Forest Street, Nelson
BB9 7NB; *t* (01282) 694471
Worship, language classes, Islamic studies. Centre run by
local branch of UK Islamic Mission, but Council of Mosques
seeks to represent all local Muslim organisations. »95

✺ **Portsmouth Muslim Society**
90 Westbourne Avenue, Emsworth, Hampshire   »94
✺ **Preston Hanfi Sunni Muslim Society** and Masjid-e-Aqsa
Haji Sandal Hussain, Secretary: 95-97 Fishwick Parade,
Preston PR1 4XR; t (01772) 764644
Society of the Hanafi *madhhab* (rite). Urdu classes.   »94
✺ **Preston Muslim Cultural Centre**
Farook Hasangee: 21 Fishergate Hill, Preston PR1 8JB;
t (01772) 824357   »94
✺ **Preston Muslim Society** and Jamia Masjid
Osman Monshi, Honorary Secretary: 18 Clarendon Street,
Preston PR1 3YN; t (01772) 257127   »94
✺ **Preston and West Lancashire Council of Mosques**
Ibrahim Kabir, Chair: 4 Varley Street, Preston PR1, Lancs.»94
● **Q News**
Faud Nahdi, Editor: Washington House, 40-41 Conduit Street,
London W1R 9FB; t (0171) 734 4887, f 734 4891
English-language liberal newspaper (52/yr), founded 1992.»95
✺ **Quba Culra Mosque**
120 Worksop Road, Attercliffe, Sheffield S9, Yorkshire;
t (0114) 244 0235   »94
✺ **Quwat-ul-Islam Mosque**
A.E. Qureshi, Chair: 97 Florence Rd, Smethwick, Warley B66
Worship, advice, adult education, social/leisure activities. »94
✺ **Quwatul Islam Masjid**
Haji Misri Khan: 99 Fennel Crescent, Broadfield, Crawley
RH11 9DT; t (01293) 526895
Mosque associated with the local Jamiat ul Muslemeen.   »95
✺ **Quwwat-ul-Islam Mosque and Islamic Society**
Maulana Osman Adam: 62-66 Upton Lane, London E7 9LN;
t (0181) 472 1072, 534 4248
South Asian mosque.   »94
✺ **Quwwatul Islam Markazi Jamia Mosque Mehria Ghosia**
Khadam Hussain: Hill Crest, 150 St Albans Hill, Bennetts End,
Hemel Hempstead HP3 9NH; t (01442) 43785
Organising society for mosque at 262 Correrells.   »94
✺ **Quwwatul Islam Mosque** and Preston Muslim Society
Peelhall Street, Deepdale, Preston PR1 6QQ; t (01772)
254578
Worship, educational and social facilities.   »94
✺ **The Raza Academy**
M.I. Kashmiri, Chairperson: 138 Northgate Road, Edgeley,
Stockport SK3 9NL, Lancashire; t (0161) 477 1595
Dr Muhammad Haroon director. Sunni publishing house and
conference organisation. *The Islamic Times* (12/yr).   »95
✺ **Raza Jamiah Mosque and Islamic Centre**
Haji F. Ellahi, Chairman: 229 Blackburn Road, Accrington
BB5, Lancashire; t (01254) 233740
Also listed (1994) at Grimshaw Street.   »94
✺ **Raza Mosque**
41 Selbourne Street, Chuckery, Walsall; t (01922) 31586
Sunni mosque. Possibly same as the Jame Ghosia listed
(1994) at 14 Selbourne Street.   »94
✺ ≡ and Muslim Welfare Society: I. Sulliman, Secretary: 71
Blade Street, Lancaster LA1 1TS; t (01524) 32087
Worship, education, welfare and funeral service.   »94
✺ ≡ and Hanfi Sunni Muslim Circle: 44-48 Alton Street,
Blackburn BB1 7NG; t (01254) 52608
Mosque of the Hanafi *madhhab*, the largest of the four Sunni
schools of law.   »94
✺ **Reading Federation of Muslim Organisations** and Islamic
Society
Dr A. Razzak: 26 Apple Close, Tilehurst, Reading RG3 6UR»95
✺ **Reading Islamic Centre**
A.H. Khan, Secretary: 52 South Street, Reading RG1 4RA;
t (01734) 504756
Religious, cultural and educational centre.   »94
✺ **Reading Muslim Women's Association**
Mrs Abdulla, President: 24 Shepherds House Lane, Earley,
Reading RG6, Berkshire; t (01734) 666606
Social, leisure and cultural activities for Muslim women. »94
✺ **Rochdale Muslim Society**
A. Rauf: 47 Norford Way, Bamford, Rochdale OL11 5QS   »94
✺ **Rowley Regis Muslim Welfare Association**
Umar Faruq: 99 Beeches Road, Rowley Regis, Warley B65,
West Midlands; t (0121) 559 7954   »94
✺ **Rugby Mosque Committee**
Grosvenor Hall, 88 Grosvenor Road, Rugby CV21; t (01788)
543680   »94
✺ **Saddam Hussein Mosque**
Birchfield Road, Perry Barr, Birmingham B20   »94
✺ **St Catherine Street Mosque Committee**
M. Mughal: 169 Agbrigg Road, Wakefield WF1 5BN;
t (01924) 71469
Manages nearby mosque at 26 St Catherine Street.   »94

✺ **Salford Mosque**
4 Harris Avenue, Davyhulme, Manchester M31; t (0161)
748 9261
See also Dar-ul-Aman Housing Association, p93.   »94
✺ **Sandwell Central Mosque Trust** and Ittehad-ul-Muslemeen
S.J. Shah: 49 Barker Street, Oldbury, Warley B68, West
Midlands; t (0121) 552 6775, 552 8679   »94
✺ **Savile Town Muslim Jamaat** and Tabligi Markaz
Yusuf Adam Patel: Thornleigh, 7-11 Savile Grove, Savile
Town, Dewsbury WF12 9LB; t (01924) 464609, 461427,
457111
Also listed (1994) at Zakaria Mosque, 2 Chapel Street, Savile
Town, WF12 9NQ. Founded 1967; social centre, weddings,
funerals; educational/community welfare activities.   »94
✺ **Shah Jalal Mosque**
H. Rahman, Chair: 32-33 Mount Street, Walsall WS1, West
Midlands; t (01922) 647624
Mosque established 1985, some 300 members.   »94
✺ ≡ and Islamic Centre: 112-114 Burns St, Burnley BB12 0AJ
See also Bangladesh Welfare Association mosque, p17.   »94
✺ ≡ and Islamic Centre: 1a Eileen Grove, off Platt Lane,
Rusholme, Manchester M14 5WE; t (0161) 248 7115   »94
✺ ≡ and Islamic Cultural Centre: 13a Longholme Road,
Rawtenstall, Rossendale BB4 7NG   »94
✺ **Shair-E-Rabbani Islamic Centre**
33 Granby Street, London E2 6DR; t (0171) 739 6046   »94
✺ **Sheffield Islamic Centre** and Madina Mosque
M. Nazir, Secretary: 24-32 Wolseley Rd, Sheffield S8 0ZU;
t (0114) 258 5021, 255 0391
Worship, Islamic education, social and welfare activities,
elderly day care.   »94
✺ **Sheffield, Rotherham and District Council of Muslims**
Dr A.K. Admani: 1 Derriman Glen, Silverdale Road, Sheffield
S11 9LQ; t (0114) 236 0465   »94
✺ **Shepherd's Bush Mosque** and Muslim Community Centre
Dr Ahmed Badat, Chair: 302 Uxbridge Road, Shepherd's
Bush, London W12 7LJ; t (0181) 740 0463, f 742 9070
Worship, cultural, educational and social activities for
multinational congregation.   »95
✺ **Shepherd's Bush Mosque Committee**
112 Godolphin Rd, London W12 7EY; t (0181) 740 0463 »94
✺ **Shi'a Islamic Centre**
Nazir Hussain, Secretary: 143 Preston New Road, Blackburn
BB2 6BJ; t (01254) 26559
Shi'ite mosque, library, educational and community group. »94
✺ **Shia Ithna-Asheri Jama'at Mosque**
127 Loughborough Rd, Leicester LE4 5LQ; t (0116) 268 2828
Khoja Twelver mosque.   »94
✺ **Shia Ithna Asheri Mosque**
Mahmood Huda: 2 Burton Street, Peterborough PE2 5HD;
t (01733) 62187
Khoja Twelver community from East Africa.   »94
✺ **SI Education Society**
Moulana S.S.S. Rizvi: 133 Rowan Road, London SW16 5HU;
t (0181) 679 7778 admin, 679 2188 info; f 679 6363
Produces and disseminates educational material, including
audiovisual resources, on Islam; courses and seminars.   »94
✺ **Slough Islamic Trust** and Jame Masjid Ghousia
29 Diamond Road, Slough SL1 1RX; t (01753) 512994   »94
✺ **Small Heath Mosque**
6 Johnson Close, Birmingham B8 2RF; t (0121) 784 3930»94
✺ **Smethwick Mosque**
89 Edgbaston Road, Smethwick, Warley B66 4LF; t (0121)
558 4077   »94
✺ **Smethwick Pakistani Muslims Association** and Anwar-ul-
Uloom Mosque
Mohammed Azad, Chair: 1-7 Corbett Street, Smethwick,
Warley B66 3PY; t (0121) 555 6047
Sunni community group, advisory/educational activities. »94
✺ **South-East Islamic Society**
Dr Taleeb Dugahee, Secretary: 209 Kings Drive, Eastbourne
BN21 2UJ; t (01323) 638755   »94
✺ **South East London Muslim Association** and Mosque
51 Elm Grove, off Rye Lane, Peckham, London SE15 5DB;
t (0171) 639 4589
Sunni religious and welfare society.   »94
✺ **South London Islamic Centre**
Abdur Rahman Bazmi, Convenor: 19 Tremaine Road, London
SE20 7UA; t (0181) 659 1303   »94
✺ ≡ A.R. Lone, Manager: 8 Mitcham Lane, Streatham, London
SW16 6NN; t (0181) 677 0588
Worship, religious and language teaching, welfare and advice
service, youth and women's groups, funeral service.   »95
✺ **South London Muslim Association**
M.I. Mohamed: 76 Elmwood Rd, West Croydon CR0 2SJ »94

✧ **Southend Islamic Trust** and Mosque; Southend Muslim
Association; Young Muslim Organisation
191 Westborough Road, Westcliff-on-Sea SS0 9DH;
t (01702) 347265   »94
✧ **Southwark Muslim Association** and Southwark Muslim
Women's Association
Zafar Iqbal: Bellenden Old School, Bellenden Road, London
SE15; *t* (0171) 732 8053
Community and resource centre for Pakistanis and others.»94
✧ **Sparkbrook Islamic Centre** and Islamic Book House
Mohammed Azfal: 179-187 Anderton Road, Sparkbrook,
Birmingham B11 1ND; *t* (0121) 773 8651, 772 5352
Large mosque; community centre, with social, welfare,
educational and inter-faith activities; incorporates bookshop
and Birmingham Central branch of UK Islamic Mission.   »95
✧ **Stepney Mosque**
25 Tunis House, Harford Street, London E1 4RP;
t (0171) 790 1807   »94
✧ **Stirling Islamic Centre**
39 Bannockburn Road, St Ninian, Stirling FK7 0BU, Scotland;
t (01786) 74324   »94
✧ **Stoneyholme Jamia Masjid and Islamic Centre**
M.S. Qadri: 102 Rectory Road, Burnley BB12 0BP; *t* (01282)
422358   »94
✧ **Student Islamic Society**
48 Shaftesbury Road, Bournemouth BH8 8SZ   »94
● **Sufi Order of the Chisti**
Sufi House, Barton Farm, Bradford-upon-Avon, Wiltshire;
t (01221) 64174
One of the largest South Asian Sufi orders, with distinctive
practices including devotional music and song.   »94
● **Sufi Order (International)**
Sufi House, 6 Parkwood Road, Wimbledon, London SW19»94
● **Sufi Order of the West**, London Sufi Centre for Holistic
Studies
21 Lancaster Road, London W11; *t* (0171) 221 3215
Also listed (1994) at 58 St Stephen's Gardens, W2. One
of a large number of mystical orders within Islam, this
group engages in meditation, retreat, dance and worship in
line with the teachings of Hazrat Inayat Khan.   »95
✧ **Sufi Way**
Wendy Rose-Neil: Four Winds, High Thicket Road,
Dockenfield GU10 4HB; *t* (01251) 253990
A 'non-sectarian' grouping within the Sufi spiritual tradition,
followers of the late shaikh Hazrat Inayat Khan.   »94
✧ **Sughra Mosque**
Bashir Ahmed, Secretary: back Granville Street, Farnworth,
Bolton BL4 7LD; *t* (01204) 73497
See Madina Mosque, p64, and Masjeed-e-Quba, p65.   »94
✧ **Sunderland Mosque**
Syed Jamil Miah: 75 Chester Road, Sunderland SR2; *t* (0191)
565 8708
Was (1993) 21 Westernhill Rd, off Chester Rd, SR2 7PH. »94
✧ **Sunni Mosque**
60 Cromwell Rd, Peterborough PE1 2EB; *t* (01733) 67285»94
✧ **Sunni Muslim Association**
12 Ansdale Street, Cheetham Hill, Manchester M8
Mainly Pakistani membership; advice and liaison service funded
by City Council. May be same as the Associations listed
(1994) at 20 Bridesoak St and 27 Greenstead Drive, M8. »94
✧ **Sunni Muslim Jamat**
H.S. Majothi, Chairperson: 14 Lanbourne Street, Leicester
LE2 6HL; *t* (0116) 288 4505
Religious, cultural, social group of women and men.   »94
● **Supreme Council of British Muslims**
Ishtiaq Ahmed, Chairman: 13 Mannheim Road, Bradford BD9
Established 1991 at conference of 200 imams and other
leaders; opposed UK involvement in the Gulf war.   »95
✧ **Surati Muslim Khalifa Society**
Mustafa F. Karim, Co-ordinator: 127 Mere Road, Leicester LE5
5GQ; *t* (0116) 251 1120, 262 5919
Religious, social, cultural, educational and welfare group. »94
✧ **Surti Khalifa Sunatwal Society** and Mosque
27 (or 127?) Ventnor St, off Leeds Rd, Bradford BD3 9JZ »94
✧ **Sussex Muslim Society** and Muslim Ladies Circle
Imam Dr Abduljalil Sajid, Director: 8 Caburn Road, Hove
BN3 6EF; *t* (01273) 505247, 722438, *f* 540058
Rafique Miah chair, Mahir Choudhury secretary; founded 1962;
30 affiliates. See Muslim Community Centre, p67, Brighton
Islamic Mission, p56, World Islamic Forum, p72. Ladies Circle
founded 1983; Yasmin Ahmed secretary. Bulletin (4/yr). »94
✧ **Sutton Islamic Centre**
Misdiq Zaida: 62 Oakhill Road, Sutton, Surrey   »94
✧ **Swindon Ismaili Community**
A.A. Moledina: 32 County Road, Swindon SN1 2EW   »94

✧ **Ta Ha Publishers Ltd**
1 Wynne Road, London SW9 0BB; *t* (0171) 737 7266, *f* 737
7267
Distributes Islamic books; see Al-Furqan Trust, p55.   »94
✧ **Taiyabah Mosque and Community Centre**
31a Draycott Street, Bolton BL1 8HD; *t* (01204) 35997
Mosque of the same name was listed (1994) at 3 Eckersley
Road, BL1 8EA (I. Patel).   »94
✧ **Taiyyibah Mosque and Madressa**, also known as Penfield
Mosque
84 Lime St, Wolverhampton; *t* (01902) 773870, 711831
Member of Confederation of Sunni Mosques, p57, although
name suggests Musta'li minor branch of Isma'ili Shi'ism. »94
✧ **Taleem ul Islam Trust**
28 Chelsea Park, Bristol BS5 6AG; *t* (0117) 955 8155   »94
✧ **Talim-ul-Qur'an** and Mosque
Mr Sadiq: 1 Ashford Street, Shelton, Stoke-on-Trent ST1,
Staffordshire; *t* (01782) 416179
Religious education, worship, community welfare.   »94
✧ **Tamilmul Quran Mosque and Madressa**
G. Mustaffa, Imam: 63 Severn Road, off Cowbridge Road,
Centon, Cardiff, Wales; *t* (01222) 397640   »94
✧ **Tawakkulia Islamic Society and Mosque**
48 Cornwall Road, Bradford BD8; *t* (01274) 734563   »94
✧ **Tehrik-i-Nizam-i-Qurran e Sunnah** *(Movement for the
Qu'ran and the Way?)*
H.I. Faryad, Director: 395 Sydenham Road, West Croydon
CR0 2EH; *t* (0181) 689 3870   »94
✧ **Thamesdown Islamic Association**
19 Broomfield, Chippenham, Wiltshire   »94
✧ ≡ K.A. Nawaz: 12 Don Close, Greenmeadow, Swindon,
Wiltshire; *t* (01793) 693569   »94
✧ **Tipton Muslim Trust Association** and Mosque
Montaz Ali: 17 Wellington Road, Tipton DY4 8RS; *t* (0121)
557 2692
Mainly-Bangladeshi mosque and community association. »94
✧ **Tipton and Tividale Islamic Centre**
24 Gate Street, Tipton DY4; *t* (0121) 520 5357
Sunni community centre.   »94
✧ **Tipton and Tividale Muslim Welfare Association**
R.A. Qayyum: 10 Gate St, Tipton DY4; *t* (0121) 520 5832
Also listed (1994) at 92 Tividale Road, Tividale.   »94
✧ **Torbay Islamic Centre**
130 Avenue Road, Torquay TQ2 5LQ; *t* (01803) 211818 »94
● **Union of Muslim Families in Great Britain**
Faizullah Khan: 55 Balfour Road, London N5 2HD; *t* (0171)
226 0934   »94
♦ **Union of Muslim Organisations of the United Kingdom and
Éire**, UMO, and National Muslim Education Council of the UK
Dr Syed Aziz Pasha, Secretary: 109 Campden Hill Rd, Notting
Hill Gate, London W8 7TL; *t* (0171) 792 2130, 221 6608
Links 200 mosques and societies concerned with education,
family law, mosques; founded 1970, aspires to represent all
Muslims in UK and Ireland; member of EU Migrants Forum,
p131. Education Council, founded 1978, works on Islamic
schools, and Islamic content in state school curriculum. »95
● **United Kingdom Action Committee**
Iqbal Sacranie: 2a Crown Road, New Malden KT3 3UW   »95
✧ **UK Islamic Academy**, also known as Madressa e Ramiyah
147 Mere Road, Leicester LE5 5GQ   »94
♦ **UK Islamic Mission**: Central Office and North London Branch
Syed Sharif Ahmed: 202 North Gower Street, London NW1
2LY; *t* (0171) 387 2157, 380 0465, *f* 383 0867
Network of 50 missionary centres throughout Britain, founded
1962; derives from the Pakistan-based Jama'at-i Islami.
Objectives include establishment of Islamic social order in UK;
co-ordination with other Islamic bodies, development of Islamic
education, supply of speakers to schools. Some branches are
listed below; see also Muslim Solidarity Committee, p68;
Islamic Youth Movement, p62; Islamic Centre, Jamia Mosques
and Pargham-e-Islam Trust, Birmingham, pp60, 63, 69; Jame
Masjid-e-Noor, p62; Madrasa Al Arabia Al Islamia, p65;
Mosque and Islamic Centre, Glasgow and Walsall, p67;
Blackheath Islamic Community Centre, p56; Hull Mosque and
Islamic Centre, p59; Islamic Book Centre and Masjid-e-Bilal,
London, pp60, 65; Madina Masjid, Luton and Manchester,
p64; Neeli Masjid, p69. (North London Branch also listed
(1993) at 148 Liverpool Road, N1.)   »95
✧ ≡ 3 Byron Street, Bradford BD3 0AD; *t* (01274) 306299
See also Marlborough Road Mosque, p65.   »95
✧ ≡ 54 Hebrew Road, Burnley BB10 1NQ; *t* (01282) 426245
Also listed (1994) at 52 Gordon St, BB12 0AX, *t* 421430.»95
✧ ≡ 1 Tydfil Pl., Roath Park, Cardiff CF2; *t* (01222) 495587
Also listed (1993) at 3 Crwys Road, Cathays, and 21 Glenroy
Street, Roath, both in Cardiff.   »95

✧ **UK Islamic Mission**: Stockton-on-Tees
9 Kenley Gardens, Norton, Clydeland TS20 1QF; *t* (01642)
556512   »95
✿ ≡ 66 Kilnmead, Northgate, Crawley RH10 2BE; *t* (01293)
528485   »94
✿ ≡ 11 Ailsa Close, Broadfield, Crawley RH11 9DW   »94
✿ ≡ and Mosque, Madrassa: M. Iqbal: 10-12 Belgrave Road,
Keighley BD21; *t* (01538) 680914   »95
✿ ≡ Glynbedw, Cwmamm, Lampeter, Dyfed, Wales;
t (01570) 423105   »95
✿ ≡ 12 Wentworth Crescent, Leeds LS17 7TW; *t* (0113)
268 4560   »95
✿ ≡ Sadiq Khokar, Chair: 41 Gwendolen Road, Leicester LE5
5SL; *t* (0116) 273 0043
Also listed (1994) at 8 Palmerston Boulevard, Leicester LE2
3YR, *t* 288 1129.   »95
✿ ≡ and Islamic Society of Britain: Dr A.Z. Khan: 119 Queen's
Drive, Mossley Hill, Liverpool L18 1JL; *t* (0151) 733 2940»95
✿ ≡ London South: 72 Holmdene Avenue, London SE24 9LE;
t (0171) 274 2979   »95
✿ ≡ London West: 121 Oaklands Road, Hanwell, London W7
2DT; *t* (0181) 579 2185 mosque, 567 5898   »95
✿ ≡ Manchester North; and Islamic Book Centre: Qari
Badruddin: 443 Cheetham Hill Road, Cheetham, Manchester
M8 7PF; *t* (0161) 740 3351
See also Al Hilal Community Project, p93; Madrassa Talim-ul-
Islam, p68. The Mission is also listed (1994) at 3 Walcott
Close, M13 9AP; 371 Wilmslow Road, Fallowfield, M14 6AH,
t 224 5479. See also Madina Masjid, M19, p64.   »95
✿ ≡ 2 Firtree Avenue, Mitcham, Surrey   »94
✿ ≡ Oldham East: 77 Retford Street, Glodwick, Oldham OL4
1BL; *t* (0161) 678 6772   »95
✿ ≡ Oldham South: A. Butt: 44 Manchester Road, Werneth,
Oldham OL9 7AP; *t* (0161) 678 6772   »95
✿ ≡ and Mosque: Karamat Hussain: 311 Cromwell Road,
Peterborough PE1 2HP; *t* (01733) 51759, 54425   »95
✿ ≡ F. Culasy, Secretary: 4 Palmerstone Rd, Earley, Reading
RG6 1HL; *t* (01734) 661894   »95
✿ ≡ 537 Abbeydale Rd, Sheffield S7 1TA; *t* (0114) 250 8695
See also Pakistan Chhachhi Association, p94.   »95
✿ ≡ 106 St Paul's Ave., Slough SL2 5ER; *t* (01753) 520607»95
✿ ≡ Wasim Darr, President: 186 Priory Road, St Denys,
Southampton SO2 1HS; *t* (01703) 584798   »95
✿ ≡ and Islamic Youth Movement: 52a Milton Street, Pleck,
Walsall WS1 4JS; *t* (01922) 20461
Mosque also listed (1994) at 25 Corporation Street, WS1
4HW, *t* 20982.   »94
✿ ≡ and Mosque: 6 Lockwood Path, Sheerwater, Woking
GU21 5RH; *t* (01932) 345416   »95
✿ ≡ and Young Muslims Wolverhampton: M. Hanif: 213
Newhampton Road East, Whitmore Reans, Wolverhampton
WV1 4BB; *t* (01902) 711304
Also listed (1993) at 35-38 Austin Street, Whitmore Reans;
and 9 Shaw Road, Wolverhampton.   »95
✿ ≡ and Mosque: S. Khan: Bull Lane Compound, Hull Road,
York YO1 3EN; *t* (01904) 413123   »95
✧ **UK Islamic Trust**
9-15 Shacklewell Lane, London E8; *t* (0181) 254 0431   »94
✧ **United Kingdom Muslim Women Association**
M. Hussain: 83 Denison Rd, Rusholme, Manchester M14 5RN
Mainly Pakistani membership.   »93
✧ **United Moslem Organization**
Dr Mohammed Kauser, Chairman: [address unknown]
Strathclyde, Scotland   »88
✧ **United Muslim Committee**
14 Victoria Road, Halesowen B26, West Midlands   »94
✧ **UWAIS Foundation**
Malik Chaudhry: 126 Ladykirk Road, Fenham, Newcastle-
upon-Tyne NE4; *t* (0191) 232 7639
Muslim charitable trust.   »94
✧ **Victoria Park Mosque** also known as South Manchester
Jamia Mosque
Dr Bashir Ahmed: 32 Upper Park Road, Victoria Park,
Manchester M14 5RU; *t* (0161) 224 4119
Mainly Pakistani membership.   »94
✧ **Waltham Forest Muslim Welfare Society** and Masjid Al-Aqsa
Z.A.R. Oomerjee, Secretary: 79 Queens Road, Walthamstow,
London E17; *t* (0181) 520 2658
Mosque, social centre, religious education and welfare. »94
✧ **Washwood Heath Muslim Centre** and Madrassah Qasim Ul-
Uloom
Qari Tassawar Ul-Haq, Director: 790 Washwood Heath Road,
Washwood Heath, Birmingham B8 2JG; *t* (0121) 327 7434
Mosque, madrassah and community centre. See also Muslim
Welfare Association, Sparkbrook, p68.   »94

✧ **Wembley Mosque and Islamic Centre**
5 Stanley Avenue, near Alperton Station, Wembley,
Middlesex; *t* (0181) 902 3258   »94
✧ **Werneth Mosque and Urdu School**
M. Khan: 48 Hereford Street, Oldham OL9 7RQ; *t* (0161)
652 8018   »94
✧ **Wessex Shi'a Ithna 'Asheri Jamat**
Jaffer Dharamsi: 42 Beechwood Close, Chandler's Ford SO5
1DB; *t* (01705) 550142
A Twelver Shi'ite society (i.e. holds that the clergy represent
the unrevealed twelfth Imam, to emerge as the Mahdi). »94
✧ **West End Mosque**
10 Berwick Street, London W1; *t* (0171) 437 8840   »94
✧ **West London Islamic Centre**
A. Vora, Secretary: 120 North Road, Southall UB1 2JR;
t (0181) 574 8037
Cultural/educational activities, welfare/immigration advice.»94
✧ **West Lothian Mosque and Community Centre**
Anwar ul-Haq: 14 Gleneagles Way, Deans South, Livingston,
Edinburgh EH54 8DP, Scotland   »94
✧ **Wimbledon Mosque**
M.A. Hamid, Chair: 264 Durnsford Road, Wimbledon Park,
London SW19 8DS; *t* (0181) 946 3350
Worship, religious education, community centre.   »94
✧ **Woking Muslim Association** and Shah Jehan Mosque
149 Oriental Rd, Woking GU22 7BA; *t* (014862) 60679 (?)»94
◆ **World Ahl Ul-Bayt (A.S.) Islamic League**
Mohsin Jaffer: 57 Church Drive, North Harrow HA2 7NR;
t (0181) 954 9881, 868 9972
International Shi'a community organisation; religious, social
and economic concerns, inter-Muslim and inter-faith under-
standing; conferences, publishing. See also World Federation
of Khoja Shia Ishna Ath'ari Communities, below.   »94
✧ **World Ahl Ul-Bayt League**
Yusuf Al Khoei: Stone Hall, Chevening Rd, London NW6 6TN
Shia organisation. See also Al Khoei Foundation, p55; British
Shia Muslim Action Committee, p57.   »95
● **World Assembly of Muslim Youth**
PO Box 3239, London NW6 1LH
Also at 46 Goodge Street, W1, *t* (0171) 636 7010. Youth
branch of the (Saudi-backed) World Muslim League.   »95
● **World Council of Muslim Youth**
47 Wellington Road, Edgbaston, Birmingham B15 2EP   »94
■ **World Federation of Khoja Shia Ithna Ash'ari Muslim
Communities**, and (local) Khoja Shia Ithna Ash'ari Muslim
Community
Dr A.G. Lakha/Mohsin Jaffer: PO Box 60, Warren House,
Wood Lane, Stanmore HA7 4LQ; *t* (0181) 954 9881, 954
6247, *f* 954 9034, 954 8028
Education and welfare alliance of Khoja Twelver Shi'ite groups,
those in UK mainly Ugandan Asians. The World Centre
maintains links with Khoja groups in Canada and elsewhere.
See World Ahl Ul-Bayt (A.S.) Islamic League, above.   »95
● **World Islamic Council**
PO Box 1736, London E10 6NF   »94
● **World Islamic Forum** and Khatme Nubuwwat Centre
Moulana Zahid ur Rashdi, Chairman: 35 Stockwell Green,
London SW9 9HZ; *t* (0171) 737 8199, *f* 978 9067-78
Mohammed Essa Mansuri, Alhaj Abdur Rahman Bawa. Mainly
Pakistani Muslims; correspondents in Denmark, USA, Canada
and elsewhere. Khatme Nubawwat Centre is a place of
worship (possibly of Khatmiya/Mirghaniya Sufi order?). »94
✧ **World Islamic Mission**
G. Haider, General Secretary: 28 Essex Road, Manor Park,
London E12 6RE; *t* (0181) 552 9050
East London Branch of a da'wa movement.   »94
✿ ≡ Mohummed Iqbal: 156 Biscot Road, Luton LU3,
Bedfordshire; *t* (01582) 480881   »94
● **World Islamic Mission (UK)**
M.J. Siddiqui, Director: 17 Burston Drive, Park Street, St
Albans, Hertfordshire; *t* (01727) 72511
Propagation of Islam, relations with other faith communities,
education; books, journals in Urdu, Arabic, English; over
20,000 members. See Jamiyat Tabligh-ul-Islam, p63. *Hijaz;
Message International* (both 12/yr).   »94
◆ **World Muslim League**, London Office
Dr Bassim Alim, Director: 46 Goodge St, London W1P 1FJ
One of the main (Saudi-based) international Islamic bodies, see
p54. See Darul Ifta UK, p58; Council of Mosques (UK and
Éire), p57; Institute of Muslim Minority Affairs, p60.   »94
✧ **Worthing Muslim Society**, also known as Islamic Society of
Worthing
Shafiat Hussain Khan: 157 Tarring Rd, Worthing BN12 2JG;
t (01903) 231192
An offshoot of the Muslim Community Centre, p67.   »95

✧ **York Muslim Association**
A. Karbani: 75 Dodsworth Avenue, Heworth, York YO3 7TZ;
t (01904) 426261   »94
✧ **Yorkshire Muslim Association**
Adambhai Davi: [address unknown] Dewsbury WF12   »94
✧ **Young Muslim Association**
J.A. Sharif: 95 Beulah Road, Thornton Heath, Croydon CR4
8JG; *t* (0181) 653 0957   »94
● **Young Muslim Organisation**
Mussadiq Ahmad, President: 54 Fieldgate Street, London E1
1ES; *t* (0171) 247 7918
Educational, cultural and leisure group; also in Birmingham.»94
✧ **Young Muslim Women's Group**
Nina Akhter: c/o 11 Peartree Crescent, Derby DE3 8RN;
t (01332) 766225
Meets at the Madeley Centre, Rosehill Street.   »94
✧ **Young Muslims**
Ahtisham Ali: Markfield Conference Centre, Ratby Lane,
Markfield, Leicester LE6 0RN
Same as National Association of Muslim Youth (UK), p69?»95
● **Young Muslims**
Nasir Nazar: 443 Cheetham Hill Road, Cheetham, Manchester
M8 7TF; *t* (0161) 740 3351
Mainly Pakistani youth religious education group. Possibly
same as Young Muslim (or Muslims) Organisation.   »94
✧ **Young Muslims (Girls Section)**
Tahira Baig/Bushra Abu Tayeeb: 141 Montgomery St, Hove
BN3 5FP; *t* (01273) 771309, 608292   »94
✧ **Young Muslims Loughborough**
Mahboob-ur-Rashid Chowdhury, President: 79 Empress Road,
Loughborough LE11 1RH; *t* (01509) 212942, *f* 210912   »94
✧ **Young Muslims Organisation**
A. Hannan, President: 2 Kimberley Road, Smethwick, Warley
B66, West Midlands; *t* (0121) 558 7581
Islamic education, leisure and welfare activities for Muslim
youth. See also Bangladeshi Eshat-Ul-Islam (UK), p17.   »94
✧ **Zahra Trust UK**
Aliya Haeri: PO Box 1021, London W2 4JQ
Sufi educational and publishing organisation.   »94
✧ **Zakaria Mosque**
Ayoob Limbada: 20 Peace Street, Bolton BL3 5LJ; *t* (01204)
350002   »94
✧ ≡ and Madressa: M. Iqbal Yusuf: 22-24 Clarendon Road,
Whalley Range, Manchester M16 8LD; *t* (0161) 881 9976,
881 7277, 881 9860
Mainly Pakistani membership.   »94
✧ **Zakariya Muslim Girls' High School**
111 Warwick Road, Batley WF17 6AJ; *t* (01924) 444217
Fee-paying secondary school opened 1982; 150 pupils.   »94
✧ **Zawiya Islamic Centre**
Cllr S. Abdi: 126 Pershore Road, Edgbaston, Birmingham B5
7NY; *t* (0121) 440 1347
Social, welfare, women's and youth activities.   »94
✧ **Zawiya Mosque**, also known as Birmingham Islamia
Allaouiazwya
Sheikh Mohamed Kassam: 294 Edwards Road, Edgbaston,
Birmingham B5 7PH; *t* (0121) 440 1758, 440 5746
Founded 1943 as Birmingham's first mosque.   »94

◎ **NORTHERN IRELAND** *44*

✧ **Belfast Islamic Centre**
Dr Mamoun, President: 38 Wellington Park, Belfast BT9 6DN;
t (01232) 664465
Religious, educational and cultural centre.   »95

ISRAELI

see also Arab/Arabic, Jewish, Middle Eastern, Palestinian.
Note: the words israelita/israélite, *in the names of French,*
Portuguese or Spanish organisations, generally mean Jewish

◎ **FRANCE** *33*

● **Association France Israël**
63 boulevard Sébastopol, 75001 Paris; *t* (1) 4233 3682,
4508 4661   »90

◎ **NETHERLANDS** *31*

● **Centrum Informatie en Documentatie over Israël**, CIDI
R.A. Levisson/R.M. Naftaniel: Postbus 11646, 2502 AP Den
Haag; *t* (070) 364 6862, *f* 365 3372
Established in 1974 to combat racism, antisemitism and anti-
Zionism; library and archive, access by appointment; research,
publishing, public speaking. *Anti-semitisme onderzoek*. »94

◎ **UNITED KINGDOM** *44*

● **Anglo-Israel Association**, AIA
Cedric Mercer, Director: 9 Bentinck Street, London W1M 5RP;
t (0171) 486 2300, 935 9505
Dr Henri Stellman. Friendship, cultural exchanges and
educational grants; founded 1949.   »95
● **Joint Israel Appeal**
Alan Fix, Executive Chairman: Balfour House, High Road,
North Finchley, London N12
Promotes economic and political interests of Israel.   »94

ITALIAN

see also European, Slovene

◎ **BELGIUM** *32*

✧ **L'Aquilone** *(The North Wind; or The Kite)*
N. Briale: Rue du Laveu 102, 4000 Liège; *t* (041) 522143»94
✧ **Association Leonardo da Vinci Culturelle, Récréative et
Sportive Italo-Belge**
Mario Pusceddu: Rue Cockerill 86, 4100 Seraing; *t* (041)
369259, 369188, *f* 374092
Rights/interests/culture of migrant workers. *Bulletin* (6/yr).»94
✧ **Association Sarde Eleonora d'Arborea** *(Sardinian Society)*
Rue de Belle-Vue 161, 7100 La Louvière; *t* (064) 281228»94
✧ **Associazione Calabresi Emigrati** *(Association of Calabrian
Emigrants)*
Sintelstraat 16, 3600 Genk   »94
✧ **Associazione Cristiana di Lavoratori Italiani**, ACLI *(Christian
Association of Italian Workers)* Beverlo
Gaston Oomslaan 150, 3581 Beringen; *t* (011) 424410
Social and cultural activities.   »94
✧ ≡ Brabant: Epifanio Guarneri: Rue de Pavie 22, 1040
Bruxelles; *t* (02) 359436
Training, employment, social activities. *Il Circolo* (12/yr). »94
✧ ≡ Limburg: Fernando Marzo: Rondpuntlaan 25, 3600 Genk;
t (089) 359050   »94
✧ ≡ La Louvière: Vincenzo Frieri: Rue St Alexandre 14, 7100
Haine St Pierre; *t* (064) 220949   »94
✧ ≡ Enzo Graci: Avenue Champs de Bataille 553, 7012
Jemappes; *t* (065) 824338   »94
✧ ≡ Michele Galella: Quai St Léonard 44, 4000 Liège; *t* (041)
279085   »94
✧ ≡ Charleroi: G.P. Murgia: Rue de Mons 68, 6031 Monceau-
sur-Sambre; *t* (071) 310418
Alternative (12/yr).   »94
✧ **Associazione Cristiana Limburgo**, ACLB *(Christian
Association of Limburg)*
Postbus 263, 3600 Genk; *t* (089) 384384
Cross-cultural social activities. *Encuentro* (12/yr).   »94
✧ **Associazione Nazionale Famiglie Emigrati**, ANFE *(National
Association of Emigrant Families)*
Bloemenlaan 73, 3640 Maasmechelen; *t* (011) 765254
Information, social activities.   »94
✧ **Associazione Siciliani nel Mondo** *(World Association of
Sicilians)*
Oude Baan 79, 3630 Maasmechelen; *t* (011) 761058   »94
✧ **Associazione Umbra dei Lavoratori Emigrati e loro Famiglie**
(Umbrian Association of Emigrant Workers and their Families)
Bosrandstraat 3, 3600 Genk   »94
✧ **Centre Culturel Italien** *(Italian Cultural Centre)*
Abramo Seghetto: Rue Courtenay 20, 5000 Namur; *t* (081)
225468
Culture, research, documentation.   »94
✧ **Centre de Documentation Italien**
Roberta Gandus: Rue de Montigny 45, 6000 Charleroi;
t (071) 313511
Historical and sociological research on migration.   »94
✧ **Centro di Animazione Italiano Basse-Sambre**, CAIBS: Centre
d'Animation des Italiens de la Basse-Sambre *(Italian
Community Development Centre of Basse-Sambre)*
Nicola Iachini, Co-ordinator: Rue des Glaces 145, 5060
Auvelais; *t* (071) 761492, 776001
Employment and welfare advice; training, education, social
activities. *Fermento*.   »94
● **Centro di Azione Sociale Italiana, Università Operaia** *(Italian
Social Action Centre, Workers' University)*
Rue A. Willemyns 211, 1070 Bruxelles; *t* (02) 521 2125 »90
♦ **Federazione Italiana Lavoratori Emigrati e Famiglie**, FILEF
(Federation of Italian Emigrant Workers and Families)
Fédération Italienne Travailleurs Emigrés et Familles
Rue Brialmont 21, 1030 Bruxelles; *t* (02) 217 1331
Information, welfare, leisure activities.   »94

✧ **Groupe Italien d'Action Socioculturelle** *(Italian Socio-Cultural Action Group)*
Martina Ruffini: Rue de l'Etoile 9, 5000 Namur; *t* (081) 211193
Cultural and welfare activities. »94
✧ **Gruppo Italiano de Molenbeek**
Rue d'Ostende 37, 1080 Bruxelles
Neighbourhood association. »90
● **Istituto per l'Istruzione Professionale dei Lavoratori e l'Assistenza degli Emigrati** *(Workers' Training and Emigrant Assistance Institute)*
[address uncertain] Ave. de Cortenberg 31, 1040 Bruxelles»90
● **Missione Cattolica Italiana** *(Italian Catholic Missions)*
Delegazione
Elia Ferro: Rue Rogier 32, 1030 Bruxelles; *t* (02) 241 1670
Co-ordination of pastoral services to Italian communities in Belgium. *Antenna* (4/yr). »94
● *Missione—Migrazione*
Route de Moro 73, 6030 Marchienne-au-Pont; *t* (071) 313410
Magazine (8/yr). »95
● *Sole d'Italia*
Siobespe SA, Rue St Laurent 26, 1000 Bruxelles; *t* (02) 478 3300, *f* 478 3502
Magazine (50/yr). »95

◎ **DENMARK** *45*

✧ **Circolo degli Italiani** *(Italian Circle)* Italiensk Center
Valby Langgade 77, 1., 2500 Valby; *t* 3117 4577 »89
● **Club degli Amici—Circolo degli Italiani in Dinamarca** *(Friends' Club—Circle of Italians in Denmark)*
L. Matagni: Hakonsvej 9, Bagsværd, 2880 København
Culture and leisure activities, information. »94
✧ **Italiensk-Dansk Forening i Århus** *(Italian-Danish Society)*
Domenico Pinna: Klostergade 37, 1., 8000 Århus C; *t* 8617 4740 »89
● **Missione Cattolica Italiana**, MCI *(Italian Catholic Mission)*
Lorenzo Del Zanna: Stenosgade 4a, 1616 København V; *t* 3131 7822, 3121 8588, *f* 3325 0738
Pastoral care, advice, cultural activities for migrants. »94

◎ **FRANCE** *33*

● **Association Franco-Italienne**
2 rue de l'Eperon, 75006 Paris; *t* (1) 4627 3400 »90
● **Associazione Cristiana di Lavoratori Italiani**, ACLI:
Association Chrétienne des Travailleurs Italiens *(Christian Association of Italian Workers)*
Raffaele Fiore: 26-28 rue Claude Tillier, 75012 Paris; *t* (1) 4372 6529, *f* 4372 5828
Welfare advice, social activities. *Focus* (12/yr). »94
✧ **Associazione Regionale Sarda** *(Sardinian Regional Society)*
168 rue Losserand, 75014 Paris; *t* (1) 4543 6212 »90
✧ **Centre d'Etudes et de Recherches sur la Culture Italienne Contemporaine**, CERCIC: Université Stendhal
Gilbert Bosetti: BP 25 X, 38040 Grenoble Cedex 9; *t* 7682 4316, exts. 3380/3434, *f* 7682 4351
Research on Italian culture and society. »94
● **Comité d'assistance italien**, COASIT *(Italian Welfare Committee)*
32 place St Ferdinand, 75017 Paris; *t* (1) 4574 2283
Advice, information, social work. »90
◆ **Institut National Confédéral d'Assistance et de Défense des Travailleurs Italiens**, INCA-F: Istituto Nazionale Confederale di Assistenza ai Lavoratori *(National Confederal Institute for Aid to and Defence of Workers)* also known as Associazione italo-francese di tutela e assistenza ai lavoratori
60 boulevard de Strasbourg, 75010 Paris; *t* (1) 4607 7351, *f* 4607 7334
An agency of the CGIL trade union confederation in Italy; supports Italian migrant workers and their families. »94
● **Istituto Fernando Santi** *(Santi Institute)*
10 rue Solférino, 75007 Paris
Main Italian migration research organisation, based in Rome, p144. *Avanti nel Mondo*. »90
✧ **Lycée italien Dante Alighieri**
12 rue Sédillot, 75007 Paris; *t* (1) 4705 1626
Italian secondary school. »94
● **Missioni Cattoliche Italiani—Delegazione:** Délégation des Missions Catholiques Italiennes *(Italian Catholic Missions National Office)*
Orfeo Ferrarese: 48 rue de Montreuil, 75011 Paris; *t* (1) 4372 0406 »94
● **Société Dante Alighieri**
12 rue Sédillot, 75007 Paris; *t* (1) 4705 1626
Cultural group. »90

◎ **GERMANY** *49*

● **Associazione Cristiana di Lavoratori Italiani**, ACLI *(Christian Association of Italian Workers)* ACLI-Germania: Bavaria
Pettenkoferstraße 8/IV, 80336 München; *t* (089) 554876
Youth welfare, education, employment issues. »94
✧ ≡ Weite Gasse 5, 86150 Augsburg; *t* (0821) 315 3599 (?), *f* 315 2263 »94
✧ ≡ Humboldtstraße 42, 44787 Bochum; *t* (0234) 16695 »94
✧ ≡ Luciano Fazi: Vilbelerstraße 36, 60313 Frankfurt am Main; *t* (069) 287814, *f* 289057
Il Giornale dei Lavoratori. »94
✧ ≡ Schwarzwaldstraße 6, 79102 Freiburg im Breisgau, Baden-Württemberg; *t* (0761) 700201, *f* 701712 »94
✧ ≡ Friedenstraße 24, 76133 Karlsruhe; *t* (0721) 816381, *f* 816006 »94
✧ ≡ Nikolaus-Groß-Straße 8, 50670 Köln; *t* (0221) 735678, *f* 772 0565
Same address for regional branch, ENAIP-NRW, of the Ente Nazionale ACLI Istruzione Professionale. »94
✧ ≡ Haagstraße 28, 47441 Moers; *t* (02841) 29528 »94
✧ ≡ Rheinstraße 30, 66113 Saarbrücken; *t* (0681) 71027 »94
✧ ≡ Schillerstraße 34, 89077 Ulm; *t* (0731) 64747 »94
✧ ≡ Lower Saxony, ACLI-Niedersachsen: Heßlingerstraße 11, 38440 Wolfsburg; *t* (05361) 15270, *f* 23965 »94
✧ ≡ Normannenstr. 26, 42275 Wuppertal; *t* (0202) 660571»94
✧ **Associazione Famiglie Italiane** *(Italian Families Association)*
Halverstraße 3, 58579 Schalksmuhle; *t* (0355) 6679
Cultural and welfare group. »90
✧ **Associazione Italiana Tutela Emigrati e Famiglie**, AITEF-CALE: Italienische Vereinigung für Kulturelles Wesen und Sozialrecht *(Italian Society for Protection of Emigrants and Families)*
Carmelo Sciacca: Postfach 1509, Hinter der Stadtmauer 50, 34346 Hann-Münden; *t* (0554) 12342 »94
✧ **Centro Documentazione Migratoria**, Cedom
Fr Carlo Marzoli, Director: Lindwurmstraße 143, 80337 München; *t* (089) 773968
Eva Schneider secretary, Pietro Rubin; founded 1975 by Missione Cattolica Italiana; research and documentation on Italian migrant workers in Germany. See also Ufficio Documentazione e Pastorale, p75. »94
● **Comitati Tricolori Italiani nel Mondo** *(Tricolour Committees of Italians Abroad)*
Urbanstraße 62a, 70182 Stuttgart; *t* (0711) 297117
Information, cultural and welfare activities. *Oltreconfine*. »94
✧ **Comitato Culturale Italiano**
Kampstraße 1, 58540 Meinerzhagen; *t* (02354) 2266
Social and cultural group. »94
✧ **Ente Nazionale ACLI Istruzione Professionale**, ENAIP:
Baden-Württemberg
Duilio Zanibellato: Mörikestraße 5, 70178 Stuttgart; *t* (0711) 602954, 603198, 600946, *f* 640 8949
Welfare, training, education, employment; see also ACLI in Cologne, above (for ENAIP NRW) and ENAIP in Italy, p144. »94
✧ **Ente Pro Italia e.V.**, EPI
Luigi Betelli: Speyererstraße 2, 60327 Frankfurt am Main; *t* (069) 732011, *f* 739 1370
An information service of the Missioni Cattoliche Italiane. *Corriere d'Italia*. »94
✧ **Federazione di Associazioni Italiane Emigrati in Germania**, FAIEG *(Federation of Italian Emigrant Societies in Germany)*
Stefano De Candia: Frankfurter Str. 69, 64293 Darmstadt; *t* (0651) 781401 »94
✧ ≡ Elbestraße 9, 63303 Dreieich; *t* (06103) 67709 »94
✧ **Federazione Italiana Lavoratori Emigrati e Famiglie**, FILEF *(Federation of Italian Emigrant Workers and Families)* Baden-Württemberg
[address uncertain] Kimmichstraße 13, 7000 Stuttgart; *t* (0711) 888138
Emigrazione Oggi. »90
● **Istituto Fernando Santi** *(Santi Institute)*
Mario Tamponi: Sybelstraße 69, 10629 Berlin; *t* (030) 882 5271
German branch. Distributes *Avanti nel Mondo* from the Institute's headquarters in Rome, p144. »94
▌ **Missione Cattolica Italiana** *(Italian Catholic Mission)*
Delegazione in Germania e Scandinavia
Luigi Betelli/Mons. Luigi Petris: Speyrerstraße 2, 60327 Frankfurt am Main; *t* (069) 732011, *f* 739 1370
Co-ordinates pastoral care of Italian Catholic migrant workers and families in Germany, Denmark and Scandinavia; sponsors Cedom, above; see also UDEP, p75, and EPI, above. »94
✧ **Sozialdienst für Italiener** *(Social Service for Italians)*
Meister-Gerhard-Straße 10-14, 50674 Köln; *t* (0221) 201 9268-69 »94

- **Ufficio Documentazione e Pastorale, Missione Cattoliche Italiane in Germania**, UDEP *(Italian Catholic Missions Documentation and Pastoral Office)*
P. Angelo Negrini: Kettelerallee 49, 6000 Frankfurt am Main 60; *t* (069) 459856
Research, documentation, information, co-ordination of pastoral work. See also Cedom, and main listing for Missione Cattolica Italiana, both p74. »90
- ♦ **Unione Nazionale Associazioni Italiani Emigrati**, UNAIE *(National Union of Italian Emigrant Associations)*
Paolo Fontanella: Ostwallstraße 98, 47798 Krefeld; *t* (02151) 21101
Links Italian organisations throughout Germany. Affiliated to Rome UNAIE, p145. *Presenza UNAIE.* »94

◎ IRELAND 353

- ✿ **Club Italiano Ltd**
Tibradden, Rathfarnham, Dublin 16; *t* (01) 493 6690
Social club. »94
- ● **Comitato dell'Emigrazione Italiana**, COEMIT *(Committee for Italian Emigrants)*
Liberato Santoro: 11 Lad Lane Lr, Dublin 2; *t* (01) 676 0691
Social, cultural, religious interests of Italian community. »94
- ● **Italian Cultural Institute**
Dr Angela Baroni, Director: 11 Fitzwilliam Square, Dublin 2; *t* (01) 676 6662
Founded 1954; promotion of Italian language and culture. »95

◎ LUXEMBOURG 352

- ● **Amitiés Italo-Luxembourgeoises**
110 ave. Gaston Diederich, 1420 Luxembourg; *t* 443935 »95
- ● **Association Italo-Luxembourgeoise**
44 rue de la Ferme, 3235 Bettembourg; *t* 516852
Cultural, employment and welfare concerns. »94
- ✿ **Associazione Bellunesi nel Mondo (Triveneti)** *(World Association of Belluno People)*
Adriano Piccolin: 1 rue de Limana, 7235 Walferdange; *t* 331728
Society of emigrants from Belluno, a town in the Dolomites. *Bellunesi nel Mondo.* »94
- ♦ **Associazione Cristiana di Lavoratori Italiani**, ACLI: Patronato
Lucia Berti: 40 rue Zénon Bernard, 4031 Esch-sur-Alzette; *t* 540189, 495747, *f* 486663
Main Italian emigrant welfare organisation. *Sole d'Italia* (52/yr). »94
- ● **Associazione Fagolar Furlan**
BP 2435, 1024 Luxembourg; *t* 330813
Cultural and leisure activities. »94
- ✿ **Associazione Gran Sasso Abruzzesi in Lussemburgo**, AGSAL *(Gran Sasso Association of Abruzzi People in Luxembourg)*
Giuseppe Filauro: 93 rue F. Mertens, 3258 Bettembourg; *t* 513084
Emigrants from south central Italy. *Abruzzo nel Mondo.* »94
- ✿ **Associazione Italiana Tutela Emigrati e Famiglie**, ACEF-AITEF *(Italian Association for Protection of Emigrants and Families)*
U. Scalise: 55 rue de la Moselle, 6683 Mertert; *t* 74133 »90
- ✿ **Associazione Lavoratori Emigrati e loro Famiglie del Friuli-Venezia Giulia** *(Friulian Emigrant Workers and Families Association)*
Renato Miserini: 13 rue St-Fiacre, 1519 Luxembourg
Migrants from Trieste and region. »90
- ✿ **Associazione Lucani in Lussemburgo** *(Association of Lucca People in Luxembourg)*
Vicenzo Ditomaso: 69 rue des Charbons, 4053 Esch-sur-Alzette; *t* 546995
Migrants from Tuscany. »90
- ✿ **Associazione la Maiella Emigrati in Lussemburgo** *(La Maiella Emigrant Association in Luxembourg)*
Romano Barbarrossa: [address unknown] 4951 Differdange; *t* 585629
Emigrants from the area around Monte la Maiella, a mountain in Abruzzo. »90
- ✿ **Associazione Monte Raut, Amici di Andreis nel Lussemburgo**
Flora Khon de Zorzi: 91 rue F. Martens, 3258 Bettembourg; *t* 510164
Possibly emigrants from Andria, in Apulia? »94
- ● **Associazione Nazionale Famiglie Emigrati**, ANFE *(National Association of Emigrant Families)*
Antonio De Letizia: 31 rue de Turin, 4337 Esch-sur-Alzette
Emigrant welfare, cultural and social activities. »94
- ✿ **Associazione Puglia-Lussemburgo**
Geremia Sibilio: 68 Grand-Rue, 9051 Ettelbruck; *t* 818991, 810697
Education and welfare of migrants; Italian culture. »94

- ✿ **Associazione Regionale Campani in Lussemburgo** *(Campania Regional Association in Luxembourg)*
Franco Avena: 29 rue de la Libération, 8031 Strassen; *t* 318791
Neapolitan immigrants. »94
- ✿ **Associazione Regionale Emigrati del Lazio** *(Regional Association of Emigrants from Latium)*
Antonio Ceccacci: 1 rue des Artisans, 3812 Schifflange; *t* 544422
Emigrants from region around Rome. »94
- ✿ **Associazione Regionale Emigrati Marchigiani e loro Famiglie**, AREMF *(Regional Association of Emigrants from the Marches and their Families)*
Bernardo Furio/Luigi Fiorani: 48 rue de Mamer, 8081 Bertrange; *t* 312575
Cultural activities, welfare of emigrants from Ancona region; formed 1980. »94
- ✿ **Associazione Regionale Pugliesi Emigrati in Lussemburgo**, ARPEL *(Regional Association of Apulian Emigrants)*
Vittori Giovanni: BP 2785, 1027 Luxembourg; *t* 470851
Emigrants from Bari and region. »94
- ✿ **Associazione Regionale Umbra Lavoratori Emigrati e loro Famiglie**, ARULEF *(Regional Association of Umbrian Emigrant Workers and Families)*
Marcello Moretti: 16 rue Fort Bourbon, 1249 Luxembourg; *t* 488176
Migrants from central mountain region. »94
- ✿ **Associazione Tre Frontiere Abruzzesi in Lussemburgo**, ATFAL *(Three Borders Abruzzi Association in Luxembourg)*
Mirko de Felice: 52 rue Phillipart, 4845 Rodarge; *t* 508585
Migrants from Aquila and surrounding region. »94
- ✿ **Associazione Trentini del Lussemburgo**
67 rue des Trevires, 2628 Luxembourg; *t* 496158
Tyrolean emigrants. »90
- ✿ **Associazione Trevisani nel Mondo** *(World Association of Treviso People)*
Giovanni Lovadina: 4 rue Titelberg, 4887 Lamadeleine; *t* 500506
Migrants from northern Veneto region. Also meets at Centro Culturale Italiano in Esch, below. »94
- ✿ **Associazione Veronesi nel Mondo** *(World Association of Veronese)*
115 avenue Grande-Duchesse Charlotte, 4531 Obercorn; *t* 586027
Migrants from Verona and Veneto. »90
- ✿ **Associazione Vincentini nel Mondo**
7 cité Cerrabati Mertet, Luxembourg »90
- ✿ **Centre Culturel Catholique Italien** *(Italian Catholic Cultural Centre)*
P. Louis Mella: Paroisse Italienne, 19 boulevard Petrusse, 2320 Luxembourg; *t* 400031 »90
- ✿ **Centro Culturale Italiano**
Walter Tonon: 5 boulevard Prince Henri, 4035 Esch-sur-Alzette; *t* 253250
See also Associazione Trevisani nel Mondo, above. »94
- ✿ **Cercle Italo-Luxembourgeois** *(Italian-Luxembourg Circle)*
Robert Hoegener: 19 rue de la Croix, 4435 Soleuvre »94
- ✿ **Circolo Amici dell'Unità** *(Circle of Friends of L'Unità)*
Nello Vignarelli/Silvana Sincini: 8 rue Kennedy, 4599 Differdange; *t* 589326
Aligned with the Italian Democratic Party of the Left, PDS; formed 1980; social conditions, union organisation of migrant workers. »94
- ✿ ≡ Giovanni Grilli: 109 rue de l'Alzette, 4011 Esch-sur-Alzette; *t* 542922 »94
- ✿ **Circolo Culturale e Ricreativo Eugenio Curiel** *(Curiel Cultural and Leisure Circle)*
Franco Barilozzi: Centre Curiel, 107 route d'Esch, 1471 Luxembourg; *t* 491750, 480169
Formed 1972; employment, civil rights advice. »95
- ✿ **Circolo Culturale e Ricreativo Italiano Antonio Gramsci**, CCRIAG *(Gramsci Italian Cultural and Leisure Circle)*
Pietro Schettini: 80 rue de Bastogne, 9011 Ettelbruck; *t* 818841
Social, cultural, employment rights group, formed 1981. »94
- ✿ **Circolo Alcide de Gasperi**
Mario Tommasi: 66 bvd Baden-Powell, 1211 Luxembourg
Christian democratic association. »94
- ✿ **Circolo Sardu d'Europa**
Antonio Dessi: BP 298, 4003 Esch-sur-Alzette; *t* 552606
Sardinian emigrants. »94
- ✿ **Circolo Vicentini del Lussemburgo**
Claudio Cortese: 4 B rue des Muguets, 2167 Luxembourg; *t* 435205
Emigrants from Vicenza region. »94

♦ **Comitato dell'Emigrazione Italiana**, COEMIT *(Italian Emigrants' Committee)*
Renato Miserini: 56 rue Adolphe Fischer, 1520 Luxembourg; *t* 4300 2857 work, 319754 home   »90
✿ **Comitato degli Italiani all'Estero**, ComItEs *(Committee of Italians Abroad)*
4 rue Wurth Paquet, 2737 Luxembourg; *t* 440134   »95
✿ **Comitato Italiano di Assistenza**, COM.IT.AS *(Italian Welfare Committee)*
Giuseppe Rocchi: 23 Domaine des Ormilles, 8088 Bertrange; *t* 319169
Formed 1988; labour rights, aid to migrant workers.   »94
✿ **Comitato Scolastico per l'Assistenza e l'Istruzione degli Immigrati Italiani**, CAFLI: Educational Welfare and Training Committee for Italian Migrants
Armando Cavotta: 145 rue de l'Alzette, 4011 Esch-sur-Alzette; *t* 549512, *f* 546942
Founded 1987; educational welfare, adult education. Also known as Comitato Scolastico Italiano.   »94
● **Istituto Italiano di Cultura**
7 rue Marie-Adelaide, 2128 Luxembourg; *t* 45560, 252274»95
● **Istituto Nazionale Confederale di Assistenza** *(National Confederal Welfare Institute)*: Patronato INCA-CGIL
Griziano Pianaro: Bureau d'Assistance Sociale pour les Italiens, 130 rue de l'Alzette, 4010 Esch-sur-Alzette; *t* 540678
Welfare agency of the Italian CGIL trade unions. See also Italia Libera, below. *Notiziario INCA*.   »95
✿ **Istituto di Tutela e Assistenza ai Lavoratori** *(Workers' Protection and Welfare Institute)*: Patronato ITAL-UIL
60 boulevard Kennedy, 4170 Esch-sur-Alzette; *t* 540545
Migrant worker welfare agency of the Unione Italiana del Lavoro trade unions.   »94
✿ **Italia Libera** *(Free Italy)* and Federazione Italiana Lavoratori Emigrati e loro Famiglie
Angelo Barboni/Luigi Peruzzi: 2 rue du Moulin, 4251 Esch-sur-Alzette; *t* 540678
Was listed (1990) as 130 rue de l'Alzette: see INCA-CGIL, above. Affiliated to FILEF in Italy, p144. Founded as an anti-fascist pressure group, later concerned with welfare and integration of migrant workers.   »94
✿ ≡ Elvio Tarsi: 79 rue du Cimetière, 3715 Rumelange; *t* 566166   »94
✿ **Missione Cattolica Italiana** *(Italian Catholic Mission)* Mission Catholique Italienne: Bonnevoie
25 rue de l'Hippodrome, 1730 Luxembourg; *t* 486235
Includes mother-tongue school. See also Schieren office, listed with the Missão Católica Portuguêsa, p100.   »95
✿ **Umbri nel Mondo** *(Umbrians Abroad)*
Giuseppe Mariani: 9 rue Sainte Barbé, 4021 Esch-sur-Alzette; *t* 593524 (?)
Tiber valley emigrants.   »94
✿ **Unione Donne Italiane nel Lussemburgo**, UDI *(Union of Italian Women)*
Flora Pitico/Pepita Orlanda: 25 avenue de la Gare, 4131 Esch-sur-Alzette; *t* 543391
Defence of women's rights, social and political mobilisation; formed 1944. See also INCA-CGIL and Italia Libera, above (along with which the UDI is affiliated to FILEF).   »94
♦ **Unione Nazionale Associazioni Italiani Emigrati**, UNAIE *(National Union of Italian Emigrant Associations)*
18 rue de l'Eau, 1449 Luxembourg; *t* 22194   »90
✿ **Unione Pugliesi Emigrati e Famiglie**, UPE *(Union of Apulian Emigrants and Families)*
Vito Cassone: 5 rue Kôpecht, 3321 Berchem; *t* 455995
Emigrants from Adriatic coastal region.   »94
✿ ≡ Franco Castellana: 10 rue de la Rotonde, 2448 Luxembourg   »94

🔲 **NETHERLANDS** *31*

✿ **Delegazione Missioni Cattoliche Italiani** *(Italian Catholic Missions Administration)*
Zeerstraat 92, 1942 AT Beverwijk; *t* (0251) 223987
Catholic pastoral care; cultural activities.   »95
● **Federazione Italiana Lavoratori Emigrati e Famiglie**, FILEF-Olanda *(Federation of Italian Emigrant Workers and Families)*
Gianfranco Saba, Secretary: Burgemeester Raymakerslaan 144, 5361 KJ Grave; *t* (0486) 474098, *f* 476516
Richard Scatzo. Major federation of Italian migrant groups; employment advice, liaison with authorities, welfare, youth and women's issues. *Notiziario FILEF*.   »95
✿ **Istituto Italiano di Cultura** *(Italian Cultural Institute)*
Keizersgracht 564, 1017 EM Amsterdam   »94
✿ **Italiaanse Federatie**
Eisenhowerstraat 45, 6224 XH Maastricht   »94

🔲 **PORTUGAL** *351*

✿ **Igreja Italiana do Loreto** *(Italian Church of Loreto)*
Pe. Dino Gottardi: Rua da Misericóridia, 1200 Lisboa; *t* (01) 342 3655   »95
● **Instituto Italiano de Cultura em Portugal** *(Italian Cultural Institute in Portugal)*
Salitre 146, 1250 Lisboa; *t* (01) 388 4172, *f* 385 7117   »95

🔲 **SPAIN** *34*

● **Instituto Hispano-Italiano de Cultura** *(Hispano-Italian Cultural Institute)*
calle Mayor 86, Madrid; *t* (91) 247 8603   »90
✿ **Parrochia degli Italiani** *(Italian Parish)*
Travesia del Biombo 1, Madrid
Catholic church.   »90
✿ **Parroquia San Nicolás de Bari** *(Parish of St Nicholas of Bari)*
plaza de San Nicolás, Madrid; *t* (91) 248 8314
Servite church and pastoral care centre.   »90

🔲 **SWITZERLAND** *41*

● **Corriere degli Italiani** (Italian Courier)
Bruchstr. 47, Postfach 143, 6000 Luzern; *t* (041) 225776
Community newspaper for Swiss and immigrant Italians.   »90

🔲 **UNITED KINGDOM** *44*

● **Anglo-Italian Society**
Yvonne Barlow, Secretary: Italian Consulate, Norfolk House, Smallbrook Queensway, Birmingham B5 4LJ; *t* (0121) 643 7794, 643 6226
Friendship, cultural exchanges; founded 1985. *Messaggero* (12/yr).   »90
● **Associazione Cristiana di Lavoratori Italiani**, ACLI *(Christian Association of Italian Workers)* Patronato
Lorenzo Losi/Pietro Molle: 134 Clerkenwell Road, London EC1R 5DL; *t* (0171) 278 0060, 278 0083-84
Employment and welfare issues.   »94
✿ ≡ Sr Giuseppina Cittadini: 69 Union Street, Bedford MK40, Beds.; *t* (01234) 357889   »90
✿ ≡ Regional Office: Giovanni Lallo: 2 Vivian Avenue, Sherwood Rise, Nottingham NG7 6JQ; *t* (0115) 960 2097»90
● **Associazione Italiana Tutela Emigrati e Famiglie**, AITEF: Italian Society for Protection of Emigrants and their Families: and Movimento Cristiano Lavoratori, MCL
Raphael Iannucci: 160 Ifield Road, London SW10; *t* (0171) 370 5227
National office of welfare and advisory agency based in Italy, p142, and of the Christian Workers' Movement.   »94
● **Associazione Liguri di Gran Bretagna** *(Ligurian Association of Great Britain)*
Wax Chandlers Hall, Gresham Street, London EC2V 7AD; *t* (0171) 606 8225
Emigrants from North-Western Italy.   »94
● **Associazione Lungianesi in Gran Bretagna** *(Association of Lungiana People in Great Britain)*
Pr Tosca Bertolini: 45 Wyatt Park Road, London SW2
Emigrants from Lungiana district. *Lungiana* (4/yr).   »94
● **Associazione Nazionale Famiglie Emigrati**, ANFE *(National Association of Emigrant Families)*
Benedetto Longinotti: Flat 31, Warrent Court, Euston Road, London NW1 3AA; *t* (0171) 387 2586   »94
● **Associazione Piemontesi nel Mondo** *(World Association of Piedmontese)*
8 Cambridge Road, North Harrow HA2, Middlesex; *t* (0181) 439 9159
Migrants from Turin region.   »94
● **British Italian Society**
21 Grosvenor Square, London W1; *t* (0171) 495 5536   »95
✿ **Centro Regionale di Assistenza e Tutela ai Emigrati**, CRATE *(Regional Centre for Emigrant Aid and Advice)*
Antonino Dragotta: 31 Hilton Road, Ipswich IP3 9RQ; *t* (01473) 715784
Migrant welfare, cultural and social activities.   »94
✿ **Centro Scalabrini**, CSER *(Scalabrini Centre)*
Gaetano Parolin: 20 Brixton Road, London SW9 6BU; *t* (0171) 735 8235, 735 5164, *f* 793 0385
Italian emigration research and documentation centre linked with Centro Studi Emigrazione Roma, p239. *La Voce degli Italiani*.   »94
● **Circolo Campani nel Mondo** *(World Association of Campania People)*
Stuart Low Nurseries, Theobalds Park Road, Enfield, Middlesex; *t* (0181) 363 0104
Neapolitan emigrants.   »90

- Circolo Politico-Culturale Gramsci *(Gramsci Political-Cultural Circle)*
80a Dean Street, London W1; *t* (0171) 437 4138
Socialist group associated with the Italian Democratic Party of the Left, PDS, see right. »90
- Circolo Trentino di Gran Bretagna *(Trentino Circle of Great Britain)*
7 Brookdale, London N11 3PP; *t* (0181) 368 1159
Migrants from Trentino-Alto Adige region. »94
✿ Club Italia
14 Alexandra Road, Bedford MK40; *t* (01234) 353135 »90
- Comitato di Coordinamento delle Associazione Italo-Scozzesi, CoCAIS *(Co-ordinating Committee of Italian-Scots Associations)*
Leandro Franchi: Lion Chambers, 170 Hope Street, Glasgow G2 2TW, Scotland; *t* (0141) 332 4297, *f* 332 3547 »94
- Ente Nazionale ACLI Istruzione Professionale, ENAIP *(National ACLI Body for Work Training)*
143 Clerkenwell Road, London EC1; *t* (0171) 278 0139
National office of the Italian-based migrant training and employment information body, p144. »90
- Federation of Italian Centres
18 Churton St, London SW1V 2LL; *t* (0171) 821 5144 »90
- Federazione di Associazioni e Comitati Scuola-Famiglia, FASFA *(Federation of Parent-Teacher Associations)*
Giuseppe Giaconi: 5 Southern Street, London N1 9AY; *t* (0171) 837 1966
Youth welfare, education, cultural concerns. »94
- Federazione di Associazioni Italiani Emigrati, FAIE *(Federation of Italian Emigrant Associations)*
Benedetto Longinotti: 248 Vauxhall Bridge Road, London SW1V 1AU; *t* (0171) 834 8869
Shares address with Patronato INAS-CISL and MAIE. »94
- Federazione di Associazioni Scuola-Famiglia, FASFA *(Federation of Parent-Teacher Associations)*
Pr Remo Finaldi, General Secretary: 42 Bromley Road, London SE6; *t* (0181) 690 0478 »90
- Federazione Italiana Lavoratori Emigrati e Famiglie, FILEF *(Federation of Italian Emigrant Workers and Families)*
Presidenza Centrale
96-98 Central Street, London EC1V 8AJ; *t* (0171) 608 0125, *f* 490 0938
British section of international migrant welfare group based in Italy, p144. *Il Punto* (6/yr). »95
✿ Istituto Nazionale di Assistenza Sociale, INAS *(National Social Welfare Institute)* Confederazione Italiana dei Sindicati del Lavoro
Luciano Rapa: 248 Vauxhall Bridge Road, London SW1V 1AU; *t* (0181) 804 2307
Social welfare agency of the trade union body Confederazione Italiana dei Sindicati del Lavoro. Advice, information. See also MAIE, right, and FAIE, above. »94
✿ Istituto Nazionale Confederale di Assistenza, INCA-CGIL *(National Confederal Welfare Institute)*
Marisa Pompei: 124 Canonbury Road, London N1 2UT; *t* (0171) 359 3701, *f* 354 4471
Social welfare agency of the trade union body Confederazione Generale Italiana del Lavoro. Advice, information. »94
✿ Istituto Fernando Santi
Gregorio Chiparo: 46 Linden Avenue, London NW10 5RA; *t* (0181) 969 0938
British section of Rome-based social work, research and information institute serving Italian migrants, p144. »94
✿ Istituto di Tutela e Assistenza ai Lavoratori, ITAL-UIL *(Workers' Aid and Advice Institute)*
Norma Gianquinto: Morley House, 1st Floor, Room 18, 320 Regent Street, London W1R 5AB; *t* (0171) 323 2710
Welfare service of the Unione Italiana del Lavoro trade union confederation. »94
✿ Italian Association of Leamington Spa
49 High St, Leamington Spa CV31; *t* (01926) 832401 »90
- Italiani nel Mondo *(Italians Abroad)*
Raffaele Sistina: 27 Brentmead Gardens, London NW10 7DT; *t* (0181) 961 4019
Catholic welfare, cultural and information service. »94
- Italiani in Scozia *(Italians in Scotland)*
P. Pietro Zorza, newsletter publisher: 62 Langlands Road, Glasgow G51 3BD, Scotland; *t* (0141) 440 1534
Newsletter. »91
- Missione Cattolica Italiana *(Italian Catholic Mission)*
Delegazione: Bedfordshire
Fr Mario Dalla Costa: 10 Woburn Road, Bedford MK40 1EG; *t* (01234) 359515
Co-ordination of pastoral care of Italian migrant workers. »94
✿ ≡ 197 Durants Rd, Enfield EN3 7DE; *t* (0181) 804 2307 »90

- Movimento Anziani Italiani, England, MAIE *(Movement of Italian Elders, England)*
Gino Biasi: 248 Vauxhall Bridge Road, London SW1V 1AU; *t* (0171) 834 2157
Interests of pensioners in organisations affiliated to FAIE. See also INAS-CISL, left. »94
- Partito Democratico della Sinistra, PDS *(Democratic Party of the Left)*
80a Dean Street, London W1
London branch of the former Italian Communist Party, PCI, which organised among emigrants. »90
✿ Unione Nazionale delle Associazioni degli Immigrati ed Emigrati, UNAIE *(National Union of Immigrant and Emigrant Associations)*
Giuseppe Franco: 151 Marsham Court, Marsham Street, London SW1P 4LB; *t* (0171) 323 0080 »94

◎ **NORTHERN IRELAND** *44*

✿ Italian Association of Northern Ireland
Seamus Diffin, Secretary: [address unknown] Belfast; *t* (01232) 693255
Formed 1992, mainly representing Italian families involved in the hospitality industry; may also be contacted through Leo d'Agostino, Italian Consul in Belfast. »92

IVORIAN

see also African, Islamic, West African

◎ **FRANCE** *33*

✿ Akwaba-Jeunesse ivorienne de Rennes *(Ivorian Youth of Rennes)*
chez M Gadou Daydro: 6 allée de Brno, 37500 Rennes
Solidarity among Ivorian community, help in settling. »89
✿ Amicale des Elèves et Etudiants Ivoriens de Lille *(Ivorian Scholars' and Students' Club of Lille)*
1-51 rue de Jules-Verne, 59260 Hellemmes
Focus for contact, meetings and integration of students. »89
✿ Association des Ivoriens à Dijon *(Dijon Ivorian Society)*
appt 318, Fontaine d'Ouche, 29 avenue Edouard-Belin, 21000 Dijon »89
- Association des Ivoriens de la région de Kani en France, AIRKF *(Association of Ivorians from Kani Region in France)*
Metié Vazoumana: 17 rue Robert-Blache, 75010 Paris »89
- Nayoua—Association des Femmes Ivoriennes en France, NAFIF *(Nayoua Association of Ivorian Women in France)*
Christine Zékou: ISM, 12 rue Guy de la Brosse, 75005 Paris; *t* (1) 4535 2710, *f* 4337 9741
Confidente (4/yr). »94
✿ Union des travailleurs ivoriens en France *(Union of Ivorian Workers in France)*
[address unknown] Clichy »90

◎ **ITALY** *39*

✿ Associazione Immigrati Costa d'Avorio
via Lamaticci 26, 60126 Ancona »90
✿ Associazione Lavoratori Costa d'Avorio *(Association of Ivorian Workers)*
via Conteverde 58, 00185 Roma; *t* (06) 446 7676, *f* 678 1182
Same address listed (1994) for Associazione Studenti Ivoriani a Roma e nel Lazio, ASSEIR (Daniel Djedjed). »94
✿ Associazione Lavoratori e Studenti Ivoriani nelle Marche, ASSORIM *(Ivorian Workers and Students Association of the Marche Region)*
via Podesti 10, 60100 Ancona; *t* (071) 206502 »94
- Associazione Studenti Ivoriani
piazza Sempione 19b, 00141 Roma; *t* (06) 686 1019
Possibly superseded by via Conteverde address (1994: see Associazione Lavoratori Costa d'Avorio, above). »90
✿ Union de la Jeunesse Ivorienne—Casa dello Studente, UJI *(Ivorian Youth Union—Student Home)* also known as UJI *de l'Umbria*, UJIDU
Arthur Bieri: CP 307, Posta Centrale, 06100 Perugia; *t* (075) 692 9811, 572 2931, *f* 573 3666
Location (1990): via Faina 4. »94

◎ **UNITED KINGDOM** *44*

- Anglo-Ivorian Society
J.D. Gravell, Honorary Secretary: 60 Worship Street, London EC2 2DJ; *t* (0171) 377 9134, *f* 377 2654
Trade, friendship, cultural exchanges; founded 1972. »90

- **Ivorian Relief Action Group**, also known as Ivorian Refugee Action Group
c/o Greenwich CRE, 115 Powis Street, London SE18 6JL
Member of National Network against Detentions and
Deportations, p177, and other migrant rights campaigns. »96

JAIN

see also Hindu, Indian

◎ **UNITED KINGDOM** *44*

✧ **Jain Community**
Kantilal Damji Joshi: 11 Clifton Hill, Brighton BN1 3HQ;
t (01273) 779056 »94
- **Jain Samaj Europe**
Dr Natubhai K. Shah, President: 69 Rowley Fields Avenue,
Leicester LE3 2ES; *t* (0116) 289 1077
Promotion of Jainist principles of Ahimsa (non-violence),
Anukampa (service to humanity), Jiv Daya (welfare of living
beings); research, publications. *Jain Quarterly* (4/yr). »88
- **Oshwal Association of the United Kingdom**
S.S. Shah: 23 Sudbury Court Road, Harrow, Middlesex »86

JAMAICAN

*see also African Caribbean, Afro-Caribbean, Anglo-Caribbean,
Caribbean, Rastafarian, West Indian*

◎ **UNITED KINGDOM** *44*

- **Association of Jamaicans**
[address unknown] »88
- *The Gleaner*
Ventura House, 176-188 Acre Lane, London SW2 5UL;
t (0181) 733 7014
Weekly newspaper of Caribbean and UK black community
news, based on the Jamaican paper *The Daily Gleaner*. »93
✧ **Jamaica Caribbean Society**
G.M. Burton: West Indian Centre, Carmoor Road, Chorlton-
on-Medlock, Manchester M13 0FB; *t* (0161) 881 5753
Advice on immigration and welfare; charity fundraising; social
events; cultural promotion inc. Jamaica Folk Ensemble. »93
✧ **Jamaica Community Services Group**
78 Heathfield Road, Handsworth, Birmingham B20 »90
✧ **Jamaica Society**
277 Chapeltown Rd, Leeds LS7 3HA; *t* (0113) 262 6435 »90
✧ **People's National Party, PNP**
285 Healy Road, Selly Oak, Birmingham B29
Governing party of Jamaica; several branches in UK. »90

JAPANESE

see also Asian

◎ **BELGIUM** *32*

✧ **Centre de Culture Japonaise**
Rue des Augustines 44, 1090 Bruxelles; *t* (02) 426 5000 »88

◎ **DENMARK** *45*

- **Dansk-Japansk Selskab**
Esplanaden 50, København; *t* 3363 3363 »95
✧ **Japanske Kvinders Kultur Sammenslutning** *(Japanese
Women's Cultural Collective)*
Takako Lyngesen: Bakkevej 22b, 2830 Virum; *t* 4242 4282 »89

◎ **FRANCE** *33*

- **Association Culturelle Franco-Japonaise de Tenri** *(Tenri
Franco-Japanese Cultural Association)*
9 rue Victor Considérant, 75014 Paris; *t* (1) 4335 1186 »90
- **Fondation du Japon** *(Japan Foundation)*
42 avenue Kléber, 75016 Paris; *t* (1) 4704 2863 »90

◎ **GREECE** *30*

- **Japanese Women in Foreign Countries**
PO Box 19233, 11710 Athinai »90

◎ **SPAIN** *34*

- **Asociación de Empresarios Japoneses de España** *(Japanese
Businesspeople's Association of Spain)*
plaza Mostenses s/n, Madrid; *t* (91) 547 6904 »95

- **Asociación de Intérpretes Nipones** *(Association of Japanese
Interpreters)*
calle Preciados 29, Madrid; *t* (91) 521 6105 »95

◎ **UNITED KINGDOM** *44*

- **Centre for Japanese Studies**, University of Sheffield
School of East Asian Studies, The University, Western Bank,
Sheffield S10 2TN
Teaching and research on language, culture and history. »94
- **Daiwa Anglo-Japanese Foundation**
Lord Roll of Ipsden, Chairman: Daiwa Foundation Japan House,
13-14 Cornwall Terrace, London NW1 4QP; *f* (0171) 486
2914
Development, funding and encouragement of Japanese studies
and Japanese cultural activity in the United Kingdom, and of
educational and cultural exchanges. »95
✧ **Japan Information and Cultural Centre**, JICC
Embassy of Japan, 101-104 Piccadilly, London W1V 9FN;
t (0171) 465 6572
Official information and cultural relations service. »95
- **Japan Society**
314-322 Regent Street, London W1; *t* (0171) 636 3029 »95
✧ **Japanese Community Centre**
Instrument House, 205-217 Kings Cross Road, London
WC1X 9DB; *t* (0171) 833 0031 »90
- **Nippon Club**
64 Queen Street, London EC4; *t* (0171) 248 7471 »95
- **Scottish Centre for Japanese Studies** University of Stirling
Department of Japanese Studies, Stirling FK9 4LA, Scotland;
t (01786) 467000
Postgraduate research on all areas of Japanese history and
culture. »95

JEWISH

*see also East European, Israeli, Middle Eastern, Polish; this is
not intended to be a comprehensive listing of Jewish
organisations, covering only national and regional associations,
representative bodies and media believed to have a significant
interest in migrants and refugees, or in anti-racist work. Local
and regional groups, synagogues, purely religious bodies and
national organisations for indigenous (EU-citizen) Jewish
communities are generally not listed. The reason for the
different treatment of Jewish and, for example, Islamic groups
is that the latter tend to represent mainly-migrant communities.*

◎ **BELGIUM** *32*

- **Centraal Beheer Joodse Weldadigheid en Maatschappelijk
Hulpbetoon** *(Central Jewish Welfare and Mutual Aid Bureau)*
Jacob Jacobstraat 2, 2018 Antwerpen; *t* (03) 232 3890
Social solidarity, refugees. »95
▌ **European Union of Jewish Students**, EUJS
Chaussée de Vleurgat 89, 1050 Bruxelles; *t* (02) 647 7279,
f 648 2431
Confederation of national Jewish student organisations;
opposes racism, fascism, antisemitism at European level. »94
- **Service Social Juif**: Joodse Sociale Dienst *(Jewish Social
Service)*
Avenue Ducpétiaux 68, 1060 Bruxelles; *t* (02) 538 8180,
f 534 6226
Welfare agency, concerns include refugees and immigrants;
member of Comité belge d'aide aux réfugiés, p130. »95
- **Unie der Joodse Oud-Weerstanders** *(Union of Jewish
Resistance Veterans)*
R. Szyffer/S. Wanderer: Chaussée d'Ixelles 148, 1050
Bruxelles »91
- **Union des Progressistes Juifs de Belgique**, UPJB *(Union of
Progressive Jews of Belgium)*
Rue de la Victoire 16, 1060 Bruxelles
Points critiques. »88

◎ **DENMARK** *45*

- **Forbundet af Polske Jøder i Danmark** *(Association of Polish
Jews in Denmark)* also known as Forbundet af Jøder fra Polen
Nørre Farimagsgade 74, 1, 1364 København K; *t* 3314
3092 »94
- **Klubben af Danmarks Jiddishister** *(Yiddish Club of Denmark)*
Guldbergsgade 118, St., 2200 København N
Yiddish-speaking Polish Jews. »90
- **Mosaisk Troessamfund** *(Danish Jewish Community)*
Ny Kongensgade 6, 1472 København K; *t* 3312 8868
Member of Dansk Flygtningehjælp, p132. »94

◎ **FRANCE** *33*

♦ **Alliance Israélite Universelle** *(World Jewish Alliance)*
45 rue La Bruyère, 75009 Paris; *t* (1) 4280 3500
The first international Jewish organisation, founded in 1860
CE. Zionist policies; philanthropic and educational activities,
mainly in France.   »94

• **Amicale des anciens déportés juifs de France** *(French Jewish Society of Former Deportees)*
14 rue Paradis, 75010 Paris; *t* (1) 4770 0483   »90

• **L'Arche** and **Radio Communauté Judaïque**, RCJ
14 rue Georges Berger, 75017 Paris; *t* (1) 4766 0335,
4622 5351, RCJ *t* (1) 4763 4358   »90

✿ **Association culturelle israélite Rachi** *(Rachi Jewish Cultural Association)*
6 rue Ambroise Thomas, 75009 Paris; *t* (1) 4824 8694   »90

• **Association Socio-culturelle Educative Juive**, ASCEJ
(Jewish Social, Cultural and Educational Association)
24 rue Tanger, 75019 Paris; *t* (1) 4038 1818   »90

• **Centre pédagogique juif de diffusion et documentation**
19 boulevard Poissonière, 75002 Paris; *t* (1) 4236 9579 »90

✿ **Comité des Israélites de l'Algérois** *(Committee of Jews of the Algiers Region)*
18 rue St Lazare, 75009 Paris; *t* (1) 4878 3880   »90

• **Comité juif d'action sociale et de reconstruction**, COJASOR
(Jewish Social Action and Reconstruction Committee)
6 rue Rembrandt, 75008 Paris; *t* (1) 4359 0363
Counselling and practical help to Jewish refugees.   »95

• **Conseil Représentatif des Institutions Juives de France**, CRIF:
Representative Council of Jewish Institutions in France
Jean Kahn, President: 19 rue Téhéran, 75008 Paris; *t* (1)
4561 0070
National umbrella organisation for Jewish community groups.
Involved in anti-racist campaigns. Same address houses other
groups including: Fonds Social Juif Unifié, FSJU, *t* 4563 1728;
AUJF, *t* 4563 0610; coopération féminine, *t* 4563 5341,
4563 4181.   »90

✿ **Institut UCJFP**
12 bis rue Georges Berger, 75017 Paris; *t* (1) 4763 8338 »90

• *Le Monde Juif* *(Jewish World)*
17 rue Geoffroy l'Asnier, 75004 Paris
Newspaper.   »88

• **Solidarité des réfugiés israélites** *(Jewish Refugee Solidarity)*
14 rue St-Lazare, 75009 Paris; *t* (1) 4526 5817   »90

• **Union des Etudiants Juifs de France**, UEJF *(Union of Jewish Students in France)*
47 rue Chabrol, 75010 Paris; *t* (1) 4523 4569   »90

• **Union des juifs du Maroc** *(Union of Jews from Morocco)*
18 rue Galvani, 75017 Paris; *t* (1) 4574 5181   »90

• **Union des juifs pour la résistance et l'entraide** *(Jewish Union for Resistance and Mutual Aid)*
14 rue Paradis, 75010 Paris; *t* (1) 4770 9047
Social work; same address as Amicale des anciens déportés
juifs de France.   »90

▌**World Jewish Congress**, WJC: Congrès mondial juif, CMJ:
European Section
Jean Kahn: [address unknown] Paris
International representative body of Jewry; campaigns against
antisemitism and racism. See also in Switzerland, right. »94

◎ **GERMANY** *49*

• *Allgemeine Jüdische Wochenzeitung* (Jewish Weekly News)
[address unknown] 5300 Bonn
Newspaper (52/yr).   »90

• **Zentrale Wohlfahrtspflege der Juden in Deutschland**
(Central Jewish Welfare Agency) also known as Zentrale
Wohlfahrtsstelle der Juden in Deutschland
Hebelstraße 17, 60318 Frankfurt am Main; *t* (069) 430206;
(611) 555958, 550139
Services to Jewish immigrants and refugees coming from
Eastern Europe, or via Israel; member of ZDWF documentation
centre, p238.   »94

• **Zentralrat der Juden in Deutschland** *(Central Council of Jews in Germany)*
Ignatz Bubis/Heinz Galinski: Rüngsdorferstraße 6, 53173
Bonn; *t* (0228) 357023, *f* 361148
Main representative body for Jewish organisations and
communities in Germany.   »95

◎ **GREECE** *30*

• **United Hebrew Immigration Aid Service**
Odos Nikis 4, Athinai; *t* (01) 323 1034
US-based group assisting Jewish refugees and emigrants from
Eastern Europe to re-emigrate.   »83

◎ **IRELAND** *353*

♦ **Jewish Representative Council**
c/o Dublin Hebrew Congregation Synagogue, Adelaide Road,
Dublin 2; *t* (01) 661 2408 office, 676 1734 synagogue
The Council is the main representative body for the small
Jewish population (about 1,500) in Ireland. There are also
Jewish Community Offices, including the Office of the Chief
Rabbi, in Dublin 6, *t* (01) 967351, and a Progressive
Synagogue, 7 Leicester Avenue, Dublin 6; *t* (01) 973955. »95

◎ **ITALY** *39*

• **American Joint Distribution Committee**, AJDC, and Hebrew
Immigrant Aid Society, HIAS
via Messina 15, 00198 Roma; *t* (06) 855 1741-43
Assistance to East European Jews in transit to Israel. May
have superseded listing for United Hebrew Immigration Aid
Service, below.   »94

• **Organisation for Rehabilitation through Training**
via S. Francesco di Sales 5, 00165 Roma; *t* (06) 655504
Vocational training of Jewish emigrants.   »83

• **United Hebrew Immigration Aid Service**, also known as
Hebrew Immigrant Aid Society, HIAS
Ente Assistenza Immigrazioni o Emigrazione, viale Regina
Margherita 269, 00198 Roma; *t* (06) 844 1041-43, 844 0810
US-based group assisting Jewish refugees and emigrants from
Eastern Europe to re-emigrate.   »90

◎ **NETHERLANDS** *31*

• **Jewish Social Aid Agency**
[address unknown]
A member agency of VluchtelingenWerk, p147.   »83

• **Joods Historisch Museum** *(Museum of Jewish History)*
Postbus 16737, 1011 RE Amsterdam; *t* (020) 626 9945,
f 624 1721
National museum and archive of Jewish history, tradition,
religion and culture.   »94

• **Joodse Studenten en Jongeren Vereniging**, IJAR *(Jewish Student and Youth Association)*
De Lairessestraat 13, 1071 NR Amsterdam; *t* (020) 676
8226   »94

◎ **POLAND** *48*

✿ **Centre for Jewish Culture**
[address unknown] Kazimierz, Krakow   »94

◎ **PORTUGAL** *351*

• **Centro Israelita de Portugal** *(Jewish Centre of Portugal)*
Rua Roça Araújo 10, Lisboa 12; *t* (01) 572041   »95

◎ **RUSSIA** *7*

♦ **Jewish Organisation of Prisoners of Fascist Concentration
Camps**, ROOF
ulitsa Panfilova d.4/5, kv.173, Moskva 125080; *t* (095) 198
6001, *f* 235 5181   »94

◎ **SPAIN** *34*

✿ **Casa de la Comunidad Hebrea de Madrid** *(House of the Jewish Community of Madrid)*
calle Balmes 3, Madrid; *t* (91) 445 9835
Community centre, synagogue.   »90

✿ **Comunidad Israelita** *(Jewish Community)*
Sinagoga, calle Judíos, Córdoba, Andalucía   »94

✿ ≡ calle Manuel Montilla 13, Madrid   »90

◎ **SWITZERLAND** *41*

▌**United Hebrew Immigration Aid Service**, HIAS, and American
Joint Distribution Committee
route de Lyon 75, 1211 Genève 13; *t* (022) 459350
US-based group assisting Jewish refugees and emigrants from
Eastern Europe to re-emigrate.   »93

• **Verband Schweizerischer Jüdischer Fürsorgen**, VSJF *(Swiss Jewish Welfare League)*
Postfach 514, 8039 Zürich; *t* (01) 201 5850, *f* 202 5877
Welfare services include assistance to Jewish refugees.   »95

▌**World Jewish Congress**, WJC: Congrès mondial juif
Case postale 191, 1202 Genève
See also Paris office, left.   »93

◎ **UNITED KINGDOM** *44*

✿ **Agudas Israel Housing Association Ltd**
Solomon Tescher: 97 Stamford Hill, London N16 5DN;
t (0181) 802 3819, *f* 800 5000   »94

- **Association of Jewish Ex-Servicemen and Women**, AJEX
Harry Farbey, Secretary: AJEX House, East Bank, London
N16 5RT; *t* (0171) 800 2884
Mutual aid, combat racism and intolerance; founded 1930 CE,
65 branches. *Action Briefing* (4/yr), *Exit Visa* (4/yr). »90
- **Association of Jewish Refugees in Great Britain**, AJR, and
Council of Jews from Germany
Laura Howe: [address uncertain] Karminski House, 9 Adamson
Road, London NW3 3HX; *t* (0171) 431 6161
Name and number 1995, address 1990. Mutual aid, welfare,
mainly of elderly refugees. *AJR Information* (12/yr). »95
- **B'Nai B'rith**
1-2 Endsleigh Street, London WC1H; *t* (0171) 387 5278,
387 5336, 387 5954 »90
- ♦ **Board of Deputies of British Jews**
Hayim Pinner, General Secretary: Woburn House, Tavistock
Square, London WC1H 0EP; *t* (0171) 387 3952, *f* 383 5848
Eldred Tabachnik QC president, Aubrey Rose vice-president;
Neville Nagler. Founded 1760 CE, recognised 1835 as repres-
entative body of British Jewry (currently 300,000 people); 420
Deputies from 250 congregations and 50 community bodies;
anti-fascism, Holocaust education (through Yad Vashem
Committee, Ben Helfgott chairman). *On Board* (10/yr).
   There are five main religious federations: the largest (with
around 135,000 adherents) is the orthodox United Synagogue,
t (0171) 387 4300 (Jonathan Sacks, Chief Rabbi; Jonathan
Kestenbaum, executive director of the Chief Rabbi's Office).
Others are the Federation of Synagogues, *t* (0181) 202 2263;
the Union of Liberal and Progressive Synagogues (Rabbi Hugo
Grynn, leader), *t* (0171) 580 1663; the Reform Synagogues of
Great Britain, *t* (0181) 349 4731 (Rabbi Tony Bayfield, chief
executive); and the Spanish and Portuguese Jews Congreg-
ation, *t* (0171) 289 2573. »96
- **Centre for the Study of Judaism and Jewish-Christian
Relations**
Rabbi Dr Norman Solomon, Director: Selly Oak Colleges,
Bristol Road, Birmingham B29 6LQ; *t* (0121) 472 4231
Research on Judaism and Christianity, promotion of tolerance
and understanding; newsletter, occasional papers. »90
- **Committee for the Welfare of Iranian Jews in Great Britain**
D. Elias, Secretary: 17 Arden Road, London N3 3AB; *t* (0181)
346 3121
S. Mehdi, chairman; founded 1981 CE to assist refugees. »89
- **Community Security Trust**
Mike Whine: Board of Deputies of British Jews, Woburn
House, Tavistock Square, London WC1H 0EP
Charity established 1994 CE; runs a volunteer security force to
protect Jewish lives and property and to counter racism. »95
- **Czechoslovak Jewish Aid Trust**
31 Craven Street, London WC2N 5NP; *t* (0171) 839 7481
Advice, assistance in emigration, settlement, education,
employment, welfare of elderly. »89
- ■ **European Council of Jewish Communities**
74 Gloucester Place, London W1; *t* (0171) 224 3445 »95
- **Holocaust Educational Trust**
Greville Janner MP, Chairman: BCM Box 7892, London
WC1N 3XX
Educational packs on the Holocaust and related themes. »95
- ♦ **Institute of Jewish Affairs Ltd**, IJA, and Institute of Jewish
Studies
Anthony Lerman, Executive Director: 79 Wimpole Street,
London W1M 7DD; *t* (0171) 935 8266
Lena Clamp. Research and publishing centre on Jewish affairs
worldwide, racial and religious prejudice. Sponsored by Anti-
Defamation League of B'Nai Brith and World Jewish Congress;
founded in New York in 1941 CE. Publishes *Christian-Jewish
Relations*, *East European Jewish Affairs* and *Antisemitism
World Report* (both 1/yr), and *Patterns of Prejudice* (4/yr).»95
- **Institute for Yiddish Studies**
Dr Dovid Katz: c/o St Antony's College, Oxford
Gennady Estraikh, Dr Dov-Ber Kerler. Established in 1995 CE
to further the study and teaching of the Yiddish language.
Publishes academic and reference books through Oksforder
Yidish Press, and literature through Three Sisters Press. »95
- ♦ **Jewish Care**, formerly Jewish Welfare Board
Stuart Young House, 221 Golders Green Road, London NW11
9DW; *t* (0171) 458 3282
Largest Jewish welfare charity. Counselling and casework for
elderly, for mentally ill (through Shalom Mental Health Centre
and outreach work), for people with learning difficulties
(Shavla centre, Judith Hassan director), and for Holocaust
victims (Holocaust Survivors Centre, Parson Street, NW4, *t*
(0181) 202 9844, J. Hassan chair). The Michael Sobell
Community Centre, Golders Green, London NW11, provides
recreational and leisure services for 1,000 members. »95

- *Jewish Chronicle*
Ned Temko, Editor: 25 Furnival Street, London EC4; *t* (0171)
405 9252
Main newspaper (52/yr) of the British Jewish community,
founded in 1840s CE; controlled by Kessler Foundation. »94
- **Jewish Community Action**, JCA
Harry Rich: 11 Christchurch Avenue, London NW6 7QP
Recruits volunteers for Jewish communal organisations. »94
- **Jewish Council for Community Relations**, JCCR
Dr Edie Friedman, Organising Secretary: 33 Seymour Place,
London W1N 6AT; *t* (0181) 455 9339
Anti-racism, migration rights, refugees, family reunion. »94
- **Jewish Council of Racial Equality**
Richard Stone: [address unknown] London
Same as, or superseding, the JCCR? »96
- **Jewish Feminist Group**
[address unknown] London »90
- *Jewish Gazette*
1 Shaftesbury Avenue, Leeds, Yorkshire; *t* (0113) 266 8273,
266 6000
Newspaper mainly serving the Leeds Jewish community of
10,000; published Leeds and Manchester since 1924 CE. »93
- ✿ *Jewish Herald*
[address unknown]
Newspaper. »88
- **Jewish Memorial Council**
Woburn House, Upper Woburn Place, London WC1H;
t (0171) 387 3081 »90
- *The Jewish People*
Yehuda Lisky, Editor: [address unknown] London
Yiddish newspaper. »88
- **Jewish Refugees Committee** and Central British Fund for
World Jewish Relief, CBF
Patricia Pinchon, Administrator: Drayton House, 30 Gordon
Street, London WC1H 0AN; *t* (0171) 387 3925, *f* 383 4810
The Committee provides advice and assistance to Jewish
refugees in the UK. The Fund is involved in information
activities, negotiation, resettlement assistance, casework on
immigration problems, liaison with Jewish and other agencies
on refugees within and outside the UK. »95
- ✿ **Jewish Representative Council**
[address unknown] Glasgow, Scotland
Represents local Jewish community. »94
- ✿ **Jewish Representative Council of Greater Manchester and
Region**
Rita Rosemarine: Jewish Cultural Centre, Bury Old Road,
Manchester M8 6FY; *t* (0161) 720 8721
Represents social, welfare and cultural organisations in the
local Jewish community of about 35,000. »94
- **Jewish Socialist Group**
BM Box 3725, London WC1N 3XX
Anti-racist, anti-fascist group. »94
- *Jewish Telegraph* Ltd
4A Roman View, Leeds, Yorkshire; *t* (0113) 269 5044 »90
- **Jewish Women's Network**
Sharon Lee, Co-ordinator: [address unknown] London »96
- ✿ **Leeds Jewish Representative Council**
151 Shadwell Lane, Leeds, Yorkshire; *t* (0113) 269 7520 »90
- ✿ **Manchester Jewish Community Council**
Henry Gutterman: [address unknown] Manchester »88
- ✿ **Manchester Jewish Socialists**
Judith Emmanual: [address confidential] Manchester;
t (0161) 203 4101
Socialist perspectives on the Middle East, anti-racism,
immigration, personal politics and other issues. »93
- *New Moon*
Matthew Kalman, Editor: [address unknown] London
Founded 1990 CE as magazine (12/yr) for younger Jews;
second only to *Jewish Chronicle* in circulation. »94
- ✿ **Oxford L'Chaim Society**
[address unknown] Oxford
Student society at Oxford University; social gatherings,
meetings, fellowship between Jews and non-Jews. »94
- **Poale Zion**
[address unknown]
Zionist socialist society affiliated to British Labour Party. »96
- **Polish Jewish Ex-Servicemen's Association**
L. Feit: 66 Chambers Lane, London NW10 2RL; *t* (0181) 459
7440
Founded 1945 CE; welfare of ex-servicemen and other Polish
Jews in Britain. »89
- **Polish Jewish Refugee Fund**
W. Schindler, Chairman: 143-145 Brondesbury Park, London
NW2 5JL; *t* (0181) 451 3425
R. Gluckstein, secretary. »89

- **Spiro Institute for the Study of Jewish History and Culture**
Nitza Spiro: The Old House, c/o King's College London, Kidderpore Avenue, London NW3 7SZ
Courses on Jewish culture, social history, classical and modern Hebrew studies; courses for children and teachers on the Holocaust, school visits by survivors, and development of Holocaust education resources. »95
- **Study Centre for Christian-Jewish Relations**
Sr Margaret Shepherd NDS, Director: 17 Chepstow Villas, London W11 3DZ; *t* (0171) 727 3597
Resource centre, courses on Jewish-Christian relations, religious tolerance and inter-faith dialogue, run by the Catholic Sisters of Sion. »88
- **Union of Jewish Students, UJS**
Paul Solomon, President: Hillel House, 1-2 Endsleigh Street, London WC1H 0DS; *t* (0171) 387 4644, *f* 383 0390
Interests of Jewish students; combats antisemitism, racism and discrimination. See also Campus Watch, p177. »95
- **Union of Liberal and Progressive Synagogues, ULPS**
Sharon Silver-Myer, Administrator: The Montagu Centre, 21 Maple Street, London W1P 6DS; *t* (0171) 580 1663
Representative body of Liberal and Progressive Judaism; co-ordinates a number of national religious and community welfare resources and services. »94
- **United Kingdom Jewish Aid and International Development, UKJAID**
The Director: 33 Seymour Place, London W1H 6AT
Founded 1989 as Jewish-led humanitarian, non-sectarian relief and Third World development charity. »94
- **United Kingdom Standing Council on Central and East European Jewry**
[address unknown]
Researches problems of Jewish minorities in, and migrants from, the former Soviet bloc, and lobbies in their interests.»95
- **Wiener Library**
Dr David Cesarani, Director: 4 Devonshire Street, London W1; *t* (0171) 636 7247
Library on Jewish history, culture, religion, Holocaust studies and related issues. »94
- **Women's Campaign for Soviet Jewry**
Margaret Rigal, Secretary: Pannell House, 779-781 Finchley Road, London NW1
Rights of Soviet Jews, including right to emigrate. »91
- **World Organization of Former Czechoslovak Jews**
F. Leitner, Secretary: 273 Green Lanes, London N4 2EX; *t* (0181) 800 2996
M.R. Springer chairman; founded 1939 CE; welfare of wartime and post-war refugees. »89
- **World Zionist Organization, WZO, and Jewish Agency for Israel**
741 High Road, Finchley, London N12 0BQ; *t* (0181) 446 1477
Department for Immigration promotes *Aliyah*, migration to Israel; Jewish Agency for Israel promotes immigrant welfare in Israel. »89

◙ **NORTHERN IRELAND** *44*

✧ **Belfast Hebrew Congregation**
The Wolfson Centre, 49 Somerton Road, Belfast; *t* (01232) 777974
Also Chevra Kadisha, *t* 773139. Main religious and social centre for Northern Ireland's small Jewish community; other centres at 5 Fortwilliam Gardens, Belfast BT15, *t* 775013; Chevra Kadisha, 55 Dunlambert Drive, BT15, *t* 774258. »94

JORDANIAN

see also Arab/Arabic, Islamic, Middle Eastern, Palestinian

◙ **ITALY** *39*

- **Unione Generale Studenti Giordani** *(General Union of Jordanian Students)*
[address unknown] »90

KAMPUCHEAN

see Asian, Cambodian, Khmer, South-East Asian

KANAK

see French: DOM/TOM, Pacific

KASHMIRI

see also Chinese, Hindu, Indian, Islamic, Pakistani

◙ **DENMARK** *45*

- **Kashmir Society in Denmark**
Rådmandsgade 86-2, 2200 København N »90

◙ **ITALY** *39*

- **Associazione di Solidarietà dei Kashmiri in Italia**
M. Farooq Tabassum: via Conteverde 58, 00185 Roma; *t* (06) 466 7676, *f* 678 1182 »94

◙ **UNITED KINGDOM** *44*

✧ **All Jammu and Kashmir Muslim Conference**
A.H.M. Younis Khan: 59 Shepherd Street, Bury BL8 »94
✧ **Azad Kashmir Muslim Association**
Mohammed Amin Qureshi, General Secretary: 11 Farcliffe Place, Bradford BD8 8QD; *t* (01274) 498677
Family welfare and charitable organisation, founded in the 1970s and serving Muslim and non-Muslim communities. »94
✧ **Azad Kashmir Welfare Association**
13 Muntz Street, Birmingham B10 9SN
Pakistani Kashmiris. »90
✧ **Azadi Resource and Research Project**
141 Sneinton Dale, Sneinton, Nottingham NG2 4LW; *t* (0115) 924 3228
Resource centre, research, advice work. »94
- **British Kashmir Group**
House of Commons, Westminster, London SW1A 0AA
All-party parliamentary committee of MPs and peers. »95
- **British Kashmiri Association, BKA**
Khalid Mahmood: 10 Downet Close, off Claremont Road, Sparkbrook, Birmingham B11 1LF; *t* (0121) 773 2790
Advice agency for Kashmiri Muslims, founded 1972. »90
- **Jammu and Kashmir Council for Human Rights**
Nazir Gilani, Secretary General: [address unknown] »95
- **Jammu Kashmir Liberation Front UK**
Azmat A. Khan: 108 Killinghall Road, Bradford BD3 8HN
Supports Kashmiri self-determination. »95
✧ **Kashmir Book Centre**
523 Stratford Rd, Birmingham B11 4LP; *t* (0121) 773 6634»94
✧ **Kashmir Muslim Welfare Association** and Kashmir Muslim Community Centre; Mosque
1 Hardy St, Leeds LS11 6BJ; *t* (0113) 271 4837 (4873?)»94
✧ **Kashmir Workers' Association**
[address uncertain] 131 Alum Rock Rd, Saltley, Birmingham B8
Also listed (1990) at 50 St Joseph's Road, Saltley. »90
✧ **Kashmir Youth Project**
Muhammed Rashid: Belfield Road, Rochdale OL16 2UR; *t* (01706) 30140, 30150
Advice, casework; Kashmiris, Pakistanis. »94
- **World Kashmir Freedom Movement, Kashmir Centre**
41 Monsell Road, London N4 2EF; *t* (0171) 354 5305, *f* 354 0840
Campaigns for self-determination; arms embargo, sanctions to force implementation by India of UN resolutions. »93

KENYAN

see African, Asian, East African

KHALISTANI

see Punjabi, Sikh

KHMER

see also Asian, Cambodian, South-East Asian

◙ **FRANCE** *33*

- **Association aide aux femmes khmères, AAFK** *(Khmer Women's Aid Association)*
11 rue Tourneux, 75012 Paris; *t* (1) 4347 5063 »90
- **Association Générale des Khmèrs à l'Etranger, AGKE** *(General Association of Khmers Abroad)*
Paul Pak: 18 avenue Marcel-Cachin, 69200 Vénissieux
Humanitarian and social work, friendship and integration of Cambodians in the Rhône-Alpes region. »90

✿ **Association des jeunes musiciens khmères, AJMK**
(Association of Young Khmer Musicians)
9 rue des Cordeliers, 95300 Pontoise
Friendship, mutual assistance, traditional music and culture
among Khmer youth. »89
✿ **Association des réfugiés khmers en Limousin**
22 rue des Azalées, 87280 Limoges »89
✿ **Centre de Documentation et de Recherche sur la Civilisation
Khmère, CEDORECK**
218 rue St-Jacques, 75005 Paris; *t* (1) 4329 9394 »94
✿ **Comité d'Entraide Khmère de Bordeaux** *(Khmer Mutual Aid
Committee of Bordeaux)*
Sarith Touch: 35 rue Sabarèges, 33440 Ambares-et-Lagrave;
t 5677 5047, 5677 7250 »94

KITTITIAN

*i.e. from St Christopher (St Kitts) and Nevis; see also African
Caribbean, Afro-Caribbean, Anglo-Caribbean, Caribbean, West
Indian*

◎ **UNITED KINGDOM** *44*

● **St Kitts, Nevis and Anguilla Association**
56 Frederick Road, Birmingham B33 »90

KOREAN

see also Asian

◎ **GERMANY** *49*

✿ **Sozialdienst für Koreaner** *(Social Service for Koreans)*
Georgstraße 7, 50676 Köln; *t* (0221) 201 0127 »94
● **Verband der Koreaner in Deutschland e.V.** *(League of
Koreans in Germany)*
Königstraße 37, 5300 Bonn; *t* (0228) 261066 »90

◎ **UNITED KINGDOM** *44*

● **Centre for Korean Studies:** School of East Asian Studies
Information Officer: University of Sheffield, Western Bank,
Sheffield S10 2TN; *t* (0114) 276 8555
Postgraduate research and publishing on Korean topics.
Library holdings, bibliographies. »95

KURDISH

see also Iranian, Iraqi, Middle Eastern, Turkish

◎ **BELGIUM** *32*

✿ **Institut Kurde de Bruxelles** *(Kurdish Institute of Brussels)*
Pervine Jamil: Rue Bonneels 4, 1040 Bruxelles; *t* (02) 230
8930, *f* 230 3402
Support for Kurdish rights; research and documentation;
culture; welfare of migrants and refugees. *Bulletin* (4/yr). »94

◎ **DENMARK** *45*

● **Dansk-Kurdisk Kultur- og Solidaritetsforening** *(Danish-
Kurdish Cultural and Solidarity Society)*
Klostergade 37, 8000 Århus C »89
● **Dansk-Kurdisk Kulturcenter** *(Danish-Kurdish Cultural Centre)*
Vesterbrogade 24 A-3, 1620 København V; *t* 3122 8998
Founded 1988; cultural and social events. »90
● **Foreningen af Arbejdere fra Kurdistan i Danmark, KOMKAR**
(Association of Kurdish Workers in Denmark) and
Co-ordination of Kurdish Associations in Europe
H. Kizilocak: Vesterbrogade 27 E, 1620 København V;
t/f 3124 7556
Founded 1986; solidarity with the Kurdish people in Turkey
and elsewhere, cultural events, seminars. Bulletin. »94
✿ **Foreningen af Demokrater fra Kurdistan** *(Society of
Democrats from Kurdistan)*
M. Gur: Dyringparken 84, st.tv., 2660 Brøndby Strand »89
✿ **Den Kurdiske Forening i Aalborg** *(Kurdish Society of Aalborg)*
v./ Nashad Amin: [address uncertain] Thulevej 38, 9210
Aalborg Sø »89
✿ **Den Kurdiske Kulturcenter i Danmark** *(Denmark Kurdish
Cultural Centre)*
Postbox 2059, 1013 København K »90
● **Patriotic Union of Kurdistan, PUK**
Mohammed Ibrahim: [address uncertain] Dalslandsgade 8,
D 701, 2300 København S; *t* 3296 2614 »90

◎ **FRANCE** *33*

✿ **Association culturelle et de solidarité franco-kurde** *(Franco-
Kurdish Cultural and Solidarity Association)*
Tildirim Nurettin: 10 rue Guy-Ropartz, 54000 Nancy
Social, music, folk dancing. »90
● **Association des Travailleurs du Kurdistan en France,
KOMKAR** *(Association of Kurdish Workers in France)*
74 rue du Faubourg Poissonière, Paris
Interests of refugees; supports liberation movement. »91
● **Association des travailleurs patriotes du Kurdistan**
(Association of Patriotic Workers of Kurdistan)
36 rue Enghien, 75010 Paris; *t* (1) 4523 5337 »90
*Comité de Kurdistan: dissolved by order of the French cabinet
on 31.11.93, along with the Federation of Kurdistan Cultural
Associations and Patriotic Workers, because of alleged links
with the Kurdistan Workers' Party, PKK.*
✿ **Institut Kurde de Paris** *(Kurdish Institute of Paris)*
106 rue Lafayette, 75010 Paris; *t* (1) 4824 6464, *f* 4770
9904
Kurdish culture, information, solidarity. »94

◎ **GERMANY** *49*

● **Confederation of Kurdish Associations, YEK-KOM**
[address unknown]
Umbrella group for Kurdish refugee societies. »95
● **Europavertretung der Nationalen Befreiungsfront Kurdistans**
(European Bureau of the Kurdistan National Liberation Front)
[address uncertain] Serxwebûn, Postfach 101683, 5000
Köln 1
Address is from 1990. Support group for Kurdistan National
Liberation Front, ERNK, which seeks an independent homeland
in Turkey and neighbouring states. *Kurdistan Report*.
Groups aligned with the ERNK or its major component, the
PKK, and present in Germany include YKWK, YXK, YJWK,
YRWK (respectively Union der patriotischer Arbeiter/Jungen/
Frauen/Intellektuellen aus Kurdistan), Kurdistan-Komitees in
Europa, Feyka-Kurdistan (Föderation der patriotischen Arbeiter-
und Kulturvereine aus Kurdistan) and HUNERKOM (Verein der
patriotischen Künstler aus Kurdistan).
In 1993 the German government banned the PKK and 35
other Kurdish organisations (details not available). By 1995
400 Kurds were in prison in Germany pending deportation.
Kani Yilmaz, EU representative of the PKK, travelled to London
in 1994 and was arrested for extradition to Germany. »95
● **Föderation der Arbeitervereine aus Kurdistan in Deutschland,
KOMKAR** *(Federation of Kurdish Workers' Unions in Germany)*
and Co-ordination of Kurdish Associations in Europe
Abubekir Saydam, President: Hansaring 28-30, 50670 Köln;
t (0221) 123376, *f* 123485
Member of EU Migrants Forum, p131; supports national
liberation and represents interests of refugees. »94
● **Föderation der Demokratischen Arbeitervereine Kurdistans,
KKDK** *(Kurdistan Federation of Democratic Workers' Unions)*
also known as Kurdische Gemeinde in Deutschland
A. Tuku: Hohenzollernring 5, 50672 Köln; *t* (0221) 251551»94
✿ **Föderation der Kurdisch Türkischen Arbeitervereine e.V.,
AKTIF** *(Federation of Turkish Kurd Workers' Unions)*
Dogan Göçmen: Ebelingenstraße 2/543, 21073 Hamburg;
t (0211) 748 8469 »94
✿ **Initiative 'Human Rights in Kurdistan'**
Sertaq Bucak: [address uncertain] Postfach 104551, 2800
Bremen 1; *t* (0421) 703932 »90
● **Kurdistan-Komitee e.V.** *(Kurdistan Committee)*
Hansaring 66, 5000 Köln 1 »90
✿ **Union der Demokraten Kurdistans, WDK**
c/o Abidin Sonmez: Linienstraße 102, 4000 Düsseldorf »90
✿ **Verein der Arbeitnehmer Kurdistans in Köln und Umgebung**
(Kurdish Employees' Union of Cologne and District)
Robertstraße 5, 5000 Köln; *t* (0221) 870 3091 »90

◎ **GREECE** *30*

● **Kurdistan Committee, EK**
Sinan Dogan: Odos Arachovis 19, 10681 Athinai; *t* (01) 363
6905 (or 4905?)
Founded 1983; self-determination for Kurdish people, asylum
advice, cultural activities for refugees. »94

◎ **ITALY** *39*

● **Associazione Studenti Kurdi in Europa, KSSE**
Fatah Hasti: [address uncertain] piazza Bianco 2, 10137
Torino; *t* (011) 308 1240, 787185
Also listed (1990) as c/o M. Sirwan, via Borgo Dora 30,
10152 Torino, *t* 521 2080. Founded 1956. »94

◎ NETHERLANDS *31*

- **Koerdische Arbeidersunie** *(Kurdish Workers Union)*
Avny Kesem/Halim Sahbudah: Stortenbekerstraat 216, 2161
Den Haag   »90
- **Koerdische Arbeidersvereniging Nederland, KKKH** *(Kurdish Workers Association of the Netherlands)*
Ali Akyar: Postbus 25965, 2502 HZ Den Haag; *t* (070) 389
5025
Member of EU Migrants' Forum, p131.   »94

◎ SPAIN *34*

- **Asociación de Amistad Hispano-Kurda** *(Spanish-Kurdish Friendship Society)*
calle General Alvarez Castro 16, Madrid; *t* (91) 594 3174 »95
- **Asociación Cultural Kurda, ACK** *(Kurdish Cultural Society)*
Mohamed Rashid Aref: avenida Costa Brava 57-59, 1° 3ª,
08380 Malgrat de Mar; *t* (93) 765 4313   »94

◎ SWEDEN *46*

- **Swedish Committee for the Human Rights of Kurdish People**
Boks 27320, 10254 Stockholm   »93

◎ SWITZERLAND *41*

- **Association Suisse-Kurdistan**
Rocher 12, 2300 La-Chaux-de-Fonds
Founded 1985; culture, information, Swiss-Kurdish contact. »96

◎ UNITED KINGDOM *44*

- **Day-Mer**
Old Library, Howard Rd, London N16 8PR; *t* (0171) 275 8440
Kurdish and Turkish support group.   »95
- ✿ **Kurdish Centres**
Selby Centre, Selby Rd, London N17; *t* (0181) 365 1889 »95
- ✿ **Kurdish Cultural Centre, KCC**
Fazil Kawani/Sarbast Aram: 14 Stannary Street, London SE11
4AA; *t* (0171) 735 0918, 820 9999, *f* 582 8894
Social, cultural and welfare centre for exiles; supports self-
determination for all peoples. Advice and casework on rights,
immigration, housing and welfare.   »95
- **Kurdish Relief Association**
BM Box 456, London WC1N 3XX   »88
- ✿ **Kurdish Society of Manchester**
Mouf Jafar: 18 Keppel Rd, Chorlton-cum-Hardy, Manchester
M21 1AT; *t* (0161) 973 6095
Social and cultural gatherings.   »93
- **Kurdistan Human Rights Project, KHRP**
Room 236, Linen Hall, 162-168 Regent Street, London W1R
5TB; *t* (0171) 287 2772, *f* 734 4927
Protection of the human rights of all Kurds; lobbies UN, CSCE
and governments, prepares ECHR cases.   »95
- ✿ **Kurdistan Information Centre**
Mizgin Sen/Mark Campbell: 10 Glasshouse Yard, London EC4
4JN; *t* (0171) 250 1315, *f* 250 1317
Also at 129 St John's Way, N19 3RQ, *t* 272 9499.
Information on North-West Kurdistan/Eastern Turkey;
contacts for media. *Kurdistan Human Rights Bulletin* (26/yr);
Kurdistan Report (6/yr).   »95
- **Kurdistan Solidarity Committee**
44 Ainger Road, London NW3 3AT
Campaigns for the creation of an independent Kurdish state.
Defends rights of Kurdish exiles and political prisoners in
Western Europe, including the PKK spokesman Kani Yilmaz,
who was arrested in Britain in 1994.   »95
- **Kurdistan Workers' Association, KWA,** also known as
Kurdish Workers Association
The Co-ordinator: Fairfax Hall, 11 Portland Gardens, London
N4 1HU; *t* (0181) 880 1804, 809 0743
Community centre; English language and vocational training,
cultural activities, advice and support for refugees.   »95
- **MED TV**
Haluk Sayan, Managing Director: [address unknown] London
Satellite TV broadcasting to Kurdish regions and communities.
Seeks to counter censorship of nationalist views.   »95

KUWAITI

see also Arab/Arabic, Islamic, Middle Eastern

◎ UNITED KINGDOM *44*

- **Free Kuwait Campaign**
41 Porchester Terrace, Bayswater, London W2 3TS
Kuwaiti government propaganda agency.   »91

LAOTIAN

see also Asian, South-East Asian

◎ FRANCE *33*

- **Association des femmes Lao en France, AFLF** *(Association of Lao Women in France)*
chez Mme Thong Sy Sonerajvong: 3 rue de l'Amiral-Roussin,
75015 Paris   »90
- ✿ **Association Laotienne—Lao Dok Champa**
54 rue du Jeudi, 61000 Alençon   »89
- ✿ **Association Mittaphab Lao de la Savoie**
401 avenue Georges-Clemenceau, 73000 Chambéry
Non-political; aid to refugees, promotion of Lao culture. »90
- ✿ **Association des réfugiés Lao-Hmong, ARLHM**
15 rue des Azalées, 87280 Limoges   »90
- ✿ **Association de solidarité des réfugiés laotiens de Nogent-sur-Seine**
168 bis rue Henri-Millet, 10100 Romilly-sur-Seine
Contacts among Laotians and with the French community. »90
- ✿ **Entraide Lao-Hmong** *(Lao-Hmong Mutual Assistance)*
9 rue des Vaneaux, apt 24, 45500 Gien
Integration of refugees, friendship with wider community. »89

LATIN AMERICAN

see also Antillean, Argentinian, Bolivian, Brazilian, Caribbean, Central American, Chilean, Colombian, Cuban, Dominican Republic, French: DOM/TOM, Guatemalan, Guyanese, Honduran, Mexican, Nicaraguan, Paraguayan, Peruvian, Puerto Rican, Salvadorean, Spanish, Uruguayan

◎ BELGIUM *32*

- **Centre d'Etudes d'Amérique Latine** *(Centre for Latin American Studies)* Université Libre de Bruxelles
María Olga Lutz: Institut de Sociologie, Avenue Jeanne 44,
1050 Bruxelles; *t* (02) 642 3182   »90
- ✿ **Vlaamse Werkgroep Indianen Zuid-Amerika, WIZA** *(Flemish Working Group on South American Indians)*
Rood Kruisstraat 43, 8800 Roeselare   »93

◎ DENMARK *45*

- ✿ **Dansk-Latinamerikansk Kvindeforening, DLK** *(Danish-Latin American Women's Committee)*
Birthe Nielsen: Humleslippen 31, 2620 Albertslund   »93
- ✿ **Latinamerikansk Kulturcenter**
Klostergade 37, 8000 Århus C; *t* 8615 9032   »89
- ✿ **Latinamerikanske Børneværksteder** *(Latin American Youth Workers)*
c/o Daghøjskolen, Blågårdsgade 15 B, 4.sal, 2200
København N; *t* 3139 6208   »89

◎ FRANCE *33*

- ✿ **Amitiés Lot-Amérique latine, Lot-AL** *(Lot-Latin America Friendship Association)*
Jean Claude Nowodworsky: Hotel de Ville, 46600 Martel;
t 6532 1481, 6537 3929
Latin American cultural events, international solidarity.   »94
- **Association Diffusion de l'Information sur l'Amérique Latine, DIAL** *(Association for Information on Latin America)*
47 quai Grands Augustins, 75006 Paris; *t* (1) 4633 4247 »90
- ✿ **Association de Solidarité avec les Peuples d'Amérique Latine, ASPAL**
La Croix Guillaud, 16440 Mouthjiers-sur-Boeme; *t* 4567
8847, *f* 4567 8129
Solidarity, human rights, rural development in Latin America;
supports craft industries among refugees in Mexico.   »93

◎ GERMANY *49*

- **Deutsch-iberoamerikanischer Kulturkreis** *(German-Latin American Cultural Circle)*
[address unknown] Berlin   »88
- **Dokumentations- und Informationszentrum Menschenrechte in Lateinamerika, DIML** *(Latin America Human Rights Documentation Centre)*
Fürther Straße 22, 8500 Nürnberg 80; *t* (0911) 267942,
f 265974
Support for human rights NGOs in Latin America; information
and lobbying on human rights protection and violations.   »93
- ✿ **Informationsstelle Lateinamerika, ILA**
Heerstraße 205, 5300 Bonn 1   »93

◎ **IRELAND** *353*

● **Latin America Solidarity Committee**
Matty Ryan: 97 Upper Newcastle Street, Galway; *t/f* (091)
21088
International solidarity, human rights.   »94

◎ **ITALY** *39*

✧ **Associazione dei Cittadini Latino-Americani, ACLA**
(Association of Latin American Citizens)
[address uncertain] via delli Sabelli 185, 00185 Roma;
t (06) 495 8626
Also listed (1990) as same street but no. 187; or via Alpi
Apuane 54, 00141 Roma; or via Milazzo 3, 00185 Roma.»90
✧ **Associazione della Comunità dei Latino Americani in Veneto,**
ACLAV *(Veneto Latin American Community Association)*
Rodrigo Díaz: via Trieste 22 bis, 35121 Padova; *t* (041) 549
7854, 549 7858
International and inter-cultural solidarity, anti-racism, migrant
welfare.   »94
✧ **Associazione per la Promozione della Cultura Latino**
Americana in Italia, APCLAI *(Association for the Promotion of*
Latin American Culture)
Marcia Flores: via Peschiera 5, 30174 Venezia; *t* (041) 549
7854, 549 7858, *f* 974331
Promotion of Latin American visual arts. See ULEV, p145.»94
● **Centro Ecclesiale Italiano America Latina, CEIAL** *(Italian*
Church Centre on Latin America) and Centro Documentazione
Oscar Romero, CEDOR
Bacilieri 1a, 37139 Verona
Catholic missionary and documentation centre.   »93
✧ **Circolo Latino-Americano** *(Latin American Circle)*
[address unknown] Genova   »90
✧ **Coordinamento Latino-Americani Democratici in Umbria**
(Umbrian Co-ordination of Latin American Democrats)
[address unknown] Perugia   »90
✧ **Gruppo Latino-Americano** *(Latin American Group)*
via Rosina 13, 31011 Asolo, TV; *t* (0423) 564280   »90
● **Servizio Informazione América Latina, SIAL** *(Latin America*
Information Service)
[address unknown]
News service, bulletin (6/yr).   »90

◎ **NETHERLANDS** *31*

● **Central Latinoamericana de Trabajadores, CLAT**
Nieuwegracht 47, 3512 LE Utrecht; *t* (030) 231 9675,
f 236 7185
Solidarity with the labour movement in Latin America.   »93

◎ **NORWAY** *47*

● **Latin America Groups in Norway**
Fredenborgveien 39, 0177 Oslo 1   »93

◎ **PORTUGAL** *351*

● **Grupo de Solidariedade com America Latina, GSAL** *(Latin*
America Solidarity Group)
Rua Pinheiro Chagas 77, 2° E, 1000 Lisboa   »93

◎ **SPAIN** *34*

● **Asociación de la Comunidad Iberoamericana en Cataluña,**
ACIC *(Latin American Community Association of Catalonia)*
Samuel Fernández Z.: carrer Caspe 44-2°, 08010 Barcelona,
Catalunya; *t* (93) 318 7383, 319 2086, *f* 319 6244
Refugee and migrant welfare advice, solidarity with Latin
America; cultural activities. *Colaboramos*.   »94
● **Asociación de Estudiantes Latinoamericanos, AELAS**
(Association of Latin American Students)
Félix Coicou: Galerna 1-4° D, Barrio Las Avenidas 1a fase C,
41004 Sevilla, Andalucía; *t* (954) 231777, 235293   »87
● **Asociación de Investigación y Especialización sobre temas**
iberoamericanos *(Latin American Specialist Research*
Association)
calle Claudio Coello 101, Madrid; *t* (91) 577 0640   »95
✧ **Asociación Latinoamericana de Baleares** *(Latin American*
Association of the Balearics)
calle Ramón Severa Moyá 42, 07015 Palma, Mallorca   »87
✧ **Asociación de Mujeres Latinoamericanas** *(Association of*
Latin American Women)
Casa de la Mujer, calle Almagro 28, 28004 Madrid; *t* (91)
308 6585   »94
✧ **Casal Latinoamericano en Catalunya, CLACA** *(Latin*
American Centre in Catalonia)
carrer Diputació 215, entresol 1a, 08007 Barcelona,
Catalunya; *t* (93) 453 (253?) 1903   »94

● **Centro Español de Estudios de América Latina, CEDEAL**
(Latin American Studies Centre of Spain) and Instituto de
Cooperación Iberoamericana
avenida de los Reyes Católicos 4-5°, 28040 Madrid; *t* (91)
243 3088, 544 6375
Research, documentation, academic and cultural exchange;
development co-operation; both agencies are sponsored by
the Agencia Española de Cooperación Internacional, p212.»94
✧ **Centro de Información y Orientación para la Mujer**
Iberoamericana Refugiada, Asilada o Inmigrante *(Latin*
American Women Refugee, Asylum-Seeker and Immigrant
Information Centre)
Yvonne David: calle Núñez Morgado 4, of. 92, 28036 Madrid;
t (91) 733 7474, 314 5193
Boletín Informativo.   »90
● **Centro de Investigaciones y Promoción Iberoamérica-Europa,**
CIPIE *(Latin America-Europe Research and Promotion Centre)*
calle Núñez Morgado 9-6° C izq., 28036 Madrid; *t* (91) 733
7474
Cuadernos CIPIE.   »93
✧ **Centro Latinoamericano** *(Latin American Centre)*
calle Diputado José Ribas s/n, 07080 Ibiza   »94
✧ **Comité Latinoamericano**
calle S. Cosme y S. Damián 24-2° 2, 28012 Madrid; *t* (91)
522 9161, 741 4216   »94
● **Consejo de Investigación y Documentación Europa y**
América Latina, CIDEAL *(Europe and Latin America Research*
and Documentation Council)
calle Cea Bermúdez 14-4° A, Madrid; *t* (91) 254 5081
Associated with Centro de Inmigrantes, Refugiados y Asilados,
p150. *Boletín CIDEAL*.   »90
● **Fundación para el Desarollo del Cooperativismo y la Economía**
Social, FUNDESCOOP *(Foundation for the Development of the*
Co-operative Movement and the Social Economy)
calle San Bernardo 20-5ª, 28015 Madrid; *t* (91) 522 3155,
f 532 9379
International development agency of the Spanish co-operative
movement, supporting numerous projects in Latin America
including refugee reintegration work.   »93
● **Instituto de Relaciones Europeo-Latinoamericanos** *(Institute*
for European-Latin American Relations)
calle Pedro de Valdívia 10, 28002 Madrid; *t* (91) 261 7200
Government-funded.   »90
✧ **Unidad Hispano Latina**
Pez 27-2° dcha, of. 207, 28204 Madrid; *t* (91) 522 5318»94

◎ **SWEDEN** *46*

● **Svalorna i Sverige Latin Amerika Sectionen**
Barnängsgatan 23, 11641 Stockholm   »93

◎ **UNITED KINGDOM** *44*

● **Carila Latin American Resource Centre** and Latin American
Welfare Group
Stefanie Borkum: Manor Gardens Centre, 6-9 Manor Gardens,
London N7 6LA; *t* (0171) 272 4231
Solidarity with Latin America; advice work, interpretinng,
casework with refugees and migrants in London; housing,
benefits, immigration law.   »95
● **Centre for Latin American Studies**, University of Cambridge
Dr David Cleary: History Faculty Building, West Road,
Cambridge CB3 9EF; *t* (01233) 335390   »94
✧ **Clwyd Latin America Human Rights Group**
[address unknown] Clwyd, Wales   »92
✧ **Edinburgh Latin America Solidarity Campaign**
[address unknown] Edinburgh, Scotland   »92
● **Hispanic and Luso-Brazilian Council**
2 Belgrave Square, London SW1; *t* (0171) 235 2303
Fosters cultural, economic and political relations between the
UK and the Spanish- and Portuguese-speaking world.   »95
● **Institute of Latin American Studies, ILAS**
Dr Elizabeth Allen: University of Glasgow, 69 Oakfield Ave.,
Glasgow G12 8QH; *t* (0141) 339 8855
Postgraduate research and teaching centre.   »94
● ≡ Dr W. Little: University of Liverpool, PO Box 147,
Liverpool L69 3BX; *t* (0151) 794 3079, *f* 794 3080
Postgraduate study and research on history, postgrad,
international relations, politics, sociology, economics.   »95
● ≡ University of London: 31 Tavistock Square, London WC1H
9HA; *t* (0171) 387 5671, *f* 388 5024, *e* ilas@sas.ac.uk   »95
✧ **La Gaitana Housing Co-op Ltd**
Room 7, 2nd Floor, Docklands Enterprise Centre, 11
Marshalsea Road, London SE1 1EP; *t* (0171) 717 1250
Co-operative managing over 40 properties in London, housing
Latin American migrants and refugees.   »95

- **Latin America Bureau**, LAB: Research and Action on Latin America and the Caribbean
Dr Jenny Pierce/James Ferguson: 1 Amwell Street, London EC1R 1UL; *t* (0171) 278 2829
Research, production of educational resources, books and booklets. Solidarity, development issues.   »95
- **Latin America Newsletters**
61 Old Street, London EC1; *t* (0171) 251 0012
Commercial publishing operation.   »91
- **Latin American Advisory Committee**
Rosa Gómez, Co-ordinator: Latin American House, Kingsgate Place, London NW6 4TA; *t* (0171) 372 6567-68
Rigoberto Pizarro. Current affairs documentation, refugees, welfare, casework, advice, anti-discrimination work. See also Latin American Association, below: same organisation?   »94
- **Latin American Arts Association**
Canning House, 2 Belgrave Square, London SW1X; *t* (0171) 245 6661   »90
- **Latin American Association**, LAA; also Latin American Community Health Group, Latin American Cultural Centre
Enrique Saenz/Pilar Charlie: Latin American House, Kingsgate Place, London NW6 4TA; *t* (0171) 624 6409, *f* 372 5244
Community centre, cultural and other activities extended 1994 to include free Legal and Social Advice Service, now with a large immigration caseload.   »96
- **Latin American Centre**, Oxford University
St Antony's College, Oxford OX2 9JF; *t* (01865) 59651   »94
- ✿ **Latin American Co-operative Development Project Ltd**
38 Mount Pleasant, London WC1X; *t* (0171) 278 8377   »90
- ✿ **Latin American Disabled Group**
[address unknown] London; *t* (0181) 964 2441, 960 2690
Volunteer service providing support, transport and social activities for Spanish, Portuguese and Latino disabled.   »94
- **Latin American Refugee Organisations against the Asylum Bill**
[address unknown] London   »96
- ✿ **Latin American Research and Socio-Cultural Studies Centre**
Jorge Salgado Rocha, Director: 299b Westbourne Park Road, London W11 1EE   »90
- ✿ **Latin American Women's Aid**, LAWA
Box 40, 136-138 Kingsland High St, Hackney, London E8 2NS
Support for women/children fleeing domestic violence.   »96
- ✿ **Latin American Women's Rights Service**, LAWRS
Julia Zalazar: Wesley House, Wild Court, London WC2B 4AU; *t* (0171) 831 4145
Advice to women students, refugees and immigrants.   »96
- ✿ **Machitún Theatre**
Nicky Parker: 46 Wilberforce Road, London N4 2SR
Lila Conde artistic director; women's theatre group.   »90
- **Research Unit on European-Latin American Relations**
Roberto Espíndola: University of Bradford, Bradford BD7 1DP; *t* (01274) 383823, *f* 305340   »94
- **Society for Latin American Studies**, SLAS
Peter Beardsell, Secretary: Department of Hispanic Studies, University of Hull, Hull HU6 7RX; *t* (01482) 465360
Founded 1964, 400 members; promotes study of all aspects of Latin American history and society. *Bulletin of Latin American Research*; *Newsletter* (3/yr).   »94
- **Solidarity with Latin America**
[address unknown] London   »92

LATVIAN

see also Baltic, East European, European

◎ **UNITED KINGDOM** *44*

- **Association of Latvian Youth in Europe, GB Branch**
[address unknown]   »90
- **Latvian Welfare Fund** Head Office
72 Queensborough Tce, London W2; *t* (0171) 229 1652   »90
- ✿ ≡ 2 Mexborough Avenue, Leeds; *t* (0113) 262 9940   »90
- ✿ ≡ The Hall, Rugby Road, Wolston; *t* (01203) 542701   »90

LEBANESE

see also Arab/Arabic, Islamic, Middle Eastern

◎ **DENMARK** *45*

- **Stottekomiteen for Ghassan Kanafanis Kultur Fond** *(Kanafani Cultural Foundation Support Committee)*
Sættedammen 16, 3400 Hillerød; *t* 4226 1524
Educational and medical charity providing aid to Palestinians and Lebanese in Lebanon.   »93

◎ **FRANCE** *33*

- **Fondation libanaise pour la paix civile permanente** *(Lebanese Foundation for a Permanent Civil Peace)*
Georges Dagher: 58 rue d'Issy, 92170 Vanves; *t* (1) 4642 8797, 4427 1625
Solidarity with Lebanese people, human rights, peace, economic development and reconstruction.   »93
- ✿ **Foyer libanais** *(Lebanese Home)*
[address unknown] 75005 Paris
Attached to Maronite church of Notre Dame du Liban.   »90

◎ **ITALY** *39*

- ✿ **Associazione Studenti Libanesi** *(Association of Lebanese Students)*
c/o CISCAST, via Principi d'Acaia 42, 10138 Torino; *f* (011) 447717   »90
- **Unione Generale degli Studenti e Lavoratori Libanesi in Italia** *(General Union of Lebanese Students and Workers in Italy)*
[address unknown] Roma   »90

◎ **SPAIN** *34*

- **Comité de Solidaridad Cataluña-Líbano** *(Catalonia-Lebanon Solidarity Committee)*
Rosa María Girbau i Vila: carrer Xifre 54, 08026 Barcelona, Catalunya; *t* (93) 210 2483, *f* 219 9453
International solidarity, culture, welfare.   »94

LIBERIAN

see also African, West African

◎ **UNITED KINGDOM** *44*

- **Liberian Association**
c/o IBO Community Centre, Parkway, Liverpool L8   »91
- ✿ **Liberian Association of Manchester**
S.K. Kajue: St Wilfrid's Presbytery, Birchvale Close, Hulme, Manchester M15 5BJ; *t* (0161) 226 2042
Cultural and social activities; welfare advice, immigration matters, anti-racism, care of elderly.   »93
- ✿ **Liberian Women Association of Manchester**
J.B. Kajue: 17 Holdgate Close, Hulme, Manchester M15 5EP; *t* (0161) 226 0701
Social and self-help group for women of Liberian origin or from other oppressed groups; equal opportunities, anti-racism. »93

LIBYAN

see also African, Arab, Islamic, Maghrebi, Middle Eastern, North African

◎ **UNITED KINGDOM** *44*

- **Jama'a al-Islamiya** *(Islamist Movement)*
Milad Hasadi: [address unknown] London
Probably the largest Libyan opposition grouping in the UK.»95
- **National Salvation Front**
[address unknown] London
Secular opposition coalition.   »95

LITHUANIAN

see also Baltic, East European, European

◎ **UNITED KINGDOM** *44*

- **Lithuanian Youth Association in Great Britain**
[address unknown]   »90

MACEDONIAN

this term is employed, in line with the usage of the groups referred to and with no political significance, to refer both to the Greek region and the Former Yugoslav Republic; see also East European, (Ex-)Yugoslav, Greek, South-East European

◎ **DENMARK** *45*

- ✿ **Jugoslaviske Forening Makedonija** *(Macedonia Yugoslavian Association)*
Stojan Nestorov: Frederikssundsvej 111, 2.th., 2400 København NV   »89

✿ Jugoslaviske Klub Makedonia *(Macedonia Yugoslavian Club)*
Postbox 42, 3500 Værløse   »90
✿ Makedonija *(Macedonia)*
Postbox 151, 2750 Ballerup; *t* 4444 2382
Listed by CIEMI as Greek, but may be the FYR of Macedonia;
cultural and information group.   »94

◎ FRANCE *33*

✿ Groupe Culturel et Artistique Nova Makedonija *(New
Macedonia Cultural and Artistic Group)*
[address unknown] Paris   »90

MADAGASCAN

see also African

◎ UNITED KINGDOM *44*

● Anglo-Malagasy Society
Hobsons, Croft Road, Chalfont St Peter SL9 9AF; *t* (01753)
884006
Friendship, cultural exchanges.   »90

MAGHREBI

*see also African, Algerian, Arab/Arabic, Islamic, Libyan, Middle
Eastern, Moroccan, North African, Saharan, Tunisian*

◎ BELGIUM *32*

✿ Centre Belgo-Maghrébin d'Expression et de Communication
'Mosaïque', CBMEC *(Mosaic Centre for Belgian-Maghrebi
Expression and Communication)*
Abdel Fargaoui, President: Rue Victor Greyson 24, 1050
Bruxelles; *t* (02) 513 9602
Social and welfare activities.   »90
● Fédération des Institutions Socio-Culturelles, FISC
(Federation of Social and Cultural Institutions)
Place de Dinant 6, 1000 Bruxelles; *t* (02) 512 2840, 511
2906
Welfare of immigrants; intercultural contact.   »94
● Jeunesse Maghrébine *(Maghrebi Youth)*
Rachida Boughanem: Centre Jeunes, Rue de Flandre 127,
1000 Bruxelles; *t* (02) 219 6991
Mohamed Said Azami, Zian Khalid, Amidou Si M'hammed;
youth, women's issues, immigrant employment; research and
information work.   »94

◎ FRANCE *33*

✿ Amitiés et Liens France-Maghreb, ALIF *(France-Maghreb
Friendship Links)*
Chadli Daoud: 1 rue Hauquelin, 38000 Grenoble; *t* 7642
3889, *f* 7642 5379
Cross-cultural and international solidarity, social activities,
employment issues. This address was (1990) that of
Association Dauphinoise de Coopération Franco-Algérienne,
ADCFA, from which ALIF may be derived.   »94
● Association des Cadres d'Origine Maghrébine d'Europe
(European Association of Managers of Maghrebi Origin)
Abdesselam Kleiche: 133 avenue de Stalingrad, 93240
Stains; *t* (1) 4827 7111, *f* 4664 2882   »94
✿ ≡ Mohamed Cherfaoui: 3 rue de Metz, 92700 Colombes
ACADOME info.   »94
✿ Association culturelle franco-maghrébine, ACFM
13 rue de l'Angleterre, 44000 Malakoff
Objects include repatriation of bodies.   »89
✿ ≡ 21 allée Baco, 44000 Nantes; *t* 4089 1567, 5182 0251
Malkoktail.   »94
✿ Association culturelle maghrébine des Ardennes *(Maghrebi
Cultural Association of Ardennes)*
9 place Winston-Churchill, 08000 Charleville-Mézières
Education, sport, culture, anti-racism, integration.   »90
✿ Association culturelle maghrébine de Caussade, ACMC
(Maghrebi Cultural Association of Caussade)
Mairie, 82300 Caussade
Religion, culture, mutual understanding.   »90
✿ Association culturelle des maghrébins de Sarcelles, ACMS
(Maghrebi Cultural Association of Sarcelles)
Messaouden Brahim: 11 bvd Bergson, 95200 Sarcelles »91
✿ Association franco-maghrébine, AFM
BP 105, 54408 Longwy Cedex; *t/f* 8225 8582
Location: 7 rue Abbé-Mussey. Defence of Maghrebi interests,
cultural and leisure activities.   »94

● Association franco-maghrébine pour le développement rural,
AFMDR *(Franco-Maghrebi Association for Rural Development)*
24 rue Chaligny, 75012 Paris   »89
✿ Association d'Information et de Réflexion sur la Culture
Maghrébine en Ariège, AIRCM
Mustapha Cherrou: [address unknown] 09100 Limbrassac;
t 6160 0757   »94
✿ Association pour l'Insertion des Femmes Originaires du
Maghreb et Jeunes, APIFOMEJ *(Association for the
Integration of Maghrebi Women and Youth)*
Khelladi Mama: rue des Mouettes, 31400 Toulouse; *t* 6153
5234   »94
✿ Association des Jeunes Maghrébines, AJM *(Young
Maghrebi Women's Association)*
Samia Nassiri: 50 Groupe Eisenhower, 17 rue Paul Taittinger,
51100 Reims; *t* 2608 7310   »94
✿ Association maghrébine de Clermont, AMC
chez M Chibouni: appt 196, 13 rue Victor-Hugo, batiment
Maine, 60600 Clermont
Islamic education, culture, inter-cultural contact.   »90
✿ Association des Maghrébins Intégrés *(Association of
Integrated Maghrebis)*
36 boulevard de Verdun, 92400 Courbevoie
Integration in French and European host communities.   »90
✿ Association des Maghrébins sparnaciens *(Epernay Maghrebi
Association)*
chez M Laghmar: 10 ave. de Middelkerke, 51200 Epernay»89
● Association nationale des élus originaires du Maghreb,
ANEOM *(National Association of Maghrebi Elected Officials)*
BP 213, 75011 Paris   »96
✿ Association des psychologues, psychothérapeutes et
animateurs maghrébins, APPAM *(Association of Maghrebi
Psychologists, Psychotherapists and Group Leaders)*
10 ter. boulevard Gambetta, 38000 Grenoble
Professional and social association.   »90
✿ Association Sociale, Educative et Culturelle de Solidarité
avec les Maghrébins *(Maghrebi Solidarity Social, Educational
and Cultural Society)*
G. Chaumont: 20 rue Eric Satie, 31100 Toulouse; *t* 6140
3243   »94
✿ Association Socioculturelle et Sportive des Maghrébins de
Joué-les-Tours *(Maghrebi Social, Cultural and Sports Society)*
maison pour tous, rue A. Bourdelle, 37300 Joué-lès-Tours »89
✿ Association Voyage Echange culturel euro-maghrébin
(Euro-Maghrebi Travel and Cultural Exchange Society)
112 rue de Géole, 14300 Caen
Cultural exchanges between Europe and the Maghreb.   »89
✿ Club Europe Maghreb
2 rue Vauban, 59140 Dunkerque
Individual and community-level contacts for Euro-Maghrebi
communication and co-operation.   »89
● Comité d'aide aux maghrébins agés en France, CAMAF
(Committee for Aid to Maghrebi Elders in France)
49 rue Mirabeau, 75016 Paris   »90
✿ Conseil consultatif des populations d'origine maghrébine de
Franche-Comté *(Franche-Comté Maghrebi Communities
Consultative Council)*
centre Pierre-Mendès-France, 3 rue Beauregard, 25006
Besançon
Moral and legal rights and interests of Franche-Comté
Maghrebis, full integration.   »90
✿ Esperance maghrébine monsoise *(Mons Maghrebi Hope)*
7-10 rue René-Coty, 59370 Mons-en-Baroeul   »90
✿ Etoile maghrébine *(Maghrebi Star)*
La Rocade, batiment A1, 91160 Longjumeau
Sporting, social and cultural, second-generation youth.   »89
✿ Expressions Maghrébines au Féminin, EMAF *(Maghrebi
Women's Self-Expression)*
Halima Theiry-Boumedienne: 29 rue Godefroy-Cavaignac,
75011 Paris; *t* (1) 4348 6237   »90
✿ Groupe Chants et Danses du Maghreb *(Maghreb Song and
Dance Group)*
Lahcen Khacime: 29 rue Jean Perrin, 18000 Bourges; *t* 4870
5806
Culture, educational welfare.   »94
✿ Institut franco-maghrébin pour la jeunesse *(Franco-Maghrebi
Youth Institute)*
38 rue Edmond-Darbois, 92230 Gennevilliers   »90
✿ Jeunesse Maghrébine *(Maghrebi Youth)*
3 chemin de la Ville, Puyvineux, 17220 La Jarrie
Culture, sport, communication, integration in host country. »89
✿ Rassemblement des Etudiants Maghrébins en Savoie, REMS
(Union of Maghrebi Students in Savoy)
Stan Larbi: 23 rue Jean-Gérard-Madoux, 73000 Chambéry
Legal advice, mediation with authorities, solidarity.   »90

◉ ITALY *39*

✿ **Association Maghrébarab Valdotaine, AMAV** *(Maghreb Arab Association of the Val d'Aosta)*
Rachid Tarhia: c/o ARCI-UISP, pza Cavalieri di Vittorio Veneto 11, 11100 Aosta; *t* (0165) 331342, 265640, *f* 235640
Welfare, housing, cultural interests of Maghrebi immigrants.»94

✿ **Associazione Culturale Italo-Maghrebina, ACIM**
Driss Liateni: via del Zeffro 45, 00054 Fiumicino Paese, RM;
t (06) 645 3186　　　　　　　　　　　　　　　　　　»90

◉ NETHERLANDS *31*

✿ **Stichting Samenwerkingsverband Marokkaanen en Tunisiërs, SMT** *(Moroccan and Tunisian Co-operative Union)* also known as Inspraakorgaan Marokkaanen en Tunisiërs
Ahmed Lamnadi, Chair: Keistraat 4, 3512 HV Utrecht; *t* (030) 236 7327, *f* 236 9118
Umbrella group affiliated to national LAO forum, p146.　　»95

◉ SPAIN *34*

✿ **Asociación Magrebí Al Tifk**
Salinas 15, pta 4, 46003 Valencia　　　　　　　　　　　»94

✿ **Centre M. Abdelkrim El Khatabi d'Estudis i Documentació, CADE** *(Abdelkrim Research and Documentation Centre)*
Solimán H. Elmorabet: vía Laietana 23, e/s C, 08003 Barcelona, Catalunya; *t/f* (93) 268 4925
Lettre de Abdelkrim.　　　　　　　　　　　　　　　　»94

✿ **Comunidad del Pueblo Magrebí**
pza del Callao 1-6°, of. 9, 28013 Madrid; *t* (91) 523 2197»94

MALAGASY

see Madagascan

MALAYSIAN

see also Asian, Islamic, South-East Asian

◉ AUSTRIA *43*

✿ **Vienna Malayalee Association**
Türkenstrasse 3, 1090 Wien　　　　　　　　　　　　　»93

◉ IRELAND *353*

✿ **Malaysia Hall**
31 Leeson Park, Dublin 6; *t* (01) 660 5598, 660 4738
Student residence?　　　　　　　　　　　　　　　　　»94

◉ UNITED KINGDOM *44*

● **British Malaysian Society, BMS**
Janet Taylor, Honorary Secretary: 9 Artillery Passage, London E1 7LJ; *t* (0171) 375 0085, *f* 247 9467
Friendship, culture, trade relations; founded 1983.　　»90

✿ **Malaysian Centre**
Abdul Halim Ab Wahid, Warden: 12-13 Burlington Street, Brighton BN1, Sussex; *t* (01273) 687960
Mainly concerned with housing and welfare of students.　»94

● **Malaysian Islamic Study Group**
90 St Thomas' Road, Finsbury Park, London N4 2WQ;
t (0181) 345 2318　　　　　　　　　　　　　　　　　»94

✿ **Muslim Youth Movement of Malaysia**
63 Humphrey Road, Old Trafford, Manchester M16 9DE
Based at Masjid-e-Hidayah Sunni-Shafi'i mosque, p59.　»94

◉ NORTHERN IRELAND *44*

✿ **Malaysian Students' Centre**
Mohd Zin Mohd Sel, Warden: 22 Adelaide Park, Belfast BT9;
t (01232) 683439　　　　　　　　　　　　　　　　　»94

MALIAN

see also African, West African

◉ FRANCE *33*

✿ **Association pour le développement de Sidibela**
56 rue Anian-Cavillon, 93350 Le Bourget
Development aid to home district.　　　　　　　　　　»89

✿ **Association des ressortissants gorysiens en France, ARGF** *(Association of Gorysian People in France)*
Amara Konté: 9 rue Bailly-de-Suffren, 93600 Aulnay-sous-Bois
Locality-based social and welfare group.　　　　　　　»90

● **Association des Travailleurs Maliens en France** *(Association of Malian Workers in France)*
120 rue Ambroise Croisat, 93200 Saint-Denis; *t* (1) 4820 5837　　　　　　　　　　　　　　　　　　　　　　»90

✿ **Bénévoles franco-maliens pour l'aide au développement du village de Samantara** *(Franco-Malian Voluntary Group for Development Aid to Samantara)*
résidence Charles-de-Gaulle, 16 route de Montreuil, 93230 Romainville
Development charity helping home village.　　　　　　»90

✿ **Bokoura: Entraide et amitié** *(Bokoura Mutual Aid and Friendship)*
Mairie, 86190 Chiré-en-Montreuil
Village affinity group, supports rural development projects in Mali.　　　　　　　　　　　　　　　　　　　　　»89

● **Organisation des travailleurs maliens du Cercle de Diema en France, OTMCDF**
23 rue du Retrait, 75020 Paris; *t* (1) 4358 7505
Social and cultural activities, welfare advice and return migration counselling for Malians in France; small-scale development projects in Mali.　　　　　　　　　　　　»93

✿ **Regroupement des Travailleurs Maliens en France, RTMF** *(Malian Workers' Group in France)*
Maison de Quartier D. Balavoine, 18 avenue Léon Blum, 92140 Bondy; *t* (1) 4847 0490　　　　　　　　　　»94

MALVINAS

see under Falkland Islands, p35 (in accordance with the usage of the one group listed)

MAPUCHE

see Chilean

MARTINIQUAIS

see Caribbean, French: DOM/TOM, Latin American

MAURITANIAN

see also African, West African

◉ FRANCE *33*

Association culturelle et sociale des ressortissants sénégalais et mauritaniens des Vosges Halpoulare: see p104

✿ **Association des ressortissants mauritaniens de Bouanze et ses environs en France, ARMBF** *(Society of Mauritanians from Bouanze and District in France)*
41 rue Robespierre, 93170 Bagnolet
Aid to home village.　　　　　　　　　　　　　　　　»90

● **Union des Travailleurs Mauritaniens en France, UTMF** *(Union of Mauritanian Workers in France)*
Mamadou Samba: 3-9 rue Marc Séguin, 75018 Paris; *t* (1) 4607 1142, 4205 5174　　　　　　　　　　　　　　»94

MAURITIAN

see also African, Asian, Hindu, Islamic

◉ UNITED KINGDOM *44*

● *Mauritian International*
Jacques Lee, Editor: 2a Vant Road, London SW17 8TJ;
t (0181) 767 2439
Magazine (12/yr).　　　　　　　　　　　　　　　　　　»88

✿ **Mauritian Muslim Welfare Association**
21 Harlesden Road, St Albans, Herts.; *t* (01727) 31193　»94

● **Mauritius Association of Great Britain**
44 Peckham Road, London SE5 8PX; *t* (0171) 703 1071, 701 5600　　　　　　　　　　　　　　　　　　　　　　»95

✿ **Mauritius Community**
Abdullah Feroze Peersaib: 6 Hurst Road, Eastbourne BN21 2PL; *t* (01323) 22139　　　　　　　　　　　　　　　»94

● *Mauritius News*
Peter Chellen: [address uncertain] PO Box 26, London SE17 1EG; *t/f* (0171) 703 1071
Also listed (1994) at 583 Wandsworth Road, SW8 3JD,
t 498 3066.　Magazine (12/yr).　　　　　　　　　　　»95

MESOPOTAMIAN

see Arab/Arabic, Assyrian, Iraqi, Kuwaiti, Middle Eastern

MEXICAN

see also Latin American

◎ ITALY *39*

● Associazione Italia-Messico *(Italy-Mexico Association)*
via Marche 23, 00187 Roma; *t* (06) 474 2484, 481 9037
International friendship, culture, welfare of migrants.   »90

◎ SPAIN *34*

● Asociación de Investigadores y Estudiantes Mexicanos en
España *(Association of Mexican Researchers and Students)*
Fernando el Católico 86, Madrid; *t* (91) 549 9221
Welfare of Mexican students and employees in Spanish
universities.   »95

◎ UNITED KINGDOM *44*

● British Mexican Society
Nora Kevans, Secretary: 17 Appletree Close, Biggleswade
SG18 8NF
Cultural, social activities, promotion of Mexican studies.   »93
● Mexico Support Group
c/o Dr Neil Harvey: [address uncertain] ILAS, 31 Tavistock
Square, London WC1H 9HA
Address 1989; same as Mexico Solidarity Group (1992)? »92

MIDDLE EASTERN

*see also African, Algerian, Arab/Arabic, Armenian, Assyrian,
Egyptian, Iranian, Iraqi, Islamic, Israeli, Jewish, Jordanian,
Kurdish, Kuwaiti, Lebanese, Libyan, Maghrebi, Moroccan,
North African, Palestinian, Syrian, Tunisian, Turkish, Yemeni*

◎ UNITED KINGDOM *44*

● Labour Middle East Council
21 Collingham Road, London SW5 0NU; *t* (0171) 370 7793
Recognized society within the British Labour Party pursuing
interests in the Middle East.   »95
● *Middle East Economic Digest*, MEED
Edmund O'Sullivan, Editor: 21 John St, London WC1N 2BP
Business magazine.   »95

MOLUCCAN

see also Asian, Dutch, Indonesian, South-East Asian

◎ NETHERLANDS *31*

*Gabungan Jajasan Maluku: a national association of Moluccan
welfare groups, which merged with other bodies in 1995 to
create the Nederlands Expertisecentrum over de Multiculturele
Samenleving, subsequently renamed FORUM—Instituut voor
Multiculturele Ontwikkeling, see p146.*
*Stichting Inspraakorgaan Welzijn Molukkers, IWM (Moluccan
Welfare and Representative Body) and Netwerk Onderwijs en
Werkgelegenheid Molukkers: a Utrecht-based national
federation of groups representing South Moluccan immigrants,
with networks on employment and education issues; a member
of the ADO, p208. Education section, Landelijk Steunpunt
Edukatie Molukkers, LSEM, has or had a separate address:
Postbus 13375, 3507 LJ Utrecht; t 233 3900, f 231 6275;
and sub-office at Collardslaan 12a, 9401 GZ Assen. In 1995
the IWM and other groups merged as the Nederlands
Expertisecentrum over de Multiculterele Samenleving, which
subsequently became FORUM, see p146.*

MONGOLIAN

see also Asian, Chinese

◎ UNITED KINGDOM *44*

● Anglo-Mongolian Society
c/o 44 Rooks Street, Cambridge CB4 4RB
Culture, history; founded 1963.   »90

MONTSERRAT

*see also African Caribbean, Afro-Caribbean, Anglo-Caribbean,
Caribbean, West Indian*

◎ UNITED KINGDOM *44*

● Montserrat Overseas People's Progressive Alliance
[address unknown]   »88

MOROCCAN

*see also African, Arab, Islamic, Jewish, Maghrebi, Middle
Eastern, North African, Saharan*

◎ BELGIUM *32*

✿ Al Manar
Abdesalam Sarie: Rue de Liedekerk 134, 1030 Bruxelles
Advice; social and cultural activities.   »94
✿ Amicale des Travailleurs et Commerçants Marocains
(Moroccan Workers' and Traders' Society)
Noordlaan 6a, 3600 Genk
Employment, training, social activities.   »94
✿ ≡ M. Boumedienne Ahmed: Rue de l'Avenir 14, 4000
Liège; *t* (041) 535088   »95
✿ Association Emergences
Ahmed Najem: Rue du Val Benoit 127, 4031 Angleur;
t (041) 671503   »95
● Association des Jeunes Marocains, AJM *(Moroccan Youth
Association)* Vereniging van Marokkaanse Jongeren
Mohamed Boukourna: Rue de la Vermicellerie 10, Molenbeek,
1080 Bruxelles; *t* (02) 410 7846
Culture, education, information.   »94
✿ Association de Solidarité Marocaine *(Moroccan Solidarity
Association)*
[address unknown] Bruxelles   »90
✿ Association Sportive de la Communauté Marocaine
M'Hamed Tamir: Rue du Pont 50, 4000 Liège;
t (041) 422502   »95
✿ Association Sportive et Culturelle des Jeunes Marocaines
(Moroccan Youth Sporting and Cultural Association)
Dr Benmouna Mohamed: Rue des Pampres 76, 4000 Liège;
t (041) 415502, 526804
Covers Wallonia and Brussels.   »95
✿ Avicenne
Mohamed Alami: Rue Haberman 15, 1070 Bruxelles; *t* (02)
521 0030
Education, culture, minority rights.   »94
✿ Centre Islamique pour les Travailleurs Marocains *(Moroccan
Workers' Islamic Centre)*
Wildekerslaan 5, 3600 Genk
Religious and cultural centre.   »94
✿ Centrum Marokkaanse Arbeiders, CMA: Centre des
Travailleurs Marocains, CTM *(Moroccan Workers' Centre)*
Mohamed Bazi: G. Belliardstraat 8/10, 2000 Antwerpen;
t (03) 232 5402
Social, educational and religious welfare.   »94
✿ Dar al Amal, Association Coopérative de Femmes
Immigrées *(Immigrant Women's Co-operative Society)*
Rue de Ribaucourt 51, 1080 Bruxelles; *t* (02) 428 5444
Education and integration of Moroccan and other Arab
women and young people.   »94
✿ Dar al Maghrib, Association de l'Immigration Marocaine
(Association of Moroccan Immigrants)
Fadi Bennadi: Rue du Croissant 4, 1060 Bruxelles
Social solidarity, anti-racism, information.   »94
✿ L'Entraide *(Mutual Assistance)*
Mme Derfoufi: [address unknown] Liège; *t* (041) 279193
Women's welfare group.   »95
● Fédération des Associations Démocratiques Marocaines,
FADM *(Federation of Moroccan Democratic Associations)*
Rue de Liedekerk 134, 1030 Bruxelles
Information, welfare.   »94
✿ Femmes Traits d'Union
Khadija Tamir: Rue du Cheval Blanc 84, 4000 Rocourt;
t c/o CCILg, (041) 218358
Women's welfare group.   »95
✿ Ibn Sina
Omar Benammar: Dieplaan 19, 3600 Genk
Sport, leisure, cross-cultural activities.   »94
✿ Iligh
Rue Goswin 24, Liège
A Berber Soussi organisation.   »95

✿ **Marokkaanse Culturele Vereniging, MCV** *(Moroccan Cultural Union)*
Ahmed Aoufi: Kapelstr. 6, 2830 Willebroek; *t* (03) 886 5630
Youth welfare, leisure, cultural activities.   »94
✿ **Solidarité Arabe**
Aziz Saidi/Mustafa Sabiki: Rue Herman Reuleaux 52, 4020 Liège; *t* (041) 434705   »95
✿ **Solidariteitsvereniging Marokkaanse Werknemers** *(Moroccan Workers' Solidarity Association)*
Bosrandstraat 47, 3600 Genk
Social and cultural group.   »94
✿ **Union des Marocains à l'Etranger** *(Union of Moroccans Abroad)*
Mansouri Lahsen: Rue des Ecoliers 11, 4020 Liège; *t* (041) 251108   »95

◎ DENMARK *45*

● **Foreningen af Marokkanske Arbejdere i Danmark** *(Moroccan Workers' Society of Denmark)*
c/o Amtals Mohammed: Bevtofgade 6A, 2.th., 1736 Kφbenhavn V   »89
● **Den Marokkanske Forening i Danmark**
Rantzausgade 62-64, opg. A og B, 2200 Kφbenhavn N; *t* 3135 6398, 3139 6241
Welfare, advice, cultural activities.   »94

◎ FRANCE *33*

✿ **Amicale des travailleurs et commerçants marocains, ATCM**
28 rue de l'Ecole, 25000 Besançon
See also national FATCMF, right.   »90
✿ ≡ Département de l'Ain: 34 rue Bourgmeyer, 01000 Bourg-en-Bresse   »90
✿ ≡ Mossaic: Carré Haut, 82210 Castelmayran   »90
✿ **Association Al Amal des Marocains de Bourges**
Mohammed Bryaj: 29 rue Louise Michel, 18000 Bourges; *t* 4865 7540
Cultural, social and leisure activities.   »94
✿ **Association culturelle et cultuelle des marocains d'Amiens-Nord** *(North Amiens Moroccan Cultural & Religious Society)*
1 rue Messager, appt 525, 80080 Amiens   »90
✿ **Association culturelle des marocains français** *(Cultural Association of French Moroccans)*
M.A. Zahir: 1 rue d'Alger, 84000 Avignon   »90
● **Association défense des droits de l'homme en Maroc**
269 bis, rue du Faubourg Saint Antoine, 75011 Paris   »93
✿ **Association des Etudiants marocains de Saint-Etienne**
CERCOOPE, UFR de lettres, 2 rue de la Tréfilerie, 4200 Saint-Etienne   »90
✿ **Association de la fédération des français d'origine marocaine**
140 galerie de l'Arlequin, 38100 Grenoble   »90
● **Association de l'Immigration Marocaine**
37 avenue de la Résistance, 93100 Montreuil   »91
♦ **Association des Marocains en France, AMF:** Head Office
Karim Messaoudi: 10 rue Affre, 75018 Paris; *t* (1) 4255 9182
Represented in EU Migrants Forum, p131; possibly same as Association des Travailleurs Marocains en France. This address may have been superseded by the Puteaux one. »90
✿ ≡ 35 rue Saint Exupéry, 49000 Angers; *t* 4186 0171   »94
✿ ≡ 14 ave. Laure de Noves, 84000 Avignon; *t* 9085 4074 »94
✿ ≡ Maison du Tiers Monde, 27 avenue Louis Blanc, 34000 Montpellier; *t* 6772 2438   »94
✿ ≡ 42 rue de la Fédération, 93100 Montreuil; *t* (1) 4857 7233, 4857 6855   »94
✿ ≡ 56 rue Fontaine au Roi, 75011 Paris; *t* (1) 4806 7031 »94
✿ ≡ 13 rue des Trois Rois, 86000 Poitiers; *t* 4941 1340, *f* 4960 4682
Based in Centre socio-culturel Le Toit du Monde.   »94
✿ ≡ Karim Messaoudi: 20 rue du Bicentenaire, 92800 Puteaux; *t* (1) 4204 2919, 4772 6518, *f* 4204 7161
See also CEDAM (European network), right. *Jossour* (6/yr).»94
✿ **Association Socio-culturelle Marocaine**
13 allée du Tage, 35200 Rennes; *t* 9935 0046   »94
♦ **Association des Travailleurs Marocains en France, ATMF** *(Association of Moroccan Workers in France)* Head Office and documentation centre
Abdullah Zniber: 10 rue Affre, 75018 Paris; *t* (1) 4223 4111, *f* 4255 9182, 4252 6061
See also Association des Marocains en France, above (may be the same organisation); see also CADIM, right. National body representing migrant workers. Member of EU Migrants Forum, p131. Many local sections, some listed below.   »94
✿ ≡ Sarthe: 4 rue d'Arcole, 71200 Le Mans   »91
✿ ≡ 9 boulevard Marcel-Paul, 93450 L'Ile-Saint-Denis   »91
✿ ≡ Marne: 3 allée des Picards, 51100 Reims   »91

✿ **Attadamoun—Solidarité des Marocains à l'Etranger** *(Solidarity among Moroccans Abroad)*
Maison des associations saint-germanoises, 3 rue de la République, 78100 Saint-Germain-en-Laye   »90
▮ **Conseil Européen des Associations Marocaines, CEDAM** *(European Council of Moroccan Associations)*
c/o AMF, 20 rue du Bicentenaire, 92800 Puteaux; *t* (1) 4204 2919, 4772 6518, *f* 4204 7161
Includes the French AMF, left. See also CADIM, below. »94
▮ **Coordination des Associations Démocratiques des Immigrés Marocains en Europe, CADIM** *(Co-ordinating Committee of Democratic Associations of Moroccan Immigrants in Europe)*
c/o ATMF, 10 rue Affre, 75018 Paris; *t* (1) 4223 4111, *f* 4252 6061
See also CEDAM, above. European network of Moroccan immigrant associations, including the ATMF, left. »94
✿ **Fédération des Associations de Travailleurs et Commerçants Marocains en France, FATCMF** *(Federation of Moroccan Workers' and Traders' Associations in France)*
16 rue de l'Orillon, 75011 Paris; *t* (1) 4338 6395   »94
✿ **Fédération Nationale des Marocains de France, FNMF** *(National Federation of Moroccans in France)*
450/4 rue Paul Eluard, 93000 Bobigny; *t* (1) 4832 7985
See also the Islamic FNMF, at same address, p53.   »94
♦ **Union des amicales marocaines en France, UAMF** *(Union of Moroccan Clubs in France)*
5 rue d'Argenson, 75008 Paris   »90
✿ **Union des Travailleurs et Commerçants Marocains** *(Union of Moroccan Workers and Traders)* Région Parisienne
33 rue Charles-de-Foucauld, 78300 Poissy
Youth and community work, group travel, integration.   »89

◎ GERMANY *49*

✿ **Freundschaftskreis der Marokkanischen Arbeiter e.V.** *(Friendship Circle of Moroccan Workers)*
Zimmerstraße 27 b, 44145 Dortmund; *t* (0231) 838933 »94
✿ **Marokkanischer Arbeiterverband e.V., MAV** *(Moroccan Workers' Union)*
Said Charchira/M. Seruali: Postfach 103609, 40027 Düsseldorf; *t* (0211) 771515, *f* 771068
Advice, social centre. Address listed (1990) as Duisburger-straße 66. See also Vereinigung der Marokkanischen Emigranten, below.   »94
● **Vereinigung der Marokkanischen Emigranten in der BRD** *(Association of Moroccan Emigrants in the FRG)*
Said Charchira: Postfach 105125, Oberbilker Allee 1, 40215 Düsseldorf; *t* (0211) 312093, *f* 312094   »94

◎ GIBRALTAR *350*

✿ **Moroccan Workers' Association**
Mohd Sarsri: 15 Casemates, Gibraltar   »95

◎ ITALY *39*

✿ **Associazione di Amicizia Italo-Marocchina** *(Italo-Moroccan Friendship Association)*
corso San Martino 2, 10122 Torino; *t* (011) 57171, 771 0382
See also Centro Islamico Torino, p54.   »90
✿ **Associazione El Bari Moulay**
via Valdibrana 54, 51100 Pistoia; *t* (0573) 975435
Solidarity, anti-racism, cultural and social activities. »94
✿ **Associazione Immigrati Marocchini**
via Mura Interne 3, 60020 Sirolo   »90
✿ ≡ Abruzzo: Youssef Hmich: via Roio 57/9, 67100 L'Aquila; *t* (0862) 419563, *f* 410981   »94
✿ **Associazione Marocchina Bologna**
via G. Alvisi 6, 40138 Bologna   »90
✿ **Associazione Marocchini**
c/o Coordinamento Immigrati Extracomunitari, Salita S. Francesco 4, 16122 Genova; *t* (010) 880403
Was listed (1990) as via Adolfo di Passano 4A, 16148 Genova.   »94
✿ **Associazione dei Marocchini in Italia, Sezione Sarda** *(Association of Moroccans in Italy, Sardinian Branch)*
via Manara 1, 09045 Quartu S. Elena, CA   »90
✿ **Associazione Marocco**
Aqio Mabjouda: via Tiepolo 1, 20129 Milano; *t* (02) 742 6173   »94
✿ **Centro Jerry Masslo**
Giampiero Daglio: via Rosa Rognoni 2, 27035 Meda; *t* (0384) 820063, *f* 822133   »94
✿ **Comunità dei Gruppi Marocchini a Roma e nel Lazio** *(Alliance of Moroccan Groups in Rome and the Lazio)*
presso Calisti: Circonvallazione Appia 31, 00179 Roma; *t* (06) 676 6601, 785 4221   »94

✿ **Unione Marocchini El Massira**
Miloud Moukafih: via Ghidoni, 25035 Ospitaletto, BS   »94

◎ **LUXEMBOURG** *352*

● **Amicale des travailleurs et commerçants marocains**
(Moroccan Workers' and Traders' Society)
Chahbi Bouchaib: 55 rue Glesener, 1631 Luxembourg;
t 490291
Training, employment, education, youth integration.   »94

◎ **NETHERLANDS** *31*

✿ **Amazigh Cultureel Werk Stichting**
Postbus 2530, 3500 GM Utrecht
A Berber Rifan cultural group.   »95
✿ **Association des Migrants Marocains à Utrecht, AMMU**
Driss el Benissi: Postbus 13027, 3507 LA Utrecht
Advice, information; welfare of migrants, anti-racism.   »94
✿ **Culturele Vereniging Adrar**
Postbus 16, 6500 AA Nijmegen
Berber Rifan organisation.   »95
✿ **Haagse Marokkaanse Vereniging** *(The Hague Moroccan Association)*
Korte Lombardstraat 11, 2512 Den Haag   »94
✿ **Stichting Ifoudar**
Postbus 15132, 3501 BC Utrecht
Berber Rifan foundation.   »95
✿ **Stichting Izouran**
Mohamed Chacha: [address unknown] Amsterdam; *t* (020) 673 6793
Also a Berber Rifan group.   »95
✿ **J Projekt, Marokkaanse Contact Functionarissen:**
Humanitas Rotterdam
Pieter de Hoochweg 110, 3024 BM Rotterdam; *t* (010) 425 0118, 425 0125, *f* 477 2658
Youth integration, anti-racism.   »94
✿ **KMAR**
Postbus 81057, 3068 BD Rotterdam   »90
● **Komitee Marokkaanse Arbeiders in Nederland, KMAN**
(Committee of Moroccan Workers in the Netherlands)
Abdou Menehbi/Amin Mouden: Ferdinand Bolstraat 39, 1072 LB Amsterdam; *t* (020) 664 0445, *f* 675 8386
Interests of migrant workers and families; anti-racism; member of MAINE network, p146, and EU Migrants Forum, p131.»94
● **Komitee Marokkaanse Arbeiders in Nederland—Jongeren, KMAN-J**
Postbus 88555, Amsterdam; *t* (020) 675 2116 (?)   »90
✿ **KVAN**
Mauritsweg 20, 3012 JR Rotterdam; *t* (010) 413 1886   »90
✿ **Marokkaans WAO Komitee, MWAOK**
M. Amanzou: Anie Biedmonstraat 109a, 1054 PD Amsterdam; *t* (020) 122490 (?)   »94
✿ **Marokkaanse Jongeren Vereniging Dordrecht-Zwijndrecht**
(Dordrecht-Zwijndrecht Moroccan Youth Union)
Mustafa Elfounti/Karim Tohouss: Wijnstraat 121, 3311 BV Dordrecht   »94
● **Marokkaanse Vrouwenvereniging in Nederland, MVVN**
(Moroccan Women's Union in the Netherlands)
Bachra Dahhan: Hemoniusstraat 14, 1074 BP Amsterdam; *t* (020) 664 7954, 881746   »94
● **Platform Marokkaanse Jongeren** *(Moroccan Youth Representation)*
Postbus 15132, 3501 BC Utrecht; *t* (030) 262 1166 (?)
Not exclusively Berber, although it shares an address with Ifoudar.   »95
✿ **Safax Vereniging voor Tamazight Cultuur**
Postbus 2530, 3500 GM Utrecht
Berber Rifan community group.   »95
✿ **Stedelijke Raad van Marokkaanse Gemeenschap in Amsterdam, SMR** *(Municipal Council of the Moroccan Community in Amsterdam)*
Postbus 55588, 1007 NB Amsterdam; *t* (020) 664 0445
Representation of Moroccan migrant workers and families.»94
✿ **Union des Mosquées Marocaines, UMMON**
M. Echarouti: Newtonstraat 12 F, 1098 HD Amsterdam; *t* (020) 692 5599 (?)
Umbrella organisation for the (almost all Maliki Sunni) Moroccan mosque societies in Holland.   »94

◎ **SPAIN** *34*

✿ **Al Manzil—Centro para Marroquíes** *(Moroccan Community Development Centre)*
calle La Bañeza 26, 28029 Madrid; *t* (91) 739 8753
Cultural activities, information, youth integration. See also Centro de Inmigrantes Al Manzil, p150.   »94

✿ **Asociación Rosalía de Castro**
Consuelo Toscano: avenida Ferrol 23, 28029 Madrid; *t* (91) 378 1072, 323 0756   »94
● **Asociación Cultural Terra Omnium** *(Land of All Cultural Association)*
A.M. Dudú: calle Ejército Español s/n, Edificio Monumental 1°, 29802 Melilla; *t* (952) 686337   »87
● **Asociación de Emigrantes Marroquíes en España, AEME** *(Association of Moroccan Emigrants in Spain)*
M. Anwar: Esgrima 7-4° E, 28012 Madrid; *f* (91) 235 6507
Employment, welfare and culture. Also listed (1994) at Club de Amigos de la Unesco, plaza Tirso de Molina 8-1°, 28012 Madrid, *t* 369 0842.   »94
✿ ≡ Radwan Asouik: Apartado de Correos 6, Colmenar Viejo, 28770 Madrid   »94
✿ **Asociación de Inmigrantes Marroquíes de Cataluña—Dar al Maghrib** *(Society of Moroccan Immigrants in Catalonia)*
carrer Sant Pau 17, 08001 Barcelona, Catalunya   »90
✿ **Asociación de Mujeres Inmigrantes Marroquíes, AMIM** *(Association of Moroccan Immigrant Women)*
Zohra El Guennouni: Casa de la Mujer, calle Almagro 28, 28010 Madrid; *t* (91) 308 1847, *f* 308 6585
Women's cultural and social group; anti-racist work.   »94
✿ **Asociación de Trabajadores y Comerciantes Marroquíes Amical** *(Friendship Society of Moroccan Workers and Traders)*
also known as Federación de Amigos y Comerciantes Marroquíes
carrer Balmes 13-3°, 08007 Barcelona, Catalunya; *t* (93) 318 6769 (6709?)   »94
♦ **Asociación de Trabajadores Inmigrantes Marroquíes en España, ATIME** *(Association of Moroccan Immigrant Workers in Spain)*
S. Kebir/Radwan Zido: calle Jesús 14-3° izq., 28014 Madrid; *t* (91) 429 4170, *f* 366 4139 (?)
Employment and training issues, social activities, residence and labour rights of the 100,000 Moroccans in Spain. Member of EU Migrants Forum, p131.   »94
● ≡ A. Hamid Beyuki, President: avenida Deportes 50, 28935 Mostoles, Madrid   »91
✿ ≡ Pais Valencia, ATIME-PV: Sagunt 114, pta 6, 46009 Valencia   »94
✿ **Centre Avaroes** *(Averroës Centre)*
Edif. Piramidón, carrer Empordá 33, Despatx 908, Barri la Pau, 08020 Barcelona, Catalunya; *t* (93) 278 0294, 278 0174, *f* 323 2859
Social, welfare and anti-racist centre named after the Spanish-Moroccan medieval philosopher. See also Federació de Col.lectivus d'Inmigrants, p151, and ETANE, p4.   »94
✿ **Centro de Acción Social San Rafael Al-Mourad** *(St Raphael Social Action Centre)*
calle Isla Saipán 35, 28035 Madrid; *t/f* (91) 316 6972
Youth welfare, information and advice.   »94
✿ **Centro Sociocultural María Inmaculada** *(Immaculate Mary Socio-Cultural Centre)*
Antonia Maldonado Martín: calle Río Llobregat 2, 29802 Melilla; *t* (952) 268 1053
Educational and youth centre run by the nuns of the RMI order (Religiosas de María Inmaculada).   »94
✿ **Centro Sociocultural San Agustín** *(St Augustine Socio-Cultural Centre)*
calle Ceuta 1, 29802 Melilla; *t* (952) 684574   »87

◎ **UNITED KINGDOM** *44*

✿ **Al-Hasaniya Moroccan Women's Centre**
Co-ordinator: Bays 4&5 Trellick Tower, Golborne Road, London W10 5PL; *t* (0181) 969 2292
Counselling, health promotion, welfare advice and other community-based services for Arabic-speaking women in North Kensington.   »96
✿ **Moroccan Information and Advice Centre Association, MIACA**
Fawwaz Zeidan, Co-ordinator: 61 Golborne Road, London W10 5NR; *t* (0181) 960 6654, 960 6672
Advice service (welfare rights, immigration, housing and employment); information service; liaison with other agencies to improve opportunities for Moroccans in west London.   »94
✿ **Moroccan Islamic Association**
Mohammed Hamid: 5 St Benedicts Road, Small Heath, Birmingham B10 9DP; *t* (0121) 772 4391   »94

MOSLEM

see Islamic

MOZAMBICAN

see also African, Southern African

◎ **IRELAND** *353*

● **Irish Mozambique Solidarity**
[address unknown] Dublin
Solidarity with Mozambique; support for Frelimo; public
education, media monitoring, international exchanges. »89

◎ **PORTUGAL** *351*

● **Aero-Associação de Espoliados de Moçambique** *(Air
Association of Mozambique Dispossessed)*
Calçada Palma Baixo 25 r/c E, Lisboa; *t* (01) 726 5757
Union of ex-colonials. »90
◆ **Associação Africana de Moçambique em Portugal** *(African
Association of Mozambique in Portugal)*
Amanibo Nala: Travessa do Possolo 13-1° E, 1300 Lisboa;
t (01) 410 4778
Cultural and welfare activities. »94
◆ **Associação dos Naturais e Ex-Residentes de Moçambique,
ANERM** *(Association of Natives and Ex-Residents of
Mozambique)*
Rua Bernardo Costa 40-2°, Lisboa; *t* (01) 346 9519
Post-colonial returnees. »90
✧ **Casa de Moçambique** *(Mozambique House)*
Carolina Matos Sara: Rua de Ceuta 32-5° C, 2975 Linda-a-
Velha
Founded 1972. »90
✧ ≡ Beneficência 111-2°, 1600 Lisboa; *t* (01) 796 4471 »95
✧ ≡ Flora Ferreira: Rua Marquesa de Alorna 26, c/d, Alvalade,
1700 Lisboa »94

◎ **SPAIN** *34*

✧ **Asociación de Colaboración y Amistad con Mozambique,
ACAM** *(Society for Co-operation and Friendship with
Mozambique)*
Junta de Comercio 24, prpal 1ª, 08001 Barcelona; *t* (93)
412 3880 »94

◎ **UNITED KINGDOM** *44*

● **Mozambique Angola Committee, MAC**
Peter Brayshaw/Margaret Ling, Co-chairs: [address unknown]
London
Solidarity with the peoples of Mozambique and Angola. In
1994, linked with the Anti-Apartheid Movement to launch the
Angola Emergency Campaign, which raised funds to assist in
the international effort to restore peace. »94
● **Mozambique Information Service**
7a Caledonian Road, London N1 9DX; *t* (0171) 278 8691,
Tx 918023 GEONET G, first line: box:geo2:mozambique-info
News review (24/yr). »90

MUSLIM

see Islamic

MYANMAR

see Asian, Burmese, South-East Asian

NAMIBIAN

see also African, Southern African

◎ **FRANCE** *33*

● **Amis de la Namibie** *(Friends of Namibia)*
80 rue Faubourg St Antoine, 75012 Paris; *t* (1) 4346 8600 »90

NEPALESE

see also Asian, Hindu

◎ **FRANCE** *33*

● **Aide Médicale et Sanitaire au Népal** *(Medical and Health Aid
to Nepal)*
144 rue Grenelle, 75007 Paris; *t* (1) 4555 8593 »90

◎ **UNITED KINGDOM** *44*

● **Britain Nepal Society**
C. Brown, Honorary Secretary: 1 Allen Mansions, Allen St,
London W8 6UY
Friendship, cultural awareness. »90
● **Gurkha Welfare Trusts**
Archway North, Old Admiralty Building, Spring Gardens,
London SW1A; *t* (0171) 218 4395 »90
● **Nepal Kingdom Foundation**
c/o Diorama Arts, 14 Peto Place, London NW1; *t* (0171) 935
7770
Culture. »90
● **Nepalwatch UK**
6 School Terrace, Reading RG1 3LS; *t* (01734) 663 781
Public education, lobbying on human rights and development
issues in Nepal, including impact of tourism. »93

NEW ZEALAND

see also Asian, Pacific

◎ **UNITED KINGDOM** *44*

*Australia and New Zealand Emigrants and Families Association:
believed defunct (1992)*
● *New Zealand News UK*
25 Royal Opera Arcade, London SW1Y 4UY; *t* (0171) 930
6451
Expatriate community newspaper (52/yr), with home news
summary. »95

NICARAGUAN

see also Central American, Latin American

◎ **BELGIUM** *32*

● **Comité Europa-Nicaragua** *(Europe-Nicaragua Committee)*
Philippe Cosyn, President: [address unknown] Bruxelles
Dossier Nicaragua. »88
● **Comité Nicaraguayen des Droits de l'Homme** *(Nicaraguan
Human Rights Committee)*
Esteban González: [address unknown] Bruxelles
Anti-Sandinista. »88

◎ **DENMARK** *45*

● **Nicaragua-Komiteen**
Kulturhuset Cikaden, Griffenfeldsgade 35, 2200 København
N; *t* 3537 1430, *f* 3537 1980 »95

◎ **FRANCE** *33*

● **Comité France-Nicaragua**
14 rue de Nanteuil, 75015 Paris »88

◎ **GERMANY** *49*

✧ **Infobüro Nicaragua** *(Nicaragua Information Bureau)*
Postfach 101320, 42013 Wuppertal
Solidarity, information work. »94
● **Nicaragua Gesellschaft** *(Nicaragua Society)*
[address unknown] 5300 Bonn
Right-wing anti-Sandinista group. »88

◎ **IRELAND** *353*

● **Irish Nicaragua Support Group**
10 Upper Camden Street, Dublin 2; *t* (01) 478 0321
Solidarity with the Sandinista movement and the Nicaraguan
people. »95

◎ **ITALY** *39*

● **Associazione Italia-Nicaragua** *(Italy-Nicaragua Association)*
via dei Sabelli 185, 00185 Roma; *t* (06) 492528 »90

◎ **LUXEMBOURG** *352*

● **Association de Solidarité Luxembourg-Nicaragua**
93 rue de Strasbourg, BP 1766, 1017 Luxembourg »93

◎ **SWEDEN** *46*

● **Vänskapsförbundet Sverige-Nicaragua** *(Swedish Nicaragua
Support Society)*
Östgötagatan 49, 11625 Stockholm »93

⊙ UNITED KINGDOM *44*

● **Nicaragua Health Fund, NHF**
83 Margaret Street, London W1N 7HB; *t* (0171) 580 4292
Raises funds to support health programmes in Nicaragua. »91
● **Nicaragua Solidarity Campaign, NSC**
Anna Keene/Peter Frankental: 129 Seven Sisters Road,
London N7 7QG; *t* (0171) 272 9619   »94

NIGERIAN

see also African, Islamic, West African

⊙ IRELAND *353*

● **Nigerian-Irish Friendship Association, NIFA**
15b Temple Road, Dublin 6; *t* (01) 496 2412   »94

⊙ ITALY *39*

✿ **Associazione Nigeria-Italia di Lavoratori, NILSA** *(Nigeria-Italy Workers' Association)*
Pola 33, Francavilla al Mare, 66023 Chieti; *t* (085) 816380»90
✿ **Comunità Nigeriana a Firenze e Province, CNFP**
Fidelis Ekundayo: Centro La Pira, via Pescione 3, 50125
Firenze; *t* (055) 257 9630   »94
✿ **Nigerian Students Union**
[address unknown] Perugia   »90

⊙ SPAIN *34*

✿ **Asociación Nigeriana de Barcelona**
Ade Akinfenwa: Apartado de Correos 34191, 08080
Barcelona, Catalunya; *t* (93) 373 8283, 219 9892
Cultural activities, advice and information.   »94

⊙ UNITED KINGDOM *44*

● **Justice Nigeria**
Michael Ogunseye, Chair: PO Box 172, Feltham TW13 6XF;
t (0181) 384 2935
Campaigns for human rights of Nigerians worldwide, including
immigration and asylum rights in the UK.   »96
● *Nigeria Now*
Dr Kayode Fayemi, Editor: 19b Bellingham Road, London
SE6 2PN
Opposition-aligned current affairs magazine.   »95
● **Nigeria Welfare and Monitoring Council**
1st Floor, 44 Lewisham High Street, London SE13 5JH;
t/f (0181) 318 5839
Community welfare/refugee rights group, founded 1995. »96
● **Nigerian Citizens' Association**
305 Hospital Street, Birmingham B19   »90
● **Nigerian Community Trust in the United Kingdom**
30 Ambleside Road, London NW10 3VJ   »94
✿ **Nigerian Muslim Association**
Mustafa Akande: 7 Widnes House, Palmer Pl., London N7 »94
✿ **Nigerian National Union, NNU; and NNU Women's Group;**
Nigerian Youth Group; Nigerian Elderly Group
L.O. Ibekwe/H. Emeadi: Appleby House, Platt Lane, Rusholme,
Manchester M14 5NE; *t* (0161) 256 1059, 224 2404
Information, seminars, meetings; elderly day care; advice on
immigration, housing and welfare; social support to Nigerian
women and women with Nigerian partners; youth club.   »93
● **Ogoni Community Association**
Lazarus Tamana/Cliff Ettridge: [address unknown] *t* (01903)
844244
Migrants from, and people in solidarity with, the Ogoni
region where land has been devastated by oil pollution. »95
✿ **Overseas Fellowship of Nigerian Christian Women**
Dr Titi Sodipo: c/o 9 Wadesmill Walk, Chorlton-on-Medlock,
Manchester M13 9UX; *t* (0161) 273 4268   »93

NORTH AFRICAN

see also African, Algerian, Arab/Arabic, Chadian, Egyptian, Islamic, Libyan, Maghrebi, Mauritanian, Middle Eastern, Moroccan, Saharan, Sudanese, Tunisian

⊙ FRANCE *33*

✿ **Association culturelle nord-africaine, ACNA**
19 rue de la Fontaine-du-Bac, 63000 Clermont Ferrand   »90
✿ **Service social familial nord africain** *(North African Family Social Service)*
5 rue Saulnier, 75009 Paris; *t* (1) 4523 1428   »90

⊙ ITALY *39*

♦ **Associazione Immigrati Nordafricani in Italia, AINAI**
(Association of North African Immigrants in Italy)
Kamel Belaitouche: via Farini 62, int. 4, 00185 Roma; *t* (06)
474 7517, 488 2374, *f* 482 0974
Maghrebi social, cultural and welfare organisation.   »94
✿ **Unione Immigrati Nordafricani, UINA**
Noureddine Aoicha: via Riserva Reale 19, 90129 Palermo,
Sicilia; *t* (091) 668 1130   »90

NORTH AMERICAN

see Canadian, Mexican, Québécois, United States

NORWEGIAN

see also European, Scandinavian

⊙ UNITED KINGDOM *44*

● **Anglo-Norse Society**
Mrs Aud Dixon, Secretary: 25 Belgrave Square, London
SW1X 8QD; *t* (0171) 235 7151
Friendship, cultural exchanges; founded 1918.   »90
✿ **Norwegian Club**
21-24 Cockspur Street, London SW1; *t* (0171) 930 4084»95

OROMO

see also African, Ethiopian

⊙ ITALY *39*

● **Associazione Oromo in Italia** *(Oromo Association in Italy)*
presso Comunità San Egidio, via della Paglia 14c, 00153
Roma; *t* (06) 589 5945, 585530   »90

PACIFIC

see also Australian, French: DOM/TOM, New Zealand, Tahitian

⊙ FRANCE *33*

● **Institut du Pacifique**
102 rue Lourmel, 75015 Paris; *t* (1) 4577 9248   »90

⊙ GERMANY *49*

✿ **Pazifik-Informationsstelle** *(Pacific Information Centre)*
Postfach 68, 8806 Neuendettelsau
Information and documentation on Pacific island affairs. »90

⊙ UNITED KINGDOM *44*

● **Pacific Islands Society of the UK and Ireland**
[address unknown]
The Outrigger (4/yr).   »89

PAKISTANI

see also Asian, Islamic, Kashmiri, Punjabi, Urdu

⊙ DENMARK *45*

● **All Pakistan Society**
Sommerstedsgade 29, st.tv., 1718 København V   »89
● **Pakistan, Pashtun and Baluch Society**
Prinsesse Charlottes Gade 31-33, kld.th., 2200 København
N; *t* 3139 2732   »89
● **Pakistan Peoples Society**
Viktoriegade 18, 1655 København V; *t* 3123 4633
See also Pakistanske Forening i Danmark, p93.   »89
✿ **Pakistani Social Welfare Committee**
Muhammed Sawar: Åwården 3, 2.tv., 2635 Ishøj   »89
✿ **Pakistansk Forening** *(Pakistani Society)*
Abdul Qayum: Åsebro 67, 3300 Frederiksværk; *t* 4212
4758   »89
✿ ≡ Klostergade 37, 8000 Århus C   »89
✿ **Pakistansk Forening i Ishøj** *(Ishøj Pakistani Society)*
c/o Kamal: Vejlgården 3, 2635 Ishøj   »94
✿ **Pakistansk Indvandrerforening i Taastrup** *(Pakistani Immigrant Society of Taastrup)*
Abdul Shakir: Leen b4, st., 2630 Taastrup, København   »90

Pakistansk Kulturforening: see Indvandrernes Kulturforening i Lyngby, p133

✿ **Pakistansk Ungdomsforening** *(Pakistani Youth Society)*
Havnegade 3, 5000 Odense C; *t* 6591 1560 »89

● **Pakistanske Forening i Danmark** *(Pakistan Society in Denmark)*
Bashy Quraishy, Chairman: c/o Blegdamsvej 4, st., 2200 København N; *t* 3116 6962
Possibly same as Pakistan Peoples Society, p92. Founded 1975; information, meetings, radio broadcasts, cultural festivals, employment and welfare advice service. »94

✿ **Den Pakistanske Studiekreds** *(Pakistani Study Circle)*
Palnatokesgade 3-2, 1733 København V »90

◉ FRANCE *33*

✿ **Association des Travailleurs Pakistanis en France** *(Association of Pakistani Workers in France)*
121 rue de St-Sébastien, 78300 Poissy; *t* (1) 4747 7625 »90

◉ ITALY *39*

✿ **Associazione degli Studenti Pakistani**
via Ostiense 110-D, 00154 Roma »90

✿ **Comunità Lavoratori Pakistani in Puglia** *(Community of Pakistani Workers in Apulia)*
Jalil Kalyal: via Caroli 15, 73039 Tricase, LE; *t* (0833) 542707
Was listed (1990) at via Redipuglia 3, 73100 Lecce. »94

✿ **Comunità Pakistana** *(Pakistani Community)*
corso Garibaldi 46, 42017 Novellara »90

● **Pakistan Association of Italy**
[address uncertain] via della Camilluccia 368, 00136 Roma
Also listed (1990) at via della Camilluccia 591. »90

◉ SPAIN *34*

● **Asociación de Paquistaníes**
Iqbal Raja: Minas del Cobre La Cruz, Linares, Jaen »90

◉ UNITED KINGDOM *44*

✿ **Al Hilal Community Project**, also known as Muslim Advice Centre
S.A.H. Zaidi: 443 Cheetham Hill Road, Cheetham, Manchester M8 7PF; *t* (0161) 740 3351
Immigration, nationality and welfare advice; youth club; sports, Urdu and Arabic classes. »93

✿ **All Pakistani Women's Association**
Rehana Yasmin/Shamin Akhtar: Slade Lane Neighbourhood Centre, 642 Stockport Road, Longsight, Manchester M13 0RZ; *t* (0161) 248 8243, 431 5664
Welfare, health and educational work with black girls and women. »93

✿ **Baluch Community Association**
Murad Baksh Baluch: 1 Fairbourne Road, Levenshulme, Manchester M19 3HY; *t* (0161) 224 4639
Welfare, housing and health advice; English classes; social and cultural activities. »93

● **Baluch Refugee Association**
190 Walm Lane, London NW2; *t/f* (0181) 450 3812
Member of the Confederation of Refugee Groups and Ethnic Minorities, p154. »92

✿ **Birmingham Pakistani Scout Development Project**
Scout Association, Centenary House, 81-91 Hatchett Street, Birmingham B19 3NY; *t* (0121) 446 4642, *f* 446 4410
Promotes minority participation in youth organisations. »94

✿ **Birmingham Pakistani Sports Forum**
Makhdoom A. Chisti: 180 Belgrave Middleway, Birmingham B12 0XS; *t* (0121) 446 4642, *f* 446 4410
Youth sports group; member of Migrants Forum, p131. »94

✿ **British Pakistani Muslim Welfare Association**
Nadir Hussein: 11 Brompton Street, Glodwick, Oldham OL14 1AB »94

✿ ≡ F. Subadar, Advisor: 6 Beeby Road, Leicester LE5 3LE »93

● **Council of British Pakistanis, CBP**, and Pakistan Forum
A. Salam, General Secretary: CBP House, 1 Dora Road, Small Heath, Birmingham B10 9RF; *t* (0121) 772 5930
A. Quayyum Choudhury. CBP is a member of EU Migrants Forum, p131; promotes community organisation, racial equality; advisory service. The local Pakistan Forum (*t* 771 4456) represents the interests of Birmingham Pakistanis in relation to the City Council and other bodies. »94

✿ **Dar-ul-Aman Housing Association**
Elizabeth Coady: Mazda House, 40b Raby Street, Manchester M16 7EB; *t* (0161) 226 6527-28
Provision of social housing for local Asian community. See Council of Mosques and Welfare Association, p65. »93

✿ **Derby Pakistan Community Centre**, also known as Pakistan Community Centre
S.G.S Jaffery, Manager: Harrington Street, Peartree, Derby DE3 8PG; *t* (01332) 774055
Founded 1983; social and welfare needs of all members of the local Pakistani community. »94

✿ **Elland Mosque Association**
F.R. Tariq, Chair: 26-34 Elizabeth Street, Elland, Halifax HX5 0JH; *t* (01422) 378808, 515311, *f* 517985
Religious and cultural society established 1972. »94

● **Federation of Pakistani Organisations**
Dr Z.U. Khan: 45 Streatham Common North, London SW16 3HS »95

✿ **Greenwich Pakistan Muslim Welfare Association** & Mosque
Asghar Hamid, Chair: 12 Victoria Way, Charlton, London SE7 7QS; *t* (0181) 858 2415
Association also listed (1993) at 53 Delafield Road, Charlton, SE7. See also Charlton Mosque, p57. »94

✿ **Hackney Pakistan Women's Welfare Centre**
25 Martaban Road, London N16; *t* (0181) 809 7039 »91

✿ **Hamdard Day Centre**
N.A.K. Kahloon: 18 Buller Road, Longsight, Manchester M13 0PP; *t* (0161) 225 6764
Day care, social and cultural activities, resources for Pakistani and other elderly people. »93

✿ **Ibadur Rahman Trust and Jamia Mosque**
Dr Bashir Ahmed, Trustee: 3 Woodlands Road, Cheetham Hill, Manchester M8 7LF; *t* (0161) 740 3696, 643 5499
Management of North Manchester Mosque, p69. »94

✿ **Islamic Pakistani Community Centre**
Riaz Bhatti: 98a Colwyn Road, Northampton NN1 3PX; *t* (01604) 21125, 585505 »94

✿ **Karmand Community Centre** and Karmand Centre Association
Shahnaz Siddique: Barkerend Road, Bradford BD3 9EP; *t* (01274) 669593
Community association; concerns include ethnic minority unemployment. »95

✿ **Khilari Group**
481 Stockport Road, Longsight, Manchester M12 4NN; *t* (0161) 224 5235, 248 6283
Sports, playscheme, youth activities. »93

✿ **Manchester Pakistani Welfare and Information Centre**
Maureen Marfani/Pashe Stott: [address uncertain] 1 Great Marlborough Street, Manchester M1 5NJ; *t* (0161) 237 1125
Address also listed (1994) as Ashburton Road West, Strafford Park, Manchester M17 1RW, *t* (0161) 872 5646. Formed 1964. Advice and information service: health, housing, discrimination, women's issues, personal problems. »94

● **Minhaj-ul-Qur'an Movement**
Javiad Akhtar: 164a Gibbet Street, Halifax HX1, West Yorkshire; *t* (01422) 357313
UK section of the Pakistan-based Minhaj-ul-Qur'an Institute International (founded 1980), which promotes family values, community spirit and interfaith understanding. »94

● **Mohajir Qoumi Movement, MQM**
4 Hale Grove Gardens, Mill Hill, London NW7 3LP; *t* (0181) 959 3111, *f* 959 1455
Support group for an opposition movement among the Mohajirs of Sindh. Concerns include human rights, welfare of political prisoners. »94

✿ **Noor-ul-Quran: Zainab Languages School**
M. Salim: 83 Hamilton Road, Longsight, Manchester M13 0PD; *t* (0161) 224 0774
Mainly Pakistani Muslim women. Translation, interpreting, language classes, welfare work, advice, cultural events. »93

✿ **North Manchester Pakistan Community Association**
M. Yasin: 443 Cheetham Hill Road, Cheetham, Manchester M8 7PT; *t* (0161) 740 3351
Cultural events, e.g. Urdu poetry evenings; Islamic burial society. See also Al Hilal Community Project, left. »93

✿ **Pak-Pakhtoon Association**
33 Nansen Road, Birmingham B11 4DR »90

✿ **Pakistan Association of Edinburgh and the East of Scotland** and Mosque Anwar-e-Madina; Community Centre
Abdul Ghafoor, Imam: Zetland Hall, 11 Pilrig Street, Edinburgh EH6, Scotland; *t* (0131) 554 9904
Sunni mosque, Urdu and Koranic education, social and leisure activities, promotion of community relations and interfaith understanding. »94

✿ **Pakistan British Social Association** and Mosque
G.Y. Kayai, President: 104 Gladstone Street, Peterborough PE1 2BL; *t* (01733) 64325
Sunni mosque, religious and community welfare group; weekly advice sessions. »94

✡ **Pakistan Chhachhi Association**
Mohammad Ilyas, Chair: 29 Firth Park, Firvale, Sheffield S5
6WL; *t* (0114) 244 4457
Community welfare group founded 1980; interpreting,
mediation with public services, rights advice.   »94

● **Pakistan Christian Women's Association**, PCWA
C.J. Gill, Secretary: 20 St Martin's Close, Erith DA8 4DZ;
t (0181) 310 3370   »94

✡ **Pakistan Community Centre**
Saijad Hussain: 481 Stockport Road, Longsight, Manchester
M12 4NN; *t* (0161) 224 5235, 248 6283
Immigration and welfare advice; community and cultural
activities; liaison with public services; Khilari youth group.»93

✡ ≡ Munir Lone: [address unknown] Reading, Berkshire   »94

✡ **Pakistan Cultural Institute**
17 Briery Road, Coventry CV2 1RS   »90

✡ **Pakistan Enterprise Centre Ltd**, PEC
Shahid R. Malik, Chief Executive: Woodbourn Road, Sheffield
S9 3LQ; *t* (0114) 243 6091, *f* 261 9330
A commercial organisation (part of the PMC Group) providing
vocational training, workspace and other services aimed at
promoting enterprise and economic regeneration within the
minority ethnic community in Sheffield; includes specialist
business training programme for Pakistani women.   »95

● **Pakistan Ex-Servicemen's Association**
54 Yardley Green Road, Birmingham B9 5QE   »90

● **Pakistan Institute**
71 Wellington Road, Edgbaston, Birmingham B15 3ET   »90

✡ **Pakistan Islamic Centre**
Mohammed Safdar, Chair: 18 Peter Street, Rawtenstall,
Rossendale BB4 7NR; *t* (01706) 216603   »94

✡ **Pakistan/Kashmir Death Committee**
K. Hussain: 48 Portland Street, Accrington BB5 1RH
Provides assistance with Islamic funeral arrangements.   »94

✡ **Pakistan Longsight United Association**
Zafar Elahi Mir: 80 Slade Grove, Longsight, Manchester M13
0SJ; *t* (0161) 205 9124
Immigration, housing, education and welfare advice and
advocacy; family counselling; interpreting and translation
service.   »93

✡ **Pakistan Moslem Centre**
[address unknown] Sheffield
Houses Support Project for Asian Women and Families with a
Child with a Disability, p15.   »94

✡ **Pakistan Muslim Association** and Madni Jamia Masjid
North Gate, Dewsbury WF12, West Yorkshire; *t* (01924)
461700
Religious and welfare association, and mosque.   »94

✡ ≡ 1a Sackville Street, Ravensthorpe, Dewsbury WF13   »94
✡ ≡ and Mosque: 45 Asa Leigh Road, Keighley BD21   »94
✡ ≡ 10 Nursery Lane, Leeds LS17 7HN   »94
✡ ≡ 137 Gipton Wood Road, Leeds LS8, Yorkshire   »94
✡ ≡ 64 Dumfries Street, Luton, Bedfordshire   »94
✡ ≡ and Newcastle Central Mosque: Z.J. Khan, Chairperson:
Malvern Street, off Elswick Road, Newcastle-upon-Tyne NE4
6SU; *t* (0191) 226 0562
Religious/community centre; welfare and social activities. »94
✡ ≡ 10 Radford Road, Hyson Green, Nottingham NG7 5FS;
t (01602) 701558   »94
✡ ≡ Mohammad Salas Khan: 2 Angler Road, Ramleaze,
Swindon SN5 9SX
Social and welfare work, anti-racism, Urdu language and
Pakistani cultural promotion.   »94
✡ ≡ Barking and Ilford: 75 Mayfair Avenue, Ilford IG1   »94

✡ **Pakistan Muslim Community Association**
R.T. Khan, Chairperson: Muslim Community Centre, Old
Boys School, 28 Melbourne Road, Leicester LE2 0GU
Religious and community welfare group; housing, immigration,
rights advice.   »94

✡ **Pakistan Muslim Welfare Association**
9 Madeley Street, Derby DE3 8EX; *t* (01332) 365845
Community welfare group; interpreting, translating, advice,
information; leisure, cultural and educational activities.   »94
✡ ≡ 110 Attercliffe Common, Sheffield S9, Yorkshire   »94
✡ ≡ 62 Dalkeith Street, Birchills, Walsall WS2 8QB; *t* (01922)
640787
Also listed (1994) at 64 Farringdon Street, Birchills (Ashiq
Hussain). See Ghousia Mosque and Community Centre. »94
✡ ≡ and Jamia Mosque: M. Quazi, Secretary: 197 Waterloo
Road, Wolverhampton WV1 4RA; *t* (01902) 24138, 312232,
f 714450
Worship, educational and cultural activities, welfare work. »94
✡ ≡ and Community Centre; Anwar-ul-Quran Mosque: 153
Walsall Road, Darlaston WS10 8BD; *t* (0121) 526 5167
Community association and Sunni mosque.   »94

✡ **Pakistan Muslim Welfare Society** and Mosque
M.B. Jee, General Secretary: Jeremy Lane, Heckmondwike,
Dewsbury WF16 9HN; *t* (01924) 402602
Mosque, community and educational centre, associated with
the Barelvi movement of Hanafi orthodox Sunnis.   »94

● **Pakistan Overseas Euro Association**
Stephen Joseph: 57 Dale Road, Luton, Bedfordshire   »94

● **Pakistan Pathans Association** and Pakistan Writers'
Association
3 Beech Avenue, Runcorn Road, Birmingham B12 8QS   »90

● **Pakistan Peoples Party**, PPP: and Pakistan Sports and
Welfare Association
31 Court Road, Birmingham B12 9LQ
The PPP is a support group for one of the main Pakistani
political parties.   »90

✡ **Pakistan Social Institute**
14 Ivy Bridge Road, Styvechale, Coventry CV3 5PH   »90

✡ **Pakistan Society**
58 Beach Road, Sparkhill, Birmingham B11 4QL   »90
✡ ≡ 9 Annandale Street, Edinburgh EH7 4AN, Scotland;
t (0131) 557 4266   »94
✡ ≡ Azmat Ullah Choudhary/Dr A.R. Alvi: 292 Mauldeth Rd
West, Manchester M21 2RF; *t* (0161) 881 5064, 928 2686
Immigration, housing and welfare advice; interpreting and
translation service.   »93

✡ **Pakistan Welfare Association**
32 Malmsbury Road, Birmingham B10 0JQ   »90
✡ ≡ Bashir Ahmed, Secretary: Muslim Community Centre, 150
Dyke Road, Brighton BN1 1AN; *t* (01273) 325471, 722438
Associated with Sussex Muslim Society, p71.   »94
✡ ≡ 181 Haydon's Road, London SW19   »91
✡ ≡ and Mosque: 47-49 Mill Bank, Wellington, Telford;
t (01952) 55389   »94

✡ **Pakistan Women's Association**
5 Salisbury Road, Birmingham B13 8JS   »90

✡ **Pakistan Women's Welfare Association**
20 Blackstock Road, London N4 2DW; *t* (0171) 266 4427»95

✡ **Pakistan Workers' Association**
56 Phipson Street, Sparkhill, Birmingham B11   »90
✡ ≡ 102 St Georges Road, Stoke, Coventry CV1 2DL
Either or both of these may be the same as the Pakistani
Workers Association (Britain), below.   »90

✡ **Pakistan Youth Forum**, PYF
Khalid Mahmood, Chairman: 147 Kirwicks Lane, Sparkbrook,
Birmingham B11 1SS; *t* (0121) 771 1808
Integration of Muslim youth in Birmingham; formed 1987.»94

● **Pakistan Youth League**
32 Richmond Hill Road, Birmingham B15 3RP   »90

✡ **Pakistani Business Executives Club**
Zahid Yaqoob: c/o Halal Meat Company [address unknown]
Birmingham
Forum for local business executives together employing over
1,000 people in various industrial sectors. Meets monthly.»94

✡ **Pakistani Community Centre**
Oliver Street, Oldham, Lancashire   »95

✡ **Pakistani Cultural Centre** and Mosque
S.H. Raza, Secretary: 8 St Helens Road, Bellevue, Doncaster
DN4 5EH; *t* (01302) 361941   »94

✡ **Pakistani Muslim Community Centre**
Mohammed Saeed: 205 Cheshire Road, Smethwick, Warley
B66, West Midlands; *t* (0121) 555 6047   »94

✡ **Pakistani Muslim Welfare Association**
37 Punch Copse Road, Three Bridges, Crawley RH10 1RB»94
✡ ≡ M.A. Rajah: 32 Beckett Lane, Langley Green, Crawley
RH11 7SP; *t* (01293) 515341, 517201   »94

✡ **Pakistani Social and Cultural Society**
Hamidi Abas: 57 Woodlands Road, Crumpsall, Manchester
M8 7WQ   »93

✡ **Pakistani Social and Welfare Society**
Mohammad Latif Khan: 16 Lower Park Road, Victoria Park,
Manchester M14 5RN; *t* (0161) 225 5974
Advice on immigration, discrimination, education, welfare
rights and other matters.   »93

✡ **Pakistani Welfare Association**
Arif Hussain: 23 Willow Row, Longton, Stoke-on-Trent ST3
4NH   »94

✡ **Pakistani Workers Association (Britain)**, PWA(B)
PO Box 128, Birmingham B5 6DP
Anti-racist, anti-fascist, anti-race relations establishment.
Paikaar (4/yr).   »90
✡ ≡ PO Box 9, South-East PDO, Manchester M13 0LH   »90

✡ **Reading Federation of the Pakistani Community**
Dr M. Elahi: 31 Green Road, Reading, Berkshire; *t* (01734)
661578
Advice service, anti-racism.   »94

✧ **Sandwell Pakistan Muslim Women's Association** and
Sandwell Muslim Education Association
Uzra Butt: 130 Vicarage Road, Oldbury, Warley B76 8HR;
t (0121) 553 3460
Women's Association also listed (1994) c/o Z. Durrani, 1
Rectory Gardens, Vicarage Street, Oldbury, *t* 552 6775. »94
✧ **Sandwell Pakistani Muslim Welfare Association**
R.G. Khan: 46 Grange Road, Cradley Heath, Warley B64;
t (0121) 561 4250   »94
✧ **Tameer-e-Pakistan Tanzeem**
1 Woodfield Road, Birmingham B12 8TD   »90
✧ **United Kingdom Pakistani Welfare Society**
J.C. Choudhary: 3 Turnbull Road, Longsight, Manchester
M13 0PZ; *t* (0161) 225 2628
Social and welfare activities, play scheme.   »93
✧ **Waltham Forest Pakistan Muslim Welfare Association**
6 Exeter Road, London E17   »94

PALESTINIAN

see also Arab, Islamic, Israeli, Jordanian, Middle Eastern

◉ **AUSTRIA** *43*

● **Komitee für medizinische und soziale Hilfe für Palästinenser**
(Committee for Medical and Welfare Aid to Palestinians)
Mariahilferstrasse 91, 1060 Wien   »93

◉ **BELGIUM** *32*

✧ **Amitiés Belgo-Palestiniennes** *(Belgian-Palestinian Friendship)*
André Verlaine: Rue Houte 4, 5340 Gesves
Intercultural friendship, solidarity.   »94

◉ **DENMARK** *45*

● **Palæstinensiske Arbejderes Forbund, PAF** *(Palestinian
Workers' Union)*
Baggesensgade 4 C, 2.sal, 2200 København N; *t* 3537 7565
Formed 1974; information, culture, solidarity.   »90
✧ **Palæstinensiske Forening i Aalborg** *(Palestinian Society of
Aalborg)*
Østerbro 38-40, 9000 Aalborg   »89

◉ **FRANCE** *33*

● **Association France-Palestine**
BP 18404, 75160 Paris Cedex 04   »93

◉ **GREECE** *30*

● **General Union of Palestinian Students, GUPS**
Bassam Mussa: Odos Marathonodromo 31, Paleio Psychico,
15452 Athinai; *t* (01) 672 6061
Founded 1974.   »94

◉ **IRELAND** *353*

● **Al-Sadaqa Ireland-Palestine Friendship Society**
David Woodworth/Rev. Ray Maher: [address uncertain] 52
Lower Rathmines Road, Dublin 6   »90
● **General Union of Palestinian Students, GUPS**, and Palestine
Information Office
Saeb Shaeth, President: PO Box 2050, 79 Merrion Square,
Dublin 2; *t* (01) 676 2959   »94

◉ **ITALY** *39*

✧ **Associazione Culturale Palestinesi**
[address unknown]   »90
✧ **Associazione Palestinese**
Hani Gaber: via Bagutta 12, 20121 Milano; *t* (02) 877993,
910 4957   »94
✧ **Associazione Palestinesi in Liguria**
Saleh Zaghloul: Vico Tana 1, 16126 Genova; *t* (010) 240
6252, *f* 281518
Social conditions for migrant workers and students, defence
of rights. *Lettere di Collegamento* (4/yr).   »94
✧ **Comunità Palestinese** *(Palestinian Community)*
piazza Guerrazzi 3, 57023 Cecina   »90
● **General Union of Palestinian Students, GUPS**: Unione
Generale Studenti Palestini
Hakim A. Ialila/Rehbi Mohamed: via dei Latini 69, 00185
Roma; *t* (06) 445 3699
Founded 1969; information, solidarity.   »90
✧ ≡ via F. Crispi 233, 70123 Bari   »90
✧ ≡ Zingarelli, via B. Panizza 5, 10137 Torino; *t* (011) 308
0060   »90

● **Unione Generale dei Medici e Farmacisti Palestinesi in Italia**
(General Union of Palestinian Doctors and Pharmacists in Italy)
via dei Latini 69, 00185 Roma; *t* (06) 230 1633, 445 3669»90

◉ **NETHERLANDS** *31*

● **Algemeen Palestijnse Arbeiders Vereniging** *(General Union of
Palestinian Workers)*
Berends Muslimani: [address unknown]   »90

◉ **PORTUGAL** *351*

● **Organização pela Libertação de Palestina, OLP**: Palestine
Liberation Organization, PLO
42 Edifício Noronhal, Lisboa 17; *t* (01) 848 3263
Representative organisation of the Palestinian people in
Palestine and the diaspora.   »90

◉ **UNITED KINGDOM** *44*

● *Al Quds al Arabi* (Arab Jerusalem)
[address uncertain] 165 King Street, London W6 0QU;
t (0181) 748 7637
Arabic daily newspaper.   »95
● **Friends of Birzeit University**
Profs. I. Brownlie/M. Robertson: c/o 21 Collingham Road,
London SW5
Solidarity with the Palestinian academic community.   »92
● **General Union of Palestinian Students, GUPS**
[address unknown] London
International student group aligned with PLO.   »89
● **Islamic Council on Palestine**
Abdus Salam Abushukeidam: 110 Shepherd's Bush Road,
London W6
Also listed (1993) at 46 Goodge Street, W1P 1FJ: see
Council of Mosques, p57.   »95
● **Jerusalem and Peace Service Consultancy Office**
Uri Davis, Director: 1a Highbury Grove Court, Highbury
Grove, London N5; *t* c/o (0171) 226 7050   »91
● **Joint Committee for Palestine**
[address unknown] London
Solidarity, boycott Israeli goods.   »90
● **Lawyers for Palestinian Human Rights**
Hilary Belchak/Pierre Makhlouf: Box BMJP1, London WC1
Solidarity with the Palestinian people and with refugees;
support for international standards of human rights.   »92
● **Medical Aid for Palestinians, MAP**
Mary King: 33a Islington Park Street, London N1 1QB;
t (0171) 226 4114
Charity providing volunteer staff and medical aid to displaced
Palestinian communities throughout the Middle East, and
supporting development of Palestinian health services.   »95
● **Palestine Liberation Organization, PLO**
4 Clareville Grove, London SW7; *t* (0171) 370 3244
Representative organisation of the Palestinian people in
Palestine and the diaspora.   »90
● *The Palestine Post*
PO Box 1EQ, London W1A 1EQ
Pro-PLO publication, founded 1983.   »90
● **Palestine Solidarity Campaign, PSC**
[address uncertain] BM PSA, London WC1N 3XX
Address from 1990. Supports PLO, founded 1982; also
PSC Women's Network. *Palestine Solidarity* (6/yr).   »92
● **Palestinian Lebanon Relief Fund**
Essam Mustafa: PO Box 542, London E13 0QW   »95
● **RETURN Group**
Roland Rance, Editor: BM RETURN, London WC1N 3XX;
t (0171) 226 7050, *f* 226 2027
Campaigns for Palestinian right to return to homeland.
RETURN.   »90
● **Trade Union Aid for Palestine**
[address unknown] London
Possibly same as Trade Union Friends of Palestine.   »90
● **Trade Union Friends of Palestine, TUFP**
PO Box 1EQ, London W1A 1EQ
Same address as *The Palestine Post*; affiliates include major
unions—ACTT, FBU, GMB, NUM, NUCPS.   »90

PARAGUAYAN

see also Latin American

◉ **UNITED KINGDOM** *44*

● **Paraguay Committee for Human Rights**
[address unknown] London   »88

PERUVIAN

see also Latin American

◎ BELGIUM *32*

✧ **Aide et Coopération au Développement d'Arequipa**, ACDA *(Arequipa Development Aid and Co-operation)*
Neuve Chausée 80, 7600 Peruwelz; *t* (069) 774344, *f* 775772
Development aid (primarily through sponsorship of poor children) to Arequipa region; assistance to migrants.   »93

◎ ITALY *39*

✧ **Associazione Peruana della Liguria**, APL *(Peruvian Association of Liguria)*
c/o FCEI, via Curtatone 2, 16126 Genova; *t* (010) 366406»90
✧ **Comunidad Peruana de Residentes en Milano** *(Peruvian Community of Residents in Milan)*
Teofilo Pozo: viale Monza 9, 20125 Milano; *t* (02) 289 6513   »94
✧ **Comunità Peruviana in Italia**
Jaime Hidalgo Rodrigo: via Conteverde 58, 00185 Roma; *t* (06) 446 7676, *f* 678 1182   »94

◎ SPAIN *34*

✧ **Asociación Alma Peruana** *(Peruvian Soul Association)*
Eduardo Oscanoa Pinto: carrer Olzinelles 30, Barcelona
Social, cultural; welfare of Peruvian migrants.   »94
✧ **Asociación de Amigos Peruano-Hispanos** *(Peruvian-Spanish Friends' Association)*
Jorge Mújica: calle Ave María 50, 28012 Madrid; *t/f* (91) 530 0485
Information and welfare group for migrants and refugees. »94
✧ **Asociación de Mujeres Peruanas** *(Association of Peruvian Women)*
calle Barquillo 44-2° izq., 28004 Madrid; *t* (91) 319 3689»94
✧ **Asociación Peruana Ollantay**
Apartad de Correus 2175, 46080 Valencia   »94
● **Asociación de Peruanos**
avenida Diagonal 441-5°, Barcelona, Catalunya; *t* (93) 321 8445
Peruvian migrant workers.   »87
✧ **Asociación de Refugiados e Inmigrantes Peruanos** *(Association of Peruvian Refugees and Immigrants)*
López de los Hoyos 98-1°, 28002 Madrid; *t* (91) 562 6927»94

◎ UNITED KINGDOM *44*

● **Peru Support Group**
[address uncertain] 20 Compton Terrace, London N1; *t* (0171) 359 2270
Address from 1990. Human rights, solidarity with Peruvian people and with refugees from Peru.   »92
● **Sol-Peru**
[address unknown] London
Solidarity group sympathetic to the Sendero Luminoso (Shining Path) guerrilla movement.   »93

PHILIPPINES

see Asian, Filipino, South-East Asian

POLISH

see also East European, Jewish

◎ BELGIUM *32*

✧ **Polonez Laan op Vurten**
3581 Beringen; *t* (011) 425392
Social and cultural group.   »94
✧ **Pools Schoolcomité** *(Polish School Committee)*
Sleutelbloomstraat 12, 3600 Genk
Educational welfare, youth integration.   »94

◎ DENMARK *45*

✧ **Dansk-Polsk Forening i Aalborg** *(Aalborg Danish-Polish Society)*
Vestergade 93, 9400 Norresundby; *t* 9838 1742   »89
✧ **Den Polske Forening Ognisko** *(Ognisko Polish Society)*
Ravnsborggade 12, 2200 København N; *t* 3135 3025   »90

◎ FRANCE *33*

● **Les Amis de la Pologne** *(Friends of Poland)*
26 rue Chalgrin, 75006 Paris; *t* (1) 4500 4254   »90
● **Association d'entraide des anciens combattants polonais en France** *(Mutual Aid Association of Polish Veterans)*
20 rue Legendre, 75017 Paris; *t* (1) 4763 1092, 4766 2352   »90
● **Comité de Soutien Polonais en France** *(Polish Support Committee in France)*
13 rue Daubenton, 75005 Paris   »90
✧ **Séminaire polonaise à Paris** *(Polish Seminary in Paris)*
Père Wolynski: Collège des Irlandais, 5 rue des Irlandais, 75005 Paris
Training centre for Catholic priests; some pastoral work.   »91

◎ IRELAND *353*

● **Polish Social and Cultural Association**, POSK
Ursula Retzlaff O'Carroll/Henryk Lebioda: 20 Fitzwilliam Place, Dublin 2; *t* (01) 676 2515, *f* 235 6507
In EU Migrants Forum, p131. Newsletter (6/yr).   »94

◎ ITALY *39*

● **Centro Pastorale dell'Emigrazione Polacca** *(Polish Migrants' Pastoral Centre)*
Wesoly Szczepan: presso Chiesa S. Stanislao, via Botteghe Oscure 15, 00186 Roma; *t* (06) 679 5347
Pastoral service based in a Polish Catholic church.   »94
● **Comitato dei Profughi Polacchi** *(Polish Refugees Committee)*
Krysztof Kanclerz: via Conteverde 58, 00185 Roma; *t* (06) 676 6601   »94
● **Fraternità Italo-Polacca**
via XX Settembre 26, 00187 Roma; *t* (06) 494 0583   »90
● **Solidarnosc** *(Solidarity)*
via Po 24, 00198 Roma; *t* (06) 638 4370
Anti-communist movement.   »90

◎ LUXEMBOURG *352*

✧ **Mission Catholique Polonaise** *(Polish Catholic Mission)*
Conrad Felix Stolarek: 2 Beiwerwiss, 6230 Bech; *t* 79161»95

◎ SPAIN *34*

✧ **Asociación Polaca Aguila Blanca** *(White Eagle Polish Society)*
calle Arlabán 7, oficina 46, 28014 Madrid; *t* (91) 316 8531, 523 1618   »94
✧ **Centro de Polacos** *(Polish Centre)*
calle Desengaño 26, 28004 Madrid; *t* (91) 522 7266   »94

◎ UNITED KINGDOM *44*

● **Anglo-Polish Society** (possibly defunct)
[address unknown] London   »90
✧ **Dom Polski** *(Polish House)*
18-20 Ashburnham Rd, Bedford MK40; *t* (01234) 353310»90
✧ **Manchester Polish Club**
J. Cameron: 433 Cheetham Hill Road, Manchester M8; *t* (01706) 36681
Social and cultural society; festivals, dances, weekend restaurant, elderly care.   »93
● **Medical Aid for Poland Fund**
16 Warwick Road, London SW5; *t* (0171) 373 5464   »90
● **Polish Air Force Association** and Polish Naval Association
14 Collingham Gardens, London SW5 0HT; *t* (0171) 373 1085, 370 2659
Also listed (1988) as address of the East European Media Project, which may be defunct.   »95
✧ **Polish Association in Slough**
Vacuna Church Lane, Stoke Poges, Slough; *t* (01753) 25668   »90
✧ **Polish Catholic Association**
Millennium House, Bordesley Street, Birmingham B5   »91
✧ ≡ 54 High Street, Leamington Spa CV31, Warwickshire; *t* (01926) 335818 office, 425073 social club   »91
✧ **Polish Catholic Centre**
Springfield Road, Coventry, Warwickshire; *t* (01203) 222186 centre, 229868 club   »90
✧ ≡ Woodfield, Newton Hill Road, Leeds, Yorkshire; *t* (0113) 262 8019, 262 0586, 262 1551   »90
✧ ≡ 1 Battison Crescent, Trentham Road, Longton, Stoke-on-Trent ST3, Staffordshire; *t* (01782) 312864, 343455   »90
✧ **Polish Catholic Church**
81 London Road, Reading, Berkshire; *t* (01734) 507370   »90
✧ **Polish Catholic Club**
17 Victoria Street, Dunstable, Kent; *t* (01582) 663241   »90

- **Polish Citizens' Committee for Refugees**
55 Princes Gate, London SW7; *t* (0171) 584 6992 »90
- ✿ **Polish Club**
67 Thornhill Road, Dewsbury WF12; *t* (01924) 461864 »90
- ✿ ≡ Old Police Station, High Street, Leamington Spa CV31, Warwickshire; *t* (01926) 429829 »90
- ✿ **Polish Clubhouse**
33 Alexandra Road, Bedford MK40; *t* (01234) 261970 »90
- ✿ **Polish Ex-Servicemen's Club**
Raans Road, Amersham, Buckinghamshire; *t* (01494) 727441, 727173 »90
- ✿ ≡ Whitefriars Lane, Coventry, Warwickshire; *t* (01203) 220752, 228926 »91
- ✿ ≡ 68 New Bedford Road, Luton; *t* (01582) 29110 »90
- ✿ ≡ The Manager: 181 Shrewsbury Street, Brooks Bar, Old Trafford, Manchester M16; *t* (0161) 226 3622 »93
- ✿ ≡ Cowley Parish Hall Annexe, Between Towns Road, Cowley, Oxford; *t* (01865) 778886 »90
- ✿ ≡ 26 Oliver Street, Rugby CV21; *t* (01788) 576183 »91
- ✿ **Polish Parish Club**
R. Filbrandt: 196 Lloyd Street North, Manchester M14 4QB; *t* (0161) 226 2544, 881 4838
Catholic social and religious organisation. »93
- ✿ **Polish Parish Social Club**
107 London Road, Northwich, Greater Manchester; *t* (01606) 43265 »95
- ✿ **Polish Social Club**
81 London Road, Reading, Berkshire; *t* (01734) 582288 »90
- ✿ **Polonia Polish Club**
231 Chesterton Road, Cambridge; *t* (01223) 65854 »90

PORTUGUESE

see also European, Timorese, and entries for Portuguese-speaking ethnic or national identities: Angolan, Brazilian, Cape Verdean, Goan, Guinea Bissau, Mozambican, São Tomé etc.

◎ **BELGIUM** *32*

- ● **Associação dos Portuguêses Emigrados na Bélgica:**
Association des Portugais Emigrés en Belgique *(Association of Portuguese Emigrants in Belgium)*
José Mendes Chuva: Rue du Belgrade 120, 1060 Bruxelles; *t* (02) 539 1884
Culture, welfare, education. *Bulletin informatif* (4-6/yr). »94
- ✿ **Association des Portugais de la Région du Centre et de Charleroi**
Rue du Marché 26, 7100 La Louvière »90
- ✿ **Clube Desportivo Português de Antuérpia** *(Portuguese Sports Club of Antwerp)*
[address unknown] Antwerpen »90
- ✿ **Clube dos Trabalhadores Portuguêses de Liège, CTPL:** Club des Travailleurs Portugais de Liège *(Portuguese Workers' Club of Liège)*
António Moura, President: Rue St Léonard 137, 4000 Liège; *t* (041) 881255
Community welfare, employment, rights advice, leisure. »94
- ✿ **Clube dos Trabalhadores Portuguêses 25 de abril, CTP** *(25 April Portuguese Workers' Club)*
Bevrijdingslaan 18, 3600 Genk; *t* (089) 386358
Workers' rights, information, advice, cultural activity. »94
- ✿ **Comissão Cultural e Recreativa de Bruselas** *(Brussels Cultural and Leisure Committee)*
Rue du Sceptre 30, 1050 Bruxelles »90
- ✿ **Communauté Portugaise d'Emmaüs** *(Portuguese Community of Emmaüs)*
A.L. Rodrigues Fernandes: Rue du Belvédère 26, 1050 Bruxelles; *t* (02) 640 4291
Social, cultural and information centre. *O Elo* (6/yr). »94
- ● **Conselho de Pais dos Portuguêses na Bélgica** *(Council of Portuguese Parents in Belgium)*
BP 56, 1050 Bruxelles
Cultural and educational interests. »94
- ✿ *Encontro* (Encounter)
[address unknown] Limburg
Emigrant newsletter. »90
- ● **Missão Católica Portuguêsa:** Mission Catholique Portugaise *(Portuguese Catholic Mission)*
Père Etienne Strojwas, National Director: CEM, Rue Brabant 174, Boite 9, 1210 Bruxelles; *t* (02) 218 4586
Pastoral care of Portuguese Catholic migrant workers and their families. National Delegate: Padre Policarpo Lopes, Avenue Général de Gaulle 15, 1050 Bruxelles; *t* (02) 640 4291, 647 6190. »90

- ✿ **Missão Católica Portuguêsa**
Kasteelstraat 32, 2000 Antwerpen; *t* (03) 237 5963
Para a Frente. »90
- ✿ ≡ Rue de la Poste 111, 1030 Bruxelles
O Elo. »90
- ✿ ≡ Henri Forirstraat 3, Zwartberg, 3600 Genk; *t* (011) 384384 »90
- ✿ ≡ Rue des Combles 1, 6080 Montignies-sur-Sambre; *t* (071) 410379 »90

◎ **DENMARK** *45*

- ✿ **Den Portugisiske Forening og Klub** *(Portuguese Society and Club)*
Ryesgade 103 B, kld., 2100 København ø; *t* 3138 6376 »90

◎ **FRANCE** *33*

- ✿ *Albatroz*
BP 458, 75161 Paris; *t* (1) 4656 8628
Bulletin. »88
- ✿ **Amicale des amis français-portugais** *(French-Portuguese Friendship Society)*
Mairie, place de l'Hôtel-de-Ville, 60400 Noyon »90
- ✿ **Amicale Portugaise Lavalloise** *(Laval Portuguese Club)*
32 rue Mortier, 53000 Laval
Football. »90
- ✿ **Association des Amis Portugais de Gerzat** *(Gerzat Portuguese Friendship Association)*
A. Afonso: Cité de l'Amitié, 63360 Gerzat; *t* 7325 2947 »94
- ✿ **Association Coordinatrice des Associations des Portugais de Seine et Marne, ACAP 77** *(Co-ordinating Group of Seine and Marne Portuguese Societies)*
Daniel Lacerda: rue des Frères Thibault, 77190 Dammarie-les-Lys; *t* (1) 6439 7969 »94
- ✿ **Association de culture populaire du Portugal Nouveau** *(New Portugal Popular Culture Association)*
[address unknown] 92700 Colombes »90
Association culturelle espagnole-portugaise: see p111
- ✿ **Association Culturelle France-Portugal Azulejo**
Marie Thérèse Freitas: 14 ter. rue Sainte Catherine, 45000 Orléans; *t* 3853 2024 »94
- ✿ **Association Culturelle Portugaise**
E. Fontes: 11 bis Faubourg de Besançon, 70400 Héricourt; *t* 8446 1943, *f* 8476 1354 »94
- ✿ **Association Culturelle Portugaise de Strasbourg, ACPS**
António Martins: 4 rue de l'Arc-en-ciel, 67000 Strasbourg; *t* 8837 3208 »94
- ✿ **Association culturelle et récréative d'Amiens Saudades de Portugal** *(Memories of Portugal Cultural and Leisure Society of Amiens)*
CSC d'Etouvie, avenue de Picardie, 80000 Amiens »90
- ✿ **Association Culturelle Récréative et Sportive Portugaise**
23 rue Ernest Lepot, 59400 Cambrai; *t* 2783 2414 »94
- ✿ **Association Culturelle O Sol do Portugal**
2 place Saint-Pierre, 33000 Bordeaux; *t* 5601 0419, 5645 5410
Music, folk dance, other cultural activities. »94
- ✿ **Association culturelle et sportive des portugais**
34 square des Terres-Noires, bat. B, 77410 Claye »90
- ✿ **Association culturelle et sportive portugaise**
26 rue de la Giraudière, 69530 Brignais »90
- ✿ ≡ Manuel Vieira: 56 avenue de Valenton, 94190 Villeneuve-Saint-Georges »90
- ✿ ≡ Antonio Antunes Mourão: [address uncertain] résidence Fontaine-Mallet, batiment Normandie 5, 93420 Villepinte
Also listed (1990) as parc de la Noue, batiment 4. »90
- ✿ **Association Franco-Portugaise d'Argenteuil, AFPA**
BP 184, 95105 Argenteuil; *t* (1) 3076 2608
Location: 92 boulevard Héloïse. »94
- ✿ **Association franco-portugaise de Vigneux-sur-Seine**
18 rue Henri-Charon, tour C, logement 61, 91270 Vigneux-sur-Seine »89
- ✿ **Association franco-portugaise de Viroflay**
Mairie, 2 place du Général-de-Gaulle, 78220 Viroflay »90
- ✿ **Association pour l'information et l'aide à la communauté portugaise, APIAC**
chez M Mario Coelho De Oliveira: 21 boulevard Claude-Bernard, 63000 Clermont Ferrand »90
- ✿ **Association des Originaires du Portugal** *(Association of Portuguese Nationals)*
6 rue Parmentier, 95870 Bezons »90
- ✿ **Association des Portugais de Bellegarde, APB** *(Bellegarde Portuguese Association)*
4 rue Louis Dumont, 01200 Bellegarde-sur-Valserine; *t* 5048 4368 »94

✿ **Association des Portugais de Franconville**
centre socioculturelle de l'Epine-Guyon, 2 rue des Hayettes,
95130 Franconville   »89
✿ **Association des Portugais Tous**
10 bis rue de Pontoise, 91600 Montmorency   »90
✿ **Association portugaise de Bienfaisance** *(Portuguese
Benevolent Association)*
3 allée des Espaliers, 93340 Le Raincy   »89
✿ **Association Portugaise Culturelle et Sociale**, APCS
Mario Castilho: 62 avenue Lucien Brunet, 77340 Pontault-
Combault; *t* 6029 0744, *f* 6029 3974   »94
✿ **Association portugaise culturelle et sportive de Portovecchio**
Poretta, route de Bastia, 20137 Portovecchio   »90
✿ **Association Portugaise Culturelle de Valentigney**
Francisco Da Costa: 6 rue Victor Hugo, 25700 Valentigney;
t 8130 4696   »94
✿ **Association Portugaise de Domont**
Horacio Gonçalves: BP 19, 95330 Domont; *t* (1) 3935
0597   »94
✿ **Association Portugaise d'Entraide et de Culture**, APEC
(Portuguese Cultural and Mutual Aid Association)
Luciano Cobbeia: 69-71 rue Boissière, 75116 Paris;
t (1) 4500 9526   »94
✿ **Association portugaise de La Fare**
route d'Aix, La Pomme de Pin et les Cinq, 13580 La-Fare-
les-Oliviers   »90
✿ **Association portugaise de Mauléon**
Paula de Souza: 29 rue Jean-Jaurès, 64130 Mauléon   »90
✿ **Association portugaise de Moissac**
7 rue des Pénitents, 82200 Moissac   »90
✿ **Association Portugaise de Montpellier**, APM
Carlos Miranda: 19 rue du Père Fabre, 34000 Montpellier;
t 6792 3241, 6787 3312
O Emigrante (52/yr), *TV Guia* (12/yr).   »94
✿ **Association Portugaise Serra e Val**
Mario Alves: place de l'Eglise, 25500 Morteau; *t* 8167 2267,
f 8167 3444
O Sol do Portugal.   »94
✿ **Association Portugaise Socio-Culturelle et Récréative de
Champigny-sur-Marne**, APSCR
Adilia Carvalho: 23 rue Albert Thomas, 94500 Champigny-
sur-Marne; *t* (1) 4880 3756, 4983 8756   »94
✿ **Association portugaise des travailleurs en France**
(Portuguese Workers' Association of France)
8 rue Derain, 93370 Montfermeil
Community welfare, repatriation of bodies.   »89
✿ **Association Récréative et Amicale des Portugais de
Cambrai-Esnes**, ARAP
Manuel De Sousa: 6 rue Danbon, 59400 Cambrai; *t* 2778
2660   »94
✿ **Association sportive-culturelle des Portugais du Gard** *(Gard
Departement Portuguese Cultural and Sports Association)*
3 bis, rue Saint-Gilles, 3000 Nimes   »89
✿ **Association sportive et culturelle des Portugais de Lure**
6 rue du Failly, 70200 Lure   »90
✿ **Association sportive portugaise—Basket-ball**
chez M Antonio Bernardino: 12 rue Saint-Vincent-de-Paul, La
Vannelière, 79140 Cerizay   »89
✿ **Association des Travailleurs Portugais** *(Portuguese
Workers' Association)*
3 place de Joinville, 75019 Paris   »90
● **Centre d'action sociale et d'acceuil franco-portugais**, CASA
(Franco-Portuguese Social Action and Reception Centre)
13 rue des Ecluses St Martin, 75483 Paris Cedex 10; *t* (1)
4452 4914-00, *f* 4452 4918   »94
✿ **Centre Lusophile de Bourges**, CLB
Antônio Garcia: BP 3021, 35 avenue des Bagatelles, 18027
Bourges; *t* 4850 2322
Bulletin (4/yr).   »94
✿ **Centre Sportif, Social, Culturel et Récréatif des Portugais
de Vierzon**
R. Nunes: rue Henri Barbusse, 18100 Vierzon; *t* 4875 0561 »94
✿ **Club portugais Camões**
zone industrielle B5, avenue Pierre-et-Marie-Curie, 06700
Saint-Laurent-du-Var   »90
✿ **Clube Juvenil Português**: Club des jeunes portugais
Centre Roquette, 51 bis rue de la Roquette, 75011 Paris;
t (1) 4806 4383
Youth welfare and recreation. See also Association Solidarité
français migrants at same address, p135.   »90
● **Collectif d'Etudes et de Dynamisation de l'Emigration
Portugaise**, CEDEP *(Portuguese Migration Research and
Community Development Group)*
Manuel Dias/F. da Silva: 24 rue Saint-Ambroise, 75011 Paris;
t (1) 4355 4606   »94

♦ **Conseil des Communautés Portugaises en France**, CCPF
(Council of Portuguese Communities in France) Head Office
8 rue Popincourt, 75011 Paris; *t* (1) 4700 5822
Interests of Portuguese migrant workers and their families.
See also regional sections, and Coordination des Collectivités
Portugaises en France, below.   »90
✿ ≡ **Région Toulouse** (also known as Fédération des
Associations Portugaises de la Région de Toulouse): José Da
Silva: 18 rue des Canavières, 81000 Albi; *t* 6338 4262   »94
✿ ≡ **Région Tour**: impasse de la Poissonnerie, 18000 Bourges;
t 4870 3358   »90
✿ ≡ **Région Nord**: 5 rue Marc Sagnier, 59400 Cambrai;
t 2781 2888   »90
✿ ≡ **Région Marseille**: 2 avenue de la Borde, 06150 Cannes-
la-Bocca; *t* 9347 7520   »90
✿ ≡ **Région Strasbourg**: 14 rue Noyer, 68000 Colmar   »90
✿ ≡ **Région Reims**: 8a rue Jules-Guesde, 08170 Fumay;
t 2441 0673   »90
✿ ≡ **Région Versailles**: 3 rue Severine, 78800 Houilles   »90
✿ ≡ **Banlieue Paris**: 104 rue de Sarrail, 10600 La
Chapelle-Saint-Luc; *t* 2574 6979   »90
✿ ≡ **Région Nancy**: 2 rue Daniel Sognet, 54460 Leverdun;
t 8324 5192   »90
✿ ≡ **Région Rouen**: 7 rue Jean Paul Marat, 14120 Mardeville;
t 3183 3088   »90
✿ ≡ **Région Centre**: 22 rue du 14 Juillet, 63200 Menetrol;
t 7373 0155   »90
✿ ≡ **Région Nantes**: 56 rue de Chalâtres, 44000 Nantes   »90
✿ ≡ **Région Orléans**: 1 rue Max Jacob, 45000 Orléans
Possibly superseded by listing for Orléans office of Fédération
des Associations Portugaises en France.   »90
✿ ≡ **Région Paris**: 92 rue Clignancourt, 75018 Paris;
t (1) 4262 8828   »90
✿ ≡ **Région Lyon**: 3 chemin du Vallon, 69160 Tassin; *t* 7834
7537   »90
✿ **Coordination des Collectivités Portugaises en France**, CCPF
(Co-ordination of Portuguese Groupings in France)
António Garcia: 20 rue Henri Barbusse, 93300 Aubervilliers;
t (1) 4834 7267, *f* 4937 1598
Information, cultural and leisure activities: may be part of the
other CCPF. *Correio Associativo* (4/yr).   »94
✿ **Encontro Português** *(Portuguese Encounter)* Rencontre
Portugais
Fernando Da Silva: 2 rue Charles Chenu, 92800 Puteaux;
t (1) 4778 9322   »94
✿ **Fédération des Associations d'Expression Portugaise de
Lorraine**, FAEPL
Fernando Da Silva: 29 rue Saint Julien, 54000 Nancy; *t* 8335
0466, *f* 8337 9206   »94
✿ **Fédération des Associations Portugaises de l'air consulaire
de Marseille** *(Federation of Portuguese Associations,
Marseilles Consular Region)*
chemin Gruyes, La Provence, 13090 Aix-en-Provence   »90
✿ **Fédération des Associations Portugaises de l'air consulaire
de Nantes** *(Federation of Portuguese Societies, Nantes
Consular Region)*
72 boulevard Meusnier de Queslon, 44000 Nantes; *t* 4076
7269   »90
✿ **Fédération des Associations Portugaises en France**
(Federation of Portuguese Associations in France)
14 rue Sainte-Anne, 45000 Orléans; *t* 3854 8515   »94
✿ **Fédération des Associations Portugaises du Nord** *(Northern
Federation of Portuguese Associations)*
11 bis rue Holden, 59170 Croix   »90
✿ **Fédération des Associations Portugaises des Vosges**, FAPV
(Vosges Federation of Portuguese Associations)
Carlos Cordeiro: 12 rue Jean Moulin, 88140 Contrexéville;
t 2908 4849   »94
● **Fondation Calouste Gulbenkian**
Centre culturel portugais, 51 avenue d'Iéna, 75116 Paris;
t (1) 4720 8684, 4070 9879
Cultural and social activities; promotion of cultural relations
with Portugal.   »94
✿ **Foyer St-Fridolin**
Père Marcel Danner: 9 rue des Pins, 68200 Mulhouse;
t 8942 4112
Centre run by Portuguese Catholic Mission.   »90
✿ **Groupe culturel et récréatif des Portugais de Franconville**
(Franconville Portuguese Cultural and Leisure Group)
Mairie, rue de la Station, 95130 Franconville   »89
✿ **Groupe folklorique portugais de Bourgoin-Jallieu 'Les Etoiles
Dorées'** *(Gilded Stars Portuguese Folk Group)*
chez Mme Marie-Alice Santo: 15 boulevard Jean-Jacques-
Rousseau, Le Plein Soleil, 38300 Bourgoin-Jallieu
Traditional music and dance.   »89

✿ **Groupe folklorique Souvenir du Portugal** *(Memories of Portugal Folk Group)*
39 rue Gambetta, 60180 Nogent-sur-Oise
Folk music and dance.   »90

✿ **Groupe typique et folklorique portugais de Meudon-la-Forêt** *(Portuguese Traditional Folk Group of Meudon)*
1 allée Gabriel-Voisin, 92290 Châtenay-Malabry   »90

● **Interaction France-Portugal**, IFP: Interacção França-Portugal
52 rue du Four, 75006 Paris; *t* (1) 4222 0399
International friendship, information, cultural promotion; see also IFP in Portugal, p36. *Interaction* (4/yr).   »94

◆ **Missão Católica Portuguêsa**: Mission Catholique Portugaise *(Portuguese Catholic Mission)* National Office
Père Jean-Claude Lucquin, SNPM, National Director: 269 bis rue du Faubourg Saint-Antoine, 75011 Paris; *t* office 4372 4721, chaplaincy 4566 6327
Pastoral care of Portuguese Catholic immigrants in France; governed by a 5-member Conselho Nacional, and managed by the 11-member Equipa de Amimação e de Coordenação da Capelania Portuguêsa em França. See also Service Interdiocésain des Travailleurs Immigrés and Service National de la Pastorale des Migrants, both p137, and (in Portugal) Obra Católica Portuguêsa de Migrações, p148.   »90

✿ ≡ **Região Sudoeste**: Padre António José Ribeiro: Presbytère, 5 bis rue du Noviciat, 33800 Bordeaux; *t* 5694 3050
Team of 32 in 27 centres, including two convents.   »90

✿ ≡ **Região Midi**: Ir. Paulette Delon, Co-ordinator: 3 place de la Verrerie, 46000 Cahors; *t* 6535 4711
Team of 31 in 23 centres including a monastery.   »90

✿ ≡ **Região Este**: Yvette Prudhomme, Co-ordinator: 20 chemin de la Justice, 88000 Epinal; *t* 2934 0135
Team of 30 in 21 centres. Joint co-ordinator: Père Pierre Broussole, 9 bis bvd Voltaire, 21000 Dijon; *t* 8065 2908.   »90

✿ ≡ **Região Provença-Mediterrâneo**: Père Joseph Recordier: 5 chemin du Cros de la Carrière, 13800 Istres; *t* 4256 3378
Team of 9 in 8 centres.   »90

✿ ≡ **Região Centro**: Père Pierre Millet, Co-ordinator: 14 rue Marceau, 28630 Le Coudray; *t* 3728 6513
Team of 30 priests, religious and lay workers in 23 centres, including Tours where there is a bulletin (*O Arauto*, Padre Constantino Ferreira da Silva, 5 allée de Cangé, App. 47, 37000 Tours).   »90

✿ ≡ **Região Ilha de França**: Père Claude Simeon, Co-ordinator: 18 rue Camille-Lemoine, 77290 Mitry-Mory; *t* 6427 1102
Team of 106 in Paris and 71 other centres, including Clichy and Gentilly where there are bulletins (*O Girassol*, Père René Ramondec, 3011 Cité Bois du Temple, 93390 Clichy; *Mais Além*, Padre José Maria Marques, 111 avenue Paul Vaillant Couturier, 94250 Gentilly). Co-ordinator for Versailles: Père Miguel Dalla Vecchia, 32 rue Gabriel-Péri, 78420 Carrières-sur-Seine; *t* 3914 6831.   »90

✿ ≡ **Região Oeste**: Père André Daugan, Co-ordinator: 65 rue Bigot de Prémeneu, 35100 Rennes; *t* 9951 5833
Team of 26 in 17 centres.   »90

✿ ≡ **Região Norte**: Père Philippe Gricourt, Co-ordinator: 2 bis rue Henri Plantagenêt, 76100 Rouen; *t* 3573 3245
25 centres. Joint co-ordinator: Père Jean-Marie Desreumaux, 18 rue Newcommen, 59100 Roubaix; *t* 2070 4330.   »90

✿ ≡ **Região Centro-Este**: Père Jean-Luc Darode, Co-ordinator, Lyons: 1 place Favard, 69800 Saint-Priest; *t* 7820 1145
Team of 53 in 42 centres. Other regional co-ordinators: Père Marcel Baroux, 2 place de 11 Novembre, 69330 Meyzieu; *t* 7831 7468; Père Guy Duret, 10 avenue de Gran, 74000 Annecy; *t* 5057 3493.   »90

✿ **Serviço Católico dos Portuguêses** *(Portuguese Catholic Service)*
8 Cloître Saint-Paul, 45000 Orléans; *t* 3853 5140
Regional religious and pastoral centre for immigrant workers and families.   »90

● **Testemunho** (Witness)
7 rue Paul-Lelong, 75002 Paris
Portuguese-language supplement (6/yr) to *Témoignage*, the journal of Action Catholique.   »90

✿ **Union portugaise de Lens et environs** *(Portuguese Union of Lens and District)*
296 rue du Bois, 62136 Richebourg   »90

◙ **GERMANY** *49*

✿ **Associação Portuguêsa**: Portugiesische Verein *(Portuguese Association)*
Venloerstraße 476, 50823 Köln; *t* (0221) 550 1825
Migrant welfare, training and employment.   »94

✿ ≡ Breitgasse 3A, 41460 Neuss; *t* (02131) 21334
Portuguese culture; migrant welfare, employment.   »94

✿ **Associação Portuguêsa do Pais de Remscheid**: Portugiesische Verein von Remscheid *(Remscheid Portuguese Association)*
Hackenbergerstraße, 42897 Remscheid, Lennep
Youth welfare, cultural events.   »94

✿ **Casa Portuguêsa de Augsburg** *(Augsburg Portuguese House)*
Zollernstraße 7b, 8900 Augsburg   »90

✿ **Centro Cultural Português**: Portugiesisches Kulturzentrum
Ederstraße 14, 6000 Frankfurt am Main; *t* (069) 708075 »90

✿ ≡ Heinrichstr. 14, 22769 Hamburg; *t* (040) 439 9344   »94

✿ **Centro Português**: Portugiesisches Zentrum
[address unknown] Bad Liebenzell   »90

✿ ≡ Schulstraße 3, Postfach 347, Borghorst   »90

✿ ≡ Berlinerstraße 125, 5800 Hagen 7; *t* (02331) 463081
Social centre; includes local Missão Católica Portuguêsa.   »90

✿ ≡ [address uncertain] Banhofstraße 13, 4320 Hattingen an Ruhr   »90

✿ ≡ [address uncertain] Heideweg 15, 4460 Nordhorn   »90

✿ ≡ [address unknown] Ravensburg-Weingarten   »90

✿ ≡ Stephanstraße 41, 42897 Remscheid, Lennep; *t* (02191) 349 763
There is also a Portuguese Catholic Mission in Remscheid.»90

✿ **Centro Português de Marburg**: Portugiesisches Zentrum Marburg
Postfach 1251, 35260 Stadt Allendorf
Culture, youth welfare.   »94

✿ **Centro Português de Mittenberg**: Portugiesisches Zentrum Mittenberg
Mainstraße, 87569 Mittenberg am Main
Culture, education, youth welfare.   »94

✿ **Centro Português de Osnabrück**: Portugiesisches Zentrum Osnabrück
Bünderstraße 6, 49084 Osnabrück; *t* (0541) 586897
Educational welfare, cultural activities.   »94

✿ **Centro Português no Taunus** *(Taunus Portuguese Centre)*
Hunoldstaler Weg, 6392 Neu Anspach   »90

✿ *Diálogo do Emigrante* (Emigrant Dialogue) Administration
A. Salvador Cabral, Editor: Harsewinkelgasse 4, 4400 Münster; *t* (0251) 44785
Newspaper (52/yr) for Portuguese communities in Europe.»90

✿ ≡ Editorial office: Hintere Bleiche 53, 6500 Mainz 1; *t* (06131) 227672   »90

● **Missão Católica Portuguêsa** *(Portuguese Catholic Mission)*
Portugiesisch Pfarrkommission: National Office
Mgr Dr Raimund Amann, National Director: Kaiserstr. 163, 5300 Bonn 1; *t* (0228) 103220
Some 30 priests, 7 nuns and 20 lay workers, mostly Portuguese, provide pastoral care to the large community in Germany; see also, in Portugal: Obra Católica Portuguêsa de Migrações, p148. National delegate for Germany: Padre Rui Cortiço Prates, Hackenbergerstraße 6C, 5630 Remscheid 11 (Lennep); *t* (02191) 62611, 63847. Heinsberg office: Regionalstelle PPK, Apfelstraße 55, 5138 Heinsberg. See also branches, below, and Centro Português de Hagen, above. »90

✿ ≡ Klosterplatz 7, 5100 Aachen   »90

✿ ≡ Linke Brandstraße 52, 8900 Augsburg; *t* (0821) 705283 residence, 311949 mission
A Ponte.   »90

✿ ≡ Waldalgesheimerstraße 26, Postfach 1108, 6550 Bad Kreuznach; *t* (0671) 31414 residence, 33181 mission
A Caminho.   »90

✿ ≡ Stresemannstr. 66, 1000 Berlin 61; *t* (030) 261 1676»90

✿ ≡ Meckenheimer Allee 97, 5300 Bonn 1; *t* (0228) 695106   »90

✿ ≡ Reuterstraße 41, 2800 Bremen 1; *t* (0421) 396 2297 home, 363 0560 mission
Folha Informativa.   »90

✿ ≡ Holsteinerstraße 33, 4600 Dortmund 1; *t* (0231) 813815, 593886   »90

✿ ≡ Kölnstraße 62, Postfach 100529, 5160 Duren; *t* (02421) 16015   »90

✿ ≡ Immermannstraße 20, 4000 Düsseldorf 1; *t* (0211) 354242   »90

✿ ≡ Meersternweg 11, 4300 Essen 12 (Karnap); *t* (0201) 382399   »90

✿ ≡ Mathildenstr. 30A, 6000 Frankfurt am Main 1; *t* (069) 654452 residence, 282696 mission   »90

✿ ≡ Schmallenbachhaus, Hirschberg 5, 5758 Frondenberg; *t* (02373) 751152   »90

✿ ≡ Wallstraße 6, 6114 Gross-Umstadt; *t* (06078) 2154   »90

✿ ≡ Danzigerstraße 62, 2000 Hamburg 1; *t* (040) 280110, 280140   »90

✿ ≡ Bennostraße 3, 3000 Hannover 91 (Linden); *t* (0511) 210 5283 home, 454009 mission   »90

✿ ≡ Teutonenstr. 47, 7100 Heilbronn; *t* (07131) 483327 »90

✿ ≡ Engelsgasse 1, 6570 Kaiserslautern; *t* (0631) 64011 »90

✿ **Missão Católica Portuguêsa**
Lutherplatz 20, 4150 Krefeld; *t* (02151) 390187   »90
✿ ≡ Klosterstraße 90, 5000 Köln; *t* (0221) 497263 residence, 122382 mission
Publishes *Boletim Paroquial de Colónia*.   »90
✿ ≡ Kernerstr. 24, 7140 Ludwigsburg; *t* (07141) 28761   »90
✿ ≡ Westring 245, 6500 Mainz; *t* (06131) 681461 residence, 227672 mission
Comunidade Cristiana.   »90
✿ ≡ Kampstraße 16-18, 5778 Meschede; *t* (0291) 2867   »90
✿ ≡ Kurfürstenstraße 3, 4950 Minden; *t* (0571) 20210
Voz Viva.   »90
✿ ≡ Burgbongert 8, 4050 Mönchengladbach 3; *t* (02166) 602834 home, (0511) 454009 mission   »90
✿ ≡ Theresienstraße 156, 8000 München 2; *t* (089) 523 3179   »90
✿ ≡ Verspoel 20, 4400 Münster; *t* (0251) 44785   »90
✿ ≡ Rheinstraße 8, 4040 Neuss; *t* (02131) 222860 home, (0251) 44785 mission   »90
✿ ≡ Gildehauserweg 72A, 4460 Nordhorn; *t* (05921) 16165
O Papagaio de Nordhorn.   »90
✿ ≡ Krefelderstraße 5B, 8500 Nürnberg 10; *t* (0911) 345902 residence, 367208 mission   »90
✿ ≡ Berlinerstraße 270, 6050 Offenbach am Main; *t* (069) 817655 residence, 845740 mission   »90
Comunidade Cristiana.   »90
✿ ≡ Hindenburgstraße 10, 7600 Offenburg/Baden; *t* (0781) 37522   »90
✿ ≡ Grosse Domsfreiheit 13, 4500 Osnabrück; *t* (0541) 318442 home; 29343, 47690 mission   »90
✿ ≡ Hackenbergerstraße 6C, 42897 Remscheid; *t* (02191) 63847
Folha Informativa.   »90
✿ ≡ Liebenzellerstraße 44, 7032 Sindelfingen; *t* (07031) 801188, 803791
Voz da Missão.   »90
✿ ≡ Hegaustraße 37, 7700 Singen; *t* (07731) 67508 residence, 64544 mission   »90
✿ ≡ Sattlerstraße 4, 7000 Stuttgart 1; *t* (0711) 226 1126 home, 605317 mission
Voz da Missão.   »90
✿ ≡ Hasslerstraße 11, 7900 Ulm am Donau; *t* (0731) 30979 residence, 385968 mission   »90
✿ ≡ Bergstr. 6, 5757 Wickede am Ruhr; *t* (02377) 3838   »90
✿ *O Portal* (The Doorway)
[address unknown] Offenbach am Main
Magazine for and by young Portuguese in Germany.   »90
✿ **Portugiesischer Elternverein** *(Union of Portuguese Elderly)*
Bruchfeldstraße 65, 6000 Frankfurt am Main   »90
✿ **Sozialdienst für Portugiesen** *(Social Service for Portuguese)*
Palanterstraße 2-4, 50937 Köln; *t* (0221) 414070   »94

🔾 **GREECE** *30*

● **Associação Cultural da Comunidade Portuguêsa** *(Portuguese Community Cultural Association)*
Libânio Forte: Mihalakopoulou 125, 11527 Athinai; *t* (01) 775 5032
Cultural interests; welfare of migrants and their families. »94

🔾 **IRELAND** *353*

● **Ireland Portugal Society**
Col. Michael Moriarty, Chairman: Upper Kilmacud Road, Blackrock, Co. Dublin
International friendship and cultural exchange.   »95

🔾 **ITALY** *39*

✿ **Igreja de Santo António dos Portuguêses** *(Catholic Church of St Anthony of the Portuguese)*
via dei Portoghesi 1, Roma; *t* (06) 654 3525   »90
● **Instituto das Cooperadoras da Família** *(Institute of Family Assistants)*
via Martino V 38, 00167 Roma
Catholic social work agency.   »90
✿ **Scuola Portoghese in Roma** *(Portuguese School of Rome)*
via dei Portoghesi 2, 00186 Roma; *t* (06) 654 2496
Educational facility for the children of migrants.   »90

🔾 **LUXEMBOURG** *352*

✿ **Amizades Portugal-Luxembourg—Amitiés Portugal-Luxembourg** *(Portugal-Luxembourg Friendship Society)*
Lucien Huss: 25 rue Léon Metz, 4238 Esch-sur-Alzette; *t* 556604
International and inter-cultural solidarity. *O Contacto*. »94

✿ **Assembleia de Deus de Lingua Portuguêsa** *(Portuguese-Language Assembly of God)*
9 route de Diekirch, Walferdange
Evangelical church.   »90
✿ **Associação Académica de Coimbra**
57 rue du Fort Neipping, 2230 Luxembourg; *t* 292209
Cultural society.   »95
✿ **Associação Cultural Radio Viriatu**
Maria José Monteiro: 63 Grand-Rue, 4575 Differdange; *t* 584127   »90
✿ **Associação de Defesa dos Interesses dos Alunos Portuguêses do Norte**, ADIAP *(Northern Society for the Interests of Portuguese Students)* and Associação dos Pais dos Alunos da Escola Portuguêsa de Diekirch
Antônio Marques Marinho: BP 120, 8 impasse St Antoine, 9205 Diekirch; *t* 808806
Educational welfare and cultural federation of Portuguese parent/teacher groups in northern Luxembourg; constituent groups include the local society (also known as Association des Parents d'Elèves de l'Ecole Portugaise de Diekirch). »94
✿ **Associação Grupo Folclórico Cantares Populares da Mocidade Portuguêsa** *(Portuguese Youth Folk and Popular Music Society)*
José Figueiredo: BP 2752, 1027 Luxembourg; *t* 438379
Cultural and social activities; folk music and dance.   »94
Associação Luso-Caboverdeana: see Cape Verdean listing, p26
✿ **Associação da Mulher Emigrante** *(Emigrant Women's Society)*
18 rue William Turner, 2634 Luxembourg; *t* 408770   »95
✿ ≡ 15 montée de Clausen, 1343 Luxembourg; *t* 466685   »95
✿ **Associação Social e Recreativa Popular Portuguêsa**
BP 1417, 1014 Luxembourg; *t* 400845   »90
✿ **Association des Portugais Emigrés au Luxembourg** *(Association of Portuguese Emigrants in Luxembourg)*
68 rue de Peppange, Bettembourg   »90
✿ **Centro de Apoio Social e Assistência**, CASA *(Social Support and Assistance Centre)* Centre d'Appui Social et Associatif
15 montée de Clausen, 1343 Luxembourg; *t* 432749
Welfare centre associated with the CAPL federation.   »94
✿ **Centro Assistencial e Recreativo** *(Welfare and Recreational Centre)*
9a rue de Luxembourg, Grevnmacher   »90
✿ **Centro Cultural Os Tondolenses**
124 rue de Hollerich, 1740 Luxembourg; *t* 487911   »95
● **Centro de Estudos da Emigração** *(Centre for Emigration Studies)*
José Francisco Marques: 34 rue Adolphe Fischer, 1520 Luxembourg; *t* 494752
Research into Portuguese migration to Luxembourg.   »94
✿ **Centro Social e Cultural Português**
Lucien Huss: 3 rue du Curé, 1368 Luxembourg
Social, cultural and religious meeting-place.   »90
✿ ≡ 32 rue d'Orchimont, 2268 Luxembourg; *t* 484473   »95
✿ ≡ and Missão Católica Portuguêsa—Região do Sul: 17 rue des Boers, 4035 Esch-sur-Alzette; *t* 540669, 544101 »94
✿ **Centro União Portuguêses** *(Portuguese Union Centre)*
45 rue de Bastogne, Ettelbruck   »90
✿ **Club CB Amizade** *(Citizen's Band Friendship Club)*
51 rue Anatole France, 1530 Luxembourg; *t* 482711   »95
◆ **Commission des Communautés Portugaises au Luxembourg**, CCP
Antonio Trinidade: CASA, 15 montée de Clausen, 1343 Luxembourg; *t* 469070   »95
◆ **Confederação das Associações Portuguêsas do Luxembourg**, CAPL: Confédération des Associations Portugaises au Luxembourg, also known as *Federação* APL
BP 2146, 1021 Luxembourg
See also Centro Apoio Social e Assistência, above.   »94
◆ **Missão Católica Portuguêsa**, MCP: Mission Catholique Portugaise *(Portuguese Catholic Mission)*
Pe Belmiro Narino Figueira: 3 rue du Curé, 1368 Luxembourg; *t* 471552
Outreach agency of the Catholic Church in Portugal. See also regional bases, including one at Centro Social e Cultural Português, Esch, above. *O Mensagem*.   »95
✿ ≡ Região do Norte (Northern Region): Pe Pedro Cerantola: Presbytère, 79a route de Luxembourg, 9125 Schieren; *t* 817312, 819860
Shares premises with Missione Cattolica Italiana (Mario Tessarotto).   »94
✿ **Portugal FM**
Manuel Chora: 71 rue du Fort Niepperg, 2230 Luxembourg; *t* 494150   »90
✿ **Portuguêses Unidos de Beaufort** *(United Portuguese of Beaufort)*
Rubén Teixeira de Sousa: 51 rue du Château, 6313 Beaufort; *t* 86747   »94

✪ **Radio Club de Esch**
83 rue du Canal, 4051 Luxembourg; *t* 544534   »90
✪ **Radio Norte Emissora Portuguêsa** *(Radio North Portuguese Station)*
Norberto Sansana: BP 93, 9201 Diekirch   »90
♦ **Service Social pour les Immigrés Portugais** *(Portuguese Immigrant Welfare Service)* Caritas Luxembourg
Amilcar Monteiro: 29 rue Michel Welter, 2730 Luxembourg; *t* 402131 ext. 540   »95
✪ **União Centro Cooperativo** *(Co-operative Centre Union)*
José Correia Trovão: 7 rue J.B. Gellé, 1620 Luxembourg; *t* 407649   »94
✪ **Union Amicale des Portugais d'Echternach** *(Echternach Portuguese Friendship Society)*
3 rue Maximilien, Echternach   »90

◎ **NETHERLANDS** *31*

✪ **Centro Português de Roterdão:** Portugees Centrum *(Portuguese Centre of Rotterdam)*
's Gravendijkwal 76, 3014 EG Rotterdam; *t* (010) 436 3303
Social and cultural group.   »94
✪ **Conselho Paroquial Português em Haia** *(Portuguese Parish Council of The Hague)*
Heilige Hartkerk, Tenierstraat 17, 2526 NX 's Gravenhage; *t* (070) 3806 4497
Luiza Nobre Duarte president (*t* (070) 347 3013); parish council for the Portuguese parish of The Hague (Paróquia do S.C. de Jesus, Haia).   »90
● **Federação das Comunidades Portuguêses na Holanda,** FCPH *(Confederation of Portuguese Communities in the Netherlands)*
José Camacho: Postbus 61319, 1005 HH Amsterdam
Employment advice, youth welfare and education.   »94
♦ **Missão Católica Portuguêsa** *(Portuguese Catholic Mission)*
Dr Rijk Jan, Director: Allochtonenpastoraat Cura Migratorium, Jan Luybenstraat, 's Hertogenbosch; *t* (073) 614 5159   »90
✪ ≡ The Hague: Pe Walter Blondeel: Kade 23, 4703 GA Roosendaal; *t* (0165) 534616 home; (070) 3806 4497   »90
✪ ≡ Nosemanstraat 10-12, 3023 TN Rotterdam; *t* (010) 425 9114 office, 436 5867 home
O Elo.   »90
✪ ≡ Amsterdam: Perim 140, 1503 GB Zaandam NH; *t* (075) 615 5901; (020) 685 2504, 686 5427
O Galo.   »90

◎ **SPAIN** *34*

✪ **Acolhimento, Centro de Portuguêses** *(Portuguese Reception Centre)*
calle Salitre 31, 28012 Madrid; *t* (91) 468 3374   »90
✪ **Asociación Cultural Portuguesa de Laciana** *(Laciana Portuguese Cultural Association)*
Antiguo Ayuntamiento, Caboalles de Arriba, León   »87
✪ **Asociación Luso-Cantabra, ALC** *(Luso-Cantabrian Association)*
Manuel J. Lousada Lopes: calle Alte 46 B, 39008 Santander, Cantabria; *t* (942) 371383
Social and cultural group.   »94
✪ **Associação Portuguêsa:** Asociación Portuguesa
Cáritas, Rio Ebro 33, 09200 Miranda; *t* (947) 311439   »94
✪ **Associação Portuguêsa do Norte:** Asociación Portuguesa del Norte *(Northern Portuguese Association)*
José António Silva: avenida Santa Bárbara 5 part., Torre del Bierzo, León   »94
✪ **Associação Portuguêsa em Pamplona:** Asociación Portuguesa en Pamplona
calle Descalzos 65-4° izq., 31001 Pamplona, Nafarroa   »87
✪ **Associação Portuguêsa 25 de Abril** *(April 25 Portuguese Association)*
Amandio José dos Santos: Apartado de Correos 55, Mieres, 33680 Oviedo, Asturias
Location: Calle Oñón 44.   »94
● **Centro Acolhimento—Assistência Religiosa** *(Reception Centre—Religious Welfare Service)*
calle Villaviciosa 24, 28000 Madrid; *t* (91) 218 2640
See Instituto Secular de Cooperadoras da Família, right.   »94
✪ **Centro Português:** Centro Portugés *(Portuguese Centre)*
Mario Soares da Conceição: calle Romil 12-1°, Apartado de Correos 322, 36200 Vigo, Pontevedra; *t* (986) 434542   »94
✪ **Comunidad Portuguesa de Madrid**
calle Zurbano 67-5°, 28010 Madrid; *t* (91) 442 2300   »87
✪ **Comunidade Portuguêsa de Tremor de Arriba**
calle Escabalón s/n, Tremor de Arriba, León   »90
● **Fundación San Juan de Tremanes**
Campo de la Iglesia s/n, Gijón, Asturias; *t* (985) 328035 »90

● **Instituto Secular de Cooperadoras da Família** *(Secular Institute of Family Assistants)*
Glória Marques Antunes: calle Villaviciosa 24, 28024 Madrid; *t* (91) 218 2240, 218 2241, 218 2242
Social work agency; see also Assistência Religiosa, left.   »90
● **Missão Católica Portuguêsa:** Misión Católica Portuguesa
Padre Pedro Fuente Fernandes, CCEM, National Director: calle Añastro 1, 28033 Madrid; *t* (91) 766 5500   »90
✪ ≡ Pe. José Coelho Matias: Parroquia de San Lorenzo, calle Salitre 33, 28024 Madrid; *t* (91) 468 3374   »90

◎ **UNITED KINGDOM** *44*

● **Anglo-Portuguese Foundation**
36 Eastcastle St, London W1N 7PE; *t* (0171) 631 4645   »90
● **Anglo-Portuguese Society**
2 Belgrave Square, London SW1X 8PJ; *t* (0171) 245 9738
Friendship, cultural exchanges; founded 1938.   »95
✪ **Centro Católico Português** *(Portuguese Catholic Centre)*
165 Arlington Road, Camden Town, London NW1 7EX; *t* (0171) 267 9612
Catholic social and pastoral centre. *Folinha Portuguêsa.*   »90
✪ **Portuguese Community Centre**
Antonio J. Rodrigues da Silva: 7 Thorpe Close, London W10 5XL; *t* (0181) 969 3890   »94

◎ **CHANNEL ISLANDS** *44*

✪ **Portuguese Club of Jersey**
14 James Street, St Helier JE2 4TT; *t* (01534) 37213   »95

PUERTO RICAN

see also Caribbean, Latin American, United States

◎ **UNITED KINGDOM** *44*

● **Puerto Rico Support Group**
[address unknown] London   »88

PUNJABI

or Panjabi; see also Asian, Indian, Pakistani, Sikh

◎ **UNITED KINGDOM** *44*

✪ *Awaze Qaum International*
Raghbir Singh/Zorawar Singh Rai: Gate 2, Unit B, Booth St, Smethwick, Warley B66 2PF; *t* (0121) 555 5921
Journal (52/yr) aligned with the International Sikh Youth Federation, p107, and the Khalistan movement. Its editor, Raghbir Singh Johal, was in 1995 imprisoned pending deportation on alleged security grounds. Address 1991. »95
● **British Sikh Punjabi Literary Society**
S.S. Sangha, Convenor: 29 Europa Avenue, Sandwell Valley, West Bromwich B70, West Midlands; *t* (0121) 553 1172 »91
● *The Daily Awaz International*
Shirley Rizvi: Unit K, Middlesex Business Centre, Bridge St, Southall UB2 4AB; *t* (0181) 813 9933 ext. 234, *f* 813 8822
Daily newspaper founded 1992.   »95
● *Des Pardes* (At Home and Abroad)
Gurbux Singh Virk, Editor: 8 The Crescent, Southall, Middlesex; *t* (0181) 571 1127-29
The main Panjabi tabloid newspaper (52/yr), sympathetic to the cause of Khalistan. Its founding editor, Tarsem Singh Purewal, was murdered in January 1995.   »95
● *Des Vides*
Ajit Singh Bagha, Editor: 78 Hayesbridge Court, Uxbridge Road, Hayes UB4, Middlesex; *t* (0181) 569 3720
Panjabi-English review (52/yr), launched 1991.   »91
● *Ghazal & Beat*
20 Dagmar Road, Southall, Middlesex; *t* (0181) 571 1224
Magazine (12/yr) on Bhangra and other Panjabi music.   »91
● **International Panjabi Literary Society**
Dr Pritam Singh Kambo: 367 Katherine Road, Forest Gate, London E7 8LT; *t* (0181) 470 7834
Literary evenings, promotion of Panjabi language.   »91
● *Khalistan News*
[address uncertain] 44 Norfolk Road, Gravesend DA12 2RX; *t* (0181) 724 1674
Sikh nationalist newspaper.   »91
● **National Council for Panjabi Teaching, NCPT**
c/o Surinder Singh Attariwala: High Cross Education Centre, High Rd, Tottenham, London N17 6QP; *t* (0181) 801 2302
Founded 1989 to promote Panjabi language teaching.   »91

- **Panjab Research Group**, PRG, and **Association for Punjab Studies in Great Britain**
c/o Shinder S. Thandi: Department of Economics, Coventry University, Priory St, Coventry CV1 5FB; *t* (01203) 838238
Darshan Singh Tatla secretary; founded 1984; academic and professional research on East and West Punjab and the diaspora; meetings, newsletter, discussion papers.   »91
- *Panjabi Darpan* (Punjab Mirror)
J. Kaushal: 36 Trent Ave., London W5; *t* (0181) 579 2091
Newspaper (52/yr).   »88
- ✧ **Panjabi Parents' Association of East London**
Gurcharan Singh Gahir, President: 135 Byron Avenue, Manor Park, London E12; *t* (0181) 470 6572
Naranjan Singh, secretary.   »91
- **Panjabi Progressive Writers' Association**
N.S. Noor: [address unknown] Bilston, West Midlands   »91
- ✧ **Panjabi Writers' Association, Southall**
Shivcharan Singh Gill: 67 Thorncliffe Road, Southall, Middlesex; *t* (0181) 574 5594   »91
- *Perdesan* (Emigrant Woman)
Kuldeep Kaur, Editor: 478 Lady Margaret Road, Southall UB1 2NW; *t* (0181) 575 8694, 575 8659
Magazine (12/yr).   »88
- **Punjab Human Rights Organization**
Manjit Singh, Co-ordinator: 70 Staines Road, Hounslow TW3 3LF; *t* (0181) 572 4571
Harjeet Singh, president; human rights in Punjab.   »91
- *Punjab Mail*
Gurdeep Singh, Editor: [address unknown] East Ham, London E6
Journal (12/yr) launched 1991.   »91
- *Punjab Times*
G.K. Sahni, Editor: 30 Featherstone Road, Southall UB2 5AB; *t* (0181) 571 2751, 571 5102
See also *Asian Chronicle*, p12. Newspaper (52/yr).   »91
- ✧ **Punjab Welfare Association**
40 Wyverne Rd, Chorlton-cum-Hardy, Manchester M21 1ZN
Welfare, housing, immigration advice; translation service.   »93
- ✧ ≡ Women's Group: Amina Dar: 50 Turnbull Road, Longsight, Manchester M13 0PY; *t* (0161) 225 5782
Social, cultural and educational activities for Pakistani and other black and ethnic minority women.   »93
- ✧ **Punjabi Cultural Society**
G.S. Atwal: 129 Soho Road, Handsworth, Birmingham B21 9ST
Panjabi school, cultural activities.   »91
- ✧ **Punjabi Group**
S. Gajjan Bansall: 57 Powell Street, Wolverhampton   »90
- *Punjabi Guardian*
Inderjit Singh Sangha, Editor: 129 Soho Road, Handsworth, Birmingham B21 9ST; *t* (0121) 554 3995
Panjabi-English periodical (26/yr).   »91
- **Punjabi Language Development Board**
Surjit Singh Kalra, Secretary: 2 St Anne's Close, Handsworth Wood, Birmingham B20 1BS; *t* (0121) 551 5272
Book distribution; promotes Panjabi language teaching.   »91

PUSHTO

or Pushtu, Pashto: see Afghan, Pakistani

QUÉBÉCOIS

see also Canadian

◎ **FRANCE** *33*

- ✧ **Association Paris Québec**
100 rue de la Roquette, 75011 Paris; *t* (1) 4373 7581   »90

RASTAFARIAN

see also African Caribbean, Afro-Caribbean, Caribbean, Jamaican, West Indian

◎ **UNITED KINGDOM** *44*

- **Ethiopian World Federation Inc.**
28 St Agnes Place, London SE11 4BE; *t* (0171) 735 0905
Production of educational materials on Ras Tafari, Rasta culture and Ethiopia. *Rasta Living*.   »94
- ✧ **Rastafarian Advisory Service**
17a Netherwood Rd, London W14 0BL; *t* (0171) 602 3767»91

RÉUNION

see also French, French: DOM/TOM

◎ **FRANCE** *33*

- **Comité national des réunionais** (National Committee of Réunion People)
39 rue Gauthey, 75017 Paris; *t* (1) 4228 6614   »90
- ✧ **La Maison de la Réunion** (House of Réunion)
39 rue Gauthey, 75017 Paris; *t* (1) 4627 2828   »90

ROMANIAN

see also East European, European, German 'National', Gypsy, South-East European, Transylvanian

◎ **DENMARK** *45*

- **Danish Action for Romania**
Florica Dejan: [address uncertain] Skt Annægade 15, 1416 København K; *t* 3154 0909, 4369 2045   »90
- **Dansk-Rumænsk Forening**
Kristian Steensgard, Frederiksbergvej 13A, 4180 Sorφ; *t* 5363 3400   »95

◎ **FRANCE** *33*

- **Opération Villages Roumains-France**
67 avenue République, 75011 Paris; *t* (1) 4357 3673   »90

◎ **GERMANY** *49*

- ✧ **Verband der Freien Rumanen und Deutschen aus Rumanien** (League of Free Romanians and Germans from Romania)
Vorgebirgstraße 178, 5000 Köln; *t* (0221) 366776   »90

◎ **IRELAND** *353*

- **Irish Romanian Adoptive Parents Group**
Derek Singleton: 21 Watson Avenue, Killiney, Co. Dublin   »91

◎ **ITALY** *39*

- ✧ **Comunità Romena Ortodossa in Torino** (Romanian Orthodox Community of Turin)
Pr. Gheorghe Vasilescu: S. Paraschiva, via Cottolengo 26, 10152 Torino; *t* (011) 216 5319   »94

◎ **LUXEMBOURG** *352*

- **Association Luxembourg-Roumanie**
23 rue Edward Steichen, 3324 Bivange; *t* 369048   »95

◎ **SPAIN** *34*

- **Asociación de Amistad Hispano-Rumana Mihail Eminescu** (Mihail Eminescu Spanish-Romanian Friendship Association)
Carmen Stefañescu: calle Arlabán 7-4°, of. 46, 28014 Madrid; *t* (91) 523 1618, *f* 523 3491
Refugee and migrant welfare, cultural activities, women's group. See also FEDORA refugee umbrella group, p151.   »94
- **Asociación Cultural Rumana Mota Marin** (Mota Marin Cultural Association)
calle Anita Vindel 29, Madrid; *t* (91) 307 0167   »90
- ✧ **Iglesia Ortodoxa Rumana** (Romanian Orthodox Church)
calle Félix Boix 13, Madrid; *t* (91) 250 8218   »90

◎ **UNITED KINGDOM** *44*

- **British Romanian Friendship Association**
Harry Gold, Secretary: 3 Dartmouth Chambers, 8 Theobalds Road, London WC1; *t* (0171) 405 3045
Friendship, cultural exchange; founded 1947.   »90
- ✧ **ORFAN**
c/o Foxden, Crow Lane, Great Bourton, Banbury OX16, Oxfordshire; *t* (01295) 750730, 265476
Volunteer workers, funding for orphanages in Romania.   »95
- **Romanian Orphanage Trust**
Donald McCready, Chief Executive: 21 Garlick Hill, London EC4V 2AU; *t* (0171) 248 5419
A charity (with an associated organisation, The European Children's Trust) operating through local partner agencies in Romania to develop care for children and families.   »95

◎ **NORTHERN IRELAND** *44*

- ✧ **Comber Romanian Orphanage Appeal Ireland**
28a Castle St, Comber, Co. Down; *t* (01247) 874052   »94

ROMANY

or Roma, Romani; see also Gypsy, Traveller

◎ BOSNIA HERCEGOVINA *387*

✿ **Braca Romi**
Adema Buce 286, 71000 Sarajevo »94

◎ FRANCE *33*

● **Romani Union** *(Romany Union)*
Annette Zahrai: [address uncertain] 23 rue de l'Abruvall,
78/70 allée St-Claud, Paris »90

◎ GERMANY *49*

✿ **Dokumentations- und Kulturzentrum Deutscher Sinti und
Roma** *(German Sinti and Romany Documentation and
Cultural Centre)*
Herbert Heuss/E. Bamberger: Zwingerstraße 18, 69117
Heidelberg; *t* (06221) 161026
Centre run by the Zentralrat Deutscher Sinti und Roma. »94
▌ **Internationale Roma-Union**
[address unknown]
Held fourth world Romany congress in Warsaw, April 1990,
delegates from 18 countries including Denmark, France,
Germany, Ireland, Netherlands, UK. »90
● **Roma- und Cinti-Union, RCU** *(Romany and Sinti Union)*
Rudko Kawczinski: Simon von Utrechtstraße 85, 20359
Hamburg; *t* (040) 310521, *f* 310475
See also Roma National Congress at same address, below.»94
▌ **Roma National Congress—European Central Office, RNC**
Rudko Kawczynski, President: Simon von Utrechtstraße 85,
20359 Hamburg; *t* (040) 319 4249, *f* 310475
International federation of Romany organisations; German
member is the Roma- und Cinti-Union, above. Defence of civil
rights of Roma in Europe, prevention of deportation of
stateless or displaced persons; training for community work
and civil rights activities; links the political work of Roma
groups through the Standing Conference for the Co-ordination
and Co-operation of the Romani Associations in Europe. »94
● **Roma Union**
H.G. Böttcher/Alfred Erdölli: Wingertstrasse 12, 6000
Frankfurt am Main
Founded 1988 to assist Romany asylum seekers, mainly from
Romania; campaigning against 1992 accord on repatriation by
Germany of 43,000 Romanians, mainly of Romany origin.»92
✿ **Romano Jekhetanipe**
c/o Lidija Mirkovic, Rheydterstraße 165, 41462 Neuss;
t (02131) 273113, *f* 272083
Campaigns against racism and intolerance and for minority
and refugee rights. »94
▌ **Standing Conference for the Co-ordination and Co-operation
of the Romani Associations in Europe**
[address unknown]
Seeks to establish an efficient Roma network throughout
Europe. »95
✿ **Verein Rom e.V.** *(Romany Union)* also known as Rom e.V.
Bobstraße 6-8, 50676 Köln; *t* (0221) 242536, *f* 240 1715
Anti-racism, support for migrant and refugee rights. »94
♦ **Zentralrat deutscher Sinti und Roma** *(Central Council of the
German Sinti and Romanies)*
Zwingerstraße 18, 69117 Heidelberg; *t* (06221) 981101,
f 981190
Representative body of the Romany communities in Germany.
See also Dokumentations- und Kulturzentrum, and Roma- und
Cinti-Union, above. »94

◎ HUNGARY *36*

✿ **Roma Parliament in Hungary**
Tavasmező útca 6, 1084 Budapest
Represents and defends Romany minority; human rights, anti-
racism, solidarity with Romany refugees. »94

◎ ITALY *39*

✿ **Associazione Rom Rasim Sejdic**
Kasim Cizmic: Vicolo Savini 63, 00146 Roma; *t* (06) 559
2893, 446 9309, *f* 687 8498 »94

◎ SLOVAKIA *42*

● **Romani National Party**
Emil Sarkezi, Leader: [address unknown]
Represents the interests of the sizeable Romani minority;
campaigns against racist violence. »95

◎ UNITED KINGDOM *44*

● **British Rommani Union**
Oggi Thomas Odley: The Reservation, Hever Road,
Edenbridge TN8 5DJ; *t* (01732) 866139 »90
▌ **International Romany Union**
Pete Mercer: [address unknown]
Possibly same as Internationale Roma-Union (Germany). »94
▌ **World Romany Congress**
[address unknown]
Affiliates include Association of Gypsy Organisations, p41.»90

RUSSIAN

see also East European, Jewish, former Soviet nationalities

◎ BELGIUM *32*

✿ **Eglise Orthodoxe Russe de la Résurrection**: Russische
Orthodoxe Kerk van de Verrijzenis *(Russian Orthodox Church
of the Resurrection)*
P. Spaakstraat 18, 1050 Brussel »90
✿ **Eglise Orthodoxe Russe de St-André**: Russische Orthodoxe
Kerk van St-Andreas *(Russian Orthodox Church of St Andrew)*
Mommaertstraat 39, 1000 Brussel »90
✿ **Eglise Orthodoxe Russe de St-Job**: Russische Orthodoxe
Kerk van St Job *(Russian Orthodox Church of St Job)*
Avenue Defré 19, 1180 Bruxelles »90
✿ **Eglise Orthodoxe Russe de St-Nicolas**: Russische Orthodoxe
Kerk van St Niklaas *(Russian Orthodox Church of St Nicholas)*
Rue des Chevaliers 29, 1050 Bruxelles »90
✿ **Eglise Orthodoxe Russe de St-Pantaleimon et St-Nicolas**:
Russische Orthodoxe Kerk van SS Pantaleimon en Niklaas
(Russian Orthodox Church of St Pantaleimon and St Nicholas)
Rue Jean-André de Mot 47, 1040 Bruxelles »90
✿ **Eglise Orthodoxe Russe de Ste-Anne**: Russische Orthodoxe
Kerk van St Anna *(Russian Orthodox Church of St Anne)*
Avenue des Trembles 4, 1020 Bruxelles »90

◎ FRANCE *33*

✿ **Action Chrétienne des Etudiants Russes** *(Russian Christian
Student Action)*
91 rue Olivier de Serres, 75015 Paris; *t* (1) 4250 5366 »90
● **Narodny Trudovniy Soyuz** *(People's Labour Union)*
[address unknown] Paris
Right-wing emigré group. »88

◎ ITALY *39*

✿ **Centro Russia Ecumenica**
Sergio Mercanzin: Vicolo del Farinone 30, 00193 Roma;
t (06) 689 6637, *f* 687 9355 »94
✿ **Comitato dei Russi in Italia**
Vladimir Keidan: via Conteverde 58, 00185 Roma; *t* (06)
446 7676, *f* 678 1182 »94

◎ LUXEMBOURG *352*

✿ **Centre Culturel A.S. Pouchkine**, formerly Association
Luxembourg-URSS
32 rue Goethe, 1637 Luxembourg; *t* 220147 »95

◎ PORTUGAL *351*

● **Associação Portugal-Russia** (presumed to be the new name
of the former Associação Portugal-URSS)
São Caetano 30, 1200 Lisboa; *t* (01) 601124 »95
✿ ≡ Rua 9 Abril 961-1°, 4200 Porto; *t* (02) 825277 »94

◎ UNITED KINGDOM *44*

● **Britain-Russia Centre**
14 Grosvenor Place, London SW1; *t* (0171) 235 2116 »95
✿ *Londonskiy Kurier* (London Courier)
Natalia Shuvayeva, Editor-in-Chief: [address unknown] London
Publication founded 1994, aimed at visiting and resident
Russians. »95

RWANDESE

see also African, Central African

◎ ITALY *39*

✿ **Agrippine Bakamurera**
via G. Rossini 9, 09128 Cagliari; *t* (070) 43196 »90

✿ **Associazione Studenti Ruandesi Italia Meridionale—Sezione Torino**, ASRIM *(Southern Italy Society of Rwandese Students—Turin Section)*
Jean-Marie V. Tshotsha: via B. Drovetti 6, 10138 Torino;
t (011) 447 4057   »94

◉ **UNITED KINGDOM** *44*

● **Rwanda-Burundi Action Group**
Nicole Lieger/Anders Ravn: Institute of Development Studies, University of Sussex, Brighton BN1, Sussex
Paolo Verme, James Fairhead; solidarity with Rwanda and Burundi; peaceful resolution of ethnic conflict.   »94
● **Rwanda Development Trust**
Hugh Jones: [address unknown] Bromley, Kent
Development aid, information.   »95

SAHARAN; SAHRAWI

see also African, Arab/Arabic, Maghrebi, Moroccan, North African

◉ **FRANCE** *33*

✿ **La Ralha, Amicale des Sahariens** *(La Ralha Sahrawi Society)*
4 rue Coëtlogon, 75006 Paris; *t* (1) 4222 6741   »90

◉ **GERMANY** *49*

● **Gesellschaft der Freunde des Sahrauischen Volkes**, GFSV *(German Society of Friends of the Sahrawi People)*
Quedlinburger Weg 3, 3000 Hannover 21   »93

◉ **SPAIN** *34*

✿ **Amigos de la República Árabe Saharaui Democrática en Aragón** *(Friends of the Sahrawi Arab Democratic Republic in Aragón)*
calle Urrea 21-1°, 50001 Zaragoza; *t* (976) 231349
Polisario solidarity movement.   »93
● **Asociación de Amigos del Pueblo Saharaui** *(Association of Friends of the Sahrawi People)*
calle Pez 27-2° izq., 28004 Madrid; *t* (91) 531 2829   »95

ST VINCENT

see Vincentian

SALVADOREAN

see also Central American, Latin American

◉ **FRANCE** *33*

● **Radio Venceremos** *(Radio We Shall Overcome)*
52 rue de Crimée, 75019 Paris
FMLN support group.   »88

◉ **IRELAND** *353*

● **Irish El Salvador Support Committee**, IESC
Brendan Butler, Chairperson: Pennock Hill, Swords, Co. Dublin; *t* (01) 840 5469, *f* 840 7026
Solidarity with progressive forces in El Salvador, welfare of refugees and returnees; information, campaigns, emergency relief. *Newsletter* (2/yr).   »94

◉ **ITALY** *39*

✿ **Associazione di Salvadoregni in Lombardia**, ASL *(Association of Salvadoreans in Lombardy)*
Daydamia Morán: via Copernico 1, 25019 Milano; *t* (02) 687 8354   »94
✿ **Comunità Salvadoregna** *(Salvadorean Community)*
via G. Mulat 78, 20159 Milano   »90

◉ **UNITED KINGDOM** *44*

● **El Salvador Committee for Human Rights**
Belisario Nieto/Deborah Knight: 83 Margaret Street, London W1N 7HB; *t* (0171) 631 4200, 631 4203   »92
● **El Salvador Solidarity Campaign**, ELSSOC
Niki Johnson: 129 Seven Sisters Road, London N7 7QG; *t* (0171) 272 4580
Solidarity with progressive forces in El Salvador, and with Salvadorean refugees.   »94

SÃO TOMÉ

see also African, Portuguese, West African

◉ **PORTUGAL** *351*

✿ **Associação Cultural e Recreativa Santomense** *(São Tomé Cultural and Leisure Association)*
Alberto Neto Rosa: Esperança 69-3° D, 1200 Lisboa   »94

SAUDI ARABIAN

see also Arab/Arabic, Islamic, Middle Eastern

◉ **UNITED KINGDOM** *44*

● **Advisory and Reformation Committee**
Khaled al-Fauwaz/Osama bin Ladin: [address unknown] Wembley, London
Pressure group opposed to the Al-Saud regime.   »94
● *al-Hayat*
[address unknown] London
Daily newspaper published in London for distribution in Saudi Arabia and elsewhere.   »95
● *Ashraq al-Aswat* and *Al-Eqtisadiah*; *Al Majalla*
Saudi Research & Publishing Co., Arab Press House, 184 High Holborn, London WC1V 7AP; *t* (0171) 831 8181, *f* 831 2130
Daily newspaper; daily business paper; magazine (52/yr), all produced in London and based in Jeddah.   »95
● **Committee for the Defence of Legitimate Rights**, CDLR
Dr Mohammed al-Mas'ari: [address unknown] Willesden, London NW10; *t* (0181) 830 2910, *f* 830 4716
Islamist, anti-monarchist, anti-corruption Saudi opposition movement; formed in Riyadh, but represented in exile by Mas'ari after his release from a Saudi prison in 1994; he has been threatened with deportation to Dominica because his political activities were embarrassing the UK government. »96
● **Saudi Arabian Educational Office**
Dr Abdullah Al-Nasser, Director: 29 Belgrave Square, London SW1 8QB
The Saudis also maintain an Information Centre and an Islamic Affairs Unit in London.   »94

SCANDINAVIAN

see also European, Finnish, Icelandic, Norwegian, Swedish; and see Danish

◉ **FRANCE** *33*

● **Cercle suédois et norvégien** *(Swedish and Norwegian Circle)*
242 rue Rivoli, 75001 Paris; *t* (1) 4260 7667   »90

◉ **IRELAND** *353*

● **Irish Scandinavian Club**
c/o Trude Visser: Ulverton Road, Dalkey, Co. Dublin; *t* (01) 280 0284
Frode Dahl, Monika Lauder; founded as Irish-Swedish Society 1946; members mostly Swedish, Irish and Danish; has absorbed Irish Norwegian Society. *Newsletter* (4-5/yr).   »94

SCOTTISH

see British, European

SENEGALESE

see also African, Islamic, West African

◉ **FRANCE** *33*

✿ **Amicale des Etudiants Sénégalais de Lille** *(Senegalese Students' Society of Lille)*
6-3 rue de Trudaine, 59650 Villeneuve-d'Ascq   »89
✿ **Association culturelle et sociale des ressortissants sénégalais et mauritaniens des Vosges Halpoulaire** *(Senegalese and Mauritanian Cultural and Social Association)*
batiment Anjou E/78, Kelermann, 88100 Saint-Dlé   »89
✿ **Association des Etudiants sénégalais de Caen** *(Association of Senegalese Students in Caen)*
305 Grand-Parc, appt 1204, 14200 Hérouville   »89

- **Association Générale des Travailleurs Sénégalais en France**
  (General Association of Senegalese Workers)
  28 rue d'Haute Paul, 75019 Paris
  See also the Union Générale, below. »90
- ☼ **Association des jeunes ressortissants sénégalais à Bordeaux** *(Bordeaux Association of Young Senegalese Nationals)*
  cité du Grand Parc, appt 209, 26 rue des Géneraux-Duche, 33300 Bordeaux »89
- ☼ **Association des Ressortissants Sénégalais à Marseille, ARSM** *(Association of Senegalese Nationals in Marseilles)*
  M'baye Diop: 93 La Canebière, 13001 Marseille; *t* 9154 0056, 9155 3950, *f* 9133 6075
  Cultural and anti-racist activities. »94
- ☼ **Association Sabar Horizons—Compagnie Doudou N'Diaye Rose Junior**
  5 rue de Tomboctou, 75018 Paris
  Music and dance. »90
- ☼ **Association des sénégalais stagiaires et étudiants à Pau** *(Pau Senegalese Students' and Trainees' Association)*
  54 avenue du Loup, 64000 Pau »90
- ☼ **Mouvement des Etudiants Socialistes Sénégalais de Rennes** *(Senegalese Socialist Students' Movement of Rennes)*
  cité universitaire de Beaulieu, chambre 193 D, 33 avenue des Buttes-de-Coesmes, 35000 Rennes »89
- ☼ **Sénégalais du pays de Montbéliard** *(Montbéliard Senegalese)*
  3 rue des Frères-Lumière, 25700 Valentigney
  Students and migrant workers in Burgundy. »89
- ☼ **Tufnde Endam (Solidarités villageoises)** *(Village Solidarity)*
  Ousmane Sow, President: 6 rue François-Pizzarre, 78200 Mantes-La-Jolie
  Fundraising for rural development projects in six Senegalese villages. »90
- ☼ **Union Générale des Travailleurs Sénégalais en France, UGTSF** *(General Union of Senegalese Workers in France)*
  12 rue Rouget de l'Isle, 92110 Clichy; *t* (1) 4731 5714, 4773 5411
  See also Association Générale, above. »94
- ☼ **Union des ressortisants sénégalais de l'Eure** *(Union of Senegalese Nationals of the Eure)*
  20 rue Molière, 27000 Evreux-La-Madeleine
  Departmental social and welfare society. »89
- ☼ **Union des Travailleurs Sénégalais en France—Action Revendicative, UTSF-AR** *(Union of Senegalese Workers in France—Affirmative Action)*
  Djiby Sy: 43 rue des Terres au Curé, 75013 Paris; *t* (1) 4880 4070, 6494 9576 »94

◎ **ITALY** *39*

- ☼ **Associazione Culturale dei Senegalesi della Provincia de Pistoia** *(Senegalese Cultural Association of Pistoia Province)*
  Association Culturelle des Sénégalais de Pistoia
  Moussa Dieng: via Veneto 7/3, 51106 Montecatini Terme; *t* (0573) 975435; (0572) 913054
  Social solidarity, anti-racism. »94
- ☼ **Associazione Senegalesi**
  c/o Coordinamento Immigrati Extracomunitari, Salita S. Francesco 4, 16122 Genova; *t* (010) 206207 »94
- ☼ ≡ Apulia: via Luigi Carbone 46, 73100 Lecce »90
- ☼ **Associazione Senegalesi di Lombardia, ASL**
  Feydou Bâ Feydou: c/o CeSIL, via Benedetto Marcello 18, 20124 Milano; *t* (02) 204 7704 »94
- ☼ **Associazione Senegalesi di Parma e Provincia, ASPP**
  Mactar Seck: via Emilia Est 22, 43100 Parma; *t* (0521) 40840 »94
- ☼ **Associazione Senegalesi di Ravenna, ASSRA**
  Mamadou Gueye: via Montanari 13, 48200 Porto Corsini, RA; *t* (0544) 447444, *f* 32528 »94
- ☼ **Associazione dei Senegalesi in Sardegna** *(Association of Senegalese in Sardinia)*
  via G. Asproni 24, 09123 Cagliari; *t* (070) 670711 »90
- ☼ **Club Amicale des Sénégalais de Treviso, CAST**
  Khaly Ndiaye: via Dandolo 2D, 31100 Treviso; *t* (0422) 409111, 409252, *f* 403731
  Cultural and social society; advice service. »94
- ☼ **Comitato Senegalese in Toscana, COMSET** *(Senegalese Committee of Tuscany)*
  Fallou Faye: via Giovanni Pacini 2, 50122 Firenze; *t* (055) 754688 »90
- ☼ **Comunità Senegalese**
  Cheikh Ndiareme Gueye: via Camillo Rosalba 47/e n° 10, 70124 Bari »90
- ☼ ≡ via F. de Sanctis 2, 40132 Bologna »90
- ☼ ≡ Isola Ponti 23, 20062 Cassano d'Adda; *t* (0363) 62152 »90

☼ **Comunità Senegalese**
via dell'Olivuzzo 33, 50143 Firenze »90
☼ **Comunità Senegalese di Livorno e Province**
Mbaye Diop/Tutti Coundoul: viale Carducci 27, 57100 Livorno; *t* (0586) 427127, *f* 429968 »94
♦ **Coordinamento Associazioni Senegalesi in Italia** *(Co-ordination of Senegalese Associations in Italy)*
Yossouph Baro: via F. Giallo 218 C/8, 00144 Roma; *t* (06) 847 6405
Represented in EU Migrants Forum, p131. »94
- **Coordinamento Nazionale Senegalesi**
  via Domenico Cavalla 58, 56100 Pisa; *t* (050) 21536 »94
☼ **Società Mutuo Soccorso tra Senegalesi a Bergamo** *(Mutual Aid Society for Senegalese in Bergamo)*
Assane Mboupp: via Carnovali 88, 24100 Bergamo; *t* (035) 324112, *f* 324113
Housing and welfare advice, cultural and social functions. »94

◎ **SPAIN** *34*

- **Asociación Catalana de Residentes Senegaleses** *(Catalan Association of Senegalese Residents)*
  Aïssata N'Doye: Assaonadors 10-2° 2ª, 08003 Barcelona, Catalunya; *t* (93) 319 6507
  Welfare, solidarity. »94
- ☼ **Asociación de Inmigrantes Senegaleses** *(Association of Senegalese Immigrants)*
  Mesón de Paredes 50, 28012 Madrid; *t* (91) 539 9936 »94
- ☼ **Asociación de Senegaleses en Valencia**
  paseig Petxina 74, pta 22, 46018 Valencia »94

SERBIAN

see also Bosnian, Croatian, European, South-East European, (Ex-)Yugoslav

◎ **FRANCE** *33*

☼ **Zabavno Rekreatiuni Club Beograd**: Association Artistique de Belgrad *(Belgrade Cultural and Recreational Club)*
9 rue Félix-Terrier, 75020 Paris
Musical club. »89

◎ **UNITED KINGDOM** *44*

- **Serbian National Organisation**
  N. Krunic, President: 106 Baker Street, London W1
  D. Novakovic. Solidarity with Serbia, and with Serbs in Croatia and elsewhere. »92
- ☼ **Serbian National Welfare Centre**
  128 Chapeltown Road, Leeds LS7; *t* (0113) 262 3429 »90
- ☼ **Serbian Orthodox Church**
  89 Lancaster Road, London W11; *t* (0171) 727 8367 »95
- ☼ **Serbian Orthodox Church of St Lazar**
  Griffins Brook Road, Birmingham B31 »90

SHIA; SHI'ITE

see Islamic

SIERRA LEONEAN

see also African, Islamic, West African

◎ **SPAIN** *34*

☼ **Sierra Leone National Union**
carrer Trinxant 65-1° 2ª, 08026 Barcelona, Catalunya »94

◎ **UNITED KINGDOM** *44*

- ☼ **Association for Sierra Leonean Refugees**
  Suite D, Building B, MacBean Centre, MacBean Street, London SE18 6LW »96
- **Sierra Leone Association**
  145 Cramlington Road, Great Barr, Birmingham B42 2EF »90
- ☼ **Sierra Leone Community**
  Sylvester During/Yomie Lewis: 186 The Fairway, New Moston, Manchester M10 0NJ; *t* (0161) 682 1010, 860 7734
  Social and cultural events. »93
- ☼ **Sierra Leone Friendship Association of Manchester**
  W. Shubu-Jones: 8 Slade Hall Road, Longsight, Manchester M12 4QF; *t* (0161) 224 7867, 436 1854
  Cultural activities, arts and crafts, self-help. »93

SIKH

see also Asian, Indian, Punjabi. Most of the bodies listed below are temples (Gurdwaras) which also function as community centres and are managed by Gurdwara Committees, usually with community representation and welfare responsibilities. The term Sikh is used here for convenience to cover not just the mainstream Sikh Panth but the Namdharis, Nirankaris, Sahajadhari and Ravidasis, not all of whom are accepted as Sikh by the khalsa mainstream.

◎ DENMARK 45

● **Sikh Foundation Denmark**
Amar Singh: Scandiagade 16-19, 2400 København SV   »89

◎ UNITED KINGDOM 44

✿ **Akhand Kirtani Jatha**
[address unknown] Birmingham
Works for the reconversion of Patit (lapsed) Sikhs.   »91

● **Babar Khalsa International**
Gurdip Singh: 153 Winson Street, Winson Green, Birmingham B18 4JW; *t* (0121) 454 2996
Society of khalsa Sikhs (devotees of Guru Gobind Singh). Welfare, human rights in Punjab. *Wangar* (12/yr).   »94

✿ **Bawa Balak Nath Temple**
9 Proffitt Avenue, Coventry; *t* (01203) 686590   »90

✿ **Bebe Nanki Gurdwara**
89 Rookery Road, Handsworth, Birmingham B21; *t* (0121) 551 3489   »90

✿ **Bhatra Singh Sabha Sikh Temple**
30-32 Cumberland Road, Reading, Berkshire   »88

✿ **Bradford Sikh Parents' Association**
2 Luther Way, King's Park, Bradford BD2 1EK; *t* (01274) 44932, 390069   »91

✿ **Bristol Sikh Cultural Centre**
Gurmit Singh/T.S. Bahra: 114 St Mark's Road, Easton, Bristol BS5 6JD; *t* (0117) 952 1318
Resource centre, community development work.   »94

◆ **British Sikh Federation**
Kashmir Singh: [address unknown]
Representation of the interests of the UK's 500,000 Sikhs; anti-racism, campaigning against religious discrimination.   »95

✿ **Central Gurdwara**
142 Berkeley Street, Glasgow; *t* (0141) 221 6698   »88
✿ ≡ 62 Queensdale Road, Shepherd's Bush, London W12; *t* (0171) 603 2789   »88

● **Dal Khalsa (UK)**
Ranjit Singh Rana: PO Box 1427, Handsworth, Birmingham B21 8BA; *t* (0121) 523 4453
Khalistan nationalist movement. *Sikh Parivaar* (12/yr).   »91

✿ **Dashmesh Darbar Sikh Temple**
Harjinder Singh, President: 97 Rosebery Avenue, Manor Park, London E12; *t* (0181) 472 5248   »95

✿ **Dashmesh Singh Sabha Bhatra Gurdwara**
80-82 Ninian Park Road, Cardiff, Wales; *t* (01222) 75916   »88

✿ **Demesh Sikh Temple**
98 Hayward Street, corner of Huxley Avenue, Cheetham Hill, Manchester M8; *t* (0161) 205 5273   »93

● **Federation of Sikh Gurdwaras and Organizations**
Dr Jaswant Singh Sohal: [address uncertain] Soho Road, Handsworth, Birmingham B21   »91

✿ **Greater Manchester Sikh Community**
Gyani Sundar Singh Sagar: 246 Brooklands Road, Sale, Cheshire; *t* (0161) 962 5200   »93

✿ **Gurdwara Ajit Darbar (UK)**
Lockhurst Lane, Coventry; *t* (01203) 662448   »90

✿ **Gurdwara Amrit Parchar Dharmak Diwan**
Harris Street, off Leeds Road, Bradford BD3, West Yorkshire; *t* (01274) 724853   »88

✿ **Gurdwara Grays**
6 Maidstone Road, Grays Thurrock; *t* (01375) 376086   »90

✿ **Gurdwara Guru Granth**
Villiers Rd, Southall UB1, Middlesex; *t* (0181) 574 7700   »88

✿ **Gurdwara Guru Har Rai Sahib**
126-128 High Street, West Bromwich B70, West Midlands; *t* (0121) 525 3275   »88

✿ **Gurdwara Guru Nanak Parkash**
Harnall Lane West, Coventry; *t* (01203) 220960   »90

✿ **Gurdwara Khalsa Mero Roop Hai Khas**
2 Dean Tce, South Shields NE33 5LL; *t* (01632) 555697   »88

✿ **Gurdwara Nanak Darbar**
136 High Road, New Southgate, London N11 1PJ; *t* (0181) 368 7104   »88

✿ **Gurdwara Nanaksar**
3 Peterborough Road, Southampton, Hampshire   »88
✿ ≡ Bath Road, Stafford; *t* (01785) 58590   »88
✿ ≡ 4 Wellington Street, Walsall; *t* (01922) 641040   »88

✿ **Gurdwara and Sikh Community Centre**
Wellington Avenue, Liverpool L15; *t* (0151) 733 0076   »88

✿ **Gurdwara Sikh Sangat**
71 Francis Road, Leyton, London E10 6PL; *t* (0181) 539 3818, 556 4732   »88
✿ ≡ 1a Campbell Road, London E3; *t* (0181) 980 2281   »88
✿ ≡ Harley Grove, Bow, London E3; *t* (0181) 980 8861   »88

✿ **Gurdwara Singh Sabha**
27-29 Spencer Rd, Crawley RH11 7DE; *t* (01293) 30163   »88
✿ ≡ 128-130 Northumberland Road, Southampton SO2 0ER; *t* (01703) 333016   »88
✿ ≡ and Sikh Temple Association: 100 North Street, Barking IG11 8JD; *t* (0181) 594 3940, 594 5834   »94

✿ **Gurdwara Sri Guru Singh Sabha**
Hibernia Road, Hounslow TW3; *t* (0181) 577 2793   »90
✿ ≡ Tindale Close, Newcastle-upon-Tyne; *t* (01632) 738011   »90
✿ ≡ Waxham Court, Sheehy Way, Slough SL1, Berkshire; *t* (01753) 526828, 31826 (?)   »90

✿ **Guru Arjan Dev Gurdwara**
49-51 Shaftesbury Street, Derby; *t* (01332) 35539
Temple named after the fifth Guru.   »88

✿ **Guru Gobind Singh Gurdwara**
Malvern/Ventnor Street, off Leeds Road, Bradford BD3, West Yorkshire; *t* (01274) 727928
Temple named after the tenth earthly Guru, Gobind Singh, who founded the khalsa religious community in 1699 CE.   »88
✿ ≡ 15 Rosamond Street, Manchester M15   »88

✿ **Guru Kaldighar Gurdwara**
78 St James Street, Waterdale, Doncaster DN1   »88

✿ **Guru Nanak Darbar Gurdwara**
31 Crabtree Manor Way, Belvedere, Erith DA8, Kent; *t* (013224) 32847   »88
✿ ≡ [address unknown] Gravesend DA12, Kent; *t* (01474) 534121, 50611   »88
✿ ≡ Old Mill Road, Plumstead, London SE18   »88

✿ **Guru Nanak Gurdwara**
72 Ford End Road, Queens Park, Bedford MK40; *t* (01234) 350092
One of many Sikh temples in Britain named after Guru Nanak, the founder of Sikhism in 1499 CE.   »88
✿ ≡ 18 Salisbury Street, Bedford MK40, Beds.   »88
✿ ≡ H. Singh Panesar: 629-631 Stratford Road, Sparkhill, Birmingham B11 4LS; *t* (0121) 771 0092   »94
✿ ≡ 219 Mary Street, Balsall Heath, Birmingham B12   »90
✿ ≡ Wakefield Road, Bradford BD4 7AH; *t* (01274) 723557, 725849   »90
✿ ≡ 27 Otago Street, Kelvinbridge, Glasgow G12 8JJ, Scotland; *t* (0141) 334 9125   »90
✿ ≡ Prospect Street, Huddersfield; *t* (01484) 423773   »90
✿ ≡ 62 Tong Rd, Armley, Leeds LS12; *t* (0113) 263 6525   »90
✿ ≡ 5 New Walk, Leicester LE1 6TE; *t* (0116) 254 0101   »90
✿ ≡ 12-16 Portland Road, Luton; *t* (01582) 571629   »90
✿ ≡ 59-61 Park Ave., Nuneaton CV11; *t* (01203) 386524   »90
✿ ≡ 5 Margate Road, Portsmouth PO2, Hampshire   »90
✿ ≡ 4 Craven Road, Rugby CV21; *t* (01788) 543192   »90
✿ ≡ 41 Normandy Road, Scunthorpe DN15, Lincolnshire   »90
✿ ≡ 22 Dale Street, Scunthorpe DN15, Lincolnshire   »90
✿ ≡ Tithe Barn Road, Stafford   »90
✿ ≡ 61 Liverpool Rd, Stoke-on-Trent; *t* (01782) 415670   »90
✿ ≡ Hadley Park Road, Hadley, Telford; *t* (01952) 51734   »90
✿ ≡ West Bromwich St, Walsall; *t* (01922) 22199   »90
✿ ≡ 130 High Street, Smethwick, Warley B66 3AP; *t* (0121) 558 2527   »90
✿ ≡ 8 Edward Street, West Bromwich B70, West Midlands; *t* (0121) 553 1242   »90
✿ ≡ 65-67 Walsall Road, Willenhall, West Midlands   »90
✿ ≡ Vernon Street, Wolverhampton; *t* (01902) 26325   »90
✿ ≡ Lea Road, Wolverhampton, West Midlands   »90
✿ ≡ Sedgeley Street, off Dudley Road, Wolverhampton WV2, West Midlands; *t* (01902) 50285, 870914   »90

✿ **Guru Nanak Nishkam Sewak Jatha**
14-20 Soho Road, Handsworth, Birmingham B21; *t* (0121) 551 1123   »90
✿ ≡ Ladypit Lane, Leeds; *t* (0113) 276 0270, 276 0261   »90

✿ **Guru Nanak Parkash Sikh Temple**
8 St Mark's Road, Bristol BS5; *t* (0117) 955 2447   »88

✿ **Guru Nanak Sat Sang Gurdwara**
31 Rutland Road, Maidenhead SL6; *t* (01628) 23507   »88
✿ ≡ 62 Forest Road, Nottingham NG7 4EP; *t* (0115) 978 1394   »88
✿ ≡ 204 Cannock Rd, Wolverhampton; *t* (01902) 50453   »88

✿ **Guru Ravidas Gurdwara**
495 Moseley Road, Balsall Heath, Birmingham B12
A temple of the Ravidasi Panth, a Punjabi 'untouchables'
movement which views the mystic Ravidas (16th-C CE) as a
Guru: mainstream Sikhs regard him as a *bhakta* (hymnist).»90
✿ ≡ Union Row, Handsworth, Birmingham B21; *t* (0121) 523
9593   »88
✿ ≡ 19 Jesmond Road, Coventry; *t* (01203) 220997   »90
✿ **Guru Teg Bahadur Gurdwara**
23 East Park Road, Leicester; *t* (0116) 276 5715   »88
● **International Sikh Youth Federation, ISYF**
Surinder Singh: [address unknown] Smethwick, Birmingham
Supports the creation of an independent Sikh state, Khalistan,
in the Punjab; see also *Awaze-Quam* magazine, p101.   »95
● **International Supreme Council of Sikhs**
Mayerwaan Singh Sardar, General Secretary: 28 Recreation
Road, Southall UB2 5PE; *t* (0181) 574 0428   »94
✿ **Kalgi Dhar Gurdwara Sahib Ji**, also known as Ramgharia
Gurdwara
138 Chapeltown Road, Leeds LS7; *t* (0113) 262 5645   »90
✿ **Medway Towns Gurdwara**
Cossack Street, Rochester ME1 2EF; *t* (01634) 49782   »88
♦ **Namdhari Sikh Sangat UK**: Gurdwara Namdhari Sangat
96 Upton Lane, Forest Gate, London E7; *t* (0181) 471 6826
Association of Kuka or reformist Sikhs, who regard the 19th-C
CE leader Baba Balak Singh as a Guru (mainstream Sikhs hold
that the 10th, Gobind Singh, was the last earthly Guru). »94
♦ **Nanak Sar Thakht**
7 Gernon Walk, Letchworth; *t* (01462) 684153
Temple and community centre (of the Sant Baba Nand Singh
movement). The name suggests the designation of Nanaksar
as a 'throne' of Sikhism in addition to the five historic centres
of Amritsar, Anandpur, Bhatinda, Nanded and Patna.   »92
♦ **Nanaksar Gurdwara Gursikh Temple**
224 Foleshill Road, Coventry CV6, Warwickshire; *t* (01203)
220434, 220805
The Nanaksar movement was established by followers of the
Punjabi sant Baba Nand Singh after his death in 1943 CE.»90
♦ **Nanaksar Ishar Darbar**
Mander Street, Wolverhampton WV; *t* (01902) 29379   »88
♦ **Nanaksar Sikh Temple**
4 Darlaston Road, Pleck, Walsall WS1, West Midlands   »88
✿ **Ramgarhia Circle**
Prem Singh Kalsi, Convenor: 205 The Broadway, Perry Barr,
Birmingham B20   »91
✿ **Ramgarhia Community Centre Hall**
1061-63 Foleshill Road, Coventry CV6, Warwickshire;
t (01203) 662594, 687658
Sikh temple and community centre.   »90
✿ **Ramgarhia Gurdwara**
69 Victoria Road, Bedford MK40, Beds.   »88
✿ ≡ Graham Street, Handsworth, Birmingham B1; *t* (0121)
236 5435   »88
✿ ≡ 27-29 Waverley Rd, Small Heath, Birmingham B10 0HG»90
✿ ≡ Bolton Road, Bradford BD2; *t* (01274) 632761   »90
✿ ≡ 1103 Foleshill Road, Coventry CV6, Warwickshire;
t (01203) 688208, 663048   »90
✿ ≡ Bearton Avenue, Hitchin SG5, Hertfordshire   »90
✿ ≡ 51 Meynell Road, Leicester; *t* (0116) 276 0765   »90
✿ ≡ 10-14 Neville Road, London E7; *t* (0181) 471 0335,
472 3738   »90
✿ ≡ Willmount Street, Masons Hill, Woolwich, London SE18;
t (0181) 854 1786, 854 4694   »90
✿ ≡ 53-57 Oswald St, Southall UB1 1HN; *t* (0181) 574 5635
Incorporates Ramgarhia Sports Club. *Sikh Sewak* (4/yr). »90
✿ ≡ Westbury Street, Wolverhampton, West Midlands   »90
✿ **Sabha Ramgarhia Sikh Temple**
Baylis Road, Woodland Avenue, Slough SL1, Berkshire;
t (01753) 525458, 30258 (?)   »90
✿ **Sanatan Temple and Community Centre**
281 Chapeltown Road, Leeds LS7, Yorkshire; *t* (0113) 262
2358, 262 9073
The Sanatan Sikhs are those who regard Sikhism as a broad
religion with much in common with Hinduism, rather than
insisting on a distinct khalsa tradition.   »94
✿ **Sangat Singh Sabha Gurdwara**
11 Summers Hill Street, St George, Bristol BS5   »88
✿ **Sant Nirankari Mandal**
236 Marston Road, Oxford; *t* (01865) 240229
Temple of a movement, also known as the Nakali (false)
Nirankaris, which arose in the 1930s CE from Sikhism but is
regarded as non-Sikh by the khalsa mainstream.   »93
● **Shiromani Akali Dal UK**
c/o 100 North Street, Barking IG11 8JD; *t* (0181) 517 0249
Support group for one of the main Sikh factions.   »90

✿ **Shri Dashmesh Sikh Temple**
305 Wheeler Street, Lozells, Birmingham B19; *t* (0121) 440
2358   »90
✿ **Sikh Association**
P.S. Ahluwalia: Europasonic Building, 12 Sherborn St, off Bury
New Rd, Strangeways, Manchester M3; *t* (0161) 861 8278
Religious activities, Panjabi classes, sports and leisure. »93
✿ **Sikh Bhatra Temple**
186 Cromwell Road, Peterborough PE1; *t* (01733) 65133»88
● *Sikh Bulletin*
Dr Owen Cole, Editor: West Sussex Institute of Higher
Education, Bishop Otter College, College Lane, Chichester
PO19 4PE
Review (2/yr).   »91
● **Sikh Committee for Interfaith Relations**
Indarjit Singh, Chairman: 43 Dorset Road, Merton Park,
London SW19 3EZ; *t* (0181) 540 4148
20 Sikh member organisations; interfaith dialogue and
understanding. *The Sikh Messenger* (4/yr).   »88
✿ **Sikh Community**
Dr Harbijahn Singh Mangat: 80 The Brow, Woodingdean BN2
6LN; *t* (01273) 300534   »94
✿ **Sikh Community Centre** and Gurdwara Parbhandak
Committee
1 Mill Street, Leamington Spa CV31, Warwickshire; *t* (01926)
421653, 883128   »90
✿ **Sikh Cultural Society of Coventry**
c/o Dr J.S. Sihota: Broad St Health Centre, Coventry CV6 »91
● **Sikh Cultural Society of Great Britain** and Guru Nanak
Foundation UK
Amar Singh Chhatwal, General Secretary: 88 Mollison Way,
Edgware HA8 5QW; *t* (0181) 952 1215
The Sikh Courier International (4/yr).   »94
● **Sikh Doctors' Association UK**
[address unknown]
Interests of Sikh medical practitioners.   »91
● **Sikh Educational Council**
Dr B.S. Bagga: PO Box 18, Hitchin SG5, Hertfordshire
Promotion of academic study and teaching on Sikhism.   »91
✿ **Sikh Gurdwara**
53-57 Crown St, Newcastle-upon-Tyne; *t* (01642) 45309 »88
✿ **Sikh Gurdwara South London**
142 Merton Road, Southfields, London SW18 5SP; *t* (0181)
874 3518   »88
● **Sikh Human Rights Group**
Dr J.S. Rai, Convenor: PO Box 45, Southall UB2 4SP;
t (0181) 577 5834
Founded 1988 CE.   »95
● **Sikh Human Rights Internet**
Iqbal Singh: [address unknown]
Human rights issues internationally, but especially in the
Punjab and in relation to Sikhs abroad and refugees.   »96
✿ **Sikh Missionary Resources Centre**
Ranjit Singh Wahiwala: [address unknown] Birmingham   »91
● **Sikh Missionary Society (UK)**
Teja Singh Manget, Hon. Gen. Secretary: 10 Featherstone
Road, Southall UB2 5AA; *t* (0171) 574 1902
Advancement of Sikhism, publishing, lectures.   »88
✿ **Sikh Parents' Society, Leicester**
Rashwel Singh: 69 Chamber Road, Leicester LE5; *t* (0116)
276 7041   »91
● **Sikh Study Forum**
R.S. Dhesi, Convenor: 85 Inglehurst Gardens, Redbridge,
Ilford IG4 5HA; *t* (0181) 550 5778
Meetings, seminars.   »91
✿ **Sikh Temple**
4 Kingshill Road, Basingstoke RG21 3JE   »88
✿ ≡ Churchill Road, Handsworth, Birmingham B20   »90
✿ ≡ 22 Goldshill Road, Birmingham B21   »88
✿ ≡ 20 Newburn Street, Bradford BD7; *t* (01274) 75916 »90
✿ ≡ 71-75 Fishponds Road, Eastville, Bristol BS5; *t* (0117)
951 1609   »90
✿ ≡ 212a Pearl Street, Cardiff, Wales   »88
✿ ≡ 4 Edit Road, Croydon, Surrey   »90
✿ ≡ Louisa Street, Darlington DL1 4ED   »90
✿ ≡ Cromwell Road, Derby; *t* (01332) 35239   »90
✿ ≡ 118 Wellington Road, Dudley DY1 1UB   »90
✿ ≡ 10 Taylors Lane, Dundee, Angus; *t* (01382) 645770 »90
✿ ≡ 11 Academy Street, Leith, Edinburgh EH6, Scotland;
t (0131) 554 4703   »90
✿ ≡ 128 McCulloch Street, Glasgow G1, Scotland   »90
✿ ≡ 96-100 New Street, Leamington Spa CV31   »90
✿ ≡ 25 St Mary's Road, Leamington Spa CV32   »90
✿ ≡ 16 Sholebroke Place, Leeds LS7, Yorkshire   »90
✿ ≡ 151 Southfield Street, Middlesbrough, Cleveland   »90

✿ **Sikh Temple**
53 Queens Park Parade, Northampton »90
✿ ≡ 26 Nottingham Road, Sherwood Rise, Nottingham NG7;
t (0115) 962 2132 »90
✿ ≡ 2 Clarendon Road, Preston PR1, Lancashire »90
✿ ≡ Ellesmere Road, Sheffield S4; *t* (0114) 242 0108 »90
✿ ≡ Blackwells Row, Cobridge, Stoke-on-Trent »90
✿ ≡ North Street, Swindon, Wiltshire »90
✿ ≡ 18 Granville Road, Watford, Hertfordshire »90
✿ **Sikh Temple Sewakjatha Sangat Bhadra Manchester**, also
known as Guru Nanak Devji Gurdwara
Manjit Singh: Monton Street, Moss Side, Manchester M14;
t (0161) 226 1131 »93
✿ **Sikh Union of Manchester**
Ujjal D. Singh: 31 Burford Road, Whalley Range, Manchester
M16 8EW; *t* (0161) 881 7067
Central representative body for Sikhs in Manchester. »93
✿ **Sikh Welfare Mission**
3 Hatfield Road, Lozells, Birmingham B19 »90
● **Sikh Youth International**
Rajinder Singh, Editor: 193 Wollaton Road, Wollaton,
Nottingham NG8 1FU
Sikh Youth International magazine (6/yr). »91
● **Sikh Youth Service**
Ranjit Singh Dhanda: 303 Soho Road, Handsworth,
Birmingham B21 9SA; *t* (0121) 523 0147
Youth welfare, culture, exhibitions, educational visits. »91
✿ **Singh Sabha** *(Sikh Association)*
32 St Andrew's Drive, Glasgow, Scotland
Temple and religious association; name derives from a
missionary movement of the late 19th century CE. »88
✿ ≡ 163 Nithsdale Road, Pollokshields, Glasgow G1,
Scotland; *t* (0141) 423 8288 »88
✿ ≡ 33 Laggen Square, Maidenhead, Berkshire »88
✿ ≡ 50 Lees Hill Street, Nottingham »88
✿ **Singh Sabha Bhatra Gurdwara**
221 Mary Street, Balsall Heath, Birmingham B12 9RN »90
✿ **Singh Sabha Gurdwara**
68 Gloucester Drive, London N4; *t* (0181) 800 9923 »88
✿ **Sri Guru Gobind Singh Gurdwara**, also known as Sangat
Bhadra Temple
Mahindar Singh, President: 61 Upper Chorlton Road, Whalley
Range, Manchester M16; *t* (0161) 226 7233, 226 2423 »93
✿ **Sri Guru Nanak Gurdwara**
1-3 Nilson Street, Dundee, Angus; *t* (01382) 23383 »90
✿ ≡ Sikh Community Centre, 30 Cumberland Road, Reading,
Berkshire; *t* (01734) 868353 »90
✿ **Sri Guru Nanak Singh Gurdwara**
26 Wellington Road, Dudley DY1; *t* (01384) 53054 »88
✿ **Sri Guru Ravidas Sabha**
282 Western Road, Southall, Middx.; *t* (0181) 574 0245 »88
✿ **Sri Guru Singh Gurdwara**
Clarence Street, Blackburn, Lancashire »88
✿ **Sri Guru Singh Sabha**
48 Way Avenue, Cranford, Hounslow TW3, Middlesex »88
✿ ≡ Hill House, Fartown, Huddersfield HD2; *t* (01484)
542982 »88
✿ ≡ 1 Wavil Close, Kettering; *t* (01536) 87436 »88
✿ ≡ Havelock Road, Southall UB2; *t* (0181) 574 8476 »88
✿ **Sri Guru Singh Sabha Gurdwara**
Radcliffe Road, Hitchin SG5; *t* (01462) 432993 »90
✿ **Sri Guru Teg Bahadur Sikh Temple**
8 Clovelly Road, Southampton; *t* (01703) 224744 »88

SINHALESE

see Sri Lankan

SINTI

see Gypsy, Romany, Traveller

SLAV

*see also Bulgarian, East European, Hungarian, Polish, Russian,
Serbian, South-East European, Ukrainian, (Ex-)Yugoslav*

◉ **LUXEMBOURG** *352*

✿ **Mission Catholique Slave et Hongroise** *(Slav and Hungarian
Catholic Mission)*
7 rue Nicolas Pletschette, 3743 Rumelange; *t* 567135 »94

SLOVENE

*see also East European, Italian, South-East European,
(Ex-)Yugoslav*

◉ **BELGIUM** *32*

✿ **Nas Dom** *(Our House)*
Gouv. A. Galopinstraat 15, 3600 Genk; *t* (089) 383080
Information, advice and cultural centre. »94

◉ **ITALY** *39*

● **Slovenski Raziskovalni Institut, SLORI** *(Slovene Ethnological
Institute)*
Prof. A. Volcic/Bratina Darko: via G. Gallina 5, 34122 Trieste;
t (040) 61183
Founded 1974; sociological, political, legal aspects of Slovene
minority population in Italy. »94

SOMALI

see also African, East African, Islamic

◉ **DENMARK** *45*

● **Somali Danish Friendship Association**
Mohamed Dahir Farah: Åkandevej 53, 1.tv., 2700 Brønshøj;
t 3128 7098 »89
✿ **Somalia Community**
Klostergade 37, 8000 Århus C »89

◉ **ITALY** *39*

✿ **Associazione Comunità Somala di Arezzo e Provincia**
(Arezzo Provincial Association of the Somali Community)
Ibrahim Asir Abdullahi: via Michelangelo 8, 52100 Arezzo;
t (0575) 352914
Refugee welfare, solidarity. »94
✿ **Associazione della Comunità Somala di Torino** *(Turin
Somali Community Association)*
Hussen Mohamed Ibrahimi: via Bogino 1, 10123 Torino;
t (011) 812 3914 »90
✿ **Associazione Culturale Italo-Somala**
Mehamed Gelani: via Sergente Maggiore 14, 80132 Napoli;
t (081) 404115, 551 1266
Social and cultural interests. »94
✿ **Associazione Italo-Somala Shabel**
Sterlin Abdi Arush/Maria Viarengo: via Bonfante 11, Torino;
t (011) 304454 »90
✿ **Associazione Somala in Liguria**
Hilole A. Moallim: via S. Bernardo 9/R, 16123 Genova;
t (010) 205425 »94
✿ **Associazione di Somali**
via Bazzini 21, 20135 Milano; *t* (02) 231838 »90
✿ **Comunità Somala** *(Somali Community)*
via Ser Ventura Monachi 8, 50125 Firenze; *t* (055) 681
1024 »90
✿ ≡ Fatuma Yassin Hagi: via Ostiense 150, 00154 Roma;
t (06) 575 3405, 446 7676, *f* 678 1182
Refugee welfare group. May be same as that listed (1990) at
via Cherso 58, 00177 Roma. »94
✿ **Comunità dei Somali Dhambaal**
Saidi Ali Ahmed/Ali Hashi: [address uncertain] via di Villa
Serventi 9, 00176 Roma; *t* (06) 27721, 832 2315
Also listed (1990) at via dei Salentini 3, 00185 Roma. »90

◉ **UNITED KINGDOM** *44*

✿ **Avon and Bristol Somali Community Group**
c/o BBVS DU, The Inkworks, 20-22 Hepburn Road, St Pauls,
Bristol BS2 8UD; *t* (0117) 942 3960 »96
✿ **Bolton Somali Muslims**
J. Ibrahim: 48 Langdon Close, Bolton BL1 2QN »94
✿ **Hove Somali Community**
Samir Ali Abdullah, President: Basement Flat, 52b Lansdowne
Place, Hove BN3 1FG; *t* (01273) 724315 »94
✿ **Islington Somali Community**
65 Halliford Street, London N1 3HF; *t* (0171) 354 9895 »95
✿ **Liverpool Somali Community**
137 Upper Hill Street, Liverpool L8 »91
✿ **Merseyside Somali Association**
24 Eversley Street, Liverpool L8 »91
✿ **Newham Somali Association**
Abdullah Yusuf: [address unknown] Newham, London
Welfare of 16,000 refugees and migrants in London. »95

- **Oxford House**
Doreen Emmet: Derbyshire Street, Bethnal Green, London
E2 6HG; *t* (0171) 729 3351
Also listed (1990) as Somalia Relief Association. Services,
including immigration casework, to East London Somalis. »96
✪ **Somali Anglo British Association of Manchester**
Dahir Othman: 25 Kippax Street, Rusholme, Manchester
M14 4EX; *t* (0161) 226 6384
Welfare, immigration advice and advocacy, social events. »93
✪ **Somali Association of Greater Manchester**
Omar Barud: 23 Arden Close, Beswick, Manchester M12
6WH; *t* (0161) 273 8533
Immigration/welfare advice, interpreting, cultural events. »93
✪ **Somali Community Association**
2 Zangwill House, Carr Street, London E14 7FZ; *t* (0171)
790 6164
Advice and welfare group for Somalis in Tower Hamlets. »91
✪ **Somali Community (Central London)**
Osman Seguleh: Abbey Community Centre, 222c Belsize
Road, London NW6 4DJ; *t* (0171) 624 8378   »94
✪ **Somali Community and Cultural Association**
Selby Centre, Selby Road, London N17; *t* (0171) 265 8335
Also listed (1991) at 12 Wickford Street, E1. Mainly
northern Somalis.   »95
✪ **Somali Community Manchester**
Ali Hassan/Ali Hussine: 302 Greater Western Street,
Rusholme, Manchester M14 4LA; *t* (0161) 227 9867
Social, cultural, welfare group; translation, interpreting. »93
✪ **Somali Education Project**
8 Newell Street, London E14 7HR; *t* (0171) 987 8848
Cultural, social, advice centre, language/literacy work. »91
✪ **Somali Health Advocacy Project**
Yvonne Riedel: International Childcare Trust, D16 Peabody
Estate, Wild St, London WC2B 4AG; *t* (0171) 379 4947
Interpreting, advice and other assistance to allow local
Somali-speaking people to access health care.   »94
✪ **Somali Islamic Circle Organisation**
16 Settles Street, London E1 1JP; *t* (0171) 377 5003
See also Islamic College, p60.   »94
✪ **Somali Mental Health Project**
Mind in Tower Hamlets, 13 Whitethorn St, London E3 4DA
Project aims to improve accessibility and appropriateness of
mental health care for Somali migrants and refugees. »94
- **Somali Progressive Association**
Abdel Karim Abdiadan: 8 West Bute Street, Butetown,
Cardiff CF1 6EP, Wales; *t* (01222) 499916   »94
✪ **Somali South London Community**
Bermondsey Village Hall, Kirby Grove, London SE1;
t (0171) 403 3530
Mainly southern Somalis.   »91
✪ **Somali Women's Cultural and Care Group**
Lula Ahmed: c/o 157 Yew Tree Road, Fallowfield,
Manchester M14
Support, advice, interpreting and cultural activities. »93
✪ **Somali Women's Group**
Amina Warsame: 29 Ruskin Avenue, Rusholme, Manchester
M14 4DP; *t* (0161) 226 7183
Translation, interpreting, adult education, health advice, care
of elderly.   »93

SOUTH AFRICAN

see also African, Namibian, Southern African

◎ **DENMARK** *45*

- **African National Congress**, ANC
Landgreven 7/3 th., 1301 København K
Overseas section of South African government party.   »90

◎ **FRANCE** *33*

- **African National Congress**, ANC
28 rue des Petites Ecuries, 75010 Paris   »90
- **CIDAA**
44 rue d'Hauteville, 75010 Paris
Solidarity with southern Africa. Acronym possibly stands for
Centre d'Information et de Documentation Anti Apartheid?
L'Afrique du Sud en Direct.   »88

◎ **GERMANY** *49*

- **Anti Apartheid Bewegung**, AAB *(Anti-Apartheid Movement)*
Blücherstraße 14, 53115 Bonn; *t* (0228) 211355
Former solidarity movement with resistance groups; now
presumably reforming in support of democratic regime. »94

◎ **IRELAND** *353*

- **Ireland South Africa Association**, ISAA: succeeds Irish Anti-
Apartheid Movement, IAAM
Gearóid Kilgallen: PO Box 38, Dún Laoghaire, Co. Dublin;
t (01) 284 4070
The IAAM, founded 1964, supported the struggle against the
apartheid regime; the ISAA, launched 1994, promotes
friendship with democratic South Africa.   »95

◎ **ITALY** *39*

- **African National Congress**, ANC: Congresso Nazionale
Africano
via S. Prisca 15a, 00153 Roma   »90

◎ **NETHERLANDS** *31*

- **African National Congress**, ANC
Postbus 16657, 1001 RD Amsterdam   »90
- **Stichting Anti-Apartheids Beweging Nederland**, AABN
(Dutch Anti-Apartheid Movement Foundation)
Postbus 10500, Lauriergracht 116/1, 1001 EM Amsterdam;
t (020) 626 7525, *f* 623 7335
Formerly supported the opposition to the apartheid regime;
now reorganising as a solidarity movement for democratic
South Africa and for progressive movements in the region.»94

◎ **PORTUGAL** *351*

✪ **Movimento Português contra o Apartheid**
Rua Rodrigo da Fonseca 56-2°, 1200 Lisboa
Formed to support the ANC and other progressive forces
resisting the minority regime in South Africa.   »94

◎ **SPAIN** *34*

- **African National Congress**, ANC: Congreso Nacional Africano
calle Hermanos García Noblejas 41-8°, 28037 Madrid   »90

◎ **SWITZERLAND** *41*

- **Anti-Apartheid Bewegung der Deutschen Schweiz**, AAB
(German Swiss Anti-Apartheid Movement)
Postfach 1022, Merkurstrasse 45, 8032 Zürich; *t* (01) 261
5424, *f* 261 5138
Solidarity with the ANC and other democratic groups. »94

◎ **UNITED KINGDOM** *44*

- **African National Congress**, ANC
PO Box 38, 28 Penton Street, London N1 9PR; *t* (0171) 837
2012, 837 1930   »94
- **Commonwealth Non-Governmental Office for South Africa**
Richard Bourne, Director: 28 Russell Square, London WC1
Organisation promoting involvement of Commonwealth NGOs
in South African development projects.   »95
- **Education for Democracy in South Africa**
Anne Harries Brown, Chair: [address unknown]
Promotes international educational development aid.   »94
✪ **South African Research Group**
Chris Jones: 68 Grange Street, St Albans, Hertfordshire
Research on educational policy and other matters.   »92

SOUTH AMERICAN

*see Argentinian, Bolivian, Brazilian, Caribbean, Central
American, Chilean, Colombian, Guyanese, Latin American,
Mexican, Paraguayan, Peruvian, Surinamese, Uruguayan*

SOUTH ASIAN

*see Asian, Bangladeshi, Bengali, Gujarati, Hindi, Hindu, Indian,
Kashmiri, Nepalese, Pakistani, Punjabi, Sikh, South-East Asian,
Sri Lankan, Tamil, Urdu*

SOUTH-EAST ASIAN

*see also Asian, Burmese, Cambodian, Filipino, Indonesian,
Khmer, Laotian, Malaysian, Moluccan, Thai, Timorese,
Vietnamese*

◎ **FRANCE** *33*

- **Aide aux réfugiés de l'Asie du Sud-Est** *(Aid to South-East
Asian Refugees)*
4 place de Barcelone, 75016 Paris   »90

✧ **Association Calvados Sud-Est Asiatique, ACASEA** *(Calvados South-East Asia Association)*
Jean Obation: 4 rue George Sand, 14000 Caen; *t* 3173 0677
Welfare of Indochinese refugees in Normandy. *Bulletin de l'ACASEA*.
»94

✧ **Association Franco-Asiatique d'Echanges et de Loisirs, AFA** *(French-Asian Exchange and Leisure Association)*
Françoise Bouré: 32 rue du Dauphiné, 57070 Metz; *t* 8774 6949
Cultural and social activities.
»94

✧ **Association Marnasia**
Mairie, 11 esplanade Droits-de-l'Homme, 77185 Lognes »89

● **Centre de solidarité et de fraternité franco-indochinois**
8 boulevard Kellermann, 75013 Paris; *t* (1) 4580 9758, 4580 9775
»90

● **Comité national d'entraide franco-cambodgien, franco-laotien et franco-vietnamien, CNE** *(National Committee for Franco-Cambodian, Franco-Laotian & Franco-Vietnamese Mutual Aid)*
42 rue Cambronne, 75740 Paris cedex 15; *t* (1) 4567 0120»93

● **Groupe de Recherche sur l'Immigration du Sud-Est Asiatique, GRISEA** *(Research Group on South-East Asian Immigrants)*
Lee Huu Khoa: 24 rue des Terres au Curé, 75013 Paris; *t* (1) 5379 0646, *f* 5379 0646
»94

✧ **Soutien à l'Initiative Privée pour l'Aide à la Reconstruction du Sud-Est Asiatique, SIPAR** *(Support for Private Initiatives in Reconstruction Aid for South-East Asia)*
Magali Petitmengin, President: 42 bis rue Saint Charles, 78000 Versailles; *t* (1) 3902 3252, *f* 3021 9264
Educational and social welfare assistance to refugees in Indochina, in camps and after voluntary repatriation, and in France where SIPAR supports 100 local voluntary groups which assist with settlement. *Par SIPAR Là* (4/yr).
»94

◎ **GERMANY** *49*

✧ **Doc-Lap-Zentrum**
Vu Ngoc Yen: Reinsburgerstraße 56, 70178 Stuttgart; *t* (0711) 627031
Founded 1980; documentation centre, research on and resettlement services to South-East Asian refugees; sponsored by Diakonisches Werk der EKD, p201.
»94

✧ **Südostasien-Informationsstelle** *(South-East Asia Information Centre)*
Josephinenstraße 71, 4630 Bochum 1
»93

● **Verein der Indochina-Flüchtlinge, Chinesischer Abstammung** *(Union of Indochina Refugees of Chinese Descent)*
Jürgen Fachinger: Gutleutstraße 94, 60329 Frankfurt am Main; *t* (069) 232376
»94

◎ **UNITED KINGDOM** *44*

● **Association of South-Eastern Asian Studies in the UK**
[address unknown]
Possibly defunct.
»90

✧ **Community Centre for Refugees from Vietnam, Laos and Cambodia**
Vo Ngoc Giao: Whiston Road, Haggerston, London E2 8BN; *t* (0171) 739 3650
»95

● **Medical and Scientific Aid for Vietnam, Laos and Cambodia**
98 St Pancras Way, London NW1; *t* (0171) 267 4398
Humanitarian and development aid.
»90

SOUTH-EAST EUROPEAN

see also Bosnian, Bulgarian, Croatian, Cypriot, East European, Greek, Macedonian, Romanian, Serbian, Slav, Slovene, Transylvanian, Turkish, (Ex-)Yugoslav

◎ **GERMANY** *49*

● **Südosteuropa Gesellschaft** *(South-East Europe Society)*
Science Centre, Steinplatz 2, 1000 Berlin 12 »90

SOUTH EUROPEAN

see Greek, Italian, Portuguese, South-East European, Spanish, Turkish

SOUTH MOLUCCAN

or Maluku: see Asian, Dutch, Indonesian, Moluccan, South-East Asian

SOUTHERN AFRICAN

see also Angolan, Cape Verdean, Comoros, Mozambican, Namibian, Rwandese, South African, Zairean, Zimbabwean

◎ **NETHERLANDS** *31*

● **Komitee Zuidelijk Afrika, KZA** *(Southern Africa Committee)*
Oude Zijds Achterburgwal 173, 1012 DJ Amsterdam; *t* (020) 627 0801, *f* 627 0441
Solidarity with progressive movements in Southern Africa, including return assistance to former refugees.
»94

● **Eduardo Mondlane Stichting** *(Mondlane Foundation)*
Hoogte Kadyk 145, 1018 BH Amsterdam; *t* (020) 623 7263, *f* 624 2721
Volunteers and funding for projects in South Africa, Angola, Mozambique and Cape Verde; refugee resettlement.
»93

◎ **SWEDEN** *46*

● **Afrikagrupperna** *(Africa Groups)*
Barnängsgatan 23, 11641 Stockholm
Solidarity with and aid to progressive governments in Southern Africa. Founded 1992 by merger of Afrikagruppen i Sverige with Afrikagruppernas Rekryberingsorg.
»93

◎ **UNITED KINGDOM** *44*

◆ **Action for Southern Africa, ACTSA: succeeds Anti-Apartheid Movement, AAM**
28 Penton Street, London N1 9SA; *t* (0171) 833 3133, *f* 837 3001
The AAM for 35 years opposed the apartheid regime; ACTSA, founded 1994, is a solidarity movement for South Africa and other southern African countries, lobbying in UK and EU. »95

● **Centre for Southern African Studies**
Dr Colin Stoneman: [address unknown]
»94

● **Southern Africa Economic Research Unit**
[address unknown]
Research and documentation on economic affairs.
»94

SPANISH

including miscellaneous Spanish-speaking; see also Basque, Catalan, European, Gypsy, Latin American

◎ **BELGIUM** *32*

● **Asociación Belgo-Española de Promoción Cultural** *(Belgian-Spanish Cultural Promotion Society)*
Place Jourdan 38, BP 3, 1040 Bruxelles »90

✧ **Centre Espagnol: Centro Español** *(Spanish Centre)*
Place Ferrer 10, 6060 Gilly; *t* (071) 415499 »94

✧ **Centre Espagnol de Formation et d'Action—Université Ouvrière, CEFA-UO: Centro Español de Formación y Acción—Universidad Obrera** *(Spanish Training and Action Centre—Workers' University)*
Julio Fierro Iribarren: Avenue Van Volxem 525, 1060 Bruxelles; *t* (02) 537 0508, *f* 537 0487
Founded 1980; education, training, employment, advice, welfare, women's issues. *Génération E* (4/yr).
»94

✧ **Centre Espagnol El Guión** *(The Leader Spanish Centre)* and **Association Culturelle des Artistes Espagnols de Namur**
Luis Suzo: Rue du Beffroi 15, 5000 Namur; *t* (081) 224286, 734337
Culture, leisure, social activities.
»94

✧ **Club Belgo-Español Federico García Lorca**
Juan Latorre: Rue des Foulons 47-49, 1000 Bruxelles; *t* (02) 512 5511
Cultural and social club.
»94

● **Coordinadora Nacional del Movimiento Asociativo de los Emigrantes en Bélgica** *(National League of Emigrant Societies in Belgium)*
Boulevard Schmidt 105, 1040 Bruxelles; *t* (02) 733 5272
Co-ordination of Spanish migrant and cultural groups.
»94

● **Fédération des Associations de Parents d'Elèves Espagnols en Belgique, FAPEB** *(Federation of Spanish Parents' Associations in Belgium)*
Senen Pinilla Fernández: Rue Emile Féron 56, 1060 Bruxelles; *t* (02) 538 6750
Employment advice, cultural activities, family welfare.
»94

✧ **Groupe Espagnol d'Action Culturelle**
Hollandstraat 14, 1060 Brussel »90

✧ **Hogar Español Altas Torres de Waterschei**
Hoevezavellaan 22, 3600 Genk; *t* (089) 383394 »94

• **Sociedad Hispano-Belga de Ayuda Mutua:** Association de Familles Espagnoles Emigrées *(Spanish-Belgian Mutual Aid Society)*
María Jara Fernández: Chaussée de Forest 246, 1060 Bruxelles; *t* (02) 539 1939
Social and cultural group; educational welfare, youth integration.   »94

◙ **DENMARK** *45*

✿ **Círculo Gallego** *(Galician Circle)*
Oscar C. Paredes: Vejlebrovej 102, 3.th., 2635 Ishøj; *t* 4273 5434   »89
✿ **Den Spanske Forening** *(Spanish Society)*
José Pulido Santana: Nærumgårdsvej 96, 2850 Nærum, København; *t* 4280 6343   »89

◙ **FRANCE** *33*

✿ **Amicale Espagnole** *(Spanish Friends Society)*
José García: 19 rue de la Poterie, 68250 Rouffach
Cultural and social activities.   »94
✿ ≡ 91 rte des Romains, 67200 Strasbourg; *t* 8829 3837»94
✿ **Amicale des espagnols de Chaumont**
bourse du travail, rue Decrès, 52000 Chaumont   »90
✿ **Amitié Franco-Espagnole** *(Franco-Spanish Friendship Association)*
Maison du Quartier, 8 rue Lt Godineau, 41000 Blois; *t* 5474 3889
Cultural and welfare activities.   »94
✿ **Amitié Franco-Espagnole Cambrésienne, AFEC** *(Cambrai Franco-Spanish Friendship Association)*
Carlos Gonsálvez: 2 rue de Londres, 59400 Cambrai; *t* 2781 5452, *f* 2785 9707
International friendship, Spanish culture.   »94
✿ **Asociación Andaluz Duende** *(The Goblin Andalusian Association)*
48 Cours de la République, salle 2, 69100 Villeurbanne; *t* 7803 5991
Social and cultural.   »94
✿ **Asociación Cultural Española Livry-Clichy** *(Livry-Clichy Spanish Cultural Association)* also known as Association culturelle espagnole
57 rue Lafayette, 01200 Bellegarde-sur-Valserine; *t* 5048 2961
Educational welfare, culture. Affiliated to APFEEF, below. »94
✿ **Asociación Francisco de Goya**
7 avenue de la Redoute, batiment 2, 92600 Asnières; *t* (1) 4798 9075   »94
✿ **Asociación Miguel Hernández**
313 avenue du Président Wilson, 93200 Saint-Denis; *t* (1) 4820 1833   »94
✿ **Asociación Iberia Cultura:** Association Ibéria Culture
Carmen Marhuenda: 198 rue Saint Jacques, 75005 Paris; *t* (1) 4325 5580
Also known as Iberia Cultura de Paris. Bookshop and cultural rendezvous. See other Iberia Cultura centres, p112.   »94
✿ **Asociación de Jubilados y Pensionistas Españoles de la Gironde, AJPEG** *(Gironde Association of Spanish Pensioners and Retirees)*
59 rue Carpenteyre, 33800 Bordeaux; *t* 5691 4523
See also AFATE, right, and LMIGE, p112.   »94
✿ **Asociación Federico García Lorca**
6 rue P. Vaillant Couturier, 93130 Noisy-le-Sec; *t* (1) 4845 0612   »94
• **Asociación de Padres de Familias Españolas Emigrantes en Francia, APFEEF:** Association de parents de familles espagnoles emigrées en France *(Association of Spanish Emigrant Parents in France)*
33 rue Linné, 75005 Paris; *t* (1) 4331 8828
Educational welfare, interests of Spanish schoolchildren and families. Regional branches and affiliates throughout France, often with different names such as Asociación Cultural Española Livry-Clichy, above. Other branches include (1990): Association de parents de familles espagnoles immigrées de l'Ariège, 23 avenue Léon-Blum, 09300 Lavelanet; 124 rue Dubourdieu, 33800 Bordeaux; 55 ave. du Dauphiné, 69330 Meyzieu; 56 rue de la Fontaine-au-Roi, 75011 Paris.   »91
✿ **Association culturelle espagnole-portugaise** *(Spanish and Portuguese Cultural Association)*
13 rue Cuiraterie, 26200 Montelimar   »89
✿ **Association pour la Diffusion des Langues et Cultures d'Espagne, ALCE** *(Association for Promoting the Languages and Cultures of Spain)*
59 rue Sébastopol, 29200 Brest; *t* 9841 5566, *f* 9802 3883
See Centre de Recherches Interculturelles du Finistère, p234.»94

✿ **Association Espagnole**
4 impasse Léon Fouriner, 38130 Echirolles; *t* 7622 0782 »94
✿ **Association Espagnole Federico García Lorca**
4 rue des Erables, 91390 Morsang-sur-Orge; *t* 6916 4063»94
✿ **Association Espagnole Sol de España**
44 bis rue du Mont Bart, 25200 Montbéliard; *t* 2580 5981»94
✿ **Association de Familles Espagnoles** *(Spanish Families Association)*
23 avenue Léon Blum, 09300 Lavelanet; *t* 6101 4751
Youth and family welfare, education, culture.   »94
✿ **Association Française d'Aide aux Travailleurs Espagnols, AFATE** *(French Association for Aid to Spanish Workers)*
M. Presal: 59 rue Carpenteyre, 33800 Bordeaux; *t* 5691 4523
See also AJPEG, left, and LMIGE, p112.   »94
✿ **Association France Espagne**
211 rue de Paris, 59800 Lille; *t* 2088 1146
Cultural and intercultural activities.   »94
✿ **Association des Parents d'Elèves de la section espagnole des Lycée et Collège Internationaux de Ferney-Voltaire** *(Spanish Parents' Society of the International Schools)*
1 avenue des Sports, 01210 Ferney-Voltaire   »90
✿ **Association des Travailleurs Espagnols** *(Spanish Workers' Association)*
16 boulevard de la Corniche, 74200 Thonon-les-Bains; *t* 5071 5818   »94
✿ **Associations Franco Espagnoles** *(Franco-Spanish Associations)*
Centre Régional de Documentation Pédagogique, 55 rue N-D de la Recouvrance, 45000 Orléans   »90
✿ **Casa de España:** Maison d'Espagne *(House of Spain)*
240 rue Francis Tonner, 06150 Cannes-la-Bocca; *t* 9347 1012
Cultural activities, welfare and housing assistance.   »94
✿ ≡ 24 rue Pierre Loti, 17000 La Rochelle; *t* 4641 7449   »94
✿ ≡ BP 2146, 9 rue de la Petite Loge, 34026 Montpellier; *t* 6760 4417   »94
✿ ≡ chez Mme Marie-Carmen Romero: 68 avenue de XXe-Corps, 54000 Nancy   »89
✿ ≡ 15 rue Séguier, 30000 Nîmes; *t* 6667 9678   »94
✿ ≡ 8 rue Nantes, 75019 Paris; *t* (1) 4037 7063, 4034 0353
See also FACEEF, p112.   »94
✿ ≡ 48 rue de Curé, 59100 Roubaix; *t* 2073 3889   »94
✿ ≡ 11 bis rue de l'Apprentissage, 42100 Saint-Etienne; *t* 7721 8077   »94
✿ ≡ Francisco Ruiz: 3 Petite Rue Marangis, 77670 Saint-Mammes; *t* 6423 0846   »94
✿ ≡ 41 rue Arches, 83700 Saint-Raphaël; *t* 9553 7530   »94
✿ **Centre Culturel Espagnol La Bigorre**
6 place de la Claverie, 65000 Tarbes; *t* 6293 3539   »94
✿ **Centre Culturel Franco-Espagnol**
9 Cité du Prieuré, 54350 Mont Saint-Martin; *t* 8225 4192»94
✿ **Centre culturel et récréatif hispano-français de Saint-Priest** *(Franco-Spanish Cultural and Recreational Centre)*
10 rue de l'Abbé-Pierre, 69800 Saint-Priest   »90
✿ **Centre Culturel et Sportif Espagnol**
M. Torres: 13 ave. Joffre, 68000 Colmar; *t* 8924 3162   »94
✿ **Centre Hispano-Français, CHF**
4 impasse Laurent Bonnevay, 69400 Villefranche-sur-Sâone; *t* 7468 8897   »94
✿ **Centro Alegría Belfort**
2 avenue Laurencie, 90000 Belfort; *t* 8428 0647   »94
✿ **Centro Cultural Español:** Centre Culturel Espagnol *(Spanish Cultural Centre)*
2 place Caillo, 32000 Auch; *t* 6205 3872   »94
✿ ≡ 85 rue René Nicod, 01100 Oyonnax; *t* 7477 4704
CIEMI (1994) lists a Centre Espagnol at Eglise de la Plaine, salle 6, 6 place Leclerc: same telephone.   »94
✿ **Centro Cultural y Recreativo Español, CCRE** *(Spanish Cultural and Leisure Centre)*
Pedro López: 41 rue Berbisey, 21000 Dijon; *t* 8030 1244 »94
✿ **Centro Español:** Centre Espagnol *(Spanish Centre)*
2 Petite rue de l'Est, 64100 Bayonne; *t* 5955 2155
Cultural and social centre.   »94
✿ ≡ Mairie de Beaune, 21200 Beaune; *t* 8022 2080   »94
✿ ≡ 2 rue du Docteur Gestin, 29200 Brest; *t* 9849 5040   »94
✿ ≡ 8 rue Jules Ferry, 62100 Calais; *t* 2134 5699   »94
✿ ≡ 59 rue du Général Compère, 51000 Châlons-sur-Marne; *t* 2665 2822   »94
✿ ≡ Tour P2, 10 boulevard Bennevy, 74500 Evian-les-Bains; *t* 5070 7382   »94
✿ ≡ Maison des Associations, 40 Route Nationale, 59760 Grande Synthe; *t* 2821 8567   »94
✿ ≡ BP 101, 61 rue de la Forêt, 57240 Le Konacker Hayange; *t* 8285 7970   »94
✿ ≡ 358 bvd National, 13003 Marseille; *t* 9162 6243   »94
✿ ≡ 10 rue du Canal, 03100 Montluçon; *t* 7028 2928   »94

✿ **Centro Español:** Centre Espagnol
Maison Municipale des Eduens, 1er étage, bur. 7, 58000
Nevers; t 8659 0823   »94
✿ ≡ José Sánchez: 32 quai du Châtelet, 45000 Orléans;
t 3854 1901   »94
✿ ≡ 47 rue Pierre Semart, 42300 Roanne; t 7770 3519   »94
✿ ≡ 12 ave. Gabriel Péri, 69190 Saint-Fons; t 7867 7966 »94
✿ ≡ 31 rue des Châlets, 31000 Toulouse; t 6162 3037   »94
✿ ≡ 1 rue des Cordeliers, 10000 Troyes; t 2580 5981   »94
✿ ≡ 10 rue des Dahlias, 57270 Uckange; t 8257 1095   »94
✿ ≡ 100 impasse de la 40ème, 69400 Villefranche-sur-
Saône; t 7465 5311   »94
✿ ≡ rue André Sentue, 69200 Vénissieux; t 7250 1791   »94
✿ **Centro Español Cultural y Recreativo** *(Spanish Cultural and
Recreational Centre)* Centre espagnol culturel et récréatif
67 rue Pradelle, 63000 Clermont Ferrand; t 7331 1543   »94
✿ **Colonia Española de Béziers**
1 rue Vieille Citadelle, 34500 Béziers; t 6749 1303, f 6728
0821   »94
✿ **Espagnols de Reims**
33 rue Jeanne d'Arc, 51100 Reims; t 2640 6346   »94
♦ **Federación de Asociaciones Culturales de Españoles
Emigrados en Francia,** FACEEF *(Federation of Spanish
Immigrant Cultural Associations)* Federation des Associations
Culturelles Espagnoles Emigrantes
José María Salazar, President: Casa de España, 8 rue de
Nantes, 75019 Paris; t (1) 4037 7117, f 4037 4644
Advice, advocacy, youth affairs, culture. *Boletín FACEEF.* »94
✿ **Foyer Espagnol** *(Spanish Home)*
4 ch. de la Coudre, 71100 Châlon-sur-Sâone; t 8543 3895
Housing; welfare, social centre for Spanish migrants.   »94
✿ ≡ 35 rue Renan, 13600 La Ciotat; t 4208 3183   »94
✿ ≡ 10 rue Cristino Garcia, 93210 La Plaine-Saint-Denis;
t (1) 4820 8677   »94
✿ ≡ 18 rue Gassicourt, 78200 Mantes-La-Jolie; t (1) 3094
7207   »94
✿ ≡ 13 avenue Loche, 71000 Mâcon; t 8538 1682   »94
✿ ≡ 3 rue Marcel Barthe, 64000 Pau; t 5906 3938   »94
✿ ≡ Francisco Martínez: 114 Grande Rue, 92310 Sèvres;
t (1) 4507 1841   »94
✿ ≡ 55 rue de la République, 69120 Vaulx-en-Velin; t 7879
2571   »94
✿ **Foyer Sportif**
1 bis rue de la Faisanderie, 78300 Poissy; t (1) 3074 4942
Housing; leisure activities.   »94
✿ **Iberia Cultura**
70 ave. de la République, 82000 Montauban; t 6320 0152
Spanish culture, educational welfare of migrants' children.»94
✿ ≡ 7 ave. de Nîmes, 34000 Montpellier; t 6772 5070   »94
✿ ≡ 28 rue Mareschal, 30000 Nîmes; t 6621 1708   »94
✿ ≡ 2 cité Clauzier, 65000 Tarbes; t 6244 8163   »94
✿ **Juventud Obrera Cristiana Emigrante,** JOC *(Young Emigrant
Christian Workers)* Jeunesse Ouvrière Chrétienne Espagnole
246 boulevard St-Denis, 92400 Courbevoie; t (1) 4333 6198
Catholic social movement founded in Belgium, see p191. »90
✿ **Liga de Mutilados e Invalidos de la Guerra de España,**
LMIGE *(League of Spanish Civil War Disabled Veterans)*
59 rue Carpenteyre, 33800 Bordeaux; t 5691 4523
Welfare of anti-fascist veterans; see AFATE, AJPEG, p111. »94
● **Mission Catholique Espagnole pour les Familles Immigrées**
(Spanish Catholic Mission for Immigrant Families)
51 bis rue de la Pompe, 75016 Paris; t (1) 4504 2334   »94

◉ **GERMANY** *49*

✿ **Asociación Cultural Juvenil,** ACJ *(Youth Cultural
Association)* Spanischer Jugendverein
Antonio Perea: Siemenstraße 39, 42857 Remscheid; t (02191)
33904
Youth welfare, leisure, cultural activities. *Mundo Juvenil.* »94
✿ **Asociación Española de Padres de Familia en la RFA**
(Spanish Parents' Association in the FRG)
Postfach 480209, 4400 Münster
Carta a los Padres.   »90
✿ ≡ Katharinenstraße 2A, 7000 Stuttgart 1   »90
✿ **Asociación de Padres de Alumnos de Bremen** *(Bremen
Association of Parents of School Students)*
Francisco Rodríguez de Sola: Kornstraße 283, 28201
Bremen; t (0421) 550955
Youth welfare, education, leisure and cultural activities. *Carta
a los Padres.*   »94
✿ **Asociación de Padres de Alumnos Españoles en Münster**
(Münster Association of Parents of Spanish Students)
Boelckeweg 25, 48155 Münster
Youth welfare, education, integration; language, culture. »94

✿ **Asociación de Padres de Familias y Alumnos Españoles**
Postfach 104522, 40213 Düsseldorf   »94
✿ **Asociación de Padres de Familias y Alumnos en Hamburgo
y alrededores** *(Hamburg Area Association of Parents of
Families and Students)*
Adolfo Fernández: Amandastraße 58, 20357 Hamburg;
t (040) 432 2052   »94
✿ **Asociación de Padres de Familias de Bonn**
Königswinter Straße 115, 53227 Bonn   »94
✿ **Asociación de Padres de Familias Españolas**
Friedrich-Ebert-Straße 50, 33102 Paderborn   »94
✿ **Asociación de Padres de Familias de Leverkusen**
(Leverkusen Parents' Association)
Reushenberger Straße 61, 51379 Leverkusen   »94
✿ **Bund Spanischer Eltervereine** *(League of Spanish Elders'
Unions)*
Mainzerstr. 174, 53179 Bonn; t (0228) 341399, f 858354
See also the Landesverband, in Kassel, below.   »94
● **Bundesverband Spanischer Sozialer und Kultureller Vereine
e.V.** *(Federal Union of Spanish Social and Cultural Societies)*
Schönberger Straße 17A, 34128 Kassel
Umbrella group for Spanish voluntary sector. Training,
employment, cultural and welfare concerns.   »94
✿ ≡ Landesgeschaftstelle NRW, Allee 27, 42897 Remscheid;
t (02191) 291448   »90
♦ **Confederación de Asociaciones Españolas de Padres de
Familia en Alemania,** CAEPF *(Confederation of Spanish
Parents' Associations in Germany)*
Vicente Riesgo: Mainzerstraße 172, 53179 Bonn; t (0228)
341399, f 858354
Youth welfare, education, culture and language, training and
employment. *Carta a los Padres* (4/yr).   »94
● **Coordinadora Europea de Asociaciones de Emigrantes
Españoles,** CEAEE *(European League of Spanish Emigrant
Associations)*
Ramón Tiscar Astasio, President: Schmerfeldstraße 4, 34130
Kassel; t (0561) 41001
Forum for discussion and co-ordinated action on problems
facing Spanish migrant communities in Europe.   »94
● **Federación de Asociaciones Juveniles y de Alumnos,** FAJA
(Federation of Spanish Youth and Student Associations)
Bundesverband Spanischer Jugend- und Schülervereine
Doormannsweg 12, 20259 Hamburg; t (040) 490 4647
Youth integration, cultural identity, political rights.   »94
✿ **Federación de Asociaciones de Padres de Familias y
Alumnos en Alemania, NRW** *(North Rhine-Westphalia
Federation of Parents' Associations)*
Postfach 480209, 48165 Münster; t (0251) 16390, 4031,
f 24222
Location: Patronats Straße 18.   »94
✿ **Jóvenes Españoles Organizados en Hamburgo:** Spanische
Jugendinitiative Hamburg e.V. *(Spanish Youth Movement of
Hamburg)*
Doormannsweg 12, 2000 Hamburg 20; t (040) 389 3405
Youth, education, training, employment, women's rights. »90
✿ **Juventud Obrera Cristiana Emigrante,** JOC *(Young Emigrant
Christian Workers)* Spanische Christliche Arbeiterjugend, CAJ
Ramón Roberto Alcalde: Hüttmannstraße 52, 45143 Essen;
t (0201) 621065, 626422, f 626671
Spanish migrant workers' section of the international Catholic
movement which arose in Belgium. *Juventud Obrera.*   »94
✿ **Landesverband der Spanischen Eltervereine in der BRD**
(State Federation of Spanish Elders' Unions in the FRG)
Postfach 100323, 34128 Kassel
Migrant welfare, employment and pension rights. See also
Bund Spanischer Eltervereine, above.   »94
✿ **Spanisches Gemeindezentrum** *(Spanish Community Centre)*
Rheinischestraße 176, 44147 Dortmund   »94
✿ **Spanisches Zentrum** *(Spanish Centre)*
An Groß St Martin 10, 50667 Köln; t (0221) 257 7925   »94

◉ **IRELAND** *353*

● **Instituto Cervantes,** formerly Spanish Cultural Institute
58 Northumberland Road, Dublin 4; t (01) 668 2024
Promotion of Spanish language and culture; interests of
migrant community. Mainly funded by foreign ministry in
Madrid. Newsletter.   »95
✿ **Spanish Society Dublin**
[address unknown] Dublin; t (01) 497 5359 (?)   »90

◉ **ITALY** *39*

✿ **Chiesa Spagnola** *(Spanish Church)*
via Giulia 151, 00186 Roma; t (06) 656 5861
Catholic church.   »90

◎ **LUXEMBOURG** *352*

✪ **Centro Cultural y Recreativo Real Madrid** *(Real Madrid Cultural and Recreational Centre)*
Alfonso Blanco: 60 boulevard Prince Henri, 4280 Esch-sur-Alzette; *t* 546419, 557350
Founded 1970; youth, sport.　　　　　　　　　　»94

✪ **Círculo Cultural Antonio Machado** *(Machado Cultural Circle)*
Pablo Sánchez: 107 route d'Esch, 1471 Luxembourg; *t* 491750, 480231, *f* 481229
Founded 1974; educational welfare of Spanish children in Luxembourg, cultural events. Address shared by Italian cultural circle, p75.　　　　　　　　　　»94

✪ **Comisiones Obreras, CCOO** *(Workers' Commissions)*
Commissions Ouvrières Espagnoles
Francisco Laredo Raya: 28 rue du Curé, 3221 Bettembourg; *t* 511458
Spanish-based trade union.　　　　　　　　　　»94

● **Fédération des Associations Démocratiques Espagnoles à Luxembourg, FADEL** *(Federation of Democratic Spanish Associations)*
Eladio Ruiz, Secretary: 37 rue M. Mantz, 3251 Bettembourg; *t* 512597　　　　　　　　　　»94

◆ **Fédération des Associations Espagnoles des Emigrés à Luxembourg, FAEEL** *(Federation of Spanish Emigrant Associations)*
J. Santiago: 34 rue du Stavelot, 9280 Diekirch; *t* 808672 »90

✪ **Fédération des Associations Espagnoles au Luxembourg, FAEL** *(Federation of Spanish Associations)*
28 rue Robert Schuman, 5751 Frisange　　　　　»94

✪ **Hogar Español** *(Spanish Home)*
124 rue de Hollerich, Luxembourg　　　　　　　»90

● **Mission Catholique Espagnole** *(Spanish Catholic Mission)*
52 rue Glesener, 1630 Luxembourg; *t* 400534　　»94
✪ ≡ c/o Caritas, 29 rue Michel Welter, 2730 Luxembourg; *t* 402131 ext. 10　　　　　　　　　　»95

✪ **Unión General de Trabajadores, UGT** *(General Workers' Union)*
Galiano Serafín: 7 rue de la Chapelle, 3378 Livange; *t* 517359
Spanish trade union confederation; employment, welfare rights, education and training, social/cultural activities.　»94

◎ **NETHERLANDS** *31*

● **Federación de Asociaciones de Emigrantes Españoles en Holanda, FAEEH** *(Federation of Spanish Emigrant Associations in Holland)*
Curaçaostraat 82 I, 1058 CA Amsterdam
Main umbrella group for Spanish migrant organisations.　»94

● **Federación de Asociaciones de Padres de Alumnos Españoles en Holanda** *(Federation of Spanish Parents' Associations in Holland)*
Overstraat 5, 5632 EM Eindhoven
Parents of school students; Spanish community social and economic welfare, cultural identity.　　　　　　»94

✪ **Molinos de Viento** *(Windmills)*
Utrechtsedwarstraat 13 I, 1017 WB Amsterdam
Cultural society.　　　　　　　　　　　　　　　»94

✪ **Unión General de Trabajadores, UGT** *(General Workers' Union)*
R. Cabrera: Lorentzstraat 38, 3817 XM Amersfoort
External section of Spanish national trade union federation; employment, welfare rights, education/training, social and cultural activities for migrant workers.　　　　　　»94

◎ **PORTUGAL** *351*

✪ **Comunidade Católica Espanhola** *(Spanish Catholic Community)*
Igreja de São José da Anunciada, Largo da Anunciada, 1100 Lisboa; *t* (01) 327537　　　　　　　　　　»90
✪ ≡ Mons. Jesus Rodrigues Otero: Capela da Beneficiência Espanhola, Avenida D. Rodrigo da Cunha 1, 1700 Lisboa; *t* (01) 890714　　　　　　　　　　»90

● **Instituto Cervantes**
Santa Maria 43 E r/c, 1150 Lisboa; *t* (01) 315 1073　»95

◎ **UNITED KINGDOM** *44*

● **Agrupación de Centros y Asociaciones de Españoles** *(Federation of Spanish Centres and Associations)*
67 Brands Hill Avenue, High Wycombe HP13, Buckinghamshire; *t* c/o (0181) 876 1146　　　　»90

● **Anglo-Hispanic Society**
I. Pirie, Honorary Secretary: 82 Bunbury Road, Northfield, Birmingham B31 2DW
Friendship, cultural exchanges.　　　　　　　　»90

● **Anglo-Spanish Society** and Spanish Club
Margaret McCall, Secretary: 5 Cavendish Square, London W1M 9HA; *t* (0171) 580 7537, 580 2750
Friendship, cultural exchanges; founded 1958.　　»95

● *Bulletin of Hispanic Studies*: University of Liverpool
D.S. Severin/A.L. Mackenzie: 2 Abercrombie Square, PO Box 147, Liverpool L69 3BX; *t* (0151) 794 2774, *f* 708 6502
Academic journal (4/yr), founded 1923, covering all aspects of the field. See Institute of Latin American Studies, p84.»95

✪ **Centro Galego** *(Galician Centre)*
4 Woodfield Place, London W9; *t* (0171) 266 3968　　»95

● **Federación de Asociaciones de Emigrantes Españoles en el Reino Unido** *(UK Federation of Spanish Emigrant Societies)*
3 Canalside House, 383 Ladbroke Grove, London W10 5AA; *t* (0181) 960 8485　　　　　　　　　　»94

✪ **Iberian Switchboard Committee**
16b Waterlane, London SW2 1PB; *t* (0171) 729 3898
Welfare and employment advice.　　　　　　　　»94

● **Instituto Cervantes**
23 Manchester Sq., London W1M 5AP; *t* (0171) 486 4350
Spanish state-funded centre offering language courses.　»95

✪ **Spanish Pensioners' Day Centre**
St George's Hall, Kensington Place, London W8; *t* (0171) 229 8281　　　　　　　　　　　　　　　»95

SRI LANKAN

see also Asian, Buddhist, Hindu, Islamic, Tamil

◎ **FRANCE** *33*

● **Association défense internationale des Sri-Lankais, ADISL**
14 boulevard Montmartre, 75019 Paris
Meetings and assistance for Sri Lankans and friends.　»90

◎ **GERMANY** *49*

● **German Society for the Proclamation of the Doctrine**, also known as German Dhammaduta Society
[address unknown] Buddhist House, Berlin
Theravada Buddhist society, active since the 1950s, whose mainly-German membership provides a base for Sri Lankan monks and their missionary outreach.　　　　　　»93

◎ **ITALY** *39*

● **Associazione dei Patrioti dello Sri-Lanka in Italia** *(Association of Sri Lankan Patriots in Italy)*
Ananda Seneviratne: via Conteverde 58, 00185 Roma; *t* (06) 446 7676
Welfare of migrants and refugees.　　　　　　　»94
✪ ≡ Provincia di Roma: via S. Eufemia 19, 00187 Roma; *t* (06) 676 6669　　　　　　　　　　　　　　　»90

✪ **Associazione Sri-Lanka**
Roy Cangaboda: via Barrili 20, 20141 Milano; *t* (02) 849 1102　　　　　　　　　　　　　　　　　　　»94

● **Associazione della Sri-Lanka in Italia**
via Castenedolo 109, 00188 Roma; *t* (06) 5797 3940 (Nowfer)　　　　　　　　　　　　　　　　　»90

● **Associazione di Sri Lanka in Italia**
Lakshman Condegama: via Conteverde 58, 00185 Roma; *t* (06) 446 7676, *f* 678 1182
Cultural and welfare activities.　　　　　　　　»95

◎ **NORWAY** *47*

✪ **Sri Lanka Resource Centre**
[address uncertain] Grensen 18, 0159 Oslo 1
Address as for Norwegian Institute of Human Rights, p210.»93

◎ **UNITED KINGDOM** *44*

● **Maha Bodhi Society of Sri Lanka (UK), MBS (UK)**
Ven. Pandith M. Vajiragnana, Abbot: London Buddhist Vihara, 5 Heathfield Gardens, Chiswick, London W4 4JU; *t* (0171) 996 9493
Instruction, retreats, reference library. The MBS was founded in Calcutta in 1891 and is now the main Sinhala Buddhist group in Sri Lanka, with many missions in other countries.»92

● **Sri Lanka Association for Peace and Democracy**
Suite 22, Unit 239, Elephant & Castle Centre, London SE1 6TE
Centre promoting the views of the Sri Lankan government on the ethnic conflict, and opposing Tamil separatism.　»92

● **Sri Lanka Islamic UK Association**
A. Azahim Mohamed, General Secretary: 62 Rose Glen, Colindale, Kingsbury, London NW9 LJS; *t/f* (0181) 952 2105
Sunni body founded 1973; Koranic studies, youth work.　»94

- *Sri Lanka Monitor*
Malcolm Rodgers, Editor: [address unknown]
Current affairs magazine.   »95
✿ Sri Lanka-UK Friendship Association
B.T. Indran Segarajasinghe: 11 Kent Road West, Rusholme,
Manchester M14 5RF; *t* (0161) 224 5019, 860 4609
Deirdre McConnell. Promotion of Sri Lankan culture,
intercultural relations; English classes.   »93
✿ *Sri Lankans*
28 Walton Drive, Harrow, Middlesex; *t* (0181) 861 1855
Magazine (12/yr).   »88

SUDANESE

*see also African, Arab/Arabic, East African, Islamic, North
African*

⊙ ITALY *39*

- Associazione dei Sudanesi in Italia
via Firenze 38, 00184 Roma; *t* (06) 673 0909   »94

⊙ SPAIN *34*

✿ Mundri Relief and Development Association, MRDA
carrer Córsega 707 e/s, 08026 Barcelona, Catalunya   »94

⊙ UNITED KINGDOM *44*

✿ Christian Coptic Refugees Group
Fr Zakaria Butros: St Mary and St Abram Church, Davigdor
Road, Hove BN3 1RF; *t* (01273) 736636, 701477
Sudanese and Egyptian Copts.   »94
✿ Southern Sudanese Welfare Association
Lino Gwaki: 2 Cringleford Walk, Longsight, Manchester M12
4PN; *t* (0161) 274 4461
Community welfare, employment and training, culture.   »93
- Sudan Human Rights Organization, SHRO
Abdek Salaam Hassan: BM Box 8238, London WC1N 3XX;
t (0171) 378 8008, *f* 378 8029
Pressure group on human rights in Sudan (formed in Sudan,
banned 1989, reformed London 1991); support for refugees
and asylum seekers; research on refugees in Africa.   »94
- *Sudan Monitor*
Emma Sharp: 7 Bury Place, London WC1
Journal on human rights in Sudan.   »91
- Sudan Musicians Association
Mohamed Wardi: [address unknown]
Promotion of Sudanese culture, and of cultural and
intellectual freedoms in Sudan.   »94
- Sudan Relief and Rehabilitation Association, SRRA
Helen Murshali: Interchange Studios, Dalby Street, London
NW5 3NQ; *t* (0171) 209 5859
Refugee welfare, humanitarian aid.   »96
- *Sudan Update*
Peter Verney, Editor: PO Box 10, Hebden Bridge HX7 6UX
Newsletter on human rights and political developments.   »95
✿ Sudanese Association of Sussex
Abubaker Abuelbashar: 41 Swanborough Drive, Brighton
BN2 5PJ; *t* (01273) 604714, 624564
Welfare of some 1,500 Sudanese refugees in Sussex.   »95
✿ Sudanese Coptic Association
Dr Alfi Andrews, Chair: 23 Embassy Court, King's Road,
Brighton BN1 2PL; *t* (01273) 328833
Religious and social organisation for Sudanese Christians. »94
✿ Sudanese Victims of Torture Group
[address unknown] London; *t* (0171) 704 0021   »96
✿ Sudanese Women's Association
Minal Ahmed/Hanan Shammi: c/o 18 Findon Road, Brighton
BN2 5NT; *t* (01273) 692925, 749793   »94

SUNNI; SUNNITE

see Islamic

SURINAMESE

see also Dutch, Hindu, Islamic, Latin American

⊙ NETHERLANDS *31*

*Stichting Lalla Rookh: a Utrecht-based cultural and social group
for Surinamese Muslims and Hindus, which merged with other
groups to create what in 1996 became FORUM: see p146.*

- Stichting Landelijke Federatie Surinaamse Vrouwenzaken,
LFSV *(National Federation on Surinamese Women's Issues)*
Albert Schweitzerlaan 142, 2552 PJ Den Haag; *t* (070) 397
1120   »95
*Stichting Landelijke Federatie van Welzijnsorganisaties voor
Surinamers, SLFWS (National Federation of Surinamese
Welfare Groups Foundation), also known as Landelijke
Federatie voor Surinamers: until 1995, one of the main
national umbrella groups of immigrants, and a member of
the EU Migrants Forum, p131, and of ADO, p208. The
Utrecht-based Stichting and eight other groups merged in
1995 as the Nederlands Expertisecentrum over de Multi-
culturele Samenleving, subsequently renamed FORUM—
Instituut voor Multiculturele Ontwikkeling, see p146.*
- Landelijke Organisatie Surinaamse Vrouwen, LOSV *(National
Organisation of Surinamese Women)*
W. Esayas/R.A. Naloop: Postbus 4062, 3502 HB Utrecht
Federation of women's groups.   »90
✿ Migranten-werkwinkel Amsterdam voor Surinamers en
Antillianen *(Amsterdam Labour Exchange for Surinamese and
Antilleans)*
Stadhouderskade 130, 1074 AW Amsterdam; *t* (020) 662
1496, *f* 673 9129
An experimental service providing specialist employment and
training advice to migrant workers from Surinam and the
Caribbean territories.   »95
- Stichting Surinaams Inspraakorgaan, SIO *(Surinamese
Representative Body)*
Postbus 13187, 3507 LD Utrecht; *t* (030) 231 6014, *f* 234
3836
Location: Nachtegaalstraat 72. Umbrella group for Surinamese
organisations; affiliated to national LAO forum, p146.   »95
- Surinaamse Arbeiders en Werkers Organisatie, SAWO
(Surinamese Workers and Labourers Organisation)
M. André: Postbus 5008, 3502 JA Utrecht; *t* (030) 246
0961   »95
- Surinaamse Stichting *(Surinam Foundation)* also known as
Surinameisische Grundung
Postbus 1226, 9701 Groningen   »90

SWEDISH

see also European, Scandinavian

⊙ UNITED KINGDOM *44*

- Anglo-Swedish Society
Helen Wolff, Secretary: 5 Mansfield Street, London W1M
9FH; *t* (0171) 580 5952
Promotion of friendship, cultural exchanges and co-operation;
founded 1919.   »90

SWISS

see also European

⊙ SPAIN *34*

- Asociación Económica Hispano Suiza
calle José Lázaro Galdiano 6, Madrid; *t* (91) 457 8726   »90

⊙ UNITED KINGDOM *44*

- Anglo-Swiss Society
F. Cobb, Secretary: 2 The Mill Yard, Wickhambreaux,
Canterbury CT3 1RQ
Friendship, cultural exchanges; founded 1948.   »90
✿ Swiss Benevolent Society
31 Cowley Street, London W1; *t* (0171) 387 2173   »95

SYLHETI

see Bangladeshi

SYRIAN

*see also Arab/Arabic, Assyrian, Islamic, Kurdish, Middle
Eastern*

⊙ FRANCE *33*

✿ Centre Culturel Arabe Syrien *(Syrian Arab Cultural Centre)*
12 avenue Tourville, 75007 Paris; *t* (1) 4705 3011   »90

- Comité pour la Défense des Libertés Démocratiques et des Droits de l'Homme en Syrie *(Committee for the Defence of Democratic Liberties and Human Rights in Syria)*
[address unknown] Paris
Campaigns for the release of political prisoners, including some of its members, and on other human rights issues. »95

◎ ITALY *39*

- Unione Nazionale Studenti Siriani
presso Consulta Cittadina dell'Immigrazione, via Merulana 123, 00185 Roma »90

◎ UNITED KINGDOM *44*

✧ Syrian Arab Association
48 Queen's Gate, London SW7; *t* (0171) 589 0334 »95

TAHITIAN

see also French: DOM/TOM, Pacific

◎ FRANCE *33*

- Association des Etudiants de Tahiti *(Association of Tahitian Students)*
63 rue Monsieur le Prince, 75006 Paris; *t* (1) 4633 7280 »90

TAIWANESE

see Chinese

TAMIL

see also Asian, Indian, Sri Lankan

◎ DENMARK *45*

✧ Dansk-Tamilsk Forening i Aalborg *(Danish-Tamil Association of Aalborg)*
Somaseharan Ratnasingham: Vesterbro 119, 4.th., 9000 Aalborg; *t* 9810 3159 »89
✧ Dansk-Tamilsk Venskabsforening *(Danish-Tamil Friendship Association)*
Turasingam Selvakumar: Porsvænget 7, 2sal, 7400 Herning; *t* 9712 5593, *f* 9716 4277
Member of EU Migrants Forum, p131. *Newsletter* (4/yr). »94
- Federation of Danish Tamil Organisations
Fladbrovej 4, 8900 Randers »94
- Tamilsk-Dansk Venskabsforening, TDV
Danmarksgade 10, 7500 Holstebro; *t* 9742 9043 »90
✧ Tamilsk Forening i Vejle *(Vejle Tamil Society)*
c/o Dansk Flygtningehjælp, Gormagade 2, 7100 Vejle »90

◎ FRANCE *33*

- Association culturelle tamoule mondiale *(Tamil World Cultural Association)*
15 allée de Taffignon, 69110 Sainte-Foy-lès-Lyon
Mutual aid; language, literature, culture; French classes. »89
✧ Centre Parisien d'Education de Tamouls
108 rue Bomet, 75015 Paris »90

◎ GERMANY *49*

✧ Liberation Tigers of Tamil Eelam, Germany
P. Sivarajah: Postfach 1302, 5170 Jülich
Tamil separatist group; unsure if it is legal in Germany. »90

◎ NETHERLANDS *31*

- Tamil Dutch Solidarity Association
Albert Neuhuysstr. 8, 3583 SW Utrecht; *t* (030) 251 7242 »90

◎ UNITED KINGDOM *44*

✧ The London Tamil Sangam
M. RajanSethupathy, Chairman: 369 High Street North, Manor Park, London E12 6PG
Cultural, educational, advice activities for Tamils in Newham. »96
✧ Newham Tamil Welfare Association
33a Station Road, London E12 5BP; *t* (0181) 478 0577
Possibly succeeded by the Sangam, above? »91
✧ Northern Tamil Association
Dr T. Sivaganam: 44 Crescent Grove, Didsbury, Manchester M20 8NH
Promotion of Tamil culture and language; refugee welfare. »93

✧ South London Tamil Welfare Group
76-78 Queens Rd, London SW19 8NR; *t* (0181) 879 7716 »91
- Tamil Action Committee
73 Green Lanes, London SE9; *t* (0181) 859 3600 »91
✧ Tamil Information Centre Ltd
V. Shyla, Documentalist: Thamil House, 720 Romford Road, London E12 6BT; *t* (0181) 514 6390
Documentation and resource centre on Tamil issues. »93
✧ Tamil Refugee Action Group
335-337 Grays Inn Road, London WC1X 8PX; *t* (0171) 833 2020
Welfare advice, defence of refugees and asylum seekers. »93
✧ Tamil Refugee Centre
Plevna Road, London N9; *t* (0181) 887 0644 »95
✧ Tamil Refugee Housing Association
K. Kuhan: 2nd Floor, Millmead Business Centre, Millmead Rd, London N17 9QU; *t* (0181) 365 0892-94, *f* 801 3822
Provision of social housing for Tamil refugees. »94
- Tamil Rehabilitiation Organisation, TRO, and International Tamil Foundation
79 Hoe Street, Walthamstow, London E17 4SA; *t* (0181) 520 5876
Charity raising funds for relief of Tamils in Sri Lanka. »95

TANZANIAN

including Zanzibar; see also African, East African

◎ DENMARK *45*

✧ Umoja wa Wazanzibari Skandinavia: Foreningen af Zanzibarier i Skandinavien *(Society of Zanzibaris in Scandinavia)*
Postbox 545, 2620 Albertslund »89

◎ FRANCE *33*

- Amitiés Franco-Tanzaniennes, AFT *(Franco-Tanzanian Friendship Association)*
Jean-Paul Desgranges: 20 rue de Rochechouart, 75009 Paris; *t* (1) 4878 5554
Solidarity, intercultural activities. *Urafriki Tanzania*. »94

TELUGU

see Indian

TERRITOIRES D'OUTRE-MER

i.e. French Overseas Territories; see French: DOM/TOM

THAI

see also Asian, South-East Asian

◎ DENMARK *45*

- Dansk-Thai Forening
Nydamsvej 22, København; *t* 4498 3701 »95
✧ Thailandsk Kulturcenter
Klostergade 37, 8000 Århus C »90

◎ UNITED KINGDOM *44*

- Anglo-Thai Society
Hugh Docherty, Secretary: 22 Ulster Court, Albany Park Rd, Kingston-upon-Thames KT2 5SS; *t* (0181) 546 3048
Trade, friendship; founded 1962. »90
✧ Temple Buddhapaeipa
19 Calonne Road, Parkside, Wimbledon, London SW19; *t* (0181) 946 1357 »95

TIBETAN

see also Asian, Chinese

◎ IRELAND *353*

- Tibet Support Group
Anthony O'Brien/Neil Steedman: 14a Ailesbury Road, Ballsbridge, Dublin 4
Solidarity with Tibet, human rights, self-determination. »91

◎ **NETHERLANDS** *31*

• **Tibet Support Group**
Postbus 1756, 1000 BT Amsterdam; *t* (020) 623 7699,
420 5438
Location: shop at Spuistraat 185a.   »95

◎ **UNITED KINGDOM** *44*

• **Appropriate Technology for Tibetans**, ApTibeT
General Secretary: 117 Cricklewood Broadway, London NW2
3JG; *t* (0181) 450 8090
Supports relief and development projects for Tibetan
refugees in India.   »95
✧ **Brighton Tibet Link**
24 Freshfield Street, Brighton BN2 2ZG; *t* (01273) 675803
Solidarity with Tibet; human rights.   »94
• **Office of Tibet**
Tsewang Topgyal, Representative: 1 Culworth Street,
London NW8 7AF; *t* (0171) 722 5378, *f* 722 0362
Official office of Dalai Lama for Northern Europe; information,
documentation.   »95
✧ **Samye Ling Tibetan Centre**
Eskdalemuir, Langholm, Dumfriesshire, Scotland; *t* (013873)
73232
Promotes study of Tibetan Buddhism.   »95
• **Tibet Foundation**
10 Bloomsbury Way, London WC1A 2SH; *t* (0171) 404
2889, *f* 404 2366
Promotes Tibetan culture, the works of the Dalai Lama, and
the interests of Tibetan refugees; raises charitable funds. »95
• **Tibet Information Network**
[address unknown] London
Documentation and campaigns on human rights and national
self-determination.   »94
• *Tibet News Review*
125 St Helen's Road, Hastings TN38, East Sussex
Preserves and promotes Tibetan culture, disseminates
teachings of Dalai Lama.   »87
• **Tibet Society and Tibet Relief Fund of the United Kingdom**
Ugyan Norbu, Secretary: 114-115 Tottenham Court Road,
London W1P 9HL
Promotes understanding of Tibetan culture and channels
educational and training funds to exile communities. »95
• **Tibet Support Group UK**
Paul Golding: 9 Islington Green, London N1 2XH; *t* (0171)
359 7573
Campaigns for the right of the Tibetan people to self-
determination, and against human rights abuses.   »96
• **Tibetan Community in Britain**
Kelsang R. Frasi, Secretary: 16 Oakmead Road, Balham,
London SW12 9SL; *t* (0181) 675 7839
Mutual assistance, relief of poverty, education of exiles;
since 1986 has run the Tibetan Refugee Charitable Trust to
gather and administer relief funds.   »91

TIGRAY; TIGRÉ

see also African, East African, Ethiopian

◎ **GERMANY** *49*

✧ **Relief Society of Tigray Deutsches Unterstützungskomitee,
REST** *(German Support Committee)*
[address unknown] 5000 Köln   »90

◎ **ITALY** *39*

✧ **Associazione Lavoratori del Tigrai** *(Tigray Workers'
Association)*
via Principe Amadeo 148, 00185 Roma; *t* (06) 731 6557 »90
• **Women's Association of Tigray in Europe**, WATE
Almas Irgao: via Principe Amadeo 148, int. 20, 00185
Roma; *t* (06) 731 6557   »94

◎ **SWEDEN** *46*

• **Stodforening till Relief Society of Tigray i Sverige**, REST
(Support Group in Sweden)
Runslingan 24a, 22477 Lund; *t* (046) 132560, 146648
Solidarity with the Tigray region, relief and development aid
to refugees.   »93

◎ **UNITED KINGDOM** *44*

• **Relief Society of Tigray**, REST
211 Clapham Road, London SW9 0QH; *t* (0171) 738 3197,
738 3327   »95

• **Tigray Development Association**
211 Clapham Rd, London SW9 0QH; *t* (0171) 924 0191 »95
• **Tigrayan People's Liberation Front**, TPLF
211 Clapham Rd, London SW9 0QH; *t* (0171) 737 5585 »95

TIMORESE

see also Asian, Indonesian, Portuguese, South-East Asian

◎ **FRANCE** *33*

• *Agir pour Timor* (Struggle for Timor)
Carlos Semedo: 22 bis rue Jouvenet, 75016 Paris; *t* (1)
4589 7022
Bulletin (6/yr) in solidarity with the people of occupied East
Timor.   »94

◎ **IRELAND** *353*

• **East Timor Ireland Solidarity Campaign**
Tom Hyland: PO Box 3800, Dublin 10; *t* (01) 623 3148
Support for Timorese self-determination and human rights,
opposition to Indonesian occupation. See also Northern
Ireland group, below.   »94

◎ **PORTUGAL** *351*

✧ **Comunidade de Refugiados de Timor** *(Timor Refugee
Community)*
Rua Fernão Mendes Pinto 29, 1400 Lisboa; *t* (01) 301 6913
Listed (1990) at Rua Pedro del Negro 4, r/c Dt°, Reboleira,
2700 Amadora, *t* (01) 495 2413; but this may be a separate
organisation.   »94
✧ **Núcleo Apoio a Timorenses** *(Timorese Support Group)* in
Centro Regional de Segurança Social—Lisboa
Avenida Visconde Valmor 77-1° D, 1000 Lisboa; *t* (01)
770768
Section of the Lisbon social security office providing welfare
and support services for Timorese migrants and refugees. »90
• **A paz é possível en Timor Leste** *(Peace is Possible in East
Timor)*
[address unknown]
Human rights, decolonisation. *Timor Oriental*.   »90

◎ **UNITED KINGDOM** *44*

• **British Coalition for East Timor**, BCET: also known as
Coalition for East Timor
Maggie Helwig: PO Box 2349, London E1 3XH; *t* (0171)
639 4700; (0181) 771 2904 (?)
Solidarity with the people of East Timor; opposition to the
Indonesian occupation; publishes leaflets, booklets. »95

◎ **NORTHERN IRELAND** *44*

✧ **East Timor Solidarity Campaign (Northern Ireland)**
John Price: c/o One World Centre, 4 Lower Crescent, Belfast
BT7 1NR
Opposition to the Indonesian invasion and occupation of East
Timor; human rights, solidarity with Timorese people. »94

TOGOLESE

see also African, West African

◎ **FRANCE** *33*

✧ **Association Multi-Assistance Togolaise**, AMAT *(Togolese
Comprehensive Assistance Association)*
Joseph Cakpo: 8 Groupe Eisenhower, 51100 Reims; *t* 2604
4045   »94
✧ **Espoir Togo-Bénin Organisation Amitié**, OTOA *(Hope for
Togo and Benin Friendship Organisation)*
chez Mme Nicole Mautalen: 16 rue Jean-Zay, 76620 Le Havre
Development assistance, exchanges.   »90

TRANSYLVANIAN

see also East European, Romanian, South-East European

◎ **DENMARK** *45*

• **Scandinavian Center for Monitoring Human Rights in
Transylvania**
Elisabeth Fabricius/Jozsef Varga: Sundkrogen 1, 6400
Sønderborg; *t* 7448 8713   »90

TRAVELLER

see also Gypsy, Irish, Romany, Spanish. Note: this category does not specifically include 'New Age' travellers, although some of the listed groups are not limited to ethnic Travellers. 'Settled' is used below in the sense that it has for the Irish Travellers, i.e. persons no longer on the road but who retain their Traveller identity.

◎ FRANCE *33*

✻ **Association d'aide matérielle et morale aux gens du voyage** *(Society for Material and Moral Support of Travellers)*
31 rue de l'Arquebuse, 51100 Reims »90

✻ **Association des gens du voyage, nomades et sédentaires** *(Society of Settled and Travelling People)* Département du Lot chez M Christian Cagniac: terrain de camping de Saint-Georges, 46000 Cahors »90

✻ ≡ Beziers: chez M Marcel Baptiste: lotissement La Guillotte, 34440 Colombiers
Rights of travelling people, on the road or settled; respect for their ethnic identity, mediation with the authorities. »90

✻ ≡ Cournonterral and district: chez M Jacob Bauer: coste des Cormmiers, 34660 Cournonterral
Covers the *communes* of Cournonterral, Pignan, Montbazin, Cournonsec, Possan, Fabregues and Saint-Jean-de-Vedas.»90

✻ ≡ Département des Alpes-de-Haute-Provence: chez M Fernand Solan: quartier Les Isnards, 04000 Digne »90

✻ ≡ Département de la Loire: chez Mme Lucienne Scheid: La Chassagne, 42720 La Bénisson-Dieu »90

✻ ≡ Département de Tarn-et-Garonne: chez M Georges Daumas: chemin du Quart, Verlhaguet, 82000 Montauban»90

✻ ≡ Département de Vaucluse: chez M Georges Naveri: 148 avenue Sousperoux, 84140 Montflavet »90

✻ ≡ Département des Alpes-Maritimes: chez M Bruno Jennaro: 35 rue Pastorelli, 06300 Nice »90

✻ ≡ Département des Pyrénées-Orientales: 16 rue du Sentier, 66000 Perpignan
Same address as Association gitane Saint-Jacquoise et du Roussillon, p40; same organisation? »90

✻ ≡ Département de l'Ardeche: chez M Jean Pyre: Les Fontaines, 07400 Rochemaure »90

✻ ≡ Département de l'Aveyron: chez M Michel Duculty: Saint-Cloud, 12000 Rodez »90

✻ ≡ Département du Gard: chez M François Santiago: 131 impasse des Lilas, 30380 St-Christol-les-Alès »90

✻ ≡ Tarascon (Bouches-du-Rhône): chez M Paul Patrac: 12 rue Arc-Moneon, 13150 Tarascon »90

✻ ≡ Département de la Haute-Garonne: chez M Octave Zigler, 31620 Villeneuve-lès-Bouloc »90

✻ **Association des gens du voyage, nomades et sédentaires d'Aubenas et environs** *(Aubenas District Society of Settled and Nomadic Travellers)*
chez M Florian Zigler: quartier des Bruyères, 07200 St-Etienne-de-Fontbellon
Rights of travelling people, whether on the road or settled; respect for ethnic identity, mediation with authorities. »90

✻ **Association des gens du voyage sédentaires du Pays d'Aix** *(Aix Association of Settled Travellers)*
Le Sagittaire, n° 1, la ZUP, 13090 Aix-en-Provence
Integration of travelling people. »90

✻ **Esperance gens du voyage Arras** *(Arras Travellers' Hope)*
maison des sociétés, rue Aristide-Briand, 62000 Arras
Living conditions of travellers in Arras district, respect for their traditions. »90

✻ **Mare Pral, Association d'entraide des gens du voyage de l'Indre et des environs** *(Travellers' Mutual Aid Society of Indre and District)*
54 rue Montaigne, 36000 Châteauroux
Tsigane identity, culture and economic activity, better relations between travelling people and the settled community. »89

◎ IRELAND *353*

✻ **Clondalkin Travellers Development Group**
Sandyford Community Centre, Lambs Cross, Sandyford 18, Dublin; *t* (01) 295 9149
Community development, advice, information. Also at Clondalkin Leisure Centre, Nangor Road, Dublin 22, *t* (01) 575124. »94

✻ **Dublin Travellers Education and Development Group**, DTEDG
Dr John O'Connell, Director: Pavee Point, 46 North Great Charles Street, Dublin 1; *t* (01) 873 2802, *f* 874 2626
Martin Collins, Gearóid Ó Riáin. Formed 1985; self-determination for Travellers, anti-racism, human rights. »95

✻ **Dublin Travellers Inter-Cultural Project**
Anastasia Crickley: 39 Upper Gardiner Street, Dublin 1
EU-funded project addressing the multiple forms of marginalisation (poverty, discrimination, poor education, poor services, political exclusion) experienced by Travellers. »91

● **European Centre for Travellers Ltd**
Sister Colette Dwyer: [address unknown]
A company established to develop a European Centre for the Advanced Training of Travellers in Coolarne, Co. Galway; aiming to provide courses for 20 to 50 Travellers from around Europe, and museum, library, research activities. »91

♦ **Irish Traveller Movement, ITM**
Thomas McCann: c/o St Joseph's Training Centre, Barry Rd, Dublin 11; *t* (01) 834 8018 (?), *f* 834 0959 (?)
Founded 1990 after split in NCTP, below; network of Travellers and settled people; campaigns for recognition and protection of Ireland's 21,000 Travellers, and 15,000 Irish Travellers in Britain, as ethnic minorities. Newsletter. »95

♦ **Minceir Misli**
[address unknown]
A Traveller-only organisation campaigning for human and civil rights for Travellers. »94

♦ **National Council for Travelling People**, NCTP, and Dublin Committee for Travelling People, DCTP
Victor Foley: 4-5 Eustace Street, Dublin 2; *t* (01) 679 8358
Founded 1964; civil rights, education, employment of settled and mobile travellers; youth, leisure, cultural activities. »94

✻ ≡ NCTP Galway: Mary Moriarty: 53 New Estate, Dublin Road, Tuam, Co. Galway; *t* (093) 28640
Moriarty has been Irish rapporteur for MAINE, p146. »90

✻ **St Kieran's School for Traveller Children**
Michael O'Reilly: Old Connaught Road, Bray, Co. Wicklow
One of three schools in Ireland for Traveller children. »95

◎ UNITED KINGDOM *44*

✻ **Brent Travellers Support Group**
c/o BIAS, Electric House, 296 Willesden Lane, London NW2; *t* (0181) 459 6286
Advice and information for travelling people. Address may have changed: see Brent Irish Advisory Service, p47. »90

✻ **Camden Travellers Support Group**
c/o Race Relations Department, Town Hall, Camden, London NW1; *t* (0171) 278 4444 »90

✻ **Ealing Travellers Bashley Road Project**
Michael Pitchford, 27 St Johns Hill, Clapham, London SW11 2RF; *t* (0171) 738 1039
Group of Travellers and settled people working to improve all aspects of the lives of Travellers. »95

✻ **Greenwich Travellers Support Group**
Housing Rights, Hare Street, Woolwich, London SE18; *t* (0181) 854 8848 »90

✻ **Haringey Travellers Support Group**
c/o Haringey Irish Community Care Centre, 72 Stroud Green Road, London N4 3ER; *t* (0171) 272 9230, *f* 263 6641 »90

✻ **Islington Travellers Support Group** (possibly defunct)
c/o Irish in Islington Project, Caxton House, St John's Way, London N19; *t* (0171) 281 3225 »90

London Gypsy Traveller Unit: see Save the Children, p227

✻ **London Travellers Forum**
c/o 5 Britannia Street, London WC1; *t* (0171) 837 1436
Representation of travellers' needs to authorities. »90

● **National Association of Teachers of Travellers**
c/o WMESTC, Broad Lanes, Bilston, West Midlands; *t* (01902) 353925
Liaison and support for teachers, improved provision. »90

● **Traveller Research Unit** and Telephone Legal Advice Service for Travellers, TLAST
Cardiff Law School, University of Wales, PO Box 427, Museum Avenue, Cardiff CF1 1XD; *t* (01222) 874580. »90

✻ **Travellers Community Social Workers**
Haringey Area 6 Office, Willoughby Road, London N8; *t* (0181) 341 1100
Social services specialist team. »90

✻ **Travellers Resource Centre**
Jadwin House, 205-211 Kentish Town Road, London NW5 2JU; *t* (0171) 267 6723
Information and advice on education, site provision and social welfare of Travellers. »90

● **Travellers Rights Organization**
S. Cauley: 4 Toneborough Estate, Abbey Rd, London NW8 »90

● **Travelling Mission to the Travelling People**
Fr Eltin Daly: St Joseph's House, Leopold Street, Oxford OX4 1PS; *t* (01865) 240325
Catholic catechetical and pastoral work throughout Britain.»90

◉ **NORTHERN IRELAND** *44*

✿ **Advisory Committee on Travellers in Northern Ireland**, ACT
Elis Gallagher, Chairman: [address unknown] Belfast
Paul Noonan. Improvement of service delivery to travellers;
increased provision of sites; liaison with other agencies.   »92
✿ **Armagh Travellers Support Group**, ATSG
Mariena Kelly-Lyth, Development Worker: Jenny's Project,
Jenny's Row, Armagh BT61 9AP; *t* (01861) 523963,
f 528445
Campaigns for provision of a serviced site for Traveller
families in the Armagh area, and promotes well-being of
Travelling people; resource unit on Travellers and health,
education, anti-racism, Traveller history and other topics. »95
✿ **Barnardo's Travellers Project**
Gerard Barton/Marie Cafolla: 542 Upper Newtownards Road,
Belfast BT4; *t* (01232) 672366, *f* 672399
Specialist project of generalist childcare charity; involved in
research project on families and racism.   »95
✿ **Belfast Travellers Association**
Michael Mongan: [address unknown] Belfast
Local organisation formed 1994 to represent the interests of
Travellers in and around the city; campaigns on housing,
halting sites and services.   »94
✿ **Belfast Travellers Education & Development Group**, BTEDG
Paul Noonan: Unit 4, Owenvarragh Building, 106
Andersonstown Road, Belfast BT11; *t* (01232) 621333   »94
✿ **Belfast Travellers Sites Project**, BTSP
Glenand Training Agency, Kennedy Way Industrial Estate,
Blackstaff Road, Belfast BT11 9DT; *t* (01232) 623297
Development of serviced sites and other social provision for
the Traveller community in Belfast. A sub-committee runs
the Belfast Travellers Youth Project which employs two youth
workers.   »94
✿ **Craigavon Travellers Support Committee**, CTSC (also known
as C T S *Agency*)
Marie Crawley/Jacqueline Kilfeather: 520 Burnside,
Brownlow, Craigavon BT65 5DE, Co. Armagh; *t* (01762)
342673, 342089
Consultation, advice and service provision to Travellers,
policy development, site provision, community relations, inter-
agency liaison.   »95
● **Northern Ireland Council for Travelling People**
Paul Noonan: 30 University St, Belfast; *t* (01232) 237372
Education and welfare of Travellers, campaigns for provision
of sites and for anti-discrimination legislation. Name also listed
as Northern Ireland Council for Travellers; see also Advisory
Committee on Travellers, above.   »94
✿ **West Belfast Travellers Project**
c/o Moyard Family Centre, Moyard Park, Belfast; *t* (01232)
438981   »94

TRINIDADIAN and TOBAGAN

*see also African Caribbean, Afro-Caribbean, Anglo-Caribbean,
Caribbean, West Indian; for East Indians, see also Asian*

◉ **UNITED KINGDOM** *44*

✿ **Trinidad and Tobago Association**
56 Frederick Road, Stechford, Birmingham   »90
✿ ≡ 380 Green Lanes, London N4; *t* (0181) 800 5857   »88

TSIGANE

see Gypsy, Romany, Traveller

TUNISIAN

*see also African, Arab/Arabic, Islamic, Maghrebi, Middle
Eastern, North African*

◉ **FRANCE** *33*

✿ **Amicale des Etudiants Tunisiens de Montpellier** *(Tunisian
Students' Society of Montpellier)*
4 bis rue Edouard-Marsal, 3400 Montpellier
Sport, culture.   »90
✿ **Amicale franco-tunisienne en France** *(Franco-Tunisian
Society of France)*
Mairie, 91860 Epinay-sous-Sénart
Interests of migrants, second generation; social, cultural
activity; international friendship.   »90

✿ **Amicale des travailleurs tunisiens** *(Tunisian Workers' Society)*
salle des Combettes, 39300 Champagnole
Social events, language classes, information and leisure
activities for workers and families.   »89
✿ ≡ 25 rue Fortuny, 75008 Paris; *t* (1) 4763 4189
Social, cultural and welfare activities.   »90
✿ **Amicale des Tunisiens de la Charente**
Maison des peuples et de la paix, 6 bis rue Marengo, 16000
Angoulême
Social, cultural and welfare activities.   »90
✿ **Amicale des Tunisiens de la Côte-d'Azur**
Moncef Zaguia: 4 rue Miralhéti, 06300 Nice; *t* 9392 2646
Cultural and leisure activities; education, youth welfare.   »94
✿ **Amicale des Tunisiens en France** Section de Commentry
chez M Habib Badry: 18 rue Molière, 03600 Commentry
Dialogue, integration, sport, culture.   »90
✿ **Amicale des Tunisiens du Havre et sa Région**
16 rue du Commandant-Chef-d'Hôtel, 76600 Le Havre
Solidarity and friendship among local Tunisians, material
interests of their community, Arab and Islamic culture.   »90
✿ **Amicale des Tunisiens d'Orléans**
18 allée du Clos-du-Chat, 45760 St-Pryvé-St-Mesmin
Cultural, sporting and social events for the Tunisian
community, inter-community contact and integration.   »90
✿ **Amicale des Tunisiens de Provence**
26 boulevard des Dames, 13002 Marseille; *t* 9191 4590
Social and welfare.   »90
✿ **Association des commerçants et des artisans tunisiens de
Provence-Languedoc**, ACATPL *(Association of Tunisian
Tradespeople of Provence-Languedoc)*
2 rue Jemmapes, 13001 Marseille
Rights of Tunisian artisans and traders in France.   »90
✿ **Association de Culture Berbère Tiddukla**
37 bis rue des Maronites, 75020 Paris; *t* (1) 4358 2325,
f 4358 4975
Tunisian arts and culture. *Tiddukla, Lettre de Tiddukla.*   »94
✿ **Association Culturelle Berbère Tiwizi**
BP 96, 75691 Paris Cedex 20
Tunisian arts and culture.   »90
● **Association de Douirets en France**, ADF
261 rue des Pyrénées, 75020 Paris
Berber youth, culture, mutual aid, integration.   »90
✿ **Association familiale tunisienne de la Nièvre** *(Tunisian
Family Association of Nevers District)*
Aux Eduens, bureau n° 8, 58000 Nevers
Material and moral interests of immigrant families.   »89
♦ **Association des Tunisiens en France**, ATF
Lala Lakhdar: 24 rue Pierre Sémard, 75009 Paris; *t* (1) 4596
0406, *f* 4596 0397
Information and welfare service. Member of EU Migrants
Forum, p131.   »94
● **Centre d'Etudes et de Recherches Amazigh**, CERAM
Tassadit Yacine: 4 rue de Chevreuse, 75006 Paris;
t (1) 4633 0434
Research and documentation on Berber culture and history.
Awal—cahier d'études berbères.   »94
✿ **Club des Etudiants Tunisiens en France**, CETF *(Tunisian
Students' Club of France)*
152 rue de Flandres, 75019 Paris
Culture, sport, learning.   »90
✿ **Fel et Yasmine—Association des jeunes tunisiens à
Grenoble** *(Association of Tunisian Youth in Grenoble)*
3 rue Docteur-Valois, 38406 Saint-Martin-d'Hères
Support and assistance to young Tunisians, inter-cultural
exhanges.   »89
✿ **Organisation franco-tunisienne d'action sociale**, OFTAS
128 rue Aristide-Briand, 92300 Levallois-Perret
Social action, cultural services, tourism, leisure,
communication.   »89
● **Rassemblement des Tunisiens en France**, RTF
36 rue Botzaris, 75019 Paris; *t* (1) 4206 9285   »94
✿ ≡ Délégation du Grand Sud: Lazhar Dhifi: 2 rue Jemmapes,
13001 Marseille; *t* 9195 6730, *f* 9164 7005
Publishes *Echos de Tunisie*.   »94
✿ **Union des jeunes tunisiens d'Orléans** *(Tunisian Youth
Association of Orleans)*
10 rue des Bouchers, 45000 Orléans
Cultural exchanges, seminars, information on Tunisian
politics, culture and society.   »90
● **Union des Travailleurs Immigrés Tunisiens**, UTIT *(Union of
Tunisian Immigrant Workers)*
Kamel Jendoubi: 70 rue de la Fraternité, 93170 Bagnolet;
t (1) 4988 1634, 4988 1657, *f* 4988 1635
Member of EU Migrants Forum, p131, and MAINE, p146. »94
✿ ≡ 21 rue des Messageries, 75010 Paris   »90

◎ **GERMANY** *49*

✿ **Tunesische Vereinigung** *(Tunisian Association)*
Ostermannstraße 19, 44147 Dortmund; *t* (0231) 837233
Welfare, solidarity.   »94
• **Vereinigung der Tunesier in Deutschland** *(Association of Tunisians in Germany)*
Zentmarkweg 30, 6000 Frankfurt am Main 90; *t* (069) 788767   »90

◎ **ITALY** *39*

• **Association Amicale Tunisienne** *(Tunisian Friendship Association)*
Albergo del Popolo, via degli Apuli 39, 00185 Roma
Friendship and solidarity.   »90
• **Associazione di Amicizia Italia-Tunisia**
via della Scrofa 117, 00186 Roma; *t* (06) 654 4240
International friendship, aid to immigrants.   »90
✿ **Comitato Tunisino** *(Tunisian Committee)*
[address unknown] 42100 Reggio Emilia   »90

◎ **NETHERLANDS** *31*

✿ **Association Tunisienne**
Postbus 53173, 2505 AD Den Haag
Interests of Maghrebis in Netherlands.   »90

◎ **UNITED KINGDOM** *44*

• **El Nahdha** *(Renaissance)*
Rachid Ghannouchi, leader: [address unknown]
Radical Islamist party banned in Tunisia, being accused of involvement in violence. Many members exiled in Europe. »95

TURKISH

see also Armenian, Asian, Cypriot, Islamic, Kurdish, South-East European

◎ **BELGIUM** *32*

✿ **Association Culturelle et d'Aide aux Travailleurs Turcs de la Region du Centre** *(Turkish Workers' Cultural and Assistance Association)* Central Region
Mustafa Kavak: Rue de Bouvy 82, 7100 La Louvière; *t* (064) 280025
Training, employment, cultural matters.   »94
✿ **Association de Solidarité des Travailleurs Turcs** *(Turkish Workers' Solidarity Association)*
Rue G. Boël 144, 7100 La Louvière; *t* (064) 220671
Cultural and social.   »94
✿ **Eenheid en Samenwerking** *(Unity and Co-operation)*
Herenstraat 16, 3600 Genk; *t* (089) 384203
Cultural and social group.   »94
• **Federatie van Turkse Islamitische Kulturele Verenigingen in Belgie**, TIKF *(Federation of Turkish Islamic Societies in Belgium)*
Stationstraat 43, 3582 Beringen; *t* (011) 432314
Cultural and religious affairs.   »94
• **Fédération des Associations de Travailleurs Turcs de Belgique**, FATTB/BTIDF *(Belgian Federation of Turkish Workers' Associations)*
Zeki Usta: Rue Masni 97, 1210 Bruxelles; *t* (02) 216 2007
Employment, training, welfare advice; social and religious activities; represented in EU Migrants Forum, p131.   »94
✿ ≡ Rue E. Urbain 208, 7111 La Louvière; *t* (064) 280025
Migrant workers' information, advice and welfare centre. »94
• **Info-Türk**
Dogan Özgüden/Inci Tugsavul: Ateliers du Soleil, Rue des Eburons 38, 1040 Bruxelles; *t* (02) 230 2783, 230 3472, *f* 230 9542
Counselling, language training, cultural and welfare work for Turkish migrants and refugees and their families in Belgium; defence of human rights in Turkey. Founded 1974.
Info-Türk (12/yr).   »94
✿ **Türk-Danis—Centre Turc d'information, d'animation culturelle et d'aide sociale** *(Turkish Information, Cultural Promotion and Welfare Centre)*
Muharrem Karaman, President: Rue de la Senne 35, 1000 Bruxelles; *t* (02) 512 9866, 512 9667, *f* 512 9556
Member of EU Migrants Forum, p131; welfare, employment aid. *Türk-Danis*, *Dominot* (both 4/yr); *Emek* (12/yr).   »94
✿ ≡ Muharrem Karaman: Rue Vauban 5, 6000 Charleroi; *t* (071) 333964   »90
✿ **Turk Kultur Dengi** *(Turkish Cultural Union)*
Rue des 600 Frachimontois 113, 4821 Andrimont   »90

✿ **Turkse Culturele Vereniging Waterschei** *(Waterschei Turkish Cultural Association)*
A. Dumontlaan 90, 3600 Genk; *t* (089) 380016   »94
✿ **Turkse Culturele Vereniging Winterslag** *(Winterslag Turkish Cultural Association)*
Hoefstadstraat 12, 3600 Genk; *t* (089) 380016   »94
✿ **Turkse Democratische Culturelle Volksvereining**, DHKD: Association populaire démocratique culturelle turque *(Turkish People's Democratic Cultural Association)*
F. Pehlivan/Kani Yavas: Wetervliesstraat 8, 9000 Gent; *t* (09) 224 3749   »94
✿ **Turkse Eenheid van Beringen** *(Beringen Turkish Union)*
Koolmijnlaan 240, 3582 Beringen; *t* (011) 432606   »94
✿ **Turkse Rangers Waterschei**
Steenbeuckstraat 20 A, 3600 Genk; *t* (089) 386348
Sporting and social club.   »94
• **Union des Travailleurs Turcs en Belgique** *(Union of Turkish Workers in Belgium)*
Haber Bulteni: [address uncertain] Rue de la Poste 38, 1030 Bruxelles; *t* (02) 520 8064
Also listed (1990) as Rue Jourdain 141, 1060 Bruxelles. »94
✿ **Werking met Kansarme Jeugd vzw** *(Action to Improve Youth Opportunities)*
Filip Ramakers: Europaplein 38, 3630 Maasmechelen; *t* (089) 764734
Name is literally Action with Youth Lacking in Opportunities. Youth employment, integration; youth social work (through Jeugdzorg Eisden), meeting place (Jeugdhuis Oke).   »94

◎ **DENMARK** *45*

✿ **Anatolsk Kulturforening** *(Anatolian Cultural Society)*
Gudrunsvej 48, kld., Postbox 1458, 8220 Brabrand, Århus; *t* 8625 3898
Cultural exchange, youth integration.   »94
✿ **Dansk-Tyrkisk Arbejder Forening** *(Danish-Turkish Workers' Society)*
φsterbro 40, 9000 Aalborg; *t* 9810 1706   »89
✿ **Dansk-Tyrkisk Forening i Herning** *(Herning Danish-Turkish Society)*
Izzet Yava: H.C. Orstedsvej 49, 7400 Herning
Training, employment, welfare.   »94
✿ **Dansk Tyrkisk Ungdomsforening**, DTU *(Danish Turkish Youth Society)*
φstre Stationsvej 38, 5000 Odense C; *t* 6611 3174   »89
• **Forbundet af Arbejdere fra Tyrkiet**, FAT *(League of Turkish Workers)*
Akif Erdem: [address uncertain] Istedgade 52, 1650 Kφbenhavn V; *t* 3131 8488
Also listed (1990) as Blegdamsvej 4, st., 2200 Kφbenhavn N, or Vesterbrogade 20-3, 1620 Kφbenhavn V, *t* 3121 8213. Founded 1975; welfare of Turks in Denmark, solidarity, advice; member of EU Migrants Forum, p131. »90
✿ **Foreningen af Arbejdere fra Tyrkiet**, TU-DER
Y. Bulut: Pollemagerporlen 128, 2650 Hvidovre; *t* 3124 3405
Cultural and welfare group.   »94
✿ **Foreningen af Tyrkiske Arbejdere** *(Association of Turkish Workers)*
Vendersgade 30, 7000 Fredericia   »89
• **Foreningen af Tyrkiske Demokratiske Arbejdere i Danmark**, TUDID *(Union of Turkish Democratic Workers in Denmark)*
and Foreningen af Arbejdere fra Tyrkiet, TU-DER
c/o IFD, Vesterbrogade 40, 1.tv., 1620 Kφbenhavn V; *t* 3124 3405, 3124 6630   »89
✿ **Istanbul Klub**
Ryttergade 4, 5000 Odense C   »89
✿ **Jyllands Tyrkiske Ungdoms Indvandrerforening** *(Jutland Turkish Immigrant Youth Society)*
Klostergade 37, 8000 Århus C   »89
• **Sammenslutning af Tyrkiske Arbejderforeninger i Danmark**, STAD *(Federation of Turkish Labour Groups in Denmark)*
H. Serefoglu: Hundshojvej 19, Ganlose, 3660 Stenlose; *t* 4218 1320
Migrant labour rights.   »94
✿ **Tyrkisk-Dansk Forening** *(Turkish-Danish Society)*
Klostergade 37, 8000 Århus C; *t* 8612 7379   »89
✿ **Tyrkisk-Dansk Venskabsforening i Ikast**
Sφnderparken 10, 7430 Ikast   »90
✿ **Tyrkisk Klub**
Frederiksgade 24 B, 5000 Odense C
Social club.   »89
✿ **Tyrkisk Kultur- og Undervisningscenter**
Postbox 171, 8900 Randers; *t* 8643 9003
Founded 1985; community welfare, employment and legal advice.   »90

☼ **Tyrkisk Kulturforening** (Turkish Cultural Society)
Kanalens Kvarter 186, 1, 2620 Albertslund »90
☼ ≡ Postbox 1461, 8220 Brabrand »90
☼ ≡ Ballerup: Måløv Hovedgade 129, 2760 Måløv,
København »89
☼ **Tyrkiske Arbejderes Solidaritetsforening** (Turkish Workers'
Solidarity Association)
Østergade 6, 8900 Randers »90
● **Den Tyrkiske Forældreforening**
c/o Cengiz Karakus: Hans Tavsensgade 33, 2.th., 2200
København N »89
☼ **Den Tyrkiske Forening i Farum** (Farum Turkish Society)
Nygårdsterrasserne 206, 3520 Farum »89
☼ **Tyrkiske Uzbek Tyrkeres Familieforening** (Turkish and
Turkish-Uzbekistan Family Association)
S. Willumsensvej 16, st.th., 2800 Lyngby; t 4287 9284 »89

◉ **FRANCE** 33

☼ **A Ta Turquie**
46 rue St Jean, 54000 Nancy; t 8337 9228, f 8335 8069
Cultural and social interests. Oloçum/Genèse (6/yr). »94
☼ **Amicale des Turcs à Digne** (Digne Turkish Society)
32 allée des Fontainiers, 04000 Digne
Cultural, sporting and social events, solidarity, mutual aid,
settlement and integration of Turkish families. »90
☼ **Amicale des Turcs et des Français** (Franco-Turkish Club)
Murat Kilic: 2 rue Goustav-Courbet, 25700 Valentigney »89
☼ **Association culturelle franco-turque**
6 place Fernand-Rey, 69001 Lyon
Franco-Turkish cultural understanding. »89
☼ **Association culturelle islamique turque**
59 rue Pierre-Butin, 95300 Pontoise »90
☼ **Association culturelle et islamique turque Angers Trelaze**
(Turkish Islamic Cultural Association)
113 chemin des Longs-Boyaux, 49000 Angers »90
☼ **Association culturelle et sportive des jeunes Turcs de**
Belfort (Belfort Turkish Youth Cultural and Sporting Society)
Ali Gedikoglu: 1 rue d'Amsterdam, 90000 Belfort
Sporting and cultural. »90
● **Association culturelle des travailleurs de Turquie en France,**
ACTTF (Cultural Association of Turkish Workers in France)
formerly Union CTTF
17 rue de l'Echiquier, 75010 Paris; t (1) 4022 9925, 4523
4739, f 4800 9925
Turkish culture, welfare, solidarity, anti-racism. »94
☼ **Association culturelle turque de Haute-Savoie**
10 rue des Camps, 74100 Annemasse
Cultural and leisure activities. »89
● **Association démocratique des travailleurs de Turquie**
(Turkish Democratic Workers' Association)
45 rue Enghien, 75010 Paris; t (1) 4523 4640 »90
☼ **Association des Ouvriers Turcs** (Turkish Workers'
Association)
Mehmet Akinci: 16 rue Claude Kogan, 38100 Grenoble;
t 7622 5201 »94
☼ **Association des Parents d'Elèves Turques de Goussainville**
(Goussainville Society of Parents of Turkish Schoolchildren)
2 allée Maurice-Ravel, 95190 Goussainville
Educational, cultural, sporting. »89
☼ **Association socioculturelle turque de Valentigney**
Mustafa Firinci: 1 rue Proudhon, 25700 Valentigney
Cultural, sporting and social life of the local Turkish
community. »90
☼ **Association de solidarité et culturelle des travailleurs de**
Turquie, ASCTT (Turkish Workers' Cultural and Solidarity
Association)
29 rue Parisis, 28100 Dreux
Solidarity and integration of Turkish immigrant workers, social
and cultural activities. »90
☼ **Association de Solidarité avec les Travailleurs Turcs**
(Turkish Workers Solidarity Association)
Yilmaz Necati: 2a rue de Koenigshoffen, 67000 Strasbourg;
t 8832 9832 »94
☼ **Association des travailleurs turcs de la région d'Eure-et-Loire,**
ATT (Eure-et-Loire Region Turkish Workers' Association)
Ecole Pierre-Mendès-France, avenue de Lattre de Tassigny,
28100 Dreux »89
● **Association des Travailleurs de Turquie, ATT** (Turkish
Workers' Association)
35 bvd de Strasbourg, 75010 Paris; t (1) 4246 5970-72 »94
☼ ≡ U. Metin/Hasan Altundag: 55 rue de Réaumur, 75002
Paris; t (1) 4039 0743
Represented in EU Migrants Forum, p131; advice, training,
cultural activity. Branches in Paris, Metz, elsewhere. »91

● **Comité de Défense des Droits Politiques en Turquie**
(Committee for the Defence of Political Rights in Turkey)
7 rue Leclerc, 75014 Paris
Solidarity group. »90
☼ **Udumuz Çocuklar ou Les enfants de l'espoir** (Children of
Hope)
5 rue Roger-Martin-du-Gard, immeuble Cerès, appt 28,
52100 Saint-Dizier
Cultural activities, integration of Turkish women and children
in French and European life by language classes, workshops,
conferences. »90
☼ **Union des familles turques de Grigny** (Union of Turkish
Families of Grigny)
26 rue des Radars, 91350 Grigny »89

◉ **GERMANY** 49

☼ **Arbeiterverein der Türkei** (Turkish Workers' Union)
Neusserstraße 81, 50670 Köln; t (0221) 732580
Employment, training, culture of migrants; anti-racism. »94
☼ **Arkadas**
Mehmet Isbilir: Friedrich-Ebertstraße 7, 65510 Idstein;
t (06126) 54970
Culture, information. »94
☼ **Avrupa Milli Görüs Teskilatlari, AMGT:** Islamische
Vereinigung der neuen Weltsicht in Europa (Islamic Alliance
for the New World-View in Europe)
Osman Yumakogullari/Ali Yüksel: Merheimerstraße 229-231,
50733 Köln; t (0221) 728360, 722536, f 739 3700
Cultural, social, religious and welfare group. »94
☼ **Berlin Türk Bilim ve Teknoloji Merkezi e.V.,** BTBTM:
Türkisches Wissenschafts- und Technologie-Zentrum (Berlin
Turkish Science and Technology Co-ordination Bureau)
Straße des 17. Juni 135, 1000 Berlin 12; t (030) 3142 4800
Educational and training advice. »90
☼ **Berlin Türk Cemaati:** Türkischer Gemeinde zu Berlin e.V.,
TGB (Turkish Community of Berlin)
Husnu Ozkanli/M.T. Çakmakoglu: Adalbertstraße 4, 10999
Berlin; t (030) 615 5967, f 615 1583
Also listed as Bundnis Türkischer Eniwanderer. Member of EU
Migrants Forum, p131; community enterprise, training. »94
☼ **Berliner Gesellschaft Türkischer Mediziner e.V.,** BTSE
(Berlin Society of Turkish Doctors) also known as
Gesellschaft Türkischer Mediziner
Ali Savarer/Dr Umut Uygun: Skalitzerstraße 138, 10999
Berlin; t (030) 614 9073
Founded 1986; training and employment of Turkish and
other foreign medical personnel; health centre. »94
☼ **Bund der Einwanderer/innen aus der Türken in Berlin,**
BETB (League of Turkish Immigrants in Berlin)
Kenan Kolat: Langenscheldtstraße 11, 10827 Berlin; t (030)
787 5150, 782 5076, f 787 5063
Education, youth integration and employment issues. »94
☼ **Bürgerhaus** (Citizens' House)
Büffelsheinerstr. 24, 6550 Bad Kreuznach; t (0671) 30723
Culture, information. »91
☼ **Demokratik Isçi Dernekleri Federasyonu,** DIDF: Föderation
der Demokratischen Arbeitervereine (Federation of
Democratic Labour Groups)
Jägerstr. 77, 47166 Duisburg; t (0203) 53289, f 53804 »94
☼ ≡ Käsenstraße 15, 5000 Köln 1; t (0221) 327972 »90
♦ **Demokratik Yurtseverler Birligi Federasyonu,** DYBF:
Föderation für Demokratischen Patriotenbunde (Federation of
Democratic Patriotic Societies)
Kottbusser Damm 74, 1000 Berlin 61; t (030) 691 9099
Advice, assistance, cultural promotion. »90
☼ **Dortmund Türkischer Volksverein, HTB** (Dortmund Turkish
People's Union)
In der Tenfe 3, 44329 Dortmund; t (0231) 892265 »94
☼ **Federation of Western Thrace Turks' Associations in**
Germany
[address uncertain] Dessauer Straße 8, 4790 Paderborn
Contacts in Munich: Cafer Alioglu, Özkan Hüseyin. »90
☼ **Föderation der Volksvereine Türkischer Sozialdemokraten**
e.V., HDF (Federation of Turkish Social Democratic Leagues)
and Föderation Progressiver Volksvereine in Europa e.V.
Aydin Sayilan: Oranienstraße 40, 47051 Duisburg; t (0203)
336437, f 338159
Publishes Halkci. »94
☼ ≡ Halis Durdu: Prittwitzstraße 44, 89075 Ulm; t (0713)
67942 »90
● **Freiheitlich Türkisch-Deutscher Freundschaftsvereine, HUR-**
TURK (Turkish-German Liberal Friendship Association)
G. Boyacioglu: Bornheimerstraße 20, 53111 Bonn; t (0228)
693525, f 696181 »94

✿ **Gesellschaft zur Förderung Behinderte Türkische Kinder**
(Society for Aid to Disabled Turkish Children)
Stiftstraße 3, 30159 Hannover; *t* (0511) 17478   »94
✿ **Immigrantengemeinschaft der Türkei** *(Turkish Immigrant Association)*
Postfach 1308, 7320 Goppingen; *t* (07163) 7190
Culture, information.   »91
✿ **Immigrantenverband der Türkei in Oldenburg Umgebung**
(Oldenburg District Turkish Immigrants' Union)
Hayrullah Tiyekli: Plaggenhau 26, 26135 Oldenburg;
t (0441) 12949   »94
✿ **Immigrantenverein aus der Türkei Nürnberg Umgebung**
(Nuremburg District Turkish Immigrant Association)
Nejat Yalcin: Adam Kleinstraße 6, 90429 Nürnberg;
t (0911) 555289   »94
✿ **Saz Rock e.V.**
Bachmanstraße 2-4, 60488 Frankfurt am Main; *t* (069)
788319   »94
✿ **Solidaritätsvereine Bremerhaven** *(Bremerhaven Solidarity League)*
Sadik Sahin: Arndtstraße 8-10, 27570 Bremerhaven;
t (0471) 21587   »94
✿ **Türk Halkevi**: Volkshaus der Türkei *(Turkish People's House)*
Cumali Corbaci: Adalbertsteinweg 103, 52070 Aachen 1;
t (0241) 54825
Culture, information, social action.   »94
✿ ≡ Sinasi Sari: Elisenstraße 5, 63739 Aschaffenburg;
t (06021) 12856   »94
✿ ≡ Yalçin Dal: Baselerplatz 6, 60329 Frankfurt am Main;
t (069) 253208, *f* 230582
Culture, information, anti-racism, social action. See also
Ideen für antirassistische Arbeit, p166.   »94
✿ ≡ Necat Suicmez: Neuer Kamp 31, 20357 Hamburg;
t (040) 439 1311   »94
✿ ≡ Dogan Erdogan: Engelsgrube 55, 23552 Lübeck;
t (0451) 78655   »94
✿ ≡ Ertugrul Sarikaya: Rohrlachstraße 117, 67059
Ludwigshafen; *t* (0621) 522818   »94
● **Türk Iscileri Dernegi**: Verein der Türkischen Arbeitnehmer
(Union of Turkish Employees)
Kölnstraße 3, 5300 Bonn; *t* (0228) 639124   »90
✿ ≡ Cevdet Demirkapi: Schiffbauerweg 4, 2800 Bremen 21;
t (0421) 613345   »90
✿ ≡ Konkordiastr. 28, 4000 Düsseldorf; *t* (0211) 161721 »90
✿ ≡ Herrenberg Umgebung: Selahattin Reisoglu: Marienstraße
21, 71083 Herrenberg; *t* (07033) 26074   »94
✿ **Türkei-Informationsbüro** *(Turkey Information Office)*
R. Öncan: Postfach 910843, 3000 Hannover 91   »90
✿ **Türkei-Zentrum** *(Turkey Centre)*
Mehmet Mümker: Schinkestraße 8-9, 12047 Berlin; *t* (030)
691 1028   »91
✿ ≡ Erkratherstr. 338, 40231 Düsseldorf; *t* (0211) 733 2060»94
✿ **Türkische Beratungsstelle der Arbeiterwohlfahrt** *(Turkish Consultative Office of Labour Assistance)*
Hahnofstraße 2, 35260 Stadt Allendorf; *t* (06428) 0655
Employment and welfare advice and representation.   »94
✿ **Türkische-Islamische Union**, DITIB *(Turkish-Islamic Union)*
Mehmet Yildirim: Venloerstraße 160, 50823 Köln; *t* (0221)
513849, 525432   »94
✿ **Türkischer Arbeiter- und Studentenverein**, TASV *(Turkish Workers' and Students' Union)*
Keskin Akyol: Lutherstr. 81, 34117 Kassel; *t* (0561) 18219»94
✿ ≡ Ali Sevine: Bremerstraße 57, 48155 Münster; *t* (0251)
664009   »94
✿ **Türkischer Arbeiterverein** *(Turkish Workers' Union)*
Mustafa Kizmaz: Rothauserstraße 5, 45879 Gelsenkirchen;
t (0209) 23691, 23692   »94
✿ ≡ Alte Landstraße, 6940 Weinheim; *t* (06201) 15288   »91
✿ **Türkischer Arbeitnehmerverein in München** *(Turkish Employees' Union of Munich)*
[address unknown] 8000 München   »90
✿ **Türkischer Arbeitsverein** *(Turkish Labour Union)*
Honuldstraße 1, 3250 Hameln   »90
✿ **Türkischer Frauenverein Kassel e.V.** *(Turkish Women's Union of Kassel)*
Hauptfeldweg 6, 34131 Kassel; *t* (0561) 35694   »94
✿ **Türkischer Verein für Wissenschaft und Kultur**, TÜBIKS
(Turkish Union for Science and Culture)
Schlüterstraße 39, 1000 Berlin 12; *t* (030) 883 7718   »90
✿ **Türkischer Volksverein**, HDB *(Turkish People's Union)* also
known as Progressive Volkseinheit der Türkei
Oranienstr. 22, 10999 Berlin; *t* (030) 614 7552, *f* 615 9272
Anti-racism, welfare, politics; *Unregelmassige Info-Blatter.*»94
✿ ≡ In der Taufe 3, 4600 Dortmund 14; *t* (0231) 892265 »90
✿ ≡ Buschingstraße 43, 81677 München; *t* (089) 913516»94

✿ **Türkiye Göçmenler Birligi**, TGB: Bundnis Türkischer
Einwanderer e.V. *(Turkish Immigrants' League)*
Prof. Hakki Keskin: Hospitalstraße 111, Haus 7, 22767
Hamburg; *t* (040) 380 9171, 380 5831, *f* 380 5728
Founded 1978; employment, social welfare of Turks, anti-
racism, intercultural contact, women's interests.   »94
✿ **Türkiyeli Göçmen Dernekleri Federasyonu**, GDF *(Federation of Turkish Immigrant Societies)* Föderation der
Immigrantenvereine aus der Türkei
Ataman Aksöyek/Loris Favero: Lichtstraße 31, 40235
Düsseldorf; *t* (0172) 260 3215, (0211) 664284, 678556,
f 683945
Training, employment information, anti-racism. Member EU
Migrants Forum, p131; European Co-ordination for Right to
Family Life of Immigrants, p136 (Zerin Sakalsiz contact). »94
✿ **Verein Arbeiter und Studenten aus Türkei** *(Union of Turkish Workers and Students)*
Fatih H. Ömeroglu: Sohlbacherstraße 34, 57078 Siegen;
t (0271) 89127   »94
✿ **Verein von Arbeiter aus Türkei—Essen** *(Turkish Workers' Union of Essen)*
Hatun Kaya: Friedrich-Ebert-Straße 37, 45127 Essen;
t (0201) 223662   »94
● **Verein zur Förderung des Deutsch-Türkischen Sportjugend-austausches e.V.** *(Society for German-Turkish Youth Sporting Contacts)*
Otto-Fleck-Schneise 12, 60528 Frankfurt am Main; *t* (069)
670 0331
Inter-cultural friendship, leisure activities.   »94
✿ **Verein der Sozialberater für Türken in Nordrhein-Westfalen**,
VSBT-NRW *(Union of Social Workers for Turks in North Rhine-Westphalia)*
c/o Gürcan: Grenzstraße 65, 45881 Gelsenkirchen; *t* (0209)
409412, 44432, *f* 409 4134
Founded 1979; inner-city employment and welfare issues.»94
● **Zentrum für Türkeistudien**, ZFT *(Institute for Turkish Studies)*
Dr Faruk Sen, Director: Gesamt-Hochschule Essen, Overberg
Straße 27, 45141 Essen; *t* (0201) 311041-42, *f* 311043
Research on Turkish affairs and on the emigrant population,
especially the 1.8 million in Germany. Sen was formerly at the
Bonn Centre, below. *Zeitschrift für Turkeistudien* (2/yr).   »94
● **Zentrum für türkische Studien**, Universität Bonn
Ahrstraße 45, 5300 Bonn C; *t* (0228) 302168   »91

◎ **GREECE** *30*
● **Greek-Turkish Solidarity Union**
Huseyin Bobrek: Odos Solomou 25a, 10681 Athinai; *t* (01)
362 5281
Founded 1984; rights of migrant workers, anti-racism.   »94
● **Turkish Democrats Union**
Odos Aghio Constantinou 12, 4th floor, Omonoia, 10431
Athinai; *t* (01) 523416
Welfare, anti-racism, job discrimination issues.   »90

◎ **NETHERLANDS** *31*
✿ **Comité Yildrirum Sport**
Keertberglaan 246, 1974 XC Ijmuiden
Leisure and social group.   »94
● **Demokratik Isçi Dernekleri Federasyonu**, DIDF: Federatie
Demokratische Verenigingen Arbeiders uit Turkije *(Federation of Democratic Labour Groups)*
Hasan Ayhan: Postbus 15372, 1001 MJ Amsterdam; *t* (020)
616 0930, *f* 689 1101
Labour rights, training/employment advice, culture.   »94
✿ ≡ Ismail Demir: Offenbachstraat 15, 6961 CA Eerbeek
Dutch section of international DIDF.   »90
● **Demokratik Sosyal Dernekler Federasyoni**, DSDF
M. Polab: Postbus 5425, 3008 AK Rotterdam; *t* (010) 485
0984 (?)
Founded 1982; rights and welfare of migrant workers,
unemployed, families.   »94
✿ **Fatih Moskee Turks Islamitisch Centrum** *(Fatih Mosque and Turkish Islamic Centre)*
Rozengracht 146-148, 1016 NJ Amsterdam   »94
✿ **Gurbuz Yabas**, ATIDG
Weesperstraat 17, 1018 DN Amsterdam
Welfare, cultural activities.   »94
✿ **Ideal Turks Werknemersvereniging**
Westluidenstraat 3, 4001 ND Tiel; *t* (0344) 613475   »95
● **Stichting Inspraakorgaan Turken in Nederland**, IOT
Noordeinde 142-144, 2515 GP Den Haag; *t* (070) 365 4492,
f 364 5630
Umbrella group for Turkish community organisations,
affiliated to national LAO forum, p146.   »95

✿ **Turkish Islamic Cultural Federation**
Burgemeester Slicherstraat 12, 2381 XJ Zoeterwonde
Religious, community welfare and social activities. »94

✿ **Turks Jongerenkomitee Voorst** (Turkish Youth Committee)
Van den Duyn Maesdamstraat 18, 7391 VM Twello »94

✿ **Turks Komitee Beverwijk**
Merwedestraat 26, 1946 TP Beverwijk »94

● **Turkse Arbeidersvereniging Nederland, HTIB** (Turkish
Workers' Society of the Netherlands)
Yücel Yildirim: 1. Wetering Plantsoen 20, 1017 SJ
Amsterdam; t (020) 622 1820
Member of EU Migrants Forum, p131; founded 1974;
immigration problems, unemployment, social conditions. »94

● **Turkse Vereniging, HTOB** (Turkish Association)
Kinderdijkstraat 102, II, 1079 GR Amsterdam »94

✿ ≡ [address uncertain] Postbus 21232, Rotterdam »94

● **Turkse Vrouwenvereniging Nederland, HTKB** (Association
of Turkish Women in the Netherlands)
Mavia Koronas: Mauritskade 22 D, 1091 DD Amsterdam;
t (020) 694 1854
Women's rights and welfare group founded 1978. »95

◎ **UNITED KINGDOM** 44

● **Anglo-Turkish Society**
43 Montrose Place, London SW1X 7DT
International friendship, study of Turkey, exchanges. »90

✿ **Association of Western Thrace Turks in London**
Erhan Imamoglu: [address uncertain] 4 Stuart House, Leroy
Street, London SE1; t (0171) 407 3713 »90

● **Britain Turkish Committee, BTC**
Mehmed Salaheddin Horoz: 27 Coniston Road, London N10
2BL; t (0181) 801 6712
Employment, welfare, social conditions; founded 1977. »94

● **Grey Wolves**
Aslan Aganoglu: [address unknown] Stoke Newington, London
Extreme right-wing nationalist movement. »95

✿ **Halkevi Turkish Community Centre**
Nafiz Bostanci/Olcay Aniker: 92-100 Stoke Newington Road,
London N16 7XB; t (0171) 275 8192, 275 8234
Mixed Kurdish and Turkish clientele. »95

✿ **Health Advocacy Services for Turkish and Kurdish
Speaking Communities**
Yildiz Biray: The Lawson Practice, St Leonards, Nuttall
Street, London N1 5LZ; t (0171) 613 5944
Counselling, group therapy and assistance in accessing
health care for refugees and migrants in Hackney. »95

● *Hürriyet*
M. Belge: 9 Maddox St, London W1; t (0171) 491 7597 »88

● **Ingiltere Türkiyeli Kibrisli Kadinla Birligi** (Union of Turkish
and Cypriot Women in England)
G. Erol, Chair: 110 Clarence Road, London E5 8JA;
t (0181) 986 1358 »94

✿ **Islington Turkish Cypriot and Turkish Elderly Group** and
Islington Turkish Women's Group
2 Newington Green Road, London N1; t (0171) 354 9661
Women's Group t 354 9895. »95

✿ **London Islamic Turkish Association**
16 Green Lanes, London N16 9ND; t (0181) 249 5417 »94

✿ **London Turkish Radio**
185b High Road, Wood Green, London N22 6BA »96

● *Milliyet*
Nuri Colakaglu, Editor: 16 South Close, London N6 5UQ
Newspaper. »88

✿ **Narool Islam Turkish Mosque**
99 Cobourg Road, off Old Kent Road, Peckham, London
SE5; t (0171) 703 0985 »94

✿ **Sussex Turkish Community**
Haji Hussain Omer: c/o Muslim Community Centre, 150
Dyke Road, Brighton BN1 5PA »94

✿ **Turkish Education Group**
2 Newington Green Road, London N1; t (0171) 226 8467,
249 8605 »96

✿ **Turkish and Kurdish Women's Group**
Manor Gardens Centre, 6-9 Manor Gardens, London N7
6LA; t (0171) 272 4231, f 263 0596 »95

✿ **Turkish Mosque**
9-15 Shacklewell Lane, London E8; t (0181) 249 9172
See also UK Islamic Trust, p72. »94

✿ ≡ 1a Clissold Road, off Albion Road, Newington Green,
London N16; t (0171) 241 5425 »94

● **Union of Turkish Progressives in Britain**
[address unknown] London
Associated with the *Isçinin Sesi* (Workers' Voice) wing of
the Turkish Communist Party, TKP. *Turkey Today*. »88

● **Union of Turkish Workers** and Committee for the Defence
of Democratic Rights in Turkey
A. Hassan: 84 Balls Pond Road, London N1 4AJ; t (0171)
923 1202, 254 0387
The Union is a member of the EU Migrants Forum, p131. »95

● **United Kingdom Turkish Islamic Association** and Azizia (or
Azizye) Mosque
Imam Ismail/Ahmet Ali: 117-119 Stoke Newington Road,
London N16; t (0171) 254 0046
Large mosque; welfare and advice service, women's and
youth groups, education, sports. »95

✿ **United Kingdom Turkish Islamic Centre**
212-216 Kingsland Road, London E2; t (0171) 739 6587 »95

✿ **United Kingdom Turkish Islamic Cultural Centre**
5 Hayling Close, London N16; t (0181) 254 0373 »94

TURKMEN; TURKMENISTANI

see Iraqi

UGANDAN

see also African, Asian, East African, Indian

◎ **DENMARK** 45

✿ **Ugandas Forening for Forældre og Rehabilitering**
Postboks 1853, 2300 København S »89

◎ **UNITED KINGDOM** 44

● **Association of Ugandan Youth and Students**
28 George Lane, London SE13 6HH »92

● **Uganda AIDS Action Fund, UAAF**
The Secretary: PO Box 62, London SE1 5AB
Provides education, prevention and support services in the
health field with particular reference to HIV and AIDS for
the African community in the UK. »95

✿ **Uganda Asylum Seekers Association**
Channelsea Business Centre, Canning Road, Abbey Lane,
London E15 3ND; t (0181) 519 0893
Refugee rights. »91

● **Uganda Community Relief Association**
Co-ordinator: Selby Centre, Selby Road, White Hart Lane,
London N17 8JN; t (0181) 808 6221, f 880 3988
Interests of Ugandan refugees and immigrants; five staff,
several volunteers. »94

● **Uganda Welfare Action Group**
NCRP, 170 Harold Road, Plaistow, London E13 0SE;
t (0181) 470 5541 »91

UKRAINIAN

see also East European, Slav

◎ **BELGIUM** 32

✿ **Narodniy Dim Oekraniens Cultureel Centrum** (People's
House Ukrainian Cultural Centre)
Torenlaan 96, 3600 Genk; t (089) 362568
Social and cultural centre. »94

✿ **Poltava—Oekrainse Volksdansgroep** (Poltava Ukrainian
Folk Dance Group)
Nieuwe Kempen 20, 3600 Genk
Ukrainian music, dance and culture. »94

◎ **GERMANY** 49

● **Zentralverband der Ukrainischer Emigration in Deutschland**
(Confederation of Ukrainian Emigrés in Germany)
[address unknown] 8000 München »90

◎ **ITALY** 39

● **Associazione di Amicizia Italia-Ucrania** (Italy-Ukraine
Friendship Association)
Hrihor Ovad: via Conteverde 58, 00185 Roma; t (06) 446
7676, f 678 1182
Social and cultural group; shares premises with Kashmiri,
Sri Lankan and other migrant groups. »94

◎ **SPAIN** 34

✿ **Ukrajinska Parochia** (Ukrainian Catholic Parish)
calle Donoso Cortés 63, Madrid; t (91) 243 0804 »90

UNITED KINGDOM 44

● **Association of Ukrainians in Great Britain, AUGB**
Head Office, 46 Linden Gardens, Notting Hill Gate, London
W2 4HG; *t* (0171) 229 8392
Also at Ukrainian Social Club, 154 Holland Park Avenue,
W11, *t* 603 0016. Welfare, culture; founded 1949. »95
✿ ≡ 170 Bower St, Bedford MK40; *t* (01234) 351928 »90
✿ ≡ 16 Cromwell Hill, Luton, Beds.; *t* (01582) 24835 »90
✿ ≡ 15 Little Church St, Rugby CV21; *t* (01788) 542810 »90
✿ **Manchester Ukrainian Association**
Bohdan Ratych: 31 Smedley Lane, Cheetham Hill,
Manchester M8 6XB; *t* (0161) 430 4391
Language, music, history, culture; aid to Ukraine. »93
● **Ukrainian Association of Great Britain**
5 Newton Grove, Leeds; *t* (0113) 262 0061, 262 1458 »90
✿ **Ukrainian Association and Social Club**
Leicester Causeway, Coventry CV1; *t* (01203) 225962 »90
✿ **Ukrainian Religious Society of St Sophia**
79 Holland Park, London W11; *t* (0171) 221 1890, 229
4419 »90
✿ **Ukrainian Social Club**
185 Buxton Road, Stockport SK2; *t* (0161) 483 7826 »95

UNITED STATES

see also Puerto Rican

◎ BELGIUM 32

✿ **American Lutheran Church of Brussels**
Avenue Salomé 7, 1150 Bruxelles »90
✿ **American Protestant Church**
Kattenberg 19, 1170 Bruxelles »90

◎ FRANCE 33

✿ **American Church**
65 quai d'Orsay, 75007 Paris; *t* (1) 4705 0799 »90
● **France-Louisiane**
17 quai Grenelle, 75015 Paris; *t* (1) 4577 0968 »90

◎ ITALY 39

✿ **Chiesa Americana** *(American Church)*
[address unknown] Roma »90

◎ SPAIN 34

● **Asociación Cultural Hispano-Norteamericano** *(Spanish
North American Cultural Association)*
calle San Bernardo 107, Madrid; *t* (91) 447 1900 »90
● **Comisión de Intercambio Cultural entre España y Estados
Unidos** *(Commission for Spanish-US Cultural Exchanges)*
paseo del Prado 28, Madrid; *t* (91) 420 0889 »90
✿ **North American Catholic Church**
avenida Alfonso XIII 165, Madrid; *t* (91) 250 8707 »90

◎ UNITED KINGDOM 44

✿ **American Church in London**
79 Tottenham Court Road, London W1P 9HB; *t* (0171) 580
2791 »95
● **American Indian Movement Committee**
6 Woodland Road, Birmingham B31 »90
✿ **American Women's Club Ltd**
68 Old Brompton Road, London SW7; *t* (0171) 589 8292 »95
● **Anglo-American Families Association Ltd**
V. Lancaster: 7 The Retreat, Wooton Wawen, Solihull »90
● **Fulbright Commission**
62 Doughty Street, London WC1N 2LS; *t* (0171) 405 4039,
f 404 6874
US-UK academic and cultural exchange programmes. »95

◎ NORTHERN IRELAND 44

✿ **Northern Ireland Indian American Society**
c/o NICEM, 17 Eblana Street, Belfast BT7 1LD »96

URDU

see also Asian, Indian, Islamic, Pakistani

◎ UNITED KINGDOM 44

✿ *Akhbar-e-Watan* (Land of Akbar the Great)
261 Hoe Street, London E17; *t* (0181) 521 6633, 521 6634
Magazine (52/yr). »88

● *Daily Jang* (Daily Battle)
Zahoor Niazi: 1 Sanctuary Street, London SE1 1ED;
t (0171) 403 4122 (?)
Newspaper. »95
✿ **Hove Urdu Speaking Group**
Abdul Khaliq: Portland Bakery, 174 Portland Road, Hove
BN3 5QN; *t* (01273) 329603 »94
● *The Khyber*
S.K. Hasan-Shah, Editor: 18 Winston Mount, Leeds LS6
3JY; *t* (0113) 278 3351
Magazine (12/yr). »88
● *Milap*
R. Soni, Editor: 307a North End Road, London W14 9NS;
t (0171) 385 8966
Journal (12/yr). See also Hindi *Navin Weekly*, p41. »88
✿ *Ravi* (The Sun)
Farida Sheikh, Editor: 123 Grattan Road, Bradford BD1
2JA; *t* (01274) 721227
Magazine (52/yr). »88
✿ **RNB Enterprises**
70 Queens Road, Walthamstow, London E17 8QP; *t* (0181)
521 6380
Urdu and Islamic bookshop. »94
● *Shafaq*
M. Malik, Editor: 37 Chichester Road, Edmonton, London
N9 9DL; *t* (0181) 803 5225
Magazine (12/yr). »88
✿ **Urdu Society Mosque**
Nasar Ullah Khan: 18 March Street, Burnley BB12 0BT »94

URUGUAYAN

see also Latin American, Spanish

◎ FRANCE 33

● **Association amitiés France Uruguay** *(France-Uruguay
Friendship Association)*
14 rue de Nanteuil, 75015 Paris; *t* (1) 4828 5617 »90

◎ SPAIN 34

● **Asociación de Amigos del Uruguay** *(Friends of Uruguay
Association)*
Diputació 215, 08011 Barcelona; *t* (93) 253 1903 »87
✿ **Asociación de Mujeres Uruguayas Lourdes Pintos, AMULP**
(Lourdes Pintos Uruguayan Women's Association)
Salvador del Mundo 3-2° B, 28025 Madrid; *t* (91) 525
4935, *f* 525 3927
International solidarity, welfare of migrant women. »95

◎ UNITED KINGDOM 44

● **British Uruguayan Society**
Jill Quaife, Secretary: Shreelane, Brooklands Road, Weybridge
KT13 0RJ; *t* (01932) 847455
Culture, friendship; founded 1945. *El Hornero* (4/yr). »90

VANIK; VEDIC

see Gujarati, Hindu

VENEZUELAN

see also Latin American, Spanish

◎ PORTUGAL 351

✿ **Centro Social Luso Venezolano**
Portela-Nogueira Regedoura, Porto; *t* (02) 764 0186 »94

VIETNAMESE

see also Asian, Chinese, South-East Asian

◎ AUSTRIA 43

● **Gesellschaft Österreich-Vietnam** *(Austria-Vietnam Society)*
E. Ringhoffer: Cottagegasse 21, 1180 Wien; *t* (01) 470
6887, *f* 360 5224
International solidarity, information on Vietnam. Founded
1975. *Viet Nam* (4/yr). »93

◎ BELGIUM *32*

• Comité International pour un Vietnam Libre, CIVIL
(International Committee for a Free Vietnam)
[address unknown] Bruxelles
Right-wing group. »88

◎ DENMARK *45*

✿ Foreningen af Vietnamesiske Flygtninge *(Association of Vietnamese Refugees)*
c/o Phung Ho: Æblets Kvarter 33, 2990 Nivå »90
✿ Hjemstavnsforeningen for Vietnamesere i Aalborg
Kastelvej 24, 9000 Aalborg »89
✿ Vietnamesisk Ungdomsforening i København *(Vietnamese Youth Society of Copenhagen)*
Taastrupgårdsvej 111, 1.tv., 2630 Taastrup; *t* 4252 6557 »89
✿ Den Vietnamesiske Buddhistiske Forening i Århus
(Vietnamese Buddhist Society of Aarhus)
Rosenhøj 18A, 2.th., 8260 Vilby 7, Jylland »94

◎ FRANCE *33*

• Association d'Amitié Franco-Vietnamienne *(Franco-Vietnamese Friendship Association)*
Charles Fourniau: 44 rue Alexis Lepere, 93100 Montreuil;
t (1) 4287 4434 »94
✿ Association d'Entraide des Vietnamiens d'Aix-Marseille,
AEVAM *(Aix-Marseilles Vietnamese Mutual Aid Association)*
Louis Tailhandier: 19 rue Peyssonnel, 13003 Marseille;
t 9108 9722, 9164 5732, *f* 9108 5940
Refugee welfare, advice. »94
• Association fraternité Viet Nam
18 rue Cardinal Lemoine, 75005 Paris; *t* (1) 4329 0427 »90
✿ Association Générale des Etudiants Vietnamiens de Paris
(General Association of Vietnamese Students in Paris)
51 rue Damesme, 75013 Paris; *t* (1) 4589 4279 »90
• Association Socio-Culturelle Franco-Vietnamienne
Joseph Mai Duc Vinh: 15 rue Boissonnade, 75014 Paris;
t (1) 4335 2072 »94
✿ Association des Vietnamiens libres de l'Aube *(Society of Free Vietnamese of the Aube Department)*
4 place de Soest, 10000 Troyes
Solidarity, traditions, culture and mutual contact among
Vietnamese refugees. »90
✿ Bibliothèque Dien-Hong
269 rue St Jacques, 75005 Paris; *t* (1) 4329 0415
Vietnamese library. »90
• Chien-Huu—Association pour la vulgarisation de la culture
vietnamienne *(Association for the Popularisation of Vietnamese Culture)*
Nguyen Huu Ich: 22 rue Nationale, 75013 Paris »89
• CID Vietnam Association
11 rue Pierre et Marie Curie, 75005 Paris; *t* (1) 4325 1495»90
✿ Comité des Laïcs Vietnamiens de la Diaspora *(Committee of Vietnamese Lay People of the Diaspora)*
Nguyen Dang Truc: 2 bis rue de las Bruche, 67116 Reichstett-
Strasbourg; *t* 8820 5822, 8820 3177, *f* 8820 1334
Cultural/welfare group for refugees. *Dinh Huong* (4/yr). »94
• Enfants du Mékong *(Children of the Mekong)*
5 rue de la Comète, 92600 Ansières; *t* (1) 4794 0084,
f 4733 4044
Advice and assistance to migrants from Vietnam and
Cambodia in France; short-term aid, and longer-term
development projects assisting returned refugees in both
countries, and children in Laos and Thailand. *Enfants du Mékong* (4/yr). »93
✿ Entraide franco-vietnamienne *(Franco-Vietnamese Mutual Aid)*
40 rue des Neuf-Arpents, 95400 Villiers-le-Bel
Dance, music, traditional festivals, cultural exchanges. »90
• Union Générale des Vietnamiens de France, UGVF
Lam Ba Chau: 16 rue du Petit Musc, 75004 Paris; *t* (1) 4272 3944, *f* 4277 7348
Doan ket (6/yr). »94
✿ Union Générale des Vietnamiens du Rhône
38 rue Sainte Geneviève, 69006 Lyon; *t* 7852 4630
Thing Tin. »94

◎ GERMANY *49*

✿ Deutsch-Vietnamesische Freundschaftskreis Reistrommel
(Rice Drum German-Vietnamese Friendship Association)
[address unknown]
Campaigns against proposals to involuntarily repatriate the
approximately 40,000 Vietnamese in Germany, mainly migrant
workers. »95

• Verein der Vietnamesischen Flüchtlinge *(Union of Vietnamese Refugees)*
Bachmanstr. 2-4, 60488 Frankfurt am Main; *t* (069) 252326»94
✿ ≡ Bei der Hofen 21, 2000 Hamburg 70; *t* (040) 654 6924»90

◎ IRELAND *353*

• Vietnamese Irish Association
Sarah Kenny, Administrator: 45 Hardwicke Street, Dublin 1;
t (01) 874 2331
Voluntary group assisting in resettlement of Vietnamese
quota refugees; premises also used by Bosnian refugees. »95

◎ ITALY *39*

✿ Chiesa Vietnamita
c/o Pontificio Collegio S. Paolo, via di Torre Rossa 40, 00165
Roma; *t* (06) 622 8004
Catholic church. »90
✿ Comunità Vietnamita
viale Molise 52, 20137 Milano; *t* (02) 5318 5410
May be same as that listed (1990) at piazza A. Fuzina 1,
20133 Milano, *t* 742 7965. »94
• Co-ordination Office for the Vietnamese in the Diaspora
Philip Tran Van Hoai: via Monte del Gallo 60/2, 00165
Roma; *t* (06) 638 1221
Cultural and advice service. »94

◎ LUXEMBOURG *352*

• Association d'aide aux réfugiés vietnamiens au Luxembourg,
AREL *(Association for Aid to Vietnamese Refugees)*
BP 1337, Luxembourg
Many types of assistance on arrival, and in settlement and
integration, to quota refugees from South-East Asia; works
with Croix Rouge Luxembourgeoise, p207. »90

◎ UNITED KINGDOM *44*

✿ An Viet Housing Association Ltd
12-14 Englefield Road, London N1 4LS; *t* (0171) 328 9777,
275 7780, 275 7521, *f* 275 8510
Small housing association for South-East Asian people; 100
properties in London, Northampton and Southampton; works
in partnership with Ujima Housing Association, p158. »95
✿ Avon Vietnamese Refugee Community
c/o BBVS DU, The Inkworks, 20-22 Hepburn Road, St Pauls,
Bristol BS2 8UD; *t* (0117) 942 3960 »96
• Boat People Home Trust
Rev. R.A. Lindley, Chairman: Rectory, Beckingham Road,
Guildford GU2 6BU; *t* (01483) 504228
Small charity founded 1980, supporting Vietnamese
immigrants. »90
✿ Community of Refugees from Vietnam
West Library, Bridgeman Road, London N1; *t* (0171) 607
6271 »90
✿ Leeds Vietnamese Community Association
53 Louis Street, Leeds, Yorkshire; *t* (0113) 262 2389 »90
✿ Manchester Vietnamese Community Association, MVCA
Woodville Resource Centre, Shirley Road, Cheetham,
Manchester M8 7NE; *t* (0161) 740 7899
Refugee settlement assistance; welfare, education, training
and employment advice; culture; language classes. »93
✿ Manchester Vietnamese Housing Project
Hoi Dong: Woodville Resource Centre, Shirley Road,
Cheetham, Manchester M8 7NE; *t* (0161) 740 6710
Development of housing provision for Vietnamese refugees;
housing advice and representation, translation, interpreting
services. »93
✿ Manchester Vietnamese Interpreters Group
My Tu Phung/Minh Bui: Woodville Resource Centre, Shirley
Road, Cheetham, Manchester M8 7NE; *t* (0161) 740 6711
Interpreting and translation services to statutory sector. »93
✿ Midlands Vietnamese Community Association, MVCA
The Secretary: 8 Charleville Road, Birmingham B19 1DA;
t (0121) 554 9685
A charity developing employment opportunities, training and
community services for local Vietnamese people. Luncheon
club for elderly, welfare advice. Part-funded by Birmingham
City Council. »94
✿ New Life Women's Group
Evette Phan/Gillian Wilson: Woodville Resource Centre,
Shirley Road, Cheetham, Manchester M8 7NE; *t* (0161) 720
7150, 740 6705
Welfare of refugee women, and women with Vietnamese
partners; adult education, language classes, playgroup, social
and cultural events. »93

❖ **Optimum Health Services NHS Trust Deptford Vietnamese Community Project**
Louise Upton/Mary Gosden: Elizabeth Blackwell House, Wardall's Grove, Avonley Road, London SE14 5ER; *t* (0181) 691 4621
Social services and health service partnership, employing a specialist worker to facilitate access to health services.   »95

❖ **Refugee Action**
Minh Bui/Gillian Wilson: Woodville Resource Centre, Shirley Road, Cheetham, Manchester M8 7NE; *t* (0161) 740 6711, 740 6705
See also national Refugee Action, p157. Training/employment issues, community development, liaison with public sector.»93

❖ **South Wales Vietnamese Community**
Kim Le Riding: 8 Williams Court, Trade Street, Cardiff CF1 5DQ, Wales; *t* (01222) 220181, *f* 229339   »93

❖ **Southwark Vietnamese/Chinese Refugee Community**
Thomas Calton Centre, Alpha Street, London SE15; *t* (0171) 635 0022   »90

● **Vietnam Refugee National Council**
St Mary's Hall, Whiston Road, London E2 8BN; *t* (0171) 613 0819
Also listed (1990) as North Peckham Estate Community Hall, Hordle Promenade East, SE15 6JB, *t* 703 0036; or 11 Walkford Way, North Peckham Estate, SE15, *t* 708 5175. »94

❖ **Vietnamese Assistance Service**
Vietnamese Club, 3 Ravensdale Gardens, London SE19 3QD; *t* (0181) 771 5199   »90

● **Vietnamese Catholic Association**
130 Poplar High Street, London E14 0AG; *t* (0171) 537 3071, (0181) 852 8056, *f* (0171) 537 3071
Also listed (1990) c/o St James' Church, 45 Elm Grove, SE15, *t* 732 2587. Catholic pastoral care.   »94

❖ **Vietnamese Cultural Association**
Toan P. Nguyen/T.V. Tran: 165 Elvate Crescent, Cheetham Hill, Manchester M8; *t* (0161) 834 0335, 205 9619
Cultural events, Vietnamese language classes.   »93

❖ **Vietnamese Elderly People's Club**
Lan Kin Bui: Woodville Resource Centre, Shirley Road, Cheetham, Manchester M8 7NE; *t* (0161) 740 3134 ext. 224
Luncheon club, social and cultural activities, liaison with housing, social and health services.   »93
Vietnamese Refugee Children and Young People's Project: see Save the Children, p227

VINCENTIAN

see also African Caribbean, Afro-Caribbean, Anglo-Caribbean, Caribbean, West Indian

◎ **UNITED KINGDOM 44**

● **St Vincent and the Grenadines Association**
Sandra Samuel, Secretary: 40 Westernville Gardens, Ilford IG2 6AL   »91

WEST AFRICAN

see also African, Beninese, Burkinabe, Cameroon, Cape Verdean, Gabonese, Ghanaian, Guinea Bissau, Guinean, Ivorian, Liberian, Malian, Mauritanian, Nigerian, Saharan, São Tomé, Senegalese, Sierra Leonean, Togolese

◎ **UNITED KINGDOM 44**

❖ **West African Senior Citizens Centre**
315 White Hart Lane, London N17; *t* (0181) 808 9213   »95

❖ **West African Welfare Association**
Mark Mdego: 98 Craven Park, London NW10 8QE; *t* (0181) 453 0299   »95

WEST INDIAN

see also African, African Caribbean, Afro-Caribbean, Anglo-Caribbean, Antillean, Black, Caribbean, Dominican, French: DOM/TOM, Grenadian, Guadeloupean, Guyanese, Jamaican, Kittitian, Montserrat, Puerto Rican, Surinamese, Trinidadian and Tobagan, Vincentian

◎ **UNITED KINGDOM 44**

❖ **Bedford West Indian Club**
2 Woburn Rd, Bedford MK40, Beds.; *t* (01234) 352298   »90

❖ **Coventry West Indian Community Association**
Community Centre, Spon Street, Coventry, Warwickshire; *t* (01203) 552929, 225967   »90

❖ **Derby West Indian Community Association, DWICA**
George Mighty: Carrington Street, Derby DE1 2ND; *t* (01332) 371529, 347427   »94

❖ **Rookery Road West Indian Youth Club**
49 Halewell Road, Edgbaston, Birmingham B16   »90

❖ **Telford West Indian Association**
Gerry Brown, Chairman: [address unknown] Telford   »91

❖ **West Indian Community Centre**
Ian Charles, Secretary: 10 Laycock Place, Leeds LS7 3HS; *t* (0113) 262 9465, 262 9496   »94

● *West Indian Digest*: Hansib Publishing Ltd
Ken Campbell, Editor: Tower House, 3rd floor, 139-149 Fonthill Road, London N4 3HF; *t* (0171) 281 1911
Magazine (12/yr).   »88

● **West Indian Ex-Servicemen's and Women's Association (UK)**
Laurent Philpotts, PR Officer: 165-167 Clapham Manor St, London SW4 6DB
Represents the interests of Caribbean ex-members of British and home forces.   »95

● **West Indian Family Counselling Service**
Chapeltown Road, Leeds LS7; *t* (0113) 262 5131   »90

● **West Indian Family and Educational Council**
195 Bevington Road, Aston, Birmingham B6   »90

● **West Indian League**
22 Linden Grove, London SE15 3LF; *t* (0171) 277 8313   »95

❖ **West Indian Organisation Co-ordinating Committee**
L. Smith: West Indian Centre, Carmoor Road, Chorlton-on-Medlock, Manchester M13 0FB; *t* (0161) 257 2092
Youth club, services for elderly; immigration, employment, welfare advice/representation, liaison with other agencies.»93

❖ **West Indian Progressive Association**
295 Wharfedale Road, Birmingham B27   »90

❖ **West Indian Sports Club and Community Centre**
Aston Douglas/Berry Edwards: Westwood Street, Moss Side, Manchester M14 4SW; *t* (0161) 226 7236
Immigration and nationality, legal and welfare advice and information; social and sporting activities; youth activities.»93

❖ **West Indian Sports and Social Club**
West Indian Centre, Carmoor Road, Longsight, Manchester M13   »90

♦ **West Indian Standing Conference, WISC**
William I. Trant: 5 Westminster Bridge Road, London SE1 7XW; *t* (0171) 928 7861-62, *f* 928 0343
Represented in EU Migrants Forum, p131.   »94

WESTERN SAHARA

see Saharan/Sahrawi

YEMENI

see also Arab/Arabic, Islamic, Middle Eastern

◎ **UNITED KINGDOM 44**

❖ **Yemeni Community Association**
[address unknown] Sheffield, Yorkshire   »88

❖ **Yemeni Workers' Association**
c/o Sparkbrook Association, Farm Road, Birmingham B11 »90

YUGOSLAV (and Former Yugoslav Republics)

Older entries in this section are likely to be out of date; where ex-Yugoslav groups have become identified with a particular republic, they are listed under the relevant heading: see also Bosnian, Croatian, East European, Macedonian, Serbian, Slav, Slovene, South-East European

◎ **DENMARK 45**

❖ **Jugoslaviske Forening** *(Yugoslavian Association)*
Jasna Ravn: Brondby Nord Vej 237-2, 2610 Rødovre   »90

● **Jugoslaviske Forening i Danmark** *(Yugoslav Society in Denmark)*
Vlado Rajovic: Kornevænget 15, st., 2750 Ballerup   »90

● ≡ Boris Keseric: Hørsevænget 35, 2.tv., 3400 Hillerød   »89

❖ **Jugoslaviske Forening Dzemal Bijedic**
Drasko Rajovic: Jyllingevej 90, 2720 Vanløse   »89

✷ Den Jugoslaviske Forening Edward Kardelj
Lundegade 5, 3000 Helsingør   »94
✷ Jugoslaviske Forening Liria
Haran Musilo: Sennepshaven 60, 1.th., 2730 Herlev   »89
✷ Jugoslaviske Forening Prespa
Frederikssundsvej 34, butik 5, 2400 København NV;
t 3110 5949   »89
✷ Jugoslaviske Klub Besa
Ravnsborggade 19, 1., 2200 København N   »89
✷ Den Jugoslaviske Klub Branko Copic
Krudtværsksaleen 10, 3300 Frederiksværk; t 4212 3742
Founded 1984; culture, leisure, welfare.   »94
✷ Den Jugoslaviske Klub Djerdap
Grønnegade 10, 4700 Næstved   »89
✷ Den Jugoslaviske Klub Ivo Lolo Ribar
Ivan Tufekovic: Engvej 3 A, 2680 Solrød Strand   »89
✷ Jugoslaviske Klub Kadinjaca
Postbox 66, 5100 Odense C   »89
✷ Den Jugoslaviske Klub Timok
Skansevej 15, 3400 Hillerød   »94
✷ Jugoslaviske Klub Veljko Vlahovic
Præstevænget 16, 2750 Ballerup, København   »90
✷ Den Jugoslaviske Kvindeklub Nada Dimic (Nada Dimic
Yugoslavian Women's Club)
Beba Jovic: Peder Skramsvej 16, st.th., 3000 Helsingør;
t 4921 7938   »89
✷ Klub 70 Jugoslaviske Klub
Goran Milanovic: [address uncertain] c/o Enghavevej 8-2,
8600 Silkeborg
Also listed (1989) c/o Stanimir Jovanovic, Daltoften 32, or
c/o Obrad Malbasic, Resedavej 29, 1 th., t 8681 3239.   »90
✷ Mødregruppen for Jugoslaviske Kvinder (Yugoslavian
Mothers' Group)
Sundhedsplejerskerne, Legeteket, Strandvejen 25 A, 3300
Frederiksværk; t 4212 1029
Health and welfare.   »89

◎ FRANCE 33

✷ Amicale des Yougoslaves de Paris, Club Kostana
(Yugoslavian Society of Paris, Kostana Club)
72 bis rue Philippe-de-Girard, 75018 Paris
Social, folk music.   »89
✷ Association des Jeunes Yougoslaves (Association of
Yugoslavian Youth)
386-392 avenue de la Division Leclerc, 92290 Chatenay
Malabry   »90
✷ Association yougoslave Trepca
12 rue Pierre Levée, 75011 Paris; t (1) 4338 6391   »90
✷ Centre Culturel Yougoslave (Yugoslav Cultural Centre)
123 rue St Martin, 75003 Paris; t (1) 4272 5050   »90
✷ Club Yougoslave Bratstvo-Jedinstvo
Mairie, 89100 Sens   »89
● Union des Clubs et Associations Yougoslaves
12 rue de Pierre Levée, 75011 Paris; t (1) 4338 6397(91?)»90

◎ GERMANY 49

✷ Gemeinschaft der Vereine Jugoslawischer Bürger e.V.
(Union of Yugoslavian Citizen's Associations)
Postfach 160328, 6000 Frankfurt am Main; t (069)
490500   »90
✷ Kulturno-Umetnicko Drustvo Boro i Ramiz, KUD: Kultur-
Künstlerische Gesellschaft Boro i Ramiz (Boro i Ramiz
Cultural and Artistic Society)
Mischa Pepaz: Alt-Moabit 43, 1000 Berlin 21; t (030) 392
8043
Cultural and social club.   »90
✷ Sozialdienst für Mitbürger aus dem ehemaligen Jugoslawien
(Welfare Service for Citizens of Former Yugoslavia)
Am Rinkenpuhl 12, 50676 Köln; t (0221) 201 9266   »94
✷ Verein der Jugoslawischen Bürger (Union of Yugoslavian
Citizens)
Alt-Moabit 105, 1000 Berlin; t (030) 392 1091   »90
✷ Zentrum der Jugoslawen in München (Munich Yugoslavian
Centre)
Schwantalerstraße 80, 8000 München; t (089) 536636   »90

◎ ITALY 39

✷ Comunità Jugoslava (Yugoslav Community)
c/o via Flaminina 1612, 00188 Roma; t (06) 691 2742   »94

◎ LUXEMBOURG 352

✷ Association Jugoslavija
154 rue de Treves, 2630 Luxembourg; t 431046   »95

✷ Association des Yougoslaves de Wiltz
12 avenue de la Gare, 9540 Wiltz   »94

◎ NETHERLANDS 31

● Federatie Joegoslavische Verenigingen (Federation of
Yugoslavian Associations)
Bemuurdeweerd wz 4, 3513 BH Utrecht
Rights of migrant workers.   »94
✷ Joegoslavisch Komitee
Verschuur 11, 4878 AB Etten-Leur   »94

◎ UNITED KINGDOM 44

● British Yugoslav Society
John Burns, Honorary Secretary: 121 Marsham Street,
London SW1P 4LX; t (0171) 828 2762
Friendship, culture, languages; founded 1949.   »90
✷ Lifeline
J.B. Louveaux: 7 Carlton Gardens, London SW1Y 5AE
Small charity sending humanitarian aid to ex-Yugoslavia.   »94
● Women's Aid to Former Yugoslavia
20 Tennyson Road, Southampton SO17 2GW
Solidarity and material aid for women in ex-Yugoslavia.   »94
✷ Yugoslav Royal Draza Mihailovic Association
3 Ladbroke Gardens, London W11; t (0171) 727 9780   »95
● Yugoslav Studies Research Group, University of Bradford
John Allcock: European Studies Department, Richmond Rd,
Bradford BD7 1DP; t (01274) 733466 ext. 3993, f 305340
Social science perspectives on current affairs in former
Yugoslavia; network of contacts with academic institutions in
the region; services Yugoslav Information Unit, which deals
with media, business, political and educational queries.
Significant library holdings.   »91

ZAIREAN

see also African, Central African, Southern African

◎ BELGIUM 32

● Comité Zaïre
BP 51, 1050 Bruxelles   »93
● Zaire Digest
Sicotrad SC, Rue de l'Abbaye 109, 1050 Bruxelles; t (02) 346
1281, f 346 2387
News magazine (6/yr).   »95

◎ FRANCE 33

✷ Association des femmes zaïroises de l'Isère pour l'entraide
et l'animation culturelle, AFEZIECA (Isère Mutual Aid and
Cultural Society of Zairean Women)
1 rue Belledonne, 38400 Saint-Martin-d'Hères
Mutual assistance, culture, development aid.   »89
● Association France-Zaïre
33 boulevard Pasteur, 75015 Paris; t (1) 4566 6997   »90
✷ Association zaïroise de Lille (Lille Zairean Association)
[address unknown] Lille   »90
● Communauté Zaïroise de France (Zairean Community of
France)
3 rue de Ménilmontant, 75020 Paris; t (1) 4636 3719   »90

◎ ITALY 39

● Association des Médecins Zaïrois de Formation Italienne,
AMEZAFI (Association of Italian-Trained Zairean Doctors)
M.Z. Nyamowala: via A. Tebaldi 25, int. 8, 00168 Roma;
t (06) 3550 1460
Information, social activities. Communications (12/yr),
Journal AMEZAFI (4/yr).   »94
✷ Associazione Studenti Zairesi (Association of Zairean
Students)
Kalongo Tshimanga: via del Circo Massimo 7, 00153 Roma;
t (06) 574 2993-97   »94
✷ Associazione Zairese in Italia, AZI
via U. Grosso 34, 00100 Roma; t (06) 569 5657   »94
✷ Associazione dei Zairesi in Toscana di Firenze e Province,
AZAT
Tshikalandanda Kambanj: via della Chiesa 21, 50041
Settimello; t (055) 887 7213   »94
✷ Comunità Zairese in Piemonte (Zairean Community of
Piedmont)
Wilondja Lunanga: piazza Emanuele Filiberto 4, 10122
Torino; t (011) 436 3298
Presumably same as that listed (1990) at via C. Lorenzini
39, 18147 Torino.   »94

◉ UNITED KINGDOM *44*

• **Communauté des Réfugiés Zaïrois en Grande Bretagne,**
COREZAG *(Community of Zairean Refugees in Great Britain)*
M.C. Kukwikila, Chairperson: 728 Romford Road, London
E12 6BT; *t* (0181) 514 5657 ext. 110, 478 2337
Refugee welfare, asylum rights.   »95
✿ **ZAIRAG**
46 Crouch Hall Court, Sparsholt Road, London N19; *t* (0171)
281 2376
Mainly asylum-seekers.   »91
✿ **Zairean Community Association, ZACA**
Selby Centre, Selby Road, Tottenham, London N17; *t* (0181)
365 1665   »95

ZANZIBARI

see Tanzanian

ZIGEUNER; ZINGARO

see Gypsy, Romany, Traveller

ZIMBABWEAN

see also African, Southern African

◉ UNITED KINGDOM *44*

• **Britain Zimbabwe Society,** also known as British Zimbabwe
Society
Marieke Faber Clarke: 5a Crick Road, Oxford OX2 6OJ
International friendship and solidarity. Support for democracy
and self-determination in Southern Africa.   »94
• **Committee for Justice in Zimbabwe**
H. Stanton: 100 Oakfield Road, Birmingham B12   »90
✿ **Zimbabwe Society**
Conway Mothobi: 45 Brighton Grove, Birch-in-Rusholme,
Rusholme, Manchester M14 5JG
Social, cultural, welfare and information group for
Zimbabweans in Greater Manchester.   »93

ZOROASTRIAN

see Indian, Iranian

Part Two

Support and Service Organisations

The Support and Service Organisations category covers bodies, almost all voluntary sector (non-governmental) organisations, which support, serve, advise or defend migrants, refugees or ethnic minorities of more than one ethnic origin. It includes, for example, umbrella organisations for minority community groups; refugee welfare and resettlement services; immigration advice agencies; and community groups in ethnic minority neighbourhoods which are not identified with one particular minority.

AUSTRIA 43

♦ **Asylkoordination Österreich** *(Austrian Asylum Co-ordination)*
Herbert Langthaler: Trattnerhof 2/14, 1010 Wien; *t/f* (01) 532 1291
Also listed (1995) c/o ÖIE, Tuchlau 8/16, *t* 533 3755-12, *f* 533 3755-21. Lobbying/information network of migrant and refugee welfare, anti-racist and other NGOs, formed 1991.»95
✿ ≡ Regionalbüro West (Western Regional Bureau): Graben 22, 4690 Schwanenstadt; *t* (07673) 4868, *f* 4823   »94
✿ **Beratungsstelle für Migrant/innen** *(Migrant Information Centre*; also known as Beratungs*zentrum* für Migrant/innen)
Am Modenapark 6/8, 1030 Wien; *t* (01) 712 5604, *f* 712 5607
Advice, information, anti-racist work.   »95
● **Deserteursberatung** *(Deserters' Advice Centre)*
Schottengasse 3a-1/59, 1010 Wien; *t* (01) 535 9109
Counselling and support to deserters and conscientious objectors.   »94
♦ **European Legal Network on Asylum, ELENA**
Dr Ulrike Brandl, Co-ordinator: University of Salzburg, Department of International Law, Churfürststrasse 1, 5020 Salzburg; *t* (0662) 8044 3652, *f* 848738
National contact for asylum lawyers' network, p154.   »95
✿ **Flüchtlingsbeauftragte der Stadt Graz** *(Graz Municipal Commissioner for Refugees)*
Schmiedgasse 26, 8010 Graz; *t* (0316) 872 3075, *f* 872 3029   »95
♦ **Flüchtlingsbetreuung der Evangelischen Kirche in Österreich** *(Refugee Care Service of the Austrian Protestant Churches*; also known as Flüchtlings*beratung* der EK in Ö)
Dr Gertrude Hennefeld: Otto-Glöckl-Strasse 16, 2514 Traiskirchen; *t* (02252) 57426, 53557   »95
♦ **Fonds zur Integration von Flüchtlingen** *(Refugee Integration Fund)*
Dr Karin Konig: Bräunerstrasse 5, 1010 Wien; *t* (01) 53216-5588, *f* 53126-5595   »95
♦ **Helping Hands—Koordinationsbüro für Flüchtlingshilfe** *(Co-ordination Bureau for Refugee Assistance)*
Liechtensteinstrasse 13, 1090 Wien; *t* (01) 3108 88010, *f* 3108 88037
Practical assistance to refugees; anti-racist work.   »94
✿ **Romano Centro**
Schneidergasse 15, 1110 Wien; *t/f* (01) 749 6336   »94
✿ **SOS-Arbeitskreis** *(SOS Working Group)*
Republikanischer Klub Neues Österreich, Rockgasse 1, 1010 Wien; *t* (01) 535 9962, *f* 535 9963
Anti-racism, anti-fascism, promotion of equality of opportunity in employment and other fields.   »94
♦ **SOS Mitmensch** *(SOS Fellowship)*
Münzwardeingasse 2/2, 1060 Wien; *t* (01) 586 0132, *f* 586 0131
Anti-racism, support to migrants and refugees.   »94
✿ **Verband für Ausländerhilfe in Kärnten und Osttirol** *(League for Aid to Foreigners in Carinthia and East Tyrol)*
Italienerstrasse 28, 9500 Villach; *t* (04242) 218441   »95

✿ **Verein ISOP—Flüchtlingsbetreuung, ISOP** *(ISOP Refugee Care Service)*
Pestalozzistrasse 3/pt, 8010 Graz; *t* (0316) 817828   »94
● **Verein Zebra** *(Zebra Union)* and Zebra Zentrum zur sozial-medizinischen, rechtlichen und kulturellen Betreuung von Ausländer/innen in Österreich *(Zebra Centre for Medico-Social, Legal Rights and Cultural Support to Foreigners in Austria)*
Daniela Stöcklmair/W. Gulis: Pestalozzistrasse 59/II, 8010 Graz; *t* (0316) 835630, *f* 815339
Practical assistance (housing, employment, rights advice, therapy and medical services) to displaced persons and refugees in Austria, solidarity, anti-racism; founded 1986.»95
● **Zentralstelle für Asylanten- und Flüchtlingsbetreuung** *(Centre for Asylum Seeker and Refugee Welfare)*
Lusthandlgasse 52, 1060 Wien; *t* (01) 319 9441, *f* 319 9445   »95

BELGIUM 32

✿ **Accueil et Promotion des Immigrés** *(Reception and Advancement of Immigrants)*
Jean-Marie Georgery: Rue Léon Bernus 35, 6000 Charleroi; *t* (071) 313370
Legal advice to refugees and migrants.   »94
✿ **Accueil et Promotion au Service des Immigrés** *(Reception and Advancement Service for Immigrants)*
Place du Chef-Lieu 11, 6040 Jumet; *t* 355773   »90
● **Action Immigrées—Vie Féminine, Mouvement Chrétien d'Action Culturelle et Sociale** *(Immigrant Action—Women's Life, Christian Cultural and Social Action Movement)*
Marisa Fella/Mary Malevej: Rue de la Poste 111, 1210 Bruxelles; *t* (02) 217 2952, *f* 223 0442
International and intercultural solidarity among women; immigrant women's employment, education, training issues; aid to refugee and other women in developing countries. *Vie Féminine* (12/yr); *Informer pour Agir* (6/yr).   »94
✿ **Action Immigrés** *(Immigrants Action)*
Alain Mensier: Foyer Culturel d'Amay, Rue aux Chevaux 7, 4540 Ampsin, Amay; *t* (085) 312446
Advice, employment assistance, culture.   »94
▌ **Agenor**: Dialogue for European Alternatives Network
Rue de Toulouse 22, 1040 Bruxelles; *t* (02) 304777 (?)
Network developing socialist perspectives on European integration issues, including migration and minority rights. *Agenor* bulletin (irregular).   »95
● **Aide aux personnes déplacées, APD** *(Aid to Displaced Persons)* Head Office
Catherine Noël, General Secretary: Rue du Marché 35, 4500 Huy; *t* (085) 213481, *f* 230147
Support and legal advice to refugees and asylum seekers. For Flemish counterpart see Hulpverlening aan ontheemden, p131; member of CBAR, p130, and of COLARCH, p28; activities include sponsorship of refugee children abroad, and settlement or repatriation assistance especially for refugees in Liège province. Founded 1950, 25 staff. *Réfugiés d'hier/ Réfugiés d'aujourd'hui*.   »95

✧ **Aide aux personnes déplacées**, APD
Rue Père Damien 14, 7090 Braine-le-Comte; *t* (067)
555967, *f* 554416   »95
✧ **Alternatief** *(Alternative)*
Sonja Bylois: Runkstersteenweg 134, 3500 Hasselt; *t* (011)
273713
Advice, training, employment.   »94
● **Amitiés Belgo-Immigrées** *(Belgian-Immigrant Friendship)*
St-Gilles Midi: Rue de la Prague 47, 1060 Bruxelles; *t* (02)
539 2283   »90
♦ **Association de Défense des Droits des Etrangers**, ADDE
(Association for the Defence of Foreigners' Rights) also
known as Association pour le droit des étrangers
François Bienfait: Avenue de Stalingrad 24, 1000 Bruxelles;
t (02) 511 9517, 511 7957, *f* 513 8228
Anti-racism, legal advice, campaigning and documentation
centre. See also Centre Bruxellois d'Action Interculturelle,
p231. *Revue du Droit des Etrangers* (5/yr).   »95
● **Association de Femmes Belges et Immigrées Nadi** *(Nadi
Association of Belgian and Immigrant Women)*
Pascale Desrumaux, Co-ordinator: Rue du Danemark 19,
St-Gilles, 1060 Bruxelles; *t* (02) 537 8365
Intercultural solidarity among women.   »94
● **Association Pédagogique d'Accueil aux Jeunes Immigrés**,
APAJI *(Educational Reception Association for Young
Immigrants)*
Aubry: Chaussée de Haecht 146, 1030 Bruxelles; *t* (02)
216 6408
Youth integration, education, training; research and
documentation.   »94
✧ **Bruxelles Accueil—Porte Ouverte**, BA-PO *(Open Door
Reception Brussels)*
Marie-Paule Moreau: Rue de Tabora 6, 1000 Bruxelles;
t (02) 511 2715, 511 8178, *f* 502 7696
Refugee solidarity, humanitarian aid.   »94
▌ **Caritas Europa**: Euro-Caritas
Rue de Pascal 4-6, 1040 Bruxelles
Solidarity with migrants, Catholic social action, information.
See also Secours international de Caritas Catholica, p192.»94
✧ **Centre d'Alphabétisation pour Travailleurs Immigrés**, CATI
(Literacy Centre for Immigrant Workers)
Anne-Marie Lotin: Rue Potagère 157, 1030 Bruxelles;
t (02) 384 0994
Adult and youth education, information, socio-economic
integration. See also Le Piment, p232.   »94
✧ **Centre d'Education Permanente et des Loisirs des Immigrés
de Burenville** *(Burenville Immigrants' Adult Education and
Leisure Centre)*
Avenue G. Truffaut 30/53, 4000 Liège   »90
✧ **Centre Familial Belgo-Immigrés** *(Belgian-Immigrant Family
Centre)*
Rachida el Idrissi: Rue de l'Eglise 59, 1060 Bruxelles; *t* (02)
537 2800
Education/training, youth integration; mainly Arab clients. »94
✧ **Centre de Formation des Etangs Noirs** *(Etangs Noirs
Training Centre)* Service Social des Etrangers
Jak Pjetri: SSE, Rue des Etangs Noirs 85, 1080 Bruxelles;
t (02) 426 8912
Advice, education, training, culture.   »94
✧ **Centre d'Immigration de Charleroi**, CIC *(Charleroi
Immigrants Centre)*
Drossia Bouras: Rue Zenobe Gramme 57, 6000 Charleroi;
t (071) 324527
Welfare advice, social/cultural work, youth integration. »94
✧ **Centre des Immigrés** *(Immigrant Centre)*
Rue des Blenets 7, 6900 Marche en Famenne
Social centre, advice, housing.   »94
✧ **Centre des Immigrés Namur-Luxembourg** *(Namur-
Luxembourg Immigrant Centre)*
Rue du Beffroi 15, 5000 Namur; *t* (081) 224286
Information, advice, social activities.   »95
♦ **Centre d'Initiation pour Réfugiés et Etrangers**, CIRE
(Refugee and Foreigner Settlement Centre) Head Office
Veronique Semoulin: Chaussée de Wavre 205, 1050
Bruxelles; *t* (02) 644 1717, *f* 646 8591
Umbrella group for agencies assisting refugees in the
Communauté française (Francophone community); integration
assistance, mainly language courses. Flemish counterpart is
OCIV, p131. *Répertoire/Guide*.   »95
✧ ≡ Ecole/School: Rue de Dublin 9, 1050 Bruxelles; *t* (02)
512 3951   »90
✧ **Centre International pour Etudiants Etrangers**, CIEE
(International Centre for Foreign Students)
Rue Wallons 16, 1348 Louvain-la-Neuve; *t* (010) 450251
Integration of foreign students.   »94

✧ **Centre Mouvement Ouvrier Chrétien de Charleroi**, CIEP
(Charleroi Christian Workers Movement Centre)
Philippe Pepin: Boulevard Tirou 167, 6000 Charleroi;
t (071) 312256, *f* 320376
Information, employment, training advice.   »94
● **Centre social protestant—Service oecuménique auprès
des réfugiés** *(Protestant Social Centre, Ecumenical Refugee
Service)* Protestants sociaal centrum, Oecumenische
vluchtelingendienst
Rue Cans 12, 1050 Bruxelles; *t* (02) 513 5182
Main Protestant refugee assistance agency; member of CIRE,
left, and CBAR, below.   »95
✧ **Centre Socio-Culturel des Immigrés de la Province de
Namur**, CSCIN
André Chapotte: Rue Dr Haibe 2, 5002 St Servais-Namur;
t (081) 737176, 730441
Training, health, welfare, employment, cultural and leisure
activities. *Horizons 2000*.   »94
✧ **Centrum voor Buitenlandse Arbeidersgezinnen vzw**,
CEBAG: Centre pour Familles des Travailleurs Etrangers
(Centre for Foreign Workers' Families)
Andrea Meire: Waarlooshofstraat 5, 2020 Antwerpen;
t (03) 238 3267
Culture, education, training and employment advice.   »94
✧ **Centrum Buitenlandse Werknemers vzw**, CBW: Centre
pour Travailleurs Etrangers *(Foreign Workers' Centre)*
Piet Janssen: Van Daelstraat 32-35, 2140 Borgerhout,
Antwerpen; *t* (03) 235 3265, 235 3406
Migrant education, training, integration; anti-racism. *CBW
Krant* (12/yr).   »94
✧ **Centrum Integratie Migranten**: Centre d'Intégration pour
Migrants: Provincie Oost-Vlaanderen
Konigin Maria Hendrikaplein 65, 9000 Gent; *t* (091)
211571   »90
✧ **Centrum Jonge Migranten Jongerenwerk**: Centre pour
Jeunes Migrants *(Migrant Youth Work Centre)*
Heirburgstraat 144, 9100 Lokeren; *t* (091) 487959   »90
▌ **Churches' Commission for Migrants in Europe**, CCME:
Commission des Eglises auprès des Migrants en Europe,
CEME: Kommission der Kirchen für Migranten in Europa
Dr Jan Niessen, General Secretary: Ecumenical Centre, Rue
Joseph II, 174, 1000 Bruxelles; *t* (02) 230
2011, *f* 231 1413
Formed 1964 as Churches' Committee on Migrant Workers in
Europe. Conferences, research, campaigns on migration
policy, migrants' rights, irregular migration, racism,
xenophobia, Islam in Europe, refugees, asylum seekers.
Affiliates include Interights, p224, ECWS, p240, NCB, p146,
and LBR, p171. Formerly published *Migration Newssheet*,
p232, which is now independent.   »95
● **Comité d'appel pour le droit d'asile** *(Right to Asylum
Appeal Committee)*
LBDH, Passage de Linhout 26-28/34, 1200 Bruxelles;
t (02) 735 2145, (085) 213481 (weekends)
Emergency help for asylum-seekers; based at Ligue belge
pour la défense des droits de l'homme, p191.   »89
♦ **Comité Belge d'Aide aux Réfugiés**, CBAR: Belgisch
Comité voor hulp aan de vluchtelingen, BCHV *(Belgian
Committee for Aid to Refugees)*
Gilbert Jaeger, President: Rue Defacqz 1, Boite 10, 1050
Bruxelles; *t* (02) 537 8220, *f* 537 8982
Umbrella group for refugee assistance and information
agencies; working parties on refugee reception, world-wide
refugee problems. Founded 1968; CBAR deals with national
issues; CIRE, left, and OCIV, p131, co-ordinate work in
respectively the French- and Dutch-speaking communities;
some member agencies work mainly in other countries.   »95
✧ **Comité de Liaison des Centres de Formation Immigrée de
l'Agglomération de Bruxelles** *(Greater Brussels Immigrant
Training Centres Liaison Committee)*
[address unknown] Bruxelles   »90
● **Comité national d'accueil**, CNA: Nationaal Kommitee voor
Onthaal *(National Reception Committee)*
Rue de Laeken 76, 1000 Bruxelles; *t* (02) 218 3167   »90
♦ **Commission Episcopale des Migrations**, CEM *(Episcopal
Commission on Migration)*
Rue Brabant 174, Boite 9, 1210 Bruxelles; *t* (02) 218 4586
Catholic Church agency responsible for the pastoral care of
immigrants, emigrants and refugees.   »90
▌ **Commission Européenne Immigrés asbl**, Comeurim
(European Commission for Immigrants)
Micheline Six, Administrator: Avenue Everard 19, 1190
Bruxelles; *t* (02) 344 4479
Founded 1972; immigration, migration in Europe, citizenship,
refugees; resource centre. *Objectif immigrés* (6/yr). »93

- **Community Help Service**
Rue St-Georges 102, Bte 20, 1050 Bruxelles; *t* (02) 647 6780
Multicultural health service; therapy in English, French,
Dutch, Hebrew and German; serves Benelux countries.   »90
- ✿ **Contre-Poing**
Antoinette Russo: Rue Omer Lefèvre 4, 6000 Charleroi;
t (071) 422361
Training, employment, youth integration.   »94
- ✿ **Coordination Bruxelloise pour l'Emploi et la Formation des Femmes**, COBEFF *(Brussels Co-ordination for Women's Employment and Training)*
Rue Potagère 157, 1030 Bruxelles
Women's work issues; see CAIT, p130; Le Piment, p232. »94
- ✿ **De Poort-Beraber Begeleidingheid**
Johan Devreese: Sleepstr. 87, 9000 Gent; *t* (091) 230254
Education, employment, training, advice. *Berichtenblad de Poort-Beraber.*   »94
- **Enfants Déplacés**, ESD *(Displaced Children)*
Richard Beya: Rue de Dublin 20, 1050 Bruxelles; *t* (02) 502 2369
Child health, education.   »94

Entraide et Solidarité Protestante, ESOP (Protestant Assistance and Solidarity): *see Service Social des Etrangers, right*

- ◆ **European Legal Network on Asylum**, ELENA
Gilbert Jaeger: Avenue George Bergmann 116/9, 1050
Bruxelles; *t* (02) 640 4505
National contact for network of asylum lawyers, p154.   »95
  - ● ≡ Dutch-speaking network: Luc Denys: Paleizenstraat 154, 1210 Brussel; *t* (02) 215 2336, *f* 241 7693   »95
  - ● ≡ Francophone network: Jean-Yves Carlier: Rue de Ways 21, 1470 Genappe; *t* (067) 773026, *f* 773687   »95
- ● **Exil: Centre médico-psychosocial pour réfugiés**, EXIL *(Exile—Psychosocial and Medical Centre for Refugees)*
Rue du Collège 43, 1050 Bruxelles; *t* (02) 649 9880
Specialist medical care for refugees.   »95
- ✿ **Gastvrij Antwerpen**
[address unknown] Antwerpen   »88
- ● **Groupe d'Animation et de Formation des Femmes Immigrées**, GAFFI *(Immigrant Women Training and Activity Group)*
Yeter Yildirim: Rue de la Fraternité 7, 1210 Bruxelles;
t (02) 219 6282   »94
- ✿ **Groupe des Immigrés de Tubize** *(Tubize Immigrants' Group)*
Moor Istvan: Rue de la Déportation 37, 1480 Tubize;
t (02) 355 4532, 355 9829
Training and employment issues, anti-racism, culture.   »94
- ✿ **Groupe Santé Josaphat** *(Jehosaphat Health Group)*
Nuran Cicekciler: Rue Royale Sainte Marie 70, 1030
Bruxelles; *t* (02) 241 7671
Migrant health, health education, youth welfare.   »94
- ✿ **Hand in Hand voor Demokratie en Verdraagzamheid** *(Hand in Hand for Democracy and Tolerance)*
Breugelstraat 31-33, 2018 Antwerpen; *t* (03) 281 1505,
f 218 5085
International solidarity, anti-racism, human rights including migrant and refugee rights.   »94
- ◆ **Hulpverlening aan ontheemden** *(Aid to Displaced Persons)* formerly Belgische Hulp aan Verplaatste Personen
Waversesteenweg 205, 1040 Brussel; *t* (02) 644 2701
Francophone counterpart is Aide aux personnes déplacées, p129; resettlement assistance, counselling, advice to refugees and asylum-seekers.   »95
- ✿ **Integratiecentrum Mozaïk Onthaal voor Gastarbeiders** *(Mosaic Reception & Integration Centre for Foreign Workers)*
Herman Montesinos: Leopoldstraat 25, 2850 Boom;
t (03) 888 7665
Social and educational centre. Possibly a successor to Onthaalcentrum Gastarbeiders Boom, see right.   »94
- ✿ **Jeugdatelier Gastarbeiders** *(Immigrant Youth Workshop)*
Linnauestraat 40, Borgerhout, 2200 Antwerpen; *t* (03) 325 1980
Sports, leisure, youth integration.   »94
- ✿ **vzw Migranten Kultureel en Sociaal Trefpunt**, MIKST: Point de Rencontre Culturelle et Social des Migrants asbl *(Migrant Social and Cultural Meeting-Place)*
Willy Wouters/Nadine Buyse: Mechelstraat 9, 1800
Vilvoorde; *t* (02) 251 1033
Multicultural youth and community centre.   »94
- ▌**Migrants Forum of the European Union**: Forum des Migrants de l'Union Européenne
Tara Mukherjee, President: Rue de Trèves 33, 1040
Bruxelles; *t* (02) 230 1414, 230 2412, *f* 230 1461
Umbrella body created 1990-91 for associations, and where possible national federations of associations, representing migrants, especially those of non-EU nationality. Funded through DG V of the European Commission, p189.   »95

- ▌**Migreurope**
Michèle Decat: Rue Stévin 115, 1040 Bruxelles; *t* (02) 230 4621
Lobbying group formed 1988 by migrant, refugee and foreign student groups. Currently inactive.   »94
- ✿ **Onthaalcentrum Gastarbeiders Boom** *(Boom Immigrant Workers Reception Centre)*
Antwerpsteenweg 15, 2650 Boom; *t* (03) 888 0632   »88
- ✿ **Onthaalcentrum voor Gastarbeiders van Brussel**, OCGB *(Brussels Reception Centre for Migrant Workers)* Centre d'Accueil pour les Travailleurs Migrants
Gallaitstraat 80, 1030 Brussel; *t* (02) 216 7830
Reception centre; advice, information.   »94
- ✿ **Onthaalcentrum Molenbeek**: Centre d'Accueil Foyer Molenbeek *(Molenbeek Reception Centre)*
Loredana Marchi: Rue des Ateliers 23, 1080 Bruxelles;
t (02) 426 7495
Advice centre, social and cultural activities; education, employment, training.   »94
- ● **Open Grenzen** *(Open Borders)*
Jan Fermon: [address unknown] Brussel
Human rights of migrants and refugees; campaigns on inhumane conditions in asylum-seeker detention centres. »95
- ◆ **Overlegcentrum voor integratie van vluchtelingen**, OCIV *(Co-ordination Centre for Refugee Integration)* formerly Voorlichtingscentrum Vluchtelingen en Vreemdelingen
Gaucherestraat 164, 1210 Brussel; *t* (02) 201 0353, *f* 201 0376
Umbrella group of refugee agencies operating in the Vlaamse gemeenschap (Flemish community); integration assistance, mainly language courses; Francophone counterpart is Centre d'initiation pour réfugiés et étrangers, p130.   »95
- ✿ **Du Pain sur la Planche** *(Bread on the Table)*
Dider Urbain: Place du Béguinage 4, 4000 Liège; *t* (041) 224871
Training, employment, social activities.   »94
- ◆ **Plate-Forme de Vigilance pour les Réfugiés** *(Refugee Protection Coalition)*
c/o LDH, Rue Watteau 6, 1000 Bruxelles
Alliance of anti-racist and refugee rights groups including the Ligue des Droits de l'Homme, p191.   »94
- ◆ **Platform Migrantenorganisaties Vlaanderen** *(Flanders Council of Migrant Organisations)*
Vlaams Overlegcomité Migratie, Poststraat 156, 1030
Brussel; *t* (02) 217 1138   »90
- ✿ **Protestants sociaal centrum—Oecumenische vluchtelingendienst** *(Protestant Welfare Centre—Ecumenical Refugee Service)*
Groeningenplein 19, 2140 Antwerpen; *t* (03) 235 3405 »95
- ✿ **Regional Integratiecentrum Migranten Oost-Vlaanderen** *(East Flanders Regional Migrant Integration Centre)* formerly Migrantenwerking Waasland
K. Demuynck/Jean-Pierre de Bock: Plezantstraat 60, 9100
Sint Niklaas; *t* (033) 778 0081   »94
- ✿ **Le Relais** *(The Staging Post)*
Paul Crickx, Secretary: Rue de l'Union 10, 1030 Bruxelles;
t (02) 220 2820
Legal and employment advice, problems of youth and women, anti-racist work; mainly serves Moroccan community.   »94
- ✿ **Service d'Accueil et d'Aide à la Main-d'Oeuvre Immigrée** *(Immigrant Workers' Reception and Advice Service)*
Place A. Rijekmans, 5000 Namur; *t* (081) 27981   »90
- ● **Service d'Accueil et de Formation pour Immigrés et Réfugiés** *(Immigrant and Refugee Reception and Training Service)*
Bvd de l'Abattoir 37, 1000 Bruxelles; *t* (02) 512 5858   »94
- ✿ **Service d'Accueil des Immigrés** *(Immigrant Reception Service)*
Avenue De Gaulle 102, 7000 Mons   »90
- ◆ **Service Social des Etrangers**, ESOP-SSE: Sociale Dienst voor Vreemdelingen *(Social Service for Foreigners)*
Mauro Sbolgi: Rue de la Croix 22, 1050 Bruxelles; *t* (02) 649 9958, *f* 649 4324
Protestant agency (part of Entraide et Solidarité Protestante, ESOP) helping refugees and economic immigrants with legal and other problems; legal advice (M. Sbolgi); works closely with ADDE, p130. Has programme for Middle Eastern Christian refugees, *t* 230 0777, 230 8166; see also Centre de Formation des Etangs Noirs, p130.   »95
  - ✿ ≡ Jocelyne Daras: Rue Comm. Lemaire 13, 7033 Cuesmes; *t* (065) 349867
Social service, education, migrant workers' rights.   »94
  - ✿ ≡ Michel Malherbe: Rue Lambert le Bègue 8, 4000 Liège; *t* (041) 235889   »94
  - ✿ ≡ M. Bulcke: Leon Spilliaerstraat 10, 8400 Oostende; *t* (059) 507851, *f* 512268   »95

◆ **Service des Travailleurs Migrants de la FGTB:** Dienst der Gastarbeiders ABVV *(Trade Union Service for Migrant Workers)*
Rue Haute 42, 1000 Bruxelles; *t* (02) 511 6466
Immigrant workers' section of the main trade union body, the Fédération générale du travail de Belgique/Algemeen Belgisch Vakverbond, ABVV; member of CIRE, p130.   »85
◆ **Service des Travailleurs Migrants et Réfugiés de la CSC:** Dienst voor migrerende arbeiders en vluchtelingen ACV *(Trade Union Migrant Workers and Refugees Service)*
Rue de la Loi 121, 1040 Bruxelles; *t* (02) 233 3411
A department of the Confédération des Syndicats Chrétiens/ Algemeen Christelijk Vakverbond (Confederation of Christian Trade Unions); member of CIRE, p130.   »85
● **Solidarité Etudiants Etrangers,** SEE *(Foreign Students Solidarity)*
Pierre Galand: Rue de la Tulipe 34, 1050 Bruxelles; *t* (02) 511 5595, 344 4479
Information leaflets.   »90
✿ **Specifieke Migranten Initiativen Foyer vzw**
Werkhuizenstraat 25, 1080 Bruxelles
Information, advice, solidarity.   »94
✿ **Transithuis** *(Transit House)*
Meibloemstraat 96, 9000 Gent; *t* (091) 275824
Accommodation assistance for refugees and migrants.   »95
✿ **Turnhoutse Buurt- en Wijkwerking** *(Turnhout Community Action)*
Kongostraat 76, 2300 Turnhout; *t* (014) 418922
Anti-racism, local economic and community development.»94
✿ **Tweede Generatie—Provinciaal Overleg Migranten Jeugdwellzijnswerk** *(Second Generation—Provincial Migrant Youth Welfare Service)*
Angelo Bruno: Rondputlaan 25, Winterslag, 3600 Genk; *t* (011) 356714
Research, documentation on youth issues, training, employment.   »94
● **Vereniging der Vlaamse Onthaaltehuizen,** VVO *(Union of Flemish Reception Facilities)*
Waterloostraat 27, 2600 Berchem; *t* (03) 239 7353   »89
✿ **Vlaams Centrum voor Integratie van Migranten,** VCIM *(Flemish Centre for the Integration of Migrants)*
Emile Vervliet/L. Van Loock: Gaucheretstraat 164, 1210 Bruxelles; *t* (02) 201 0300, *f* 201 0339
Anti-racist and intercultural work, advice and assistance to migrants and refugees. See also Overlegcentrum voor Integratie van Vluchtelingen, p131.   »94
◆ **Vlaams Overlegcomité Migratie,** VOCOM: Comité Flamand de Reflexion sur les Migrations *(Flemish Committee for Migration Questions)*
Lode van Loock: Poststraat 156, 1030 Brussel; *t* (02) 217 1114
Legal advice (Veerle Hobin), pressure group, research and study centre. *Bareel*.   »89
✿ **vzw de Vrienden van El Kantra** *(Friends of El Kantra)*
Herman Fenners/Liebrecht Salen: Kan. De Deckerstraat 66, 2800 Mechelen; *t* (015) 218024, 201125
Education, culture. *El Kantra* (12/yr).   »94
✿ **Werkgroep Integratie Vluchtelingen** *(Working Group on Refugee Integration)*
Katelynestraat 52, 2800 Mechelen; *t* (015) 218077   »95
✿ **Werklozen-Jongerenwerking Waterschei** *(Waterschei Unemployed Youth Action)*
Binnenlaan 50, Waterschei, 3600 Genk
Youth training, employment, education.   »94
✿ **Zells Info- en Adviescentrum** *(Zele Information and Advice Centre)*
De Deckerstraat 19, 9149 Zele; *t* (052) 446131   »90

CYPRUS *357*

▌ **European Federation of Overseas Cypriots**
Evangelos Mavroummatis, President: [address unknown] Nicosia
Federation of national representative bodies of (mainly Greek) Cypriots in Europe; affiliated to POMAK.   »95
▌ **World Federation of Overseas Cypriots,** POMAK
George Christophides, Acting President: [address unknown] Nicosia
Federation of national representative bodies of Cypriots abroad. Discusses problems of second and subsequent generations of migrants, problems of repatriation, promotes international awareness of the illegal Turkish occupation of 40 per cent of Cyprus.   »95

DENMARK *45*

✿ **Aalborg Kommune Flygtningerådgivningen** *(Aalborg Municipality Refugee Advice Service)*
Tinghusgade 5, 9400 Nørresundby; *t* 9811 2211   »94
✿ **Center for Indvandrer- og Flygtningekvinder** *(Immigrant and Refugee Women's Centre)*
Lene Søndberg: Gammelgårdsvej 73, 3520 Farum; *t* 4295 6634   »94
◆ **Council of Europe Minority Youth Committee—Danmark,** CEMYC-DK
Kingosgade 15-kld., 1818 Frederiksberg C; *t* 3123 2130
Migrant, refugee and ethnic minority youth umbrella group; see CEMYC in Germany, p200.   »94
● **Danmarks Radio—Indvandrerredaktionen** *(Danish Radio—Immigrant Community Programmes Office)*
Rosenorns Allé 22, 1970 Frederiksberg C; *t* 3135 0647   »94
● *Danmarksposten*
Kristianiagade 8, 2100 København ∅; *t* 3138 2500
Magazine (10/yr) for Danish emigrants.   »95
◆ **Dansk Flygtningehjælp:** Danish Refugee Council, DRC
Arne Piel Christensen, Secretary General: Postboks 53, 1002 København K; *t* 3391 2700, *f* 3332 8448
Location: Borgergade 10/3. sal, 1300 København. Bo Bruun, René Albeck, Finn Slumstrup; formed 1956; refugee reception, counselling, determination of status (with Ministry of Justice), legal advice and protection, family reunion, resettlement, economic and social integration (with Ministry of Social Affairs), employment (with Labour Exchanges), education, interpreting, advice on re-migration. Documentation, information, fund-raising for overseas refugee projects. Provides 24-hour emergency service; works with 12 member agencies, solidarity groups and lawyers; local consultant (since 1974) of the UNHCR, p217; Jacob Gammelgård of the DRC is the contact for the European Legal Network on Asylum, ELENA, p154. *Exil* (4/yr), *Flygtningenyt* (6/yr).   »95
✿ ≡ Fredens Torv 12, 8000 Århus C; *t* 8613 7588   »95
✿ ≡ Sct. Jørgens Park 52, 4700 Næstved; *t* 5577 2666 »95
✿ ≡ Bullerup Skovgaard, Brolandsvej 11, 5320 Agedrup; *t* 6610 7660   »95
✿ ≡ Kastevej 26, Postboks 207, 9100 Ålborg; *t* 9816 9044»95
✿ ≡ Olaf Ryes Gade 7K, 6000 Kolding; *t* 7550 2533   »95
✿ ≡ Kirkestræde 9-1, 7500 Holstebro; *t* 9740 3122   »95
European Legal Network on Asylum: see Dansk Flygtningehjælp
✿ **Fællesklubben for Indvandrere og Danskere** *(Danes and Immigrants Joint Social Club)*
Bymuren 100, 2650 Hvidovre; *t* 3149 8383   »90
✿ **Foreningen af Indvandrerarbejdere i Taastrup** *(Taastrup Immigrant Workers Association)*
Medborgerhuset, Køgevej 71, 2630 Taastrup   »90
✿ **Holstebroegnens Indvandrerforening** *(Holstebro Immigrant Society)*
Kulturhuset, Danmarksgade 10, 7500 Holstebro; *t* 9747 3718
Founded 1985; advice, public information, social events. »90
✿ **Indvandrer Kvindecentret** *(Immigrant Women's Centre)*
Hardarshan Gill: Elmegade 21, 2200 København N; *t* 3139 6985
Major social welfare organisation.   »90
✿ **Indvandrer Kvindeprojektet i Hvidovre Kommune** *(Hvidovre Municipality Immigrant Women's Projects)*
Trædejerporten 5 A, 2650 Hvidovre; *t* 3178 1211, 3677 1876
Advice, social work.   »94
✿ **Indvandrercentret** *(Immigrant Centre)* and Vicaria Solidaritet-Støttegruppe
Klostergade 37, 1., 8000 Århus C; *t* 8612 7379
Advice, welfare, social centre for immigrants; and the Vicariat for Solidarity, a church-based social justice group.   »89
✿ **Indvandrerforeningen i Horsens** *(Horsens Immigrant Society)*
Kildegade 8-10, 8700 Horsens   »90
◆ **Indvandrerforeningernes Sammenslutning i Danmark,** IND-sam *(Immigrant Societies Federation)* also known as Etniske Mindretals Sammenslutning *(Ethnic Minorities Federation)*
Joseph Obeng, Chairman: [address uncertain] Blegdamsvej 4 st., 2200 København N; *t* 3139 2143, 3139 2568, *f* 3537 7273 (H. Dam)
Address also listed (1994) as Bredgade 36 C, 4.tv., 1260 København, *t* 3332 0526, *f* 3332 0824. Also known as Indvandrernes Sammenslutning i Danmark. Gitte Vesterlund, Joseph Obeng, Selvakumar Turasingham; member of EU Migrants Forum, p131; main umbrella group of immigrant associations, formed 1980. Sub-groups include IND-sam's Kvindegruppe (women's group) and legal affairs, anti-racist, employment, education and housing groups.   »94

✿ **Indvandrerkvinde-Klub i Hillerød** *(Hillerød Immigrant Women's Club)*
Frederiksværkgade 19, 3400 Hillerød; *t* 4225 4253　　》89
● **Indvandrerkvindeforeningen Soldue** *(Soldue Immigrant Women's Association)*
Hardashan Kaur Gill: Kingasgade 15, kld., 1818 Frederiksberg C; *t* 3131 4134, 3116 8464　　》94
● ≡ Hf Kalvebod 16, 2450 København SV　　》90
✿ **Indvandrernes Fællesklub i Brøndby Strand** *(Brondby Strand Immigrant Social Club)*
Kisumparken 73, 3, 2660 Brøndby Strand　　》90
◆ **Indvandrernes Fællesråd i Danmark**, IFD *(Denmark Immigrants' Council)*
Vesterbrogade 40, 1.tv., 1620 København V; *t* 3124 6330, 3124 3405
Advice to individuals, policy development, public information, cultural events; formed 1975.　　》90
✿ **Indvandrernes Kultur og Solidaritetsforening**, IKSF *(Immigrant Cultural and Solidarity Society)*
Muhammed Celim: Nyvej 53, 3.th., 2620 Albertslund; *t* 4264 4948
Youth and educational welfare, training, employment, mainly Turks; founded 1983.　　》94
✿ **Indvandrernes Kulturforening i Lyngby** *(Lyngby Immigrant Cultural Society)* and Pakistansk Kulturforening
v./ Imdad Ali: S. Willumsensvej 12, 2800 Lyngby　　》89
✿ **Indvandrernes Velfærds- og Kulturkomite** *(Immigrant Welfare and Cultural Committee)* Copenhagen
[address uncertain] Værebrovej 44, 2880 Bagsværd　　》90
✿ **Indvandrernes Velfærds- og Kulturkomite Hillerød**
Østervang 97, 3400 Hillerød　　》90
◆ **Indvandrerrådet** *(Immigrant Council)*
c/o Indenrigsministerriet, Christiansborg Slotsplads 1, 1218 København K; *t* 3392 3380
Interior ministry advisory body on policy towards immigrants and minorities.　　》94
✿ **Indvandrerrådgivning** *(Immigrant Counselling)*
Albertslund Rådhus, 2620 Albertslund; *t* 4264 9610, lokal (extension) 2304
Municipal advice service.　　》89
✿ **Indvandrersolidaritet**, IS *(Immigrant Solidarity)* also known as Silkeborg Indvandrersolidaritet, SI
Frederiksberggade 26, 8600 Silkeborg; *t* 8681 6260
Founded 1982; services immigrant associations.　　》94
✿ **Informationskontoret for Udlændinge** *(Foreigners' Information Service)*
Fiskergade 33-37, 8000 Århus C; *t* 8612 5013　　》89
■ **International Rehabilitation Council for Torture Victims**, IRCT
Dr Inge Genefke: [address uncertain] Postboks 2107, 1014 København K; *t* 3376 0600, *f* 3376 0500
Location: Borgergade 13. Also listed (1994) as Postboks 2672, Juliane Maries Vej 34, 2100 København ø, *t* 3139 4694. Human rights pressure group; support for refugees and asylum seekers who have suffered torture; research, lobbying, public information. See also the associated Rehabiliterings- og Forskningscentret for Torturofre, right. *Torture* (4/yr).　　》94
✿ **Ishøj Indvandrerforening** *(Ishøj Immigrant Society)*
[address uncertain] Vejlegården 1, 2635 Ishøj　　》90
● **Katolsk Informationscenter** *(Catholic Information Centre)*
Bredgade 67, st., 1260 København K; *t* 3332 1049
Church-sponsored advice agency.　　》89
✿ **Kirkens Korshærs Sociale Indvandrerrådgivning**
Drejervej 6, 2400 København NV; *t* 3181 2880
Church-funded migrant advice agency.　　》89
✿ **Klubben for Indvandrerarbejdere i Ishøj**, KIA *(Ishøj Immigrant Workers' Club)*
Erol Taskiran: [address uncertain] Østergade 1,2, 2635 Ishøj
May be the same as the Indvandrerklubben Ishøj listed (1990) at Gildebrovej 18-3 (Mehmet Ozdemir).　　》90
✿ **Københavns Kommunes Indvandrerrådgivning** *(Copenhagen Municipal Immigrants' Advice Service)*
Skole, Sct. Hans Gade 27, 2200 København N; *t* 3135 6354
Immigrant, employment and welfare advice.　　》89
● **Komiteen for Udlændinges Retssikkerhed** *(Committee for the Protection of Foreigners' Rights)*
Fredscentret i Århus, Fredsbutikken, Nørregade 6, 8000 Århus C; *t* 8619 5423
Advice on legal and welfare rights; campaigning on international human rights issues.　　》94
✿ **Kristelig Studenter-Settlements Rådgivning for Indvandrere** *(Christian Students' Settlement Immigrant Advice Service)*
Dybbølsgade 41, 1721 København V; *t* 3122 8820, 3122 8835
Immigrant welfare, rights advice, youth integration.　　》94

● **Landsforeningen af Danske Flygtningevenner** *(Danish National Refugee Assistance Society)* Københavnerkontoret
Dronningensgade 14, 1420 København K; *t* 3195 2003
Information, advice and social support for refugees.　　》94
✿ ≡ North Jutland: Aggersundvej 44, 9690 Fjerritslev; *t* 9821 3435　　》89
● **Mødestedet for Indvandrere og Danskere**
Oehlenschlægersgade 26, kld.th., 1663 København V; *t* 3121 2703　　》89
● *Nyt fra Danmark* (News from Denmark)
Allan Aistrup, Publisher: Ny Oestergade 5, 1101 København K; *t* 3391 2566
Magazine (4/yr) for Danish expatriates; founded 1981.　　》95
✿ **Odense Flygtningevenner** *(Odense Refugee Service)*
v./ Knud Scheel-Hincke: Reventlowsvej 9, 5000 Odense C; *t* 6591 6048　　》89
✿ **Rådgivningskontor for Indvandrer i Ishøj Kommune** *(Ishøj Municipality Immigrant Advisor)*
Ishøj Storetorv 20, 2635 Ishøj; *t* 4254 2174, 4254 1211 exts. 122/126　　》89
● **Rehabiliterings- og Forskningcentret for Torturofre**, RCT:
Rehabilitation and Research Centre for Torture Victims
Postboks 2672, Juliana Maries Vej 34, 2100 København ø; *t* 3139 4694, *f* 3139 5020
Medical treatment of torture victims; research into torture and training in treatment methods. See also the International Rehabilitation Council for Torture Victims, left.　　》93
✿ **Ringsted Gæstearbejderklub** *(Ringsted Guest-Workers'Club)*
Køgevej 61, 4100 Ringsted; *t* 5361 9037　　》89
✿ **Roskilde Kommunes Indvandrerklub** *(Roskilde Municipality Immigrants' Club)* Administration
c/o Flemming Petersen: Socialforvaltningen, Køgevej 90, 4000 Roskilde; *t* 4237 3300 ext. 2283　　》89
✿ ≡ Club: Blågårdsstræde 8, 4000 Roskilde　　》89
✿ **Silkeborg Indvandrersamvirke** *(Silkeborg Immigrant Co-operative)*
Karen Goul Andersen: [address uncertain] Thorsoskvanten 14, Vinklund, 8600 Silkeborg; *t* 8681 1399
Also listed (1990) c/o M. Christensen, Kak Muksvej 30, or at Baggensvej 10, 1 th. Solidarity work, public education, employment advice, counselling.　　》94
● **Udlændinges Aktionsforening** *(Foreigners' Action Group)*
c/o Peter Lind: H.A. Clausensvej 20 B, 2820 Gentofte; *t* 3165 8820　　》89

ESTONIA 372

● *The Baltic Independent*
Box 45, Pärnu Mnt 67a, 0090 Tallinn; *t* (2) 683074, 681269
Newspaper (52/yr) aimed at Baltic emigré communities in 50 countries.　　》95
✿ **Romale**
Box 694, 0026 Tallinn
Anti-racism, anti-fascism, refugee rights; Romany group? 》94

FINLAND 358

◆ **Pakolais Neuvonta** *(Refugee Advice Centre)* and European Legal Network on Asylum, ELENA
Kirsi Tarvainen/Pertti Rauhio: Ludviginkatu 3-5 B 42, 00130 Helsinki; *t* (90) 644104, 644106, *f* 644109
Advice and information centre of by the Refugee Council. Legal aid except in criminal cases, research, information on court decisions, lobbying, documentation on refugee and migrant issues. Tarvainen is the national co-ordinator for ELENA, see p154. *Pakolaistiedote* (Refugee News, 4/yr). 》95
✿ ≡ Anna-Maija Toukkari: Huoltokatu 7, 45100 Kouvola; *t* (951) 371 3111, *f* 371 3115　　》95
✿ ≡ Ria Tulonen: Pohjolankatu 25a, 33500 Tampere; *t* (931) 219 7569, *f* 219 7524　　》95
✿ ≡ Kristina Stenman: Uddnäsvägen, 65170 Vasa; *t* (961) 3127 188　　》95
◆ **Suomen Pakolaisapu**: Finnish Refugee Council
Ludviginkatu 3-5 B 42, 00130 Helsinki; *t* (90) 644100, *f* 644109
National NGO providing advice (through Pakolais Neuvonta), support and settlement services to refugees and asylum seekers. Extensive aid programme for refugees and returnees abroad, especially in Africa and Asia; raises funds for UNHCR, p217, and UNRWA, p188. *Pakolainen* (Refugees, 6/yr). 》95

FRANCE 33

- **Accueil des Etudiants Etrangers** *(Foreign Students Reception)*
13 rue de Santeuil, 75005 Paris   »90
- **Accueil Familiale des Jeunes Etrangers** *(Family Reception for Foreign Youth)*
23 rue du Cherche-Midi, 75006 Paris; *t* (1) 4222 5034,
4222 1334
Youth exchange, au pair, paying guest services for foreign
young people (14-30).   »94
- **Accueil des Jeunes en France, AJF** *(France Youth Reception)*
16 rue du Pont-Louis-Philippe, 75004 Paris; *t* (1) 4272 7209,
f 4027 0871, *Tx* 240909
Central booking service for youth accommodation (30,000
beds across France). This office deals with group bookings;
individual service is available at three other offices in Paris,
tels. 4277 8780, 4354 9586, 4285 8619.   »94
- **Accueil et Promotion** *(Reception and Advancement)*
Christine Devaud: Centre de Préformation, 21 rue de la
Fontaine au Roi, 75011 Paris; *t* (1) 4338 0081
Teaching materials, visual archive; education, youth
integration. Address also listed (1990) as 51 bis rue Piat,
75020 Paris, *t* (1) 4366 0900.   »94
- ✣ **Accueil et Promotion Echanges Hainaut-Cambresis, APE**
(Reception, Advancement and Exchanges)
André Ival: BP 17, 59301 Valenciennes Cedex; *t* 2746 6892
Location: 26 avenue de Saint-Amand. Formerly Accueil et
Promotion des Etrangers. Training, employment, culture,
education. *APE informations*.   »94
- **Action Coordonnée pour le Développement Urbain Concerté,
ACDUC** *(Co-ordinated Action for Planned Urban Development)*
Assane Ba: 32 rue des Epinettes, 75017 Paris; *t* (1) 4263
2100
Town planning, local politics, information.   »94
- **Aide à l'Enfant Réfugié** *(Aid to Refugee Children)*
5 rue Gassendi, 75014 Paris; *t* (1) 4327 8188
Emergency aid overseas, educational assistance, family
placements in France for refugee and displaced children. »93
- ✣ **Alphabétisation et promotion des migrants de
l'agglomération rouennaise, APMAR** *(Literacy and
Advancement of Rouen District Migrants)*
immeuble Castor, escalier B, appt 13, 29 rue Galilée, 76000
Rouen   »90
- ✣ **Amicale des Nords-Africains et des Résidents Etrangers en
France, ANAREF** *(North African & Foreign Residents' Society)*
175 rue de la Mertzau, 68100 Mulhouse; *t* 8945 7457
Housing and welfare group; mainly Maghrebi.   »94
- ✣ **Amis de la Délégation des Migrations, ADM** *(Migration
Office Friendship Group)*
Pe. José Maria de Antonio: 15 promenade du Pradeau, 65000
Tarbes; *t* 6293 4135, *f* 6251 0713
Social, cultural and welfare group supporting the work of the
Catholic SNPM, p138.   »94
- ✣ **Aquitaine Education Intégration**
2 rue Paul-Bert, 33000 Bordeaux
Education; immigrants, unemployed, others.   »89
- ✣ **Association d'accueil des femmes immigrées et françaises
de Saint-Cloud, AFIF** *(French and Immigrant Women's
Reception Society)*
10 rue des Tennerolles, 92210 Saint-Cloud
Welfare and settlement of refugee and migrant women.   »89
- ✣ **Association pour l'Accueil et la Formation des Travailleurs
Etrangers, AAFTE** *(Society for the Reception and Training of
Foreign Workers)*
Pierre Groult: Centre Jim Valliant, 19 bis, rue du Pré de la
Bataille, 76000 Rouen; *t* 3588 5894   »94
- **Association pour l'Accueil et la Formation des Travailleurs
Migrants, AFTAM** *(Society for the Reception and Training of
Migrant Workers)*
Jacques Dierckens: 122 rue Nollet, 75017 Paris; *t* (1) 4226
6313, *f* 4263 4587
Migrant housing, training, employment.   »94
- ✣ **Association pour l'Accueil et l'Hébergement des Travailleurs
Migrants et de leurs Familles, AAHTMF** *(Association for the
Reception and Housing of Migrant Workers and their Families)*
rue du Pré Gené, 03100 Montluçon; *t* 7029 0303   »94
- **Association d'accueil aux médecins et personnel de santé
réfugiés en France, AMPSRF** *(Reception Society for Refugee
Doctors and Health Workers)*
Pavillon Benjamin Balt, Hôpital Ste-Anne, 1 rue Cabanis,
75014 Paris; *t* (1) 4565 8750
Reception and employment services to refugees in the
medical professions. Founded 1973.   »95

- **Association pour l'accueil et la préformation des travailleurs
migrants** *(Society for the Reception and Training of Migrant
Workers)*
239 rue de Percy, 75012 Paris; *t* (1) 4346 1198
Possibly the same as AFTAM, left.   »83
- ✣ **Association d'Accueil des Travailleurs Etrangers et Migrants**
(Association for the Reception of Foreign and Migrant Workers)
22 rue Mégevand, 25000 Besançon; *t* 8182 1078   »90
- ✣ **Association d'accueil des travailleurs migrants, AATM**
(Association for the Reception of Migrant Workers)
13 rue Chevalier-au-Lion, 10000 Troyes   »90
- ✣ **Association d'Aide aux Travailleurs Etrangers de la Région
Rouennaise, AATERR** *(Rouen Region Foreign Workers' Aid
Association)*
Jean-Claude Tubeuf: 21 rue de l'Eglise, 76120 Grand-
Quevilly; *t* 3569 2521
Housing and welfare advice.   »94
- **Association des Amis de *Passages* pour l'Education, la
Formation Professionelle et la Solidarité avec l'Immigration**
(Friends of Passages *in Solidarity with Migrants)*
17 rue Simone-Veil, 75013 Paris
Society for the education and training of, and solidarity with,
migrant workers; linked with journal *Passages*.   »89
- ✣ **Association Antiboise pour l'Alphabétisation, AAA** *(Antibes
Literacy Association)*
Jérôme Bracq: 11 avenue du Mas Ensoleillé, 06600 Antibes;
t 9334 3603, 9333 4787
Literacy and cultural work with migrants.   »94
- ✣ **Association corse pour la promotion et la formation des
migrants, ACPFM** *(Corsican Society for Training and
Advancement of Migrants)*
chez M Antoine Ettori: résidence A.-Mandarina 2, bât. 1,
chemin du Finosello, 20090 Ajaccio, Corse
Adult and community education for immigrants.   »90
- **Association Culturelle et Amicale des Familles d'Outre-Mer
et Migrants, ACAFOM** *(Cultural and Friendship Association
of Overseas French and Migrant Families)*
Suzanne De Dives Gueydon: 42 rue des Sept Arpents, 93500
Pantin; *t* (1) 4844 4808
Migrant solidarity, anti-racism.   »94
- ✣ **Association culturelle orthodoxe de l'eglise Saint Séraphin
de Sarow** *(Orthodox Cultural Association of the Church of St
Seraphin)*
91 rue Lecourbe, 75015 Paris; *t* (1) 4273 0503
Orthodox religious group, ethnicity uncertain.   »90
- ▌**Association démocratique des Français à l'étranger, ADFE**
(Democratic Association of French People Abroad)
[address unknown]
See also ADFE in Italy and Luxembourg, p36.   »90
- ✣ **Association 2ème G** *(Second Generation Association)*
[address unknown]   »90
- **Association pour le Développement de la Formation des
Immigrés, ADFI** *(Association for the Development of
Immigrant Training)*
Christian Negre: [address uncertain] boulevard de Sébastopol,
75003 Paris; *t* (1) 4271 0874
Forum on migrant training issues.   »90
- ✣ **Association Douaisienne pour l'Accueil des Travailleurs
Migrants, ADATMI**
137 boulevard Faidherbe, 59500 Douai; *t* 2788 9293
Housing and welfare assistance.   »94
- ♦ **Association pour l'Enseignement et la Formation des
Travailleurs Immigrés et de leurs Familles, AEFTI** *(Association
for the Education & Training of Migrant Workers & Families)*
16 rue de Valmy, 93100 Montreuil; *t* (1) 4287 0220
Also known as Association *nationale* EFTI; see p135.   »94
- **Association Entraide Formation Travailleurs Migrants,
ASSEFTA** *(Migrant Workers' Mutual Aid and Training
Association)*
44 rue Traversière, 75012 Paris; *t* (1) 4347 1913, 4343
5299   »90
- ✣ **Association d'entraide et de solidarité, AES** *(Mutual Aid
and Solidarity Association)*
25 rue Eugène-Voisin, 94340 Joinville-le-Pont
Advice, assistance, education, self-help, information work
with immigrants.   »89
- ✣ **Association pour l'établissement des réfugiés** *(Refugee
Settlement Association)*
21 bis, rue de la Pérouse, 75116 Paris   »93
- ✣ **Association des Etudiants Franc-comtois issus de
l'Immigration** *(Franche-Comté Society of Students of
Immigrant Origin)*
11 rue du Luxembourg, 25000 Besançon
Social, economic and professional interests of students;
integration in all spheres of life.   »90

● Association pour les Etudiants, les Stagiaires et les Travailleurs des Pays en Voie de Développement *(Society of Students, Trainees and Workers from Developing Countries)*
6 rue Jean Dolent, 75014 Paris; *t* (1) 4336 3666 »90

● Association Familiale pour la Protection des Etudiantes Etrangères *(Family Association for the Protection of Foreign Female Students)*
45 rue de Vaugirard, 75006 Paris; *t* (1) 4548 8254 »90

✿ Association des femmes de la Casamance Adeane
Chartreuse, appt 17, 2 rue Anatole-France, 27000 Evreux-La-Madeleine
Leisure activity, meetings of women. »89

● Association des femmes réfugiées, AFR *(Association of Refugee Women)*
14 rue de Nanteuil, 75015 Paris »89

✿ Association Haut-Marnaise pour les Immigrés, AHMI *(Haute-Marne Immigrants' Association)*
Mario Nemer: 9 bvd Thiers, 52000 Chaumont; *t* 2503 4506
Housing and welfare issues. »94

● Association Internationale Accueil Santé *(International Health and Reception Society)*
68 boulevard Davout, 75020 Paris; *t* (1) 4009 8888
Presumably migrant health and welfare activities. »90

● Association des jeunes méditerranéens en France, AJMF *(Association of Mediterranean Youth in France)*
[address unknown] »90

✿ Association pour le Logement des Travailleurs Immigrés de Clermont, ALTIC *(Clermont Immigrant Workers Housing Association)*
Claude Portal: 7 rue de l'Ange, 63000 Clermont Ferrand; *t* 7330 8410, 7336 2392 »94

♦ Association pour le Logement des Travailleurs Immigrés et de leurs Familles, ALTIF *(Housing Association for Immigrant Workers and their Families)*
42 rue de Cambronne, 75740 Paris Cedex 15; *t* (1) 4566 9315 »94

✿ Association maison des travailleurs immigrés de Puteaux, AMTIP *(Puteaux Immigrant Workers' Centre Association)*
[address unknown] 92800 Puteaux »90

✿ Association pour le Mieux-être et le Logement des Isolés, AMLI *(Association for the Welfare and Housing of the Marginalised)*
G. Bernard: 1 rue Chambière, 57000 Metz; *t* 8732 6077, *f* 8732 8969 »94

▌Association Mondiale pour les Réfugiés, AMR: World Refugee Association
Monique Coursier: 35 boulevard Murat, 75016 Paris; *t* (1) 4651 5300
Asylum rights, refugee welfare. »94

♦ Association nationale d'assistance aux frontières pour les étrangers, ANAFE *(National Association for Aid to Foreigners at Borders)*
c/o Inter-Service Migrants, 2 cité de l'Ameublement, 75011 Paris; *t* c/o CIMADE (1) 4008 0534, *f* 4008 0527
A network of 17 advice agencies, trade unions and other groups providing legal assistance to asylum claimants and others at points of entry. »95

♦ Association nationale pour l'enseignement et la formation des travailleurs immigrés et de leurs familles, AEFTI *(National Association for the Education of Immigrant Workers and their Families)*
Claude Vankeirbilck: 46 rue de Montreuil, 75011 Paris; *t* (1) 4367 1155
See also Association pour l'enseignement et la formation des travailleurs immigrés, p134, and Confédération générale du travail—Section immigration, p196. *Savoirs et Formation.*»94

✿ ≡ Valence: also known as Association drômoise pour l'enseignement et la formation des travailleurs immigrés, AEFTI-26: UD-CGT, 17 rue Georges-Bizet, 26000 Valence »90

✿ Association Nejma
Khélil Belheine: 57 rue de Bucarest, 13300 Salon-de-Provence; *t* 9053 3437
Research, documentation, migrant welfare. See also Association Wejmaa, right. »94

✿ Association pour la promotion culturelle des immigrés de Stains *(Society for the Cultural Promotion of Immigrants)*
salle polyvalente Max-Jacob, allée Max-Jacob, 93240 Stains
Cultural, social, artistic activities. »90

✿ Association pour les Réfugiés du Calvados
F. Lugand: 19 rue Mélingue, 14300 Caen; *t* 3150 3289 »94

✿ Association Régionale pour la Formation et l'Education des Migrants, ARFEM *(Regional Association for Migrant Training and Education)*
BP 1352, 115 rue du Molinel, 59015 Lille Cedex; *t* 2054 6712 »94

✿ Association Régionale du Théâtre de l'Emigration, ARETE
Fatiha Sid/Madtib Mabouche: 4 rue Rembrandt, 25000 Besançon; *t* 8151 4780, *f* 8151 3001
Name also listed (1994) as Association Régionale Echanges, Théâtre et Education. Immigrant drama and culture. *La Feuille du Baobab* (6/yr). »94

✿ Association pour la Santé des Migrants—Loire-Atlantique, ASAMLA *(Migrant Health Association of the Loire Atlantique)*
Geneviève Morinière: 7 rue de Gigant, 44100 Nantes; *t* 4069 8676, 4008 4670 »94

● Association Service Sociale Familial Migrants, ASSFAM *(Migrant Family Social Service Association)*
Ghislaine de Preville, Dr: 5 rue Saulnier, 75009 Paris; *t* (1) 4523 1428, *f* 4523 3807
Welfare advice, social work. »94

✿ Association de solidarité pour l'accueil et l'assistance des réfugiés, ASAAR *(Solidarity Society for Reception and Assistance to Refugees)*
275 route de l'Empereur, 92500 Rueil-Malmaison »90

✿ Association de solidarité des femmes immigrées *(Immigrant Women's Solidarity Association)*
centre interculturel, 28 rue de Laghouat, 75018 Paris
Active solidarity, integration of Senegalese and other immigrant women and children. »90

♦ Association Solidarité français migrants *(French-Migrant Solidarity Association)* Head Office
4 square Vitruve, 75020 Paris; *t* (1) 4360 5870
See also Solidarité français migrants, p138. »90

✿ ≡ Centre Roquette, 51 bis rue de la Roquette, 75011 Paris; *t* (1) 4355 4320 »90

✿ ≡ 44 cité Fleurs, 75017 Paris; *t* (1) 4263 2375 »90

✿ Association de solidarité pour l'intégration des immigrés, ASI *(Solidarity Association for the Integration of Immigrants)*
13 rue de Vaugirad, 92190 Meudon
Study and help to resolve the range of problems relating to integration of immigrants in France or, if desired, in the countries of origin. »90

♦ Association de solidarité avec les travailleurs immigrés, ASTI *(Association for Solidarity with Immigrant Workers)*
42 avenue du Bas-Meudon, 92130 Issy-les-Moulineaux »89

✿ ≡ 11 impasse Sainte-Croix, 71100 Chalon-sur-Saône »89

✿ ≡ cité Formanoir, bat. 02, entrée D, appt 124, 33600 Pessac »89

✿ ≡ Anne Marie Leridon: 27 rue Félibre Gaut, 13100 Aix-en-Provence; *t* 4226 4689
Welfare, housing advice, anti-racist work. »94

✿ Association de solidarité avec les travailleurs migrants, ASTM *(Association for Solidarity with Migrant Workers)*
David Rocheblave: résidence les Asphodèles, 30 rue Fontaine-St-Berthomieu, 34070 Montpellier; *t* 6727 8822 »94

✿ Association Vauclusienne d'Aide et d'Insertion, AVAI *(Vaucluse Aid and Integration Association)*
Edouard Guignard: 68 rue des Lices, 84000 Avignon; *t* 9086 5314
Welfare, educational and integration assistance to (primarily Asian) migrants and refugees. »94

✿ Association Wejmaa
7 rue de Sofia, Local Prince Nasi, 13300 Salon-de-Provence; *t* 9053 3437
Same as Association Nejma, left? »90

✿ CEFISEM Paris, Pour les Enfants de Migrants *(For Migrants' Children)*
97 rue de Balard, 75015 Paris; *t* (1) 4554 0497 »90

✿ Centre d'Animation pour Femmes d'Origine Etrangère *(Foreign Women's Community Centre)*
Warda Benarab: [address uncertain] 10 boulevard Eugène-Decros, 93260 Les Lilas; *t* (1) 4897 1324 »90

✿ Centre d'orientation sociale, COS *(Social Orientation Centre)*
52 rue de l'Arbre Sec, 75001 Paris; *t* (1) 4260 1152
Social work with elderly refugees. »83

✿ Centre Régionale de Préformation des Migrants en Languedoc-Roussillon *(Regional Centre for Migrant Job Training)*
Mas Prunet, route de Pont de Lavérun, 34000 Montpellier; *t* 6267 3928 »90

✿ Collectif d'Accueil pour les Solliciteurs d'Asile à Strasbourg, CASAS *(Strasbourg Reception Collective for Asylum Seekers)*
Pascale Adam: 13 quai Saint-Nicolas, 67000 Strasbourg; *t* 8825 1303, *f* 8825 7663
Solidarity, advice and assistance to refugees. »94

✿ Comité d'Accueil Régional des Apatrides, Réfugiés et Déplacés, CARARD *(Regional Reception Committee for the Stateless, Refugees and Displaced Persons)*
Le Peyrouat, bat. 13, rue Adjt. Jean Luxey, 40000 Mont-de-Marson; *t* 5806 0977 »94

✣ Comité d'Action Sociale en faveur des Travailleurs Migrants, COTRAMI *(Migrant Worker Welfare Committee)*
72 rue Logelbach, 68000 Colmar; *t* 8979 6172
Advice and information.   »94

● Comité d'aide exceptionelle aux intellectuels réfugiés, CAIR *(Refugee Intellectuals Emergency Aid Committee)*
43 rue de Cambronne, 75015 Paris; *t* (1) 4306 9302
Financial and practical help to refugee writers, artists and academics.   »95

✣ Comité d'Aide aux Réfugiés, CAAR *(Refugee Aid Committee)*
31 bis rue du Général Leclerc, 92270 Bois-Colombes; *t* (1) 4242 7048, *f* 4760 1441
Bulletin de liaison.   »94

♦ Comité Catholique contre la Faim et pour le Développement, Service Migrants, CCFD *(Catholic Committee on Hunger and Development Migrants Service)*
Claude Baehrel/Claude Calliere: 4 rue Jean Lantier, 75001 Paris; *t* (1) 4482 8000, 4482 8177, *f* 4482 8145
International aid and development agency of the Church, with around 700 current projects; Service Migrants funds agencies providing welfare assistance to migrants and refugees in France. Member of the European Co-ordination for the Right to Family Life of Immigrants, right (contact Adelino de Sousa).
Faim et Développement (12/yr).   »94

♦ Comité Intergouvernemental auprès des Evacués, Service oecumenique d'entraide, CIMADE: Intergovernmental Committee on Evacuees, Ecumenical Aid Service
Jacques Geneviève/L. Giovannoni: 176 rue de Grenelle, 75007 Paris; *t* (1) 4418 6050, 4550 3443, *f* 4556 0859
Publicly-funded agency (generally known by its acronym), founded 1939 and linked to Protestant and Orthodox churches; solidarity with migrants, emergency help, refugee reception, counselling in detention centres, education, language training, legal advice to asylum seekers; some overseas development aid. Branches in Paris, Lyons, Marseilles, Montbéliard, Montpellier (*t* 6747 1415) and Strasbourg. *CIMADE informations* (12/yr).   »94

● ≡ Development Office: Département développement, 8 boulevard Bonne Nouvelle, 75010 Paris; *t* (1) 4523 2377 »90

● ≡ Batignolles: Délégation de Paris et Service Etrangers: Hélène Rubak: 46 boulevard des Batignolles, 75017 Paris; *t* (1) 4008 0534, *f* 4008 0527
Affiliated to European Co-ordination for the Right to Family Life for Immigrants, right.   »95

✣ ≡ Regional Office: CIMADE-Lyon, 3 rue Diderot, 69001 Lyon; *t* 7828 4789
Address uncertain (1990); number confirmed (1995).   »95

✣ ≡ Centre international: 80 rue du 8 Mai 1945, 91300 Massy; *t* 6920 2332, *f* 6920 0041   »93

♦ Comité de Liaison et d'Alphabétisation pour la Promotion, CLAP *(Committee for Liaison and Literacy Work for Advancement)* Head Office
Gérard Lutier: 7 impasse Charretière, 75005 Paris; *t* (1) 4633 5555, *f* 4633 9210
Literacy and language classes, cultural, social and welfare services for migrants. See also regional sections, below, and ISMM at same address, p164. *Alpha et Promotion; Bulletin des Ateliers d'Ecriture*.   »94

✣ ≡ Aquitaine: Lahbib Mouhoub: Cité Lumineuse, batiment D, 1er étage, rue Jean Brunet, 33300 Bordeaux; *t* 5650 6674, *f* 5669 0554   »94

✣ ≡ Rhône-Alpes: Rahim Alkoum: 5 rue Sala, 69002 Lyon; *t* 7837 7089, *f* 7842 7616   »94

✣ ≡ Mediterranean coast: Nabil ben M'rad: 4 rue du Docteur Combalt, 13006 Marseille; *t* 9181 5087, *f* 8153 5937
Réseau CLAP Méditerranée.   »94

✣ ≡ Lorraine, CLAP-est: Guy Didier: 17 G Laurent Bonnevay, 54100 Nancy; *t* 8398 5920, *f* 8396 6457
See also Strasbourg office.   »94

✣ ≡ Ile de France, CLAP-IDF: Pierre Moreau: Centre de Préformation, Tour Rimini, 8 avenue de Choisy, 75643 Paris Cedex 13; *t* (1) 4585 3602, 4406 8333, *f* 4406 8339   »94

✣ ≡ Normandy: 33 ter. rue de Fontenelle, 76000 Rouen, Normandie; *t* 3588 5737, *f* 3515 9823   »94

✣ ≡ Alsace (CLAP-est): Bernard Rolet: 76 avenue des Vosges, 67000 Strasbourg; *t* 8835 7244, 8862 1312, *f* 8852 1821
CLAP-est covers Alsace and Lorraine; see also Nancy office.
Alpha et Promotion Alsace Lorraine (4/yr).   »94

✣ ≡ Midi-Pyrénées: Catherine Mouton: Local 602, 1er étage, 1 cheminement L. Auriacombe, 31100 Toulouse; *t* 6214 4445, *f* 6244 2772   »94

● Comité de Liaison pour la Promotion des Migrants, CLP *(Liaison Committee for the Advancement of Migrants)*
15 rue Réaumur, 75003 Paris; *t* (1) 4804 9770
Possibly a local branch of CLAP, above?   »94

● Comité médical pour les exilés, COMEDE
78 rue du Général Leclerc, BP 31, 94272 Le Kremelin Bicêtre Cedex; *t* (1) 4521 3840
Free medical and psycho-social care services for refugees and asylum seekers, including torture victims.   »93

● Comité Médico-Social pour la Santé des Migrants, CMSSM *(Medico-Social Committee for Migrant Health)* also known as Migrations Santé
C. Huraux-Rendu, President: 23 rue du Louvre, 75001 Paris; *t* (1) 4233 2474, 4233 6403, *f* 4233 2973
Mohamed El Moubaraki, Antoine Lazarus; formed 1968; researches migrant and refugee health issues, co-ordinates medical treatment of refugees in reception centres and the community; documentary resources. See also Migrations Santé—Languedoc, p137. *Migrations Santé* (6/yr).   »94

✣ ≡ J.C. Guiraud: 26 impasse Vitry, 31200 Toulouse; *t* 6157 8951, 6227 2462, *f* 6147 1184   »94

● Comité National contre la Double Peine *(National Committee against Double Punishment)* and Collectif des Femmes contre la Double Peine
21 ter rue Voltaire, 75011 Paris
See also CEDIDELP, p233. Campaigns against deportation of immigrants convicted of criminal offences.   »94

✣ Comité Rhodanien d'Accueil des Réfugiés et de Défense des Droits d'Asile, CRARDDA *(Rhône Refugee Reception and Asylum Rights Defence Committee)*
O. Brachet: BP 1054, 19 rue de la Baïsse, 69612 Villeurbanne; *t* 7803 7445, *f* 7885 5530
Housing and welfare of refugees and asylum-seekers. *Bref CRARDDA* (12/yr).   »94

● Comité unitaire français-immigrés *(United French-Immigrant Committee)*
14 rue de Nanteuil, 75015 Paris
Solidarity and pressure group.   »90

♦ Commission de Sauvegarde du Droit d'Asile, CSDA *(Commission to Safeguard the Right of Asylum)*
c/o FTDA, 4-6 passage Louis Philippe, 75011 Paris; *t* (1) 4807 1010, *f* 4807 2650
Umbrella group for 35 NGOs, defends legal rights of refugees and asylum seekers. See also France Terre d'Asile, p137.»95

▌Conseil des Associations des Immigrés en Europe, CAIE: Council of Immigrant Associations in Europe
46 rue de Montreuil, 75011 Paris; *t* (1) 4372 7585, *f* 4372 9090
See CAIE in Switzerland, p152, and CAIF, below.   »94

♦ Conseil des Associations d'Immigrés en France, CAIF: Council of Immigrant Associations in France
Hamouda Hertelli: 46 rue de Montreuil, 75011 Paris; *t* (1) 4372 7585, 4372 2871, *f* 4372 9090
Antonio Barao, Kader Galit. Legal advice and information, solidarity. Umbrella group of immigrant associations; member of EU Migrants Forum, p131. See CAIE, above. »94

▌Coordination européenne pour le droit des étrangers de vivre en famille: European Co-ordination on the Right to Family Life for Immigrants
Dominique Lahalle: 25 boulevard de Bonne Nouvelle, 75002 Paris; *t* (1) 4041 0165, *f* 4041 0359
International coalition of organisations (pp121, 136, 138, 149, 155, 160, 189, 199, 205, 234) campaigning for the right to family reunion for migrants settled in the EU.   »95

✣ Ecole de formateurs et d'animateurs en milieux migrants, EFAM *(School for Migrant Trainers and Community Workers)*
3 rue Père-Chevrier, 69007 Lyon
Immigrant adult education, social and cultural work.   »89

● Enfants réfugiés du monde, ERM *(Refugee Children of the World)*
Dr Mireille Szatan, President: [address uncertain] 2 impasse de la Providence, 75020 Paris; *t* (1) 4348 3132, *f* 4348 5160
Also listed (1994) as 34 rue Gaston Lauriau, 93100 Montreuil: *t* (1) 4859 6029, *f* 4859 6488. Assistance to refugee children and families in the Third World. *Bulletin ERM* (4/yr).   »94

✣ Equilibre
BP 7124, 69548 Lyon Cedex; *t* 7869 6141, 7273 0414, *f* 7273 0576, *Tx* 375066
Location: 14 bis boulevard de l'Artillerie. Economic and social development in Africa, Asia and eastern Europe; emergency aid; projects aimed at reintegration of returning refugees. »94

♦ Fédération des associations de solidarité avec les travailleurs immigrés, FASTI *(Federation of Immigrant Worker Solidarity Associations)*
Mohsen Dridi, Secretary General: 4 square Vitruve, 75020 Paris; *t* (1) 4031 8441, *f* 4364 0473
Carlos Bravo, president. Anti-racism; solidarity campaigns, advice for immigrants and refugees. *Expression immigré(e)s-français(es)* (4/yr).   »95

▌ **Fédération des Exilés en Europe**, FEE: Federation of Exiles in Europe
M Assumali Nyembo: 9 place des Cardères, 95200 Sarcelles; *t* 3994 1897
Umbrella group of organisations representing refugees and political exiles.   »94
◆ **Fédération Nationale des Associations de Réception et de Réadaption Sociale**, FNARS *(National Federation of Associations for Reception and Social Adaptation)*
Bernard Quaretta, Vice-President: [address unknown]
National umbrella group co-ordinating local migrant welfare societies.   »95
✿ **Fédération pour l'Unité des Réfugiés** *(Refugee Unity Federation)*
Palais de l'Etoile, 1 rue Sylvain, 83000 Toulon; *t* 9446 5167   »94
● **Femmes inter associations**, FIA-ISM *(Women's Voluntary Sector Group)*
Adolé Ankrah/M. Schneider: 12 rue Guy de la Brosse, 75005 Paris; *t* (1) 4337 6128
Intercultural solidarity amongst women. See also Inter Service Migrants, below, and Interferences Culturelles, p164.
Regards, Femmes d'ici et d'ailleurs.   »94
✿ **Formation, Recherche, Animation auprès des Travailleurs Etrangers**, FRATE *(Training, Research and Community Development with Migrant Workers)*
Christian Dufay: 44 Grande Rue, 25000 Besançon; *t* 8182 2175, *f* 8183 3447
Name alternatively listed (1994) as Formation, Recherche, Animation *pour le Travail et l'Education*.   »94
◆ **France Terre d'Asile**, FTDA *(France, Country of Asylum)*
Gérard Millet, Director: 4-6 passage Louis Philippe, 75011 Paris; *t* (1) 4807 1010, *f* 4807 2650
Fadela Amrani; information, emergency aid, legal advice, housing in over 50 reception centres, employment assistance, social services to refugees and asylum seekers throughout France; founded 1971. Works through a network of regional and local committees. See also Commission de sauvegarde du droit d'asile, p136. *Lettre d'information* (6/yr), *Tour d'horizon* (52/yr).   »95
◆ **Groupe d'Information et de Soutien aux Travailleurs Immigrés**, GISTI *(Immigrant Workers Information and Support Group)*
Patrick Mony/Claire Rodier: 30 rue des Petites Ecuries, 75010 Paris; *t* (1) 4247 0760 advice, 4247 0709 main; *f* 4247 0747
Founded 1972; Danièle Lochak, Nathalie Ferre. Rights of migrant workers in France and the European Union. Research, documentation, campaigns, legal advice.   »95
✿ **Groupe Orsay**
Jacqueline Babut: [address uncertain] 47 rue de Clichy, 75009 Paris   »90
✿ **Institut pour la Promotion des Travailleurs Etrangers**, IPTR *(Institute for the Advancement of Foreign Workers)*
45 rue des Vinaigriers, 75010 Paris; *t* (1) 4607 9037   »90
◆ **Inter Service Migrants**, ISM: Union nationale (ISM-U, also known as Union Inter Service Migrants)
Michel Sauvetre: 12 rue Guy de la Brosse, 75005 Paris; *t* (1) 4535 5757, 4337 6252, *f* 4337 9741
Services to migrants and refugees including translation, interpreting, housing and legal advice, information and liaison with public services; see also ISM-Information and local branches, below, CLISMA, right, Femmes inter associations, above, and Interferences Culturelles, p164.   »94
● ≡ ISM-Information (also known as Inter migrants information): Julien Neri: 27 rue Linné, 75005 Paris; *t* (1) 4336 6666, 4331 7955, *f* 4707 2815
Information and legal advice service of ISM-U. *Fiches juridiques et pratiques* (3/yr).   »94
● ≡ ISM-Traduction Information, ISM-TI: Nasser Bounazou: Les Argonautes, 2-4 cité de l'Ameublement, 75011 Paris; *t* (1) 4356 2050, *f* 4356 1810   »95
● ≡ ISM—Formation: 116 rue de Belleville, 75020 Paris; *t* (1) 4349 4445, *f* 4349 5602
Training, educational issues.   »94
✿ ≡ ISM Nord-Pas-de-Calais: 13 rue Edouard Delesalle, 59800 Lille; *t* 2040 1985   »94
✿ ≡ ISM Rhône-Alpes (also known as ISM Sud-est): Christian Arnaud: 32 cours La Fayette, 69003 Lyon; *t* 7860 0900, *f* 7860 0203   »94
✿ ≡ ISM Méditerranée: Nourredine Abouakil: 1 boulevard Garibaldi, 13001 Marseille; *t* 9192 5644, *f* 9192 5647   »94
✿ ≡ ISM-Est: 2D avenue de Blida, 57000 Metz; *t* 8732 1155, *f* 8730 4940
Prismes (2/yr).   »94

✿ **Comité de Liaison Inter Service Migrants Auvergne**, CLISMA
Luc Pomares: 8 rue Bons Enfants, 63000 Clermont Ferrand; *t* 7391 4657, *f* 7391 7020
Local branch of Inter Service Migrants, left: housing, education, welfare advice.   »94
✿ **Interassociations pour l'Insertion des Immigrés et Réfugiés en Moselle** *(Moselle Umbrella Group for Immigrant and Refugee Integration)*
Békir Gunes: Maison des Associations, Quartier Lahitolle, 57500 Saint Avold; *t* 8791 0850
Refugee solidarity, welfare assistance.   »94
● **Intercapa—Solidarité Etudiants Etrangers**
Brima Conteh: 9 rue Devaria, 75020 Paris; *t* (1) 4343 6100, 4462 9060   »93
✿ **Le Cana, Centre de Formation et de Préparation à l'Emploi** *(Le Cana Centre for Employment Training and Preparation)*
Alain David/J-L. Boissezon: 514 chemin de la Madrague-Ville, 13344 Marseille Cedex 15; *t* 9160 9301, *f* 9103 2939
Also listed (1990) as La Cana, Centre de Préformation Professionnelle pour Femmes Etrangères (Foreign Women's Job Training Centre).   »94
✿ **Maison de l'Etranger** *(International House)*
Spyros Theodorou: 9 rue du Général Leclerc, 13003 Marseille Cedex 03; *t* 9128 2404, *f* 9128 2417
Welfare advice, information.   »94
✿ **Migrations Santé—Languedoc**
David Nicoladze: 2 avenue E. Bertin Sans, 34259 Montpellier Cedex 5
See Comité Médico-social pour la Santé des Migrants, p136.»94
✿ **Mission et service parmi les migrants**, MISSERM *(Mission and Service among Migrants)*
Champ-Blanc 20, 69570 Dardilly   »89
✿ **Mouvement pour la défense des droits de la femme noire**, MODEFEN *(Movement for the Defence of the Rights of Black Women)*
Lydie Dooh-Bunya: 94 boulevard Masséna, 9, Villa d'Este, 75624 Paris Cedex 13; *t* (1) 4585 5952, *f* 4584 1345
Anti-racism; rights of migrant and refugee women.   »94
✿ **MRASH**
Centre Pierre-Léon, 14 ave Berthelot, 69361 Lyon cedex 07»90
✿ **Promotion Sociale des Travailleurs Immigrés**, PSTI *(Social Advancement of Immigrant Workers)*
112 avenue Jean-Jaurès, 94800 Villejuif; *t* (1) 4677 2988»90
Rencontre Internationale sur le droit de vivre en famille des immigrés en Europe: see Coordination européen pour le droit des étrangers de vivre en famille, p136
● **Reperes**
161 bis rue Saint-Jacques, 75005 Paris; *t* (1) 4354 5427
See also Algerian student group REALE, p9.   »90
✿ **Réseau Accompagnement Actions Médiations Interculturels Saônois**, AAMIS *(Saône Network for Intercultural Mediation and Action)* formerly Association Saônoise d'Aide aux Travailleurs Etrangers
A. Dorafi/Françoise Levecque: 5 cours François Villon, 70000 Vesoul; *t* 8475 3627, *f* 8476 6921
Welfare advice, advocacy, mediation, research and information. *Autre Regard* (3/yr).   »94
◆ **Réseau juridique européen pour l'asile**: European Legal Network on Asylum, ELENA
Gilles Piquois, Co-ordinator: 11 rue Soufflot, 75005 Paris; *t* (1) 4325 5300, *f* 4325 3613
French contact for ELENA international network of immigration and refugee law practitioners, see p154.   »95
✿ **Santé et Communication** *(Health and Communication)*
Jean-Claude Gorriquer: 153 rue de Charonne, 75011 Paris; *t* (1) 4356 2515   »94
✿ **Service des immigrés** *(Immigrant Service)* Région d'Orsay
10 rsd. de Vancoleurs, 91940 Les Ulis; *t* 6928 4228
Catholic chaplaincy to Portuguese and other immigrants. »90
◆ **Service Interdiocésain des Travailleurs Immigrés**, SITI *(Interdiocesan Service for Immigrant Workers)*
Mgr Roger Menteur, Director: Archevêché de Paris, 8 rue de la Ville l'Evêque, 75384 Paris Cedex 08; *t* (1) 4924 1079, 4266 9015, 4924 1111, *f* 4924 1192
Yves de Mallmann. Inter-cultural and inter-faith relations, solidarity, pastoral care of Catholic immigrants; study papers. *Presença Portuguêsa, SITI info* (both 12/yr).   »94
◆ **Service National de la Pastorale des Migrants**, SNPM *(National Migrants Pastoral Service)* Head Office
Père Jean-Claude Luquin, Director: 269 bis rue du Faubourg Saint Antoine, 75011 Paris; *t* (1) 4372 4721
Jean-François Berjonneau. Founded 1966; community relations, Islam in France, pastoral care of immigrants. *Migrations et Pastorale* (8/yr), *Cahiers de la Pastorale des Migrants* (4/yr), *Evangelho e Vida* (4/yr), monographs.   »94

✿ **Service National de la Pastorale des Migrants, SNPM** *(National Migrants Pastoral Service)* and Equipes Pastorales des Migrants *(Migrant Pastoral Teams)*
1 place des Tilleuls, 38000 Grenoble; *t* 7642 5425 »90
✿ ≡ Délégués Diocesain de la Pastorale des Migrants, Créteil: Thérèse Begin: 10 rue P. Roger, 94370 Sucy en Brie; *t* (1) 4590 2667
The *délégués diocesains* and the *équipes pastorales* are lay people, religious or priests designated to co-ordinate pastoral work among Catholic migrants in some dioceses; there are also *délégués* for particular communities such as the Portuguese. »90
✿ ≡ Délégué Diocesain, Tarbes et Lourdes: Pe. José Maria de Antonio: 15 promenade du Pradeau, 65000 Tarbes; *t* 6293 4135, *f* 6251 0713
See also ADM support group, p134. »90
✿ ≡ Délégués Diocesain, Versailles: Père Pierre Brunetti: 26 rue du Maréchal Joffre, 78000 Versailles; *t* (1) 3021 1484 »90
◆ **Service Social d'Aide aux Emigrants, SSAE** *(Social Service for Aid to Emigrants)* part of Service Social International
Monique Moreira: 72 rue Régnault, 75640 Paris Cedex 13; *t* (1) 4077 9450, 4077 9446, 4367 0407, *f* 4584 4305
State-funded agency providing counselling, support and assistance to refugees and migrants in the community, and liaising with international welfare agencies; offices or correspondents in 47 départements. A member of the European Co-ordination for the Right to Family Life of Immigrants, p136. *Accueillir* (6/yr). »95
● **Solidarité français migrants** *(French-Migrant Solidarity)*
[address uncertain] 43 rue Borrego, 75020 Paris; *t* (1) 4364 9304
Also listed (1990) at 4 square Vitruve, 75020 Paris. See also Association solidarité français migrants, p135. »90
✿ ≡ 12 rue Dagobert, 92110 Clichy; *t* (1) 4731 1332 »90
✿ **Solidarité immigrés Epône-Mezieres** *(Immigrants' Solidarity)*
Mairie, 78680 Epône
Joint French-immigrant campaign for foreign workers' rights and interests. »90
✿ **Solidarité Migrants, Solida'Mis**
Chantal Vermet: BP 553, 51069 Reims Cedex; *t* 2686 4735
Advice centre, founded 1987. »90
✿ **SOS Refoulement** *(SOS Deportation)*
I. Régnier: CSF, 15 rue Vaillant, 21000 Dijon; *t* 8067 1676
Legal assistance, campaigns against return of asylum claimants to countries of orign or unsafe third countries, and against administrative deportations of immigrants. »94
● **Terre des Hommes, TDH** *(Land of Mankind, literally; only French name is used)*
4 rue Franklin, 93200 Saint-Denis; *t* (1) 4809 0976
Child welfare development charity affiliated to FITDH in Switzerland, p217; some refugee assistance work. »94
✿ **Union des Associations Immigrées de Rennes, UAIR**
30-32 quai Saint Syr, 35000 Rennes; *t* 9933 0103
Representation of migrant groups; multicultural activities. »94
✿ **Union des Immigrés de l'Eure**
Ali Saidi: 1 rue Michelet, 27000 Evreux-la-Madeleine; *t* 3228 8363 »94
● **Union Mutuelle des Communautés Issues de l'Immigration, UMCII** *(Mutual Aid Union of Immigrant-Origin Communities)*
Thierry Fabre: 22 rue d'Aumale, 75009 Paris; *t* (1) 4280 6922, 4995 7730, 4995 7700
Solidarity, health and welfare. »94
◆ **Union Nationale d'Associations pour l'Accueil de l'Enfant Réfugié, AER** *(National Union of Refugee Children Reception Societies)*
41 avenue René Coty, 75014 Paris; *t* (1) 4327 8188 »91
● **Union nationale déportés de Rawa Ruska** *(National Union of Rava Russkaya Deportees)*
28 boulevard Strasbourg, 75010 Paris; *t* (1) 4206 7760
No definite information, but this may be group of survivors of concentration camps in Rava Russkaya (near Lvov in Ukraine, just across the Polish border). »90
◆ **Union Nationale des Associations Gestionnaires des Foyers de Travailleurs Migrants, UNAFO** *(National Union of Migrant Workers' Housing Associations)*
Annick Brun: 13 rue Brochant, 75017 Paris; *t* (1) 4627 2399, *f* 4627 9595 »94
✿ **Union des travailleurs immigrés de Sevran, UTIS** *(Sevran Immigrant Workers' Union)*
16 rue Pierre-Brossolette, 93270 Sevran
Social, cultural, information work. »90
✿ **Vous et Nous** *(You and Us)*
16 avenue du Maréchal Foch, 95100 Argenteuil
Social and literacy work with immigrants and others. »90

GERMANY *49*

✿ **AKARSU e.V. Gesundheitsetage, AKARSU**
Sevim Celebi: Oranienstraße 25, 10999 Berlin; *t* (030) 614 7031
Founded 1983; employment, welfare, education, training of migrants. »94
✿ **Aktion Noteingang** *(Emergency Entry Action)*
c/o Club Alpha 60, Pfarrgasse 3, 74523 Schwäbisch Hall
Anti-racist youth group; solidarity with refugees and immigrants. »94
✿ **Arbeiterwohlfahrt Kreisverband Düsseldorf e.V.**
Thomas Döring: Oberbilker Allee 287, 40227 Düsseldorf 1; *t* (0211) 770010, 770136
Activities include Projekt Schulsozialarbeit (educational social work project); general youth welfare interests, multi-culturalism, education, training; publishes a German-Turkish youth magazine, *Merhaba die Neue Brücke* (Greetings/the New Bridge). »94
✿ **Arbeitsgemeinschaft der Ausländerbeiräte in Hessen, AGAH** *(Hesse Immigrant Counsellors' Liaison Group)*
Murat Gakir: Kaiser Friedrich-Ring 31, 65185 Wiesbaden; *t* (0611) 989950
Network of public and voluntary organisations providing information and advice to migrant workers and families. »94
✿ **Arbeitsgemeinschaft der Kommunalen Ausländer-vertretungen Niedersachsens** *(Lower Saxony Forum of Municipal Agencies for Foreigners)*
Julio Molina: Postfach 4460, 49034 Osnabrück; *t* (0541) 323 2595, *f* 323 4201
Location: Bierstraße 32A. Co-ordinates services for migrants, promotes intercultural contact. »94
✿ **Asylpfarramt Baden-Württemberg** *(Baden-Württemberg Refugee Pastorate)*
Pfarrer Werner Baumgarten: Vogelsangstraße 60, 70197 Stuttgart; *t* (0711) 631355, 636 5435, *f* 636 9737
Legal advice, support services for asylum seekers. This may succeed, or may have been a constituent of, the Arbeitskreis Asyl Baden-Württemberg (Working Group on Asylum) listed (1990) at the same address. »94
✿ **Ausländerinitiative Freiburg e.V.** *(Freiburg Foreigners' Initiative)*
Lorettostraße 42, 79100780 Freiburg
Migrant welfare, employment rights. »94
● **Basso Tribunal**
c/o AStA TU, Marchstraße 6, 10587 Berlin; *t* (030) 314 24437, *f* 312 1398
Permanent People's Tribunal set up in the 1970s as a successor to the Russell War Crimes Tribunal, investigating a range of human rights issues; held inquiry in Berlin in 1994 into the right of asylum in Europe, focussing on Germany, France, Switzerland and Spain. See Fondazione Lelio Basso, Italy, p206 (the German address may relate only to the Berlin session). »95
● **Behandlungszentrum für Folteropfer, BZFO** *(Treatment Centre for Torture Victims)*
Spandauer Damm 130, Haus 6, 1000 Berlin 19; *t* (030) 3035 3591, *f* 3035 3482
Psycho-social and medical care of refugees and others recovering from torture; information, lobbying and education on torture. »93
✿ **Bund für Soziale Verteidigung, BSV** *(Social Defence League)*
Postfach 2110, Friedensplatz 1a, 32378 Minden; *t* (0571) 29456, *f* 23019
Anti-racist; supports rights of migrants and refugees. No further information. »94
◆ **Bundesarbeitsgemeinschaft der Immigrantenverbände, BAGIV** *(Federal Working Group of Immigrant Groups)*
H.G. Hecker: Poppelsdorfer Allee 19, 53115 Bonn; *t* (0228) 224610, *f* 265255
Major umbrella group of immigrant bodies; member of EU Migrants Forum, p131; civil and political rights, employment, training, youth welfare, anti-racism. »94
✿ ≡ Duisburger Straße 66, 4000 Düsseldorf 30
Also listed (1990) as Lichenstr. 31, 4000 Düsseldorf 1. »90
● **Bündnis 90/Die Grünen—Referat für Asyl- und Einwandererfragen** *(Green Party Asylum and Immigration Department)*
Hochhaus Tulpenfeld, 53090 Bonn; *t* (0228) 167739
Policy forum, advice, interventions on behalf of asylum-seekers and migrants. »94
✿ **Deutsche Flüchtlingshilfe Bonn, DFHB**
Colmantstraße 5, 5300 Bonn 1 »93

- **Deutsche Stiftung für UNO-Flüchtlingshilfe** *(German Foundation for UN Refugee Aid)*
c/o Deutsche Ausgleichbank, Wielandstraße 4, 5300 Bonn 2; *t* (0228) 831683, *f* 831638
Raises funds for refugee counselling, resettlement and support services in Germany and abroad, in association with the UNHCR, p201, UNRWA, p188, and other agencies. »93
- ♦ **Deutscher Gewerkschaftsbund Bundesvorstand Ausländische Arbeitnehmer, DGB** *(German Trade Unions Federal Executive for Foreign Employees)*
Hans-Böckler-Straße 39, 40476 Düsseldorf; *t* (0211) 43010, *f* 430 1409
Migrant worker bureau of the DGB labour federation; concerns include anti-racism, migrant worker rights. See also DGB-Jugend, p200. »94
- **Carl-Duisberg-Gesellschaft e.V.**, **CDG** *(Duisberg Society)*
Hohenstaufenring 30-32, 50674 Köln; *t* (0221) 20980, *f* 209 8111
Educational charity concerned largely with vocational training; helps to administer the EU LINGUA programme on language learning, and aspects of the PETRA programme, p192, promoting international links in vocational training (*t* 209 8365). Has funded training for refugees. »94
- ✿ **Einwanderer-Treff** *(Migrant Rendezvous)*
Kasseler Straße 13, 60486 Frankfurt am Main; *t* (069) 772160, *f* 706323
Social centre; anti-racist journal. *Fremden-Info* (Visitors' Information). »94
- ✿ **Exil—Kulturkoordination** *(Exiles' Cultural Co-ordination Group)*
Friederikenstraße 41, 45130 Essen; *t* (0201) 777176, *f* 779762
Migrant and refugee cultural expression. »94
- **Flüchtlingsrat** *(Refugee Council)*
Handjerystraße 19-20, 1000 Berlin 41 »90
- ✿ **Flüchtlingsrat NordRhein—Westfalen** *(North Rhine Westphalia Refugee Council)*
Frauenstraße 25, 48143 Münster; *t* (0251) 511184 »94
- ✿ **Frankfurter Rechtshilfekomitee für Ausländer** *(Frankfurt Immigrant Legal Aid Committee)*
Sigrid Abrigada: c/o Evangelische Studentengemeinde, Lessingstraße 2, 60325 Frankfurt am Main; *t* (069) 729161
Legal and welfare advice. »94
- ✿ **Frauenaktion Scheherazade** *(Sheherazade Women's Action Group)*
Johanniterstraße 35-37, 51065 Köln; *t* (0221) 696357, *f* 693741
Feminist group including minority and refugee women. »94
- ✿ **Gesellschaft zur Förderung Ausländischer Jugendlichen e.V.** *(Society for Aid to Immigrant Youth)*
Elisenstraße 20, 3000 Hannover 91 »90
- **Immigranten Politisches Forum, IPF** *(Immigrants' Political Forum)*
Oranienstraße 159, 10969 Berlin; *t* (030) 615 8716
Co-ordination of immigrant associations. »94
- ✿ **Initiative für Menschenrechte** *(Human Rights Initiative)*
Bärbel Stechel, Chairperson: [address unknown] Wischhafen, Niedersachsen
Campaigns against racist violence; supports refugee rights.»94
- ♦ **Interessengemeinschaft der mit Ausländern Verheirateten Frauen e.V.**, **IAF: Association of Binational Marriages, Families and Partnerships** *(literally Alliance of Women with Foreign Husbands)*
Elisabeth Machhour: Goethestraße 53, 8000 München
Pressure group and support network, founded 1972 by German women married to Palestinians who were deported from Germany; immigration rules, nationality, right to family reunion, anti-racism, racial equality, minority rights, other matters affecting cross-national partnerships. See also Verband bi-nationaler Familien und Partnerschaften, p140.»95
- ✿ ≡ E. Grunowstraße 2, 2800 Bremen; *t* (0421) 76076 »94
- ✿ **Kirklich Beauftragter für Ausländerarbeit** *(Church Commissioner for Social Work with Foreigners)* Evangelische Kirche in Berlin—Brandenburg Konsistorium
Thomas Venske: Neue Grünstraße 19/22, 10179 Berlin; *t* (030) 278 02169, *f* 279 1176 »95
- **Kulturkomitee für ausländische Arbeitnehmer** *(Cultural Committee for Foreign Employees)*
[address unknown] »90
- ✿ **Landesarbeitsgemeinschaft ausländische Flüchtlinge in Nordrhein-Westfalen, LAF** *(North Rhine-Westphalia Working Group on Refugees)*
Kronprinzenstraße 62, 4000 Düsseldorf 1; *t* (0211) 372008
Welfare, integration of refugees in the Land; information; co-ordination of refugee associations. »83

- ✿ **Lower Saxony Refugee Council**
Kai Weber: [address unknown] »94
- ✿ **MaterialDienst Asyl, MD Asyl** *(Asylum Practical Help)*
c/o Obere Holtener Straße 28, 47167 Duisburg; *t* (0203) 590226, *f* 501122
Research, service development, archive and resource centre for refugee and migrant assistance, anti-racism and anti-fascism. »94
- ▌ **Network of National Minorities Youth in Western Europe**
Atilla Vurgun: Koloniestraße 33, 1000 Berlin 6; *t* (030) 493 9756
Vurgun is national rapporteur for MAINE information group, p146. This Network may be linked with/same as Council of Europe Minority Youth Committee, p200. »90
- **Ökumenischer Vorbereitungsausschuß zur Woche der ausländische Mitbürger** *(Ecumenical Preparatory Board for Foreign Residents' Week)*
Neue Schlesingergasse 22-24, 6000 Frankfurt am Main 1
See also Pro Asyl, below. »90
- ♦ **Pro Asyl—Bundesweite Arbeitsgemeinschaft für Flüchtlinge** *(Pro-Asylum—Federal Working Group for Refugees)*
Günther Burkhardt: Postfach 101843, Neue Schlesingergasse 22, 60018 Frankfurt am Main; *t* (069) 230688, 293160, *f* 230650, 280370
Rev. Herbert Leuninger. Refugee rights group, made up of representatives of eight NGOs active on protection issues; its founding in 1986 was aided by the UNHCR, p201, which aids its public information activities including the annual Refugee Day: see Ökumenischer Vorbereitungsausschuß, above. »94
- ✿ ≡ Rainer M. Hofmann: Elsaß-Straße 51, 52068 Aachen; *t* (0241) 501021, *f* 534411
Pressure group on asylum rights; services to refugees. »95
- ✿ **Project AQUA**
An St. Urban 2, 51063 Köln; *t* (0221) 811386, *f* 818935
Training, employment and welfare concerns. »94
- ✿ **Psychologischer Dienst für Italiener und Spanier** *(Psychological Service for Italian and Spanish People)*
Dr Urso: Mittelstr. 52-54, 50672 Köln; *t* (0221) 257 3141
Specialist mental health counselling/treatment service. »94
- **Psychosoziales Zentrum für ausländische Flüchtlingen, PSZ** *(Psycho-Social Centre for Foreign Refugees)*
Jean Claude Diallo: Hinter den Ulmen 15, 60433 Frankfurt am Main; *t* (069) 520081-82, *f* 538435
Medical and welfare assistance to mainly Latin American and African torture victims and other traumatised refugees; funded by Diakonisches Werk Frankfurt, p201, and government. »95
- ✿ ≡ Berlinerstr. 208, 01773 Altenberg; *t* (0365) 412181 »95
- ✿ ≡ Graf-Adolf-Straße 102, 40210 Düsseldorf; *t* (0211) 353315 »95
- ✿ ≡ Diakonisches Werk Bayern *(Bavaria Pastoral Care Service)*: Pirckheimer Straße 6, 90408 Nürnberg; *t* (0911) 9354 401-406, *f* 9354 404 »95
- ✿ ≡ Dudweiler Landstraße 153, 66123 Saarbrücken; *t* (0681) 390 5005 »95
- **Psychosoziales Zentrum Dietrich Koch: Psychosoziale Hilfen für Politisch Verfolgte** *(Psycho-Social Assistance Centre for the Politically Persecuted)*
Roscher Straße 2a, 1000 Berlin 12
Dealing with the psychological and social after-effects of torture, this therapeutic counselling centre works with refugees who are experiencing the severest forms of marginalisation. Funded under EU Poverty 3 programme. »91
- ♦ **Raphaelswerk—Dienst am Menschen Unterwegs e.V.** *(St Raphael's Association—Service to People on the Move)*
Dr Victor Mohr, General Secretary: Adenauerallee 41, 20097 Hamburg; *t* (0402) 43677, 46154, 484420, *f* 484 4226
Christopher Layden. Agency founded 1871; counselling, re-migration assistance (mainly to USA and Australia) and other services to immigrants, refugees, emigrants and bi-national couples; affiliate of International Catholic Migration Commission, p217. *Jahrbuch, Jahresbericht*. »95
- ✿ **Reception and Advice Centre for Ethnic Minorities**
[address unknown] 5000 Köln »88
- ✿ **Refugio**
[address unknown] München
Support group for refugees in Munich. »95
- ✿ **Regionale Arbeitsstelle für Ausländerfragen e.V.** *(Regional Working Group on Foreigners' Issues)*
Schumannstraße 5, 10117 Berlin; *t* (030) 282 9627, *f* 238 4303 »94
- ✿ **Selbstandige Immigrantinnen**
Zekiye Sarpyel: Perlebergerstraße 29, 1000 Berlin 21; *t* (030) 461 7771
Enterprise, employment, training for young women immigrants; see Council of Europe Minority Youth Committee, p200. »90

✿ **Sozialdienst für Ausländer Theresa-von-Avila-Haus** *(Theresa of Avila House, Social Service for Foreigners)*
Spielmannsgasse 4-10, 50678 Köln; *t* (0221) 931 8100
Housing and welfare assistance.   »94

✿ **Sprachverband Deutsch für ausländische Arbeitnehmer e.V.**
(German Language Society for Foreign Employees; usually known as Sprachverband)
Gerhard Fiedler, Director: Raimundistraße 2, 55118 Mainz;
t (06131) 679021, 964440, 964444
Jochem Kahl; labour ministry-funded agency formed in 1974 to offer German language and social integration courses to immigrant workers and families; substantial resource centre; publications include *Deutsch Lernen—Zeitschrift für den Spracherunterricht mit ausländischen Arbeitnehmern* (4/yr), *Bildungsarbeit mit Ausländischen Jugendliche—Konzepte und Materialen* (3/yr).   »94

● **Stiftung Mitarbeit** *(Co-operation Foundation)*
Bornheimer Straße 37, 53111 Bonn; *t* (0228) 630023, *f* 695421
Youth welfare foundation, involved in the EU's PETRA vocational training scheme, p192. Anti-racism, migrant and refugee concerns.   »94

● **Tolstoy Hilfs- und Kulturwerk** *(Tolstoy Foundation)*
Savigny Straße 30, 6000 Frankfurt am Main; *t* (069) 520081
Help to Russian and other East European refugees, and more recently to third world refugees, seeking to emigrate to third countries, usually the United States. See also in East European listings, pp32-33.   »89

✿ **Unterkommission des Pastoralkommission—Seelsorge am Menschen unterwegs** *(Pastorate to Migrants Subcommission of the Pastoral Commission)*
Dick Klaus: Postfach 108014, Marzellenstraße 32, 50668 Köln; *t* (0221) 164 2711
Pastoral care, advice and welfare work.   »94

◆ **Verband bi-nationaler Familien und Partnerschaften, IAF:**
Association of Binational Marriages, Families and Partnerships
Sabine Kriechhammer-Yagmur: Kasseler Straße 1a, 60486 Frankfurt am Main; *t* (069) 707 5087, 737898, 732638, *f* 707 5092
Concerned with immigration, nationality and other problems of Germans with non-German partners; provides social support for such families, and campaigns for anti-racism and a multicultural perspective. See also main IAF listing, p139; AGISRA, p166, and Iranian women's group, p45, at same address; and ECB based in France, p164.   »94

◆ **Verband der Initiativgruppen in der Ausländerarbeit e.V.,**
VIA *(League of Immigrant Assistance Action Groups)* VIA-Bundesgeschäftsstelle *(Federal Head Office)*
Theaterstraße 10, 5300 Bonn 1; *t* (0228) 655553
Founded 1979; network of local non-party, secular and multi-cultural groups providing practical aid to refugees and immigrants.   »90

✿ ≡ North Rhine-Westphalia, VIA-NRW: Hernerstraße 299, 4630 Bochum 1; *t* (0234) 547 9944   »90
✿ ≡ Heinz Soremsky: Hochemmericher Straße 71, 47226 Duisburg; *t* (02065) 53346, *f* 535661
VIA-Magazin, Viaticus.   »94
✿ ≡ Hamburg, VIA-Nord: Nernstweg 25, 22765 Hamburg; *t* (040) 392690   »94
✿ ≡ Bavaria, VIA-Bayern: M. Bosl: H.-Lingg-Straße 12, 8000 München 2; *t* (089) 530 9039   »90
✿ ≡ Bavaria, VIA-Bayern: L. Scholz: Bauerngasse 29, 8500 Nürnberg 70; *t* (0911) 288477   »90
✿ ≡ Baden-Württemberg, VIA Ba-Wü: M. Bittl: Haußmann-straße 6, 7000 Stuttgart 1; *t* (0711) 263 7178   »90

✿ **Verein zur Förderung Ethnischer Minderheiten e.V.** *(Union for the Advancement of Ethnic Minorities)*
Bergmanstraße 35, 80339 München; *t* (089) 509584
Anti-racism, multiculturalism.   »94

✿ **Verein zur Förderung und Integration von Ausländische Jugendlicher** *(League for the Advancement and Integration of Immigrant Youth)*
Ikbal Berber: Försterstraße 24, 66111 Saarbrücken; *t* (06821) 33275   »94

✿ **Verein Mutter-Kind Stube e.V.** *(Mother and Child Room Association)*
Bagdat Bozhurst: Denissstraße 25, 90429 Nürnberg; *t* (0911) 269176
Employment training, education, social and cultural facilities for immigrant women.   »94

✿ **Verein für Psychische Gesundheit von Migranten e.V.**
(Union for the Mental Health of Migrants)
c/o Herr Saric: Austraße 14, 74076 Heilbronn
Research and service provison on psycho-social wellbeing of migrants.   »94

◆ **Working Group Asylum in Churches**
Dirk Vogelskamp, Director: [address unknown]
An umbrella organisation of churches providing sanctuary for refugees threatened with deportation, especially since the tightening of asylum laws in 1993. Despite the absence of a legal basis for asylum in churches, of the 1,000 or so taking refuge since 1985, for periods ranging from three months to three years, some 85 per cent have succeeded in having deportation orders revoked.   »95

◆ **Zentralstelle Pastoral Deutschen Bischofskonferenz—Referat Auslanderseelsorge** *(Migrants Pastorate Department—German Bishops' Conference Central Pastoral Service)*
Joachim Justus: Kaiserstraße 163, 53113 Bonn; *t* (0228) 103218, *f* 103219   »94

GREECE *30*

● **Agonistiki-Agonas**
Damasipou 8, Zografou, 15771 Athinai
Education, welfare, immigrant youth integration; information service.   »94

● **Association des Rapatriés d'Europe Occidentale** *(Association of Returnees from Western Europe)*
Menandrou 51, 10437 Athinai; *t* (01) 323 4952   »90

● **Athens Reception**
Vas. Konstantinou Avenue 5-7, Athinai; *t* (01) 729 0151 »90

✿ **Community Centre**
[address unknown] Egaleon
Established by NGOs including ICMC, p203, WCC, below, and YWCA, along with the IOM and the UNHCR, both p203; refugee counselling, temporary employment.   »83

◆ **European Legal Network on Asylum, ELENA**
Ioanna B. Babassika, Co-ordinator: Amfictionis 1b, 11851 Athinai; *t* (01) 345 9065, 347 7826, *f* 361 2273
National contact for the EU-wide network of practitioners in refugee law, see p154.   »95

◆ **Greek Refugee Council**
Irene Feraldis: Odos Arachovis 39, 10681 Athinai; *t* (01) 360 5029, 360 2508, 360 7645, *f* 360 3774
The main national agency for refugee advice and free legal assistance; assessment of asylum claims, material aid and social support for refugees.   »95

● **Iatriko Kentro Apokatiastasis Thymaton Vassanistirion:**
Medical Rehabilitation Centre for Torture Victims
Odos Lycavittou 9, Kolonaki, 10672 Athinai; *t* (01) 360 4967, *f* 361 2273
Medical and psychological care of traumatised refugees, campaigns for the prevention of torture.   »95

● **Inter-Church Aid**
Holy Synod of the Church of Greece, Odos P. Gennadiou 14, Athinai; *t* (01) 738671   »83

✿ **Refugee Reception Centre**
[address unknown] Lavrion
See also International Social Service, and the Centre's funders, IOM and UNHCR, all p203.   »83

● **Reintegration Centre for Return Migration, KSPM**
A. Papantoniou: Odos Deinokratous 68, 11521 Athinai   »90

◆ **Service to Refugees, World Council of Churches, WCC:**
also known as Ecumenical Refugee Programme
Mary A. Botas, Director: Odos Dodekanissou 6, Agios Panteleimon, Ana Kalamaki, 17456 Athinai; *t* (01) 991 8812, 995 5738, 991 2416, *f* 995 7813
Efthalia Pappa. One of the two main refugee services; range of activities similar to that of ICMC, p203, with which it co-operates; see also WCC international headquarters, p219.»95

● **Social Work Foundation, SWF**
Evangelia Loukadounou: Odos Mantzapou 6, 10672 Athinai; *t* (01) 360 7922, 363 5881, *f* 360 0786
Refugee and migrant welfare, housing and employment advice in Greece, along with other social work and community development concerns.   »94

HUNGARY *36*

● **Független Szövetsége**
Tolnai útca 34, 8000 Székesfehérvár
Anti-racist, anti-fascist; supports refugee rights.   »94

● **Kalyi Jag**
Barcsay útca 11, 1073 Budapest; *t* (01) 251 8263
Anti-racist, anti-fascist; refugee rights.   »94

IRELAND 353

✿ **Cork Diocesan Emigration Service**
Sr Patricia O Regan, Director: 34 Paul Street, Cork; *t* (021) 274520
Catholic church-backed advice unit for emigrants.   »94

● **Emigrant Advice**
Marie Keegan/Kate Sheehan: 1a Cathedral Street, Dublin 1; *t* (01) 873 2844, *f* 872 7003
Free advisory service for intending emigrants, covering visas, residence procedures, welfare entitlements, employment and housing. Some work with return migration and immigration; funded by the Catholic Social Service Conference, but open to all; resource centre, research, training seminars.   »95

✿ **Emigrant Advice Centre**
Sr Anthony: Social Service Centre, Castlebar, Co. Mayo; *t* (094) 22814
Advice and counselling to those planning emigration.   »94

✿ **Emigrant Advice Service**
Sr Noreen Lyons: St Mary's, Portumna, Co. Galway; *t* (0509) 41034
Emigration counselling and advice service of the (Catholic) Galway Diocesan Youth Service.   »94

✿ **Emigration Advisory Bureau**
[address unknown] Limerick
Voluntary advice service for intending emigrants.   »89

● **Emigration Research and Action Group**, ERAG
Liam Ó Cuinnegáin: c/o 16-17 Beresford Place, Dublin 1
Voluntary group created 1984; research and information on emigration and its socio-economic causes and consequences. Campaigns for voting rights for emigrants.   »93

◆ **Interdepartmental Committee on Emigration**
Derek Feely: Department of Foreign Affairs, 82 St Stephen's Green, Dublin 2; *t* (01) 478 0822, *f* 668 6518
Body, comprising representatives of relevant government departments and other agencies, co-ordinating Irish government policy on emigration and support to emigrant groups and agencies in Ireland and abroad.   »95

● **International Network for Ireland**
Donna O'Connor: [address unknown] Dublin
Encourages return migration.   »91

● **Irish Anti-Extradition Committee**
Basement, 29 Mountjoy Square Road, Dublin 1; *t* (01) 366489 (?)
Political campaign against extradition of Irish citizens to Britain; interests include welfare of prisoners abroad.   »90

◆ **Irish Commission for Prisoners Overseas**, ICPO
Nuala Kelly, Co-ordinator: 57 Parnell Square West, Dublin 1; *t* (01) 872 2511
Anne Whelan administrator; Archbishop Joseph Cassidy president, Rev. Prof. Patrick Hannon chairman. Catholic agency founded 1985 under Irish Episcopal Commission for Emigrants, below. Pastoral and social work with the 1,200 Irish people in foreign jails (including 1,000 in Britain: see London office, p49), and their families; research/information service for prisoners, families and welfare groups. Promotes penal reform, voluntary transfer of prisoners between countries, human rights of prisoners, refugees and migrants, and fair treatment of non-nationals in all judicial and prison systems. *Newsletter for Irish Prisoners Overseas* (3/yr).   »95

◆ **Irish Council for Overseas Students**, ICOS
Wendy Cox: 41 Morehampton Road, Dublin 4; *t* (01) 660 5233, *f* 668 2320
Advisory service for overseas students, including refugees. *Annual Report, Annual Statistics*.   »95

● *The Irish Emigrant*
Liam Ferris: Menlo, Galway; *t* (091) 767534, *f* 755635, *e* Ferris@iol.ie
An e-mail service of weekly news from Ireland.   »95

◆ **Irish Episcopal Commission for Emigrants**, IECE
Fr Paul Byrne OMI, Director: 3rd floor, 57 Parnell Square, Dublin 1; *t* (01) 872 3655, *f* 872 3717
Nola Young, administrator. Established by the Irish Catholic bishops in 1957 (succeeding an informal committee set up in the early 1940s); created and liaises with Irish chaplaincies in Britain, p49, continental Europe, pp46-7, and the USA. Concerned with pastoral care of Irish people abroad, and those considering emigration; prior to the establishment of state-funded services in the early 1990s, its Refugee Section helped co-ordinate settlement assistance to Vietnamese and other refugees in Ireland, and it funded the Emigrant Welfare Bureau, now superseded by the (independent) Emigrant Advice centre, above. See also ICPO, above.   »95

◆ **Irish Refugee Council**
Nadette Foley/Neasa Ní Ailegain: Arran House, 35-36 Arran Quay, Dublin 7; *t* (01) 872 4424, 872 4433, *f* 872 4411
Ken Duggan, executive director. Founded 1990 as state-funded but independent body for non-governmental agencies working with asylum-seekers, displaced persons and refugees, overseas and in Ireland. Main concerns are protecting asylum rights, and providing services to refugees including emergency relief, legal casework, repatriation assistance. Local office (dealing with Shannon Airport asylum claims) at 1 Bank Place, Ennis, Co. Clare, *t* (065) 22026.   »95

✿ **Kerry Emigrant Support Group**, KESG: Taca Eisimirceach Chiarraí
Ena McCarthy, Secretary: The Bungalow, Ballyard House, Ballyard, Tralee, Co. Kerry; *t* (066) 24234
Voluntary group providing advice and information for those intending to emigrate.   »95

● **Louvain Development Trust**
Richard Dennis/Paddy Maguire: [address unknown] Dublin
Charity funding the Irish Institute of European Affairs, in Belgium, p46. A similar body raises funds for the Irish College in Paris, also p46; both centres are former seminaries and now provide accommodation for Irish students.   »91

● **People Active Through Community Help**, PATCH
20 Mark Street, Dublin 2
Community development; some interest in migration and minorities.   »94

◆ **The Refugee Agency**: succeeds Refugee Resettlement Committee
John O'Neill, Director: Berkeley House, 17 Berkeley Street, Dublin 7; *t* (01) 830 9081, 830 9522, *f* 830 1645
Iseult O'Malley, chair; board members from Departments of Health, Education, Environment, Justice, Employment & Enterprise, Social Welfare and Foreign Affairs, with observer members representing several NGOs. State-funded agency mainly involved in the care and resettlement of some 500 Vietnamese, and around 300 Bosnian, refugees.   »95

◆ **Refugee Legal Advisory Services** and European Legal Network on Asylum, ELENA
Robert Eager: Garret Sheehan & Co., 32 Francis Street, Dublin 8; *t* (01) 453 3477, 453 3521, *f* 453 3528
Panel of lawyers providing expert advice and assistance for asylum seekers; Eager is Irish contact for ELENA, p154.   »95

● **World University Service**, WUS
33 Pembroke Street Lower, Dublin 2; *t* (01) 661 6555, *f* 676 8299
Support and advice for students from less developed countries and for refugee students. Part of international WUS, p219.»94

ITALY 39

✿ **Altre Luci** *(Other Lights)*
via T. Ciceri 5, 22100 Como; *t* (031) 306390, *f* 304420
Inter-cultural contact and solidarity.   »94

● **Asilo Politico** *(Political Asylum)*
viale Etiopia 45, Roma   »90

✿ **Associazione ADAESER Stranieri**
Zeinab Abdelazi: Polisportivo, via Independenza 11, Modena Est; *t* (059) 920242   »90

✿ **Associazione Cittadini Extracomunitari del Polesine** *(Polesine Association of Non-EU Citizens)*
via Verdi 27, 45100 Rovigo; *t* (0425) 428312, *f* 428340
Represents interests of, and provides social support for, residents other than European Union nationals.   »94

✿ **Associazione delle Comunità Straniere in Italia**, ACSI *(Association of Foreign Communities in Italy)*
Habib ben Sghaier: via Napoli 4, 71100 Foggia; *t* (0881) 48808, 41849   »90

✿ **Associazione Cristiana Lavoratori Italiani—Patronato ACLI Sportello Stranieri**, ACLI *(Italian Christian Workers' Association—Foreigners Section)*
via Falamonica 1/7, 16123 Genova; *t* (010) 203412
Foreigners' welfare.   »90

✿ **Associazione Extracomunitari** *(Non-EU Association)*
via Spani 12, 42100 Reggio Emilia; *t* (0522) 5813   »90

● **Associazione Forum**
via Santa Eufemia 19, 00187 Roma; *t* (06) 678 7926
See also Comitato Profughi Esteri, p143.   »90

✿ **Associazione Giovani 80—Comunità Paolo e Lorenzo Pernigotti** *(Youth 80 Association—Pernigotti Community)*
Anna Garaffa: piazza San Marco 2, 20121 Milano; *t* (02) 657 2476
Youth welfare, housing, education.   »94

✧ **Associazione Immigrati Extracomunitari** *(Non-EU Immigrants' Association)*
Camera del Lavoro, via del Padovanino 1, 35123 Padova; *t* (049) 664122
See also the Ufficio Lavoratori Immigrati of the CGIL trade unions, p143.   »90
✧ ≡ via Fiammie Gialle 1, 33170 Pordenone   »90
✧ **Associazione Immigrati Extracomunitari Bassanese**, AIEB *(Bassano Non-EU Immigrants Association)*
Lorentz Luboya: viale Volpato 10, 36100 Bassano del Grappa, Vicenza
Welfare and housing of non-EU migrants.   »94
✧ **Associazione Immigrati Triveneto**
pza Alcide de Gasperi 41, 35131 Padova; *t* (049) 660840»90
▌**Associazione Italiana Tutela Emigrati e Famiglie**, AITEF *(Italian Society for Protection of Emigrants and their Families)*
via Santa Maria in Via 12, 00187 Roma; *t* (06) 672 7290, 67271
May be linked with Partito Socialista Democratico Italiano, PSDI. *Umanità Europea.*   »90
♦ **Associazione Nazionale Famiglie Emigrati**, ANFE *(National Association of Emigrant Families)*
Saporito Learco, President: [address uncertain] via Federico Cesi 44-0, 00193 Roma; *t* (06) 321 3956, 317764 (?)
Also listed (1990) at via Olelia 6, 00193 Roma. Founded 1947; research, documentation, assistance to emigrants and immigrants. See branches in Belgium, p73, Luxembourg, p75, UK, p76. *Notizie fatto Problemi dell'Emigrazione.*   »90
✧ ≡ Apulia: Tommaso Iacovelli: via Luigi Sbano 16, 71100 Foggia, Puglia; *t* (0881) 639397   »94
♦ **Associazione Nazionale Oltre Le Frontiere**, ANOLF *(National Overseas Association)*
Mohamed Saady: via Medina 5, 80100 Napoli; *t* (081) 551 5120-21, *f* 551 4395
Anti-racism, welfare advice, international solidarity, cultural and social activities.   »94
✧ ≡ Lombardy: Francesco Bergamelli: c/o CISL, via Carnovali 88, 24100 Bergamo, Lombardia; *t* (035) 324200   »94
✧ ≡ Apulia: Abbas Elgouhari: via Trento 42, 71100 Foggia, Puglia; *t* (0881) 724388, *f* 671681   »94
✧ ≡ Lazio region: Abdelhafidh Oussaifi: via Guglielmo Marconi 12, 03100 Frosinone; *t* (0775) 250623   »94
✧ ≡ Friuli-Venezia Giulia region: Gregoretti Lucio: via Manzoni 5 G, 34170 Gorizia; *t* (0481) 533321, *f* 34615   »94
✧ ≡ Marches: Sammy Kunou: via S. Maria della Porta 43, 62100 Macerata; *t* (0733) 230463, 237928, *f* 235928   »94
✧ **Associazione Professori Universitari Cittadini Stranieri** *(Association of Foreign University Lecturers)*
via G. Frassinello 1/16, 16159 Genova; *t* (010) 441739
Professional and social interests.   »90
✧ **Associazione Regionale Famiglie Immigrati**, ARFI *(Regional Association of Immigrant Families)*
Mady Mandoh: [address uncertain] via Michele Amari[zo?] 30-32, 90139 Palermo, Sicilia; *t* (091) 589322
Postcode uncertain: 90142, 90129? Advice, campaigns for migrant rights.   »90
✧ **Associazione Rifugiati Politici** *(Association of Political Refugees)*
presso Comunità Europea Giornalisti, via XX Settembre 26, 00187 Roma   »90
✧ **Associazione Fernando Santi**
via Brera 18, 20121 Milano; *t* (02) 877903
See also Istituto Fernando Santi, p144.   »90
♦ **Associazione Scalabrini Profughi-Emigrati-Rifugiati**, ASPER *(Scalabrini Society for Asylum-Seekers, Refugees and Emigrants)*
P. Renzo Marcon: via Ulisse Seni 2, 00153 Roma; *t* (06) 5833 0993, *f* 5833 1092
Also listed (1990) at via del Mascherone 60, 00186 Roma, *t* 687 9943.   »94
✧ **Associazione Solidarietà Dandolo**
via degli Astalli 7, 00186 Roma; *t* (06) 301 0339   »90
✧ **Associazione Stranieri in Vicenza** *(Association of Foreigners in Vicenza)*
Borgo Scroffa 16, 36100 Vicenza; *t* (0444) 673829
Solidarity among immigrants in the Trento region.   »90
✧ **Associazione Trentina Accoglienza Stranieri**, ATAS *(Trento Association for the Reception of Foreigners)*
Dr Antonio a Beccara: via Endrici 27, 38100 Trento
Migrant reception and welfare services.   »90
✧ **Azione Comboniana Servizio Emigrati Terzo Mondo**, ACSE
Renato Bresciani: via del Buon Consiglio 19, 00184 Roma; *t* (06) 818 3717, *f* 589 8101
Welfare and housing advice, solidarity with Third World immigrants.   »94

✧ **Caritas Italiana: Caritas Diocesana, Naples: Settore Immigrati**
Rosana Ronao, Co-ordinator: Largo Donnaregina 2, 80138 Napoli; *t* (081) 454047, 451169
Migrant welfare and employment advice.   »94
✧ ≡ **Caritas Diocesana, Turin: Servizio Migranti:** Dr Gerolamo Bigo: via Principi d'Acaja 42 bis, 10138 Torino; *t* (011) 447 7178, *f* 434 2222   »94
✧ **Casa dell'Accoglienza Don Luigi Savarè** *(Don Luigi Savarè Reception Centre)*
Mario Ferrari: via S. Francesco 16, 20075 Lodi, MI; *t* (0371) 52252, 58773
Migrant housing and welfare.   »94
✧ **Casa Accoglienza Shalom** *(Shalom Reception Centre)*
Riccardo Gini: via Bonvesin de la Riva 2, 20129 Milano; *t* (02) 738 3971, 7012 5648, *f* 749 0955
Anti-racism, housing support, social activities.   »94
✧ **Centro di Accoglienza** *(Reception Centre)*
[address unknown] Perugia; *t* (075) 22880   »90
✧ **Centro Accoglienza Don Bosco per Giovani Stranieri** *(Don Bosco Reception Centre for Young Foreigners)*
E. Leonardi: via Magenta 25, 00185 Roma; *t* (06) 490071
Housing, welfare and health advice.   »94
✧ **Centro Accoglienza e Cultura Immigrati Stranieri**, CACIS *(Reception and Cultural Centre for Foreign Immigrants)*
Riccardo Zingaro: via De Anellis 46, 70031 Andria, BA; *t* (0883) 22022   »94
✧ **Centro Accoglienza Extracomunitari**, CAE *(Reception Centre for Non-EU Immigrants)*
Germano Garatto: Ufficio Stanieri, via L. Gagliardo 2, 16126 Genova; *t* (010) 257206, 516147, *f* 267768
A Catholic welfare agency under the Fondazione di Religione Auxilium. Formerly known as Ufficio Stranieri, Caritas Diocesana.   »94
✧ **Centro Accoglienza Immigrati Esteri** *(Foreign Immigrants' Reception Centre)*
Caritas, via Milano 17, 00055 Ladispoli
Catholic Church-sponsored welfare service.   »90
✧ **Centro di Accoglienza Sociale Territoriale**, CAST *(Regional Reception and Welfare Centre)*
Franco Fino: via Leone XIII 12, 20145 Milano; *t* (02) 498 4426
Housing and welfare assistance.   »94
✧ **Centro Accoglienza Straniere** *(Reception Centre for Foreigners)* also known as Ufficio Accoglienza, Caritas
Ngô Dinh Lê Quyên: via delle Zoccolette 17, 00186 Roma; *t* (06) 687 5228, 686 4460, 686 1554
Refugee and migrant reception, welfare and advice service. A service of Caritas Romana (the diocesan branch of the major Catholic charity).   »95
✧ **Centro Accoglienza per Studenti Esteri OMMS** *(Reception Centre for Foreign Students)*
via Machiavelli 50, 00185 Roma; *t* (06) 731 0868   »90
✧ **Centro Accoglimento** *(Reception Centre)*
via Pace 18, Modena   »90
✧ **Centro di Aiuto alla Vita Mangiagalli**, CAV
via Commenda 12, 20122 Milano; *t* (02) 5518 1923, *f* 546 1477
Women and families welfare centre. *Lettera ai soci* (4/yr).»94
✧ **Centro d'Ascolto Amico in Più** *(Extra Friend Attention Centre)*
Liliana Bruni: via M.A. Colonna 1, 20149 Milano; *t* (02) 3360 1729
Advice/information for Latin American and other migrants.»94
✧ **Centro d'Ascolto per la Prevenzione del Disagio Psicologico degli Immigrati** *(Attention Centre for the Prevention of Psychological Disturbance in Immigrants)*
Raffaele Bracalenti: via Arenula 21, 00186 Roma; *t* (06) 686 7495
Psychiatric health promotion, counselling and care.   »94
✧ **Centro di Assistenza agli Emigrati**
[address unknown] La Spezia
Aid, advice.   »90
✧ **Centro Collegamento per i Diritti degli Immigrati** *(Liaison Centre for Immigrants' Rights)*
Marcos Bava: via Taddea 33, 50123 Firenze; *t* (055) 287607
Legal aid. *Collegamento.*   »90
✧ **Centro Collegamento sull'Immigrazione dall'Estero** *(Liaison Centre on Foreign Immigration)*
via Baracca 91, Firenze; *t* (055) 287607, *f* 499 1753   »95
✧ **Centro di Emigrazione**
piazza San Ambrogio 3, 20123 Milano; *t* (02) 869 3304   »90
✧ **Centro Immigrati ICAS** *(Immigrants' Centre)*
via Carraia 66, 50047 Prato; *t* (0574) 34228   »90
● **Centro Informazione sui Detenuti Stranieri**, CIDSI *(Information Centre on Foreign Prisoners)*
[address unknown] Roma   »90

✿ **Centro Internazionale di Accoglienza** *(International Reception Centre)*
Lungo Tevere dei Vallati 1, 00186 Roma; *t* (06) 561019　»90

✿ **Centro Internazionale Scambi Culturali—Accoglienza Immigrati, CISCAI** *(International Immigrant Reception and Cultural Exchange Centre)*
Alfonso Bellini: via G. Petroni 121, 70123 Bari; *t* (080) 502 1730
Formerly (1990) listed c/o Caritas Diocesana, pza Odegitiria Arciv., 70122 Bari, *t* (080) 237311.　»94

✿ **Centro Internazionale per gli Studenti** also known as Centro La Pira
via Pescione 3, 50125 Firenze; *t* (055) 877 7041
Foreign students, educational welfare. Address of groups including ASAFP, p3, and CNFP, p92.　»90

✿ **Centro Lavoratori Immigrati** *(Immigrant Workers' Centre)*
Zouhir ben Hamed: presso CGIL, via Piemonte 35, 63039 San Benedetto del Tronto; *t* (0735) 83803
Trade union advice centre; see CGIL, right.　»90

✿ **Centro Lavoratori Stranieri, CELSTRA** *(Foreign Workers' Centre)*
Mehari Desbele: corso di Porta Vittoria 43, 20122 Milano; *t* (02) 549 5254
Employment and welfare advice.　»94

✿ **Centro Lavoratori Stranieri Immigrati, CELSI** *(Centre for Foreign Immigrant Workers)*
via Galilei 55, 00199 Roma; *t* (06) 731 6063, 734915
See also Cooperativa di Servizio, right.　»94

✿ **Centro Lavoratori Stranieri in Italia, CeLSI-CGIL** *(Centre for Foreign Workers in Italy)* and Centro Associazioni Immigrati in Italia
via Adua 22, 00199 Roma; *t* (06) 836636, 834466
Migrant labour support group of the CGIL trade union confederation, see right.　»90

✿ **Centro Migranti** *(Migrants Centre)*
c/o Curia Vescovile, Casella Postale 394, via Gabriele Rosa 30, 25121 Brescia　»90

✿ **Centro di Prima Accoglienza** *(Initial Reception Centre)*
Comune de Bologna
via G. Petroni 9, 40126 Bologna; *t* (051) 236136
Legal advice and assistance for refugees and foreigners; works closely with regional authorities.　»95

✿ **Centro di Prima Accoglienza per Extracomunitari** *(Initial Reception Centre for Non-EU Immigrants)*
Roberto Betti: via Brighenti 24, 47937 Rimini; *t* (0541) 704384
Founded 1988; advice, advocacy.　»94

✿ **Centro Raccolta Profughi Stranieri** *(Foreign Refugees Reception Centre)*
via Grotte S. Lazzaro, 81043 Capua (Caserta); *t* (0823) 961021
Local refugee reception centre.　»83

✿ **Centro Regionale di Assistenza e Tutela degli Emigrati, CRATE** *(Regional Centre for Aid and Protection of Emigrants)*
Antonio Peragine: viale della Repubblica 71 N, 70125 Bari; *t* (080) 557 3992, *f* 504 6598
A regional section of UNAIE, p145. Welfare and advice services for Puglian emigrants. *Puglia nel Mondo* (12/yr).　»94

✿ **Centro Regionale Migrantes**
Antonio Denisi: via T. Campanella 63, 89127 Reggio Calabria; *t* (0965) 27873, *f* 330963　»94

✿ **Centro Ricreativo e Culturale Estere** *(Foreigners' Cultural and Leisure Centre)*
via S. Maria La Nova 15, 80134 Napoli　»90

✿ **Centro Servizi per Cittadini Extracomunitari** *(Non-EU Citizens Service Centre)*
Walter Citti: via del Sale 4a, 34121 Trieste; *t* (040) 313486, *f* 313497
Welfare and legal advice service operated jointly by ACLI and Caritas, both p205.　»94

✿ **Centro Servizi Stranieri di Santa Maria della Consolazione** *(Our Lady of Consolation Foreigners' Service Centre)*
Paolo Rocca: via Vida 10, 12051 Alba (Cuneo); *t* (0173) 293110, 28350
Housing and social welfare advice.　»94

✿ **Centro di Solidarietà Internazionale Lavoratori, CeSIL** *(Centre for International Workers' Solidarity)*
Damiano Bonini, Director: via Benedetto Marcello 18, 20124 Milano; *t* (02) 204 7704, 204 9754
Luigia Alberti. Founded 1980 by Confederazione Italiana Sindicati Lavoratori trade unions, right; anti-racism, legal and welfare advice to asylum seekers and immigrants, research, publications, resource centre. Bonini is Italian contact of European Legal Network on Asylum, ELENA, p154. See also INAS-CISL, p144.　»94

✿ **Centro di Solidarietà per Lavoratori e Studenti Stranieri** *(Foreign Workers and Students Solidarity Centre)*
c/o Oasi di S. Antonio, Fontiveggie, 06100 Perugia　»90

✿ **Circolo Plotter ARCI Nova**
Angelo Mandatori: corso BTG Aosta 13a, 11100 Aosta; *t* (0165) 44262
Advice centre.　»90

✿ **Collegamento Iniziative Ecclesiale per l'Immigrazione dell'Italia Settentrionale, GEMITO** *(Liaison Service for Church Projects on Migration from Southern Italy)*
Paolo Bonetti: via Copernico 1, 20125 Milano; *t* (02) 689 7520, 688 2232, *f* 6698 1944
Co-ordinates pastoral and social work initiatives for migrants from the poor South of Italy to the industrial North.　»94

✿ **Comitato per la Difesa dei Diritti degli Immigrati, CDDI** *(Committee for the Defence of Immigrants' Rights)*
Luigi Perrone: via dei Sotterranei 2 A, 73100 Lecce; *t* (032) 22053, 646835
Rights advice, solidarity.　»94

✿ **Comitato Profughi Esteri** *(Foreign Refugees Committee)*
Caterina Estherai: presso Provincia di Roma, via Santa Eufemia 19, 00187 Roma; *t* (06) 676 6601
Asylum rights advice. See also Associazione Forum, p141.»94

● **Comitato Rifugiati Politici Antifascisti** *(Committee for Anti-Fascist Political Refugees)*
c/o Centro di Documentazione Tricontinentale, via Cesare Beccaria 94-96, 00147 Roma; *t* (06) 319589　»83

● **Comunità Impegno Servizio Volontariato, CISV** *(Voluntary Service Pledge Community)*
Rosa Maria Rondelli: corso Chieri 121/6, 10132 Torino; *t* (011) 899 3823, *f* 899 4700
Voluntary service international development agency. *Volontari per lo Sviluppo* (6/yr).　»94

✿ **Confederazione Generale Italiana del Lavoro, CGIL** *(Italian General Confederation of Labour)* Ufficio Lavoratori Stranieri *(Foreign Workers Office)*
Janneke Bor/Carlo Chiapelli: Borgo dei Greci 3, 50122 Firenze; *t* (055) 270 0472　»90

✿ ≡ Ufficio Lavoratori Stranieri: Abdallah El Masri: Camara del Lavoro, Bassa Val di Cecina, corso Mazzini 44, 57126 Livorno; *t* (0586) 825111　»90

✿ ≡ Ufficio Lavoratori Immigrati (Immigrant Workers Office): Silvano Cogo: Camara del Lavoro, via del Padovanino 1, 35123 Padova; *t* (049) 822 6370
Advice and assistance service of the CGIL trade union confederation. See Associazione Immigrati Extracomunitari, p142; Centro Lavoratori Immigrati and CeLSI-CGIL, left.　»94

✿ ≡ Ufficio Lavoratori Stranieri: Thiam Mass/Mario Mannucci: viale Bonaini 71, 56100 Pisa; *t* (050) 5152 15245, 565020, 515216, *f* 589014　»94

● **Confederazione Italiana Sindicati Lavoratori, CISL** *(Italian Confederation of Trade Unions)* Ufficio Confederale Migrazione *(Federal Migration Office)*
Roberto Magni: via Po 21, 00198 Roma; *t* (06) 841 5651, *f* 884 2357
Migrant labour section of one of the main trade union federations. The CISL has a large network of local advice centres for employment issues, the Centri per il Lavoro, and a welfare section, INAS-CISL, p144; and see CeSIL, left.　»94

● **Consulta Cittadina dell'Immigrazione**
via Merulana 123, 00185 Roma
Address of several migrant groups.　»90

✿ **Consulta Emigrazione-Immigrazione Regione Piemonte** *(Piedmont Regional Emigration-Immigration Consultative Group)*
[address uncertain] via Amedeo Peyron 16, 10143 Torino
Also listed (1990) at piazza Castello 165, 10122 Torino.　»90

✿ **Cooperativa di Servizio, COOP-DES**
Debora Leiva: via Galilei 55, 00185 Roma; *t* (06) 734915, *f* 7049 5275　»94

● **Coordinamento degli Artisti Stranieri in Italia** *(Foreign Artists' Co-ordination in Italy)*
Marinella Salerno Suárez: via Gallicano nel Lazio 65-67, Ottavia, 00135 Roma; *t/f* (06) 3081 1622　»94

✿ **Coordinamento Associazioni Straniere** *(Co-ordination of Foreigners' Associations)*
via Principi d'Acaja 42 bis, 10138 Torino　»90

✿ **Coordinamento Immigrati Extracomunitari della Liguria** *(Co-ordination of Non-EU Immigrants in Liguria)* also known as Coordinamento Ligure Extracomunitario
Ramón Rubilar/Elsa Weldeghiorgis: Salita San Francesco 4, 16122 Genova; *t* (010) 2098 2240
See also Coordinamento Immigrati Ligure, p144.　»94

✿ **Coordinamento Immigrati Jesi** *(Jesi Immigrants' Co-ordination)*
c/o CGIL, piazza Ex-Appannaggio, 60035 Jesi　»90

✿ **Coordinamento Immigrati Ligure** *(Liguria Immigrants'*
Co-ordination)
Rima Drody-Moghadam: via Curtatone 2/5, 16122 Genova;
t (010) 887225
Linked to Protestant churches through FCEI, below.   »90
◆ **Coordinamento dei Immigrati del Sud del Mondo**, CISM
(Co-ordination of Immigrants from the Southern Countries)
Head Office
Abba Danna: presso ARCI Nazionale, via Francesco Carrara
24, 00196 Roma; *t* (06) 446 5455, 361 0731, 322791,
f 446 5934, 321 6877
Represented in EU Migrants Forum, p131; umbrella group of
immigrant associations. See *Nero e non Solo!*, p169.   »94
✿ ≡ via Vittorio Veneto 85, 00010 Casape   »90
✿ ≡ via Bruxelles 57 c, Collosseo, 04100 Latina   »90
✿ ≡ piazzetta di Porta Bazzano 11, 67100 L'Aquila   »90
✿ ≡ piazza Ferretto 4, 30100 Mestre, Venezia   »90
✿ ≡ via del Bontà 64, 00100 Milano   »90
✿ ≡ via S. Uborio 33, 80100 Napoli   »90
✿ ≡ via Trapani 3, 90100 Palermo, Sicilia   »90
✿ ≡ via Montanara 69, 43100 Parma   »90
✿ ≡ Contrada S. Gennaro 2, 87036 Rende   »90
✿ ≡ via Giannelli 65, 05100 Terni   »90
✿ ≡ piazza Umberto I 3, 05030 Torre Ospina   »90
● **Coordinamento dei Lavoratori Stranieri in Lombardia**, CLSL
(Co-ordination of Foreign Workers in Lombardy)
Lucy Resischel Rojas: via Bagutta 12, 20121 Milano; *t* (02)
780811   »94
✿ **Coordinamento Migranti** *(Migrant Co-ordination)*
[address unknown] 20100 Milano   »90
✿ **Coordinamento Provinciale Immigrati**
via Pietralata 3, Bologna   »90
✿ **Coordinamento Stranieri**
c/o CERCE, via dei Leprosetti 5, 40100 Bologna   »90
✿ ≡ c/o CGIL, via Vaccari 128, 36100 Vicenza   »90
✿ **Coordinamento degli Stranieri Extracomunitari della**
Lombardia *(Co-ordination of Non-EU Foreigners in Lombardy)*
via Tadino 12, 20124 Milano; *t* (02) 2940 3274   »90
✿ **Coordinamento Studenti Stranieri della Lombardia**
(Co-ordination of Foreign Students in Lombardy)
[address unknown] Milano   »90
✿ **Delegazione Immigrati Extracomunitari Toscana** *(Tuscany*
Delegation of Non-EU Immigrants)
[address uncertain] via Pistoiese 138 H, 50145 Firenze
Also listed (1990) at via S. Egidio 8, Firenze; or via Banchelli
70, 50047 Prato; or via Pistoiese 1301, 50110 S. Donnino;
or via di S. Giusto 49, 50018 Scandicci; or via U. Foscolo,
56100 Pisa. Some of these may be private addresses, or
addresses of local branches.   »90
✿ *Duemilastagioni*
[address unknown] Torino
Anti-racist journal published by and for immigrants.   »88
✿ **Ente Milanese Assistenza Solidarietà Integrazione**, EMASI
(Milan Agency for Welfare, Solidarity and Integration)
Marisa Marchetti: via della Signora 3, 20122 Milano; *t* (02)
772 3226, *f* 780968
Extravoce (2/yr).   »94
● **Ente Nazionale ACLI Istruzione Professionale**, ENAIP *(ACLI*
National Training Body)
Silvio Peverelli: via G. Ventura 4, 20134 Milano; *t* (02) 2641
4760, 2641 5072, *f* 2641 5056
Job training, research and documentation agency of ACLI,
p205; see also in UK, p76; Germany, p74. *Skill* (2/yr). »94
✿ ≡ Salita S. Brigida 8/1, 16126 Genova; *t* (010) 293863 »90
◆ **Federazione delle Chiese Evangeliche in Italia—Servizio**
Rifugiati e Migranti, FCEI-SRM *(Federation of Protestant*
Churches—Migrant and Refugee Service) Head Office
Anne Marie Dupré: via Firenze 38, 00184 Roma; *t* (06)
483188, 483768, 475 5120, 474 3695, *f* 482 8728
Esther Haile Jacobson. Main migrant and refugee solidarity
programme of the Protestant churches. Housing, language
training, integration, employment and remigration assistance.
SRM Materiali (4/yr); *Notizie Evangeliche* (52/yr).   »94
✿ ≡ Mahmoud Mansoubi/Silvia de Carmen Esteban: via
Vittorio Veneto 85, 00010 Casape; *t* (06) 774 580703? »90
✿ ≡ Letizia Tomassone: via Curtatone 2/5, 16122 Genova;
t (010) 887225   »90
◆ **Federazione Italiana Lavoratori Emigrati e Famiglie**, FILEF
(Italian Federation of Emigrant Workers and their Families)
Armelino Milani/Dino Pelliccia: via IV Novembre 114, 00187
Roma; *t* (06) 679 5484
Founded 1967; assistance to, research and documentation on
Italian emigrant workers. See also sections in Belgium,
Germany, Luxembourg, Netherlands and UK, pp73-77.
Emigrazione (12/yr), *Emigrazione Notizie* (52/yr).   »94

◆ **Federazione delle Organizzazioni delle Comunità Straniere**
in Italia, FOCSI *(Federation of Organisations of Foreign*
Communities in Italy)
[address uncertain] c/o via Adua 22, 00188 Roma; *t* (06)
686 8328 (ab. Segr.)
Also listed (1990) as via Radicofani 97, or via Merulana
123; both 00185 Roma.   »90
● ≡ Jamal Tannir/John Nowfer: via dei Salentini 3, 00185
Roma; *t/f* (06) 445 7556
Umbrella group, advice and campaigns work; member of EU
Migrants Forum, p131.   »90
◆ **Fondazione Migrantes** *(Migrants Foundation)* and Ufficio
Centrale per l'Emigrazione Italiana, UCEI
Giuseppe Monticelli Lucrezio, General Secretary: via Aurelia
481, 00165 Roma; *t* (06) 664 0096-97, 662 2777, *f* 662
0530
Mons. Lino Belotti acting national director; agency founded
1966 by (Catholic) Conferenza Episcopale Italiana; emigration,
immigration and refugee issues, pastoral care of migrants,
counselling, emergency assistance; its refugee service
(Servizio Profughi) has offices in the Latina reception centre,
t (0773) 488910; also operates resource centre. At same
address: UCEI (possibly superseded by the Fondazione?), and
Unione Cristiana di Enti tra e per gli Emigrati Italiani, UCEMI.
Servizio Migranti 6/yr); *Migranti-press* (52/yr).   »94
● **Fondazione Franco Verga**
Giampiero Bartolucci: via Anfiteatro 14, 20121 Milano;
t (02) 869 3194, *f* 879095
Private foundation; welfare and legal assistance, solidarity
with emigrants and immigrants. *Incontro e solidarietà*. »95
✿ **Forum delle Comunità Straniere**
piazza delle Madaglie d'Oro 18, 13100 Vercelli   »90
◆ **Forum delle Comunità Straniere in Italia** *(Forum of Foreign*
Communities in Italy)
Loretta Caponi: via Gregoriana 12, 00187 Roma; *t* (06) 446
7676, *f* 678 1182
Confederation of migrant associations.   »94
◆ **Istituto per l'istruzione professionale e assistenza emigrati**
(Institute for Professional Instruction and Aid to Emigrants)
[address unknown] Roma
Helps Italian emigrants. See also Istituto Santi, below. »86
◆ **Istituto Nazionale di Assistenza Sociale**, INAS-CISL
(National Social Welfare Institute) Sede Centrale, Servizio
Emigrazione-Immigrazione
Gianni Tosini: viale Regina Margherita 83/6, 00198 Roma;
t (06) 844381-84, *f* 854 7856
A service of the CISL labour confederation, p143. General
welfare and social security advice and assistance for migrants
from or into Italy; branches throughout Italy. See also Centro
di Solidarietà Internazionale Lavoratori, p143. *Corrispondenza*
Italia; Sicurezza Sociale Oggi.   »94
◆ **Istituto Fernando Santi**, IFS: Head Office
Igor Patruno: piazza del Fanti 10, 00194 Roma; *t* (06) 360
0801, 461016
Founded 1970 under Istituto per l'istruzione professionale e
assistenza emigrati, above; research, conferences,
documentation centre on immigration and Italian emigration.
See in France and Germany, p74, and UK, p77; see also
Associazione Fernando Santi, p142. Various publications
including *Avanti nel Mondo* and *Avanti Europa*.   »90
● ≡ Servizio Immigrazione: via XX Settembre 49, 00187
Roma; *t* (06) 482 8335, *f* 482 8359   »94
✿ ≡ Sicily: via A. Pacimotti 34, 95100 Catania   »90
✿ ≡ Circolo di Taranto: Lorenzo Capodiferro: via De Cesare
74, 74100 Taranto; *t/f* (099) 452 7700   »94
● **Jesuit Refugee Service**, JRS
CP 6139, Borgo S. Spirito 5, 00195 Roma; *t* (06) 6897
7386, *f* 687 9283, *e* Geo2:czerny
Funding, staff and material aid for projects helping refugees
in Asia, Africa and Latin America; counselling of refugees
and migrants in various receiving countries including UK and
Belgium.   »94
✿ **NAGA—Associazione Volontaria Assistenza Nomadi**
Daniele Camisa: viale Bligny 22, 20136 Milano; *t* (02) 5830
1420, 580 5289, *f* 5830 0089
Welfare advice, health promotion. *Informaga* (2/yr).   »94
✿ **Progetto Inserimento per le Persone di Lingua Straniera**,
NYIAN *(Integration Project for Foreign-Language Speakers)*
Angela Scalzo: c/o UIL, via Cavour 108, 00184 Roma;
t (06) 474 1802, *f* 482 7250
Educational, labour rights and welfare assistance for foreign
workers; a project of the UIL trade union confederation, p145.
Dimensione Lavoro (6/yr).   »94
✿ **Scuola per Extra Comunitari** *(Non-EU People's School)*
via dei Quartieri, 10122 Torino   »90

✼ **Segretaria per gli Esteri, Diocesi di Milano** *(Secretariat for Foreigners, Diocese of Milan)*
Ferdinando Colombo/Nunzio Ferrante: via Copernico 1, 20124 Milano; *t* (02) 689 7520, 82232
Caritas-backed service, since 1988 has offered legal help to persons refused asylum in Switzerland. »90

✼ **Servizio Orientamento Esteri di Milano, SOEM** *(Milan Foreigners Orientation Service)*
via G. Lazzaroni 8, 20131 Milano; *t* (02) 689 9135 »90

✼ **Ufficio Accoglienza Studenti Esteri** *(Foreign Students Reception Office)*
corso Matteotti 31, 60121 Ancona; *t* (071) 51766 »90

♦ **Ufficio Centrale Studenti Esteri in Italia, UCSEI** *(Central Office for Foreign Students in Italy)* Head Office
Mgr Remigio Musaragno: via dei Monti Parioli 59, 00197 Roma; *t* (06) 360 4491, 321 8901
Publishes *Amicizia Studenti Esteri*; Catholic agency founded 1959, providing accommodation, advice and help to foreign students, including refugees. »90
• ≡ via Galilei 6, 20124 Milano »90
✼ ≡ Munah Moiguha: piazza Mariotti 1, 06100 Perugia; *t* (075) 27182 »89

✼ **Ufficio Stranieri e Nomadi** *(Foreigners' and Travellers' Office)* Comune di Torino
Olivero Fredo: via del Carmine 4, 10122 Torino; *t* (011) 436 9683, 576522 66-68, *f* 436 9631
Legal advice and assistance to foreigners, refugees and travellers in Turin. »95

✼ **Unione Italiana degli Immigrati, UNITI**
Salamon Pino: piazza Aldo Moro 14, 70122 Bari; *t* (080) 524 3681
See also regional UIL trade union office, p207. »94

♦ **Unione Italiana del Lavoro, UIL** *(Italian Labour Union)*
Coordinamento Nazionale Immigrati (National Immigrants Office)
via Lucullo 6, 00187 Roma; *t* (06) 49731
National immigrant co-ordination office of major trade union confederation, concerned with immigrant labour rights. See also ITAL-UIL, p206, and NYIAN, p144. »94

✼ **Unione Lavoratori Emigrati Veneti, ULEV** *(Venice Union of Emigrant Workers)*
Loris Andrioli: via Peschiera 5, 30174 Venezia; *t* (041) 549 7811, 549 7858, *f* 974331
Unclear whether this is a body for emigrant workers from Venice, or immigrants in Venice. See also APCLAI, p84.
Veneto Emigrazione (4/yr). »94

♦ **Unione Nazionale delle Associazioni degli Immigrati ed Emigrati, UNAIE** *(National Union of Immigrant and Emigrant Associations)*
Ferrucio Pisoni: via dei Cestari 13, 00156 Roma; *t* (06) 678 9621, *f* 648 9644
Founded 1966; research, campaigning on immigration and emigration. See in Germany, p75, and CRATE in Puglia, p143.
Presenza UNAIE (12/yr), *Informazioni UNAIE* (24/yr). »94
✼ ≡ via Buion 36, 33080 Porcia »90

✼ **UOHI**
via Marchi 29, 00100 Roma
Possibly United Office of Hebrew Immigration (which assists migration to Israel)? »90

✼ **Welcome—Centro Sociale per Famiglie Immigrate** *(Welfare Centre for Immigrant Families)*
Mariella Spaini: viale Romania 32, 00197 Roma; *t* (06) 8530 0916, *f* 854 6470
Welfare and health assistance. »94

✼ **Young Women's Christian Association—Progetto Donne Migranti e Rifugiate, YWCA** *(YWCA Migrant and Refugee Women Project)*
Dina Eroli Cautela: via Cesare Balbo 4, 00184 Roma; *t* (06) 481 4525
Advice and assistance to migrant and refugee women. »94

LUXEMBOURG *352*

♦ **Association de soutien aux travailleurs immigrés, ASTI** *(Immigrant Workers Support Association)* also known as A de *solidarité avec les* T I
Serge Kollwelter: 10 rue Auguste Laval, 1922 Luxembourg; *t* 438333, *f* 420871
Anti-racism, solidarity with migrants and refugees; see also Lëtzeburger Flüchtlingsrôt, right. Kollwelter is the national representative of Migrant Associations Information Network in Europe, MAINE, p146. See also CDAIC, p239, and CLAE, right. *Echo de l'Immigration—Ensemble*. »95

• **Centre Pastorale en Monde du Travail—Secteur Immigration, CPMT** *(Catholic Pastorate for Labour, Immigration Sector)*
Rosetta Paganotti: 5 avenue Marie-Thérèse, 2132 Luxembourg; *t* 44743, 44339
See also SESOPI below; CDPI, p169. *Breck* (12/yr). »94

♦ **Comité de Liaison et d'Action des Etrangers, CLAE** *(Foreigners' Liaison and Action Committee)*
Franco Barilozzi/Giovanni Rastrelli: 10 rue Auguste Laval, 1922 Luxembourg; *t* 432345, 438333, *f* 428610, 420871
Member of EU Migrants Forum, p131; presumably same as Comité de Liaison et d'Action des Immigrés (CLAI, listed 1990). See ASTI, left, and CDAIC, p239. *CLAE-Info*. »94

♦ **Commission Diocésaine pour la Pastorale des Migrants, CDPM**
4 rue du Génistre, 1623 Luxembourg; *t* 462023
Catholic agency for pastoral care of migrants. Possibly superseded by CDPI, p169? »90

♦ **European Legal Network on Asylum, ELENA**
Marc Elvinger, Co-ordinator: 20 rue des Franciscaines, 1539 Luxembourg; *t* 252682, *f* 252686
National section of the UK-based network of migration and refugee law practitioners, p154. »95

♦ **Lëtzebuerger Flüchtlingsrôt** *(Luxembourg Refugee Council)*
c/o ASTI, 10 rue Auguste Laval, 1922 Luxembourg; *t* 438333, *f* 420871
National umbrella organisation for the agencies and organisations serving refugees. »95

• **Service Accueil des Etrangers** *(Reception Service for Foreigners)*
9 rue Chimay, 1383 Luxembourg; *t* 4796 2751
Advice and assistance to immigrants. »94

♦ **Service d'Accueil et d'Information Juridique** *(Reception and Legal Advice Service)*
12 côte d'Eich, 1450 Luxembourg; *t* 41464
Information on the legal status of immigrants. »94

♦ **Service Socio-Pastoral Intercommunautaire, SESOPI** *(Intercommunity Social and Pastoral Service)* formerly Secrétariat Socio-Pastoral de l'Immigration
Miguel Mario Santillo: 5 avenue Marie-Thérèse, Centre Convict bloc D, 2132 Luxembourg; *t* 447432 03, *f* 447451
Renato Cescutti. Catholic agency, operational arm of the CDPI, p169, mainly providing pastoral care to Italian and Portuguese immigrants, also involved in migration and refugee rights campaigns. See also CPMT, above. »95

NETHERLANDS *31*

✼ **Allochtonen-overleg Gemeente Amsterdam** *(Amsterdam Municipal Aliens Consultative Body)*
[address unknown] Amsterdam »93

✼ **Allochtonenpastoraat Cura Migratorum** *(Migrant Pastoral Care Centre)*
Jan Luybenstraat, 's Hertogenbosch; *t* (073) 614 5159
Catholic agency responsible for pastoral care of migrants. »90

✼ **Amsterdams Centrum Buitenlanders, ACB**
Gijs von der Fuhr, Information Officer: Westermarkt 6, 1016 DK Amsterdam; *t* (020) 627 9460, 627 3197, *f* 626 2516
Advice, information, counselling, resource centre for migrants; assistance with discrimination cases. »94

✼ **Amsterdams Solidariteits Komitee Vluchtelingen, ASKV** *(Amsterdam Refugee Solidarity Committee)*
Haarlemmerplein 17, 1013 HP Amsterdam; *t* (020) 627 2408, *f* 420 3208
Advice and assistance to refugees and asylum seekers in the city. See also Platform Illegale Vluchtelingen, p146. »94

✼ **Bureau migrant en werk Rotterdam** *(Rotterdam Migrant Employment Office)*
Schiedamse Vest 79, 3012 BE Rotterdam; *t* (010) 414 1277, *f* 413 6505
Experimental service linking migrant organisations and the employment service; seeks to increase migrant and minority access to the labour market. »95

• **Centrale Opvang Asielzoekers, COA** *(Central Reception Centre for Asylum Seekers)* and Landelijk Aanmeldingspunt, LAMP *(National Entry Point)*
Postbus 3002, 2280 ME Rijswijk; *t* (070) 307 1500, 307 1700, *f* 307 1519
Location: Verrijn Stuartlaan 28, 2288 EL Rijswijk. Official agency for initial processing of asylum claims. »94

• **Stichting Centrale Opvang Vluchtelingen, COV** *(Refugee Reception Centre Foundation)*
Loolaan 32, 7315 AC Apeldoorn; *t* (015) 225275 (?), *f* 216530 (?) »95

✧ **Stichting Centrum Buitenlanders Midden-Nederland** *(Mid-Holland Foreigners' Centre Foundation)*
Bemuurde Weerd wz 4, 3513 BH Utrecht; *t* (030) 231 3833, *f* 232 8777 »95

✧ **Centrum Buitenlanders West-Brabant** *(West Brabant Foreigners' Centre)*
L. Lazaar: J.F. Kennedylaan 38, 4811 ET Breda »90

♦ **Christelijk Nationaal Vakverbond—Secretariaat Buitenlandse Werknemers,** CNV *(Christian National Labour League—Foreign Workers' Section)*
G. Pruim/G.A. Cremers: Postbus 2475, 3500 GL Utrecht; *t* (030) 291 3911, *f* 294 6544
Main Christian democrat trade union federation's specialist secretariat for migrant workers. International labour solidarity, development education, anti-racism. A member of the ADO, p208. *CNV Opinie* (12/yr), *Kom Over Magazine* (4/yr). »95

✧ **Comité Illegalen Zondebok**
Postbus 3133, 2601 DC Delft; *t* (015) 278 7289
Supports illegal immigrants, unrecognised asylum seekers.»95

European Legal Network on Asylum, ELENA: see Vluchtelingen Werk, p147.

♦ **Federatie Nederlandse Vakbewegingen—Secretariaat voor Etnische Minderheden,** FNV *(Dutch Labour Movement Federation—Ethnic Minorities Office)*
Postbus 8456, 1005 AL Amsterdam; *t* (020) 581 6300, *f* 684 4541
Location: Naritaweg 10. Bureau of the FNV, one of the main trade union federations, concerned with migrant workers, minorities and racism. A member of the ADO, p208; it supports projects helping Third World labour movements. »94

♦ **Federatie van Vluchtelingen-Organisaties in Nederland,** VON *(Federation of Refugee Organisations in the Netherlands)*
Alem Desta/S. Celik: Merelstraat 2 bis, 3514 CN Utrecht; *t* (030) 271 4505, *f* 273 3844
Founded 1985; advises national and local government, political parties and other bodies on asylum and related issues; legal advice (Thomas Hessels); research, information. See also Steunfonds Vluchtelingen Organisaties, p147. »95

♦ **FORUM—Instituut voor Multiculturele Ontwikkeling** *(Institute for Multicultural Development)*
Postbus 201, 3500 AE Utrecht; *t* (030) 294 0037, *f* 296 0050
Location: Kanalweg 84b (the former NCB offices). A national centre launched in 1996, succeeding the Nederlands Expertise-centrum over de Multiculturele Samenleving, NEMS, founded in July 1995. NEMS was a merger of Nederlands Centrum Buitenlanders, right; the Antillean group FORSA, p9; Gabungan Jajasan Maluku and Stichting Inspraakorgaan Welzijn Molukkers, p88; Stichting Lalla Rookh and Stichting Landelike Federatie van Welzijnorganisaties voor Surinamers, p114; Landelijke Samenwerking van Organisaties van Buitenlandse Arbeiders, right, and Landelijk Steunpunt Buitenlandse Vrouwencentra, below. Before the relaunch as FORUM it was joined by a ninth body, Landelijk Platform Woonwagen-bewoners en Zigeuners, p40. At its launch FORUM had 100 staff working in three main areas: Transferpunt Opvang Niewkomers (TON; immigrant reception and advice), Cross-Cultureel Management (CCM; multicultural issues at work) and Multi-culturele Wijk (the multicultural neighbourhood). »96

✧ **Huis van Migranten** *(Migrants' House)*
M. Mahjarb: V. Ostedestraat 341, 1020 Amsterdam; *t* (020) 679 4982
Founded 1986; community group of local Turks and Moroccans. »95

✧ **Interkerkelijke Werkgroep—Kerk en Asielzoekers** *(Inter-Church Working Group on Church and Asylum Seekers)*
Gedempte Oudegracht 104, 2011 GW Haarlem »94

▋**Stichting Internationaal Netwerk van lokale initiatieven voor asielzoekers,** INLIA: International Network of Local Initiatives for Asylum Seekers
Rode Weeshuisstraat 1-3, 9712 ET Groningen; *t* (050) 513 8181, *f* 514 4944 »95

● **Komitee Zelfstandig Verblijfsrechten voor Migranten Vrouwen,** KZVR *(Committee for Independent Residence Rights for Migrant Women)*
M. Buiteman: Mauritskade 22 D, 1091 GC Amsterdam; *t* (020) 694 1854, *f* 665 0880
Campaigns against sexism in immigration control. »95

Landelijk Steunpunt Buitenlandse Vrouwencentra, LSBV (National Support Centre for Immigrant Women's Groups): a national centre, based in Utrecht, co-ordinating international women's organisations formed at local level. In 1995 the centre and eight other bodies merged to create the Nederlands Expertisecentrum over de Multicuterele Samenleving, right, which subsequently became FORUM, see above.

● **Landelijke Advies- en Overlegstructuur Minderhedenbeleid,** LAO *(National Advisory and Consultative Structure on Minority Policy)*
Postbus 20011, 2500 EA Den Haag; *t* (070) 302 6192, *f* 302 7638
Forum of migrant organisations advising government on minority policy. »95

Landelijke Samenwerking van Organisaties van Buitenlandse Arbeiders, LSOBA (National Coalition of Foreign Workers' Groups): a national umbrella group of migrant associations, based in Utrecht; affiliated to the EU Migrants Forum, p131, and to ADO, p208. In 1995 it merged with other groups to create what became FORUM, see left.

✧ **Limburgse Immigratie Stichting** *(Limburg Immigration Foundation)*
José Belmar Morales: Postbus 516, 6400 AM Heerlen; *t* (045) 571 3142
Location: Akerstraat 41, 6411 GW Heerlen. Migrant solidarity, information. »95

✧ **Mama Cash**
Postbus 15686, 1001 ND Amsterdam; *t* (020) 689 3634
Multi-cultural foundation. »94

✧ **Migranten-werkwinkel Amsterdam voor mediterranen** *(Amsterdam Labour Exchange for Mediterranean Migrants)*
Stadhouderskade 130, 1074 AW Amsterdam; *t* (020) 662 1496, *f* 673 9129
Also at Nieuw-West, Baarsjeweg 301, 1058 AG Amsterdam. An experimental service providing specialist employment and training advice to migrant workers from the Mediterranean countries. »95

✧ **Migranten-werkwinkel Den Haag** *(The Hague Labour Exchange for Migrants)*
Prinsengracht 49, 2512 EX Den Haag; *t* (070) 389 3941, *f* 389 3421
Experimental service providing specialist employment advice to migrant workers. »95

✧ **Migrantenvoorlichting** *(Migrant Information)*
A. Mokhtari: Stadhuis, Sectie Voorlichting, kamer SH239, Coolsingel 40, 3011 AD Rotterdam; *t* (010) 417 3024-25
Civic office responsible for development and support of information services for migrants. »95

▋**Migrants Associations' Information Network in Europe,** MAINE: Réseau d'information pour les Associations d'Immigrés en Europe
ECWS, Postbus 3073, 6202 NB Maastricht; *t* (043) 321 6724, *f* 325 5712, *Tx* 56164 EUR CW
Location: Hoogbrugstraat 43, 6221CP Maastricht. Formed as information exchange network of organisations representing or serving migrants in Europe; produced NGO directory, *Info-MAINE* bulletin; promoted informal contact among activist groups; run by European Centre for Work and Society, p240.»91

✧ **Minderheden-werkwinkel Breda** *(Breda Labour Exchange for Minorities)*
Meerten Verhoffstraat 4, 4811 AS Breda; *t* (076) 145927
Experimental service providing specialist employment advice to ethnic minority workers. »95

Stichting Nederlands Centrum Buitenlanders, NCB: Dutch Centre for Migrants (literally Dutch Centre for Foreigners Foundation): a Utrecht-based resource centre for migrant and minority rights movements; provided information, research, advice, consultancy on matters concerning foreign workers, students and refugees in the Netherlands; published leaflets, booklets, a newsletter on minority affairs, Contrast (52/yr), and a legal newsletter Migrantenrecht (12/yr). A member of the ADO, p208; also involved in Churches' Commision on Migrants in Europe, p130. In 1990-91 it helped to form the Europees Steunpunt Migranten en Vluchtelingen, p240. In July 1995 the NCB and other migrant bodies merged to create the group, below, which became FORUM, see left.

Nederlands Expertisecentrum over de Multiculturele Samen-leving, NEMS (Dutch Expertise Centre on Multicultural Society): the name initially chosen on the merger in 1995 of the groups which subsequently became FORUM—Instituut voor Multiculturele Ontwikkeling, see left.

● **Platform Illegale Vluchtelingen,** PIV *(Platform for Illegal Refugees)*
Haarlemmerplein 17, 1013 HP Amsterdam; *t* (020) 627 2408, *f* 420 3208
Advice and assistance to refugees refused asylum; campaigns for residence rights. See also ASKV, p145. »94

● **Platform des Organisations Démocratiques des Immigrés en Europe**
F. Navarro: Herengracht 22, 1015 BL Amsterdam; *t* (020) 622 2746 (?)
Founded 1978; information, advice, campaigns. »90

✿ **Stichting Probrasa**
Marijke Frijters: Tuinstraat 49-01, 5038 DA Tilburg   »90
✿ **Project Aisa**
Oudegracht 312, Utrecht; *t* (030) 230 0210
National co-operative of black, migrant and refugee women;
development of women's voluntary sector.   »95
✿ **Project Integratie Nieuwkomers, PIN** *(Newcomers Integration Project)*
J.G.M. Breukels, Director: PIN-Centrum, Witte de Withstraat 30, 3012 Rotterdam; *t* (010) 405 5544
Assists integration of migrants through the provision of advice and support on life in Rotterdam, educational opportunities, Dutch classes and other matters.   »95
✿ **Regionaal Centrum Buitenlanders**
Houtmarkt 21, 2011 AL Haarlem; *t* (023) 359394, *f* 359164
Counselling, information, legal advice; linked to ACB, p145.»94
✿ **Saint Pasar Amsterdam**
A. Akariou: Postbus 751, 1000 AT Amsterdam; *t* (020) 625 0217
Youth training, employment.   »95
● **Sociale Dienst Scheepvaart** *(Seafarers Social Service)*
Ministerie van Sociale Zaken en Werkgelegenheid
Postbus 1024, 3000 BA Rotterdam
Specialist welfare service for mariners, operated by Ministry of Social Affairs and Employment, p209.   »95
✿ **Solidariteitsfonds X min Y**
Keizersgracht 132-II, 1015 CW Amsterdam; *t* (020) 627 9661, *f* 622 8229
Anti-racist foundation; no other information.   »94
✿ **Steunfonds Allochtone Startende Ondernemers, STASON** *(Support Fund for Immigrant Entrepreneurship)*
Heemraadsingel 245, 3023 CD Rotterdam; *t* (010) 476 2620, *f* 476 2580   »94
♦ **Steunfonds Vluchtelingen Organisaties, SVO** *(Refugee Organisations Support Fund)*
Postbus 15116, 3501 BC Utrecht; *t* (030) 271 4505, *f* 273 3844
Location: Merelstraat 2 bis. Joint welfare fund for refugees.
See also VON, p146.   »95
Stichting... if not listed here, see under next significant word of the title
● **Stichting Doen**
Van Eeghenstraat 81, 1071 EX Amsterdam; *t* (020) 664 2569, *f* 675 7397
Foundation providing services to refugees. See also Stichting Triodos-Doen, below.   »94
● **Stichting Omroep Allochtonen, STOA** *(Aliens Broadcasting Foundation)*
Postbus 1234, 3500 BE Utrecht; *t* (030) 230 2240, *f* 230 2975
Programming for ethnic minorities. See also Public Broadcasting for a Multicultural Europe, p172.   »94
✿ **Stichting Optie** *(Choice Foundation)*
Soestdijkseweg Zuid 249, 3721 AE Bilthoven; *t* (030) 225 2424 (?), *f* 225 2383 (?)
Development of education, training and employment opportunities for ethnic minorities.   »95
● **Stichting Pharos—Steunpunt Gezondheidszorg Vluchtelingen** *(The Lighthouse Foundation—Refugee Health Care Centre)*
also known as Centrum Gezondheidszorg Vluchtelingen
Postbus 13318, 3507 LH Utrecht; *t* (030) 234 9800, *f* 236 4560
Location: Herenstraat 35. Also at Sectie Geestelijke Gezondheidszorg, Prins Hendrikkade 120, 1011 AM Amsterdam; *t* (020) 627 4974, *f* 625 3589. Welfare Ministry national agency providing health care and health education to refugees and asylum seekers, including expert psycho-social services; also provides specialist training and advice.   »95
✿ **Stichting Triodos-Doen**
Postbus 55, Prins Hendriklaan 9-11, 3700 AB Zeist; *t* (030) 691 6544, *f* 691 2524
Refugee concerns. See also Stichting Doen, above.   »95
♦ **Stichting Vluchteling, SV** *(Refugee Foundation)*
Antoon Claasen, Information Officer: Stadhouderslaan 28, 2517 HZ Den Haag; *t* (070) 346 8946, *f* 361 5740
Co-ordinates Dutch refugee agencies' overseas activities in relation to solidarity, advice, funding and practical assistance to refugees in developing countries.   »94
● **Stichting voor Vluchteling-Studenten** *(Refugee Students Foundation)* and University Assistance Fund, UAF
K. Bleichrodt: Postbus 14300, Wilhelminapark 38, 3581 NJ Utrecht; *t* (030) 252 0835, *f* 252 1899
Counselling and financial assistance in educational and vocational training matters for refugees and asylum seekers; voluntarily funded; member of VluchtelingenWerk, right.   »95

■ **Unrepresented Nations and Peoples Organisation, UNPO**
Postbus 85878, Javastraat 40 A, 2508 CN Den Haag; *t* (070) 360 3318, *f* 360 3346
Campaigns for the self-determination and human rights of national minorities, tribal peoples and other peoples not represented at the United Nations.   »94
✿ **Vereniging Lau Mazirel**
Postbus 16875, 1001 RJ Amsterdam; *t* (020) 625 7377, *f* 638 6366
Migrant, refugee and anti-racist youth group.   »94
♦ **VluchtelingenWerk, VVN:** Dutch Refugee Council: formally Vereniging VluchtelingenWerk Nederland
N.V.M. Lont/Frits Florin: Postbus 2894, 1000 CW Amsterdam; *t* (020) 688 1311, *f* 688 2181, 682 3353, *Tx* 10122 vvn
Location: 3e Hugo de Grootstraat 7, 1052 LJ Amsterdam.
The main national refugee agency, with around 400 member groups and 140 staff; NGO members other than those listed separately include Federation of Women's Organisations; founded by merger of several groups in 1979. Emergency help, settlement, integration, research, documentation centre (Gerlien Harthoorn), legal advice, lobbying, public education about refugee questions; counselling, language training, social and other assistance. Operates via local groups (Vluchtelingen Werkgroepen), with around 7,000 volunteers (group addresses from VVN head office), three regional bureaux and a central rights advice service; receives state and voluntary funding. A member of the ADO, p208. Clara Fetter is Dutch contact for European Legal Network on Asylum, ELENA, p154, and secretary to Working Group on Legal Aid for Refugees, below. *VluchtelingenWerk—Nieuwsbrief Vluchtelingen* (4-6/yr).   »95
✿ ≡ Regio Noord-oost: Osterlaan 11, 8011 GC Zwolle; *t* (038) 422 3407   »90
✿ ≡ Regio West: Singel 56, 1015 AB Amsterdam; *t* (020) 622 5464   »90
✿ ≡ Regio Zuid: Konigsweg 2, 5211 BL Den Bosch; *t* (073) 613 7513   »90
✿ **VluchtelingenWerk Nieuwegein Stichting** *(Nieuwegein Refugee Service Foundation)*
Herenstraat 105, 3431 CB Nieuwegein; *t* (030) 605 0491, 604 1409   »95
✿ **VluchtelingenWerk—Rijnmond, VWR**
Weena 745, 3013 AL Rotterdam; *t* (010) 433 0099, *f* 433 0302   »94
✿ **VluchtelingenWerk Stichting** *(Refugee Service Foundation)*
J. de Bakkerstr. 2, 3441 EE Woerden; *t* (030) 682 4986 »95
✿ **VluchtelingenWerk Zeist Stichting** *(Zeist Refugee Service Foundation)*
Het Rond 6a, 3701 HS Zeist; *t* (030) 691 7768   »95
✿ **Werkgroep Rechtsbijstand Vreemdelingenzaken** *(Working Group for Legal Assistance on Alien Questions)*
[address unknown]
Network of legal advice and representation agencies. May be same as Working Group on Legal Aid for Refugees, below.»93
● **Working Group on Legal Aid for Refugees**
Clara Fetter, Secretary: 3e Hugo de Grootstraat 7, 1052 LJ Amsterdam; *t* (020) 688 1311, *f* 688 2181, 682 3353, *Tx* 10122 vvn
Walter Jansen; based in the VluchtelingenWerk head office, above; network of about 475 lawyers handling asylum claims and appeals. Full address list available from secretary.   »95
● **Stichting ZOA Vluchtelingenzorg, ZOA:** ZOA Refugee Care Netherlands
H. Huberts, Director: Postbus 10343, Sleutelbloemstraat 7, 7301 GH Apeldoorn; *t* (055) 366 3833, *f* 366 8799
Ecumenical Christian group providing emergency relief and ongoing care programmes for refugees and returnees in Africa, Asia, Latin America. Founded 1973. *ZOA Nieuws* (3/yr).»95

NORWAY 47

♦ **European Legal Network on Asylum, ELENA**
Carl K. Rieber-Mohn, Co-ordinator: Prinsensgate 14, 0152 Oslo 2; *t* 2242 0118, *f* 2242 4003
National contact for European network, p154, of lawyers experienced in handing asylum applications and appeals. »95
♦ **Norsk Organisasjon for Asylsøkere, NOAS:** Norwegian Organisation for Asylum Seekers
Postboks 8893, Youngstorget, Torggt. 26, 0128 Oslo; *t* 2220 8440-48, *f* 2220 8444
Independent association for advice and support to asylum applicants, including emergency assistance, lawyers' network, lobbying, public information activities. *Noas Ark* (4/yr). »95

♦ **Det Norske Flyktningeråd**, DNF: Norwegian Refugee Council
Postboks 6758, St Olavs plass, Pilestredet 15B, 0130 Oslo
1; *t* 2211 6500, *f* 2260 0272
Principal state-funded NGO providing advice and support
services to refugees and asylum seekers in Norway, in
co-operation with the UNHCR, p217, and the Ministry of
Foreign Affairs. Also provides emergency aid and development
assistance to refugees and returnees in developing countries.
På Flykt Bakgrunn; På Flykt Nyheter (2, 11/yr).   »94

PORTUGAL *351*

✪ **Associação de Amigos da Encosta Nascente**, AAEN
(Eastern Hill Friendship Association)
João Vivaldo Monteiro: Estrada Militar, Rua X 8, 2700
Amadora; *t* (01) 491 2419
Migrant solidarity, welfare, intercultural understanding.   »94
✪ **Associação Cultural Moinho da Juventude** *(The Mill Youth
Cultural Association)*
Maria Alice Gomes Evora: Travessa do Outeiro 1, Alto da
Cova da Moura, 2700 Amadora; *t* (01) 497 1070
Migrant advice, welfare, culture. See also African group,
Associação Moinho da Juventude, p4.   »94
● **Associação de Emigrantes Lusiadas** *(Lusitanian Emigrants'
Association)*
Apartado 5184, 1704 Lisboa Codex; *t* (01) 759 4074   »90
● **Associação de Reencontro de Emigrantes**, ARE *(Emigrants
Reunion Association)*
Alfredo Masson: Avenida António José de Almeida 22,
1000 Lisboa; *t* (01) 847 8171, *f* 847 0567
International solidarity, anti-racism, links between migrants
and home country. *Apenas Informações.*   »94
✪ **Centro de Acolhimento e Integração Social** *(Reception
and Social Integration Centre)*
P. José Antunes Vaz: Avenida da Europa, 6355 Vilar
Formoso; *t* (071) 52594, *f* 53455
Boletim de Vilar Formoso.   »94
✪ **Centro de Apoio à Reinserção de Emigrantes**, CARE
(Emigrant Resettlement Support Centre)
Campo dos Mártires da Pátria 43, r/c, 1100 Lisboa
Reintegration of returned emigrant workers; presumably a
service of one of the Catholic migrant agencies at that
address.   »94
♦ **Comissão Episcopal de Migrações** *(Episcopal Commission
for Migration)*
Padre Manuel Nobre Soares, Secretary: Campo dos Mártires
da Pátria 43-1°, 1100 Lisboa; *t* (01) 538116
Dom Teodoro de Faria president; Catholic Church body
responsible for pastoral care of migrants, mainly Portuguese
communities abroad, and of seafarers and tourists; works
through the Obra Católica Portuguêsa de Migrações and the
Obra do Apostolado do Mar, right, the Secretários Diocesanos,
right and p149, and the Pastoral do Turismo.   »95
♦ **Committee of Jurists for Aid to Refugees in Portugal**, CARP
J.A. Costa Manso: Avenida Eng. Duarte Pacheco, Emp.
Amoreiras, Torre 2, 5° and., sala 2, 1000 Lisboa; *t* (01) 387
0301, 387 1327, *f* 387 1196
Legal advocacy for asylum seekers; for European Legal
Network on Asylum, ELENA, see p154.   »95
✪ **Confederação Geral dos Trabalhadores Portuguêses—
Intersindical Nacional**, CGTP-IN *(General Confederation of
Portuguese Workers—Trade Union Congress)* Departamento
de Emigração *(Migrants Department)*
Joaquim Fernandes: Rua Victor Cordon 1, 1200 Lisboa;
t (01) 347 2181, 343 3290, *f* 342 3662 (?)
Specialist office for migrant workers within the largest
national trade union confederation.   »94
♦ **Conselho das Comunidades Portuguêsas** *(Council of
Portuguese Communities)*
[address unknown]
Possibly a consultative body of representatives of Portuguese
emigrant communities.   »82
● **O Emigrante** (The Emigrant)
Rua Vitor Cordon 19, 1200 Lisboa; *t* (01) 325157
Newspaper (52/yr) for Portuguese emigrant communities. »90
● **Fundação Lar do Emigrante Português no Mundo** *(Home
Foundation for Portuguese Emigrants Abroad)*
Com. Manuel Oliveira: Covelas, 4780 Santo Tirso; *t* (052)
51875-76   »94
✪ **Grupo Recreativo Unidos das Ilhas**, GUDI
Vitalino Santos Rodriguez: Rua do Girassol 1, r/c, Alto da
Cova da Moura, 2700 Amadora
Sporting and leisure activities: African group?

● **O Lusitano** (The Lusitanian)
Rua da Quintinha 54, 1200 Lisboa; *t* (01) 668161-66
Magazine (12/yr) serving emigrant communities.   »90
● **Obra do Apostolado do Mar** *(Apostolate of the Sea)* Head
Office
Padre Francisco António Ferreira, National Director: Rua da
Emenda 66-1°, 1200 Lisboa; *t* (01) 346 9141, 328949,
370757
Agency of the Commisão Episcopal de Migrações, left, for
pastoral care of seafarers; runs social centres for Portuguese
and foreign sailors, all called Clube "Stella Maris", in Buarcos,
Caxinas, Gafanha da Nazaré, Leixões, Lisbon, Nazaré, Peniche,
Setúbal and Sines. *Stella Maris* (12/yr).   »90
✪ ≡ Rua Fresca 78, Leça da Palmeira, 4450 Matosinhos;
t (02) 995 2756, 995 2619   »90
♦ **Obra Católica Portuguêsa das Migrações**, OCPM
(Portuguese Migration Pastorate)
P. Manuel Soares Nobre, National Director: Campo dos
Mártires da Pátria 43-1°, 1100 Lisboa; *t* (01) 353 8116,
f 715 5757
Maria Fernanda Lourenço de Gouveia secretary; agency of
Commissão Episcopal de Migrações, left, co-ordinating the
pastoral care of emigrant communities, immigrants and
refugees; founded 1962; affiliate of International Catholic
Migration Commission, p217. Information work includes radio
broadcasting; public education, counselling, social work,
welfare rights advice correspondence service; assistance to
refugees in re-emigration. See also Portuguese pastoral
centres in several European countries, pp97-101. *Migrações
Portuguêsas* (1/yr); *Cá e Lá* (4/yr).   »94
✪ **Plataforma ONED**
Avenida Visconde Valmor 35-3° D, 1000 Lisboa
Advice service.   »94
✪ **Radio Paris Lisboa SA**
Carole Medrinal: Avenida João Crisostomo 55a, 1000
Lisboa; *t* (01) 546960   »90
● **Região das Equipas de Língua Portuguêsa no Estrangeiro**,
RELPE *(Portuguese-Language Teams for Overseas)*
Avenida de Roma 96-4° E, 1200 Lisboa; *t* (01) 897889
Catholic Church body serving emigrant Portuguese
communities.   »94
✪ **Secretariado Arquidiocesano de Migração** *(Archdiocesan
Migration Secretariat)* Archdiocese of Braga
Fernando José Gomes, Assistant: Rua de Santa Margarida 8,
4700 Braga; *t* (053) 22471
Provision and arrangement at regional and local level of
pastoral care and social work services to migrants, under
direction of the Comissão Episcopal de Migrações, left, and
the OCPM, above. This is administrative office; see service
address (Secretário Diocesano de Migração), below.   »90
✪ **Secretariado Diocesano de Migração** *(Diocesan Migration
Secretariat)*
Paço Episcopal, Terreiro da Sé, 4000 Porto; *t* (02) 310578
Responsibilities as for Secretariado Arquidiocesana in Braga.
This is administrative office; see also service address
(Serviço Diocesano de Migração), p149.   »90
✪ **Secretário Diocesano de Migração** *(Diocesan Migration
Secretary)*
Pe Duarte Manuel Goncalves da Rosa: Apartado 163, 9701
Angra do Heroísmo Codex; *t* (095) 23374, 24601
Angra team has six staff.   »90
✪ Portoalegre e Castelo Branco: Pe. José da Graça: Residência
Paroquial de São Vicente, 2200 Abrantes; *t* (041) 22268
Four staff.   »90
✪ ≡ Pe. Albino Rodrigues de Pinho: Rua José Estêvão 50,
3800 Aveiro; *t* (034) 25687   »90
✪ ≡ Pe António da Silva Lima: Rua António José Lisboa 270-
1°, Montelíos, Real, 4700 Braga; *t* (053) 621678, 23118
Braga team has two members.   »90
✪ ≡ Cón. Dr Aníbal Folgado: Seminário de São José, 5300
Bragança; *t* (073) 23247
Bragança group has three members.   »90
✪ ≡ Funchal: Pe. João Ferreira: Residência Paroquial, 9135
Camacha; *t* (091) 922125   »90
✪ ≡ Pe António de Sousa: Casa Nova, Seminário, 3000
Coimbra; *t* (039) 716895, 716884, 24210, 20167
Coimbra team has three members.   »90
✪ ≡ Pe Dr Felipe Marques de Figueiredo: Largo dos Colegias
2, Apartado 54, 7000 Evora; *t* (066) 23451, 28362   »90
✪ ≡ Diocese of the Algarve: Pe. Júlio Tropa Mendes: Santa
Bárbara de Nexe, 8000 Faro; *t* (089) 90233   »90
✪ ≡ Cón. José Joaquim Cardoso: Portelo de Cambres, 5100
Lamego; *t* (054) 66153   »90
✪ ≡ Pe. Luís Inácio João: Quinta de São Batolomeu, Lote
13-2° D, 2400 Leiria; *t* (044) 31432, 32760   »90

✿ **Secretário Diocesano de Migração**
António dos Reis Rodrigues: Campo dos Mártires da Pátria
45, 1100 Lisboa; t (01) 563901
See also CARE, p148.   »90
✿ ≡ Beja: Pe. Fernandes Pereira: Avenida Domingos
Rodrigues Pablo 2 A, 7520 Sines; t (069) 622941   »90
✿ ≡ Santarém: Pe Leopoldo de Sousa Gonçalves:
Carregueiros, 2300 Tomar; t (049) 33775   »90
✿ ≡ Guarda: Pe Manuel Duarte Cándido Curto: Tortozendo,
Barco, 6215 Unhais da Serra; t (075) 96516
Guarda diocese has four staff.   »90
✿ ≡ Pe Manuel Correia Quintas: Paço Episcopal, Quinta de
São Lourenço, 4900 Viana do Castelo; t (058) 322615
Viana group has four members.   »90
✿ ≡ Pe. Norberto Pires Portelinha: Seminário, 5000 Vila
Real; t (059) 22034, 22327   »90
✿ ≡ Cón. Mercier Pereira dos Santos: Igreja dos Terceiros,
3500 Viseu; t (032) 25937   »90
● **Seminário Scalabriniano** *(Scalabrini Seminary)* and
Secretário Diocesano de Migrações, Setúbal
Pe. Ezio Ragnoli: Rua Alves Redol 257, Paivas, Amora, 2840
Seixal; t (065) 221 7929
Catholic seminary producing priests to serve migrant
communities; incorporates diocesan migrant pastorate.
Jovems sem Fronteiras (Youth without Borders; 12/yr).   »90
✿ *Serviço Diocesano de Migração* *(Diocesan Migration Service)*
Pe José María Moreira: Igreja da Trinidada, 4000 Porto;
t (02) 962576, 313001
Provision at regional and local level of pastoral care and
social work services to migrants, under the direction of the
Commissão Episcopal de Migrações and co-ordinated by the
OCPM; these, and secretariat address, p148. Four staff. »90
✿ *Voz da Queiriga* (Voice of Queiriga)
M. Donato de Almeida e Cunha, Editor: Avenida da Igreja,
3650 Vila Nova de Paiva Codex; t 54222
Bulletin for emigrants from the region, mostly in France. »90

RUSSIA 7

✿ *Moscow Magazine*
Room 303, Dom Journalista, Suvorovsky Boulevard 8A,
Moskva 121019; t (095) 291 1787, f 973 2144
Dutch-owned magazine for expatriate communities.   »95

SPAIN 34

● **Acción Familiar**, AFA *(Family Action)*
Fernando Cortázar: Lagasca 120, int. 9°, 28006 Madrid;
t (91) 411 2943, 561 0601, f 411 5840
Welfare, advice.   »94
✿ **Algeciras Acoge** *(Algeciras Welcomes)*
Ventura Morón 2, 11201 Algeciras; t (956) 663700
Reception centre for migrants in the Cadiz region.   »94
✿ **Alicante Acoge**, AA *(Alicante Welcomes)*
Miguel Martínez Sarabia: [address uncertain] calle Aguila 35-
3ª, 03006 Alacant/Alicante; t (96) 511 5285, 511 5292
Also listed (1994) at Virgen de las Nieves 4 bajo, 03009
Alicante, t 517 2661. Migrant reception centre; welfare,
housing, legal advice.   »94
✿ **Almería Acoge, Asociación de Ayuda al Inmigrante** *(Almeria
Welcomes, Immigrant Aid Society)* and Cáritas Española
Juan Sánchez Miranda: calle Alcalde Muñoz 10-2° izq.,
04004 Almería; t (951) 271575, f 270670
Anti-racist work, assistance to refugees and (mainly
Moroccan) migrants in Andalucía. Branches at San Pablo
26 bajo dcha, 04007 El Egido, t 486110; 28 de Febrero 4,
04740 Roquetas de Mar, t 321880, f 270670.   »94
✿ **Alquibla—Asociación Cultural y Social**
Antonia Sánchez Urios: calle Alberto Sevilla s/n, 30011
Murcia; t (968) 344766
Youth integration. *Sin Detenerse* (1/yr).   »94
✿ **Alternativa Solidaria**
Ant. Ricardos 15 SA 1, Apartado 5469, 08080 Barcelona,
Catalunya; t (93) 340 4362, f 830 1253   »94
● **Asistencia Pedagógica, Orientación y Apoyo al Retorno,**
APOYAR *(Educational Assistance, Orientation and Aid for
Returnees)*
Anne-Marie Meste: calle Ocaña 1-4°, Ptª 2, Esc. A, 28047
Madrid; t (91) 717 1365
Services for returning emigrants.   »90

● **Asociación de Ayuda Mútua de Inmigrantes en Cataluña,**
AMIC *(Immigrant Mutual Aid Society of Catalonia)*
María Pilar González: Rambla Santa Mónica 10 baixos,
08002 Barcelona, Catalunya; t (93) 318 7827, f 412 0373
Migrant and refugee welfare; community development,
advice, information. Based in the CITE (migrant workers'
information centre) of the UGT trade union, see below.   »94
✿ **Asociación Europea para la Formación Profesional y
Educación Intercultural de Refugiados, Asilados e Inmigrantes,**
FO-INTER: European Society for Refugee and Immigrant
Training and Intercultural Education
Luis Lizama Fuentes: avenida de la Aviación 87-89 bajo,
28044 Madrid; t/f (91) 705 1315
Training and education issues affecting refugees and
migrants; mainly Latin American.   »94
◆ **Asociación Libre de Abogados, Derechos Extranjeros y
Minorías** *(Lawyers' Collective for Immigrant and Minority
Rights)*
Andrés López Rodríguez: calle Castello 24-3° int. izq., 28001
Madrid; t (91) 435 6550, 435 6511, f 577 7450
Legal advice and assistance, campaigns on racism, migration
and minority rights.   »94
✿ **Asociación Pro Inmigrantes en Asturias**, Apia *(Asturias
Association for Immigrant Welfare)*
Angel Cuervo Arango: calle González del Valle 5, 33003
Oviedo, Asturias; t/f (98) 525 0200
Rights advice, social welfare; associated with the Delegación
Diocesana de Migraciones, p151.   »94
✿ **Asociación de Refugiados y Asilados de la Ciudad de
Valencia**, ARACOVA *(Valencia Refugees and Asylum Seekers
Association)*
Sueca 58, pta E, 46006 Valencia   »94
◆ **Asociación de Solidaridad con los Trabajadores Inmigrantes,**
ASTI *(Association for Solidarity with Immigrant Workers)*
Antonio Martínez, Director: calle Cava Alta 25-3° izq., 28005
Madrid; t (91) 365 6448, 365 6518, f 366 4139
José Valero legal advice, Teresa Sánchez; counselling on
immigration, employment, rights, concerned largely with
workers in informal sector; member of EU Migrants Forum,
p131; reception centre. Spanish contact for European Co-
ordination for the Right to Family Life for Immigrants, p136.
See also Delegación Diocesana, p151. *Inmigrante* (6/yr). »95
✿ ≡ Francisco Puértolas: calle Santa Ana 20, Majadahonda,
28220 Madrid; t (91) 638 3500   »94
◆ **Associació Catalana de Solidaritat i d'Ajut al Refugiat,**
ACSAR *(Catalan Association for Solidarity with and Aid to
Refugees)* Asociación Catalana de Solidaridad y de Ayuda a
Refugiados
Josep Ribera Pinyol: Parallel 202 b., 08015 Barcelona,
Catalunya; t (93) 423 7828, 423 9825, f 426 6803
Antoni M. Lluch, director, Montserrat López; advice and
welfare services to refugees in Catalonia; antiracism. Linked
with the Cruz Roja, pp151 & 214.   »94
✿ **Bilbo Etxezabal** *(Bilbao Open House)* Bilbao Casa Abierta
Eduardo Ruiz Vieytez: calle Príncipe de Viana 1, esq. Anselma
de Salces, 48007 Bilbo, Bizkaia, Euskadi; t (94) 446 7206,
446 1798
Voluntary body formed 1989. Reception centre for Latin
American, Portuguese, and more recently African, Filipino
and other migrants, funded by local and regional government;
associated with diocesan Commission for Justice and Peace
(see Justicia y Paz, p215); migrant advice and orientation,
legal aid, health care, language classes, cultural and
educational activities; research.   »94
✿ **Cantabria Acoge** *(Cantabria Welcomes)*
Rualasal 7-5° dcha, 39001 Santander; t (942) 364445
Migrant worker reception centre linked with the local branch
of Cáritas Española, p213.   »94
● **Catalunya Solidaria** *(Catalan Solidarity)*
carrer Avinyó 29, 08002 Barcelona, Catalunya
See also Federació de Col.lectivus d'Inmigrants de Catalunya,
p151 (possibly same organisation?).   »94
✿ **Centre d'Informació per Treballadors Estrangers**, CITE
(Information Centre for Foreign Workers) Comisiones Obreras
M. Soleyman/Ferrer Olivé: vía Laietana 16-1ª, 08003
Barcelona, Catalunya; t (93) 315 0711, 319 8466, f 312
2017
Housing and welfare advice and support service for
Moroccan and other immigrants, formed 1986 by the CCOO
trade union federation.   »94
✿ **Centre d'Informació per Treballadors Estrangers**, CITE:
Unión General de Trabajadores, UGT *(General Workers' Union)*
Rambla de Santa Mónica 10, 08002 Barcelona, Catalunya;
t (93) 318 4338
Immigrant workers' advice centre. See also AMIC, above. »94

✿ **Centre Internacional Escarré per a Minories Etniques i les Nacions**, CIEMEN *(Escarré International Centre for Ethnic Minorities and Nationalities)*
Aureli Argemi i Roca: Pau Claris 106-1er 1ª, 08009 Barcelona, Catalunya; *t* (93) 302 0144, 302 0276, *f* 412 0890
Solidarity with European and other ethnic minorities; resource centre. See also Integral, p215. *Europa de les Nacions* (4/yr), *Mercator* (12/yr).   »94

✿ **Centro de Acogida de Inmigrantes**, CEAIN *(Immigrant Reception Centre)*
María Del Mar Rodriguez: [address uncertain] calle Vicario 16, 11403 Jerez de la Frontera; *t* (956) 349585
Also listed (1994) at Edificio Mérito bloque 4 bajo B, 11401 Jerez. Refugee and migrant housing, welfare, advice.
Boletín Informativo (4/yr).   »94

● **Centro de Defensa de los Refugiados** *(Centre for the Defence of Refugees)*
Club de la Unesco de Madrid, plaza Tirso de Molina 8-1°, 28012 Madrid
See also Iranian group CEDRI, p45 (possibly same?).   »90

✿ **Centro Guía para Inmigrantes y Refugiados**, CGI-UGT *(Guidance Centre for Immigrants and Refugees)* Unión General de Trabajadores
calle Capitán Maldonado Argibay 90, 28029 Madrid; *t* (91) 314 2365, 314 2401
Advice centre operated by the UGT trade union federation; also at San Leopoldo 19, 28029 Madrid, *t* 314 6228.   »94

✿ **Centro de Información y Acogida**, CEDIA *(Reception and Information Centre)*
plaza de la Marina Española 12, 28013 Madrid; *t* (91) 541 6512, 541 6763
Advice, housing and settlement aid.   »94

✿ **Centro de Información para Trabajadores Extranjeros**, CITE *(Information Centre for Foreign Workers)* Comisiones Obreras, CCOO *(Workers' Commissions)*
Campo de Gibraltar, 11206 Algeciras; *t* (956) 650312
Local advice unit for migrant workers; labour rights, housing, welfare, social and cultural issues, participation in anti-racist campaigns. This and the CITEs listed immediately below are run by the CCOO trade union federation; these are followed by the CITEs of the UGT unions.   »94

✿ ≡ also known as C de I para T *Migrantes*, CITMI: calle Cardenal Belluga 10 bajo, 03006 Alicante; *t* (96) 512 2298-99, 592 9640-41, *f* 513 1255   »94

✿ ≡ calle Javier Sanz 14, 04004 Almería; *t* (951) 570647
Also at calle Almería 1-1° C, 04007 El Egido.   »94

✿ ≡ calle Lope de Vega s/n, 24300 Bembimbre, León; *t* (987) 510920
See also Asociación Cultural Amilcar Cabral, p39.   »94

✿ ≡ avenida Sabino Arana 20, 48013 Bilbo, Bizkaia, Euskadi; *t* (94) 442 5500   »94

✿ ≡ Carlos I 1-3, 20011 Donostia, Gipuzkoa, Euskadi; *t* (943) 470399, *f* 463366   »94

✿ ≡ Oulad Bejit Mohamed: I. Walis 1, 07800 Ibiza, Baleares; *t* (971) 315361   »94

✿ ≡ muelle Heredia 26-6°, 29001 Málaga; *t* (952) 228803-04
Also at Marbella, *t* 771116.   »94

✿ ≡ Corvalán 6, 30002 Murcia; *t* (968) 212223   »94

✿ ≡ calle Asturias 9-4°, 33004 Oviedo; *t* (984) 257199   »94

✿ ≡ Mustapha Bouliharrk: [address unknown] Palma, Mallorca; *t* (971) 726060-61   »94

✿ ≡ Navarro Villoslada 21, 31003 Pamplona, Nafarroa; *t* (948) 244200   »94

✿ ≡ Santa Clara 5, 39001 Santander; *t* (942) 227704   »94

✿ ≡ calle Trajano 1, 41002 Sevilla; *t* (954) 215205-07   »94

✿ ≡ August 48 baixos, 43003 Tarragona; *t* (977) 228396, 221809   »94

✿ ≡ Hernán Cortés 36, 36203 Vigo, Pontevedra; *t* (986) 228894   »94

✿ ≡ plaza de la Constitución 12 bajo, 50008 Zaragoza; *t* (976) 239185   »94

✿ **Centro de Información para Trabajadores Extranjeros**, CITE *(Information Centre for Foreign Workers)* Unión General de Trabajadores, UGT *(General Workers' Union)*
avenida de la Fuerzas Armadas 2, 11202 Algeciras; *t* (956) 651801
Migrant workers' advice and welfare centre; this and those listed below are operated by the UGT, one of the main labour confederations; see also Confederación de CITEs, p151, and the CCOO CITEs, above.   »94

✿ ≡ calle Sevilla 36, 04700 El Ejido; *t* (951) 570890   »94

✿ ≡ 1° de Mayo 21, 35002 Las Palmas, Gran Canaria   »94

✿ ≡ avenida La Fama 8, 30006 Murcia; *t* (968) 268727   »94

✿ ≡ Arquitecto Mora 7, 46019 Valencia   »94

✿ ≡ Costa 1, 50001 Zaragoza; *t* (976) 700100   »94

✿ **Centro de Información para Trabajadores Migrantes**, CITMI: Comisiones Obreras
plaza Nápolis i Sicilia 5, 46003 Valencia; *t* (96) 388 2100»94

✿ **Centro de Inmigrantes Al Manzil** *(Al Manzil Immigrants Centre)*
Gran Vía 2, Madrid; *t* (91) 638 3500
Men's reception centre; see also Al Manzil—Centro para Marroquíes, p90, and ASTI, p149.   »90

✿ **Centro de Inmigrantes Fuenlabrada** *(Fuenlabrada Immigrants Centre)*
calle Zamora 1, Fuenlabrada, Madrid; *t* (91) 615 1012   »94

✿ **Centro de Inmigrantes Majadahonda para Mujeres** *(Majadahonda Women Immigrants' Centre)*
calle Escudero 2-1°, 28000 Madrid   »94

✿ **Centro de Inmigrantes de Móstoles** *(Móstoles Immigrant Centre)*
María Cruz Chica: avenida Cerro Prieto 34, 28931 Móstoles, Madrid; *t* (91) 646 6061
Cultural, leisure and information centre.   »94

✿ **Centro de Inmigrantes, Refugiados y Asilados** *(Immigrant, Refugee and Asylum-Seeker Centre)*
Héctor Casanueva Ojeda: calle Núñez Morgado 4, of. 92, 28036 Madrid; *t* (91) 314 5193, 323 1763, *f* 323 3789
Centre for (mainly Latin American) refugee, migrant and solidarity activities. See also CIPIE, CIDEAL and Latin American women's Centro de Información y Orientación at same address, all p84.   »94

✿ **Centro Rural Familiar Migrante** *(Migrants' Rural Family Centre)*
La Fuensanta, 02004 Albacete   »90

♦ **Comisión Católica Española de Migración**, CCEE *(Spanish Catholic Migration Commission)* formerly CCE de *Emigración*
Ramón de Marcos Saenz, Director: [address uncertain] calle Sierra 6, Madrid; *t* (91) 554 5529
Also listed (1994) at Valenzuela 10-1° izq., 28014 Madrid, *t* 532 7478-79, *f* 532 2059. Church agency providing advice and welfare services for refugees and migrants in and from Spain. Affiliate of the International Catholic Migration Commission, p217; helps refugees to settle in third countries; see also Comisión Episcopal de Migraciones, below; and local Delegaciones Diocesanas and FAIN solidarity group, p151.»95

● ≡ Servicio de Refugiados y Migrantes: calle Guadiana 10, El Viso, 28002 Madrid; *t* (91) 261 7200
Migrant and refugee advice and welfare services.   »94

✿ **Comisión Diocesana de Migración** *(Diocesan Migration Commission)*
Prat de la Riba 35 bajo, 43001 Tarragona; *t* (977) 210655
Catholic Church pastoral agency.   »90

♦ **Comisión Episcopal de Migraciones**, CEM *(Episcopal Commission on Migration)*
Jesús Ansó/Pedro Puente: calle Añastro 1, Apartado 29075, 28033 Madrid; *t* (91) 766 5500, *f* 766 7981   »94

♦ **Comisión Española de Ayuda al Refugiado**, CEAR *(Spanish Commission for Aid to Refugees)* and European Legal Network on Asylum, ELENA
María Jesús Arsuaga, General Secretary: avenida del General Perón 32-2° dcha, 28020 Madrid; *t* (91) 555 0698, 555 2908, 555 4269, 556 9545, *f* 555 5416, *Tx* 27380 CEARM E
Juan Bandres, Ramón Munagorri Triana. Research, social service and pressure group formed by trade union, church, humanitarian and solidarity groups, part-funded by Social Affairs Ministry, p215; refugee status, legal protection, settlement help funded by UNHCR, p212; reform of asylum law, socio-economic integration, employment, counselling; anti-racist work. The CEAR is concerned with the legal position of asylum seekers, while the Red Cross, pp151 & 214, attends to welfare needs. The CEAR co-operates with the UNHCR office (same address), editing Spanish version of its magazine. Some aid to refugees abroad. Jorge Canarias Fernández Cavada of CEAR is national contact for the ELENA network, p154. *Refugiados* (12/yr, for UNHCR); *Boletín.* »95

✿ ≡ José María de Olabarri 4-1° B, 48001 Bilbo, Bizkaia, Euskadi; *t* (94) 423 9110, *f* 423 9111   »94

✿ ≡ Doctor Chil 4, 35001 Las Palmas, Gran Canaria; *t* (928) 311627, *f* 312129   »94

✿ ≡ plaza Príncipe de Asturias 30-4° 1, 41940 Tomares, Sevilla; *t* (95) 415 1606, *f* 442 0304   »94

♦ **Comité de Defensa de los Refugiados, Asilados e Inmigrantes en España**, COMRADE *(Committee for the Defence of Refugees, Asylum-Seekers and Immigrants)*
Rafael Luis Guardo Polo: Apartado de Correos 8564, 28080 Madrid; *t* (91) 377 4443, *f* 777 7814
César Torres, Abdel Hamid Beyuki. Location: Gutiérrez de Cetina 88-1° 3, 28017 Madrid. Anti-racism, aid to refugees and immigrants. Founded 1988. *Sin Fronteras* (6/yr).   »94

♦ **Confederación de Centros de Información para Trabajadores Extranjeros** *(Confederation of Foreign Worker Information Centres)*: Unión General de Trabajadores, UGT
Fernández de la Hoz 12, 28000 Madrid; *t* (91) 419 1750
Federation of advice and welfare centres (CITEs, listed p150) for foreign workers. An agency of the UGT, one of the main national labour confederations, see p152 and p216. See also Centro Guía para Inmigrantes y Refugiados, and the CITEs of the rival Comisiones Obreras union, all p150.   »94

✿ **Córdoba Acoge** *(Cordoba Welcomes)*
José María Ledesma: calle Cinco Caballeros 1-1° 1, 14007 Córdoba, Andalucía; *t* (957) 252101
Refugee and migrant reception and information centre.   »94

♦ **Cruz Roja Española**, CRE-SAE *(Spanish Red Cross)*
Servicio de Refugiados y Extranjeros
Carmen García Guijosa: calle Juan Montalvo 3, 28040 Madrid; *t* (91) 533 3102-05, *f* 533 4279
Olga Couso national director of the Refugees and Foreigners Service; Felix Barrena. The main channel for government and UNHCR funding of refugee assistance activities; these include counselling (but not legal advice: see CEAR, p150), help in settlement, social and economic integration of refugees, language training, re-migration assistance. Development education, anti-racism: published 1991 study on racism in text-books. See local CRE sections, p214, most of which provide direct services to migrants and refugees, or offer referrals to this specialist branch; see also Red Cross international, p218, and ACSAR in Catalonia, p149.   »94

✿ **Delegación Diocesana de Migraciones**, DDM *(Diocesan Delegation for Migration)*
Juan Herrera A.: calle Colegio 3, 23002 Jaén; *t* (953) 230200, 733078
The DDM co-ordinates Catholic pastoral care for migrants, working closely with charities including Cáritas, p213.   »94

✿ ≡ DDM Lérida: plaza San José 3-1°, 25002 Lérida; *t* (973) 270498   »90

✿ ≡ Antonio Martínez: calle Cava Alta 25-3° izq., 28005 Madrid; *t* (91) 365 6518, 265 6448, *f* 266 4139
See also Asociación de Solidaridad con los Trabajadores Inmigrantes, p149.   »94

✿ ≡ Macario Villalón López: calle Hospital San José 4-1°, 28901 Getafe, Madrid; *t* (91) 681 5111, *f* 681 5114
Advice and welfare services.   »94

✿ ≡ Asturias: calle Santa Ana 4-1°, 33005 Oviedo; *t* (985) 217852
See also Asociación Pro Inmigrantes en Asturias, p149.   »90

✿ ≡ plaza de la Seo 6-2°, 50001 Zaragoza; *t* (976) 294738
See also Cáritas, p213, and SOS Racismo, p174.   »94

✿ **Departament de Migració de Caritas Diocesana de Barcelona** *(Migration Department, Barcelona Diocesan Caritas)* and Comissió Diocesana de Migració
Alex Masllorens: carrer Banys Nous 16-2°, 08002 Barcelona, Catalunya; *t* (93) 317 7438, 412 4343, *f* 301 3961
The migrant welfare section (formerly known as Centro de Acogida para Extranjeros) of the local section of the Catholic charity Cáritas, see p213; advice, social services, youth integration. Address shared with Catholic diocesan commission for pastoral care of migrants.   »94

♦ **Departamento Confederal de Inmigración—Unión Sindical Obrera**, DCI-USO *(Confederal Immigration Department, Workers' Trade Union)*
Ramón Salaices Jiménez: calle Príncipe de Vergara 13-7°, 28001 Madrid; *t* (91) 577 4109, 577 4113, *f* 577 2959
National migrant labour section of the USO trade union confederation. See also Santander branch, below.   »94

✿ **Departamento de Inmigrantes—Unión Sindical Obrera**, USO *(Immigrants Department, Workers' Trade Union)*
Mercedes Pereda Puente: calle Carlos III 5, e/s, 39009 Santander, Cantabria; *t* (942) 227004
Local section of the DCI-USO, above, an information and advice service of a major labour organisation.   »94

♦ **Dirección de Relaciones con la Diáspora** *(Directorate for Relations with the Diaspora)* Gobierno Vasco, Secretaría General de Acción Exterior
Navarra 2, 01006 Vitoria/Gasteiz, Araba, Euskadi; *t* (945) 188156
Agency of the Basque government responsible for maintaining cultural relations with organisations representing Basque communities abroad.   »94

♦ **Federació de Col.lectivus d'Inmigrants de Catalunya** *(Catalan Federation of Immigrant Groups)*
Hotel d'Entitats, Edif. Piramidón 9ª planta, carrer Empordà 33, La Pau, 08020 Barcelona, Catalunya
Umbrella group for migrant and refugee organisations. See also Catalunya Solidaria, p149.   »94

● **Federación de Asociaciones y Centros de Integración y Ayuda a Marginados**, FACIAM *(Federation of Societies and Centres for Assistance to and Integration of the Marginalised)*
Camino de Guijarro 8, 28050 Madrid   »94

♦ **Federación de Asociaciones Pro-Inmigrantes Extranjeros en España**, FAIN *(Federation of Associations for Foreign Immigrants in Spain)*
José Magaña: calle Valenzuela 10-1° izq., 28014 Madrid; *t/f* (91) 523 2095
See also Comisión Católica Española de Migraciones, p150.»94

✿ **Federación de Centros de Acogida de Inmigrantes Extranjeros en Andalucía** *(Andalusian Federation of Foreign Immigrant Reception Centre)*
Juan Sánchez Miranda: calle Benito Pérez Galdós 1, 41004 Sevilla, Andalucía; *t* (95) 421 8440, 421 0600, *f* 456 0639
Based in the Sevilla Acoge centre, p152.   »94

♦ **Federación de Organizaciones para Refugiados y Asilados**, FEDORA *(Federation of Refugee and Asylum-Seeker Organisations)*
calle Arlabán 7-4°, of. 46, 28014 Madrid; *t* (91) 523 1618, *f* 523 3491
See also Asociación de Amistad Hispano-Rumana, p102.   »94

✿ **Granada Acoge** *(Granada Welcomes)*
calle Santa Paula s/n, 18001 Granada; *t* (958) 200836
Reception centre for Arab and other migrants.   »94

✿ **Huelva Acoge** *(Huelva Welcomes)*
Velarde 3 bajo, 21003 Huelva; *t* (955) 245226
Migrant workers' reception centre operated by the local branch of Cáritas, the Catholic welfare agency, p213.   »95

● **Instituto Español de Emigración**, IEE *(Spanish Emigration Institute)* Ministerio de Trabajo y Seguridad Social
paseo del Pintor Rosales 42-44, 28008 Madrid; *t* (91) 247 5200
Established 1956, under the labour ministry. Involved in the issue of certain types of work permit; contact with Spanish communities abroad, information for those intending to emigrate or to return; sociological and statistical research on immigration and emigration; welfare work; educational help for emigrants. *Memoria de la DGIEE*; *Carta de España*.   »94

✿ **Instituto Romano de Servicios Sociales y Culturales**
Cervantes 7-2 1ª, Apartad 202, 08080 Barcelona, Catalunya; *t* (93) 412 7745, *f* 412 7040   »94

✿ **Jaén Acoge**
[address unknown] Jaén
Reception centre for Arabs and others; campaigns against racism and xenophobia.   »93

✿ **Las Palmas Acoge** *(Las Palmas Welcomes)* and Cáritas Española
avenida de Escaleritas 51, 35011 Las Palmas, Gran Canaria; *t* (928) 251740, 364372
Migrant worker reception centre operated by the local section of Cáritas, the Catholic welfare agency, p213.   »95

✿ **Málaga Acoge** *(Málaga Welcomes)*
Francisco J. Sepúlveda Muñoz: calle Gigantes 1-1°, 29008 Málaga; *t* (952) 222 9772, *f* 222 9776
Migrant and refugee reception centre, linked with local section of Cáritas, p213; housing and welfare advice. Also listed (1994) at Ollerías 31-1°, 29012 Málaga.   »94

● **Médicos del Mundo—Centro de Atención Socio-Sanitario al Inmigrante**, MDM-CASSIM *(Doctors of the World—Immigrant Social and Health Care Centre)*
Corredera Baja de San Pablo 25, 28004 Madrid; *t* (91) 523 4116, *f* 522 3873
Activities include health care research and services for immigrants; published 1994 resource guide on immigrant communities. May be linked with Medicus Mundi, p215.   »94

✿ **Murcia Acoge** *(Murcia Welcomes)*
Cartagena 6, 30700 Torre Pacheco, Murcia
Migrant/refugee reception, welfare service; anti-racism.   »94

✿ ≡ Delegación de Cartagena (Cartagena Branch): Monserrat Cascante Dávila: calle Tierno Galván 38 bis, 30200 Cartagena, Murcia; *t* (968) 505301, 527256
Boletín (12/yr).   »94

✿ **Oficina de Asesoramiento para Trabajadores Extranjeros y Emigrantes Retornados**, ATE *(Advisory Office for Immigrant Workers and Returned Emigrants)* also known as Asesoría para Trabajadores Extranjeros
Cristián Quiñones: calle Lope de Vega 38-5°, 28014 Madrid; *t* (91) 536 5208, 536 5213, *f* 536 5218
Sometimes listed as Centro de Información para Trabajadores Extranjeros. Founded 1988, linked to Comisiones Obreras trade union. *Migraciones*.   »94

✿ **Oficina de Inmigración**: Unión General de Trabajadores
Carretera de Barcelona 71-73, 17000 Girona, Catalunya
Migrant worker advice centre of UGT labour union, p152.»94

✿ **Programa de Apoyo a Extranjeros**, PAEX *(Foreigners Support Programme)* and Cáritas Española
Inmaculada Barrio: Eulogio Serdán kalea 5 b., 01012 Vitoria/Gasteiz, Araba, Euskadi; *t* (945) 146483, *f* 232716
Legal, employment and welfare advice service of the Catholic welfare agency Cáritas, p213 (which has many parish sections in Araba, contactable through diocesan office, *t* 232850).»94

✿ **Promoción de Colectivos Marginados**, PROCOMAR *(Promotion of Marginalised Communities)*
Gregorio Aguado Arranz: calle Santuario 7, 47002 Valladolid; *t* (983) 220444
Local community development.   »94

✿ **La Rioja Acoge** *(Rioja Welcomes)*
Olga Mejía Torres: calle La Brava 16 bajo, 26001 Logroño; *t* (941) 263115, *f* 256623
A service of diocesan Cáritas, the Catholic welfare agency, p213. Migrant reception and settlement; welfare and cross-cultural activities.   »94

● **Servei d'Acol.liment d'Infants i Famílies els Quatre Vents**, SAI *(Four Winds Children and Families Reception Service)*
Lita Bañeres Alvarez: carrer Sant Pau 52-54, 08001 Barcelona, Catalunya; *t* (93) 412 0661
Welfare, education, family social work.   »94

✿ **Sevilla Acoge—Centro de Acogida de Inmigrantes Extranjeros** *(Seville Welcomes—Reception Centre for Foreign Immigrants)*
Fernando Reyes García de Castro: Benito Pérez Galdós 1, 41004 Sevilla; *t* (95) 421 8440, 421 0600, *f* 456 0639
Also listed (1994) at Aguilas 5. Cultural, information and advice centre. See Federación de Centros de Acogida, p151.»94

◆ **Unión General de Trabajadores—Secretaría de Emigración**, UGT *(Emigration Secretariat, General Workers' Union)*
Fernández de la Hoz 12, 28004 Madrid; *t* (91) 419 1750
Emigrant services section of major trade union confederation; see also UGT sections abroad, p113. See also Confederación de Centros de Información para Trabajadores Extranjeros and Oficina de Inmigración, p151, individual CITEs, pp149-150, and Centro Guía para Inmigrantes y Refugiados, p150.   »90

✿ **Valencia Acoge** *(Valencia Welcomes)*
calle San Juan Bosco 10, 46019 Valencia; *t* (96) 366 0168, 388 4149
Anti-racism, integration of migrants.   »94

SWEDEN 46

◆ **Flyktinggruppernas och Asylrådens Riksförbund**, FARR *(National League of Refugee Groups and Asylum Councils, also known as Forum for Asylum Seekers and Refugees)*
Box 137, 77623 Hedemora; *t* (0225) 14777, (0159) 10707, *f* (0225) 14777   »95

◆ **Immigranternas Riksförbund** *(National League of Immigrants)*
Box 22101, Katrinedalsgatan 43, 50002 Borås; *t* (033) 136070, *f* 136075
Defends interests of immigrants and refugees.   »94

▌ **International Association of Immigrant Women**, RIFFI
Norrtullsgatan 45, 11345 Stockholm; *t* (08) 302189, *f* 317011   »94

● **Internationella Arbetslag**, IAL
Barnängsgatan 23, 11641 Stockholm; *t* (08) 643 0889
Anti-racist, anti-fascist, international solidarity youth organisation. See also Afrikagrupperna, p110, and Svensk Fillipinska Foreningen, p35.   »94

✿ **Minoriteternas Intressegrupp**, MIG
Box 11069, 75011 Uppsala   »93

✿ **Rådgivningsbyrån för asylsökande och flyktingar** *(Advisory Service for Asylum Seekers and Refugees)*
Gyllenstiernasgatan 14, 11526 Stockholm; *t* (08) 660 2170, *f* 665 0940   »95

◆ **Samarbetsorganet för Invandrarorganisationer i Sverige**, SIOS *(Co-operative Council of Immigrant Organisations in Sweden)*
Vegagatan 1, 11329 Stockholm; *t* (08) 301360
National umbrella organisation for migrant and refugee community groups.   »94

◆ **Svenska Flyktingrådet**: Swedish Refugee Council, SRC, and European Legal Network on Asylum, ELENA
Ingemar Strandberg: Torstensonsgatan 6, 11456 Stockholm; *t* (08) 667 6899, 654 9720, *f* 661 6598, 667 4426
Main publicly-funded NGO for advice, information, legal and social work with refugees and asylum seekers in Sweden; founded 1971. Strandberg is national contact for the ELENA network of refugee law practitioners, p154.   »95

◆ **Youth Council of the Swedish Immigrant Organisations**
Visbyringen 36, 16373 Spånga; *t* (08) 795 7824   »94

SWITZERLAND 41

✿ **Aktion für abgewiesene Asylbewerber**, AAA *(Action for Unsuccessful Asylum Applicants)*
Waldheim, 3072 Ostermundingen; *t* (031) 931 1093
Campaign for refugee policy reform; advice and assistance to those refused asylum.   »94

◆ **Arbeitsstelle für Asylfragen** *(Working Group on Asylum)*
Postfach 6966, 3001 Bern; *t* (031) 312 4032, *f* 312 4045
Works on development of non-racist asylum policies which respect international human rights standards.   »94

◆ **Asylkoordination Schweiz**, AKS: Coordination Suisse Asile *(Switzerland Asylum Co-ordination)*
Postfach 5215, 3001 Bern; *t* (031) 312 4038, *f* 312 4045
Refugee assistance.   »94

✿ **Asylkoordination Zürich** *(Zurich Asylum Co-ordination)*
Quellenstrasse 25, 8005 Zürich; *t* (01) 272 5575
Refugee assistance, anti-racist campaigns. *Fluchtseiten*.»94

✿ **Beratungsstelle für Asylsuchende** *(Asylum Seekers' Advice Centre)*
Weite Gasse 15, Postfach 2071, 5402 Baden, Aargau; *t* (056) 217241, *f* 217624   »95
✿ ≡ Schützenmattstrasse 16a, 4057 Basel; *t* (061) 261 5749, *f* 261 5766   »95
✿ ≡ Plessurquai 53, 7000 Chur, Graubünden; *t* (081) 226918, *f* 224861   »95
✿ ≡ Im Spiegelhof 18, 8750 Glarus; *t* (058) 616701, *f* 616702
Advice service on Thursday afternoons.   »95
✿ ≡ Mario Gattiker: Löwenstrasse 3, Postfach, 6002 Luzern; *t* (041) 522385, *f* 528258
A service of the local Caritas branch; see also Caritas Schweiz main office at the same address, p217.   »95
✿ ≡ Tellstrasse 4, Postfach, 9000 St Gallen; *t* (071) 222279, *f* 225470   »95
✿ ≡ Bertastrasse 8, Postfach 828, 8003 Zürich-Lochergut; *t* (01) 451 1000, *f* 451 1139
Part-time advice service.   »95

✿ **Beratungsstelle der Hilfswerke für Asylsuchenden** *(Asylum Seekers' Assistance Project Advice Centre)*
Am Rathausbogen 15, 8200 Schaffhausen; *t* (053) 253025, *f* 249956   »95

✿ **Berner Rechstberatungsstelle für Asylsuchende** *(Berne Rights Advice Centre for Asylum Seekers)*
Lorrainestr. 6, 3013 Bern; *t* (031) 332 6405, *f* 331 8072 »95

✿ **Bureau d'aide au départ/Immigration** *(Departure/Immigration Assistance Office)* Croix-Rouge Suisse, Section genevoise
13 rue des Rois, 1204 Genève; *t* (022) 781 1438, *f* 781 1508
Offers advice on repatriation and third-country resettlement of asylum seekers and refugees.   »95

✿ **Caritas Flüchtlingshilfe Zentralschweiz** *(Central Switzerland Caritas Refugee Aid)* Beratungsstelle für Asylsuchende
Gotthardstrasse 68, Postfach 24, 6410 Goldau; *t* (041) 522385, *f* 528258
Support, advice for refugees in the Schwyz/Zug region.   »95

● **Christlicher Friedensdienst—Flüchtlingshilfe**, CFD *(Refugee Assistance Section, Christian Peace Service)*
Postfach 1274, 3003 Bern; *t* (031) 301 6006-07, *f* 302 8734
Location: Falkenhöheweg 8, 3012 Bern. Practical assistance to refugees and asylum seekers; anti-racism.   »95

● **Comité Suisse pour la Défense du Droit d'Asile**, CSDDA *(Swiss Committee for the Defence of the Right to Asylum)*
Case postal 3928, 1010 Lausanne; *t* (021) 652 6443
Refugee advice and assistance, anti-racism.   »94

▌ **Conseil des Associations des Immigrés en Europe**, CAIE: Council of Immigrant Associations in Europe
Marie-Ange Colsa: rue de Genève 44, 1004 Lausanne; *t* (021) 246239
Human rights, immigration controls, employment, welfare, cultural identity. See also CAIE in France, p136.   »90

✿ **Consultorio giuridico per i richiedenti d'asilo**, SOS *(Legal Consultancy for Asylum Seekers)*
via Besso 41, 6900 Lugano; *t* (091) 574355, *f* 575526
A part-time advice service for refugees in Ticino.   »95

▌ **European Churches' Working Group on Asylum and Refugees**, ECWGAR: Conference of European Churches, CEC
Dr Frans Bouwen, Secretary: Case postale 2100, 150 Route de Ferney, 1211 Genève 2; *t* (022) 791 6234, *f* 791 6227, *Tx* 415730 OIK CH
Lobbying, information, co-ordination of church activities on behalf of refugees, asylum seekers and related legal and policy issues. A section of the CEC, the regional counterpart of the World Council of Churches, p219. *Refugees*.   »93

● **Fraueninformationszentrum Dritte Welt, FIZ** *(Third World Women's Information Centre)*
Maud Lebert: Quellenstrasse 25, 8005 Zürich; *t* (01) 271 8282, *f* 272 5074
Solidarity, information, language training and social support for migrant women, especially those subjected to physical, emotional or sexual abuse. *Zundbrief* (2/yr).　　　»93

● **Gesellschaft Minderheiten in der Schweiz, GMS** *(Society for Minorities in Switzerland)*
Postfach 282, 8027 Zürich; *t* (01) 201 1659
Anti-racism, support for migrants and refugees.　　　»94

▋ **International Movement of Rights and Humanity**
chemin Crêts-de-Pregny 27, Grand-Saconnex, 1218 Genève; *t* (022) 788 5838, *f* 788 5857　　　»94

◆ **Organisation Suisse d'Aide aux Réfugiés, OSAR:** Schweizerische Flüchtlingshilfe, SFH *(Swiss Organisation for Aid to Refugees)*
rue Chaucrau 3, 1003 Lausanne; *t* (021) 320 5641, *f* 320 1120
The main refugee advice and assistance agency; information, lobbying, anti-racism. Operates as the OSAR from Lausanne for the French-speaking parts of Switzerland; see also SFH, below.　　　»95

✿ **Rechtsberatung für Asylsuchende** *(Asylum Seekers' Rights Advice Service)* Caritas Aargau
c/o Caritas, Postfach, 5001 Aargau; *t* (064) 248555, *f* 226305
Location: Laurenzenvorstadt 71. Service on Tuesdays.　　»95
✿ ≡ Luzernerstrasse 7, 4502 Zuchwil; *t/f* (065) 255892
A part-time servive for refugees in Solothurn.　　　»95

◆ **Schweizerische Flüchtlingshilfe, SFH:** Organisation Suisse d'Aide aux Réfugiés, OSAR *(Swiss Refugee Assistance)*
Michael Marugg: Postfach 279, Kinkelstrasse 2, 8035 Zürich; *t* (01) 368 4242, 361 9640, *f* 368 4200, 362 8710
Also known as Schweizerische *Zentralstelle für* Flüchtlingshilfe. National organisation co-ordinating legal, social and economic aid to UNHCR-registered refugees and asylum seekers; documentation (Irina Lerch-Bortoli), research, lobbying, repatriation assistance. Founded 1936; over 20 staff. Operates as the SFH in the German-speaking areas; see also OSAR, above. Marugg is the national contact for the European Legal Network on Asylum, p154. *Asyl: Schweizer-ische Zeitschrift für Asylrecht.*　　　»95

● **Schweizerisches Arbeiterhilfswerk—Flüchtlingsdienst, SAH** *(Refugee Service, Swiss Labour Assistance)*
Postfach 325, Quellenstrasse 31, 8031 Zürich; *t* (01) 271 6075, 272 1521, 271 2600, *f* 272 5550
Trade union office for advice and assistance to refugees and asylum seekers, including reception centres.　　　»95

✿ **Thurgauer Beratungsstelle für Asylsuchende** *(Thurgau Advice Centre for Asylum Seekers)*
Freiestrasse 26, 8570 Weinfelden; *t* (072) 224241　　»95

▋ **Trust Fund for Disabled Refugees**
Palais des Nations, 1211 Genève; *t* (022) 731 0261
Development and funding of care and rehabilitation services for disabled refugees; sponsored by UNHCR, p219.　　»94

✿ **Winterthurer Beratungsstelle für Asylsuchende** *(Winterthur Advice Centre for Asylum Seekers)*
Steinberggasse 18, 8400 Winterthur; *t* (052) 213 7983
Advice on asylum procedures and welfare; Wednesday afternoon service.　　　»95

UNITED KINGDOM 44

✿ **Afro-Asian Advisory Service**
53 Addington Square, London SE5 5LB; *t* (0171) 701 0141
Counselling, advice and advocacy service for Caribbeans, Africans and Asians on immigration rules, divided families, study visas and other matters.　　　»95

✿ **Afro-Asian Society**
Dr S. Ala-ud-Din: 25 Sunnybank Road, Longsight, Manchester M13 0XF; *t* (0161) 248 6844
Immigrant welfare advice; employment, housing, education, benefits.　　　»93

● **Aid for Destitute Victims of Oppression**
330 Copley House, London W7 1QF; *t* (0171) 575 6591
Human rights, aid to refugees; women's interests.　　　»94

✿ **All Saints Haque Centre**
Kulwant Bahia: 13 Vicarage Road, All Saints, Wolverhampton WV2 1DZ; *t* (01902) 50764
Advice, mainly to Caribbean and Asian clients, on immigration issues including primary purpose rule, divided families; community development.　　　»94

● **Amnesty Campaign for Refugees and Unregistered Migrants**
c/o CCRJ, Inter-Church House, 35 Lower Marsh, London SE1; *t* (0171) 924 9033　　　»95

● **Association of Visitors to Immigration Detainees, AVID**
Audrey Atter: 53 Western Road, Winchester SO22 5AH; *t* (01962) 863317
Local groups near several detention centres.　　　»95

✿ **Asylum Aid**
Alasdair Mackenzie, Co-ordinator: 244a Upper Street, Islington, London N1 1RU; *t* (0171) 359 4026, *f* 354 9187
Originated as specialist section of Rights and Justice, p227; now independent agency, providing free advice, representation and support to refugees; campaigns for fair treatment of asylum seekers. Small staff and volunteer support.　　»95

● **Asylum Rights Campaign**
Kate Allen: 46 Francis Street, London SW1P 1QN; *t* (0171) 798 9008, *f* 798 9010
Also listed (1996) c/o 3 Bondway, SW8 1SJ.　　　»96
Avon Immigration and Nationality Advice Centre: defunct (1995)

✿ **Ayesha Family Resource Centre** also known as The Ayesha Project
Yasmin Hussein: c/o 308 Brownhill Road, Catford, Lewisham, London SE8 1AU; *t* (0181) 695 6000 ext. 3010
Services for minority ethnic women facing violence.　　»94

✿ **Basle Court Refugee Hostel**
2b Fairmount Road, Brixton Hill, London SW2 1AD; *t* (0181) 671 4481-83　　　»94

✿ **The Bibini Centre for Young People**
PO Box 23, Manchester M14 4BF
Holistic residential care and support service for Black children and young people in Manchester; founded 1993.　　»96

✿ **Black and Minority Ethnic Victim Support Project**
Development Worker: Victim Support Scotland, 14 Frederick Street, Edinburgh, Scotland; *t* (0131) 225 7779
A service of Lothian Victim Support Scheme for victims of racial harassment and racially motivated crime.　　»94

✿ **Brent and Harrow Refugee Consortium**
Marianne Matthews: Northwest London TEC, 118-120 Station Road, Harrow HA1 2RL
Training and employment assistance to refugees.　　»93

● **British Afro-Asian Solidarity Organisation, BAASO**
Mohammed Arif: [address unknown] London
Associated with The Marxist Party, a Trotskyist group.　　»92

✿ **Brixton Circle Projects**
33 Effra Road, Brixton, London SW2 1BZ
Specialist resiential and day care services for African and Caribbean people living with mental health difficulties.　　»96

✿ **Brixton Refugee Health Project**
Julia Deane, Development Officer: Lambeth, Southwark & Lewisham Health Commission, 1 Lower Marsh, Waterloo, London SE1 7NT
Seeks to increase access to, and appropriateness and awareness of, primary and community health services to refugees. Outreach, training, rights advice.　　»95

✿ **Cambridge Ethnic Community Forum**
M. Mbayah: Llandaff Chambers, 2 Regent Street, Cambridge CB2 1AX; *t* (01223) 315877, 464696　　　»94

✿ **Camden Health and Race Group**
c/o Voluntary Action Camden, Instrument House, 207-215 King's Cross Road, London WC1X 9DB; *t* (0171) 837 5544
A voluntary sector forum on health and community care issues affecting black and ethnic minority people.　　»95

✿ **Camden Refugee Workers' Network**
Development Worker: Instrument House, 207-215 King's Cross Road, London WC1X 9DB; *t* (0171) 837 5544
Forum representing needs of refugee communities to statutory agencies, promoting community involvement in identifying and addressing health care, social welfare, education needs.　»94

● **Campaign Against Immigration Act Detentions, CAIAD**
[address unknown] London; *t* (0171) 254 9701
Opposes the detention of thousands of persons pending the outcome of immigration and asylum procedures.　　»95

✿ **Campaign to Close Campsfield,** also known as Close Campsfield Campaign
c/o 111 Magdalen Road, Oxford OX4 1RQ; *t* (01865) 724452, 726804, 722357
Organises pickets and leafletting in a campaign to close down Campsfield House, where asylum applicants are imprisoned pending adjudication of their cases. Also opposes detentions at Harmondsworth, Haslar, Rochester, Brixton and elsewhere, and supports European campaigns on racist treatment of refugees and migrants. *Campsfield Monitor* (4/yr).　　»96

● **Campaign for Unauthorised Migrant Workers**
c/o Camden REC, 58 Hampstead Road, London NW1　　»91

✣ **Care and Rehabilitation Centre**
99 Strathville Road, London SW18 4QR; *t* (0181) 877 9322
A project of the black-led Aladura International Church. »90

● **Catholic Church, Emigrants Pastoral**
Rt Rev. Kevin O'Connor: 12 Richmond Close, Eccleston,
St Helens WA10 5JE; *t* (01744) 23535 »90

● **Child Migrants Trust**
Margaret Humphreys: [address unknown]
Support group for adults who were deported as children to
Australia and other countries by British charities, in many
cases resulting in abuse and psychological problems. »95

● **Churches' Commission for Migrants in Europe, CCME—UK**
section
Rev. Jemima Prasadam, UK contact: All Saints Vicarage,
Shaftesbury Road, Luton LU4 8AH »90

✣ **Claiming the Inheritance**
Samuel Dolphin: 32 Dyas Avenue, Great Barr, Birmingham
B42 1HE; *t* (0121) 358 3416 »90

● **Committee for Migrants and Refugees**: Catholic Bishops'
Conference of England and Wales
John Joseet, Policy Co-ordinator: [address uncertain] 39
Eccleston Square, London SW1V 1PD; *t* (0171) 630 8279,
834 0522, *f* 630 5166
Also listed (1994) at Allington House, 1st Floor, 136-142
Victoria Street, London SWIE 5DL. Advises Catholic bishops
on policy and pastoral issues around refugees and migrants;
liaises with Church groups and agencies working for refugees
in England and Wales, and in the EU, and with other refugee
agencies, voluntary bodies and UK and EU institutions. »94

✣ **Commonwealth Welfare and Immigration Advisory Centre,**
CWIAC
A. Asabere, Chairman: 479 High Road, Leytonstone, London
E11 4JU; *t* (0181) 558 9597 »94

● **Confederation of Refugee Groups and Ethnic Minorities**
190 Walm Lane, London NW2; *t/f* (0181) 450 3812
Members include Baluch Refugee Association, p93. »94

● **Council of Europe Minority Youth Committee, CEMYC UK**
Mohammed Dhalech: PO Box 70, Gloucester GL1 4AH;
t/f (01452) 504147
Network of minority youth groups; see in Germany, p200. See
also National Association of Muslim Youth, p69. »94

✣ **Cricklefield Refugee Project**
[address unknown] London
Refugee support activities, including adult education and
training at Hackney Community College. »95

✣ **Cultural Unity Working Group, CUWG**
The Co-ordinator: c/o 69 Bellenden Road, Peckham, London
SE15 5BH
Network of minority ethnic voluntary sector bodies in
Southwark; interests in health and social service issues. »95

✣ **Detention Advice Service**
Ragnhild Witherow: 244a Upper Street, Islington, London N1
1RU; *t* (0171) 704 8007, *f* 354 9187
Advice to people held in prison or detention centres with
immigration problems. See also Asylum Aid, p153. »95

✣ **Dutch Pot Project**
Alida Ebanks: [address unknown] Westminster, London SW1;
t (0181) 960 8504
Voluntary organisation providing luncheon club, visiting and
other services to black elderly people, Afro-Caribbean and
Continental African, in Westminster. »95

✣ **Ealing Borough Council Housing Department**: Refugee
Services Officer
Perceval House, 14-16 Uxbridge Road, London W5 2HL
Housing Department employs a specialist officer to liaise
with refugee organisations and the local Homeless Persons
Unit, to assist in settlement of refugees. »95

✣ **East London Sanctuary Association**
c/o Halkevi, 92-100 Stoke Newington Road, London N16 7XB
Campaign for rights of refugees and asylum seekers.
Possibly defunct. »91

✣ **East Sussex County Council Bilingual Support Service**
Sally Handford, Team Co-ordinator: Marshlands CP School,
Marshfoot Lane, Hailsham BN27 2PH; *t* (01323) 842045
One of many specialist educational services providing for the
extra needs of ethnic minority children. This Service operates
through peripatetic area teams to support pupils for whom
English is a second or other language. »95

✣ **East West Community Project**
Depak Patel: 37 Bruce Street, Leicester LE3 0AF; *t* (0116)
254 2633 »94

✣ **EDGE**
Melvin Pemberton: 7 Farrer Road, Longsight, Manchester
M13 0QX; *t* (0161) 224 7502
Group for black people with disabilities. »93

✣ **Edinburgh Ethnic Enterprise Centre**
M. Dhall: 20 Montagu Terrace, Edinburgh EH3 5QR
Counselling new business start-ups and development,
creation of job opportunities for ethnic minorities. »95

✣ **Edinburgh Ethnic Minorities Employment Access**, EEMEA
Shenaz Bahadur/Veronica Noone: c/o Lothian REC, 12a
Forth Street, Edinburgh EH1 3LH; *t* (0131) 529 4301
Job training programmes for ethnic minorities. »95

✣ **Ekaya Housing Association**
[address unknown] London; *t* (0171) 274 4000
Provision of social housing. »94

✣ **Ektha Housing Association**
338 Commercial Rd, Portsmouth PO4 1BT; *t* (01705) 824499
Social housing for Black and ethnic minority communities.»96

● **Employment Conditions Abroad Ltd**
Adam Philpott: Anchor House, 15-19 Britten Street, London
SW3 3TY
Legal advice to emigrant workers. »86

✣ **Enfield Refugee Consortium, ERC**
c/o Enfield Voluntary Service Council, 341a Baker Street,
Enfield EN1 3LF
A recently formed agency co-ordinating and supporting the
activities of local groups providing services to refugees. »94

✣ **Essex County Council Social Services Department**
Refugee Services
Manager (Refugees): County Hall, Chelmsford CM1 1YS;
t (01245) 434131
Co-ordinates and monitors public and NGO services to
refugees, including those arriving at Stansted Airport. »95

✣ **Ethnic Alcohol Counselling in Hounslow, EACH**
Lakhvir Randhawa: Holdsworth House, 65-73 Staines Road,
Hounslow TW3 3HW; *t* (0181) 577 6059
Counselling for people from Asian communities who have
alcohol problems; day centres in Houslow and Harrow. »96

✣ **Ethnic Minorities Advice Centre**
S.M. Haque: 9 Cowley Road, Oxford OX4 1JB; *t* (01865)
240576 »94

✣ **Ethnic Minorities Advice Service**
Faten Hameed: Mackenzie House, 400 Argyle Street,
Glasgow G2 7BQ, Scotland »94

✣ **Ethnic Minorities Law Centre Ltd**
41 St Vincent Place, Glasgow G1 2ER, Scotland »94

✣ **Ethnic Minorities Representative Council, EMRC**
Cllr Tehmtan Framroze, Chair: Muslim Community Centre, 150
Dyke Road, Brighton BN1 5PA; *t* (01273) 686981, 779227
Imam Abduljalil Sajid/Arlene Hui joint secretaries. Also EMRC
Women's Section, Asmat Roe co-ordinator (79 Dale Crescent,
Patcham, Brighton BN1 8NT, *t* 554501). Represents 70
ethnic minority voluntary sector groups in Sussex. Advice
service through Brighton Citizens Advice Bureau, p220. »94

✣ **Ethnic Minority Training and Employment Project**
Kensington & Chelsea College, Hortensia Road, London
SW10 0QP; *t* (0171) 351 2357
Provides English language and vocational skills training for
refugees and migrants, primarily from the Horn of Africa. »94

✣ **Ethnic Network**
170a Heston Rd, Hounslow TW5 0QW; *t* (0181) 577 6059
Counselling service. »90

✣ **Ethnic Switchboard**
Co-ordinating Centre for Community and Health Care, 28
Lessingham Avenue, London SW17 8LU; *t* (0181) 682 0216,
682 0217
Medical interpreting and translation. »90

▌ **European Legal Network on Asylum, ELENA**
Eva Kjærgård, Co-ordinator: ECRE Secretariat, Bondway
House, 3 Bondway, London SW8 1SJ; *t* (0171) 820 1156,
582 9928, *f* 820 9725
Network of asylum and immigration law experts and services
in 18 countries (the EU, Iceland, Norway, Switzerland and
Slovenia); co-ordinated by the Legal Officer of ECRE, p244.
Promotes contact between lawyers working on asylum cases,
at national and European levels; seminars, handbooks; see
national contacts, below and pp129, 131-3, 137, 140-1,
143, 145, 147-8, 150, 152, 155, 200, 211-2, 238. »94

♦ **European Legal Network on Asylum, ELENA**
David Burgess/Chris Randall, Co-ordinators: Winstanley
Burgess Solicitors, 378 City Road, London EC1V 2QA;
t (0171) 278 7911, *f* 833 2135
UK contacts for the network of refugee law practitioners. »95

▌ **Fair Trials International**
Stephen Jakobi: Bench House, Ham St, Richmond TW10 7HR
Campaigns for harmonisation of the rules of justice in the EU,
provision of interpreting, and anti-discriminatory practices, to
ensure that non-nationals should not be disadvantaged in
dealings with police, the courts or the prison systems. »96

✧ **Faith Asylum Refuge**
[address unknown] »96
♦ **Family Immigration Rights, FAIR**
Lourdes Domingo, Secretary: c/o JCWI, 115 Old Street, London EC1V 9JR; *t* (0171) 251 8708, *f* 251 8707
Campaigns for right to family reunification of persons settling in the EU; UK contact for the European Co-ordination for the Right to Family Life for Immigrants, p136. »96
✧ **Farnworth Cultural Centre**
Iftkhar Khan: 118 Market Street, Farnworth, Bolton BL4, Lancashire; *t* (01204) 793793 »94
✧ **Greater Manchester Immigration Aid Unit, GMIAU**
Steve Cohen/Tony Openshaw: 400 Cheetham Hill Road, Manchester M8; *t* (0161) 740 7722, *f* 740 5172
Free legal advice, information, casework, advocacy and training on immigration and nationality issues; national and international campaigns. *No-one is Illegal* (4/yr). »95
✧ **Greenwich Refugee Association**
Paul Lam-Kilama: Suite D, Building B, Macbean Centre, Macbean Street, Woolwich, London SE18 6LW
Welfare of Somali, Ugandan, Eritrean and other refugees; information and counselling, including alcohol project. »96
✧ **Hackney English Language Scheme**
Rashida Laher/Margo Clark: Hackney Community College, Woodberry Down Branch, Woodberry Grove, London N4 2RH; *t* (0171) 809 7737
Classes for Asian, Middle Eastern and African adults. »94
✧ **Haringey Refugee Consortium**
Selby Centre, Selby Road, White Hart Lane, London N17 8JN
Services to refugees, including English langage teaching. »94
✧ **Hitslink Advice Agency**
39 Abingdon Road, Highfields, Leicester LE2 1HA; *t* (0116) 255 5737
Young people's advice agency in inner city; mainly serves Black communities; general welfare, housing, debt, rights advice, counselling, some immigration/nationality work. »95
● **Hosting for Overseas Students, HOST**
Jo Caesar, Joint Chief Executive: 3 New Burlington Mews, London W1R 8LU; *t* (0171) 494 2468
Vacations/weekends with families for foreign students. »95
● **Immigrants Aid Trust, IAT**
115 Old Street, London EC1V 9JR; *t* (0171) 251 8708, *f* 251 8707
Charitable trust supporting the advice work of JCWI, right.»96
● **Immigrants Welfare Association**
34 Bisson Road, Stratford, London E15 2RD
Legal rights advice, solidarity. »91
♦ **Immigration Advisory Service, IAS**
Geraldine Clerck/David Barrass: 2nd Floor, County House, 190 Great Dover Street, London SE1 4YB; *t* (0171) 357 6917, 357 7511, *f* 378 0665
Charity providing free legal advice, information and representation on immigration problems. Emergency out-of-hours service, *t* (0181) 814 1559. »95
✧ ≡ Government Buildings, Clay Lane, Yardley, Birmingham B26 1DX; *t* (0121) 706 9765, *f* 765 4640 »95
✧ ≡ South Wales Office: 211a City Road, Roath, Cardiff CF2 3JD, Wales; *t* (01222) 496662, *f* 496602 »95
✧ ≡ Room 3049, Gatwick Village, Gatwick Airport, Horley RH6 0NN; *t* (01293) 533385, *f* 568831 »95
✧ ≡ 69-71 Grove Road, Hounslow TW3 3PS; *t* (0181) 814 1115, *f* 814 1116
Also Ports and Detention Unit, *t* 814 1559, *f* 814 1578. »95
✧ ≡ Matthew Murray House, 97 Water Lane, Leeds LS11 5QN; *t* (0113) 244 2460, *f* 243 1006 »95
✧ ≡ Suite 7b, 7th Floor, Blackfriars House, Parsonage Street, Manchester M3 5JA; *t* (0161) 834 9942, *f* 832 9322 »95
♦ **Immigration Advisory Service (Scotland), IAS**
[address uncertain] 115 Wellington Street, Glasgow G2 2XT, Scotland; *t* (0141) 248 2456
Also listed (1995) at 115 Bath Street, G2 4LE, *t* 248 2956, *f* 221 5388. »95
♦ **Immigration Law Practitioners Association, ILPA**
Susan Rowlands/Ian Macdonald QC: The Basement, 38 Great Pulteney Street, London W1R 3DE; *t* (0171) 434 3690, *f* 434 3691, *e* ilpa@mcr1.poptel.org.uk
Solicitors, barristers and other experts in immigration, nationality and refugee law; most belong to private legal practices or law centres. Publishes directory of members.»95
✧ **Independent Immigration Support Agency, IISA**
John McCarthy: 14 Bell Barn Shopping Centre, Cregoe St, Lee Bank, Birmingham B15 2DZ; *t* (0121) 622 7353, *f* 622 1954
Advice, casework and representation for individuals with immigration and nationality problems; casework; partly funded by Legal Aid Board. »95

✧ **International Student House**
Carol Sutcliffe: 229 Great Portland Street, London W1N 5HD; *t* (0171) 631 8300
Charity established 1963 providing accommodation and leisure facilities for around 550 foreign students. »95
✧ **Islington Health and Race Group**
c/o Healthy Islington 2000, 159-167 Upper Street, London N1 1RE; *t* (0171) 477 3029
A voluntary sector forum on health and community care issues affecting black and ethnic minority people. »95
✧ **Islington Refugee Working Party**
c/o IVAC, 322 Upper St, London N1 2XQ; *t* (0171) 226 4862
Assessment of needs of refugees in Islington; co-ordination and improvement of service delivery. »92
✧ **Jeman Association**
J. Emanuwa: 13 Camberwell Church St, London SE5 8TR »90
✧ **Jesuit Refugee Service**
162 Stockwell Rd, London SW9 9TQ; *t* (0171) 924 9423 »95
♦ **Joint Council for the Welfare of Immigrants, JCWI**
Claude Moraes, Director: 115 Old Street, London EC1V 9JR; *t* (0171) 251 8706 advice, 251 8708 administration, *f* 251 8707, *e* jcwi@mcr1.poptel.org.uk
Ayodele Gansallo policy co-ordinator, Robert Phillips finance director, Don Flynn European projects, some 10 other staff; legal advice and services to migrants and refugees; campaigns for non-racist, non-sexist immigration policies. A member of the European Co-ordination for the Right to Family Life of Immigrants, p155; associated with ILPA, left, CCME, p130, ELENA, p154, and other UK and European campaign groups including Action Group on Immigration and Nationality and Caribbean Entry Refusal Action Group (both dormant). Deals with over 8,000 enquiries per year; publishes an advisers' handbook, commissions this Directory, is developing on-line information service and produces booklets and leaflets. See also FAIR and IAT, left. *JCWI Bulletin* (4/yr). »96
✧ **Kaamyabi**
17 North Grange Court, Leeds LS6 2BZ
Campaigns on European migration policies and other issues affecting the black community. »90
Kalayaan—Justice for Overseas Domestic Workers: see the Filipino listing, p36
✧ **KINNAT**
26 Rectory Road, Crumpsall, Manchester M8 6AE
Group for ethnic minority people with disabilities. »93
● **Labour Asylum Rights Campaign (Scotland)**
[address unknown] London »96
▌ **Labour International**
Chris Jones, Co-ordinator: John Smith House, Walworth Road, London SE1
Network of emigrant supporters of British Labour Party; established 1992; branches mainly in Europe. »94
✧ **Language Line**
18 Victoria Park Square, London E2 9PF; *t* (0181) 980 6263, 981 9911, 983 4042
Telephone interpreting for medical and other social needs.»95
✧ **Leeds Council for Overseas Student Affairs**
The Rendezvous, Brunswick Terrace Building, Merrion Way, Leeds, Yorkshire; *t* (0113) 246 0999 »90
✧ **The Local Economic Consortium**
The Consortium Managers: Islington Enterprise Centre, 64 Essex Road, London N7 8LR
A group of local ethnic minority employment and training bodies delivering European Social Fund programmes. »94
✧ **Lokamaya Press**
Bahauddeen Latif: 8 Batoum Gardens, London W6 7QD »90
✧ **London Conference on Overseas Students, LCOS**
International Students House, Regent's Park, London NW1; *t* (0171) 631 8300
Advice and support for international students at institutions of further and higher education in London. »95
✧ **London Interpreting Project, LIP**
Administrator: 20 Compton Terrace, London N1 2UN; *t* (0171) 359 6798, *f* 226 0482
Voluntary organisation; training, research, information and resource development in community interpreting and bilingual advocacy services, in the public and voluntary sectors. »95
✧ **L'Ouverture Theatre Trust**
Unit 604, Brixton Enterprise Centre, 442-444 Brixton Road, London SW9 8EJ »90
✧ **Manchester Action Committee on Health Care for Ethnic Minorities, MACHEM**
Linda FitzPatrick: Unit 28, Greenheys Business Centre, 10 Pencroft Way, Manchester M15 6JJ; *t* (0161) 232 0488
Promotes equality in employment and service provision for black and ethnic minority people in the health service. »94

✿ **Merseyside Immigration Advice Unit, MIAU**
Manneh Brown: 34 Princes Road, Liverpool L8 1TH;
t (0151) 709 8360, *f* 709 4996
Immigration rights advice; research on economic needs of
newly arriving migrants and refugees; employment, training
and educational placement services. »95

✿ **Methodist International House**
The Warden: 4 Inverness Terrace, Bayswater, London W2;
t (0171) 229 5101
Hostel for 140 students and other visitors from overseas. »95

✿ **Midlands Refugee Council**
K. Adam, Co-ordinator: Unit 204, The Argent Centre, 60
Frederick Street, Hockley, Birmingham B1 3HS; *t* (0121) 212
1435, 212 0399, *f* 212 2477
Santino M. Deng. Founded 1989; advice, refugee welfare,
health promotion. »95

✿ **Migrant Advisory Service**
14 Featherstone Rd, Southall UB2 2AA; *t* (0181) 574 4433
Immigration and rights advice. See also IWA(GB), p44. »95

✿ **Migrant Helpline**
Room 210, No. 1 Control Building, Eastern Docks, Dover,
Kent; *t* (01304) 203977 »95

✿ **Migrant and Refugee Communities Forum**
Belinda Calaguas: 1 Thorpe Close, London W10 5XL;
t (0181) 964 4815, *f* 969 5936
Development of resource centre and shared services for 27
migrant and refugee groups, including advice, translation and
interpreting, social and cultural facilities. Health promotion,
including HIV/AIDS work with Ugandan women. »95

● **Migrant Rights Action Network**
St Francis of Assisi Centre, Pottery Lane, London W11 4NQ
Umbrella group for campaigns on immigration and refugee
rights. »91

Migrant Support Unit: defunct (1995)

● **Migrant Training Company, MTC**
Vian Gunaid/Errol Smalley: 6-20 St John's Mews, London
WC1N 2NS; *t* (0171) 916 1638-41
Registered charity providing computer-based and other
employment training for migrants and refugees. »95

● **Migrants Resource Centre**
George Michaelides: 24 Churton Street, London SW1V 2LP;
t (0171) 233 9868, 834 6650, 834 2505, *f* 931 8187
Employment and other rights of migrants and refugees;
research and documentation; computer training, child care,
community services. »95

✿ **Minority Group Support Service**
Penny Hinchcliffe: South Street, Southfields, Hillfields,
Coventry CV1 5EJ »90

▌ **The Missions to Seamen**
St Michael Paternoster Royal, College Hill, London EC4R 2RL;
t (0171) 248 5202
International charity of Anglican Church, concerned with the
welfare of seafarers of all races and creeds in ports around
the world. Publishes two newspapers and a range of
information leaflets. »94

✿ **Moss Side People's Centre**
E. Edwards: St Mary's Street, Moss Side, Manchester M15
5NA; *t* (0161) 226 7015
Community development, welfare/housing advice, tribunal
representation, economic development; resource centre for
black and ethnic minority people. »93

✿ **Multi-Lingual Community Rights Shop**
12a Asylum Road, Peckham, London SE15 2RL
Advice, information for Black and minority ethnic people. »96

● **NAFSIYAT Intercultural Therapy Centre**
278 Seven Sisters Rd, London N4 2HY; *t* (0171) 264 4130
Provision of therapy and training of therapists. »90

● **National Coalition of Anti-Deportation Campaigns**
22 Berners Street, Lozells, Birmingham B19 2DR
Links local campaigns against the detention and deportation
of immigrants and refugees; associated with the National
Network against Detentions and Deportations, p177. »96

● **National Federation of Self-Help Organisations, NFSHO**
Rene Webb, General Secretary: 361 Clapham Road, London
SW9 9BT; *t* (0171) 274 9566
Venis Buckle chairperson, Dr Vince Hines director; founded
1975 as umbrella group; claims to have 1,000 affiliates;
information, training, advocacy, conferences. Sponsored
formation of Standing Conference of African and Asian
Organisations, also known as African-Asian Conference UK,
mainly to consider implications of European Union for black
people in the UK. *Self-Help News* (12/yr). »91
✿ ≡ Information Office, and Standing Conference of African
and Asian Organisations: 150 Townmead Road, Fulham,
London SW6 2RA; *t* (0171) 731 8440 »91

◆ **National Union of Refugee Organisations, NURO**
Mike Rahman, Chair: [address unknown] London
Representation and defence of refugee and asylum-seeker
rights; anti-racism. »95

✿ **Naz Project**
Kim Mujli: [address unknown] Middlesex; *t* (0181) 563 0205,
741 1879
Provides HIV education, prevention and support services for
local South Asian, Turkish, Arab and Irani communities. »96

✿ **Newham Churches Immigration Support Group**
NCRP, 170 Harold Road, Plaistow, London E13 0SE;
t (0181) 472 2785
Sanctuary, humanitarian aid for Caribbean and other persons
threatened with deportation. »91

✿ **Newham Refugees Centre**
728 Romford Road, London E12 6BT; *t* (0181) 514 5657 »95

● **North of England Refugee Service, NERS** (formerly North East
Refugee Service), and North-East Coalition for Asylum Rights
Tim Kell/Areti Sianni: 19 Bigg Market, Newcastle-upon-Tyne
NE1 1UN; *t* (0191) 222 0390, 222 0406, *f* 222 0239
Information, advice and community development work;
housing, employment, education and training help. The
Coalition (Vijay Singh Riyait) campaigns around asylum law.»96

✿ **Northern Refugee Centre**
Jew Lane, off Fitzalan Square, Sheffield S1 2BE; *t* (0114)
270 1429, *f* 276 6807
Support for refugees and asylum seekers in the Sheffield
area; educational, employment and training initiatives. »95

✿ **Nottingham Area Council for Overseas Student Affairs,**
NACOSA
61b Mansfield Road, Nottingham NG8 2QY; *t* (0115) 947
4793
Welfare of foreign students; see also UKCOSA, p158. »94

✿ **Nucleus Legal Advice Centre**
Anne McLoughlin/Neil Froom: 298 Old Brompton Road,
London SW5 9JF; *t* (0181) 373 1379
Free legal advice and representation centre; immigration and
refugee work, mainly serving African, Middle Eastern, EU
nationals in the Earls Court area. »95

● **The Ockenden Venture**
Constitution Hill, Guildford Road, Woking GU22 7UU;
t (01483) 772012, *f* 750774, *Tx* 859213
Founded 1955; settlement, advice, educational, medical and
welfare services and return assistance to refugees, displaced
and stateless persons and asylum seekers in the UK (mainly
Vietnamese and Eritreans) and in Africa and Asia. »96
✿ ≡ 28 Hampstead Road, Hockley, Birmingham B19 1DB;
t (0121) 554 9023 »95
✿ ≡ Woodleigh, Vicarage Road, Thornhill Lees, Dewsbury
WF13, West Yorkshire; *t* (01924) 461101 »90

✿ **Osprey International Students Advice Centre**
49 Bruntsfield Crescent, Edinburgh EH10 4EZ, Scotland »95

● **Overseas Doctors Association UK Ltd**
Dr S. Venugopal/Dr S. Kumar: 28-32 Princess Street,
Manchester M1 4LB; *t* (0161) 236 5594
Founded 1975; interests of UK-based medical and dental
professionals born and/or trained outside the UK; equal
opportunities in employment and training, minority health
issues. Co-ordinates the Institute of Transcultural Health
Care, p245. Based Manchester, with regional divisions
elsewhere in the UK. »94

● **Overseas Students Trust**
117 Vauxhall Bridge Road, London SW1V 1ER »90

● **Overseas Teachers Social Circle**
74 Green Lane, Birmingham B22 »90

✿ **Oxfordshire Immigration and Nationality Project**
Oxford CAB, Princes Street Advice Centre, 44b Princes St,
Oxford OX4 1DD
Project funded by the County Council providing specialist
consultancy, training and casework to eight CABx and to
other voluntary and statutory agencies in Oxfordshire. »95

✿ **Pal Platform**
111b Moray Road, London N4 3LB »90

✿ **PATH (London) Ltd** (Positive Action Training in Housing)
[address unknown] London
Combats racial discrimination in employment in housing
associations and local authorities; provides positive action
training for black and ethnic minority housing workers. »94

✿ **The People's Trust**
Wayne X/Marceeah Massop: Kingsland High Street, Hackney,
London E8
Black studies group which in 1994 worked in association
with the Nation of Islam, a US-based radical Black Muslim
group, to organise an event in London involving a satellite
link-up with that group's leader Louis Farrakhan. »94

☼ **Pitt Street Settlement**
191 East Surrey Grove, Peckham, London SE15 5PP;
t (0171) 703 4775, 701 0835
General advice centre with Afro-Caribbean, Asian, African
and Turkish clients.   »91
● **Platform Fortress Europe**
R.J. Jenkins: 125 Stonhouse Street, London SW4 6BH   »93
☼ **Praxis**
Pott Street, London E2 0EF; *t* (0171) 729 7985, *f* 729 0134
Welfare rights advice, cultural and other activities within
Somali and Latin American refugee communities.   »95
● **Prisoners Abroad**, formally National Council for the Welfare
of Prisoners Abroad
Janet Johnstone, Director: 82 Rosebery Avenue, London
EC1R 4RR; *t* (0171) 833 3467
Legal help, information, support and advice to ensure welfare
of UK residents imprisoned in other countries, and their
families; small team manages 1,100 cases in over 50
countries, from a total of 2,000-odd UK prisoners abroad.»96
● **Project Fullemploy**, formerly The Urban Trust
Daniel Levy: 91 Brick Lane, London E1 6QL
Supports black and ethnic minority voluntary-sector groups
involved in economic and community development.   »95
☼ **Redbridge Refugee Forum**
c/o Redbridge REC, Methodist Church Hall, Ilford Lane, Ilford
IG1 2JZ; *t* (0181) 478 4513, 514 0688, *f* 514 0870
Project of Redbridge Council for Voluntary Service; survey of
refugees in the area; development of a local Refugee Centre
co-ordinating public and voluntary sector support services.»96
● **Redress Trust**, also known as Redress
Keith Carmichael, Director: 6 Queen Square, London WC1N
3BG; *t* (0171) 278 9502
William Dishington. Legal charity which seeks compensation
for victims of torture.   »95
♦ **Refugee Action**: Head Office
Sheila Fox: The Cedars, Mansfield Road, Oakwood, Derby
DE21 4FY; *t* (01332) 833310, 834828, 831273, *f* 834946
Social work, community development with refugees and
asylum seekers; has worked with Vietnamese refugees in
England, see p125, Scotland and N. Ireland; has also worked
with Ugandan Asians, Tamils and Bosnians in England, and
with refugees in Nicaragua. Founded 1981, 55 staff.   »95
● ≡ Family Reunion Office, Resource Centre: 4 Cowper St,
Leeds LS7 4DS; *t* (0113) 262 2024, 262 4892   »90
☼ ≡ Reception Centre: 28 Track Road, Batley WF17,
Yorkshire; *t* (01924) 465340   »90
☼ ≡ The Coach House, 2 Upper York Street, St Pauls,
Bristol BS2 8QN; *t* (0117) 942 4613, *f* 983 4946   »94
☼ ≡ Jack Shieh/Hue Lam: 240a Clapham Road, Stockwell,
London SW9 0PZ; *t* (0171) 735 5361, *f* 587 3676   »95
♦ **Refugee Arrivals Project**, RAP
Deborah Worsley/Marie Babyanss: Room 2005, 2nd Floor,
Queen's Building, Heathrow Airport, Hounslow TW6 1DL;
t (0181) 759 5740, *f* 759 7058, 759 0482
Independent voluntary organisation providing relief for refugees
at port of entry, and ensuring effective support in their early
days in the UK; advice and assistance with housing and
welfare benefits. Founded 1988; helps several thousand
people per year. Employs about 25 interpreter-escorts; part-
funded by London boroughs, managed by refugee community
groups and refugee agencies.   »96
♦ *Refugee Community News*
4 South Lambeth Place, London SW8 1SJ; *t* (0171) 582 6922
A publication of the Refugee Council, below.   »94
♦ **The Refugee Council**, formerly British Refugee Council, BRC
Nick Hardwick, Chief Executive: Bondway House, 3-9
Bondway, London SW8 1SJ; *t* (0171) 582 6922, *f* 582 9929
The UK's main refugee charity; umbrella body of over 100
advice and assistance agencies, formed 1982. Advice and
Referral Team helps with reception, settlement, housing,
welfare benefits, training and social services, and counselling;
other sections and regional teams work on community
development, housing, research, information; working groups
on health and other issues. Provides secretariat for European
Council on Refugees and Exiles, p244, and European Legal
Network on Asylum, p154; manages the Refugee Training &
Employment Centre, right. Specialist facilities include Bosnia
Project, p23, providing housing and casework for quota
refugees in Dewsbury, Yorkshire; and Korczak House in Honor
Oak, London SE, a home for young unaccompanied (mainly
East African) refugees. See Welsh Refugee Council, p158,
Scottish Refugee Council, right. *Refugee Community News*
(12/yr), *Exile* (10/yr), handbooks, research reports.   »95
● ≡ Information Unit: 240-250 Ferndale Road, London SW9
8BB; *t* (0171) 737 1155   »91

Refugee Education and Training Advice Service, RETAS: see
World University Service (UK), p229
● **Refugee Housing**
47-49 Durham Street, London SE11 5JA; *t* (0171) 582 0038,
f 582 6065
A national housing association providing accommodation and
support services for over 1,400 refugees and asylum seekers.
Reception centres, houses and offices in Hackney, Camden,
Earls Court, Chislehurst and elsewhere; South London Region
alone (based in Kennington) employs 25 staff and manages
over 200 units. Opening a housing scheme in Sheffield for
Somali and other refugees in 1995.   »95
♦ **Refugee Legal Centre**, RLC
Barry Stoyle, Director: Sussex House, 39-45 Bermondsey
Street, London SE1 3XF; *t* (0171) 827 9090, 357 7421,
f 378 1979
Charity, with over 100 staff, providing free legal advice,
representation and long-term casework to 30,000 refugees
and asylum seekers each year, including about 6,000 appeal
cases. Advice line (*t* 378 6242), detention line (378 6243),
emergency out-of-hours service (*t* (01831) 598057). Assists
at all stages of the asylum application, determination and
appeal procedure. Funded by UNHCR, p228, and the Home
Office, p223. Established (as The New Refugee Unit) in 1992
restructuring of the UK Immigrants Advisory Service.   »96
● **Refugee Support Centre**, RSC
The Director: 47 South Lambeth Road, London SW8 1RH;
t (0171) 820 3606
Also at King George's House, Stockwell Rd, SW9. National
charity providing counselling and psychotherapy services to
refugees and asylum seekers. Several languages offered;
specialist work includes Elderly Project.   »95
☼ **Refugee Training and Employment Centre**, RTEC
240 Ferndale Road, Brixton, London SW9 8BB; *t* (0171) 737
1155
A division of The Refugee Council, left; provides employment-
related training, advice, counselling and career guidance. »95
● **Refugee Women's Association**, RWA
Print House, 18 Ashwin Street, London; *t* (0171) 923 2412
A voluntary organisation seeking to empower refugee women
to gain access to employment, education and training. »96
▍**Refugees International**
Lionel Rosenblatt, President: [address unknown]   »90
☼ **St Pauls Advice Centre**
146 Grosvenor Road, St Pauls, Bristol BS2 8YA; *t* (0117)
955 2981
Run by St Pauls Advice Service Association; Caribbean,
Pakistani, Bangladeshi immigration work.   »91
♦ **Scottish Refugee Council**, SRC: Head Office
Ted Matthews, Acting Chief Executive: 43 Broughton Street,
Edinburgh EH1 3JU, Scotland; *t* (0131) 577 8083-84,
f 556 7617
Scottish counterpart of The Refugee Council, left; specialist
advice on asylum; addresses social welfare and resettlement
needs of refugees, including several hundred Bosnian evacuees
in the community and at a North Berwick reception centre;
liaises with statutory and voluntary services.   »96
● ≡ 73 Robertson Street, Glasgow G2 8QD, Scotland;
t (0141) 221 8793, *f* 248 1835
Advice and support to refugees in the west of Scotland. »95
☼ **Shakti Women's Aid**
Mukami McCrum: 31 Albany Street, Edinburgh EH1 3QN,
Scotland; *t* (0131) 557 4010
Aid, support, refuge for Black women at risk of violence.
Employment, training, health advice.   »95
☼ ≡ 209 High Street, Linlithgow EH9 7EN, Scotland   »91
☼ **Shalom Immigration and Legal Advisory Service**
Philip O Fawale: 22 Leybourne House, Lovelinch Close,
London SE15 1HL; *t* (0171) 277 6117   »94
● **Sia—National Development Agency for the Black and**
Minority Ethnic Voluntary Sector
49-51 Bedford Row, Holborn, London WC1V 6DJ; *t* (0171)
430 0811, *f* 831 9767
Supports Black voluntary groups through training events,
seminars, networking, information, policy research.   »94
☼ **Social Action Forum**
RSGB, Manor House, 80 East End Road, London N3 5RP;
t (0181) 349 4731, *f* 343 0901
Religious (Jewish?) group promoting social change and
humanitarian assistance.   »91
☼ **Southall Rights Legal Advice Centre**
54 High Street, Southall UB1 3DB; *t* (0181) 571 4920, 843
0094
Generalist advice centre; some, mainly Asian and African,
immigration work.   »94

✿ **Southwark Refugee Project, SRP**
Mohamed Ali Salih/G. Wilson: 161 Sumner Road, Peckham, London SE15 6JL; *t* (0171) 703 4046, *f* 701 7812
Advice for refugees and asylum seekers in Southwark; funded by the Borough Council's Equalities Sub-Committee.   »96

● **Stonewall Immigration Group**
2 Greycoat Place, London SW1P 1SB; *t* (0171) 222 9007, *f* 222 0525
Immigration rights pressure group campaigning for equality of treatment for lesbian/gay and heterosexual relationships. »95

✿ **Stop the Detentions Action Group**
Morwen Tregudda, Secretary: PO Box 207, Southall UB2 5BF; *t* (0181) 571 0676
Campaigns against immigration and asylum detentions.   »94

✿ **Ujima Housing Association**
187 Kilburn High Rd, London NW6 6JE; *t* (0171) 328 9775»95

✿ **Ukaidi Advice Centre**
Elron Brown: 9 Marple Square, St Ann's, Nottingham NG3; *t* (0115) 958 3173   »90

● **UKCOSA: The Council for International Education**, formerly United Kingdom Council for Overseas Student Affairs
Olivia Goulden/Mareta Anderson: 9-17 St Albans Place, Islington, London N1 0NX; *t* (0171) 226 3762, *f* 226 3373
Neil Gaskin. Co-ordinates advice and assistance services to overseas and refugee students; information, documentation, emergency assistance; see also Leeds and Nottingham Area Councils for Overseas Student Affairs, pp155-6.   »95

✿ **Unity Helpline**
Rev. H. Kudiabor, Co-ordinator: 64 Ravenswood Road, London SW12 9PJ; *t* (0181) 673 0793
Multiracial counselling on mental health problems; training; drop-in centre. May be linked with Unity Centre of South London: see Black listing, p23.   »90

✿ **Unity Housing Association Ltd**
Philip Prasad, Director: 113-115 Chapeltown Road, Leeds LS7 3HY; *t* (0113) 262 1260
Maggie Cassidy. A black-led social housing organisation with 600 homes in management. Involved in a research project, 1994-96, on housing needs of ethnic minorities in Leeds. »95

✿ **Waltham Forest Anti-Deportation Campaign**
[address unknown] London E17
Campaigns for migrant and refugee rights, and against deportations under asylum and immigration law.   »96

✿ **Waltham Forest Immigration Aid Centre**
William Morris Community Centre, Greenleaf Road, London E17 6QQ; *t* (0181) 503 6628
Specialist legal and procedural advice and assistance with immigration, family reunion problems.   »95

✿ **Waltham Forest Refugee Project**, Redbridge and Waltham Forest Family Health Services
[address unknown] Waltham Forest, London E17
Facilitates access to primary health care for Somali, Kurdish and other refugees; seeks to improve the quality of services they receive. Research, information, liaison with service providers and refugee communities.   »95

✿ **The Welfare Centre**
A. Azad: Mazda House, 40b Raby Street, Manchester M16 7EB; *t* (0161) 226 6527-28
Mainly Pakistani clientele; advice and information on immigration, refugee status, welfare rights. See also Dar-ul-Aman Housing Association, p93.   »93

◆ **Welsh Refugee Council**
8 Williams Court, Trade Street, Cardiff CF1 5DQ, Wales
Supports the settlement of refugees and displaced persons in Wales, in association with the statutory and voluntary sectors and especially refugee representative groups. Community development and advice work.   »94

✿ **West Bowling Community Advice and Training Centre**
Jane Binns: The Portakabins, Clipstone Street, West Bowling, Bradford BD5 8EA; *t* (01274) 392896, 733770
General consumer and legal rights advice service, some immigration work.   »94

✿ **West Midlands Anti-Deportation Campaign, WMADC**
c/o The Asian Resource Centre, 101 Villa Road, Handsworth, Birmingham B19 1NH; *t* (0121) 551 4518
Campaigns against the deportation of individuals refused the right to stay in the UK, and against racist and sexist immigration laws.   »96

● **The Windsor Fellowship**
Beverley Bernard, Director: 47 Hackney Rd, London E2 7NX
Charity established 1986 to improve educational, training and employment prospects of ethnic minorities, through mentor programmes and support for minority students.   »95

CHANNEL ISLANDS 44

◆ **Jersey Rights Association, JRA**
Ron Backhouse: PO Box 552, St Helier, Jersey JE2 8XZ; *t* (01534) 80800
Civil rights pressure group; concerns around migration include restrictive policies on housing rights.   »95

NORTHERN IRELAND 44

● **Committee for the Transfer of Irish Prisoners**
Caroline McEvoy: 14 Glencolin Avenue, Belfast BT11
Campaigns for the right of transfer from British prisons to prisons in Ireland of Irish persons, including those convicted of politically-motivated offences.   »95

✿ **Derry Emigration Bureau**
22 Bridge Street, Derry; *t* (01504) 266266
Emigration advice and counselling.   »90

✿ **Emigrant Advice Unit**
Mary White: Community Support Centre, 76-78 Hamill Street, Belfast BT12 4AA; *t* (01232) 328295, *f* 327172
Advice and information to intending emigrants.   »94

✿ **Newry Emigration Advice Unit**
c/o Welfare Rights Centre, 2 Bridge Street, Newry BT35 8AE, Co. Down; *t* (01693) 67631, 67632   »94

● **Northern Ireland Council for Ethnic Minorities, NICEM**
Patrick Yu/Eleanor McKnight: c/o Chinese Welfare Association, 17 Eblana Street, Belfast BT7 1LD; *t* (01232) 314925
Umbrella group launched 1994 for minority groups and support organisations; anti-racism, community development, campaigns for legislation against racial discrimination which at present is legal in Northern Ireland.   »96

VATICAN CITY STATE 39

▌ **Pontifica Commissio de Spirituali Migratorum atque Itinerantium**: Pontifical Commission for the Pastoral Care of Migrants and Travellers
Archbishop Emmanuel Clarizio, Pro-president: piazza S. Calisto 16, 00153 Roma; *t* (06) 698 7193, 698 7275
Founded 1970; promotes welfare and Catholic pastoral care of nomads, refugees, migrants, seafarers and other people on the move; research, documentation; *Migrations, On the Move* (3/yr), *Apostolatus Maris*, *Nomads*, occasional papers.   »86

Part Three

Anti-Racism, Anti-Fascism, Multiculturalism, Internationalism and Development Education

This category covers organisations involved in campaigning against racism, discrimination, fascism, antisemitism, xenophobia and intolerance, and/or in promoting minority rights and cultures, international or cross-cultural understanding and friendship, solidarity, equity in employment and other fields, and good community or race relations. It also covers groups involved in education and campaigns about these issues and about 'Third World', minority rights or global development issues (although some such groups, those with very broad humanitarian concerns, are listed instead in the Agencies section). It includes bodies working in the development of multicultural resources for education, international solidarity or exchange groups not specific to one ethnic minority or nationality, and groups representing anti-fascist war veterans or commemorating events connected with anti-fascist struggles. Most of the groups listed are in the voluntary sector, although some are publicly funded.

3

ALBANIA 355

● **Committee for Foreign Cultural Relations**
Rruga Asim Vokshi 2, Tirana
International friendship. *Shqiperia e Re* (6/yr).   »94

AUSTRIA 43

● **Arbeitsgemeinschaft Ausländer/innenwahlrecht** *(Working Group on the Enfranchisement of Foreign Residents)*
Mühlbacherhofweg 5/7, 5020 Salzburg; *t* (0662) 881145, *f* 8709 0019
Campaigns for extension of voting rights to non-citizens. »94
✿ **Begegnungszentrum für aktive Gewaltlosigkeit** *(Centre for Non-Violent Direct Action)*
Postfach 504, Wolfgangerstrasse 26, 4820 Bad Ischl; *t* (06132) 24590
Anti-racist, anti-fascist work.   »94
● **Bund Sozialistische Freiheitskämpfer** *(League of Socialist Freedom Fighters)*
K. Schmidt: Löwelstrasse 18, 1014 Wien
Veterans of wartime resistance?   »91
● **Bundesverband Österreichischer Widerstandskämpfer und Opfer des Faschismus/KZ-Verband** *(Austrian League of Resistance Fighters and Victims of Fascism/Concentration Camp Survivors Group)*
O. Wiesflecker: 2 LaSallestrasse 40/2/II/6, 1020 Wien; *t* (01) 265389
Anti-fascist veterans' organisation.   »94
● **Europäisches Bürgerforum:** European Civic Forum: Forum Civique Européen, and Austria-Transcarpathia Friendship Association
Hof Stopar, Lobnig 16, 9135 Eisenkappel; *t* (04238) 558, *f* 8232
Anti-racist, anti-nationalist group founded 1992, and associated with the CEDRI movement; see also in France, p163, Germany, p166 and Switzerland, p175.   »92
● **Gesellschaft für bedrohte Völker**, GfbV *(Society for Threatened Peoples)*
Mariahilferstrasse 105-2/13, 1060 Wien; *t* (01) 597 1176
Rights of tribal peoples and minorities around the world. »94

● **Initiative gegen Ausländerfeindlichkeit, Rassismus und Antisemitismus**, IGARA *(Initiative against Xenophobia, Racism and Antisemitism)*
Stiftgasse 8, 1070 Wien; *t* (01) 523 3884   »94
● **Institut für interkulturelle Zusammenarbeit**, Ethnotek *(Institute for Inter-Cultural Co-operation)*
Heidi Behn Thiele: Aschenaugasse 1, 2340 Mödling; *t* (022) 362 4217
Publicly-funded body promoting cross-cultural contact through events, exhibitions and information networking; rights of immigrants, refugees and minorities. Newsletters, leaflets.»93
✿ **Interkulturelles Zentrum** *(Multicultural Centre)*
Kettenbrückengasse 23, 1050 Wien; *t* (01) 5867 5440, *f* 5867 5449
Foundation promoting cross-cultural understanding and dialogue.   »94
▌**International Federation of Resistance Movements:** Féderation Internationale de la Résistance, FIR
Kapitelgasse 4/1, 1170 Wien; *t* (01) 458850, *f* 454670
Federation of veterans of anti-fascist struggles.   »94
♦ **Kampagnekomitee Österreich, Jugendkampagne gegen Rassismus des Europarates** *(Austrian Campaign Committee, Council of Europe Youth Campaign against Racism)*
Jürgen Gangoly: Am Modenapark 1-2/326, 1030 Wien; *t* (01) 5979 73528, *f* 5979 73589
Committee, including Österreichischer Bundesjugendring and Österreichische Jungarbeiterbewegung, both p188, organising participation in the Council of Europe-sponsored anti-racist campaign year, see p197, including intercultural youth camp.»95
♦ **Katholische Aktion-Platform gegen Ausländerfeindlichkeit** *(Catholic Action Programme against Xenophobia)*
Spiegelgasse 3, 1010 Wien; *t* (01) 5152 5661   »94
● *Lotta Dura*
[address unknown]
Anti-fascist magazine.   »96
✿ **Plattform gegen Ausländerfeindlichkeit und Rassismus— Oberösterreich** *(Upper Austria Coalition against Xenophobia and Racism)*
Weingartshofstrasse 38, 4020 Linz, Oberösterreich; *t* (0732) 667363, *f* 654586   »94
● **Rote Falken Österreich** *(Austrian Red Hawks)*
Rauhensteingasse 5/5, 1010 Wien; *t/f* (01) 512 1298
Youth anti-racist, anti-fascist group.   »94
✿ **Wiener Integrationsfonds** *(Vienna Integration Fund)*
Friedrich-Schmidt-Platz 3, 1080 Wien; *t* (01) 403 6645, *f* 403 66459 (?)   »94

BELGIUM 32

- **ACW**
Wetstraat 121, 1040 Brussel; t (02) 237 3111
Anti-racist group; no further information. »94
✿ **Aktiegroep Kritisch Onderwijs** *(Critical Education Action Group)*
M. Laquere: Gebr. van Eyckstraat 50, 9000 Gent »91
✿ **Anti Faschistisch Front—Front Antifasciste, AFF-FAF**
(Anti-Fascist Front)
Kloosterstraat 5, 2000 Antwerpen; t (03) 232 0670, f 232 0670
Anti-racism, support for migrant and refugee rights. Also active in Limburg. »94
✿ **Association Interculturelle L'Aquilone** *(Aquilone Intercultural Association)*
Nicola Briale: Rue Sebastien Laruelle 2, 4000 Liège; t (041) 237460
Bulletin (6/yr). »90
✿ **Atelier d'Art Populaire** *(People's Art Workshop)*
Chaussée de Mons 26, 1070 Bruxelles; t (02) 425 1616
Multi-cultural arts workshop, mainly Spanish clientele. »90
- **Avec Vous—pour la Démocratie, contre les Exclusions**
(With You—For Democracy, Against Exclusion)
Rue de la Tulipe 34, 1050 Bruxelles; t (02) 511 3699, f 513 0255
Anti-racist migrant rights movement. »94
✿ **Blokbuster**
Postbus 3, St Lievenslaan 23, 9000 Gent 21; t (091) 232 3159, 336239
Anti-racism, anti-fascism, migrant and refugee rights, intercultural understanding, human rights information. »94
✿ **Carrefour Chantiers**
María Acedo: Boulevard de l'Empereur 25, 1000 Bruxelles; t (02) 502 6042, 511 9684, f 502 6036
International solidarity, intercultural contact, anti-racism. »94
- **CelsiuS-Belgique**
Jehan de Wangen, Editor: Mantrant, BP 2128, 1000 Bruxelles
Franco-Belgian collective; formerly published the magazine *CelsiuS* (11/yr) on extreme right and racism; now maintains documentation and book review service in same field, with occasional publications. »94
✿ **Centre pour l'Egalité des Chances et pour la Lutte contre le Racisme** *(Centre for Equal Opportunities and Anti-Racism)*
Rue de la Loi 155, 8ième étage, Résidence Palace, 1040 Bruxelles; t (02) 233 0611, f 233 0704
Public body promoting equality of opportunity; participated in the Council of Europe's 1994-95 European Youth Campaign Against Racism, p197. »95
- **Centre International**
Boulevard Maurice Lemonnier 171, 1000 Bruxelles; t (02) 513 6907
Linked to the (Marxist-Leninist) Party of Labour; see also *Solidaire*, p161. »90
✿ **Centre Jeunes de Cluys**
Eric Vandenhoek: Général Eisenhower 47, 2140 Borgerhout; t (03) 271 0782
Anti-racist youth work; information, education. »94
- **Centrum voor Etnische Gelijkheid** *(Centre for Racial Equality)*
[address unknown]
Established in 1992-93 along the lines of the Dutch Landelijk Bureau Racismebestrijding, p171. »93
- **Comité International d'Auschwitz**
M. Goldstein: Rue de la Treille 15, 1050 Bruxelles
Concentration camp survivors and others involved in maintaining Auschwitz memorial. »91
▋ **Comparative Education Society in Europe**
Rue de la Concorde 60, 1050 Bruxelles; t (02) 514 3340, f 514 1172
Promotes teaching and research in comparative and international education; founded 1961. »93
✿ **Convivence**
[address unknown] Bruxelles
Multi-culturalism. »88
- **CSC Vormingswerk—De Wereld van Anne Frank** *(CSC Education Initiative—The World of Anne Frank)*
Postbus 877, 1000 Bruxelles; t (02) 502 6401, f 548 3580
Anti-racist, anti-fascist work in association with the Anne Frank Stichting, Amsterdam, p170. »94
▋ **European Federation for Intercultural Learning, EFIL**
Rue de la Montagne 36, 1000 Bruxelles; t (02) 514 5250, f 514 2929
See also Experiment in Europe, right. »94

▋ **Experiment in Europe, EIE**
Rue de la Montagne 36, 1000 Bruxelles; t (02) 514 5930, f 514 2929
See also EFIL, left. »94
✿ **Formation et Travail en Quartier Populaire—Atelier**
(Workshop for Training and Employment in the Inner City)
Eric Delvosal: Rue des Alliés 315, 1060 Bruxelles; t (02) 537 7724
Education, training, employment, youth integration. »94
✿ **Foyer Culturel de Seraing**
Rue Renaud Strivay 44, 4100 Seraing; t (041) 373880, 375454
Intercultural contact and understanding. »94
✿ **Le Goeland, Centre d'Expression et de Créativité** *(Le Goeland Arts Centre)*
Nicole Hamande: Rue du Rivage 10, 1300 Wavre; t (010) 224001
Arts, culture, adult education and leisure activities. »94
✿ **Graffiti**
Stalingradlaan 18-20, 1000 Brussel; t (02) 511 0214, f 512 2384
Anti-racist, anti-fascist youth centre. »94
✿ **Groupe Contact Sensibilisation, GCS** *(Contact and Awareness Group)*
Ahmed Mahou: Rue de Liedekerke 134, 1030 Bruxelles; t (02) 217 9140, f 217 6267
Inter-cultural contact; Maghrebi culture; sports, leisure. »94
✿ **Les Halles de Schaerbeek**
Philippe Grombeer: Rue de la Constitution 20, 1030 Bruxelles; t (02) 218 0031, f 219 4290
Anti-racist work. »94
- *Halt*
H. Boukhriss: 4 Postbus 16, 1000 Brussel 22
Anti-racist journal. This may be a private address. »91
✿ **Interculture-Charleroi**
Silvano d'Angelo, Co-ordinator: Rue Chavannes 22, 6000 Charleroi; t (071) 312404
Local multi-cultural and community development group. »90
▋ **International Auschwitz Committee**
32, Avenue d'Italie, boite 19, 1050 Bruxelles; t (02) 672 6756, f 512 5884
Holocaust education, preservation of Auschwitz as memorial; anti-racism, anti-fascism. »94
✿ **Internationale Vrouwenwerking Flora** *(Flora International Women's Group)*
Béatrice Zelner, Co-ordinator: Borsbeekstraat 113, Borgerhout, 2140 Antwerpen; t (03) 271 1018
Women's rights, welfare; cultural activities; education. »94
♦ **Jongeren Tegen Racisme, JTR** *(Youth Against Racism)*
Poststraat 156, 1030 Brussel; t (02) 217 1114
Anti-racism, anti-fascism. »90
✿ **Jongeren Tegen Racisme—School Zonder Racisme, JTR-SZR** *(Youth Against Racism—Racism-Free Schools)*
Tony Fonteyne: Maria Theresiastraat 10, 9000 Gent; t/f (09) 233 3185
Anti-racist work with schools and youth groups; opposes minority quota systems. »95
✿ **Koloriek**
[address unknown] »88
✿ **Kontaktorgaan Internationale Solidariteit, KIS** *(International Solidarity Clearing House)*
Breughelstraat 31-33, 2000 Antwerpen; t (03) 239 0608
Third World consciousness, anti-racism. »94
✿ **Kulturen in Beweging** *(Cultures on the Move)*
Breughelstraat 31, 2018 Antwerpen; t (03) 218 6580, f 230 4540
Multi-culturalism, anti-racism, promotion of migrant cultural expression. »94
♦ **Mouvement contre le racisme, l'antisémitisme et la xénophobie, MRAX** *(Movement against Racism, Antisemitism and Xenophobia)*
Yvonne Jospa, President: Rue de la Poste 37, 1210 Bruxelles; t (02) 217 5495, 218 2371, 217 4270, f 219 6959
Major anti-racist human rights pressure group; interests of migrants and refugees. Maria Miguel is Belgian contact for European Co-ordination for the Right to Family Life for Immigrants, p136. *MRAX info* (4/yr). »95
- **Musée National de la Résistance/Front de l'Indépendance, FI** *(National Resistance Museum/Independence Front)*
Rue Van Lint 14, 1070 Bruxelles; t (02) 522 4041
Museum and archive of the wartime resistance movements; anti-fascist education. »94
✿ **Le Nouvel Espoir** *(New Hope)*
Fouad Mejloufi: Rue Jean Ekelmans 31, 1160 Bruxelles
Youth welfare, intercultural contact. »94

✿ **Objektief 479.917**: Objectif 479.917—Non au Racisme et Fascisme *(Objective 479.917—No to Racism and Fascism)*
Eddy Maes: Kazernestraat 68, 1000 Brussel; *t* (02) 513 8346, *f* 513 9831
Anti-racist, anti-fascist migrant rights campaign. *Objektief 479.917* (4/yr). »94

● **Samenwerking Verzetzdeelnemers 1940-1945** *(1940-45 Resistance Fighters League)*
J.F. Wolff, Vice-President: De Planck 7c, 3790 Voeren
Anti-fascist veterans. »91

● *Solidaire* (In Solidarity)
Boite 10, Blvd Maurice Lemonnier 171, 1000 Bruxelles; *t* (02) 513 6626
Anti-racist and minority affairs journal, possibly linked with (Marxist-Leninist) Party of Labour; see also Centre International, p160. Address is from 1990. »95

● **SOS Racisme Belgique**
Avenue de l'Armée 103, 1040 Bruxelles
Anti-racist campaigning group. »90

● **Stichting Auschwitz** *(Auschwitz Foundation)*
Rue des Tanneurs 65, 1000 Bruxelles; *t* (02) 512 7998, *f* 512 5884
Holocaust education, anti-racism, anti-fascism. »94

✿ **Vent du Nord/Vent du Sud asbl** *(North Wind/South Wind)*
Rue General Bertrand 44, 4000 Liège
Multiculturalism, anti-racism. »88

✿ **Vereniging voor Solidariteit**, VVA *(Solidarity Union)*
Hilde Kieboom: Lombardenstraat 28, 2000 Antwerpen; *t* (03) 231 4837, *f* 226 0737 »94

✿ **La Voix des Femmes** *(Women's Voice)*
Hayriye Baici: Rue de l'Alliance 18, 1030 Bruxelles; *t* (02) 218 7787, *f* 219 6085
Women's rights, intercultural understanding, anti-racism, migrant support. *Le Foulard—Solidarité*. »94

✿ **Vriendenkring Dachau** *(Dachau Fellowship)*
M. De Ghouy/Adrienne De Canck: Keistraat 52, 9830 St Martens Latem »91

CZECH REPUBLIC *42*

● *Autonomie* (Autonomy)
PS 223, 11121 Praha 1
Radical youth magazine. »94

✿ **DUHA, Kancelar pro Cechy** *(Rainbow Association, Czech Office)*
Senovázné nám. 24, 11647 Praha 1; *t* (02) 2410 2374, *f* 2410 2375
Multicultural youth group. »94

◆ **European Youth Campaign against Racism—Czech Campaign Secretariat**, and Kruh SDM *(Circle of Children's and Youth Associations)*
Senovázné nám. 24, 11647 Praha 1; *t* (02) 2410 2469, *f* 2410 2471
National secretariat for the 1994-95 Council of Europe youth campaign, p197, based at the national youth council. »94

● **Hnutí Obcanské Solidarity a Tolerance**, HOST *(Citizens' Solidarity and Tolerance Movement)*
Mr Bergmann: PS 13, 12800 Praha 2; *t/f* (02) 2491 1338
Anti-racist, anti-fascist group. Participated in the 1994-95 European Youth Campaign Against Racism, p197. »94

● **Nadace Tolerance**
c/o Libri Prohibiti, Senovázné nám. 2, 11000 Praha 1
Anti-racist, anti-fascist movement. »94

DENMARK *45*

✿ **Århus Ungdoms- og Kulturforeningen** *(Aarhus Youth and Cultural Society)*
Grønnegade 80, 8000 Århus C »89

✿ **Aktive modstandsfolk** *(People's Active Resistance)*
Nygårdsvej 52, 2100 København ø
Anti-fascist work. »94

● **Arbejderbevaegelsens Internationale Forum**, AIF *(Labour Movement International Forum)*
Teglvaersgade 27, 2100 København ø; *t* 3296 0066, *f* 3120 1768
International solidarity, anti-racism. »94

● **Dansk International Venskabsorganisation** *(Danish Organisation for International Friendship)*
Lal M. Changezi: Isafjordsgade 2, 1.tv., 2300 København S »89

● **Dokumentations- og Rådgivningcenteret om Racediskrimination**, DRC *(Documentation and Advice Centre on Racial Discrimination)*
Emmanuel Kwesi Aning: Bredgade 36C mellembygning 4.sal, 1260 København K; *t* 3332 3945, *f* 3332 0824
Anti-racist research and action; advice to victims of discrimination and harassment; support for migrant and refugee rights. Associated with IND-sam, p132. »94

● **Fællesinitiativet mod Racisme**, FIR *(Joint Initiative against Racism)*
Elmegade 27, kld, 2200 København N
Anti-racist work; see also Foreningen Demos, below. »94

● **Fagforeninger mod racisme** *(Trade Unions against Racism)*
JBF - Hestemøllestræde 5, 1464 København K »94

● **Fairplay 91**
Blegdamsvej 4 st., 2200 København N; *t* 3139 2143, *f* 3536 2410
Human rights, anti-racism. »94

◆ **Foreningen Demos** and Demos Dokumentationsgruppen
Postboks 1110, 1009 København K; *t* 3123 1391
Anti-racist, anti-fascist organisation; research, archive (Demos Dokumentationsgruppen, Elmegade 27, kld, 2200 København N), publishing. See also Fællesinitiativet mod Racisme, above. Publications include *Demos* and the anti-fascist journal *Nyhedsbrev*. »96

✿ **Foreningen for Indvandrere og Danskere** *(Association of Immigrants and Danes)*
Yussuf Sevin: Uffesvej 24, 5270 Odense N
Solidarity with migrants; human rights, legal advice, welfare work. »94

✿ **Frederikssund Fremmedarbejderklub** *(Frederikssund Foreign Workers' Club)*
Skolegade 1a, 3600 Frederikssund »89

✿ **International Venskabsklub i Taastrup** *(Taastrup International Friendship Club)* formerly International Venskabsklub Blåkildegard
L. Hansen: Grundtvigsvej 13, 2630 Taastrup; *t* 4299 1627
Social and cultural group for migrants. »94

■ **International Working Group for Indigenous Affairs**, IWGIA
Andrew Grey: Fiolstræde 10, 1171 København K; *t* 3312 4724, *f* 3314 7749
Campaigns for cultural, political and economic rights of indigenous peoples and minorities worldwide. »95

✿ **Internationale Kulturforum** *(International Cultural Forum)*
BBc Postboks 266, 1800 Frederiksberg C
Autonomi. »94

✿ **Den Internationale Kvindeforening**, DIK-AOF *(International Women's Society)*
Inge Thorup Frederiksen: Vesterbro 2, 5000 Odense C »89

✿ **Internationalt Forum**
Albert Jensen, Secretary: Griffenfeldsgade 35, 2200 København N; *t* 3537 1430, 3537 1888, *f* 3537 1980
Development education, human rights worldwide, solidarity with migrants and refugees and with progressive and popular organisations in countries of the South. *Newsletter* (52/yr), *Mañana* (5/yr). »95

✿ **Rebel**
Griffenfeldsgade 41, 2200 København N; *t* 3537 8658
Anti-racist, anti-fascist youth organisation. »94

✿ **Solidaritets- og Kulturforening i Ringsted**, SKF *(Ringsted Solidarity and Cultural Society)* formerly Venskabs- og Kulturforeningen i Ringsted
Haslevvej 6, 4100 Ringsted; *t* 5361 6700, *f* 5361 6823
Formed 1982; anti-racist activities, advice service on employment, welfare, education and training issues, cultural events, information. »94

● **SOS-Racisme**
Jaohan Horstmann: Irmingersgade 1, 2100 København ø; *t* 4294 8473 »90

✿ ≡ Vivi Torben: Mork Hojdej 134, 2K, 2730 Harlec »94

● **Sprogpædagogisk Center** *(Children's Educational Centre)*
Danmarks Pædagogiske Bibliotek, Lers Park Allé 101, 2100 København
Development of multicultural education; teaching resource centre. »94

✿ **Transcultura**
Dr Tove Skutnabb-Kangas: [address uncertain] Trønninge Mose 3, 4420 Regstrup; *t* 5346 4412 »90

✿ **Venskabsforeningen for Danskere og Indvandrere** *(Friendship Association for Danes and Immigrants)*
Pia Bødtker: Islandshøparken 60, I.4., 2990 Niva »89

✿ **Venskabsforeningen for Flygtninge-, Indvandrer- og Danske Kvinder** *(Friendship Association of Refugee, Immigrant and Danish Women)*
Mylius Erichsens Vej 1 (barakken), 9210 Aalborg Sø »89

FINLAND 358

✿ **Antifa—Helsinki**
PL 7, 00801 Helsinki
Anti-fascist action. »94
✿ **Antifa—Lohja** *(Lohja Anti-Fascists)*
c/o KMK, Kalevankatu 1, 08100 Lohja »94
▌ **International Friendship League**, IFL
Fältspasvägen 5-9/1/48, 00710 Helsinki »94
● **Suomen Ammattiliittojen Solidaarisuuskeskus**, SASK
(Finnish Trade Union Solidarity Centre)
Unioninkatu 45 H 115, 00170 Helsinki; *t* (90) 135 1833,
f 135 5703, *e* geo2:sask-finland
Development education, mainly within the trade union
movement, and aid agency of the Confederation of Finnish
Trade Unions; projects in Africa, Latin America and Asia. »93

FRANCE 33

✿ **Accents Multiples** *(Many Accents)*
Jean Pierre Gonin: 11 rue de l'Oriflamme, 84000 Avignon;
t 9082 9182
Intercultural solidarity, information. »94
● **Agence pour la Promotion des Cultures et du Voyage,**
APCV *(Agency for the Promotion of Cultures and Travel)*
Rahim Rezigat: 39 rue Pinel, 93200 Saint-Denis; *t* (1) 4813
0800
International and inter-cultural solidarity. »94
✿ **Alsace Plurielle** *(Pluralist Alsace)*
Martine Saenger: 42 rue de Bâle, 68100 Mulhouse; *t* 8966
5418, *f* 8966 4781
Multicultural group. »94
● **Amicale de Ravensbruck** *(Ravensbruck Fellowship)*
R. Guérin: 26 rue Bapst, 92600 Asnières
Possibly private address. Association of survivors of fascist
concentration camp. »91
● **Amitié Internationale des Jeunes** *(International Youth
Friendship)*
33 avenue Eylau, 75016 Paris; *t* (1) 4727 7564 »90
✿ **Amitiés Mussipontains-Immigrés**, AMI *(Pont-à-Mousson
Immigrant Friendship Group)*
Huguette Berthou: BP 191, 18 place Saint Antoine, 54706
Pont-à-Mousson; *t* 8383 1341
Anti-racist work, solidarity with immigrants, education,
integration. »94
✿ **Animations et spectacles populaires et interculturels,**
ASPIC *(Popular Intercultural Event Promotions)*
Farida Atamma: 46 rue de Ménilmontant, 75020 Paris; *t* (1)
4636 1424
Cultural and social events, promotion of minority cultures.
Le Ménilmuche. »94
● **Appel des 250 contre le Front National—Ras le Front**
*(Appeal of the 250 against the National Front—Raze the
Front)*
P. Crottet, BP 87, 75561 Paris Cedex 12; *t* (1) 4264 8025,
f 4223 8623
Anti-fascist group. »94
✿ **Arc-en-ciel** *(Rainbow)*
[address unknown] »90
✿ **Art-Culture-Communication**, ACC
Renaud Barillet: 53 rue Robert Cousin, 77176 Nandy; *t* (1)
6441 0404, *f* 6441 9772
Promotion of minority cultures in the media. »94
♦ *Article 31*: Head Office
BP 423, 75527 Paris Cedex 11; *t* (1) 4806 8800
National journal on right and racism, with regional editions.
Closely associated with MRAP, p164. »90
✿ ≡ Alsace: 7 ave. de la Foret Noire, 67000 Strasbourg »90
✿ ≡ c/o CEP, BP 5006, 69245 Lyon Cedex 05 »90
✿ ≡ [address unknown] Toulouse »90
✿ **Association Coup de Soleil** *(Sunbeam Association)*
Georges Morin: BP 328, 75001 Paris; *t* (1) 4597 7029
Also listed (1995) as Coup de Soleil, BP 2344, 75001 Paris.
Multicultural, anti-racist. *Lettre du Coup de Soleil* (4/yr). »94
✿ **Association culturelle anti-raciste**
20 rue d'Anjou, 22000 Saint-Breuc
Anti-racist work. »89
● **Association Henri Curiel**
17 rue de la Butte aux Cailles, 75013 Paris
Anti-racist. »90

✿ **Association pour le Développement des Relations
Intercommunautaires à Marseille** *(Marseilles Association for
Community Relations)*
54 rue du Paradis, 13006 Marseille; *t* 9125 0503 »90
● **Association dialogue entre les cultures** *(Association for
Inter-Cultural Dialogue)*
Jean-Yves Merian: 43 rue Richelieu, 75001 Paris »90
✿ **Association Emergence Nanterre**
[address unknown] Nanterre »90
● **Association générale métisse** *(Mixed-Race Society)*
5 rue Domrémy, 75013 Paris »89
✿ **Association Interculturelle**, ASAL
Ali Gafour: 64 rue de Viller, 54300 Luneville; *t* 8373 2915,
f 8373 0758 »94
✿ **Association interculturelle de briançonnais Mosaïque**
(Mosaic Inter-Cultural Association of Briançon Area)
MJC, rue Pasteur, 05100 Briançon
Bridge between local and foreign communities, defence of
immigrant rights, integration. »89
✿ **Association Interculturelle Carrefour** *(Crossroads Inter-
Cultural Association)*
51 rue Glacière, 75013 Paris; *t* (1) 4336 6387 »90
✿ **Association interculturelle pour la promotion et l'insertion,**
AIPI *(Inter-Cultural Association for Integration and Social
Progress)*
11 rue Nationale, 13001 Marseille »90
✿ **Association interculturelle et sportive** *(Inter-Cultural
Sporting Association)*
Hassan Haïzoun: 2 rue de Coblence, appt 545, 58000 Nevers
Social assistance and advice to immigrant families, cultural,
sporting and educational activities, exchanges. »89
✿ **Association Kaléidoscope** *(Kaleidoscope Association)*
[address unknown] »90
✿ **Association pour une meilleure intégration**, AMI
(Association for Greater Integration)
Centre socio-culturel Maison du Centre, 7 rue du Maréchal-
Maison, 93800 Epinay-sur-Seine »90
● **Association de la nouvelle génération immigrée**, ANGI
(Association of the Immigrant New Generation)
9 rue de la Maladrerie, 93300 Aubervilliers; *t* (1) 4384 8507
Mainly-*beur* (second generation) pressure group. »94
✿ **Association pluriculturelle pour la coopération et le
développement** *(Multicultural Association for Co-operation
and Development)*
Maison des societés, bureau 212, rue Saint-Jean, 26000
Valence
Inter-cultural dialogue and exchange, development aid,
humanitarian relief in the Comoros and elsewhere. »90
✿ **Association pour la recherche et l'animation culturelle,**
ARAC *(Association for Cultural Research and Promotion)*
Habib Laidi: 3 rue Mont Louis, 75011 Paris; *t* (1) 4370
5448, 4370 6533, *f* 4370 3927
Also listed (1990) as Association de Recherche et d'Action
Culturelle. »94
● **Association Rencontres Audiovisuelles** *(Audiovisual
Encounters Association)*
10 rue du Regard, 75006 Paris; *t* (1) 4549 2241 »90
✿ **Association Sans Frontières des Initiatives et Rencontres,**
ASFIR *(No Borders Association for Encounters and Initiatives)*
Gisèle Mathonnet: 21 rue Georges Ducarre, 42300 Roanne;
t 7771 2280
Maghrebi-French cross-cultural understanding. »94
✿ **Association Solidarité Etrangers Français**, ASEF *(French
and Foreigners Solidarity Association)*
[address unknown] »90
● **Association de Solidarité Familiale et Culturelle**, ASSOFAC
(Family and Cultural Solidarity Association)
50 rue Stephenson, 75018 Paris; *t* (1) 4223 1333, *f* 4223
4350
Educational materials, youth welfare. *Nadim*. »94
✿ **Association de soutien, de développement et d'amélioration
de la vie tribale** *(Association for the Support, Development
and Improvement of Tribal Life)*
René Guiart/Nicolas Furet: BP 42, 04300 Forcalquier
International solidarity group associated with the CEDRI
movement, p163; support for endangered minority groups in
Africa and elsewhere. »90
✿ **Association de soutien à l'expression des communautés
d'Amiens**, ASECA *(Association for Self-Expression of
Communities in Amiens)*
Bernard Delemotte: BP 2709, 80027 Amiens Cedex; *t* 2280
0116
Location: 74 rue des Jacobins. Citizenship, nationality, civic
participation, voting rights of migrants. *La lettre de la
citoyenneté* (6/yr). »94

✧ **Association Texture**
Ahmed Benyachi: BP 42, 32 rue Montaigne, 59022 Lille
Cedex; *t* 2085 0232
Anti-racism, advice service. *Le citoyen*.   »94

● **Association des Trois Mondes, ATM** *(Three Worlds
Association)*
Martine Leroy: 63 bis rue Cardinal Lemoine, 75005 Paris;
t (1) 4354 7869, *f* 4634 7019
Research and documentation centre on North-South and
cross-cultural issues. *Images Nord-Sud* (4/yr).   »94

● **Associations amitiés Afrique-Proche Orient** *(Africa-Middle
East Friendship Association)*
5 rue des Petites Ecuries, 75010 Paris; *t* (1) 4246 9195 »90

✧ **Atelier Contemporain de Cultures et des Echanges
Culturels** *(Contemporary Workshop for Culture and Cultural
Exchanges)*
8 rue de l'Abbaye, 75006 Paris   »90

● **CelsiuS**
Mantrant, BP 49, 75865 Paris Cedex 18
Franco-Belgian collective researching extreme right, see p160;
published magazine *CelsiuS* (11/yr), now suspended.   »94

✧ **Centre des Cultures Meditérranéennes** *(Centre for
Mediterranean Cultures)*
Tour Bastionnée, 41 rue Georges-Pompidou, 90000 Belfort;
t 8428 3810
Research, information, cross-cultural activities.   »94

✧ **Centre de Documentation et d'Information contre le
Racisme et pour l'Egalité des Droits, CEDIRED** *(Anti-Racism
and Equal Rights Information and Documentation Centre)*
3 cheminement L. Auriacombe, 31100 Toulouse; *t* 6214
6139, *f* 6214 6157   »94

● **Centre d'Etudes sur le Racisme et le Fascisme** *(Centre for
Studies on Racism and Fascism)*
30 allée Sellier, 31400 Toulouse   »90

✧ **Centre Interculturel de Documentation, CID**
Vincent Courtin: Ateliers et Chantiers de Nantes, 33 rue
Léon-Jamin, 44200 Nantes; *t* 4047 8836, *f* 4048 7834
May succeed the Collectif Vivre Ensemble (Living Together
Collective) listed (1990) at same address.   »94

✧ **Centre Interculturel Rencontre** *(Encounter Intercultural
Centre)*
Monique Van Lancker: 2 place Vaubon, 59140 Dunkerque;
t 2860 3232
Rencontre.   »91

◆ **Centre de Recherche, d'Information et de Documentation
Antiraciste, CRIDA** *(Anti-Racist Research, Information and
Documentation Centre)*
21 ter. rue Voltaire, 75011 Paris; *t* (1) 4372 4934, *f* 4372
0642, 4372 1577
Research centre which publishes the important anti-racist
journal *Reflexes*; monitors activities of the Front National,
the "naziskins" and other far-right movements in France.
Promotes co-operation between anti-racist and human rights
organisations and minorities. International associates include
Searchlight magazine (UK), p183.   »96

✧ **Centre socio-culturel Le Toit du Monde**
Bernard de Corbier: 31 rue des Trois Rois, 86000 Poitiers;
t 4941 1340, *f* 4960 4682
Migrant workers centre. *Tract d'activités* (12/yr), *Rose des
Vents* (3/yr).   »94

✧ **Citoyen et Citoyenne '89** *(Citizens '89)*
30 rue Espariat, 13100 Aix-en-Provence
Pressure group for minorities of Mediterranean origin in
Provence-Alpes-Côte d'Azur region, based on 1789 concepts
of citizenship and human rights.   »89

◆ **Club Recherches, Perspectives, Expressions et Sociétés,
RE.PER.ES** *(Research, Perspectives, Communication and
Societies Club)*
5 rue Blaise-Cendrars, 13100 Aix-en-Provence
Non-partisan group; material and moral interests, equality,
economic and social integration of youth of immigrant origin
and of their parents; Maghrebi culture and identity; opposition
to racism, xenophobia and marginalisation and isolation of
Maghrebi communities; mutual respect between French and
Maghrebis.   »89
✧ ≡ 130 cité de la Minette, 78700 Conflans-Ste-Honorine »89
✧ ≡ 30 allée des Amonts, 91940 Les Ulis   »89
✧ ≡ bat. B, résidence Les Marlières, 62820 Libercourt   »89
✧ ≡ chez M Ahmed Djellali: 1 rue Gustave-Charpentier, Val
Forré, 78200 Mantes-La-Jolie   »89
✧ ≡ 1 place Saint-Exupéry, 77110 Meaux   »89
✧ ≡ 5 tour Lavoisier, 77130 Monterau-Faur-Yonne   »89
✧ ≡ Bachir Bousba: 14 rue Pierre-Mignard, 44100 Nantes »89
✧ ≡ Union départementale des clubs RE.PER.ES: 9 rue du
Pont-Guilhemery, 31000 Toulouse   »89

✧ **Collectif Anti-Raciste et Anti-Fasciste de la Sarthe** *(Sarthe
Anti-Racist, Anti-Fascist Collective)*
Jean Thevenot: Maison des Associations, 4 place Arcole,
72015 Le Mans Cedex; *t* (1) 4328 7979, 4380 7852   »94

✧ **Collectif Anti-Raciste de Corse, AVA-BASTA** *(Corsican
Anti-Racist Collective)*
Noëlle Vincensini: BP 3, 30 cours Napoléon, 20176 Ajaccio
Cedex 1; *t* 9521 5424, 9551 1802, *f* 9551 2969   »94

✧ **Collectif Féministe contre le Racisme** *(Feminist Anti-Racist
Collective)*
Maison des Femmes, 8 cité Prost, 75011 Paris; *t* (1) 4348
2491
Human rights, anti-racist women's group.   »94

✧ **Collectif Havrais contre le Racisme et pour l'Egalité des
Droits** *(Le Havre Anti-Racist and Equal Rights Collective)*
22-24 rue Lamartine, 76600 Le Havre; *t* 3525 0502
This address was listed (1989) as that of Association pour la
promotion, l'action et la création—Génération Intégration,
which engaged in youth-led sporting, cultural and social
activities; the Collectif may be a related organisation.   »94

✧ **Collectif Tiers Monde intercommunal des cantons de
Louvers-Val-de-Reuil** *(Regional Third World Collective)*
48 voie du Lièvre, 27100 Val-de-Reuil
Solidarity, development aid, information, education.   »89

▌ **Comité Européen pour la Défense des Réfugiés et des
Immigrés, CEDRI**: European Committee for the Defence of
Refugees and Immigrants: and Forum Civique Européen
Nicolas Furet/René Guiart: BP 42, 04300 Forcalquier; *t* 9273
0598, 9275 0598, 9273 1356, *f* 9273 1818, 9273 7106
Solidarity association; Swiss, German, Austrian affiliates,
pp175, 166, 159; publishes in several languages. Several
linked organisations use this address, including European Civic
Forum, campaigning for voting and other rights for migrants;
Europäische Föderation Freier Radios, linking local independent
radio stations, and Association de soutien, de développement
et d'amélioration de la vie tribale, p162. *Archipel*.   »94

▌ **Comité International Sachsenhausen, CIS**: International
Sachsenhausen Committee
41 boulevard Gambetta, 46000 Cahors; *t* 6535 7908
Memorial committee for victims of Nazi persecution in
Sachsenhausen concentration camp.   »94

✧ **Comité de Lutte Anti-fasciste** *(Anti-Fascist Campaign
Committee)*
c/o J.A.: BP 2289, 13212 Marseille Cedex 02   »88

✧ **Communauté d'entraide et de solidarité de Villiers-le-Bel**
(Mutual Aid and Solidarity Community)
Mairie, 95400 Villiers-le-Bel   »89

● **Communautés Ethniques de Langue Française, CELF**
(French-Speaking Ethnic Communities)
103 rue Lille, 75007 Paris; *t* (1) 4753 9867   »90

● **Consortium Européen pour les Relations Nord-Sud**
(European Consortium for North-South Relations)
39 boulevard St-Germain, 75005 Paris; *t* (1) 4046 9375 »90

✧ **Coordination Information Tiers-Monde, CITM** *(Third World
Information Co-ordination)*
70 rue de Bayeux, 1400 Caen; *t* 3185 2078
Development education, anti-racism, public information
activities around immigration, minorities and human rights.
Active only in Normandy.   »93

✧ **Couleur locale** *(Local Colour)*
10 rue des Frères-Mercier, 25000 Besançon
Friendship and cultural links among multi-national student
community.   »89

✧ **Différents**
147 avenue Marcel-Maegelen, 18000 Bourges
Defence of all racial and other minorities.   »89

✧ **Echange et Promotion** *(Exchange and Promotion)*
4 place Saint Roch, 42100 Saint-Etienne; *t* 7725 1894   »90

✧ **Echanges Culturels en Méditerranée, ECUME**
O.D. Belli: 45 rue de Panier, 13002 Marseille; *t* 9156 1309,
f 9156 0050
Research, information, intercultural activities.   »94

✧ **Entreprendre Ensemble** *(Joint Enterprise)*
215 rue Jean-Jacques Rousseau, 92130 Issy-les-Moulineaux;
t (1) 4634 1981, *f* 4325 0950
Migrant youth employment, training and enterprise.   »94

✧ **Equipe Technique Interventions Interculturelles, ETNICS**
(Technical Team for Multicultural Initiatives)
Dominique Mansuy: Château d'Eau, avenue d'Epernay,
51100 Reims; *t* 2686 0802
Training and assistance for cross-cultural events.   »94

✧ **Espace Interculturel Méditerranéen, EICM**
Fatima Serrar: 23 rue de Grasse, 31400 Toulouse; *t* 6125
1645
Maghrebi culture; see also AIRCM and COFRIMI, pp233-4.»94

✧ **Espace Pluriel Amitiés sans frontières**, ESPAS *(Friendship without Borders Intercultural Venue)*
Ali Abderrahmane: 5 rue Lacharrière, 75011 Paris; *t* (1) 4700 7959
Journal *Espace*. »94

▌ **European Association for Transcultural Group Analysis**
6 bis rue Bachaumont, 75002 Paris; *t* (1) 4236 9127, *f* 4508 4536 »96

▌ **European Conference of Binational-Bicultural Relationships**, ECB
Beate Collet: 101 rue de Dessous-des-Berges, 75013 Paris; *t* (1) 4424 2849
Federation of associations representing partners in binational and intercultural relationships. »94

● **Fédération Française des Clubs UNESCO**, FFCU
2 rue Lapeyrère, 75018 Paris; *t* (1) 4258 6806, *f* 4606 2808
Development education, promotion of international solidarity and human rights; funding and material aid to Francophone Africa. »93

✧ **Femmes sans frontières** *(Women Without Borders)*
21 rue Colette, 69800 Saint-Priest
Women's solidarity and self-expression nationally and internationally, multi-cultural encounters and exchanges. »90

✧ **Fondation pour la Cohabitation des Communautés et la Coopération Internationale**, F3CI *(Foundation for Community Coexistence and International Co-operation)*
Tahar Rahmani: 14 rue des Dominicaines, 13001 Marseille; *t* 9156 0805
Multiculturalism, international friendship, youth welfare. *La lettre 3CI* (24/yr). »94

◆ **France plus**: Head Office
5 impasse Onfroy, 75013 Paris; *t* (1) 4581 2121, *f* 4581 0091
National movement formed in 1985; works through dozens of local committees. Represents *beur* and Maghrebi youth and those from overseas French *départements* and territories; anti-racism, citizenship rights, political participation; secularist, integrationist; civic education, inter-cultural exchanges, other projects to assist integration of second-generation youth. »94
✧ ≡ Aveyron: Aveyron-plus: Le Clapas, Termenoux, 12560 Campagnac »90
✧ ≡ 8 rue des Chênes, 59330 Hautmont »90
✧ ≡ Limousin: 1 rue Armand-Barbès, 87000 Limoges »90
✧ ≡ Marseilles: Mouloud Rezzaouli [address unknown] »95
✧ ≡ 18 rue Bassano, 30900 Nîmes »90
✧ ≡ Toulouse: 64 ave. de Toulouse, 31800 St-Gaudens »90

● **Frères des Hommes** *(Brothers of Mankind)* Head Office
9 rue Savoie, 75006 Paris; *t* (1) 4354 0571 »90
● ≡ Secretariat: 45 bis rue de la Glacière, 75013 Paris; *t* (1) 4707 0000
Major international development charity; solidarity with third world, especially children. »93

● **Galaxie**
Katia Lobry: 1 résidence Politzer, 93200 Saint-Denis
Exchanges, learning holidays. »89

✧ **Gardarem Lou Larzac**
c/o Daniel Darras: Cap d'Ase, 12100 Millau
Pacifism, third world. »90

✧ **Génération 2001**
1-7 rue de la Mare, 75020 Paris; *t* (1) 4349 5588 »90

✧ **Génériques**
Driss El Yazami: 34 rue de Citeaux, 75012 Paris; *t* (1) 4928 5775, *f* 4928 0930
Research, documentation and publishing on migration, minorities and intercultural relations. *Migrance* (4/yr). »94

● *Le Globe*
[address unknown]
Anti-racist journal; was bombed in 1988. »88

● **Groupement pour les Droits des Minorités**, GDM: Minority Rights Group
A. Fenet/Yves Plasseraud: 212 rue Saint Martin, 75003 Paris; *t* (1) 4277 2626, *f* 4579 8046
Human rights research and pressure group. *Lettre du GDM* (4/yr). »94

✧ **Images Spectacles et Musiques du Monde**, ISMM
François Charbonnier: 7 impasse Charretière, 75005 Paris; *t* (1) 4325 1980
Multicultural media, anti-racism, youth integration. See also CLAP, p136. »94

✧ **Information—Foi—Développement**, IFD *(Information, Faith and Development)*
21 rue du Faubourg de Saverne, 67000 Strasbourg; *t* 8832 9579
Development education, human rights, international and inter-cultural solidarity. »93

✧ **Interférences Culturelles** *(Cultural Cross-Currents)*
12 rue Guy de la Brosse, 74005 Paris; *t* (1) 4707 1158, *f* 4337 1853
Promotion of minority cultures and inter-cultural contact in Paris region; public education about migrants and the developing world. See also Inter Service Migrants, p137. »93

▌ **International Registry of World Citizens**, IRWC
66 bvd Vincent Auriol, 75013 Paris; *t* (1) 4586 0358 »94

▌ **Ligue internationale contre le racisme et l'antisémitisme**, LICRA: International League against Racism and Antisemitism: Head Office
Jean-Pierre Broch, President: 40 rue de Paradis, 75010 Paris; *t* (1) 4770 1328, *f* 4800 0399
Struggles against racism and antisemitism by uniting men and women of all opinions for peace and equality among peoples. Formed 1927. Sections in France, Hungary, Italy, Portugal, Luxembourg, Switzerland (p175) and elsewhere, providing advice to refugees and migrants as well as engaging in public information, lobbying, education and research work. »94
✧ ≡ 20 place Auban-Moet, 51200 Epernay »90
✧ ≡ 12 rue Paul-Déroulède, 06000 Nice »90
✧ ≡ Haute-Savoie: 1 rue du Port, 74200 Thonon-les-Bains »90

✧ **Maison des Cultures du Monde**
Chérif Khaznadar: 101 boulevard Raspail, 75006 Paris; *t* (1) 4544 7230, *f* 4544 7660
Multicultural artistic and media activities. *L'Internationale de l'Imaginaire*. »94

✧ **Maison de Tous les Couleurs** *(House of All Colours)*
Wadad Zebib: [address uncertain] 53 rue Beaunier, 75014 Paris; *t* (1) 4543 2977 »90

● **Le Manifeste—contre le FN et le Nationalisme**
(Manifesto—against the National Front and Nationalism)
45 rue Rébeval, 75019 Paris; *t* (1) 4803 4848, *f* 4803 1186
Group opposing Le Pen's Front National and other ultra-right racist movements. »94

● *Mémoire Fertile* (Fertile Memory)
Abdelghani Ghalfi: 44 rue Traversière, 75012 Paris; *t* (1) 4345 1310
Represented in EU Migrants Forum, p131. »90

✧ **Migrations et Développement**, M&D
Lahoussain Jamal: 9 bis chemin des Violins, 05120 L'Argentière-la-Bessée; *t* 9223 0088, *f* 9223 0509
International and intercultural solidarity. »94

✧ **Mission pour le Développement des Echanges Méditerranéens**, MDEM
Claude Lasnel: 4 rue de la Visitation, 13004 Marseille; *t* 9134 0232, *f* 9185 4214
International cultural exchanges. *Echanges et Méditerranée* (6/yr). »94

◆ **Mouvement contre le Racisme et pour l'Amitié entre les Peuples**, MRAP *(Movement against Racism and for Friendship among Peoples)* Head Office
Mouloud Aounit/Michèle Ganem: 89 rue Oberkampf, 75543 Paris Cedex 11; *t* (1) 4806 8800, *f* 4806 8801
Anti-racist, anti-fascist movement; campaigns against xenophobia, hatred and violence, and for human rights, mutual respect, dignity and understanding. Advice and support to victims of discrimination. Many local committees. See also *Article 31*, p162. *Différences* (12/yr), *Droits et Libertés*. »95
✧ ≡ 11 rue de la Prairie, 92610 Antony »90
✧ ≡ PTT, 10 rue Renault, 33200 Bordeaux »90
✧ ≡ Domaine du Barros, 47200 Marcellus »90
✧ ≡ 27 boulevard Louis-Blanc, 34000 Montpellier »90
✧ ≡ BP 3161, 31027 Toulouse Cedex »90

✧ **Mouvement pour l'Egalité et contre le Racisme**, MER
3 square Lully, 51200 Epernay; *t* 2654 6081
Anti-racism, rights advice. »94

▌ **Mouvement international Aide à Toute Détresse—Quart Monde**, ATD *(International Fourth World Relief Movement)*
107 avenue du Général Leclerc, 95480 Pierrelaye; *t* (1) 3464 6963
Solidarity with the poorest and most excluded social groups in France and abroad; support and advice to migrants. »94

✧ **Objectif Tolérance**
Nord-Isère: 20 avenue du Bourg, 38300 Domarin
Centrist, progressive, anti-racist and integrationist. »89
✧ ≡ 108 rue de l'Aisne, 45160 Olivet »89

● **Peuples solidaires**, PSO *(Solidarity between Peoples)*
17 place de l'Argonne, 75019 Paris; *t* (1) 4035 1728, *f* 4035 0620
Through 90 member groups, promotes solidarity with the peoples of the South, and awareness of their human, social and economic rights. »93

● **Pieds noirs, Pieds blancs** *(White Feet, Black Feet)*
8 avenue Philippe-Auguste, 75011 Paris »89

- **Politis**
76 rue Villiers de l'Isle Adam, 75020 Paris; *t* (1) 4636 2424
Anti-racist journal. »90
✿ **Radio Amitié** *(Radio Friendship)*
BP 134, 25200 Bethoncourt; *t* 8192 9071, 8196 6066,
f 8196 6011
Location (1990): 16 rue L. da Vinci. Station is run by the
Association Radio Amitié. »94
✿ **Radio Gazelle—Association Rencontre Amitié**, ARA
Salah-Eddine Bariki: BP 2129, 13205 Marseille Cedex 01;
t 9191 6660 »90
✿ **Rencontre plurielle** *(Pluralist Encounter)*
50 avenue de Chennevières, 94420 Le Plessis-Trévise
Promotes dialogue between Maghrebi and European cultures,
social and cultural exchanges between French and immigrant
communities. »90
▌**Sennacieca Asocio Tutmundo**, SAT: Association Mondiale
Anational *(World Stateless Association)*
67 avenue Gambetta, 75020 Paris; *t* (1) 4797 8705,
f 4797 7190
'Stateless' meaning opposed to the concept of nationality,
rather than not being entitled to a citizenship. »94
- **Solidarité Développement Pair International** *(International
Development Twinning Solidarity)*
[address unknown] Paris
Development issues, especially connected with Lebanese
reconstruction. *Nouvelles de Liban*. »90
✿ **Solidarité aux Femmes d'ici et d'ailleurs**, Safia *(Local and
Foreign Women's Solidarity)*
Nadia Zouareg/Hassina Guerrouni: 32 rue de Rivoli, 59800
Lille; *t/f* 2056 2745 »95
✿ **SOS Ça Bouge**
Sidi Sella: 48 avenue Maréchal de Lattre de Tassigny,
93140 Bondy; *t* (1) 4849 0604, 4849 6739
Migrant solidarity; cultural/social activities, anti-racism. »94
▌**SOS-Racisme**: Head Office
14 cité Griset, 75011 Paris; *t* (1) 4806 4000, *f* 4355 9463
Nora Zaidi. French and international anti-racist movement,
with strong *beur* (second-generation immigrant) influence;
originally Socialist-aligned, later linked with Les Verts; see
Stop-Racisme, below, and similarly-named SOS bodies in
Spain, p174, Germany, p166-7, Switzerland, p175, Belgium
and Denmark, p161. The French movement offers legal
advice to migrants (Service juridique: Fidèle Martoux). »94
✿ ≡ SOSR 49, 5 rue Eugénie-Mansion, 49000 Angers »90
✿ ≡ Marne-la-Valée: LCR des Tilleuls, allée Voltaire, 77186
Noisiel »90
✿ **Stop-Racisme**
salle d'activité culturelle, avenue du Père-Sylvain-Giraud,
13510 Eguilles
Non-party political humanitarian action against racism. »89
✿ ≡ Faculté de Nice adhérente de SOS Racisme: M Cuturello:
résidence Fabron-Parc, 21 avenue de Fabron, 06200 Nice »89
✿ ≡ Val d'Ol-Yerres: 2 rue Marc-Sagnier, 91330 Yerres »89
- **Survival International France**
45 rue du Faubourg du Temple, 75010 Paris; *t* (1) 4241
4762, *f* 4245 3451
Support for threatened tribal minorities worldwide; public
information and education about indigenous peoples. »93
✿ **Texture**
32 rue Montaigne, 59000 Lille; *t* 2085 0232 »95
✿ **Trait d'Union**
Suzel Faizant: BP 567, 13492 Marseille; *t* 9134 0232,
f 9185 4214
Solidarity, welfare of Maghrebi and other migrants. »94
✿ **Trans-cultures**
3 passage de Castillon, Grazailles-la-Reille, 11000 Carcassonne
Second-generation integration, inter-cultural activity. »90
✿ **Urgence** *(Emergency)*
44 rue St-Georges, 69005 Lyon
Anti-fascist group. »90
▌**Simon Wiesenthal Center**
S. Samuels: 734 rue du Faubourg St Honoré, 75008 Paris
Research, documentation and campaign group working for
prosecution of Nazi war criminals. »91

GERMANY 49

✿ **Aktion Dritte Welt Saar**, A3W *(Saarland Third World Action)*
Weiskirchener Straße 24, 66674 Losheim; *t* (06872) 6982,
f 7826
International solidarity, multiculturalism, opposition to
racism and oppression. »94

✿ **Aktion Sühnezeichen/Friedensdienste**, ASF *(Symbolic
Reparation Initiative/Peace Service)*
B. Bergmeier Uwe: Jebenstraße 1, 10623 Berlin; *t* (030)
310261, *f* 312 4651
Anti-racism, human rights, refugee support, inter-cultural
contact. »94
- **Aktionsgemeinschaft Solidarische Welt**, ASW *(Action for
World Solidarity)*
Hedemannstraße 14, 10696 Berlin; *t* (030) 251 0265,
f 251 1887
International development assistance, solidarity; supports
peace and anti-racist movements, rights of indigenous and
minority groups; development education in Germany. »94
✿ **Amt für Multikulturelle Angelegenheiten**, AMKA
Barckhausstraße 1-3, 60325 Frankfurt am Main; *t* (069)
2123 8765, *f* 2123 7946
Public body promoting multiculturalism. »94
✿ **Antifa—Landeskoordination NRW** *(North Rhine-Westphalia
Anti-Fascist Co-ordination)*
Gathe 55, 42107 Wuppertal, Elberfeld; *t/f* (0202) 450629»94
- **Antifaschistische Aktion—Bundesweite Organisation**, AFA
(Anti-Fascist Action Federal Organisation)
c/o SpinnenNetz, Werderstraße 8, 65195 Wiesbaden;
t (0611) 440887, *f* 949 0751 »94
✿ ≡ c/o Buchladen, Rote Straße 10, 37073 Göttingen
Campaigns against fascist and racist activity. »94
✿ **Antifaschistische Bildungs-, Informations- und
Dokumentationszentrum**, ABIDOZ *(Anti-Fascist Education,
Information and Documentation Centre)*
Postfach 810146, Rothenburgerstraße 106, 90429
Nürnberg; *t* (0911) 288946
See also *Rabaz*, p167. »94
✿ *Antifaschistische Nachrichten* (Anti-Fascist News)
c/o GNN-Verlag, Postfach 260226, Zülpicherstraße 7,
50674 Köln; *t* (0221) 211658, *f* 215373
Anti-racist, anti-nazi magazine. »94
✿ *Antifaschistische Zeitung*, AFZE (Anti-Fascist Newspaper)
Schweffelstraße 6, 24118 Kiel »96
✿ *Antifaschistische Zeitung NRW* (North Rhine-Westphalia
Anti-Fascist News)
c/o Infoladen, Brunnenstraße 41, 42105 Wuppertal
Documents fascist and anti-fascist activity in NRW. »94
- *Antifaschistisches Info Blatt* (Anti-Fascist Information Paper)
also known as *Antifa-InfoBlatt*
c/o L. Meyer: Gneisenaustraße 2a, Mehringhof, 10961 Berlin
Tony Dempschung. Anti-racist, anti-fascist journal, German
and Turkish editions. Also publishes and distributes (as Antifa
Versand) anti-fascist booklets. Several other names, contact
addresses and telephone numbers are listed by the Dutch
centre, United (1994): unclear whether they are local contact
points, local versions, or a support organisation. These are:
antiFA c/o IV VdN, Chausseestraße 29, 10115 Berlin, *t* (030)
281 6094; Antifaschistisches Magazin c/o VVN/BdA, Boddin-
straße 64, 12053 Berlin, *t* 681 1975 or 686 6006, *f* 687
3099; Antifa-Kontaktstelle am AStA-FU, Kiebitzweg 23,
14195 Berlin, *t* 831 5844, *f* 831 4536. »96
✿ **Anti-Rassismus-Büro Bremen** *(Bremen Anti-Racism Bureau)*
Sielwall 38, 28203 Bremen; *t* (0421) 706444, *f* 706445
Anti-racism, anti-fascism, rights of refugees including
detainees on the notorious ship *Embrica Marcel*; its opposition
to deportations led to a police raid in January 1996. »96
✿ **Anti-Rassismus Informationszentrum Berlin**
[address unknown] Berlin
Research, information and documentation centre serving the
anti-racist movement; linked with ARIC in Holland, p170. »94
✿ **Anti-Rassismus Informationszentrum NordRhein-Westfalen**,
ARIC-NRW *(North Rhine-Westphalia Anti-Racism Information
Centre)*
Haus der Katholische Jugend, Grünstraße 4, 47051 Duisburg;
t (0203) 20249, *f* 287881
Research, information and documentation centre serving the
anti-racist movement and migrant and refugee groups; linked
with ARIC in Holland, p170. See also DISS, p236. »94
✿ **Antirassistisch-Interkulturelles Informationszentrum Berlin**,
ARIC *(Anti-Racist Intercultural Information Centre, Berlin)*
c/o Regionale Arbeitsstelle für Auslanderfragen,
Schumanstraße 5, 10117 Berlin; *t* (030) 282 3079, *f* 238
4303
Anti-racism, anti-fascism; advice and assistance to refugees
and migrants; cultural and social activities. »94
✿ *Antirassistische Initiative* (Anti-Racist Initiative)
Yorckstraße 59 HH, 10965 Berlin; *t* (030) 786 5917, *f* 786
9984
Human rights, anti-racist action; help line, AR Telefon;
publishing, ZAG Redaktion. Monitors racial violence. »95

✿ **Arbeitsgemeinschaft gegen internationale sexistische und rassistische Ausbeutung**, AGISRA *(Working Group on International Sexist and Racist Exploitation)*
Kasseler Straße 1a, 60486 Frankfurt am Main; *t* (069) 777755, *f* 777757 »94

✿ **Arbeitsgruppe SOS-Rassismus NRW** *(North Rhine-Westphalia SOS Racism Working Group)*
Haus Villigst, 58239 Schwerte; *t* (02304) 755190 »94

✿ **Ausländsgesellschaft Nordrhein-Westfalen** *(North Rhine-Westphalia International Society)*
Postfach 103334, Steinstraße 48, 44033 Dortmund; *t* (0231) 838 0014, 838 0000, *f* 838 0055
Anti-racism, multicultural education, youth welfare. »94

● **Ausschuß für Entwicklungsbezogene Bildung und Publizistik**, ABP *(Committee for Development Education and Journalism)*
Kniebisstraße 29, 70188 Stuttgart; *t* (0711) 925 7740
Foundation promoting international awareness and public education on development, migration, minorities, human rights and global issues. »94

✿ **Bonner Institut für Faschismus-Forschung und Anti-faschistische Aktion**, BIFF *(Bonn Institute for Research on Fascism and Anti-Fascist Action)*
Postfach 410108, 53023 Bonn »94

✿ *Die Brücke* (The Bridge)
Riottestraße 16, 66123 Saarbrücken; *t* (0681) 390 5850, *f* 817229
Multicultural magazine. »94

✿ **BUKO Arbeitsschwerpunkt Rassismus und Flüchtlings-politik** *(BUKO Special Working Group on Racism and Refugee Policy)*
c/o Infobüro Nicaragua, Postfach 101320, 42013 Wuppertal; *t* (0202) 300030, *f* 314346
Possibly a section of the Bundeskongress Entwicklungs-politischer Aktionsgruppen, BUKO, see p200. »94

✿ **Bund der Antifaschisten**, BdA *(Anti-Fascist League)*
Fröbelstraße 48, 04463 Großpösna; *t* (0341) 211 2711
Anti-racist and anti-fascist activity. »94

✿ **Buntstift** *(Crayons)*
Groner-Tor-Straße 31-32, 37073 Göttingen; *t* (0551) 46045, *f* 42858
Anti-racist, multicultural foundation. The name conveys (in German) the notion of 'many colours' and 'charitable foundation' (Stiftung). »94

● **Christlich-Islamische Begegnung Dokumentationsleitstelle**, CIBEDO *(Christian-Muslim Encounter Central Documentation Office)*
Hans Vöcking: Postfach 170427, Guiolettstraße 35, 60325 Frankfurt am Main; *t* (069) 726491, *f* 723052
Intercultural understanding, public education, research and documentation. *CIBEDO* (4/yr). »94

✿ **Cultur Cooperation**, CUCO
Nernstweg 32-34, 22765 Hamburg; *t* (040) 394133, *f* 390 9866
Promotion of inter-cultural exchange and understanding; see also BUKO, p200, and *IKA* magazine, p237. »94

✿ **Dachverband der Ausländischekulturvereine in Bremen e.V.**, DAB *(Umbrella Group of Foreigners' Cultural Societies in Bremen)*
Zeki Alptekin: Mosaik Kulturhaus, Schiffbauerweg 4, 28237 Bremen; *t* (0421) 613345, 612071, *f* 617950
Die Stimme. »94

● **Deutscher Volkshochschul-Verband**, DVV *(German Public High School Union)*
Obere Wilhelmstraße 32, 53225 Bonn
Research, promotion of multicultural education. See also the Pädagogische Arbeitsstelle, in the Institut für Erwachsenen-bildung, p237. »94

◆ **Deutsches Komitee der Jugendkampagne des Europarates**: German Committee of the Council of Europe Youth Campaign
Andrea Lummert: Haager Weg 44, 53127 Bonn; *t* (0228) 910 2131, *f* 910 2122
National organising committee for events within the Council of Europe Youth Campaign against Racism, p197. Led by Deutscher Bundesjugendring, p200. »95

✿ **Dritte Welt Haus Bielefeld**, DWH *(Bielefeld Third World House)*
August-Bebel-Straße 62, 33602 Bielefeld; *t* (0521) 62802, *f* 63789
Multicultural, anti-racist centre; refugee support. »94

● **Edelweiss-Piraten**
Gneisenaustraße 2a, Mehringhof, 10961 Berlin
Anti-racist youth group linked with *AntiFa InfoBlatt*, p165.»94

✿ **Eine Welt für alle** *(One World for All)*
Adenauerallee 37, 53113 Bonn; *t/f* (0228) 267 9818
Anti-racist, multicultural internationalist movement. »94

✿ **Europa-Bro**
Jannis Sakellariou: Oberanger 38/1 V, 8000 München 2 »90

● **Europäisches Bürgerforum**: European Civic Forum: Forum Civique Européen
Postfach 102, 1026 Berlin
Anti-racist, anti-nationalist group founded 1990, associated with the CEDRI movement; see also in France, p163, Austria, p159 and Switzerland, p175. »92

▌ **Europe at School**
Bachstraße 32, 53115 Bonn; *t* (0228) 729 0040, *f* 695734
Promotes cultural exchange, multicultural education in European schools. »94

● **European Youth Exchange**, EYE
Dr-Külz-Straße 4, 01445 Radebeul; *t/f* (0351) 74684 »94

✿ **Farbe Bekennen—Eine grün-offene Initiative in NRW** *(Showing our Colours—A Green/Non-Party Initiative in NRW)*
Volksgartenstraße 35, 40227 Düsseldorf; *t* (0211) 770080, *f* 726550
Multicultural anti-racist social and campaigning group in North Rhine-Westphalia. »94

✿ **FIJD** *(Dachau International Youth Centre?)*
S. Stadler: Zur Alten Schiesstatt 1, 8060 Dachau »91

● **Forum Buntes Deutschland—SOS Rassismus** *(Multicoloured Germany Forum—SOS Racism)*
Postfach 2644, 53016 Bonn; *t* (0228) 213061, *f* 262978
Campaigns on racism, fascism and nationalism; for migrant, minority and refugee rights. See SOS Rassismus, p167. »94

✿ **Frauen in der Einen Welt**
Meral Akkent: Bulmannstraße 31, 8500 Nürnberg 40; *t* (0911) 455653
Women's enterprise, training, research, education. »90

✿ **Friedenszentrum Martin-Niemöller-Haus** *(Niemöller House Peace Centre)*
Pacelliallee 61, 1000 Berlin 33; *t* (030) 832 5497, *f* 831 6153
International solidarity, development education, anti-racism, support for refugee rights. »93

● **Germanwatch**
Reifenbergerstraße 26, 53227 Bonn; *t* (0228) 440343
Monitors racist and neo-fascist activity. »94

● **Gesellschaft für bedrohte Völker**, GbV: Society for Threatened Peoples: Association pour les peuples ménacés: Asociación para la defensa de los pueblos amenazados
Robin Schneider/Annelore Hermes: Postfach 2024, 37073 Göttingen; *t* (0551) 499060, 499066, 55822, 55823, *f* 58028
Office location listed (1994) as Düstere Straße 20a or Gronerstraße 40. Campaign group for the survival of tribal and other minority groups worldwide; see also in Luxembourg, p169, Austria, p159. *Mayday* (6/yr), *Pogrom* (6/yr). »94

✿ **Haus der Kulturen der Welt** *(House of World Cultures)*
John-Foster-Dulles-Allee 10, 1000 Berlin 21; *t* (030) 394031
Cultural centre, exhibitions, conferences. »90

● **Ideen für antirassistische und antifaschistische Arbeit** *(Ideas for Anti-Racist and Anti-Fascist Work)*
c/o ASF, Hauptstraße 2, 38154 Königslutter
Resource for anti-racist education and campaigning. *Ideen*.»94

✿ **Informations, Dokumentations und Aktionszentrum für eine multikulturelle Zukunft**, IDA *(Information, Documentation and Action Centre for a Multicultural Future)*
Charlottenstraße 55, 40210 Düsseldorf; *t* (0211) 164 9432, *f* 351326
Anti-racism, anti-fascism, migrant and refugee rights. »94

✿ **Initiative Antirassistische Politik** *(Anti-Racist Policy Initiative)*
[address uncertain] Postfach 443, 09004 Chemnitz »95

● **Institut für Kulturelle Weiterbildung** *(Institute for Cultural Exchange)*
Dr Rose Haferkamp: Postfach 101193, Stammstraße 90, 5000 Köln 30; *t* (0221) 519500, *f* 525882
Intercultural exchange, development education; integration assistance for migrants in Germany and abroad; co-operation with similar organisations in other European countries. »93

✿ **Interkulturelles Projekt Babylon** *(Babylon Multicultural Project)*
Weißenhöher Straße 73-89, 12683 Berlin; *t* (030) 524 3940, *f* 524 9214
Multicultural centre; anti-racist, anti-nazi activities; migrant and refugee support; social and cultural activities. »94

▌ **International Christian Youth Exchange**, ICYE, International Office
Goethe Straße 85-87, 10623 Berlin; *t* (030) 428 3214, *f* 428 3215 »94

● **International Communication Project**
c/o AStA, Universität Hannover, Welfengarten 1, 30167 Hannover; *t* (0511) 762 5061, *f* 717441
Newsletter. »94

- **Internationale Begegnung in Gemeinschaftsdiensten, IBG**
(*International Encounter in Community Service*)
Schloßerstraße 28, 70180 Stuttgart; *t* (0711) 649 0263,
f 640 9867
Multicultural, anti-racist group.   »94
- ✿ **Internationale Initiative Hochfeld, IIH**
Karoline Steiger: Immendal 29, 47053 Duisburg; *t* (0203)
69595
Migrant rights; welfare work. *Arbeitsbericht* (1/yr).   »94
- **Internationale Solidaritätsfonds von Bündnis 90/Die Grünen**
(*Green Party International Solidarity Fund*)
Postfach 1227, 53309 Bornheim; *t* (0221) 249394
Supports anti-racist, anti-fascist, human rights, development
education and international solidarity work.   »94
- ✿ **Internationaler Arbeitskreis Sonnenberg** (*Sonnenberg International Working Group*)
Internationales Haus Sonnenberg, Postfach 2654, 38016
Braunschweig; *t* (0531) 49242, *f* 42512
Anti-racism, migrants' rights. Organised 1993 European
conference on these issues.   »94
- ✿ **Internationaler Kulturkreis Moers, IKM** (*Moers International Cultural Circle*)
Tullio Virdis: Kirschenallee 35, 47443 Moers; *t* (02841)
504564, *f* 2215
Social, cultural and welfare group for Italian and other
migrant workers.   »94
- ✿ **Internationales Begegungszentrum Friedenshaus, IBZ**
(*Peace House International Encounter Centre*)
Teutoburgerstraße 106, 33607 Bielefeld; *t* (0521) 69874,
f 170121
Multicultural meeting place, migrant and refugee resource
centre.   »94
- ✿ **Internationales Bildungs- und Begegnungswerk, IBB**
(*International Education and Encounter Initiative*)
Reinoldistraße 2-4, 44135 Dortmund; *t* (0231) 952 0960,
f 521233
Anti-racist, multicultural education.   »94
- **IVVdN**
K.J. Goldstein: Chausseestrasse 29, 1040 Berlin
Represented at European anti-racist conference (1991), no
further information. International arm of VVN-BdA, right? »91
- **Jugend gegen Rassismus in Europa—Deutsche Sektion,**
JRE (*Youth against Racism in Europe—German Section*)
Postfach 300629, 50776 Köln; *t* (0221) 811886, *f* 137280
Socialist youth anti-racist, anti-fascist movement.   »94
- **Junge Europäische Föderalisten Deutschlands, JEF**
(*European Federalist Youth—Germany*)
Berliner Platz 1, 53111 Bonn; *t* (0228) 639328, *f* 694984»94
- **Komitee für eine Welt** (*One World Committee*)
Eberhardshofstr. 20, 90429 Nürnberg; *t* (0911) 666867   »94
- ✿ **Kontakt International Magdeburg** (*Magdeburg International Contact*)
Breiter Weg 250, 39104 Magdeburg; *t* (0391) 33102
Anti-racism, refugee concerns.   »94
- ✿ **Mahnwache Deutzer Brücke**
Deutzer Werft, 50679 Köln; *t* (0221) 810264, *f* 885371
Anti-nationalist, anti-racist group; refugee rights.   »94
- **Medien gegen Rassismus** (*Media against Racism*)
c/o RTL TV, Aachener Straße 1036, 50858 Köln; *t* (0221)
456 2752, *f* 456 4290   »94
- ✿ **Millerntor Roar! Antifaschistische Fußball-Fans**
Thadenstraße 94, 22767 Hamburg; *t* (040) 439 6961,
f 430 5119
Anti-nazi football fans' group.   »94
- ✿ **Morgengrauen** (*Daybreak*)
c/o SoZ Verlag, Dasselstrasse 75-77, 50674 Köln;
t (0221) 211555, *f* 214137
Anti-racist, anti-nazi magazine, also serving migrant and
refugee communities.   »94
- ✿ **Nationale Mahn- und Gedenkstätte Buchenwald**
(*Buchenwald National Memorial and Warning Centre*)
F. Seidel/U. Schneider: 5301 Buchenwald
Anti-fascist memorial and educational centre based at the
former Nazi concentration camp.   »91
- ✿ **Netzwerk gegen Gewalt und Rassismus** (*Network against Violence and Racism*)
Breite Str. 15, 14467 Potsdam; *t* (0331) 21454, *f* 27548»94
- **Partei des Demokratisches Sozialismus—Arbeitsgemein-schaft Antirassismus, PDS** (*Party of Democratic Socialism Anti-Racist Working Group*)
Kleine Alexanderstraße 28, 10178 Berlin; *t* (030) 2840 9447,
f 2840 9310
Anti-racist, anti-fascist policy development and action group
within one of the main socialist parties. Also deals with
migration and refugee issues.   »94

- ✿ **Projekt Multikulturelle Feministische Bildungsarbeit**
(*Multi-Cultural Feminist Development Project*)
Toksöz Gulay: Kienstraße 111, 1000 Berlin 44
Group for German and immigrant women.   »90
- ✿ ***Rabaz***
[address unknown] Nürnberg
Local anti-fascist magazine; linked with ABIDOZ, p165?   »96
- **Referendum Doppelte Staatsbürgerschaft** (*Dual Citizenship Referendum Campaign*)
Oranienstraße 25, 10969 Berlin; *t* (030) 6150 0536,
f 6150 0599
Campaign for full voting and civil rights for foreign-born
residents, and for entitlement to German nationality without
the requirement to renounce the original citizenship.   »94
- ✿ **Rheinisch Westfälische Auslöndsgesellschaft und Auslandsinstitut** (*Rhine-Westphalia International Society and Institute*)
[address uncertain] Prinz Friedrich-Karl-Straße 38, 4600
Dortmund   »90
- ✿ ***Schwarzer Faden*** (Black Threads)
Postfach 1159, 71117 Grafenau; *t* (07033) 44273, *f* 45264
Anti-racist journal.   »94
- ✿ **Solinger Appell** (*Solingen Appeal*)
Werwolf 57a, 42651 Solingen; *t* (0212) 200740, *f* 12404
Migrant and minority rights campaign group.   »94
- ✿ **SOS Rassismus—Berlin** (*SOS Racism, Berlin*)
Haus der Demokratie, Friedrichstraße 165, 10117 Berlin;
t (030) 200 2540, *f* 609 3721
Also known as Bürgerinitiative SOS-Rassismus. Anti-racist,
anti-fascist work; legal and practical assistance to migrants
and refugees. Branches, including (1991) c/o J. del Pozo/E.
Stiesch, Rotlindtstraße 58, 6000 Frankfurt 1; and Steinbach.
See also Forum Buntes Deutschland—SOS Rassismus, p166.»94
- **Stiftung Umverteilen** (*Fair Shares Foundation*)
Mehringdamm 50, 10961 Berlin; *t* (030) 785 9844, *f* 786
5224
Funds anti-racist work, and assistance to migrants and
refugees.   »94
- ✿ **Stop Rassismus** (*Stop Racism*)
Borriesstraße 28, 30519 Hannover; *t* (0551) 838 7177
Human rights, anti-racist and anti-fascist campaigns in Hanover
and district.   »94
- ✿ **Stoppt Nazi-Zeitungen** (*Anti-Nazi Press*)
c/o Le Sabot Nr. 7, Breite Straße 76, 53111 Bonn
Youth-oriented anti-fascist media group.   »94
- ✿ **SUSI Interkulturelles Frauenzentrum** (*SUSI Multicultural Women's Centre*)
Monbijouplatz 4, 10178 Berlin; *t* (030) 282 6627, *f* 208 8367
Anti-racist, multi-ethnic women's centre; campaigns, meetings,
resources.   »94
- ✿ ***Thüringer Antifa Nachrichten*** (Thuringian Anti-Fascist News)
c/o Joseph Grüne, Eislebenerstraße 3-71, 99086 Erfurt;
t (0361) 673 8293
Local anti-racist journal.   »94
- ✿ **Verein Menschen in der Stadt, VMS** (*Civic Communities*)
Doris Schäfer: Textorstraße 15, 97070 Würzburg; *t* (0931)
18644-45, *f* 57835
Organisation promoting solidarity with migrants and refugees,
intercultural contact.   »94
- ♦ **Vereinigung der Verfolgten des Naziregimes/Bund der Antifaschisten, VVN-BdA** (*Union of Victims of the Nazi Regime/Anti-Fascist League*)
Frauenlobstraße 24/1, 80337 München; *t* (089) 535533,
f 538 9464
Anti-fascist group; VVN was originally for concentration camp
survivors, but now has a broader anti-racist agenda. Branches
elsewhere including (1991) c/o E. Bejarano, Brödermannsweg
73a, 2000 Hamburg 61; c/o P. Gingold, Reichsforststraße 3,
6000 Frankfurt 71.   »94
- ✿ **Werkstatt 3** (*Workshop 3*)
Nernsberg 32-34, 22765 Hamburg; *t* (040) 392191, *f* 390
9866   »96
- **WIR—Forum für ein besseres Verständnis zwischen Deutschen und Ausländern, WIR e.V.** (*Forum for Better Understanding between Germans and Foreigners*)
Elsa-Brandström-Straße 6, 50667 Köln; *t* (0221) 739·3730,
f 735070
Intercultural and antiracist work. Also in Bonn?   »94
- ▌**Youth for Exchange and Understanding, YEU**
Kirchfeldstraße 85, 40215 Düsseldorf; *t/f* (0211) 333946
Promotes international, intercultural youth exchange
programmes through a network of affiliated groups.   »94
- ✿ ***ZAP***
Postfach 1007, 66441 Bexbach; *t* (06826) 81572, *f* 6047
Magazine with anti-racist, anti-fascist content.   »94

GREECE 30

♦ **Citizens' Movement Against Racism**
Costas Protakis: c/o Prof. M. Stathopoulos, Odos Ippokratous 33, 10680 Athinai; *t* (01) 360 5388, *f* 363 9640   »94
● **Cross-Cultural Association**
c/o Zoe Loukopoulos: Idomeneos 23, Nea Liossa, 13122 Athinai   »94
♦ **SOS Ratsismos** *(SOS Racism)*
Yannis Ferris: Odos Emmanuel Benaki 6, 10564 Athinai; *t* (01) 325 0665
Human rights, anti-racist and anti-fascist campaigns, defence of migrants and refugees.   »94

HUNGARY 36

● **Antifasiszta Akció, AFA** *(Anti-Fascist Action)*
Postafiok 13, 1360 Budapest
Anti-racist, anti-nazi campaigns.   »94
● **Fédération Internationale des Résistants, FIR** *(International Federation of Resisters)*
E. Lakatos: Radneti Miklos U 34, 1134 Budapest   »91
✧ **Hungarian Federation of Resisters and Antifascists, HFRAF**
Postafiok 38, Szabadsag ter 16, 1363 Budapest V; *t* (01) 118844
Anti-fascist veterans' organisation.   »94
✧ **Martin Luther King Organization, MLKO**
Zsombolyai útca 3, 1113 Budapest; *t/f* (01) 135 6865
Anti-racism, anti-fascism; migrant and refugee rights.   »94

IRELAND 353

● **Action from Ireland**
Joe Murray: The Cottage, 63 Harold's Cross Road, Dublin 6W; *t* (01) 496 6880, *f* 496 6388
Peace, human rights, development education; interest in refugee issues. *Peacemaker* (3/yr).   »95
● **Anti-Nazi League, ANL**
[address unknown] Dublin
Anti-racist, anti-fascist group linked with UK ANL, p176. »95
● **Comhlámh,** Association of Returned Development Workers
10 Upper Camden Street, Dublin 2; *t* (01) 478 3490
Development education/third world support group. Global solidarity, human rights, anti-racism, anti-sexism. *Focus on Ireland and the Wider World* (3/yr).   »95
✧ **Dublin Anti-Fascist Action, AFA**
PO Box 3355, Dublin 7
Monitors and combats fascist and racist activity.   »94
♦ **Harmony**
Tony Ffrench, Chairperson: 41 Morehampton Road, Donnybrook, Dublin 4; *t* (01) 490 6196
Phil Lawlor secretary, Rebecca Rahman PR officer. Founded 1986. Promotes inter-ethnic understanding, equality and goodwill. Cultural and anti-racist activities, media monitoring. Campaigns for legal action against racial discrimination and incitement to hatred. Newsletter (irregular).   »95
✧ **Das Haus—La Maison—The House**
356 South Circular Road, Dublin 8
Multicultural centre; newsletter of the same name.   »94
● *Ireland and the Wider World*
John Walsh: 55 Grand Parade, Cork; *t* (021) 275881
Journal (4/yr) on foreign affairs, economic development, politics and culture, and on Irish affairs from a global perspective. Superseded by *Focus*: see Comhlámh, above?»94
● **Refugee Trust,** also known as Irish Refugee Trust; formerly Refugee Year Trust
Rev. Norman Fitzgerald CSSp, National Director: 4 Dublin Road, Stillorgan, Co. Dublin; *t* (01) 283 4256
Bro. Tom O'Grady. Founded 1989; emergency relief and long-term assistance to refugees and displaced people in Africa, Bosnia, Turkey, especially disabled, elderly, women, children. Public education, seminars, newsletter (4/yr).   »96
♦ **Trocaire** *(Mercy, literally; only the Irish name is used)*
Andy Storey: 169 Booterstown Avenue, Blackrock, Co. Dublin; *t* (01) 288 5385, *f* 288 3577
Catholic development aid, refugee relief, and development education charity; international and intercultural solidarity. *One World* (6/yr), *Development Review* (1/yr).   »94

ITALY 39

✧ **Arco IRIS**
Stefano Panzetta: c/o ACLI, via Ferrari 9, 22100 Como; *t* (031) 304880, *f* 305180
Anti-racism, solidarity, social activities.   »94
● **Associazione Culturale Assistenza Popolare, ACAP** *(Popular Welfare Cultural Association)* also known as Comunità San Egidio
Dra Milena Santerini: Comunità San Egidio, piazza San Egidio 3a, 00153 Roma; *t* (06) 589 5945, 580 3548, 581 3053, *f* 580 0197
Solidarity with migrants; training, employment, welfare, legal and housing issues. Books, other publications; a member of the EU Migrants Forum, p131.   »95
✧ **Associazione Interculturale Soweto**
Angelo Proto: via XXI Aprile 2, 00042 Anzio, RM; *t* (06) 983 1237, *f* 984 8392
Anti-racism, international solidarity.   »94
✧ **Associazione Interetnica Shangrillà** *(Shangri La Inter-Ethnic Association)*
Adel Jabbar: via S. Francesco d'Assisi 1a, 38100 Trento; *t* (0461) 237787, *f* 230397
Anti-racism, multiculturalism, refugees; *Colori* (12/yr).   »94
● **Associazione Nazionale Ex-Deportati Politici nei Campi Nazisti, ANED** *(National Association of Ex-Deportees from the Nazi Camps)*
T. Ducci: via Bagutta 12, 20121 Milano; *t* (02) 790637
Anti-fascist association of concentration camp survivors; shares address with several immigrant groups.   »94
✧ **Associazione Stop Razzismo**
Giancarlo Brunatto: via Ugo Bassi 2, 20159 Milano   »94
✧ **Centro Culturale Internazionale Giovanni XXIII** *(Pope John XXIII International Cultural Centre)*
Lungo Tevere dei Vallati 1, via del Conservatorio 1, 00185 Roma; *t* (06) 686 4460, 686 1019   »90
✧ **Centro di documentazione contro il razzismo—Gridalo Forte** *(Shout it Out Anti-Racist Documentation Centre)*
via dei Sabelli 18, 00185 Roma; *t/f* (06) 445 0615
Anti-racist, anti-fascist research, documentation and campaigning centre.   »94
● **Centro Informazione e Educazione allo Sviluppo, CIES** *(Centre for Information and Education on Development)*
via Palermo 36, 00184 Roma; *t* (06) 474 6246, *f* 486419
Development education and Third World solidarity work in Italy; financial and material aid for development/emergency relief projects, including work with refugees; migrant and refugee advice in Italy.   »93
✧ **Centro per Iniziative Popolari di Solidarietà Internazionale, CISPI** *(Centre for Popular Initiatives in International Solidarity)*
Rosario Lembo: via F. Baldelli 41, 00146 Roma; *t* (06) 541 4894, 541 5730, *f* 5960 0533
Research and documentation centre; anti-racism, international solidarity. *Solidarietà internazionale* (4/yr).   »94
✧ **Centro Internazionale Crocevia, CIC** *(Crossroads International Centre)*
Antonio Onorati: via F. Ferraironi 88 G, 00172 Roma; *t* (06) 241 3976, *f* 242 4177
International solidarity, development education. *Territorio* (4/yr), *Risorse* (4/yr).   »94
✧ **Centro Multiculturale Internazionale**
Giuseppe Spedicato: via Nicola Cataldi 34, 73100 Lecce; *t* (0832) 315519, *f* 315606
Advice service, solidarity. May be the same as the Centro Informazione Terzo Mondo, CTM, listed (1993) at via Nicola Cataldi 21.   »94
✧ **Centro di Solidarietà San Martino, CDS**
Walter Izzo: via Giovanni della Casa 19, 20151 Milano; *t* (02) 3801 0589, *f* 3801 0789
Migrant and refugee health and welfare.   »94
✧ **Centro Sviluppo Terzo Mondo, CESVITEM** *(Third World Development Centre)*
via L. Mariutto 36, 30035 Mirano, VE; *t/f* (041) 570 0843
Development education, support for development and relief projects in the Third World; advice to migrants in Italy.   »93
✧ **Circolo Terzo Mondo, CTM** *(Third World Circle)*
Giovanni Giusti: via XX Settembre 47, 55045 Pietrasanta; *t/f* (0584) 792769
International solidarity.   »94
● **Comitato Italiano per l'UNICEF**
via Ippolito Nievo 61, 00153 Roma; *t* (06) 588971, *f* 589 9334
Development education, fundraising for UNICEF, p219.   »93

✿ **Comitato Chico Mendes**
Andrea Panzavolta: via G. Guidarelli 7, 48100 Ravenna;
t (0544) 404626, 414188
Third World solidarity and development education group.
Prospettive Nord-Sud. »94

♦ **Conferenza Permanente per l'Uguaglianza Razziale in
Europa**: Standing Conference for Racial Equality in Europe,
SCORE
via Farini 16, 00185 Roma; *t* (06) 488 1010
Pressure group for non-racist immigration policies and
promotion of race equality in EU; see SCORE (UK), p184. »94

✿ **Cooperativa Proficua**
Lucy Resischel Rojas: via Bagutta 12, 20121 Milano;
t/f (02) 780811
Migrant women's collective. »94

● **Cooperazione Internazionale**, COOPI
via De Lemene 50, 20151 Milano; *t* (02) 308 4856, 308
5057, *f* 3340 3570
Funding and volunteer personnel for development and relief
projects in the South, including refugee aid in Somalia; aid to
African migrants in Italy, including housing, employment and
training advice and repatriation assistance. »93
✿ ≡ Felice Spingola: via G. de Chirico 217, 87030 Saporito
Dirende; *t* (0984) 462052, *f* 461554
International solidarity. »94

● **Cooperazione per lo Sviluppo dei Paesi Emergenti**, COSPE
(Development Co-operation for Emerging Countries)
Luciana Sassatelli, President: via della Colonna 25, 50121
Firenze; *t* (055) 234 6511, *f* 234 6514
International and intercultural solidarity, development of
popular organisations in the South, development education,
human rights, aid to refugees in Africa/Latin America. »94

● **Cooperazione Terzo Mondo**, CTM *(Third World Co-operation)*
Heinrich Grandi: via Marcello 18, 39100 Bolzano; *t* (0471)
975333, *f* 977599
International solidarity, development education. *L'Altro
Mercato* (6/yr). »94

● **Coordinamento di Iniziative Popolari di Solidarietà
Internazionale**, CISPI
via Ferdinando Baldelli 41, 00146 Roma; *t* (06) 541 4894,
f 5960 0533
Development education, training, co-ordination of 24 Italian
NGOs working on (mainly African) development issues. »93

● **Eurocultura**
via A. Rossi 7, 36100 Vicenza; *t* (0444) 964770, *f* 567682
Inter-cultural contact and understanding. »94

● **Gruppo di Volontariato Civile**, GVC *(Civilian Volunteering
Group)*
Villa Aldini, via dell'Osservanza 35/2, 40136 Bologna;
t (051) 585604, *f* 582225
Volunteers for development and relief projects in Africa,
the Middle East and Latin America, including refugee aid;
language training, welfare of migrants in Italy. »93

✿ **Istituto di Cooperazione Economica Internazionale**, ICEI
Luisa Lanzanuova, Director: via Salvini 3, 20122 Milano;
t (02) 784723, 799144, *f* 7600 0101
International/intercultural solidarity, development education,
information and documentation on ethnic minorities, North-
South issues. *Tam-Tam* (4/yr). »94

♦ **Italia Razzismo** *(Racism Italy)*
[address uncertain] via del Corso 173, 00186 Roma;
t (06) 679 7441
Also listed (1994) at via del Parlamento 9, 00186 Roma;
t (06) 6760 9325. Anti-racist and migrant rights campaign,
linked with magazine *Nero e non solo*, below. Same as SOS
Razzismo, right? »94

● **Lega Internazionale per i Diritti e la Liberazione dei Popoli**,
LIDLIP *(International League for the Rights and Freedom of
Peoples)* Ligue Internationale pour les Droits et la Libération
des Peuples
Luciano Ardesi, Secretary: Fondazione Lelio Basso, via della
Dogana Vecchia 5, 00186 Roma; *t* (06) 686 4640, *f* 333
6732
International solidarity, social and economic justice, human
rights worldwide, anti-racism, migrant and refugee issues.
See also the Ligue in Switzerland, p175. *UNACT* (3/yr). »94
✿ ≡ pza Campeto 7/4a, 16123 Genova; *t* (010) 291493 »90

✿ **Mondo Unico** *(One World)*
Pablo Salazar/Abucar Moallim: c/o COSPE, via della Colonna
25, 50121 Firenze; *t* (055) 247 9587, 234 6511, *f* 234 6514
Global solidarity, migrant welfare; see COSPE, above. »94

✿ **Nero e non Solo!** (Black and not Alone!)
via dei Mille 23, 00185 Roma; *t* (06) 446 5455, *f* 446 5934
Magazine for migrant, refugee and anti-racist movements.
See also CISM-ARCI, p144, and Italia Razzismo, above. »94

✿ **Nero e non Solo! Bologna** (Black and not Alone! Bologna)
c/o ANPPIA, via Rizzoli 9, 40125 Bologna; *t* (051) 291274,
f 291290
Regional office (or edition?) of the anti-racist journal. »94

♦ **Osservatorio Nazionale sulla Xenofobia**, ONX *(National
Monitoring Office on Xenophobia)*
Aster Carpanelli/Mauro Valeri: Forum delle Comunità
Straniere in Italia, via Conteverde 58, 00185 Roma; *t* (06)
446 7676, *f* 678 1182
Also listed (1994) at via Arenula 21, 00186 Roma; *t*
687503, *f* 686 7495. Monitors and analyses racial attacks
and other manifestations of hostility towards foreigners and
minorities. *ONX News* (6/yr). »94

✿ **Progetto Domani—Cultura e Sviluppo**, ProDoCS
(Tomorrow Project on Culture and Development)
Dr Anna Maria Donnarumma, President: via Etruria 14 c,
00183 Roma; *t* (06) 708 1171-72, *f* 700 3710
International solidarity, multiculturalism, co-operation with
development projects in Latin America. Journal *Cultura e
Solidarietà* (4/yr). »94

● **Solidarietà Nomade** *(Traveller Solidarity)*
Dr Susanna Placidi: piazza S. Egidio 3, 00153 Roma; *t* (06)
580 6883
An initiative of the Comunità San Egidio. Anti-racism,
solidarity with migrants and minorities. »90
✿ ≡ Luciano Rosasco: piazza San Bernardo 30/1, 16123
Genova; *t* (010) 208712-82, *f* 203764 »94

♦ **SOS Razzismo—Italia** *(SOS Racism—Italy)*
via del Leone 13, 00186 Roma; *t* (06) 482 0965, *f* 687
5184
Anti-racist, anti-fascist, migrant rights campaign group. See
also Italia Razzismo, left. »94

LUXEMBOURG *352*

● **Action Solidarité Tiers Monde**, ASTM *(Third World Solidarity
Action)* and Centre d'Information Tiers Monde, CITMI
39 rue du Fort Niepperg, 2230 Luxembourg; *t* 400427

● **Association Luxembourgeoise pour les Nations Unies**, ALNU
(Luxembourg United Nations Association)
99 route d'Arlon, 1140 Luxembourg; *t* 454606
Also listed (1994) at 5 rue Notre Dame, 2240 Luxembourg;
t 478248. Promotes the principles of the United Nations in
respect of international relations, human rights, peace and
other matters. General interest in refugee problems. »95

● **Commission Diocésaine pour la Pastorale Intercommun-
autaire**, CDPI
Renato Cescutti: 5 avenue Marie-Thérèse, Centre Convict,
2132 Luxembourg; *t* 447432 01-03, *f* 447451
Catholic migrant and refugee solidarity organisation. See
SESOPI and CPMT, both p145. »94

● **Fédération des Victimes du Nazisme Enrolées de Force**
5 rue de la Déportation, 1415 Luxembourg; *t* 48232
Represents wartime forced labour survivors. »95

● **Iwerliewen fir Bedreete Volleker**: Society for Threatened
Peoples: Société pour les Peuples Menacés: Gesellschaft für
bedrohte Völker
A. Rollinger: 1 rue Heldestein, 1723 Luxembourg; *t* 403291,
f 405849
National affiliate of German-based organisation, p166,
campaigning for tribal and minority peoples. »93

✿ **Pädagogik der Gastarbeiter Kinder** *(Education of Migrant
Workers' Children)*
Karl Glocknerstraße 21, haus B, 5400 Gessen
Multicultural training for teachers of immigrant children. »90

♦ **SOS Racisme**
Mme Pastove: BP 2443, 1024 Luxembourg; *t* 572134,
482965
Anti-racist campaign group. »94

● **Union Européenne des Fédéralistes** *(European Federalists
Union)*
Vittorio Cidone: 16 avenue du Grand-Duc Jean, 1842
Howald; *t* 43013 2954, *f* 43013 4129 »94

NETHERLANDS *31*

● **AFS Interculturele Programma's**
Marnixkade 65a, 1015 XW Amsterdam; *t* (020) 626 9481
Study and work placements abroad for young people.
Possibly linked to AFSIU in Sweden, p175? »94

▌ Anne Frank Stichting, AFS: Anne Frank Foundation
Jan Erik Dubbelman, international office: Postbus 730,
1000 AS Amsterdam; *t* (020) 556 7100, *f* 620 7999
Major anti-racist institution founded to commemorate a
young victim of the Nazi occupation; museum at Anne Frank
Huis (Prinsengracht 263-265), events, seminars. Operates
worldwide with a travelling exhibition and sister organisations
in several countries. Promotes anti-racist and anti-fascist
work, and initiatives combatting discrimination, intolerance
and prejudice of all kinds. Publishing, advice on educational
and training materials, library, documentation centre. »94

✿ **Anti-Discriminatie Bureau**, ADB: Amersfoort *(Amersfoort
Anti-Discrimination Bureau)*
Soesterweg 9, 3812 AA Amersfoort, Utrecht; *t/f* (033) 463
8070
Local agency handling all types of discrimination cases,
including race and sex; legal advice, advocacy, referrals to
specialist services. The other ADBs listed below provide
similar services; some are part-time or voluntarily run, but
most, including ADB Amersfoort, have professional staff. »95
✿ ≡ Amsterdam: Vijzelstraat 77-11, 1017 HG Amsterdam;
t (020) 638 5551, *f* 620 1401 »94
✿ ≡ Amsterdam-Noord: Hagendoornplein 11, 1031 BV
Amsterdam; *t* (020) 637 0737, *f* 632 2139 »94
✿ ≡ Arnhem: Sonsbeeksingel 151a, 6822 BM Arnhem;
t (026) 443 0903 »95
✿ ≡ Dronten: and Stichting de Schoof: Postbus 9, 8250 AA
Dronten, Flevoland; *t* (0321) 316266, *f* 310080
Location: Vooronder 2, 8251 XD Dronten. »95
✿ ≡ Ede: Postbus 8028, 6710 AA Ede, Gelderland; *t* (0313)
441616, *f* 440753 (?) »95
✿ ≡ Enschede/Twente: Espoorstraat 7, 7511 CD Enschede,
Overijssel; *t* (053) 430 2299
The other ADB serving the Enschede-Hengelo conurbation is
the ADB Hengelo/Twente, at Schalkburgerstraat 25, 7551
GS Hengelo, *t* (074) 242 4848. »95
✿ ≡ Gouda: Postbus 1086, 2800 BB Gouda; *t* (0182)
588100, *f* 588464
Location: Agnietenstraat 24, Gouda. »95
✿ ≡ Groningen: Postbus 929, 9700 AX Groningen; *t* (050)
312 6212
Location: Oude Ebbingestraat 6c, 9712 HH Groningen. »95
✿ ≡ Haarlem: Postbus 284, 2000 AG Haarlem; *t* (023) 531
5842
Location: Bakenessergracht 8, Haarlem. »95
✿ ≡ Heerlen: Postbus 3, 6400 AA Heerlen, Zuid-Limburg;
t (045) 571 8501 »95
✿ ≡ Hilversum: Neuweg 31, 1211 LV Hilversum; *t* (035)
621 6985 »95
✿ ≡ Maastricht: Cortenstraat 4, 6211 HT Maastricht;
t (043) 325 0938, *f* 325 1505 »95
✿ ≡ Meppel: Weerdstraat 78, 7941 XH Meppel; *t* (0522)
252789, *f* 251623 »95
✿ ≡ Nijmegen: De Ruyterstraat 17, 6512 GA Nijmegen;
t (024) 324 0400 »95
✿ ≡ Regio Noord-Kennemerland: Postbus 3095, 1801 GB
Alkmaar; *t* (072) 515 4400, *f* 515 4143
Location: Geesterweg 21, Alkmaar. »95
✿ ≡ Roermond: Postbus 568, 6040 AN Roermond; *t* (0475)
315002 »95
✿ ≡ Schiedam: Van Swindensingel 40, 3112 RJ Schiedam;
t (010) 426 4406, *f* 473 1916 »94
✿ ≡ Tilburg: also known as Tilburgs meldpunt discriminatie:
Stationsstraat 39, 5038 EC Tilburg, Noord-Brabant; *t* (013)
543 8917, *f* 535 0253 (?), 543 7096
See also COS/VWW, right. »95
✿ ≡ Waterland: Postbus 377, 1440 AJ Purmerend; *t* (0299)
436988 »95
✿ ≡ Zeeland: Brouwenaarstraat 4, 4382 LK Vlissingen;
t (0118) 486427, *f* 486450 »95
✿ ≡ Zoetermeer: Postbus 7226, 2701 AE Zoetermeer;
t (079) 316 5659, 316 9644
Location: Dorpstraat 36a, Zoetermeer. »95

✿ **Anti-Discriminatie Bureaus Assen en Drenthe**, ADB *(Assen
and Drenthe Anti-Discrimination Bureaux)*
Postbus 701, 9400 AS Assen; *t* (0592) 313978
Small local agencies with professional staff assisting victims
of racial discrimination; legal advice, advocacy, referrals. »95
Anti-Discriminatie Overleg, ADO: see p208

✿ **Anti-Discriminatie Raad Dordrecht**, ADRD *(Dordrecht Anti-
Discrimination Council)*
Postbus 1136, 3300 BC Dordrecht; *t* (078) 614 3332
Location: Hof 10, 3311 XG Dordrecht. Small, professionally-
staffed local agency for assistance to victims of racial
discrimination; legal advice, advocacy, referrals. »95

✿ **Antifa Leiden—Politiek Info Centrum De Invalshoek** *(Leiden
Anti-Fascists—Angle of Attack Political Information Centre)*
Koppenhinksteeg 2, 2312 HX Leiden; *t* (071) 512 7619
Local anti-racist, anti-fascist group participating in national
Anti-Fascistische Actie, below. »95

✿ **Anti Fascisme Overleg Groningen**, AFO *(Groningen Anti-
Fascist Consultative Group)*
Postbus 1027, 9701 BA Groningen
Local action against racism and the far right. »94

◆ **Anti-Fascistische Actie**, AFA *(Anti-Fascist Action)*
Landelijk Secretariaat, Postbus 31420, 6503 CK Nijmegen;
t (024) 323 8162, *f* 322 3267
A coalition of some 20 independent local and regional groups
engaged in campaigning, research and direct action against
ultra-right parties, narrow nationalism and racial prejudice.»95
✿ ≡ Postbus 14710, 1001 LE Amsterdam »94
✿ ≡ Postbus 626, 6800 JE Arnhem »94
✿ ≡ Postbus 10061, 5200 EB Den Bosch »94
✿ ≡ Postbus 2210, 5600 CE Eindhoven; *t* (040) 244 4707»95
✿ ≡ Hengelo-Enschede: Postbus 1264, 7500 BG Enschede»94
✿ ≡ Postbus 2374, 1620 EJ Hoorn »94
✿ ≡ Postbus 224, 8901 BA Ljouwert (Leeuwarden), Friesland
See also FAFK, p171. »94
✿ ≡ Postbus 28546, 3003 JA Rotterdam; *t* (010) 467 8822»94
✿ Zaanstreek: Postbus 414, 1500 EK Zaandam »94

● **Antifascistische Oud Verzetsstrijders Nederland** *(Anti-
Fascist Resistance Veterans of Holland)*
J.G. Smidt: Vict. Regiadreef 17, 3563 GD Utrecht »91

✿ **Anti-fascistische telefoonlijn** *(Anti-Fascist Helpline)*
Postbus 60233, 6800 JE Arnhem; *t* (026) 361 5363
Operates a 24-hour reporting service and telephone chain to
enable anti-fascist activists in the Arnhem area to organise in
response to activities of racist and ultra-right groups. »95

● **Anti-Racisme Groep**, ARG *(Anti-Racist Group)*
Gerard de Bondtstraat 25, 5017 GS Tilburg, Zuid-Holland;
t (013) 535 7041
Established 1982; disseminates own and other groups' anti-
racist publications in meetings, schools, youth centres and
so on; organises meetings and demonstrations. »94

● **Stichting Anti-Racisme Informatie Centrum**, ARIC
M.A. Kreuger: Postbus 1812, 3000 BV Rotterdam; *t* (010)
414 3434, 411 3911, *f* 412 8433
Location: Grotekerkplein 5, 3011 GC Rotterdam (shared with
RADAR advice centre). Information, resources for anti-racist
and multi-cultural work; collaborates with ADO, p208, in
publication of *Anti-Racisme Gids*. Library of 10,000 volumes,
training workshops, production of campaign materials; sister
organisations in Berlin and Duisburg, see p165. »94

✿ **Anti-Racisme Initiatief Wageningen** *(Wageningen Anti-
Racism Initiative)*
Burgtstraat 3, 6701 DA Wageningen
Local anti-racist, anti-fascist group participating in national
Anti-Fascistische Actie. »94

✿ **ARAFK**
Koninginnenweg 15, 1075 CK Amsterdam; *t* (020) 614 2799
Promotes mutual respect and coexistence among different
ethnic groups in southern Amsterdam; opposes racism and
fascism; organises meetings, discussions, cross-cultural
events. Possibly an acronym for Anti-Racist, Anti-Fascist
Committee? »94

● **Avise Foundation**
Rooseveltlaan 197, 1079 AP Amsterdam; *t* (020) 642 2788,
f 646 4247
Helps Third World journalists and film-makers to prepare and
market television programmes on development, human rights,
cultural and North-South issues. »93

✿ **Breed Platform Tegen Racisme** *(Breda Anti-Racist Coalition)*
Postbus 703, 5201 AS Den Bosch; *t* (073) 613 6927
Anti-racism, anti-fascism. *Kleintje Muurkrant*. »95

✿ **Bureau Rassendiscriminatie Lelystad** *(Lelystad Racial
Discrimination Bureau)*
Postbus 563, 8200 AN Lelystad; *t* (0320) 252929
Location: Veluwemerrstraat 252, 8233 XD Lelystad. Small,
voluntary local centre against racial discrimination; legal
assistance, referrals to other agencies. »95

✿ **Centrum voor Internationale Samenwerking**, COS/VWW
(Centre for International Co-operation)
Stationsstraat 39, 5038 EC Tilburg, Noord-Brabant; *t* (013)
535 1523, *f* 543 7096
Anti-racism, multiculturalism. See also ADB Tilburg, left. »95

● **Centrum Ontwikkeling der Volkeren** *(Centre on the
Development of Peoples)*
Rijksweg 8, 6267 AG Cadier en Keer; *t* (04407) 2333 (?),
f 3183
Development education for intending volunteer workers. »93

- Comité voor Aanbeveling van Oud Verzetsdeelnemers (*Committee for the Recognition of Resistance Veterans*)
A. Ploeg: Breitnerstraat 3, 6813 HN Arnhem
Possibly a private address.   »91
✷ Comité Herdenking Februaristaking 1941 (*February 1941 Strike Commemoration Committee*)
T. IJisberg/A. Van Dijk-Stol: Grebbebos 18, 2134 KV Hoofddorp; *t* (023) 562 5230
Organises annual commemorative march and exhibition marking the Amsterdam dock strike of 25 February 1941, which was held to protest at the persecution of Jews by German occupation forces and Dutch collaborators.   »95
- Comité Vrouwen van Ravensbruck (*Ravensbruck Women's Committee*)
S. Pratomo-Gret: Frankendaalstraat 2, 1759 VD Callantsoog
Represents concentration camp survivors.   »91
- Contactgroep van den Heul Oud Verzetsdeelnemers (*Poppy League of Resistance Veterans*)
J. Bussink: J. v.d. Waalstraat 24hs, 1098 PL Amsterdam
Possibly a private address; also listed (1991) c/o J. Vlietman, Jisperveldstraat 245, 1024 Amsterdam. Anti-fascist war veterans group.   »91
✷ Derde Wereld Informatiehuis (*Third World Information Centre*)
Postbus 750, 5201 AT Den Bosch; *t* (073) 621 8970, *f* 621 8512
Location: Simon Stevinweg 17. International solidarity, development education, cultures. *Bijeen* (Together).   »95
✷ Discriminatie Meldpunt Tegelen (*Tegelen Discrimination Reporting Centre*)
Bongerdstraat 229, 5931 NE Tegelen; *t* (077) 373 7777, *f* 374 0333
Small local centre with professional staff aiding victims of racial discrimination; legal advice and assistance, referrals to other agencies.   »95
- Dwars-Antifa—groenlinkse jongerenorganisatie (*Hard-line Anti-Fascists—Green/Left Youth Organisation*)
Postbus 267, 1000 AG Amsterdam; *t* (020) 626 7374, *f* 627 0693
Anti-racist, anti-nazi youth movement.   »94
- Stichting Europa Centrum, SEC (*Europe Centre Foundation*)
Postbus 30402, 2500 GK Den Haag; *t* (070) 360 2273, *f* 356 3348
Promotes European integration among young people, within and outside the educational system.   »94
▌ European Local Authorities Information Network on Ethnic Minority Policies, ELAINE: European Centre for Work and Society
ECWS, Postbus 3073, 6202 NB Maastricht; *t* (043) 321 6724, *f* 325 5712, *Tx* 56164 EUR CW
An initiative of the ECWS, p240; information exchange on multicultural initiatives and minority issues at civic level. »95
- Fascisme Onderzoeks Kollektief, FOK (*Collective for Research on Fascism*)
Postbus 10748, 1001 ES Amsterdam; *t* (020) 693 6211
Anti-fascist network which researches activities and links of ultra-right and racist groupings in the Netherlands.   »94
- Frysk Anty-Fassisme Komitee, FAFK (*Friesian Anti-Fascist Committee*)
Postbus 566, Haniasteeg 57, 8901 BJ Ljouwert (Leeuwarden), Friesland; *t* (058) 215 5455
Anti-fascist group established 1975 (the first in modern Holland). Seeks to inform Friesian people of the dangers of fascist resurgence in Holland and abroad; publications, meetings, demonstrations; library, press archive, materials in Dutch and Friesch. FAFK promotes the use of the red triangle as a symbol of the anti-fascist movement. See also AFA Leeuwarden, p170.   »95
✷ Gemeentelijk Discriminatie Meldpunt Leeuwarden (*Leeuwarden Municipal Reporting Centre for Discrimination*)
Postbus 21000, 8900 JA Ljouwert (Leeuwarden), Friesland; *t* (058) 233 8555, *f* 215 3949
Civic agency with professional staff aiding victims of racial discrimination; legal advice and assistance, referrals to other agencies.   »95
- Germany Alert
Postbus 59165, 1040 KD Amsterdam; *f* (020) 686 5661 »94
✷ Haags Initiatief tegen Fascisme en Discriminatie, HIFD (*The Hague Initiative against Fascism and Discrimination*)
Postbus 73859, 2500 AJ Den Haag; *t* (070) 389 3540, *f* 388 9892
Group established in 1984, taking its objectives from Article 1 of the Constitution; promotes equity in employment and other fields, equal opportunities; combats all forms of racism, fascism and discrimination in the region.   »94

✷ Stichting Haags Meld- en Registratiepunt Discriminatie Zaken (*The Hague Reporting and Monitoring Centre on Discrimination Issues*)
Postbus 15687, 2554 EM Den Haag; *t* (070) 389 8141, *f* 380 9900
Location: Stationsweg 88, Den Haag. Local anti-discrimination foundation; monitoring of harassment, legal advice and assistance, referrals to other agencies.   »94
✷ Haarlem Release
Postbus 734, 2003 RX Haarlem; *t* (023) 531 3428
Local anti-racist, anti-fascist group participating in national Anti-Fascistische Actie, p170.   »95
✷ The Hague Anti-Racist and Discrimination Team
Dr Polls Hagenaars: [address uncertain] Oosteinde 33, 2271 EB Voorburg; *t* (070) 306 2255   »90
✷ Informatie-Actiecentrum Assata (*Assata Information and Action Centre*)
Begijnenstraat 34, 6511 WP Nijmegen; *t* (024) 323 8162, *f* 322 3267
Compilation and dissemination of information for anti-racist movement; archive, seminars; computer networks and bulletin-boards. Provides national secretariat for AFA, p170.   »95
▌ International Fellowship of Reconciliation, IFOR
Spoorstraat 38, 1815 BK Alkmaar; *t* (072) 512 3014, *f* 515 1102
Interfaith and intercultural understanding; see also p188. »95
- Jeugdvoorlichting 1940-1945 (*1940-45 Youth Education Group*)
A.J. Guling: Julianaweg 6a, 6062 ZP Oosterbeek
Education about the war, the resistance and anti-fascism. »91
✷ Jongeren Tegen Racisme Breda, JTR (*Breda Youth against Racism*)
Van Goorstraat 29, 4811 HH Breda; *t* (076) 514 5084
Anti-fascist, anti-racist group; member of national AFA.   »95
- Jongeren Tegen Racisme in Europa, JTRE: Youth against Racism in Europe
Postbus 11561, 1001 GN Amsterdam; *t* (020) 692 5382, *f* 618 0032
Organises youth to oppose racial prejudice, discrimination and ultra-right activity nationally and internationally. See also JRE in Germany, p167, and YRE in UK, p185.   »94
✷ Jongerenbond (*Union of Youth*)
Hooghuisstraat 29-III, 5611 GS Eindhoven; *t* (040) 246 4403
A range of anti-racist activities including multicultural events, removal of racist graffiti, publications and research.   »95
✷ Kerken en Multi-Culturele Samenleving (*Churches and Multicultural Society*)
Luybenstraat 17, 5211 BR Den Bosch; *t* (073) 614 3032, *f* 614 5159
A foundation which supports local churches and voluntary groups organising anti-racist and multicultural activities, including an annual Migrants Week.   »95
✷ Komitee Utrecht tegen Racisme en Fascisme, KURF (*Utrecht Anti-Racist and Anti-Fascist Committee*)
Postbus 2709, 3500 GS Utrecht
Location: Lauwerecht 55, Utrecht. Local anti-racist, anti-fascist group participating in national Anti-Fascistische Actie, p170. Research, public demonstrations, educational work.»94
- Kontakt der Kontinenten, KDK (*Continents in Contact*)
Amersfoortsestraat 20, 3769 AS Soesterberg; *t* (034) 635 1755, *f* 635 4735
Development education, solidarity between Netherlands and developing countries; advice and assistance work with refugees and migrants in Holland.   »93
◆ Landelijk Bureau Racismebestrijding, LBR: National Bureau against Racial Discrimination
Drs Marcel Zwamborn, Director: Postbus 517, 3500 AM Utrecht; *t* (030) 233 1421, *f* 232 8294
Location: Drieharingstraat 35/2, 3511 BH Utrecht. L.Y. Gonçalves chair, Drs Leo Balai, Drs Leyla Hamidi, H. Pos. Agency funded by Justice Ministry, national lottery, European Commission and others; seeks to prevent and combat racial discrimination; legal advice and representation, promotion of equal opportunities, development of advice services. Offers training and expert assistance, supports Anti-Discriminatie Bureaus (through Landelijk vereniging, p172); involved with national and international anti-racist and migrant rights groups. *LBR Bulletin* (6/yr), *Jaarverslag* (1/yr).   »95
- Landelijk Kontakt Groep Verzetsgepensioneerden, LKG (*National Contact Group for Resistance Veterans*)
C.F.W. Van Dillen: [address uncertain] Haarlemmerstraat 125, 1058 JW Amsterdam
Possibly a private address; also listed (1991) c/o W.G. Kop, Assinklanden 17, 7452 BA Enschede. Federation of anti-fascist resistance pensioners.   »91

♦ **Landelijke Vereniging van Anti-Discriminatie Bureaus en Meldpunten, LV** *(National Union of Anti-Discrimination Bureaux and Centres)*
c/o Landelijk Bureau Racismebestrijding, Postbus 517, 3500 AM Utrecht; *t* (030) 233 1421, *f* 232 8291
Co-ordinates activities of local ADBs, mostly p170; shares knowledge and expertise in combatting discrimination on grounds including race, gender and sexual orientation. »95

✤ **Magenta**
Nieuwe Achtergracht 101, 1018 WR Amsterdam; *t* (020) 623 6756, *f* 623 5929
Anti-racist, anti-fascist group; no further information. »94

✤ **Meldpunt Discriminatie Apeldoorn** *(Apeldoorn Discrimination Reporting Centre)*
Stationstraat 8, 7311 NS Apeldoorn; *t* (055) 522 5555
Local office with professional staff handling race and sex discrimination cases; legal advice and assistance, referrals to other agencies. »95

✤ **Meldpunt Discriminatie Leiden**
L. Smit/P. van Eer: Herengracht 48, 2312 LE Leiden; *t* (071) 512 0903, *f* 512 8802 »95

✤ **Meldpunt Discriminatie Vlaardingen**
[address unknown] Vlaardingen; *t* (010) 248 4000, *f* 248 4250
Small, volunteer-run centre aiding victims of racial discrimination. »94

✤ **Meldpunt Discriminatie Zaanstreek**
Postbus 361, 1500 EJ Zaandam; *t* (075) 612 5696
Small local centre handling racial discrimination cases. »95

✤ **Meldpunt Discriminatie Zwolle**
Grote Kerkplein 15, 8011 PK Zwolle; *t* (038) 498 2375, *f* 498 2041
Local centre with professional staff handling all types of discrimination cases. »95

✤ **Meldpunt Rassendiscriminatie Delft** *(Delft Racial Discrimination Reporting Centre)*
Phoenixstraat 66, 2611 AM Delft; *t* (015) 214 7463
Small, professionally-staffed local office aiding victims of racial discrimination. »95

✤ **Meldpunt Utrecht tegen Discriminatie, MUTD** *(Utrecht Reporting Centre against Discrimination)*
Postbus 1541, 3500 BM Utrecht; *t* (030) 296 1103, 233 3996
Location: Kanaalstraat 215, 3531 CH Utrecht. Local voluntary agency for advice, assistance, advocacy for victims of racial and sexual discrimination. »95

● **Nationaal Comité 4 en 5 mei** *(National Committee for 4 and 5 May)*
J.C.E. Belinfante: Rapenburgstraat 109, 1011 VL Amsterdam; *t* (020) 620 9688, *f* 620 5620
Postbus 16737, 1001 RE Amsterdam. Organises annual national commemorative events marking the liberation of Holland in 1945, and youth education about World War II and the themes of equality and non-discrimination. »94

● **Nederland bekent Kleur—Comité 21 maart, NBK** *(21 March Committee—Holland Shows its Colours)*
Postbus 55588, 1007 NB Amsterdam; *t* (020) 676 6710, *f* 676 3931
Location: Ferdinand Bolstraat 39. The name puns on the Dutch term for 'following suit' in a card game, thus offering the alternative meanings that Holland is 'showing off' its multi-colour society, or that it is 'playing its part' (in combatting racism). The group promotes anti-racist and anti-fascist activity, including marking the UN day against racism (21 March); it works with similar groups abroad and promotes the Dutch version of the 'European Passport Against Racism'.»94

✤ **Nederlands Auschwitz Comité**
Postbus 74131, 1070 BC Amsterdam; *t/f* (020) 672 3388
Survivors group; supports maintenance of Auschwitz concentration camp as anti-fascist memorial. »94

● **Overlegorgaan van Joden en Christenen in Nederland, OJEC** *(Jewish-Christian Consultative Committee for Holland)*
Keizersgracht 104b, 1015 CV Amsterdam; *t* (020) 620 5605, *f* 625 4452
Committee of Jewish community and Christian church representatives to discuss all matters of mutual concern. Involved in combatting antisemitism, fascism and racism through public events, provision of information, publishing, organisation of projects. »94

✤ **Platform Anti-Racisme Eindhoven, PARE**
c/o Stichting Balans, Postbus 6287, 5600 HG Eindhoven; *t* (040) 244 4477, *f* 244 4031
Broad coalition of political, social and church-based groups opposed to racism and fascism, formed as a response to racist arson attacks in 1993. See Stichting Balans, right. »95

● **Policy Group on Anti-Racism Awareness**
Desiree Ooft: [address uncertain] Charlotte Brontestraat 289, 1102 XD Amsterdam »90

✤ **Stichting Pop against Racism** *(Pop against Racism Foundation)*
Nieuwe Kerkstraat 37, 1018 DX Amsterdam; *t* (020) 627 7766, *f* 420 5446
The foundation, created in 1993, promotes inter-cultural contact, tolerance, solidarity and understanding through the Racism Beat It rock festival, and in youth media. »94

▌ **Public Broadcasting for a Multicultural Europe, PBME**
Postbus 1234, 3500 BE Utrecht; *t* (030) 230 2240, *f* 230 2975
Development of programming about ethnic minorities, anti-racism and multicultural education. See also the Stichting Omroep Allochtonen, p147. »95

✤ **Rotterdamse anti-discriminatie actieraad, RADAR** *(Rotterdam Anti-Discrimination Action Council)* also known as Stichting RADAR
C. Triesscheijn: Postbus 1812, 3000 BV Rotterdam; *t* (010) 412 6212, *f* 412 8433
Head office location: Grotekerkplein 5, 3011 GC Rotterdam. Also operates RADAR-Meldpunt Spijkenisse (Spijkenisse Reporting Centre), *t* 411 3911. Local anti-discrimination centres; legal advice and assistance, including migration and asylum problems. See also ARIC Rotterdam, p170. »95

● **Samenwerking Verzet 1940-1945** *(1940-45 Resistance League)*
R.W. Hemmes: Thorbeckelaan 74, 2564 BS Den Haag
Commemorates anti-fascist resistance. »91

● **School Zonder Racisme** *(School without Racism)*
Willemstraat 59, 5611 HC Eindhoven; *t* (040) 359999, *f* 445712
Promotes adoption of anti-racist policies and multicultural education by schools. »94

✤ **SOS Racisme**
Aziz Bakri: Kariboestraat 111, 3523 PC Utrecht; *t* (030) 251 3751
Anti-racist advice and campaigns work. »95

✤ **Steunpunt Anti-Rassen Discriminatie, STARD** *(Assistance Centre on Racial Discrimination)*
Koekoekstraat 28, 3514 CW Utrecht; *t* (030) 271 0377, 271 2723
Small local agency with professional staff, for advice, legal assistance and support to victims of racial discrimination. »95

● **Stichting 1940-1945** *(1940-45 Foundation)*
E.G.T. Van der Wall/R. De Gast: Postbus 41809, 1009 DA Amsterdam
Anti-fascist group to commemorate war and resistance. »91

✤ **Stichting Balans** *(Balance Foundation)*
Willem Arts, Co-ordinator: Postbus 6287, 5600 HG Eindhoven; *t* (040) 244 4477, *f* 244 4031
Local anti-discrimination foundation; monitors racism; legal advice and assistance, referrals to other agencies. Provides secretariat for Platform Anti-Racisme Eindhoven, left. »95

● **Stichting ter Bestrijding van het Antisemitisme, STIBA** *(Foundation to Combat Antisemitism)*
Postbus 2009, 3000 CA Rotterdam; *t* (010) 420 2315
Research/campaigning against fascism and antisemitism. »94

● **Stichting Burgerschapskunde, SBK** *(Foundation for Citizenship Education)*
Frank Elbers: [address unknown]
Has been involved in anti-racist education work. »94

✤ **Stichting Provinciaal Platform Antiracisme, SPPAR** *(Provincial Anti-Racist Coalition Foundation)*
Turfmarkt 30, 2801 HA Gouda; *t* (0182) 524802, *f* 583825
Information, campaign materials and resources for local anti-racist movements in the province of Zuid-Holland; organises activities for the UN International Day for the Elimination of Racial Discrimination (21 March). »95

● **Stichting Uitwisseling, SU** *(Exchange Foundation)*
Duinweg 7, 1860 AB Bergen; *t* (02208) 94144, *f* 94008
Promotes international exchanges of young workers and unemployed people; works with similar groups abroad. »94

● **Subsidiefonds Plaatselijke Aktiviteiten, SPA** *(Subsidy Fund for Local Activities)*
Oranje Nassaulaan 51, 1075 AK Amsterdam; *t* (020) 673 2543
Supports development education and international solidarity work by local voluntary groups. »93

✤ **TREF Charlois**
Postbus 55054, 3008 EB Rotterdam; *t* (010) 485 3450, *f* 486 6455
Local anti-discrimination centre for southern Rotterdam; legal advice and assistance, referrals to other agencies. »94

▌ **United for Intercultural Action, UNITED: European Network Against Nationalism, Racism, Fascism and in support of migrants and refugees**
Postbus 413, 1000 AK Amsterdam; *t* (020) 683 4778, 623 4902, *f* 683 4582, *e* united@antenna.nl
Pan-European network of 260 anti-racist, anti-fascist, migrant, minority, pacifist and other organisations; promotes international and intercultural co-operation, defends migrant and refugee rights; listings of groups and events, conferences, mailing lists, label runs, other services. *Directory of Internationalism* (1/yr), bulletin (6/yr).   »96

▌ **United Nations of Youth, UNOY**
Venedien 25, 1441 AK Purmerend; *t* (0299) 436093, *f* 427126
Global awareness, multicultural education, anti-racism.   »95

● **Verenigd Verzet 1940-1945** *(United Resistance 1940-45)*
M.Ph. Vlaskamp-Kwak: J. van den Waalstraat 36, 1098 PM Amsterdam
Represents anti-fascist war veterans.   »91

✿ **Vereniging Kinderen van Verzetsdeelnemers 1940-45** *(Union of Children of Resistance Members)*
M. Aukes-Paalvast: [address uncertain] Maritsa 5, 1189 LD Amstelveen
Families of anti-fascist veterans. Also listed (1991) c/o W. Diemer, Charlotte de Bourbonlaan 21a, 3062 GB Rotterdam.»91

✿ **Vervolgingsslachtoffers NVT** *(Organisation of Victims of Persecution)*
W.B. Meyer-Biet: Stadionkade 10 hs, 1077 VH Amsterdam»91

✿ **De Vonk** *(The Spark)*
Postbus 60233, 6800 JE Arnhem; *t/f* (026) 445 5996
Anti-fascist, anti-racist, anti-sexist, internationalist group; in national Anti-Fascistische Actie, p170. Cultural events, graffitti overpainting, educational/campaigning materials. »94

✿ **Vrienden van Kerwin** *(Friends of Kerwin)*
Spuistraat 47a, 1012 SR Amsterdam; *t* (020) 622 5799
Organises annual public commemoration of the racist murder on 20 August 1983 of Kerwin Duinmeijer, of Amsterdam.»94

● **Vriendenkring Mauthausen** *(Mauthausen Fellowship)*
M. Ohringer: Borssenburgstraat 35, 1078 VB Amsterdam
Foundation representing concentration camp survivors. See also Spanish Amical de Mauthausen, p174.   »91

● **Werkgroep Migranten en Media** *(Migrants and Media Working Group)* Nederlandse Vereniging van Journalisten
Olaf Stomp: Johan Vermeerstraat 22, 1071 DM Amsterdam; *t* (020) 676 6771, *f* 662 4901
Group within the NVJ (Dutch National Union of Journalists) promoting fair reporting of race, minority and immigration issues, and equity of treatment for minority journalists.   »94

✿ **Werkgroep tegen Fascisme en Racisme, WTFR** *(Working Group against Fascism and Racism)*
[address uncertain] Grasbroekerweg 166, 6412 BJ Heerlen, Limburg; *t* (045) 572 3806
Address also listed (1994) as Ruys de Beerenbroucklaan 47, 6417 CC Heerlen, *t* 571 4150. Regional group established 1982 to combat fascism and the far right in Limburg, in Holland and internationally. Educational activities.   »95

✿ **Werkgroep tegen Racisme** *(Working Group against Racism)*
Albrechtsveld 17, 2804 WB Gouda; *t* (0182) 535502
Regional anti-racist group; victim support, erasure of racist graffiti, educational activities.   »95

▌ **World Organisation of Young Esperantists, TEJO**
Nieuwe Binnenweg 176, 3015 BJ Rotterdam; *t* (010) 436 1044, *f* 436 1751
Promotes international and intercultural friendship and communication through Esperanto.   »94

▌ **Youth for a Europe Without Borders, YEWB**
St Jacobsstraat 10-20, 1012 NC Amsterdam; *t* (020) 625 9272, *f* 620 3774
Anti-racist, anti-fascist youth movement sharing address with the Dutch Socialist Workers' Party.   »94

NORWAY 47

◆ **Antirasistisk Senter** *(Anti-Racist Centre)*
Khalid Salimi: Postboks 244, Sentrum, 0103 Oslo; *t/f* 2211 6000
Location: Hausmannsgate 27. National anti-racist, anti-fascist, migrant rights centre; assists individuals who experience persecution and discrimination, campaigns against Progress Party and other racist groups. *Samora* magazine.   »95

● **Blitz Infogroup**
Pilestredet 30-c, 0164 Oslo; *f* 2211 2349
Anti-fascist centre; bombed on 21 August 1994.   »94

● **Humanist Association**
[address unknown] Oslo
Has produced anti-racist educational materials. *Humanist*.»95

◆ **Monitor**
Postboks 4406, Nygårdstangen, 5028 Bergen
Scandinavian anti-fascist magazine, founded 1994 and produced in co-operation with *Searchlight* (UK), p183, *Reflexes* (France), p163, and *Antifa Info-Blatt* (Germany), p165.   »96

● **Organisasjonen Mot Offentlig Discriminering, OMOD** *(Anti-Discrimination Organisation)*
Postboks 2832, Toyen, 0608 Oslo; *t* 2220 8737, *f* 2220 8444
Combats racial discrimination and harrassment.   »94

◆ **SOS Rasisme Norway**
Postboks 297, 5501 Haugesund; *t/f* 5271 2175
Anti-racist, anti-fascist campaigns including one around the 1995 local elections.   »95

✿ **Yes to a Colourful Community**
Komunes Sentralforbund, Postboks 1378, Vika, 0114 Oslo 1
Local anti-racist initiative.   »93

POLAND 48

✿ **Anti-Nazi Front, ANF**
PO Box 771, 50900 Wroclaw 2; *t* (071) 216702, *f* 557426
Anti-fascist youth group.   »94

✿ **Anti-Nazi Group**
[address unknown] Bydgoszcz   »94

✿ **Auschwitz Information and Meetings Centre**
ul. sw. m. Kolbego 1, 32600 Oswiecim; *t* (0381) 31000, *f* 31001   »94

● **Stefan Batory Foundation**
ul. Flory 9, 00586 Warszawa; *t* (022) 488055, *f* 493561
Opposes racism and fascism.   »94

▌ **International Auschwitz Committee, IAC**
ul. Turecka 3, 00957 Warszawa; *t* (022) 414755
Maintains Auschwitz (Oswiecim) concentration camp as a memorial to the victims of fascism.   »94

● **Polish Anti-Nazi League**
[address unknown]
Anti-fascist youth group reported to be active in 1994. »94

● **Radical Anti-Fascist Action, RAAF**
Also an anti-fascist group reportedly active in 1994.   »94

PORTUGAL 351

✿ **Cooperação e Desenvolvimento, OIKOS**
João Antonio Silva: Avenida Visconde Valmor 35-3° D, 1000 Lisboa; *t* (01) 796 4719, 796 0363, *f* 793 9791
Oikos (6/yr).   »94

● **Frente Anti-Racista** *(Anti-Racist Front)*
Rua Rodrigo da Fonseca 56-2°, 1200 Lisboa   »94

✿ **Leigos para o Desenvolvimento, LD** *(Laity for Development)*
Manuel Sousa Guedes: Estrada da Torre 26, 1750 Lisboa; *t* (01) 752 4278, *f* 759 9616 (?)
Christian development aid and humanitarian relief group, focussing on Lusophone Africa; refugee aid in Malawi.   »95

◆ **SOS Racismo**
José Falcão, President: Apartado 22508, 1146 Lisboa Codex; *t* (01) 847 8064, *f* 809628
Location: Avenida Guerra Junqueiro 19-5° E, 1000 Lisboa. Campaign against racism, for migrant and refugee rights. »95

✿ **União das Cidades Capitais Luso-Afro-Américo-Asiáticas, UCCLA** *(Union of Portuguese-Speaking Capital Cities)*
Avenida 24 de Julho 118, 1300 Lisboa; *t* (01) 395 5309, *f* 608155
International friendship and solidarity.   »94

ROMANIA 40

◆ **Asociatia Studentil de Lupta Impotriva Rasismului din Romania, ASLIR** *(Romanian Student Association for Fighting against Racism)* and Youth Association for European Friendship, ATPE
Serban Nicolae: Str. Dr Burghelea 10 A, Bucuresti, Sector 2; *t/f* (01) 312 5097
Anti-racist, anti-fascist campaigns; ATPE (Anca Crîngasu, *t* 650 1236, *f* 667 2285) promotes international exchanges.»94

✿ **Association for Fighting against Racism**
St. 6 Noiembrie 36, bloc T6, ap.34, 5800 Suceava; *t* (030) 216840
Possibly a regional branch of ASLIR, p173?   »94
♦ **Romanian Group for Intercultural Action**, GRAI
St. Eminescu 81, Bucuresti; *t* (01) 610 8472
Migrant solidarity, multiculturalism.   »94

RUSSIA 7

✿ **Antifascist Centre of Moscow**
Yevgeny Proshechkin: ulitsa Ger. Panfilovcev 17-korp. 4/kv. 62, Moskva 123480; *t* (095) 928 7113, *f* 923 5412
Monitors extreme right; campaigns for rigorous enforcement of the law against incitement to racial discord.   »95
▌**International Association of Former Prisoners of Concentration Camps**
Gogolevsky bulevar 4, Moskva 119885; *t* (095) 202 5552»94
● **Russian Charitable Antifascist Fund**
ulitsa Udaltsova 11-1, Moskva 117415; *t* (095) 131 8890»94
● **Russian Union of Former Prisoners of Fascist Concentration Camps**
Victory Square, pl. Podedy 173, Novgorod 173000; *t* (81600) 92468
See also Jewish Organisation of Prisoners of Fascist Concentration Camps, p79.   »94

SPAIN 34

● **Amical de Mauthausen** *(Mauthausen Fellowship)*
J. Escuer Gomis: c/o Aragón 312-5° 6ª, 08009 Barcelona, Catalunya
Anti-fascist group of concentration camp survivors. See also Dutch Vriendenkring Mauthausen, p173.   »91
✿ **Araña** *(Spider)*
calle Larra 16-2° izq., 28004 Madrid; *t* (91) 594 4980, *f* 445 2707
See also Plataforma Jóvenes contra la Intolerancia, right. »94
● **Asociación de Ex-presos y Refugiados Políticos Antifascistas** *(Association of Anti-fascist Ex-Political Prisoners and Refugees)* also known as Asoc. de Ex-presos y *Represaliados* Políticos
J.G. Puerta García: calle Campomanes 8-2, 28013 Madrid; *t* (91) 559 5234   »95
● **Asociación de Formación Socio-Educativa—Intercultura**, AFSE *(Intercultural Society for Social and Educational Development)*
Ferraz 56-2°, 28004 Madrid; *t* (91) 559 6331, *f* 547 9101»94
● **Ayuda en Acción** *(Aid in Action)*
Españoleto 13-1°, 28010 Madrid; *t* (91) 447 5211   »94
✿ **Club de Amigos de la Unesco de Madrid**, CAUM *(Madrid Friends of Unesco Club)*
Eloy Terrón Abad: plaza Tirso de Molina 8-1°, 28012 Madrid; *t* (91) 227 0557, 369 1652, 369 0842, *f* 429 6356
Global solidarity, intercultural events; see Unesco, p219. »94
✿ **Coordinación de Asociaciones Culturales de Madrid**, COACUM *(Madrid Cultural Associations Network)*
calle Clavel 5-4° dcha, 28004 Madrid; *t* (91) 523 9662, *f* 521 2340
Information and co-ordination group for migrant, minority and neighbourhood cultural organisations. *Agenda de la Red* (12/yr).   »94
✿ **Ecos do Sur** *(Southern Echos)*
Juan Manuel Galán Suárez: Apartado de Correios 677, 15080 A Coruña; *t* (981) 624133, *f* 267837
International solidarity, development education.   »94
✿ **Entrepueblos**
carrer Diputació 215, entresol 1°, 08011 Barcelona, Catalunya; *t* (93) 253 1903   »90
● **Fundación Internacional Olof Palme**, FIOP *(Olof Palme International Foundation)*
plaça Assemblea de Catalunya 8, 08911 Badalona; *t* (93) 384 5133, *f* 384 5338
Human rights, international solidarity, anti-racism.   »94
✿ ≡ José Baeza Castilla: Apartad de Correus 171, 17300 Blanes, Catalunya; *t* 330852, *f* 331320   »94
✿ **Intermon**
carrer Roger de Lluria 15, 08010 Barcelona, Catalunya; *t* (93) 301 2936   »94
✿ **Iuventus**
calle Príncipe 26-3° izq., 28012 Madrid; *t/f* (91) 369 3418
Anti-racist youth organisation.   »94

● **Jóvenes contra la Intolerancia**, JCI *(Youth against Intolerance)*
avenida del General Perón 32-2° dcha, 28020 Madrid; *t* (91) 555 0698, *f* 555 5416
Anti-racist journal associated with CEAR, p150; solidarity with migrants and refugees. See also PJCI—Secretaría Técnica, below. *Jóvenes contra la Intolerancia* (6/yr).   »94
✿ **Manos Unidas** *(Hands Together)*
calle Barquillo 38-2°, 28004 Madrid; *t* (91) 308 2020, 410 7500, *f* 308 4208
International development, humanitarian aid; raising of awareness, development education; focus on famine relief and prevention.   »94
● **Paz y Cooperación**, PYC *(Peace and Co-operation)*
Joaquín Antuña: calle Meléndez Valdés 68-4° 1, 28015 Madrid; *t/f* (91) 543 5282
International solidarity, development education, peace, disarmament, anti-racism; support for migrant and refugee rights; international volunteering and development aid programme has included work with refugees.   »94
✿ **Plataforma Jóvenes contra la Intolerancia—Secretaría Técnica**, PJCI *(Youth Against Intolerance, Secretariat)*
calle Larra 16-2° izq., 28004 Madrid; *t* (91) 594 4920, 445 1140, *f* 445 2707
Anti-racism, refugee and immigrant solidarity. See also JCI, above, Araña, left, and Solidaridad 2000, below.   »94
✿ **Red Intercultural de Innovación Social** *(Cross-Cultural Network for Social Innovation)*
Apartad de Correus 94205, 08080 Barcelona, Catalunya; *t/f* (93) 881 1321   »94
✿ **Solidaridad 2000**
calle Larra 16-2° izq., 28004 Madrid; *t* (91) 445 1140, *f* 445 2707
Anti-racist campaign of Jóvenes contra la Intolerancia, above. See also Araña, left.   »94
● **SOS Arrazakeria**: SOS Racismo
Santa Catalina 3 bajo, 20004 Donostia, Gipuzkoa, Euskadi; *t* (943) 423138
Basque anti-racist organisation. Research and documentation centre which in 1994 produced a resource book for minority, migrant and anti-racist work throughout the Spanish State *(Guía de recursos contra el racismo*, published at Pt1500 by Gakoa, Calle Peña y Goñi 13-1°, 20002 Donostia, Gipuzkoa, Euskadi). Multicultural events, Arabic classes.   »95
✿ ≡ Zumarraga kalea 3 b., 48006 Bilbo, Bizkaia, Euskadi; *t* (94) 479 0310
Anti-racist education, campaigns, events; pursues individual cases of racism and discrimination.   »94
✿ **SOS Arrazakeria Araba**: SOS Racismo Alava
Francia 11-2° dcha, 01004 Vitoria/Gasteiz, Araba, Euskadi; *t* (945) 265909
Anti-racist campaigns and information, rights advice to immigrants and assistance in dealing with officialdom, language classes.   »94
✿ **SOS Arrazakeria Nafarroa**: SOS Racismo Navarra
Estafeta, 31001 Iruñea-Pamplona; *t* (948) 825857, *f* 212758
Also at Apartado 399, 31500 Tudela, *t/f* 825857.   »95
♦ **SOS Racisme**
Isidoro Barba Camara: carrer Escudellers Blancs 12 bajos, 08002 Barcelona, Catalunya; *t* (93) 301 0597, 412 0034, *f* 301 0147
Anti-racism; defence of migrant and refugee rights.   »94
✿ **SOS Racisme Lleida**: SOS Racismo Lérida
Prat de la Riba 40-2° 1, 25008 Lleida, Catalunya   »95
✿ **SOS Racisme Pais Valencia**
Juan de Mena 4-2ª, 46008 Valencia; *t* (96) 385 2848   »95
✿ **SOS Racismo Baleares**
plaza del Bastión 10, 07703 Maó/Mahón, Menorca; *t* (971) 363844   »95
✿ ≡ Casal d'Entitats de la Ciutat, Montenegro 8, 07012 Palma, Mallorca   »95
✿ **SOS Racismo Madrid**
plaza Tirso de Molina 5-1° A, 28012 Madrid; *t* (91) 429 3070, *f* 369 2603   »95
✿ **SOS Racismo Zaragoza**
pza de la Seo 6, 50001 Zaragoza; *t* (976) 290214, *f* 591994
See also Cáritas Española, p213, and Delegación Diocesana de Migraciones, p151.   »95
● **Universiteris pel Tercer Mon**, Mon-3 *(University Third World Group)* Federación de Universitarios Solidarios
Facultad de Ciencias Económicas, avenida Diagonal 690, 08034 Barcelona, Catalunya; *t* (93) 280 5161, 402 4325, *f* 280 2378
Third World solidarity, anti-racism.   »94

SWEDEN 46

☼ **AFS Interkulturell Utbildning, AFSIU**
Box 17517, Timmermannsgatan 8, 11891 Stockholm;
t (08) 668 8956, *f* 668 4018
Youth NGO; possibly linked with AFS Interculturele
Programma's in Netherlands, p169? »94
● **Arbetsgruppen för en ungdomskampanj mot rasism**
(Working Group for a Youth Campaign Against Racism)
[address unknown] Stockholm
Contact for 1994-95 European Youth Campaign, see p197.»94
● *Expo*
Box 1031, 11479 Stockholm
New anti-fascist magazine. »96
☼ **Fredligt Arbete till Insikt Medmänsklighet Ansvar Unionen,**
FATIMA *(Peace Work through Insight and Responsibility)*
Box 2078, Lillåvägen 47, 10312 Stockholm; *t* (08) 659
8521, 659 2768
International and intercultural solidarity, development
education, welfare/integration of refugees and migrants. »94
☼ **Institute for Intercultural Relations—Simply Human**
Box 17201, Stockholm City Council, 10462 Stockholm;
t (08) 737 4327, *f* 737 4266
Multicultural civic events. »94
● **Internationella Kulturutbyte, IKU** *(International Cultural
Exchange)*
Box 2156, 10314 Stockholm; *t* (08) 201675
Youth exchange organisation. »94
● **Platform Fortress Europe, PFE**
Blomstervägen 7, 79133 Falun; *t/f* (023) 26777
Campaigns against exclusionist and racist migration and
refugee policies in Europe. »94
♦ **Riksförbundet Stoppa Rasismen** *(National Stop Racism
Movement)*
Box 4002, 10261 Stockholm »94

SWITZERLAND 41

♦ **Anti-Racism Information Service, ARIS**
avenue Trembley 14, 1209 Genève; *t* (022) 740 3530,
f 740 3565 »94
▮ **Association Mondiale pour l'Ecole Instrument de Paix, EIP:**
World Association for the School as an Instrument of Peace
Rue du Simplon 5, 1207 Genève; *t* (022) 735 2422, *f* 736
4863
Promotion of and training in education about peace, conflict
resolution, human rights, anti-racism, related topics; founded
1967; affiliates in African and American countries. »93
● **Bewegung für ein Offene, Demokratische und Solidarische
Schweiz, BODS** *(Swiss Openness, Democracy and Solidarity
Movement)*
Postfach 8553, 3001 Bern; *t* (031) 381 3930, *f* 381 6014
Pressure group for a liberal, multicultural society, supports
migrant and refugee rights. »94
☼ **Centre de Contact Suisse-Immigrés** *(Swiss-Immigrant
Contact Centre)*
Gravelone 1, 1950 Sion; *t* (027) 231216
Multicultural events, migrant/refugee solidarity in Valais. »95
● **Centre Europe-Tiers Monde, CETIM** *(Europe-Third World
Centre)*
quai Wilson 37, 1201 Genève; *t* (022) 731 5963
Development education, publishing on North-South economic
relations, migration, refugees and human rights. »93
▮ **Comité Européen pour la Défense des Réfugiés et des
Immigrés, CEDRI:** European Committee for the Defence of
Refugees and Immigrants, and Forum Civique Européen:
European Civic Forum
François Bouchardeau, President: Missionstrasse 35,
Postfach 2780, 4002 Basel; *t* (061) 446619, *f* 446620,
Tx 964310 EKOLM
Solidarity with migrants and third world; against racism and
nationalism. See also CEDRI in France, p163, and Europä-
isches Bürgerforum in Austria, p159 and Germany, p166. »94
▮ **Committee on the Elimination of Racial Discrimination, CERD**
c/o UN Centre of Human Rights, Palais des Nations, 1211
Genève 10; *t* (022) 734 6011 »94
● **Forum gegen Rassismus:** Forum contre le racisme: Anti-
Racist Forum
Case postal 95, 1000 Lausanne 9; *t/f* (021) 311 8057
Alliance of anti-racist groups. »94

● **Forum Schule für eine Welt:** Forum Ecole pour un seul
monde *(One World Education Forum)*
Aubrigstrasse 23, 8645 Jona; *t/f* (055) 284082
Promotion of global vision, and awareness of development,
human rights and solidarity issues, in schools; themes
addressed include migration and minority rights. »93
▮ **International Movement Against All Forms of Discrimination
and Racism, IMDAR**
Case postale 2100, route de Ferney 150, 1211 Genève 2;
t (022) 791 6263, *f* 791 0361
Sponsored by the World Council of Churches, p219. »94
▮ **International Organisation for the Elimination of All Forms
of Racial Discrimination, EAFORD**
Case postale 2100, Bureau 475, 1211 Genève 2; *t* (022)
788 6233, 732 5534, *f* 788 6245, 732 5082
Office: route des Morillons 5, Grand-Saconnex, 1218
Genève. Connected with the World Council of Churches
Program to Combat Racism. »94
♦ **Ligue Internationale Contre le Racisme et l'Antisémitisme,**
LICRA: International League against Racism & Antisemitism
Case postal 1754, 1211 Genève 1; *t* (022) 757 6033,
f 757 6064
See also French LICRA, p164. »94
▮ **Ligue internationale pour les droits et la libération des
peuples:** International League for the Rights and Freedom of
Peoples
Case postal 315, 1211 Genève 4; *t* (022) 798 7707, *f* 788
0277
International solidarity; human rights, including refugee issues.
See LIDLIP and Fondazione Basso in Italy, pp169, 206. »94
☼ **Le Printemps de l'antiracisme** *(Anti-Racist Spring)*
Case postal 2507, 1211 Genève 2 Dépôt; *t* (022) 320 7811,
f 329 8994 »94
♦ **SOS Racisme**
Case postale 779, passage du Cardinal 2d, 1701 Fribourg 1;
t (037) 242125, *f* 244541
Anti-racist campaigns; see French SOS Racisme, p165. »94
♦ **Stiftung gegen Rassismus und Antisemitismus, GRA**
(Foundation to Combat Racism and Antisemitism)
Schweizergasse 6, 8001 Zürich
Anti-racist, anti-fascist work. »94
☼ **Vivre Ensemble** *(Living Together)*
Case postal 177, 1211 Genève 8; *t* (022) 320 6094
Anti-racism, migrant support, multiculturalism. »94
▮ **Women's International League for Peace and Freedom,**
WILPF: Sub-Committee on Racism
Case postal 28, rue de Varembé 1, 1211 Genève 20;
t (022) 733 6175, *f* 740 1063
International progressive women's organisation; anti-racist,
pro-migrant, pro-refugees. »94

UNITED KINGDOM 44

☼ **Action Against Racism, AAR**
Unity Café [address unknown] Oldham, Lancashire
Anti-racist campaigning; multi-cultural meeting place. »94
● **Action Against Racism in Training, AART**
7 Frederick Street, Hockley, Birmingham B1 3HE
Development of equal opportunities for black people both as
trainers and as trainees. »90
☼ **All Faiths for One Race—All Fight Fascism, Oppression and
Racism, AFFOR**
27 Weston Road, Handsworth, Birmingham B19 1EH;
t (0121) 523 8076
Inter-faith and inter-ethnic understanding and solidarity,
practical action to combat racism and intolerance. »94
☼ **Anglo-Asian-Afro-Caribbean Friendship and Cultural
Association**
62 River Dale Road, Erith DA8, Kent; *t* (013224) 38929 »90
● **Anne Frank Educational Trust**
Gillian Walnes, Executive Director: Garden Floor, 43 Portland
Place, London W1N 3AJ
Anti-fascist, anti-racist educational charity linked with the
Anne Frank Stichting (Netherlands), p170. Touring exhibition
on the Holocaust, antisemitism and intolerance. »95
♦ **Anti-Fascist Action, AFA**
BM Box 1734, London WC1N 3XX; *t* (0171) 409 0429
Formed 1985, this is a coalition of local direct action groups
which monitor and oppose fascist and racist organisations at
ideological and street level, by all necessary means. See local
AFA groups in Bradford, Cleveland, Edinburgh, Exeter, Halifax,
Hertfordshire, Leeds, Liverpool, Manchester, Norwich, York;
several of these form the AFA Northern Network. »95

◆ **Anti Nazi League, ANL**
Paul Holborow: PO Box 2566, London N4 2HG; *t* (0171) 924 0333, *f* 924 0313
Anti-fascist, anti-racist group campaigning against movements such as the National Front and British National Party. Activities include rallies and the distribution of leaflets. Many leading members are in the Labour Party (including some MPs and MEPs) or the Socialist Workers' Party, but the ANL is a non-party group open to all anti-fascists. »95

✿ **Anti-Racist Action**
Box 83, South-West PDO, Manchester M15 5NJ
Anti-racist campaigns. Possibly same as or successor to Manchester Anti-Fascist Action, p181. »93

◆ **Anti-Racist Alliance, ARA**
Narendra Makanji, Chair: PO Box 150, London WC1X 9AT; *t* (0171) 278 6869, *f* 278 6886
National Black-led anti-racist, anti-fascist campaign, launched 1991; one of the main UK anti-racist groups, but has suffered internal divisions. Advice, information, co-ordination of Black organisations, trade unions and community groups. Major affiliates include Indian Workers Association, p44, Society of Black Lawyers, p23, and National Black Caucus, p22. »95

▌ **Associated Country Women of the World**
H. McGrigor, General Secretary: 50 Warwick Square, London SW1V 2AJ; *t* (0171) 834 8635
Founded 1930; international association of 302 women's organisations in 71 countries, totalling 9m members; international goodwill, understanding, welfare of rural women, development and women's issues at global level. *The Countrywoman* (4/yr). »85

● **Association of British Civilian Internees, Far East Region**
Keith Martin, Chairman: [address unknown]
Represents survivors of Japanese fascist internment and concentration camps. »95

✿ **Aylesbury Vale Racial Equality Council**
Harkishan Lal Wadhwa, Director: 23a Walton St, Aylesbury HP20 1TZ; *t* (01296) 25334, 27660
Promotes racial equality in Buckinghamshire; casework with individuals includes divided families, visitor visas, refusals of entry, primary purpose, accommodation; mainly Asian, Caribbean client groups. »95

✿ **Banbury Racial Equality Council**
Fred Riches, Secretary: 22 Church Street, Banbury OX16 9ND; *t* (01295) 264518
Location: 33a Crouch Street, OX16 9PR. Promotion of racial equality, elimination of discrimination. Not CRE-funded. »95

✿ **Barking and Dagenham Anti-Fascists**
PO Box 3212, London E6 »94

✿ **Barking and Dagenham Racial Equality Council**
Sheila Delaney, Director: 1st Floor, Methodist Church Building, London Road, Barking IG11 8AL; *t* (0181) 594 2773
Promotion of race equality; works with local Pakistani, Caribbean and Indian communities. Not funded by CRE. »95

✿ **Barnet Racial Equality Council**
A.B.E. Magba-Kamara, Director: 1 Friern Park, North Finchley, London N12 9DE; *t* (0181) 445 6051-57, *f* 446 0445
Promotes racial equality in Barnet; community development, Asian/Caribbean immigration casework, refugee work. »95

✿ **Bath Racial Equality Council**
Monira Ahmed, Director: 1st Floor, 24 Westgate Street, Bath BA1 1EP; *t* (01225) 442352, *f* 481912
Promotion of race equality, elimination of discrimination. »95

✿ **Bedford Racial Equality Council**
Buddhev Pandya, Director: 36 Mill Street, Bedford MK40 3HD; *t* (01234) 350459, 340728, *f* 327487
Elimination of racial discrimination, promotion of equality; advice work including Asian and Caribbean immigration, primary purpose, DNA tests. »95

✿ **Bexley and Greenwich Campaign Against Fascism**
Cllr Geoff Dickson, Chair: PO Box 46, Bexleyheath Sorting Office, 2 Glengall Road, Bexleyheath DA7 4BS »88

✿ **Bexley Racial Equality Council**
J. Haider, Acting Director: Library Building, 3 Walnut Tree Road, Erith DA8 1RA; *t* (01322) 340316
Promotion of race equality, elimination of discrimination. »95

✿ **Birmingham Anti-Fascist Action, AFA**
PO Box 2414, Handsworth, Birmingham B21 0TZ
Organises local anti-fascist and anti-racist research, demonstrations, leafletting and other activity. »94

✿ **Birmingham City Council Race Relations Unit**
Khurshid Ahmed, Assistant Chief Executive: Council House Extension, 3 Congreve Passage, Birmingham B3 3DA; *t* (0121) 235 2545
Ahmed has been UK rapporteur for the MAINE information network, p146. »94

✿ **Birmingham Fellowship of Faiths**
Caroline Wallace, Secretary: 72 Cartland Road, Stirchley, Birmingham B30 2SE; *t* (0121) 443 2934
Mutual understanding among people of different faiths. »88

✿ **Birmingham Inter-Faiths Council**
Rev. Michael Walters: [address uncertain] Central Hall, Corporation Street, Birmingham B4
Also listed (1988) at 141 Heathfield Road, Handsworth, B19 1HL, *t* (0121) 233 4302 (David Forbes, secretary), or (1990) Christ Church Vicarage, 34 Grantham Road, Sparkbrook, B11 1LU. Promotes dialogue among major faiths in the city. »90

✿ **Birmingham Racial Attacks Monitoring Unit, BRAMU**
Steve Batchelor, Chairman: Afro-Caribbean Resource Centre, 339 Dudley Road, Winson Green, Birmingham B18 4HB; *t* (0121) 455 9500
Maxie Hales director. Monitoring of racial attacks in the city; research and analysis. Produces reports, assists in victim support, participates in policy development. »96

● **Black-Jewish Forum**
Anthony Julius: [address unknown] London
Promotes contact and solidarity among minorities. »95

✿ **Blackburn Ethnic Minorities Development Association, EMDA**
St John's Centre, St John's Place, Victoria Street, Blackburn BB1 6DW; *t* (01254) 680757
Umbrella group for 35 mainly Asian voluntary bodies. »95

✿ **Blackburn Racial Equality Council, BREC**
M. Rafique Malik, Director: St John's Centre, St John's Place, Victoria Street, Blackburn BB1 6DW; *t* (01254) 261924
Works for a just society, racial equality and the elimination of racial discrimination, prejudice, harassment and violence. »96

✿ **Blackley Anti-Racist Group, BARG**
Walt Crowson, Chair: Neighbourhood Adult Education Centre, Plant Hill Road, Blackley, Manchester M9 2WP; *t* (0161) 795 6010
Anti-racist campaigns, victim support, multicultural events.»93

✿ **Blackpool Anti-Fascist Action, AFA**
c/o PO Box 63, Lancaster LA1 4GP
Anti-fascist, anti-racist campaigns. »95

✿ **Bolton Racial Equality Council**
Jo Hall, Director: Room 39, 2nd Floor, Civic Centre, Le Mans Crescent, Bolton BL1 1UF; *t* (01204) 528087, 391567
For race equality, against discrimination. Advice service; small immigration caseload, family reunion, visitor visa issues. »95

✿ **Borough of Charnwood Community Relations Council,**
also known as Charnwood Community Relations Council
D. Beal/Amu Devani, Directors: 66 Nottingham Road, Loughborough LE11 1EU; *t* (01509) 261651
Promotion of racial equality, elimination of discrimination. »95

✿ **Bradford Anti-Fascist Action, AFA**
PO Box 127, Leeds LS3 1TS; *t* (0113) 242 4680
Local anti-racist and anti-fascist activities; participation in national campaigns. »96

✿ **Bradford Concord Inter-Faith Society**
Norman Collins, Co-ordinator: 9 Westview, Undercliffe Old Road, Bradford BD2 4RQ; *t* (01274) 634387
Inter-faith contacts, co-operation. Newsletter (6/yr). »88

✿ **Bradford Racial Equality Council, and/or West Yorkshire Racial Equality Council**
Ishtiaq Ahmed, Director: Oakwell House, 8 Oak Avenue, Bradford BD8 7AQ; *t* (01274) 541358, *f* 483422
Promotion of racial equality, elimination of discrimination; advice work, mainly with Pakistani migrants. Unclear what is the relationship of Bradford REC to West Yorkshire REC, listed (1995) by CRE at same address (Mohammad Naeem director, *t* 492400). »95

✿ ≡ Keighley Office: Zafar Ali: Albert Street, near Highfield Lane, Keighley BD21 2AT; *t* (01535) 607717, *f* 690561
Sometimes known as Keighley REC, this is in fact a sub-office of Bradford REC. »95

✿ **Brent Campaign Against Racial Discrimination**
Guy Elliston, Secretary: [address unknown] London NW6 »88

✿ **Brent Racial Equality Council, BREC:** succeeds Brent Community Relations Council
[address unknown] London NW; *t* (0181) 937 3421
Promotion of race equality, elimination of discrimination. Launched 1995 to succeed the CRC, located at 11 Brondesbury Road, Kilburn, NW6, *t* (0171) 372 2000. »95

✿ **Brighton Anti-Fascist Action, AFA**
c/o Brighton Unemployed Centre, 6 Tilbury Place, Brighton BN1, Sussex
Organises local anti-fascist and anti-racist research, demonstrations, leafletting and other activity. »94

✿ **Bristol Anti-Fascist Action, AFA**
c/o London AFA, BM 1734, London WC1N 3XX
Local anti-fascist/anti-racist research and action. »94

✿ **Bristol Racial Equality Council**
Peter Courtier, Director: Colston House, Colston Street,
Bristol BS1 5AQ; *t* (0117) 929 7899, *f* 922 7713
Promotion of racial equality, elimination of discrimation;
services to local Caribbean, Asian communities.　　»95

✿ **Bromley Racial Equality Council**
S.N. Hussain: 114 Maple Road, Penge, London SE20 8JB;
t (0181) 776 8838
Promotion of racial equality, elimination of discrimination. »95

✿ **Burnley and Pendle Racial Equality Council**, formerly North
East Lancashire Community Relations Council
Aziz A. Chaudhury, Director: 19 Market Square, Nelson BB9
7LP; *t* (01282) 692474, *f* 619129
Promotion of racial equality in North East Lancashire, and
elimination of discrimination.　　»95

✿ **Bury Metro Racial Equality Council**
Nasrullah Khan JP, Director: 12 Tenterden Street, Bury BL9
0EG; *t* (0161) 761 4533
Combats race discrimination, promotes equal opportunity. »95

✿ **Cable Street Beat**
[address unknown]
Anti-Fascist Action pop music wing.　　»88

✿ **Calderdale Racial Equality Council**
M.A. Bismil, Director: 7-8 Wards End, Halifax HX1 1BX;
t (01422) 366804, *f* 360975
Promotion of race equality and good community relations,
campaigning against discrimination and disadvantage in
employment/other fields. Some immigration casework.　　»95

✿ **Cambridge City Council Racial Harassment Service:**
Community Services Department
Neil Stott: [address unknown] Cambridge; *t* (01223) 358977
ext. 3833
Investigates and acts against racial harassment, especially in
relation to council housing.　　»95

✿ **Cambridge Council of Christians and Jews**
[address unknown] Cambridge　　»88

✿ **Cambridge Inter-Faith Group**
David Yarham, Convenor: 47 Priam's Way, Stapleford,
Cambridge CB2 5DT; *t* (01223) 842007
Inter-faith understanding; meetings, visits, retreats.　　»88

✿ **Camden Council Equalities Unit**
Town Hall, Judd Street, London WC1H 9JE
Promotion of equality of opportunity in the Council workforce,
and equality in service provision, in this multicultural area.»95

*Camden Monitoring Project: defunct (1995); see Bengali
Workers' Association, p19*

✿ **Camden Racial Equality Council**, CREC
Dharmendra Kanani, Director: 58 Hampstead Road, London
NW1 2PY; *t* (0171) 383 3588
Organisation opposing racism, promoting equal opportunities
and good community relations in Camden; advice, assistance
to individuals; monitoring racial violence.　　»95

✿ **Camden Racial Harassment Initiative**
Co-ordinator: Town Hall, Judd Street, London WC1H 9JE
A partnership co-ordinated by Camden Council and involving
the police, Camden REC, community and voluntary groups, to
develop policies and practices to deal with racial harassment in
Camden and to achieve the best outcomes for victims.　　»95

✿ **Camden Unity**
c/o Searchlight, 37b New Cavendish St, London W1M 8JR
Monitors and campaigns against racism, discrimination and
racial violence.　　»96

✿ **Campaign Against Double Punishment**
Geoff Pleasance: c/o POPS, St Mark's Cheetham, Tetlow
Lane, Cheetham, Manchester M8 7HF; *t* (0161) 740 8600
Campaigns against deportation of immigrant offenders who
have served their prison sentence.　　»93

● **Campaign Against Fascism in Europe**, CAFE
PO Box 30, London SE15 5EP; *t/f* (0171) 703 3423
Opposes racist and extreme-right organisations and policies
in European countries and institutions.　　»94

◆ **Campaign Against the Immigration and Asylum Bill**, CAIAB
28 Commercial Street, London E1; *t* (0171) 247 9907
Broad-based coalition opposing restrictive legislation.　　»96

◆ **Campaign Against Racism and Fascism**, CARF: and
National Network against Detentions and Deportations
BM Box 8784, London WC1N 3XX; *t* (0171) 837 1450
Research, information and campaigns against racism and
fascism in UK and Europe. Monitors racial attacks, the far
right, policing and immigration controls. Its magazine (*CARF*,
6/yr, published from 1977 in association with the Institute of
Race Relations, p245, and independently from 1991), is one of
the main anti-racist publications in Britain. The national anti-
deportation network (also in Manchester, *t* (0161) 740 7722)
co-ordinates local campaigns against deportations.　　»95

● **Campaign Against Racist Laws**, CARL
Prem Singh/Harpal Brar: 15 Kenton Avenue, Southall UB1
3QF; *t* (0181) 571 1437
Godfrey Cremer; campaigns on Immigration and Nationality
Acts, primary purpose rule.　　»95

● **Campaign for Anti-Racist Education**, CARE
229 Seven Sisters Road, London N4 2DA
Organised in six regional groups.　　»90

● **Campus Watch**
[address unknown]; *t* (01426) 942826
Campaign against racism in third-level education, established
1994 by *Searchlight*, p183, the Union of Jewish Students,
p81, and the National Union of Students, p226.　　»96

✿ **Cardiff Anti-Fascist Action**, AFA, formerly South Wales Anti-
Fascist Action
PO Box 368, Cardiff CF2 1SQ, Wales
Organises local anti-fascist/anti-racist demonstrations,
research, leafletting and other activity.　　»94

✿ **Cardiff Interfaith Association**
J. Harding, Chairperson: 37 Donald Street, Roath, Cardiff
CF2 4TJ, Wales; *t* (01446) 732361
Understanding and tolerance among people of different
religious traditions.　　»88

● **Catholic Association for Racial Justice**, CARJ
Molly Porter: St Vincent's Community Centre, Talma Road,
Brixton, London SW2 1AS; *t* (0171) 274 0024
Anti-racism, youth welfare, refugees; national membership
organisation.　　»96

✿ **Central Race Equality Unit**: London Borough of Greenwich
Chief Executive's Department, Greenwich Council, 37
Wellington Street, Woolwich, London SE18 6PW; *t* (0181)
854 0055 ext. 6406, 854 8888
Local authority unit for the development, co-ordination and
implementation of policies to eliminate discrimination and
ensure equality in the provision of council services.　　»95

✿ **Central Scotland Racial Equality Council**
Pek Yeong Berry, Director: Room 32-34, Cape Unicentre,
Kerse Road, Stirling FK7 7SG, Scotland; *t* (01786) 450025
Elimination of racial discrimination in Central Scotland,
promotion of racial equality.　　»95

● **Centre for Anti-Racist Education and Anti-Racist Strategies**
Mawbey School, Coopers Road, London SE1; *t* (0171) 237
3824
Multicultural educational resource centre.　　»94

● **Centre for International Briefing**
Patrick Lloyd, Director: Farnham Castle, Farnham, Surrey;
t (01252) 21194
50 staff; founded 1953; resource centre, briefing courses on
living and working abroad and for visitors to Britain.　　»90

● **Centre for International Studies**
Meadowlea House, 86 Littleham Road, Exmouth EX8 2QT;
t (01395) 264902, *f* 268031
Development education, including migration and refugee
issues; conferences, courses, publishing.　　»93

● **Centre for Multicultural Education**, CME
Crispin Jones/Alice Henfield/Dr Jagdish Gundara: Institute of
Education, University of London, 20 Bedford Way, London
WC1H 0AL; *t* (0171) 612 6722, 636 1500, *f* 612 6733
Research and resource development in multicultural and anti-
racist education. See Bangladeshi TADCO project, p18.　　»95

● **Centre for World Development Education**
Derek Walker, Director: 128 Buckingham Palace Road, London
SW1W 9SH; *t* (0181) 730 8332
Founded 1977; resource centre, publications, seminars on
development, North-South interdependence.　　»90

✿ **Chesham Racial Equality Council**
Peter W. Yerrell, Honorary Secretary: 35 Birch Way, Chesham
HP5 3JL; *t* (01895) 446561
Voluntary agency (not CRE-funded) which promotes race
equality and the elimination of discrimination in the locality.»94

✿ **Chesterfield Community Relations Steering Committee**
Bernard Cummins, Secretary: 18 Dorest Drive, Brimington,
Chesterfield S43 1DS; *t* (01245) 206711　　»90

● **Christians Against Racism and Fascism**
[address uncertain] PO Box 48, London E2 0HH; *t* (0171)
739 3938　　»90

● **Christians for Europe**
10 Holland Park Avenue, London W11; *t* (0171) 792 3938 »90

● **Churches' Commission for Racial Justice**, CCRJ
Rev. David Haslam, Moderator: CCBI, Inter-Church House,
35-41 Lower Marsh, London SE1 7RL; *t* (0171) 620 4444,
f 928 0010
Rev. Theo Samuel. National inter-church body promoting interracial equity and equality of opportunity. Activities include
research, lobbying, publishing. *Church and Race* (3/yr).　　»96

✧ **Cleveland Anti-Fascist Action**, AFA
Box 13, c/o St Mary's Centre, Corporation Road,
Middlesbrough, Cleveland
Local anti-fascist/anti-racist research, demonstrations,
leafletting and other activity. »96

✧ **Cleveland Racial Equality Council**, also known as Racial
Equality Council Cleveland
Harbhajan Singh Jagra: 51a Kings Road, North Ormesby,
Middlesbrough TS3 6NJ; t (01642) 222563, f 251783
Combatting racial discrimination, promoting equality. »96

✧ **Cobridge Multicultural Project**
[address unknown] Stoke-on-Trent, Staffordshire
With Stoke Citizens Advice Bureau, p228, provides advice
service to an area with a large Caribbean community. »94

● **Committee for Community Relations**: Catholic Bishops'
Conference of England and Wales
Richard Zipfel, Secretary: [address uncertain] 39 Eccleston
Square, London SW1V 1PD; t (0171) 834 8692
Advises on ethnic minority and human rights issues. »91

● **Committee for Other Faiths**: Catholic Bishops' Conference
of England and Wales
Rt Rev. Charles Henderson, Chairman: Park House, 6a
Cresswell Park, London SE3 9RD; t (0171) 318 1094
Church agency promoting understanding and goodwill among
people of different religious; various publications. »88

● **Committee for Relations with People of Other Faiths**:
Council of Churches in Britain and Ireland
Rev. Clinton Bennett, Secretary: Inter-Church House, 35-41
Lower Marsh, London SE1 7RL; t (0171) 620 4444 ext. 2120
Promotes good relations between the major Christian churches
of Britain and Ireland and other faith communities; *Document:
a Christian journal of inter-religious encounter* (4/yr). »88

✧ **Community Action for Police Accountability**, CAPA
Oxford House, Derbyshire Street, London E2 6HG; t (0171)
729 1404, 729 2652
Also listed (1996) at St Hilda East Community Centre, Club
Row, E2. Pressure group on racial harrassment and other
policing issues in Tower Hamlets, Islington and Hackney. See
also Civil Rights Advice and Support Group, p222. »96

*Community and Race Relations Unit: see Council of Churches
for Britain and Ireland, p222*

● **Council of Christians and Jews**, CCJ
Paul Mendel, Deputy Director: 1 Dennington Park Road, West
End Lane, London NW6 1AX; t (0171) 794 8178, 794 8179,
f 431 3500
Dialogue between Christians and Jews, eradication of
prejudice including anti-semitism, public education; publishes
Common Ground (3/yr), *Newsletter*. »88
✧ ≡ 325 Pershore Road, Birmingham B5 »90

✧ **Council for Racial Justice**
14 Millstone Lane, Leicester LE1 5JN »90

✧ **Coventry Anti-Harassment and Attacks Network**, CAHAN
CREC, Fleet House, Corporation Street, Coventry CV1 1EG;
t (01203) 520646 »90

✧ **Coventry Inter Faith Group**
Rev. Dr Christopher Lamb, Convenor: Coventry Cathedral,
Priory Row, Coventry CV1 5ES; t (01203) 227597
Meetings, mutual understanding among people of different
faiths. *The Rainbow* (4/yr). »88

✧ **Coventry Racial Equality Council**, CREC
Cllr A.J. Waugh, Director: Fleet House, Corporation Street,
Coventry CV1 1EG; t (01203) 633236, f 632441
Promotion of racial equality in Warwickshire, elimination of
discrimination; six staff. Advice services; Job Club for
minority unemployed, t 633900. »95

✧ **Crewe Central Community Group**
The Senior Officer: Camm Street Centre, Camm Street,
Crewe CW2 7DW; t (01270) 587429
Non-CRE-funded voluntary group with aims and functions
equivalent to those of a Racial Equality Council. »95

✧ **Croydon Racial Equality Council**, CREC
The Director: 70 Park Lane, Croydon CR0 1JE; t (0181) 686
8014, 686 8524
Vallin Miller. Promotion of race equality, elimination of
discrimination; casework including practical and emotional
support to victims of racial harassment or attacks. Some
immigration advice work. »95

✧ **Dartford Racial Equality Council**
Dev Sharma, Director: Enterprise House, 8 Essex Street,
Dartford DA1 2AU; t (01322) 287251
Promotion of race equality, elimination of discrimination. »95

✧ **Derby Campaign Against Racism and Fascism**, CARF,
formerly Derby Anti-Fascist Action
PO Box 70, Derby DE1 9JW
Anti-fascist/anti-racist research and action. »95

✧ **Derby Open Centre Multi-Faith Group**
Canon Richard Orchard: 24 Kedleston Road, Derby DE3
1GU; t (01332) 41201
Understanding among ethnic and religious groups. »88

✧ **Derby Racial Equality Council**
Tony Walsh, Director: 31 Normanton Road, Derby DE1 2GJ;
t (01332) 372428
Promotion of racial equality, elimination of discrimination;
education and youth work. »95

● **Development Education Association**, DEA
The Director: 29-31 Cowper Street, London EC2A 4AP
Promotes international awareness, fair trade, social justice,
sustainable development, through development education.»95

✧ **Doncaster Council for Racial Equality**
Saroj Verma, Director: 1 Chequer Road, Doncaster DN1 2AA;
t (01302) 735201
Promotion of racial equality, elimination of discrimination. »95

✧ **The Drum** and Newtown Cultural Project Ltd
Unit 205b, 120 Vyse Street, Hockley, Birmingham B18 6NF;
t (0121) 693 3613, 693 3618
Newtown Cultural Project is a charity preparing for the 1996
launch of The Drum, a performing and media arts centre
dedicated to the artistic and cultural expression of African,
Asian and Caribbean communities. The centre, successor to
The Cave, is financed by the City Council, the regional Arts
Board and other agencies. »95

✧ **Dudley Racial Equality Council**
G.S. Dhanjal, CRO: 16a Stone Street, Dudley DY1 1NS;
t (01384) 456166
Promotion of racial equality, elimination of discrimination;
advice services. Works with local Indian, Pakistani
communities. »95

✧ **Durham County Racial Equality Council**, also known as
Durham Council for Racial Equality
Dr S.P. Singh, Chair: 192 Carmel Road North, Darlington DL3
8RH; t (01325) 380100 ext. 3411
Voluntary body (not CRE-funded) promoting racial equality
and the elimination of discrimination. »95

✧ **Ealing Racial Equality Council**
Godfrey Cremer, Director: 2 The Green, High Street, Ealing,
London W5 5DA; t (0181) 579 3861, f 566 5581
Daphne Stewart. Promotion of equal opportunities in Ealing,
elimination of racial discrimination. »95

✧ **East Staffordshire Racial Equality Council**
Amir Kabal JP, Director: Centre for Voluntary Service, off
Union Street Car Park, Burton-on-Trent DE14 1AA; t (01283)
510922, f 510456
Promotion of racial equality, elimination of discrimination. »95

✧ **Eastbourne Racial Equality Council**
Brian Burt, Secretary: 3 Ashburnham Place, Hailsham BN27
3AX
Voluntary body (not CRE-funded) promoting equality of
opportunity and the elimination of racial discrimination in
Eastbourne district. »95

✧ **Ecowas Womens Group**
Victoria Mambu/Caroline Cocker: 4 Beamish Cose,
Chorlton-on-Medlock, Manchester M13 9SU; t (0161) 226
6586, 273 8745
Multicultural women's group. »93

✧ **Edinburgh Anti-Fascist Action**, AFA
PO Box 474, Edinburgh EH11, Scotland
Organises local anti-fascist and anti-racist monitoring,
research, demonstrations, leafletting. »96

✧ **Enfield Racial Equality Council**, EREC
Chandra Bhatia, Director: The Cottage, 258a Hertford Road,
Enfield EN3 5BN; t (0181) 805 6121, f 805 2560
Elimination of racial discrimination, promotion of equality
initiatives throughout the borough. »96

✧ **Equality at Work**
Ann Simpson: Blackburn College, Feilden Street, Blackburn
BB2 1LH; t (01254) 57155
Training and consultancy in equal opportunities, development
of positive action programmes; provision of vocationally-
related English language training. »94

✧ **Equality Works Consultancy and Training**
Jane Farrell: 11 Carleton Gardens, Brecknock Road, London
N19 5AQ; t (0171) 284 2574 »94

✧ **Essex Racial Equality Council**
Marion Press, Director: Civic Centre, 3rd Floor, Victoria
Avenue, Southend SS2 6EG; t (01268) 724119
Promotion of racial equality, elimination of discrimination in
Southend area. »95
✧ ≡ Basildon Office: Gary Price, Race Equality Officer: Council
Offices, Felmore End, Pitsea, Basildon SS13 1PN; t (01268)
724119, f 724131 »95

● **Evangelical Christians for Racial Justice**, ECRJ
Raj Patel/Elaine Smith, Administrators: 12 Bell Barn Shopping
Centre, Cregoe Street, Lee Bank, Birmingham B15 2DZ;
t (0121) 622 5799, 622 6807
Paul Grant, David Mallard; founded 1972, was Evangelical
Race Relations Group until 1985; anti-racism, resources,
conferences. *Racial Justice* (3/yr). »94

✿ **Exeter Anti-Fascist Action**, AFA
c/o The Flying Post, PO Box 185, Exeter EX4 4EW
Organises local anti-fascist/anti-racist activities. »96

✿ **Fife Racial Equality Council**
May Fong, Director: 2 Acorn Court, Glenrothes KY7 5LZ,
Scotland; *t* (01592) 610211
Elimination of racial discrimination, promotion of equality and
good race relations; confidential advice to anyone who has
faced racial discrimination or harassment. »95

● **Football Supporters Association**
Roger Scoon, Anti-Racism Officer: [address unknown]
Fans' organisation which runs the CRE-funded "Let's kick
racism out of football" campaign against racist chanting and
other manifestations of racism in football. *United Colours of
Football* fanzine. »94

● **Friends Community Relations Committee**, also known as
Quaker Community Relations Committee
Pam Hughes/Paula Harvey: Friends House, Euston Road,
London NW1 2BJ; *t* (0171) 387 3601
Section of Quaker Social Responsibility and Education, SRE;
advisory role to the Religious Society of Friends, raising
awareness of racial discrimination and good practice; books,
films, directory, videos. *Quakers and Race* newsletter. »95

● **Gap Activity Projects Ltd**, GAP
Trisha West: GAP House, 44 Queen's Rd, Reading RG1 4BB
International youth exchanges; 90 voluntary staff; over 1300
volunteers go from or come to the UK each year to work in a
variety of ecological, educational or caring contexts. »95

✿ **Glasgow Sharing of Faiths Group**
Rosemary Eldridge, Convenor: International Flat, 20 Glasgow
Street, Glasgow G12 8JP, Scotland; *t* (0141) 339 6118
Friendship and understanding among local religious groups;
monthly open meetings; *Sharing of Faiths* (4/yr). »88

✿ **Gloucestershire Race Advice Service**: Gloucestershire
County Council
Tony Gómez/Juliet Morefield: Widden Old School, Widden
Street, Gloucester GL1 4AQ; *t* (01452) 20483 (?)
Based at Gloucester Law Centre, p223. »94

✿ **Gloucestershire Race Equality Council**, GLOSREC: succeeds
Gloucester Council for Racial Equality
G. Child, Director: [address uncertain] 15 Brunswick Road,
Gloucester GL1 1HG; *t* (01425) 411961
Also listed (1995) at 75-81 Eastgate Street, GL1 1PN.
Established 1994-95 to work alongside voluntary groups and
statutory agencies to develop initiatives to address community
needs, eliminate discrimination, and promote racial equality
and anti-discriminatory practices. »95

✿ **Grampian Racial Equality Council**
Barney Crockett, Director: 9a Little Belmont Street, Aberdeen
AB1 1JB, Scotland; *t* (01224) 625895
Elimination of racial discrimination, promotion of equality. »95

✿ **Grays Anti-Fascist Action**
PO Box 16, Ilford IG1 1R2 »89

● **Greater London Action for Racial Equality**, GLARE
Patrick Edwards, Director: London Voluntary Sector Resource
Centre, 356 Holloway Road, London N7 6PA; *t* (0171) 700
0100 ext. 281; 700 8135
Caroline Holder, administrator; independent body promoting
race equality policy development; represents and co-ordinates
all 26 London Racial Equality Councils on issues such as
immigration controls, race relations, refugees, Europe. »96

✿ **Greater Manchester Anti-Racist Alliance**
Cllr Iqbal Stram: Frontline Books, Box 17, 1 Newton Street,
Piccadilly, Manchester M1 1HM
Anti-racist and anti-fascist campaigns; see ARA, p176. »93

● **Green Party Anti-Racist and Anti-Fascist Network**, GPARAFN
[address uncertain] 1a Waterloo Road, London N19 5NJ
Network of anti-fascist and anti-racist activists; advances anti-
racist agenda within the ecology movement and its allies. »94

✿ **Greenwich Council for Racial Equality** and Greenwich
Campaign Against Racial Attacks, GCARA
Makhan Singh Bajwa, Director: 2nd Floor, 115-123 Powis
Street, Woolwich, London SE18 6JL; *t* (0181) 855 7191,
855 7194, *f* 317 3707
Dev Barra. The Council promotes race equality and works for
the elimination of discrimination. The (separate) Campaign,
also known as Greenwich Action Committee, monitors and
opposes racial violence and harassment in the area. »96

✿ **Gwent Racial Equality Council**
Jill Peterson, Admin Officer: 124 Commercial Street,
Newport NP9 1HB, Wales; *t* (01633) 250006
Elimination of discrimination, promotion of racial equality.
Advice work with Asian, African, Caribbean communities.»94

✿ **Hackney Community Defence Association**
Colin Roach Centre, 56 Clarence Road, London E5; *t* (0181)
533 7111
Anti-racist campaigns, especially on policing issues. »96

✿ **Hackney Race Equality Unit**
Head of Unit: Town Hall, Mare Street, London E8 1EA
Unit which monitors and contributes to policy and practice in
the delivery of Borough services to ensure racial equity. »95

✿ **Hackney Racial Equality Council**, HREC
Trevor Carter/Alan Badman: 17-19 Dalston Lane, London E8;
t (0171) 241 0097, *f* 923 4180
Promotes racial equality, elimination of disadvantage. Works
with Asian, African, Turkish, Caribbean communities. »95

✿ **Halifax Anti-Fascist Action**, AFA
PO Box 127, Leeds LS3 1TS; *t* (0113) 242 4680
Local anti-racist and anti-fascist activities; participation in
national campaigns. »96

✿ **Hammersmith and Fulham Racial Equality Council**
James Barzey, Acting Director: Palingswick House, 241 King
Street, London W6 9LP; *t* (0181) 741 5717
Promotion of racial equality in the district, elimination of
discrimination. »95

✿ **Haringey Racial Equality Council**
Sabes Sugunasabesan, Director: 14a Turnpike Lane, Hornsey,
London N8 0PT; *t* (0181) 889 6871-74, *f* 889 6455
Promotes racial equality, combats discrimination; advice work
with Asians, West Indians, Cypriots and other groups. »95

✿ **Haringey Racial Harassment Monitoring Project**
c/o Haringey Council, 40 Cumberland Road, Wood Green,
London N22 4SG
Joint project of Haringey Council, Haringey REC, the local
police and Haringey Community Police Consultative Group;
monitors reports of and co-ordinates response to racial
harassment and racist incidents in the borough. »95

✿ **Harlow Community Relations Council**
Latton Bush Centre, Southern Way, Harlow, Essex; *t* (01279)
641075 »90

✿ **Harrow Inter-Faith Council**
Rev. Hazel Whitehead, Secretary: 55 Warrington Road,
Harrow HA1 1SZ; *t* (0181) 427 3872
Dialogue and understanding among different faiths. »88

✿ **Harrow Racial Equality Council**, HREC
Rose-Marie Adams, Director: 64 Pinner Road, Harrow HA1
4HZ; *t* (0181) 427 6504
Independent voluntary charity. Promotion of racial equality
and justice, elimination of discrimination; K. Raleigh chair,
Prem Pawar; immigration, asylum, harassment casework.»95

✿ **Hertfordshire Anti-Fascist Action**, Herts AFA
PO Box 245, St Albans, Hertfordshire
Organises local anti-fascist/anti-racist activity including
research, demonstrations, leafletting. »96

✿ **Hillingdon Race Equality Development Project**
London Borough of Hillingdon, Civic Centre, Uxbridge UB8
1UW; *t* (01895) 250394
Project to establish a successor body to Hillingdon Community
Relations Council. Managed by the borough's Race Equality
Steering Group, the project will use consultants working with
local community representatives and official bodies. »95

● **Hit Racism for Six Campaign**
c/o Centre for Sport Development Research, Department of
Sports Studies, Roehampton Institute, London SW15 3SN;
t (0171) 561 1606
Campaigns against racism in cricket. »96

✿ **Hounslow Monitoring Project**, HMP
Bali Gill: [address unknown] Hounslow TW3, Middlesex;
t c/o (0181) 572 8656
A branch of Southall Monitoring Group, p183, a community
organisation providing legal, moral and practical support to
people suffering racial harassment and domestic violence.
Provides Asian women's counselling service in association
with West London Asian Health Agency, p15. »95

✿ **Hounslow Racial Equality Council**
Permjeet Panesar, Director: 45 Treaty Centre, Hounslow
TW3 1ES; *t* (0181) 570 1168
Charity promoting racial equality, combatting discrimination
in the district. »95

✿ **Hounslow Voluntary Action**
51 Grove Road, Hounslow TW3 3PR; *t* (0181) 577 3226
Community development, refugee work with Asian, African,
Indian Ocean communities. »91

✿ **Hull and District Racial Equality Council**
Minnie Southwick: 2nd Floor, Ferensway Chambers, 120-122 George Street, Hull HU1 3AA; *t* (01482) 227601, *f* 225166
Anti-racism, promotion of equality; not CRE-funded. »95

✿ **Hyndburn and Rossendale Racial Equality Council:** Head Office
Derek Loney, Director: 2nd Floor, Regency House, Blackburn Road, Accrington BB5 1HF; *t* (01254) 395719; (01706) 224525
Campaigns for racial equality and against discrimination. Advice work including some Pakistani, Bangladeshi immigration casework. Has a sub-office at 33 Kay Street, Rawtenstall, Rossendale BB4 7LS. »95

✿ **Interfaith Action**
Renu Begum: [address uncertain] 20 West Street, Rochdale OL16 2EN; *t* (01706) 53347
Sheila A. Lee *t* (0706) 345346. »90

● **Inter Faith Network for the United Kingdom**
Brian Pearce, Director: 5-7 Tavistock Place, London WC1H 9SS; *t* (0171) 388 0008, *f* 387 7968
Formed 1987 to promote dialogue and mutual understanding among different religions; governed by a Council representing the affiliated bodies. »94

✿ **Interim Cheshire Racial Equality Council,** ICREC
Lily Ho: c/o The Professional Centre, Woodford Lodge, Woodford Lane West, Winsford CW7 4EH; *t* (01606) 557328
Preparing for the establishment of an REC to promote equality of opportunity and good relations between persons of different racial groups in Cheshire, and to work towards eliminating unlawful discrimination. »95

▎**International Centre for Multicultural Education**
Dr Derek Cherrington: [address uncertain] City of Birmingham Polytechnic, Edgbaston, Birmingham B15 3TN »90

✿ **International Society**
84 Plymouth Grove, Manchester
International friendship and solidarity; provides meeting place for migrant organisations. »93

✿ **International Solidarity Tower Hamlets**
Oxford House, Derbyshire Street, London E2 6HG; *t* (0171) 739 1786
Anti-racist education and campaigning. See also CAPA, p178, Somalia Relief Association, p109, and Civil Rights Advice and Support Group, p222. »91

● **Interracial Solidarity**
[address unknown] Leicester »88

✿ **Ipswich and Suffolk Council for Racial Equality**
Elaine Graham Walters: 17 Woodbridge Road, Ipswich IP4 2EA; *t* (01473) 221954
Promotion of racial equality in Suffolk, elimination of discrimination; monitors racist attacks in the area (170 in 1994). »95

✿ **Islington Anti-Racist and Anti-Fascist Action,** ARAFA
Anna Sullivan/Hafitz Rahman: c/o Box 11, Centerprise, Kingsland High Street, London E8
Local anti-racist work, linking with national campaigns. (Contact names 1989, address 1996.) »96

✿ **Islington Council Race Equality Unit**
Zak Stavrinos: Town Hall, Upper St, Islington, London N1 »94

● **Japanese Labour Camp Survivors' Association**
Arthur Titherington, Secretary: 100 Pinewood Avenue, Eastwood, Leigh-on-Sea SS9 5PB
Represents British survivors of fascist prison camps. »95

✿ **Kensington and Chelsea Racial Equality Council**
Rumman Ahmed, Director: Westway Information Centre, 140 Ladbroke Grove, London W10 5ND; *t* (0181) 969 2433 ext. 7729
Promotion of community relations, combatting discrimination in this multi-ethnic district in which over 90 languages are spoken. Funded by Borough Council, not CRE. »95

✿ **Kent Anti-Fascist Action Committee,** AFA
PO Box 88, Rochester ME1 1AU
Organises local anti-fascist/anti-racist monitoring, research, demonstrations, leafletting and other activity. »96

✿ **Kingston Group for Racial Understanding**
Ajit Singh, Chair: 107 Whitton Road, Hounslow TW3 2EJ »88

✿ **Kingston Racial Equality Council**
John Azah, Director: Welfare House, 53 Canbury Park Road, Kingston-upon-Thames KT2 6LQ; *t* (0181) 547 2332
Promotion of race equality in Kingston, combatting discrimination and harassment; community development. »95

✿ **Kirklees and Calderdale Inter-Faith Fellowship**
Bill Jones, Secretary: 316 Huddersfield Road, Mirfield WF14 9PY; *t* (01924) 495303
Informal dialogue, understanding among different faith communities. *Inter-Faith Matters* (4/yr). »88

✿ **Kirklees Metropolitan Council Equal Opportunities Unit**
R. Patel: Civic Centre, 1 High Street, Huddersfield HD1 2BA; *t* (01484) 422133 exts. 2309, 2288, 2310
Local authority policy advice on immigration, refugees, nationality, racial equality. »94

✿ **Kirklees Racial Equality Council,** KREC: Dewsbury Office, formerly Kirklees Steering Committee for Community Relations
Satish Malik, CRO: Ground Floor, Town Hall, Dewsbury WF12 8DG; *t* (01924) 465151 ext. 348
Promotion of racial equality and equal opportunities, combatting discrimination and harassment in the area. »95

✿ ≡ Huddersfield Office, formerly South Kirklees Community Relations Council: Maqsood Ahmad, Director: 24 Westgate, Huddersfield HD1 1NU; *t* (01484) 540225-26, *f* 429828 »95

✿ **Lanarkshire Campaign Against Racism and Fascism,** CARF
PO Box 981, Hamilton ML3 8EL, Scotland
Local anti-racist and anti-fascist activities; participation in national and UK campaigns. »96

✿ **Shiji Lapite Memorial Committee**
PO Box 273, London E7; *t* (0181) 555 8151
Campaigns for an independent inquiry into the death of Oluwashiji Lapite, who was unlawfully killed in December 1994 by Stoke Newington police. »96

✿ **Leeds Alliance against Racism and Fascism**
c/o Leeds AFA, PO Box 127, Leeds LS3 1TS; *t* c/o (0113) 242 4680
Coalition including Leeds AFA and local branches of the Anti-Nazi League, Anti-Racist Alliance, Youth against Racism in Europe, the Labour Party and the Trades Council. Anti-racist demonstrations and campaigns. »95

✿ **Leeds Anti-Fascist Action,** AFA
PO Box 127, Leeds LS3 1TS; *t* (0113) 242 4680
Organises local anti-fascist/anti-racist research, demonstrations, other activity. See also Leeds Alliance against Racism and Fascism, above. *Attitude*. »96

✿ **Leeds Concord Inter-Faith Fellowship**
Dr Peter Bell, Secretary: 19 Gledhow Park Drive, Leeds LS2 4JT; *t* (0113) 262 9140
Inter-faith understanding and respect; resource centre, newsletter, meetings, community events. »88

✿ **Leeds Divided Families Campaign**
c/o Fiona Callow: 48 Stratford Street, Leeds LS11, Yorkshire
Opposes racist and sexist immigration rules. »91

✿ **Leeds Fans United Against Racism**
[address unknown] Leeds, Yorkshire
Campaigns against racist and fascist activity at football matches, including racist chanting. »95

✿ **Leeds Racial Equality Council**
John Roberts, Director: 29 Harrogate Road, Chapel Allerton, Leeds LS7 3PD; *t* (0113) 237 4663 (?), *f* 237 4872 (?)
Elimination of discrimination, promotion of racial equality; advice work with Asian, West Indian community issues including immigration rules, DNA tests. »95

✿ **Leicester Anti-Fascist Alliance,** AFA, also known as Leicester Anti-Fascist Action
PO Box 368, Leicester LE2 7YZ
Anti-fascist/anti-racist research, demonstrations, leafletting and other activity. »96

✿ **Leicester City Council Race Relations Unit**
Ms Rashni: New Walk Centre, Welford Place, Leicester LE1 6ZG; *t* (0116) 254 9922 exts. 6070-72
Local authority policy unit advising on matters affecting Gujarati, Vietnamese, Bengali, Caribbean, Irish, Chinese, Pakistani, Punjabi and African residents. »93

✿ **Leicester Council of Faiths**
Rev. Michael Walls, Secretary: The Vicarage, Oakham Road, Tilton-on-the-Hill, Leicester LE7 9LB; *t* (0116) 254244 (?)
Mutual understanding, co-operation among different faiths.»88

✿ **Leicester Racial Equality Council,** LREC
Dave Purdey, Director: 4th Floor, 13-15 Belvoir Street, Leicester LE1 6LS; *t* (0116) 254 5918, *f* 254 5921
Promotion of racial equality and good community relations in the county; elimination of discrimination; advice to individuals; support to community groups; education, training. »95

✿ **Leicester Racism Awareness Consortium**
3 Hill Street, Leicester LE1 3PT »90

✿ **Leicestershire Steering Group for Racial Justice**
11 The Market Place, 4th floor, The Jetty, Leicester LE1 2ZL; *t* c/o (0116) 254 9922 ext. 6074 »88

● **Lesbian and Gay Coalition against Racism**
[address unknown] London »96

✿ **Lewisham Action on Policing,** LAP
192 Evelyn Street, Deptford, London SE8 5DB
Research, advice, casework, information and campaigning on racial harassment, other issues in policing South London. »96

✧ **Lewisham Racial Equality Council, LREC**
Asquith Gibbes, Director: 48 Lewisham High Street, London
SE13 5JH; *t* (0181) 852 9808
Sue Mead, Richard Backes; promotes equal opportunities,
elimination of race discrimination. Research on racial
harassment and violence. Advice work including immigration,
refugees, exclusion from school of black students. »96

● **Liberation**, formerly Movement for Colonial Freedom
490 Kingsland Road, London E8 4AE; *t* (0171) 254 6223
Stan Newens MEP, chair; third world solidarity and anti-racist
society; NGO status at UN. »96

✧ **Liverpool Anti-Fascist Action, AFA**, formerly Merseyside
Anti-Fascist Action
PO Box 110, Liverpool L69 8DP
Organises local anti-fascist and anti-racist research,
demonstrations, leafletting and other activity. »96

✧ **Liverpool Anti-Racist Community Arts Association**
Ibrahim Thompson: 23 Clarence Street, Liverpool L3 5TN »96

✧ **London Alliance Against Racism and Fascism, LAARF**
BM Box LAARF, London WC1N 3XX
Anti-Racist Bulletin. »91

✧ **London Anti-Fascist Action, AFA**
BM 1734, London WC1N 3XX
Anti-fascist research, demonstrations and campaigns. »94

✧ **London Equal Opportunities Federation Ltd**
23 Lewisham High Street, London SE13 5AF
A voluntary organisation promoting equal opportunities for
minorities, women and people with disabilities in the
construction activities of 80 housing associations. »95

✧ **London Society of Jews and Christians**
Doreen Davenport: 1 Greenham Road, Eltham, London SE9
1UQ; *t* (0171) 850 9000
Promotes mutual respect; lectures, discussions, events. »88

✧ **Longsight and Levenshulme Anti-Racist Group**
Balijit Badesha: c/o South Manchester Law Centre, 584-586
Stockport Road, Manchester M13 0RG; *t* (0161) 225 5111
admin, 248 8348 helpline
Anti-racist campaigns; support for victims of harassment,
including 24-hour helpline. »93

✧ **Lothian Racial Equality Council**
The Director: 14 Forth Street, Edinburgh EH1 3LH, Scotland;
t (0131) 556 0441, *f* 556 8577
Promotion of racial equality, elimination of discrimination,
assistance to anyone who experiences racial harassment or
discrimination. Advice work: primary purpose and family
reunion cases, mainly Pakistanis, Chinese, other Asians. »96

✧ **Luton Community Relations Council**
M.S. Khan, CRO: 58 Stuart Street, Luton, Bedfordshire »90

✧ **Manchester Against Immigration Controls, MAGIC**
Mark Abrahams: 168 Egerton Road North, Whalley Range,
Manchester M16 0DB; *t* (0161) 881 9747 »94

✧ **Manchester Anti-Fascist Action**
[address unknown] Manchester
A local section of Anti-Fascist Action. See also Greater
Manchester Anti-Racist Alliance, p179. »88

✧ **Manchester Council for Community Relations, MCCR**,
formerly Manchester Council for Racial Equality, MCRE
Nasrullah Khan Moghul, Director: 4th Floor, Peter House,
2-14 Oxford Street, Manchester M1 5AG; *t* (0161) 228
0710, *f* 228 0745
Sayed Ahmed, Lynne Sutton. Promotes equal opportunities,
combats racism; liaises with national and local government,
with the private sector and with ethnic minority community
groups. Advice work on matters including immigration. »96

✧ **Manchester Inter-Faith Group**
John Wilson, Secretary: The Sacred Trinity Centre, Chapel
Street, Salford M3 7AJ; *t* (0161) 832 3709
Inter-faith contact, co-operation and respect. »88

✧ **Mandela Centre**
Chapeltown Road, Leeds LS7; *t* (0113) 262 2816 »90

● **Media Workers Against the Nazis, MWAN**
NUJ, Acorn House, 314 Grays Inn Road, London WC1X 8DP
Pressure group within the National Union of Journalists and
other media trade unions; opposes uncritical or excessive
coverage of the British National Party and other nazi groups;
promotes anti-racist and anti-fascist policies in the media. »95

✧ **Medway and Gillingham Racial Equality Council**
Margot Kane, Director: 16 New Road Avenue, Chatham ME4
6BA; *t* (01634) 403001
Elimination of discrimination, promotion of equal opportunities,
advice; mainly Asian, East African Asian communities. »95

✧ **Medway Inter-Faith Group**
Margaret Narborough, Secretary: 35 Leeward Road,
Rochester ME1 2NE; *t* (01634) 407120
Inter-faith understanding and friendship. »88

✧ **Merseyside Action Against Racial Terrorism, MAARTG**
Jane Eme, Chair: c/o Merseyside REC, 64 Mount Pleasant,
Liverpool L3 5SH; *t* c/o (0151) 709 6858
Works with housing agencies and victims of harassment. »90

✧ **Merseyside Interfaith Group**
Vida Barnett, Chairwoman: 81 St Mary's Road, Huyton,
Liverpool L36 5SR; *t* (0151) 489 2294
Friendship, trust, understanding among all major faiths. »88

✧ **Merseyside Racial Equality Council, MREC**
c/o Town Hall, Brighton Street, Wallasey, Wirral L44 8ED
Reconstituted 1996; promotion of racial equality in Knowsley,
Liverpool, Sefton, St Helens and Wirral. »96

✧ **Merton Racial Equality Council**
Lloyd Thomas, Director: 36 High Street, Colliers Wood,
London SW19 2AB; *t* (0181) 540 7386
T. Mahmud. Works for elimination of racial discrimination,
promotion of equality. »95

✧ **Milton Keynes Racial Equality Council**
Rev. Barney Pityana, Chair: Acorn House, 377 Midsummer
Boulevard, Central Milton Keynes MK9 3HP; *t* (01908)
606828, *f* 200979
Paul Clifford director. Promotion of racial equality and
elimination of racial prejudice and violence; some casework
with Pakistani, other Asian groups. »95

✧ **Mosaic**
Jill Howes: 9 Rugby Rd, Brighton BN1 6EA; *t* (01273) 502620
Social grouping for families of mixed ethnic origins. »94

✧ **Multi-Agency Racial Harassment Project**
Chief Executive's Department, Manchester City Council,
Town Hall, Manchester M60 2LA; *t* (0161) 234 3077
Combats racial harassment through local victim support
schemes, improving and co-ordinating responses of public
agencies (police, housing, education, social services, courts),
publicising the problem and the city's response. »92

✧ **Multicultural Support Service**: London Borough of Waltham
Forest
Cathy Syer, Administrator: Education Centre, Queens Road,
Walthamstow, London E17; *t* (0181) 521 3311 ext. 284,
f 509 9668
Assisting teachers and schools to develop specialist provision
for refugee and minority children; curriculum materials, staff
training, pastoral support, liaison with other services. »95

✧ **Multicultural Support Service Resource Unit**
[address uncertain] The Bordesley Centre, Stratford Road,
Birmingham; *t* (0121) 772 5917 (?)
Educational resources, specialist teaching and training. »90

✧ **Multi-Racial Project**
University of Keele, Keele ST5 5BG; *t* (01782) 621111 »90

● **National Anti-Racist Movement in Education, NAME**
Clancy Etienne: 41 Strawberry Lane, Carshalton SM5 2NG;
t (0161) 442 2673
Membership organisation supporting the development of anti-
racist and multicultural education. *Arena*. »95

♦ **National Assembly against Racism**
Kumar Murshid/Rokhsana Fiaz: 22 Hanbury St, London E1
Established in 1995; affiliates include Newham Monitoring
Project, p182; sponsors include Labour MPs Diane Abbott and
Ken Livingstone. Promotes charter against racism. »96

● **National Association of Development Education Centres,**
NADEC
Graham Cahle: 6 Endsleigh Street, London WC1H 0DX;
t (0171) 388 2670
International social justice. »90

● **National Association for Multiracial Education**
[address uncertain] 71 Rogbon Gardens, Oxhey, Watford »90

♦ **National Association of Racial Equality Councils, NAREC**:
Head Office
Clifford Boam: 1st Floor, 8-16 Coronet Street, London N1
6HD; *t* (0171) 739 6658-59, *f* 739 1528
Umbrella body for local RECs, all of which are listed
separately. Formerly National Association of Community
Relations Councils; member of EU Migrants Forum, p131. »95
✧ ≡ Northern office: 231-235 Chapeltown Road, Leeds LS7;
t (0113) 262 8726 »90

● **National Federation of Far East Prisoners of War**
Harold Payne: [address unknown]
Represents survivors of Japanese fascist prison camps. »95

● **National Institute for Social Work Race Equality Unit, REU**
Juliet Gardner/Audrey McLeod: 5 Tavistock Place, London
WC1H 9SN; *t* (0171) 387 9681
Jabeer Butt. The REU is the only national organisation set up
(in 1987) to work with and for social services and related
agencies on promoting better social care for black and ethnic
minority communities. Funded by the Department of Health;
six staff. »95

3

● **New Internationalist**
55 Rectory Road, Oxford OX4 1BW; *t* (01685) 728181,
f 793152
Development education, third world solidarity magazine
(12/yr); educational materials.   »95

✿ **Newham Association of Faiths**
Margaret Williams, Secretary: 234 Upton Lane, Forest Gate,
London E7 9NP; *t* (0181) 552 4776
Social justice, tolerance, inter-faith understanding.   »88

✿ **Newham Community Renewal Programme Ltd**, NCRP
S. Agyeman-Mensah: 170 Harold Road, Plaistow, London
E13 0SE; *t* (0181) 472 2785
Community development, employment and training.   »95

✿ **Newham Council for Racial Equality**, NCRE: also known as
Newham Racial Equality Council, NREC
Director: 175 Upton Lane, Forest Gate, London E7 9PJ;
t (0181) 471 4621, *f* 522 8933
Promotes equal opportunities for ethnic minorities, combats
racial discrimination; funded by CRE and borough council.»95

✿ **Newham Council Social Services Department Race
Equality Section**
99 The Grove, Stratford, London E15 1HR
Ensures equity in delivery of Council services; operates Action
Plan for Refugees involving community development, advice
services and joint initiatives with other agencies.   »95

✿ **Newham Monitoring Project**, NMP
Unmesh Desai, Chair: PO Box 273, Forest Gate, London E7;
t (0181) 552 6284, *f* 552 7467
Jasbir Singh. Monitors and combats racial violence, fascism
and police harassment; promotes community organisation, and
work within the white working class; provides advice, support
and information; runs Newham Unity Festival. Five staff. »96

✿ **North Staffordshire Racial Equality Council**
Roy Davis, Director: 1st Floor, Tontine Buildings, 56 Tontine
Street, Hanley, Stoke-on-Trent ST1 1LY; *t* (01782) 214061
Promotion of race equality, elimination of discrimination; small
REC, works with South Asian/Caribbean communities.   »95

✿ **North West Monitoring Group**
[address confidential] *t* (0370) 392414, noon to midnight
Local anti-fascist campaigning and research.   »96

✿ **North Yorkshire Racial Equality Council**, formerly York and
District Council for Community Relations
10 Priory Street, York YO1 1EX; *t* (01904) 610810
Elimination of discrimination and promotion of racial equality
in the County of North Yorkshire. Not CRE-funded.   »95

✿ **Northampton Racial Equality Council**
Richard Davis, Director: 64 Charles Street, Northampton
NN1 3BG; *t* (01604) 32231
Promotion of racial equality, elimination of discrimination,
advice service: small Asian immigration caseload.   »95

✿ **Norwich Anti-Fascist Action**, AFA
PO Box 73, Norwich NR1 2EB
Organises local anti-fascist/anti-racist research, monitoring,
demonstrations, leafletting and other activity.   »96

✿ **Norwich and Norfolk Racial Equality Council**, REC
Ann Matin: The Advice Arcade, 4 Guild Hall Hill, Norwich
NR2 1JH; *t* (01603) 617541
Small REC working for equality of opportunity and against
racial discrimination. Conducted 1994 survey of racism in
Norfolk and is developing programme in response.   »95

✿ **Nottingham City Council Race and Housing Project**
Errol Hemans, Co-ordinator: [address unknown] Nottingham
Monitors and responds to the racial harassment of council
tenants; promotes equality in housing provision.   »95

✿ **Nottingham and District Racial Equality Council**, NDREC
Milton Crosdale, Director: 67 Lower Parliament Street,
Nottingham NG1 3BB; *t* (0115) 958 6515, *f* 959 0624
Laurence Platt. Works for racial equality, against
discrimination; advice service, some immigration work;
research (1981, 1994) into employment discrimination.   »95

✿ **Nottingham Inter-Faith Group**
John Crawley, Secretary: White Cottage, 1a Stanton Road,
Sandiacre NG10 5DE; *t* (0115) 939 5106
Friendship, co-operation among faith communities.   »88

✿ **Nottinghamshire Anti-Fascist Alliance**, AFA: also known as
Nottingham Anti-Fascist Alliance
Ross Bradshaw: PO Box 179, Nottingham NG1 3AQ
Organises local anti-fascist/anti-racist research,
demonstrations, leafletting and other activity.   »96

✿ **Oldham Action Against Racism**
c/o Brian Davis, MP, GMB Offices, 108 Union Street, Oldham
OL1 1DY
May be a successor to Oldham Campaign Against Racism and
Fascism (1988). Organises local activities; participates in
national campaigns, against racism and the ultra-right.   »96

✿ **Oldham Racial Equality Council**, OREC, formerly Oldham
Council for Racial Equality
Sabiha Shazad: 2nd Floor, Metropolitan House, Hobson St,
Oldham OL1 1QD; *t* (0161) 911 4744, *f* 911 4743
Re-established 1994; promotion of racial equality and harmony
in Oldham; advice work including immigration issues.   »95

● **One World Group of Broadcasters**, Secretariat
Room 302, 152 Great Portland Street, London W1N 6AJ;
t (0171) 765 5035, *f* 765 5459
Media workers' group promoting development education,
global awareness, anti-racism, concern for human rights. »94

● **Open Eye**
John Murray/Matthew Kalman: [address unknown]
Magazine monitoring extreme right-wing movements, bizarre
cults and conspiracy theorists around the world.   »95

✿ **Oxford Round Table of Religions**
Rev. Sidney Hinkes, Chair: St Mary's Vicarage, Headington,
Oxford OX3 9EY; *t* (01865) 61886
Inter-faith contact, mutual education and support.   »88

✿ **Oxfordshire Racial Equality Council**
Cesar A. Guidi, Joint Secretary: Macclesfield House, New
Road, Oxford OX1 1NA; *t* (01865) 815449, *f* 791637
Promotion of racial equality, elimination of discrimination. »95

✿ **Partnership against Racial Harassment in Somerset**
Rev. Mark Ellis: [address unknown] Yeovil
Founded 1995 in response to particular problems of rural
racism in the south-west of England.   »95

✿ **Peterborough Inter-Faith Council**
Lesley Mathias: 18 West Street, Kings Cliffe, Peterborough
PE8 6XR; *t* (01780) 87355
Understanding and co-operation between different
communities of faith; meetings, worship, public education.»88

✿ **Peterborough Racial Equality Council**
Hermesh Lakanpaul, Director: 32 Russell Street, Peterborough
PE1 2BQ; *t* (01733) 54630, 341061
Works for racial equality and elimination of discrimination.
Advice service; divided families, primary purpose rule.   »95

✿ **Plymouth and District Racial Equality Council**
Bengie Parker, Chair: 4th Floor, Civic Centre, Plymouth PL1
2AA; *t* (01752) 668000 exts. 4907, 4127
Peter Aley. Promotion of race equality, elimination of
discrimination; community development; not CRE-funded. »95

✿ **Preston and Western Lancashire Racial Equality Council**
M.F. Desai, Director: Town Hall Annexe, PO Box 10, Birley
Street, Preston PR1 1RL; *t* (01772) 266422
Promotion of racial equality, elimination of discrimination and
disadvantage, support to victims of harassment.   »95

✿ **Pwyllgor Cyslltiadau Cymdeithas de Morgannwg**: South
Glamorgan Race Equality Council, SGREC
Jaginder Basi Singh, Director: 8 Williams Court, Trade Street,
Cardiff CF1 5DQ, Wales; *t/f* (01222) 224097
Promotion of racial equality, elimination of discrimination and
harassment; advice on immigration, asylum, other matters;
Somali, South Asian, Caribbean, Chinese communities.   »96

✿ **Race Equality Consultative Forum**
Julie Klukarski: 6 York Court, Wilder Street, Bristol BS2 8QQ;
t (0117) 924 4474
Provides a mechanism for consultation between Black and
minority ethnic communities, local government and other
public bodies.   »94

*Race Equality Units, Equal Opportunities Units: see parent
body, e.g. National Institute for Social Work, Newham Council*

● **Race for Opportunity Campaign**
Robert Ayling, Chairman: [address unknown] London
Public education campaign launched in 1995 by Business in
the Community, a group founded in 1981 to promote
community involvement by British private enterprise.   »96

✿ **Racial Attacks Monitoring Project**, RAMP
6 Seymour Street, Highfields, Leicester LE2 0LB; *t* (0116)
262 1727
Established 1986.   »88

*Racial Discrimination Legal Defence Fund, RDLDF: believed
defunct (1995)*

*Racial Equality Councils (Community Relations Councils or
Committees, Councils for Racial Equality, Associations for
Racial Equality, Councils for Community Relations): these are
local voluntary organisations throughout the UK (except in
Northern Ireland), most funded by the Commission for Racial
Equality, CRE, or by local authorities (some are unfunded).
They promote good community relations and equality of
opportunity, and combat racial discrimination in their locality.
They include representatives of public and voluntary bodies,
employers and others. Many provide advice and advocacy
services, others offer referral services. See separate entries
for some 88 CRE-funded RECs and several equivalent bodies.*

✧ **Reading Campaign Against Racism and Fascism**, CARF
4 Silver Street, Reading, Berkshire
Local anti-racist and anti-fascist activities; participation in
national campaigns. »96

✧ **Reading Inter-Faith Group**
J.W. Talbot, Secretary: 84 Waverley Road, Reading RG3
2PY; *t* (01734) 590233
Inter-faith harmony and understanding. »88

✧ **Reading Racial Equality Council**
Rajinder Sohpal, Director: 2-4 Silver Street, Reading RG1
2ST; *t* (01734) 868755, *f* 314786
Kevin Durham. Race equality, elimination of discrimination.
Works with local Asian and Afro-Caribbean populations. »95

✧ **Redbridge Council of Faiths**
Peter Baker, Chairman: The Lodge, Coppice School, Manford
Way, Chigwell IG7 4AL; *t* (0181) 500 4736
Sharing of religious experience, opposition to racism and
sectarianism; visits, services. »88

✧ **Redbridge Racial Equality Council**
M. Nunoo, Director: Methodist Church Hall, Ilford Lane, Ilford
IG1 2JZ; *t* (0181) 514 0688, *f* 514 0870
Promotion of race equality in Redbridge, elimination of
discrimination. Involved in the development of a Refugee
Centre through Redbridge Refugee Forum. »95

✧ **Redditch Community Relations Council**
Cllr Madge Tillsley: Town Hall, Alcester Street, Redditch B98
8AH; *t* (01527) 64252
Voluntary body, not CRE-funded; promotion of racial equality
and combatting discrimination. »95

✧ **Religious Advice Centre**
Yunus U. Patel: 223-225 Whalley Range, Blackburn BB1
6NN; *t* (01254) 582141
Centre providing information and advice on religious matters,
and promoting Christian-Muslim understanding. »94

● **Returned Volunteer Action**, RVA
Rod Leith/Gail Lewis: 1 Amwell Street, London EC1R 1UL;
t (0171) 278 0804
Third world support, anti-racism, development education
pressure group consisting mainly of former overseas workers
with CIIR, p221, VSO, p228, UNAIS and other agencies. »94

✧ **Richmond Inter-Faith Group**
Rev. Anne McClelland, Secretary: 12 Hillmont Road, Hinchley
Wood, Esher KT10 9BA; *t* (0181) 398 3706 »88

✧ **Rochdale Campaign Against Racism and Fascism**, CARF
Shahida Dolan, Chair: c/o Brian Davis MP, GMB Offices, 108
Union Street, Oldham OL1 1DY
Monitors and opposes racist violence; victim support. »96

✧ **Rochdale Interfaith Action**
Stanley Hope: 445 Bury Road, Rochdale OL11 5EU; *t* (01706)
58491
Social justice, right to family life, interfaith understanding. »88

✧ **Rochdale Racial Equality Council** and Rochdale Employment
Advice Project, REAP
D. Codner, Acting Director: 1st Floor, Champness Hall, Drake
Street, Rochdale OL16 1PB; *t* (01706) 352374, *f* 711259
Elimination of racial discrimination, promotion of equal
opportunities; immigration work, mainly Asian; assistance with
complaints under the Race Relations Acts, and tribunal cases.
REAP is specialist advice and training service for minority job-
seekers, supporting positive action programmes. »95

✧ **Rotherham Racial Equality Council**
Mohammed Almas Abbasi: Imperial Buildings, Rooms 11-13,
Corporation Street, Rotherham S60 1NP; *t* (01709) 373065
Promotion of racial equality, elimination of discrimination. »95

✧ **Rugby Racial Equality Council**
H.J. Mansoomansingh, Director: 5 Pennington Street, Rugby
CV21 1AZ; *t* (01788) 576424, *f* 560142
Promotion of racial equality in Rugby, opposition to
discrimination. Indian, Pakistani, Caribbean community issues
including divided families. »95

✧ **Sandwell Racial Equality Council**
170 High Street (Arcade), West Bromwich B70 7QS;
t (0121) 525 1488
Promotion of racial equality, elimination of discrimination.
Some immigration work: Indian, Pakistani, Bangladeshi. »95

● **Scottish Action Against Racism and Fascism in Europe**
Satwat Rehman: [address unknown] Scotland
Seeks to build a strong, coherent anti-racist movement which
recognises the impact of class and gender. »95

● **Scottish Anti-Racist Alliance**
c/o Clyde Books, 19 Parnie Street, Glasgow, Scotland »94

● **Scottish Anti-Racist Teacher Education Network**
Kifi Tordzro, Co-ordinator: Jordanhill College, Southbrae Drive,
Glasgow G13 1PP, Scotland; *t* (0141) 950 3357
Organises training workshops. »90

● **Scottish Council for Racial Equality**
N.K. Sood, Secretary: 18 Belvedere Park, Edinburgh EH6 4LR
Yousuf Inait. No further information: not CRE-funded. »94

● **Scottish Education and Action for Development**, SEAD
23 Castle Street, Edinburgh EH2 3DN; *t* (0131) 225 6550
Development education, promotion of human rights and
social justice in Scotland and worldwide. Funds several
refugee projects abroad (through other agencies). »93

✧ **Scunthorpe & South Humberside Racial Equality Council**,
formerly Scunthorpe & District Community Relations Council
Jawaid Ishaq, Chair: 20 Normanby Road, Scunthorpe DN15
6AL; *t* (01274) 867231
Promotion of racial equality, elimination of discrimination.
Not CRE-funded. »95

◆ *Searchlight*, formally Searchlight Magazine Ltd
Gerry Gable, Publisher: 37b New Cavendish Street, London
W1M 8JR; *t* (0171) 284 4040, *f* 284 4410
A major anti-racist, anti-fascist research organisation which
publishes a monthly journal in that field. Campaigning and
education through charity, Searchlight Educational Trust;
research and consultancy services to the media; participates
in UK and European anti-racist initiatives. Address given is
for postal purposes; editorial address is confidential. »95

✧ **Sharrow Action Committee Against Racism and Fascism**
c/o Horsa Hut, Sharrow Lane, Sheffield S11, Yorkshire »88

✧ **Sheffield Against Racism and Fascism**
c/o Sheffield College Students' Union, Granville Road,
Sheffield S2 2RL
Local anti-racist and anti-fascist activities; participation in
national campaigns. »96

✧ **Sheffield Racial Equality Council**, SREC
Peter Moore, Director: 108 The Moor, Sheffield S1 4PD;
t (0114) 273 6601, *f* 276 7732
Dawn Lewis. Promotion of racial equality in Sheffield,
advancing equal opportunities policies; help, advice and
support to minority ethnic complainants. »96

✧ **Sinfin Together Project**
Cllr Robin Turner: [address unknown] Sinfin, Derby
Anti-racist community group founded 1995 after a rise in the
number of racist incidents in Derby (to 202 in 1994). »95

✧ **Slough Race Equality Council**, SREC
Sajidah Chaudhary: 3rd Floor, Old Crown, Windsor Road,
Slough SL1 2DL; *t* (01753) 691266
Promotion of racial equality and equal opportunities. Not
CRE-funded. »95

✧ **South Newham Action on Policing**, SNAP
Sharon Dray: [address unknown] London
Campaigns against racism in policing in Newham. »95

✧ **South Side Monitoring Group**
[address unknown] Glasgow, Scotland
Anti-fascist group, formed 1990. »90

✧ **South Wales Divided Families Campaign**
Saba Haq: 14 Mackintosh Place, Roath, Cardiff CF2 4RQ,
Wales; *t* (01222) 498626
For right to family reunion, reform of racist and sexist
immigration rules. »91

✧ **South West London Anti-Fascist Association**
c/o Searchlight, 37b New Cavendish St, London W1M 8JR
Local anti-racist and anti-fascist activities; participation in
national campaigns. »96

✧ **Southall Monitoring Group Ltd**, SMG
6a South Road, Southall UB1 1RT; *t* (0181) 572 8656
Founded 1976; campaigning, legal casework, monitoring,
advice and resource group on racism, immigration, policing,
domestic violence, sexual attitudes. See also Hounslow
Monitoring Project, p179. *Southall Review* (4/yr). »95

✧ **Southampton Racial Equality Council**, SREC
Inayat Khan, Director: 12 Palmerston Road, Southampton
SO14 1LL; *t* (01703) 229646, *f* 337467
Julia Carette, race equality officer. Promotes race equality in
Southampton, elimination of discrimination; complainant aid
in employment and other fields. »95

✧ **Southwark Council for Racial Equality**
Hyacinth Parsons, Director: 125 Camberwell Road, London
SE5 0HB; *t* (0171) 252 7033, *f* 703 1358
Provision of services (drop-in centres, lunch clubs etc.) to the
Irish, Turkish, Cypriot, Asian and other ethnic minority groups
in Southwark. Promotion of good inter-community relations,
elimination of discrimination. »95

✧ **Southwark Council Racial Equality Unit**
East House, 35 Peckham Road, London SE5 8UH; *t* (0171)
525 7480, *f* 525 7433
Promotion of racial equality in Southwark, with special
reference to public employment and the delivery of Borough
Council services. »93

✿ **Stafford Racial Equality Council**
Avril Sinclair, Director: SDVS Centre, 131-141 Northwalls,
Stafford ST16 3AD; *t* (01785) 46471, *f* 224864
Elimination of discrimination, promotion of racial equality in
Staffordshire.   »95

● **Standing Conference on Inter-Faith Dialogue in Education,
SCIFDE**
Angela Wood: 88a Brondesbury Villas, Kilburn, London NW6
6AD; *t* (0181) 560 4513
Conferences on religious education, publications.   »88

▌ **Standing Conference of Jews, Christians and Muslims in
Europe**
Fr Gordon Marshall OP: Holy Cross Priory, 45 Wellington
Street, Leicester LE1 6HW; *t* (0116) 255 6902
Inter-faith dialogue, combatting prejudice; meetings,
conferences, mainly Britain and Germany.   »88

◆ **Standing Conference on Racial Equality in Europe (UK),
SCORE**
Basil Bollers: Chelsea Methodist Church, 155a King's Road,
London SW3 5TX; *t* (0171) 795 0227, *f* 795 0241
150 affiliated groups. Campaigns on racism and minority
rights in Europe, and against Fortress Europe policies in EU;
lobbies MPs and MEPs, liaises with SCORE groups in other
European countries, e.g. p169; launched 1990.   »95

✿ **Strathclyde Community Relations Council, SCRC**
Maggie Chetty, Director: 2nd Floor, 115 Wellington Street,
Glasgow G2 2XT; *t* (0141) 227 6048, *f* 227 6054
Derek Goh. Promotion of racial equality, elimination of
discrimination, monitoring of racial harassment, assistance to
victims. Co-ordinates the 'Let's kick racism out of football'
campaign in Scotland. *Community Voice*.   »95

● **Student Assembly Against Racism**
[address unknown] London   »96

✿ **Sussex Racial Equality Council, SREC (succeeds Crawley
Council for Community Relations)**
Erik Shopland, Director: 194 Three Bridges Road, Crawley
RH10 1LR; *t* (01293) 521058, *f* 521080
Promotion of racial equality and equal opportunities,
elimination of discrimination in the county. Advice work with
Indian, Pakistani, Moroccan and other migrant communities;
research (1995-96) on health care for minorities.   »95

✿ **Sutton Racial Equality Council, SREC**
Daphne Beaton, Director: 2 Grove Cottage, Grove Park,
Carshalton SM5 3BB; *t* (0181) 770 6199, *f* 770 6198
Promotion of race equality, race related advice work,
development of small-scale community based projects.   »95

✿ **Tameside Racial Equality Council, TREC**
Brenda Skorupa, Admin. Officer: 35a Manchester Road,
Denton, Manchester M34 3JU; *t* (0161) 336 3359
Assists statutory, private sector and voluntary bodies and
local communities to promote race equality; 12 staff, with
programmes on education, social services, employment,
health, housing, criminal justice and Europe.   »95

✿ **Tayside Community Relations Council**
John White, Director: 20 Paterson Street, Coldside, Dundee
DD3 6QR, Scotland; *t* (01382) 818806
Elimination of racial discrimination, promotion of equality.
Advice work; serves Pakistani, Bangladeshi communities.   »95

✿ **Thamesdown Racial Equality Council**
Farringdon House, 1 Farringdon Road, Swindon SN1 5AR;
t (01793) 528545, 613274, *f* 430524
Promotes race equality; combats discrimination; information
and training work on equal opportunities. Some immigration
advice to Caribbean and South Asian communities.   »96

✿ **Third World Centre**
38-40 Exchange St, Norwich, Norfolk; *t* (01603) 610993
Development education.   »90

✿ **Three Boroughs Race Equality Project, 3BREP**
[address unknown] London; *t* (0181) 640 6296
Independent voluntary organisation linking Racial Equality
Councils in Kingston, Sutton and Bromley; provides common
services in fields such as community development.   »92

● **Tools for Self Reliance, TFSR**
The Co-ordinator: Netley Marsh, Southampton SO40 7GY
Supplies tools to artisans in developing countries.   »95

✿ **Tower Hamlets Anti-Racist Committee**
Kumar Murshid, Chairperson: c/o CAG, 22 Hanbury Street,
London E1
Opposition at local and national level to racist violence, and to
racism and fascist movements such as the BNP.   »95

✿ **Tower Hamlets Association for Racial Equality**
M.A. Sayed, SCRO: 347-349 Cambridge Heath Road,
London E2 9RA; *t* (0171) 729 5775
Campaigning, advice, casework, victim support. Possibly
superseded by Tower Hamlets REC.   »90

✿ **Tower Hamlets Racial Equality Council, THREC**
Dr Cyriac Maprayil, Director: Norvin House, 45-55 Commercial
Street, London E1 6BB; *t* (0171) 377 8077, *f* 377 5299
Tackling racial discrimination and racial disadvantage in Tower
Hamlets; working with local community groups to promote
racial equality and harmony.   »95

● **Trade Union International Research and Education Group,
TUIREG**
Ruskin College, Walton Street, Oxford OX1 2HE; *t* (01865)
54599, 56564, *f* 511313
Development education and international solidarity work in
trade unions; promotes active support for human rights and
social justice.   »93

✿ **Trafford Community Relations Committee**
Trafford Community & Advice Centre, 139 Stamford Street,
Manchester M16 9LT; *t* (0161) 226 3206, 226 7613   »88

● **Transcultural Psychiatry Society**
Department of Psychiatry, The Ridgeway, Enfield EN2 8JL;
t (0181) 366 6600 ext. 452
Campaigns on racial issues in mental health care; newsletter,
conferences.   »90

✿ **Truth and Justice for Mark Harris Campaign**
[address unknown] Bristol; *t* (01222) 811178
Campaigns for full investigation of the death in police custody
in 1994 of Mark Harris, a black man from Bristol.   »95

✿ **Tyne and Wear Anti-Fascist Association, TWAFA**
Alec McFadden, Secretary: c/o 4 The Cloth Market,
Newcastle-upon-Tyne NE1 1EA; *t* (0191) 222 1660, 232
4606
Organises local anti-fascist and anti-racist activity.   »96

✿ **Tyne and Wear Community Relations Council: Inter Faith
Panel**
Margery Hammersley: 1 West Lane, Winlaton NE21 6PQ;
t (0191) 414 8892
Anti-racism, inter-faith contact; superseded by REC?   »90

✿ **Tyne and Wear Racial Equality Council**
Simon Banks, Director: MEA House, 4th Floor, Ellison Place,
Newcastle-upon-Tyne NE1 8XS; *t* (0191) 232 7639
Promotion of racial equality, elimination of discrimination. »96

◆ **United Campaign Against Racism, UCAR**
Woburn House, Tavistock Square, London WC1H 0EZ
Coalition of groups campaigning against racism, antisemitism,
fascism and xenophobia.   »95

✿ **United Nations of Youth (UK)**
4 Convent Close, Cannock WS11 3UR; *t* (01543) 577920
Internationalist youth organisation; peace, conflict resolution,
global responsibility, intercultural understanding.   »94

● **Uniting Britain—for a just society**
Louise Ansari: Campaigns Section, Commission for Racial
Equality, 10-12 Allington Street, London SW1E 5EH;
t (0171) 932 5331
A three-year campaign (1994-97) funded by the CRE. Events,
extensive media advertising, publications.   »94

● **USDAW Race Relations Committee**
Union of Shop, Distributive & Allied Workers, 188 Wilmslow
Road, Manchester M14 6LJ
Provides support for anti-racist campaigns in, or of special
interest to, the trade union movement.   »94

● **Wales Anti-Racist Alliance**
c/o WAAM, 224 City Road, Cardiff CF2 3JH, Wales
Presumably the Welsh section of UK ARA, p176.   »94

✿ **Walsall Interfaith Group**
Sr Maureen CSSP, Secretary: 14 Laing House, Walstead Rd,
Walsall WS5 4NJ; *t* (01922) 644267
Racial harmony, inter-faith dialogue, support to minority
groups, meetings, conferences.   »88

✿ **Walsall Racial Equality Council**
S.A. Khan, Director: Advice Centre, 4-6 Lower Hall Lane,
Walsall WS1 1RH; *t* (01922) 39090
Promotion of equal opportunities, elimination of racial
disadvantage. Local authority and CRE funded.   »95

✿ **Waltham Forest All Faiths Group**
Rev. Susan Armitage, Secretary: 91 Grange Park Road,
Leyton, London E10 5ER; *t* (0181) 539 8823
Inter-faith friendship and understanding.   »88

✿ **Waltham Forest Racial Equality Council**
Choudhury Anwar, Director: 25 Church Hill, Walthamstow,
London E17 3AB; *t* (0181) 521 8851-53
Jean Lambert, Allah Ditta. Promotion of racial equality,
elimination of discrimination.   »94

✿ **Wandsworth Racial Equality Group**
Abdul Chaudhary, Director: 107 Trinity Road, London SW17
7SQ; *t* (0181) 682 3201
Promotion of harmonious race relations, opposition to
discrimination and harassment. Not CRE-funded.   »95

✿ **Warwick District Racial Equality Council**
Anita Kumari, Director: 28 Hamilton Terrace, Leamington
Spa CV32 4LY; *t* (01926) 421447
Promotion of racial equality, elimination of discrimination,
advice and casework mainly with Indians. »95

✿ **Watford Racial Equality Council**
Shanaz Mirza, Director: 16 Clarendon Road, Watford WD1
1JY; *t* (01923) 237005, 256044, *f* 240398
Promotion of equality, elimination of discrimination, advice to
individuals. Small Bangladeshi and Pakistani immigration
caseload. »95

✿ **Wellingborough Anti-Fascist Alliance**
c/o Wellingborough REC, Victoria Centre, Palk Road,
Wellingborough NN8 1HT
Local anti-racist and anti-fascist activities; participation in
national campaigns. »96

✿ **Wellingborough Multi-Faith Group**
Alan Galpin, Manager: Victoria Centre, Palk Road,
Wellingborough NN8 1HT; *t* (01933) 77400
Understanding, mutual education on religious traditions. »88

✿ **Wellingborough Racial Equality Council**
Paul Crofts, Director: c/o Victoria Centre, Palk Road,
Wellingborough NN8 1HT; *t* (01933) 278000
Works for equality of opportunity, and against racial
discrimination. Advice service, including some Bangladeshi,
Gujerati family reunion cases. »95

✿ **West Glamorgan Race Equality Council**: also known as
West Glamorgan Community Relations Council
E.U. Haq, Director: 10a Mount Pleasant, Swansea SA1 6EE,
Wales; *t* (01792) 457035, *f* 459374
Dr Parvaiz Ali chair; S.S. Myrpurrey. Voluntary organisation
promoting better racial equality policy and practice by
employers and service deliverers throughout West Glamorgan.
Assists victims of discrimination and racial harassment,
monitors racial incidents (500 in South Wales in 1994). »95

✿ **Westminster Race Equality Council**, WREC
James Gordon, Director: 69-71 Praed Street, London W2
1NS; *t* (0171) 706 3014
Promotion of good ethnic relations, and of the interests of
black and ethnic minority communities in Westminster. »95

✿ **Wiltshire Racial Equality Council**, WREC
Simeon Foster, Director: Bridge House, Stallard Street,
Trowbridge BA14 9AE; *t* (01225) 766439
Promotion of racial equality in the county, elimination of
discrimination; liaison to ensure accessibility of services. »96

✿ **Woking Community Relations Forum**
Maybury Centre, Board School Road, Woking GU21 5HD
Voluntary body promoting equal opportunities and good
community relations; monitors racial harassment. »94

✿ **Wolverhampton Borough Council Race Relations Office**
Civic Centre, St Peter's Square, Wolverhampton WV1 1SH;
t (01902) 27811 ext. 4081
D.V. John race relations and equal opportunities adviser;
provides policy advice to the local authority. »91

✿ **Wolverhampton Inter-Faith Group**
Ivy Gutridge, Assistant Secretary: The Inter-Faith Centre, 43
Princess Street, Wolverhampton WV1 1HD; *t* (01902) 27601
Inter-faith dialogue, mutual respect, social justice; meetings,
community work. »88

✿ **Wolverhampton Racial Equality Council**
Earlston E. Warner: 2 Clarence Road, off Clarence Street,
Wolverhampton WV1 4HZ; *t* (01902) 773589, *f* 313348
Elimination of racial discrimination, promotion of equality. »95

✿ **Worcester Racial Equality Council**, WREC
The Director: St Swithun's Institute, The Trinity, Worcester
WR1 2PN; *t* (01905) 29283
Promotion of racial equality, elimination of discrimination
within Hereford and Worcester. »95

● **Working Group Against Racism in Children's Resources**,
WGARCR
460 Wandsworth Rd, London SW8 3LX; *t/f* (0171) 627 4594
Information, advice, consultancy, training and other services
designed to ensure equal rights for all young children. »95

▌ **World Congress of Faiths**, WCF
Tom Gulliver, Hon. General Secretary: [address uncertain]
28 Powis Gardens, London W11 1JG; *t* (0171) 727 2607
Rev. Marcus Braybrooke, chairman (1994; but the address
given dates from 1988). Mutual respect for the spiritual
values of different religions, opposition to intolerance and
exclusivism; lectures, retreats, interfaith conferences and
services. Founded 1936. *Interfaith News; World Faiths
Insight* (both 3/yr). »94

✿ **Wycombe and District Racial Equality Council**, formerly
Wycombe and District Race Equality Steering Committee
Alfred Webley, Director: 272 Desborough Road, High
Wycombe HP11 2QR; *t* (01494) 527616, 443339, *f* 448764
Elimination of discrimination in High Wycombe, promotion of
racial equality, community development, advice. »95

✿ **York Anti-Fascist Action**, AFA
PO Box 306, York YO3 7GH
Organises local anti-fascist/anti-racist monitoring, research,
demonstrations, leafletting and other activity. »96

● **Youth Against Racism in Europe**, YRE
PO Box 858, London E2 7RR; *t* (0181) 533 4533
Socialist youth movement; anti-racist, anti-fascist campaigns.
Overseas counterparts include Jugend gegen Rassismus in
Europa, Germany, p167, and YRE in Holland, p171. »94

✿ ≡ Rachel Salmon: 41 Albermarle Street, Moss Side,
Manchester M14; *t* (0161) 226 0884
Local, national and international anti-racist campaigns. »93

✿ **Youth Against Racism and Fascism**
26 Seymour Road, Cheetham, Manchester M8 6BG
Anti-fascist campaigns, demonstration, lobbies; defence of
ethnic minority families against racist violence. »93

NORTHERN IRELAND 44

✿ **Northern Ireland Community Relations Council**, NICRC: also
known as Community Relations Council, CRC
Dr Mari Fitzduff, Director: 6 Murray Street, Belfast BT1 6DN;
t (01232) 439953, *f* 235208
Dr James Hawthorne chairman, Joe Hinds development
officer, Ray Mullan information officer. Autonomous state-
funded agency promoting good inter-community relations in
Northern Ireland (primarily in terms of the Protestant-Catholic
divide); research, documentation, funding activities; supports
extension to Northern Ireland of legislation protecting ethnic
minority rights. Runs Community Relations Information
Centre, 31 Castle Lane, Belfast BT1, *t* 311881. »95

✿ **Northern Ireland Council for Ethnic Equality**, NICEE
c/o Multicultural Resource Centre, Bryson House, 28 Bedford
St, Belfast BT2 7FE; *t* (01232) 325835 ext. 52, *f* 439156
Voluntary body established 1995 to promote racial and ethnic
equality in Northern Ireland; modelled on the UK Councils for
Racial Equality. »95

✿ **Skinheads Against Racial Prejudice**, SHARP
[address unknown] Belfast
Anti-racist youth movement, possibly defunct. »91

✿ **Women's Racism Awareness Group**, WRAG
[address unknown]
Possibly a student group in Queen's University Belfast; has
campaigned against racist material in Student Union
publications. »95

Part Four

Agencies and Authorities

This category covers those official national and international agencies, national and local government offices, and major voluntary-sector groups (Non-Governmental Organisations, NGOs) which are concerned with refugees, migration and minorities. It also covers institutions and NGOs which work mainly in much broader fields, such as international development aid, humanitarian relief, human rights, religious or trade union activities, if they are known to have an active interest in refugee, migrant or minority issues within that broader context. However, specialist units of these broader-focus groups, dealing directly with migrant or minority groups in their own countries, are more likely to be found in the category covering their special concerns. For example national trade union confederations are listed here, but trade union immigrant worker bureaux will be found in the 'Support and Service' category (Part Two); some inter-church bodies are here, but special ones with multicultural concerns will be in the 'Anti-racism' category (Part Three); and government or NGO offices dealing with just one ethnic group will be listed under the appropriate ethnic heading (in Part One).

ALBANIA 355

- International Cultural Centre and Open Society Fund
Rz. Labinoti 125, Tirana; t (042) 34621, f 34223
An initiative of the US-based Soros Foundation.   »94
- United Nations High Commissioner for Refugees, UNHCR
c/o UNDP, Deshmoret E4, Shkurtit Street Villa 35, Tirana;
t (042) 28474 or c/o UNDP 33047, f c/o UNDP 34448
Refugee status and protection; see main listing, p219.   »95

AUSTRIA 43

- Amnesty International Österreichische Sektion, AI
Apostelgasse 25-27, 1030 Wien; t (01) 718 7777, f 718 7778
Human rights group, see p220, focussing on political persecution; interest in refugee issues in that context. Regional sections: Vienna, Salzburg, Oberösterreich, Tyrol.»95
- Blue Danube Radio, BDR
[address unknown]
Non-commercial radio station founded in the 1970s by ÖRF state broadcasting corporation to provide foreign-language programming for the international community in Austria.   »95
- Ludwig-Boltzmann-Institut für Menschenrechte, BIM (Boltzmann Institute of Human Rights)
Manfred Nowak, Director: Berggasse 7/2, 1090 Wien; t (01) 317 4020, f 317 4022
Human rights concerns, anti-racism, support for rights of migrants, refugees and minorities; documentation, education, research. Founded 1992. Newsletter, country reports.   »94
- Brot für Hungernde (Bread for the Hungry)
Gerhilde Merz, Executive Secretary: Blumengasse 4/6, 1180 Wien; t (0222) 408 9605
International development aid and solidarity, human rights; funds projects in Africa, Asia, Latin America, including some for refugee resettlement. Newsletters (6/yr).   »93
- Bund Europäischer Jugend—Junge Europäischer Föderalisten, BEJ-JEF (European Youth League—Young European Federalists)
Jahnweg 5, 8330 Feldbach; t (03152) 2497, f 24974   »94

♦ Caritas Österreich: and Österreichisches Kuratorium für Fluchtlingshilfe (Austrian Board of Assistance to Refugees)
Fr Helmut Schüller: Nibelungengasse 1/4/3, Postfach 114, 1010 Wien; t (01) 587 1577, f 587 1577/13
Major Catholic welfare agency; social services to refugees and asylum seekers; campaigns on racism and migrant rights. Its Refugee Department (the Kuratorium für Fluchtlingshilfe: Mag. Wolfgang Taucher, t 587 1577/33) provides legal counselling, jointly with UNHCR, p188; its Resettlement Office (Fr Moser, t 587 1577/34) advises on refugee housing and welfare. Airport office (Flughafen Caritas, t 7110-2889): emergency aid to asylum seekers; legal and practical help also given through regional Caritas Flüchtlingsreferaten: Vienna t 310 9808, Eisenstadt (02682) 62525-304, Feldkirch (05522) 71260, Graz (0316) 8015, Innsbruck (0512) 586836/13-16, Klagenfurt (0463) 503330, Linz (0732) 777851, Salzburg (0662) 435523, St Pölten (02742) 53486/30. Caritas (6/yr).   »95
▌ European Student Information Bureau, ESIB, and National Unions of Students in Europe
Liechtensteinstrasse 13, 1090 Wien; t (01) 3108 88048, f 3108 88036
Anti-racist activities.   »94
- Evangelische Arbeitsgemeinschaft für Entwicklungs-zusammenarbeit (Evangelical Working Group on Development Co-operation)
[address unknown]
Co-ordinates international humanitarian aid and development assistance work of the Protestant church agencies.   »93
- Evangelischer Arbeitskreis für Weltmission in Österreich, EAWM (Protestant Working Group on World Mission)
Heidi Prinz: Martin Luther Platz 1, 9020 Klagenfurt; t (0463) 511607 31, f 511607 33
International solidarity, missionary work, development aid, including emergency relief for refugees in Africa; development education, human rights promotion. Die Brücke (4/yr).   »93
✿ Flughafendienst (Airport Service)
Dr Dimitz: Kaunitzgasse 33/13, 1060 Wien; t (01) 567 0985, 587 2829, f 587 5999
Welfare service; some work with refugees.   »95
- Grüne-Alternative-Jugendinitiative (Green Alternative Youth Initiative)
Lindengasse 40, 1070 Wien; t (01) 5212 5242
Radical ecologist youth movement with anti-racist/anti-fascist policies.   »94

■ **International Council on Social Welfare, ICSW:** Conseil International de l'Action Social
Sirppa Utriainen, General Secretary: Koestlergasse 1/29, 1060 Wien; *t* (01) 587 8164, *f* 587 9951
Promotion of social development, including provision of NGO and public support services for refugees, migrants and minorities, globally and especially in developing countries. *ICSW Information* (4/yr). »93

♦ **International Organization for Migration, IOM,** formerly Intergovernmental Committee for Migrations, ICM
Dr Kottek: Sobieskigasse 20, 1090 Wien; *t* (01) 344554, *f* 344207-31
National office of the IOM (see Switzerland, p218). »95

● **International Progress Organisation, IPO**
Kohlmarkt 4, 1010 Wien; *t* (01) 533 2877, *f* 533 296221 (?)
Anti-racism, other issues. »94

■ **International Union of Socialist Youth, IUSY**
Neustiftgasse 3, 1070 Wien; *t* (01) 523 1267, *f* 526 1872
International federation of youth movements linked to social democratic parties; anti-racist, anti-fascist activities. »94

● **Internationaler Versohnungsbund, IVB,** Österreichischer Zweig: International Fellowship of Reconciliation, IFOR, Austrian Section
Irmgard Ehrenberger: Lederergasse 23/3/27, 1080 Wien; *t* (01) 408 5332
Promotion of peace, reconciliation, human rights and social justice worldwide; refugee assistance work in ex-Yugoslavia and elsewhere; see p171. *Spinnrad* (6/yr). »93

● **Koordinierungsstelle der österreichischen Bischofskonferenz für internationale Entwicklung und Mission, KOO** *(Austrian Bishops' Board for World Development and Mission)*
Dr Helmut Ornauer, Director: Türkenstrasse 3, 1090 Wien; *t* (01) 340321
Development education; co-ordination of foreign humanitarian aid and development activities of over 30 Catholic NGOs, including work for dispaced persons and human rights. »93

● **MitMenschen** *(Fellowship)*
Schneidergasse 15, 1110 Wien; *t* (01) 745196
Anti-racism, refugee support. »94

● **Österreichische Gesellschaft Rettet das Kind:** Save the Children
Dieter Wesenauer, General Secretary: Pouthongasse 3, 1150 Wien; *t* (01) 926216, 924418, *f* 924664
National section of International Save the Children Alliance (Switzerland, p218). Emergency humanitarian aid to refugees abroad. *Mitteilungen* (4/yr). »93

● **Österreichische Jungarbeiterbewegung, ÖJAB** *(Austrian Young Workers Movement)*
Mittelgasse 16a, 1060 Wien; *t* (01) 5979 73531, *f* 5979 73589
Youth movement participating in Austrian committee, p159, of European Youth Campaign Against Racism, p197. »94

♦ **Österreichische Rotes Kreuz:** Austrian Red Cross
Wiener Haupstrasse 32, 1040 Wien; *t* (01) 58900-125, *f* 58900-199
Activities include processing applications for refugee identity documents of the ICRC, p218. »95

● **Österreichischer Bundesjugendring, ÖBJR** *(Austrian Youth Council)*
Am Modenapark 1-2/326, 1030 Wien; *t* (01) 715 5743, *f* 712 8584
National federation of youth organisations; leading participant in the Austrian committee, p159, of the Council of Europe's Youth Campaign Against Racism, p197. »94

● **Österreichischer Informationsdienst für Entwicklungspolitik, ÖIE** *(Austrian Information Service on Development Policy)*
Helmut Hartmeyer, Director: Tuchlau 8/16, 1010 Wien; *t* (01) 533 3755-0, *f* 533 3755-21
Major international solidarity and development education organisation; supports refugee and minority rights, lobbies on humanitarian concerns in foreign political and economic relations. »93

♦ **Österreichisches Institut für Menschenrechte** *(Austrian Institute for Human Rights)*
Edmundsburg-Mönchsberg 2, 5020 Salzburg; *t* (0662) 848 7461, *f* 848 7464 »94

● **Österreichisches Komitee gegen die Folter:** Austrian Committee against Torture: and Institute of International Law and International Relations
Hans-Sachs-Gasse 3/III, 8010 Graz; *t* (01) 380 3414, *f* 381 1924
Small voluntary group; legal research, information, publishing and other activities against torture and other cruel, inhuman and degrading treatment of prisoners worldwide (excluding assistance to individuals). Founded 1981. »93

● **Österreichisches Nord-Sud Institut für Entwicklungs-zusammenarbeit** *(Austrian North-South Institute for Development Co-operation)*
Heinz Miko, Director: Möllwaldplatz 4/2, 1040 Wien; *t* (01) 505 4492, *f* 504 4679
Small development co-operation and emergency relief organisation founded 1991; activities in Latin America and Africa, including aid to Sahrawi refugees in Algeria. »93

✿ **Pfarre Schwechat** *(Schwechat Pastorate)*
Hauptplatz, 2320 Schwechat; *t* (01) 707 6475
Welfare services, including refugee assistance. »95

♦ **Service Civil International Österreich, SCI** *(International Civil Service Austria)*
Schottengasse 3a/1/59, 1010 Wien; *t* (01) 535 9108, 639 0652, *f* 532 7416
International social welfare issues, anti-racist work. See European regional office in Belgium, p188. »94

● **SOS Mitmenschschüler/innen** *(SOS Fellowship School Students)*
Schottenfeldgasse 24, 1070 Wien
Anti-racist humanitarian youth movement. »94

● **Sozialistische Jugend Österreichs, SJÖ** *(Austrian Socialist Youth)*
Neustiftgasse 3, 1070 Wien; *t* (01) 523 4123, *f* 526 1872
Youth section of the Austrian social democratic movement; anti-racist, anti-fascist policies. »94

■ **United Nations Centre for Social Development and Humanitarian Affairs, CSDHA**
Postfach 500, 1400 Wien; *t* (01) 211310, *f* 232156
Located in the Vienna International Centre, Wagramerstrasse 5; this includes the United Nations Information Centre for Austria, Hungary and Germany. »94

■ **United Nations High Commissioner for Refugees, UNHCR:** Regional Office for Austria, Poland, Czech and Slovak Republics
Staffan Bodemar/Andrea Sölkner: Postfach 550, 1400 Wien; *t* (01) 211310 0 4968, 211310 0 5306, *f* 239514, *Tx* 135612 UNO A
Location: Vienna International Centre, Building F, 8th Floor, Wagramerstrasse 5, Wien 22. Emergency assistance, legal advice, resettlement aid to refugees. See UNHCR, p219, and in Poland, Czech Republic and Slovakia, pp211, 193, 212.»95

■ **United Nations Relief and Works Agency for Palestine Refugees in the Near East, UNRWA**
Postfach 700, 1400 Wien; *t* (01) 211310, *f* 230 7487, *Tx* 135310
Founded 1950; welfare, health care, education of Palestinians in the Occupied Territories and in other countries. »93

♦ **Unterstützungskomitee für politisch verfolgte Ausländer/innen** *(Support Committee for Politically Persecuted Foreigners)*
Dr Karin König: Währingerstrasse 59/II, 1090 Wien; *t* (01) 408 5501, 408 4210, *f* 403 2737
Welfare, legal aid and language classes for refugees; assistance with asylum applications; public information campaigns and lobbying on refugee issues. »95

● **Wiener Institut für Entwicklungsfragen und Zusammenarbeit** *(Vienna Institute for Development Questions and Co-operation)*
Weyrgasse 5, 1030 Wien; *t* (01) 713 3594
Information on problems of developing countries; promotes development co-operation. Founded 1964. »93

BELGIUM *32*

✿ **Action Social au Bernalmont** *(Bernalmont Social Action)*
J.-M. Michel: Lavaniste Voie 72, 4000 Liège; *t* (041) 277442
Inter-cultural contact and solidarity. »94

● **Action Vivre Ensemble—Entraide et Fraternité** *(Action for Coexistence—Mutual Aid and Fraternity)*
Rue du Gouvernement Provisoire 32, 1000 Bruxelles; *t* (02) 219 1983, *f* 217 3259
Christian humanitarian aid agency working in the French- and German-speaking communities (its Flemish counterpart is Broederlijk Delen). Founded 1977; 24 staff; rural projects and emergency relief efforts, including some refugee work, in the Third World, and development education in Belgium. *Flash* (12/yr), *Partenaire* (4/yr), *Voix du Tiers-Monde* (4/yr). »94

● **Agence PETRA-LINGUA**
Place Surlet de Chockier 15-17, 1000 Bruxelles; *t* (02) 221 8936-37, *f* 221 8923, 238 1444
National centre for francophone Belgium in the EU's PETRA network of youth vocational guidance resource centres, p192, and the LINGUA programme for foreign language promotion.»94

- **Algemeen Belgisch Vakverbond-Jongeren**, ABVV-J *(Trade Union Youth)*
Hoogstraat 42, 1000 Bruxelles; *t* (02) 513 0774
Youth section of the national trade union federation; anti-racist activities.   »94

█ **Amnesty International European Union Association**
Willy Laes/Eric Gillet: Rue Berckmans 9, 1060 Bruxelles; *t* (02) 537 1302, *f* 537 4750
Represents the international human rights organisation (see secretariat, p220) to institutions of the European Union.   »95

♦ **Amnesty International—Belgique francophone**
Rue Berckmans 9, 1060 Bruxelles; *t* (02) 538 8177, *f* 537 3729
French-speaking section of human rights pressure group concerned with political prisoners; assistance to refugees, documentation centre; see also Dutch-speaking Amnesty, European and international offices.   »95

♦ **Amnesty International—Vlaanderen**, also known as Amnesty International Nederlandstalige Afdeling
Kerkstraat 156, 2060 Antwerpen; *t* (03) 271 1616, *f* 235 7812
Flemish (Dutch-speaking) section; details as for francophone Amnesty.   »95

- **Association Belge des Juristes Démocrates** *(Belgian Association of Democratic Lawyers)* Service d'Education Permanente des Adultes
Me. Jacques Bourgaux: Rue Berckmans 14, 1060 Bruxelles; *t* (02) 539 0314
Lawyers' pressure group; its Adult Education Service is involved in training and employment issues affecting migrants and refugees. *Journal des Juristes Démocrates*.   »94

- **Association Développement, Emploi, Formation et Insertion Sociale**, DEFIS *(Association for Development, Work, Training and Integration)*
Pierre Ansay: Avenue Clémenceau 10, 1070 Bruxelles; *t* (02) 523 2035
Training, employment and social integration of young immigrants. *Defipresse*.   »94

- **Association Europe-Tiers Monde**, ETM *(Europe-Third World Association)*
Peter Troberg, President: Rue de la Loi 170, 1048 Bruxelles; *t* (02) 234 8377, *f* 234 8378
Voluntary group, formed 1968, providing small-scale disaster relief in developing countries, including aid to refugees.   »93

█ **Association Internationale des Juristes Démocrates**, AIJD: International Association of Democratic Lawyers, IADL
Renée Bridel: Avenue Albert 263, 1180 Bruxelles; *t* (02) 345 1471, 343 3596, *f* 345 3596
Progressive lawyers' group founded 1946; defence of human rights worldwide, including refugee and migrant rights; funds refugee training and settlement activities in Europe.   »94

- **Belgian Helsinki Committee**
Dr Yvo J.D. Peters: [address uncertain] Lenoirstraat 13, 1090 Brussel   »88

♦ **Belgische Liga voor de Verdediging van de Rechten de Mens**, BLVRM *(Belgian League for the Defence of Human Rights)*
[address uncertain] Guldenvlieslaan 1, 1000 Brussel; *t* (02) 511 6088
Dutch-speaking counterpart of LBDH, p191.   »90

- **Broederlijk Delen**, BD *(Brotherly Sharing)*
Huideuettersstraat 185, 1000 Brussel; *t* (02) 502 5700, *f* 502 8101
Catholic humanitarian relief agency, Flemish counterpart of Entraide et Fraternité; founded 1961, 50 staff. Development education in Flanders, financial and technical support for development and human rights projects and emergency relief (including aid to refugees) in the Third World.   »93

█ **CARE International**
Boulevard du Régent 58/10, 1000 Bruxelles; *t* (02) 502 4333, *f* 502 8202, *Tx* 20253 CARE B
International development aid and humanitarian relief; work in Africa and Asia includes refugee and displaced persons emergency aid, resettlement and repatriation, in collaboration with UNHCR, p219; some Latin American projects. Founded 1982. *CARE International Report* (3/yr), leaflets.   »93

✿ **Centre Féminin d'Education Permanente**, CFEP *(Women's Adult Education Centre)*
Bernadette Michel: Place Quételet 1a, 1030 Bruxelles; *t* (02) 219 2802, *f* 219 2774
Education, training and employment interest of women.   »94

✿ **Centre de Formation et d'Education Familiale** *(Family Education and Training Centre)*
Marc Garcet: Rue Vert-Vinâve 60, 4041 Vottem; *t* (041) 277274, 276714
Family welfare, employment advice, training.   »94

- **Charta 91** *(Charter '91)*
Francine Mestrum: Wellingstraat 89, 9000 Gent; *t/f* (091) 252142
Civil rights pressure group; general concerns include democracy in European Union, anti-racism.   »94

█ **Christian Movement for Peace**, CMP
Avenue du Parc Royal 3, 1020 Bruxelles; *t* (02) 478 9410, *f* 478 9432
Human rights, peace and justice youth movement; anti-racism, refugee rights; see Kairos Youth Co-ordination, p191.   »94

✿ **Collectif d'Alphabétisation** *(Literacy Collective)*
Catherine Stercq: Rue de Rome 12, 1060 Bruxelles; *t* (02) 538 3657, *f* 538 2744
Literacy work, largely with immigrants; research.   »94

✿ **Collectif des Femmes** *(Women's Collective)*
Anne Forrest: Rue des Sports 17-19, 1348 Louvain-la-Neuve; *t* (010) 474769
Women's employment, training. *Pluri'elles*.   »94

- **Comité Belge pour l'UNICEF** *(Belgian Committee for UNICEF)*
Avenue des Arts 20, Boite 18, 1040 Bruxelles; *t* (02) 230 5970, *f* 230 3462
Defends rights of children worldwide; development and humanitarian aid, some refugee projects; development education; fundraising for UNICEF, p219.   »95

- **Comité pour les Relations Internationales des Jeunes d'Expression Française de la Belgique**, CRIJ *(Belgian Francophone Youth International Relations Committee)*
Boulevard Adolphe Max 13-17, 1000 Bruxelles; *t* (02) 223 1527, *f* 219 8612
Foreign affairs committee of youth council, CJEF, p190.   »94

♦ **Commissariat général aux réfugiés et aux apatrides** *(Commissioner-General for Refugees and Stateless Persons)* Commissariaat-generaal voor de vluchtelingen en de staatlozen
Boulevard E. Jacqmain 150, 1050 Bruxelles; *t* (02) 205 5111, *f* 205 5115
Government office responsible for determining applications for refugee status.   »95

█ **European Commission**: Commission Européenne: Headquarters
Rue de la Loi 200, 1049 Bruxelles; *t* (02) 235 1111, *f* 235 0129, 299 0122, *Tx* 21877 COMEU B, *Tg* COMEUR Brussels
The Commission is the administrative organ of the European Union; migration-related functions include promotion of labour mobility; many of these matters are dealt with by DG V, the Directorate-General for Employment, Industrial Relations and Social Affairs (*t* 235 4893; Annette Bosscher, head of Division "Freedom of movement migration policy"). The Human Capital and Mobility Programme supports initiatives in this area and funds research. Other relevant programmes include PETRA (for co-operation in vocational training, p192), LINGUA (promoting language learning), Youth for Europe (youth exchanges, p191), ERASMUS (mobility of students and academic staff, p190), EURES (employment services network, p190) and TEMPUS (education and Eastern Europe, p192).»94

♦ ≡ Rue Archimède 73, 1040 Bruxelles; *t* (02) 235 3844, *f* 235 0166, *Tx* 26657 COMINF B
National representative office; information on EU issues.   »94

█ **Community Programme for Education and Training in Technology**, COMETT
COMETT Technical Assistance Office, Rue Montoyer 14, 1040 Bruxelles; *t* (02) 513 8959, *f* 513 9346
European Union and EFTA programme for new technology training; promotes transnational student and staff exchanges and joint training.   »94

- **Confédération Générale des Enseignants** *(General Confederation of Teachers)*
Noëlle De Smet: Rue du Méridien 22, 1030 Bruxelles; *t* (02) 218 3450
Teachers' union; interests in migrant education, training, culture. *Echec à l'Echec, Solidarité*.   »94

█ **Confédération des Organismes Familiaux de la Communauté Européenne**, COFACE *(European Union Confederation of Family Organisations)*
Lucien Bouis, President: Rue de Londres 17, 1050 Bruxelles
Also listed (1995) at Rue du Congrès 17, 1000 Bruxelles.
A member of the European Co-ordination for the Right to Family Life of Immigrants, p136.   »95

- **Conseil Consultatif pour l'Immigration** *(Consultative Council on Immigration)* Ministère de l'Emploi et du Travail: Ministerie van Tewerkstelling en Arbeid
Rue Belliard 51-53, 1040 Bruxelles; *t* (02) 513 4090 or 233 4111 (?)
Labour ministry organ which advises the government on employment and other matters affecting immigrants. See Koninklijk Commissariaat voor het Migrantenbeleid, p191.»90

- **Conseil de la Jeunesse d'Expression Française de Belgique,** CJEF *(Belgian Francophone Youth Council)*
Boulevard Adolphe Max 13-17, 1000 Bruxelles; *t* (02) 223 0991, *f* 219 8612
National federation of youth groups; anti-racist policies. International arm is CRIJ, p189. »94
- **Coopération Internationale pour le Développement et la Solidarité,** CIDSE *(International Co-operation for Development and Solidarity)*
Rue Stévin 16, 1040 Bruxelles; *t* (02) 230 7722, *f* 230 7082, *Tx* 64208 CIDSE B
Co-ordinates 16 Belgian Christian development agencies working in Latin America, Africa and Asia, including several providing emergency aid to refugees. »93
- ▌ **Council of Europe:** Conseil de l'Europe: Brussels office Résidence Palace, Rue de la Loi 155, Service triage boite 3, 1040 Bruxelles; *t* (02) 230 4170, 230 4721, *f* 230 9462 Liaison with Brussels-based European institutions. »93
- ▌ **Council of European National Youth Committees,** CENYC Chaussée de Wavre 517-519, 1040 Bruxelles; *t* (02) 648 9101, *f* 648 9640
Forum of national councils of youth organisations. »94
- ◆ **Croix Rouge de Belgique:** Belgische Rode Kruis *(Belgian Red Cross)*
Vleurgatsesteenweg 98, 1050 Brussel; *t* (02) 627 3420, *f* 640 6408
Normal range of national Red Cross functions including a Social Service with refugee health/welfare responsibilities; member of CIRE and CBAR refugee aid groups, p130; many local sections; see also international Red Cross, p218. »95
- **Direction générale de la Sécurité Sociale—Service des relations internationales** *(Social Security Agency International Service)* Ministère de la Prévoyance Sociale
Rue de la Vierge Noire 3c, 1000 Bruxelles; *t* (02) 509 8111 International social security issues. »94
- ✿ **Ecole d'Alphabétisation Mons-Borinage** *(Mons-Borinage Literacy School)*
Rue Jules Destrée 154, 7390 Quaregnon; *t* (065) 780643»90
- ▌ **Economic and Social Committee**
Rue Ravenstein 2, 1000 Bruxelles; *t* (02) 519 9011, *f* 513 4893
Advisory body of employers, trade union and other interests from all EU member countries, consulted by EU Council of Ministers and Commission in relation to social and economic policy issues including the free movement of labour. »93
- **ERASMUS Agence francophone**
Rue d'Egmont 5, 1050 Bruxelles; *t* (02) 504 9211
National (francophone) office for the EU academic exchange programme, below. »94
- **EURES Office communautaire:** European Employment Services Network
FOREM, Boulevard de l'Empereur 3, 1000 Bruxelles; *t* (02) 510 2011, *f* 510 2267
Francophone national office of the EU-sponsored employment information network, right. »94
- ▌ **Euro Citizen Action Service,** ECAS
Tony Venables, Director: Rue Defacqz 1, 1050 Bruxelles; *t* (02) 534 5166, *f* 534 5275
Advisory, co-ordination, representation and lobbying services to some 300 human rights, minority and other NGOs dealing with European partners and institutions. Work in immigration and asylum fields included (1994: Nick Blow) compiling a directory of advice centres. *Le Citoyen Européen* (9/yr). »95
- ▌ **European Anti Poverty Network,** EAPN
Rue Belliard 205, bte. 13, 1040 Bruxelles
Forum of national and regional initiatives against poverty and unequal development; some projects deal with migrants and refugees as economically disadvantaged groups. »94
- ▌ **European Bureau for Conscientious Objection,** EBCO
Rue Van Elewyck 35, 1050 Bruxelles; *t* (02) 648 5220, *f* 840 0774
Peace movement agency supporting conscientious objectors and deserters throughout Europe. »94
- ▌ **European Community Action Scheme for the Mobility of University Students,** ERASMUS
ERASMUS Bureau, Rue Montoyer 70, 1040 Bruxelles; *t* (02) 233 0111, *f* 233 0150
Programme for promoting educational co-operation and exchange of students and staff between EU member countries. See national offices, above and pp192, 195, 200, 212. »94
- ▌ **European Community Organisation of Socialist Youth,** ECOSY
Rue Belliard 97, 113, 1040 Bruxelles; *t* (02) 284 2837, *f* 230 1766
Organisation of youth affiliates of socialist parties; concerns include anti-racism, anti-fascism. »94

- ▌ **European Co-ordination Bureau,** ECA
Rue du Marteau 19, 1040 Bruxelles; *t* (02) 217 5632, *f* 219 8396
Liaison centre for (Catholic?) youth organisations; concerns include human rights, refugees, migrants. »94
- ▌ **European Ecumenical Commission for Church and Society**
Marc Lenders: Rue Joseph II 174, 1040 Bruxelles; *t* (02) 230 1732 »90
- ▌ **European Educational Exchanges—Youth for Understanding,** EEE-YFU
Van Geertstraat 69, 2140 Borgerhout; *t* (03) 236 0636, *f* 236 1457
International non-governmental youth organisation promoting cultural and educational exchange, understanding and tolerance. »94
- ▌ **European Employment Services Network,** EURES
Colin Wolfe: European Commission, DG V, Unit D/4, Avenue de Cortenberg 80, 4-22, 1040 Bruxelles; *t* (02) 299 0477, *f* 299 0508
Network, developed from 1991, of hundreds of 'Euroadvisers' in all EU countries, mainly in state employment services but including academic, trade union and employers' groups' personnel who advise on employment opportunities in other EU countries, and living and working conditions. Advice is also given to prospective employers. A database on vacancies and other matters is hosted by the Commission but the initial contact should be with the nearest Euroadviser: see national EURES offices, left and pp192, 194-5, 200, 204, 206, 208, 215, 226. »94
- ✿ **European Foundation Centre,** EFC
Rue de la Concorde 51, 1050 Bruxelles; *f* (02) 512 3265 »94
- ▌ **Stichting European Human Rights Foundation,** EHRF
Avenue Michelange 70, 1040 Bruxelles; *t* (02) 724 9424, *f* 734 6831
Worldwide promotion and defence of human rights, including migrant, minority and refugee rights; funding of voluntary human rights groups in developing countries. In 1993 it prepared a report for the European Commission on the implementation of an EU code on equal opportunities. »94
- ▌ **European Network of Women**
Rue Blanche 29, 1050 Bruxelles; *t* (02) 537 7988, *f* 537 5596 »93
- ▌ **European Social Fund,** ESF
European Commission, Rue de la Loi 200, 1049 Bruxelles; *t* (02) 299 1111, *f* 235 0138
Funding mechanism of the EU for addressing poverty and social inequality. »94
- ▌ **European Trade Union Confederation,** ETUC
Rue Montagne aux Herbes Potagères 37, 1000 Bruxelles; *t* (022) 218 3100
A section of the ICFTU, p191, concerned, inter alia, with social aspects of European integration. »89
- ▌ **European Trade Union Confederation—Youth,** ETUC-Y
Boulevard Emile Jacqmain 155, 1210 Bruxelles; *t* (02) 224 0411, *f* 224 0454
Youth section of the ICFTU's European confederation; youth employment, training, migrant labour rights, anti-racism. »94
- ▌ **European Union Youth Exchange Bureau,** EUYEB
Place du Luxembourg 2-3, 1040 Bruxelles; *t* (02) 511 1510, *f* 511 1960
Promotion of educational and youth organisation exchanges within the EU. »94
- **Evangelisch Hulp- en Ontwikkelingsorganisatie:** Tear Fund Belgium *(literally Evangelical Aid and Development Organisation)*
Groenstr. 19, 1800 Vilvoorde; *t* (02) 251 7710, *f* 251 8252
Protestant humanitarian relief and economic development charity; activities include aid to displaced persons in Third World. »93
- **Federatie van autonome centra voor maatschappelijk werk** *(Federation of Independent Advice Centres)*
c/o Willy Vleugels: Guimardstraat 1, 1040 Brussel; *t* (02) 511 3357 »89
- **Fondation Roi Baudouin** *(King Baudouin Foundation)*
Rue Brederode 21, 1000 Bruxelles; *t* (02) 511 1840, *f* 511 5221 »94
- **Foodfirst Information and Action Network,** FIAN
Rue de la Raperie 4, 4280 Hannut; *t* (019) 511083
Development agency, part of German-based international network, supporting the human right to food; focus on minority groups, displaced people in developing countries.»93
- ✿ **Formation Insertion Jeunes** *(Youth Training and Integration)*
Viviane Delhage: Rue Franc Gaillard 2-2A, 1060 Bruxelles; *t* (02) 538 7087
Training, employment of young people. »94

✿ **Le Grès, Groupe Animation Quartier** *(Le Grès Community Development Group)*
Philippe Crucifix: Boulevard du Souverain 143, 1260 Bruxelles; *t* (02) 230 2805
Education, training, cultural activities, community work.   »94

● **Handicap International—Belgique**
Clayslaan 11, 1030 Brussel; *t* (02) 735 2008, *f* 735 2761
Humanitarian aid to disabled people in developing countries, including refugees and displaced people.   »93

▌ **Haut Commissariat des Nations Unies pour les Réfugiés:**
United Nations High Commissioner for Refugees, UNHCR: Hoge Commissaris van de Verenigde Naties voor Vluchtelingen
Michel Moussali, Director: Rue Van Eyck 11b, 1050 Bruxelles; *t* (02) 649 0153, 649 8119, *f* 641 9005, *Tx* 64352 HICOM B, *Tg* HICOMREF Bruxelles
Branch Office for Belgium, with corresponding office in Luxembourg, p207; refugee status, protection; see p219.»95

▌ **Human Rights Watch**
Rue Van Campenhout 15, 1040 Bruxelles; *t* (02) 732 2009, *f* 732 0471
EU representative office of a major (US-based) international human rights agency. Incorporates Africa Watch, Helsinki Watch and other specialist groups. See also p224.   »94

● **Humanistische Jongeren, HJ** *(Humanist Youth)*
Moretusstraat 2-4, 1060 Brussel; *t* (02) 521 7920, *f* 522 8540
Youth organisation; internationalist, anti-racist outlook.   »94

● **Institut für Aus- und Weiterbildung im Mittelstand und in kleineren und mittleren Unternehmen** *(Institute for Training & Further Education in Small & Medium-sized Enterprises)*
Loten 3a, 4700 Eupen; *t* (087) 740294, *f* 556507
Among other functions, runs the PETRA youth vocational training international exchange scheme, p192, for the German-speaking community.   »94

▌ **Institute of Cultural Affairs, ICA**
Rue Amedée Lynen 8, St Josse, 1030 Bruxelles; *t* (02) 219 0087, 219 4943, *f* 219 0406, *Tx* 62035
A progressive, multicultural centre providing accommodation and conference facilities. Associated bodies: ICA Belgium (founded 1977) and ICA International, which offer human resource programmes for voluntary groups, mainly in rural development and community empowerment, and Service Ventures, offering ICA methods to businesses. Sister organisations in the UK, Netherlands, Germany, Portugal; the ICA has a global network of directors and affiliates, and consultative status with UN, other international bodies.   »93

▌ **International Christian Youth Exchange—Europe, ICYE**
Naamsesteenweg 164, 3001 Leuven; *t* (016) 233762, *f* 295099
International non-governmental organisation promoting exchanges among Christian youth groups, anti-racism, intercultural understanding and tolerance.   »94

▌ **International Coalition for Development Action, ICDA**
Rue Stévin 115, 1040 Bruxelles; *t* (02) 231 1659, *f* 230 0348
Development education, development aid pressure group. »94

▌ **International Confederation of Free Trade Unions, ICFTU:**
Confédération Internationale des Syndicats Libres
John Vanderkeven, General Secretary: Boulevard Emile Jacqmain 155, 1210 Bruxelles; *t* (02) 224 0411, *f* 224 0454
Major international labour confederation, founded 1949; member federations in over 100 countries; concerns include migrant employment, training, social justice, human rights, anti-racism; has a specialist Equality Questions department; International Solidarity Fund for developing-country unions and oppressed labour leaders. See also ETUC, p190.   »94

▌ **International Falcon Movement—Socialist Educational International, IFM-SEI:** Mouvement International de Faucons—International de l'Education Socialiste
Rue Quinaux 3, 1030 Bruxelles; *t* (02) 215 7927, *f* 245 0083, *Tx* 25074 IFMSEI B
Founded 1922, youth and educational movement affiliated to the Socialist International, p227; anti-racism, anti-fascism, human rights concerns.   »94

▌ **International Federation of Liberal and Radical Youth, IFLRY**
BP 781, Rue de Lombard 3, 1000 Bruxelles; *t* (02) 512 4457, *f* 502 4122
Youth section of world association of liberal parties.   »94

▌ **International Young Catholic Students, IYCS-IMCS**
Rue du Marteau 19, 1040 Bruxelles; *t* (02) 218 5437, *f* 219 8396   »94

● **Jeugd voor Europa:** Youth for Europe Flemish Agency
JINT vzw, Grétrystraat 26, 1000 Brussel; *t* (02) 218 6455
European Union programme to promote the mobility of young people by supporting exchange projects. See headquarters, and Walloon and German agencies, right.   »94

✿ **Jeugdhuis Rzoezie** *(Rzoezie Youth House)*
Abdeslam Doudoub: Tinellaan 4, 2800 Mechelen; *t* (015) 206014-85, *f* 204559
Youth centre, mainly Moroccan clientele. Advice, training, education, youth welfare.   »94

▌ **Jeunesse pour l'Europe:** Youth for Europe
PETRA Youth Bureau, Place du Luxembourg 2-3, 1040 Bruxelles; *t* (02) 511 1510, *f* 511 1960
EU programme to promote the mobility of young people by supporting exchange projects; open from 1995 to EFTA countries. See also national agencies, left, below and pp194, 198, 201, 203-4, 209, 215, 221.   »94

● ≡ **Walloon Agency: Agence pour la Promotion des Activités Internationales de Jeunesse:** Boulevard Adolphe Max 13-17, 1000 Bruxelles; *t* (02) 219 0906
Belgian Francophone national office of the agency above. »94

▌ **Jeunesse Ouvrière Chrétienne, JOC** *(Christian Worker Youth)*
Rue Vanderstichelen 21, 1210 Bruxelles; *t* (02) 426 2149, *f* 426 4172
International Catholic social justice movement, founded around 1920 and recruiting mainly among young industrial workers; concerns include migrant labour rights, youth integration, anti-racism; the Spanish section has emigrant branches, p112.»94

● **Jugend für Europa Agentur:** Youth for Europe German Community Agency
Neustrasse 93, 4700 Eupen; *t* (087) 554872
National (German-speaking community) office of the EU and EFTA youth exchange service, above.   »94

▌ **Kairos Youth Co-ordination, KAIROS**
Avenue du Parc Royal 3, 1020 Bruxelles; *t* (02) 478 3470, *f* 478 9432
Human rights, social justice youth movement; anti-racism, migrant rights. See Christian Movement for Peace, p189.»94

◆ **Koninklijk Commissariaat voor het Migrantenbeleid** *(Royal Commission on Migration Policy)*
F. Saeys/H. Boukhriss: Wetstraat 155, 1040 Brussel; *t* (02) 233 0611, *f* 233 0704
Research, documentation, policy advice to government.   »94

✿ **Liga voor mensenrechten** *(Human Rights League)*
André De Becher, Preseident: Postbus 8, Universiteitsstraat, 9000 Gent; *t* (091) 646877, *f* 646999
Human rights pressure group; welfare of asylum seekers and refugees in Flanders, anti-racism.   »95

● **Ligue Anti-impérialiste** *(Anti-Imperialist League)*
Rue de la Caserne 68, 1000 Bruxelles   »90

● **Ligue belge pour la défense des droits de l'homme, LBDH** *(Belgian League for the Defence of Human Rights)*
Rue Antoine Dansaert 70, 1000 Bruxelles; *t* (02) 735 2145
Human rights group; general secretary, francophone section, Sabine Missistrano; see also BLVRM, p189, and Comité d'appel pour le droit d'asile, p130.   »90

◆ **Ligue des Droits de l'Homme, LDH** *(Human Rights League)*
Pierre Herbelq: Rue Watteau 6, 1000 Bruxelles; *t* (02) 502 1426, *f* 502 1819
Human rights pressure group; interest in refugee issues: see Plate-forme de Vigilance pour les Réfugiés, p131. Affiliate of FIDH, p197. *Chronique de la LDH* (12/yr).   »95

✿ **Ligue des Familles** *(Family League)*
Rue du Trône 127, 1050 Bruxelles; *t* (02) 513 1960
Welfare, training/employment issues, cultural activities. *Le Ligueur.*   »94

✿ **Lire et Ecrire** *(Read and Write)*
Rue d'Andenne 79, 1060 Bruxelles
Literacy work, information. *Le Journal de l'Alpha.*   »94

▌ **Médecins Sans Frontières, MSF** *(Doctors without Borders, literally: only French title used)* International Bureau
Dr Alain Destexhe, General Secretary: Boulevard Léopold II 209, 1080 Bruxelles; *t* (02) 426 5552, *f* 426 7535
International humanitarian organisation providing medical aid primarily to refugees, disaster victims and people in zones of conflict; international office established 1991; 12 national member agencies and 2,000 medical staff from 60 countries. *Lettre internationale MSF* (4/yr).   »94

● **Médecins Sans Frontières—Belgique, MSF-B:** National office
Rue Deschampheleer 26, 1080 Bruxelles; *t* (02) 425 0300, *f* 425 3460, *Tx* 63607 MSF B
Belgian section of international medical charity; serves refugees and people displaced by conflict in Africa and Asia, works for the development or reconstruction of primary health care services; refugee and migrant aid in Belgium.   »94

◆ **Ministère des Affaires Etrangères:** Ministerie van Buitenlandse Betrekkingen *(Ministry of Foreign Affairs)*
Rue des Quatre Bras 2, 1000 Bruxelles; *t* (02) 516 8111, 513 6240
Responsible for refugee status and protection.   »85

♦ **Ministère de la Communauté Française** *(Ministry for the Francophone Community)*
Boulevard Léopold II, 44, 1080 Bruxelles; *t* (02) 413 2471, *f* 413 2296
Government ministry for issues affecting the French-speaking population, including international youth exchanges. »93
♦ **Ministerie van de Vlaamse Gemeenschap—Departement Onderwijs** *(Ministry for the Flemish Community, Education Department)* Rijksadministratief Centrum
Arcadengebouw, 3e verd., 1010 Brussel; *t* (02) 210 5122-23, *f* 210 5372
Education ministry for the Flemish community; responsibilities include Belgian participation in the EU's COMETT programme for transnational training in technology, p189, and its ERASMUS university exchange programme, p190. »94
● ≡ Dienst Internationale Betrekkingen (International Service):
RAC Arcadengebouw, 3e verd., 1010 Brussel; *t* (02) 210 5419, *f* 210 5372
International educational issues affecting the Dutch-speaking population. Member of European Steering Committee for Inter-governmental Co-operation in the Youth Field, CDEJ, and participates in TEMPUS programme for EU links with Central and Eastern Europe, p192. See also the PETRA office, p193.»94
♦ **Ministerium der Deutschsprachigen Gemeinschaft** *(Ministry for the German-Speaking Community)*
Gospert 1-5, 4700 Eupen; *t* (087) 744539, *f* 552891
Government ministry for issues affecting the German-speaking minority. Its cultural office, Abteilung Kulturelle Angelegenheiten, is in the European Steering Committee for Intergovernmental Co-operation in the Youth Field, CDEJ. »94
● **Mouvement Chrétien pour la Paix**, MCP *(Christian Peace Movement)*
Rue de la Sablonnière 18, 1000 Bruxelles; *t* (02) 219 5720, *f* 223 1495
Anti-racist Christian youth movement. »94
♦ **Office des Etrangers**: Dienst Vreemdelingenzaken *(Aliens Office)* Ministère de la Justice: Ministerie van Justitie
Squâre de Meeûs 8, 1040 Bruxelles; *t* (02) 513 9400
Asylum, refugee status, protection. »83
♦ **Organisation Internationale pour les Migrations**, OIM:
International Organization for Migration, IOM (formerly Intergovernmental Committee for Migrations, ICM)
Rue Belliard 65, 1040 Bruxelles; *t* (02) 230 6055, *f* 230 0763
Branch office for Belgium and Luxembourg of the IOM, which facilitates international migration and resettlement: see main IOM listing, p218 (Switzerland). »94
● **Oxfam Belgique**: Oxfam België
Rue du Conseil 39, 1050 Bruxelles
International humanitarian relief. Member of Chilean refugee aid group COLARCH, p28. »93
▌ **Pax Christi Youth Forum International**, PCYF
Rue du Vieux Marché aux Grains 21, 1000 Bruxelles; *t* (02) 502 5550, *f* 502 4626
Catholic international solidarity, peace and human rights movement. »94
▌ **PETRA Youth Bureau** and European Network of Guidance Resource Centres
Place du Luxembourg 2-3, 1040 Bruxelles; *t* (02) 511 1510, *f* 511 1960
PETRA is an EU programme on the vocational training of young people; concerns include training and work experience placements abroad. The Network links national centres in all EU countries providing information and advice to young people about training, employment and education in other countries. See also Youth for Europe, p191, and PETRA national offices, pp139, 140, 188, 191, 193-4, 202, 204, 207, 215. »94
▌ **Phare Democracy Programme**, PHARE
Avenue Michelange 70, 1040 Bruxelles; *t/f* (02) 736 8405
European Union programme; concerns include anti-racism, migrants, refugees. »94
✿ **Provincie Limburg, Dienst Onthaal van Gastarbeiders**:
Service Provincial d'Immigration et d'Accueil de Limbourg *(Limburg Provincial Immigration and Reception Service)*
Marie-Claude Rosiers-Leonard: Thonissenlaan 19, 3500 Hasselt; *t* (011) 222986 »90
▌ **Quaker Council for European Affairs**
Square Ambiorix 50, 1040 Bruxelles; *t* (02) 230 4935, *f* 230 6370
Represents the social concerns of the Religious Society of Friends including social justice, human dignity, development, and anti-racism at European level. »94
● **Rassemblement des femmes pour la Paix**: Vrouwen-vereniging voor Vrede *(Women's Movement for Peace)*
[address unknown]
Member of COLARCH, Chilean refugee committee, p28. »83

● **Rode Jeugd—Jongerenorganisatie van de PvdA** *(Red Youth—Labour Party Youth Organisation)*
Lemonnierlaan 171, 1000 Brussel; *t* (02) 513 1095
Socialist youth movement; anti-racist, anti-fascist. »94
● **Secours International de Caritas Catholica Belgica**, SICC:
Internationaal Hulpbetoon van Caritas Catholica *(Caritas International Assistance)*
Luc Keymans/J. Cleemput: Rue du Commerce 70-72, 1040 Bruxelles; *t* (02) 511 4255, *f* 514 4867, *Tx* 25713 CARITA B
Humanitarian relief agency, founded 1948; research and documentation, lobbying, emergency aid to groups including displaced persons in Belgium and abroad; refugee welfare, settlement and repatriation assistance; Département Migration is at Rue Guimard 1, 1040 Bruxelles; member of CIRE and CBAR, p130. *Contacts* (4/yr), *Notes de documentation* (6/yr).»95
▌ **Service Civil International**, SCI *(International Civil Service)*
European office
Draakstr. 37, 2018 Antwerpen; *t* (03) 235 9473, *f* 235 2973
International welfare agency; see national sections in Austria, p188, Belgium, below, France, p199, Germany, p202, Italy, p206, and Switzerland, p219. »94
● ≡ Belgian office: Van Elewyckstraat 35, 1050 Brussel; *t* (02) 649 0738, *f* 640 0774 »94
✿ **Service d'Immigration et d'Accueil de la Province de Liège** *(Liège Provincial Immigration and Reception Service)*
Rue E. de Bavière 6, 4020 Liège; *t* (041) 423190 »90
✿ **Service Provincial d'Immigration du Hainaut** *(Hainaut Provincial Immigration Service)*
[address uncertain] Quai de Brabant 29, 6000 Charleroi »90
✿ **Socialistisch Jeugdverbond**, SJV *(Young Socialist League)*
Grasmarkt 105/47, 1000 Brussel; *t* (02) 512 2340, *f* 511 1290
Socialist youth movement; anti-racist, anti-fascist. »94
● **Solidarité libérale internationale**: Internationale Liberale Solidariteit *(International Liberal Solidarity)*
Rue de la Samaritaine 56, 1000 Bruxelles; *t* (02) 513 2134
Liberal welfare and refugee agency; member of CBAR, p130.»95
● **Solidarité socialiste—Service social**: Socialistische Solidariteit—Sociale dienst *(Socialist Solidarity—Social Service)*
Rue de Parme 28, 1060 Bruxelles; *t* (02) 537 9545 French, 537 9215 Dutch; *f* 534 6226
Socialist relief agency, providing social services to refugees and immigrants; member of CIRE and CBAR, p130. »95
▌ **Tacis Democracy Programme**, TACIS
Avenue Michelange 70, 1040 Bruxelles; *t/f* (02) 732 6653
European Union programme; concerns include anti-racism, migrants, refugees. »94
✿ **Thuislozenzorg Vlaanderen** *(Flanders Homeless Welfare)*
Diskmuidelaan 50, 1050 Berchem; *t* (03) 366 0426, *f* 366 1158
Accommodation assistance. »95
▌ **Trans-European Mobility Scheme for University Studies**, TEMPUS
TEMPUS Bureau, Avenue des Arts 194, 1040 Bruxelles; *t* (02) 212 0411, *f* 214 0400
European Union programme for promoting staff and student mobility and other forms of co-operation with Central and Eastern Europe. »94
● **Vereniging voor Technische Samenwerking** *(Society for Technical Co-operation)*
Handelsstr. 20, 1040 Brussel; *t* (02) 513 7534, *f* 512 0502
International development assistance agency founded 1985, publicly and privately funded, 60 staff plus volunteers; mainly agricultural projects in Latin America and Africa; has worked with refugees and displaced people in El Salvador. Development education, lobbying in Belgium. »93
✿ **Vlaams Platform voor International Jongerenwerk**, VPIJ *(Flemish Programme for International Youth Work)*
Grétrystr. 26, 1040 Brussel; *t* (02) 218 6455, *f* 219 4655»94
● **Vlaamse Dienst voor Arbeidsbemiddeling en Beroeps-opleiding**, VDAB *(Flemish Employment and Vocational Training Agency)* and EURES Flemish Unit
Keizerslaan 11, 1000 Brussel; *t* (02) 502 5001, *f* 502 5474
Location: M. Lemonnierlaan 131. The national employment agency for the Flemish community, with 18 sub-offices; responsibilities include administration of the EU's EURES programme, p190, for transnational employment advice and information (EURES office: *t* 506 1609, *f* 512 2474; regional contact points in Antwerp, Ghent, Kortrijk and Lanaken). »94
● **Vlaamse Kommissie Rechtvaardigheid en Vrede**, KRV *(Flemish Commission for Justice and Peace)*
Christian Savat, General Secretary: Brialmontstraat 11/05, 1030 Brussel; *t* (02) 218 6348, *f* 223 1159
Alliance, founded 1967, of some 30 development and human rights NGOs. »93

- **VPA PETRA** *(European Youth Training Network)*
Trierstraat 92, bus 3, 1040 Brussel; *t* (02) 238 1411, *f* 238 1444
Section of the Education Department of the Ministry for the Flemish Community; participates in the EU-sponsored PETRA network, p192, of youth training and guidance agencies. »94
- **Welzijnszorg asbl** *(Welfare Care)*
Koningstraat 176, 1210 Brussel
Radical Catholic group. »88
- **Wereldsolidariteit, WS: Solidarite Mondiale** *(World Solidarity)*
Wetstraat 121, 1040 Brussel; *t* (02) 237 3765, *f* 237 3300
International solidarity, links between Belgian labour and voluntary groups abroad; has assisted Chilean refugees in Belgium, and migrants returning to Sri Lanka. »93
- ▌**Young European Federalists, JEF**
Place du Luxembourg 1, 1040 Bruxelles; *t* (02) 512 0053, *f* 512 6673
Pro-European youth movement with sections in EU member countries, e.g. pp167, 187, 209; anti-racist policies. »94
- ▌**Youth Forum of the European Union, YF**
Rue Joseph II 120, 1040 Bruxelles; *t* (02) 230 6490, *f* 230 2123
Official EU-sponsored forum of national youth councils and similar bodies; concerns include anti-racism, integration of migrant youth. »94

BOSNIA HERCEGOVINA *387*

- **International Peace Centre**
Titova 7a, 71000 Sarajevo; *t* (071) 663730, *f* 663626 »94
- **Open Society Fund—Soros Foundation, OSF-SF**
Ise Jovanovica 2, 71000 Sarajevo; *t* c/o [+1] (412) 339 4736, *f* c/o 339 4724
US-based philanthropic organisation promoting human rights, democracy and international mobility. »94
- ✿ **Sarajevo Centre for Peace**
Dobrovoljascka 3, 71000 Sarajevo; *t* (071) 214884, *f* (071) 216238 »94
- ◆ **United Nations High Commissioner for Refugees, UNHCR:** Branch Office for Bosnia Hercegovina
Magistralni put 1, 71000 Pale; *t* (071) 783967; satphone (871) 1754554, *f* 785347; satfax 1754555
Technically responsible for refugee status and protection. »95

BULGARIA *359*

- **Bulgarian Helsinki Committee**
6 Gourgouliat Street, 5th Floor, 1000 Sofia; *t/f* (02) 818980 »94
- **Friends of People**
40a Strouga Street, Sofia; *t* (02) 326088, *f* 884032
Promotes international friendship and exchanges. »94
- **Open Society Fund—Soros Foundation, OSF-SF**
PO Box 114-1 Bulgaria Square, 11th Floor, NDK Boulevard, 1463 Sofia; *t* (02) 658323, *f* 658276
US-based philatropic organisation. »94
- ◆ **United Nations High Commissioner for Refugees, UNHCR**
Latinka Str. 13, Sofia; *t* (2) 727216, 720821, *f* 720849
Refugee status and protection; see main entry, p219. »95

CROATIA *385*

- **Helsinki Committee for Human Rights**
Perkovceva 2, 41000 Zagreb; *t* (041) 442229, *f* 442883
Promotion of international law and standards in human rights; particular interest in refugee protection. »94
- ✿ **Nacionalni Savez Mladezi Hrvatske** *(National Youth Union of Croatia)*
Trg. Hrvatski Velikana 4-4, 41000 Zagreb; *t* (041) 450044, *f* 435314
Main national youth NGO. »94
- **Open Society Fund—Soros Foundation, OSF-SF**
Krvavi Most 2, 41000 Zagreb; *t* (041) 272017, *f* 75741
National branch office of US-based philanthropic organisation committed to democratic development in Central Europe. »94
- ✿ **Suncokret—Centre for Grassroots Voluntary Work**
Marusevacka 8, 41000 Zagreb; *t* (041) 318576, *f* 339317
Social work with refugees and other groups. »94

- ◆ **United Nations High Commissioner for Refugees, UNHCR**
Kupska 2, 41000 Zagreb; *t* (041) 629555, *f* 530101
Refugee status and protection; see headquarters, p219. »95

CYPRUS *357*

- ◆ **Service for Overseas Cypriots**
Platonas Kyriakides: Ministry of Foreign Affairs, Nicosia
Supports community development, maintenance of cultural identity among Cypriot emigrants; advice and information on repatriation; co-ordination of policy with Greece towards the Greek-speaking diaspora. »95
- **United Democratic Youth Organisation, EDON**
PO Box 1986, Nicosia; *t* (02) 466459, *f* 365161
Youth group in the Greek-speaking community. »94
- ◆ **United Nations High Commissioner for Refugees, UNHCR**
PO Box 1642, Nicosia; *t* (02) 359026, 359043, *f* 359053
Refugee status and protection; see headquarters, p219. »95

CZECH REPUBLIC *42*

- ◆ **Amnesty International—Czech Section**
Palackého 9, 11000 Praha 1; *t* (02) 235 5996
Human rights pressure group, mainly concerned with political prisoners (see AI International Secretariat, p220) but with an interest in refugee issues. »94
- **Helsinki Committee**
Libuse Silhanova, Deputy President: [address uncertain] Mlady Horákové 103, 16000 Praha 6; *t* (02) 323259, *f* 323538
Address also listed (1994) as Panska 7, 11669 Praha, *t* 220181, *f* 220948. Promotion of international standards of human rights; anti-racism. Organised Third Helsinki Citizens' Assembly in Prague in 1993, with themes including racism, migration and minority rights. »94
- ▌**International Union of Students, IUS**
PO Box 58, 17th November Street, 11000 Praha 1; *t* (02) 2481 0438, *f* 2481 0855
International federation of national student unions; anti-racist, anti-fascist policies. »94
- ✿ **King George of Podiebrady Foundation for European Co-operation**
PS 7, 11900 Praha 1, Hrad; *t* (02) 551964, *f* 551968 »94
- **League for Human and Youth Rights** and Peace Groups Information Centre
Panská 7, 11669 Praha 1; *t* (02) 227454, *f* 236 8441
Human rights, anti-racism, anti-fascism. »94
- **Peace Union of Bohemia and Moravia**
U hranic 17, 10000 Praha 10; *t* (02) 735 7091
Anti-nationalist, anti-racist peace movement. »94
- **Rada Mládeze Cech, Moravy a Slezska, RMCMS** *(National Youth Council)*
Senovázné nám. 24, 11647 Praha 1; *t* (02) 223239, *f* (02) 228383
Umbrella group of youth organisations. »94
- ◆ **United Nations High Commissioner for Refugees, UNHCR**
PS 505, 11121 Praha 1; *t* (02) 268529, *f* 24230574
Location: Karoliny Svetle 4, 11000 Praha 1. Refugee status, protection; see p219, and regional office in Austria, p188.»95

DENMARK *45*

- ✿ **Århus Retshjælp** *(Aarhus Legal Aid)*
Bødker Balles Gård 15 I, 8000 Århus C; *t* 8619 4700 »83
- **Amnesty International—Dansk Afdeling, AI-DK**
Lars N. Joergensen, General Secretary: Dyrkøb 3, 1166 København K; *t* 3311 7541, *f* 3393 3746
Human rights, campaigns for prisoners of conscience and against death penalty, see p220; interested in refugee issues in those contexts. Member of Dansk Flygtningehjælp, p132.»95
- **Arbejdsmarkedets Center for Internationale Uddannelses- aktiviteter, ACIU** *(Labour Market Centre for International Training Programmes)* and PETRA
Hesseløgade 16, 2100 København ø; *t* 3927 1922, *f* 3927 2217
Independent agency established by government, employers and unions to extend Danish participation in international vocational training, including the EU PETRA exchange programme, p192. »94

- **Arbejdsmarkedsstyrelsen** *(Labour Market Authority)* and EURES
Blegdamsvej 56, Postbox 2722, 2100 København K; *t* 3392 5900, *f* 3312 1378
Labour Ministry agency responsible for employment and careers guidance counselling. Includes the Danish EURES office (*f* 3536 2411), part of the European network of employment information services, p190.   »94
- **ASF-Dansk Folkehjælp** *(Danish Labour Assistance)*
Max Simonsen, General Secretary: Jernbanevej 12, Postbox 206, 4960 Hedeby; *t* 5390 7400, *f* 5390 7399
Also listed (1993) at Roskildevej 147, PO Box 206, 2620 Albertslund. Trade union relief agency; member of Dansk Flygtningehjælp (refugee council), p132.   »95
- **Caritas Danmark**
Bredgade 69, 1260 København K; *t* 3312 7261
Catholic relief agency. Refugee welfare, accommodation. Member of Dansk Flygtningehjælp, p132.   »94
- **Church of Denmark Council on Inter-Church Relations**
Rev. Jens Johansen: Vesterbrogade 52/4, 1620 København V; *t* 3315 5927   »90
- **European Commission**
Højbrohus Østergade 61, Postboks 144, 1004 København K; *t* 3314 4140, *f* 3311 1203, 3314 1392, *Tx* 16402 COMEUR DK
National office of the Commission, p189; information on EU policy and related matters.   »94
- **Conference of European Churches**
Johannes Langhoff: [address uncertain] Dronninggardvej 2, 2840 Holte; *t* 4242 4065   »90
- **Danish Helsinki Committee**
Prof. E. Siesby, Chairman: [address unknown]
Focus on minorities in Europe; Fanny Gjørup, *t* 3391 3307; Margareta Kepinska Jakobsen, *t* 3162 7949.   »90
- ♦ **Dansk Røde Kors:** Danish Red Cross
Poul Jul Andersen: Postbox 1092, Landemærket 25, 1008 København K; *t* 3138 1444, *f* 3142 1186
Member of Dansk Flygtningehjælp, p132; Asylum Department involved in humanitarian assistance, housing, welfare, education of pre-asylum refugees in Denmark, international family tracing. Raises funds for refugee aid and other humanitarian work abroad; see also international Red Cross, p218. In the year to July 1993 the DRK documented 100 suicide attempts by refugees. *Dialog* (4/yr), *Hjælp* (12/yr).»95
- **Dansk Ungdoms Fællesråd**, DUF: Danish Youth Council
Anders Lade Karl, General Secretary: Scherfigsvej 5, 2100 København ø; *t* 3129 8888, *f* 3129 8382
Løvland Macko. Umbrella group for 70 youth organisations; international solidarity, youth welfare; integration of migrant and refugee youth; member of Dansk Flygtningehjælp, p132. Participated in 1994-95 European Youth Campaign Against Racism, p197. *Under Paraplyen* (4/yr), *DUF-Nyt* (12/yr).   »95
- **Dansk UNICEF Komite:** Danish Committee for UNICEF
Arne Stinus, General Secretary: Billedvej 8, 2100 København ø; *t* 3929 5111, *f* 3927 0577
International solidarity, development education; fundraising for UNICEF, p219. *UNICEF-Nyt* (4/yr).   »94
- **Det Danske Center for Menneskerettigheder:** Danish Centre for Human Rights, DCHR
Kjærum Morten, Director: Grundtvigs Hus, Studiestræde 38/2, 1455 København K; *t* 3391 1299, *f* 3391 0299
Martin Breum, Jens Vedsted-Hansen. National human rights pressure group. Research, documentation, campaigns; legal assistance to refugees and migrants. *Update* (6/yr).   »95
- **Danske Kvinders Nationalråd** *(Danish National Council of Women)*
Niels Hemmingsensgade 8-10, 1153 København K; *t* 3312 8087; *f* 3312 6740
Member of Dansk Flygtningehjælp, p132.   »95
- **Direktoratet for Social Sikring og Bistand—Internationale Afdeling** *(Social Security and Welfare Agency International Department)*
Ny Kongensgade 9, 1472 Købenshavn K; *t* 3391 2622, *f* 3391 5654
Deals with social security issues affecting migrant workers.»94
- ♦ **Direktoratet for Udlændinge** *(Aliens Administration)*
Absalonsgade 9, 1658 København V
Department of the Ministry of Justice, right; administers Law for Foreigners, maintains computerised Aliens Register used in immigration control, issues residence permits, processes asylum applications.   »95
- ▌European Confederation of Youth Clubs, ECYC
Ømevej 45, 2400 København NV; *t* 3110 8038, *f* 3110 4655
International forum of youth clubs; concerns include anti-racism, promotion of intercultural understanding.   »94

- ♦ **Flygtningenævnet** *(Refugee Board)*
[address unknown] København
Independent agency which considers appeals against asylum refusals by the Direktoratet for Udlændinge, left.   »91
- ✿ **Flygtningesekretariatet** *(Refugee Secretariat)*
Magistratens 4. afdeling, Godthåbsgade 8, 9400 Nørresundby; *t* 9811 2211 exts. 4067, 4068   »89
- **FN-Forbundet**, FNF: Danish United Nations Association
Skindergade 26, København; *t* 3312 3939
Internationalism, human rights. Member of Dansk Flygtninge-hjælp (refugee council), p132.   »95
- **Folkebevægelsen mod Fremmedhad**, FMF *(People's Movement against Xenophobia)*
Aboulevarden 18, 2200 København N; *t* 3168 2053   »95
- **Folkekirkens Nødhjælp:** Danchurchaid, Inter-Church Aid and World Service, DCA
Christian Batslev Olesen, General Secretary: Sankt Peders stræde 3, 1453 København K; *t* 3315 2800, *f* 3315 3860
Ecumenical humanitarian aid agency. Member of Dansk Flygt-ningehjælp, p132; refugee welfare, advice work in Denmark, overseas projects for refugees/returnees. *Nød* (12/yr).   »94
- **Fredsfonden** *(Peace Foundation)*
Nyhavn 21, 1051 København K; *t* 3332 4417, *f* 3315 7130   »94
- **Ibis**
Jan Birket-Smith: Nørrebrogade 68B, 2 sal., 2200 København N; *t* 3135 8788, *f* 3135 0696
Human rights, development education; support for NGOs in Africa and Latin America, including several involved refugee welfare and reintegration. Formerly, as Dansk Nationalkomite for World University Service, affiliated to WUS-International, p219. *Zig-Zag* (9/yr).   »94
- **Informationscenter for studie- og udviklingsrejser**, ICU *(Information Centre for International Study and Exchange)*
Vandkunsten 3, 1467 København K; *t* 3314 2060
Also listed (1994) at Dronningensgade 75, 1420 København K; *t* 3195 2900, *f* 3195 1533. State and voluntary agency for exchange and youth mobility; information, practical assistance; supports EU programmes including LINGUA, PETRA, p192, Youth for Europe, p191, and Teacher Exchange Scheme.   »95
- ♦ **Justitsministeriet** *(Ministry of Justice)*
Nina Holst Christensen: Slotholmsgade 10, 1216 København K; *t* 3312 0906
Overall reponsibility for policy on asylum applications, refugee status and protection; on migration matters works through Direktoratet for Udlændinge, left.   »95
- ✿ **Københavns Retshjælp** *(Copenhagen Legal Aid)*
Gammel Kongevej 10, 1610 København V
Member of Dansk Flygtningehjælp (refugee council), p132.»83
- **Labourmovements International Forum**
Bent Christensen: [address uncertain] Teglværksgade 27, 2100 København ø; *t* 3129 6066   »90
- ▌Liberal International Human Rights Committee
Grete Bille: [address uncertain] Islehusvej 36, st., 2700 Brønshôj; *t* 3128 6648   »90
- ♦ **Mellemfolkeligt Samvirke**, MS: Danish Association for International Co-operation: Association Danoise pour la Coopération Internationale
Ole Hammer: Borgergade 10-14, 1300 København K; *t* 3332 6244, *f* 3315 6243, *Tx* 15928 MS DK, *Tg* Mellemsam
Aid agency with interest in migrants and refugees; participant in MAINE network, p146, and Dansk Flygtningehjælp, p132. See also MS Indvandrerdokumentation, p233.   »94
- ▌Nordic Council of Ministers
Store Strandstræde 18, 1255 København K; *t* 3311 4711, *f* 3393 8955
Intergovernmental forum for Iceland, Norway, Sweden and (with their dependencies) Denmark and Finland. Promotes and facilitates convergence and co-operation on economic and social issues, including the free movement of labour, social security rights, training, changes of nationality, parity in marital and children's rights, and cultural exchange. Not to be confused with the Nordic Council, p216.   »93
- **Nordic Youth Committee**
Store Strandstræde, 1225 København K; *t* 3396 0200, *f* 3396 0202
International consultative body for national youth movements in the Nordic countries.   »94
- **Det Økumeniske Fællesråd i Danmark**, DOF *(Ecumenical Council of Denmark)*
Jorgen Thomsen, Secretary: Skindergade 24/1, 1159 København K; *t* 3315 5927, *f* 3311 3214
Inter-church agency promoting humanitarian co-operation, development education, Christian approach to human rights and economic justice, including migration/refugee issues.   »94

● **Red Barnet Danmark:** Danish Save the Children: also known as Landsorganisationen Red Barnet
Uffe Torm: Brogårdsvænget 4, 2820 Gentofte; *t* 3968 0888, *f* 3168 0510
International humanitarian relief; some refugee return and reintegration work. Member of Dansk Flygtningehjælp, p132; see also ISCA, p218. *Red Barnet Information* (10/yr). »95

▌ **Servas International**
Birkedals Allé 40, 5250 Odense SV; *t/f* 6617 0240 »94

● **Specialarbejderforbundet i Danmark,** SID
Claus Larsen-Jensen, International Secretary: Postboks 392, Nyropsgade 30, 1620 København V; *t* 3314 2140, *f* 3397 2460, 3332 1450, *Tx* 19596 SID DK
Trade union with human rights, development education and overseas development aid activities. *Fagbladet* (52/yr). »95

◆ **Statens Indvandrerkonsulenter** *(State Counselling Service for Immigrants)* Indenrigsministeriet (Ministry of the Interior)
Karen Andersen: Christiansborg Slotsplads 1, 1218 København K; *t* 3392 3380, *f* 3312 1513
Welfare advice, information. Works closely with Dansk Flygtningehjælp, p132. »94

◆ **Udenrigsministeriet** *(Ministry of Foreign Affairs)*
Asiatisk Plads 2, 1448 København K; *t* 3392 0000 »85

● **Undervisningsministeriet** *(Ministry of Education)*
Frederiksholms Kanal 26, 1220 København ø; *t* 3392 5000, 3392 5436 COMETT, 3392 5403 ERASMUS, *f* 3392 5075
Ministry responsible, inter alia, for participation in European exchange and co-operation programmes such as COMETT, p189, TEMPUS, p192 and ERASMUS, p190 (all run by the Rektorkollegiets Sekretariat, third-level department), and LINGUA (EF-Sekretariatet, or EU department). Other foreign relations are handled by the Internationale Afdeling, Frederiksholms Kanal 25D, *t* 3392 5300, *f* 3392 5567. »94

United Nations High Commissioner for Refugees, UNHCR: see Stockholm office, p217, and Dansk Flygtnigehjælp, p132

▌ **World Assembly of Youth,** WAY
Ved Bellahøj 4, Bronshøj, 2700 København; *t* 3160 7770, *f* 3160 5797 »94

ESTONIA 372

◆ **Commission for the Refugee Issue**
Jüri Adams, Minister of Justice: Ministry of Justice, Tallinn
Set up 1994 to advise on administrative and policy responses to arrival of third-country refugees via Russia. »95

● **Eesti Inimõiguste Institut** *(Estonian Human Rights Institute)*
Tonismägi 2, 0100 Tallinn; *t* (2) 459477, *f* 453334
Human rights monitoring and pressure group. »94

● **Eesti Noorsoouhenduste Kogu,** ENK *(Estonian Youth Council)*
Suur-Karja 23, 0001 Tallinn; *t* (2) 448552, *f* 433624 »94

● **Open Society Fund—Soros Foundation,** OSF-SF
Olevimägi 12, 0010 Tallinn; *t* (6) 313791, *f* 313796
Estonian office of a US-based philanthropic organisation promoting democracy, human rights and socio-economic progress in Central and Eastern Europe. »94

FINLAND 358

● **Amnesty International—Suomen Osasto,** AI *(Finnish Section)*
Ruoholahdenkatu 24d, 00180 Helsinki; *t* (90) 693 1488, *f* 693 1975
National section of the (UK-based, p220) human rights campaign for those persecuted for political beliefs. Provides documentation on refugees' countries of origin, and opposes improper refusals of asylum. *Amnesty Tietode* (6/yr). »95

● **Central Organisation of Finnish Trade Unions—Youth Committee**
Siltasaarenkatu 3 A, 00530 Helsinki
Specialist section of trade union confederation; concerns include rights of young migrant and minority workers. »94

● **Democratic Youth League of Finland,** SDNL
Vuorikatu 22 A 7, 00100 Helsinki; *t* (90) 663199, *f* 663225
Progressive, anti-racist and anti-fascist youth organisation.»94

● **Ihmisoikeuksien ja Kansalaisvapauksien Puolesta** *(Human Rights and Civil Liberties League)*
[address uncertain] PO Box 245, 00171 Helsinki; *t* (90) 135 1470, *f* 135 1101
Also listed (1993) as PO Box 696. Concerned with a range of human rights issues at home and abroad, including racism and refugee rights. Founded 1979. *Ihmisoikeudet* (1/yr).»94

● **Kansainvälinen Vapaaehtoistyö,** KVT
Rauhanasema, Veturitori, 00520 Helsinki; *t* (90) 144408, *f* 147297
Youth NGO with anti-racist, anti-fascist orientation. »94

● **Kirkon Ulkomaanapu:** Finnchurchaid
Satamakatu 11, 00160 Helsinki; *t* (90) 18021, *f* 180 2207
Humanitarian relief and development agency of the Lutheran church; human rights, development education; repatriation help, and other services to refugees mainly in Africa. »95

● **NADA**
Nytte Ekman: [address unknown] Helsinki
Humanitarian relief agency; concerns include position of asylum-seekers in Estonia. »95

● **Ombudsman for Aliens:** Ministry for Social Affairs & Health
Antti Seppälä: PL 267, 00171 Helsinki; *t* (90) 160 3760 »95

● **Suomen Nuorisoyhteistyö Allianssi,** Allianssi: Finnish Youth Co-operation Alliance
Olympiastadion, Eteläkaarre, 00250 Helsinki; *t* (90) 348 2422, *f* 491290
Umbrella group; participated in the 1994-95 European Youth Campaign Against Racism, p197. »94

● **Suomen Punainen Risti,** SPR/FRK: Finnish Red Cross
Jari Pirjola: Tehtaankatu 1a, PO Box 168, 00140 Helsinki; *t* (90) 12931, *f* 654149, *Tx* 121331
Humanitarian and development aid, training, help to Red Cross societies in developing countries; services to refugees, including repatriation/reintegration assistance. See p218.»95

● **Suomen Ylioppilaskuntien Liga,** SYL: Finlands Studenten Förbund *(Finnish Students' Union)*
Kalevankatu 3a 46, 00100 Helsinki; *t* (90) 680 3110, *f* 642413 »94

▌ **World Peace Council,** WPC
Lönnrotinkatu 25A 6 krs, 00180 Helsinki; *t* (90) 693 1044
Internationalist, anti-racist peace movement with national affiliates in many countries. »94

FRANCE 33

● **Action Catholique Ouvrière,** ACO *(Catholic Worker Action)*
7 rue P. Lelong, 75002 Paris; *t* (1) 4236 3611, *f* 4026 2018
International solidarity; Catholic pastorate. *Témoignage ACO; Testemunho ACO* (both 12/yr). »94

▌ **Action des Chrétiens pour l'Abolition de la Torture,** ACAT: Action by Christians for the Abolition of Torture: Fédération internationale
252 rue Saint-Jacques, 75005 Paris; *t* (1) 4329 8852, *f* 4046 0183
Campaigns against torture and inhuman treatment in any country; welfare of refugees; see pp200, 207. »93

● **Action Internationale contre la Faim,** AICF *(International Action against Hunger)*
34 ave. Reille, 75014 Paris; *t* (1) 4565 4040, *f* 4565 9250
Humanitarian aid and development assistance: agricultural, medical, craft industries; programmes include refugee aid projects in Africa and Asia. Over 30 member agencies. »93

● **Action Nord Sud** *(North-South Action)*
14 avenue Berthelot, BP ERAC, 69361 Lyon Cedex 07; *t* 7869 7991, *f* 7869 7994
International humanitarian aid agency; activities include refugee reintegration work in Near East, Asia, Balkans. »93

● **Agence de coopération culturelle et technique,** AGECOOP
13 quai André Citroën, 75015 Paris; *t* (1) 4437 3300, *f* 4579 1498
Promotes co-operation in cultural and technical areas, such as rural development, among 32 Francophone countries. »93

◆ **Agence Nationale pour l'Emploi,** ANPE *(National Employment Agency)* Ministère du Travail, de l'Emploi et de la Formation
10 place de la Défense, La Défense 4, 92080 Paris Cedex 26; *t* (1) 4996 0650, *f* 4773 8489
Agency of the Labour Ministry; runs 700 local employment offices, providing placement services, information and advice on employment and training. Open to non-nationals, as are the 518 Centres d'Information et d'Orientation, CIO, operated by the Ministry of Education. These offer careers counselling and practical information on training, including options in other EU countries. Each CIO region has an office for information on the EU, and information on France for non-nationals; it is, however, the ANPE which represents France in the EURES network of employment services, p190. »94

● **Aide et Action**
67 bvd Soult, 75012 Paris; *t* (1) 4019 0414, *f* 4019 0662
Educational charity providing funds, resources and training in the Third World, including refugee/returnee projects. »93

● **Aide sans Frontières**
9 rue Mathis, 75019 Paris   »90
● **Alliance des Unions Chrétiennes de Jeunes Gens de France,**
UCJG: Young Mens's Christian Association Alliance of
France: Service Justice et Développement
5 place de Vénétie, 75643 Paris Cedex 13; *t* (1) 4586 8432,
f 4586 6492
Development education; language courses and social
assistance to migrants and refugees in France; development
aid and volunteer programmes in Africa.   »93
◆ **Amnesty International—Section française**
4 rue de la Pierre-Levée, 75553 Paris Cedex 11; *t* (1) 4923
1111, 4338 7474, *f* 4338 2615, *Tx* Amnesty 213659 F
Human rights, political prisoners abroad, see p220; emergency
assistance, counselling to refugees and asylum seekers. »95
● **Arche de la Fraternité:** also known as Fondation Arche de
la Fraternité
Emmanuelle Parodi: 1 Parvis de La Défense, La Défense,
92040 Paris Cedex 89; *t* (1) 4907 2626, *f* 4778 8647,
4907 2621
Promotes human rights, international solidarity, anti-racism.
Founded 1989.   »94
● **Architectes sans Frontières,** ASF
38 rue des Mathurins, 75008 Paris; *t* (1) 4268 0768,
f 4017 0743
Disaster relief, emergency housing for displaced persons and
refugees, construction training and development projects.»93
● **Association des constructeurs pour la réhabilitation et
l'optimalisation de la terre,** ARCOTERRE *(Builders'
Association for Land Reclamation and Improvement)*
60 place des Géants, 38100 Grenoble; *t* 7633 0834,
f 7633 3054
Development aid group: training in and application of
appropriate technology in housing and other construction
projects; has worked with Afghan refugees in Pakistan.   »93
✿ **Association pour la Diffusion, l'Adaptation et la Préformation**
(Association for Awareness, Adaptation and Training)
M Soukhaong: 21 rue des Malmaisons, 75013 Paris; *t* (1)
4585 7312   »90
▌ **Association Européenne des Citoyens,** AEC: European
Citizens' Association
31 rue de Reuilly, 75012 Paris; *t* (1) 4379 0923   »94
● **Association Familiale Protestante** *(Protestant Family
Association)*
47 rue de Clichy, 75009 Paris   »90
● **Association française des juristes démocrates,** AFJD
(French Association of Democratic Lawyers)
59 rue Nicolo, 75016 Paris; *t* (1) 4504 9738
Lawyers' group for human rights; campaigns for citizenship
and voting rights for migrants. See AIJD, p189.   »91
● **Association Nationale des Résidents des Foyers
SONACOTRA** *(National Society of SONACOTRA Tenants)*
Bourse du Travail, Esplanade B. Frachon, 93100 Montreuil-
sous-Bois
Tenants' federation for a workers' social housing company,
p199, which has a major role in housing immigrants.   »90
● **Association des parents et des amis de détenus,** APAD
(Association of Families and Friends of Prisoners)
29 rue Stephenson, 75018 Paris
Prisoners' rights and welfare.   »90
✿ **Association pour la Réinsertion de l'Enfance et de
l'Adolescence,** ARENA *(Society for the Reintegration of
Children and Young People)*
Jean-Luc Recordon: Hameau la Pinède, Traverse Valette,
13009 Marseille; *t* 9125 0503   »90
● **Associations Populaires Familiales et Syndicales,** APFS
(Family, Union and Community Associations)
Jo Weber: 1 rue de Maubeuge, 75009 Paris; *t* (1) 4280
2705, *f* 4526 2463
Empreinte (4/yr).   »94
● **Bioforce Développement**
44 boulevard Lénine, 69200 Vénissieux; *t* 7867 3232,
f 7870 2712
Technical and logistical help to emergency relief programmes
worldwide, including refugee and migrant housing, health
care, counselling, repatriation and settlement projects. »93
● **Bureau International de Liaison et de Documentation**
(International Liaison and Documentation Bureau)
50 rue Laborde, 75008 Paris; *t* (1) 4387 2550   »90
● **Bureau International du Travail,** BIT: International Labour
Office, ILO
205 boulevard Saint-Germain, 75006 Paris
National office of Swiss-based ILO, a UN agency, p218.   »90
● **Centre des Droits de l'Homme** *(Centre for the Rights of Man)*
30 rue Gandon, 75013 Paris; *t* (1) 4582 7777   »94

● **Centre pour l'Europe des Citoyens et des Droits de l'Homme,**
CECDH: Centre for Citizens' Europe and Human Rights
6 rue Wencker, 67000 Strasbourg
Human rights issues; anti-racism.   »94
✿ **Centre de Formation pour l'insertion économique et sociale
et l'aide aux mutations,** CESAM *(Training Centre for Socio-
Economic Integration and Adaptation)*
Françoise Marin: 7 rue Mariotte, 21000 Dijon; *t* 8030 6061
Youth training and employment assistance.   »94
✿ **Centre d'Information sur les Droits de la Femme,** CIDF
(Women's Rights Information Centre)
Laurence Reiss: 5 rue Jean-Jacques Rousseau, 33000
Bordeaux; *t* 5644 3030, *f* 5601 1681
Research, information, advice, documentation on women's
rights, employment and other issues. Same address listed
(1990) for Association Régionale pour l'Obtention des Droits,
la Promotion et l'Information des Femmes en Aquitaine; this
may be the same body.   »94
● **Centre International des Avocats** *(International Lawyers'
Centre)*
Christian Wilhelm: Maison du Barreau, 2 quai Jacques-Sturm,
67000 Strasbourg   »90
● **Centre National d'Information et de Documentation des
Femmes et des Familles,** CNIDFF *(National Information and
Documentation Centre on Women and Families)*
Françoise Michaud: 7 rue du Jura, 75013 Paris; *t* (1) 4331
1234
Research, information and advice. *Nouv'elles* (4/yr).   »94
◆ **Centre de sécurité sociale des travailleurs migrants,**
CSSTM *(Social Security Centre for Migrant Workers)*
F. Bonniol, Director: 11 rue de la Tour des Dames, 75436
Paris Cedex 09; *t* (1) 4526 3341
Established 1950; information on social security rights,
pensions and related issues. *Bulletin de liaison* (4/yr); *Lettre
du CSSTM* (12/yr).   »94
✿ **Collectif d'Alphabétisation** *(Literacy Collective)*
1 place Paul Painlevé, 75005 Paris; *t* (1) 4633 4116   »90
● **Comité National des Associations de Jeunesse et
d'Education Populaire,** CNAJEP *(National Committee of Youth
and Community Education Societies)*
15 rue Martel, 75010 Paris; *t* (1) 4770 7131, *f* 4770 3001»94
● **Commission des Communautés Européennes:** Commission
of the European Communities
288 boulevard Saint-Germain, 75007 Paris; *t* (1) 4063 3800,
f 4556 9417-19, *Tx* CCEBRF 202271 F
Represents the Commission, p189; information on EU issues.»94
✿ ≡ CMCI, 2 rue Henri Barbusse, 13241 Marseille Cedex 01;
t 9191 4600, *f* 9190 9807, *Tx* 402538 EURMA   »94
● **Commission française Justice et Paix** *(French Commission
for Justice and Peace)*
71 rue Notre-Dame-des-Champs, 75006 Paris; *t* (1) 4325
9291, *f* 4329 0995
Catholic church agency. Research/action on human rights
issues; public education on migrant and refugee rights.   »93
◆ **Commission des recours** *(Appeals Commission)*
99 rue de la Verrerie, 75004 Paris; *t* (1) 4277 8086
Hears appeals on refugee status rulings of OFPRA, p199. »83
● **Confédération française démocratique du travail,** CFDT
(French Democratic Labour Confederation)
4 boulevard de la Villette, 75019 Paris
Trade union federation.   »90
● **Confédération Générale du Logement** *(General Housing
Federation)*
Frédérique Rastoll: Tour La Parisiane, 6 rue Emile Reynaud,
93300 Aubervilliers; *t* (1) 4839 8586   »90
◆ **Confédération générale du travail—Section immigration,**
CGT *(Immigrant Section, General Confederation of Labour)*
263 rue de Paris, 93516 Montreuil Cedex
Immigrant section of main labour federation; migrant workers'
rights, training, social security issues. See AEFTI, p135. »90
● **Confédération Syndicale des Familles** *(Confederation of
Family Associations)*
53 rue Riquet, 75019 Paris   »90
● **Conseil National d'Aide à la Vie Associative,** CNVA
(National Council for Aid to the Voluntary Sector)
50 rue Mouraud, 75020 Paris; *t* (1) 4372 1331   »90
◆ **Conseil National pour l'Intégration des Populations
Immigrées,** CNIPI *(National Council for the Integration of
Immigrant Populations)* formerly Conseil National des
Populations Immigrées: Ministère de la Solidarité
DPM, bureau DM2, 8 avenue de Ségur, 75350 Paris 07 SP;
t (1) 4056 5108
Government agency responsible for information and advice
on national migration policy and ethnic relations. See also
Direction de la Population et des Migrations, p197.   »94

▌ **Co-ordinating Committee for International Voluntary Service,** CCIVS: Comité de Coordination du Service Volontaire International
Maison de l'UNESCO, 1 rue Miollis, 75015 Paris; *t* (1) 4568 2731, *f* 4568 1000, 4273 0521
Forum for 130 governmental and NGO voluntary personnel agencies from over 50 countries which work in international development and humanitarian relief, development education and the promotion of global solidarity. »94

▌ **Council of Europe,** CE: Conseil de l'Europe: Europarat
BP 431 R6, 67075 Strasbourg Cedex; *t* 8841 2000, *f* 8841 2781-83, *Tx* 870943
Location: Maison de l'Europe, 67006 Strasbourg. Intergovernmental organisation founded 1949, now including all European Union member countries and many others in western and eastern Europe. Council activities and interests relevant to migrants and minorities include the work of the European Committee on Migrations, right. The Council has a Population and Training Division for research and reports on intra-European migration and migrants in Europe. It promotes parity of provision, and equal treatment of member country nationals, in social security arrangements; its Community Relations Programme supports integration of immigrant and minority communities; see also the European Commission of Human Rights, right, and CEMYC, p200. The Council's Youth Directorate sponsored the 1994-95 European Youth Campaign against Racism, right. See also European Commission against Racism and Intolerance, right, International Institute for Democracy, p198, European Science Foundation, p235, and several other Council-sponsored or related bodies. »94

▌ ≡ Directorate of Human Rights: Conseil de l'Europe, Palais des Droits de l'Homme, 67075 Strasbourg Cedex; *t* 8841 2000, *f* 8841 2793 »94

▌ ≡ Resettlement Fund: 55 avenue Kléber, 75784 Paris Cedex 16; *t* (1) 4755 5500, 4704 3865, *f* 4755 0338, 4727 3647 »94

♦ **Croix Rouge Française,** CRF: French Red Cross: Service réfugiés-migrants
André Delaude: 1 place Henry Dunant, 75008 Paris; *t* (1) 4443 1100, *f* 4443 1101
Reception, housing, integration assistance and welfare advice for refugees, notably from South-East Asia, and migrants; tracing service, placement of unaccompanied minors. Works through local sections throughout France, and in partnership with national Red Cross societies in developing countries. *Présence Croix Rouge*. See international bodies, p218. »95

● **Culture et Liberté, Association nationale pour le développement culturel du monde du travail** *(Culture and Liberty, National Society for the Cultural Development of Working Life)*
Alain Mamac'h/Joël Jamet: BP 92, 9-11 rue Louis David, 93172 Bagnolet; *t* (1) 4360 7490, *f* 4360 9799
Inter-cultural solidarity. *Infordoc*. »94

● **Délégation Catholique pour la Coopération** *(Catholic Delegation for Co-operation)*
86 rue de Rennes, 75006 Paris »90

♦ **Direction de la Population et des Migrations,** DPM *(Directorate for Population and Migration)* Secrétariat d'état chargeé des immigrés, Ministère de la Solidarité
Gérard Moreau: 1 place de Fontenoy, 75007 Paris; *t* (1) 4056 4148, 4056 4072, *f* 4056 5042
Division of ministry responsible for research and development of policy on social and economic integration of immigrants and refugees; there are also DPMs with similar responsibilities at *département* level; see also CNIPI, p196. *Notes et documents* (12/yr), *Lettre de la DPM*. »94

✿ **Droits de l'Homme et Solidarité,** DHS *(Human Rights and Solidarity)*
127 rue Notre-Dame-des-Champs, 75006 Paris; *t* (1) 4326 8030
Legal advice and information. »94

● **Enfance Espoir** *(Childhood Hope)*
30 rue de l'Epargne, 94600 Choisy-Le-Roi; *t* (1) 4890 9571, *f* 4892 0159
Emergency relief and development aid projects in developing countries; migrant welfare advice in France; reintegration assistance for returnees. »93

● **Enfance et Partage**
7 rue Guy Deverre, 61200 Argentan; *t* 3367 1195, *f* 3339 3472
Health, educational, food and development aid to benefit children mainly in Africa, Latin America and ex-Yugoslavia; autonomous local branches engage in their own partnership projects abroad, and activities in France sometimes including migrant welfare work. »93

● **Enfants du Monde** *(Children of the World)*
126 boulevard Vauban, 59800 Lille; *t* 2030 0492
Development education; funds development projects abroad, emergency assistance to refugees and people displaced by war. Founded 1975; international Enfants du Monde (24 rue Jean Martin, 13005 Marseille, *t* 9148 2919), founded 1980, provides technical support for development projects. »93

✿ **Eurologement** *(Eurohousing)*
Teulet: 110 rue Lemercier, 75017 Paris; *t* (1) 4485 8148, *f* 4627 2197
Advice and information on housing. »94

▌ **European Commission of Human Rights**
Kersten Rogge: Council of Europe, BP 431 R 6, 67075 Strasbourg Cedex; *t* 8861 4961
Considers complaints from organisations, governments and individuals alleging violations of human rights law. »93

▌ **European Commission against Racism and Intolerance,** CRI
Conseil de l'Europe, Maison de l'Europe, BP 431 R6, 67075 Strasbourg Cedex; *t* 8841 2348, *f* 8841 2793
Organ of the Council of Europe, left, responsible for proposing and reviewing legislative changes concerning racism and intolerance in member states. »94

▌ **European Committee on Migrations,** CEM
John Murray, Secretary: Conseil de l'Europe, Maison de l'Europe, BP 431 R6, 67075 Strasbourg Cedex; *t* 8841 2167, 8861 4961, *f* 8836 7057
Council of Europe organ co-ordinating research, information and policy development on migration; promotes equality of opportunity, community relations and the 1983 European Convention on the Legal Status of Migrant Workers. »94

▌ **European Court of Human Rights**
Conseil de l'Europe, Maison de l'Europe, BP 431 R6, 67075 Strasbourg Cedex; *t* 8861 4961, *f* 8837 3265
International court which decides human rights cases against governments, after consideration by the Commission, p189, under the terms of the European Convention. »94

▌ **European Cultural Fund**
c/o Conseil de l'Europe, Maison de l'Europe, BP 431 R6, 67075 Strasbourg Cedex; *t* 8841 2000, *f* 8841 2781
Council of Europe organ promoting cultural co-operation and exchange and the protection of cultural heritage. »94

▌ **European Federation of Youth Service Organisations,** EFYSO
3 rue Récamier, 75341 Paris Cedex 07; *t* (1) 4358 9797, *f* 4358 9788
National affiliates include the French Jeunesse pour l'Action Démocratique en Europe, p198. »94

▌ **European Youth Campaign against Racism, Xenophobia, Antisemitism and Intolerance** ("All Different—All Equal")
Ulrich Bunjes, Director: Youth Campaign Secretariat, Conseil de l'Europe, 67065 Strasbourg; *t* 8841 2961, *f* 8841 2742
Year-long campaign by the Council of Europe, left, and national youth and anti-racist groups, see e.g. pp159-161, 166, 175, 194-5, 203-4, 207, 210, 214, 218, promoting tolerance. »94

▌ **European Youth Foundation,** EYF
European Youth Centre, 30 rue Pierre de Coubertin, 67000 Strasbourg, Wacken; *t* 8841 2300-11, 8841 2019, *f* 8841 2777-78
Council of Europe-sponsored international foundation created 1973, promoting pan-European youth activities and multi-lateral co-operation among national youth organisations. »94

▌ **European Youth Information and Counselling Agency,** ERYICA
101 quai Branly, 75740 Paris Cedex 15; *t* (1) 4065 0261 »93

● **Fédération des Centres Sociaux et Socio-culturels de France,** FCSF *(Federation of Welfare and Socio-Cultural Centres of France)*
Elisabeth Callu: 10-12 rue de la Volga, 75020 Paris; *t* (1) 4356 1259, *f* 4356 7610
Ouvertures (6/yr). »94

✿ **Fédération des Familles de France**
Jacques Bichot: 28 place St Georges, 75009 Paris; *t* (1) 4453 4590, *f* 4596 0788
See also UNAF, p199. *Cahiers d'Action Familiale; Lettre d'Action Familiale*. »94

▌ **Fédération Internationale des Droits de l'Homme,** FIDH: International Federation for Human Rights
Daniel Jacoby: [address uncertain] 27 rue Jean Dolent, 75014 Paris; *t* (1) 4332 (4331?) 9495, *f* 4336 3543
Also listed (1994) at 14 passage Dubail, 75010 Paris, *t* 4037 5426, *f* 4472 0586. International human rights federation founded 1922; its 66 members include the French Ligue des Droits de l'Homme and others in many countries, e.g. Belgian LDH, p191, Northern Ireland CAJ, p229, Italian FIDH, p205. Concerns include anti-racism, migrant, minority and refugee rights worldwide. *La Lettre de la FIDH* (52/yr). »94

▌ **Fédération Mondiale des Cités Unies et Villes Jumelées,** FMCV: United Towns Organisation, UTO
22 rue d'Alsace, 92532 Levallois-Perret Cedex; *t* (1) 4739 3686, *f* 4739 3685
International agency for inter-city relations, exchanges and twinning, especially with less developed countries; promotes human rights, integration of refugees, migrants and minorities, inter-cultural contact; 4,000 local and regional councils.   »94
● **Fédération Nationale Léo Lagrange**
21 rue de Provence, 75009 Paris; *t* (1) 4246 8292
Training.   »90
● **Fondation Soros**
38 boulevard Beaumarchais, 75011 Paris; *t* (1) 4805 2474, *f* 4021 6541
US-based philanthropic organisation primarily interested in promoting change in eastern Europe.   »94
● **Fondation pour la Vie Associatif,** FONDA *(Foundation for Voluntary Organisation)*
Anne David: 18 rue de Varenne, 75007 Paris; *t* (1) 4549 0658, *f* 4284 0484
Community development, anti-racism; resource centre.
Tribune (8/yr).   »94
◆ **Fonds d'Action Sociale pour les Travailleurs Immigrés et leurs Familles,** FAS *(Social Action Fund for Immigrant Workers and their Families)*
Tour Paris-Lyon, 209-211 rue de Bercy, 75585 Paris Cedex 12; *t* (1) 4202 7777, 4002 7300, *f* 4346 0427
Socio-economic integration, housing, welfare of migrants.»94
✿ **Fonds d'Action Sociale pour les Travailleurs Immigrés et leurs Familles,** FAS: Délégation régionale
1 rue de la Course, 67000 Strasbourg; *t* 8875 5166   »90
● **Fonds pour l'installation locale des réfugiés,** FILOR *(Fund for the Local Settlement of Refugees)*
[address unknown]
Fund established by government, UNHCR, below, and NGOs, giving grants for basic needs; succeeded by FAS, above?   »83
● **France Libertés—Fondation Danielle Mitterrand** *(France and Liberty—Danielle Mitterrand Foundation)*
Palais de Chaillot, 1 place de Trocadéro, 75116 Paris; *t* (1) 4755 8181, *f* 4755 8188
Human rights, anti-racism.   »94
● **Groupe Développement**
Batiment 106, BP 07, 93350 Le Bourget Aéroport; *t* (1) 4934 8313, *f* 4934 8310
Development aid funding to Asian, African, Latin American projects; support for refugee return and resettlement.   »93
● **Handicap International**
Espace Rhône Alpes Coopération, 14 avenue Berthelot, 69361 Lyon Cedex 07; *t* 7869 7979, *f* 7869 7994
Aid to people with physical, mental and sensory disabilities worldwide, including refugees; see also p191.   »93
◆ **Haut Commissariat des Nations Unies pour les Réfugiés:** United Nations High Commissioner for Refugees, UNHCR: Délégation en France
M. von Arnim: 9 rue Keppler, 75016 Paris; *t* (1) 4443 4858, 4070 9212, *f* 4070 0739, *Tx* 651048 UNHCR F
Refugee status and protection, emergency aid; see p219. »95
✿ **Hospitalisation Bretagne sans frontières** *(Brittany Hospital Care without Borders)*
cabinet médical, 62 rue de la Roche, 29870 Lannilis
Health assistance to children in the third world.   »90
✿ **Institut des Droits de l'Homme de Lyon** *(Lyons Institute for Human Rights)*
10-12 rue A. Fochier, 69002 Lyon; *t* 7232 5050
Research, publishing and education on international human rights issues, including refugee and minority rights.   »93
● **Institut de Formation et de Coopération Décentralisée,** IFCOD *(Institute for Training and Decentralised Co-operation)*
Adolphe Memevegni: 16 rue d'Amaillé, 75017 Paris; *t/f* (1) 4572 5039
Youth training, education. See also RIFEN, p.19.   »94
▌ **Institut international de la démocratie,** IID: International Institute for Democracy
Palais de l'Europe, BP 431 R 6, 67006 Strasbourg Cedex; *t* 8841 2541, *f* 8841 2781
Intergovernmental agency promoting democracy and human rights worldwide; sponsored by Council of Europe, p197.»94
● **Institut National de la Jeunesse et de l'Education Populaire** *(National Institute for Youth and Community Education)* and Agence national française Jeunesse pour l'Europe
BP 35, 78160 Marly-le-Roi; *t* (1) 3917 2767-68, *f* 3917 2790, 3916 5779
Location: Val Flory, rue Paul Leplat. Information on education opportunities, including transnational placements; national secretariat for Youth for Europe programmes, p191.   »94

● **International Rescue Committee,** IRC
[address uncertain] 35 boulevard des Capucines, 75008 Paris; *t* (1) 4261 6354
National office of the US-based intergovernmental body, p218, assisting refugees in many countries; see also OIM, p199.»83
▌ **Jeunesse pour l'Action Démocratique en Europe,** JADE: Youth for Democratic Action in Europe
3 rue Récamier, 75341 Paris Cedex 07; *t* (1) 4358 9797, *f* 4358 9788
See also the European Federation of Youth Service Organisations, p197, and LFEEP, p235.   »94
● **Libertés sans frontières**
René Bromane/François Jean: 8 rue Saint-Sabin, 75011 Paris
International civil rights group allied to Médecins sans Frontières, below, at the same address.   »90
◆ **Ligue des Droits de l'Homme,** LDH *(League for the Rights of Man)* also known as Ligue *pour les* droits de l'homme
Madeleine Reberioux, Vice-president: 27 rue Jean Dolent, 75007 Paris; *t* (1) 4408 8729, 4707 5635, *f* 4535 2320 (2390?)
Henri Leclerc, president. Human rights group. LDH Service Juridique provides legal assistance to refugees and asylum seekers. See also FIDH, p197.   »95
✿ **Logement et Promotion Sociale** *(Housing and Social Advancement)*
23 bis rue Pinel, 93200 Saint-Denis; *t* (1) 4243 3416   »90
✿ **Maison des Femmes du Hédas**
Thérèse Auclair: 2 rue René Fournets, 64000 Pau; *t* 5982 8254
Migrant women's cultural and information centre.   »94
✿ **Maison de la Promotion Sociale** *(House of Social Advancement)*
Domaine Universitaire, 38406 Saint-Martin d'Hères; *t* 7642 0727   »90
▌ **Médecins du Monde,** MDM *(Doctors of the World, literally: only French title is used)*
67 avenue de la République, 75341 Paris Cedex 11; *t* (1) 4929 1515, *f* 4355 9122
International charity mainly providing medical assistance to refugees and other victims of conflict and natural disaster in the developing world; some disaster relief work in industrialised countries, and medical aid to the poorest in France. See also Medicus Mundi in Spain, p215: same? »94
● **Médecins sans Frontières,** MSF-F *(Doctors without Borders, literally: only French title used)*
Dr Rony Brauman/B. Pécoul: 8 rue Saint-Sabin, 75544 Paris Cedex 11; *t* (1) 4021 2929, *f* 4806 6868
French section of international medical aid charity, see p191, which serves refugees and other groups affected by conflict or disaster, and provides help in basic health care, health promotion and sanitation in developing countries. *MSF infos* (2/yr), *Messages* (12/yr).   »94
◆ **Ministère des Affaires Etrangères** *(Ministry of Foreign Affairs)*
37 quai d'Orsay, 75007 Paris; *t* (1) 4753 5353
International aspects of migration and refugee policy.   »88
◆ **Ministère de l'Intérieur** *(Ministry of the Interior)*
[address uncertain] 13 place Beauvais, 75001 Paris
Address also listed (1990) as 11 rue des Saussaies, 75008 Paris, *t* 4522 9090. Government department responsible for registration of immigrants and for asylum applications.   »90
● **Ministère de la Jeunesse et des Sports** *(Youth and Sports Ministry Foreign Relations Department)* Département du Partenariat et des Relations Internationales
78 rue Olivier de Serres, 75739 Paris Cedex 15; *t* (1) 4045 9000, *f* 4531 8238
Department promoting youth exchange and co-operation; member of European Steering Committee for Intergovernmental Co-operation in the Youth Field, CDEJ.   »93
● **Mission de liaison interministérielle pour la lutte contre les trafics de main d'oeuvre** *(Interministerial Contact Group on Combatting Labour Exploitation)*
Ministère de la Solidarité, 1 place de Fontenoy, 75007 Paris; *t* (1) 4056 6000
Interdepartmental agency co-ordinating efforts to regulate employment, notably of migrants, in the informal sector. »88
● **Mouvement d'Action Judiciaire** *(Judicial Action Movement)*
46 rue de Vaugirard, 75006 Paris   »90
● **Oeuvres Hospitalières Françaises de l'Ordre de Malte,** OHFOM *(French Hospitaller Action of the Order of Malta)*
92 rue de Ranelagh, 75787 Paris Cedex 16; *t* (1) 4520 8020, *f* 4520 4804
International humanitarian and development aid wing of the Order, a Catholic movement with the status of a sovereign state. Mainly supports health care work in developing countries, including aid to refugee populations.   »93

● Oeuvres sociales d'outre-mer *(International Social Work)*
27 rue Oudinot, 75007 Paris; *t* (1) 4734 6157 »90
✿ Office Départemental pour l'Insertion des Communautés
Etrangères, ODICE *(Regional Office for the Integration of
Foreign Communities)*
M. Eynac: 27 rue du Colonel Roux, 05000 Gap; *t* 9251 2308
Research, information, co-ordination of public services to
migrants in the *département*. »94
◆ Office français de protection des réfugiés et apatrides,
OFPRA *(French Office for the Protection of Refugees and
the Stateless)*
[address uncertain] Tour Périphérique, 6 rue Emile-Reynaud,
93306 Aubervilliers; *t* (1) 4835 0220
Address from 1990. Official agency for the recognition of
refugee status, and the protection of refugees and stateless
persons; decisions are made by the director, with internal
appeal to the Commission des recours, p196. »95
◆ Office des Migrations Internationales, OMI *(Office for
International Migrations)*
44 rue Bargue, 75732 Paris Cedex 15; *t* (1) 4566 2600,
f 4566 0577
Successor to the Office National d'Immigration; formed 1945
to document and regulate immigration; annual *Statistiques de
l'immigration* and annexe, *Actualités-Migrations* (52/yr),
Mouvements (12/yr), books. »94
◆ Organisation Internationale pour les Migrations, OIM:
International Organization for Migration, IOM
c/o IRC, 66 rue de Provence, 75009 Paris; *t* (1) 4016 4034
See also IOM headquarters, p218. National office of the
intergovernmental agency, not to be confused with the
(French) Office des Migrations Internationales, above. »91
▌Organization for Economic Co-operation and Development,
OECD: Organisation pour la Coopération et le Développement
Economiques, OCDE
OECD Secretariat, 2 rue André Pascal, 75775 Paris Cedex
16; *t* (1) 4524 8200
Intergovernmental organisation founded 1961. Range of
economic research activities on topics including labour
migration; the Continuous Reporting System on Migration,
SOPEMI, in the Directorate for Social Affairs, Manpower
and Education, produces country studies and cross-country
comparisons of migration data; occasional reports,
conferences, library with extensive migration collection. »94
▌ ≡ Development Centre: 94 rue Chardon-Lagache, 75016
Paris; *t* (1) 4524 8200, *f* 4524 7943
Office of the OECD responsible for external co-operation and
global development issues. In 1993 the Development Centre,
along with Huridocs, p243, and the UNHCR, p219, produced a
directory of NGOs from OECD countries active in the areas of
migrants, refugees, human rights and development. »94
✿ Partages *(Sharing)*
12 résidence de la Gare, 95370 Montigny-les-Cormeilles
Youth work, especially with immigrants, anti-drug, anti-crime
work, civic education, rights advice, health information. »90
● Pharmaciens sans frontières, PSF *(Pharmacists without
Borders)*
4 voie militaire des Gravanches, 63000 Clermont-Ferrand;
t 7390 8134, *f* 7390 2725
International humanitarian aid and disaster relief, including
medical and dispensary services to refugees. »93
● Santé Sud *(Health in the South)*
200 boulevard National, bat. N, 13003 Marseille; *t* 9195
6345, *f* 9195 6805
Health and basic needs charity working mainly on long-term
development projects in Africa; has done some work with
refugees in Thailand. »93
◆ Secours Catholique *(Catholic Aid)* Caritas France
Denise Harding/Jean-Pierre Bultez: 106 rue du Bac, 75341
Paris Cedex 07; *t* (1) 4320 1414, *f* 4549 9450
Catholic humanitarian aid agency, providing funding and
material support to many emergency relief and development
projects worldwide, often involving refugees and displaced
people. Activities in France include counselling, housing,
resettlement, practical help to refugees and asylum seekers;
network of volunteer helpers; 100 offices around the country.
Emergency service: Centre Accueil, *t* (1) 4839 1092. »95
● Secours populaire *(People's Aid)* and Médecins du Secours
Populaire Français
9 rue Froissart, 75003 Paris; *t* (1) 4278 5048
Medical and other humanitarian assistance to refugees and
victims of conflict and disaster. »90
● Service Civil International, SCI
2 rue Eugène Fournière, 75018 Paris
International welfare agency; see also the European regional
office, in Belgium, p192. »93

◆ Service emploi chargé des réfugiés *(Refugee Employment
Service)* Agence national pour l'emploi
29 rue Saint-Armand, 75015 Paris; *t* (1) 4531 1690
Section of the state employment agency, p195, concerned
with the placement of refugees. »83
● Société Nationale de Construction de Logements pour les
Travailleurs, SONACOTRA *(National Company for Workers'
Housing)*
42 rue Cambronne, 74750 Paris Cedex 15; *t* (1) 4567 5540,
4061 4242
Low-cost social housing for disadvantaged groups including
migrants; offices house several migrant aid groups. »94
● Société de Saint-Vincent de Paul
5 rue du Pré-aux-Clercs, 75007 Paris; *t* (1) 4261 5025,
f 4261 7256
Catholic charity providing financial and practical assistance
to the poorest and most disadvantaged in society, at home
and abroad; refugee aid worldwide, especially in conflict
zones, and welfare activities in France including migrant and
refugee counselling, language training, employment and
housing assistance. Local branches (called conferences)
throughout France, and in over 100 other countries. »93
● Solidarités Jeunesses—Mouvement Chrétien pour la Paix,
SJ-MCP *(Youth Solidarity—Christian Peace Movement)*
38 rue du Faubourg St Denis, 75010 Paris; *t* (1) 4800 0905,
f 4770 6827
International solidarity, anti-racism; see also MCP, p192. »94
✿ SOS REPERES, SOSRE
27 rue Freycinet, 92600 Asnières
Economic, social, sporting, educational, informational,
advocacy work for needy, especially immigrants and youth. »89
✿ SOS Solidarité
HLM Les Plantes, route de Saint-Flour, 43100 Brioude
Employment, housing and other rights advice and advocacy
services for immigrants, youth and others. »90
● Syndicat des Avocats de France, SAF
21 bis, rue Victor Masse, 75009 Paris; *t* (1) 4282 0126
Lawyers' union. »90
● Syndicat de la Magistrature, SM
BP 155, 75523 Paris; *t* (1) 4805 4788
Trade union of magistrates, anti-racist policies. »90
● Témoignage Chrétien *(Christian Witness)*
Georges Montaron, Director: [address unknown] »88
● *Travail* (Labour)
64 rue de la Folie Mericourt, 75011 Paris; *t* (1) 4700 4772
Employment/trade union journal. »90
● Union Générale des Associations gestionnaires de foyers de
travailleurs *(General Union of Workers' Housing Companies)*
122 rue Nollet, 75017 Paris; *t* (1) 4627 2399 »90
▌Union internationale des organismes familiaux, UIOF
(International Union of Family Organisations)
Rubén Urrutia: 108 avenue Ledru-Rollin, 75011 Paris; *t* (1)
4700 0240
A member of the European Co-ordination for the Right to
Family Life of Immigrants, p136. See also UNAF, below. »95
● Union nationale des associations familiales, UNAF *(National
Union of Family Associations)* and Confédération Nationale
des Associations Familiales Catholiques
Roger Burnel/Régine Chataigner: 28 place St Georges, 75009
Paris; *t* (1) 4874 8074, 4995 3600, *f* 4216 1276
See Fédération des Familles de France, p197; unclear if these
are separate or linked organisations. See also the Union inter-
nationale des organismes familiaux, above. *Réalités familiales*
(4/yr); *Lettre de l'UNAF* (10/yr). »94
▌United Nations Educational, Scientific and Cultural
Organisation, UNESCO: Section of NGOs and Foundations
Ndèye Fall, Chief: 7 place de Fontenoy, 75352 Paris 07 SP;
t (1) 4568 1000, 4568 1731, *f* 4567 1690
UN agency which seeks to contribute to peace and security
by promoting collaboration among nations through education,
science and culture. Particular interest in racial problems,
prevention of discrimination, conflict research. It is involved
with UNRWA, p188, in educating Palestinian refugees.
Founded 1946; 182 member states, 2,184 staff, very large
range of publications. Several national support committees,
mainly involved in fundraising. At same address: UNESCO
Division of Human Rights and Peace (Carrie Marias). »94
▌ ≡ Youth and Sport Activities Division: 1 rue Miollis, 75015
Paris; *f* (1) 4065 9871 »94
● Vétérinaires sans frontières, VSF *(Vets without Borders)*
Espace Rhône Alpes Coopération, 14 avenue Berthelot,
69361 Lyon Cedex 07; *t* 7869 7959, *f* 7869 7956
Veterinary aid and animal husbandry training in the Third
World, including assistance to refugee communities in Africa,
Asia and Central America. »93

GERMANY 49

- **Konrad-Adenauer-Stiftung** *(Adenauer Foundation)*
[address unknown]
Has provided educational grants to refugees. »83
- **Aktion der Christen für die Abshaffung der Folter:** Action
by Christians for the Abolition of Torture, ACAT
Postfach 1114, 4710 Lüdingshausen; *t* (025) 917533
Campaigns against torture; interested in refugee and asylum
issues in that context. See also pp195, 207. »93
- **Aktionsbündnis Maastricht—So nicht! Volksentscheids-
bewegung** *(Maastricht—No Way! Referendum Action Group)*
c/o IDEE, Prinz-Albert-Straße 43, 53113 Bonn; *t* (0228)
215318, *f* 214033
Movement demanding a referendum on European integration;
opposes Fortress Europe migration policies. »94
- ◆ **Amnesty International—Deutsche Sektion,** AI-BRD
Wolfgang Grenz: Heerstraße 178, 53111 Bonn; *t* (0228)
983730, 650981, *f* 630036
Human rights worldwide, campaigns for political prisoners, see
p220; German section provides some services to refugees and
asylum seekers including counselling, information, casework,
educational assistance and campaigns for refugee rights. »95
- ◆ **Arbeiterwohlfahrt Bundesverband e.V.** *(German Labour
Assistance)* also known as Bundesverband der
Arbeiterwohlfahrt
Klaus Dittler/Wolfgang Schuth: Oppelnerstraße 130, 53119
Bonn; *t* (0228) 668 5131, 668 5152, *f* 668 5209
Service and pressure group, part of Internationales Arbeiter-
hilfswerk; its Referat Ausländische Flüchtlinge engages in
refugee social work, group counselling, legal/employment/
training advice; member ZDWF documentation centre, p238;
see Institut für Sozialarbeit und Sozialpädagogik, p236. »95
- **Arbeitsgemeinschaft der Gemeinden,** AGG *(Student
Community Working Group)*
Rheinweg 34, 5300 Bonn; *t* (0228) 234021
Catholic student movement; some informal voluntary refugee
assistance through local groups. »83
- **Arbeitsgemeinschaft Junge Genoss/innen in und bei der
PDS** *(PDS Young Comrades Working Group)*
Kleine Alexanderstraße 28, 10178 Berlin; *t* (030) 2840
9419, *f* 2480 9326
Youth group of the Partei des Demokratisches Sozialismus;
anti-racist, pro-migrant policies. »94
- ✿ **Beauftragte für Ausländerfragen** *(Commissioner for
Foreigners' Affairs)* Berlin Senate
Barbara John: Potsdamerstraße 65, 1000 Berlin 30 »90
- ✿ ≡ Berlin Magistrate: Annette Kahane: Breiterstraße 35,
1020 Berlin »90
- ✿ ≡ Dr Wolfgang Richter, Commissioner: [address unknown]
Rostock
Protection of interests of non-German residents. Active in
anti-racist/conflict resolution work since the 1992 riots. »94
- ✿ **Bildungswerk für Friedensarbeit,** BF *(Peace Work
Development Group)*
Alfred-Bozi-Straße 10, 33602 Bielefeld; *t* (0521) 175569,
f 66274
Anti-racist, anti-fascist work in the context of peace and
conflict resolution education. »94
- **Heinrich-Böll-Stiftung** *(Böll Foundation)*
Bruckenstraße 5-11, 50667 Köln; *t* (0221) 207110, *f* 207
1151
Memorial foundation for the Nobel-laureate author; funds
some anti-racist, pro-migrant work. »94
- ◆ **Bundesamt für die Anerkennung ausländischer Flüchtlinge**
(Federal Office for Recognition of Foreign Refugees)
Zollhaus Straße 95, 90469 Nürnberg; *t* (0911) 9431, *f* 9432
Government office which processes asylum requests and
determines refugee status; responsible for refugee protection;
research and documentation of refugee flows and related
issues; sub-offices in the Länder. »94
- **Bundesanstalt für Arbeit,** BA *(Federal Institute of Labour)*
and Nationale Koordinationsstelle EURES
Regensburger Straße 104, 90478 Nürnberg; *t* 911 1790,
f 91117 92123
Autonomous public agency; free careers guidance, training and
job placement; manages job subsidies, unemployment and
welfare benefits. It operates through regional offices and local
employment offices, Arbeitsamter. Each regional office liaises
with at least one country in the EURES European employment
information network, p190, which also has a central unit in the
BA (*t* 179 2286). Services are available to non-nationals. See
Institut für Arbeitsmarkt- und Berufsforschung, p237. »94

- ◆ **Bundesbeauftragte für Asylangelegenheiten** *(Federal
Commissioner for Asylum Affairs)*
[address unknown]
Federal official able to appeal against decisions of Bundesamt,
left, concerning refugee status. »83
- ◆ **Bundesbeauftragte für Ausländerfragen** *(Federal
Commissioner for Foreigners' Affairs)*
Cornelia Schmalz-Jacobsen, Commissioner: Postfach 140280,
53057 Bonn
Monitors policy and practice towards Germany's 7 million
immigrants, refugees and asylum seekers for compliance with
national and international standards of human rights. »94
- **Bundesgrenzschutz,** BGS *(Federal Border Police)*
[address unknown]
The security agency with primary responsibility for the
prevention and detection of illegal immigration. »95
- ◆ **Bundesinnenministerium** *(Federal Ministry of the Interior)*
Graurheindorferstraße 108, 5300 Bonn 1; *t* (0228) 6821
Processes asylum requests. »85
- **Bundeskongress Entwicklungspolitischer Aktionsgruppen,**
BUKO *(Federal Congress of Development Policy Action Groups)*
Nernstweg 32-34, 22765 Hamburg; *t* (040) 393156
Pressure group for increased and better-targeted international
development aid. May be the parent body of BUKO Arbeits-
schwerpunkt Rassismus und Flüchtlingspolitik, p166. »94
- **Büro für notwendige Einmischungen** *(Emergency Intervention
Bureau)*
Pulverteich 18, 20099 Hamburg; *t* (040) 241688, *f* 280 3601
Concerned with refugees/migrants; no further information.»94
- ✿ **Büro Jan-Philipp Reemtsma**
Mittelweg 36, 20148 Hamburg; *t* (040) 414 0970, *f* 410
4602
Foundation with interests in the area of migration and
community relations. »94
- ▌ **Council of Europe Minority Youth Committee,** CEMYC:
Dachverband der Minderheitenjugendlichen in West-Europa
S. Ertan/Z. Sarypel: Perleberger Straße 29, 1000 Berlin 21;
t (030) 395 8141
See also in Denmark, p132, Netherlands, p208, and UK, p154.»90
- ✿ **Council of Voluntary Agencies Working in Germany**
Mohlstraße 14, 8000 München 80
Co-ordinates US, UK, French and international agencies
assisting refugees. »83
- **CVJM-Gesamtverband in Deutschland** *(National Council of
YMCAs in Germany)*
Im Drustel 8, Postfach 410149, 3500 Kassel-Wilhelmshöhe;
t (0561) 308 7250, *f* 308 7270
International relief activities include work for refugees,
returning migrants and displaced persons in Third World. »93
- **Deutsche Friedensgesellschaft—Kriegsdienstverweigerer,**
DFG-KV *(German Pacifist Association—Military Service
Resisters)*
Schwanenstr. 16, 42551 Velbert; *t* (02051) 4217, *f* 4210
Peace group; protection of conscientious objectors from
Germany and abroad. »94
- **Deutsche Gewerkschaftsbundjugend,** DGB-Jugend *(German
Trade Union Confederation Youth)*
Hans-Böckler-Straße 39, 40476 Düsseldorf; *t* (0211) 43010,
f 430 1409
Youth section of the DGB labour federation; concerns include
anti-racism, training and integration of young migrant workers.
See also DGB migrant worker bureau, p139. »94
- ◆ **Deutsche Rechtsberaterkonferenz,** DRK *(German Legal
Advisers' Conference)* and European Legal Network on
Asylum, ELENA
Rudolf Klever: Brahmsallee 16, 20144 Hamburg; *t* (040) 410
7351-52, *f* 410 2885
Founded by Diakonisches Werk and Caritas, and supported by
the Red Cross and UNHCR, all p201; network of 60 lawyers
offering specialist services to refugees; Klever is the national
contact for ELENA, p154. »95
- **Deutscher Akademischer Austauschdienst,** DAAD *(German
Academic Exchange Service)* and ERASMUS
Kennedyallee 50, 53175 Bonn; *t* (0228) 8820, *f* 882444
Information, documentation, funding of academic exchange
programmes for the German Foreign Office; administers the
EU's ERASMUS exchange programme, p190, in Germany. Has
given educational grants to refugees. Also funds German
studies abroad, as at Institute for German Studies, p37. »95
- **Deutscher Bundesjugendring,** DBJR *(German Federal Youth
Movement)*
Haager Weg 44, 53127 Bonn; *t* (0288) 910210, 910 2131,
f 910 2122
National confederation of youth organisations. See also
Deutsches Komitee der Jugendkampagne, p166. »94

◆ **Deutscher Caritasverband, DCV** *(Caritas Germany)* Referat
Flüchtlings- und Aussiedlerhilfe
Hermann Uehlein: Postfach 420, 79104 Freiburg i. Breisgau;
t (0761) 200362, 200475, *f* 200572
Location: Karlstraße 40; Dieter Schäfers, Wolfgang Kopp.
Catholic relief agency offering range of reception, legal advice
through the Deutsche Rechtsberaterkonferenz, p200,
counselling and other services to immigrants and refugees;
560 sections covering all Länder. Involved in many overseas
relief projects assisting refugees, migrants and displaced
persons. See Caritas Internationalis, p230, and the
International Catholic Migration Commission, p217. Member
of the ZDWF documentation centre, p238. *KLD-Brief*
Ausländische Flüchtlinge/Aussiedler (25/yr). »95

✧ **Deutscher Paritätischer Wohlfahrtsverband, DPWV**
(German Egalitarian Welfare League)
Harald Löhlein/Christine Nawrath: Heinrich-Hoffmann-Str. 3,
60528 Frankfurt am Main; *t* (069) 6706-0 (201), *f* 6706-204
Member of ZDWF documentation centre, p238. See also
Paritätischer Wohlfahrtsverband Europabüro, p202. »95
✧ ≡ Loherstraße 7, 42283 Wuppertal; *t* (0202) 28220
Welfare and advice service. »94

✧ **Deutsches Jugendinstitut** *(German Youth Institute)*
Saarstraße 7, 8000 München 40; *t* (030) 3183 2405 »90

◆ **Deutsches Rotes Kreuz:** German Red Cross Society
Heinz Knoche/Bernhardt Döveling: Postfach 1460, 53113
Bonn; *t* (0228) 541491, 541493/487, *f* 541500
Location: Friedrich-Ebert-Allee 71. Reception, counselling,
repatriation assistance, other services to refugees; development and humanitarian aid projects. Member of ZDWF
documentation centre, p238, and international Red Cross
movement, p218. *Flüchtlingsforum* (2/yr). »94

✧ **Diakonisches Werk Duisburg** *(Duisburg Pastoral Service)*
Am Burgarker 14-16, 47051 Duisburg
Migrant welfare, employment assistance. »94

● **Diakonisches Werk der Evangelischen Kirche in Deutschland,
EKD** *(Pastoral Service of the German Protestant Churches)*
Peter von Bethlenvalvy, head of refugee service: Stafflenberg-
str. 76, 70184 Stuttgart; *t* (0711) 215 9533, *f* 2159 1288
Gerhard Railh, Axel Führ. Relief agency formed 1957;
information, counselling, legal advice through Deutsche
Rechtsberaterkonferenz, p200; some educational assistance,
employment advice and other services to refugees, including
grants from its Stipendienfonds; research on refugee problems;
other human rights and development aid/education work;
branches at Länder and local level. Affiliated to WCC, p219,
and Lutheran World Federation, p218; member of ZDWF
documentation centre, p238. Founded Psychosoziales
Zentrum für ausländische Flüchtlingen, p139; see also
Doc-Lap-Zentrum, p110. *Infoblatt* (6/yr), reports. »95

✧ **Diakonisches Werk der Evangelische-Lutherische Kirche in
Thüringen** *(Thuringen Evangelical Lutheran Church Pastoral
Care Service)*
Karl-Marx-Straße 8, 99817 Eisenach; *t* (03691) 203611,
f 75328 »95

✧ **Diakonisches Werk in der Pommerschen Evangelische
Kirche** *(Pomeranian Evangelical Church Pastoral Care Service)*
H. Kummerow: Rudolf-Petershagen-Allee 38, 17489
Greifswald; *t* (03834) 87610, *f* 876114 »95

● **Europäische Bewegung Deutschland—Europa-Zentrum**
(Europe Centre of the German European Movement)
Postfach 1529, 53005 Bonn »94

● **Europäische Kommission,** Vetretung in der BRD: European
Commission, Representation in Germany
Zitelmannstraße 22, 53113 Bonn; *t* (0228) 530090,
f 5300950/12, *Tx* 184015 EUROP D
National representative office of the Commission, p189;
provides information on EU policy, legislation and related
matters. »94
✧ ≡ Kurfürstendamm 102, 10711 Berlin; *t* (0430) 896 0930,
f 892 2059, *Tx* 184015 EUROP D »94
✧ ≡ Erhardtstraße 27, 80331 München; *t* (089) 202 1011,
f 202 1015, *Tx* 5218135 »94

▌ **European Peace Research Association, EuPRA**
Beethovenallee 4, 53173 Bonn; *t* (0288) 356032, *f* 356050
Promotes and co-ordinates research, conferences and
exchanges on peace and conflict resolution. »94

● **Evangelische Studentengemeinde, ESG** *(Protestant Student
Community)*
Kniebisstr. 29, 7000 Stuttgart 1; *t* (0711) 281034, 281035
Protestant student movement, branches throughout Germany,
many of which have special focus on assistance to refugees,
including counselling, scholarships, legal aid, information. »83

✧ **Evangelisches Missionzentrum** *(Protestant Mission Centre)*
Gerhard Hoffmann: Saalgasse 15, 6000 Frankfurt/Main 1 »90

✧ **Flughafensozialdienst Berlin-Schönefeld** *(Berlin Airport
Social Services)*
Frau Olsen-Konitz: Flughafen, 12527 Berlin-Schönefeld;
t (030) 609157 50-52, *f* 609157 53
This, and the two offices listed below, provide emergency
assistance to asylum claimants and other travellers. »95

✧ **Flughafensozialdienst Frankfurt**
Gudrun Petasch-Molling: Flughafen Frankfurt, Zimmer 2175,
Postfach 174, 60549 Frankfurt; *t* (069) 690 50201, 690
47131, *f* 690 54341 »95

✧ **Flughafensozialdienst München II**
B. Zepf: Postfach 241, 85334 München; *t* (089) 975909 32,
f 975909 30 »95

✧ **Fonds Soziokultur** *(Socio-Cultural Fund)*
Hohenhof, Stirnband 10, 58013 Hagen; *t* (02331) 58501,
f 56824 »94

▌ **Goethe-Institut**
Helene-Weber-Allee 1, 80637 München; *t* (089) 159210,
f 1592 1450
Promotion of German language and culture, and exchange
programmes; many offices abroad. »94

✧ **Heilig-Kreuz-Gemeinde** *(Holy Cross Student Community)*
Jurgen Quandt: Nostitzstraße 6-7, 1000 Berlin 61 »90

◆ **Hoher Flüchtlingskommissar der Vereinten Nationen:**
United Nations High Commissioner for Refugees, UNHCR:
Vertreter in der BRD (Representative in Germany)
Gesche Karranbrock: Rheinallee 6, 53173 Bonn; *t* (0228)
957090, 364011-013, *f* 362296, 363588, *Tx* 885529
UNHCR, *Tg* HICOMREF Bonn 2
Rene van Rooyen; national Branch Office responsible for
refugee status and protection; see head office, p219. »95
✧ ≡ Zirndorf sub-office: Postfach 1129, 90505 Zirndorf;
t (0911) 699743-44, *f* 64461, *Tx* 626816 UNHCR D
Location: Rothenburgerstraße 29, 90513 Zirndorf; based at
main refugee reception centre. »95

● **Humanistische Union, HU** *(Humanist Union)*
Bräuhausstraße 2, 80331 München; *t* (089) 226141,
f 226442 »94

▌ **International Association for Religious Freedom**
[address unknown] Frankfurt am Main
Freedom of conscience and of religion, cross-cultural
exchange, international social service. See also p224. »88

▌ **International Council of Christians and Jews, ICCJ**
Sir Sigmund Sternberg (UK), Chairman: Postfach 1129,
Werléstr. 2, 64629 Heppenheim; *t* (06252) 5041, *f* 68331
Interfaith dialogue, anti-racism, anti-fascism. »94

◆ **International Organization for Migration, IOM**
Koblenzstraße 99, 5300 Bonn 2; *t* (0228) 820940
Intergovernmental body, p218, promoting planned migration;
also provides selective assistance for re-emigration. »91

● **International Rescue Committee**
[address uncertain] Holbeinstraße 12/1, 8000 München 80;
t (089) 477286, 475427
National office of the US-based refugee aid body, p218. »83

▌ **Internationale Gesellschaft für Menschenrechte, IGFM:**
International Society for Human Rights, ISHR
Robert Chambers, General Secretary: Kaiserstr. 7R, 60325
Frankfurt am Main; *t* (069) 236971, 722369, *f* 234100
Human rights pressure group, identified from its foundation
in 1972 with conservative causes; see also p224. »94

● **Internationale Liga für Menschenrechte** *(International
League for Human Rights)*
Alisa Fuss, Vice-president: Mommsenstraße 27, 10629
Berlin; *t* (030) 324 3688, *f* 324 0256 »94

◆ **Internationaler Sozialdienst—Deutscher Zweig, IS:**
International Social Service, ISS, German Section
Ursula Rölke: Am Stockborn 5-7, 60439 Frankfurt am Main;
t (069) 58031, *f* 580 3465
Ingrid Baer, Helga Jochenhövel-Schieke. See main entry,
p218; German branch has special interest in unaccompanied
minors. See Institut für Sozialarbeit und Sozialpädagogik,
p236. *IS in Brief, Coordination Région Europe*. »95

● **Jugend für Europa Deutsches Büro:** Youth for Europe
German Bureau
Hochkreuzallee 20, 53175 Bonn; *t* (0228) 950 6214, *f* 950
6222
Foundation promoting European awareness and exchanges
among young people; see p191. »94

● **Jungdemokraten—Junge Linke, JD-JL** *(Young
Democrats—Left Youth)*
Chausseestraße 8, 10115 Berlin; *t/f* (030) 283 3245
Radical youth movement; anti-fascist, anti-racist policies. »94

● **Justitia et Pax** *(Justice and Peace)*
Kaiserstraße 163, 5300 Bonn 1; *t* (0228) 103318
Catholic social justice group. »93

- **Kairos Europa**
Hegenichstraße 22, 69124 Heidelberg; t (06221) 72610,
f 781183
Progressive, anti-racist Christian movement.   »94
- **Katholisch-Akademischer Austauschdienst, KAAD**
(Catholic Academic Exchange Service)
Reuterstraße 39, 5300 Bonn; t (0228) 216051, 226241
Assistance to refugee students. May be the body listed
(1983) as Katholischer Akademischer Ausländerdienst.   »83
- **Katholische Zentralstelle für Entwicklungshilfe** *(Catholic
Central Agency for Development Aid)* and Misereor—Aktion
gegen Hunger und Krankheit
Postfach 1450, Mozartstraße 9, 5100 Aachen; t (0241)
4420, f 4421 88
The Zentralstelle, with 130 staff, manages the Church's
overseas development programme, sponsoring projects for
government funding including refugee relief and resettlement
projects in Latin America and Africa. Misereor is the bishops'
aid agency, with 500 staff channelling donated and public
funds to long-term development and emergency relief work,
often aiding refugees and displaced people. Both agencies
also engage in development education in Germany.   »93
- ✿ **Kinderhaus des deutschen Kinderschutzbundes** *(Children's
Home of the German Children's Protection Society)*
Markt 16, 25524 Itzehoe; t (04821) 62773
Youth welfare, education and culture.   »94
- ✿ **Komitee für Grundrechte und Demokratie e.V.** *(Committee
for Constitutional Rights and Democracy)*
Bismarckstr. 40, 50672 Köln; t (0221) 523056, f 520559
Civil/human rights, anti-racism, equality before the law.   »94
- ✿ ≡ An der Gasse 1, 64759 Sensbachtal
Human rights, legal advice.   »94
- **Medico International**
Obermainanlage 7, 60314 Frankfurt am Main; t (069)
944380, f 436002
International medical charity; assists migrants and refugees
abroad.   »94
- **Friedrich-Naumann-Stiftung, FNST** *(Naumann Foundation)*
Postfach 4027, 5330 Königswinter 41; t (022) 237010,
f 237011 88
Promotion of human rights and political liberalism worldwide,
funding educational and devlopment projects in Africa, Asia,
Latin America. Has made educational grants to refugees. »93
- **Netzwerk Friedenskooperative** *(Pacifist Co-operatives
Network)*
Römerstraße 88, 53111 Bonn; t (0228) 692904, f 692906
Network of local peace groups with interests including anti-
racism and refugee rights.   »94
- **Netzwerk Menschenrechte e.V.** *(Human Rights Network)*
Postfach 301125, 10722 Berlin; t (030) 448 3671, 262
3085, f 262 9503
Human rights in Europe and the Third World, international
refugee and immigration issues; world refugee information
handbook; member of European Migration Centre, p237. »94
- **Ohne Rüstung leben—Ökumenische Aktion für Frieden und
Gerechtigkeit, ORL** *(Living Unarmed—Ecumenical Action for
Peace and Justice)*
Furtbachstraße 10, 70178 Stuttgart; t (0711) 640 9620,
f 640 7980
Progressive internationalist pacifist organisation.   »94
- ✿ **Ökumenisches Studienwerk** *(Ecumenical Study Service)*
Girondelle 80, 4630 Bochum; t (0234) 73011
Some educational grants to refugees.   »83
- **Pädagoginnen und Pädagogen für den Frieden, PPF**
(Teachers for Peace)
Kölner Straße 11, 57072 Siegen; t (0271) 20596, f 484494
Peace education, including anti-racist/anti-fascist work.   »94
- **Paritätischer Wohlfahrtsverband** *(Egalitarian Welfare League)*
Harald Löhlein: Heinrich Hoffmannstraße 3, 60528 Frankfurt-
am-Main; t (069) 6706 0 201, f 6706 204   »95
- ● ≡ Europabüro: José Povedano Sánchez: Endenicher Straße
125, 53115 Bonn; t (0228) 985 9910, 985 9911
See Deutscher Paritätischer Wohlfahrtsverband, p201.   »94
- **Pax Christi—Deutsche Sektion**
Feststrasse 9, Postfach 1345, 61118 Bad Vilbel; t (06101)
2073, f 65165
Catholic humanitarian organisation; anti-racist work.   »94
- ✿ **Regionale Arbeitsstelle zur Förderung ausländischer Kinder
und Jugendlicher, RAA** *(Regional Working Group for the
Advancement of Foreign Youth)*
Barbara Schlotmann, G. Dresen: Heßlerstraße 208-210,
45329 Essen; t (0201) 369185-86, 358996, f 340345
Anti-racism, cultural action, research, documentation, youth
integration; offices in Dortmund and Stuttgart. *Zeitschrift
Gemeinsam* (2/yr), *Informationen* (6/yr).   »94

- ♦ **Service Civil International—Deutscher Zweig, SCI**
(International Civil Service, German Section)
Blücherstraße 14, 53115 Bonn; t (0228) 212086, f 219329
International welfare agency; see also European office in
Belgium, p192.   »94
- **Stiftung Entwicklung und Frieden, SEF** *(Development and
Peace Foundation)*
Gotenstraße 152, 53175 Bonn; t (0228) 376935, f 375636
Development education, peace education; anti-racist work in
those contexts.   »94
- **Stipendienfonds des Landeskirchen** *(National Church
Scholarship Fund)*
[address unknown]
Some educational grants to refugees.   »83
- **Stipendienfonds der Universitäten** *(Universities' Scholarship
Fund)*
[address unknown]
Some educational grants to refugees.   »83
- **Terre des Femmes (Menschenrechte für die Frau)** *(World of
Women—Human Rights for Women)*
Postfach 2531, 72015 Tübingen; t (07071) 24289,
f 550352, 27063
Information work and campaigns on women's human rights
issues worldwide, especially concerning women refugees,
women in conflict zones. Funding and support for women's
centres in Asia, Africa, Latin America; some counselling and
training for refugees in Germany.   »94
- **Terre des Hommes Deutschland e.V.—Hilfe für Kinder in
Not** *(People's World Germany—Aid to Children in Need)*
Heiko Kauffmann: Postfach 4126, Ruppenkampstraße 11a,
49031 Osnabrück; t (0541) 71010, f 707 2233
Children's welfare; see FITDH, p217. Postcode uncertain: may
be 49084. Journal (6/yr), leaflets.   »94
- **Volkswagen-Stiftung** *(Volkswagen Foundation)*
Postfach 810509, Kastanienallee 35, 30505 Hannover;
t (0511) 83810, f 838 1344
Philanthropic foundation; particular interest in anti-racist
projects.   »94
- **Weltfriedensdienst, WFD** *(World Peace Service)*
Hedemannstraße 14, 10696 Berlin; t (030) 2539 9019,
f 251 1887
Peace movement with anti-racist and anti-fascist concerns.
See also ASW, p165.   »94
- **World University Service—Deutschland, WUS**
Goebenstraße 35, 65195 Wiesbaden; t (06121) 446648,
f 446489
Funds educational assistance, mainly to refugees, in Germany
and abroad; based in Switzerland, p219.   »94
- ▌ **World University Service—International Student Network,
WUS**
Goebenstraße 35, 65195 Wiesbaden; t (06121) 446648,
f 446489
Provides a forum for students supporting or directly benefitting
from the international educational and scholarship programmes
of WUS, p219, including those in Germany.   »94
- ♦ **Zentralstelle für Arbeitsvermittlung** *(Central Job Placement
Office)* and PETRA
Feuerbachstraße 42, 60325 Frankfurt am Main; t (069)
71110, f 7111 1555
Deals with requests for employment and training placements
from persons outside Germany, including training under the
EU's PETRA scheme, p192.   »94

GREECE 30

- ♦ **Aliens Department**, Ministry of Public Order
Odos 3 September 48, Athinai; t (01) 823 6011
Deals with asylum requests, and with refugee status and
protection.   »85
- ♦ **Amnesty International—Greek Section**
Odos Sina 30, 10672 Athinai; t (01) 360 0628, f 363 8016
Human rights group focussing on political prisoners abroad;
see International Secretariat listing, p220; Greek Section has
interest in refugee and asylum questions.   »94
- **Anti-War Campaign—Anti-Nationalist Campaign, AAC**
Odos Valtetsiou 35, 10681 Athinai; t (01) 361 3928, f 361
9397
Pacifist, anti-racist, anti-fascist movement.   »94
- ♦ **Caritas Hellas**
V. Chrysemtlopoulos: Odos Kapodistriou 52, 10432 Athinai;
t (01) 247879, 639 9147
Catholic welfare agency; international solidarity, refugee
services. See also ICMC, p203. Information bulletin (1/yr).»94

♦ **European Commission**
Vassilissis Sofias 2, PO Box 11002, 10674 Athinai; *t* (01) 724 3982-84, *f* 724 4620, *Tx* (0601) 219324 ECAT GR
National office of the Commission, p189; information on EU policy and related matters. »94

● **Elleniko Instituto Allilengyis ke Synergasias me tis Anaptyssomenes Chores,** HELINAS *(Greek Institute for Solidarity and Co-operation with Developing Countries)*
Pantelis Sklias, General Secretary: Odos Orminiou 9, 15528 Athinai; *t* (01) 723 4456, *f* 723 7662
International development aid, mainly in Africa; development education in Greece. *Co-operation North-South* (4/yr). »94

● **Ethnikon Symboulion Organoseon Neon Ellados,** ESONE
Ms Kyziridou: Odos Amerikis 11, 10672 Athinai; *t* (01) 361 1596, *f* 362 2400
National youth umbrella group. Participated in the 1994-95 European Youth Campaign Against Racism, p197. »94

● **General Secretariat for Equal Rights**
Odos Moussiou 2, Plaka, 10555 Athinai; *t* (01) 321 8044, 321 5622, *f* 324 6900, 323 0473
Women's rights agency. »94

● **General Secretariat for Youth** and Youth for Europe
Odos Acharnon 417, 11143 Athinai; *t* (01) 253 2312, *f* 253 1349
National umbrella group; see also Youth for Europe, p191.»94

● **Greek Anti-Poverty Network**
Odos Dinokratous 68, 11521 Athinai
Part of the European Union anti-poverty programme. »94

✿ **Greek Committee for International Democratic Solidarity,** EEDDA
Spirou Trikoupi 25, 10683 Athinai; *t* (01) 361 3052, *f* 363 1603
Internationalism, anti-racism, migrant and refugee rights. »94

♦ **Greek Red Cross**
Odos Lycavittou 1, 10672 Athinai; *t* (01) 361 7048
Humanitarian aid, advice, other services to refugees; see also international Red Cross bodies, p218, and see Idrima Marangopoulou gia ta Dikeomata tou Athropou, below. »94

● **Idrima Marangopoulou gia ta Dikeomata tou Anthropou:**
Marangopoulos Foundation for Human Rights, MFHR
Joanne Petropoulos, Secretary: Odos Lycavittou 1, 10672 Athinai; *t* (01) 363 7455, *f* 362 2454
Human rights promotion, research and documentation; advice to refugees and asylum seekers. »94

▍ **International Alliance of Women**
Odos Lycavittou 1, 10672 Athinai; *t* (01) 362 6111, *f* 362 2454
Federation of 75 national women's organisations in 65 countries; human rights, social justice concerns. »93

♦ **International Catholic Migration Commission,** ICMC
Odos Kapodistriou 52, 10432 Athinai; *t* (01) 523 0521, 523 1473
Swiss-based agency, see p217; of two main refugee services in Greece, mainly aimed at overseas resettlement; counselling, mediation, documentation; works closely with WCC, p140, UNHCR, right and p219, and government offices in receiving countries; see also Caritas, p202. »94

● **International Organization for Migration,** IOM (formerly Intergovernmental Committee for Migrations, ICM)
Odos Dodekanissou 6, Agios Panteleimou, Ana Kalamaki, Alimos, 17456 Athinai; *t* (01) 991 9040-44
Greek national office of the international IOM, p218; often referred to as ICM. Assists planned migration. »94

♦ **International Social Service,** ISS
Chris Kondoyanni: Kolonaki, Odos Mantzarou 6, 10672 Athinai; *t* (01) 363 6191, 361 7710
International NGO, see p218, which assists individuals and families to resolve social welfare problems involving more than one country, especially those arising from voluntary or forced migration. Counselling at Lavrion refugee centre, p140. »94

● **Ministry of Foreign Affairs**
Odos Zalokosta 10, Athinai; *t* (021) 361 0581
Refugee status and protection. »85

● **Ministry of Labour**
Odos Piraeus 40, 10182 Athinai; *t* (01) 523 3111, 523 3146, *f* 524 1977
Concerned with the regulation of employment, vocational training, careers guidance and related matters, directly and through the Hellenic Manpower and Employment Organisation, OAED, which operates local employment offices. »94

● **National Security Service,** Ministry of Public Order
Odos Katehaki 1, Holargos, Athinai; *t* (01) 692 9210
Asylum requests, refugee status and protection. »83

● **National Welfare Organisation**
K. Tsatsos, President: Odos Ipatias 6, Athinai TT7 »90

♦ **United Nations High Commissioner for Refugees,** UNHCR:
Branch Office for Greece
Skoufa 59, 10672 Athinai; *t* (01) 361 0295-98, 363 3607, *f* 362 8440, *Tx* 222650 HCR GR, *Tg* HICOMREF Athens
Refugee status, protection, economic integration; see p219.»95

● **Youth Committee of the Coalition of Left and Progress**
Themistocleous and Gamveta Street 7, 10677 Athinai; *t* (01) 3619 2324, *f* 363 9252
Socialist youth group with anti-racist policies. »94

▍ **Youth for the World:** Jeunes pour le Monde
El. Axiomaticon 29, 16233 Athinai; *t/f* (01) 725 5646
Internationalist youth organisation; anti-racist, multicultural.»94

HUNGARY *36*

✿ **Hungarian Peace Association**
Postafiok 113, Europa Ház, Dezsö utca 3, 1395 Budapest 62; *t* (01) 156 8440, *f* 156 8499
Internationalism, anti-racism. »94

● **Magyarországi Ifjúsági Szervezetek Országos Tanácsa,** MISZOT
Rosenberg hp. útca 1, 1054 Budapest; *t/f* (01) 131 8588
Youth NGO umbrella organisation. »94

♦ **United Nations High Commissioner for Refugees,** UNHCR
Törökvész útca 30, 1022 Budapest; *t* (1) 250 4444, 250 4654, *f* 250 2701, *Tx* 202708 HCR H
Refugee status and protection; see headquarters, p219. »95

✿ **World Federation of Democratic Youth,** WFDY
Postafiok 147, Frangepán útca 16, 1389 Budapest; *t* (01) 270 1202, *f* 129 5226
International alliance of socialist youth organisations. Anti-racist, anti-fascist. »94

ICELAND *354*

● **Aeskulyossamband Islands,** AESI
PO Box 1426, Laugarvegur 162, 121 Reykjavik; *t* (91) 623035, *f* 623052
Youth NGO. »94

● **Hitt Husid**
Brautarholt 20, 105 Reykjavik; *t* (91) 624320, *f* 624341
Foundation listed by United directory of anti-racist organisations (1994); no further information. »94

♦ **Hjalparstofnun Kirkjunnar** *(Churches' Aid Foundation)*
Tjarnagata 10, 150 Reykjavik; *t* (91) 26440 (?), *f* 624495
Funding and material aid agency of the national Protestant church; development and emergency relief, mainly in Africa; includes Kurdish and African refugee projects. »93

♦ **Rauoi Kross Islands:** Icelandic Red Cross
Rauòarástíg 18, PO Box 5450, 105 Reykjavik; *t* (91) 626722, *f* 623150
Settlement, integration and repatriation assistance to refugees; overseas humanitarian relief and development activities through international Red Cross movement, p218. »93

IRELAND *353*

♦ **Amnesty International—Irish Section**
Des Hogan, Refugee Co-ordinator: 48 Fleet Street, Dublin 2; *t* (01) 677 6361, *f* 677 6392, ebclark@amnesty.gn.apc.org
Mary Lawlor, Director. Irish section of international human rights movement, p220; campaigns for political prisoners abroad. Works for the reform of Ireland's refugee procedures, which result in the imprisonment of some asylum applicants, and the refusal or non-determination of most applications.»96

● **Christian Aid Ireland**
Rev. Michael Begg: Christ Church, Rathgar Road, Dublin 6; *t* (01) 496 6184, *f* 497 3880
Fundraising for international humanitarian aid, development education and solidarity activities. An offshoot of Christian Aid (UK). *Christian Aid News* (4/yr). »95

● **Church Missionary Society Ireland,** CMSI
Rev. Cecil Wilson, General Secretary: Overseas House, 3 Belgrave Road, Rathmines, Dublin 6; *t* (01) 497 0931, *f* 497 0939
Christian missionary work in Africa and Asia, and relief work there with refugees and other groups; intercultural dialogue, international solidarity. *Transmission* (4/yr). »94

4

◆ **European Commission**
Jean Monnet Centre, 39 Molesworth Street, Dublin 2; *t* (01) 671 2244, *f* 671 2657
National representative office of the Commission, p189; information on EU policy and related matters. »94

◆ **Concern**
Fr Aengus Finucane, Chief Executive: 52 Lower Camden Street, Dublin 2; *t* (01) 475 4162, *f* 475 7362
Founded 1968, Third World relief agency; working with refugees mainly in in Africa and Asia, training and employing local personnel in development projects and responding to emergencies. Also Belfast branch. *Concern News* (3/yr), *World Poverty Review* (1/yr). »95

◆ **Department of Education**: An Roinn Oideachais: Refugee Primary Education Project
Michael O'Quinn: Marlborough Street, Dublin 1
The Department also has interests in Traveller and migrant education, and operates the Leargás Youth Exchange Bureau, right (the agency for the EU's PETRA scheme in Ireland). »94

◆ **Department of Justice**: Office of the Minister & Secretariat 72-76 St Stephen's Green, Dublin 2; *t* (01) 678 9711; visa enquiries 678 9466
Immigration and Citizenship Division deals with immigration and nationality matters and with asylum applications. »95

◆ **European Anti-Poverty Network**: Irish office
8 Great Georges Street North, Dublin 1; *t* (01) 874 5737
National co-ordination of EU-funded anti-poverty projects. »95

▌ **European Bureau for Lesser-Used Languages**: Biuró Eorpach do Teangacha Neamhshorleathana: Bureau Européen pour les langues moins répandues
Dónall Ó Riagáin, General Secretary: 10 Sráid Haiste Iocht., Báile Atha Cliath 2; *t* (01) 661 2205, 661 8743, *f* 676 6840
Diarmaid Breathnach. Concerned with survival and status of minority languages in Europe. Governmental, private and intergovernmental funding. *Contact Bulletin* (4/yr). »95

◆ **Foras Aiseanna Saothair**, FAS: National Training and Employment Authority, and EURES
Kevin Quinn, EURES Manager: 27-33 Upper Baggot Street, Dublin 4; *t* (01) 668 5777, *f* 660 9093
The state agency (always known by its acronym, FAS) for employment advice, placement and training; supports special training projects for members of the Traveller minority; provides emigration counselling and advice via 80 local offices, some with 'Euroadvisers' (in the EURES network, p190, advising people who migrate within the EU). Services of all state bodies are equally available to foreign residents. »95

◆ **Free Legal Advice Centres Ltd**, FLAC
49 South William Street, Dublin 2; *t* (01) 679 4239, *f* 679 1554
Also at 6 Camden Place, Cork. Founded 1969; campaigns for comprehensive scheme of civil legal aid and advice, offers assistance to those unable to pay for legal services. »95

✿ **Immigration Office**
Garda Station, Union Quay, Cork; *t* (021) 275759
Regulates immigration; part of the Department of Justice. »90
✿ ≡ Ringaskiddy, Co. Cork; *t* (021) 371179 »90
✿ ≡ The Pier, Rosslare, Co. Wexford; *t* (053) 33149 »90

● **Institiúid Teangeolaíochta na hEireann**, ITE: Linguistics Institute of Ireland
31 Fitzwilliam Place, Dublin 2; *t* (01) 662 0446, *f* 661 0004
Research into and promotion of language teaching, learning and maintenance, and linguistics; involved in the LINGUA scheme (co-ordinated in Ireland by the Department of Education, above, which funds ITE) to increase access to the languages of other EU countries. »94

▌ **Ireland Funds**
Kinnear Court, 16 Cumberland Street South, Dublin 2; *t* (01) 671 4677
Seek to raise funds for development and reconciliation projects, mainly among Irish emigrant communities in North America, Australia and Britain. »90

◆ **Irish Commission for Justice and Peace**, ICJP
Pauline Eccles: 169 Booterstown Avenue, Blackrock, Co. Dublin; *t* (01) 288 4853, *f* 283 4161
Catholic agency, promotes Christian precepts in domestic and international policy areas; public education about Third World development, human rights, refugees, poverty. »94

◆ **Irish Council for Civil Liberties**, ICCL
John McDermott: 35-36 Arran Quay, Dublin 7
Main Irish domestic human rights organisation. »88

● **Irish Peace Council**
[address uncertain] 29 Lower Baggot Street, Dublin 2; *t* (01) 661 1661
Promotion of peace and justice in Ireland and in the world order. »90

◆ **Irish Red Cross Society**: Head Office
Martin Good, General Secretary: PO Box 1312, 16 Merrion Square, Dublin 2; *t* (01) 676 5135-37, *f* 661 4461, *Tx* 32746
Also at Ennis, Co. Clare. International humanitarian relief, mostly through international Red Cross and Red Crescent movement, p218; development education in Ireland. Prior to the establishment of the Refugee Agency, p141, the Irish Red Cross participated in an NGO committee co-ordinating refugee reception, health and social care and resettlement, including Vietnamese quota refugees and more recent arrivals from Somalia and elsewhere. *Newsletter* (6/yr). »95
✿ ≡ Refugee Home: St Andrews, 50 Merrion Road, Dublin 4; *t* (01) 668 5307 »90

● **Leargás Exchange Bureau** and PETRA National Co-ordination Unit; Youth for Europe
John McCarthy: Avoca House, 189-193 Parnell Street, Dublin 1; *t* (01) 873 1411, *f* 873 1316
Management and development of services promoting of international youth, student, teacher and trainee exchanges and intercultural understanding, including the PETRA scheme for vocational training, p192, and Youth for Europe, p191. »94

● **National Campaign for the Homeless**
[address unknown] Dublin
Travellers Sub-Committee produced 1990 report on accommodation policies for Travellers. »91

◆ **National Youth Council**: Comhairle Naisiúnta na nOíge
Melissa Butcher: 3 Montague Street, Dublin 2; *t* (01) 478 4122, *f* 478 3974
A national confederation of youth organisations. The Council co-ordinated the Irish response to the 1994-95 Council of Europe Youth Campaign against Racism, p197; in 1995 it issued a report on racism in Ireland. »95

● **Pax Christi**
Tony D'Costa: 52 Lower Rathmines Road, Dublin 6; *t* (01) 496 5293, *f* 496 5492
Catholic pressure group for social justice and human rights. *Olive Branch: Peace and Justice Issues*. »94

● **Voluntary Service International**, VSI
Tom Ryder: 30 Mountjoy Square, Dublin 1; *t* (01) 855 1011, *f* 855 1012
Recruitment and funding of voluntary personnel for overseas development projects. »95

● **Women in Development, Europe**, WIDE
Pauline Eccles: 169 Booterstown Avenue, Blackrock, Co. Dublin; *t* (01) 288 4853, *f* 283 4161
Campaigns on gender issues in human rights, international development, migrant women; supported by the Irish Commission for Justice & Peace, left. *WIDE Bulletin* (4/yr). »94

ITALY 39

● **Agenzia Gioventù per l'Europa**: Youth for Europe Agency, Ministero degli Affari Esteri
piazzale della Farnesina 1, 00194 Roma; *t* (06) 323 6218, *f* 323 3552
Promotes non-school youth exchanges and European consciousness among young people; see also p191. »94

◆ **Alto Commissariato delle Nazioni Unite per i Rifugiati**, ACNUR: United Nations High Commissioner for Refugees, UNHCR
via Caroncini 119, 00197 Roma; *t* (06) 807 8155, 807 7119, *f* 808 2338, *Tx* 622430 UNHCR I, *Tg* HICOMREF Roma
Asylum applications, recogniton of 'mandate' refugee status, refugee protection; see p219. Assumed advisory role in the Italian government's Commissione di Elegibilità, which deals with asylum claims, during the 1991 Albanian refugee influx.»95

● **Amnesty International—Sezione Italia**, AI
viale Mazzini 146, 00195 Roma; *t* (06) 3751 4860, *f* 3751 5406
Human rights pressure group mainly concerned with political prisoners, see International Secretariat, p220; provides advice and counselling for asylum seekers and refugees. »94
✿ ≡ Maurizio Ruaprio: via Ugo Foscolo 2, 20121 Milano; *t* (02) 7200 3901, *f* 878176
Human rights, refugee support, research/documentation. »94

◆ **Associazione Cristiana di Lavoratori Italiani**, ACLI *(Italian Christian Workers' Association)* Ufficio Nazionale
Giovanni Ascani: via Giuseppe Marcora 18-20, 00153 Roma; *t* (06) 584 0485, 58401, *f* 584 0436
International solidarity, welfare of migrants (including emigrants from Italy) and refugees. Offices throughout and outside Italy. See also MNM, p4, and ENAIP, p144. *ACLI Oggi* (52/yr), *AESSE Azione Sociale* (6/yr). »94

✿ **Associazione Cristiana di Lavoratori Italiani:** Collaboratrici Familiari, ACLI-COLF *(Family Aides)*
[address uncertain] piazza Castellino 56, 80128 Napoli; *t* (081) 241332
Social work with migrants. »90
✿ ≡ Collaboratrici Familiari, ACLI-COLF: via Roma 57, 38100 Trento; *t* (0461) 32251 »90
✿ **Associazione Fratelli dell'Uomo** *(Brotherhood of Man Association)*
Rodolfo Canciani: via Varesina 214, 20156 Milano; *t* (02) 3340 4091, *f* 3800 9194
International solidarity, development education. »94
● **Associazione Interventi Cooperazione allo Sviluppo,** AICOS *(Association for Development Co-operation Initiatives)*
Roberto Girola: via Martiri Oscuri 5, 20125 Milano; *t* (02) 284 1423, *f* 2614 3638
International development, especially in health field; solidarity, development education. »94
● **Associazione per la Partecipazione allo Sviluppo,** APS *(Association for Participation in Development)*
corso Regina Margherita 163, 10144 Torino; *t* (011) 437 4936, 437 5049, *f* 437 5267
Development aid to, development education about, and assistance to migrants and refugees from Africa and Asia.»93
● **Associazione Professionale Italiana Collaboratrici Familiari,** API-COLF *(Italian Professional Association of Family Aides)*
P. Erminio Crippa: piazza Cairoli 2, 00186 Roma; *t* (06) 686 9262, 579 3940
Family social work; employment. Also listed (1990) at via Casale S. Pio V 20, 00165 Roma, *t* 622 1534 (as national headquarters). See also FEDER-COLF, p206. »94
✿ ≡ corso Alcide De Gasperi, 70125 Bari »90
✿ ≡ via 1° Settembre 117, 98122 Messina; *t* (090) 35547»90
✿ ≡ Clementina Barili: Sede Provinciale, via C. Salerio 53/A, 20151 Milano; *t* (02) 308 7649 »90
✿ ≡ Pasqualino Pizzo: via A.F. Bonborti 12, 35141 Padova; *t* (049) 39585 »90
✿ ≡ Sicily: Rizalina Santiago: via Duca della Verdura 27, 90141 Palermo, Sicilia; *t* (091) 250763 »90
✿ ≡ via Chini 2, 38100 Trento; *t* (0461) 311509 »90
✿ ≡ Campo S. Maurizio, 30124 Venezia; *t* (041) 711356 »90
♦ **Caritas Italiana:** Head Office
Mons. Giuseppe Pasini, Director: via F. Baldelli 41, 00146 Roma; *t* (06) 541 2435, 541 0286, *f* 541 0300
Catholic humanitarian relief and development aid organisation; development education; services to immigrants, refugees and asylum seekers; see diocesan sections, and special migrant units (e.g. Centro Accoglienza Straniere, Centro Accoglienza Extracomunitari, p142; Segretaria per gli Esteri, p145). »93
✿ ≡ Germano Garatto: via Gagliardo 2, 16126 Genova; *t* (010) 257606, *f* 267768
Italian contact for the European Co-ordination for the Right to Family Life for Immigrants, p136. »95
✿ ≡ Pr Gaetano Tornese: [address unknown] Lecce
One of the main local agencies providing emergency help to refugees and asylum seekers in Lecce, a major transit point for migrants from Albania, Kurdistan and elsewhere. »95
✿ ≡ Caritas Diocesana, Pisa: piazza Arcivescovado 18, 56100 Pisa; *t* (050) 25162 »90
✿ ≡ Caritas Diocesana, Rome: main office: Caritas Romana, Largo Agosta 10, 00171 Roma; *t* (06) 688 6465
See also diocesan Centro Accoglienza Straniere, p142. »90
● **Catholic Relief Services**
via Boezio 21, 00192 Roma; *t* (06) 318051 »83
● **Centro di Informazione sulla mobilità e le equivalenze accademiche,** CIMEA *(Centre for Information on Mobility and Recognition of Qualifications)*
Fondazione RUI, viale Ventuno Aprile 36, 00162 Roma; *t* (06) 8632 1281, *f* 8632 2845
Promotes international mobility of students, researchers and teachers; part of the EU's NARIC network on recognition of qualifications. Information for Italians intending to work or study abroad, and foreigners intending to do so in Italy. »94
● **Centro Internazionale di Cooperazione allo Sviluppo,** CICS: International Centre for Development Co-operation
via Crescenzio 82, 00193 Roma; *t* (06) 687 4328, *f* 683 7508
Emergency relief for refugees and displaced people abroad; development co-operation programmes, mainly in Africa and Latin America; development education. »93
● **Centro Missionario Pontificio Istituto Missioni Estere,** PIME: Missionary Centre, Pontifical Institute for Foreign Missions
P. Gianfranco Vianello: via Mosé Bianchi 94, 20149 Milano; *t* (02) 498 0741
Catholic missionary training centre with interest in migration issues. »90

✿ **Centro Raccolta Profughi Stranieri** *(Reception Centre for Foreign Refugees)*
via XXIV Maggio, 04100 Latina; *t* (0773) 488910 c/o UCEI
Official reception point for refugees and asylum seekers; accommodation, social services; relevant government departments and some NGO services, including UCEI, p144, IRC, p206, and WCC, p207, have offices in the Centre. »83
✿ **Comitato Italiano Giovanile per le Relazione Internazionale,** CIGRI *(Italian Youth Committee for International Relations)*
via Pietro Cartoni 4, 00152 Roma; *t* (06) 537 0332, *f* 5820 1442
Promotes youth exchange programmes. »94
● **European Commission**
via Poli 29, 00187 Roma; *t* (01) 678 9722, *f* 679 1658, 679 3652, *Tx* 610184 EUROMA I
National office of the Commission, p189; information on EU policy and related matters. »93
✿ ≡ corso Magenta 59, 20123 Milano; *t* (02) 4801 2505, *f* 481 8543, *Tx* 316200 EURMIL I »93
● **Confederazione Generale Italiana del Lavoro,** CGIL *(Italian General Confederation of Labour)*
corso d'Italia 25, 00198 Roma; *t* (06) 841 5651, *f* 884 2357
Major trade union confederation; services, equally available to migrant workers, include advice on employment and training, and welfare work: see INCA-CGIL, p206. Its research service is the Istituto Ricerche Economiche e Sociali, IRES (via S. Teresa 23, 00198 Roma, *t* 855 1055). See also the CGIL's specialist Uffici Lavoratori Stranieri, p143. »94
✿ ≡ Oscar Barchiesi: via G. Oberdan 10, 60122 Ancona; *t* (071) 203923, 203924 »90
♦ **Consiglio Italiano per i Rifugiati,** CIR: Italian Refugee Council
Valeria Biscardi: via S. Tommaso d'Aquino 116, 00136 Roma; *t* (06) 397357 52-53, 310 9955, *f* 397357 58, 310942
National co-ordinating body of refugee assistance agencies and NGOs; establishment was promoted by the UNHCR, p204.»95
● **Cooperazione Giuridica Internazionale** *(International Legal Co-operation)*
[address uncertain] via Fibreno 28, 00199 Roma; *t* (06) 831 0155 »90
✿ **Coordinamento delle ONG per la Cooperazione Internazionale allo Sviluppo,** COCIS *(NGO Co-ordination for International Development Co-operation)*
Gildo Baraldi, President: [address uncertain] via Urbana 156, 00184 Roma; *t* (06) 485974, *f* 474 1762
Also listed (1993) at via Correnti 17, 20123 Milano, *t* (02) 8940 1705. Umbrella group for around 25 Italian non-governmental organisations involved in development aid, emergency relief and development education. »94
● **Coordinamento degli Studenti Democratici,** CSDI *(Co-ordination of Democratic Students)*
via Bucaneve 3, int.5, 00172 Roma; *t* (06) 287 4456 »90
♦ **Croce Rossa Italiana:** Italian Red Cross
via Toscana 12, 00187 Roma
Humanitarian relief agency; some services to refugees and displaced people. See international bodies, p218. »93
● **Dipartimento per l'informazione e l'editoria Sportello immigrati** *(Immigrants Desk, Information & Publishing Department)*
Presidenza del Consiglio dei Ministri, via Po 14, 00198 Roma
Cabinet Office department for official publications concerning migrants. »90
● **Esercito della Salvezza:** Salvation Army
David Cavanagh: via P. Sarpi 44, 20154 Milano; *t* (02) 331 9942
Uniformed militant Christian fundamentalist sect with a range of welfare services. *Il Grido di Guerra* (12/yr). »94
● **Federazione Internazionale dei Diritti dell'Uomo,** FIDH: Fédération Internationale des Droits de l'Homme: International Federation for Human Rights
Pasquale Bandiera: corso Vittorio Emanuele II 18, 00186 Roma; *t* (06) 678 5814, 678 6048, *f* 994 2224
National office of the FIDH, a French-based international human rights association, p197. *Le Nuove Libertà* (12/yr).»94
● **Federazione Organizzazioni Cristiani per il Servizio Internazionale Volontario,** FOCSIV *(Federation of Christian Organisations for Voluntary International Service)*
Luca Jahier: via del Conservatorio 1, 00186 Roma; *t* (06) 687 7796, 687 7867, *f* 687 2373
International solidarity, development assistance through the provision of voluntary workers. *Voluntari e Terzo Mondo* (4/yr); *Piccolo Pianta* (12/yr). »94
● **Fondazione Giovanni Agnelli** *(Agnelli Foundation)*
Marcello Pacini: via Giacosa 38, 10125 Torino; *t* (011) 658666, 650 3434, *f* 650 2777
A major charity funded by the Fiat tycoon. *Altreitalie* (2/yr), *Notizie dall'Italia* (4/yr). »94

■ **Fondazione Lelio Basso**
via della Dogana Vecchia 5, 00186 Roma; t (06) 6880 1468,
f 687 7774
International human rights organisation, with a range of
concerns including migration and asylum rights: see Basso-
Tribunal (Germany), p138, and LIDLIP, p169.   »95
● **Fondazione Italiana per il Volontariato**, FIVOL *(Italian*
Foundation for the Voluntary Sector)
Cesare Graziani: via Nazionale 39, 00184 Roma; t (06) 481
4991, f 481 4617
Research, educational work, promotion of voluntary service.
Revista del Volontariato (12/yr).   »94
● **Alcide de Gasperi Foundation for Peace and International**
Co-operation
via della Camilluccia 420, 00135 Roma; t (06) 3550 7023,
f 305 0556
Foundation in memory of the leading post-war Christian
Democrat; international relations, Italians abroad. »94
● **Guardia di Finanza** *(Revenue Guard)*
[address unknown] Roma
Customs police agency involved in detection and prevention
of illegal immigration.   »95
♦ **International Organization for Migration**, IOM (formerly
Comitato Intergovernativo per le Migrazione Europei)
via Nomentana 62, 00161 Roma; t (06) 854 0151-55
National office of the Swiss-based IOM, p218; planned
migration, including return migration of skilled workers. »90
♦ **International Rescue Committee**, IRC
piazza Collegio Romano 1B, 00186 Roma; t (06) 679 6635
National office of the New York-based intergovernmental
body, p218. Advice and assistance for re-emigration of
refugees; office in Latina Refugee Centre, p205.   »94
■ **Isis International**
via San Saba 5, 00152 Roma; t (06) 574 6479
Women's rights and welfare issues worldwide.   »94
● **Istituto Nazionale Confederale di Assistenza**, INCA-CGIL
(National Confederal Welfare Institute)
via Buonarroti 29-37, 00185 Roma; t (06) 738611
Welfare section of the Confederazione Generale Italiana del
Lavoro trade unon confederation; branches throughout Italy.
See also CGIL, p205; Uffici Lavoratori Straniere, p143. »94
✿ **Istituto Salesiano dello Sacro Cuore** *(Salesian Institute of*
the Sacred Heart)
via Marsala, 00185 Roma; t (06) 491497
Catholic organisation concerned with youth welfare. »94
● **Istituto di Tutela e Assistenza ai Lavoratori**, ITAL-UIL
(Institute for Workers' Protection and Welfare)
Giampiero Bonifazi: via Po 62, CP 162, 00198 Roma; t (06)
675471 (677471?), 845 0285, f 854 7992
Labour welfare agency of the Unione Italiana del Lavoro trade
union confederation, p145; branches in Italy and abroad.
Lavoro Italiano nel Mondo (6/yr); *ITAL notizie* (4/yr). »94
● **Mani Tese '76** *(Reaching Out '76)*
via Cavenaghi 4, 20149 Milano; t (02) 4800 8617, f 481
2296
Development education; agricultural development and human
rights in Third World; refugee resettlement in El Salvador. »93
● **Ministero degli Affari Esteri** *(Ministry of Foreign Affairs)*
Palazzo della Farnesina, 00194 Roma; t (06) 36911, 323 6218
Ministry formerly responsible for refugee status and protection,
still handles aspects of migration and refugee policy. The
Direzione Relazioni Culturali promotes cultural relations with
other countries, and educational exchanges (in liaison with the
Direzione Generale per gli Scambi Culturale in the education
ministry). See also Agenzia Gioventù per l'Europa, p204. »94
● **Ministero dell'Interno** *(Ministry of the Interior)*
Direzione Generale Servizi Civili, via Sforza 14, 00184 Roma;
t (06) 4827 2090 (?)
Relevant responsibilities include the regulation of foreign
residents; determination of applications for refugee status;
emergency assistance to asylum applicants.   »94
♦ **Ministero del Lavoro e della Previdenza Sociale** *(Ministry*
of Labour and Social Security) Direzione Genenerale per
l'Impiego *(Employment Directorate)*
via Flavia 6, 00187 Roma; t (06) 484587
Ministry responsible for employment policy, job placement,
unemployment, labour statistics, national insurance and
participation in the EURES information network, p190.
Operating through provincial bureaux (Uffici Provinciali del
Lavoro, UPLMO; for addresses t 497911) and local offices
(Sezioni Circonscrizionali per l'Impiego), it assists job-seekers
including legal immigrants, who form a preferential category
from which larger employers are theoretically obliged to take
on a quota. See also Servizio per i problemi dei lavoratori
extracomunitari e delle loro famiglie, right.   »94

● **Movimento Studentesco per l'Organizzazione Internazionale**,
MSOI *(Student Movement for International Organisation)*
Palazzetto di Venezia, via San Marco 3, 00186 Roma;
t (06) 679 3949, f 621641   »94
♦ **Osservatorio sull'immigrazione** *(Immigration Information*
Office)
Vice Presidenza del Consiglio dei Ministri, Palazzo Chigi,
piazza Colonna 366, 00187 Roma
Section of Cabinet Office responsible for monitoring
immigration and refugee questions.   »90
✿ **Questura, Ufficio Stranieri** *(Police Headquarters, Aliens*
Office)
via S. Vitale, 00184 Roma; t (06) 4686
Aliens police, responsible for receipt of asylum applications,
issue and renewal of residence permits, and registration of
addresses; there are 95 Questure throughout Italy. »90
● **Servizio Civile Internazionale—Italia**, SCI *(International Civil*
Service—Italy)
via dei Laterani 28, 00184 Roma; t (06) 700 5367
International welfare agency; see also European office, in
Belgium, p192.   »94
♦ **Servizio per i problemi dei lavoratori extracomunitari e delle**
loro famiglie *(Service for the Problems of Non-EU Workers and*
their Families) Ministero del Lavoro e della Previdenza Sociale
via Flavia 6, 00187 Roma
Department of the Ministry of Labour and Social Security, left,
responsible for training, employment, labour rights and the
welfare of non-EU workers.   »90
♦ **Servizio Sociale Internazionale—Sezione Italiana**, SSI:
International Social Service, ISS; Italian Section: Head Office
Graziella Praturlon: via Vittorio Veneto 96, 00187 Roma;
t (06) 488 1090, 488 4640, f 481 7605
Legal and social services, liaison with UNHCR, p204, social
work, counselling and assistance to refugee students; national
section of the INGO, p218, which intervenes in social welfare
problems involving more than one country, especially those
arising from voluntary or forced migration.   »94
✿ ≡ Fanny Marchese: Delegazione regionale, via Napo Torriani
30, 20124 Milano; t (02) 669748   »90
♦ **Sindacato dei Collaboratori Familiari**, FEDER-COLF *(Union of*
Family Aides)
piazza Cairoli 117, 00186 Roma
Family social work, welfare advice; see API-COLF, p205. »90
● ≡ Luciana Bertelli: via M. Melloni 49 a, 20129 Milano;
t (02) 749 0448   »94
✿ **Ufficio Emigrazione-Immigrazione** *(Regional Emigrant and*
Immigrant Service) Marche
Assessorato al lavoro e formazione professionale, via Gentile
da Fabriano 9, 60125 Ancona; t (071) 8061
The Uffici Emigrazione-Immigrazione delle Regioni are official
agencies dealing with the welfare of migrant workers and
families, whether Italians abroad, returnees or foreigners. »94
✿ ≡ Val d'Aosta: Ufficio Stranieri, presso Questura, corso
Battaglione, 11100 Aosta   »90
✿ ≡ Apulia: Assessorato Servizi Sociali e Lavoro Puglia,
piazza Aldo Moro 37, 70122 Bari; t (080) 401111   »94
✿ ≡ Emilia Romagna: Consulta per l'Emigrazione e
l'Immigrazione, viale Aldo Moro 38, 40127 Bologna; t (051)
284111, f 283923   »94
✿ ≡ Trentino Alto Adige: Provincia Autonoma di Bolzano:
Ufficio Mercato del Lavoro, Casa del Lavoro, via Leonardo da
Vinci, 39100 Bolzano   »90
✿ ≡ Sardinia: Assessorato Lavoro Regionale, via XXVIII
Febbraio 1, 09100 Cagliari, Sardegna; t (070) 6061   »94
✿ ≡ Molise: Assessorato Regionale Emigrazione e Lavoro,
via D'Amato 1, 86100 Campobasso; t (0874) 4291   »94
✿ ≡ Calabria: Assessorato al Lavoro, via Repubblica Marinara
2, 88100 Catanzaro Lido; t (0961) 8511   »94
✿ ≡ Tuscany: Assessorato al Lavoro, Regione Toscana,
piazza della Libertà 16, 50129 Firenze; t (055) 438 2111 »94
✿ ≡ Liguria: Assessorato al Lavoro, via Fieschi 15, 16121
Genova; t (010) 54851   »94
✿ ≡ Lombardy: Assessorato al Lavoro Lombardia, via Fabio
Filzi 22, 20124 Milano   »90
✿ ≡ Campania: Assessorato al Lavoro, via Don Bosco 4f,
80132 Napoli; t (081) 796 1111   »94
✿ ≡ Sicily: Gruppo 21°, Assessorato Regionale Lavoro, via
Pernice 3, 90144 Palermo, Sicilia; t (091) 696 1111 »94
✿ ≡ Servizio Immigrazione-Cooperazione Umbria: Ufficio
Relazioni Esterne e Rapporti Communitari, corso Vannucci,
06100 Perugia   »90
✿ ≡ Abruzzo: Giunta Regionale, viale Bodio 423, 65100
Pescara   »90
✿ ≡ Basilicata: Dipartimento per le attività produttive, via
Anzio, 85100 Potenza   »90

✿ **Ufficio Emigrazione-Immigrazione**: Lazio
Assessorato al Lavoro, via Rosa Raimondi Garibaldi 7,
00145 Roma; *t* (06) 54571
For activities see the first Ufficio listed on p206. »94
✿ ≡ **Provincia di Roma**: Ufficio Immigrazione, via Santa
Eufemia 19, 00187 Roma »90
✿ ≡ **Piedmont**: Assessorato al Lavoro/Movimenti Migratori
Piemonte, via Magenta 12, 10100 Torino; *t* (011) 43211 »94
✿ ≡ **Trentino Alto Adige**: Provincia Autonoma di Trento:
Assessorato al Lavoro, via Torre Verde 27, 38100 Trento;
t (0461) 234830 »94
✿ ≡ **Friuli-Venezia Giulia**: Direzione Regionale del Lavoro, via
Battisti 18, 34100 Trieste »90
✿ ≡ **Veneto**: Dipartimento Emigrazione-Immigrazione, Palazzo
Sceriman, Cannaregio 168, 30121 Venezia »90
✿ **Ufficio Rifugiati** *(Refugee Office)* Comune di Milano
Giancarla Boreatti: via Tadino 12, 20100 Milano; *t* (02) 552
10277 »95
✿ **Unione Italiana del Lavoro—Sindacato Regionale**, UIL
(Italian Labour Union—Regional Section)
Salamon Pino: piazza Aldo Moro 14, 70122 Bari; *t* (080)
524 0392, *f* 524 2655
Regional office of a major trade union confederation; see also
UIL Coordinamento Nazionale Immigrati and UNITI, p145. »94
● **World Council of Churches**, WCC
piazza Sallustio 24, 00187 Roma; *t* (06) 564279, 475 9130
Italian office of the Swiss-based WCC, p219; activities include
advice and assistance to refugees in Rome and at the Latina
Refugee Centre, p205, *t* (0773) 40691. »83
● **Young Men's Christian Association**, YWCA
Cautela Dina: via Cesare Balbo 4, 00184 Roma; *t* (06) 481
4525
Christian humanitarian agency; some refugee welfare
activities. »94

LATVIA 371

● **Soros Foundation**, SF
Kr. Barona 31, 1722 Riga; *t* (2) 280641, *f* 882 8160
National office of the US-based philanthropic institution
promoting democracy and freedom of movement. »94
● **Youth Council of Latvia**, LJP
L. Pils iela 6, 1050 Riga; *t* (2) 226463, *f* 224785
Umbrella organisation for the Latvian youth NGO sector. »94

LIECHTENSTEIN 41

◆ **Amt für Soziale Dienste** *(Social Services Department)*
Herr Gstöhl: Postfach 197, 9494 Schaan; *t* (075) 236 7284,
f 236 7219
Social welfare, integration; participated in the 1994-95
European Youth Campaign Against Racism, p197. »94

LITHUANIA 370

● **Council of Lithuanian Youth Organisations**, LiJOT
PO Box 2193, 2049 Vilnius; *t* (2) 352270, *f* 355651
Umbrella group for the Lithuanian youth sector. »94
◆ **Immigration and Asylum Administration**
Ministry of Social Affairs and Labour, Vilnius
Agency created in 1995 to handle migration issues. »95
● **Open Society Fund—Soros Foundation**, OSF-SF
Jaksto 9, 2600 Vilnius; *t* (2) 629003, *f* 221419
National office of a US-based philanthropic organisation
promoting democratic transformation in Central Europe. »94

LUXEMBOURG 352

● **Action des Chrétiens pour l'Abolition de la Torture**, ACAT:
Action by Christians for the Abolition of Torture
23 ave. G. Diderich, 1420 Luxembourg; *t* 250457, *f* 251820
National section of French-based campaign, p195, on torture
and the death penalty; refugee issues in this context. »95
● **Actioun Lëtzebuergesch**
Henri Rinnen: BP 98, 2010 Luxembourg; *t* 470612
Training, employment, education, youth welfare. »95

◆ **Administration de l'Emploi, Ministère du Travail**
(Employment Division, Ministry of Labour)
38a rue Philippe II, 2340 Luxembourg; *t* 478 5300, *f* 464519
Government agency responsible for employment matters: job
placement, training, careers guidance; participates in the
PETRA vocational training network, p192. Offices at Diekirch
and Esch-sur-Alzette. Services are equally available to non-
nationals (who form a third of the workforce). »95
◆ **Amnesty International Luxembourg**, AI
Georges Wivenes: BP 1914, 1019 Luxembourg; *t* 481687,
f 483680
Location: 23 rue des Etats Unis. Human rights pressure
group, see p220; pre-asylum assistance to refugees. »95
◆ **Caritas Luxembourg**
BP 1721, 1017 Luxembourg; *t* 402131 exts. 530-531,
f 402131 exts. 26, 409
Location: 29 rue Michel Welter, 2730 Luxembourg. Major
Catholic charity providing welfare and housing assistance and
other services to refugees and asylum seekers through its
Service Réfugiés (Agnès Rausch), which co-operates with the
Lëtzebürger Flüchtlingsrôt, p145; refugee reception centre
(Flüchtlingshaus Eisenborn, 1 rue du Forêt, *t* 788062); welfare
service (Sozialinstitut Mersch, *t* 326644). Aid to immigrants
through Service Accueil (Michèle Besch-Kridel); special service
for Portuguese immigrants; and Service Aide à l'Etranger
(Fränz Jacobs, ext. 340). Also supports migrant and refugee
welfare projects in Eastern Europe and the South. »95
● **Centre d'Information et d'Echanges de Jeunes** *(Youth
Information and Exchange Centre)* and Jeunesse pour l'Europe
M. Putzeys: 76 boulevard de la Pétrusse, 2320 Luxembourg;
t 405552, *f* 405556
A service of the CGJL (youth council, below); promotes
international exchanges; see also Youth for Europe, p191. »95
● **Centre de Pastorale Familiale** *(Family Pastorate Centre)*
Ernest Jacoby: 3 place du Théatre, 2613 Luxembourg;
t 474544
Catholic welfare service. »95
● **Comité Luxembourgeoise pour l'UNICEF**
99 route d'Arlon, 1140 Luxembourg; *t* 448715, 449674
Fundraising for refugee relief and other activities of the UN
Children's Fund, p219; development education. »95
◆ **Commissariat du Gouvernement aux Etrangers** *(Government
Standing Commission on Aliens)* Ministère de la Famille
14 avenue de la Gare, Luxembourg; *t* 478 ext. 6572 »95
● **Commission des Communautés Européennes**: Commission
of the European Communities
bât. Jean Monnet, rue Alcide De Gasperi, 2920 Luxembourg;
t 4301-1, *f* 4301-4433, *Tx* 3423/3446 COMEUR LU
National office of the Commission, p189; information on EU
policy and related matters. »95
● **Conseil Général de la Jeunesse Luxembourgeoise**, CGJL
(General Youth Council of Luxembourg)
BP 657, 2016 Luxembourg; *t/f* 406090
Location: 76 bvd de la Pétrusse, 2320 Luxembourg. Umbrella
organisation of youth voluntary sector. See also Centre
d'Information et d'Echanges de Jeunes, above. »94
◆ **Conseil National de l'Immigration** *(National Council on
Immigration)* Ministère de la Famille
Gaston J. Raus, President: 14 avenue de la Gare, Luxembourg;
t 478 ext. 384
Founded 1977; research and policy formation on social,
educational, political aspects of immigrant integration. »90
■ **Court of Justice of the European Union**
BP 1406, Palais de la Cour de Justice, 2925 Luxembourg;
t 43031, *f* 433766, *Tx* 2510
Supreme judicial organ of the EU; ensures compliance with
the Treaties and rules in disputes on their interpretation. »94
◆ **Croix-Rouge Luxembourgeoise**: Luxembourg Red Cross
Jacques Hansen: BP 404, boulevard Joseph II, 2014
Luxembourg; *t* 450202, *f* 457269
Humanitarian activities; works with AREL, p124, and other
agencies, on refugee welfare; special Service Réfugiés, *t*
221639. See global bodies, p218. *Revue de la Jeunesse.* »95
◆ **Haut Commissariat des Nations Unies pour les réfugiés**:
United Nations High Commissioner for Refugees, UNHCR
Correspondant au Luxembourg: 34 rue de Crécy, 2419
Luxembourg; *t* 47911, *Tx* 3626 BIL LU
Refugee status and protection; see UNHCR in Switzerland,
p219, and Belgium-based regional office, p191. »95
● **Kathoulesch Manneractioun**, KMA *(Catholic People's Action)*
5 avenue Marie-Thérèse, Centre Convict, 2132 Luxembourg;
t 44743-251
Assists refugees at Caritas' Mersch reception centre to find
housing and employment, and raises funds for African and
Latin American development and relief projects. »95

✧ **Lëtzebuerger Scouten** *(Luxembourg Scouts)*
Guy Weis: 5 avenue Marie-Thérèse, Centre Convict, 2132
Luxembourg; *t* 44743 ext. 254
Youth movement; anti-racist, pro-human rights policies.   »95
● **Médecins sans Frontières—Luxembourg, MSF** *(Doctors
without Borders)*
17 route de Luxembourg, 7240 Bereldange; *t* 332515
Also listed (1993) at BP 777, 110 avenue Gaston Diderich,
2017 Luxembourg; *t* 458812, *f* 459239. Emergency
medical aid to refugees, displaced persons and victims of
disaster, mainly in developing countries; see p191.   »95
● **Ministère des Affaires Etrangères** *(Foreign Ministry)*
BP 1602, 5 rue Notre Dame, 1016 Luxembourg; *t* 478 ext. 1
Responsibilities include refugee status and protection.   »95
◆ **Service des Etrangers** *(Aliens Service)*
Ministère de la Justice, 16 boulevard Royal, 2449
Luxembourg; *t* 478 ext. 4533, *f* 227661
Deals with naturalisations, ID cards for foreign residents,
receives asylum requests.   »95
◆ **Service de l'Immigration**, Ministère de la Famille
(Immigration Service, Ministry of the Family)
14 avenue de la Gare, 1610 Luxembourg; *t* 484159
Also listed (1995) at 12-14 avenue Emile Reuter, 2919
Luxembourg; *t* 478 ext. 6500, *f* 478 ext. 6570. Economic
and social integration of immigrants and refugees; see also
Conseil National de l'Immigration, p207. Runs Centre
d'Accueil (reception centre), *t* 478 ext. 6524.   »95
● **Union Nationale des Etudiant(e)s du Luxembourg, UNEL**
(Luxembourg National Union of Students)
BP 324, 2013 Luxembourg; *t* 253123, *f* 253122
Location: 13 avenue Gaston Diderich, 1420 Luxembourg.
Student organisation with anti-racist policies.   »95

MALTA 356

● **Kunsill Nazzjonali Taz-Zghazagh, KNZM** *(National Youth
Council?)*
St Francis Ravelin, Floriana; *t* 234305, *f* 234376   »94
● **Zghazagh Hbieb in-Natura, ZHIN** *(Youth Ecologist
Movement?)*
PO Box 339, Valletta; *t* 239091, *f* 240717
Youth movement; anti-racist policies.   »94

NETHERLANDS 31

▮ **Action for Solidarity, Equality, Environment and Development,**
A SEED: European Office
Postbus 92066, 1090 AB Amsterdam; *t* (020) 668 2236,
f 665 0166
Human rights education; refugee concerns.   »94
✧ **Airport Chaplaincy**
Schiphol Amsterdam Airport, Amsterdam; *t* (020) 601 2666
KLM, 601 2567 airport
Welfare service which provides emergency help to incoming
refugees and asylum seekers.   »95
● **Algemeen Nederlands Jeugd Verbond, ANJV** *(Dutch
General Youth Union)*
Spuistraat 47a, 1012 SR Amsterdam; *t* (020) 622 5799
Co-ordinating body for youth sector. Anti-racist policies.   »94
◆ **Amnesty International—Nederlandse Afdeling, AI-NL**
Kees Bleichrodt: Keizersgracht 620, 1017 ER Amsterdam;
t (020) 626 4436, *f* 624 0889
Campaigns on political prisoners and death penalty, see p220;
Dutch section works on refugee issues, as a member of
VluchtelingenWerk, p147; documentation centre (Petra Catz).
Wordt Vervolgd (12/yr), *Verdrukt* (3/yr), *Globaal* (4/yr).   »95
◆ **Anti-Discriminatie Overleg, ADO** *(Anti-Discrimination Forum)*
Drs Carmelita W.M. Serkei: Postbus 596, 3500 AN Utrecht;
t (030) 234 1264, *f* 234 0231
J. Lahaise, H. Wentholt. Location: Nieuwe Kade 291, 3511
RW Utrecht. Research, media archive; anti-discrimination
training, expert advice to media personnel; promotion of
multiculturalism in the workplace; co-ordination of anti-racist
campaigns and organisations; multi-cultural media projects,
media awards. Publicly funded (through Ministerie van WVC)
co-operative agency of trade unions, churches, refugee groups
including VluchtelingenWerk, p147, and immigrant groups and
centres such as the NCB and LSOBA, p146, IWM, p88, and
Forsa, p9. Founded 1987. Co-publishes a directory of anti-
racist groups *(Anti-racisme gids)*. *ADO-Journaal* (4/yr).   »95

● **Artsen Zonder Grenzen Nederland** *(Doctors without Borders)*
Médecins sans Frontières Pays-Bas, MSF
Postbus 10014, Max Euweplein 40, 1001 EA Amsterdam;
t (020) 520 8700, *f* 620 5170
National affiliate of the international emergency medical aid
charity MSF, p191. Provides services to refugees and victims
of conflict and disaster abroad.   »94
▮ **Association des Etats Généraux des Etudiants de l'Europe,**
AEGEE *(European Association of National Student
Organisations)*
Postbus 244, Mijnbouwplein 11, 2600 AE Delft; *t* (015)
278 6933, *f* 278 6425   »95
✧ **Autonoom Centrum** *(Autonomous Centre)*
Kinkerstraat 48 huis, 1053 DX Amsterdam; *t* (020) 612
6172, *f* 616 8967
Anti-racism, anti-fascism, migrant and refugee support.   »94
● **Bureau Internationale Arbeidsbemiddeling en Stagiaires, IABS**
(Bureau for International Placement and Work Experience) in
the Centraal Bureau voor de Arbeidsvoorziening, CBA
Postbus 437, 2280 AK Rijswijk; *t* (070) 313 0911, *f* 313
0250
Branch of the Central Employment Board (which operates the
national job placement service through regional and local
offices): information and assistance with placements abroad.
Partner in EURES employment information network, p190.»94
✧ **Buro voor Rechtshulp** *(Rights Assistance Bureau)*
Spuistraat 10, 1012 TS Amsterdam; *t* (020) 626 4477
Consumer, housing, labour and migrant rights advice service;
free initial consultations. Offices in the east of the city, *t*
599 9333, south, 676 7011, and west, 616 5036.   »94
● **Caritas Nederlandica/Mensen in Nood**
Hekellaan 6, Postbus 1041, 5200 BA 's-Hertogenbosch
Catholic welfare charity, a member agency of Vluchtelingen
Werk, p147; see also Caritas Internationalis, p230.   »93
● **Christelijk Nationaal Vakverbond Jongerenorganisatie, CNV-j**
(Christian National Labour League Youth Organisation)
Theo Nelissen: Postbus 2475, Ravellaan 1, 3500 GL Utrecht;
t (030) 291 3715, 291 3911, *f* 294 6544
Youth section of one of the main trade union confederations.
International and inter-cultural solidarity; development
education; youth welfare. See also the CNV's Secretariaat
Buitenlandse Werknemers, p146.   »95
● **Commissie Justitia et Pax** *(Justice and Peace Commission)*
Dr V.M. Scheffers/Michael Peters: Rhijngeesterstratweg 40,
Postbus 1031, 2340 BA Oegstgeest; *t* (071) 517 5901,
f 517 5391
Catholic pressure group; human rights, humanitarian aid;
refugee assistance at parish level. *JP Bulletin* (4/yr).   »95
▮ **Council of Europe Minority Youth Committee, CEMYC**
Postbus 9683, 2003 LR Haarlem; *t* (0255) 537438, *f* (010)
435 3978
This committee represents the interests of migrant and
minority youth on a range of matters including education,
employment, civil rights, social integration, anti-racist/anti-
fascist organisation, refugees. See Council of Europe, p197;
CEMYC in Germany and UK, pp200 & 154; IIMI, p240.   »95
● **Defence for Children International—Afdeling Nederland,**
DCI-NL
Postbus 75297, 1070 AG Amsterdam; *t* (020) 663 4550,
f 663 4236
Human rights group focussing on refugee children.   »94
● **Diaconal Office of the Reformed Churches in the Netherlands**
[address unknown]
A member agency of VluchtelingenWerk, p147.   »83
◆ **Directie voor de Emigratie** *(Emigration Service)* Ministerie
van Sociale Zaken en Werkgelegenheid
Postbus 1024, 3000 BA Rotterdam; *t* (010) 453 3410
Part of the Ministry of Social Affairs and Employment, p209;
research, documentation on migration; repatriation help.   »89
◆ **Directie voor Vluchtelingen, Minderheden en Asielzokers**
(Directorate for Refugees, Minorities and Asylum Seekers)
Ministerie van Welzijn, Volksgezondheid en Cultuur
A.J. Van Gils: Postbus 5406, Sir Winston Churchilllaan 368,
2280 HK Rijswijk
Government department (within the Ministry of Welfare,
Public Health and Culture) responsible for development and
implementation of refugee and minority policy.   »94
◆ **Directie Vreemdelingenzaken** *(Directorate for Alien Affairs)*
Ministerie van Justitie, Schedeldoekshaven 100, 2511 EX
Den Haag; *Tx* 34554
Aliens section, includes department for emergency service to
refugees; local Vreemdelingendienst (Aliens Service) offices,
e.g. p210, are responsible for processing asylum applications,
and for refugee status and protection. See also main Ministry
entry, p209, which may supersede this data.   »89

● **Emancipatieraad** *(Council for Emancipation)* Ministerie van Sociale Zaken en Werkgelegenheid
Postbus 90806, 2509 LV Den Haag; *t* (070) 361 4371 (?), *f* 361 5448 (?)
A body formed under the Social Affairs and Employment Ministry, right; concerned with the integration of marginalised groups. »94

● **Europese Commissie**: European Commission
Korte Vijverberg 5, Postbus 30465 (30456?), 2500 GL 's Gravenhage; *t* (070) 346 9326, *f* 364 6619, *Tx* 31094 EURCO NL
National representative office of the Commission, p189, providing information on EU policy and related matters. *Europa van Morgen.* »95

● **Europese Culturele Stichting**, ECS: European Cultural Foundation, ECF
V. Fonville: Jan van Goyenkade 5, 1075 HN Amsterdam; *t* (020) 676 0222, *f* 675 2231
International friendship, anti-racism, multiculturalism. »94

✿ **EXIS Centrum voor Internationale Jongerenactiviteiten** *(EXIS International Youth Activity Centre)* and Youth for Europe
Postbus 15344, 1001 MH Amsterdam; *t* (020) 626 2664, 626 1276, *f* 622 8590, 626 2664
Location: Prof. Tulpstraat 2. Information on international youth exchanges, work placements, au pair work and language courses. See Netherlands Committee for Multilateral Youth Work, p210; Youth for Europe, p191. *Reisweg* (1/yr). »94

✿ **De Expeditie—Centrum voor geweldloze verandering** *(The Expedition—Centre for Non-Violent Change)*
Schimmelpenninckkade 30, 3813 AE Amersfoort; *t* (033) 475 3001
Anti-racism, pacifism, social transformation. »95

✿ **Federatie Nederlandse Vakbewegingen Jongeren**, FNV-J *(Trade Union Youth)*
Postbus 8022, 3503 RA Utrecht
Youth section, with anti-racist/anti-fascist policies, of the FNV labour confederation, see p146. »94

● **Stichting Fonds Vredesprojekten** *(Peace Projects Fund)*
Postbus 1080, 3500 BB Utrecht »94

✿ **Gemeentelijk Allochtonen Overleg**, GAO *(Municipal Consultancy on Aliens)*
Carlien Kortram: Stadskantoor, kamers 361-363, Rodezand 18, 3011 AN Rotterdam; *t* (010) 417 3547
Provides advice and consultancy within the city council structures to assist in service delivery to minority citizens.»95

● **General Diaconal Council of the Dutch Reformed Church**
[address unknown]
A member agency of VluchtelingenWerk, p147. »83

● **Groen Links** *(Green Left)*
Postbus 700, Hoogte Kadijk 145, 1000 AS Amsterdam; *t* (020) 620 2212, *f* 625 1849
Socialist-ecologist movement with anti-racist policies. »94

● **Stichting Helsinki Citizens' Assembly Projekten**
Johan Bussiosstraat 35, 6708 MR Wageningen; *t* (0317) 415336, *f* 425682
Human rights concerns, including anti-racism, refugees. »95

◆ **Hoge Commissaris voor Vluchtelingen van de Verenigde Naties**: United Nations High Commissioner for Refugees, UNHCR: Branch Office for the Netherlands
Vertegenwoordiger in Nederland, Stadhouderslaan 28, 2517 HZ Den Haag; *t* (070) 346 8810-11, *f* 346 8812, *Tx* 34418 UNHCR NL
Works under the Brussels-based Benelux Regional Office, p191, and head office, p219; refugee status, protection. »95

● **Humanistisch Overleg Mensenrechten**, HOM *(Humanist Forum on Human Rights)*
Postbus 114, 3500 AC Utrecht; *t* (030) 231 8145, *f* 236 7104
Education, action and lobbying activities around social, economic, cultural and political aspects of human rights, with a particular focus on women's rights. »95

● **Interkerkelijk Vredesberaad**, IKV *(Interchurch Peace Consultative Council)*
Postbus 85893, Celebesstraat 60, 2508 CN Den Haag; *t* (070) 350 7100, *f* 354 2611
International solidarity, promotion of peace and reconciliation. See also hCa Balkan Project, p23. »94

● **Interkerkelijke Organisatie voor Ontwikkelingssamenwerking**, ICCO *(Inter-Church Development Co-operation Organisation)*
A.J. Sijpkes: Postbus 151, 3700 AD Zeist; *t* (030) 692 7811, *f* 692 5614
Location: Zusterplein 22A. International development aid and emergency relief; around 1,000 current projects in some 80 countries, including aid to refugees and migrants in the South; development education in Holland. »95

▌ **International Association for the Exchange of Students for Technical Experience**, IAESTE
Rotterdamseweg 145, 2628 AL Delft; *t* (015) 788030, 571051
Promotes international work placements for agriculture and technology students. »94

▌ **International Court of Justice**, ICJ
Peace Palace, Carnegieplein 2, 2517 KJ Den Haag; *t* (070) 392 4441, *f* 364 9928, *Tx* 32323
Hears disputes only between states. »94

▌ **International Humanist and Ethical Union**, IHEU
Nieuwegracht 69a, 3512 LG Utrecht; *t* (030) 231 2155, *f* 236 7104
Confederation of 64 national humanist organisations; joint humanitarian relief and development funding work aiding marginalised and powerless social groups in Asia, Africa and Latin America. »95

● **International Social Service—Nederlandse Afdeling**, ISS
Elly van Eeuwijk: Laan Copes van Cattenburch 139, 2585 GA 's Gravenhage; *t* (070) 356 0967
National section of the international NGO, p218, which helps individuals and families with international social welfare problems arising from voluntary or forced migration. »94

● **Internationale Christelijke Vredes Dienst**, ICVD *(International Christian Peace Service)*
M. van Bouwdijk Bastiaansestraat 56, 1054 SP Amsterdam; *t* (020) 689 2735, *f* 618 4469
Christian pacifist organisation with human rights, anti-racist, refugee concerns. See also VIA, p210. »94

◆ **Internationale Organisatie voor Migratie**, IOM: International Organization for Migration
Postbus 10796, 2501 HT Den Haag; *t* (070) 361 5166, *f* 310 6622
National office of the intergovernmental body, p218, providing advice and assistance in connection with emigration and return migration. Library and documentation centre. »95

● **Jonge Democraten**, JD *(Young Democrats)*
Noordwal 10, 2513 EA Den Haag; *t* (070) 362 2162, *f* 364 1917
Youth political movement with anti-racist policies. »94

● **Jonge Europese Federalisten**, JEF *(Young European Federalists)*
Postbus 11063, 2301 EB Leiden; *t* (071) 513 2918
Dutch section of the pan-European youth movement, p193.»95

● **Landelijk Werkgroep Consumentenrecht** *(National Working Group on Consumer Rights)*
[address unknown]
Network of legal and consumer rights advice agencies. »93

◆ **Liga voor de Rechten van de Mens** *(Human Rights League)*
Herengracht 218, 1016 BT Amsterdam; *t/f* (020) 638 4567
Human rights concerns, including migrant, minority and refugee rights, discrimination and racism. »94

◆ **Ministerie van Binnenlandse Zaken**, BiZa *(Ministry of Home Affairs)*
[address unknown]
Directs minorities policy. »89

● **Ministerie van Buitenlandse Zaken** *(Ministry of Foreign Affairs)*
Postbus 20081, Plein 23, 2500 EA Den Haag; *t* (070) 614941
Responsible for asylum applications, refugee status, protection. »85

◆ **Ministerie van Justitie—Immigratie en Naturalisatiedienst** *(Ministry of Justice, Immigration and Naturalisation Service)*
[address unknown] Amsterdam; *t* (020) 654 3132
Processes immigration and naturalisation cases; provides emergency service for asylum applicants and entry refusal cases. See also Directie Vreemdelingenzkaen, p208. »95

◆ **Ministerie van Sociale Zaken en Werkgelegenheid**, SoZaWe *(Ministry of Social Affairs and Employment)* Centrale Directie Voorlichting, Bibliotheek en Documentatie
Postbus 90801, 2509 LV Den Haag; *t* (070) 333 4443-44, *f* 333 4033
Government department responsible for a range of economic and social matters; its local social security and employment offices deal with welfare benefit queries affecting non-nationals; management of refugee and asylum-seeker reception services; provision of advice and information to foreigners, including social security and employment advice leaflets in minority languages. See also Emancipatieraad, left; Directie voor de Emigratie, p208; Sociaal Wetenschappelijke Afdeling, p210; Sociale Dienst Scheepvaart, p147. »95

✿ **MiZaMir** *(We for Peace)*
Groen van Prinstererstraat 90-94, 1051 EP Amsterdam; *t* (020) 681 4885, *f* 684 7635
Peace group with migrant/refugee membership. »94

● **Nederlands Juristen Comité voor de Mensenrechten**, NJCM
(Dutch Lawyers' Committee for Human Rights)
J. Steenbergen/E.M. Peeters: Postbus 9520, Hugo de
Grootstraat 27, 2311 XK Leiden; *t/f* (071) 527 7748
Human rights pressure group, affiliated to International
Commission of Jurists, p217; anti-racism, refugee and minority
rights. *NJCM Bulletin* (8/yr). »95

◆ **Nederlands Migratie Instituut**, NMI
Noordeinde 142-144, 2514 GP Den Haag; *t* (070) 360
2927, *f* 361 4512
Advice and assistance to individuals and groups about return
migration. See also RIC, below. »95

✿ ≡ Regiokantoor Noordwest (North-West Regional Office):
Saskiahuis, Jodenbreestraat 8, 1011 NK Amsterdam;
t (020) 552 2116 »95

✿ ≡ Regiokantoor Den Haag (The Hague Regional Office):
Tenierstraat 13, 2526 NX Den Haag; *t* (070) 388 9408 »95

✿ ≡ Regiokantoor Zuidoost (South-East Regional Office):
Willemstraat 59, 5611 HC Eindhoven; *t* (040) 246 4826 »95

✿ ≡ Regiokantoor Zuidwest (South-West Regional Office):
Hoogstraat 110, 3011 PL Rotterdam; *t* (010) 417 2928 »95

◆ **Nederlandse Rode Kruis**: Dutch Red Cross
M.P.L. Vergeer: Leeghwaterplein 27, Postbus 28120, 2502
KC Den Haag; *t* (070) 384 6868, *f* 384 6643
Humanitarian relief agency, over 500 local branches; funds
overseas aid projects; involved in caring for refugees in the
Netherlands. See also international Red Cross, p218. *Rode
Kruis Koerier* (6/yr). »94

● **Netherlands Committee for Multilateral Youth Work**
Suzette Dumfries: Postbus 15344, 1001 MH Amsterdam;
t (020) 626 2664, *f* 622 8590
Location: Prof. Tulpstraat 2. Anti-racist, multicultural
approaches to youth work; associated with EXIS international
youth centre, p209. »94

● **NIVON Jeugd en Jongeren**, NIVON JJ
Nieuwe Herengracht 119, 1011 SB Amsterdam; *t* (020) 626
9661, *f* 638 8511
Anti-racist youth NGO; no further information. »94

▌ **Organising Bureau of European School Student Unions**,
OBESSU
Nieuwezijds Voorburgwal 21-II, 1012 RC Amsterdam;
t (020) 623 4713, *f* 625 5814
International federation of youth movements. »94

● **Pax Christi**
Postbus 19318, 3501 DH Utrecht; *t* (030) 233 3346
Catholic humanitarian aid group. »95

● **Raad van Kerken** *(Council of Churches)*
[address unknown]
Main ecumenical forum; social policy concerns include
migrants, refugees, minority rights and ethnic relations. A
member of the ADO, p208. »93

✿ **Rotterdams Informatie Centrum**, RIC *(Rotterdam Information
Centre)*
Hoogstraat 110, 3011 PV Rotterdam; *t* (010) 417 2929
General information service on culture, employment,
accommodation, welfare and education; includes specialist
migrant information desk provided by Nederlands Migratie
Institut, above. »95

● **Sociaal en Cultureel Planbureau**, SCP *(Social and Cultural
Planning Office)*
Erna Hooghiemstra/Paul Tesser: Postbus 37, 2280 AA
Rijswijk; *t* (070) 319 8700, *f* 396 3000
Location: J.C. van Markenlaan 3. Documentation and research
on social affairs, including minorities' housing and socio-
economic status. *Sociaal en cultureel rapport*. »95

● **Sociaal Economische Raad**, SER *(Social and Economic
Council)*
[address unknown] 's Gravenhage
Government think tank. Research co-ordination, analysis,
advice on socio-economic policy; interests include migration,
minority employment. »94

● **Sociaal Wetenschappelijke Afdeling** *(Department of Social
Science)* Ministerie van Sociale Zaken en Werkgelegenheid
Dr Ruben Gowricharn: Postbus 1024, 3000 BA Rotterdam;
t (010) 453 3486, *f* 543 0646
Research division of the Ministry of Social Affairs and
Employment, p209; labour market, migration and ethnic
minority research. »94

● **Stichting Oecumenische Hulp**, SOH: Dutch Interchurch Aid
H. Zomer: Cornelis Houtmanstraat 17, Postbus 13077,
3507 LB Utrecht; *t* (030) 271 0614, *f* 271 7814
Overseas development aid, humanitarian relief, development
education; counselling and welfare services for refugees and
displaced persons in the Netherlands and abroad. A member
agency of VluchtelingenWerk, p147. *SOH Berichten* (4/yr).»95

● **Stimulering Internationale Uitwisseling Horeca**, SIH *(Horeca
International Exchange Promotion)*
Jacob Bellamyhove 34, 2717 WR Zoetermeer; *t* (079) 711725
Promotes cross-national temporary employment and training
placements for Dutch and foreign workers in the hotel and
catering trades. »94

● **Terre des Hommes**, TdH
Van Speijkstraat 3, 2518 EV Den Haag; *t* (070) 363 7940
Dutch affiliate of a Swiss-based humanitarian organisation,
p217, with an interest in refugee issues. »94

● **Bernard Van Leer Foundation**
Postbus 82334, 2508 EH Den Haag; *t* (070) 351 2040,
f 350 2373
Childcare and educational charity targetting socially and
culturally disadvantaged children, including migrants and
refugees, in Belgium, France, Germany and Holland, and in
some 30 other countries where the parent multinational
corporation operates. »93

◆ **Vereniging voor Rechtshulp** *(Union for Rights Advice)*
T.L. Tan: [address unknown]
National network of legal and consumer rights, including
immigration rights, advice agencies. »93

✿ **Vreemdelingendienst** *(Aliens Service)*
Doelwater 5, 3011 AH Rotterdam; *t* (010) 424 2581
Official agency responsible for handling residence permit
applications, processing asylum applications, monitoring
foreign residents and liaison with national and ethnic
organisations; see Directie Vreemdelingenzaken, p208. »95

● **Vrijwillige Internationale Aktie**, VIA *(Voluntary International
Action)*
M. van Bouwdijk Bastiaansestraat 56, 1054 SP Amsterdam;
t (020) 689 2760, *f* 618 4469
Anti-racist voluntary service group. See ICVD, p209. »94

✿ **Wereldfederalisten Beweging Nederland**, WFBN *(World
Federalist Movement, Holland)*
Postbus 77846, 1070 AK Amsterdam; *t* (020) 620 1613,
f 664 3246 »94

● **Working Group Indigenous Peoples**
Jacques de Kort: [address uncertain] Postbus 4098, 1009
AB Amsterdam; *t* (020) 693 8625 »90

▌ **Youth for Development and Co-operation**, YDC
Overschiestraat 9, 1062 HN Amsterdam; *t* (020) 614 2510,
f 617 5545 »94

NORWAY 47

● **Amnesty International Norge**, AI
Maridalsveien 87, 0461 Oslo 4; *t* 2238 0032
Human rights pressure group mainly concerned with political
prisoners abroad, see p220, and with asylum rights in Norway
in that context; provides information and documentation on
refugees' countries of origin. »95

● **Development Aid from People to People**, DAPP: and
Travelling High School
Box 394, 2601 Lillehammer
International solidarity; development education, volunteer
training and placements in community-based projects in
Mozambique. »95

● **Institutt for Menneskerettigheter**: Norwegian Institute of
Human Rights
Grensen 18, 0159 Oslo 1; *t* 2242 1360, *f* 2242 2542
General human rights concerns, including refugee and minority
rights. »94

● **Landsrådet for Norske Ungdomsorganisasjoner**, LNU
(Norwegian National Youth Council) and Atlantis Youth
Exchange
Rolf Hofmosgate 18, 0655 Oslo; *t* 2267 0043, *f* 2268 6808
Umbrella group for youth organisations; participated in the
1994-95 European Youth Campaign Against Racism, p197.
The Atlantis foundation promotes international and inter-
cultural youth exchange programmes. »94

● **National Peace Council**
Fredrik S. Heffermehl: [address unknown] Oslo
Internationalism, human rights, conflict resolution. »94

◆ **Norges Rode Kors**: Norwegian Red Cross
Holberggt. 1, Postboks 6875, St Olavs plass, 0130 Oslo 1
Normal range of national Red Cross humanitarian activities;
housing for asylum seekers, lobbying for migrant and refugee
rights. See international movement, p218. »95

● **Norsk Folkehjelp** *(Norwegian People's Aid)*
Torggt. 16, 0181 Oslo 1; *t* 2240 1050
Humanitarian aid agency; provides housing and welfare
support to asylum seekers. »95

- **Det Norske Menneskerettighetsfond** *(Norwegian Human Rights Foundation)*
c/o AIS/LO, Youngsgt. 11, 0181 Oslo 1; *t* 2240 1104, *f* 2240 1100
International protection of human rights, especialy in conflict situations and in developing countries. Founded 1988 to act as an umbrella group for the LO labour federation, the Red Cross, Save the Children and other national organisations.»93
- **Det Norske Menneskerettighetshuset** *(Norwegian Human Rights Centre)* and Helsingforskomitee: Helsinki Committee
Urtegate 50, 0608 Oslo; *t* 2257 1220, *f* 2257 0088
Promotion and defence of international standards of human rights.   »94

POLAND 48

- **Polska Rada Mlodziezy**, PRM *(Polish Youth Council)*
ul. Litewska 2-4, 00581 Warszawa; *t* (02) 628 4222, *f* 628 2315
National umbrella organisation for youth movements.   »94
- ▌ **Swiatowy Zwiacek Miast Pokuje**, SZMP: World Union of Citizens for Peace
ul. Miodowa 6-8, 00251 Warszawa; *t* (02) 635 0908, *f* (022) 201178
Internationalism, cross-cultural understanding.   »94
- ♦ **United Nations High Commissioner for Refugees**, UNHCR
2 Aleja Roz, 00556 Warszawa; *t* (02) 628 6930, 912 1448, *f* 625 6124
Refugee status and protection. See also regional office in Vienna, p188, and head ofice, p219.   »95

PORTUGAL 351

- ♦ **Alto Comissariado das Nações Unidas para os Refugiados,** ACNUR: United Nations High Commissioner for Refugees, UNHCR: Branch Office for Portugal
Adelmo Risi Valdettaro, Protection Officer: Rua Latina Coelho, Edifício Avis, Bloco A3, 17° esq., 1050 Lisboa; *t* (01) 579862, 579717, *f* 579812, *Tx* 41812 UNHCR, *Tg* HICOMREF Lisboa
Refugee status, protection and welfare; see p219.   »95
- **Amnistia Internacional—Secção Portuguêsa**
Carla Grijo: Fialho Almeida 13-1° D, 1070 Lisboa; *t* (01) 386 1652, *f* 386 1782
Address also listed (1994) as Rua Martens Ferrão 34-3° D, 1016 Lisboa. National section of human rights organisation focussing on political prisoners and capital punishment, see p220; Portuguese section active on refugee issues.   »95
- **Assembleia da República:** Emigrant representatives
Largo das Cortes, 1200 Lisboa; *t* (01) 395 3620
Four seats in the Chamber of Deputies are reserved for the emigrant vote, of which two are for emigrants within Europe; these have recently been held by Fernando Figueiredo (Partido Social Democrata), *t* (01) 600855, 600687, and Caio Roque (Partido Socialista), *t* 660141, 673224, 673424.   »95
- **Assistencia Médica Internacional**, AMI *(International Medical Aid)*
Dr Fernando Nobre, President: José Patrocín 49, 1900 Lisboa; *t* (01) 837 1667
International emergency medical aid; development projects, often involving refugees and displaced people.   »95
- **Associação de Cooperação e Amizade**
Avenida da Liberdade 232-1° D, Lisboa; *t* (01) 560912   »90
- **Associação Portuguêsa dos Direitos Cidadãos** *(Portuguese Association for Citizens' Rights)*
Augusto Rosa 66-2° D, 1100 Lisboa; *t* (01) 888 3349   »95
- **Associação Portuguêsa para o Serviço Social Internacional,** APSSI *(Portuguese Association for International Social Service)*
Camilo Cesaltina Lopes: Rua da Boavista 81-4° dta, 1200 Lisboa; *t* (01) 396 8700
Branch of international welfare agency; see ISS, p219.   »95
- ♦ **Cáritas—União de Caridade Portuguêsa** *(Caritas, Portuguese Charity Union)* Sector Social Emigração *(Emigration Division)*
Maria Delfino Trinidade: Estrada do Forte de Ameixoeira 19, 1750 Lisboa; *t* (01) 759 6046, *f* 759 6240
Catholic relief agency, see p230; concerns include emigrant welfare, and the needs of immigrants and refugees.   »95
- ✿ ≡ Cáritas Diocesana de Lisboa: Avenida Sid Pais 20-5° D, 1050 Lisboa; *t* (01) 573386   »95
- ✿ ≡ Centro Acolhimento: Lt 13 A/B Manuela Porto, 1500 Lisboa; *t* (01) 714 0054   »95

- ▌ **Centro Norte-Sud:** North-South Centre: Centre Nord-Sud: European Centre for Global Interdependence and Solidarity
Avenida da Liberdade 229-4°, 1250 Lisboa; *t* (01) 522903, *f* 353 1329
Agency of the Council of Europe, p197. Promotes global citizenship education, both in the formal educational system and through twinning and exchange programmes between schools, towns and NGOs. Opposes racism, xenophobia, antisemitism and intolerance and promotes inter-cultural understanding and international solidarity. Has liaison offices in Tunis and Nicosia.   »95
- ✿ **Centro Regional de Segurança Social—Lisboa** *(Lisbon Regional Social Security Centre)* Serviço de Apoio a Refugiados, SAR *(Refugee Support Service)*
Avenida Estados Unidos de América 37, 1700 Lisboa; *t* (01) 847 0410
Under the Ministério dos Assuntos Sociais; welfare and social integration of refugees, working in liaison with UNHCR, left. See Núcleo Apoio a Timorenses, p116.   »95
- **Civitas—Associação da Defesa e Promoção dos Direitos dos Cidadãos** *(Society for Defence and Promotion of Civil Rights)*
Helena Cidade Moura: Rua de S. Marçal 77-79, 1200 Lisboa; *t* (01) 342 4528, 468 1374, *f* 346 0554
Human rights pressure group. Information, educational materials, campaigns. *Boletim Civitas* (4/yr).   »95
- **Comissão Europeia:** European Commission
Centro Europeu Jean Monnet, Largo Jean Monnet 1-10°, 1250 Lisboa; *t* (01) 541144, 315 1360, *f* 554397, *Tx* 18810 COMEUR P
National representative office of the Commission, p189; provides information on EU policies, legislation and programmes.   »95
- **Conselho Português para a Paz e a Cooperação**
Rua Rodrigo Fonseca 56-2°, 1250 Lisboa; *t* (01) 386 3375»95
- ♦ **Conselho Português para os Refugiados**, CPR: Portuguese Refugee Council, and European Legal Network on Asylum, ELENA
Tito de Morais Mendes: Rua Viriato 27-2° A, 1050 Lisboa; *t* (01) 315 9847, 353 7692, *f* 387 1196
Deals with asylum requests, refugee status and protection; succeeds the Comissão Consultativo para os Refugiados established by 1981 Decree. Legal advice and support group co-ordinated by Susana Carvalho Amador, who is the national contact for the ELENA lawyers' group, p154.   »95
- **Departamento para os Assuntos Europeus e Relações Externas** *(European Affairs and External Relations Division)*
Ministério de Emprêgo e Segurança Social
Plaça de Londres 2-10°, 1000 Lisboa; *t* (01) 847 0021
Labour and Social Security Ministry office handling intra-EU mobility of labour issues.   »95
- **Departamento de Relações Internacionais e Convenções de Segurança Social**, DRICSS *(International Relations and Social Security Conventions Department)*
Rua da Junqueira 112, 1399 Lisboa Codex; *t* (01) 362 1633
Government office responsible for social security of emigrant and returning workers. *Boletim.*   »95
- **Federação de Mulheres para a Paz Mundial** *(Women's Federation for World Peace)*
Artilharia 39-4°, 1250 Lisboa; *t* (01) 388 9110
Peace, civil rights, social justice pressure group.   »95
- ♦ **Instituto de Apoio á Emigração e as Comunidades Portuguêsas**, IAECP *(Institute for Support to Emigrants and Portuguese Communities)*
Dra Maria Rita Andrade Gomes, President: Avenida Visconde Valmor 19, 1000 Lisboa; *t* (01) 763081-82
Maria Luísa Pinto. Founded 1980 by Ministério dos Negócios Estrangeiros, foreign ministry; researches emigration from Portugal, and supports Portuguese migrant workers and communities abroad; there is a Serviço Informativo, ext. 47, and a Serviço de Apoio Jurídico e Social, exts. 20, 22; local *delegações* in Aveiro, Braga, Bragança, Chaves, Coimbra, Faro, Guarda, Porto (English: Oporto), Viseu, Madeira (at Funchal) and the Azores (at Angra). *Migrações* (occasional).   »94
- **Instituto Português da Juventude** *(Portuguese Youth Institute)*
Avenida Liberdade 194, 1250 Lisboa; *t* (01) 315 1961, *f* 315 1959
National youth agency; Gabinete de relacões comunitárias e internacionais handles relations with foreign counterparts.»95
- **Ministério da Administração Interna** *(Ministry of Home Affairs)*
Praça do Comércio, 1100 Lisboa; *t* (01) 364521
Responsible for welfare and protection of refugees.   »85
- **Ministério da Justiça** *(Ministry of Justice)*
Praça do Comércio, 1100 Lisboa; *t* (01) 360786
Asylum requests, decisions on refugee status.   »85

✧ **Movimento Cristão para a Paz**, MCP *(Christian Peace Movement)*
Praça da Republica 18-3°, 3000 Coimbra; *t* (039) 27459, *f* 34336
Concerns include racism, human rights, refugees. »94
● **Organização Internacional para as Migrações**, OIM: International Organization for Migration, IOM (formerly Comité Intergovernamental para as Migrações)
Rua Cámara Pestana 23, 1198 Lisboa Codex; *t* (01) 520011, 547691
National office of the planned migration agency, p218. »90
✧ ≡ Rua Alexandre Herculano 296-2°, 4000 Porto »90
◆ **Polícia de Estrangeiros**
Rua Conselheiro José Silvestre Ribeiro, Lote 22, 1600 Lisboa; *t* (01) 714 1144 »90
✧ **Presbyterian Church Women's Group**
M.A. da Conceição Marcelino: Avenida d. Afonso Henriques, 28 r/c esq., 2870 Moutijo; *t* (01) 231 0708 »90
◆ **Secretaria de Estado da Emigração e Comunidades Portuguêsas** *(Ministry for Emigration and Portuguese Abroad)*
Dr Manuel Correia de Jesus, Secretary of State: Palácio das Necesidades, Largo do Rilvas, 1300 Lisboa; *t* (01) 675795, 672818
Government department for emigration policy and relations with emigrant communities; works through IAECP, p211. »90
◆ **Serviço de Estrangeiros** *(Aliens Service)*
Avenida António Augusto de Aguiar 18, 1000 Lisboa; *t* (01) 554040, 554047, 554049
Asylum requests, refugee status and protection. »83
◆ **Serviço de Fronteiras e Imigração** *(Borders and Immigration Service)*
[address unknown] Lisboa
Controls immigration, manages the registration of aliens. »94
✧ **União das Instituções de Solidariedade Social**
Rua Oliveira Monteiro 356, 4000 Porto »94

ROMANIA 40

● **Asociatia Pentru Apararea Drepturilor Omuli in Romania**
Calea Victoriei 120, Bucuresti; *t* (01) 312 4528, *f* 312 1528
A youth NGO listed in the United directory of anti-racist groups; no further information. »94
● **Soros Foundation for an Open Society**
Narcisa Cimpoca: PO Box 22196, Bv. Ana Ipatescu, 71102 Bucuresti, Sect. 1; *t* (01) 650 3473, *f* 312 7053
National office of the US-based philanthropic trust promoting democratic reform in Central Europe. »94
◆ **United Nations High Commissioner for Refugees**, UNHCR
Strada Mihai Eminescu 124, Corpul A, apt. 3, 79362 Bucuresti; *t* (1) 210 1596, 611 0057, *f* 210 1594
Refugee status and protection; main listing p219. »95
● **Young Generation Society of Romania**, STGR
Dristorului 102, bloc 10, et. 8, ap. 79, Bucuresti, Sect. 3
Anti-racist, anti-fascist youth NGO. »94

RUSSIA 7

◆ **United Nations High Commissioner for Refugees**, UNHCR
Seleznevskaya ul. 11a (1), 101489 Moskva; *t* (095) 284 3220, 284 3292, *f* 973 1960
Refugee status and protection; see headquarters, p219. »95

SAN MARINO 39

✧ **Consiglio Nazionale della Gioventù Sammarinese**, CNGS *(San Marino National Youth Council)*
via Ca' dei Lunghi, 47031 Cai Lungo; *t* (0549) 903970, *f* 882301
Umbrella organisation for the republic's youth movements. »94

SERBIA 381

✧ **Council for the Defence of Human Rights and Freedoms**
[address unknown] Pristina, Kosovo
Information, campaigns on human rights issues, including rights of ethnic Albanians in Kosovo. »93

◆ **United Nations High Commissioner for Refugees**, UNHCR: Office in the Former Republic of Yugoslavia
58 Proleterskih Brigada, 11000 Beograd; *t* (11) 444 3746, 444 4244, *f* 444 9707, *Tx* 12458 UNHCR YU, *Tg* HICOMREF Belgrade
Refugee status and protection; based Switzerland, p219. »95

SLOVAKIA 42

◆ **United Nations High Commissioner for Refugees**, UNHCR
PO Box 39, 81011 Bratislava; *t* (7) 210 3637-38, *f* 210 3686, *Tg* HICOMREF Bratislava
Location: Pribinova 25. Refugee status and protection. See also regional office in Austria, p188; head office, p219. »95

SLOVENIA 386

◆ **Civic Link Center for Human Rights** and European Legal Network on Asylum, ELENA
Renata Marmulaku: Ciril Metodov Trg 7, 61000 Ljubljana; *t* (061) 133 4191, *f* 133 5111
Broad range of human rights concerns, including minority and refugee rights. Tanja Petovar is national contact for the ELENA network of asylum law practitioners, p154. »95
● **Drustvo za prostovoljno delo MOST—SCI Slovenia**
Breg 12, 61000 Ljubljana; *t* (061) 125 3244, *f* 224943
Concerns include anti-racism and refugee rights. »94
◆ **United Nations High Commissioner for Refugees**, UNHCR
Trg Republika 3/12, 61000 Ljubljana; *t* (061) 156133, 156142, *f* 125 6170
Refugee status and protection; see main listing, p219. »95

SPAIN 34

✧ **Abogados sin Fronteras** *(Lawyers without Borders)*
Conde de Arana 2-3ª, 46004 Valencia
Human rights group. »94
● **Agencia Española para Becas ERASMUS** *(Spanish Agency for ERASMUS Grants)*
Secretaría General, Consejo de Universidades, Ciudad Universitaria s/n, 28071 Madrid; *t* (91) 549 6678, 549 7700, *f* 543 4550
Administers the system promoting mobility of students and academic staff between EU countries, see p190. »94
● **Agencia Española de Cooperación Internacional**, AECI *(Spanish Institute for International Co-operation)*
Miguel Angel Moratinos: avenida de los Reyes Católicos 4, 28040 Madrid; *t* (91) 244 0600, 583 8310
An agency of the foreign ministry's Secretaría de Estado para la Cooperación Internacional; co-ordinates development assistance and emergency relief, promotes cultural exchange and scientific co-operation with developing countries. See Instituto Hispano-Arabe de Cultura, p11. »94
◆ **Alto Comisionado de las Naciones Unidas para los Refugiados**, ACNUR: United Nations High Commissioner for Refugees, UNHCR
Guilherme Da Cunha: Apd° de Correos 36121, 28020 Madrid; *t* (91) 556 3649, 556 3503, emergencies 555 8631-32, *f* 555 8632, *Tx* 23255 ACNUR, *Tg* HICOMREF Madrid
Location: avenida General Perón 32, 28034 Madrid; Refugee status and protection, anti-racism, human rights, social and economic integration; funds refugee aid programmes via Red Cross, p214, and CEAR, p150. See headquarters, p219. »95
● **Amnistía Internacional Sección Española** *(Amnesty International Spanish Section)*
[address uncertain] Donoso Cortés 22-1°, 28015 Madrid; *t* (91) 593 0233, *f* 594 1953
Also listed (1994) at Gran Vía 6-5°, 28013 Madrid, *t* 531 2509, *f* 531 7114. Human rights pressure group, see p220, focussing on political prisoners; Spanish section also works on refugee issues. Branches throughout the Spanish State. »94
● **Asociación contra la Tortura**, ACT *(Association Against Torture)*
Fernando Salas, President: calle Dr Esquerdo 22-4° izq., 28028 Madrid; *t* (91) 309 3454
Defence of civil liberties, campaigns against the use of torture and inhuman or degrading treatment. In 1993 it monitored 267 cases, involving 448 officials. »95

● **Asociación Española de Cooperación Europea e Intercambio Cultural** *(Spanish Association for European Co-operation and Cultural Exchange)*
avenida Gran Vía 43, Madrid; *t* (91) 541 3205   »95

● **Asociación Medicus Mundi de España**
calle Sánchez Barcaiztegui 38, Madrid; *t* (91) 552 2063, *f* 552 5438
International medical aid charity serving refugees and victims of disaster.   »95

✿ **Asociación Pro-Derechos Humanos de Bizkaia**, APDH *(Vizcaya Human Rights Association)*
Alameda de Relkade 6-1° dcha, 48003 Bilbo, Bizkaia, Euskadi; *t* (94) 423 5848
Human rights information, public education, campaigns and assistance to individuals, including migrants and refugees.»95

● **Asociación Pro Derechos Humanos de España**, APDHE *(Spanish Association for Human Rights)*
Carmen Sacristais Zundo: calle José Ortega y Gasset 77-2° A, 28006 Madrid; *t* (91) 402 2312, 402 3204, 404 2231, *f* 402 8499
Human rights pressure group; anti-racism, legal advice, international solidarity.   »95

✿ **Asociación Pro Derechos Humanos**
calle Angel 13 bajo, 18002 Granada; *t* (958) 520023   »95
✿ ≡ Cristobal Morales 10, 41001 Sevilla; *t* (95) 421 2122»95

✿ **Asociación para la Promoción e Inserción Profesional** *(Association for Integration and Employment)*
Trentch 25-3ª-3ª, 46110 Valencia
Promotes training and employment opportunities for immigrants and other marginalised groups.   »94

● **Associació Catalana d'Amistat i Cooperació**, ACAC *(Catalan Association for Friendship and Co-operation)*
José María Acero Gallego: Comtessa de Sobradiel 1-2° B, 08002 Barcelona, Catalunya; *t* (93) 301 7476
International solidarity, development education.   »94

♦ **Cáritas Española**: Servicios Centrales
calle San Bernardo 99, 28015 Madrid; *t* (91) 455 5300, *f* 593 4882
Catholic relief agency with a wide range of welfare activities generally directed at the poorest and most marginalised in society; consequently many of its activities benefit migrant and refugee communities. These include refugee legal advice, housing and welfare assistance through CEAR, p150, and on its own account, assistance with form-filling and relations with official bodies, language classes and orientation of immigrants, visits to foreign prisoners, emergency financial assistance. It has many diocesan and local sections: addresses not listed below available from this office. See Caritas Internationalis, p230; and local migrant services such as Almería Acoge, p149, and Huelva Acoge, La Rioja Acoge, Las Palmas Acoge, and the Delegaciones Diocesanas de Migraciones, all p151.»94

✿ ≡ plaza de Recife s/n, 15004 A Coruña, Galicia; *t* (981) 269066, 269549, 269839
Also at Magdalena 221, 15402 El Ferrol, *t* 352339; and at plaza de la Inmaculada 5, 15704 Santiago de Compostela, *t* 581542.   »94

✿ ≡ avenida de Aguilera 65, 03007 Alacant/Alicante, Valencia; *t* (96) 511 4836, 511 4971   »94

✿ ≡ Hermanos Jiménez 13, 02004 Albacete; *t* (967) 222600, 221246   »95

✿ ≡ San Juan de la Cruz 8, 05001 Avila; *t* (918) 221847 »94

✿ ≡ avenida Antonio Mesa Campos 13 bajo, 06005 Badajoz; *t* (924) 231157, 231172   »94

✿ ≡ plaza Nueva 1, 08002 Barcelona; *t* (93) 301 3550
Also at Vic, *t* 886 1752; and see Departament de Migració de Cáritas Diocesana, p151.   »94

✿ ≡ Lersundi kalea 13-1°, 48009 Bilbo, Bizkaia, Euskadi; *t* (94) 423 4518
Has worked since 1992 with immigrants; welfare, training and employment advice and information, housing aid, small grants, language classes through Bilbo Etxezabal, p149. Parish branches throughout Bizkaia.   »94

✿ ≡ Eduardo Martínez Campo 10, 09003 Burgos; *t* (947) 202214, 204841   »94

✿ ≡ Cuesta de Aldana 1, 10003 Cáceres; *t* (927) 248739
Also at Plasencia, *t* 411553.   »94

✿ ≡ Hospital de Mujeres 26, 11001 Cádiz; *t* (956) 214885
Also at Jerez, *t* (956) 320181.   »95

✿ ≡ plaza Africa s/n, 11701 Ceuta; *t* (956) 515554
Branch in Spanish North African territory.   »94

✿ ≡ Caballeros 7, 13003 Ciudad Real; *t* (926) 251213, 251290   »94

✿ ≡ pza Colón 3, 2ª-4°, 14001 Córdoba; *t* (957) 481875 »95

✿ ≡ avenida de la República Argentina 25, 16002 Cuenca; *t* (966) 222515   »94

✿ **Cáritas Española**: Donostia (San Sebastián)
paseo Salamanca 2, entreplanta, 20003 Donostia, Gipuzkoa, Euskadi; *t* (943) 421661, 424049
Migrant services include information, employment advice, small grants. Parish branches throughout Gipuzkoa.   »94

✿ ≡ Francisco Ciurana 10, 17002 Girona, Catalunya; *t* (972) 204980   »94

✿ ≡ Dr Azpitarte 3, 18012 Granada; *t* (958) 202611, 201261
Also at Guadix, *t* (958) 660430.   »95

✿ ≡ avenida de Venezuela 7, 19005 Guadalajara; *t* (911) 220027   »94

✿ ≡ Costanilla de Ricafort s/n, 22002 Huesca; *t* (974) 223179
Also at Barbastro, *t* 310031, and Jaca, *t* 360188.   »95

✿ ≡ Carlos III, 27-1°, 07800 Ibiza; *t* (971) 311762   »95

✿ ≡ Generalísimo 7, 24003 León; *t* (987) 255457
Also at Astorga, *t* 616796.   »94

✿ ≡ plaza San José 2, 25002 Lleida; *t* (973) 268705
Also at episcopal offices, Seo de Urgel, *t* 351263; and sub-office at Solsona, *t* 312501.   »94

✿ ≡ Cáritas Diocesana: calle Hospital Viejo 13, 26001 Logroño; *t* (941) 252340, 247529
See also La Rioja Acoge, p152.   »94

✿ ≡ pza El Ferrol 3-3° izq., 27001 Lugo; *t* (982) 242009 »94

✿ ≡ Cáritas Diocesana: calle Martín de los Heros 21, 28008 Madrid; *t* (91) 247 1403, 542 0100   »94

✿ ≡ Rampa de La Aurora 1-3ª, 29015 Málaga; *t* (952) 228 7250
See also Málaga Acoge, p151.   »95

✿ ≡ Sagrado Corazón de Jesús, 29802 Melilla; *t* (952) 684200
Branch in Spanish North African territory.   »94

✿ ≡ Barahundillo 2, 30001 Murcia; *t* (968) 211186   »94

✿ ≡ plaza Obispo Cesáreo s/n, 32005 Ourense, Galicia; *t* (988) 236819   »94

✿ ≡ Rosal 63 bajos, 33009 Oviedo; *t* (985) 210627   »95

✿ ≡ pza Carmelitas 2 b, 34005 Palencia; *t* (988) 743035 »94

✿ ≡ Seminario 4, 07001 Palma, Mallorca; *t* (971) 716288»95

✿ ≡ San Antón 8-1° izq., 31001 Pamplona; *t* (948) 225908
Also at Muro 8, 31500 Tudela, *t* 826859.   »94

✿ ≡ Benito Corbal 17-2° izq., 36002 Pontevedra, Galicia; *t* (986) 844259, 852417
Also at Edificio Alegre, 36201 Vigo, *t* 223086.   »94

✿ ≡ Monroy 2, 37001 Salamanca; *t* (923) 269698, 269785
Also at Ciudad Rodrigo, *t* 460693.   »94

✿ ≡ 18 de Julio 23 e/s, 38004 Santa Cruz, Tenerife; *t* (922) 277212   »95

✿ ≡ Rualasal 4 e/s, 39001 Santander; *t* (942) 227809
See also Cantabria Acoge, p149.   »95

✿ ≡ pza Obispo Ahedo 2, 12400 Segorbe; *t* (964) 110199»94

✿ ≡ San Agustín 4, 40001 Segovia; *t* (911) 432227   »94

✿ ≡ Don Remondo 15, 41004 Sevilla; *t* (954) 227216   »95

✿ ≡ San Juan 4, 42003 Soria; *t* (975) 212455   »94

✿ ≡ plaza de Palau 2, 43003 Tarragona; *t* (977) 233412
Also at Tortosa, *t* 441143.   »94

✿ ≡ San Pedro 9, 44001 Teruel; *t* (974) 602089   »95

✿ ≡ Castilla-La Mancha: Aljibes 12, 45002 Toledo; *t* (925) 223600   »94

✿ ≡ Cáritas Diocesana: Valencia, Departamento Migración: Fani Raga: Trinitarios 3, 46002 Valencia; *t* (96) 331 9205
See also Mesa de Entidades, an NGO umbrella group, p215.»94

✿ ≡ Simón Aranda 15, 47002 Valladolid; *t* (983) 202301 »94

✿ ≡ plaza Viriato 1, 49001 Zamora; *t* (988) 532629   »94

✿ ≡ plaza de la Seo 6-1°, 50001 Zaragoza; *t* (976) 294730
See also SOS Racismo, p174; Delegación Diocesana de Migraciones, p151. Sub-office at Calatayud, *t* 881130.   »95

✿ **Centro de Acogida a Refugiados** *(Refugee Reception Centre)* Instituto Nacional de Servicios Sociales, INSERSO
Julián Zamora Alonso: calle Luis Buñuel 2, Vallecas, 28038 Madrid; *t* (91) 777 7814, 777 7898
Part of INSERSO, p215; there is also a Centro de Acogida (reception centre) at Alcobendas, and a detention centre at Moratalaz.   »94

♦ **Centro Estatal de Servicio Social de Asilados y Refugiados**, CESSAR *(State Centre for Social Services to Asylum Applicants and Refugees)*
Teresa de Benavides Castro, Director: calle Andrés Mellado 31, 28015 Madrid; *t* (91) 243 4805
Formerly (or also) known as Centro de Servicio Social de Refugiados, Asilados y Desplazados, CESERAD; established 1984 by the Ministerio de Trabajo y Seguridad Social as part of the Instituto Nacional de Asistencia Social; specialist centre for social work, research, information, counselling and social integration of refugees and asylum seekers; *Estudios del CESSAR* (2/yr), *Refugiados* (12/yr), *Hoja del CESSAR* (24/yr), special studies, documentation.   »90

✿ **Centro Juventud y Europa** *(European Youth Centre)*
calle Doctor Zamenhoff 54 bajo, 46008 Valencia; *t* (96) 382
4395, *f* 382 4227
Promotes European awareness and internationalism.			»94
◆ **Comisaría General de Documentación** *(Commissariat-*
General for Documentation) Dirección General de Policía
Ministerio del Interior, calle General Pardiñas 90, 28006
Madrid; *t* (91) 402 8100, 402 8012
Police office responsible for the national identity document
system and other matters including registration of and
documentation on foreign residents, expulsion and arrest of
aliens, prevention and detection of illegal immigration, border
policing including ports and airports, and initial receipt of
asylum requests. The Comisaría operates through its Servicio
de Fronteras y Extranjeros (Borders and Foreigners Service),
which comprises sections for Foreign Residents, Passports,
Movements of Foreigners, and Asylum and Refugee matters.
Memoria (1/yr).			»94
● **Comisión Católica de Justicia y Paz** *(Catholic Commission*
for Justice and Peace) Comisión Diocesana de Madrid
calle Bailén 8, Madrid; *t* (91) 542 3190			»90
● **Comisión Europea:** European Commission
calle de Serrano 41-5°, 28001 Madrid; *t* (91) 435 1700,
f 576 0387, 577 2923, *Tx* 46818 OIP E
National representative office of the Commission, p189;
provides information on EU policy, legislation, programmes and
related matters.			»94
✿ ≡ Edificio Atlántico, planta 18, avenida Diagonal 407 bis,
08008 Barcelona, Catalunya; *t* (93) 415 8177, *f* 415 6311,
Tx 97524 BDC E			»94
● **Comisión Española de Cooperación con la UNESCO**
paseo Juan XXIII 5, 28040 Madrid			»90
Comisión Interministerial de Asilo y Refugio (Inter-Ministerial
Commission on Asylum and Refuge): see Dirección General
de Extranjería y Asilo, right
Comisiones Obreras, CCOO (Workers' Commissions labour
confederation): see p150, Centros de Información para
Trabajadores Extranjeros (CITEs; but do not confuse with
CITEs of UGT union); see also p151, Oficina de Asesoramiento
para Trabajadores Extranjeros y Emigrantes Retornados
● **Comité Internacional de Rescate**, CIR: International Rescue
Committee, IRC: also known as Oficina Internacional de
Rescate, OIR
calle Luchana 36-4° dcha, 28010 Madrid; *t* (91) 447 2872,
f 447 2321
A US-based intergovernmental organisation, p218, which
assists re-emigration of refugees to third countries.			»95
● **Confederación General del Trabajo**, CGT *(General Labour*
Confederation)
Xavier Carda: avenida del Cid 154 bajo, 46014 Valencia
Major trade union confederation, with migrant worker
members. *Libre Pensamiento* (4/yr), *Rojo y Negro* (12/yr).»94
◆ **Confederación Nacional de Trabajo**, CNT *(National*
Confederation of Labour)
avenida de Epalza 12-2°, 48005 Bilbo, Bizkaia, Euskadi;
t/f (94) 415 3880
Regional welfare office of one of the main trade union
confederations.			»94
● **Consejo de la Juventud de España**, CJE *(Spanish Youth*
Council)
plaza Comendadores 6, 28015 Madrid; *t* (91) 521 2619,
f 532 6529
Umbrella group for national youth organisations. Partner in
the 1994-95 European Youth Campaign Against Racism, p197.»94
● ≡ Grupo de Trabajo Emigración Europea: Alicia Manzana, Co-
ordinator: Monte Esquinza 42, 28010 Madrid; *t* (91) 419 7789
Study, advice and information on socio-economic and political
impact of emigration on youth, women and families.			»90
◆ **Consell General de l'Inmigració, Generalitat de Catalunya**
(Catalan Government General Council on Immigration)
plaza Sant Jaume s/n, 08002 Barcelona, Catalunya
Main Catalan government agency concerned with formulation
of regional policy towards migrants, and the provision or
adaptation of services.			»94
● **Consell Nacional de la Joventut de Catalunya**, CNJC
(Catalan National Youth Council)
Diagonal 430, 1er, 08037 Barcelona, Catalunya; *t* (93) 416
1685, *f* 415 2186
Umbrella organisation of youth agencies and organisations.»94
● **Coordinadora de ONGs para el Desarrollo** *(Co-ordination of*
Development NGOs)
calle Cartagena 22-2° izq., 28028 Madrid; *t* (91) 361 1096,
f 361 1145
Co-ordinates Spanish NGOs in development education,
humanitarian assistance to refugees and other fields.			»94

◆ **Cruz Roja Española** *(Spanish Red Cross)*: Asamblea Suprema
avenida Dr Federico Rubio y Gali 3, 28039 Madrid; *t* (91)
254 6986
Major national humanitarian aid agency; has specialist service
for refugees and migrants with its own Madrid office, see
p151, which also operates through a large number of local and
provincial branches and sections, some of which are listed
below. The branches also offer a range of other welfare and
medical services to the general public and particular groups,
and organise fundraising and voluntary relief work. See also
Gurutze Gorria, p151, and international Red Cross, p218. »94
✿ ≡ C. Enríquez s/n, 15004 A Coruña; *t* (981) 206490			»94
✿ ≡ avenida Novelda 28, 03010 Alacant/Alicante, Pais
Valenciá; *t* (96) 524 4811
Local branches in 15 suburbs and neighbouring towns,
including Altea, Benidorm, Javea and Villajoyosa.			»94
✿ ≡ Asamblea Provincial, San Antonio 19, 02004 Albacete;
t (967) 242977			»95
✿ ≡ N. Salmerón 28, 04004 Almería; *t* (951) 255325			»95
✿ ≡ carrer Joan d'Austria 120-124, 08002 Barcelona,
Catalunya; *t* (93) 485 2512
Also at avenida Vallvidrera 73, *t* 205 6215; and at
L'Hospitalet, *t* 333 4543.			»94
✿ ≡ avenida Delicias s/n, 10004 Cáceres; *t* (927) 210599»94
✿ ≡ Santa María de la Soledad 10, 11001 Cádiz; *t* (956)
270521			»95
✿ ≡ San José s/n, 12004 Castelló; *t* (964) 227597			»94
✿ ≡ P. Victoria s/n, 14001 Córdoba; *t* (957) 296483			»95
✿ ≡ plaza C. Sotelo 6, 16002 Cuenca; *t* (966) 229420			»94
✿ ≡ Escoriaza 8, 18002 Granada; *t* (958) 228740			»95
✿ ≡ Asamblea Provincial, avenida Venezuela 1, 19005
Guadalajara; *t* (911) 232043			»94
✿ ≡ pasaje C. Loarre s/n, 22002 Huesca; *t* (974) 242954 »95
✿ ≡ calle Alcalde M. Castaño 108, 24005 León; *t* (987)
216969			»94
✿ ≡ Beneficencia s/n, 26005 Logroño; *t* (941) 204064			»94
✿ ≡ avenida Madrid s/n, 27001 Lugo; *t* (982) 241908			»94
✿ ≡ P. Farola s/n, 29015 Málaga; *t* (952) 217009, 220188,
276312, 483023
Telephone numbers are: city office (address shown), the
provincial assembly, two local offices.			»95
✿ ≡ avda General Mola 21, 29804 Melilla; *t* (952) 682989
Covers the Spanish enclave on the Moroccan coast.			»94
✿ ≡ plaza de la Cruz Roja 1, 30003 Murcia; *t* (968) 220260
Also branch office, *t* 220451.			»94
✿ ≡ Asamblea Provincial de Asturias, Martínez Vigil 36,
33009 Oviedo; *t* (985) 229280			»95
✿ ≡ avenida Gaspar B. Arquitecte 73, 07120 Palma, Mallorca;
t (971) 760780, 752689			»95
✿ ≡ Yanguas y Miranda 3, 31002 Pamplona, Nafarroa;
t (948) 222766			»94
✿ ≡ Padre Gaite s/n, 36002 Pontevedra; *t* (986) 863386 »94
✿ ≡ Asamblea Provincial de Canarias, San Lucas 60, 38004
Santa Cruz, Tenerife; *t* (922) 246744			»95
✿ ≡ calle Marqués Hermida 23, 39009 Santander; *t* (942)
210703			»95
✿ ≡ A. Dios 6, 41004 Sevilla; *t* (95) 438 8231			»95
✿ ≡ calle Santo Domingo de Silos 1, 42002 Soria; *t* (975)
228977			»94
✿ ≡ avenida María Cristina 17, 43002 Tarragona; *t* (977)
223411			»90
✿ ≡ San Miguel 3, 44001 Teruel; *t* (974) 600386
Also Alcañiz sub-office, *t* 830204.			»95
✿ ≡ General Moscardó 6, 45001 Toledo; *t* (925) 216014 »94
✿ ≡ Cirilo Amorós 6, 46004 Valencia; *t* (96) 394 0257			»94
✿ ≡ Hernán Cortés 42, 49001 Zamora; *t* (988) 511842			»94
✿ ≡ Zaragoza, Asamblea Provincial: calle Sancho y Gil 8,
50001 Zaragoza; *t* (976) 216960, 224884
Among other humanitarian activities, provides advice and
assistance to refugees.			»94
◆ **Dirección General de Extranjería y Asilo** *(Directorate*
General for Alien Affairs and Asylum) Ministerio del Interior
[address unknown] Oficina de Asilo y Refugio, Madrid;
t (900) 150000
The Interior Ministry division responsible for the administration
of law in relation to foreigners, refugees and asylum seekers.
Processes asylum claims received through the Asylum and
Refuge Office in Madrid, and through provincial police stations
or Oficinas de Extranjería; issues temporary ID cards and, if
appropriate, Geneva Convention travel documents. Asylum
claims which are initially assessed as well founded are passed
up to the Comisión Interministerial de Asilo y Refugio (a body
representing the Interior and Justice ministries) for the drafting
of a recommendation, and eventually for final determination at
ministerial level.			»94

◆ **Dirección General de Migraciones** *(Migration Directorate)*
Ministerio de Asuntos Sociales
paseo del Pintor Rosales 44, 28071 Madrid; *t* (91) 547 5200
Now a branch of the Ministry of Social Affairs (formerly in the Ministry of Labour and Social Security). Information, policy development, programmes on migration and migrants; separate Subdirecciones Generales for immigration (*t* 548 0200) and Spanish emigration. Provides some funding for educational and welfare aid, advice, other services to (legal) immigrants. Priorities are reintegration of returning emigrants, in self-employment, employment or co-operative ventures; and the mobility of young workers, including participation in the EU's PETRA vocational training scheme, p192.   »94

● **Federación de Iglesias Evangélicas de España** *(Federation of Protestant Churches of Spain)*
José Cardoni Gregori: [address uncertain] calle Trafalgar 32, 28010 Madrid; *t* (91) 247 3170   »90

◆ **Foro de Inmigrantes** *(Immigrants Forum)*
[address unknown] Madrid
Officially-funded body created under the 1994 Plan for the Social Integration of Immigrants to co-ordinate government, NGO and migrant organisations' work.   »95

● **Fundació per la Pau** *(Peace Foundation)*
[address unknown] Barcelona, Catalunya   »90

● **Fundación Española para la Cooperación** *(Spanish Foundation for Co-operation)* and Solidaridad Internacional, SI
Angeles Yañez Barnuevo, Director: Glorieta de Quevedo 7-6° dcha, 28015 Madrid; *t* (91) 593 1113, 593 1141, *f* 448 4469
International development and humanitarian aid projects, including emergency assistance to refugees in Latin America, Turkey and Iraq. *Solidaridad Internacional* (3/yr).   »94

✿ **Gobernación Civil de Madrid, Sección Extranjeros** *(Aliens Section, Madrid Civil Administration)* (possibly obsolete)
paseo de las Delicias 76, 28045 Madrid   »83

✿ **Gurutze Gorria**: Cruz Roja: Red Cross
José María Olabarri kalea 6, 48001 Bilbo, Bizkaia, Euskadi; *t* (94) 424 7617, 423 3129
Humanitarian aid agency; see Cruz Roja Española, p214. Material and social aid to refugees and asylum seekers, including assistance with housing and employment.   »94
✿ ≡ paseo Zorroaga s/n, 20011 Donostia; *t* (943) 471267
Many branches elsewhere in Gipuzkoa.   »94

● **Institut de Drets Humans de Catalunya** *(Catalonia Human Rights Institute)*
[address unknown] Barcelona, Catalunya
Human rights group, with international concerns; sponsored conference with Council of Europe, p197. *Informatiu*.   »90

● **Instituto de la Juventud** *(Youth Institute)* and Youth for Europe
calle Ortega y Gasset 71, 28006 Madrid; *t* (91) 347 7800, *f* 402 2194
A body under the Ministerio de Asuntos Sociales, right; advises young people on employment matters, including working and training abroad. Youth for Europe, p191, promotes non-school exchanges and youth projects.   »94

● **Instituto Nacional de Empleo, INEM** *(National Institute for Employment)* Ministerio de Trabajo y Seguridad Social
calle Condesa de Venadito 9, 28027 Madrid; *t* (91) 585 9785, *f* 377 5887
Branch of the Ministry of Labour responsible (except in Euskadi and Catalunya) for employment and training issues, including production of labour market statistics, the local employment exchanges, careers counselling, job placement and unemployment benefits. Its services are available to all, including foreigners (but only if legally entitled to work) and returning emigrants. Participates in the EURES information network of EU employment services, p190. *Estadística de Empleo* (12/yr).   »94

● **Instituto Nacional de Servicios Sociales, INSERSO** *(National Institute of Social Services)*
calle Ginzo de Lima 58 c/ avenida Ilustración, 28049 Madrid; *t* (91) 347 8592-94, *f* 347 8595
Also listed (1990) at calle María de Guzmán 54, 28003 Madrid, *t* 534 6591, 534 3658. Agency of the Ministerio de Asuntos Sociales, right, responsible for delivery of social welfare services to the elderly, disabled people and refugees; works with ACNUR, p212, and CEAR, p150, on refugee counselling, integration, vocational guidance and employment issues. See also Centro de Acogida a Refugiados, p213. »94

✿ **Integral**
a/c CIEMEN, carrer Pau Claris 106 1er 1a, 08009 Barcelona, Catalunya; *t* (93) 302 0144, *f* 412 0890
Human rights organisation concerned with threatened tribal and other minorities worldwide. See CIEMEN, p150.   »94

● **Justícia i Pau** *(Justice and Peace)*
Arkady Oliveras: carrer Rivadeneyra 6, 10, 08002 Barcelona, Catalunya; *t* (93) 317 6177, *f* 412 5384
North-south relations, refugees, anti-racism.   »94
✿ ≡ Palau 2, 46001 Valencia   »94

◆ **Justicia y Paz** *(Justice and Peace)*
calle Francisco Silvela 77 bis-1° dcha, 28028 Madrid; *t* (91) 261 1214
Catholic episcopal agency; human rights, welfare advice, anti-racism.   »94
● ≡ and Coordinadora de ONGs de Euskadi: M. Fernández: calle Príncipe de Viana 1, esq. Anselma de Salces, 48007 Bilbo, Bizkaia, Euskadi; *t* (94) 446 7206
Catholic diocesan agency concerned with social justice questions; it operates an advice and welfare service. See also Bilbo Etxezabal, p149. The Coordinadora (*t* 437 8042) is an umbrella body for Basque voluntary groups.   »94

● *Kontrola Kontrolpean*
[address unknown] Donostia, Gipuzkoa, Euskadi
Basque human rights journal; concerns include policing, torture, migrant and refugee rights.   »95

● **Médicos Sin Fronteras, MSF-E** *(Doctors without Borders)*
Médecins sans Frontières Espagne
avenida Portal del Angel 1-1, 08002 Barcelona, Catalunya; *t* (93) 412 5252
Spanish section of international MSF, see p191; emergency medical aid around the world, especially to refugees and victims of conflict.   »94

◆ **Medicus Mundi**
Hnos García Noblejas 49, 28037 Madrid; *t* (91) 327 2535»94
✿ ≡ Elisa 14, 08023 Barcelona   »94
✿ ≡ calle Monasterio de Irache 44, 31001 Pamplona, Nafarroa; *t* (948) 277062
See also Asociación Medicus Mundi de España, p213.   »90

✿ **Mesa de Entidades—Colectivo de Organizaciones no Gobernamentales** *(Board of Associations—Collective of Voluntary Bodies)*
Trinitarios 3, 46014 Valencia; *t* (96) 391 9205
Co-ordination of local voluntary sector, including migrant, minority and solidarity groups. See also the local Cáritas Española, p213.   »94

● **Ministerio de Asuntos Sociales** *(Ministry of Social Affairs)*
calle José Abascal 39, 28003 Madrid; *t* (91) 347 7000
Asylum requests, refugee welfare; see also Centro de Acogida a Refugiados, p213, CEAR, p150, and Dirección General de Migraciones and INSERSO, left.   »90

● **Movimiento de Hermandad de Trabajadores, MHT** *(Workers' Brotherhood Movement)*
María Teresa Martín: calle Juan de Austria 9, 28010 Madrid; *t* (91) 447 3000, 445 2315, *f* 446 4292
Catholic workers' movement; solidarity, human rights. *A Hombros de Trabajadores; Más*.   »94

● **Movimiento por la Paz, el Desarme y la Libertad, MPDL** *(Movement for Peace, Disarmament and Freedom)*
calle Santa Catalina 8-2° dcha, 28014 Madrid; *t* (91) 429 7644, *f* 429 7373, 402 7110
Peace movement; internationalist, anti-racist policies; its journal had in 1992 a special edition on racism and xenophobia. *Tiempo de Paz* (4/yr).   »94

● **Oficina de Derechos Humanos** *(Human Rights Office)*
Ministerio de Asuntos Exteriores *(Foreign Ministry)*
plaza de la Provincia 1, 28011 Madrid; *t* (91) 266 4800, 266 5000
Formerly concerned with refugee and asylum casework, now handled by Asuntos Sociales; still concerned with broad migration and refugee policy issues.   »90

● **Organización Internacional para la Migración, OIM:** International Organization for Migration, IOM (formerly Comité Intergubernamental para las Migraciones)
calle San Bernardo 99 bis 7°, 28015 Madrid; *t* (91) 445 7116
Spanish section of the Swiss-based international body, p218, promoting planned migration.   »94

● **Prosalus: ONG para la Promoción de la Salud en Países en Desarrollo** *(Non-Governmental Organisation for Health Promotion in Developing Countries)*
Herreros de Tejada 3, 28016 Madrid; *t* (91) 564 9959
Promotion of health care, provision of medical staff and equipment to developing countries; some emergency relief work with refugees.   »94

✿ **Secretaría de Relaciones Culturales** *(Cultural Relations Secretariat)*
Josep M. Huguet y Reverter: Rambla de Santa Mónica 8, 08002 Barcelona, Catalunya; *t* (93) 318 5004, *f* 301 2234
Promotion of intercultural events; information, documentation, anti-racism.   »94

● Servicio Exterior de la Iglesia Evangélica *(External Service, Protestant Church)*
calle Noviciado 5a, 28008 Madrid; *t* (91) 231 3947
Activities include educational and other social assistance to refugees, partly through CEAR, p150. »83

♦ Servicio Social Internacional, SSI: International Social Service, ISS: Spanish Section
María Jesús Pérez: calle Condesa de Venadito 34, 28027 Madrid; *t* (91) 347 8171-74
National section of the INGO, p218, which assists individuals and families to resolve welfare problems involving more than one country, especially in cases of forced migration. »94

✷ Sindicat de Treballadors de l'Ensenyment, STEI
(Educational Workers' Union)
Pedro Polo Fernández: carrer Vinyassa 14, 07005 Palma, Mallorca; *t* (971) 460888, 467646, *f* 771200
Teachers' union with an interest in multicultural education. *Pissara* (6/yr). »94

● Fundación Solidaridad Democrática, SD *(Democratic Solidarity Foundation)*
paseo de las Delicias 59-2° dcha, 28045 Madrid; *t* (91) 239 3496
Also listed (1994) at calle Fuencarral 121-6°, 28004 Madrid, *t* 445 1310. *Boletín Informativo SD*. »94

● Solidaridad para el Desarrollo y la Paz, SODEPAZ *(Solidarity for Development and Peace)*
Francisco Calderón, Chairman: calle Pizarro 5, 28004 Madrid; *t* (91) 522 8091, *f* 523 3832
International solidarity; anti-racism, development education, aid projects in Latin America and Western Sahara, support for refugee rights and for returnees in El Salvador. *Cuadernos Africa-América Latina* (4/yr). »94
✷ ≡ La Nau 7-1ª C, 46003 Valencia »94

● Solidaridad, Educación y Desarrollo, SED *(Solidarity, Education and Development)*
Pepe Acal: calle Hnos García Noblejas 158, pto 3 1° A, 28037 Madrid; *t* (91) 327 2385, *f* 754 5970 »94

● Subdirección de Cooperación Internacional *(Sub-Directorate for International Co-operation)* Ministerio de Educación y Ciencia
paseo del Prado 28-2°, 28014 Madrid; *t* (91) 420 0889, 420 1659, *f* 420 3325
Education Ministry section for international affairs, including Spanish participation in the EU programmes LINGUA (language learning), NARIC (validation of foreign qualifications) and TEMPUS (East-West co-operation, p192), all of which are designed to assist international labour mobility. »94

● Unión General de Trabajadores—Sección Juventud, UGT *(Youth Section, General Workers' Union)*
calle Hortaleza 88, 28004 Madrid; *t* (91) 589 7600, *f* 589 7603
Trade union youth wing; concerns include anti-racism, and solidarity with migrants and refugees—see CITEs, p150. »94

SWEDEN 46

♦ Aliens Board
[address unknown] Stockholm
Makes final decisions on applications for asylum or right of residence. »95

● Amnesty International Sverige, AI
Box 23400, 10435 Stockholm; *t* (08) 729 0200, *f* 341608
Human rights, especially of those persecuted for political beliefs; asylum and refugee rights. See p220. »95

● Diakonia *(Pastoral Work)*
Älvsjö Gårdsväg 3, 12530 Älvsjö; *t* (08) 644 0425, *f* 640 3660
Protestant humanitarian relief/development agency; funding and practical help for projects involving refugees, displaced people, minorities and marginalised groups in Latin America, Asia, Africa; refugee/migrant settlement help in Sweden. »93

● Elevorganisationen i Sverige
Box 26064, 10041 Stockholm; *t* (08) 233393, *f* 213393
National youth NGO. »94

● Foundation for Human Rights
Artillerigatan 59, 11445 Stockholm »93

● Frivilligorganisationernas Fond för Mänskliga Rattigheten *(Voluntary Organisations' Fund for Human Rights)*
Karin Rohlin: Drottninggatan 101, 11360 Stockholm; *t* (08) 303150, *f* 303031
Financial and practical aid for human rights groups in developing countries, and for South-South NGO networking; anti-racism, refugee rights; scholarships for refugees. »95

● Hoppets Stjarna: Star of Hope International
Kärrsjö, 8954 Trehörningsjö; *t* (0662) 41060, *f* 41039
Humanitarian aid agency assisting refugees, displaced persons, street children, people with disabilities and others in Latin America, Africa, Asia and Eastern Europe. »93

♦ Indvandraverket *(State Immigration Board)*
[address unknown] Stockholm
Makes preliminary rulings on applications for asylum or right of residence. »95

● Landsrådet för Sveriges Ungdomsorganisationer, LSU: National Council of Swedish Youth Organisations
Kungsgatan 48-3tr, 11135 Stockholm; *t* (08) 201122, *f* 203530
Umbrella group for national youth NGOs; international solidarity and development education work involves co-operation with South African youth bodies. »94

♦ Ministry of Housing, Culture and Immigration
Leif Blomberg, Minister: [address unknown] Stockholm
Ministry responsible for all aspects of migration and refugee policy. »95

▌Nordic Council
Box 19506, Tyrgatan 7, 10432 Stockholm; *t* (08) 143420, *f* 117536
Organisation of delegates from the Nordic countries (Iceland, Norway, Sweden, Finland, Denmark and associated territories of the last two). Promotes co-operation and convergence in many areas; works through six standing committees, including one on legal matters which deals with refugee and asylum issues. See also Nordic Council of Ministers, p194. »93

✷ Olof Palmes Internationella Centrum
Box 3221, 10364 Stockholm; *t* (08) 210739, *f* 102375
Multicultural, anti-racist centre. »94

● Olof Palmes Minnesfond för internationella Förståelse
Sveavägen 68, 11134 Stockholm; *t* (08) 700 2600
Foundation promoting humanitarian and anti-racist causes.»94

● Pingst Missionens U-Landshjalp, PMU: Pentecostal Mission Aid for Developing Countries
Krossgatan 15, 12626 Vällingby; *t* (08) 739 0465, *f* 387315
Humanitarian aid and development agency active mainly in Africa and Asia; some of its projects involve Ethiopian, Afghan and Kurdish refugees. »93

● Rädda Barnen: Save the Children
Torsgatan 4, 10788 Stockholm; *t* (08) 698 9000, *f* 698 6829
Humanitarian aid targeted at needs of children; services to refugees in developing countries; see ISCA, p218. »95

✷ Saminourra
Nomadskolev. 26, 98235 Gällivare; *t* (0970) 16605, *f* 15555
Listed in the United directory (1994) as concerned with migrants. Possibly represents the Sami (Laplander) nomads of the north? »94

● Stiftelsen för Internationelt Ungdomsutbyte, SIU *(Foundation for International Youth Exchange)*
Kungsgatan 48, 11135 Stockholm; *t* (08) 201980, *f* 203530
Foundation associated with the national youth council. »94

● Svenska FN-Förbundet: Swedish United Nations Association
Skolgränd 2, Box 15115, 10465 Stockholm; *t* (08) 644 9835, *f* 641 8876
International solidarity, human rights, development education; 150 local branches. »93

● Svenska Kyrkans Mission, SKM: Church of Sweden Mission
Sysslomansgatan 4, Box 297, 75105 Uppsala; *t* (018) 169500, *f* 169640
Lutheran missionary society with extensive humanitarian relief and development aid activities, including assistance to refugees and migrants in the Middle East, Africa and Central America. »93

● Svenska Röda Korsets Ungdomsförbund: Swedish National Red Cross Society
Östhammarsgatan 70, Box 27316, 10254 Stockholm; *t* (08) 665 5600, *f* 783 6692
Humanitarian aid at home and abroad, including refugee welfare assistance. See international Red Cross, p218. »95

● Sveriges Frikyrkosamråd: Free Church Council of Sweden
Box 1770, 11187 Stockholm; *t* (08) 453 6830, *f* 453 6829
Represents social concerns of the Church, including migrant, refugee and minority rights and welfare. »95

● Sveriges Socialdemokratiska Ungdomsförbund, SSU *(Swedish Social Democratic Youth League)*
Box 11544, 10061 Stockholm; *t* (08) 714 4800, *f* 714 9508
Youth wing of the labour party, with anti-racist, anti-fascist and human rights concerns. »94

● Ung Vänster *(Left Youth)*
Box 12660, 11293 Stockholm; *t* (08) 654 3200, *f* 650 8557
Location: Kungsgatan 84, 11135 Stockholm. Socialist youth group; anti-racism, refugee issues, human rights. »94

● **Ungdomsriksdag '94—För vår gemensamma framtid**
Box 7177, 10388 Stockholm; *t* (08) 453 5253, *f* 453 5254
Involved in organisation of a Youth Parliament. »94

▮ **United Nations High Commissioner for Refugees, UNHCR:**
Sweden, Nordic Countries and Baltic Republics office
Styrmansgatan 4, 11454 Stockholm; *t* (08) 783 5920, *f* 783
5903, *Tx* 8106198 UNHCR, *Tg* HICOMREF Stockholm
Refugee status and protection across the Nordic and Baltic
regions. In Denmark the UNHCR operates through its local
consultant, Dansk Flygtningehjælp, p132, which runs a
resettlement programme. See main UNHCR listing, p219.»95

SWITZERLAND *41*

● **Amnesty International—Schweizer Sektion/Section Suisse**
Alain Bovard, Refugee Co-ordinator: Postfach 1051,
Monbijoustrasse 26, 3001 Bern; *t* (031) 381 7966, *f* 382
3647, *Tx* 351327
Human rights pressure group founded 1971, focussing on
political prisoners, torture and the death penalty, but with an
interest in refugee issues and anti-racism. Documentation
centre on refugee countries of origin. See AI International
Secretariat, based in London, p220. *AI-Magazin* (German);
Liberté (French). »95
✿ **Anlaufstelle Baselland** *(Basle Starting Point)*
Oberfeldstrasse 11a, 4133 Pratteln; *t* (061) 821 4477, *f* 821
4583
Advice agency; asylum and refugee counselling service. »95
● **Antenna Internationale**
rue Grenus 10, 1201 Genève; *t* (022) 731 8036, *f* 731 9786
Promotion of human rights in developing countries;
international solidarity. »93
● **Brot für Alle**, BfA *(Bread for All)* and Evangelische Missions-
gesellschaft in Basel, EMG
Missionsstrasse 21, 4003 Basel; *t* (061) 268 8333 BfA,
268 8111 EMG; *f* 268 8268, *Tx* 963315 KEM CH
Both BfA, which raises money for Swiss Interchurch Aid, and
the larger parent organisation, the Basle Evangelical Mission
Society, support Third World projects involving refugees, and
engage in development education in Switzerland. »93
♦ **Caritas Schweiz/Suisse**
Jürg Krummenacher, Director: Postfach, Löwenstrasse 3,
6002 Luzern; *t* (041) 522222, *f* 512064
Major Catholic humanitarian and development aid agency
(over 500 staff) with projects in many countries, including
several working with refugees and returnees. In Switzerland,
many local or regional sections provide advice and practical
assistance to migrants and refugees, either as part of their
general charitable activities or through specialist services such
as the Beratungsstellen: see pp152-153. »95
✿ **Caritas Genève**
53 rue de Carouge, Case postale 148, 1211 Genève 4;
t (022) 320 2144, *f* 329 4745
Catholic charity; asylum advice service Monday and Friday
mornings. »95
✿ **Caritas Jura**
8 chemin de Bellevoie, Case postale 51, 2800 Delémont;
t (066) 225622, *f* 222340
Catholic charity, offers part-time asylum advice service. »95
✿ **Caritas Suisse—Fribourg**
rue de Botzet 2, 1705 Fribourg; *t* (037) 824171, *f* 824173
Catholic charity; asylum advice service on Mondays. »95
✿ **Caritas Valais**
19 rue de Loèche, 1950 Sion; *t* (027) 233502
Services to asylum seekers. »95
✿ **Caritas Vaud**
8 rue César-Roux, Case postale 237, 1000 Lausanne 17;
t (021) 320 3461, *f* 320 3401
Services to asylum seekers and refugees. »95
✿ **Centre Social Protestant, CSP** *(Protestant Welfare Centre)*
Case postale 177, 14 rue du Village Suisse, 1211 Genève 8;
t (022) 320 7811, *f* 329 8994
Charity; activities include support and advice for asylum
seekers. »95
✿ ≡ 11 rue Centrale, 2740 Moutier; *t* (032) 933221, *f* 932282
Social services in the Berne area, including assistance to
asylum seekers. »95
✿ ≡ 11 rue des Parcs, 2000 Neuchâtel; *t* (038) 251155,
f 213969
Welfare service; support for asylum seekers. »95
▮ **Commission on Global Governance**
Case postal 184, avenue Joli-Mont 11, 1211 Genève 28;
t (022) 798 2713, *f* 798 0147 »94

♦ **Croix-Rouge Suisse, CRS: Schweizerisches Rotes Kreuz,**
SRK: Swiss Red Cross
avenue de Rumine 2, 1005 Lausanne; *t* (021) 323 3131,
f 320 9557
Repatriation and third-country advice to asylum seekers. »95
▮ **Defence for Children International, DCI:** International
Secretariat
Case postal 88, rue de Varembé 1, 1211 Genève 20; *t* (022)
734 0558, *f* 740 1145, *Tx* 414128 DCI CH
Promotion of children's rights worldwide; 40 national member
organisations. Conferences, information, lobbying on issues
including refugee and migrant families. »94
✿ **Entraide Protestante Suisse, EPER** *(Evangelical Church
Social Services)*
Montmeillan 15, 1005 Lausanne; *t* (021) 312 6977
French-speaking counterpart of the HEKS, below; services
include support for asylum seekers. »95
▮ **Fédération Internationale Terre des Hommes, FITDH**
*(International Land of Mankind Federation, literally; only the
French name is used)*
rue Michel-Chauvet 22, 1208 Genève; *t* (022) 736 3372,
f 736 1510
International federation, and UN representative office, of nine
national TDH charities which fund child-centred development
and relief projects in the Third World and Eastern Europe,
including some work with refugees. Some welfare work with
migrants in Germany and France. (Affiliates include Swiss
TDH, Case postale 912, 1000 Lausanne 9, *t* (021) 653 6666;
has worked with Kurdish and Rwandese refugee children.)»96
● **Friedensbrugg—Friedensförderung Projekte in Konfliktgebiete**
(Bridge of Peace—Peace-Building Projects in Conflict Zones)
Florastrasse 12, 4057 Basel; *t* (061) 693 3160, *f* 691 5528
Conflict resolution group; its interests include racism and
refugee flows. »94
● **Hilfswerk der Evangelischen Kirchen der Schweiz, HEKS/
EPER** *(Swiss Evangelical Churches' Social Services)*
Flüchtlingsdienst (Refugee Service)
Anita Biedermann: Postfach 168, 8029 Zürich; *t* (01) 422
4455, *f* 422 4448
Location: Forchstrasse 282, 8027 Zürich. Church-funded
social work body; refugee assistance, reception centres. »95
✿ **Inter-Active**
Bahnhofstrasse 8, 6045 Meggen; *t/f* (041) 373991
Youth organisation, anti-racist activities. »94
*Intergovernmental Committee for Migration: see International
Organization for Migration, p218*
● **Intermundo**
Schwarztorstrasse 69, 3007 Bern; *t* (031) 382 3231, *f* 382
0988
International awareness, anti-racist youth organisation. »94
▮ **International Catholic Migration Commission, ICMC:**
Commission Internationale Catholique pour les Migrations
Elizabeth Winkler, Secretary General: Case postale 96, 1211
Genève 20; *t* (022) 733 4150, *f* 734 7929
Location: rue de Vermont 37-39. Founded 1951; research on
refugees and migration, co-ordination of agencies assisting
migrants, displaced persons and refugees irrespective of
religion or origin; pre- and post-migration counselling, training,
voluntary repatriation, resettlement and other services in many
countries, involving over 1,500 staff. Public information,
lobbying; *Menschen Unterwegs* (4/yr), *ICMC Migration News*
(4/yr), *Migrations* (French, irregular), newsletters (4/yr), annual
report. The 85 member bodies include ICMC in Greece, p203,
and Turkey, p219; Deutscher Caritasverband, p201, and
Raphaelswerk, p139; Obra Católica Portuguêsa das Migrações,
p148; Comisión Católica Española de Emigración, p150. »94
▮ **International Commission of Jurists, ICJ:** Commission
Internationale de Juristes
chemin de la Joinville 26, Case postale 160, 1216 Cointrin,
Genève; *t* (022) 788 4747, *f* 788 4880
Research and monitoring of legal aspects of human rights.»94
▮ **International Council of Voluntary Agencies, ICVA:** Conseil
International des Agences Bénévoles
Delmar Blasco/Anthony Kozlowski: rue J.-A.-Gautier 13,
Case postale 216, 1211 Genève 21; *t* (022) 732 6600,
f 738 9904
Forum for 84 international voluntary agencies and national
umbrella groups involved in humanitarian and development aid,
development education and human rights, refugee and migrant
assistance and protection of minorities. »94
▮ **International Federation of Catholic Parochial Youth
Communities, FIMCAP**
St Karliquai 12, 6000 Luzern 5; *t* (041) 511806, *f* 514857
Catholic pastoral and social concerns, including anti-racist
work at local level. »94

■ **International Federation of Red Cross and Red Crescent Societies,** IFRCS: Fédération Internationale des Sociétés de la Croix Rouge et du Croissant Rouge
George Webber, Secretary General: chemin des Crêts 17, Case postale 372, Petit-Saconnex, 1211 Genève 19; t (022) 730 4222, f 733 0395
Co-ordinates 150 national societies in peacetime humanitarian aid, disaster relief and support of refugees and displaced people; research, training programmes, resource development. Founded 1919; staff of 400. See International Red Cross and Red Crescent Movement, below, and national societies.
Weekly News (52/yr); *Red Cross—Red Crescent* (4/yr). »95

■ **International Labour Organization,** ILO: Bureau International du Travail, BIT: Migrant Service
W.R. Bohning, Chief: International Labour Office, route des Morillons 4, 1211 Genève 22; t (022) 799 6111, 799 6369, f 788 3894
R. Harari, C. Castro Almeyda; founded 1919, UN agency since 1946; 168 member states, 1,900 staff; improvement of working and living conditions, human rights, productive employment. Promotes equality of opportunity and treatment for migrant workers and their families, and equal treatment of nationals and non-nationals in social security matters.
Conducts research (International Institute for Labour Studies, at same address); periodicals, reports, library on international labour migration; see also BIT in France, p196. »94

■ **International Organization for Migration,** IOM: Organisation internationale pour les migrations, OIM: Organización Internacional para las Migraciones, OIM
Case postale 71, route des Morillons 17, Grand-Saconnex, 1211 Genève 19; t (022) 717 9111, f 798 6150, Tx 415722
Founded 1951 (as Intergovernmental Committee for European Migration, subsequently Intergovernmental Committee on Migrations, since 1989 IOM); over 60 country representative offices, see index. Statistical, legal and policy information on migration; financial and practical help in planned migration, with schemes for professionals moving or returning to developing countries; assists UNHCR, p219, in transport, health care and settlement of refugees and displaced persons; refugee repatriation assistance in Vietnam, Latin America and the Kurdish regions. *International Migration* (4/yr). »94

■ **International Peace Bureau,** IPB
rue de Zürich 41, 1201 Genève; t (022) 731 6429, f 738 9419 »94

■ **International Red Cross and Red Crescent Movement:** and International Committee of the Red Cross, ICRC
avenue de la Paix 19, 1202 Genève; t (022) 734 6001; information office 730 2421, f 734 8280, 733 2057
Non-governmental humanitarian movement consisting of 150 national societies, the International Federation, above, which provides disaster relief and other services in peacetime, and the ICRC, which operates in zones of conflict and is directed by a committee of 25. »94

■ **International Rescue Committee Inc.,** IRC: Europe Office
rue J.-A.-Gautier 7, 1201 Genève; t (022) 731 3360, f 738 9268
New York-based body providing re-emigration help for refugees. See national offices, p198, 201, 206 and 214.»94

■ **International Save the Children Alliance,** ISCA: Alliance Internationale d'Aide à l'Enfance
rue de Lausanne 147, 1202 Genève; t (022) 731 7016, f 738 0585 (0858?), Tx 412675 RBI CH
Federation of 24 national humanitarian relief agencies with particular interest in child welfare; many also support refugee projects. Members include Save the Children, p227, Rädda Barnen, p216, Österreichische Gesellschaft Rettet das Kind, p188, and Red Barnet, p195. *Alliance Newsletter* (2/yr). »94

■ **International Service for Human Rights:** Service International pour les Droits de l'Homme
rue de Varembé 1, Case postale 16, 1211 Genève 20; t (022) 733 5123, f 733 0826
A small agency which facilitates access for human rights NGOs to the UN lobbying and information processes. *Human Rights Monitor* (4/yr), newsletters. »94

■ **International Social Service,** ISS: International Headquarters
Marcelle Brisson: General Secretariat, quai du Seujet 32, 1201 Genève; t (022) 731 7454, f 738 0949
An international non-governmental organisation, INGO, which assists in the resolution of social welfare problems involving more than one country, often arising from voluntary or forced migration. It supports migrant/refugee reception, integration, welfare, training, settlement and repatriation projects in Europe and Asia. See SSI in Geneva, p219, ISS or SSI offices in other countries, pp201, 203, 206, 209, 216, 224, SSAE in France, p138, and APSSI in Portugal, p211. *ISS in Brief* (3/yr). »94

■ **International Youth and Student Movement for the United Nations,** ISMUN
Palais des Nations, 1211 Genève 10; t (022) 798 5850, f 733 4838
Federation of internationalist youth organisations. »94

● **Jungsozialisten Schweiz, Juso** *(Swiss Socialist Youth)*
Postfach 8208, 3001 Bern; t (031) 311 5272, f 301 0065
Socialist youth movement with anti-racist orientation. »94

● **Komitee Schluss mit dem Schnüffelstaat** *(Committee to End State Snooping)*
Catherine Weber: Postfach 6948, 3001 Bern; t (031) 312 4030, f 312 4045
Pressure group opposed to oppressive and over-zealous policing, notably of foreign residents and refugees. »95

● **Ligue Suisse des Droits de l'Homme** *(Swiss League for Human Rights)*
avenue Ste. Clotilde 9, 1205 Genève; t (022) 282844
General human rights concerns; anti-racism. »94

■ **Lutheran World Federation:** Department for World Service
route de Ferney 150, Case postale 2100, Grand-Saconnex, 1211 Genève 2; t (022) 791 6111, f 798 8616, Tx 415546
Federation of 107 Protestant churches; very large budget for international humanitarian relief projects, including services to refugees and displaced people in Third World countries, and migrants in North America and Australia; information and education on development and humanitarian issues. »94

● **Medair**
rue de Genève 77 bis, 1004 Lausanne; t (021) 245533, f 252560
Emergency medical aid to refugees, displaced persons and disaster victims; has been active in Iraq and Africa. »93

● **Médecins sans Frontières—Suisse,** MSF-CH *(literally Doctors without Borders; only French name is used)*
clos de la Fonderie 1, Carouge, 1227 Genève; t (022) 300 4445, Tx 421927 MSF CH
National section of the (Belgium-based, p191) international charity providing emergency medical teams to disaster areas, war zones, refugees and displaced people. International MSF has a separate office (rue des Cordiers 14b, 1207 Genève) for liaison with the UN system and other international bodies.»93

♦ **Office Fédéral des Réfugiés:** Bundesamt für Flüchtlinge *(Federal Refugee Office)*
J. Grüter: Taubenstrasse 16, 3003 Bern; t (031) 325 9511, 325 9350, 311 4059
The federal agency responsible for formulation and implementation of policy and practice towards refugees and asylum seekers; provides emergency service for new arrivals. It also maintains the Central Foreigners Register, which prepares and publishes monthly statistics on the foreign population in Switzerland by nationality, location, residency status, occupation, sex and so on. »95

■ **Organisation Mondiale contre la Torture,** OCMT: World Organization against Torture, also known as SOS-Torture
Eric Sottas, Director: rue de Vermont 37-39, Case postale 119, 1211 Genève 20; t (022) 733 3140, f 733 1051, e geonet2:omct
Information clearing house for world-wide network of 162 human rights NGOs campaigning on torture; activities include publishing, information, emergency financial help to refugees anywhere who are fleeing from torture. *SOS-Torture* (6/yr); *OMCT News* (6/yr). »94

■ **Quaker United Nations Office,** QUNO, and Friends World Committee for Consultation
avenue du Mervelet 13, 1209 Genève; t (022) 733 3397, f 734 0015
Represents Quaker bodies worldwide; lobbies UN system on human rights, refugee and migrant issues, other peace and justice concerns. *QUNO Reporter* (4/yr). »93

✿ **RAD—Genossenschaft der Landstrasse** *(RAD—Co-operative of the Highways)*
Postfach 1647, 8048 Zürich; t (01) 492 5477
Anti-racist policies; no further information. »94

● **Schweizerische Arbeitsgemeinschaft der Jugendverbände, SAJV** *(Swiss Coalition of Youth Groups)* Conseil suisse des associations de la jeunesse, CSAJ
Schwarztorstrasse 69, 3007 Bern; t (031) 382 2225, f 382 4493
Forum of youth groups, with anti-racist stance; see also Intermundo. Participated in the 1994-95 European Youth Campaign Against Racism, p197. »94

● **Schweizerisches Komitee für UNICEF:** Comité suisse pour l'UNICEF: Swiss Committee for UNICEF
Werdstrasse 36, 8021 Zürich; t (01) 241 4030, f 241 4038
Supports development projects of UNICEF, p219; children's rights campaigns, including for migrants in Switzerland. »93

♦ **Schweizerisches Rotes Kreuz, SRK:** Croix-Rouge Suisse,
CRS: Swiss Red Cross
Hubert Bucher, General Secretary: Postfach 2699, 3001
Bern; *t* (031) 667111, *f* 222793, *Tx* 911102 CRSB CH
Among other activities of a national Red Cross society, offers
language training, housing and rights advice, other assistance
to migrants, refugees and asylum seekers; operates reception
centres. Supports numerous aid projects abroad. See also
Francophone CRS, p217, and international bodies, p218. »95

♦ **Service Civil International—Schweiz, SCI:** *(International
Civil Service—Switzerland)*
Gerbergasse 21a, 3000 Bern 13; *t* (031) 311 7727
International social welfare agency; see also Austrian, Belgian,
French, German, and Italian sections, and European office in
Belgium, p192. Activities include anti-racist work. »94

♦ **Service Social International—Section Suisse, SSI:**
International Social Service, ISS (Swiss Section)
Leslie Moussalli, Refugee Co-ordinator: 10 rue Dr Alfred-
Vincent, 1201 Genève; *t* (022) 731 6700, *f* 731 6765
See also international headquarters of ISS, p218. The national
SSI office mainly provides legal and welfare services to
asylum-seekers registered with the UNHCR, below, in the
French-speaking parts of Switzerland. »95

● **Stiftung Kinderdorf Pestalozzi, SKIP:** Pestalozzi Children's
Village Foundation
rue Guillaume 12, 1700 Fribourg; *t* (037) 232636, *f* 225043
Maintenance of an international children's village in
Switzerland, and (through Abteilung Kinderhilfe Dritte Welt,
Third World Children's Aid Department) aid to refugee,
displaced and abandoned children in developing countries.»93

▌ **United Nations Centre for Human Rights**
Rooms D406-416, Palais des Nations, 1211 Genève 10;
t (022) 917 1234, *f* 917 0212 »94

▌ **United Nations Children's Fund, UNICEF**
Palais des Nations, 1211 Genève 10; *t* (022) 798 5850,
f 791 0822
UN agency created 1946, focussing on rights and needs of
children worldwide; almost 7,000 staff, and thousands of
volunteers in over 30 national committees (mainly in Western
countries, and mainly involved in fundraising, lobbying and
development education). Concerns include health, literacy,
education, elimination of child labour, protection of children
affected by conflict including refugee children. Numerous
publications. »94

▌ **United Nations Commission on Human Rights**
Palais des Nations, 1211 Genève 10; *t* (022) 734 6011 »94

▌ **United Nations High Commissioner for Refugees, UNHCR:**
including NGO Liaison Section
Sadako Ogata, High Commissioner: Case postale 2500,
1211 Genève 2 Dépôt; *t* (022) 739 8111, *f* 739 8618;
magazine *t* 739 8502, *f* 739 8449, *Tx* 415740 HCR CH,
Tg HICOMREF Geneva
Location: Centre William Rappard, 154 rue de Lausanne,
1202 Genève. Santiago Romero Pérez, NGO Co-ordinator
(*t* 739 8193, *f* 739 8789). International headquarters, and
Swiss national office, of the UN agency founded 1951,
succeeding the International Refugee Organization founded
1946 to help persons displaced by war in Europe; mandate
renewed thereafter every five years and broadened to include
all refugees forced to leave their own country because of a
well-founded fear of persecution; 4,125 employees in 108
offices covering 171 countries. Emergency aid, welfare and
protection of refugees, promotion of asylum, assistance with
voluntary repatriation, integration in receiving countries or
resettlement in third countries, seeks solutions to refugee
problems; conducts research; budget of US$1,200m (1994)
financed mainly by voluntary contributions from 47 member
states; runs International Refugee Documentation Network.
See index for regional and country offices; see also Dansk
Flygtningehjælp, p132, CEAR, p150, and Centre for
Documentation on Refugees, p243. Periodicals, databases,
bulletin board. Collaborates with over 200 NGOs, including
national refugee councils and humanitarian aid agencies.
Refugees (12/yr, 6 editions), *Refugee Abstracts* (4/yr). »95

▌ **United Nations Non-Governmental Liaison Service, UN-NGLS**
Dr Tony Hill, Co-ordinator: Palais des Nations, 1211 Genève
10; *t* (022) 798 5850, *f* 488 7366
Development of effective two-way communication between
the UN system and national and international NGOs. »94

▌ **United Nations Voluntary Fund for Victims of Torture,
UNVFVT:** United Nations Centre for Human Rights
Palais des Nations, 1211 Genève 10; *t* (022) 734 6011 »94

▌ **Women's World Summit Foundation**
Hotel Beau-Rivage, quai Mt-Blanc 13, 1201 Genève; *t* (022)
738 6619, *f* 738 9847 »94

▌ **World Alliance of Young Men's Christian Associations**
quai Wilson 37, 1201 Genève; *t* (022) 732 3100, *f* 738 4015
Co-ordination and strengthening of humanitarian programmes
of over 100 national YMCA bodies worldwide, including aid
to refugees, migrants, returnees and displaced people. »93

▌ **World Council of Churches, WCC**
Case postale 2100, route de Ferney 150, 1211 Genève 2;
t (022) 791 6111, *f* 791 0361, *Tx* 23423 OIK CH
Alliance of 335 Protestant and Orthodox churches in 100
countries, promoting ecumenical Christian perspectives on
social issues. Various WCC organs have interests in refugee
and migrant rights, racial equality, minorities and related
topics, including Commission on Inter-Church Aid, Refugee &
World Service, WCC-CICARWS; Migration Secretariat led by
Patrick Taran, publishes *Migration Today* (2-3/yr), booklets;
Programme to Combat Racism, WCC-PCR (Melaku Kikle,
Nathalie Africa, Thandi Bengu, Monika Grob, Rev. N. Barney
Pityana, Dr Jeane Sindab, Sabine Ododesku); also Commission
on the Churches' Participation in Development, CCPD, and
WCC Communication and WCC Language Service; see WCC in
Greece and Italy, pp140 & 207, and ECWGAR, p152. »94

▌ **World Federation of United Nations Associations**
Annexe du Petit-Saconnex, Palais des Nations, 1211 Genève
10
Alliance of national UN Associations (see e.g. Denmark, UK,
Sweden) which promote awareness of and support for the
principles and activities of the UN, engage in development
education and promote North-South solidarity. »93

▌ **World Student Christian Federation**
chemin des Crêts de Pregny 27, Grand-Saconnex, 1218
Genève; *t* (022) 988953
Federation of over 60 national student Christian movements;
humanitarian concerns including refugee issues. »85

▌ **World University Service—International, WUS**
Nigel Hartley, General Secretary: chemin des Iris 5, 1216
Genève; *t* (022) 798 8711, *f* 798 0829, *Tx* 415537 WUS CH
Development charity which promotes university participation in
the resolution of social problems; educational support to
refugees, returned migrants, women and other disadvantaged
groups, especially those in or from zones of conflict. Founded
1920; 53 national committees, including Germany, Ireland,
UK, pp202, 141, 229; and see Ibis, p194. »94

▌ **World Vision International, WVI:** Vision Mondiale
Internationale
chemin de la Tourelle 6, 1209 Genève; *t* (022) 798 4183,
f 798 6547
Christian humanitarian relief agency, with 65 national sections;
some of its projects involve refugees, displaced people and
returning migrants in Africa and Asia. »93

▌ **World Young Women's Christian Association, WYWCA:**
Alliance Mondiale des Unions Chrétiennes Féminines
quai Wilson 37, 1201 Genève; *t* (022) 732 3100, *f* 731 7938
A humanitarian aid agency supported by over 90 national
YWCA bodies; its priorities include direct aid to refugees and
migrants in European, African and Asian countries. »93

TURKEY 90

● **Human Rights Association of Turkey**
[address unknown] Istanbul
General human rights concerns. In 1994 four of its members
faced criminal charges arising from its publications on the
repression of the Kurdish minority. »95

● **Human Rights Foundation of Turkey**
Yanus Onen, Chair: Menekse 2 sokak 16/6, Kizilay, 06440
Ankara
Fevzi Argun, research director. Also at Cumhuriyet Bulvari
212/3, Alsancak, 35220 Izmir. Seeks to defend human rights
in accordance with international standards. In 1994 Onen and
Argun were charged with disseminating anti-state propaganda
by publicising torture of Kurds. »95

● **International Catholic Migration Commission, ICMC**
Kalipci sokak 146/2, Tesvikiye, Istanbul
National section of Swiss-based international agency, p217;
reception and welfare services for migrants and refugees. »93

● **Turkish Red Crescent Society**
Genel Baskanligi, Karanfil sokak 7, Wizilay, 06650 Ankara
Humanitarian agency with a wide range of services, including
emergency assistance to refugees and displaced people. »93

♦ **United Nations High Commissioner for Refugees, UNHCR**
Abidin Daver sokak 17, Cankaya, 06680 Ankara; *t* (312)
440 9337, 439 6615-18, *f* 438 2702
Refugee status, protection; see Swiss headquarters, left. »95

UNITED KINGDOM 44

● **ActionAid**
Hamlyn House, Archway, London N19 5PG; *t* (0171) 281 4101, *f* 272 0899
Rural development aid in Africa, Asia and Latin America; development education in UK; some of its projects benefit refugees and populations displaced by war.   »93

● **Action Health**
Maureen Smith: The Gatehouse, 25 Gwydir Street, Cambridge CB1 2LG
International solidarity; support and development personnel for primary health care projects in Africa and Asia.   »95

● **Action for Peoples in Conflict, AfPiC**
Freepost, PO Box 3259, London SW10 0YY
Charity providing humanitarian aid, including emergency assistance to Bosnian refugees.   »95

✿ **Acton Legal Rights Advice Panel**
Acton Hill Church Centre, Woodlands Avenue, Acton, London W3 9BY
General advice work, includes some immigration work with Asians and West Indians.   »91

● **ADAPT Support Unit, ECOTEC Ltd**
Priestley House, 28-34 Albert Street, Birmingham B4 7UD; *t* (0121) 616 3670
UK managers of the EU's ADAPT transnational employment initiative, linking development projects in member states. »96
Advice Bureaux, Citizens' Advice Bureaux, Advice Centres: Britain has many independent agencies offering advice and advocacy in consumer rights, welfare and legal matters; we have listed those with a known interest in migration, asylum or minority issues. Where bureaux have worked with particular client groups these may be mentioned in the entries: this does not mean that they work exclusively with such groups. See also Federation of Independent Advice Centres, p223, Law Centres, p225, and National Association of CABx, p226.

✿ **Advice Centre in the Blue**
190 Southwark Park Road, London SE16 4RP; *t* (0171) 231 2472-74
General advice work, includes some immigration work with Vietnamese, Somalis, Maghrebis.   »94

● **Advice on Individual Rights in Europe, AIRE**
Nuala Mole: 74 EuroLink Business Centre, 49 Effra Road, London SW2 1BZ; *t* (0171) 924 0927, *f* 733 6786
Advice and information on European legal and rights issues, including migration.   »95

♦ **Aliens Registration Office**
10 Lamb's Conduit Street, London WC1X 3MX; *t* (0171) 230 1208
UK government agency for monitoring foreign residents. »95

● **All-Party Parliamentary Group on Race and Community**
Baroness Flather, Chair: 11 Carteret Street, London SW1H 9DL; *t* (0171) 222 8178, *f* 233 0161
Robert Hughes MP, Greville Janner MP secretaries; Clifford Headley director. Members of House of Lords and House of Commons concerned with policy issues affecting minorities; meetings, conferences, reports. Associated with charities such as Runnymede, Rowntree and Cadbury Trusts.   »95

▌ **Amnesty International, AI: International Secretariat**
Pierre Sané, Secretary General: 1 Easton Street, London WC1X 8DJ; *t* (0171) 413 5500, *f* 956 1157, *Tx* 28502
Maggie Maloney. International secretariat (not the UK section) of a human rights organisation working for the release of those imprisoned for their beliefs, for fair trials for political offences, for freedom of speech and belief, against torture and the death penalty. Interested in problems of refugees in the context of political persecution; advises on the use of international standards for the protection of refugees, and intervenes with governments on specific refugee cases and issues. AI, founded 1961, has a staff of 250, and 500,000 members in 150 countries. Documentation centre; country studies, occasional papers; see national sections and EU Association, in index. *Newsletter* (12/yr), *Report* (1/yr).   »95

♦ **Amnesty International—British Section, AIBS**
David Bull, Director: 99-119 Rosebery Avenue, London EC1R 4RE; *t* (0171) 814 6200, *f* 833 1510, *Tx* 917621 AIBS
Human rights pressure group focussing on political prisoners, see above; information, documentation; AIBS Refugee Office (Richard Dunstan) provides country information to the Home Office, p223, makes representations to the Asylum Division, right, monitors policy and practice in relation to international standards; can arrange specialist medical and other assistance for refugees; over 300 local groups. *Amnesty* (6/yr).   »95

▌ **Anti-Slavery International, ASI (formerly Anti-Slavery Society for the Protection of Human Rights)**
Lesley Roberts, Director: The Stableyard, Broomgrove Road, London SW9 9TL; *t* (0171) 924 9555, *f* 738 4110
David Ould. World's oldest human rights organisation, founded 1787; research, lobbying and campaigning for the elimination of slavery and related practices (debt bondage, child labour, forced labour, servile marriage, exploitation of indigenous groups). Currently working on 18 countries; lobbies UN and EU, engages in public education, disseminates research through affiliates around the world. Voluntary and governmental funding from several countries.   »95

● **Article 19**
Dr Frances D'Souza, Director: Lancaster House, 33 Islington High Street, London N1 9LH; *t* (0171) 278 9292, *f* 713 1356, *e* article19@gn.apc.org
International campaigns for freedom of expression and information; interested in minority, refugee and other human rights issues in that context.   »94

● **Association of Metropolitan Authorities, AMA**
Rashmi Patel: 34 Great Smith Street, London SW1P 3BJ; *t* (0171) 222 8100, *f* 222 0878   »95

♦ **Asylum Division, Home Office Immigration and Nationality Department**
Quest House, 11 Cross Road, Croydon CR9 2BY; *t* (0181) 686 0688
A section of the Home Office, responsible for the management of applications for asylum and refugee status. See also the Immigration Service which initially processes claims. »95

✿ **Avon and Bristol Community Law Centre, A&BCLC**
Jo McDonald: 2 Moon Street, Bristol BS2 8QE; *t* (0117) 924 8662
Free legal advice and representation; specialisms include immigration law and race discrimination cases.   »95

✿ **Bellenden Neighbourhood Advice Centre**
Copleston Centre, Copleston Road, Peckham, London SE15 4AN; *t* (0171) 639 8447, 639 2745
Independent advice centre; immigration and policing work with Turkish, African, Asian and Caribbean communities.   »95

● **Benefits Agency Overseas Branch, Department of Social Security**
Benton Park Road, Longbenton, Newcastle-upon-Tyne NE98 1YX; *t* (0191) 213 5000
Deals with social security cases involving migrant workers.»95

✿ **Blackfriars Settlement Advice Centre, also known as Blackfriars Advice Centre**
Chris Beringer/Terri Jones: 44-47 Nelson Square, London SE1 0QA; *t* (0171) 928 9521
Welfare and rights advice, some immigration work.   »95

✿ **Blakenhall Community Advice Centre**
St John's Methodist Church, 164 Dudley Road, Wolverhampton WV2 3DN; *t* (01902) 453861
General advice service, including immigration problems. »94

● **Board for Social Responsibility, BSR: Church of England**
Rev. John Gladwin, General Secretary: Church House, Great Smith Street, London SW1P 3NZ; *t* (0171) 222 9011
David Skidmore; 15 staff; founded 1958; organ of the General Synod, promoting Church reflection and action on many issues including race and minorities; publishes a social services yearbook. *Crucible* (4/yr), *BSR News* (4/yr).   »95

✿ **Bradford Citizens Advice Bureau**
Shirley Ginever: 17 Canal Road, Mill Street, Bradford BD1 4AT; *t* (01274) 370500
General legal and consumer advice; some immigration and benefits work with Asians, West Indians.   »95

✿ **Bradford Law Centre**
Cath Beresford: 31 Manor Row, Bradford BD1 4PX; *t* (01274) 306617, *f* 390939
Legal advice and assistance, some immigration work.   »95

✿ **Brent Community Law Centre, BCLC**
389 High Road, Willesden, London NW10 2JR; *t* (0181) 451 1122-25, *f* 830 2462
General legal advice and representation centre.   »95

✿ **Brighton Citizens Advice Bureau**
Vinay Mushiana: 39-41 Surrey Street, Brighton BN1 3PB; *t* (01273) 204543
Generalist advice agency. Houses the Brighton Area Race Project of the local EMRC, see p154, advising on legal rights, racial harassment and related issues, and a Black and Minority Ethnic Women's Counselling Project.   »96

✿ **Brighton Housing Trust Housing Aid and Legal Centre, BHT-HALC**
144 London Road, Brighton BN1 4PH; *t* (01273) 672015
Large legal and housing aid centre with 17 staff; developing a specialist immigration and employment advice service.   »95

✿ **Brighton Rights Advice Centre**
M. Martin/Veronica Kofman: 102a North Road, Brighton BN1
14E; *t* (01273) 600972, *f* 674127
Generalist rights advice agency, some immigration work. »95

✿ **Bristol City Council Race Equality Unit**
Museji A. Takiola: Room 242, Council House, College Green,
Bristol BS1 5TR; *t* (0117) 922 2661
Local authority policy unit. »91

● **British Agencies for Adoption and Fostering, BAAF**
Skyline House, 200 Union Street, London SE1 0LY; *t* (0171)
593 2000, *f* 593 2001
Inter-agency group; interests include problems of transnational
and intercultural adoptions. »95

● **The British Council and Youth Exchange Centre**
10 Spring Gardens, London SW1A 2BN; *t* (0171) 389 4030,
930 8466, *f* 389 4033, 493 5035
Administers assistance programmes for foreign students;
promotes educational, scientific and cultural exchanges. Its
Overseas Student Services Department, and the UK NARIC
centre, for recognition of foreign qualifications, is based in
Manchester: Medlock Street, M15 4PR, *t* (0161) 957 7000.
There are other regional, and overseas, offices. »95

♦ **British Red Cross, BRC:** Head Office
Marion Lowe, Operations Director: 9 Grosvenor Crescent,
London SW1X 7EJ; *t* (0171) 235 5454, *f* 245 6315
M.R. Whitlam director general, John Gray, director of public
relations. Humanitarian relief agency with 89 branches and
90,000 volunteers. Its International Division participates in
overseas emergency operations, often working with refugees
and displaced persons. See BRC Bosnian Programme, p23,
and international Red Cross bodies in Switzerland, p218. »96

✿ ≡ London Branch: Lucy Bishop: 28 Worple Rd, Wimbledon,
London SW19 4EE; *t* (0181) 944 8909
Voluntary organisation of 4,000 members, with a range of
services and fund-raising activities in Greater London. Work
with refugees and asylum-seekers includes a Family Tracing
and Message Service operated by volunteers. »95

● **British Youth Council, BYC**
Ade Ademuyiwa: 57 Chalton Street, London NW1 1HU;
t (0171) 387 7559, *f* 383 3545
National representative body for youth organisations. »95

✿ **Brixton Community Law Centre Ltd, BCLC,** also known as
Brixton Law Centre
T. Okunola/C. Oliver: 506-508 Brixton Road, London SW9
8EN; *t* (0171) 737 0440, 733 4245, *f* 326 1397
General advice and casework, representation, campaigning;
some Caribbean, West African, other immigration work. »95

▌**Building a Europe of Solidarity Together, BEST,** also known
as Solidarity
49 Green Road, Reading RG6 2BS; *t* (01734) 662291
A campaign to draw together European citizens concerned
with social justice issues, including homelessness, poverty,
unemployment, industrial conversion, economic development,
labour and trade union rights. »94

● **CAFOD,** formally Catholic Agency for Overseas Development
Nick Richards/Louise Illingworth: 2 Romero Close, Stockwell
Road, London SW9 9TY; *t* (0171) 733 7900, *f* 274 9630
George Gelber head of public policy. Humanitarian aid and
development agency of the Catholic Church in England and
Wales, funding 1,000 projects in 75 countries; interest in
refugee and other human rights issues. »96

✿ **Cambridge Citizens Advice Bureau**
2 Pikes Walk, Cambridge CB1 1LF
General consumer and legal advice; some immigration and
related work. Also listed (1995) at 72-74 Newmarket Road,
CB5 8DZ, *t* (01223) 361418. »95

✿ **Camden Community Law Centre**
2 Prince of Wales Road, Kentish Town, London NW5 3LG;
t (0171) 485 6672-73, *f* 267 6218
Founded 1973; collective of 18 workers. General legal,
housing, education, welfare, immigration and asylum advice
and casework; specialist Afro-Caribbean community welfare
rights worker. »95

✿ **Camden Local Education Authority Social Work Service**
The Crowndale Centre, 216-220 Eversholt Street, London
NW1 1BD
Educational welfare service. Employs specialist social worker
supporting access to education of children from homeless and
refugee backgrounds. »95

✿ **Canning Town Information Centre Ltd**
57 Barking Road, London E16 4HB; *t* (0171) 474 0931
General advice centre; some work with Asian and other
communities on immigration, housing, welfare benefits. »95

✿ **Cardiff City Council Race and Housing Section**
Fowzia Ali: Central Square, Cardiff CF1, Wales »93

✿ **Cardiff Law Centre**
15 Splott Road, Splott, Cardiff CF2 2BU, Wales; *t* (01222)
498117, *f* 498118
Community legal advice and representation centre; some
immigration work. »95

✿ **Carlisle Law Centre**
43 Cecil Street, Carlisle CA1 1NS; *t* (01228) 515129,
f 515819
Legal advice and assistance. »95

● **Catholic Institute for International Relations, CIIR**
Dr Ian Linden: Unit 3, Canonbury Yard, 190a New North Road,
London N1 7BJ; *t* (0171) 354 0883, *f* 359 0017
Educational and humanitarian aid; promotes development,
democracy, economic justice and human rights, and public
understanding of international affairs; has supported refugee
and migrant aid projects abroad. Has 2,500 members. »95

● **Central Bureau for Educational Visits and Exchanges** and
Youth for Europe; LINGUA
Seymour Mews House, Seymour Mews, London W1H 9PE;
t (0171) 725 9461, 486 5101, *f* 935 1017
Promotes international exchange placements of students and
teachers, and the EU's LINGUA programme on language
learning; a partner in Youth for Europe, p191. »94

✿ **Central London Law Centre**
Baljinder Bhopal/Tamara Lewis: 47-49 Charing Cross Road,
London WC2H 0AN; *t* (0171) 437 5854, *f* 734 3563
Bobby Chan. Collective of seven workers providing legal
advice and assistance; some immigration, asylum, housing,
discrimination and other work with minority communities. »95

✿ **Centre 70 Advice Centre**
138 Christchurch Road, Tulse Hill, London SW2 3DQ
General consumer and legal advice; immigration work. »96

● **Charter '87**
Dr Louise M. Pirouet: 8 Geldart Street, Cambridge CB1 2LX;
t (01223) 314655
Human rights pressure group, campaigning for constitutional
and legal reform. Includes Charter for Refugees, which
demands fair treatment for asylum seekers. »96

● **Charter 88**
Andrew Puddephat: Exmouth House, 3-11 Pine Street, London
EC1R 0JH; *t* (0171) 833 1988, *f* 833 5895
Promotion of constitutional reform in the interests of human
rights and participatory democracy. »96

✿ **Chelsea Citizens Advice Bureau**
Michael Haran, Solicitor: Chelsea Old Town Hall, Kings Road,
London SW3 5EE; *t* (0171) 351 0019, *f* 351 5240
Consumer and legal advice; some immigration work. »94

✿ **Chesterfield Law Centre**
Russ de Haney/Steve Taylor: 44 Park Road, Chesterfield S40
1XZ; *t* (01246) 550674, *f* 551069
Legal advice, including immigration and nationality. »95

● **Children's International Summer Villages, CISV**
MEA House, Ellison Place, Newcastle-upon-Tyne NE1 8XS;
t (0191) 232 4998, *f* 261 4710
Organises international, multicultural summer camps. »94

● **Children's Legal Centre,** University of Essex
Wivenhoe Park, Colchester CO4 3SQ; *t* (01206) 873820
Children's rights charity; research and campaigns; migration
and refugee rights policy issues affecting children. Part-time
telephone advice line, no casework. *Childright* (12/yr). »96

● **Christian Action**
Canon Eric James: 125 Kennington Road, London SE11 6SF;
t (0171) 735 2372 »91

▌**Christian Aid**
Rev. Michael Taylor, Director: PO Box 100, London SE1 7RT;
t (0171) 620 4444, *f* 620 0719
Location: Inter-Church House, 35-41 Lower Marsh, SE1 7RG.
Development aid and development education charity, working
in 70 countries; advocacy in Europe for the poor of the world.
Founded 1948 as Inter-Church and Refugee Service of British
Council of Churches. Third world refugee aid, scholarships in
UK and Ireland, refugee counselling/welfare work. Resources
for multi-cultural education. *Christian Aid News* (4/yr). »95

● **Christian Outreach**
Martin Lee, Director: 1 New Street, Leamington Spa CV31
1HP; *t* (01926) 315301, *f* 885786
Charity founded 1967; material aid mainly to refugees and
displaced people in South-East Asia and Africa. »93

✿ **Church of God of Prophecy**
H.C. Lawrence: College Chapel, Hamilton Road, Longsight,
Manchester M13 0NG; *t* (0161) 225 0813, 432 7421
Black-led Christian church; drop-in centre, community
activities. »93

✿ ≡ Alan Simpson: 300 Moss Lane East, Moss Side,
Manchester M14 4LZ; *t* (0161) 226 9012 »93

✿ **Citizens Advice Bureau (Scotland)**
26 George Square, Edinburgh EH8 9LD, Scotland
Consumer and legal advice, some immigration work.   »94

✿ **Citizens Rights Office**
43 Broughton Street, Edinburgh EH1 3JU, Scotland; t (0131)
557 0213, 557 3887
Independent advice centre; immigration work.   »91

✿ **Civil Rights Advice and Support Group**
c/o CAPA, Oxford House, Derbyshire Street, London E2 6HG;
t (0171) 729 1264, f 729 0435
Advice on civil rights issues, including immigration problems,
racial discrimination. Associated with Community Action on
Police Accountability, p178.   »94

● **Civil Rights (UK)**
Rudy Narayan/Saeeda Shah: Justice House, 400-402 Brixton
Road, London SW9 7AW; t (0171) 978 8545
Legal advice and campaigning organisation of radical black
lawyers.   »90

● **European Commission**
Jean Monnet House, 8 Storey's Gate, London SW1P 3AT;
t (0171) 973 1992, f 973 1900, 973 1973
National office of the Commission, p189; information on EU
policy and related matters. Regional offices: Windsor House,
9-15 Bedford Street, Belfast BT2 7EG, t (01232) 240708, f
248241, Tx 74117 CECBEL G; 4 Cathedral Road, Cardiff
CF1 9SG, t (01222) 371631, f 395489, Tx 497727 Europa
G; 9 Alva Street, Edinburgh EH2 4PH, t (0131) 225 2058,
f 226 4105, Tx 727420 EUEDIN G.   »94

◆ **Commission for Racial Equality**, CRE: Head Office
Herman Ouseley, Chair: Elliot House, 10-12 Allington Street,
London SW1E 5EH; t (0171) 828 7022; press office 932
5354, f 630 7605
Sukhdev Sharma, executive director. Autonomous agency
with 200 staff, reporting to the Home Office; established by
the 1976 Race Relations Act, to promote racial equality of
opportunity and good community relations; research, policy
advice, investigative and enforcement work, funding of
initiatives on race relations, employment, education, housing,
justice; legal advice and advocacy for individuals in race
discrimination cases; funds local Councils for Racial Equality.
Regional offices in England, Scotland and Wales; the CRE has
no presence in Northern Ireland, where racial discrimination is
not illegal. Connections, booklets, leaflets, handbooks.   »95

✿ ≡ Colin Rice: Alpha Tower, 11th Floor, Suffolk Street,
Queensway, Birmingham B1 1TT; t (0121) 632 4544, f 643
1592
Base (with sub-office in Leicester) of the CRE Midlands
regional team; also responsible for Wales until the opening of
the Cardiff office in 1995.   »95

✿ ≡ Yorkshire Bank Chambers, 1st Floor, Infirmary Street,
Leeds LS1 2JP; t (0113) 243 4413, f 244 3213   »95

✿ ≡ Haymarket Hse, 4th Floor, Haymarket Shopping Centre,
Leicester LE1 3YG; t (0116) 251 7852, f 251 5359   »94

✿ ≡ Jane Abdulla: Maybrook House, 5th Floor, 40 Blackfriars
Street, Manchester M3 2EG; t (0161) 831 7782, 831 7788,
f 833 2186   »95

◆ ≡ Wales/Cymru: Comisiwn dros Gydraddoldeb Hiliol, CGH:
[address unknown] Cardiff/Caerdydd
New regional office for Wales opened in 1995, initially with
five staff.   »95

◆ ≡ Scotland: Martin Verity: Hanover House, 45-51 Hanover
Street, Edinburgh EH2 2PJ; t (0131) 226 5186, f 226 5243
Moussa Jogee, CRE Commissioner for Scottish Affairs.   »95

▮ **Commonwealth Institute**
Sir Michael Caine, Director: 230 Kensington High Street,
London W8 6NQ; t (0171) 603 4535, f 602 7374,
Tx 8955822
Information, documentation, education, exhibitions on
Commonwealth affairs; promotion of Commonwealth co-
operation and cultural exchange. Founded 1887 as Imperial
Institute. What's On (24/yr).   »95

✿ **Community Fellowship Pentecostal Church**
E. Poyser: 61 Fouracres Road, Manchester M32 8EP
Black-led Christian church.   »93

● **Community Service Volunteers**, CSV
Elisabeth Hoodless: 237 Pentonville Road, London N1 9NJ;
t (0171) 278 6601
Also Volonteurope network of community service
organisations. Volonteurope (4/yr).   »94

● **Concern Universal**
14 Manor Road, Chatham ME4 6AN; t (01634) 813942,
f 402942
Promotes sustainable development through partnership with
Third World NGOs; provides emergency aid and resettlement
support to refugees and displaced people abroad.   »95

● **Council of Churches for Britain and Ireland**, CCBI, formerly
British Council of Churches, BCC
Rev. David Haslam, Director, CRRU: Inter-Church House,
35-41 Lower Marsh, London SE1 7RL; t (0171) 620 4444,
f 620 0719
Rev. John Reardon general secretary. Promotes Christian
social policy development, ecumenism, other campaigns in
churches and society. The Community and Race Relations
Unit, CRRU, addresses racism and inequality; the Council is
also involved in the sanctuary movement, and Action by
Christians Against Torture, p195. See also Committee for
Relations with People of Other Faiths, p178.   »95

● **Council for Education in World Citizenship**, CEWC
Seymour Mews House, Seymour Mews, London W1H 9PE;
t (0171) 935 1752, f 935 5548
Promotion of global awareness and responsibility; environmental, development, peace education; multiculturalism and
anti-racism.   »94

● **Council for International Educational Exchanges**, CIEE
33 Seymour Place, London W1H 6AT; t (0171) 224 8896
Arranges exchange placements of students and teachers
between UK and foreign educational establishments.   »94

● **Council for Social Responsibility**
C.J. Lees/Guy Harlings: 53 New St, Chelmsford CM1 1NG
Church of England advisory body.   »90

✿ **Coventry Income and Legal Rights Service**, also known as
Coventry Law Centre
2nd floor, Broadgate House, The Bridge, Broadgate, Coventry
CV1 1NG; t (01203) 223051-53, f 220157
Generalist law centre, some Asian immigration work.   »95

✿ **Creative Support Ltd**
Kath Dawson: 5th Floor, Dale House, 35 Dale Street,
Manchester M1 2HF; t (0161) 236 0829
A mental health charity providing a range of housing and
support services in the Greater Manchester area, including
(1995) an Asian Women's Mental Health Service in Bolton,
and a residential project for African-Caribbean men in Hulme,
central Manchester.   »95

✿ **Ealing Borough Law Centre**, formerly Southall Community
Law Centre
Madhav Patil: 11b King Street, Southall UB2 4DF; t (0181)
574 2434, f 843 9165
Generalist rights advice centre; some immigration work with
Punjabi and other client groups.   »94

✿ **Earls Court Advice Centre**
Gemma Bukowska: 282 Earls Court Road, London SW5;
t (0171) 835 2151
Legal advice, some immigration work.   »94

✿ **City of Edinburgh District Council**
Shenaz Bahadur, Race Relations Officer: 6 Cockburn Street,
Edinburgh EH1 1NY, Scotland; t (0131) 529 4301
City council activities in relevant fields include monitoring
equity in the delivery of civic services, and assistance to
Edinburgh Ethnic Enterprise Centre, p154.   »95

● **Educational Grants Advisory Service**
501 Kingsland Road, London E8 2DY
Provides advice on study opportunities in the UK.   »95

✿ **Emmanuel Pentecostal Church**
Pastor Ron Phillips: Brennon Close, off Arnott Crescent,
Boundary Lane, Hulme, Manchester M15; t (0161) 427 6261
Black-led Christian church.   »93

✿ **Equal Access Project**: Parkside Health
Rachel Hughes: Parkside Health NHS Trust, Woodfield Road,
London W9 2BB; t (0181) 961 9005
Project (funded to March 1997) to identify and help remove
barriers to accessing health care in Brent for marginalised
groups including ethnic minorities.   »95

● **Equal Opportunities Commission**, EOC
Julie Cornwall: Overseas House, Quay Street, Manchester
M3 3HN; t (0161) 833 9244, f 835 1657
Promotes, monitors and helps to enforce equal rights and
opportunities for women in England, Scotland and Wales,
mainly in employment issues. Has published some research on
ethnic minority women in the labour market.   »95

▮ **European Contact Group on Urban Industrial Mission**, ECG:
Communauté Européenne de Travail sur Eglise et Société
Industrielle
48 Peveril Crescent, Manchester M21 1WS; t/f (0161) 881
6031
Co-ordinates 20 European national church bodies involved in
urban mission and economic and social justice issues; several
of these (in Austria, Finland, France, Germany, Italy, the
Netherlands, Portugal and Switzerland) are involved in directly
providing migrant and refugee counselling and support
services.   »93

■ **European Counter Network—London**
c/o Infoshop, 56a Crampton Street, London SE17; *f* (0171)
326 0353
Alliance of radical, anti-racist and civil rights groups.　»94
● **European Movement—United Kingdom**
Stephen Woodard, Director: 11 Tufton Street, Westminster,
London SW1P 3QB; *f* (0171) 799 2817
Campaigns for full British participation in European Union;
interested in pan-European social issues.　»95
■ **European Solidarity Towards Equal Participation of Peoples,**
EuroStep
Lindsay Judge, c/o Oxfam, 274 Banbury Road, Oxford OX2
7DZ; *t* (01865) 311311　»95
■ **European Young Homelessness Network, EYHN**
88 Old Street, London EC1V 9HU; *t* (0171) 253 0202, *f* 608
3325
Alliance of national and local agencies providing emergency
accommodation and social housing for young people in need,
including migrants and refugees, throughout the EU.　»94
✿ **Family Welfare Association**
501-505 Kingsland Road, London E8 4AU; *t* (0171) 254
6521　»90
◆ **Federation of Independent Advice Centres, FIAC**
Becky Green: 13 Stockwell Road, London SW9 9AU; *t* (0171)
274 1839, 274 1878
Umbrella body providing training, recruitment and other
services to several hundred advice centres, many working in
immigration, nationality, minority rights and related fields. »96
● **Feed the Children**
David H.W. Grubb: [address unknown] Reading, Berkshire
International humanitarian relief, including aid to refugees and
disaster victims in Africa and elsewhere.　»95
● **Female Prisoners Welfare Project Hibiscus, FPWP/Hibiscus**
3b Aberdeen Studios, 22 Highbury Grove, London N5 2EA;
t (0171) 226 7727, *f* 226 1850
Charity working on behalf of all women prisoners, with
particular reference to foreign women.　»95
◆ **Foreign and Commonwealth Office, FCO:** Migration & Visa
Department; Nationality & Treaty Department
Clive House, Petty France, London SW1H 9HD; *t* switchboard
(0171) 270 3000, visa enquiries 270 4056, application forms
270 4043, FCO Correspondence Unit 270 4038, 270 4012,
270 4198
The UK ministry of external affairs; responsibilities in migration
and refugee matters include treaty and visa questions and
protection of UK migrants, while the Home Office, right, deals
with domestic aspects such as immigration and asylum.　»95
✿ **Free Representation Unit, FRU**
Kathleen McGivern: Room 140, 1st Floor, 49-51 Bedford
Row, London WC1R 4LR; *t* (0171) 831 0692
Legal advice and representation before tribunals, including
immigration matters.　»95
✿ **Gateshead Law Centre**
Pat Hannard, Administrator: Swinburne House, Swinburne
Street, Gateshead NE8 1AX; *t* (0191) 477 1109
General legal advice and services; some (mainly South Asian)
immigration casework.　»95
■ **Global Computer Network for Environment, Peace and
Human Rights, GreenNet**
23 Bevenden Street, London N1 6BH; *t* (0171) 608 3040,
f 253 0801
Provides e-mail, bulletin board and other electronic
communication services to NGOs. Includes many migrant,
refugee and human rights organisations around the world.»94
✿ **Gloucester Law Centre**
Widden Old School, Widden Street, Gloucester GL1 4AQ;
t (01452) 423492, *f* 387594
General legal advice; immigration and minority rights work,
with Gloucester CRE and Gloucestershire Racial Advice
Service, both p179.　»95
✿ **Granby Advice and Information Project, GAIP**
Project Manager: c/o NACAB Merseyside & West Cheshire
Area Office, Concourse House, Lime Street, Liverpool L1
1NY; *t* (0151) 708 8762
Community outreach generalist advice service operated by
Citizens Advice Bureau in a multi-racial inner city area.　»95
✿ **Gravesend Citizens Advice Bureau**
The Manager: 8-9 Parrock Street, Gravesend DA12 1ET
General legal and consumer advice centre, developing services
for the (mainly Indian) ethnic minorities in the locality.　»94
✿ **Greenwich Community Law Centre**
187 Trafalgar Road, Greenwich, London SE10 9EQ; *t* (0181)
853 2550, 858 7397, *f* 858 5253
Legal advice and assistance collective, some immigration
casework; funded by borough council.　»95

✿ **Hackney Citizens Rights Group**
Centerprise, 136-138 Kingsland High Street, Hackney,
London E8 2NS; *t* (0171) 359 8998
Legal and welfare rights; some work with immigrants.　»95
✿ **Hackney Law Centre**
Carol Blakemore: 236-238 Mare Street, Hackney, London E8
1HE; *t* (0181) 985 8364, 986 9966, 985 5236, *f* 533 2018
Pierre Makhlouf, A. Jackman. Legal advice and advocacy,
including immigration and racial discrimination work.　»95
✿ **Hammersmith and Fulham Community Law Centre**
142-144 King Street, London W6 0QU; *t* (0181) 741 4021,
f 741 1450
Legal assistance, some immigration work.　»95
● **Hand in Hand Trust**
Worton Hall, Worton Road, Isleworth TW7 6ER
Charity which has supported work on migrant rights.　»95
✿ **Handsworth Law Centre**
220 Soho Road, Birmingham B21 9LR; *t* (0121) 554 0868,
551 1969
Legal advice and assistance agency in a multi-racial area. »95
✿ **Harehills and Chapeltown Law Centre**
263 Roundhay Road, Leeds LS8 4HS; *t* (0113) 249 1100,
f 235 1185
Legal assistance, some immigration work.　»95
✿ **Harlesden Advice Centre, HAC**
2 Tavistock Road, Harlesden, London NW10 4ND; *t* (0181)
965 2590, 965 7305
General advice centre, some Asian immigration work.　»91
✿ **Hayes Citizens Advice Bureau**
David Henderson, Manager: 16 Botwell Lane, Hayes UB3
2AA; *t* (01895) 811207, *f* 237940
Generalist consumer and welfare rights advice and counselling
centre, attached to Hillingdon CAB; some Asian-language
services, and specialist worker for the Somali community.»95
● **Health Unlimited**
Lucy Medd: 3 Stamford Street, London SE1 9NT; *t* (0171)
928 8105, *f* 928 7736
Charity working in less developed countries to improve the
health of communities affected by conflict; 12 current
programmes in Latin America, Asia and Africa.　»96
● **The Terrence Higgins Trust**
S. Viinikka/A. Holt: 52-54 Grays Inn Road, London WC1X
8JU; *t* (0171) 831 0330, *f* 242 0121
HIV and AIDS advice, including immigration matters.　»95
✿ **Highfields and Belgrave Community Law Centre, HBCLC**
Namza F.B. Mohamed/Kamlesh Modi: 6 Seymour Street,
Highfields, Leicester LE2 0LB; *t* (0116) 253 2928, *f* 253 8894
General legal advice and representation centre; social security,
housing, employment, civil liberties; immigration/nationality
work with Asian, African and Caribbean families.　»95
✿ **Hillingdon Legal Resource Centre, HLRC**
12 Harold Avenue, Hayes UB3 4QW; *t* (0181) 561 9400,
561 9262, *f* 756 0837
General legal advice centre near Heathrow Airport; immigration
and nationality, discrimination, welfare rights work.　»96
■ **HMD International:** Humanitarian Aid Medical Development
1a Beethoven Street, London W10 4LG
Disaster relief, medical services to refugees and victims of
war; current programmes include Bosnia.　»95
◆ **Home Office**
50 Queen Anne's Gate, London SW1H 9AT; *t* (0171) 273
3000, *f* 273 2190
The ministry of internal affairs only for England and Wales,
but with responsibility for all UK immigration, refugee and
nationality policies and procedures, and many policy matters
affecting minorities. See Asylum Division, p220; Nationality
Division, p226; Immigration Service, local Immigration Offices,
Immigration and Nationality Department and Immigration
Appellate Authority, p224, and Commission for Racial Equality,
p222. Headed by the Home Secretary, one of the four senior
members of the UK Cabinet. Immigration, passports and
refugee issues are dealt with one of the Home Office's four
junior ministers. Its Community Programmes Department
funds many projects in ethnic minority communities.　»95
✿ **Hounslow Council Housing Services Department**
Director: Civic Centre, Lampton Road, Hounslow TW3 4DN
Public housing provision. The Department has one principal
and three area-based Race Equality Advisers, to help ensure
equality in service delivery and employment practice.　»95
✿ **Hounslow Law Centre**
Dhira Wickramanayake: 51 Lampton Road, Hounslow TW3
1JG; *t* (0181) 570 9505, 572 6347, *f* 572 0730
Law centre with immigration, refugee and employment
discrimination caseload, largely Asian clientele. Specialist
refugee employment advice.　»96

✿ **Huddersfield Citizens Advice Bureau**
Ravinder Chana/Sue Gee: 6-8 St Peter's Street, Huddersfield
HD1 1DH; *t* (01484) 512346, 545683
Large town centre advice agency; some, mainly Asian and
Caribbean, immigration advice work.   »95

◆ **Human Rights Watch**
2nd Floor, Lancaster House, 33 Islington High Street, London
N1 9LH; *t* (0171) 713 1995, *f* 713 1800
Campaigns on human rights worldwide; migration and refugee
issues in that context. Specialist sections include Human
Rights Watch Africa. See also in Belgium, p191. *Searchlight*,
formerly *Africa Watch*.   »95

✿ **Humberside Law Centre**
Janine S. Swindells, Co-ordinator: 95 Alfred Gelder Street,
Hull HU1 1EP; *t* (01482) 211180, *f* 589036
General legal advice centre, some immigration work.   »95

◆ **Immigration Appellate Authority**, formerly Immigration
Appeals Office
Thanet House, 231-232 Strand, London WC2R 1DA; *t* (0171)
353 8060, *f* 583 1976
Considers, through tribunal system, appeals against decisions
of the Immigration and Nationality Department, below, of the
Home Office. Regional offices: Birmingham *t* (0121) 706
4382, Cardiff (1st Floor, 2 Park Street, CF1 1ET), Feltham *t*
(0181) 893 1000, Glasgow *t* (0141) 221 3489, Leeds *t*
(0113) 244 9898, and Manchester *t* (0161) 837 1000.   »95

◆ **Immigration and Nationality Department**, Home Office
Lunar House, 40 Wellesley Road, Croydon CR9 2BY; *t* (0181)
686 0688
Develops and administers policy on immigration, nationality,
refugee status and protection; see also Nationality Division,
p226, Asylum Division and Aliens Registration Office, p220,
Immigration Appellate Authority, above, and Immigration
Service and Immigration Offices, below.   »95

✿ **Immigration Office**
Terminal Building, Gatwick Airport, Horley RH6 0NN;
t (01293) 502019 South Terminal switchboard, casework
502654, *f* 553643; North Terminal switchboard 892500,
casework 892545; asylum cases 892515, *f* 892560;
detention centre 524284.   »95
✿ ≡ Queen's Building, Heathrow Airport, Hounslow TW6 1DL
The largest port-of-entry immigration office. Arrivals control,
Immigration Service administration and detention areas, with
the following contact numbers (all beginning (0181) 745):
Terminal 1: arrivals control 6800, casework 6809, *f* 6814;
Terminal 2: general 6850, casework 6860, *f* 6877; Terminal
3: general 6900, casework 6932, *f* 6943; Terminal 4: general
4700, casework 4724, *f* 4705; Detention Centre 6484; for
detainees *t* (0181) 564 9726-27.   »95
✿ ≡ Terminal Building, Leeds/Bradford Airport, Yeadon, Leeds,
Yorkshire; *t* (0113) 250 2931, *f* 250 0949   »95
✿ ≡ Luton Airport, Luton; *t* (01582) 421891, *f* 405215 »95
✿ ≡ Terminal Building, Stansted Airport, Stansted; *t* (01279)
680118, enforcement office 680692, detention centre
681548, *f* 680041.   »95

◆ **Immigration Service**, formally Her Majesty's Immigration
Service
C. Manchip, Director: Lunar House, 40 Wellesley Road,
Croydon CR9 2BY
Operational agency of the Immigration and Nationality
Department, above; runs local Immigration Offices, detention
centres and surveillance and enquiry units; makes initial
decisions on whether entry should be granted: appeals may be
made to the Immigration Appellate Authority. The main
London office of the Service is Becket House, 66-68 St
Thomas' Street, SE1 3QU, *t* (0171) 238 1000, asylum cases
238 1331-32, *f* 378 9107 (duty officer) and 378 9100
(casework). The Service's Intelligence and Investigation Unit
is at Harlington, Middlesex (*t* (0181) 745 2400). See also the
major airport Immigration Offices at Heathrow, Gatwick,
Stansted, Luton and Leeds/Bradford. Other regional Public
Enquiry Offices: Birmingham Airport, *t* (0121) 782 3600;
Glasgow Airport, *t* (0141) 887 2255; Norwich Airport, *t*
(01603) 408859; Harwich port, *t* (01255) 504371; Liverpool,
t (0151) 236 8974; and Belfast, see Northern Ireland. These
cities (apart from Norwich) also have local Immigration Offices
(contact numbers from the Enquiry Offices). Other
Immigration Offices, holding centres and specialist
units—numbers from Enquiry Offices, Home Office or
JCWI—include Bristol, Cardiff, Cheriton (for Channel Tunnel),
Dover, East Midlands Airport, Edinburgh, Gravesend, London
City Airport, Manchester, Newcastle and Ramsgate; detention
centres and prisons used by the Service include Campsfield
House, Doncaster, Harmondsworth (Middlesex), Haslar
(Southampton), Rochester, Winson Green (Birmingham).   »95

● **Immunity Legal Centre**
Helen Tyrrell/Jeremy Gibb: 32-38 Osnaburgh Street, London
NW1 3ND; *t* (0171) 388 6776, *f* 388 6371
Immigration advice (and other legal services) for people
affected by HIV.   »95

✿ **Independent Living Alternatives, ILA**
Tracey Jannaway: Fulton House, Fulton Road, Wembley Park
HA9 0TF; *t* (0181) 902 8998
A service promoting independent living for disabled persons;
currently (1994-95) developing an Ethnic Project to target
support to disabled people from London's ethnic minorities in
ways appropriate to their cultural and religious needs. »94

● **Inquest—United Campaign for Justice**
Debbie Coles/Helen Shaw, Co-Directors: 330 Seven Sisters
Road, London N4 2PJ; *t* (0171) 802 7430
Campaigns around deaths in detention; these cases often
involve black people in police custody, or held under
immigration and asylum law.   »95

▮ **Interights**: International Legal Centre for the Protection of
Human Rights
John Musgrave: 33 Islington High Street, London N1 9LH;
t (0171) 278 3230, *f* 278 4344
Research and documentation on human rights, including
refugee and migration law and policy matters. Involved in
Migration Newssheet. Bulletin (4/yr), booklets.   »95

▮ **International Alert**
Kumar Rupesinghe, General Secretary: 1 Glyn Street, London
SE11 5HT; *t* (0171) 793 8383, *f* 793 7975, *Tx* 94017974
INTA G
Information and documentation on conflict and human rights,
with special interest in early identification of major conflicts,
promoting mediation and dialogue, development of standards
of conduct that avoid violence and help resolve conflict. It has
an associated charity, the Standing International Forum on
Ethnic Conflict, Genocide and Human Rights.   »96

● **International Association for Religious Freedom** British Group
Rev. Peter Godfrey: 41 Bradford Drive, Ewell, Epsom KT19
0AJ; *t* (0181) 313 9122
125 individual members and many Unitarian congregations;
freedom of conscience, freedom of religion, cross-cultural
exchange, social service. See also in Germany, p201.   »88

✿ **International Community Service**
Z. Adam/B. Ogienderi: 336 Chester Road, Sutton Coldfield
B73 5BY; *t* (0121) 384 3841   »94

● **International Health Exchange, IHE**
8-10 Dryden Street, London WC2E 9NA; *t* (0171) 836 5833,
f 379 1239 (?)
Provision and training of health workers for overseas relief and
development agencies, including those involved in emergency
aid to refugees and displaced people.   »96

● **International Organization for Migration, IOM**
26 Westminster Palace Gardens, Artillery Row, London
SW1P 1RR
National office of the intergovernmental body, p218, assisting
planned migration, notably the return of African professionals
to their own countries.   »96

✿ **International Pentecostal City Mission Church Inc.**
Gainsborough Bridge, Fillebrook and Colworth Road,
Leytonstone, London E11
Black-led Christian church; community activities; hosts
Waltham Forest Afro-Caribbean Senior Citizens Club, p7. »94
✿ ≡ Deacon L. Edwards: 1 Epping Walk, Hulme, Manchester
M15   »93

◆ **International Social Service (UK), ISS UK**
Peter Fry: Cranmer House, 39 Brixton Road, London SW9
6DD; *t* (0171) 735 8941-44, *f* 582 0696
An INGO, p218, which helps with problems requiring social
work intervention in more than one country; liaises with
statutory and voluntary sectors in UK and world-wide.
Assistance and counselling for elderly refugees.   »95

▮ **International Society for Human Rights, ISHR**
Glenn Calderwood, Campaigns Officer: St George's House,
14 Wells Street, London W1P 3FP
Pressure group associated with conservative causes; see
German headquarters, p201.   »95

✿ **Into Business**
Kanu Maher: Leicester City Council, 30 New Walk, Leicester;
t (0116) 255 4464
Enterprise agency with special interest in ethnic minority
business development.   »91

✿ **Islington Women's Counselling Centre, IWCC**
Eastgate Building, 131b St John's Way, London N19 3RQ
A multi-ethnic organisation offering individual psycho-analytic
counselling and therapeutic groupwork. Special projects for
refugee women and for Irish women.   »95

● **Justice**
Anne Owers, Director: 59 Carter Lane, London EC4V 5AQ;
t (0171) 329 5100, *f* 329 5055
Helen Bamford. Human rights and law reform group; its
concerns include inhumane treatment of asylum-seekers.
Affiliate of the International Commission of Jurists, p217. »96

✿ **Kensington Citizens Advice Bureau**
Carlos Dabezies, Solicitor: 140 Ladbroke Grove, London W10
5ND; *t* (0181) 969 2433
General consumer and legal advice; immigration work: family
reunion, refugees, other issues. »95

✿ **Kirklees Community Law Centre**
Solveig Rawlings: 5 Lion Chambers, John William Street,
Huddersfield HD1 1ES; *t* (01484) 518525, 542883, *f* 543006
Law centre founded 1994; specialist advice on matters
including immigration, nationality and discrimination. »95

✿ **Kush Housing Association Ltd**
98 Stoke Newington High Street, London N16 7NY
Black-led social housing group; 500 homes in five London
boroughs, mainly African-Caribbean tenants. »96

✿ **Lambeth Welfare Rights Unit**
7th Floor, International House, Canterbury Crescent, London
SW9 7QE »94
*Law Centres: the 50 or so listed here are independent agencies
offering free legal advice and representation services, often
including some immigration and asylum work. All can provide
referrals to specialist services. Where Centres have worked
with particular ethnic groups these are often mentioned: this
does not mean that the Centres work only with such groups.
See Law Centres Federation, below, and Advice Bureaux,
p220.*

● **Law Centres Federation**, LCF
Duchess House, 18-19 Warren Street, London W1P 5DP;
t (0171) 387 8570, *f* 387 8368
Network of legal advice and assistance centres, many (listed
separately) having substantial caseloads in immigration,
nationality, refugee and race relations areas. Regional office:
3rd Floor, Arundel Court, 117 Arundel Street, Sheffield S1
2NU; *t* (0114) 278 7088, *f* 787004. »95

✿ **Leeds Citizens Advice Bureau**, CAB
Richard Norton: Westminster Buildings, 31 New York Street,
Leeds LS2 7DT; *t* (0113) 245 7679, 245 3037
General legal and consumer advice centre in an inner city.
Works with many ethnic minorities and travellers. »94

● **Legal Action Group**, LAG
Roger Smith, Director: 242-244 Pentonville Road, London N1
9UN; *t* (0171) 833 3931, *f* 837 6094
Graham Davies. A charity whose purpose is to promote equal
access to justice. Publications include *Immigration and
asylum: emergency procedures*, journal (12/yr), books;
courses, conferences. »95

✿ **Legal Defence and Monitoring Group**
BM Box HAVEN, London WC1X 3NN
Provides observers and legal back-up for public protests and
demonstrations; founded 1995. »96

✿ **Leicester Rights Centre**
Madhu Gurung: 2nd Floor, Burdett House, 122-124 Granby
Street, Leicester LE1 1DL; *t* (0116) 255 3781, *f* 255 6431
Law centre with immigration and nationality work including
East African Asians, Gujaratis. »94

✿ **Lewisham Council Housing Race Equality Unit**
Race Equality Manager: Capital House, 47 Rushey Green,
Catford, London SE6 4BA
Development, implementation and management of housing
policies and services to meet the needs of the multi-racial
population in the area, including measures to combat racial
harassment. Local agencies, such as Silwood Community
Forum, also have specialist Council-employed officers to deal
with racial harassment and community safety issues for the
housing service. »95

◆ **Liberty**, formerly National Council for Civil Liberties, NCCL:
also Civil Liberties Trust; Cobden Trust
John Wadham, Director: 21 Tabard Street, London SE1 4LA;
t (0171) 403 3888, *f* 407 5354
Hillary Ransom, office manager. The leading campaigning
organisation on all UK civil rights matters. The Civil Liberties
Trust publishes information on civil rights; the Cobden Trust
funds research on such issues and produced, with JCWI, a
report (1995) on migrant and asylum rights. »96

✿ **Liverpool 8 Law Centre**
34-36 Princes Road, Liverpool L8 1TH; *t* (0151) 709 7222,
f 709 4996
General law centre; interests include African, Bangladeshi,
Chinese immigration cases, family reunion, DNA testing,
refugees. »95

▌ **Local Government International Bureau**
David Herbert, Assistant Director: 35 Great Smith Street,
London SW1P 3BJ; *t* (0171) 222 8100
The international and European affairs arm of the local
authority Associations; representation and advice. »95

✿ **London Advice Services Alliance**
Margi Butler: 2nd Floor, Universal House, 88-94 Wentworth
Street, London E1 7SA; *t* (0171) 377 2798, *f* 247 4725 »94

✿ **London Voluntary Service Council**, LVSC: London Voluntary
Sector Resource Centre
356 Holloway Road, London N7 6PA; *t* (0171) 700 8114,
700 8107, 700 0010
Co-ordination and support services for the 30,000 voluntary
bodies in London. *Voluntary Voice* (12/yr), directories. »95

✿ **Longsight and Moss Side Community Project**
Mohina Puri: Pastoral Centre, 95A Princess Road, Moss Side,
Manchester M14 4TH; *t* (0161) 225 8583, 226 4632
Resource centre; mental health drop-in centre, family welfare
casework, work with Asian elderly. »93

✿ **Luton Law Centre**
Balbir Dutt: 2a Reginald Street, Luton LU2 7QZ; *t* (01582)
481000 part-time, *f* 482581
Generalist legal advice centre; Asian, Caribbean, Middle
Eastern immigration, DNA testing, asylum, family reunion.»95

✿ **Manchester Citizens Advice Bureau**
Ray Forbes, District Manager: Swan Buildings, Swan Street,
Manchester M4 5JW
Generalist consumer advice service through several local
offices; some immigration work. »94

✿ **Maternity Links**
Shaheen Chaudry: The Old Co-op, 38-42 Chelsea Road,
Easton, Bristol BS5 6AF; *t* (0117) 955 8495 »94

● **Médecins sans Frontières (UK)**, MSF-UK *(literally Doctors
without Borders; only French name is used)*
Anne-Marie Huby: 124-132 Clerkenwell Road, London EC1R
5DL; *t* (0171) 329 6939, *f* 329 6936
Also listed (1994) as 3-4 St Andrew's Hill, EC4V 5BY.
National section of the medical aid charity, see p191; serves
refugees and victims of conflict and disaster. »95

● **Medical Emergency Relief International**, MERLIN
Sue Harper/Annie Macklow-Smith: 1a Rede Place, London
W2 4TU; *f* (0171) 243 1442
A humanitarian agency providing medical volunteer teams in
the first phase of international emergencies. »96

◆ **Medical Foundation for the Care of Victims of Torture**,
MFCVT, also known as The Medical Foundation
Helen Bamber, Director: 96-98 Grafton Road, London NW5
3EJ; *t* (0171) 813 7777, *f* 813 0011
Provides direct medical, psychological and social care and
treatment for, and campaigns on behalf of, victims of torture
including refugees; serves over 2,500 people per year;
promotes human rights, fair treatment of asylum seekers. »96

✿ **Merton Council Translation Services Project Team**
Chief Executive's Department, Merton Civic Centre, London
Road, Morden SM4 5DX
Provides interpreting and translation service for minority-
language users of public services. »95

● **Methodist Church Division of Social Responsibility**
Ivan Weekes/Carolyn Maynard: Central Hall, Storey's Gate,
Westminster, London SW1H 9NH; *t* (0171) 222 8010
Regional office in York (Stanley Platt). Advises and represents
the Church in matters of social justice and community affairs.
The Methodists' Secretary for Racial Justice is also secretary
to the Churches Commission for Racial Justice, p177. »95

✿ **Middlesbrough Law Centre**
St Mary's Centre, 82-90 Corporation Road, Cleveland TS1
2RW; *t* (01642) 223813, *f* 241495
Generalist legal advice and advocacy service; immigration and
nationality work accounts for half of its caseload. »95

✿ **Millen Advice Point**
Salisbury Street, Swindon, Wiltshire; *t* (01793) 487934
Consumer rights advice; Asian-language services. »95

▌ **Minority Rights Group**, MRG
Alan Phillips, Director: 379 Brixton Road, London SW9 7DE;
t (0171) 978 9498, *f* 738 6265
Robert Webb. International educational and campaigning
charity; research, publishing, campaigning on human rights of
ethnic, religious and linguistic minorities around the world, and
on ethnic conflict as background to refugee flows. *Outsider*
newsletter (4/yr); over 80 country reports (adding 5/yr). »96

✿ **Mitcham Citizens Advice Bureau**
326 London Road, Mitcham CR4 3ND
Generalist rights advice agency serving a multi-racial area of
south-west London; specialist services include outreach to
Asian women. »95

✿ **Moss Side and Hulme Forum**
Hartley Hanley, Chairman: [address unknown] Manchester
Community group in a mainly-black area. Concerns include
anti-racism, policing.   »95

✿ **Mutual Community Care Association, MCCA**
50 Bellott Street, Manchester M8
Welfare, immigration, educational and personal advice,
counselling and casework.   »93

♦ **National Association of Citizens Advice Bureaux, NACAB**
Fernando Ruz: Myddleton House, 115-123 Pentonville Road,
London N1 9LZ; *t* (0171) 833 2181, *f* 833 4371
Umbrella organisation of local CABx—generalist legal and
consumer advice centres, with volunteer and professional
staff, many of which have significant caseloads on
immigration, refugee and nationality issues; those known
to be particularly active in such fields are listed separately.
NACAB, which provides a range of central support services
(recruitment, training) to the local Bureaux, has a number of
regional offices.   »95

● **National Council for Voluntary Organisations, NCVO**
(formerly National Council of Social Service)
Regent Wharf, 8 All Saints Street, London N1 9RL; *t* (0171)
713 6161, *f* 713 6300
Umbrella group for 600 NGOs, including many in the advice,
community development, minorities, welfare rights fields. »95

● **National Liaison Committee of Diocesan Justice and Peace
Groups**
[address unknown]
Co-ordination of the church's approach to social and human
rights issues.   »94

● **National Union of Students, NUS**
Jim Murphy, President: Nelson Mandela House, 457-461
Holloway Road, London N7 6LJ; *t* (0171) 272 8900, *f* 263
5713
Federation of third-level student unions; separate national
offices in Scotland (Edinburgh) and Wales (Swansea). Anti-
racist campaigns; see also Campus Watch, p177.   »95

♦ **Nationality Division**, Home Office Immigration and
Nationality Department
3rd Floor, India Buildings, Water Street, Liverpool L2 0QN;
t (0151) 236 4723, *f* 255 1160
The division of the Home Office, p223, which processes
applications for naturalisation and citizenship. See also
Immigration and Nationality Department, p224.   »95

● **New Testament Church of God Community Project**
Rev. Rudolph Parkinson, National Secretary: 179 High Road,
London NW10 2SD; *t* (0181) 459 5345, 459 1142
Largest of the black-led churches in Britain; congregations in
many areas.   »94

✿ **Newcastle Law Centre**
Maureen Foster: 279 Westgate Road, Newcastle-upon-Tyne
NE4 6AJ; *t* (0191) 230 4777, *f* 233 0295
Generalist law centre; immigration work includes divided
families, primary purpose, refugees; mostly South Asian
clients.   »95

✿ **Newham Citizens Advice Bureau Legal Service**
Edmund Jankowski: 13 Albert Road, London E16 2DW;
t (0171) 473 3131
Generalist rights advice, some work on immigration. »96

✿ **Newham Rights Centre, NRC**: also known as Newham
Rights Law Centre
Haleem Thomas/Laurel Gregg: 285 Romford Road, Forest
Gate, London E7 9HJ; *t* (0181) 519 4870, 555 3331,
f 519 7348
Inner-city legal advice and representation centre with asylum,
nationality and immigration caseload. Also campaigning,
training, publishing in these fields.   »95

✿ **North East London Advocacy**
The Administrator: Alpha Business Centre, South Grove,
Walthamstow, London E17 7NX; *t* (0181) 521 7603
Human rights based citizen advocacy, with professional and
volunteer staff; includes specialist Asian advocacy work. »94

✿ **North Islington Law Centre**
161 Hornsey Road, London N7 6DU; *t* (0171) 607 2461,
f 700 0072
Legal advice and advocacy; specialist Immigration Unit with
case load including Turkish, Cypriot, Kurdish, Caribbean,
Indian, Pakistani, Bangladeshi, Filipino and West African
immigration and asylum work.   »96

✿ **North Kensington Law Centre, NKLC**
Karen D'Rozario/Jay Sharma: 74 Golborne Road, London
W10 5PS; *t* (0181) 969 7473, *f* 968 0934
Generalist legal advice and assistance centre; all aspects of
immigration except business/work related; European social
security issues.   »95

✿ **North Lambeth Law Centre**
14 Bowden Street, Kennington, London SE11 4DS; *t* (0171)
582 4372-73, 582 4425, *f* 582 2148
General legal and welfare advice and representation; some,
mainly African and Caribbean, immigration work.   »95

✿ **North Lewisham Law Centre**
Barbara Ledgister/Amir Hamzavi: 28 Deptford High Street,
London SE8 3NU; *t* (0181) 692 3217, 692 5355, *f* 694 2516
Legal assistance, some immigration and nationality work. »95

✿ **North Manchester Law Centre**
K. Ashcroft: Community Services Centre, Paget Street,
Collyhurst, Manchester M10 7UX; *t* (0161) 205 9031, 205
5040
General legal advice and advocacy, anti-discrimination work,
some refugee and immigration/deportation work.   »95

✿ **Notting Hill Housing Group**
26 Paddenswick Road, London W6 0UB
Housing trust with some 12,000 properties; developing four
housing projects for young refugees in conjunction with the
London Borough of Hillingdon.   »95

✿ **Nottingham and District Citizens Advice Bureau**
Mohammed Tufail: Castlegate House, 24-30 Castle Gate,
Nottingham NG1 7AT
Generalist rights advice centre.   »94

✿ **Nottingham Law Centre**, also known as Hyson Green Law
Centre
Jane Bramley: 119 Radford Road, Hyson Green, Nottingham
NG7 5DU; *t* (0115) 978 7813, *f* 979 2969
General law centre; family reunion, other immigration rights
work with Indians, Pakistanis, Bengalis.   »95

✿ **Oldham Law Centre**
Paul Johnson: 2nd Floor, Prudential Buildings, 79 Union
Street, Oldham OL1 1HL; *t* (0161) 627 0925
Legal assistance, all areas of immigration work; employs a
specialist Asian Women's Rights Officer.   »95

● **One World Action**
Jane Winder, Director: Floor 5, Weddel House, 13-14 West
Smithfield, London EC1N 9HY; *t* (0171) 329 8111
Andy Rutherford. Development education charity, campaigns
with and for poor and exploited people, especially women, in
the South, for a better, more equal world.   »95

● **Overseas Placing Unit**, also known as the Overseas Labour
Service: Department for Education and Employment, DEE
Porterbrook House, W5 Moorfoot, Sheffield S1 4PQ; *t* (0114)
275 3275, *f* 259 3728, 275 8316
Processes applications for work, and requests for information
about work, relating to other EU countries or to non-nationals
seeking work in the UK. Does not deal directly with the
public, but through local Jobcentres (employment information
offices) and partner agencies in the EURES information
network, p190. Work permit applications: *t* (0117) 924 4730.»95

▌**Oxfam**
274 Banbury Road, Oxford OX2 7DH; *t* (01865) 311311,
f 312600
Major international charity (1,800 staff, 2,000 projects in 70
countries). Development education, humanitarian aid, disaster
relief; works with refugees and returnees worldwide. »94

✿ **Paddington Law Centre**
439 Harrow Road, London W10 4RE; *t* (0181) 960 3155,
f 968 0417
A general law centre; some welfare and immigration/refugee
work with Asian, Caribbean, African, Middle Eastern and
other client groups.   »95

✿ **Parkside Health Equal Access Project**
Woodfield Road, London W9 2BB
Two-year Project (1995-97) to identify barriers to accessing
health care and to influence change in the patterns of service
use and service delivery, to improve the health of marginalised
groups in Brent. It employs outreach workers, based in High
Street, Harlesden, for the major ethnic communities. »95

● **Peace Brigades International, PBI**
83 Margaret Street, London W1N 7HB; *t* (0171) 636 7644
Pacifist human rights organisation which sends international
civilian peace volunteer teams to areas of conflict. »96

● **Physicians for Human Rights**
Dr Andrew J. Carney/Dr Peter Hall: 57 Parliament Hill, London
NW3
Concerned with international human rights issues, especially
those with a public health or welfare aspect.   »94

✿ **Piccadilly Advice Centre**
John Lowery: 100 Shaftesbury Avenue, London W1V 7DH;
t (0171) 734 8678   »94

✿ **Pitsmoor Citizens Advice Bureau**
30 Spital Hill, Sheffield S4 7LG; *t* (0114) 273 8838
Generalist advice centre; immigration/nationality work. »95

✿ **Plumstead Community Law Centre**
105 Plumstead High Street, London SE18 1SB; *t* (0181) 855 9817, *f* 316 7903
General legal and consumer rights advice, including immigration problems. »95

✿ **Pottery Lane Advice Centre**
Fiona Nijaye: St Francis of Assisi Community Centre, Pottery Lane, London W11 4NQ; *t* (0171) 792 9011
Generalist community advice centre; see also Kalayaan (domestic workers group), p36. »94

✿ **Princes Street Advice Centre**, Oxford Citizens Advice Bureau
44b Princes Street, Oxford OX4 1DD
Extension office of the CAB, dealing mainly with the local Asian community's welfare rights, employment and immigration problems; see also Oxfordshire Immigration and Nationality Project, p156. »95

● **Quaker Committee on Government Openness**
Friends House, Euston Road, London NW1 2BJ; *t* (0171) 387 3601
Organ of the Religious Society of Friends which promotes freedom of information and responsive government, opposing official secrecy and bureaucratism. »94

● **Quaker Peace and Service**, QPS: Religious Society of Friends
Mary Hogan, General Secretary: Friends House, Euston Road, London NW1 2BJ; *t* (0171) 387 3601, *f* 388 1977
36 staff; founded 1979; educational work and voluntary service on global peace and development issues, including support (not funding) for refugee relief and development projects; publications including *QPS Reporter* (4/yr). »95

● **Race Relations Employment Advisory Service**, RREAS:
Southern Division: London, SE and SW England
236 Grays Inn Road, London WC1X 8HL; *t* (0171) 211 4566
Part of the Department for Education and Employment. »95

✿ ≡ Northern Division: Birmingham (West Midlands & Wales): Cumberland House, 14th Floor, 200 Broad Street, Birmingham B15 1TA; *t* (0121) 643 8144 ext. 201 »95

✿ ≡ Northern Division: Leeds (Yorkshire, Humberside, North): Jubily House, 33-41 Park Place, Leeds LS1 2RJ; *t* (0113) 244 6299 »95

✿ ≡ Northern Division: Nottingham (East Midlands): Birbeck House, 14-16 Trinity Square, Nottingham NG1 4AX; *t* (0115) 958 1224 »95

✿ ≡ Northern Division: Manchester (North-West & Scotland): Employment Service, Ontario House, 2 Furness Quays, Salford M5 2XZ; *t* (0161) 873 1000 »95

✿ **Reading International Support Centre**, RISC
103 London Street, Reading RG1 4QA; *t* (01734) 586692
Development education charity, promoting awareness of human rights and social justice issues. »94

● **Rights and Justice**
Mary Dines: 305a Aberdeen House, 22 Highbury Grove, London N5 2EA; *t* (0171) 704 6028, *f* 704 6026
Civil rights pressure group; see also Asylum Aid, p153. »95

✿ **The Rights Office**
Lucie Mackenzie: 12 Picardy Place, Edinburgh EH1 3JT
Generalist advice centre, including migrant and minority rights questions. See also Shakti Women's Aid, p157. »93

✿ **The Rights Shop**
296 Bethnal Green Rd, London E2 0AG; *t* (0171) 739 4173
Welfare, consumer and other legal advice; Asian language services. »96

✿ **Rochdale Law Centre**
Audrey MacDonald/Chris Cunningham: Smith Street, Rochdale OL16 1HE; *t* (01706) 341674, 57766
Generalist legal advice and representation service; some immigration work. »96

✿ **Rochdale Metropolitan Borough Council Equal Opportunities Unit**
Municipal Offices, Smith Street, Rochdale OL16 1YA
The Council's three-member EO Unit, in the Chief Executive and Town Clerk's Department, assists in development and monitoring of Council policies and services as they relate to race issues, disabled people and women. »95

● **Royal College of Nursing Immigration Advisory Service**
20 Cavendish Square, London W1M 0AB; *t* (0171) 629 3870, *f* 355 1379
The national body for the nursing profession in the UK; offers advice on immigration and recognition of qualifications to foreign nurses. »95

● **Bertrand Russell Peace Foundation**, BRPF
Bertrand Russell House, Gamble Street, Nottingham NG7 4ET; *t* (0115) 970 8318, *f* 942 0433
Funds work on international understanding, peace education, human rights, anti-racism. »94

✿ **Salford Law Centre**
Sajida Ismail: 498 Liverpool Street, Salford M6 5QZ; *t* (0161) 736 3116 including minicom, *f* 745 9257
General rights and welfare advice, immigration work with Pakistani, Yemeni, Iranian and other families. Briefing papers on migration issues including disability. »95

✿ **Saltley Action Centre**, SAC
Abdul Malik, Chair: 2 Alum Rock Road, Saltley, Birmingham B8 1JB; *t* (0121) 328 2307, *f* 327 7486
Nur ul-Haq vice-chair, Sajid Malik advice worker. Generalist law centre with Bangladeshi, Mirpuri, other Asian immigration cases. Established 1977. See also Minorities Resource Centre, p245. »95

▌ **Save the Children**, SCF
Mike Aaronson, Director: Mary Datchelor House, 17 Grove Lane, London SE5 8RD; *t* (0171) 703 5400, *f* 793 7610
International development and emergency aid charity with focus on child and family welfare; 80 UK and European projects, relief work in 50 countries including some refugee work in Africa and Asia. Projects of SCF in the UK (formerly separate from the international SCF, merged 1996) include Vietnamese and South East Asian refugee resettlement, a London Gypsy Traveller Unit, production of development education resources, funding of community groups including Hopscotch Asian Women's Centre. See also Österreichische Gesellschaft Rettet das Kind (Austria), p188, Rädda Barnen (Sweden), p216, Landsorganisationen Red Barnet (Denmark), p195, and International Save the Children Alliance (Switzerland), p218. »96

✿ **SCDC**
Helen Carter: 45 Newcombe House, Notting Hill Gate, London W11; *t* (0171) 229 1234 »90

● **Scottish Catholic International Aid Fund**, SCIAF
Duncan MacLaren, Executive Director: 5 Oswald Street, Glasgow G1 4QR, Scotland; *t* (0141) 221 4447
Official aid and development agency of the Catholic Church in Scotland; promotion of international solidarity and North-South economic justice. »95

● **Scottish Council for Civil Liberties**, SCCL
Alan Miller, Chair: 146 Holland Street, Glasgow G2 4NG, Scotland; *t* (0141) 332 5960
Defence of human rights and civil liberties in Scotland. »95

● **Scottish European Aid**, SEA
Liz McLaughlin/Pepy Turnbull: 18 Hanover Street, Edinburgh EH2 2EN, Scotland; *t* (0131) 225 4465
Humanitarian infrastructural, social work and health care projects in Bosnia and Romania. »95

✿ **SEA Housing Co-operative Ltd**
163a Knight's Hill, London SE27 0PZ; *t* (0181) 761 7981 »90

✿ **The Selby Centre**
The Director: Selby Road, Tottenham, London N17 8JN
Multicultural business and leisure facility. »95

✿ **Sheffield Law Centre**
Lesley Rawlins/Derek McConnell: Waverley House, 10 Joiner Street, Sheffield S3 8GW; *t* (0114) 273 1888, *f* 273 1501
General advice and representation; some immigration, DNA tests, asylum work with Pakistani, Bangladeshi, Somali, Yemeni, Caribbean clients. Developing specialist services to the Black communities of Sheffield. »95

✿ **Shiloh Youth Development Project**
Lawrence Road, London SE25 5AV; *t* (0181) 771 8525 »90

● **Single Parent Action Network**, SPAN
L. Dixon: Millpond, Baptist Street, Easton, Bristol BS5 0YJ
Welfare rights campaign, supports black self-help groups. »96

✿ **Social and Pastoral Action**
Michael Feeney: 46 Francis Street, London SW1P 1QN
Catholic church agency. »95

▌ **Socialist International**, SI
Luis Ayala, General Secretary: Maritime House, Old Town, Clapham, London SW4 0JW; *t* (0171) 627 4449
World-wide alliance of socialist and social democratic parties. *Socialist Affairs* (4/yr). »94

✿ **South Islington Law Centre**
131-132 Upper Street, London N1 1QP; *t* (0171) 354 0133, 350 3207, *f* 354 8155
General law centre with some EU, Turkish, Nigerian, Bangladeshi immigration work. Base for the (dormant) London Divided Families Campaign on immigration rules. »95

✿ **South Manchester Law Centre**
584-586 Stockport Road, Longsight, Manchester M13 0RQ; *t* (0161) 225 5111, *f* 225 0210
General legal advice and advocacy, including immigration matters; Pakistani, Somali, Bangladeshi, West African, Far Eastern, Latin American cases. See also Longsight and Levenshulme Anti-Racist Group, p181. »95

✣ **Southampton Citizens Advice Bureau**
Zahid Arain/John Clarke: 3 Kings Park Road, Southampton
SO1 2AS; *t* (01703) 223659, 331675, 333868, *f* 237284
General consumer, legal and welfare rights work; some Asian
and Caribbean immigration and related cases. »94

✣ **Southwark Law Centre**
Hanover Park House, 14-16 Hanover Park, Peckham, London
SE15 5HS; *t* (0171) 732 2008, *f* 732 2034
Free legal advice and representation. »95

✣ **Southwark Law Project**
2 East Dulwich Grove, London SE22 8PP; *t* (0181) 229 1024
Law centre with generalist housing, welfare, employment
caseload; Nigerian, Asian, Caribbean immigration work. »95

✣ **Southwark Victim Support Scheme**
Delia Mitchell: 62 Borough High Street, St Margaret's Court,
London SE1 1XF
Support to victims of crime, including racial harassment. »96

✣ **Stockton and Hartlepool Law Centre**
Simon Daly: 76 Norton Road, Stockton-on-Tees TS18 2DE;
t (01642) 605060, *f* 618616
Legal assistance, some immigration work. »95

✣ **Stockwell and Clapham Law Centre**
Rachel Cooper: 57-59 Old Town, Clapham, London SW4 0JQ;
t (0171) 720 6231, *f* 498 6760
Legal advice, including immigration and nationality cases. »95

✣ **Stoke-on-Trent Citizens Advice Bureau**
Tontine Buildings, 56 Tontine Street, Hanley, Stoke-on-Trent
ST1 1LY; *t* (01782) 261157
General advice centre; inner-city service in partnership with
Cobridge Multicultural Project, p178. »94

▌ **Marie Stopes International**
Patricia Hindmarsh: 62 Grafton Way, London W1P 5LD
Reproductive health care worldwide. Currently (1995)
developing initiatives for refugees and displaced persons. »95

▌ **Survival International**
Honor Drysdale/Stephen Corry: 11-15 Emerald Street, London
WC1N 3QL; *t* (0171) 723 5535 (?)
Campaigns for self-determination of tribal peoples, and helps
to protect their lives, lands and rights. Founded 1969. »95

● **Tear Fund**
100 Church Road, Teddington TW11 8QE; *t* (0181) 977
9144, *f* 943 3594
Evangelical Christian humanitarian aid agency, supporting
numerous development and emergency relief projects, often
involving refugees, in Africa, Asia and Latin America. »93

✣ **Thamesdown Community Law Centre**
26 Victoria Rd, Swindon SN1; *t* (01793) 486926, *f* 432193
General legal and welfare advice. »95

● **Third World First**, 3W1
217 Cowley Road, Oxford OX4 1UH; *t* (01865) 245678,
f 200179
Development education, anti-racism; campaigns among
students on a range of issues including refugees, overseas
students, deportation, racism and sexism. »95

✣ **Tottenham Legal Advice Centre**
Helen Garner: 15 Bramshill Gardens, London NW5 1JJ;
t (0171) 272 8662
New law centre; services include immigration advice. »96

✣ **Tottenham Neighbourhood Law Centre**
M.K. Mukherjee: 15 West Green Road, Tottenham, London
N15 5BX; *t* (0181) 802 0911, *f* 809 7078
Generalist legal advice centre; some immigration work. »95

✣ **Tower Hamlets Council Social Services Directorate
Equalities Unit**
Ghulum Morshed: [address unknown] London E; *t* (0171) 512
4200 ext. 4873
Unit reviews design and delivery of social services to ensure
that they do not discriminate against groups or individuals.»95

✣ **Tower Hamlets East Citizens Advice Bureau**
Alea Ismail: 86 Bow Rd, London E3 4DL; *t* (0181) 981 6826
Welfare rights, housing, employment, immigration and
nationality advice; special service to Bengali community. »95

✣ **Tower Hamlets Law Centre**
Maria Davidson/Habib Rahman: 341 Commercial Road, London
E1 2PS; *t* (0171) 791 0741, *f* 702 7301
Lilian Byrnes. Legal, welfare and employment rights advice
and representation; specialist team for immigration, nationality,
welfare rights and refugee work. Monitors racist attacks.»96

◆ **Trades Union Congress**, TUC
Congress House, Great Russell Street, London WC1B 3LS;
t (0171) 636 4030, *f* 636 0632
National confederation of trade unions; its Equal Rights
Department conducts research and develops policy on a wide
range of race equality, migration and minority issues.
Organised National Unite Against Racism rally in 1995. »95

✣ **Turnpike Lane Advice Bureau**
16 Turnpike Lane, Hornsey, London N8 0PT; *t* (0181) 888
4233
General legal and consumer rights advice; Cypriot,
Bangladeshi, Turkish, Eritrean, Somali, Kurdish immigration and
refugee concerns. »94

✣ **United Evangelical Project Legal Centre**
David Alcock: 29 Trinity Road, Aston, Birmingham B6 6AJ;
t (0121) 523 0965, *f* 554 4894
General legal and welfare rights advice centre operated by
Christian community project. See also Black-Led Churches
Liaison, p20. »94

● **United Kingdom Committee for UNICEF**, UNICEF-UK
Robert D. Smith: 55 Lincoln's Inn Fields, London WC2A 3NB;
t (0171) 405 5592, *f* 405 2332
Support, publicity and fundraising for UNICEF, the United
Nations Children's Fund, p219, a leading international
development agency working for children. »95

● **United Nations Association—UK**, UNA-UK
Malcolm Harper, Director: 3 Whitehall Court, London SW1A
2EL; *t* (0171) 930 2931, *f* 930 5893
Promotes the principles of the United Nations concerning
peaceful co-existence of nations, conflict resolution through
negotiation and mediation, equitable trading and political
relations, self-determination of peoples, international standards
on human rights, humanitarian relief, and other matters. »94

▌ **United Nations High Commissioner for Refugees**, UNHCR:
Branch Office for the UK
Philippe Lavanchy: 21st Floor, Millbank Tower, 21-24 Millbank,
London SW1P 4QP; *t* (0171) 828 9191, *f* 630 5349,
Tx 8951252 HCRLDN G, *Tg* HICOMREF London
The national office of the Swiss-based UN agency, p219,
responsible for refugee status and protection; this office also
serves Ireland when the need arises. »95

✣ **Vauxhall Law Centre**
Multi-Services Centre, Silvester Street, Liverpool L5 8SE;
t (0151) 207 2004, 207 3502
Free legal advice and representation service covering all areas
including immigration. »95

● **Voluntary Service Overseas**, VSO (usually known by the
acronym)
317 Putney Bridge Road, London SW15 2PN; *t* (0181) 780
1331
Development agency providing 1,700 skilled volunteer workers
to 55 African, Caribbean and Pacific countries, and, through
the East European Partnership, EEP, to 12 countries in Central
and Eastern Europe. »95

✣ **Waltham Forest Social Justice Unit**
Walthamstow Town Hall, Forest Road, London E17 4JF;
t (0181) 527 5544
Local council unit establishing (1996) a new contracted-out
agency, developed from a Project Against Racial Attacks and
Harassment, to provide advice, advocacy and support for racial
minorities, women, gay people, elders, youth, people affected
by HIV/AIDS and the economically disadvantaged. »96

✣ **Walthamstow Citizens Advice Bureau**
Hilary Plews: 167 Hoe Street, London E17 3AL; *t* (0181) 520
2649, 521 5414, 520 0939, *f* 509 9611
Generalist advice bureau, some immigration-related work. »95

✣ **Wandsworth Interpreting Service**: Wandsworth Council
[address unknown] London SW
Interpreting and translation services to racial minority
communities in Wandsworth. »95

✣ **Wandsworth Law Centre Ltd**
Morris Assaf: 248 Lavender Hill, London SW11 1LJ; *t* (0171)
228 9462, 228 2566, *f* 738 9638
Generalist legal advice and representation centre; specialist
services on race discrimination, racial harassment and issues
affecting asylum seekers. »95

▌ **War Resisters International**, WRI
5 Caledonian Road, London N1 9DX; *t* (0171) 278 4040,
f 278 0444
Peace movement providing political and practical assistance to
persons deserting military service or refusing conscription.»94

● **War on Want**, WoW
Giampi Alhadeff, Director: 37 Great Guildford Street, London
SE1 7PJ; *t* (0171) 620 1111, *f* 261 9291
Third World development charity with a strong campaigning
focus. Interested in human rights issues and international
solidarity work. The associated political campaigning group is
War on Want Campaigns. »95

✣ **Warrington Law Centre**
64-66 Bewsey Street, Warrington WA2 7JQ; *t* (01925)
651104, *f* 444736
Free legal representation and advice. »95

✿ **Watford Citizens Advice Bureau**
Carol Firman, Deputy Manager: St Mary's Churchyard, High
Street, Watford WD1 2BE
Generalist consumer advice; has outreach programme for
minority communities, including Urdu-speaking women. »95

✿ **Watford Council Corporate Equality Advice Team**
Race Equality Adviser: Strategic Development Department,
Town Hall, Watford WD1 3EX; *t* (01923) 240175
Develops and monitors the local authority's Equality Strategy,
and policies for combatting racial harassment; promotes racial
equality in Watford, and advises Council staff on how best to
meet the needs of ethnic minority citizens. »95

✿ **Wesleyan Holiness Church**
Pastor K. Charles: 50 Boundary Lane, Hulme, Manchester
M15; *t* (0161) 226 9685
Black-led Christian church. »93

✿ **West Hertfordshire Community Health NHS Trust**
99 Waverley Road, St Albans AL3 5TL
General health care trust within the National Health Service;
employs a Cross Cultural Services Organiser (based at The
Avenue Clinic, Watford) to develop services offered to people
from ethnic minorities. »94

● **Wilberforce Council**
Salisbury Hall, Park Road, Hull HU3 1TD; *t* (01482) 26848,
f 568756
Support for international standards of human rights, including
rights of minorities, migrants and refugees. A small
campaigning group founded 1980. »93

▌**Women's International League for Peace and Freedom**, WILPF
157 Lyndhurst Road, Worthing BN11 2DG; *t* (01903) 205161
Promotes human rights, development education, international
solidarity. »96

● **World Development Movement**, WDM
Jean Rowland: 25 Beehive Place, London SW9 7QR; *t* (0171)
737 6215, *f* 274 8232
Lobbying and pressure group on Third World issues. Engages
in development education; challenges aid and trade policies.
Non-profit organisation, refused charitable status because of
its campaigning activities. »96

◆ **World University Service (UK)**, WUS UK, and Refugee
Education and Training Advisory Service, RETAS
Sam Clarke, Director: 20-21 Compton Terrace, London N1
2UN; *t* (0171) 226 6747, *f* 226 0482
Hermione Murrell, Parvin Paidar. National committee of WUS
International, p219, a development agency specialising in
education; legal and educational advice, assistance and
scholarships, for refugees, asylum seekers and third world
students in the UK and abroad, and related campaigning,
development education and information work; students mainly
from Middle East, Africa and Latin America. Manages RETAS,
t 288 4604, whose 15 staff, in three teams, provide advice
and technical training programmes for refugees, refugee
organisations and service providers. »96

✿ **Worlds End Neighbourhood Advice Centre**
2 Worlds End Place, London SW10 0HE; *t* (0171) 351 5749
General advice service; Filipino, Latin American, Moroccan,
Bangladeshi visa and settlement work. »91

✿ **Wythenshawe Law Centre**
260 Brownley Road, Wythenshawe, Manchester M22 5EB;
t (0161) 498 0905-06, *f* 498 0750
Free legal advice and representation; immigration and
nationality advice. »95

NORTHERN IRELAND 44

✿ **Amnesty International—Northern Ireland Region**, AI
Carolyn Mason, Regional Representative: c/o Corrymeela
House, 8 Upper Crescent, Belfast BT7
Regional section of Amnesty International UK, p220. General
human rights concerns; focus on death penalty and victims of
political oppression. There are local groups in at least 8
districts. »94

✿ **Central Community Relations Unit**, CCRU: Department of
Finance and Personnel
Brian Morrow: Parliament Buildings, Stormont, Belfast BT4;
t (01232) 520700
A civil service unit monitoring, analysing and informing the
development of policy and administrative practice as they
impact on community relations within the region. Although it
is mainly concerned with the relationship between and relative
positions of the Catholic minority and Protestant majority
communities, it also deals with ethnic minorities in Northern
Ireland (where racial discrimination is legal). »95

● **Committee on the Administration of Justice**, CAJ
Martin O'Brien, Information Officer: 45-47 Donegall Street,
Belfast BT1 2FG; *t* (01232) 232394, *f* 333522
Campaigns for the highest standards of justice and civil rights
in Northern Ireland; particular interest in minority rights, and
has called for legislation on racial discrimination, harassment
and equal opportunities. Affiliated to FIDH, p197. *Just
News* (12/yr). »95

✿ **Council for Education in World Citizenship (Northern
Ireland)**, CEWC
c/o Banbridge Academy, Lurgan Road, Banbridge BT32 4AQ,
Co. Down; *t* (018206) 24462
Internationalist, multicultural youth organisation; see UK
CEWC, p222. »94

✿ **Immigration Office**
Belfast International Airport, Aldergrove, Antrim; *t* (01849)
422500
Immigration control; part of UK Home Office, p223. »94
✿ ≡ and Home Office regional Public Enquiry Office: Olivetree
House, Fountain Street, Belfast BT1 5ER; *t* (01232) 322547
enquiries, 232951 general, *f* 244939
Advice, assessment and enforcement in immigration and
nationality matters. »95

✿ **International Voluntary Service (Northern Ireland)**, IVS
122 Great Victoria Street, Belfast BT2 7BG; *t* (01232)
238147, *f* 244356
Recruits and funds voluntary personnel for overseas
development projects; promotes development education, global
awareness. »94

● **Irish Methodist World Development Fund**
6 Lester Park, Magherafelt BT45 6HD, Co. Derry; *t* (01648)
33691
Church agency fundraising for development aid and emergency
relief, including numerous refugee assistance projects
overseas. »93

✿ **Law Centre (NI)**, formerly Belfast Law Centre
Anne Grimes: 7 University Road, Belfast BT7 1NA; *t* (01232)
321307, *f* 236340
Les Allemby, Jill Girvan, R. McEvoy. Charity which promotes
development of social welfare law, and of rights advice and
advocacy services. Legal advice and assistance, casework,
some immigration work; associated office in Derry (9
Clarendon Street, *t* (01504) 262433). »95

✿ **Northern Ireland Association of Citizens Advice Bureaux**
11 Upper Crescent, Belfast BT7; *t* (01232) 231120
Umbrella organisation for local consumer advice centres; these
do not normally deal with immigration or (in the absence of
anti-racist legislation) ethnic minority rights matters, but can
provide referral to specialist services. »94

✿ **Northern Ireland Centre in Europe**
22 Great Victoria Street, Belfast BT2; *t* (01232) 312323
Information and liaison services for Northern Ireland voluntary
organisations, public sector bodies and businesses in their
dealings with European Union partners and institutions;
maintains an office in Brussels. »95

✿ **Northern Ireland Council for Voluntary Action**, NICVA
Edwin Graham/Paula Casey: 127 Ormeau Road, Belfast BT7
1SH; *t* (01232) 321224, *f* 438350
Support and co-ordination agency for voluntary organisations;
has engaged in anti-racist work. »94

✿ **Northern Ireland Voluntary Trust**, NIVT
22 Mount Charles, Belfast BT7; *t* (01232) 245927, *f* 329839
Independent charitable trust, supporting development of
voluntary sector. »94

✿ **Standing Advisory Commission on Human Rights**, SACHR
Aiden Sherrard: Temple Court, 39 North Street, Belfast BT1
1NA; *t* (01232) 243987, *f* 247844
Official body monitoring human rights issues in Northern
Ireland; commissions research and issues reports on issues
such as majority-minority community differentials and
emergency legislation. Has taken some interest in the lack of
legal protection of ethnic minorities in Northern Ireland, and
has made recommendations for legislation. »96

✿ **Training and Employment Agency**, Work Permits Section
Room 304, Clarendon House, 9-21 Adelaide Street, Belfast
BT2 8DJ; *t* (01232) 541771, *f* 541546
Deals with work permit applications relating to employment in
Northern Ireland, largely following the criteria of the (UK)
Overseas Labour Service, p226. »95

✿ **Welfare Rights Unit**
5a Ann Street, Enniskillen BT74, Co. Fermanagh; *t* (01365)
327267
Generalist legal, consumer and social security rights advice
service. »94

VATICAN CITY STATE *39*

▌ **Caritas Internationalis**
Dr Gerhardt Meier, General Secretary: Palazzo San Calisto, Città del Vaticano, 00120 Roma; *t* (06) 6988 7197, 6988 7235, *f* 6988 7237
International Catholic welfare and humanitarian aid agency, with voluntary services to refugees and migrants in many countries. Founded 1950; 125 national bodies including those indexed under Caritas or (France) Secours Catholique.   »93

▌ **Pontifica Commissio Justitia et Pax:** Pontifical Commission for Justice and Peace
piazza S. Calisto 16, 00153 Roma; *t* (06) 698 7191
Central committee for the development and co-ordination of the Catholic Church's response to social justice, human rights, peace and development issues.   »85

Part Five

Research and Documentation Centres

This category covers research groups and associations, university departments, voluntary-sector documentation centres, institutes, libraries and other places and organisations which carry out research or teaching, or provide information or research resources, on migration, minorities, race relations and related issues. Some are solely devoted to such topics, while others are interested in them as part of a wider academic or social agenda. This listing does not include centres specific to one ethnic or national group, which are listed under the appropriate Part One ethnic heading; nor does it include undergraduate teaching departments unless they also engage in research. We have not tried to make this a comprehensive listing of research centres, partly because university centres in particular are easily located through other reference publications, and through formal and informal networks. We would draw attention to the existence of specialist international academic and NGO centres and umbrella groups such as the Ethnic Studies Network, MERGER (based at ERCOMER in Utrecht), and the Scalabrini federation. Users of the Directory who are having difficulty in locating research expertise in a particular field are advised to make contact with such centres and networks.

AUSTRIA 43

■ **Association for the Study of the World Refugee Problem,** AWR
Prof. Dr Henn-Jüri Uibopuu: University of Salzburg, Department of International Law, Churfürststrasse 1, 5020 Salzburg; *t* (0662) 8044/3655
Founded 1954, 10 member organisations; academic society for the study of international aspects of refugee law and related issues, asylum rights, minority rights, settlement and integration of refugees; conferences, seminars; publishing programme, research centre. *AWR Bulletin* (4/yr). »95
● **Dokumentationsarchiv des Österreichischen Widerstandes,** DÖW *(Documentary Archive of the Austrian Resistance)*
Altes Rathaus, Wipplingerstrasse 8, 1010 Wien
Archives of the anti-fascist resistance movement. »94
■ **Europäisches Zentrum: European Centre: Centre Européen**
Berggasse 17, 1090 Wien; *t* (01) 319 4505-0, *f* 319 4505-19
International social science research, training and information centre, founded 1974 (as the European Centre for Social Welfare Training and Research) under UN sponsorship. It works mainly through co-operative research teams of social scientists in two to 20 countries. International Migration, Social Integration and Human Rights is one of seven current research strands. The Centre publishes a range of books, reports and journals in English, German and French, including *EUROSOCIAL Bulletin d'Information/Newsletter/Nachrichten; Journal für Sozialforschung; Annual Report.* »95
♦ **Institut für Hohere Studien** *(Institute for Advanced Studies)*
Dr Rainer Bauböck: Stumpergasse 56, 1060 Wien; *t* (01) 59991, *f* 597 0635
Dr August Gächter, D. Cinar. Research centre with migration-related activities in its political science department, Abteilung Politische Wissenschaften. Conducting (1994) comparative study of naturalisation of immigrants in 12 countries. »94
■ **International Concentration Camp Committee, ICCC:** Comité International des Camps
H. Langbein: Weigandhof 5, 1100 Wien; *t* (01) 644 9585
Represents survivors of fascist concentration camps. »94
● **International Futures Library—Robert Jungk Foundation**
Imbergstr. 2, 5020 Salzburg; *t* (0662) 873206, *f* 848153 »94

BELGIUM 32

● **Antwerps Centrum voor Migrantenstudies** *(Antwerp Centre for Migration Studies)* Departement Sociologie en Sociale Beleid
Prof. Dr Jan Vranken: Universiteit Antwerpen, Prinsstraat 13, 2000 Antwerpen
Sociological research into migration and ethnicity; member of the Utrecht-based MERGER group, p240. »94
✿ **Centre Bruxellois d'Action Interculturelle** *(Brussels Centre for Intercultural Action)* formerly Centre Socio-Culturel des Immigrés de Bruxelles
Bruno Ducoli, President: Avenue de Stalingrad 24, 1000 Bruxelles; *t* (02) 513 9602, 513 9576, *f* 512 1796
Massimo Bortolini, Javier Leunda. Race relations research, information and action. See ADDE, p130. Affiliated to the MAINE network, p146. *Agenda Interculturel* (6/yr). »94
● **Centre d'Etude du Développement de l'Ethnicité et des Migrations** *(Centre for Research on Migration and the Development of Ethnicity)* Université de Liège au Sart-Tilman
Marco Martiniello: Faculté de Droit, Politologie Générale, Boulevard Rectorat 7, bte 43 bat 31, 4000 Liège; *t* (041) 663040, 663035, *f* 662983 »95
✿ **Centre d'Etudes et de Documentation Sociale** *(Centre for Social Studies and Documentation)*
Rue Louvrex 47, 4000 Liège »90
● **Centre d'Information sur les Pratiques Associatives, CIPA** *(Information Centre on Practical Integration)*
Serge Cols, President: Rue de la Sablonnière 18, 1000 Bruxelles; *t* (02) 217 1495
Community development in Belgium and abroad, civil rights, anti-racism; information, public education campaigns, documentation. Has assisted voluntary repatriation and resettlement projects in Vietnam. *Virages, Critiques et Perspectives* (both 4/yr). »94
● **Centre pour la Recherche Interdisciplinaire sur le Développement** *(Centre for Interdisciplinary Research on Development)*
Jacques Dorselaer: Rue Vaduc 152, 1160 Bruxelles; *t* (02) 672 4172
Bulletins, reports, studies. »94

- **Centre de Sociologie et d'Economie Régionale**, Institut de Sociologie
Mateo Alaluf: Université Libre Bruxelles, Campus du Solbosch, Avenue Jeanne 44, 1050 Bruxelles; *t* (02) 650 3431 »95

✿ **Centre Tricontinental**
Avenue Sainte Gertrude 5, 1348 Ottignies, Louvain-la-Neuve; *t* (010) 453152
Documentation, information, research on developing countries' sociology, culture, economics, politics; international solidarity, human rights. »93

- **Centrum voor Bevolkings en Gezinsstudien**: Centre d'Etude de la Population et de la Famille *(Centre for the Study of Population and the Family)*
K. Pauwels: Markiesgebouw, Markiesstraat 1, 1000 Brussel; *t* (02) 507 3583, *f* 507 3419
Research and information on demographic issues. Founded 1962 under Health Ministry auspices. Reports and journals on (mainly internal) migration and related matters. »94

✿ **Centrum Etnische Minderheden en Gezondheid** *(Centre for Ethnic Minority Health)*
Doornzelestraat 32, 9000 Gent; *t* (091) 232923
Research and information on health issues affecting migrants and ethnic minorities. »94

✿ **Centrum voor Informatie en Samenlevingsopbouw**, CISO-Zuid: Centre d'Information et de Développement de la Vie Sociale *(Centre for Community Information and Development)*
[address uncertain] Belegstraat 69, 2018 Antwerpen; *t* (03) 237 7139 »90

✿ **Centrum voor Interculturalisme en Migratie-onderzoek**: Centre pour l'Interculturalisme et Recherche sur Migrations *(Centre for Multiculturalism and Migration Research)*
Prof. Dr Eugeen Roosens: Katholieke Universiteit te Leuven, Blide Inkpomstr. 7, 3000 Leuven; *t* (016) 285398, *f* 285360
Academic research and documentation centre; see also Centrum voor Sociale en Culturele Antropologie, below. »94

✿ **Centrum voor Sociale en Culturele Antropologie**, Katholieke Universiteit te Leuven: Centre pour l'Anthropologie Sociale et Culturelle, Université Catholique de Louvain
Prof. Dr Eugeen Roosens: Tiensestraat 102, 3000 Leuven; *t* (016) 286047, *f* 286000
Felice Dassetto, see also GREM, below; and see Centrum voor Interculturalisme en Migratie-onderzoek, above. »94

- **Cultures et Santé** *(Cultures and Health)*
Thérèse Claeys Bouvaert, Co-ordinator: Avenue de Stalingrad 24, 1000 Bruxelles; *t* (02) 513 5699
Health, welfare, employment and integration of immigrants; research and information. »94

▌ **European Trade Union Institute**, ETUI
Boulevard de l'Impératrice 66, 1000 Bruxelles; *t* (02) 512 3070
The research and information service of the European Trade Union Confederation, p190; reports on social dimension of the single market. »89

- **Fonds National de la Recherche Scientifique**, FNRS *(National Scientific Research Fund)*
Rue Melpomene 4, 1080 Bruxelles
Funds some migration-related research. »94

◆ **Groupe d'Etude des Migrations et des Relations Interethniques**, GREM *(Migration and Ethnic Relations Study Group)* Département des Sciences Politiques et Sociales
Dr Felice Dassetto: Université Catholique de Louvain, Place Montesquieu 1, Boite 21, 1348 Louvain-la-Neuve; *t* (010) 474251, 474247, *f* 474603
Formerly Groupe de Recherche et d'Etude sur les Migrations. Inter-disciplinary research on migration and minorities. Has responsibility for Système Bibliographique et Documentaire relatif à l'Immigration, SYBIDI, a research and documentation exercise established in 1980. (There may also be a SYBIDI office in Brussels: CIEMI lists it (1994) at Rue du Méridien 22b, 1030 Bruxelles; *t* (02) 537 1971, contact P. Targosz).
Sybidi périodique, Sybidi papers. »94

- **Groupe de Recherche sur l'Histoire de l'Immigration**, Université Libre de Bruxelles
Anne Morelli/J.-P. Schreiber: Faculté de Philosophie et Lettres, ULB, Avenue F.D. Roosevelt 17, 1050 Bruxelles; *t* (02) 650 3848, 650 3346 »95

- **Info-Diffusion Immigrés** *(Immigration Information and Documentation)*
Abderrahmane Cherradi: Rue du Méridien 15, 1030 Bruxelles; *t* (02) 217 9782
Research, information, publishing on rights and interests of migrant workers. *Tribune Immigrée.* »94

- **International Human Relations**
Faith Yvonne Mohammed: [address uncertain] Rue de Pologne 35, 1060 Bruxelles; *t* (02) 537 7434 »90

▌ **International Union for the Scientific Study of Population**, IUSSP: Union Internationale pour l'Etude Scientifique de la Population
William Brass, President: Rue des Augustins 34, 4000 Liège; *t* (041) 224080
Founded 1928; study of demography and international and internal migration; publishes journal and research papers.
IUSSP Newsletter (3/yr). »86

✿ **Katholieke Universiteit te Leuven—Université Catholique de Louvain** *(Catholic University of Louvain)* Département de Pédagogie et Sociologie
Dekenstraat 28-30, 3000 Leuven »90

✿ **Migrantenoverleg Mechelen**, MOM *(Mechelen Migrants Consultative Group)*
Wollemarkt 21, 2800 Mechelen; *t* (015) 206483 »90

▌ *Migration Newssheet*
Antonio Cruz, Editor: Rue Joseph II, 174, 1000 Bruxelles; *t* (02) 230 3750, *f* 230 3750
Founded as an information project under the Churches' Committee for Migrants in Europe, p130, now an independent publication (12/yr) with an international editorial network. Migration, refugees, nationality and asylum law, racism, government policies, EU developments, related topics. »95

- **Le Piment Collectif Pédagogique** *(Pepper Teacher Training Collective)*
Dominique Fievez: Rue Potagère 157, 1030 Bruxelles; *t* (02) 218 2729
Multicultural education and training issues. See also COBEFF, p131, and CAIT, p130. »94

Système Bibliographique et Documentaire relatif à l'Immigration, SYBIDI: see Groupe d'Etude des Migrations et Relations Interethniques, left

- *Tijdschrift voor Vreemdelingenrecht* (Journal on Aliens Law)
[address unknown]
Professional journal for the study of law on migration and related issues. »93

✿ **Université Libre de Bruxelles** *(Free University of Brussels)*
Avenue Franklin D. Roosevelt 50, 1050 Bruxelles; *t* (02) 649 0030 »94

- **Université de Paix** *(Peace University)*
Bvd du Nord 4, 5000 Namur; *t* (081) 226102, *f* 231882
Peace and development education; intercultural understanding, conflict resolution training, human rights, international solidarity. Founded 1960; 13 staff. »93

BULGARIA *359*

- **Bulgarian Society for Regional Cultural Studies**
Dr Yulian Konstantinov: PO Box 59, 1233 Sofia; *t* (02) 800992, *f* 316017 »94

DENMARK *45*

✿ **Aalborg Universitetcenter**, AUC *(University of Aalborg)* Department of Social Studies
Prof. Dr Helge Hilding Mansson/Prof. Per Salomonsen: Krogh-stræde 7, 9220 Aalborg *φ*
Migration and minority research, education. »94

✿ **Center for Kulturforskning** *(Centre for Cultural Research)*
Universitet Århus, Finlandsgade 26, 8200 Århus N; *t* 8616 3611
Research on cultural diversity. »94

- **Center for Peace and Conflict Research**
Pierre Lemaître/Elzbieta Tromer: Vadkunsten 5, 1467 København K; *t* 3332 6432
Research in ethnic and other fields of conflict. »94

- **Danmarks Lærerhøjskole** *(Royal Danish School for Educational Studies)*
Christian Horst/Anne Holmen: Emdrupvej 101, 2400 København NV; *t* 3169 6633
Studies on schooling of immigrant children, language acquisition, training and integration. »94

- **Foundation for International Understanding**
Postboks 85, Kultorvet 2, 1003 København K; *t* 3313 9418 »94

- **Institut for Samfunds- og Erhvervsudvikling**
Dr Jan Hjarnö: Sydjysk Universitetscenter, Glentevej 7, 6705 Esbjerg *φ*
Research on migration, minorities and ethnic relations. Member of Netherlands-based MERGER network, p240. »94

● **Institute of Political Science**, Universitet Århus
Dr Charlotte Hamburger: Universitetsparken, 8000 Århus C;
t 8613 0111, *f* 8613 9839
C. Hamburger conducts research on immigration and inter-
ethnic relations; φystein Gaasholt researches minorities;
colleagues are engaged in related work.   »94
◆ **MS Indvandrerdokumentation** *(MS Migrant Documentation)*
Ole Hammer, Head: Borgergade 10-14, 1300 København K;
t 3332 6244, *f* 3315 6243, *Tx* 15928 MS DK
Inger Bruun documentalist; founded 1977 by Mellemfolkeligt
Samvirke development agency, p194; documentation, inter-
cultural studies, seminars. *Nyhedsbrev om Indvandrere og
Flygtninge* (Migrant and Refugee Newsbrief), *Dokumentation
om Indvandrere* (Immigrant Documentation), books.   »94
✿ **Roskilde Universitetscenter**, RUC: International Development
Studies
Tue Magnussen: PO Box 260, 4000 Roskilde; *t* 4675 7711
Research on ethnic relations.   »94
◆ *Samspil*
Arly Christensen: Bredgade 31, Baghuset, 4.sal, Postbox
1098, 1009 København K; *t* 3311 0744
Monthly journal subtitled "et tidsskrift om og for indvandrere"
(the newspaper by and for immigrants). Also *På Let Dansk*
(4/yr).   »94
● **Socialforskiningsinstituttet**, SFI: Danish National Institute of
Social Research
Prof. Svend Aage Hansen, Chairman: Borgergade 28, 1300
København K; *t* 3313 9811, *f* 3313 8992, *Tx* RESEARCHDAN
Jan Magnussen director, Jacob Vedel-Petersen executive
director, Kirsten Just Jeppesen; independent centre founded
1958 by Ministry of Social Affairs, over 100 staff; social
research for national and international bodies. Its Research
Department 1, social policy, works on refugees and migration
issues; publications include *SFI-Nyt* (4/yr).   »94
✿ **Third World Voice**
c/o Nyelandsvej 53, 2000 Frederiksberg F; *t* 3888 1977
Archive and resource centre on global development, migration
questions, refugees, anti-racism.   »94
✿ **University of Copenhagen**: Minority Studies
Jette Kofoed: [address uncertain] Nφrre Allé 19A, st.2, 2200
København N; *t* 3537 5535
Others involved in the field include Vibeke Andersson *t* 4444
1747, Connie Jul Pedersen *t* 3174 6821, Helen Krag *t* 3154
2211, Inge Lassen, Kira Polack Wickström *t* 3393 0194,
Kirsten Hvenegaard *t* 3185 8445.   »90

FINLAND 358

● **Centre for International Mobility**, CIMO
PO Box 343, 00530 Helsinki; *t* (90) 7747 7033 (?), *f* 774
7064
Foundation promoting freedom of movement of labour.   »94
● **Finland Futures Research Centre**
PO Box 110, 20521 Turku; *t* (921) 638311, *f* 233 0755
Research on national and international social and political
issues.   »94

FRANCE 33

◆ **Agence pour le Développement des Relations Inter-
culturelles**, ADRI
Michèle Monteiller: 4 rue René Villermé, 75011 Paris; *t* (1)
4348 4919, *f* 4348 2517
Socio-economic integration of migrants, cultural identity,
promotion of good relations between migrants and French;
documentation centre established 1976, and funded by the
Ministère des Affaires Sociales. Produces directories of
migrant organisations, and a range of journals including
Migrations Etudes, *ADRI-info*, *ADRI-biblio*, *Insertions*. »94
● **Agence Im'média**
Mogniss Hamed Abdallah: 26 (38?) rue des Maronites,
75020 Paris; *t* (1) 4636 0145, *f* 4636 7258
Anti-racist media agency, focussing on Maghreb and its
migrants. *Quo Vadis*, *Lettre de l'Agence Im'média*.   »95
● **Association Amana—Hommes et Migrations**
Jacques Ghys, Director: 40 rue de la Duée, 75020 Paris;
t (1) 4797 2605, *f* 4797 9977
Philippe Dewitte. Founded 1947; research on migration in
Europe; literacy manuals, research papers, resource centre.
Hommes et Migrations: documents (12/yr).   »94

● **Association pour l'Etude des Sciences Humaines en Afrique
du Nord et au Proche-Orient** *(Association for the Study of
the Social Sciences in North Africa and the Middle East)*
Pierre Robert Baduel: Maison de la Méditerranée, 3-5 avenue
Pasteur, 13100 Aix-en-Provence; *t* 4221 5988, *f* 4221 5275
Research on the Maghreb and the Islamic world. See also
IREMAM, p235, CEHMC, below, and associated bodies.
Revue du Monde Musulman et de la Méditerranée.   »94
✿ **Association d'Information et de Réflexion sur la Culture
Maghrébine**, AIRCM *(Society for Information and Study on
Maghrebi Culture)*
Mimoun Houbaine: Espace interculturel méditerranéen, 23
rue de Grasse, 31400 Toulouse; *t* 6125 1645
See also COFRIMI, p234.   »94
● **Association interculturelle de production, de diffusion et de
documentation audiovisuelle**, AIDDA *(Intercultural Society for
Audiovisual Production, Distribution and Documentation)*
Hédi Chenchabi: 21 rue Simart, 75018 Paris; *t* (1) 4255
0686, *f* 4259 2420
Multicultural media research and production. *Entre autres*
(2/yr).   »94
✿ **Association pour la recherche sur l'insertion des
communautés étrangères** *(Society for Research on the
Integration of Foreign Communities)*
20 avenue Danglade, 33600 Pessac
Study and development of better means for integrating
populations of foreign origin.   »89
✿ **Banlieuescopies** *(Urban Investigations)*
Adil Jazouli: 91 bis rue du Cherche Midi, 75006 Paris; *t* (01)
4222 4823, *f* 4222 8850
Postcode uncertain. Studies the sociology of outer cities
(where in France minorities tend to live, in contrast with the
UK model of inner-city concentrations).   »95
✿ **Bibliothèque Interuniversitaire de Lille** *(Lille Inter-University
Library)*
J.L. Margue: BP 99, 59653 Villeneuve d'Ascq Cedex; *t* 2067
1717
Extensive migration-related holdings.   »94
✿ **Centre d'animation Johary Ravalson Projets Culturels**
36 rue du Colonel P. Avis, 75015 Paris; *t* (1) 4557 9697
Film, artistic and cultural projects on immigration, youth,
French Arabs.   »91
● **Centre de Documentation Internationale sur le Développe-
ment, les Libertés et la Paix**, CEDIDELP: International
Development, Rights and Peace Documentation Centre
Suzanne Humberset: 21 ter. rue Voltaire, 75011 Paris;
t (1) 4531 1808, 4531 4338, *f* 4372 1577, 4531 0310
World affairs and human rights archive associated with the
anti-racist centre CRIDA, p163; see also CEDETIM, below.
Le Bibliotin, *Profil*, *Passerelles* (all 4/yr).   »94
● **Centre d'Etude des Sociétés du Commonwealth et des Iles
Britanniques** *(Centre for Study of Commonwealth and British
Isles Societies)*
Université Paris VIII, Vincennes-Saint-Denis, Paris
Themes at annual conference have included study of British
expatriate communities in Europe.   »92
● **Centre d'Etudes Anti-Impérialistes**, CEDETIM *(Centre for
Anti-Imperialist Studies)*
Karine Barrere: 21 ter. rue Voltaire, 75015 Paris; *t* (1) 4531
4338
Documentation on global development and social justice
issues. See also CEDIDELP, above, and CRIDA, p163.   »94
✿ **Centre d'Etudes Historiques sur la Méditerranée
Contemporaine**, CEHMC *(Centre for the Modern History of
Mediterranean Countries)*
G. Chastagnaret: Université de Provence, Centre d'Aix, 29
avenue Robert Schumann, 13621 Aix-en-Provence; *t* 4220
2825, *f* 4220 5111
Research on North Africa, the Middle East and the
Mediterranean region.   »94
● **Centre d'Etudes sur les Migrations et les Relations
Interculturelles**, CEMRIC
Université des sciences humaines, 8 rue de Londres, 67000
Strasbourg; *t* 8860 2050   »94
✿ **Centre d'Etudes de l'Orient Contemporain**, CEOC *(Centre
for Contemporary Middle Eastern Studies)*
Paul Balta: 13 rue de Santeuil, 75231 Paris Cedex 05; *t* (1)
4587 4165
Research on the Arab world. *Maghreb-Machrek* (4/yr).   »94
✿ **Centre d'Etudes et de Recherches sur l'Innovation Sociale
et Educative**, CERISE *(Research and Study Centre on Social
and Educational Innovation)*
Mireille Couhe: 77 rue des Haies, 75020 Paris; *t* (1) 4009
0671
Multicultural education, youth integration.   »94

♦ Centre d'Etudes et de Recherches Internationales, CERI
(International Research and Study Centre) Fondation
Nationale des Sciences Politiques, FNSP
Cathérine Withol de Wenden, Director: 27 rue St-Guillaume,
75341 Paris Cedex 07; t (1) 4249 5130, 4249 5134,
f 4549 0610
Also listed (1993) at 4 rue de Chevreuse, 75006 Paris; name
also given (1990) as Centre d'Etudes et de Recherches sur
l'Immigration. Jean-Luc Domenach, Rémy Leveau, Anne de
Tinguy. Interdisciplinary centre, with 55 researchers on
international political science topics; recognised by the CNRS,
below, as a Centre of Excellence in 1993. Research group
Migrations studies South-North and East-West migration,
European migration policies, nationality and citizenship, and
other issues. Cahiers d'études (4/yr), Nouvelles du CERI. »94
✿ Centre d'Etudes et de Recherches sur l'Orient Arabe
Contemporain, CEROAC (Research and Study Centre on the
Modern Arab Middle East)
Jean-François Rycx, Head of Research: 3-5 avenue Pasteur,
13100 Aix-en-Provence; t 4221 5988
Part of IREMAM institute, p235; sociology, anthropology,
geography, modern history of the Arab world. See also
Association pour l'Etude des Sciences Humaines en Afrique du
Nord et au Proche-Orient, and CEHMC, both p233.   »90
● Centre d'Etudes et de Recherches sur les Relations
Interethniques et les Minorités, CERIEM (Study and Research
Centre on Ethnic Relations and Minorities) Université de Haut-
Bretagne-Rennes 2
6 avenue Gaston Berger, 35043 Rennes Cedex   »89
● Centre de Formation et d'Information pour la Scolarisation
des Enfants Migrants, CEFISEM: Training and Information
Centre on Migrant Children's Schooling
26 rue Boursault, 75017 Paris; t (1) 4387 5060, 4387
6115   »94
✿ Centre des Hautes Etudes sur l'Afrique et l'Asie Modernes,
CHEAM (Centre for Advanced Study of Modern Africa & Asia)
Philippe Decraene: 13 rue du Four, 75006 Paris; t (1) 4326
9690, f 4051 0358
L'Afrique et l'Asie Modernes (4/yr), bulletin (2/yr).   »94
♦ Centre d'Information et d'Etudes sur les Migrations
Internationales, CIEMI (Information and Study Centre on
International Migrations)
Lorenzo Prencipe, Director: 46 rue de Montreuil, 75011 Paris;
t (1) 4372 4934, 4372 0140, f 4372 0642
Voluntary-sector documentation centre on migration, founded
1977; economic, political, cultural, educational aspects; its
former focus on Italian migration (and politics of Italians in pre-
1944 France) has broadened, and most work is now on non-
EU migrants in Europe. Archives, bibliographies, monographs,
press surveys (Migrations Europe, 12/yr); published (1991,
1994) French-language directories of migrant associations in
Europe, similar in scope to JCWI's directories. Member of
Coordination européenne pour le droit des étrangers de vivre
en famille, p136. Migrations Société (6/yr; Pierre Toulat). »95
✿ Centre Interdisciplinaire Méditerranéen d'Etudes et de
Recherches en Sciences Sociales, CIMERSS (Mediterranean
Interdisciplinary Centre for Research and Study in the Social
Sciences)
Gérard Neyrand: rue Fernand Canobio, 13320 Bouc Bel Air;
t/f 4222 9981   »94
♦ Centre national de documentation pédagogique, CNDP
(National Centre for Educational Documentation) Head Office
Jean-Paul Tauvel: 29 rue d'Ulm, 75230 Paris Cedex 05;
t (1) 4329 2164
Documentation centre on education and training, founded
1973 under Ministère de l'Education Nationale; publications,
bibliography, library; specialist CNDP-Migrants centre.   »94
● ≡ CNDP-Migrants: 91 rue Gabriel-Péri, 92120 Montrouge;
t (1) 4657 1167, f 4657 1060
Migrants Formation (4/yr), Migrants Nouvelles (10/yr).   »94
♦ Centre national de la recherche scientifique, CNRS
(National Centre for Scientific Research)
295 rue Saint-Jacques, 75005 Paris; t (1) 4634 7990
National research co-ordination and funding body, supporting
several specialist centres with interests in migration and
minorities; these include IRESCO, IREMAM, and Observatoire
des Migrations Internationales dans la Région Nord-Pas-de-
Calais, all p235.   »90
✿ Centre de Recherche et de Documentation sur l'Immigration,
CRDI
BP 1188, 9 Petite rue de Feuillants, 69202 Lyon Cedex 01»94
● Centre de Recherche sur l'Histoire des Mouvements Sociaux
(Research Centre on the History of Social Movements)
9 rue Mahler, 75004 Paris
Researches trade unions and other social movements.   »90

✿ Centre de Recherches et d'Etudes sur les Sociétés
Méditerranéennes, CRESM (Centre for Study and Research
on Mediterranean Societies)
M. Camau: Maison de la Méditerranée, 3-5 avenue Pasteur,
13100 Aix-en-Provence; t 4223 0386, 4296 2781
Member of IREMAM institute, p235; socio-economic, political,
bibliographical, other studies in Aix and Marseille universities
related to Algeria, Libya, Morocco, Tunisia. Les Cahiers du
CRESM, Recherches sur les sociétés méditerranéennes. »90
✿ Centre de Recherches et d'Informations des Africains et
Arabes, CRIAA (Research and Information Centre for Africans
and Arabs)
65 avenue du Maine, 75014 Paris; t (1) 4327 0028
Research and documentation, mainly on the Maghreb and
Mashraq and migrants from there.   »94
✿ Centre de Recherches Interculturelles du Finistère, CRIF
(Finistère Intercultural Research Centre) also known as Centre
de Relations Internationales du Finistère
Roger Sade: 59 rue de Sébastopol, 29200 Brest; t 9841
5566, 9803 5616, f 9802 3883
International solidarity and cross-cultural understanding. See
also ALCE, p111. Lettre d'information (12/yr).   »94
♦ Centre de Recherches Migratoires, CERM
64 boulevard Auguste Blanqui, Paris   »90
✿ Centre Universitaire de Recherches et de Documentation sur
les Migrants (Research & Documentation Centre on Migrants)
Université de Provence, Centre d'Aix, 29 avenue Robert
Schumann, 13621 Aix-en-Provence
See also CEHMC, p233, and the IREMAM centres, p235. »90
♦ Club de réflexion sur l'immigration, la démocratie et
l'intégration, CRIDI (Club for the Study of Immigration,
Democracy and Integration)
78 avenue Secrétan, 75019 Paris
Publishes journal on social, juridical, political and cultural
aspects of immigration. Bulletin (24/yr).   »94
✿ Collectif d'Etudes et de Recherches sur le Fascisme, CERF
BP 4131, 31031 Toulouse
Documentation on racism and ultra-right.   »90
▮ Comité international de Coopération dans les Recherches
Nationales en Démographie, CICRED: Committee for
International Co-operation in National Demographic Research
Jean Bourgeois-Pichat, President: 27 rue du Commandeur,
75675 Paris Cedex 14; t (1) 4320 1345, f 4327 7240
Founded 1971; co-ordinates, supports demographic research
undertaken at national level; publishes directories, research
reports. Review of Population Reviews (4/yr).   »86
✿ Conseil et Formation sur les Realités de l'Immigration et de
l'Interculturel, COFRIMI (Advice and Training on Immigration
and Multiculturalism)
Mimoun Houbaine: 23 rue de Grasse, 31400 Toulouse;
t/f 6226 7115
See also AIRCM, p233, and EICM, p163. Les Cahiers du
COFRIMI.   »94
● CREDOC
Annette Jobert: 142 rue du Chevaleret, 75634 Paris   »90
✿ CRESAB
Sylvie Le Bars: Université de Nancy II, BP 3397, 54015
Nancy Cedex   »90
● Culture et Politique en Méditerranée (Mediterranean Culture
and Politics)
c/o IRESCO, 59-61 rue Pouchet, 75849 Paris Cedex 17;
t (1) 4025 1025   »90
♦ Documentation réfugiés, DR (Refugee Documentation):
formally Centre interassociatif francophon d'information et
de documentation sur le droit d'asile et les réfugiés (French-
Speaking Voluntary Sector Information and Documentation
Centre on Refugees and the Right to Asylum)
Pedro Vianna, Director: 11 rue Ferdinand Gambon, 75020
Paris; t (1) 4348 1566, f 4348 1722
Archive, research and information centre on refugee issues,
right to asylum, countries of origin; advice to refugees and
those assisting them. Documentation réfugiés (24/yr).   »95
✿ Editions Arcantiere
8 passage Folie Regnault, 75020 Paris; t (1) 4348 1728 »90
● Equipe de recherches Migrations internationales du travail
et sociétés d'origine, MIGRINTER (Research Team on Inter-
national Labour Migration and Societies of Origin)
Prof. Gildas Simon, Director: Dépt. Géographie, Université de
Poitiers, 95 ave. du Recteur Pineau, 86022 Poitiers; t 4945
3257, 4945 1266, 4946 2577, f 4945 3286, 4945 3322
J. Alves; research group under CNRS, left; sociological,
economic and political studies of migrations and minorities.
Also listed (1994) as Migrations Internationales Espaces et
Société; research papers, library, conferences. Revue
Européenne des Migrations Internationales (3/yr).   »94

▌ Fondation Européenne de la Science: European Science
Foundation
1 quai Lezay-Marnésia, 67000 Strasbourg; *t* 8835 3063
Founded 1974; an agency of the Council of Europe, p197,
which promotes European co-operation in scientific research,
including social sciences; extensive work on migration and
ethnicity; research papers, conferences, proceedings.   »86
● Fondation René Seydoux pour le Monde Méditerranéen
(Seydoux Foundation for the Mediterranean World)
Geneviève & René Seydoux: 5 boulevard Malesherbes, 75401
Paris; *t* (1) 4924 4041, *f* 4924 4043
Research on the Maghreb, Arab culture and related themes.
Répertoire Méditerranéen.   »94
**● Groupe de recherche et d'analyse des Migrations
Internationales, GRAMI** *(Research and Analysis Group on
International Migrations)*
Jeanne Singer-Kerel: 4 rue Michelet, 75006 Paris; *t* (1) 4354
5066
Research on international labour market, migration, return
migration of Maghrebis; papers, seminars; library.   »86
✧ Groupe de Recherche sur le Développement Rural, GRDR
8 rue Paul Bert, 93300 Aubervilliers; *t* (1) 4834 9594
Sociology, economic development of rural areas.   »94
**✧ Groupe de Recherches et d'Etudes sur le Proche Orient,
GREPO** *(Middle East Study and Research Group)*
D. Panzac: 3-5 avenue Pasteur, 13100 Aix-en-Provence;
t 4221 5988
Human geography and sociology of Middle East; part of
IREMAM institute, right. Possibly connected with the
Association pour l'Etude des Sciences Humains en Afrique du
Nord et au Proche-Orient, p233.   »89
**✧ Groupement d'Etude et de Recherche des Méthodes Actives
d'Education, GERMAE** *(Research and Study Group on Active
Education Methods)*
Bernard Andros: [address uncertain] 67 rue de Dunkerque,
75009 Paris; *t* (1) 4874 8608   »90
**♦ Groupement de Recherches Coordonnées sur les Migrations
Internationales, GRECO 13**
George Abou Sada, Director: 59-61 rue Pouchet, 75017
Paris; *t* (1) 4025 1025
Part of IRESCO, right; large research centre formed 1978
under CNRS, p234; documentation, bibliography, research co-
ordination; see IDERIC, below; founded REMISIS, p236.
GRECO 13 review, microfiches, papers.   »90
**✧ Groupement de Recherches d'Echanges et de
Communication, GREC** *(Exchange and Communication
Research Group)*
Marius Apostolo: 172 avenue de Paris, 94300 Vincennes;
t (1) 4398 3861, *f* 4328 0283
Research on intercultural relations and minorities.   »94
**● Histoire des identités nationales, du racisme et des migrations
en Europe, HINARME**
Gérard Noiriel: ENS, 45 rue d'Ulm, 75230 Paris Cedex 05;
t (1) 4432 3164, *f* 4329 7369   »96
▌ Human Rights Documentation Centre, HRDC
c/o Conseil de l'Europe, Maison de l'Europe, BP 431 R6,
67075 Strasbourg Cedex; *t* 8861 4961, *f* 8825 0166
Archive and documentation centre of the Council of Europe,
p197, on international and national human rights issues.   »94
▌ Human Rights Information Centre
c/o Conseil de l'Europe, Maison de l'Europe, BP 431 R6,
67075 Strasbourg Cedex; *t* 8841 2024, *f* 8841 2704
Information on international and national human rights issues.»94
**● Institut d'Etudes et de Recherches Interethniques et
Interculturelles, IDERIC** *(Interethnic and Intercultural Research
and Study Institute)*
Michel Oriol, Director: 63 boulevard de la Madeleine, batiment
A, 06000 Nice; *t* 9344 8244
Formed 1965, later came under GRECO 13 research group,
above; migration and culture, education, family, religion;
information centre. *Bulletin de l'IDERIC* (1/yr).   »94
▌ Institut International des Droits de l'Homme, IIDH:
International Institute for Human Rights
Jean-Bernard Marie, General Secretary: 1 quai Lezay-
Marnésia, 67000 Strasbourg; *t* 8835 0550, *f* 8836 3855
Archive, research centre, pressure group on all aspects of
human rights; activities in Africa and Central Europe.   »94
**● Institut International de Recherche et de Formation sur
Education, Cultures et Développement, IRFED** *(International
Institute for Research and Training on Education, Cultures
and Development)*
Ruth Padrun: 49 rue de la Glacière, 75013 Paris; *t* (1) 4331
9890, *f* 4337 5433
Research on social aspects of development, and multicultural
approach to development education and training.   »94

♦ Institut National d'Etudes Démographiques, INED *(National
Institute for Demographic Studies)*
Gérard Calot, Director General: 27 rue du Commandeur,
75675 Paris Cedex 14; *t* (1) 4320 1345, *f* 4327 7240
Demography, social research; academic journals including
Population (5/yr); pamphlets, working papers, documentation
centre. *Population et Sociétés* (12/yr).   »94
**✧ Institut de Recherches et d'Etudes sur le Monde Arabe et
Musulman, IREMAM** *(Research and Study Institute on the
Arab and Islamic World)*
Prof. André Raymond, Director: Maison de la Méditerranée,
3-5 avenue Pasteur, 13100 Aix-en-Provence; *t* 4296 2781,
4221 5988, *f* 4221 5275
Françoise Lorcerie, Gilbert Beaugé, Jocelyne Césari; study
centre established 1985 by Aix-Marseille university and the
CNRS, p234; five constituent bodies including CEROAC and
CRESM, p234, GREPO, left, LAPMO, below; see CEHMC and
Association pour l'Etude des Sciences Humaines en Afrique du
Nord, p233. Bibliographic databases, research on migration in
the Maghreb and other areas. *Annuaire de l'Afrique du Nord,
Maghreb contemporain, Archives maghrébines*.   »94
✧ Institut de Recherches sur le Monde Arabe Contemporain
(Research Institute on the Modern Arab World)
Maison de l'Orient Méditerranéen, 7 rue Raulin, 69635 Lyon
Cedex 07   »89
**♦ Institut de recherches sur les sociétés contemporaines,
IRESCO** *(Contemporary Societies Research Institute)*
René Gallissot, Director: 59-61 rue Pouchet, 75849 Paris
Cedex 17; *t* (1) 4025 1118, 4025 1025, *f* 4025 1221
Dr Mirjana Morokvasic (*t* 4025 1220), Paul Vielle; a CNRS
sociology and demography research centre, home to the
GRECO 13 unit, left; see also REMISIS, p236. *Peuples
méditerranéens*, other journals.   »94
✧ Interface migrants
11 rue Bordier, 93300 Aubervilliers   »89
**✧ Laboratoire d'anthropologie et de préhistoire des pays de la
Mediterranée Occidentale, LAPMO** *(Research Centre on the
Anthropology and Prehistory of Western Mediterranean
Countries)*
M. Gast: 3-5 avenue Pasteur, 13100 Aix-en-Provence; *t* 4221
5988
Part of IREMAM, above; social anthropology of North Africa.»89
● Laboratoire d'anthropologie urbaine *(Urban Anthropology
Research Centre)*
Jacques Gutwirth/Collette Petonnet, Research Directors:
Musée de l'Homme, Palais du Trocadéro, 75116 Paris;
t (1) 4355 7267
Several current research themes involving migration and
minorities.   »89
✧ Laboratoire Population/Environnement, LPE *(Population and
Environment Research Centre)*
Faculté des Sciences, Centre St-Charles, place Victor Hugo,
13331 Marseille Cedex 03; *t* 9195 9071
Academic research into internal and international migration,
health, urbanisation; working papers; sponsored by the
Université de Provence and ORSTOM, p236.   »90
**✧ Laboratoire de Recherches Economiques et Sociales,
LABORES** *(Economic and Social Research Centre)*
Michel Falise, Director: 1 rue Norbert Segard, BP 109, 59046
Lille Cedex; *t* 2057 1177
Socio-economic research consortium funded by the CNRS,
p234; see also OMINOR, below.   »89
✧ Laboratoire des sociétés pluriethniques et pluriculturelles
(Multi-Ethnic and Multi-Cultural Societies Research Centre)
Université Paul Valéry Montpellier 3, BP 5043, route de
Mende, 34032 Montpellier   »89
**✧ Ligue Française de l'Enseignement et de l'Education
Permanente, LFEEP** *(French League for Teaching and Adult
Education)*
Jean-Marie Roirant: 3 rue Récamier, 75007 Paris; *t* (1) 4358
9738-39, *f* 4358 9734
Anti-racism, adult education, internationalism; see also JADE,
p198. *Les idées en mouvement* (12/yr).   »94
● Maison des Sciences de l'Homme *(Human Sciences Centre)*
54 boulevard Raspail, 75006 Paris
Social science research.   »89
**✧ Observatoire des Migrations Internationales dans la Region
Nord-Pas-de-Calais, OMINOR** *(Regional Research Centre on
International Migrations)*
1 rue François Baes, 59046 Lille Cedex; *t* 2054 1120
Georges Abou Sada délégué général; formed 1980 by Centre
National de la Recherche Scientifique, p234; research into
socio-economic aspects of migration, documentation centre;
one of three centres forming the Laboratoire de recherches
économiques et sociales, above.   »90

- **ORSTOM/Démographie**
Michel Picouet: 213 rue La Fayette, 75480 Paris Cedex 10;
t (1) 4803 7777
Small research centre under Institut Français de Recherche
Scientifique pour le Développement en Coopération; internal
and international migration; monographs, library.   »86
☼ **Pan-African News Agency**
44 boulevard Michelet, 13008 Marseille   »90
☼ **Radio Pays—Le contact avec les pays** *(Country Radio—
Contact with the Nations)*
CAP 118, 93558 Montreuil Cedex; *t* (1) 4859 2212, *f* 4859
2078
Programming and broadcasting for migrant and minority
communities.   »94
- **Rapporteurs sans Frontières, RSF** *(Reporters without Borders)*
17 rue Abbé de l'Epéc, 34000 Montpellier; *t* 6779 8182,
f 6779 6080
Human rights, freedom of information worldwide.   »94
☼ **Réalisation d'Etudes Projets Originaux et Nouveaux
Services, REPONSE**
6 place d'Angleterre, 54500 Vandeouvre-les-Nancy; *t* 8356
9270, *f* 8353 4447
Intercultural solidarity, information, research. *Bulletin
REPONSE* (4/yr).   »94
☼ **Recherches et Etudes sur les Migrations et les Pathologies**
(Migration and Health Research and Studies)
537 avenue Notre-Dame-de-Santé, 84200 Carpentras
Medical studies in relation to migration.   »90
☼ **Recherches et Formations** *(Research and Training)*
Gilles Verbunt: 153 rue de Rome, 75017 Paris   »90
- **Réseau d'Etude des Migrations et des Relations Euro-
méditerranéennes** *(Migration and European-Middle Eastern
Relations Study Network)*
Claude Liauzu: Tour 24/34, 2 place Jussieu, 75251 Paris
Cedex 05; *t* (1) 4427 6355, *f* 4427 6964
Research, promotion of Euro-Arab cultural exchange.   »94
♦ **Réseau d'Information sur les Migrations Internationales,
REMISIS:** Information Network on International Migrations
Armelle Chervel: 59-61 rue Pouchet, 75849 Paris Cedex 17;
t (1) 4025 1025, 4025 1118, *f* 4228 9544
Collates and disseminates research and bibliographies on
migration topics; sponsored by CNRS, p234, and based at
IRESCO, p235. *REMISIS: revue bibliographique* (4/yr).   »94
- **Réseau d'Information Tiers Monde des Centres de
Documentation pour le Développement, RITMO** *(Third World
Information Network of Development Documentation Centres)*
8 bvd Roger Salengro, 38100 Grenoble; *t/f* 7670 2767   »94
☼ **RIC-CERDIC**
2 rue Goethe, Palais Universitaire, 67083 Strasbourg   »90
- **Société Africaine de Culture**
25 bis rue des Ecoles, 75005 Paris; *t* (1) 4354 1558
A centre funded by UNESCO, p199, promoting cultural and
academic co-operation and exchange among African countries;
journal describes itself as a "cultural review of the negro
world". *Présence Africaine* (4/yr).   »93
☼ **Société pour l'Education, la Formation et le Recherche
Interculturelles, SIETAR** *(Society for Cross-Cultural Education,
Training and Research)*
André Cresson: 5 rue Adel, 93250 Villemomble; *t/f* (1) 4528
5827   »94
- **Unité de recherche Anthropologie des populations
contemporaines et préhistoriques** *(Research Unit on the
Anthropology of Modern and Prehistoric Populations)*
F. Raveau: Laboratoire d'anatomie, Université de Paris V, 45
rue des Sts-Pères, 75270 Paris Cedex 06; *t* (1) 4260 3720
Social adaptation of immigrants.   »89
☼ **Université de Lyon 2**
Isaac Joseph: avenue Pierre Mendes-France, 69500 Bron »90

GERMANY *49*

- **Aktives Museum Faschismus und Widerstand** *(Educational
Museum on Fascism and Resistance)*
R.W. Zeiler: Brunsbütteler Damm 223 B, 1000 Berlin 20   »91
☼ **Arbeitsbereich Ausländersozialarbeit** *(Immigrant Social
Work Team, Institute for Social Work)* Institut für Sozialarbeit
und Sozialpädagogik
Dr Gerd Stüwe: Am Stockborn 5-7, 60439 Frankfurt am Main;
t (069) 582025-28, *f* 582029
Sociological and educational research into migrants and the
second generation; books, research papers; founded 1974,
sponsored by the Arbeiterwohlfahrt Bundesverband, p200.
Informationsdienst zur Ausländerarbeit (4/yr).   »94

☼ **Ausbildung von Lehrern für Ausländerkinder** *(Training
Centre for Teachers of Immigrant Children)*
Pädagogische Hochschule, Krekelderstr. 33, 4040 Neuss »90
- *Das Ausländer—Magazin im deutschsprachigen Raum,*
DAMID *(The Foreigner—Magazine for German-Speaking Areas)*
Talstraße 3-6, 13189 Berlin; *t* (030) 4700 7201, *f* 4700
7251
Journal serving migrant communities.   »94
- **Otto-Benecke-Stiftung, OBS** *(Benecke Foundation)*
Ute Heinen/Helga Geisler-Scholl: Postfach 190163, 53113
Bonn; *t* (0228) 81630, *f* 816 3400
Location: Kennedy Alee 105-107, 53175 Bonn. Independent
state-funded agency; language training, educational counselling
and scholarships for refugees and others from countries with
human rights problems; information, publishing, conferences,
grants; educational development and returnee integration
projects in Africa.   »95
♦ **Berliner Institut für Vergleichende Sozialforschung e.V.,
BIVS:** Berlin Institute for Comparative Social Research
Dr Jochen Blaschke: Postfach 301125, 10722 Berlin; *t* (030)
444 1088, *f* 444 1085
Dr Thomas Schwarz. Location: Potsdammerstraße 91, Berlin;
academic research centre, founding member of the European
Migration Centre, p237; editorial department (Verlagsabteilung)
publishes bibliographies and research papers on ethnicity and
migration themes, mainly through Edition Parabolis, below.
Current projects are on ethnic minorities in Germany,
migration-related statistics, construction of a worldwide
network of refugee organisations, the impact of East-West
migration, racism and discrimination, health and migration,
refugees and development issues, migration in the Middle East;
electronic archive of European press, databases of statistics,
bibliography, addresses, graphics.   »94
- **blick nach rechts—Sozialdemokratischer Pressedienst** *(Look
Right—Social Democratic Press Service)*
Postfach 120408, Pressehaus 1/217, 53046 Bonn; *t* (0228)
915200, *f* 815 2012
Monitors racism, fascism, refugee and minority issues; journal
blick nach rechts.   »94
- **Bürgerrechte und Polizei—CILIP Informationsdienst** *(Civil
Rights and Policing—CILIP Information Service)*
c/o FU Berlin, Malteserstraße 74-100, 12249 Berlin; *t* (030)
779 2462, *f* 775 1073
Documentation of policing issues, with special reference to
race, minorities and fascism. *Bürgerrechte und Polizei*.   »94
- **Deutsches Institut für internationale pädagogische Forschung,
DIPF** *(German Institute for International Educational Research)*
Dr Wolfgang Mitter: Schloßstraße 29, 60486 Frankfurt am
Main; *t* (069) 770245
Research on the education of Portuguese and other guest-
workers' children.   »94
☼ **Dokumentationsstelle Migration Interkulturelle Erziehung
Hochschule** *(Documentation Centre on Migration and
Multicultural Education)*
Im Fort 7, 76829 Landau, Pfalz; *t* (06341) 280214
Teacher training resource centre.   »94
- **Duisburger Institut für Sprach- und Sozialforschung, DISS**
(Duisburg Institute for Linguistic and Social Research)
S. Jäger: Realschulstraße 51, 47051 Duisburg; *t* (0203)
20249, *f* 287881
Research on migrant integration, minority languages and
related themes. See also ARIC-NRW, p165.   »94
- **Friedrich-Ebert-Stiftung** *(Ebert Foundation)*
Godesberger Allee 149, 53175 Bonn; *t* (0228) 883212,
8830, *f* 833396, *Tx* 885479 FEST D
Humanitarian and philanthropic organisation founded 1925;
supports anti-racist and anti-fascist work; some educational
assistance to refugees through Solidarity Fund; see also
Forschungsinstitut Ausländerforschung und Ausländerpolitik,
p237. Berlin office: Knesebeckstraße 99, 10623 Berlin.   »95
♦ **Edition Parabolis**
Postfach 301125, 10722 Berlin; *t* (030) 444 1088, *f* 444
1085
Publishing arm of the Berliner Institut für Vergleichende
Sozialforschung, above, and with it a member of the European
Migration Centre, p237; publishes *Migration* (a European
journal of international migration and ethnic relations, founded
1987, 2/yr), *Archiv: Migration* (press review, 12/yr),
Bibliograph- ische Informationen zur Ethnizität und Migration
(4/yr), *Jahrbuch für Vergleichende Sozialforschung* (1/yr); also
monographs and bibliographies.   »90
▌ **Europäische Forum für Migrationstudien, EFMS:** European
Forum for Migration Studies
Prof. Dr Friedrich Heckmann: Katherinenstraße 1, 96052
Bamberg; *t* (0951) 37041, *f* 32888   »94

● **Europäisches Migrationsmuseum e.V.**: European Migration Museum
c/o BIVS, Postfach 301125, 10722 Berlin
Formed by, and now a member of, the European Migration Centre, below; exhibitions and symposia on historical and cultural aspects of migration in Europe. »90

● **Arbeitsgemeinschaft Europäisches Migrationszentrum**: European Migration Centre
Postfach 301125, 10722 Berlin; *t* (030) 448 3671, 444 1088, *f* 262 9503, 444 1085
Study and documentation of migration and ethnic relations in Europe, and refugee and world development issues; supports migrant and minority communities, and integration in host societies, opposes racism and xenophobia; conferences and seminars, consultancy, publications, cultural projects; members are the Berliner Institut für Vergleichende Sozialforschung and Edition Parabolis, p236, the Europäisches Migrationsmuseum, above, Netzwerk Menschenrechte, p202, and the Verein für Gegenseitigkeit, p238. Operates the Archiv Migration (Potsdammerstraße 91; same fax; *t* 262 3084). »94

✿ **Fachhochschule i. Verwaltung und Rechtspflege Berlin** *(Special Administrative and Judicial Training School)*
Kurfürstendamm 206-209, Berlin 15; *t* (030) 3183 2405 »90

● **Folgen der Arbeitsmigration für Bildung und Erziehung, FABER** *(Consequences of Labour Migration for Education & Training)*
Fachbereich Erziehungswissenschaft, Universität Hamburg, Von-Melle-Park 8, 20146 Hamburg; *t* (040) 4123 2170
Research grouping in education faculty. »94

● **Forschungsinstitut Ausländerforschung und Ausländerpolitik** *(Research Institute on Foreigners and Foreign Policy)*
Friedrich-Ebert-Stiftung
Dr Ursula Mehrländer: Godesberger Allee 149, 5300 Bonn 2; *t* (0228) 883212, *Tx* 885479 FEST D
Günther Schultze, Abteilung Arbeits- und Sozialforschung; immigration policy, sociological research on foreigners in Germany; research reports, library. »90

● **Forschungsstelle Arbeitsmigration, Flüchtlingsbewegungen und Migrationspolitik** *(Research Group on Labour Migration, Refugee Movements and Migration Policy)*
Margit Mayer: Freie Universität Berlin, Rüdesheimerstraße 1, 14197 Berlin; *t* (030) 821 3854 »94

✿ **Forschungsstelle Ausländischer Arbeiterkinder** *(Research Group on Foreign Workers' Children)*
Pädagogischen Hochschule, Kunzenweg 21, 79117 Freiburg-im-Breisgau; *t* (0761) 682312
Teacher training issues for work with immigrant children. »94

● **Freie Universität Berlin** *(Free University of Berlin)*
Dr Ayse S. Caglar: Bolivar Allee 9, 14050 Berlin; *t* (030) 305 0340
Some migration and minority-related research. See also Forschungsstelle Arbeitsmigration, Flüchtlingsbewegungen und Migrationspolitik, above. »94

● **Freudenberg-Stiftung**
Christian Petry: Freudenbergstraße 2, 6940 Weinheim »90

✿ **Hochschule für Wirtschaft und Politik** *(College of Economics and Politics)*
Friedrich Heckmann: Von-Melle-Park 9, 2000 Hamburg 13 »90

● **Alexander von Humboldt Stiftung** *(Humboldt Foundation)*
[address unknown]
Some educational grants to refugees. »83

✿ **Informationszentrum Dritte Welt, iz3w** *(Third World Information Centre)*
Postfach 5328, Kronenstraße 16 (Hinterh.), 79100 Freiburg; *t* (0761) 74003, *f* 709866
Development education, solidarity with minorities and refugees. *Blätter des iz3w.* »94

✿ **Informationszentrum für Fremdsprachenforschung, IFS** *(Foreign Language Research Information Centre)*
Dr Reinhold Freudenstein: Phillips-Universität, Hans Meerwein Str., Lahnberge, 35043 Marburg am Lahn; *t* (06421) 282141
Bibliographies, research papers. »94

● **Institut für angewandte Sozialforschung** *(Institute of Applied Social Studies)* Universität Köln
Hartmut Esser: Albert-Magnus-Platz, 5000 Köln 41 »90

● **Institut für Arbeitsmarkt- und Berufsforschung** *(Institute for Labour Market and Occupational Research)* Bundesanstalt für Arbeit, BA (Federal Labour Agency)
Regensburger Str. 104, 90478 Nürnberg; *t* (0911) 173016, 1790, *f* 179 3258
Research wing of the BA, p200; extensive publishing on labour market issues. »94

● **Institut für interkulturelle Erziehung** *(Institute for Multi-Cultural Education)*
Gerd Hoff: Habelschwerdterallee 45, 14195 Berlin; *t* (030) 838 5779, 838 3884, *f* 838 6366 »94

● **Institut für Migrations- und Rassismusforschung** *(Research Institute on Migration and Racism)*
Rutschbahn 38, 20146 Hamburg; *t* (040) 452162 »94

● **Institut für Migrationsforschung, Ausländerpädagogik und Zweitsprachendidaktik** *(Institute for Migration Research, Education of Foreign Children and Second-Language Teaching)*
Universität Essen
Ursula Boos-Nünning/R.S. Baur: Universitätsstraße 12, 45141 Essen; *t* (0201) 183 3248, 183 2576, *f* 183 3755
Research centre on multi-cultural education and youth integration. *Publikationsverzeichnis, Verzeichnis Forschung und Lehre.* »94

● **Institut für Migrationsforschung und interkulturelle Studien** *(Institute for Migration Research and Cross-Cultural Studies)*
Universität Osnabrück
Dr Peter Marschalck: Schloßstraße 8, 49069 Osnabrück; *t* (0541) 969 4796, *f* 969 4397 »94

✿ **Institut für Politikwissenschaft, Abteilung II** *(Institute for Political Science, Department II)*
Platz der Weissen Rose, 4400 Münster; *t* (0251) 839357 »90

● **Institut für Soziologie** *(Sociology Institute)*
Dr Czarina Wilpert: Technical University of Berlin, Hardenbergstraße 4-5, 1000 Berlin 12; *t* (030) 3142 5089, *f* 3142 7846
Some migration-related research interests. »94

▌ **Internationaler Arbeitskreis Migration und Psychische Gesundheit** *(International Working Group on Migration and Mental Health)*
c/o Antonio Norten: Darmstädterstraße 15, 50678 Köln »94

● **Internationaler Bund für Sozialarbeit und Jugendsozialwerk e.V., IBSJ** *(International League for Social Work and Youth Work)*
Ludoefusstraße 2-4, 60487 Frankfurt am Main; *t* (069) 79540, *f* 795 4203
Youth welfare, training and employment. »94

● **Internationaler Kulturaustausch, IKA** *(International Cultural Exchange)*
Nernstweg 32-34, 22765 Hamburg; *t* (040) 390 9463, *f* 390 9866
Promotes inter-cultural exchange and understanding; see also BUKO, p200, CUCO, p166, and IKU, p175. Journal *IKA*. »94

✿ **Kassel University** Department of Social Sciences
Henning Melber: Nora-Platiel-Straße 1, 3500 Kassel »90

✿ **Katholisches Sozialinstitut** *(Catholic Social Institute)*
Domberg 27, 85354 Freising »94

✿ **Landesinstitut für Schule- und Weiterbildung** *(Regional Institute for Schooling and Further Education)*
Paradieser Weg 64, 59494 Soest; *t* (02921) 6831 »94

● **Lupe e.V.** *(Magnifying Glass)*
Postfach 360123, 10971 Berlin; *t* (030) 615 6680, *f* 614 4762
Archive of the anti-racist, anti-fascist movement. »94

✿ **Nomos Verlagsgesellschaft**
Postfach 610, 76530 Baden-Baden
Documentation, publishing on refugee and migration issues. *Zar Aktuell* (3/yr). »94

✿ **Off Limits**
c/o Haus für Alle, Amandastraße 58, 20357 Hamburg; *t* (040) 431587, *f* 430 4490
Multicultural journal; migrant and refugee issues. »94

● **Pädagogische Arbeitsstelle—Institut für Erwachsenenbildung des DVV, PAS-DVV** *(German Public High School Union Adult Education Institute Teacher Training Working Group)*
Holzhausenstraße 21, 60322 Frankfurt am Main; *t* (069) 154005 0, *f* 154005 174
Research and publishing on adult education in a multicultural context. See also Deutscher Volkshochschul-Verband, p166. »94

✿ **Wilhelm-Pieck-Universität Rostock**: History Section (Sektion Geschichte)
Lothar Elsner: Wilhelm-Külz-Platz 4, 2500 Rostock 1
Also Dirk Köhler, Christine Schildhauer, Wolf Pansow. »90

♦ **Der Rechte Rand** (The Right Fringe)
Postfach 1324, Rolandstraße 16, 30013 Hannover; *t* (0511) 341036
Journal, researches far-right and racist activity. »94

✿ **Ruhr-Universität** Fakultät für Sozialwissenschaften
Hermann Korte: Postfach 1360, 4630 Bochum 1
Sociological research. »90

✿ **Sozialinstitute der Katholische Arbeitnehmer-Bewegung**
Bernhard Eder: Postfach 1360, 8483 Vohenstrauß; *t* (09651) 3262
Location: Friedrichstraße 23. Social studies centre of KAB Suddeutschlands (Catholic Workers' Movement of Southern Germany); organises seminars and workshops on migration questions. »91

☼ **Sozialkritischer Arbeitskreis** *(Working Group for Critical Sociology)*
Frankfurterstraße 10, 64293 Darmstadt   »94
☼ **Universität Kiel**
Paul Gans: Department of Geography, Olshausenstraße 40, 2300 Kiel 1
Population geography.   »90
☼ **Universität Konstanz**
Hartmut Elsenhans: Fachbereich Politikwissenschaften, Universitätstraße 10, 7750 Konstanz 1   »90
☼ **Universität Osnabrück**
Klaus Bade: Fachbereich Kultur- und Geowissenschaften, Postfach 4469, 4500 Osnabrück
See also Institut für Migrationsforschung und interkulturelle Studien, p237.   »90
● **Verein für Gegenseitigkeit e.V.** *(Co-operative [or Mutual] Union)*
[address unknown]
Member of the European Migration Centre, p237.   »90
● **Wissenschaftszentrum Berlin für Sozialforschung** *(Berlin Sociological Research Centre)*
Prof. Hedwig Rudolph: Reichpietshufer 50, 1000 Berlin 30
General socio-economic research; one section (Forschungs-schwerpunkt I, Arbeitsmarkt und Beschäftigung) involved in migration-related work.   »94
● **Zentrale Dokumentationsstelle der freien Wohlfahrtspflege für Flüchtlinge, ZDWF** *(Central Documentation Service for Refugee Welfare Agencies)*
Ilse Bueren/Simone Wolken: Hans-Böcklerstr. 3, Postfach 301069, 53225 Bonn; *t* (0228) 462047-48, *f* 464704
Refugee law documentation and research centre founded in 1980 by six NGOs; research reports, library.   »94
☼ ≡ Karsten Lüthke/Theresa Wolff: Cecilienstraße 8, 53721 Siegburg; *t* (02241) 50001-02, *f* 50003
Unsure if this is a sub-office of the ZDWF in Bonn or a new address for it.   »95
☼ **Zentrum für Migranten und interkulturelle Studien e.V., ZIS** *(Centre for Migrants and Cross-Cultural Studies)*
Lindenhofstraße 43, 2800 Bremen 21; *t* (0421) 616 4258
Documentation and studies on migration and problems of (mainly Turkish) immigrants in Germany and EU; practical assistance, advice, language classes, integration courses, social work, campaigns for immigrant rights.   »91

GREECE 30

☼ **Aristotle University**
Prof. Georgios Tsiakalos: Department of Education, 54006 Thessaloniki; *t/f* (031) 200059
Some migration-related research.   »94
● **Ethnikon Kentron Koinonikon Erevnon, EKKE** *(National Centre for Social Research)*
Dmitris Fatouros: Odos Sophocleous 1, 10559 Athinai; *t* (01) 321 2611, *f* 321 6471
Publications include *Epitheorisi Koinonikon Erevnon*.   »94
● **Foundation for Mediterranean Studies, FMS**
Nikos Stylanidis: Odos Lycavittou 2, 10671 Athinai; *t* (01) 364 5345, 363 8461, *f* 362 9352   »94
● **Idrima Meteon Hersonesou tou Aimou, IMXA**
K. Svolopoulos: PO Box 10611, 54110 Thessaloniki
Balkan Studies (2/yr), *Balkanike Bibliografia*.   »94
● **Kentron Erevnistis Hellinikis Koinonias** *(Centre for Research on Greek Society?)*
Gregory Gizelis: Solonos 84, 10673 Athinai; *t* (01) 360 3028
Helliniki Koinonia (1/yr).   »94
● **Kentron Erevnon ya tis Gynekes tis Mesoyiou, KEGME** *(Centre for Research on Mediterranean Women?)*
Ketty Lazaris: Odos Harilaou TriKoupi 115, 11473 Athinai; *t* (01) 361 3968, *f* 361 5660
Publications include *Mediterranean Women*.   »94

HUNGARY 36

● **Ethnic and Minority Studies Programme**, Eötvös Lóránd University
György Csepeli/A. Örkény: Institute of Sociology, PO Box 394, VIII Pollack Mihaly tér. 10, 1446 Budapest
Sociological and ethnological research centre affiliated to the MERGER network, p240.   »94

IRELAND 353

● **Anthropological Association of Ireland**
Séamus Ó Siocháin: Department of Anthropology, St Patrick's College, Maynooth, Co. Kildare
Learned society; among other work on Irish and European minorities, has organised seminars on Traveller culture.   »91
● **Economic and Social Research Institute, ESRI**
4 Burlington Road, Dublin 4; *t* (01) 676 0115
Prof. Jerry Sexton labour force expert; research into social and economic questions including migration-related issues.   »94
■ **European Foundation for the Improvement of Living and Working Conditions**
[address unknown] Dublin
Conducts four-year research programmes on socal and economic issues in the EU.   »93
■ **International Political Science Association, IPSA**
John Coakley, Membership Secretary: University of Limerick, Plassey Technological, Park, Limerick
Has Research Committee on Politics and Ethnicity, which publishes bulletin, and numerous activities relevant to migration and minority studies.   »91
● **Irish Association for Migration Studies**
Ciarán Ó Maoláin: 11 Desart Lane, Armagh BT61 8AR; *t/f* [+44] (01861) 526881, *e* ciaran@mcr1.poptel.org.uk
Association open to researchers working in Ireland on migration, and overseas researchers on Irish migration.   »94
● **Irish Centre for the Study of Human Rights**
Dr Gerard Quinn, Director: University College Galway, Galway
Academic centre for research on domestic and international human rights issues.   »95
● **National Economic and Social Council**
Earl Court House, Earlsfort Terrace, Dublin 2
Has published study on emigration.   »91

ITALY 39

● **Agenzia di Stampa Disagio Pace Ambiente—Migrazioni, ASPE Migrazione** *(Migration Department, Disturbance of the Peace Press Agency)*
via Giolitti 21, 10123 Torino; *t* (011) 814 2716, *f* 839 5577
Media agency with specialist service on migrants, minorities, refugees and racism.   »94
● **Amnesty International—Centro per l'Educazione ai Diritti Umani, CEDU** *(AI Centre for Human Rights Education)*
via Castiglione 25, 40124 Bologna; *t* (051) 225186, *f* 260090
Preparation and dissemination of educational and briefing materials on human rights issues; see AI, p204.   »94
■ **Association Internationale d'Etudes des Civilisations Méditeranéennes, AIECM** *(International Association for the Study of Mediterranean Civilisations)*
Pe. Luigi Serra: via Baracca 85, 85100 Potenza; *t* (0971) 27402   »90
♦ **Associazione per gli Studi Giuridici sull'Immigrazione, ASGI** *(Association for Legal Studies on Immigration)* and European Legal Network on Asylum, ELENA
Massimo Pastori/Lorenzo Trucco: corso Vittorio Emanuele II 82, 10121 Torino; *t* (011) 562 7607, *f* 562 7416
Network of experts on migration and asylum law. Trucco co-ordinates ELENA, p154, in Italy. *Lettera ai Soci* (6/yr).   »95
● ≡ Bruno Nascimbene: Via V Bellini 12, 21122 Milano; *t* (02) 792458, *f* 793948   »96
☼ **Centro Educazione alla Mondialità, CEM** *(World Citizenship Education)*
Domenico Milani: via Piamarta 9, 25121 Brescia; *t* (03) 377 0780, *f* 377 2781
International solidarity, multicultural education. May be linked to the centre of the same name listed (1993) at viale San Martino 8, 43100 Parma. *CEM/Mondialità* (12/yr).   »94
☼ **Centro Europa per la Scuola Educazione Società, CESES** *(European Schools Centre on Education and Society)*
Giovanni Polliani: via Pantano 17, 20122 Milano; *t* (02) 5830 6797
Multicultural education research and development.   »94
● **Centro Italiano di Formazione Europea, CIFE** *(Italian Centre for European Training)*
Prof. Raimondo Cagiano de Azevedo: Salita de Crescenzi 26, 00186 Roma; *t/f* (06) 689 2715
Research, development of educational resources on cross-cultural issues. *Quaderni Federasti* (4/yr).   »94

♦ **Centro Studi Emigrazione Roma**, CSER *(Rome Centre for Emigration Studies)* also known as Centro Studi Scalabriniani
Bruno Mioli/Graziano Tassello: via Dandolo 58, 00153 Roma;
t (06) 580 9764, 589 7664, *f* 581 4651, 589 0651
Founded 1963; migration studies, especially of Italians in the Americas. Member of EU Migrants Forum, p131, and the international Federation of Migration Study Centres; documentation centre, research projects, conferences. Publications include *Studi Emigrazione/Etudes Migrations* (4/yr), *Dossier Europa Migrazione* (6/yr), other journals.   »94

● **Centro Studi Investimenti Sociali**, CENSIS
piazza di Novella 2, 00199 Roma; *t* (06) 839 0641   »90

✿ **Centro Studi Mediterranei**
Agostino Spataro: piazza Cavour 51, 92100 Agrigento;
t/f (0922) 401237
Research on the Mediterranean region including the Middle East. *Richerche e Proposte* (1/yr).   »94

✿ **Centro Studi Terzo Mondo**, CSTM *(Third World Studies Centre)*
Umberto Melotti: via G.B. Morgagni 39, 20129 Milano;
t/f (02) 2940 9041
Development education, training of volunteers for Third World projects, multicultural resources; *Terzo Mondo* (4/yr).   »94

✿ **Centro Terzo Mondo Documentazione e Informazione**, CTM *(Third World Information and Documentation Centre)*
Licio Lepore: via Pucci 34, 55049 Viareggio; *t* (0584) 46385
Solidarity; information and advice service.   »94

✿ **Collegio Universitario Aspiranti Medici Missionari**, CUAMM *(University College for Candidates for the Medical Missions)*
Luigi Mazzucato: via S. Francesco 126, 35121 Padova;
t (049) 875 1279, 875 1649
Training and education of young people intending to join religious bodies providing medical mission services to Third World countries. *CUAMM Notizie* (3/yr).   »94

● **Comitato Italiano per lo Studio dei Problemi della Popolazione**, CISP *(Italian Committee for the Study of Population)*
Nora Federici, President: via Nomentana 41, 00161 Roma;
t (06) 859555
Dr Brigmenti general secretary; founded 1928; demographic research, including foreigners in Italy. *Genus* (2/yr).   »90

✿ **Comunità Università Mediterranea**, CUM
Luigi Ambrosi: piazza Umberto I 1, 70121 Bari; *t* (080) 360786, *f* 314641
Bollettino della CUM (2/yr).   »94

✿ **Cooperativa Dedalus Studi e Ricerche Sociali** *(Dædalus Collective for Social Studies and Research)*
Elena De Filippo: via Michelangelo da Caravaggio 52, 80126 Napoli; *t/f* (081) 526 5884   »94

● **Emigrazione/Immigrazione Centro Studi**, EMIM *(Emigration/Immigration Study Centre)*
Stefan Heiner/Karin Bechtle: via della Consulta 50, 00186 Roma; *t* (06) 483044, 581 6512
Research on Italian return migration.   »86

✿ *Etnie: scienza politica e cultura dei popoli minoritari* (Ethnic Groups: political science and culture of minorities)
Miro Mirelli: viale Bligny 22, 20136 Milano; *t* (02) 5830 0530
Journal (5/yr) on minorities. See also NAGA, p144.   »90

● **Fondazione Leone Caetani—Accademia Nazionale dei Lincei**
Francesco Gabrieli: via della Lungara 10, 00165 Roma;
t (06) 650831   »94

● **International Documentation and Communication Centre**, IDOC
via S. Maria dell'Anima 30, 00186 Roma; *t* (06) 686 8332, *f* 683 2766, *e* Geo2:idoc
Archive, information centre, conferences on international affairs, development, migration and ethnic minority issues.»94

▌**International Sociological Association**, ISA: Research Committee on Migration
Francesco Cerase, Secretary: via Acquileia 15, 00198 Roma;
t (06) 845 0304
Research co-ordination, conferences and symposia on migration; *International Migration Review* (4/yr).   »90

✿ **Istituto di Diffusione dalla Cultura Araba, Siciliana e Mediterranea** *(Institute for the Dissemination of Arab, Sicilian and Mediterranean Culture)*
Orio Poerio: via Libertà 34, 90141 Palermo; *t* (091) 625 6707
Cultural research, publishing. *Antologia Siciliana* (4/yr).   »94

● **Istituto di Diritto Publico** *(Institute of Public Law)*
via Mecenate 77, 00184 Roma   »90

▌**Istituto Internazionale di Diritto Umanitario**: International Institute of Humanitarian Law, IIHL
Villa Ormond, corso Cavallotti 115, 18038 San Remo, IM;
t (0184) 541848, *f* 541600
Promotion of human rights law internationally and in all jurisdictions; research; archive on legislation and cases.   »94

✿ **Istituto per l'Oriente C.A. Nallino**
Giovanni Oman: via Alberto Caroncini 19, 00197 Roma;
t (06) 804106
Research and information on the Middle East and Africa. See also Centro per le Relazioni Italo-Arabe, p10. *Oriente moderno* (12/yr), *Rassegna di studi etiopici* (4/yr).   »94

✿ **Istituto per Relazioni Italia, Africa, America Latina, Medio Oriente**, IPALMO
Carlo Guelfi: via del Tritone 62B, 00187 Roma; *t* (06) 679 2321-11, *f* 679 7849
Research and documentation on Italy's external relations, migration and international affairs. Journal *Politica Internazionale* (10/yr).   »94

✿ **Istituto di Ricerche sulla Economia Mediterranea**, IREM *(Research Institute on the Mediterranean Economy)*
Maria Rosaria Carli: viale Antonio Gramsci 5, 80122 Napoli;
t (081) 681530, *f* 761 1157
Research, bibliography on economic affairs of Mediterranean countries.   »94

● **Istituto di Ricerche sulla Popolazione**, IRP *(Institute for Population Research)*
Prof. Antonio Golini, Director: viale Beethoven 56, 00144 Roma; *t* (06) 592 1474, 592 5414
Formed 1980 under Consiglio Nazionale delle Ricerche, CNR; research on demography, internal and international migration questions in Italy; publications.   »86

● **Istituto per lo Studio della Multietnicità**, ISMU *(Institute for the Study of Ethnic Pluralism)* and Centro di Documentazione
Prof. Michele Colasanto: Fondazione Cariplo, Foro Buonaparte 22, 20121 Milano; *t* (02) 7202 3375, 7202 3398, *f* 876042
Vincenzo Cesareo, Dr Francesco Zucchini, Dr Natale Losi.
Interdisciplinary research on ethnic relations; member of Utrecht-based MERGER network, p240. *ISMU informa* (4/yr).»96

✿ **Promozione Tecnologie Esperienze Organizzazione**, PROTEO
Benedetta Cammelli: via Marconi 69, 40122 Bologna; *t* (051) 247898, 294735, *f* 251055
Research and information on educational and cultural development.   »94

▌**Society for International Development**, SID
Robert Cassani, Director: Palazzo Civiltà del Lavoro, 00144 Roma; *t* (06) 591 7897, *f* 591 9836
Provides forum for exchanges on development research, aid and education; over 100 national branches.   »94

✿ **Università degli Studi di Urbino**
Peter Kammerer: Istituto di Filosofia, via Soffi 9, 61029 Urbino   »90

✿ **University of Bologna**
[address unknown] Bologna
Giuseppe Sciortino migration research.   »90

LUXEMBOURG 352

● **Centre de Documentation et d'Animation Interculturelles**, CDAIC *(Inter-Cultural Documentation and Promotion Centre)*
Serge Kollwelter: 10 rue Auguste Laval, 1922 Luxembourg;
t 438333, *f* 420871
See also ASTI and CLAE, both p145.   »95

✿ **Flash Contacts Echanges**, FCE
BP 208, 2012 Luxembourg; *t* 490240
Radical, anti-racist magazine.   »94

NETHERLANDS 31

✿ **Activist Press Service**, APS
Postbus 6452, Fred. Hendrikstraat 111, 1005 EL Amsterdam;
t/f (020) 686 6213
Provides e-mail and other communications services to progressive voluntary-sector organisations.   »94

✿ **Afdeling Rechtssociologie** *(Department of the Sociology of Law)* Katholieke Universiteit te Nijmegen
Jan Rath/Kees Groenendijk: Postbus 9049, 6500 KK Nijmegen
Location: Thomas van Aquinostraat 6, Nijmegen. Research interests include minority policy, discrimination.   »90

● **Antropologisch-sociologisch centrum** *(Anthropology and Sociology Centre)*
Oudezijds Voorburgwal 185, 1012 DK Amsterdam; *t* (020) 525 2654, *f* 525 3010   »95

● **Averroès Stichting** *(Averroes Foundation)*
Nieuwe Keizersgracht 45, 1018 VC Amsterdam; *t* (020) 627 0111, *f* 626 0224   »95

- **Centraal Bureau voor de Statistiek**, CBS
Hoofdafdeling S1 (Bevolkingsstatistieken) [address unknown]
Voorburg
Official statistical agency; annual report on immigration
(*Jaarwerk Statistiek van de Buitenlandse Migratie*), and other
migration, refugee and aliens statistics.   »90
- **Centrum voor Onderzoek van Maatschappelijke Tegenstell-ingen**, COMT *(Centre for Research in Social Differentiation)*
C. Bouw/A.J.F. Kobben: Rijksuniversiteit Leiden, Hooigracht
15, 2312 KM Leiden; *t* (071) 514 8333 ext. 2153
Lotty Eldering; university research and documentation centre
founded 1976; study of social conflicts, discrimination; social
and political aspects of immigrant communities.   »90
- **Displaced Persons Centre Information Service**, also known
as Stichting Displaced Persons Centre
Timothy Thomason, Executive Director: Elisabethgaarde 52,
1403 KB Bussum; *t* (035) 691 8418
Founded 1978; multi-disciplinary research into the problems
giving rise to refugee flows especially in South-East Asia;
Periodic Review (18/yr), special reports (12/yr).   »86
- ▌ **European Centre for Work and Society**, ECWS: Centre
Européen 'Travail et Société'
Gabriel Fragnière: Postbus 3073, 6202 NB Maastricht; *t* (043)
321 6724, 325 5712
Location: Hoogbrugstraat 43, 6221 CP Maastricht. Research
on migration (Sarah Cooper), employment, labour markets and
other social and economic issues; library (Isolde Vaessen).
Associated with Churches' Commission for Migrants in Europe,
p130; MAINE and ELAINE information networks, pp146 &
171, and Centro Europeo 'Trabajo y Sociedad', p242.   »95
- ♦ **European Documentation Centre and Observatory on
Migration and Ethnic Relations**, EDCOMER
Marta Branco, documentalist: Universiteit Utrecht, Heidelberg-laan 2, 3584 CS Utrecht; *t* (030) 253 9220, *f* 253 9280,
e ercomer@fsw.ruu.nl
Also at Postbus 80140, 3508 TC Utrecht. Information and
documentation centre within ERCOMER, below; seeks to acquire
a collection of statistical and written material for all of Europe,
to provide information in response to requests, and to publish
bibliographical and documentation reports.   »95
- ▌ **European Research Centre on Migration and Ethnic Relations**,
ERCOMER, and Migration and Ethnic Relations Group for
European Research, MERGER
Dr Malcolm Cross, Director: Universiteit Utrecht, Heidelberg-laan 2, 3584 CS Utrecht; *t* (030) 253 9220, 253 4425, *f* 253
9280, *e* ercomer@fsw.ruu.nl
Also at Postbus 80140, 3508 TC Utrecht. A multi-disciplinary
centre founded 1993 in the Department of General Social
Studies, succeeding Werkgroep Studies van de Multi-Etnische
Samenleving (SMES, established 1982) and other research
activities in ethnicity, minorities and migration. Comparative
research in all aspects of international migration, minorities and
ethnic relations, especially in Western Europe. EU-funded
research fellowships; co-ordinates the 13-country MERGER
network of scholars active in migration and ethnic relations
fields. Developing database and documentary archive through
EDCOMER, above, a book series and a working paper series.
Associates within the University include Prof. Dr Han Entzinger
t 253 2928, Prof. Louk Hagendoorn, 253 4654, Dr Helma
Lutz, 253 4641, Dr Karen Phalet, 253 5560, and others.
ERCOMER has become the editorial base for *New Community*,
the European journal on migration and ethnic relations (4/yr)
formerly produced in the UK (M. Cross editor, Jette Johst;
published by Carfax). *Merger* bulletin (3/yr).   »95
- ▌ **Europees Steunpunt Migranten en Vluchtelingen**, ESMV:
European Support Centre for Migrants and Refugees
Postbus 201, 3500 AE Utrecht; *t* (030) 294 0037, *f* 296
0050 (?)
Location: Kanaalweg 84b. Formed 1990-91 as an initiative of
the Nederlands Centrum Buitenlanders, presumably now linked
with FORUM, see p146. Migrant and refugee rights, anti-racism, information on migration and refugees in European
context.   »95
- **Faculteit Sociale Wetenschappen, Universiteit Utrecht**
(Faculty of Social Sciences, University of Utrecht)
Dr Robert Kloosterman: Postbus 80140, 3508 TC Utrecht;
t (030) 253 1885, *f* 253 4733
See above for ERCOMER, the Utrecht-based centre for
European migration research. There are other Faculty
members with interests in migration, minorities and related
issues including Dr Jack Burgers, *t* 253 1862, Prof. Willem
Dercksen, 253 5554, Dr Gerrit-Bartus Dielissen, 253 1923,
Prof. Godfried Engbersen, 253 5475, Peter Rensch, 253 2748,
Drs Jan Veraart, 253 6734, and Dr Maykel Verkuyten, 253
5559. This is not a comprehensive listing.   »95

- ▌ **ID-Archiv**, International Institute of Social History
IISH, Cruquiusweg 31, 1019 AT Amsterdam; *t* (020) 668
5866, *f* 665 4181
Research on social and ethnic identity.   »94
- ✿ **Infowinkel Phoenix** *(Phoenix Information Exchange)*
Postbus 28546, 3003 JA Rotterdam; *t* (010) 467 8822
Information centre, archive, clippings library, bookshop,
resource and activity centre for anti-racist, anti-fascist,
refugee, animal welfare, radical left and feminist groups. »94
- ♦ **Institute for International Migration Issues**, IIMI
E.A. Ros: Postbus 227, 2000 AE Haarlem; *t* (0255) 537438,
f (072) 589 4566
Location: Mercuriusstraat 56. Research on population
movements, labour mobility, refugees and ethnic relations.
See also CEMYC, p208.   »95
- **Institute of Social Studies**, ISS
J. van Dommele/Dr Amina Mama: Postbus 29776, 2502 LT
Den Haag; *t* (070) 462 0414
Teaching and research in development studies; advisory work.
Most students come from developing countries.   »95
- **Instituut voor Migratie- en Etnische Studies**, IMES: Institute
for Migration and Ethnic Studies, Universiteit van Amsterdam
Prof. Rinus Penninx/Dr Jan Rath: Rokin 84, 1210 KX
Amsterdam; *t* (020) 525 3627, *f* 525 3628
Superseded the Centrum voor Etnische Studies.   »95
- **Instituut voor Sociale Geografie**, SGI/UvA *(Institute for
Social Geography)*
Prof. Hans van Amersfoort: Universiteit van Amsterdam,
Nieuwe Prinsengracht 130, 1018 VZ Amsterdam; *t* (020)
525 4063, *f* 525 4051
Dr Cees Cortie. Sociology of migration, and related issues.
Has produced annual Netherlands migration studies for the
SOPEMI system: see OECD, p199.   »94
- **Instituut voor Sociologisch-Economisch Onderzoek**, ISEO
(Social and Economic Research Institute) Erasmus Universiteit
Dr Justus Veenman/Theo Roelandt: Postbus 1738, 3000 DR
Rotterdam; *t* (010) 408 2776, *f* 453 1066
Location: Burgemeester Oudlaan 50. Statistical and other
research on minorities. Migration-related work is also done in
the Department of Social Sciences (Dr Wiebe de Jong, *t* 408
1607; Dr Kees Masson, *t* 408 1609; both *f* 453 2729).   »95
- **Instituut voor Toegepaste Sociale Wetenschappen**, ITS
(Institute of Applied Social Sciences) Katholieke Universiteit
te Nijmegen
H.J.M. van den Tillaart: Postbus 9048, 6500 KJ Nijmegen;
t (080) 653500, *f* 653599
Location: Toernooiveld 5. Research topics have included
ethnic enterprise.   »95
- ✿ **Inter-Cultureel Instituut**, ICI *(Cross-Cultural Institute)*
Vestdijklaan 374, 9721 VZ Groningen; *t* (050) 252422 (?)»94
- ▌ **International Association for Cross-Cultural Psychology**
Dr Y.H. Poortings: Department of Psychology, Tilburg
University, 5000 LE Tilburg   »90
- ▌ **International Association for Intercultural Education**, IAIE
Pieter Batelaan: Faculty of Education, Central Dutch
Polytechnic, Postbus 14007, 3508 SB Utrecht; *t* (030) 252
5111
Also contactable c/o P. Batelaan, Sumatralaan 37, 1217 GP
Hilversum, *t* (035) 624 7375, *f* 623 9244. *European Journal
of Intercultural Studies*.   »95
- ▌ **International Association for the Study of Racism**, IASR
Teun A. van Dijk, Universiteit van Amsterdam, Spuistraat
210, kr. 339, 1012 VT Amsterdam; *t* (020) 525 3834,
f 639 1727, *e* teun@alf.let.uva.nl
Scholarly association for the study of racist ideology,
discrimination and ethnic conflict.   »94
- ▌ **International Institute for Migration Issues**
Postbus 227, 2000 AE Haarlem   »90
- ● *Knipselkrant Minderheden, Discriminatie en Racisme*
(Clippings Journal on Minorities, Discrimination and Racism)
Postbus 93054, 2509 AB Den Haag; *t* (070) 313 8181 (?)»94
- ✿ **Kollektief Anti Fascistisch/Kapitalistisch Archief**, KAFKA
(Anti-Fascist/Anti-Capitalist Archive Collective)
Postbus 59043, 1040 KA Amsterdam   »94
- ✿ *Konfrontatie—Onafhankelijk Links Maandblad*
(Confrontation—Independent Left Monthly News)
Postbus 3249, 2601 DE Delft
Radical journal (12/yr) with anti-racist content.   »94
- ✿ **Leids Instituut voor Sociaal Wetenschappelijk Onderzoek**,
LISWO *(Leiden Institute for Social Science Research)*
Rijksuniversiteit Leiden
Leo Balai/Aydin Yenal: Postbus 9555, 2300 RB Leiden;
t (071) 527 3835, *f* 527 3788
Location: Wassenaarseweg 52. Research includes work on
racism in amateur sport, and on anti-racist policies.   »95

- *Mensen Rechten Magazine*, MRM *(Human Rights Magazine)*
Postbus 17157, 1001 JD Amsterdam; *t* (020) 638 3826,
f 625 4991
Journal on national and international human rights issues,
including minority and refugee rights. »94
- *Migranten Nieuwsblad* (Migrants Newspaper)
Postbus 639, 3500 AP Utrecht; *t* (030) 296 3688 »95
- Nationaal Oorlogs- en Verzetsmuseum *(National Museum of the War and the Resistance)*
G.M. Teuning: Museumpark 1, 5825 AM Overloon; *t* (0478) 641250, *f* 642405
Museum and archive on 1939-45 war and resistance, relating history to contemporary experience, for example in the themes of racism and discrimination. School visits, educational resources. See also Verzetsmuseum, right. »94
- Nederlands Instituut voor Zorg en Welzijn, NIZW *(Dutch Institute for Social Welfare and Care)*
Postbus 19152, 3501 DD Utrecht; *t* (030) 230 6311, *f* 231 9641
Includes specialist Sector Maatschappelijke en Culturele Ontwikkeling (Section for Social and Cultural Education) which carries out research on minorities. »95
- Nederlands Interuniversitair Demografisch Instituut, NIDI
Dr Saskia Y. Voets: Postbus 11650, 2502 AR 's Gravenhage
Jeanette Schoorl; research on population change, migration and minorities. »90
- *Nomen Nescio*, NN
Van Ostadestraat 233 N, 1073 TN Amsterdam; *t/f* (020) 676 1773
Magazine; anti-racist, anti-fascist, supports migrant and refugee rights. »94
- Programma Interdisciplinair Onderzoek Oorzaken Mensenrechten Schendingen, PIOOM: Interdisciplinary Research Programme on Root Causes of Human Rights Violations
Dr Alex Schmid: RU Leiden, Postbus 9555, Wassenaarseweg 52, 2333 AK Leiden; *t* (071) 527 3861-48, *f* 527 3788, 527 3619
Founded 1988. Academic research centre on human rights issues, including refugee questions. *PIOOM Newsletter*; *Progress Report* (both 2/yr). Based in LISWO, p240. »95
- Project Anti Racistische Evaluatie Leermiddelen, PAREL *(Project for the Anti-Racist Evaluation of Teaching Aids)*
Postbus 386, Nieuwe Kade 289, 3500 AJ Utrecht; *t* (030) 231 7387, *f* 234 0231
Educational resource consultancy; see ADO, p208. »95
- Projectgroep Evaluatie Welzijn 0-18 jarige Allochtonen *(Working Party on Evaluating the Welfare of Alien Minors)*
Wassenaarseweg 52, 2333 AK Leiden; *t* (071) 527 3905 (?)
Connected with the LISWO research centre, p240. »95
- *Rechtshulp, Maandblad voor de sociale praktijk* (Rights Advice, Social Service Monthly)
Peter Rodrigues: [address unknown]
Journal (12/yr) for rights advice agency workers. »93
- *Sectie Interculturele Pedagogiek (Section for Cross-Cultural Teacher Training)* Rijksuniversiteit Leiden
LISWO, Wassenaarseweg 52, Postbus 9555, 2300 RB Leiden; *t* (071) 527 4071, *f* 527 3619 »95
- ✿ Sinai Centrum
J. Lansen, Director: Postbus 66, 3800 AB Amersfoort »91
- ▎ Society for Intercultural Education, Training and Research, SIETAR
Postbus 614, c/o Haarlem Business School, 2003 RP Haarlem; *t* (023) 527 7345, *f* 527 7384 »95
- Sociology Centre, University of Amsterdam
Dr Hans Vermeulen: Oude Zijds Achterburgwal 185, 1012 Amsterdam; *t* (020) 525 3010
Held 1993 conference on the anthropology of ethnicity. »94
- Standing Committee of Experts on International Immigration, Refugee and Criminal Law
Aldo Kuijer: c/o FORUM, Postbus 201, 3500 AE Utrecht; *t* (030) 294 0037, *f* 296 0050 (?) »96
- Stichting Voorlichting Gezondheidszorg Buitenlanders *(Foundation for Information on Health Care for Foreigners)*
Postbus 8, 3500 CB Utrecht; *t* (030) 297 1144, *f* 297 1111
Location: Da Costakade 45. Health education materials, promoting health care provision for immigrants. »95
- Studie- en Informatiecentrum Mensenrechten, SIM *(Human Rights Research and Information Centre)* Netherlands Institute of Human Rights
Prof. P.R. Baehr: Janskerkhof 16, 3512 BM Utrecht; *t* (030) 253 8033-34, *f* 253 7168, *e* sim@pobox.ruu.nl
Archive, research on human rights, racism and related issues; in 1995 Netherlands Research School for Human Rights opened as joint venture with Limburg and Erasmus (Rotterdam) universities; *Netherlands Quarterly of Human Rights*. »95

- Trans-National Institute
20 Paulus Potterstraat, Amsterdam
Offshoot of US Institute for Policy Studies. »90
- Vakgroep Taal en Minderheden *(Working Group on Languages and Minorities)* Katholieke Universiteit Brabant
Warandelaan 2, 5037 AB Tilburg; *t* (013) 306311 »95
- ✿ Verzetsmuseum Amsterdam *(Amsterdam Resistance Museum)*
E. Habold/J.A. Koetsier: Lekstraat 63, 1079 EM Amsterdam
Museum and archives on the Dutch wartime anti-fascist resistance movement. »91

NORWAY 47

- Programmet for Menneskeretighetsstudier: Programme for Human Rights Studies
Fantoftvegen 38, 5036 Fantoft
Research and analysis on human rights, democracy and conflict worldwide. »93

PORTUGAL 351

- Centro de Estudos Africanos, Instituto Superior das Ciências do Trabalho e da Empresa
Avenida das Forças Armadas, 1600 Lisboa; *t* (01) 795 5361
Study and research on Africa, especially the Lusophone countries. »95
- Centro de Estudos Africanos e Asiáticos *(African and Asian Studies Centre)*
Avenida Ilha Madeira, Lisboa 1400; *t* (01) 615264 »94
- ≡ (in Instituto de Investigação Científico Tropical): Junqueira 30, 1300 Lisboa; *t* (01) 362 2621 »95
- Centro de Estudos e Documentação Europeia
Miguel Lupi 20-2°, 1200 Lisboa; *t* (01) 397 8207 »95
- ◆ Centro de Estudos das Migrações e das Relações Interculturais, CEMRI: Centre for the Study of Migration and Intercultural Relations, Universidade Aberta de Lisboa
Prof. Maria Beatriz Rocha-Trindade: Palácio Ceia, Rua Escola Politécnica 147, 1200 Lisboa; *t* (01) 397 2334, 397 2343, *f* 397 3229, *Tx* 16129 UNIVAB P
Research centre of the distance-learning university founded 1988, with a particular interest in Portuguese migration and emigrant communities; offices in Coimbra and Oporto, and multi-media institute (COAIS Serafim dos Anjos). CEMRI's teaching and research on multiculturalism, minorities and European topics developed from the university's Linha de Investigação: Migração (Migration Research Group). »94
- Centro de Estudos Sociais, CES *(Centre for Social Studies)*
Santos Boaventura De Souza: Apartado 3087, 3000 Coimbra; *t* (039) 26459, *f* 25841
Research and publishing. *Revista de Ciências Sociais*. »94
- ◆ Centro Europeu de Formação e Estudos sobre as Migrações, CEFEM *(European Centre for Training and Study on Migration)*
Pio Fantinato: Quinta da Escola, Foros de Amora, 2840 Seixal; *t* (01) 225 1969, *f* 225 7462
Info-Migrações. »94
- Centro de Informação e Documentação Amilcar Cabral, CIDAC *(Cabral Information and Documentation Centre)*
Rua Pinheiro Chagas 77-2°, 1000 Lisboa; *t* (01) 352 8718
International solidarity, development education. »94
- Fundação Calouste Gulbenkian *(Gulbenkian Foundation)*
Avenida de Berna 45, 1093 Lisboa Codex; *t* (01) 793 5131, *f* 793 5139
Philanthropic foundation; activities include bursaries to Portuguese students, and grants to foreign students and academic staff working in Portugal. »95
- Gabinete Emigração e Desenvolvimento *(Emigration and Development Office)*
Rua Combatentes da Grande Guerra 62-2°, 6200 Covilhã; *t* (075) 25639 »90
- Grupo de Estudo e Acção sobre a Emigração Temporária *(Temporary Emigration and Action Group)*
a/c Pe. António Francisco dos Santos, Seminário Maior, 5100 Lamego; *t* (054) 62151
Catholic research group on the pastoral care of seasonal workers and temporary emigrants. »90
- Instituto de Ciências Sociais, Universidade de Lisboa *(Social Sciences Institute, University of Lisbon)*
Prof. Maria Beatriz Rocha Trindade: Avenida das Forças Armadas, Edifício ISCTE, 1600 Lisboa; *t* (01) 793 2272 »95

5

- **Instituto de Estudos para o Desenvolvimento Internacional,** IEDI *(International Development Studies Institute)* Graça Anahory de Vasconcellos: Rua de S. Domingo à Lapa 111-3°, 1200 Lisboa; *t* (01) 609636-8, *f* 395 1570, 668064 Third World studies. Formerly *Centro* de EDI. »95
- ○ **Universidade Nova de Lisboa** *(New University of Lisbon)* Núcleo de Lingüística, Avenida de Berna, Lisboa »90

ROMANIA 40

- **Romani Center for Social Intervention and Studies,** CRISS PO Box 22-68, 70100 Bucuresti; *t/f* (01) 312 4188 Anti-racist, anti-fascist orientation. »94

SPAIN 34

- ○ **Associació Educativa de les Il.les,** AEI *(Islands Educational Association)* Tomás Martínez Miro: Ortega y Gasset 9-1°, 07008 Palma, Mallorca; *t* (971) 418626 (or 418616?), *f* 415640 Development of multicultural child and adult education; based in Escola de Formació en Mitjans Didàtics (teacher training school). »94
- **Centre d'Informació i Documentació Internacionals a Barcelona,** CIDOB *(Barcelona International Information and Documentation Centre)* and Federació Catalana d'ONG pel Desenvolupment Josep Ribera: carrer Elisabets 12, 08001 Barcelona, Catalunya; *t* (93) 302 6495, *f* 302 2118, *Tx* 99767 The Centre researches and publishes on international affairs and the Third World; particular focus on Africa; associated with the Federation of Catalan Development NGOs. *Anuario* (1/yr), *Afers Internacionals* (4/yr). »94
- **Centro de Documentación de las Naciones Unidas** *(United Nations Documentation Centre)* avenida General Perón 32-1°, 28020 Madrid; *t* (91) 555 8087, 555 8742 »90
- **Centro Estatal de Documentación e Información de Servicios Sociales,** CEDISS *(State Centre for Social Services Documentation and Information)* Modesto Lafuente 13, 28003 Madrid; *t* (91) 441 8100 »90
- ○ **Centro de Estudios y Solidaridad con América Latina y Africa,** CDSALA *(Centre for Research on and Solidarity with Latin America and Africa)* Palleter 43, 46008 Valencia »94
- **Centro Europeo Trabajo y Sociedad:** European Centre for Work and Society, ECWS Rafael Guardo, Delegado en España: calle Marquesa Viuda de Aldama 21, Alcobendas, 28100 Madrid; *t* (91) 777 7814 Interests include refugee and migrant labour issues; see the ECWS in the Netherlands, p240. »90
- **Centro de Investigaciones sobre la Realidad Social,** CIRES *(Centre for Research on Social Affairs)* calle Orense 37-5° A, 28020 Madrid; *t* (91) 556 9036 Conducted 1994 survey on attitudes to migrants and minorities throughout Spain. »94
- **Centro de Investigaciones Sociológicas,** CIS *(Sociological Research Centre)* c. Montalbán 8, 28014 Madrid; *t* (91) 580 7600, 580 7615 Conducted major 1991 survey (17,000 respondents) on attitudes to migrants and minorities across Spain. »94
- **Colectivo Ioe** Miguel Angel de Praday: calle Luna 11-1° dcha, 28004 Madrid; *t* (91) 531 0123, *f* 532 9662 Carlos Pereda, Walter Actis. Sociological studies of situation of migrant workers; also known as Centro de Intervención Sociológica. Associated with Cáritas, p213. »94
- **Colectivo de Migraciones** Millalén Morán: calle Marqués de Monteagudo 8, 28028 Madrid »90
- **Consejo Superior de Investigaciones Científicas** *(Higher Council for Scientific Research)* [address unknown] Madrid National funding and publishing agency for academic research; 1994 publications include J.L. Rodríguez's history of the far right in Spain. »95
- **Escuela de Formación Específica en Materias de Inmigración,** EFEMI *(Special Training School on Immigrant Questions)* calle Cava Alta 25, 28005 Madrid; *t* (91) 364 1266 Catholic training centre. »94

- **Federación Española de Universidades Populares** *(Spanish Federation of People's Universities)* calle los Madrazos 3-1°, 28014 Madrid Adult education; research, documentation; some work on the Maghreb. »94
- **Fundació Servei Girona de Pedagogía Social,** SER.GI *(Servei Girona Social Education Foundation)* carrer Baldiri Reixach 50, 17003 Girona, Catalunya; *t* (972) 205505 Multicultural educational research. See also GRAMC, below. *Revista SER.GI.* »94
- **Fundación Paulino Torras** Vicente Font: paseo de Gracia 58-2° 2ª, 08007 Barcelona, Catalunya; *t* (93) 487 6929, *f* 488 3617 *Itinera Anales* (1/yr), *Cuadernos.* »94
- **Gabinete de Estudios sobre la Emigración** *(Emigration Studies Bureau)* avenida del Generalísimo 76, 14 B, 28000 Madrid; *t* (91) 250 0000 ext. 68 »90
- **Grup de recerca Immigració i minories ètniques** *(Immigration and Ethnic Minorities Research Group)* Universidad Autónoma de Barcelona Prof. Carlota Solé Puig: Dept° Sociología, Universidad Autónoma, Bellaterra, Barcelona, Catalunya; *t* (93) 581 2418 Interdisciplinary study group, specialising as follows: Prof. C. Solé Puig European migration, Dr Louis Lemkow Zeterling (ext. 1383) migrant health, Dr Lluis Flaquer Villardebo, Dr Angels Pascual (Dept° de Geografía ext. 1736) return migration, Dr Alice Gail Bier (*t* 209 2211) internal migration. »94
- ○ **Grups de Recerca i Actuació sobre Minories Culturals i Treballadors Estrangers,** GRAMC *(Research and Action Groups on Cultural Minorities and Foreign Workers)* Josep M. Terricabras N.: [address uncertain] plaça Lluis Companys 7, 17030 Girona; *t* (972) 231050, *f* 213717 Research on migration-related social, cultural, educational and economic topics. Also listed (1994) as c/o the Fundació Servei Girona de Pedagogia Social, above, *t* (972) 205505, 214966. Bulletin (4/yr). »94
- **HEGOA, Centro de Documentación e Investigaciones sobre Paises en Desarrollo** *(Research and Documentation Centre on Developing Countries)* Euskal Herriko Unibersitatea avenida Lehendekari Agirre 83, Deusto, 48015 Bilbo, Bizkaia, Euskadi; *t* (94) 447 3512 Research unit within the economics faculty of the University of the Basque Country. »94
- **Institut Català d'Estudis Mediterranis,** ICEM *(Catalan Institute for Mediterranean Studies)* Maria Angels Roque: avenida Diagonal 407 bis, planta 21, 08008 Barcelona, Catalunya; *t* (93) 415 7222, *f* 415 8790 Research on the Mediterranean countries and cultures, including migration from Morocco, Tunisia and Algeria. »94
- **Instituto de Estudios Políticos para América Latina y Africa,** IEPALA *(Latin America and Africa Political Studies Institute)* Juan Carmelo García: calle Hermanos García Noblejas 41-8°, 28037 Madrid; *t* (91) 408 4112/4212/4561, *f* 408 7047 Research, information, documentation on the Third World.»94
- **Instituto Nacional de Estadística,** INE *(National Statistical Institute)* Ministerio de Trabajo y Seguridad Social [address uncertain] paseo del Pintor Rosales 44, 28071 Madrid; *t* (91) 547 5200 Also listed (1994) as a dependency of the Ministerio de Economía y Hacienda, at paseo de la Castellana 183, 28046 Madrid, *t* 572 0793, *f* 583 9158. Government service responsible for statistical research and publishing, including statistics on foreign residents in Spain (compiled by the Dirección General de Policía, p214). The Autonomous Communities each have their own statistical services. »94
- ♦ **Observatorio de la Inmigración** *(Immigration Observatory)* [address unknown] Madrid Research unit created under the 1994 Plan for Social Integration of Immigrants; measures migration flows. »95
- ○ **Recursos d'Animació internacional,** RAI *(International Cultural Promotion Resources)* Princesa 6-1°, 08003 Barcelona, Catalunya; *t* (93) 268 1321, *f* 268 3438 »94
- ○ **Universidad Pontifica de Comillas** *(Pontifical University of Comillas)* Isabel Lazaro/Javier Ezquerra: ICAI/ICADE, Alberto Aguilera 23, 28015 Madrid; *t* (91) 542 2800, *f* 248 6569 Research on international migration. »93
- ○ **Universidad Popular de Cartagena** *(People's University of Cartagena)* Basilio Galindo Salmerón: Centro Cultural de la Ciudad, 1ª planta, 30204 Cartagena, Murcia; *t* (968) 128800 ext. 106 Adult education, research, information; Maghrebi students.»94

SWEDEN 46

✿ **Barrikaden**
Box 7539, 20042 Malmö
Radical anti-fascist magazine. »94

◆ **Centrum for Invandringsforskning: Centre for Research in International Migration and Ethnic Relations**
Prof. Charles Westin, Director: Stockholms Universitet, 10691 Stockholm; t (08) 162000, f 156720
Prof. Tomas Hammar. An interdisciplinary research centre on migration, development, ethnic relations and ethnic minorities; a member of the Utrecht-based MERGER network, p240. The Centre co-ordinates a working group on research on racism and the far right in Europe. »94

● **Raoul Wallenberg Institutet for Manslika Rattigheter och Humanitar Ratt, RWI** (Wallenberg Institute for Human Rights and Humanitarian Law)
Box 207, Sankt Annegatan 4, 22100 Lund; t (046) 107000, f 104445
Research and education on human rights; assistance to and co-operation with developing country institutes, pressure groups and centres in this field. »94

SWITZERLAND 41

▌ **Centre for Documentation on Refugees, CDR**
c/o UNHCR, Case postale 2500, 1211 Genève 2 Dépôt; t (022) 739 8458, f 739 8682, 731 9546
International governmental organisation researching refugee flows to enable prompt humanitarian response. »95

✿ **Dokumentationsarchiv, DOK-WI-CH** (Documentation Centre)
Postfach 14, 8407 Winterthur
Anti-fascist documentation centre. »94

● **Entwicklungspolitischer Dokumentations- und Pressedienst** (Development Policy Documentation and Press Service) and Schulstelle 3. Welt
Postfach 1686, Monbijoustrasse 31, 3001 Bern; t (031) 382 1232, f 382 2205
Archive and press agency on global development issues, including migration, refugees and racism. The Schulstelle provides development education materials to schools. »94

● **Federal Office for Statistics**
D. Ullmann: Schwarztor 53, 3003 Bern; t (031) 618879
Conducts decennial census; compiles and publishes other social and economic statistics. »94

● **Flüchtlingsinformation** (Refugee Information)
Postfach 6175, 3001 Bern; t (031) 301 1535, f 302 8734
Magazine on refugee issues, racism, human rights and related topics. »94

▌ **Human Rights Information and Documentation Systems International, HURIDOCS:** Système international d'information et de documentation sur les droits de l'homme
rue Jean-Jaquet 2, 1201 Genève; t (022) 741 1767, f 741 1768, e geonet:geo2:huridocs
Global network of human rights organisations, established 1982. Protection of human rights worldwide, including refugee rights, and freedom from racial discrimination. Promotes research, information and documentation activities of member organisations, and development of standards and models for information management; HURIDOCS itself does not engage directly in documentation, but it co-produced (1993, with OECD, p199 and UNHCR, p219) a directory of refugee and migrant support NGOs (Human Rights, Refugees, Migrants & Development, OECD, Paris). »95

● **Infosud—Agence de presse et documentation**
chemin des Epinettes 10, 1007 Lausanne; t (021) 617 4353, f 617 4352
Press agency supplying media with articles on North-South topics, migration, refugees, demographics, development and human rights; information service, documentation centre; assistance to journalists from the South seeking access to media in the North, and to journalists, students and others from the North seeking information on the South. »93

● **Institut de recherche sur l'environnement construit** (Institute for Research on the Built Environment)
Th. Huissoud/M. Schuler: Département d'architecture, Ecole polytechnique fédérale, Case postale, 1001 Lausanne; t (021) 693 3297
Research activities include compilation of demographic statistics relevant to migration and minorities. »94

● **Sociologisches Institut** (Institute of Sociology) Universität Zürich
Dr Kurt Imhof/Gaetano Romano, Researchers: Rämistrasse 69, 8001 Zürich; t (01) 257 2141
Sociological research, including Working Group on Immigrant Populations; projects on racism and xenophobia (1993-95), and on attitudes towards foreigners in Switzerland (1994-96, with Hans-Joachim Hoffman-Nowotny, Monique Dupuis). »94

◆ **Swiss Study Group for Ethnic Research**
[address unknown]
Theme of 1993 convention was "In search of a new relationship with the alien". »94

UNITED KINGDOM 44

● **Advisory Centre for Education, ACE**
1b Aberdeen Studios, 22 Highbury Grove, London N5 2EA; t (0171) 354 8321, f 354 9069
Information on education in the UK, including multicultural issues. ACE Bulletin (6/yr). »95

● **The Afiya Foundation**
[address unknown] London
Research into ethnic minority health care issues. »96

✿ **African and Asian Resource Centre**
[address uncertain] Newman College, Gennerslane, Bartley Green, Birmingham; t (0121) 476 1181 »90

✿ **African and Asian Visual Artists Archive, AAVAA**
School of Art and Design, University of East London, Romford Road, London E15 4LZ; t (0181) 590 7722
Research, documentation, public education on the African and Asian contribution to visual arts; formerly based in Bristol.»96

● **Association of Contemporary Iberian Studies, ACIS**
Dr R. Rix, Secretary: Trinity and All Saints College, Brownberrie Lane, Horsforth, Leeds LS8 5HD; t (0113) 258 2916, f 258 1148
Fosters study of Spain and Portugal; founded 1968. »90

● **Association of Hispanists of Great Britain and Ireland**
Department of Hispanic Studies, University of Birmingham, PO Box 363, Birmingham B15 2TT; t (0121) 414 6038
Mainly Spanish and Portuguese language teachers. »90

● **Association of Social Research Organisations, ASRO**
T. Quirke, Secretary: c/o ODI, Regent's College, Inner Circle, Regent's Park, London NW1 4NS; t/f (0171) 487 7590
30 learned societies; founded 1972. »90

● **Association for the Study of Ethnicity and Nationalism, ASEN**
London School of Economics, Houghton Street, London WC2A 2AE; t (0171) 955 6801, f 955 7405
Conferences, co-operation among researchers on ethnicity, religion, nationalism and related fields. »96

✿ **Birkbeck College Department of Politics and Sociology,** University of London
Dr John Solomos: Malet Street, London WC1E 7HX; t (0171) 631 6566, 580 6622, f 436 2182 »94

✿ **Birmingham Development Education Centre**
Selly Oak Colleges, Bristol Road, Birmingham B29 6LQ; t (0121) 472 3255
Public education on Third World and development issues. »94

● **The Black Cultural Archives, BCA:** African Peoples Historical Monument Foundation
Sam Walker: 378 Coldharbour Lane, Brixton, London SW9 8LF; t (0171) 738 4591, f 738 7168
Bookshop, museum and archive dedicated to black history in UK; library of books and videos; speakers for schools. »94

✿ **Black and Ethnic Minorities Research/Development Project:** Hastings Voluntary Action
31a Priory Street, Hastings TN34 1EA; t (01424) 444010
A project seeking to identify the needs and concerns of local ethnic minorities, and to involve them in planning and delivery of local health, social care and policing services. »95

✿ **Black and Ethnic Minority Mental Health Development Team**
MIND SE Regional Office, 24-32 Stephenson Way, London NW1 2HD; t (0171) 387 9070
Research on health needs and provision. »90

✿ **Bradford Resource Centre**
31 Manor Row, Bradford BD1 4PS; t (01274) 725046
Workers' and community resource centre; helps Bangladeshi, Pakistani, Caribbean communities. See also Bradford Law Centre, p220. »94

● **The British Academy**
The Secretary: 20-21 Cornwall Terrace, London NW1 4QP; f (0171) 224 3807
National society for the humanities and the social sciences; extensive programme of overseas academic exchanges. »95

- **British Association for Soviet, Slavonic and East European Studies**
Department of Russian Studies, Bristol University, 17 Woodland Road, Bristol BS8 1TE; *t* (0117) 930 3030 exts. 3512, 3516
Academic study of Eastern Europe; founded 1988. »90

- **British Institute of Human Rights, BIHR**
School of Law, Kings College London, Strand, London WC2R 2LS; *t* (0171) 836 5454, 873 2273
Independent institute established 1970 to serve as a focal point for all aspects of the promotion of human rights in the UK. Associated with the KCL School of Law. »94

- **British International Studies Association**
Department of International Relations, University of Keele, Keele ST5 5BG; *t* (01782) 621111
Fosters development of multi-disciplinary studies in international affairs. »90

- **British Journal of Holocaust Education**
Dr John Fox, Editor: [address unknown]
Scholarly journal, founded 1992, for Holocaust studies. Part-funded by the Yad Vashem Charitable Trust, p247. »94

- **Careers Europe**
Equity Chambers, 40 Piccadilly, Bradford BD1 3NN; *t* (01274) 757521, *f* 742332
Information service on employment opportunities throughout the EU; database, newsletter, enquiry service. »94

- **Central Asian Research Centre**
8 Wakley Street, London EC1V 7LT »88

- **Central Office of Information, COI**
Hercules Road, London SE1 7DU
Government publicity agency; COI Translations produces print, audio, video and other translated material in a variety of European, Asian and African languages for government departments. Much of that work involves advice leaflets and forms in the Indic languages and Chinese for the main UK ethnic minorities. »95

- **Centre for Black and White Christian Partnership**
Rt Rev. Dr Patrick Kalilombe, Director: Selly Oak Colleges, Bristol Road, Birmingham B29 6LQ; *t* (0121) 472 7952
John Adegoke administrator, Olu Abiola. Founded 1978; education, information, contact and understanding among black and white Christians; development of theology and practice in multi-cultural society. *Newsletter*. »94

- **Centre for Caribbean Studies**, University of Warwick
Dr David Dabydeen: Coventry CV4 7AL; *t* (01203) 523523
Research and teaching on Caribbean culture and history. »96

- **Centre for Contemporary Studies**
Marilyn Herman: Ingersoll House, 202 New North Road, London N1 7BL »90

- **Centre for Equality and Discrimination**
Andrew Johnson, Director: [address unknown] Glasgow, Scotland; *t* (0141) 950 3357
Among other activities, the Centre is developing (1994) a project which promotes equality of access to university education in Scotland by ethnic minorities. »94

- **Centre for German-Jewish Studies**, University of Sussex
Prof. Edward Timms: School of European Studies, Falmer, Brighton BN1 9QN; *t* (01273) 606755
Advanced research and teaching on the history and culture of German-speaking Jews, including refugees. »96

- **Centre for Holocaust Studies**, University of Leicester
University Road, Leicester LE1 7RH; *t* (0116) 252 2522
Postgraduate study and research into the Nazi Holocaust. »94

- **Centre for Information on Language Teaching and Research**
Regent's College, Inner Circle, Regent's Park, London NW1 4NS; *t* (0171) 486 8221
Development of language teaching. »90

- **Centre for Middle Eastern and Islamic Studies**
Dr Suha Taji-Farouki: [address unknown] »94

♦ **Centre for Research in Ethnic Relations, CRER**
Prof. Zig Layton-Henry, Director: University of Warwick, Coventry CV4 7AL; *t* (01203) 523605, 523523, *f* 524324
Dr Clive Harris, Prof. John Rex. National centre for postgraduate research into migration and ethnic and race relations, part-funded by ESRC, right. Research reports, bibliographies and other publications. Current (1993-98) research programme deals with national and EU aspects of migration and citizenship, ethnic mobilisation and nationalism, and economic change and racial discrimination. »96

- **Centre for South Asian Studies** and British Association for South Asian Studies
Prof. Akbar Ahmed/Dr D.J. Smith: Selwyn College, University of Cambridge, Sidgwick Avenue, Cambridge CB3 9DQ
Postgraduate research centre, and association of academics engaged in studies relating to the Indian sub-continent. »94

- **Centre for the Study of Public Order, CSPO**: University of Leicester
John Benyon, Director: University of Leicester, 6 Salisbury Road, Leicester LE1 7QR; *t* (0116) 252 2458, *f* 252 3944
Lynn Turnbull, Tracy Simmonds. Research interests include minorities, ethnic relations, refugees, racial violence. »94

✪ **Coda International Training, CIT**
Fred Adams/Clare Caves/Kirsty Long: 7b Broad Street, Nottingham NG1 3AJ; *t* (0115) 952 6060, *e* gn:cit
Charity transferring computing, documentation, research and organisation skills to democratic organisations in developing countries in Central America and Southern Africa. »95

- **Commonwealth Information Centre**
Commonwealth Institute, 230 Kensington High Street, London W8 6NQ; *t* (0171) 603 4535
Documentation and resource centre on the affairs of the Commonwealth and its member countries. »94

- **Community Education Trust**
9 Manor Gardens, London N7 6LA; *t* (0171) 263 4675
Informal and community education. »90

✪ **Community Music Education Project**
Aniruddha Das: 60 Farringdon Road, London EC1R 3PP; *t* (0171) 490 2577
Research, documentation and education on the music of ethnic minorities, and use of music to raise consciousness of racism and community history. See Asian Dub Foundation, p12. »95

✪ **Community Religions Project**, University of Leeds
Dr Jim Knott, Co-ordinator: Department of Theology and Religious Studies, Leeds LS2 9JT; *t* (0113) 233 3646
Study of contemporary religions in Britain, especially of ethnic minorities in Yorkshire; monographs, resource centre. »88

✪ **Community Roots Resource Centre**
177 Barford Street, Highgate, Birmingham B5 6TN »90

- **Counter Information**
c/o 11 Forth Street, Edinburgh EH1, Scotland »94

- **Department of Arabic and Islamic Studies**
University of Exeter, Northcote House, Queen's Drive, Exeter EX4 4QJ; *t* (01392) 263100 »95

- **Department of Comparative Religion**
Dr Roger Ballard: University of Manchester, Manchester M13 9PL; *t* (0161) 275 2000 »90

- **Economic and Social Research Council, ESRC**
Cherry Orchard East, Kembry Park, Swindon SN2 6UG; *t* (01793) 513838
Administers government funding of social and economic research. »88

✪ **Ethnic Research**
28 Girton Road, Northolt UB5 4SR »94

✪ **Ethnic Study Group**
Co-ordinating Centre for Community and Health Care, 28 Lessingham Avenue, London SW17 8LU; *t* (0181) 682 0216, 682 0217
Multidisciplinary support/advice to mental health workers. »90

- **Ethnicity Research Group**, Lancaster University
Dr Roger Penn: Department of Sociology, Lancaster LA1 4YL; *t* (01524) 65201 ext. 4170, *f* 594256 »94

▮ **European Council on Refugees and Exiles, ECRE**: Conseil Européen sur les Réfugiés et les Exilés, and INFODOC
Philip Rudge, General Secretary: Bondway House, 3-9 Bondway, London SW8 1SJ; *t* (0171) 582 9928, *f* 820 9725
Umbrella group for research and co-ordination established in the 1970s by voluntary agencies working with refugees in Western Europe. Campaigns on asylum policy; runs European Legal Network on Asylum, p154, and INFODOC information network; publications including handbook on asylum procedures, research, conferences. Secretariat provided by the Refugee Council, p157; 60 member agencies, including 11 national refugee councils. *Asylum in Europe*. »96

▮ **European Group for the Study of Deviance and Social Control**
8 Woodland Road, Bristol BS8 1TN
Forum of European researchers into policing, criminology, the legal and penal systems and related areas. »94

- **European Research Centre, ERC**: Loughborough University
Alec G. Hargreaves: Department of European Studies, Loughborough LE11 3TU; *t* (01509) 222981, *f* 269395
Research and documentation on contemporary European affairs. »94

✪ **Fair Play Training and Consultancy Serrvices**
6a Chapel St, Potton, Sandy SG19 2PT; *t/f* (01767) 262105
Company producing anti-discrimination training resources. »96

✪ **Harambee Centre for Environmental and Development Education**
110 Regent Street, Cambridge CB2 1DP
Charity: development education, international awareness and environmental responsibility; resource centre. »95

♦ **Human Rights Centre**, University of Essex
Prof. Kevin Boyle, Director: Wivenhoe Park, Colchester CO4
3SQ; *t* (01206) 873333
Research, conferences, seminars, postgraduate studies on all
aspects of international human rights law and practice,
including minority rights.   »95

• **Human Rights Law Centre**, The University of Nottingham
Prof. D.J. Harris/Patrick Twomey: Department of Law,
University Park, Nottingham NG7 2RD; *t* (0115) 951 5697
Current research projects include the work of Frances
Nicholson, funded by the Airey Neave Trust, on British and
European refugee law.   »95

• *Index on Censorship*
Lancaster House, 33 Islington High Street, London N1 9LH;
t (0171) 278 2313, *f* 278 1878
Magazine documenting human rights violations worldwide,
principally around freedom of expression issues; publishes
the work of censored writers, many of whom are exiles. »95

✿ **Indian Teacher Training and Ethnic Minorities Recruitment
and Retention Project**, ITT
Angie Faust: Newman College, Genner Lane, Bartley Green,
Birmingham B32 3NT; *t* (0121) 476 1181, *f* 476 1196
Research and documentation project of the West Midlands
Consortium of teacher training centres, promoting ethnic
minority participation in the profession through development
of culturally-appropriate approaches and resources.   »94

• **Industrial Relations Services**
18-20 Highbury Place, London N5 1QP
Among other activities, publishes a journal on legal and
practical issues around equality of opportunity in employment,
Equal Opportunities Review (6/yr).   »96

• **Institute of Commonwealth Studies**, University of London
Dr Shula Marks, Director: 27-28 Russell Square, London
WC1B 5DS; *t* (0171) 580 5876, *f* 255 2160
Founded 1949; study of the Commonwealth, of its countries
and peoples, and of UK-Commonwealth relations; library,
seminars, publications.   »93

• **Institute of Commonwealth Studies**, University of Oxford
Arthur Hazlewood, Director: Queen Elizabeth House, 21 St
Giles, Oxford OX1 3LA; *t* (01865) 52952
Founded 1947; research, teaching, library on the developing
countries of the Commonwealth.   »90

• **Institute of Community Studies**
18 Victoria Park Square, London E2 9PF   »90

• **Institute of Development Studies**, IDS
Andrew Cohen Building, University of Sussex, Falmer,
Brighton BN1 9RE; *t* (01273) 678275, *f* 621202
Postgraduate research in a wide range of development issues,
sometimes including migration-related themes.   »94

• **Institute of Manpower Studies**
Mantel Building, University of Sussex, Falmer, Brighton BN1
9RF; *t* (01273) 606755
Some migrant labour research.   »90

• **Institute for Public Policy Research**, IPPR
Joanne Lenaghan/Sarah Spencer: 30-42 Southampton Street,
London WC2E 7RA; *t* (0171) 379 9400
Policy research and development; interested in national and
European aspects of migration and minorities policy.   »95

♦ **Institute of Race Relations**, IRR
A. Sivanandan, Director: 2-6 Leeke Street, King's Cross Rd,
London WC1X 8HS; *t* (0171) 837 0041, *f* 278 0623
Jenny Bourne, Danny Reilly, Liz Fekete; important research
and documentation centre on racism, racial violence, race
relations, immigration and related issues; extensive library.
Produces the main British radical journal on race and racism,
Race and Class (4/yr), and a European news review, *European
Race Audit* (12/yr); teaching materials, books, other
publications.   »95

• **Institute of Transcultural Health Care**, ITCH
The Chairman: 15-17 Upper Albert Road, Sheffield S8
Formerly (1991) at Edgbaston, Birmingham: Erica Beach, Dr S.
Venugopal (*t* (0121) 327 6423). Conducts and co-ordinates
interdisciplinary studies into the health of the Black and ethnic
minority populations in the UK. Associated with the Overseas
Doctors Association, p156.   »94

▌ **Institute for War and Peace Reporting**, IWPR
Margrit Bass/Rachel Valladares: Lancaster House, 33 Islington
High Street, London N1 9LH; *t* (0171) 713 7130
International charity working on conflict news, analysis and
resolution, especially in relation to the Balkans and the
Caucasus. *WarReport* magazine.   »95

✿ **Interfaith Education Centre**
City of Bradford Metropolitan Council, Liserhills Road,
Bradford, West Yorkshire
Promotion of cross-cultural education.   »90

▌ *International Journal of Refugee Law*
Prof. G.S. Goodwin-Gill (Canada), Editor: Oxford Journals,
Oxford University Press, Pinkhill House, Southfield Road,
Eynsham, Oxford OX8 1JJ; *t* (01865) 882283, *f* 882890
Academic journal (4/yr); documentation and research articles
on development of refugee law and practice worldwide.   »94

• **International Migration Project**, University of Dundee
Profs. Huw Jones/Allan Findlay: Department of Geography,
Dundee DD1 4HN, Scotland; *t* (01382) 23181
A research project funded by the ESRC, p244, studying
patterns of international migration in Asia.   »95

♦ *Journal of Refugee Studies*
Roger Zetter, Editor: Oxford Journals, Oxford University Press,
Pinkhill House, Southfield Road, Eynsham, Oxford OX8 1JJ;
t (01865) 882283, *f* 882890
Interdisciplinary international academic journal (4/yr) on all
aspects of forced population movement. Produced in
association with the Refugee Studies Programme, p246. See
also *International Journal of Refugee Law*, above.   »94

• **Judicial Studies Board**
Judith Julius: [address unknown] London
Training body for judges; includes Ethnic Minorities Advisory
Committee which oversees race awareness training.   »96

• **Kings College London Nutrition and Dietetics Department**
Jane Thomas: Campden Hill Road, London W8 7AH
Currently (1995) researching South Asian diet and health.»95

• *Lobster*
Stephen Dorrill, Editor: 135 School Street, Netherthong,
Holmfirth HD7 2YB; *t* (01484) 681388
Magazine on parapolitics, the far right and related topics;
competes with the other journal of this name.   »95

• *Lobster*
Robin Ramsay, Editor: 214 Westbourne Avenue, Hull HU5
3JB; *t* (01482) 447558
Magazine (irregular, 2/yr) on parapolitics: the far right, racist
movements, policing, intelligence agencies.   »95

♦ **Local Authorities Race Relations Information Exchange**,
LARRIE
Charmaine Gray, Information Officer: 41 Belgrave Square,
London SW1X 8NZ; *t* (0171) 259 5464, 235 6081, *f* 235
1257
Sarah Palmer, Amarjit Kaur Aluwahlia. Promotes co-operation
among British and European local government bodies on
minority issues. *What's New* (4/yr).   »95

✿ **London Research Centre**, LRC
Marian Storkey: 81 Black Prince Road, London SE1 7SZ;
t (0171) 735 4250
Conducts research projects on social and economic issues in
London; published major study by Storkey (1994) on ethnic
minorities in the capital.   »95

• **Migrant Media**
[address unknown] London; *t* (0171) 254 9701
Collective, founded 1989, producing films on migrant rights
issues in Britain and Europe.   »95

• **Migration and Ethnicity Research Centre**
Prof. Colin Holmes: Department of History, University of
Sheffield, Sheffield S10 2TN; *t* (0114) 282 6361, 236 3544
Multidisciplinary team drawn mainly from geography, history
and sociology departments; research on migration and
minorities, including Asian population of Sheffield.   »95

• **Migration Research Unit**, Department of Geography
Dr J. Salt: University College, 26 Bedford Way, London
WC1H 0AP; *t* (0171) 387 7050 ext. 5525, *f* 380 7565
Statistical, social and economic research into international
migration, especially in Britain and the EU.   »95

✿ **Minorities Resource Centre**
Abdul Malik, Secretary: 2 Alum Rock Road, Saltley,
Birmingham B8 1JB; *t* (0121) 326 6696, 328 1194
Documentation, information, advice on immigration and other
rights; Pakistani, Bangladeshi, West Indian communities. See
also Saltley Action Centre, p227.   »95

✿ **Minority Arts Advisory Service**
Julian Brutus: 4th Floor, 28 Shacklewell Lane, London E8
2EZ; *t* (0171) 254 7275, *f* 923 1596
Was listed (1990) at 25-31 Tavistock Place, WC1 9SF, *t* 388
6571. Advice on provision for ethnic minority artistic and
cultural activity; information, publishing on black literary,
performing and media arts. *Artrage* (4/yr).   »95

• *Multicultural Teaching*
Gillian Klein, Editorial Director: Trentham Books, Westview
House, 734 London Road, Oakhill, Stoke-on-Trent ST4 5NP;
t (01782) 745567, *f* 745553
Research and training journal (3/yr) focussing on multicultural
education, and dealing with relevant issues such as racism,
discrimination and Holocaust studies.   »94

✿ **Multi-Faith Centre**
Dr Mary Hall, Executive Director: Harborne Hall, Old Church Road, Harborne, Birmingham B17 0BD; *t* (0121) 427 1044
Education and training of professionals in awareness of major religious traditions, promotion of pluralism. »88

● **National Foundation for Educational Research**, NFER
Clare Burstall: The Mere, Upton Park, Slough SL1 2DQ; *t* (01753) 574123, *f* 691632
Sponsors research on issues including multicultural education; participates in EURYDICE information exchange network of EU education authorities. *Educational Research*, *NFER News*.»94

● **National Health Service Ethnic Health Unit**, also known as Ethnic Health Unit
Dr Michael Chan, Director: 7 Belmont Grove, Leeds LS2 9NP; *t* (0113) 246 7280-82
Toni Haliwell. Research and documentation unit of the NHS Executive; seeks to improve access to and quality of health care for minorities; funds research on 'best practice' standards and encourages nationwide implementation; funds local health care projects involving partnership with minority groups. »95

● **National Institute of Economic and Social Research**
2 Dean Trench Street, Smith Square, London SW1P 3HE
Sociological and economic research. »90

● **New Ethnicities Unit**, University of East London
Romford Road, London E15 4LZ; *t* (0181) 590 7722
Research and other activities relating to issues of race and ethnicity in education, culture and the community; publishing and seminar programme, major conference in 1996. »96

● **The Oriental Institute**, University of Oxford
Pusey Lane, Oxford OX1 2LE; *t* (01865) 278222
Research on China and other Asian societies and cultures.»95

● **James Parkes Library**
Dr Tony Kushner: University of Southampton, Highfield, Southampton SO9 5NH; *t* (01703) 595000
Large collection on Jewish, especially Anglo-Jewish, historical and cultural subjects. »94

● **Policy Studies Institute**, PSI
W.W. Daniel/Catherine Shaw: 100 Park Village East, London NW1 3SR; *t* (0171) 387 2171
Independent centre researching social and economic issues, including minorities in workforce; publishes research reports, books. *Cultural Trends*. »95

✿ **Queen Mary College**, QMC: University of London
Dr Shamit Shaggar: Department of Politics, Mile End Road, London E1 4NS; *t* (0171) 975 5555
Migration interests. »90

✿ **'Race' and Public Policy Research Unit**, RAPP: University of Leeds
Ian Law/Malcolm Harrison: School of Sociology and Social Policy, Leeds LS2 9JT; *t* (0113) 233 4410, 233 4430
Seminars, conferences, research, Internet activities on race-related issues including equality and anti-racist work. »96

● **Race Relations Research Unit**, University of Bradford
Dr Charles Husband: Department of Social and Economic Studies, Richmond Road, Bradford BD7 1DP; *t* (01274) 733466 ext. 4780, *f* 305340
Joint venture with Ilkley Community College; a forum for discussion, promotion, communication of research on race and racism; local, regional and national seminars; register of research; advice on research in race-related fields. »91

Race Today Collective: defunct (1995)

● **Refugee Assessment and Guidance Project**
University of North London, 166-220 Holloway Road, London N7 8DB; *t* (0171) 607 2789
Project liaising among universities, refugee organisations and funding agencies to develop means of accelerating recognition of the foreign educational and vocational qualifications of refugees, facilitating access to employment and education.»95

◆ **Refugee Studies Programme**, RSP: International Development Centre, University of Oxford
Dr Barbara Harrell-Bond, Director: Queen Elizabeth House, 21 St Giles, Oxford OX1 3LA; *t* (01865) 273600, 270722-3, 270729, *f* 270721, *Tx* 83147 attn. QEH
Dr V. Robinson, Sally Baden; founded 1982; interdisciplinary centre for research, documentation and teaching on causes, consequences and experience of forced migration, and on reintegration and related topics; summer schools and seminars for academics and practitioners. Developing an international association for refugee studies. New Director to take office mid-1996. See also *Journal of Refugee Studies*, p245. »95

● **Research Unit on Racism and Migration**
Prof. Bob Miles: University of Glasgow, Glasgow G12 8QQ, Scotland; *t* (0141) 339 8855
Research interests include East-West migration, Irish in Britain; working with BIVS, Germany, p236, on press archive project.»91

✿ **Roehampton Institute London**, Faculty of Social Sciences
Southlands College, Wimbledon Parkside, London SW19 5NN; *t* (0181) 392 3094
Institute affiliated to the University of Surrey; offers training in ethnic minority health care issues. »95

◆ **Joseph Rowntree Charitable Trust**, JRCT
The Garden House, Water End, York YO3 6LP; *t* (01904) 627810, *f* 651990
A major philanthropic foundation; funds action-oriented research into issues affecting race relations. »94

● **Royal Asiatic Society of Great Britain and Ireland**
L. Collins, Secretary: 60 Queen's Gardens, London W2 3AF; *t* (0171) 724 4742
Learned society, founded 1823, to promote study of Oriental history and cultures; about 1,000 members. »93

● **Royal Institute of International Affairs**, RIIA, informally known as Chatham House
Lord Wright of Richmond: Chatham House, 10 St James' Square, London SW1Y 4LE; *t* (0171) 957 5700, *f* 957 5710
Research, seminars on foreign affairs, since 1920. Published 1994 study *Europe and International Migration*. *International Affairs* (4/yr); *The World Today* (12/yr). »96

● **Royal Over-Seas League**
Roderick Larkin, Director, Cultural Affairs: Over-Seas House, Park Place, St James's Street, London SW1A 1LR; *t* (0171) 408 0214, *f* 499 6738
Promotion of international friendship and cultural exhange, especially between the UK and the Commonwealth; founded 1910. »95

◆ **The Runnymede Trust**
Trevor Phillips, Chair: 11 Princelet Street, London E1 6QH; *t* (0171) 375 1496, *f* 247 7695
Robin Richardson, director (to mid-1996). Founded 1968; research, information, public education on immigration, asylum, racism and race relations in Britain and Europe, conferences, reference library. *Runnymede Bulletin* (10/yr), statistical publications, pamphlets. »96

● **Russian and East European Research Centre**, University of Wolverhampton
Pete Glatter: Wulfruna Street, Wolverhampton WV1 1SB; *t* (01902) 321000 »94

● **School for Advanced Urban Studies**, SAUS, University of Bristol
Derek Hawes/Barbara Perez: University of Bristol, Grange Road, Bristol BS8 4EA; *t* (0117) 974 1117, 930 3030
Hawes and Perez published (1995) a study on Gypsies and Travellers in Britain, and organised a conference on their situation. »95

● **School of Oriental and African Studies**, SOAS, including Group for Ethnic Minority Studies
Dr Werner Menski: Thornhaugh Street, Russell Square, London WC1H 0XG; *t* (0171) 323 6339, 637 2388
The University of London centre for interdisciplinary teaching and research on Africa, Middle East and Asia; several research groups and areas of study relevant to migrants and minorities, including Group for Ethnic Minority Studies (Dr Menski) and a Saudi-funded chair in Islamic studies. »95

● **School of Slavonic and East European Studies**
Dr Karen Schönwalder: University of London, Senate House, Malet Street, London WC1E 7HU; *t* (0171) 637 4938 ext. 4084, 637 4934, *f* 436 8916
Main UK centre for research and education on Central and Eastern European countries and cultures. Includes Centre for the Study of Minorities, director Martyn Rady. »95

● **Scottish Ethnic Minorities Research Unit**, SEMRU
David Walsh: Caledonian University, 70 Cowcaddens Road, Glasgow G4 0BA, Scotland; *t* (0141) 331 3000
Inter-university, interdisciplinary research unit. »95

● **SHAP Working Party on World Religions in Education**, SHAP
Clive Lawton: c/o National Society's RE Centre, 36 Causton Street, London SW1P 4AU; *t* c/o (0171) 932 1194, *f* c/o 932 1199
Promotes study of world religions at all academic levels; produces resources for classroom use. »94

● *Statewatch*
Tony Bunyan: PO Box 1516, London N16 0EW; *t* (0181) 802 1882, *f* 880 1727, *e* statewatch-off@geo2.poptel.org.uk
Research, documentation, publishing, on-line bibliographic and text databases on the state and the individual, policing, parapolitics, human rights, migration and refugees, minorities, racism, the far right. *Statewatch* (6/yr), books, booklets. »95

✿ **Transcultural Psychiatry Unit**
Elaine Zagorski, Administrator: Lynfield Mount Hospital, Heights Lane, Bradford BD9 6DP; *t* (01274) 494194
Seminars for mental health workers, bibliography service. »90

✿ **Ujamaa Arts Project Ltd**
Ufton Centre, Ufton Road, London N1; *t* (0171) 241 2549
Black arts development. »90

University of London: see Birkbeck College, British Institute of Human Rights, Centre for Multicultural Education, Institute of Commonwealth Studies, Institute of Latin American Studies, Migration Research Unit, Muslim College, Queen Mary College, School of Oriental and African Studies, School of Slavonic and East European Studies, Sir Robert Menzies Centre for Australian Studies

✿ **Watford School of Arabic and Islamic Studies**
Dr A. Ghany Saleh, Director: 492 Whippendell Road, Watford WS1 7QJ; *t* (01923) 245670, *f* 213377
Voluntary Sunday school providing instruction to GCSE and A-Level in Arabic language and Islamic studies; promotes interfaith understanding; open to non-Muslims. »94

✿ **West Midlands Practice Development Centre**
Angus McCabe, General Manager: Birmingham Settlement, 318 Summer Lane, Birmingham B19 3RL
Promotes placements for social work students within Black managed voluntary organisations; specialist library and information resources for social work education. »96

● **Yad Vashem Charitable Trust** and National Yad Vashem Educational Trust
Woburn House, Tavistock Square, London WC1H 0EP
Seeks to perpetuate the memory of the Holocaust; Educational Trust promotes Holocaust studies; in 1992 assisted in the launch of *British Journal of Holocaust Education*, p244. »94

NORTHERN IRELAND 44

● **Centre for Research and Documentation, CRD:** Lárionad Taighde agus Doicmédúcháin
Caitríona Ruane, Co-ordinator: 89b Glen Road, Belfast BT11 8BD; *t* (01232) 626678, *f* 301708
Information and documentation on national and international issues, including refugees, migration, minorities, human rights and the Irish situation in a global perspective. *CRD News* (3/yr), factsheets, posters. »94

● **Centre for the Study of Conflict, CSC**
Information Officer: University of Ulster, Cromore Road, Coleraine BT52 1SA, Co. Derry; *t* (01265) 44141 ext. 4666, *f* 324917, *e* csc@ulst.ac.uk
Research on majority-minority relations, including the position of ethnic minorities in Northern Ireland. *Northern Ireland Research Briefing* (4/yr), research reports, seminars. »95

▮ **Ethnic Studies Network, ESN**
Prof. John Darby: University of Ulster, Cromore Road, Coleraine BT52 1SA, Co. Derry; *t* (01265) 44141, *f* 324917
A w network of academic, voluntary and other organisations and individuals investigating inter-ethnic conflict and related matters; linked with INCORE, below. *ESN Bulletin* (4/yr). »95

▮ **International Centre on Conflict Resolution and Ethnicity, INCORE:** University of Ulster/United Nations University
Prof. John Darby, Director: Aberfoyle House, Magee College, Northlands Road, Derry; *t* (01504) 265621
A joint project between the University of Ulster and the Tokyo-based UNU; research and training, conferences, development of databases and other resources on domestic and international conflict and conflict resolution techniques. »95

✿ **Multi-Cultural Resource Centre**
Fee Ching Cameron/Nooshin Hedayati: Bryson House, 28 Bedford Street, Belfast BT2 7FE; *t* (01232) 325835 exts. 52, 53, 55, *f* 439156
Rozana Huq, Mei Ying Ho. Information/resource service for minority groups, schools, social service agencies and public. Translation, interpreting, networking, events. Funders include health and social services agencies and Northern Ireland Voluntary Trust. *Bridging the Gaps* (video); *Directory*. »95

✿ **One World Centre**
Stephen McCloskey: 4 Lower Crescent, Belfast BT7 1NR; *t* (01232) 241879
Resource centre for global and Third World studies. Development education, international solidarity; teaching resources, documentation on human rights, trade, aid. »94

✿ **Queen's University Belfast**, Department of Social Anthropology
Dr Hastings Donnan, Reader: 29 University Square, Belfast BT7; *t* (01232) 245133, *f* 320668, *Tx* 74487 QUBADM
Has been involved in academic research on the position of South Asians in Northern Ireland. »94

5

Indexes

The first index gives page numbers for organisations and publications, in alphabetical order of significant words (for indexing rules see page ix). Only names and official translations are indexed. Publications are in *italic type*; generic names (*Bulletin*, *Newsletter*, etc.) are not indexed, nor are publications with the same name as the parent organisation. Names are usually given in full, but if two or more names begin in the same way, ***bold italics*** show the word(s) to be repeated after the semi-colon (;) or, in the next entry, at the symbol ≡. Association is often abbreviated to Assoc.; terms like Ltd, e.V., Inc. and so on are omitted.

The second index lists acronyms (initials and other abbreviations of names).

Country codes, as follows, are given before the page numbers. Note that names and acronyms may appear more than once on the page indicated, and that organisations with the same name or acronym, even if indexed together, are not necessarily connected.

AL	Albania	*H*	Hungary	*SM*	San Marino
AT	Austria	*IS*	Iceland	*SR*	Serbia
BE	Belgium	*IR*	Ireland (Republic)	*SK*	Slovakia
BH	Bosnia Hercegovina	*IT*	Italy	*SV*	Slovenia
BG	Bulgaria	*LT*	Latvia	*E*	Spain
CT	Croatia	*FL*	Liechtenstein	*S*	Sweden
CY	Cyprus	*LH*	Lithuania	*CH*	Switzerland
CS	Czech Republic	*LX*	Luxembourg	*TR*	Turkey
DK	Denmark	*M*	Malta	*UK*	United Kingdom
EE	Estonia	*NL*	Netherlands	*- NI*	Northern Ireland
SF	Finland	*NR*	Norway	*- CI*	Channel Islands
F	France	*PL*	Poland	*- IM*	Isle of Man
D	Germany	*PR*	Portugal	*V*	Vatican City State
GI	Gibraltar	*RO*	Romania		
GR	Greece	*RS*	Russia		

ORGANISATIONS AND PUBLICATIONS

1924 Committee *UK* 54

A & C Music Circuit *UK* 20
A comme Afrique *F* 2
A Ta Turquie *F* 120
Aalborg Flygtningerådgivningen *DK* 132
≡ Universitetcenter *DK* 232
Århus Retshjælp *DK* 193
≡ Ungdoms- og Kulturforeningen *DK* 161
Abasindi Co-operative *UK* 20
Abbeyfeale Society *UK* 47
Abruzzo nel Mondo LX 75
Abogados sin Fronteras *E* 212
Abrat Islamic Foundation *UK* 54
Abu-Bakar Mosque; Abu Bakr Mosque *UK* 54
Academy of Indian Dance *UK* 43
ACADOME info F 86

Accents Multiples *F* 162
Acceuil Cambodgien *F* 25
Acceuil des Etudiants Etrangers; Familiale des Jeunes Etrangers; des Jeunes *F* 134
Acceuil et Promotion; Echanges Hainaut-Cambresis; des étrangers *F* 134
≡ des Immigrés; au Service des Immigrés *BE* 129
Acceuillir F 138
Acción Familiar *E* 149
ACE Bulletin UK 243
Acolhimento, Centro de Portuguêses *E* 101
Action Against Racism; in Training *UK* 175
ActionAid *UK* 220
Action Briefing UK 80
Action Catholique Ouvrière *F* 195
≡ Chrétienne des Etudiants Russes *F* 103
≡ des Chrétiens pour l'Abolition de la Torture *F* 195, *LX* 207

Action by Christians for the Abolition of Torture *F* 195, *D* 200, *LX* 207
≡ Coordonnée pour le Développement Urbain Concerté *F* 134
≡ from Ireland *IR* 168
≡ Group for Irish Youth *UK* 47
≡ Health *UK* 220
≡ Immigrées—Vie Féminine; Immigrés *BE* 129
≡ Internationale contre la Faim; Nord Sud *F* 195
≡ for Peoples in Conflict *UK* 220
≡ Social au Bernalmont *BE* 188
≡ Solidarité Tiers Monde *LX* 169
≡ for Solidarity, Equality, Environment & Development *NL* 208
≡ for Southern Africa *UK* 110
≡ Vivre Ensemble *BE* 188
Actioun Lëtzebuergesch *LX* 207

Activist Press Service *NL* 239
Acton Legal Rights Advice Panel *UK* 220
Acton Mosque *UK* 54
Actualités de l'Emigration *BE F* 8
Actualités-Migrations *F* 199
ADAPT Support Unit *UK* 220
Konrad-Adenauer-Stiftung *D* 200
ADiTi: National Organisation of South
 Asian Dance *UK* 12
Administration de l'Emploi *LX* 207
Advice Bureaux; Centre in the Blue;
 Centres; on Individual Rights in Europe
 UK 220
Advisory Centre for Education *UK* 243
 ≡ Committee on Emigrant Welfare
 Services *UK* 48
 ≡ Committee on Travellers *NI* 118
 ≡ Council on the Education of Romany &
 other Travellers *UK* 41
 ≡ & Reformation Committee *UK* 104
Ægyptisk Forbund i Danmark *DK* 33
Aero-Associação de Espoliados de
 Moçambique *PR* 91
Aeskulyossamband Islands *IS* 203
AESSE Azione Soziale *IT* 204
Afdeling Rechtssociologie *NL* 239
Afers Internacionals *E* 242
Afghan National Credit & Finance; Society
 UK 1
Afghanaid *UK* 1
Afghanistan Vereniging *NL* 1
Afiya Foundation *UK* 243
Africa *IT PR* 4
africa 95 *UK* 5
Africa Analysis; Book Centre; Centre *UK* 5
Africa Confidential *UK* 5
Africa Educational Trust; Evangelical
 Fellowship *UK* 5
 ≡ Insieme *IT* 3
 ≡ Now *UK* 5
Africa Oggi *IT* 3
Africa Research & Information Bureau *UK* 5
 ≡ Society *IR* 3
Africa World Review *UK* 5
African Affairs *UK* 6
African-Asian Conference UK *UK* 156
African & Asian Resource Centre; Visual
 Arts Archive *UK* 243
African Business *UK* 6
African Caribbean Business Association;
 Community Development Unit; Develop-
 ment Network; Family Mediation Service
 UK 6
African & Caribbean Finance Forum *UK* 6
African Caribbean Leadership Council *UK* 6
African & Caribbean Music Circuit *UK* 20
 ≡ Caribbean National Artistic Centre *UK* 6
 ≡ Churches Council on Immigration &
 Social Justice *UK* 5
 ≡ Communities Council in Europe *F IT* 3
 ≡ Community of Greater Manchester *UK* 5
 ≡ Cultural Association *DK* 2
 ≡ Cultural Society *UK* 5
 ≡ European Institute *NL* 4
 ≡ Family Advisory Service; Human Rights
 Centre *UK* 5
 ≡ National Congress *DK F IT NL E UK* 109
 ≡ Peoples Historical Monument
 Foundation *UK* 243
 ≡ People's Movement *UK* 6
 ≡ Refugee Housing Action Group; Refugee
 Women's Group; Refugees & Migrants
 Monitoring Project; Reparations
 Movement; Rights; Society; Studies
 Assoc.; Welfare & Advice Centre *UK* 5
African Women's Association; Welfare
 Association; Welfare Group *UK* 5
Africans de Lleida *E* 4
Africatrack *F* 2
Afrikagrupperna *S* 110
Afrique espoir *F* 2
L'Afrique et l'Asie Modernes *F* 234
L'Afrique du Sud en Direct *F* 109
Afro-Asian Advisory Service; Society
 UK 153
Afro-Caribbean & Asian Forum *UK* 20
 ≡ Association; Care Group; Co-operative
 Society; Co-ordinating Council; Cultural
 Centre; Development Unit; Focus; Mental
 Health Association; Mental Health Project;
 Organisation; Resource Society; Self-Help
 Organization; Social Workers' Assoc.;
 Society; Teachers' Association; Youth
 Council *UK* 7
Afro-German Women *D* 19
Afro-West Indian United Council of
 Churches *UK* 7
AFS Interculturelle Programma's *NL* 169
AFS Interkulturell Utbildning *S* 175
Aga Khan Foundation *UK* 62
 ≡ Ismaili Mosque; Shia Imami Ismaili
 Jamat Khana *UK* 55

Agence de coopération culturelle et
 technique *F* 195
 ≡ pour le Développement des Relations
 Interculturelles; Im'média *F* 233
Agence Nationale pour l'Emploi *F* 195
 ≡ française Jeunesse pour l'Europe *F* 198
Agence PETRA-LINGUA *BE* 188
Agence pour la Promotion des Activités
 Internationales de Jeunesse *BE* 191
 ≡ des Cultures et du Voyage *F* 162
Agencia Centroamericana de Noticias *BE* 27
Agencia Española para Becas ERASMUS;
 de Cooperación Internacional *E* 212
Agency for Co-operation & Research in
 Development *UK* 5
Agenda Intercultural *BE* 231
Agenda de la Red *E* 174
Agenzia Gioventù per l'Europa *IT* 204
 ≡ di Stampa Disagio Pace Ambiente *IT* 238
Agir pour Timor *F* 116
Agonistiki-Agonas *GR* 140
Agrippine Bakamurera *IT* 103
Agrupación de Centros y Asociaciones de
 Españoles *UK* 113
 ≡ Chile Democrático *E* 28
 ≡ de la Comunidad Musulmana *E* 54
Agudas Israel Housing Association *UK* 79
Ahl Ul-Bayt Islamic Centre *UK* 57
Ahle Hadith Mosque *UK* 65
Ahmadiyya Muslim Association; Assoc.
 Darul-Amaan; Community Centre *UK* 55
Ahram—Associazione Egiziana *IT* 33
Al-Magazin *CH* 217
Aid for Destitute Victims of Oppression
 UK 153
Aide et Action *F* 195
 ≡ et Coopération au Développement
 d'Arequipa *BE* 96
 ≡ à l'Enfant Réfugié *F* 134
 ≡ Médicale et Sanitaire au Népal *F* 91
 ≡ aux personnes déplacées *BE* 129
 ≡ aux réfugiés de l'Asie du Sud-Est *F* 109
 ≡ sans Frontières *F* 196
 ≡ et Soutien aux Haïtiens de France *F* 41
Airport Chaplaincy *NL* 208
Ajani Centre *UK* 20
AJR Information *UK* 80
AKARSU Gesundheitsetage *D* 138
Akhand Kirtani Jatha *UK* 106
Akhbar-e-Watan *UK* 123
Akina Mama wa Afrika *UK* 5
Aktiegroep Kritisch Onderwijs *BE* 160
Aktion für abgewiesene Asylbewerber
 CH 152
 ≡ der Christen für die Abshaffung der
 Folter *D* 20
 ≡ Dritte Welt Saar *D* 165
 ≡ Noteingang *D* 138
 ≡ Sühnezeichen/Friedensdienste *D* 165
Aktionsbündnis Maastricht—So nicht!
 D 200
Aktionsgemeinschaft Solidarische Welt
 D 165
Aktive modstandsfolk *DK* 161
Aktives Museum Faschismus und
 Widerstand *D* 236
Akwaba-Jeunesse ivoirienne de Rennes
 F 77
al-Ansar *S* 54
Al Aqsa *D* 53
Al-Eqtisadiah *UK* 104
Al Falah Islamic Youth Mission; Al-Furqan
 Islamic Heritage Foundation; Al-Furqan
 Trust *UK* 55
Al-Giamia *IT* 54
Al-Hasaniya Women's Centre *UK* 90
al-Hayat *UK* 104
Al Hijra School *UK* 55
Al Hilal *UK* 60
Al Hilal Community Project *UK* 93
Al Hilal Masjid; Al-Hoda Islamic
 Booksellers; Al-Huda Bookshop; Al-Huda
 Islamic Centre; Al-Isra Islamic College
 UK 55
al-Jabha al-Islamiya li-Inqadh *BE* 8, *D UK* 9
Al Jamat-ul-Muslimin of Bangladesh *UK* 17
Al-Kashkool Bookshop; Al Khoei
 Foundation *UK* 55
Al Majalla *UK* 104
Al Manar *BE* 88
Al Manzil—Centro para Marroquíes *E* 90
Al Medina Muslim Association; Al-Medina
 Trust; Al-Muntada Al-Islami School *UK* 55
Al Muttaqiin *UK* 17
Al-Noor Bookshop; Mosque *UK* 55
Al Quds al Arabi *UK* 95
Al-Qur'an Society *UK* 62
Al-Rahmah Mosque; Al-Rahman Mosque
 UK 55
Al-Sadaqa Ireland-Palestine Friendship
 Society *IR* 95
Al-Saqi Bookshop *UK* 55

Al Usra *UK* 67
al-Watan al-Arabi *F* 10
Aladura International Church *UK* 154
Alamadina Jamia Mosque; Alazhar Mosque
 UK 55
Albanian-German Humanist Association
 AL 37
Albanian Life; Albanian Society *UK* 8
Albatroz *F* 97
Alexandra Road Mosque *UK* 55
Algeciras Acoge *E* 149
Algemeen Belgisch Vakverbond *BE* 189
 ≡ Nederlands Jeugd Verbond *NL* 208
 ≡ Palestijnse Arbeiders Vereniging *NL* 95
Algerian Community Association; Refugee
 Council *UK* 9
Alicante Acoge *E* 149
Aliens Board *S* 216
 ≡ Department *GR* 202
 ≡ Registration Office *UK* 220
All-African Council *DK* 2
All-Amhara People's Organisation *UK* 34
All-Asia Christian Consultative Group *UK* 12
All Burma Students' Democratic Front *S* 25
All Different—All Equal campaign *F* 197
All Faiths for One Race—All Fight Fascism,
 Oppression & Racism *UK* 175
All Jammu & Kashmir Muslim Conference
 UK 81
All Muslim Funeral Society; Welfare
 Association *UK* 55
All Pakistan Society *DK* 92
All Pakistani Women's Association *UK* 93
All-Party Parliamentary Group on Race &
 Community *UK* 220
All Saints Haque Centre *UK* 153
Allgemeine Jüdische Wochenzeitung *D* 79
Alliance of Asian Christians *UK* 12
 ≡ for a Better China *UK* 29
 ≡ to Defend Bosnia-Herzegovina *UK* 23
 ≡ Française *IR* 36
 ≡ Internationale d'Aide à l'Enfance *CH* 218
 ≡ Israélite Universelle *F* 79
 ≡ of Newham Muslim Associations *UK* 55
Alliance Newsletter *CH* 218
Alliance des Unions Chrétiennes de Jeunes
 Gens de France *F* 196
Allochtonen-overleg Gemeente
 Amsterdam; Allochtonenpastoraat Cura
 Migratorum *NL* 145
Almería Acoge, Asociación de Ayuda al
 Inmigrante *E* 149
Alpha et Promotion *F* 136
Alphabétisation et promotion des migrants
 de l'agglomération rouennaise *F* 134
Alquibla—Asociación Cultural y Social
 E 149
Alsace Plurielle *F* 162
Alternatief *BE* 130
Alternativa Solidaria *E* 149
Alternative *BE* 73
Alto Comisionado de las Naciones Unidas
 para los Refugiados *E* 212
Alto Comissariado das Nações Unidas para
 os Refugiados *PR* 211
Alto Commissariato delle Nazioni Unite per
 i Rifugiati *IT* 204
Altre Luci *IT* 141
Altreitalie *IT* 205
L'Altro Mercato *IT* 169
Amaana Trust *UK* 55
Amakhosikazi e Afrika *UK* 5
Aman Project *UK* 15
Amana *UK* 55
Amar Deep *UK* 41
Amazigh Cultureel Werk Stichting *NL* 90
AMEL-Espoir, Association des Algériens *F* 8
American Church *F IT UK* 123
 ≡ Indian Movement Committee *UK* 123
 ≡ Joint Distribution Committee *IT CH* 79
 ≡ Lutheran Church of Brussels; Protestant
 Church *BE* 123
 ≡ Women's Club *UK* 123
Amical de Mauthausen *E* 174
Amicale Africaine *F* 2
 ≡ des Algériens en Belgique *BE* 8
 ≡ des Algériens en Europe *F* 8
 ≡ des amis français-portugais *F* 97
 ≡ des anciens déportés juifs *F* 79
 ≡ Belgo-Héllénique *GR* 19
 ≡ des camerounais de Bordeaux *F* 25
 ≡ Chinoise Côte-d'Azur *F* 28
 ≡ des Elèves et Etudiants Ivoriens *F* 77
 ≡ Espagnole; des espagnols de Chaumont
 F 111
 ≡ des Etudiants Sénégalais de Lille *F* 104
 ≡ des Etudiants Tunisiens *F* 118
 ≡ Française des Ingénieurs et Cadres
 GR 36
 ≡ franco-tunisienne en France *F* 118
 ≡ des Institutrices et Gouvernantes
 Françaises *GR* 36

Amicale des Nords-Africains et des Résidents Etrangers en France *F* 134
≡ Portugaise Lavalloise *F* 97
≡ de Ravensbruck *F* 162
≡ des ressortissants centrafricains *F* 27
≡ des Travailleurs et Commerçants Marocains *BE* 88, *F* 89, *LX* 90
≡ des travailleurs tunisiens *F* 118
Amicale des Tunisiens de la Charente; de la Côte-d'Azur; en France; du Havre et sa Région; d'Orléans; de Provence *F* 118
Amicale des Turcs à Digne; Turcs et des Français *F* 120
≡ Yougoslaves de Paris, Club Kostana *F* 126
Amicizia Studenti Esteri IT 145
Amigos de la República Arabe Saharaui Democrática en Aragón *E* 104
Amir-e-Millat Mosque, Islamic Centre *UK* 55
Amis de la Délégation des Migrations *F* 134
≡ Haute Egypte *F* 33
≡ Namibie *F* 91
≡ Pologne *F* 96
Amitié Franco-Afghane *F* 1
≡ franco-croate Lyon *F* 31
≡ Franco-Espagnole; Franco-Espagnole Cambrésienne *F* 111
≡ Internationale des Jeunes *F* 162
Amitiés Belgo-Cambodgiennes *BE* 25
≡ Belgo-Colombiennes *BE* 30
≡ Belgo-Immigrées *BE* 130
≡ Belgo-Palestiniennes *BE* 95
≡ France-Asie *F* 12
≡ franco-chinoises *F* 28
≡ Franco-Tanzanienne *F* 115
≡ Italo-Luxembourgeoises *LX* 75
≡ et Liens France-Maghreb *F* 86
≡ Lot-Amérique latine *F* 83
≡ Mussipontains-Immigrés *F* 162
Amitiés Portugal-Luxembourg; Amizades Portugal-Luxembourg *LX* 100
Amnesty UK 220
Amnesty Campaign for Refugees & Unregistered Migrants *UK* 153
Amnesty International *AT* 187, *BE* 189, *CS* 193, *DK* 193, *D* 200, *SF* 195, *F* 196, *GR* 202, *IR* 203, *IT* 204, 238, *LX* 207, *NL* 208, *NR* 210, *PR* 211, *E* 212, *S* 216, *CH* 217, *UK* 220, *NI* 229
Amnesty Tietode SF 195
Amnistia Internacional *PR* 211
Amnistía Internacional *E* 212
Amsterdams Centrum Buitenlanders; Solidariteits Komitee Vluchtelingen *NL* 145
Amt für Multikulturelle Angelegenheiten *D* 165
Amt für Soziale Dienste *FL* 207
An-Nisa Society *UK* 55
An Teach Irish Housing Association *UK* 47
An Viet Housing Association *UK* 124
Anamchara na nGael i bPáras *F* 46
Anatolsk Kulturforening *DK* 119
Angikar UK 19
Angelou Centre *UK* 20
Anglican Church of the Holy Trinity *BE* 24
Anglo-Akanthou Aid Association *UK* 31
≡-Albanian Association *UK* 8
≡-American Families Association *UK* 123
≡-Arab Assoc.; -Argentine Society *UK* 11
Anglo-Asian-Afro-Caribbean Friendship & Cultural Association *UK* 175
≡ Cultural Assoc.; Women's Assoc. *UK* 12
Anglo-Austrian Society *UK* 16
≡-Belgian Society *UK* 19
≡-Brazilian Society *UK* 24
≡-Chilean Society *UK* 28
≡-Czechoslovak Welfare Assoc. *UK* 32
≡-Danish Society *UK* 32
Anglo-German Assoc.; Foundation for the Study of Industrial Society *UK* 37
Anglo-German Review UK 37
Anglo-Hellenic Association; League *UK* 39
Anglo-Hispanic Society *UK* 113
≡-Irish Encounter *IR* 24
≡-Israel Association *UK* 73
≡-Italian Society *UK* 76
≡-Ivorian Society *UK* 77
≡-Malagasy Society *UK* 86
≡-Mongolian Society *UK* 88
≡-Netherlands Society *UK* 32
≡-Norse Society *UK* 92
≡-Philippine Association for Real Togetherness *UK* 35
Anglo-Polish Society *UK* 96
Anglo-Portuguese Foundation; Society *UK* 101
Anglo-Spanish Society *UK* 113
≡-Swedish Society; -Swiss Society *UK* 114
≡-Thai Society *UK* 115
≡-Turkish Society *UK* 122
Angola Emergency Campaign *UK* 91
Angolan Action & Fraternity Group *UK* 9

Animations et spectacles populaires et interculturels *F* 162
Anjuman Ahle Sunnat Wal Jamaat; -e-Eshaate Islam *UK* 55
Anjuman-e-Gujerati Mosque; Muslim Association *UK* 40
Anjuman-e-Haideria; Hamidiyak; Islahul-Muslimeen; Islamia; Jaarania *UK* 55
≡ Khawateen Centre *UK* 12
≡ Khwateen; Muhibban-e-Ahl-e-Bait Hussainia Mosque; Naqibul Islam Mosque; Saifee; Taraqqi-Urdu; Zinatul-Islam *UK* 55
Anjuman Faiz-ul-Quran; Ghulaman-e-Rasool; I-Ishat e Islam; i-Tareej Taraqqi-i-Urdu *UK* 55
≡ Islah-ul-Muslemeen; Islahul Muslimin; Khuddam-ud-Din; Muhibban-e-Rasool; Noor-ul-Islam *UK* 56
Ankur Brent Asian Youth Service *UK* 12
Anlaufstelle Basselland *CH* 217
Anne Frank Educational Trust *UK* 175
≡ Foundation; Stichting *NL* 170
Ansaru Allah Community *UK* 56
Antenna *BE* 74
Antenna Internationale *CH* 217
Anthropological Association *IR* 238
Anti Apartheid Bewegung *D CH* 109
Anti-Apartheid Movement *UK* 110
Anti-Apartheids Beweging *NL* 109
Anti-Discriminatie Bureau Amersfoort; Amsterdam; Amsterdam-Noord; Arnhem; Assen en Drenthe; Dronten; Ede; Enschede; Gouda; Groningen; Haarlem; Heerlen; Hengelo; Hilversum; Maastricht; Meppel; Nijmegen; Noord-Kennemerland; Roermond; Schiedam; Tilburg; Waterland; Zeeland; Zoetermeer *NL* 170
Anti-Discriminatie Overleg *NL* 208
≡ Raad Dordrecht *NL* 170
Antifa—Helsinki *SF* 162
Antifa-InfoBlatt D 165
Antifa—Landeskoordination NRW *D* 165
Antifa Leiden *NL* 170
Antifa—Lohja *SF* 162
Anti Faschistisch Front *BE* 160
Antifaschistische Aktion—Bundesweite Organisation; Bildungs-, Informations- und Dokumentationszentrum *D* 165
Antifaschistische Nachrichten; *Antifaschistische Zeitung*; *Antifaschistisches Info Blatt D* 165
Anti Fascisme Overleg Groningen *NL* 170
Anti-Fascist Action *UK* 175
Antifascist Centre of Moscow *RS* 174
Anti-Fascistische Actie; Oud Verzetsstrijders; telefoonlijn *NL* 170
Antifasiszta Akció *H* 168
Anti-Nazi Front; Group *PL* 173
≡ League *IR* 168, *UK* 176
Anti-Racism Information Service *CH* 175
Anti-Racisme Groep; Informatie Centrum; Initiatief Wageningen *NL* 170
Anti-Racist Action; Alliance *UK* 176
Anti-Racist Bulletin UK 181
Antirasistisk Senter *NR* 173
Anti-Rassismus Büro Bremen; Informationszentrum *D* 165
Antirassistisch-Interkulturelles Informationszentrum; Antirassistische Initiative *D* 165
Anti-semitisme onderzoek NL 73
Anti-Slavery International *UK* 220
Anti-War/Anti-Nationalist Campaign *GR* 202
Antologia Siciliana IT 239
Antropologisch-sociologisch centrum *NL* 239
Antwerps Centrum voor Migrantenstudies *BE* 231
Anwar-e-Mohammedia Mosque *UK* 56
Anwar-ul-Quran Mosque *UK* 94
Anwar-ul-Uloom Mosque *UK* 70
APE informations F 134
Apenas Informações PR 148
Apna Ghar; Day Care Centre *UK* 12
Apostolatus Maris V 158
Appel des 250 contre le FN *F* 162
Appropriate Technology for Tibet *UK* 116
L'Aquilone *BE* 73
Aquitaine Education Intégration *F* 134
AR Telefon *D* 165
Arab Advice & Information Bureau; Line; Studies Society; Women's Association; Women's Group; Workers' Union *UK* 11
Arabic Language & Islamic Culture *UK* 56
Arabic Mosque; Speaking Community *UK* 11
Arabismo E 11
Arachne Greek-Cypriot Women's Group *UK* 31
Arafat Book Service *UK* 56
Araña *E* 174
Arawak Housing Association *UK* 6

Arbeiterverein der Türkei *D* 120
Arbeiterwohlfahrt Bundesverband *D* 200
≡ Kreisverband Düsseldorf *D* 138
Arbeitsbereich Ausländersozialarbeit *D* 236
Arbeitsgemeinschaft der Ausländerbeiräte in Hessen *D* 138
≡ Ausländer/innenwahlrecht *AT* 159
≡ Europäisches Migrationszentrum *D* 237
≡ gegen internationale sexistische und rassistische Ausbeutung *D* 166
≡ der Gemeinden; Junge Genoss/innen in der PDS *D* 200
≡ der Kommunalen Ausländervertretungen Niedersachsens *D* 138
Arbeitsgruppe SOS-Rassismus NRW *D* 166
Arbeitskreis Asyl Ba-Wü *D* 138
≡ von Sozialberatern für Fragen der Reintegration griechischer Arbeitnehmer und ihrer Familien in Griechenland *D* 38
Arbeitsstelle für Asylfragen *CH* 152
Arbejderbevaegelsens Internationale Forum *DK* 161
Arbejdsmarkedets Center for Internationale Uddannelsesaktiviteter *DK* 193
Arbejdsmarkedsstyrelsen *DK* 194
Arbetsgruppen för en ungdomskampanj mot rasism *S* 175
Arc-en-ciel *F* 162
L'Arche *F* 79
Arche Essalem *F* 53
Arche de la Fraternité *F* 196
Archipel F 163
Architectes sans Frontières *F* 196
Archiv: Migration D 236
Archives maghrébines *F* 235
Arco IRIS *IT* 168
Ardagh & Clonmacnois Society *UK* 47
Arena UK 181
Argentina Democrática *IT* 11
Aristotle University *GR* 238
Arkadas *D* 120
Armagh Travellers Support Group *NI* 118
Armenian Aid; Popular Movement; Relief Society of Great Britain *UK* 11
Armenian Voice *UK* 12
Armensk Kulturforening *DK* 11
Art-Culture-Communication *F* 162
Article 19 *UK* 220
Article 31 F 162
Artrage UK 245
Artsen Zonder Grenzen Nederland *NL* 208
Arya Pratinidhi Sabha; Samaj Birmingham *UK* 42
Asante Sana *UK* 20
Asesoría para Trabajadores Extranjeros *E* 151
ASF-Dansk Folkehjælp *DK* 194
ASHA Asian Women's Aid *UK* 12
Asha Women's Group *UK* 17
Ashiana Housing Association; Project *UK* 12
Ashrafia Mosque *UK* 58
Ashraq al-Aswat UK 104
ASIAN Ltd *UK* 12
Asian Action Group; Arts Group; Association; Bookshop *UK* 12
Asian Business UK 15, 40
Asian Centre; Chaplaincy *UK* 12
Asian Chronicle UK 12
Asian Community Action Group *UK* 12
≡ Care Resource Centre *UK* 15
Asian Congress on Local Affairs; Dance Group; Dub Foundation; Elderly Group of Merton *UK* 12
Asian Express UK 12
Asian Family Counselling Service; Forum *UK* 12
≡ Girls' Club; Girls' Project; Health Awareness Project; Health Group *UK* 13
Asian Herald UK 13
Asian House Cultural Association; Mental Health Team; Music Circuit *UK* 13
≡ Muslim Welfare Association *UK* 56
Asian Observer UK 13
Asian Parents *UK* 44
≡ People with Disabilities Alliance; People's National Association; Resource Centre; Resource Project; Sheltered Accommodation; Sound Radio *UK* 13
≡ Special Housing Initiative Agency *UK* 12
≡ Students Christian Trust; Teachers' Association *UK* 13
Asian Times UK 13
Asian Trader UK 40
Asian Weekly UK 13
Asian Welfare Association; Women & Girls Cultural Project; Women Writers' Collective *UK* 13
Asian Women's Adhikar Association; Advice Centre; Advisory Service; Association; Centre *UK* 13
≡ Conference UK *UK* 15

Asian Women's Health Group; Health Initiative *UK* 13
≡ Mental Health Service *UK* 222
≡ Refuge; Resource Centre; Support Group; Welfare Group *UK* 13
Asian Youth Movement; Project *UK* 13
Asilo Politico *IT* 141
Asistencia Pedagógica, Orientación y Apoyo al Retorno *E* 149
Asna Ashriyya Shia Mosque *UK* 56
Asociación Africana; de Africanos; de Africanos de Girona; Afro-Catalana; Afro-Hispana para la Integración del Marginado; Afro-Vasca *E* 4
≡ Alemana de Beneficiencia *E* 37
≡ Alma Peruana *E* 96
Asociación de Amigos de Africa *E* 4
≡ do Brasil *E* 24
≡ de China *E* 29
≡ Hispano-Iraquíes *E* 46
≡ Peruano-Hispanos *E* 96
≡ del Pueblo Saharaui *E* 104
≡ de los Pueblos de Guinea Ecuatorial *E* 33
≡ del Uruguay *E* 123
Asociación de Amistad Hispano-Arabe *E* 10
≡ Hispano-Cubana B. de las Casas *E* 31
≡ Hispano-Kurda *E* 83
≡ Hispano-Rumana Mihail Eminescu *E* 102
≡ de las Mujeres Filipinas *E* 35
Asociación Andaluz Duende *F* 111
≡ Argentina de Derechos Humanos *E* 11
≡ de Ayuda Mútua de Inmigrantes en Cataluña *E* 149
≡ Belgo-Española de Promoción Cultural *BE* 110
≡ Rosalía de Castro *E* 90
≡ Catalana de Residentes Senegaleses *E* 105
≡ Catalana de Solidaridad y de Ayuda a Refugiados *E* 149
≡ Chilena de Derechos Humanos *E* 28
≡ de Colaboración y Amistad con Mozambique *E* 91
≡ del Colegio Alemán *E* 37
≡ de la Comunidad Iberoamericana en Cataluña *E* 84
≡ contra la Tortura *E* 212
Asociación de Cubanos; La Palmera *E* 31
Asociación Cultural Bubi *E* 33
≡ Amilcar Cabral *E* 39
≡ Club Argentino *E* 11
≡ Española Livry-Clichy *F* 111
≡ Hispano-Norteamericano *E* 123
≡ Juvenil *D* 112
≡ Kurda *E* 83
≡ Maleva *E* 33
≡ Portuguesa de Laciana *E* 101
≡ Rhômbe; Riebapua *E* 33
≡ Rumana Mota Marin *E* 102
≡ Terra Omnium *E* 90
≡ de Universitarios de Guinea Ecuatorial; Viyil *E* 33
Asociación para la defensa de los pueblos amenazados *D* 166
≡ de Desarrollo Gitano *E* 41
≡ Económica Hispano Suiza *E* 114
≡ de Emigrantes Marroquíes *E* 90
≡ de Empresarios Japoneses *E* 78
≡ de Enseñantes con Gitanos *E* 41
Asociación Española de Africanistas *E* 4
≡ Amistad con los Pueblos Arabes Bayt Al-Thaqafa *E* 10
≡ Cooperación Europea e Intercambio Cultural *E* 213
≡ Integración Gitana *E* 41
≡ Padres de Familia en la RFA *D* 112
Asociación de Estudiantes Ecuato-guineanos *E* 33
≡ Latinoamericanos *E* 84
Asociación de Estudio del Mundo Arabe Contemporáneo y la Cooperación *E* 10
≡ Europea para la Formación Profesional y Educación Intercultural de Refugiados, Asilados e Inmigrantes *E* 149
≡ de Ex-presos y Refugiados Políticos Antifascistas *E* 174
≡ Familiar Mixta de Africanos *E* 4
≡ de Formación Socio-Educativa—Intercultura *E* 174
≡ Francisco de Goya; Miguel Hernández *F* 111
≡ Hispano Alemana de Enseñanzas Técnicas *E* 37
≡ Iberia Cultura *F* 111
Asociación de Inmigrantes Filipinos *E* 35
≡ Marroquíes de Cataluña—Dar al Maghrib *E* 90
≡ Senegaleses *E* 105
Asociación de Intelectuales Africanos *E* 4
≡ Intérpretes Nipones *E* 78
≡ Investigación y Especialización sobre temas iberoamericanos *E* 84

Asociación de Investigadores y Estudiantes Mexicanos en España *E* 88
≡ Jama Kafo *E* 27
≡ de Jubilados y Pensionistas Españoles de la Gironde *F* 111
≡ Juvenil de Expresión Gitana *E* 41
≡ Karibu para Refugiados Africanos *E* 4
≡ Laboral Luzvim *E* 35
≡ Latinoamericana de Baleares *E* 84
≡ Libre de Abogados, Derechos Extranjeros y Minorías *E* 149
≡ Federico García Lorca *F* 111
≡ Luso-Cantabra *E* 101
≡ Magrebí Al Tifk *E* 87
≡ Mediadora de los Problemas Africanos en España *E* 4
≡ Medicus Mundi de España *E* 213
Asociación de Mujeres Chilenas Tralun *E* 28
≡ Dominicanas en España *E* 32
≡ Españolas Gitanas; Españolas Gitanas Romi Serseni *E* 41
≡ Inmigrantes Marroquíes *E* 90
≡ Latinoamericanas *E* 84
≡ Peruanas *E* 96
≡ Uruguayas Lourdes Pintos *E* 123
Asociación Musulmana; en España *E* 54
Asociación Nacional Presencia Gitana *E* 41
≡ Pablo Neruda *E* 28
≡ Nigeriana de Barcelona *E* 92
Asociación de Padres de Alumnos de Bremen; Alumnos Españoles en Münster; Familias y Alumnos Españoles; Familias y Alumnos en Hamburgo; Familias de Bonn; Familias Españolas *D* 112
≡ Familias Españolas Emigrantes *F* 111
≡ Familias de Leverkusen *D* 112
Asociación de Paquistaníes *E* 93
≡ Peruana Ollantay; de Peruanos *E* 96
≡ Polaca Aguila Blanca *E* 96
Asociación Portuguesa; del Norte; en Pamplona *E* 101
Asociación Pro Derechos Humanos; de Bizkaia; de España *E* 213
Asociación Pro Inmigrantes en Asturias *E* 149
≡ para el Progreso de Guinea Ecuatorial *E* 33
≡ para la Promoción e Inserción Profesional *E* 213
≡ de Refugiados y Asilados de la Ciudad de Valencia *E* 149
≡ de Refugiados e Inmigrantes Peruanos *E* 96
≡ de Residentes Bolivianos *UK* 23
≡ Romapall; del Secretariado General Gitano *E* 41
≡ Las Segovias para la Cooperación con Centroamérica *E* 27
≡ de Senegaleses en Valencia *E* 105
≡ Socio-Cultural Arabe *E* 11
≡ de Solidaridad con los Trabajadores Inmigrantes *E* 149
Asociación de Trabajadores Africanos de Lleida *E* 4
≡ y Comerciantes Marroquíes Amical *E* 90
≡ Filipinos *E* 35
≡ Inmigrantes Marroquíes en España *E* 90
Asociatia Pentru Apararea Drepturilor Omuli in Romania *RO* 212
Asociatia Studentil de Lupta Impotriva Rasismului din Romania *RO* 173
ASRA Greater London Housing Association; Housing Association *UK* 13
Assembleia de Deus *LX* 100
Assembleia da República *PR* 211
Assistencia Médica Internacional *PR* 211
Assistenza Religiosa ai Cecoslovachi *IT* 32
Associação Académica de Coimbra *LX* 100
≡ Africa Solidariedade; Africana *PR* 4
≡ Africana de Moçambique *PR* 91
≡ de Amigos da Encosta Nascente *PR* 148
≡ Amigos da Mulher Angolana *PR* 9
≡ de Amizade Portugal Albania *PR* 8
≡ de Amizade Portugal-Angola *PR* 9
≡ de Amizade Portugal-Cabo Verde *PR* 26
≡ de Amizade Portugal-Cuba *PR* 31
Associação dos Antigos Alunos do Ensino Secundário de Cabo Verde; do Liceu Gil Eanes *PR* 26
Associação dos Brasileiros *PR* 24
≡ Caboverdeana de Lisboa; Caboverdeana de Sines; 5 de Julho *PR* 26
≡ de Cooperação e Amizade *PR* 211
≡ de Coordenação e Integracão dos Migrantes Angolanos *PR* 9
Associação Cultural da Comunidade Portuguêsa *GR* 100
≡ e Desportiva da Pedreira *PR* 26
≡ Moinho da Juventude *PR* 148
≡ Radio Viriatu *LX* 100
≡ e Recreativa Angolana *PR* 9
≡ e Recreativa Santomense *PR* 104

Associação de Defesa dos Interesses dos Alunos Portuguêses do Norte *LX* 100
≡ de Emigrantes Lusiadas *PR* 148
≡ de Espoliados de Angola *PR* 9
≡ Estrela d'Africa *PR* 4
≡ de Estudantes Angolanos *PR* 9
≡ dos Franceses do Norte *PR* 36
≡ Bento Gonçalves *PR* 26
≡ Grupo Folclórico Cantares Populares da Mocidade Portuguêsa *LX* 100
≡ Guineense de Solidariedade Social; de Guineenses *PR* 39
≡ Luso-Africana de Solidariedade *PR* 4
≡ Luso-Caboverdeana *LX* 26
≡ Moinho da Juventude *PR* 4
≡ da Mulher Emigrante *LX* 100
≡ das Mulheres Caboverdeanas *IT* 25
≡ dos Naturais e Ex-Residentes de Moçambique *PR* 91
≡ dos Pais dos Alunos de Diekirch *LX* 100
≡ Portugal-Bulgaria *PR* 24
≡ Portugal-Russia/URSS *PR* 103
Associação Portuguêsa *D* 99, *E* 101
≡ dos Direitos Cidadãos *PR* 211
≡ do Norte *E* 101
≡ dos Pais de Remscheid *D* 99
≡ em Pamplona *E* 101
≡ do Serviço Social Internacional *PR* 211
≡ 25 de Abril *E* 101
Associação dos Portuguêses Emigrados na Bélgica *BE* 97
≡ de Reencontro de Emigrantes *PR* 148
≡ Social e Recreativa Popular Portuguêsa *LX* 100
Associaçãos Unidas de Caboverde *PR* 26
Associació Catalana d'Amistat i Cooperació *E* 213
≡ de Solidaritat i d'Ajut al Refugiat *E* 149
Associació Educativa de les Il.les *E* 242
Associated Country Women of the World *UK* 176
Association d'acceuil des femmes immig-rées et françaises de St-Cloud *F* 134
Association pour l'Accueil et la Formation des Travailleurs Etrangers; Migrants *F* 134
Association pour l'Accueil et l'Héberge-ment des Travailleurs Migrants; d'accueil aux médecins et personnel de santé réfugiés; pour l'accueil et la préformation des travailleurs migrants *F* 134
Association d'acceuil des travailleurs étrangers et migrants; migrants *F* 134
Association aide aux femmes khmères *F* 81
Association d'aide matérielle et morale aux gens du voyage *F* 117
≡ aux réfugiés vietnamiens *LX* 124
Association pour l'aide social aux travailleurs africains *F* 2
≡ d'Aide aux Travailleurs Etrangers de la Région Rouennaise *F* 134
≡ Al Amal des Marocains de Borges *F* 89
Association algérienne pour le décès; la promotion de la culture et de la langue arabe *F* 8
Association des Algériens en Savoie *F* 8
≡ Amana—Hommes et Migrations *F* 233
≡ Amicale Tunisienne *IT* 119
Association des Amis de Passages *F* 134
≡ Portugais de Gerzat *F* 97
Association d'amitié française et africaine *F* 2
≡ Franco-Vietnamienne *F* 124
≡ Luxembourg-Cap Vert *LX* 26
Association des amitiés asiatiques *F* 12
≡ amitiés France Uruguay *F* 123
≡ Antiboise pour l'Alphabétisation *F* 134
≡ arabe des droits de l'homme *F* 10
≡ arménienne d'aide sociale *F* 11
≡ des artistes et créateurs africains *F* 2
≡ Artistique de Belgrad *F* 105
≡ Belge des Juristes Démocrates *BE* 189
≡ de Bienfaisance *GR* 36
Association of Black Churches; Clergy; Counsellors; Probation Officers; Social Workers & Allied Professions *UK* 20
Association of Blind Asians *UK* 13
≡ de la boucherie islamique *F* 53
≡ of British Internees *UK* 176
≡ des Cadres d'Origine Maghrébine d'Europe *F* 86
≡ Calvados Sud-Est Asiatique *F* 110
Association des Cap-Verdiens d'Esch; du Luxembourg; du Nord *LX* 26
Association of Caribbean Nationals *UK* 26
≡ champenoise de coopération inter-régionale *F* 2
≡ des Chinois résidents en France *F* 28
≡ Chrétienne des Travailleurs Italiens *F* 74
≡ des commerçants et des artisans tunisiens de Provence-Languedoc *F* 118
≡ de la communauté algérienne de la Sarthe *F* 8

Association congolaise Temo F 31
≡ pour la connaisance de l'Islam F 53
≡ des constructeurs pour la réhabilitation et l'optimalisation de la terre F 196
≡ of Contemporary Iberian Studies UK 243
≡ Coordinatrice des Associations des Portugais de Seine et Marne F 97
≡ corse pour la promotion et la formation des migrants F 134
≡ Coup de Soleil F 162
≡ de Culture Berbère Tiddukla F 118
≡ de culture islamique et arabe F 53
≡ de la Culture Islamique de la Région du Centre BE 52
≡ de culture populaire du Portugal Nouveau F 97
≡ Culturelle et d'Aide aux Travailleurs Turcs de la Region du Centre BE 119
Association culturelle des Algériens du Doubs; de Haute-Savoie; des Vosges F 8
Association Culturelle et Amicale des Familles d'Outre-Mer et Migrants F 134
≡ anti-raciste F 162
≡ arabo-islamique F 53
≡ des Artistes Espagnols de Namur BE 110
≡ et artistique des Asiates de France F 12
≡ Berbère Tiwizi F 118
≡ du Chili LX 28
≡ de la communauté africaine d'Orléans F 2
≡ de la communauté algérienne F 8
≡ et cultuelle des marocains F 89
≡ des Elèves et Etudiants Camerounais F 25
≡ espagnole; espagnole-portugaise F 111
≡ France-Portugal Azulejo F 97
≡ Franco Allemande F 37
≡ franco-arabe Roanne F 10
≡ Franco-Japonaise de Tenri F 78
≡ franco-maghrébine F 86
≡ franco-turque F 120
≡ et d'intégration des étudiants africains à Montpellier F 2
≡ islamique, récréative et sportive F 53
≡ islamique turque; et islamique turque Angers Trelaze F 120
≡ et islamique de Vernon F 53
≡ israélite Rachi F 79
≡ maghrébine des Ardennes F 86
≡ maghrébine de Caussade F 86
≡ des maghrébins de Sarcelles F 86
≡ des marocains français F 89
≡ La musique et l'Afrique F 2
≡ musulmane F 53
≡ nord-africaine F 92
≡ orthodoxe de l'église Saint Séraphin de Sarow F 134
≡ portugaise; portugaise de Strasbourg F 97
≡ et de promotion de la langue arabe F 10
≡ et récréative Saudades de Portugal F 97
≡ Récréative et Sportive Portugaise F 97
≡ des Sénégalais de Pistoia IT 105
≡ et sociale des ressortissants sénégalais et mauritaniens des Vosges F 104
≡ O Sol do Portugal F 97
≡ et de solidarité franco-kurde F 82
≡ et sportive des jeunes Turcs F 120
≡ et sportive des portugais; et sportive portugaise F 97
≡ tamoule mondiale F 115
≡ des travailleurs de Turquie; turque de Haute-Savoie F 120
Association Henri Curiel F 162
≡ des Danois au Luxembourg LX 32
≡ Danoise pour la Coopération Internationale DK 194
≡ Dauphinoise de Coopération Franco-Algérienne F 86
≡ décès familiale algérienne F 8
≡ de Défense des Droits des Etrangers BE 130
Association pour la défense des droits de l'homme en Afrique F 2
≡ et des libertés démocratiques dans le monde arabe F 10
≡ en Maroc F 89
Association défense internationale des Sri-Lankais F 113
Association démocratique des Français à l'étranger F 134, IT LX 36
≡ des travailleurs de Turquie F 120
Association 2ème G F 134
Association Développement, Emploi, Formation et Insertion Sociale BE 189
Association pour le Développement de la Formation des Immigrés F 134
≡ des Relations Intercommunautaires F 162
≡ de Sidibela F 87
Association dialogue entre les cultures F 162

Association pour la Diffusion, l'Adaptation et la Préformation F 196
≡ d'Information sur l'Amérique Latine F 83
≡ des Langues et des Cultures d'Espagne F 111
Association Douaisienne pour l'Accueil des Travailleurs Migrants F 134
≡ de Douirets en France F 118
≡ pour le droit des étrangers BE 130
≡ for East African Asians UK 13
≡ de l'éducation et l'enseignement des enfants islamiques en France F 53
≡ Educative et Culturelle de la Langue Arabe F 10
≡ Emergence Nanterre F 162
≡ Emergences BE 88
≡ pour l'Enseignement et la Formation des Travailleurs Immigrés F 134
≡ d'entraide des anciens combattants polonais en France F 96
≡ d'entraide des femmes africaines F 2
≡ Entraide Formation Travailleurs Migrants F 134
≡ Entraide et promotion des travailleurs algériens F 8
≡ d'entraide et de solidarité F 134
≡ des Vietnamiens d'Aix-Marseille F 124
Association Espagnole; Federico García Lorca; Sol de España F 111
Association of Estonians in GB UK 34
≡ pour l'établissement des réfugiés F 134
≡ des Etats Généraux des Etudiants de l'Europe NL 208
≡ pour l'Etude des Sciences Humaines en Afrique du Nord et au Proche-Orient F 233
Association des Etudiants Africains de la Sarthe; Africains du térritoire de Belfort; d'Afrique Centrale et de l'Ouest; d'Afrique Noire de Tours F 2
≡ Algériens d'Europe F 8
≡ Franc-comtois issus de l'Immigration F 134
≡ Grecs de Limbourg BE 38
≡ Guadeloupéens F 39
≡ islamiques, section Lyon F 53
≡ issus de l'Immigration Algérienne F 8
≡ marocains de Saint-Etienne F 89
≡ sénégalais de Caen F 104
Association pour les Etudiants, les Stagiaires et les Travailleurs des Pays en Voie de Développement F 135
≡ des Etudiants de Tahiti F 115
≡ Eurasia F 12
Association euro-africaine; d'entraide F 2
Association Euro-Arabe pour le Travail et l'Echange F 10
≡ Euro-Asie d'Education et des Echanges Culturels F 12
≡ Europe-Tiers Monde BE 189
≡ Européenne des Citoyens F 196
≡ d'Expression des Jeunes Immigrés F 10
≡ Familiale pour la Protection des Etudiantes Etrangères F 135
Association Familiale Protestante F 196
≡ tunisienne de la Nièvre F 118
Association de Familles Espagnoles F 111
≡ de Familles Espagnoles Emigrées BE 111
≡ de la fédération des français d'origine marocaine F 89
Association des Femmes Belges et Immigrées Nadi BE 130
≡ de la Casamance Adeane F 135
≡ inter cultures F 2
≡ Lao en France F 83
≡ réfugiées F 135
≡ du Sud-Sahara—Afrique Yakhareu F 2
≡ zaïroises de l'Isère pour l'entraide et l'animation culturelle F 126
Association for Fighting against Racism RO 174
≡ de Foi et Pratique de la Religion Islamique BE 52
≡ pour la formation contre le racisme et pour l'identité culturelle algérienne F 8
≡ pour la formation et la réinsertion des africains migrants F 2
≡ des français islamiques F 53
Association Française d'Aide aux Travailleurs Espagnols F 111
≡ d'Amitié et de Solidarité avec les Peuples d'Afrique F 2
≡ des juristes démocrates F 196
≡ des Volontaires du Progrès F 2
Association France-Canada F 25
≡ France Espagne F 111
≡ France Gabon F 37
≡ France Israël F 73
≡ France-Palestine F 95
≡ France Tchécoslovaquie F 32
≡ France-Zaïre F 126
≡ Franco-Asiatique d'Echanges et de Loisirs F 110

Association Franço-Britannique F 24
≡ franco-écossaise UK 36
≡ franco-ghanéenne F 38
≡ Franco-Italienne F 74
Association franco-maghrébine; pour le développement rural F 86
Association Franco-Portugaise d'Argenteuil; de Vigneux-sur-Seine; de Viroflay F 97
Association fraternité Viet Nam F 124
Association Générale pour l'Enseignement et la Culture Peul Langue Poular F 2
≡ des Etudiants Algériens d'Aix F 8
≡ des Etudiants Vietnamiens de Paris F 124
≡ des femmes algériennes en Europe F 8
≡ des Khmèrs à l'Etranger F 81
≡ métisse F 162
≡ des Travailleurs Sénégalais F 105
Association génération future F 27
Association des gens du voyage, nomades et sédentaires F 40, 117
≡ nomades et sédentaires d'Aubenas; sédentaires du Pays d'Aix F 117
Association of Ghanaian Immigrants IT 38
≡ gitane Saint-Jacquoise; des Gitans d'origine espagnole; des Gitans sédentaires d'Aix-en-Provence F 40
≡ des Grecs LX 39
≡ of Guyanese Nationals UK 40
≡ of Gypsy Organisations UK 41
≡ Haut-Marnaise pour les Immigrés F 135
≡ of Hispanists of GB & Ireland UK 243
≡ Ibéria Culture F 111
≡ de l'Immigration Marocaine F 89
≡ pour l'information et l'aide à la communauté portugaise F 97
Association d'Information et de Réflexion sur la Culture Maghrébine F 233
≡ en Ariège F 86
Association pour l'Insertion des Femmes Originaires du Maghreb et Jeunes F 86
Association Interculturelle F 162
≡ L'Aquilone BE 160
≡ de briançonnais Mosaïque; Carrefour F 162
≡ de production, de diffusion et de documentation audiovisuelle F 233
≡ pour la promotion et l'insertion; et sportive F 162
Association Internationale Acceuil Santé F 135
≡ d'Etudes des Civilisations Mediteranéennes IT 238
≡ des Juristes Démocrates BE 189
Association irlandaise F 46
Association Islah F 53
Association islamique; culturelle sunnite des français musulmans rapatriés; des jeunes musulmans de la Charente; pour le progrès des femmes; de Rieux-Minervois F 53
Association Italo-Luxembourgeoise LX 75
Association des Ivoiriens à Dijon; de la région de Kani en France F 77
Association of Jamaicans UK 78
Association des jeunes cambodgiens de l'Ile-de-France F 25
≡ français musulmans F 53
≡ Maghrébines F 86
≡ Marocains BE 88
≡ méditerranéens en France F 135
≡ musiciens khmères F 82
≡ musulmans français F 53
≡ ressortissants sénégalais F 105
Association des Jeunes Yougoslaves F 126
≡ Jeunesse congolaise en France F 31
≡ of Jewish Ex-Servicemen/Women; of Jewish Refugees UK 80
≡ Jugoslavija LX 126
≡ Kaléidoscope F 162
≡ Laotienne Lao Dok Champa F 83
≡ of Latvian Youth UK 85
≡ Leonardo da Vinci Culturelle, Récréative et Sportive Italo-Belge BE 73
≡ locale des femmes algériennes F 8
Association pour le Logement des Travailleurs Immigrés de Clermont; et de leurs Familles F 135
Association loisirs, entraide de la communauté algérienne de Pompey F 8
≡ Luxembourg-Chine LX 29
≡ Luxembourg-Roumanie LX 102
≡ Luxembourg-URSS LX 103
≡ Luxembourgeoise pour les Nations Unies LX 169
≡ Maghrébarab Valdotaine IT 87
≡ maghrébine de Clermont IT 86
Association des Maghrébins Intégrés; sparnaciens F 86
Association maison des travailleurs immigrés de Puteaux F 135

Association Marnasia F 110
≡ des Marocains en France F 89
≡ pour la médecine et la recherche en Afrique F 2
≡ des Médecins Zaïrois de Formation Italienne IT 126
≡ pour une meilleure intégration F 162
≡ of Metropolitan Authorities UK 220
≡ pour le Mieux-être et le Logement des Isolés F 135
≡ des Migrants Marocains à Utrecht NL 90
≡ Mira Femmes Musulmanes BE 52
≡ Mittaphab Lao de la Savoie F 83
Association Mondiale Anational F 165
≡ pour l'Ecole Instrument de Paix CH 175
≡ pour les Refugiés F 135
Association Multi-Assistance Togolaise F 116
Association of Muslim Lawyers; Researchers; Scholars in Britain UK 56
≡ Schools UK 60
≡ Youth & Community Workers UK 56
Association musulmane d'Albi F 53
≡ musulmane culturelle d'enseignement de langue arabe F 10
≡ musulmane culturelle de la paix F 53
≡ des musulmans de Montluçon F 53
≡ Les Nanas Beurs F 19
Association nationale d'assistance aux frontières pour les étrangers F 135
≡ des élus originaires du Maghreb F 86
≡ pour l'enseignement et la formation des travailleurs immigrés F 135
≡ Résidents des Foyers Sonacotra F 196
Association Nejma F 135
≡ noire africaine d'Elancourt F 2
≡ de la nouvelle génération immigrée F 162
≡ des Originaires du Portugal F 97
≡ des Ouvriers Turcs F 120
Association des parents et des amis de détenus F 196
≡ d'Elèves de la section espagnole des Lycée et Collège Internationaux F 111
≡ d'Elèves Turques de Goussainville F 120
≡ de familles espagnoles emigrées F 111
Association Paris Québec F 102
≡ Pédagogique d'Acceuil aux Jeunes Immigrés BE 130
≡ du Peuple Gitan F 40
≡ pour les peuples ménacés D 166
≡ pluriculturelle pour la coopération et le développement F 162
≡ populaire démocratique culturelle turque BE 119
Association des Portugais de Bellegarde F 97
≡ Emigrés en Belgique BE 97
≡ Emigrés au Luxembourg LX 100
≡ de Franconville F 98
≡ de la Région du Centre BE 97
≡ Tous F 98
Association portugaise de Bienfaisance; Culturelle et Sociale; culturelle et sportive de Portovecchio; Culturelle de Valentigney; de Domont; d'Entraide et de Culture; du Gard; de La Fare; de Mauléon; de Moissac; de Montpellier; Serra e Val; Socio-Culturelle et Récréative de Champigny-sur-Marne; des travailleurs en France F 98
Association pour la promotion culturelle des immigrés de Stains F 135
≡ de l'enseignement de la langue arabe F 10
≡ et l'insertion de la communauté algérienne F 8
≡ de la langue et de la culture du Soninké; du Soninké F 2
Association des psychologues, psycho-thérapeutes et animateurs maghrébins F 86
Association for Punjab Studies UK 102
Association Radio Amitié F 165
Association des Rapatriés d'Europe Occidentale GR 140
≡ français d'origine marocaine F 89
Association de Recherche et d'Action Culturelle; pour la recherche et l'animation culturelle F 162
≡ pour la recherche sur l'insertion des communautés étrangères F 233
≡ Récréative et Amicale des Portugais de Cambrai-Esnes F 98
≡ pour les Réfugiés du Calvados F 135
≡ des réfugiés cambodgiens de l'Aube F 25
≡ des réfugiés khmers en Limousin F 82
≡ des réfugiés Lao-Hmong F 83
Association Régionale pour la Formation et l'Education des Migrants F 135
≡ Provence d'Amitié Franco-Chinoise F 28
≡ du Théâtre de l'Emigration F 135

Association pour la Réinsertion de l'Enfance et de l'Adolescence F 196
≡ Rencontres Audiovisuelles F 162
≡ des résidents d'origine chinoise F 28
Association des ressortissants gorysiens F 87
≡ guinéens de Toulouse-Midi-Pyrenées F 39
≡ mauritaniens de Bouanze F 87
≡ Sénégalais à Marseille F 105
Association of Returned Development Workers IR 168
≡ for the Rights of Britons Abroad LX 24
≡ Sabar Horizons—Compagnie Doudou N'Diaye Rose Junior F 105
≡ Sans Frontières des Initiatives et Rencontres F 162
≡ pour la Santé des Migrants F 135
≡ Saônoise d'Aide aux Travailleurs Etrangers F 137
≡ Sarde Eleonora d'Arborea BE 73
≡ des sénégalais stagiaires et étudiants à Pau F 105
≡ Service Sociale Familial Migrants F 135
≡ for Sierra Leonean Refugees UK 156
≡ of Social Research Organisations UK 243
≡ Sociale, Educative et Culturelle de Solidarité avec les Maghrébins F 86
Association socioculturelle africaine Drome-Ardèche F 2
≡ des Angolais BE 9
≡ Educative Juive F 79
≡ Franco-Vietnamienne F 124
≡ Marocaine F 89
≡ et Sportive des Maghrébins F 86
≡ turque de Valentigney F 120
Association socio-éducative et culturelle franco-musulmane Rabita F 53
Association de solidarité pour l'acceuil et l'assistance des réfugiés F 135
≡ africaine; des Africains en France F 2
≡ et culturelle des travailleurs de Turquie F 120
≡ Etrangers Français; Familiale et Culturelle F 162
≡ de femmes immigrées; français migrants F 135
≡ franco-cambodgienne F 25
≡ de l'immigration algérienne F 8
Association pour la solidarité et l'insertion des femmes africaines du Havre F 2
Association de solidarité pour l'intégration des immigrés F 135
≡ Luxembourg-Nicaragua LX 91
≡ Marocaine BE 88
≡ avec les Peuples d'Amérique Latine; des réfugiés laotiens de Nogent F 83
≡ des travailleurs algériens F 8
≡ avec les travailleurs immigrés F 135, LX 145
≡ avec les travailleurs migrants F 135
≡ avec les Travailleurs Turcs F 120
≡ des Travailleurs Turcs BE 119
Association of South-Eastern Asian Studies in the UK UK 110
Association de soutien, de développement et d'amélioration de la vie tribale; de l'expression des communautés d'Amiens F 162
≡ aux travailleurs immigrés LX 145
Association Sportive de la Communauté Marocaine BE 88
≡ et Culturelle des Etudiants Africains F 2
≡ Culturelle des Jeunes Marocaines BE 88
≡ et culturelle des Portugais du Gard; et culturelle des Portugais de Lure; portugaise—Basket-ball F 98
Association des Stagiaires et Etudiants Camerounais de Bordeaux F 25
Association for the Study of Ethnicity & Nationalism UK 243
≡ the World Refugee Problem AT 231
Association Suisse—Kurdistan CH 83
≡ of Sunni Muslims UK 56
≡ Texture F 163
Association des Travailleurs Africains de la Somme F 2
≡ algériens en France F 8
≡ Arabes du Mans et de la Sarthe F 10
≡ Espagnols F 111
≡ et familles algériennes du Sud de la France F 8
≡ du Kurdistan en France F 82
≡ Maliens en France F 87
≡ Marocains en France F 89
≡ Noirs de la Région Toulonnaise F 19
≡ Pakistanis en France F 93
≡ patriotes du Kurdistan F 82
≡ Portugais F 98
≡ turcs de la région d'Eure-et-Loire; de Turquie F 120
Association des Trois Mondes F 163

Association Tsholo Nkese F 3
≡ Tunisienne NL 119
≡ des Tunisiens en France F 118
≡ of Ugandan Youth & Students UK 122
≡ of Ukrainians in Great Britain UK 123
≡ de l'Union Islamique en France F 53
≡ of Upper Egypt F 33
≡ Vauclusienne d'Aide et d'Insertion F 135
≡ des Vietnamiens libres de l'Aube F 124
≡ of Visitors to Immigration Detainees UK 153
≡ Voyage Echange culturel euro-maghrébin F 86
≡ Wejmaa F 135
≡ of Western Thrace Turks UK 122
≡ yougoslave Trepca F 126
≡ des Yougoslaves de Wiltz LX 126
≡ zaïroise de Lille F 126
Associations amitiés Afrique-Proche Orient F 163
≡ Franco Espagnoles F 111
≡ Populaires Familiales et Syndicales F 196
Associazione ADAESER Stranieri IT 141
≡ Africa Insieme; Africa Oggi; degli Africani in Piemonte IT 3
≡ Algerina IT 9
≡ di Amicizia Italia-Tunisia IT 119
≡ di Amicizia Italia-Ucrania IT 122
≡ di Amicizia Italo-Marrochina IT 89
≡ Argentini in Campania IT 11
≡ Bangladesh IT 17
≡ Baobab per la Promozione Culturale IT 3
≡ Bellunesi nel Mondo LX 75
≡ Bolivia Italia; Boliviana della Liguria IT 23
≡ Calabresi Emigrati BE 73
≡ Camerunesi in Italia IT 25
≡ Capoverdiana; Capoverdiana a Firenze IT 25
≡ Cile Lombardia IT 28
≡ dei Cinesi a Milano IT 28
Associazione Cittadini Algerini IT 9
≡ Egiziani IT 33
≡ Extracomunitari del Polesine IT 141
≡ Latino-Americani IT 84
≡ di Solidarietà con Bosnia IT 23
Associazione della Comunità Egiziana IT 33
≡ Etiopi in Italia IT 34
≡ dei Latino Americani in Veneto IT 84
≡ Somala di Arezzo e Provincia; Somala di Torino IT 108
≡ Straniere in Italia IT 141
Associazione Cristiana di Lavoratori Italiani BE 73, F D 74, IT 204-5, LX 75, UK 76
≡ Patronato ACLI Sportello Stranieri IT 141
Associazione Cristiana Limburgo BE 73
Associazione Culturale Africana Samory Touré IT 3
≡ Assistenza Popolare IT 168
≡ Italo-Maghrebina IT 87
≡ Italo-Somala IT 108
≡ Palestinesi IT 95
≡ dei Senegalesi di Pistoia IT 105
≡ di Studenti Africani a Bari IT 3
Associazione Democratica Francese all'Estero IT 36
≡ Donne Africane IT 3
≡ Donne Arabe e Straniere IT 10
≡ Donne Cilene Esuli IT 28
≡ Donne Immigrate Africane IT 3
≡ Egiziana IT 33
≡ El Bari Moulay IT 89
≡ Eritrei IT 34
≡ Extracomunitari IT 141
≡ Fagolar Furlan LX 75
≡ Famiglie Italiane D 74
≡ Filippina IT 35
≡ Forum IT 141
≡ Fratelli dell'Uomo IT 205
≡ Giovani 80 IT 141
≡ Gran Sasso Abruzzesi LX 75
≡ Hararki Etiopia IT 34
Associazione Immigrati Arabi IT 10
≡ Costa d'Avorio IT 77
≡ Etiopia, Eggito, Oromo IT 34
≡ Extracomunitari; Extracomunitari Bassanese IT 142
≡ Marrochini; Marrochini in Abruzzo IT 89
≡ Nordafricani in Italia IT 92
≡ Triveneto IT 142
Associazione Interculturale Soweto; Interetnica Shangrillà IT 168
≡ Interventi Cooperazione allo Sviluppo IT 205
≡ Iraniani in Liguria IT 45
≡ Italia-Algeria IT 9
≡ Italia-Argentina IT 11
≡ Italia Colombia IT 30
≡ Italia-Messico IT 88
≡ Italia-Nicaragua IT 91
≡ Italiana Tutela Emigrati e Famiglie D 74, IT 142, LX 75, UK 76
≡ Italo-Capoverdiana a Napoli IT 25

Associazione Italo Egiziana in Piemonte
    IT 33
≡ Italo-Somala Shabel *IT* 108
Associazione Lavoratori Costa d'Avorio
    IT 77
≡ Donne e Studenti Eritrei a Torino *IT* 34
≡ Egiziana *IT* 33
≡ Emigrati e loro Famiglie del F-VG *LX* 75
≡ Eritrea *IT* 34
≡ Filippini in Italia; Filippini in Piemonte
    IT 35
≡ e Studenti Ivoriani nelle Marche *IT* 77
≡ del Tigrai *IT* 116
Associazione Liguri di Gran Bretagna *UK* 76
≡ Lucani in Lussemburgo *LX* 75
≡ Lungianesi *UK* 76
≡ la Maiella Emigrati *LX* 75
≡ Marocchina Bologna; Marocchini; dei
    Marocchini in Italia, Sezione Sarda;
    Marocco *IT* 89
≡ Monte Raut, Amici di Andreis in
    Lussemburgo *LX* 75
Associazione Nazionale di Amicizia e di
    Cooperazione Italo-Araba *IT* 10
≡ Ex-Deportati Politici nei Campi Nazisti
    IT 168
≡ Famiglie Emigrati *BE* 73, *IT* 142, *LX* 75,
    UK 76
≡ Oltre Le Frontiere *IT* 142
Associazione Nigeria—Italia di Lavoratori
    IT 92
≡ Oromo in Italia *IT* 92
≡ Palestinese; Palestinesi in Liguria *IT* 95
≡ Panafricana *IT* 3
≡ per la Partecipazione allo Sviluppo *IT* 205
≡ dei Patrioti dello Sri-Lanka *IT* 113
≡ Peruana della Liguria *IT* 96
≡ Piemontesi nel Mondo *UK* 76
≡ Popolo di Capo Verde *IT* 26
≡ Professionale Italiana Collaboratrici
    Familiari *IT* 205
≡ Professori Universitari Cittadini Stranieri
    IT 142
≡ per la Promozione della Cultura Latino
    Americana in Italia *IT* 84
≡ Puglia-Lussemburgo *LX* 75
Associazione Regionale Campani; Emigrati
    del Lazio; Emigrati Marchigiani *LX* 75
≡ Famiglie Immigrati *IT* 142
≡ Pugliesi Emigrati in Lussemburgo *LX* 75
≡ Sarda *F* 74
≡ Umbra Lavoratori Emigrati *LX* 75
Associazione Residenti Argentini *IT* 11
≡ Rifugiati Etiopici per l'Autoassistenza
    IT 34
Associazione Rifugiati Politici *IT* 142
≡ Etiopi in Italia *IT* 34
Associazione Rom Rasim Sejdic *IT* 103
≡ di Salvadoregni in Lombardia *IT* 104
≡ Fernando Santi *IT* 142
≡ Sao del Ciad *IT* 28
≡ Scalabrini Profughi-Emigrati-Rifugiati
    IT 142
Associazione Senegalesi; di Lombardia; di
    Parma; di Ravenna; in Sardegna *IT* 105
Associazione Siciliani nel Mondo *BE* 73
≡ Solidarietà Dandolo *IT* 142
≡ di Solidarietà dei Kashmiri *IT* 81
≡ Somala in Liguria; di Somali *IT* 108
≡ Sri Lanka *IT* 113
≡ Stop Razzismo *IT* 168
≡ Stranieri in Vicenza *IT* 142
Associazione di Studenti Africani di
    Firenze; Africani a Roma *IT* 3
≡ Camerunesi a Firenze; Camerunesi in
    Italia *IT* 25
≡ del Congo *IT* 31
≡ Ivoriani; Ivoriani a Roma *IT* 77
≡ Kurdi in Europa *IT* 82
≡ Libanesi *IT* 85
≡ Pakistani *IT* 93
≡ Ruandesi *IT* 104
≡ Zairesi *IT* 126
Associazione per gli Studi Giuridici
    sull'Immigrazione *IT* 238
≡ dei Sudanesi in Italia *IT* 114
≡ Tre Frontiere Abruzzesi *LX* 75
≡ Trentina Accoglienza Stranieri *IT* 142
≡ Trentini; Trevisani nel Mondo *LX* 75
≡ Umbra dei Lavoratori Emigrati *BE* 73
≡ Veronesi nel Mondo; Vincentini nel
    Mondo *LX* 75
≡ Volontaria Assistenza Nomadi *IT* 144
≡ Zairese in Italia; Zairesi in Toscana di
    Firenze e Province *IT* 126
Assurisk-Armensk Forening i Horsens
    DK 11
Assyrian Culture & Advice Centre;
    Refugees Relief Foundation; Society of GB
    UK 16
*Asyl: Schweizerische Zeitschrift für
    Asylrecht* *CH* 153

Asylkoordination Österreich *AT* 129
≡ Schweiz; Zürich *CH* 152
Asylpfarramt Baden-Württemberg *D* 138
Asylum Aid *UK* 153
Asylum Division *UK* 220
Asylum in Europe *UK* 244
Asylum Rights Campaign *UK* 153
Atelier d'Art Populaire *BE* 160
Atelier Contemporain de Cultures et des
    Echanges Culturels *F* 163
Athenry Society *UK* 47
Athens Reception *GR* 140
Atlantis Youth Exchange *NR* 210
Attadamoun—Solidarité des Marocains à
    l'Etranger *F* 89
Attitude *UK* 180
Aubergenville Intégration Fraternité
    Africaine *F* 3
Aughagower & Cushlaigh Society *UK* 47
Aujourd'hui l'Afrique *F* 2
Aumenier des Irlandais de Paris *F* 46
Ausbildung von Lehrern für Ausländer
    Kinder *D* 236
Auschwitz Information & Meetings Centre
    PL 173
Das Ausländer—Magazin *D* 236
Ausländerinitiative Freiburg *D* 138
Ausländsgesellschaft NRW *D* 166
Ausschuß für Entwicklungsbezogene
    Bildung und Publizistik *D* 166
Ausschuß der Kirchen für Ausländerfragen
    in Europa *BE* 130
Austin House Hotels *UK* 47
Austria-Transcarpathia Friendship
    Association *AT* 159
Austrian Catholic Centre *UK* 16
Austrian Red Cross *AT* 188
Autograph—Association of Black
    Photographers *UK* 20
Autonome Iranische Frauenbewegung *D* 45
Autonomi *DK* 161
Autonomie *CS* 161
Autonoom Centrum *NL* 208
Autre Regard *F* 137
Avanti Europa *IT* 144
Avanti nel Mondo *F* 74, *IT* 144
Avec Vous—pour la Démocratie, contre les
    Exclusions *BE* 160
Averroès Stichting *NL* 239
Avicenne *BE* 88
Avise Foundation *NL* 170
Avon & Bristol Asian Women's Network
    UK 14
≡ Community Law Centre *UK* 220
≡ Somali Community Group *UK* 108
Avon Immigration & Nationality Advice
    Centre *UK* 153
≡ Vietnamese Refugee Community *UK* 124
Avrupa Milli Görüs Teskilatlari *D* 120
Awaaz *UK* 14
Awal—cahier d'études berbères *F* 118
Awaze-Quam International *UK* 101
Awraq *E* 11
Ayesha Family Resource Centre; Project
    UK 153
Aylesbury Central America Group *UK* 27
≡ & District Irish Society *UK* 47
≡ Vale Racial Equality Council *UK* 176
Ayuda en Acción *E* 174
Azad Kashmir Muslim Association; Welfare
    Association *UK* 81
Azad Youth Club *UK* 57
Azadi Resource & Research Project *UK* 81
Azeemia Foundation *UK* 56
Azione Comboniana Servizio Emigrati Terzo
    Mondo *IT* 142
Azizia (or Azizye) Mosque *UK* 122

Babar Khalsa International *UK* 106
BACEE Journal *UK* 33
Baha'i International Community *CH* 16
Baha'i National Centre *UK* 16
Bahay Kubo Housing Association *UK* 36
Balham Mosque *UK* 56
Balita ng Malayang Pilipinas *NL* 35
Balkan Studies *GR* 238
Balkanike Bibliografia *GR* 238
Ballycroy Society *UK* 47
Ballyhaunis Mosque *IR* 53
Baltic Association of GB; Council *UK* 16
Baltic Independent *EE* 133
Baltic Research Unit *UK* 16
Baluch Community Association; Refugee
    Association *UK* 93
Banbury Mosque *UK* 56
Banbury Racial Equality Council *UK* 176
Bangla Educational & Cultural Centre *UK* 17
Bangladesh Allaya Mosque & Islamic
    Centre; Association *UK* 17
≡ Association in Italy *IT* 17
≡ Caterers' Association; Centre *UK* 17

Bangladesh Centre Association; Cultural
    Society; Eshat-Ul-Islam; International
    Women's Association; Islamic
    Association; Islamic Centre *UK* 17
Bangladesh Islamic Consultative
    Committee; Organisation *UK* 62
≡ Cultural Assoc.; Organisation *UK* 17
≡ Society *UK* 17-18
Bangladesh Jubok Somity; Medical
    Association; Muslim Association; Muslim
    Organisation; People's Association;
    People's Solidarity Centre *NL* 17
≡ Porishad *UK* 18
≡ Residents' Welfare Assoc.; Shomity;
    United Muslim Society; Welfare Assoc.;
    Women's Association; Women's Assoc.
    in GB; Workers Association; Youth &
    Cultural Shamiti; Youth League *UK* 17
Bangladeshi Advice Centre; Islamic
    Education Centre; Medical Association;
    Mosque *UK* 17
≡ Muslim Association; Workers
    Association; Youth Association *UK* 18
Banlieuescopies *F* 233
Baobab *IT* 3
Barbados Assoc.; Overseas Assoc. *UK* 18
Bareel *BE* 132
Barking & Dagenham Anti-Fascists; &
    Dagenham Racial Equality Council *UK* 176
≡ Muslim Social & Cultural Society *UK* 56
Barnardo's Chinese Health Project *NI* 30
≡ Greater Manchester Asian Women's
    Project *UK* 14
≡ Travellers Project *NI* 118
Barnet African-Caribbean Association *UK* 7
≡ Asian Women's Association *UK* 14
≡ Racial Equality Council *UK* 176
Barrikaden *S* 243
Basera Asian Women's Aid *UK* 14
Basildon Irish Club *UK* 47
Basildon Muslim Association *UK* 56
Basingstoke Irish Society *UK* 47
Basle Court Refugee Hostel *UK* 153
Bassera Women's Project *UK* 14
Basso Tribunal *D* 138
Bath Islamic Centre & Mosque *UK* 56
≡ Racial Equality Council *UK* 176
≡ Sufi Healing Order *UK* 56
Stefan Batory Foundation *PL* 173
Battersea Mosque *UK* 61
≡ & Wandsworth Irish Group *UK* 47
Bawa Balak Nath Temple *UK* 106
Bazm-e-Adab Manchester *UK* 14
Bazmi-i-Tafreeh *UK* 56
Beara Society *UK* 47
Beauftragte für Ausländerfragen *D* 200
Beaumont Leys Muslim Association *UK* 56
Bebe Nanki Gurdwara *UK* 106
Bedford Afro-Caribbean Self-Help
    Association *UK* 7
≡ Racial Equality Council *UK* 176
≡ Study Centre *UK* 56
≡ West Indian Club *UK* 125
Begegnungszentrum für aktive Gewaltlosig-
    keit *AT* 159
Behandlungszentrum für Folteropfer *D* 138
Belfast Hebrew Congregation *NI* 81
≡ Islamic Centre *NI* 73
≡ Law Centre *NI* 229
Belfast Travellers Association; Education &
    Development Group; Sites Project *NI* 118
Belgian Helsinki Committee *BE* 189
Belgian Red Cross *BE* 190
Belgisch Comité voor hulp aan de
    vluchtelingen *BE* 130
Belgische Hulp aan Verplaatste Personen
    BE 131
≡ Liga voor de Verdediging van de
    Rechten van de Mens *BE* 189
≡ Rode Kruis *BE* 190
Belgrave Baheno *UK* 14
Bellenden Advice Centre *UK* 220
Bellunesi nel Mondo *LX* 75
Benburb Base *UK* 47
Otto-Benecke-Stiftung *D* 236
Benefits Agency Overseas Branch *UK* 220
Bénévoles franco-maliens pour l'aide au
    développement de Samantara *F* 87
Bengali Association of the West Midlands;
    Community Education Project; Muslim
    Mosque & Community Centre; Women's
    Group; Workers' Action Group; Workers'
    Association *UK* 19
Beratungsstelle für Asylsuchende; der
    Hilfswerke für Asylsuchenden *CH* 152
Beratungsstelle/Beratungszentrum für
    Migrant/innen *AT* 129
Berichtenblad de Poort-Beraber *BE* 131
Berlin Institute for Comparative Social
    Research *D* 236
≡ Türk Bilim ve Teknoloji Merkezi; Türk
    Cemaati *D* 120

Berliner Gesellschaft Türkischer Mediziner
  D 120
  ≡ Institut für Vergleichende Sozial-
    forschung *D* 236
Berner Rechstberatungsstelle für
  Asylsuchende *CH* 152
Bethnal Green Asian Children & Women's
  Association *UK* 14
Bewegung für ein Offene, Demokratisch
  und Solidarische Schweiz *CH* 175
Bexley & Greenwich Campaign Against
  Fascism; Racial Equality Council *UK* 176
Bharat Sevaf Samaj; Bharatiya Vidya
  Bhavan *UK* 43
Bhatra Singh Sabha Sikh Temple *UK* 106
Bhavan *UK* 14
Bibini Centre for Young People *UK* 153
*Bibliographische Informationen zur
  Ethnizität und Migration D* 236
Bibliothèque Dien-Hong *F* 124
  ≡ Interuniversitaire de Lille *F* 233
Le Bibliotin F 233
Bijeen NL 171
Steve Biko Housing Association *UK* 20
Bilbao Casa Abierta; Bilbo Etxezabal *E* 149
*Bildungsarbeit mit Ausländische
  Jugendliche D* 140
Bildungswerk für Friedensarbeit *D* 200
Bioforce Développement *F* 196
Birkbeck College *UK* 243
Birmingham Anjumane Islam Trust *UK* 56
  ≡ Anti-Fascist Action *UK* 176
  ≡ Black Oral History Project *UK* 20
  ≡ Central Mosque *UK* 56
Birmingham Chinese Society; Youth
  Association; Youth Project *UK* 29
Birmingham City Council Race Relations
  Unit *UK* 176
  ≡ Development Education Centre *UK* 243
  ≡ Fellowship of Faiths; Inter-Faiths
    Council *UK* 176
  ≡ Irish Forum; Irish Welfare & Information
    Centre *UK* 47
  ≡ Islamia Allaouiazwya *UK* 73
  ≡ Mosque Trust *UK* 56
  ≡ Pakistani Scout Development Project;
    Pakistani Sports Forum *UK* 93
  ≡ Racial Attacks Monitoring Unit *UK* 176
Bishop Ho Ming Wah Association *UK* 29
Maurice Bishop Patriotic Movement *UK* 39
Biuró Eorpach do Teangacha Neamhshor-
  leathana *IR* 204
Black Action; Advice Workers Forum; Arts
  Alliance; Arts Network; & Asian Police
  Association *UK* 20
Black Beauty & Hair UK 20
Black Business Development Assoc. *UK* 20
  ≡ Businesses in Birmingham *UK* 6
  ≡ Children Counselling Project;
    Community Forum; Community Safety
    Project *UK* 20
  ≡ Cultural Archives *UK* 243
  ≡ Direct Action for Equal Rights & Justice;
    Elderly Group Southwark; Employment
    Institute; Environment Network *UK* 20
Black & Ethnic Minorities Research &
  Development Project; Minority Mental
  Health Development Team *UK* 243
Black Europe Concern; European Media
  Project; Family Coalition *UK* 20
  ≡ German Women *D* 19
Black HIV & AIDS Forum; Network; South
  East London *UK* 20
Black Housing UK 21
Black-Jewish Forum *UK* 176
Black-Led Churches Liaison *UK* 20
Black Lesbian & Gay Centre; Group *UK* 20
Black Mental Health Resource Centre;
  Migrant & Refugee Women's European
  Network *UK* 21
  ≡ & Minority Ethnic Victim Support
    Project *UK* 153
  ≡ Music Assoc.; People's Entertainment;
    Perspectives in Volunteering Group;
    Research Workers Network; Roof Housing
    Co-op; Socialist Society; Star Housing
    Assoc.; Theatre Co-operative; Training &
    Enterprise Group *UK* 21
Black Voices UK 21
Black Women & Europe Network; & Mental
  Health Group; for Wages for Housework
  UK 21
Black Women's Action Group; Co-
  operative; Creativity Project; Editorial &
  Consultancy Collective; Family Support
  Group; Group; Support Group *UK* 21
Black Workers' Association; Group *UK* 21
Black Youth & Community Workers
  Association; Movement *UK* 21
Blackburn Council of Mosques *UK* 56
  ≡ Ethnic Minority Development
    Association *UK* 176

Blackburn Irish Society *UK* 47
Blackburn Racial Equality Council *UK* 176
Blackfriars Advice Centre; Settlement
  Advice Centre *UK* 220
Blackheath Bangladesh Association *UK* 18
  ≡ Islamic Community Centre; Jamia
    Mosque *UK* 56
Blackley Anti-Racist Group *UK* 176
Blackliners *UK* 21
Blackpool Anti-Fascist Action *UK* 176
Blackpool Irish Society *UK* 47
Blackpool Islamic Community *UK* 56
Blakenhall Community Advice Centre
  UK 220
Blätter des iz3w D 237
blick nach rechts *D* 236
Blitz Infogroup *NR* 173
Blokbuster *BE* 160
Blue Danube Radio *AT* 187
B'Nai B'rith; Board of Deputies of British
  Jews *UK* 80
Board for Social Responsibility *UK* 220
Boat People Home Trust *UK* 124
Bohra Jamaat *UK* 40
Bokoura: Entraide et amitié *F* 87
Boletim Paroquial da Colónia D 100
Boletim de Vilar Formoso PR 148
Boletín de las Asociaciones Gitanas E 41
Heinrich-Böll-Stiftung *D* 200
Bolton Bangladesh Association *UK* 18
  ≡ Irish Community Association *UK* 47
  ≡ Muslim Community Association *UK* 56
  ≡ Racial Equality Council *UK* 176
  ≡ Somali Muslims *UK* 108
  ≡ Surti Sunni Vohra Muslim Assoc. *UK* 56
  ≡ West Indian Association *UK* 6
Ludwig-Boltzmann-Institut für Menschen-
  rechte *AT* 187
Bonner Institut für Faschismus-Forschung
  und Antifaschistische Aktion *D* 166
Books from India *UK* 43
Bordesley Green Mosque *UK* 56
Borough of Charnwood Community
  Relations Council *UK* 176
Bosnia & Herzegovina Fund of Britain;
  Project; Solidarity Campaign *UK* 23
Bosnian Advisory Centre; Students Appeal
  UK 23
Bournemouth Islamic Centre *UK* 56
Bournemouth & Poole Irish Society *UK* 47
Braca Romi *BH* 103
Bradford Anti-Fascist Action *UK* 176
  ≡ Bangladeshi Parishad *UK* 18
  ≡ Citizens Advice Bureau *UK* 220
  ≡ Concord Inter-Faith Society *UK* 176
  ≡ Council of Mosques; Khalifa Muslim
    Society *UK* 56
  ≡ Law Centre *UK* 220
  ≡ Muslim Welfare Society & Mosque
    UK 56
  ≡ Racial Equality Council *UK* 176
  ≡ Resource Centre *UK* 243
  ≡ Sikh Parents' Association *UK* 106
Brahma Kumaris Centre *UK* 42
Brasilieninitiative Freiburg *D* 23
Brazilian Arts & Community Centre;
  Support Centre *UK* 24
Breck *LX* 145
Breed Platform Tegen Racisme *NL* 170
Bref CRARDDA F 136
Brent Campaign Against Racial
  Discrimination *UK* 176
  ≡ Chinese Centre *UK* 29
  ≡ Community Law Centre *UK* 220
  ≡ Community Relations Council *UK* 176
  ≡ & Harrow Refugee Consortium *UK* 153
  ≡ Indian Association *UK* 43
Brent Irish Advisory Service; Cultural &
  Community Centre; Mental Health Group;
  Society; Women's Group *UK* 47
Brent Islamic Bureau *UK* 56
  ≡ Racial Equality Council *UK* 176
  ≡ Travellers Support Group *UK* 117
Bridges Project *UK* 21
Brief CH 218
Brighton Anti-Fascist Action *UK* 176
  ≡ Asian Circle *UK* 14
  ≡ Citizens Advice Bureau; Housing Trust
    Housing Aid & Legal Centre *UK* 220
  ≡ Irish Society *UK* 47
  ≡ Islamic Centre & Mosque *UK* 67
  ≡ Islamic Mission *UK* 56
  ≡ Rights Advice Centre *UK* 221
  ≡ Tibet Link *UK* 116
Bristol Anti-Fascist Action *UK* 176
  ≡ & Avon Black Dance Project *UK* 23
  ≡ & Avon Chinese Women's Group *UK* 29
  ≡ & Avon Muslim Association *UK* 56
  ≡ Black Business; Black Voluntary Sector
    Development Unit *UK* 21
  ≡ City Council Race Equality Unit *UK* 221
  ≡ Irish Society *UK* 47

Bristol Mosque Committee *UK* 56
  ≡ Racial Equality Council *UK* 177
  ≡ Roscommon Association *UK* 47
  ≡ Sikh Cultural Centre *UK* 106
Britain-Australia Society *UK* 16
  ≡ Cuba Resource Centre *UK* 31
  ≡ Nepal Society *UK* 91
  ≡-Russia Centre *UK* 103
  ≡ Turkish Committee *UK* 122
  ≡ Zimbabwe Society *UK* 127
British Academy *UK* 243
  ≡ Afro-Asian Solidarity Organisation
    UK 153
  ≡ Agencies for Adoption & Fostering
    UK 221
British Association for Canadian Studies
  UK 25
  ≡ for Central & Eastern Europe *UK* 33
  ≡ for Chinese Studies *UK* 29
  ≡ for Irish Studies *UK* 47
  ≡ for South Asian Studies *UK* 244
  ≡ for Soviet, Slavonic & East European
    Studies *UK* 244
British Bangla Alliance *UK* 19
  ≡ Bulgarian Friendship Society *UK* 24
  ≡ Coalition for East Timor *UK* 116
  ≡ Council *IR* 24, *UK* 221
  ≡ Council of Churches *UK* 222
  ≡ Historical Society of Portugal *PR* 24
  ≡ Hungarian Friendship Society; Indian
    Councillors Association *UK* 43
  ≡ Institute of Human Rights *UK* 244
  ≡ Institute in Paris *F* 24
  ≡ Institute of Persian Studies *UK* 45
  ≡ International Studies Association *UK* 244
  ≡ Irish Assoc.; Irish Rights Watch *UK* 47
  ≡ Islamic Academy *UK* 56
  ≡ Italian Society *UK* 76
*British Journal of Holocaust Education
  UK* 244
British Kashmir Group; Kashmiri
  Association *UK* 81
  ≡ Ladies Club of Luxembourg *LX* 24
  ≡ Malaysian Society *UK* 87
  ≡ Mexican Society *UK* 88
British Muslim Action Front; Assoc. *UK* 56
  ≡ Council; Engineers & Scientists
    Association; Forum; Solidarity *UK* 57
British Pakistani Muslim Welfare
  Association *UK* 93
British Red Cross UK 221
  ≡ Bosnian Refugee Programme *UK* 23
British Refugee Council *UK* 157
  ≡ Romanian Friendship Association *UK* 102
  ≡ Rommani Union *UK* 103
  ≡ School of Brussels *BE* 24
  ≡ Shia Muslim Action Committee *UK* 57
  ≡ Sikh Federation *UK* 106
  ≡ Sikh Punjabi Literary Society *UK* 101
  ≡ Uruguayan Society *UK* 123
British Workers' Association; Union *DK* 24
British Youth Council *UK* 221
  ≡ Yugoslav Society *UK* 126
  ≡ Zimbabwe Society *UK* 127
Brixton Black Women's Centre *UK* 21
  ≡ Circle Projects *UK* 153
  ≡ Law Centre *UK* 221
  ≡ Mosque *UK* 57
  ≡ Refugee Health Project *UK* 153
Broad African Representative Council *UK* 5
Broadfield Mosque *UK* 57
Broederlijk Delen BE 189
Bromley Asian Community Organisation;
  Muslim Council *UK* 14
  ≡ Racial Equality Council *UK* 177
Brot für Alle *CH* 217
Brot für Hungernde *AT* 187
Die Brücke AT 187, *D* 166
Bruff & District Society *UK* 47
Bruxelles Acceuil—Porte Ouverte *BE* 130
Building a Europe of Solidarity Together
  UK 221
BUKO Arbeitsschwerpunkt Rassismus und
  Flüchtlingspolitik *D* 166
Bulgarian Helsinki Committee *BG* 193
Bulgarian Society for Regional Cultural
  Studies *BG* 232
The Bulletin BE 24
Bulletin des Ateliers d'Ecriture F 136
Bulletin of Hispanic Studies UK 113
Bulletin of Latin American Research UK 85
Bulletin REPONSE F 236
Bund der Antifaschisten *D* 166
  ≡ Einwanderer/innen aus der Türken *D* 120
Bund Europäischer Jugend *AT* 187
  ≡ für Soziale Verteidigung *D* 138
  ≡ Sozialistische Freiheitskämpfer *AT* 159
  ≡ Spanische Elternvereine *D* 112
Bundesamt für die Anerkennung ausländ-
  ischer Flüchtling *D* 200
Bundesamt für Flüchtlinge *CH* 218
Bundesanstalt für Arbeit *D* 200, 237

Bundesarbeitsgemeinschaft der
Immigrantenverbände *D* 138
Bundesbeauftragte für Asylangelegen-
heiten; Ausländerfragen *D* 200
Bundesgrenzschutz; Bundesinnen-
ministerium; Bundeskongress Entwick-
lungspolitischer Aktionsgruppen *D* 200
Bundesverband der Arbeiterwohlfahrt
D 200
≡ Österreichischer Widerstandskämpfer
und Opfer der Faschismus *AT* 159
≡ Spanischer Jugend- und Schülervereine;
Spanischer Sozialer und Kultureller
Vereine *D* 112
Bündnis 90/Die Grünen—Referat für Asyl-
und Einwandererfragen *D* 138
≡ Türkischer Einwanderer *D* 120-1
Buntstift *D* 166
Bureau d'aide au départ/Immigration
CH 152
Bureau Européen pour les langues moins
répandues *IR* 204
Bureau International Afghanistan *F* 1
≡ de Liaison et de Documentation *F* 196
≡ du Travail *F* 196, *CH* 218
Bureau Internationale Arbeidsbemiddeling
en Stagiaires *NL* 208
≡ migrant en werk Rotterdam *NL* 145
≡ Rassendiscriminatie Lelystad *NL* 170
Bürgerhaus *D* 120
Bürgerinitiative SOS-Rassismus *D* 167
Bürgerrechte und Polizei *D* 236
Burhani Community Centre *UK* 57
Burma Action Group UK *UK* 25
Burnley Council of Mosques *UK* 57
≡ & Pendle Racial Equality Council *UK* 177
Büro für notwendige Einmischungen *D* 200
Buro voor Rechtshulp *NL* 208
Büro Jan-Philipp Reemtsma *D* 200
Bury Metro Racial Equality Council *UK* 177
Bury Park Masjid *UK* 57
Business in the Community *UK* 182

Cá e Lá *PR* 148
Cable Street Beat *UK* 177
CAFOD *UK* 221
Cahiers d'Action Familiale *F* 197
Les Cahiers du COFRIMI; *Les Cahiers du
CRESM*; *Cahiers d'Etudes* *F* 234
Cahiers de la Pastorale des Migrants *F* 137
Cairde; na nGael *UK* 47
An Caisleán *UK* 49
Calamus Foundation *UK* 57
Calderdale Racial Equality Council *UK* 177
Cambodia Trust *UK* 25
Cambridge Citizens Advice Bureau *UK* 221
≡ City Council Racial Harrassment
Service; Council of Christians & Jews
UK 177
≡ Ethnic Community Forum *UK* 153
≡ Inter-Faith Group *UK* 177
≡ Muslim Welfare Society & Mosque
UK 57
Camden Black Parents & Teachers Group;
Black Sisters *UK* 21
≡ Chinese Community Centre *UK* 29
≡ Community Law Centre *UK* 221
≡ Council Equalities Unit *UK* 177
≡ Cypriot Women's Group *UK* 31
≡ Health & Race Group *UK* 153
≡ Irish Centre *UK* 50
≡ Local Education Authority Social Work
Service *UK* 221
≡ Monitoring Project *UK* 19
≡ Racial Equality Council; Racial
Harassment Initiative *UK* 177
≡ Refugee Workers' Network *UK* 153
≡ Travellers Support Group *UK* 117
≡ United Asian Youth *UK* 14
≡ Unity *UK* 177
A Caminho *D* 99
Campaign Against Double Punishment;
Fascism in Europe *UK* 177
≡ Immigration Act Detentions *UK* 153
≡ the Immigration & Asylum Bill; Racism
& Fascism; Racist Laws *UK* 177
≡ Repression & for Democratic Rights in
Iraq *UK* 46
Campaign for Anti-Racist Education *UK* 177
≡ to Close Campsfield *UK* 153
≡ for Democratic Opposition in Iraq *UK* 46
≡ for Unauthorised Migrant Workers
UK 153
Campsfield Monitor *UK* 153
Campus Watch *UK* 177
Canadian American Overseas Association;
Women's Club *UK* 25
Canning Town Information Centre *UK* 221
≡ Islamic Centre; Mosque & Welfare
Association *UK* 57
Cantabria Acoge *E* 149

Canterbury Islamic Centre *UK* 57
Capellania della Comunità Etiope-Eritrea
IT 34
Capilla Británica *E* 24
Cara Irish Housing Association; *Cara
Newsletter* *UK* 47
A Caravana *PR* 40
Cardiff Anti-Fascist Action *UK* 177
≡ City Council Race & Housing Section
UK 221
≡ Interfaith Association *UK* 177
≡ Law Centre *UK* 221
≡ Law School *UK* 117
Cardinal Hume's Committee for the
Caribbean *UK* 26
CARE International *BE* 189
Care & Rehabilitation Centre *UK* 154
Careers Europe *UK* 244
Caribbean Centre; Communication Project;
Community Centre; Council for Europe
UK 26
≡ Crafts Circle; Cricket Club; Cultural
International; Development Project
Foundation *UK* 27
≡ Entry Refusal Action Group *UK* 155
≡ Golden Age Club; Heritage Group *UK* 27
Caribbean Insight *UK* 27
Caribbean Labour Solidarity; Links
Organisation; Pensioners & Friends;
Peoples Association *UK* 27
≡ Scandinavian Association *DK* 26
≡ Sunrise Social Club; Teachers
Association *UK* 27
Caribbean Times *UK* 27
Caribbean Women's Association *UK* 27
Carila Latin American Resource Centre
UK 84
Caritas *AT* 187
Caritas Aargau *CH* 153
≡ Danmark *DK* 194
≡ Diocesana *IT* 142, 205, *E* 213
Cáritas Diocesana de Lisboa *PR* 211
≡ Valencia, Departamento Migración *E* 213
Cáritas Española *E* 149, 151-2, 213
Caritas Europa *BE* 130
≡ Flüchtlingshilfe Zentralschweiz *CH* 152
≡ France *F* 199
≡ Genève *CH* 217
≡ Hellas *GR* 202
≡ Internationalis *V* 230
≡ Italiana *IT* 142, 205
≡ Jura *CH* 217
≡ Luxembourg *LX* 207
≡ Nederlandica/Mensen in Nood *NL* 208
≡ Österreich *AT* 187
≡ Romana *IT* 142
≡ Schweiz/Suisse *CH* 217
Cáritas—União de Caridade Portuguêsa
PR 211
Caritas Valais; Vaud *CH* 217
Carlisle Law Centre *UK* 221
Carn *UK* 47
Carrefour Chantiers *BE* 160
Carta de España *E* 151
Carta a los Padres *D* 112
Casa dell'Accoglienza Don Luigi Savarè;
Shalom *IT* 142
Casa Africana *PR* 4
≡ de Angola do Algarve *PR* 9
≡ do Brasil de Lisboa *PR* 24
≡ Chile *BE* 28
≡ de la Comunidad Hebrea de Madrid *E* 79
≡ della Cultura Islamica di Milano *IT* 54
≡ de España *F* 111
≡ de Goa *PR* 38
≡ de Moçambique *PR* 91
≡ de la Palabra, Centro de Africanos *E* 4
≡ Portuguêsa de Augsburg *D* 99
≡ Retruco Solidaridad con Argentina *E* 11
Casal Latinoamericano en Catalunya *E* 84
Roger Casement Irish Centre *UK* 47, 49
Catalunya Solidaria *E* 149
Catholic Agency for Overseas
Development *UK* 221
≡ Association for Racial Justice *UK* 177
≡ Bishops' Conference *UK* 154, 178
≡ Church, Emigrants Pastoral *UK* 154
≡ Institute for International Relations
UK 221
≡ Relief Services *IT* 205
≡ Union of Filipinos in Athens *GR* 35
Cavan Association *UK* 47
CBW Krant *BE* 130
CEFISEM Paris, Pour les Enfants de
Migrants *F* 135
CelsiuS *BE* 160, *F* 163
Celtic League *UK* 47
CEM/Mondialità *IT* 238
Center for Indvandrer- og Flygtningekvinder
DK 132
Center for Kulturforskning; for Peace &
Conflict Research *DK* 232

Centraal Beheer Joodse Weldadigheid en
Maatschappelijk Hulpbetoon *BE* 78
≡ Bureau voor Arbeidsvoorziening *NL* 208
≡ Bureau voor de Statistiek *NL* 240
Central Ahl-e-Sunnat wa Jamat *UK* 57
Central America Human Rights Committee;
Co-ordination *UK* 27
Central America Report *UK* 27
Central America Week; Women's Network
UK 27
Central Asian Research Centre *UK* 244
≡ British Fund for World Jewish Relief
UK 80
≡ Bureau for Educational Visits &
Exchanges *UK* 221
≡ Community Relations Unit *NI* 229
≡ European University *UK* 33
≡ Gurdwara *UK* 106
≡ Hanafiyah Mosque *UK* 63
≡ Jamia Masjid *UK* 57
≡ Latinoamericana de Trabajadores *NL* 84
≡ London Law Centre *UK* 221
≡ Mosque of Brent *UK* 57
≡ Office of Information *UK* 244
≡ Organisation of Finnish Trade Unions—
Youth Committee *SF* 195
≡ Race Equality Unit; Scotland Racial
Equality Council *UK* 177
≡ Valmik Sabha Ashram *UK* 42
Centrale Opvang Asielzoekers;
Vluchtelingen *NL* 145
Centre M. Abdelkrim El Khatabi d'Estudis i
Documentació *E* 87
≡ d'Acceuil Foyer Molenbeek; d'Acceuil
pour les Travailleurs Migrants *BE* 131
≡ d'Acol.liment per Africans Sant Pau *E* 4
≡ d'action sociale et d'acceuil franco-
portugais *F* 98
≡ d'Alphabétisation pour Travailleurs
Immigrés *BE* 130
Centre d'Animation pour Femmes d'Origine
Etrangère *F* 135
≡ des Italiens de la Basse-Sambre *BE* 73
≡ Johary Ravalson Projets Culturels *F* 233
Centre pour l'Anthropologie Sociale et
Culturelle *BE* 232
≡ for Anti-Racist Education & Anti-Racist
Strategies *UK* 177
≡ d'Appui Social et Associatif *LX* 100
≡ for Arab Gulf Studies *UK* 11
≡ Arabe d'Accueil et d'Information *BE* 10
≡ Arabe de l'Art et de la Littérature *BE* 10
≡ for Armenian Information & Advice
UK 12
≡ for Asian Women *UK* 14
≡ Avaroes *E* 90
≡ Belgo-Maghrébin d'Expression et de
Communication 'Mosaïque' *BE* 86
≡ for Black & White Christian Partnership
UK 244
≡ Bruxellois d'Action Interculturelle *BE* 231
≡ for Caribbean Studies *UK* 244
≡ Catalá de Luxembourg *LX* 27
≡ for Citizens Europe & Human Rights
F 196
≡ de Contact Suisse-Immigrés *CH* 175
≡ for Contemporary Studies *UK* 244
≡ de Culture et d'Information sur le
Monde Arabe *F* 10
≡ de Culture Japonaise *BE* 78
Centre culturel africain *F* 3
≡ Arabe Syrien *F* 114
≡ et Artistique France-Grèce *F* 38
≡ Assyro-Chaldéen *BE* 16
≡ Belgique Chine *BE* 28
≡ Catholique Italien *LX* 75
≡ Chinois *F* 28
≡ Egyptien *F* 33
≡ Espagnol; Espagnol La Bigorre *F* 111
≡ franco-chinois *F* 28
≡ Franco-Espagnol *F* 111
≡ Grec *BE* 38
≡ Indo-Français *F* 43
≡ Irlandais *F* 46
≡ Islamique *LX* 54
≡ Italien *BE* 73
≡ A.S. Pouchkine *LX* 103
≡ et récréatif hispano-français *F* 111
≡ et Sportif Albanais *BE* 8
≡ et Sportif Espagnol *F* 111
Centre Culturel Yougoslave *F* 126
≡ des Cultures Méditérranéennes *F* 163
Centre de Documentation et d'Animation
Interculturelles *LX* 239
≡ et d'Information contre le Racisme et
pour l'Egalité des Droits *F* 163
≡ Internationale sur le Développement, les
Libertés et la Paix *F* 233
≡ Italien *BE* 73
Centre de Documentation et de Recherche
sur la Civilisation Khmère *F* 82
≡ for Documentation on Refugees *CH* 243

Centre des Droits de l'Homme *F* 196
≡ d'Education Permanente et des Loisirs
  des Immigrés de Burenville *BE* 130
≡ pour l'Egalité des Chances et pour la
  Lutte contre le Racisme *BE* 160
≡ for Equality & Discrimination *UK* 244
Centre Espagnol *BE* 110, *F* 111
≡ culturel et récréatif *F* 112
≡ de Formation et d'Action; El Guión
  BE 110
≡ d'Estudis Africans *E* 4
Centre d'Etude du Développement de
  l'Ethnicité et des Migrations *BE* 231
≡ de la Population et de la Famille *BE* 232
≡ des Sociétés du Commonwealth et des
  Iles Britanniques *F* 233
Centre d'Etudes d'Amérique Latine *BE* 83
≡ Anti-Impérialistes *F* 233
≡ et de Documentation Sociale *BE* 231
≡ Historiques sur la Méditerranée
  Contemporaine; sur les Migrations et les
  Relations Interculturelles; de l'Orient
  Contemporain *F* 233
≡ sur le Racisme et le Fascisme *F* 163
≡ et de Recherches Amazigh *F* 118
Centre d'Etudes et de Recherches sur la
  Culture Italienne Contemporaine *F* 74
≡ sur l'Innovation Sociale et Educative
  F 233
≡ Internationales; sur l'Orient Arabe
  Contemporain; sur les Relations
  Interethniques et les Minorités *F* 234
Centre pour l'Europe des Citoyens et des
  Droits de l'Homme *F* 196
≡ Europe-Tiers Monde *CH* 175
≡ Européen *AT* 231
≡ Européen 'Travail et Société' *NL* 240
≡ Familial Belgo-Immigrés *BE* 130
≡ pour les Familles des Travailleurs
  Etrangers *BE* 130
≡ Féminin d'Education Permanente *BE* 189
Centre de Formation et d'Education
  Familiale *BE* 189
≡ des Etangs Noirs *BE* 130
≡ et d'Information pour la Scolarisation
  des Enfants Migrants *F* 234
≡ pour l'insertion économique et sociale et
  l'aide aux mutations *F* 196
Centre France Asie *F* 12
≡ for German-Jewish Studies *UK* 244
≡ des Hautes Etudes sur l'Afrique et l'Asie
  Modernes *F* 234
≡ Hellénique de Culture et de Formation
  BE 38
≡ Hispano-Français *F* 111
≡ for Holocaust Studies *UK* 244
≡ d'Immigration de Charleroi; des
  Immigrés; des Immigrés Namur-
  Luxembourg *BE* 130
≡ for Indian Studies *UK* 43
Centre d'Informació i Documentació
  Internacionals a Barcelona *E* 242
≡ per Treballadors Estrangers *E* 149
Centre d'Information et de Développement
  de la Vie Sociale *BE* 232
≡ sur les Droits de la Femme *F* 196
≡ et d'Echanges de Jeunes *LX* 207
≡ et d'Etudes sur les Migrations
  Internationales *F* 234
≡ Guadeloupe, Guyane, Martinique *F* 36
Centre for Information on Language
  Teaching & Research *UK* 244
≡ d'Information sur les Pratiques
  Associatives *BE* 231
≡ d'Information Tiers Monde *LX* 169
≡ d'Initiation pour Réfugiés et Etrangers;
  d'Intégration pour Migrants *BE* 130
≡ interassociatif francophone
  d'information et de documentation sur le
  droit d'asile et les réfugiés *F* 234
≡ Interculturel de Documentation;
  Interculturel Rencontre *F* 163
≡ pour l'Interculturalisme et Recherche sur
  Migrations *BE* 232
≡ Interdisciplinaire Méditerranéen d'Etudes
  et de Recherches en Sciences Sociales
  F 234
≡ Internacional Escarré per a Minories
  Etniques i les Nacions *E* 150
≡ International *BE* 160
≡ International des Avocats *F* 196
≡ for International Briefing *UK* 177
≡ International pour Etudiants Etrangers
  BE 130
≡ for International Mobility *SF* 233
≡ for International Studies *UK* 177
≡ for Islamic Studies *UK* 57
Centre Islamique *BE* 52
≡ pour les Travailleurs Marocains *BE* 88
Centre for Japanese Studies *UK* 78
≡ Jeunes de Cluys *BE* 160
≡ pour Jeunes Migrants *BE* 130

Centre for Jewish Culture *PL* 79
≡ for Korean Studies *UK* 82
≡ for Latin American Studies *UK* 84
≡ Lusophile de Bourges *F* 98
≡ for Middle Eastern & Islamic Studies
  UK 244
≡ Mouvement Ouvrier Chrétien de
  Charleroi *BE* 130
≡ for Multicultural Education *UK* 177
Centre national de documentation
  pédagogique *F* 234
≡ d'Information et de Documentation des
  Femmes et des Familles *F* 196
≡ de la recherche scientifique *F* 234
Centre Nord-Sud *PR* 211
≡ d'orientation sociale *F* 135
≡ Parisien d'Education de Tamouls *F* 115
≡ de Pastorale Familiale *LX* 207
≡ Pastorale en Monde du Travail—Secteur
  Immigration *LX* 145
≡ pédagogique juif de diffusion et
  documentation *F* 79
Centre de Recherche et de Documentation
  sur l'Immigration; sur l'Histoire des
  Mouvements Sociaux *F* 234
≡ d'Information et de Documentation
  Antiraciste *F* 163
Centre pour la Recherche Interdisciplinaire
  sur le Développement *F* 163
Centre de Recherches et d'Etudes sur les
  Sociétés Méditerranéennes; et d'Infor-
  mations des Africains et Arabes; Inter-
  culturelles de Finistère; Migratoires *F* 234
≡ Tsiganes *F* 40
Centre Régionale de Préformation des
  Migrants en Languedoc-Roussillon *F* 135
≡ de Relations Internationales du Finistère
  F 234
≡ for Religious Learning & Instruction
  UK 63
Centre for Research & Documentation
  NI 247
≡ in Ethnic Relations *UK* 244
≡ in International Migration & Ethnic
  Relations *S* 243
Centre de sécurité sociale des travailleurs
  migrants *F* 196
≡ de Service de la Docherie *BE* 10
≡ 70 Advice Centre *UK* 220
Centre Social et Culturel Africain *BE* 2
≡ Protestant *CH* 217
≡ protestant—Service oecuménique
  auprès des réfugiés *BE* 130
Centre Socio-Culturel des Immigrés de
  Bruxelles *BE* 231
≡ des Immigrés de Namur *BE* 130
≡ Le Toit du Monde *F* 163
Centre de Sociologie et d'Economie
  Régionale *BE* 232
≡ de l'Islam *BE* 52
Centre de solidarité et de fraternité franco-
  indochinois *F* 110
≡ for South Asian Studies *UK* 244
≡ for Southern African Studies *UK* 110
≡ Sportif, Social, Culturel et Récréatif des
  Portugais de Vierzon *F* 98
Centre for the Study of Conflict *NI* 247
≡ Islam & Christian-Muslim Relations
  UK 57
≡ Judaism & Jewish-Christian Relations
  UK 80
≡ Migration & Intercultural Relations
  PR 241
≡ Minorities *UK* 246
≡ Public Order *UK* 244
Centre pour Travailleurs Etrangers *BE* 130
≡ des Travailleurs Marocains *BE* 88
≡ Tricontinental *BE* 232
≡ Universitaire de Recherches et de
  Documentation sur les Migrants *F* 234
≡ for World Development Education
  UK 177
Centrepoint *UK* 5
Centro de Acción Social San Rafael *E* 90
Centro di Accoglienza; Don Bosco per
  Giovani Stranieri; e Cultura Immigrati
  Stranieri; Extracomunitari; Immigrati
  Esteri; Sociale Territoriale; Straniere; per
  Studenti Esteri *IT* 142
Centro Accoglimento *IT* 142
Centro de Acogida de Inmigrantes *E* 150
≡ Quisqueya *E* 32
≡ a Refugiados *E* 213
≡ Santa Luisa de Marillac *E* 31
Centro Acolhimento *PR* 211
≡ Assistência Religiosa *E* 101
≡ e Integração Social *PR* 148
Centro di Aiuto alla Vita Mangiagalli *IT* 142
≡ Alegría Belfort *F* 111
≡ di Animazione Italiano *BE* 73
≡ de Apoio à Reinserção de Emigrantes
  PR 148

Centro de Apoio Social e Assistência
  LX 100
≡ Argentino de Asturias *E* 11
Centro d'Ascolto Amico in Più; per la
  Prevenzione del Disagio Psicologico degli
  Immigrati *IT* 142
Centro Assistencial e Recreativo *LX* 100
≡ Assistenza Capoverdiani *IT* 26
≡ di Assistenza agli Emigrati *IT* 142
≡ Associazioni Immigrati in Italia *IT* 143
≡ de Atención Socio-Sanitario al
  Inmigrante *E* 151
≡ di Azione Soziale Italiana, Università
  Operaia *BE* 73
≡ Católico Português *UK* 101
Centro Collegamento per i Diritti degli
  Immigrati; sull'Immigrazione dall'Estero
  IT 142
Centro Comunità Araba *IT* 10
≡ Cubano de España *E* 31
Centro Cultural Africano Mabana *E* 4
≡ Brasileiro *PR* 24
≡ Español *F* 111
≡ de Guinea Ecuatorial *E* 33
≡ Hispano-Francés *E* 36
≡ Ismaelita *PR* 54
≡ Português *D* 99
≡ y Recreativo Español *F* 111
≡ y Recreativo Real Madrid *LX* 113
≡ Os Tondolenses *LX* 100
Centro Culturale Internazionale Giovanni
  XXIII *IT* 168
≡ Islamico in Italia *IT* 54
≡ Italia-Iran *IT* 45
≡ Italiano *LX* 75
≡ Italo-Arabo *IT* 10
≡ Nelson Mandela *IT* 3
Centro de Defensa de los Refugiados *E* 150
≡ Defensa de los Refugiados Iraníes *E* 45
≡ Documentación de las Naciones Unidas
  E 242
Centro di documentazione contro il
  razzismo—Gridalo Forte *IT* 168
≡ Documentazione Migratoria *D* 74
≡ Documentazione Oscar Romero *IT* 84
≡ Ecclesiale Italiano America Latina *IT* 84
≡ Educazione alla Mondialità *IT* 238
≡ di Emigrazione *IT* 142
≡ de Encuentro y Acogida El Cobre *E* 31
Centro Español *BE* 110, *F* 111-2
≡ Cultural y Recreativo *F* 112
≡ de Estudios de América Latina *E* 84
≡ de Formación y Acción *BE* 110
Centro Estatal de Documentación e
  Información de Servicios Sociales *E* 242
≡ de Servicio Social de Asilados y
  Refugiados *E* 213
Centro de Estudios Africanos *E* 4
≡ Salvador Allende *E* 28
≡ y Solidaridad con América Latina y
  Africa *E* 242
Centro de Estudos Africanos; Africanos e
  Asiáticos; e Documentação Europeia
  PR 241
≡ da Emigração *LX* 100
≡ das Migrações e das Relações
  Interculturais; Sociais *PR* 241
Centro Europa per la Scuola Educazione
  Società *IT* 238
≡ Europeo Trabajo y Sociedad *E* 242
≡ Europeu de Formção e Estudos sobre as
  Migrações *PR* 241
≡ Galego *UK* 113
≡ Guía para Inmigrantes y Refugiados
  E 150
≡ Immigrati ICAS *IT* 142
≡ de Informação e Documentação Amilcar
  Cabral *PR* 241
Centro de Información y Acogida *E* 150
≡ Cultural de Colombia *E* 30
≡ y Documentación Africanas *E* 4
≡ y Orientación para la Mujer
  Iberoamericana Refugiada, Asilada o
  Inmigrante *E* 84
≡ para Trabajadores Extranjeros; para
  Trabajadores Migrantes *E* 150
Centro Informazione sui Detenuti Stranieri
  IT 142
≡ e Educazione allo Sviluppo *IT* 168
≡ sulla mobilità e le equivalenze
  accademiche *IT* 205
≡ Terzo Mondo *IT* 168
Centro per Iniziative Popolari di Solidarietà
  Internazionale *IT* 168
Centro de Inmigrantes Al Manzil;
  Fuenlabrada; Majadahonda para Mujeres;
  de Móstoles; Refugiados y Asilados *E* 150
≡ Interafricano de Iniciativas Culturales *E* 4
≡ de Intercambio Cultural Argentino-
  Catalán *E* 11
Centro Internazionale di Accoglienza *IT* 143
≡ di Cooperazione allo Sviluppo *IT* 205

Centro Internazionale Crocevia *IT* 168
≡ Scambi Culturali—Accoglienza
Immigrati; per gli Studenti *IT* 143
Centro de Intervención Sociológica *E* 242
Centro de Investigaciones y Promoción
Iberoamérica-Europa *E* 84
≡ sobre la Realidad Social; Sociológicas
E 242
Centro Islamico *IT* 54
≡ Islámico; Islámico para España *E* 54
≡ Islamico Torino *IT* 54
≡ Israelita de Portugal *PR* 79
≡ Italiano di Formazione Europea *IT* 238
≡ Juventud y Europa *E* 214
≡ La Pira *IT* 143
≡ Latinoamericano *E* 84
Centro Lavoratori Immigrati; Stranieri;
Stranieri Immigrati; Stranieri in Italia *IT* 143
Centro Jerry Masslo *IT* 89
≡ Migranti *IT* 143
≡ Missionario Pontificio Istituto Missioni
Estere *IT* 205
≡ Multiculturale Internazionale *IT* 168
≡ Norte-Sud *PR* 211
≡ Pastorale dell'Emigrazione Polacca *IT* 96
≡ de Polacos *E* 96
Centro Português *D* 99, *E* 101
≡ de Marburg; de Mittenburg; de
Osnabrück *D* 99
≡ de Roterdão *NL* 101
≡ no Taunus *D* 99
Centro di Prima Accoglienza; di Prima
Accoglienza per Extracomunitari *IT* 143
≡ Raccolta Profughi Stranieri *IT* 143, 205
≡ Regional de Segurança Social *PR* 116,
211
Centro Regionale di Assistenza e Tutela
degli Emigrati *IT* 143, *UK* 76
≡ Migrantes *IT* 143
Centro per le Relazioni Italo-Arabe *IT* 10
≡ Ricreativo e Culturale Estere *IT* 143
≡ Rural Familiar Migrante *E* 150
≡ Russia Ecumenica *IT* 103
≡ Santa Isabel *E* 32
≡ Scalabrini *UK* 76
Centro Servizi per Cittadini Extracomunitari
IT 143
≡ Stranieri di Santa Maria della
Consolazione *IT* 143
Centro Social e Cultural Português *LX* 100
≡ Luso Venezuelano *PR* 123
Centro Sociocultural María Inmaculada;
San Agustín *E* 90
Centro di Solidarietà Internazionale
Lavoratori; per Lavoratori e Studenti
Stranieri *IT* 143
≡ San Martino *IT* 168
Centro Studi Emigrazione Roma;
Investimenti Sociali; Mediterranei;
Scalabriniani; Terzo Mondo *IT* 239
≡ Zingari Romano Sicharimesko Than *IT* 40
Centro Sun Yat Sen *E* 29
≡ Sviluppo Terzo Mondo *IT* 168
≡ Terzo Mondo Documentazione e
Informazione *IT* 239
≡ União Portuguêses *LX* 100
Centrum voor Bevolkings en Gezinsstudien
BE 232
≡ Buitenlanders Midden-Nederland;
Buitenlanders West-Brabant *NL* 146
≡ voor Buitenlandse Arbeidersgezinnen;
Buitenlandse Werknemers *BE* 130
Centrum voor Etnische Gelijkheid *BE* 160
≡ Minderheden en Gezondheid *BE* 232
Centrum Gezondheidszorg Vluchtelingen
NL 147
Centrum voor Informatie en Documentatie
over Israël *NL* 73
≡ en Samenlevingsopbouw *BE* 232
Centrum Integratie Migranten *BE* 130
≡ voor Interculturalisme en Migratie-
onderzoek *BE* 232
≡ Internationale Samenwerking *NL* 170
≡ for Invandringsforskning *S* 243
≡ Jonge Migranten Jongerenwerk *BE* 130
≡ Marokkaanse Arbeiders *BE* 88
≡ voor Onderzoek van Maatschappelijke
Tegenstellingen *NL* 240
≡ Ontwikkeling der Volkeren *NL* 170
≡ voor Sociale en Culturele Antropologie
BE 232
Cercle africain des entrepreneurs de France
F 3
≡ franco allemand *F* 37
≡ Italo-Luxembourgeois *LX* 75
≡ suédois et norvégien *F* 104
Chapelle Orthodoxe Grècque de la Ste-
Trinité et St-Côme et Damien *BE* 38
Charlestown & District Society *UK* 47
Charlton Mosque *UK* 57
Charnwood Community Relations Council
UK 176

Charta 91 *BE* 189
Charter '87; Charter 88 *UK* 221
Chashma-e-Rahmat Mosque *UK* 57
Chatham House *UK* 246
Cheetham Asian Girls Project; Asian
Women's Association *UK* 12
≡ Electronic Village *UK* 21
Chelsea Citizens Advice Bureau *UK* 221
Chesham Racial Equality Council *UK* 177
Chesterfield Community Relations Steering
Committee *UK* 177
≡ Law Centre *UK* 221
≡ Muslim Association; Muslim Women
Welfare Group *UK* 57
Chien-Huu—Association pour la vulgar-
isation de la culture vietnamienne *F* 124
Chiesa Americana *IT* 123
≡ Bulgara *IT* 24
≡ Cilena *IT* 28
≡ Croata *IT* 31
≡ Etiope *IT* 34
≡ Francese *IT* 36
≡ Inglese *IT* 24
≡ Nazionale Germanica *IT* 37
≡ Portoghese e Capoverdiana *IT* 26
≡ Spagnola *IT* 112
≡ Tedesca *IT* 37
≡ Ungherese *IT* 43
≡ Vietnamita *IT* 124
Child Migrants Trust *UK* 154
Children's International Summer Villages;
Legal Centre *UK* 221
Childright *UK* 221
Chile Democrático *UK* 28
Chilean Society *UK* 28
Chilensk-Dansk Solidaritetsforening *DK* 28
China Magazine *UK* 30
China Appeal; Cultural Funds *UK* 29
China Quarterly *UK* 29
China Society *UK* 29
Chinese Advisers Forum; Arts Centre; Arts
For All; Association; Christian Fellowship;
Community Association; Community
Centre *UK* 29
Chinese Community Newsletter *UK* 29
Chinese Cultural Centre; Cultural
Development Centre; Education, Culture
& Community Centre; Health Information
Centre; Information & Advice Centre;
Information Centre Co-op; Mental Health
Association; Professional Association;
Solidarity Campaign *UK* 29
≡ Welfare Association *NI* 30
Chinese Women's Domestic Violence
Helpline; Group; Refuge Group; Research
& Health Project *UK* 29
Christelijk Nationaal Vakverbond Jongeren-
organisatie *NL* 208
≡ Secretariaat Buitenlandse Werknemers
NL 146
Christian Action; Aid *UK* 221
≡ Aid Ireland *IR* 203
≡ Coptic Refugees Group *UK* 114
≡ Movement for Peace *BE* 189
≡ Outreach *UK* 221
Christians Against Racism & Fascism; for
Europe *UK* 177
Christlich-Islamische Begegnung
Dokumentationsleitstelle *D* 166
Christlicher Friedensdienst—Flüchtlingshilfe
CH 152
Chronique de la LDH *BE* 191
Church of Denmark Council on Inter-
Church Relations *DK* 194
≡ of England *UK* 220, 222
≡ of God of Prophecy *UK* 221
≡ Missionary Society Ireland *IR* 203
Church & Race *UK* 177
Church of Sweden Mission *S* 216
Churches' Commission for Migrants in
Europe *BE* 130, *UK* 154
≡ for Racial Justice *UK* 177
CID Vietnam Association *F* 124
Cigány Ház *H* 40
CILIP Informationsdienst *D* 236
Il Circolo *BE* 73
Circolo Amici dell'Unità *LX* 75
≡ Campani nel Mondo *UK* 76
≡ Culturale Africa Insieme *IT* 3
Circolo Culturale e Ricreativo Eugenio
Curiel; Italiano Antonio Gramsci *LX* 75
Circolo Alcide de Gasperi *LX* 75
≡ degli Italiani *DK* 74
≡ Latino-Americano *IT* 84
≡ Plotter ARCI Nova *IT* 143
≡ Politico-Culturale Gramsci *UK* 77
≡ Sardu d'Europa *LX* 75
≡ di Taranto *IT* 144
≡ Terzo Mondo *IT* 168
≡ Trentino di Gran Bretagna *UK* 77
≡ Vicentini del Lussemburgo *LX* 75
Círculo Cultural Antonio Machado *LX* 113

Círculo Gallego *DK* 111
Citizens' Advice Bureau—Scotland *UK* 222
≡ Advice Bureaux *UK* 220
≡ Movement Against Racism *GR* 168
≡ Rights Office *UK* 222
Le citoyen; Citoyen et Citoyenne '89 *F* 163
Le Citoyen Européen *BE* 190
Civic Link Center for Human Rights *SV* 212
Civil Liberties Trust *UK* 225
≡ Rights Advice & Support Group;
Rights—UK *UK* 222
Civitas—Associação da Defesa e Promoção
dos Direitos dos Cidadaos *PR* 211
Claiming the Inheritance *UK* 154
Clann na hEireann *UK* 47
Clare Association *UK* 48
Cleveland Anti-Fascist Action; Racial
Equality Council *UK* 178
Clondalkin Travellers Development Group
IR 117
Clonfert Society *UK* 48
Club Afrique-France *F* 3
≡ Amicale des Sénégalais *IT* 105
≡ degli Amici *DK* 74
≡ de Amigos de la UNESCO *E* 174
≡ Belgo-Español F. García Lorca *BE* 110
≡ Británico *E* 24
≡ CB Amizade *LX* 100
≡ Cheoil *UK* 48
≡ de Culture et Danse Hélléniques *LX* 39
≡ des Etudiants Tunisiens en France *F* 118
≡ Europe Maghreb *F* 86
≡ Italia *UK* 77
≡ Italiano *IR* 75
≡ des jeunes portugais; portugais Camões
F 98
≡ Recherches, Perspectives, Expressions
et Sociétés *F* 163
≡ de réflexion sur l'immigration, la
démocratie et l'intégration *F* 234
≡ des Travailleurs Portugais de Liège *BE* 97
≡ Yougoslave Bratstvo-Jedinstvo *F* 126
Clube Desportivo Português de Antuérpia
BE 97
≡ de Empresários do Brasil *PR* 24
≡ Juvenil Português *F* 98
≡ Marítimo Africano de Lisboa *PR* 4
Clube dos Trabalhadores Portuguêses de
Liège; 25 de abril *BE* 97
Clwyd Latin America Human Rights Group
UK 84
Coalition for East Timor *UK* 116
Cobden Trust *UK* 225
Cobridge Multicultural Project *UK* 178
Coda International Training *UK* 244
Colaboramos *E* 84
Coláiste na nGael *F* 46
Colectivo Ioe; de Migraciones *E* 242
Collaboratrici Familiari *IT* 205
Collectif d'Acceuil aux Réfugiés du Chili
BE 28
≡ d'Accueil pour les Solliciteurs d'Asile à
Strasbourg *F* 135
≡ Africain de Solidarité *F* 3
≡ d'Alphabétisation *BE* 189, *F* 196
≡ Anti-Raciste et Anti-Fasciste de la
Sarthe; Anti-Raciste de Corse *F* 163
Collectif d'Etudes et de Dynamisation de
l'Emigration Portugaise *F* 98
≡ et de Recherches sur le Fascisme *F* 234
Collectif Féministe contre le Racisme *F* 163
Collectif des Femmes *BE* 189
≡ contre la Double Peine *F* 136
Collectif Haïti de France *F* 41
≡ Havrais contre le Racisme et pour
l'Egalité des Droits; Tiers Monde
intercommunal; Vivre Ensemble *F* 163
Collegamento *IT* 142
Collegamento Iniziative Ecclesiale per
l'Immigrazione dell'Italia Settentrionale
IT 143
Collège des Irlandais *F* 46
Collegio Universitario Aspiranti Medici
Missionari *IT* 239
Colombia Committee for Human Rights;
Solidarity Committee *UK* 30
Colombian Refugee Association *UK* 30
Colonia Española de Béziers *F* 112
Colori *IT* 168
Comber Romanian Orphanage Appeal
Ireland *N* 102
Comhairle Naisiúnta na nOíge *IR* 204
Comhaltas Ceoltóirí Eireann *LX* 46, *UK* 48
Comhlámh *IR* 168
Comisaría General de Documentación *E* 214
Comisión Católica Española de Migración
E 150
≡ Católica de Justicia y Paz *E* 214
≡ de las Comunidades Europeas *E* 214
≡ de Derechos Humanos de Guatemala
E 39
≡ Diocesana de Justicia y Paz *E* 214

Comisión Diocesana de Migración; Episcopal de Migraciones; Española de Ayuda al Refugiado *E* 150
≡ Española de Cooperación con la Unesco *E* 214
≡ de Intercambio Cultural entre España y Estados Unidos *E* 123
Comisiones Obreras *LX* 113, *E* 149-150, 214
Comisiwn dros Gydraddoldeb Hiliol *UK* 222
Comissão Caboverdiana de Setubal *PR* 26
≡ das Comunidades Europeias *PR* 211
≡ Cultural e Recreativa de Bruselas *BE* 97
≡ Episcopal de Migrações *PR* 148
Comissão Pró-Associação Caboverdiana do Algarve; do Porto; do Seixal *PR* 26
Comitati Tricolori Italiani nel Mondo *D* 74
Comitato Cile *IT* 28
≡ di Coordinamento delle Associazione Italo-Scozzesi *UK* 77
≡ Culturale Italiano *D* 74
≡ per la Difesa dei Diritti degli Immigrati *IT* 143
≡ dell'Emigrazione Italiana *IR* 75, *LX* 76
≡ Intergovernativo per le Migrazione Europei *IT* 206
≡ degli italiani all'Estero; Italiano di Assistenza *LX* 76
≡ Italiano Giovanile per le Relazione Internazionale *IT* 205
≡ Italiano per lo Studio dei Problemi della Popolazione *IT* 239
≡ Italiano per l'UNICEF *IT* 168
≡ Chico Mendes *IT* 169
≡ Profughi Esteri *IT* 143
≡ dei Profughi Polacchi *IT* 96
≡ Rifugiati Politici Antifascisti *IT* 143
≡ dei Russi in Italia *IT* 103
Comitato Scolastico per l'Assistenza e l'Istruzione degli Immigrati; Italiano *LX* 76
Comitato Senegalese in Toscana *IT* 105
≡ Tunisino *IT* 119
Comité voor Aanbeveling van Oud Verzetsdeelnemers *NL* 171
≡ d'Accueil Régional des Apatrides, Réfugiés et Déplacés *F* 135
≡ d'Action Sociale en faveur des Travailleurs Migrants *F* 136
Comité d'aide exceptionelle aux intellectuels réfugiés *F* 136
≡ aux maghrébins agés en France *F* 86
≡ aux Réfugiés *F* 136
Comité d'appel pour le droit d'asile *BE* 130
≡ d'assistance italien *F* 74
≡ Belge d'Aide aux Réfugiés *BE* 130
≡ Belge pour l'UNICEF *BE* 189
≡ Catholique contre la Faim et pour le Développement *F* 136
≡ de coordination africaine pour la démocratie *F* 3
≡ de Defensa de los Refugiados, Asilados e Inmigrantes en España *E* 150
≡ pour la Défense des Droits de l'Homme en Pays-Basque *F* 18
≡ de Défense des Droits Politiques en Turquie *F* 120
≡ pour la Défense des Libertés Démocratiques et des Droits de l'Homme en Syrie *F* 115
≡ pro Derechos Humanos en Cuba *E* 31
≡ d'Entraide Khmère de Bordeaux *F* 82
≡ Europa-Nicaragua *BE* 91
≡ Européen pour la Défense des Réfugiés et des Immigrés *F* 163, *CH* 175
≡ Exterior Mapuche *UK* 28
≡ des Femmes Arabes Immigrées *F* 10
≡ Flamand de Reflexion sur les Migrations *BE* 132
≡ France-Colombie pour les Droits de l'Homme *F* 30
≡ France-Irlande *F* 46
≡ France-Nicaragua *F* 91
≡ Herdenking Februaristaking 1941 *NL* 171
≡ Illegalen Zondebok *NL* 146
≡ Inter-Africain sur les pratiques traditionelles ayant effet sur la santé des femmes et des enfants *CH* 5
≡ Intergouvernemental auprès des Evacués *F* 136
≡ Intergovernamental para as Migrações *PR* 212
≡ Intergubernamental para las Migraciones *E* 215
≡ Internacional de Rescate *E* 214
Comité International d'Auschwitz *BE* 160
≡ des Camps *AT* 231
≡ de Coopération dans les Recherches Nationales en Démographie *F* 234
≡ d'Entraide Humanitaire pour la Population Khmère *F* 25
≡ Sachsenhausen *F* 163
≡ de soutien aux intellectuels algériens *F* 9
≡ pour un Vietnam Libre *BE* 124

Comité des Israélites de l'Algérois *F* 79
≡ des jeunes de Vénissieux *F* 53
≡ juif d'action sociale et de reconstruction *F* 79
≡ de Kurdistan *F* 82
≡ des Laïcs Vietnamiens de la Diaspora *F* 124
≡ Latinoamericano *E* 84
Comité de Liaison et d'Action des Etrangers *LX* 145
≡ d'Alphabétisation pour la Promotion *F* 136
≡ des Centres de Formation Immigrée de l'Agglomération de Bruxelles *BE* 130
≡ Inter Service Migrants Auvergne *F* 137
≡ pour la Promotion des Migrants *F* 136
Comité de Lutte Anti-fasciste *F* 163
≡ Luxembourgeoise pour l'UNICEF *LX* 207
≡ médical pour les exilés; Médico-Social pour la Santé des Migrants *F* 136
Comité national d'acceuil *BE* 130
≡ des Associations de Jeunesse et d'Education Populaire *F* 196
≡ contre la Double Peine *F* 136
≡ d'entraide franco-cambodgien, franco-laotien et franco-vietnamien *F* 110
≡ des réunionais *F* 102
Comité Nicaraguayen des Droits de l'Homme *BE* 91
≡ Pro Derechos Humanos de Colombia *E* 30
≡ pour les Relations Internationales des Jeunes d'Expression Française *BE* 189
≡ Rhodanien d'Acceuil des Réfugiés et de Défense des Droits d'Asile *F* 136
≡ de Solidaridad Cataluña-Líbano *E* 85
≡ de Soutien Polonais en France *F* 96
≡ Suisse pour la Défense du Droit d'Asile *CH* 152
≡ suisse pour l'UNICEF *CH* 218
≡ des travailleurs algériens *F* 9
≡ unitaire français-immigrés *F* 136
≡ Vrouwen van Ravensbruck *NL* 171
≡ Yildrirum Sport *NL* 121
≡ Zaïre *BE* 126
Commissió Diocesana de Migració *E* 151
Commissariaat-generaal voor de vluchtelingen en de staatlozen *BE* 189
Commissariat général aux réfugiés et aux apatrides *BE* 189
≡ du Gouvernement aux Etrangers *LX* 207
Commissie Justitia et Pax *NL* 208
Commission des Communautés Européennes *BE* 189, *F* 196, *LX* 207
≡ Portugaises au Luxembourg *LX* 100
Commission Diocésaine pour la Pastorale Intercommunautaire *LX* 169
≡ des Migrants *LX* 145
Commission des Eglises auprès des Migrants en Europe *BE* 130
≡ Episcopale des Migrations *BE* 130
≡ of the European Communities *BE* 189, *DK* 194, *F* 196, *D* 201, *GR* 203, *IR* 204, *IT* 205, *LX* 207, *NL* 209, *PR* 211, *E* 214, *UK* 222
≡ Européenne Immigrés *BE* 130
≡ for Filipino Migrant Workers *IT NL* 35, *UK* 36
≡ Française de la Culture de l'Agglomération Bruxelloise *BE* 36
≡ française Justice et Paix *F* 196
≡ on Global Governance; Inter-nationale Catholique pour les Migrations; Internationale de Juristes *CH* 217
≡ for Racial Equality *UK* 184, 222
≡ des recours *F* 196
≡ for the Refugee Issue *EE* 195
≡ de Sauvegarde du Droit d'Asile *F* 136
≡ for Spanish-United States Cultural Exchanges *E* 123
Commissions Ouvrières Espagnoles *LX* 113
Committee on the Administration of Justice *NI* 229
≡ for Bangladeshi Rights in the UK *UK* 18
≡ for Black Affairs *UK* 21
≡ for Community Relations *UK* 178
Committee for the Defence of Democratic Rights in Turkey *UK* 122
≡ Legitimate Rights *UK* 104
Committee on the Elimination of Racial Discrimination *CH* 175
≡ for Foreign Cultural Relations *AL* 159
≡ for Human Rights in Honduras *UK* 43
≡ on International Co-operation in National Demographic Research *F* 234
≡ for Italian Emigrants *IR* 75
≡ of Jurists for Aid to Refugees *PR* 148
≡ for Justice in Zimbabwe *UK* 127
≡ for Migrants & Refugees *UK* 154
≡ for Other Faiths; for Relations with People of Other Faiths *UK* 178
≡ for the Transfer of Irish Prisoners *NI* 158
≡ for the Welfare of Iranian Jews *UK* 80

Common Ground *UK* 178
Commonwealth Information Centre *UK* 244
≡ Institute *UK* 222
≡ Non-Governmental Office for South Africa *UK* 109
≡ Welfare & Immigration Advisory Centre *UK* 154
Commonword *UK* 21
Communauté antillo guyanaise *F* 26
≡ Camerounaise de France *F* 25
≡ Catholique Française *PR* 36
≡ d'entraide et de solidarité de Villiers-le-Bel *F* 163
≡ Européenne de Travail sur Eglise et Société Industrielle *UK* 222
≡ Hellénique de Liège *BE* 38
≡ Portugaise d'Emmaüs *BE* 97
≡ des Réfugiés Zaïrois *UK* 127
≡ Zaïroise de France *F* 126
Communautés Ethniques de Langue Française *F* 163
Communications *IT* 126
Community Action for Police Accountability *UK* 178
≡ Centre *GR* 140
≡ Centre for Refugees from Vietnam, Laos & Cambodia *UK* 110
≡ Education Trust *UK* 244
≡ Fellowship Pentecostal Church *UK* 222
≡ Help Service *BE* 131
≡ Music Education Project *UK* 244
≡ Programme for Education & Training in Technology *BE* 189
≡ of Refugees from Vietnam *UK* 124
≡ Relations Council *NI* 185
≡ Religions Project; Roots Resource Centre *UK* 244
≡ Security Trust *UK* 80
≡ Service Volunteers *UK* 222
Community Voice *UK* 184
Community of Zairean Refugees *UK* 127
Comparative Education Society in Europe *BE* 160
Comunidad Israelita *E* 79
≡ Musulmana *E* 54
≡ Peruana de Residentes en Milano *IT* 96
≡ Portuguesa de Madrid *E* 101
≡ del Pueblo Magrebí *E* 87
Comunidade Católica Caboverdeana *PR* 26
≡ Espanhola *PR* 113
≡ Irlandesa e Inglesa *PR* 46
Comunidade Cristiana *D* 100
Comunidade Hindú; de Portugal *PR* 42
Comunidade Islâmica; de Oeiras *PR* 54
Comunidade Portuguêsa de Tremor de Arriba *E* 101
≡ de Refugiados de Timor *PR* 116
Comunità Argentina *IT* 11
≡ Azerbagiana in Italia *IT* 16
Comunità Brasiliana in Italia; di Roma *IT* 23
Comunità Cilena; Cilena di Roma *IT* 28
≡ Cinese *IT* 28
≡ Cristiana Afro-Araba in Lombardia *IT* 3
≡ Cristiana Filippine di Bologna *IT* 35
≡ Egitto; Egiziana *IT* 33
≡ Eritrea; Eritrea a Genova *IT* 34
≡ Europea Giornalisti *IT* 34
≡ Filippina *IT* 35
≡ Ghanese *IT* 38
≡ dei Gruppi Marocchini a Roma *IT* 89
≡ Impegno Servizio Volontariato *IT* 143
≡ Iraniana in Italia *IT* 45
Comunità Islamica di Brescia; in Italia; e Moschea di Napoli; del Trentino Alto Adige *IT* 54
Comunità Isola Capo Verde *IT* 26
≡ Italo-Argentina *IT* 11
≡ Jugoslava *IT* 126
≡ Lavoratori Pakistani in Puglia *IT* 93
≡ Lavoratrici di Capoverde in Piemonte *IT* 26
≡ dei Musulmani in Piemonte *IT* 54
≡ Nigeriana a Firenze e Province *IT* 92
≡ Pakistana *IT* 93
≡ Palestinese *IT* 95
≡ Paolo e Lorenzo Pernigotti *IT* 141
≡ Peruviana in Italia *IT* 96
≡ Romena Ortodossa in Torino *IT* 102
≡ Salvadoregna *IT* 104
≡ San Egidio *IT* 34, 168-9
≡ Senegalese; Senegalese di Livorno *IT* 105
≡ Somala; dei Somali Dhambaal *IT* 108
≡ Università Mediterranea *IT* 239
≡ Vietnamita *IT* 124
≡ Zairese in Piemonte *IT* 126
Concern *IR* 204
Concern Universal *UK* 222
Confederação das Associações Portuguêsas do Luxembourg *LX* 100
≡ Geral dos Trabalhadores Portuguêses—Intersindical Nacional *PR* 148

Confederación de Asociaciones Españolas de Padres de Familia en Alemania *D* 112
≡ de Centros de Información para Trabajadores Extranjeros *E* 151
≡ General del Trabajo; Nacional del Trabajo *E* 214
Confederation of African Nationals & Descendants *UK* 5
≡ of Asian Organisations *UK* 12
Confédération des Associations Portugaises au Luxembourg *LX* 100
Confederation of Bangladeshi Organisations *UK* 18
Confédération française démocratique du travail *F* 196
≡ Générale des Enseignants *BE* 189
≡ Générale du Logement; Générale du Travail—Section immigration *F* 196
Confederation of Indian Organisations *UK* 44
≡ of Kurdish Associations *D* 82
Confédération des Organismes Familiaux de la Communauté Européene *BE* 189
Confederation of Refugee Groups & Ethnic Minorities *UK* 154
≡ Sunni Mosques—Midlands *UK* 57
Confédération Syndicale des Familles *F* 196
Confederazione Generale Italiana del Lavoro *IT* 143, 169
≡ Italiana Sindicati Lavoratori *IT* 143, *UK* 77
Conference of European Churches *DK* 194, *CH* 152
Conferenza Permanente per l'Uguaglianza Razziale in Europa *IT* 169
Confidente F 77
Congrès mondial juif *F CH* 79
Congreso Nacional Africano *E* 109
Congresso Nazionale Africano *IT* 109
Connections UK 222
Connolly Association *UK* 48
Conseil des Associations d'Immigrés en Europe *F* 136, *CH* 152
≡ en France *F* 136
Conseil des Communautés Africaines en Europe *BE* 2, *F IT* 3
≡ Portugaises en France *F* 98
Conseil Consultatif pour l'Immigration *BE* 189
≡ des populations d'origine maghrébine de Franche-Comté *F* 86
Conseil Européen des Associations Marocaines *F* 89
≡ sur les Réfugiés et les Exilés *UK* 244
Conseil de l'Europe *BE* 190, *F* 197
≡ des Femmes Francophones *BE* 2
≡ et Formation sur les Realités de l'Immigration et de l'Interculturel *F* 234
≡ Général de la Jeunesse Luxembourgeoise *LX* 207
≡ International de l'Action Social *AT* 188
≡ de la Jeunesse d'Expression Française de Belgique *BE* 190
Conseil National d'Aide à la Vie Associative *F* 196
≡ des Français Musulmans *F* 53
≡ de l'Immigration *LX* 207
≡ pour l'Intégration des Populations Immigrées; des Populations Immigrées *F* 196
Conseil Représentatif des Institutions Juives de France *F* 79
≡ des Instituts et Communautés Croates de France *F* 31
Conseil suisse des associations de la jeunesse *CH* 218
Consejo de Investigación y Documentación Europa y América Latina *E* 84
≡ de la Juventud de España *E* 214
≡ Superior de Investigaciones Científicas *E* 242
Conselho das Comunidades Portuguêsas *PR* 148
≡ de Pais dos Portuguêses *BE* 97
≡ Paroquial Português em Haia *NL* 101
≡ Português para a Paz e a Cooperação; Português para os Refugiados *PR* 211
Consell General de l'Inmigració; Nacional de la Joventut de Catalunya *E* 214
Consiglio delle Comunità Africane in Europa *IT* 3
≡ Italiano per gli Rifugiati *IT* 205
≡ Nazionale della Gioventù Sammarinese *SM* 212
Consortium Européen pour les Relations Nord-Sud *F* 163
Consulta Cittadina dell'Immigrazione; Emigrazione-Immigrazione Regione Piemonte *IT* 143
Consultorio giuridico per i richiedenti d'asilo *CH* 152
Contact Bulletin IR 204
Contactgroep van den Heul Oud Verzetsdeelnemers *NL* 171

O Contacto LX 100
Contacts BE 192
Contre-Poing *BE* 131
Convience *BE* 160
Convoy of Mercy *UK* 23
Conway House *UK* 49
Cooperação e Desenvolvimento *PR* 173
Coopération Internationale pour la Développement et la Solidarité *BE* 190
Co-operation Ireland *UK* 48
Co-operation North-South GR 203
Cooperativa Dedalus Studi e Ricerche Sociali *IT* 239
≡ Proficua *IT* 169
≡ di Servizio *IT* 143
≡ di Solidarietà Africana *IT* 3
Cooperazione Giuridica Internazionale *IT* 205
≡ Internazionale; per lo Sviluppo dei Paesi Emergenti; Terzo Mondo *IT* 169
Coordinación de Asociaciones Culturales de Madrid *IT* 174
Coordinadora de Asociaciones Gitanas *E* 41
≡ Europea de Asociaciones de Emigrantes Españoles *D* 112
≡ Nacional del Movimiento Asociativo de los Emigrantes en Bélgica *BE* 110
≡ de ONGs para el Desarrollo *E* 214
≡ de ONGs de Euskadi *E* 215
Coordinamento degli Artisti Stranieri in Italia *IT* 143
≡ Associazioni Senegalesi in Italia *IT* 105
≡ Associazioni Stranieri *IT* 143
≡ della Baia Domizia *IT* 3
Coordinamento Immigrati Extracomunitari della Liguria; Jesi *IT* 143
≡ Ligure; del Sud del Mondo *IT* 144
Coordinamento di Iniziative Popolari di Solidarietà Internazionale *IT* 169
≡ Latino-Americani Democratici in Umbria *IT* 84
≡ dei Lavoratori Stranieri in Lombardia *IT* 144
≡ dei Lavoratori, Studenti e Rifugiati Iraniani in Italia *IT* 45
≡ Ligure Extracomunitario *IT* 143
≡ Migranti *IT* 144
≡ Nazionale Immigrati *IT* 145
≡ Nazionale Senegalesi *IT* 105
≡ delle ONG per la Cooperazione Internazionale allo Sviluppo *IT* 205
≡ Provinciale Immigrati; Stranieri; degli Stranieri Extracomunitari della Lombardia *IT* 144
≡ degli Studenti Democratici *IT* 205
≡ Studenti Stranieri della Lombardia *IT* 144
Co-ordinating Committee for International Voluntary Service *F* 197
Coordination des Associations Démocratiques des Immigrés Marocains en Europe *F* 89
≡ Bruxelloise pour l'Emploi et la Formation des Femmes *BE* 131
≡ des Collectivités Portugaises *F* 98
≡ des Comités Chili *F* 28
≡ européenne pour le droit des étrangers de vivre en famille *F* 136
≡ of Greek Immigrants in Europe *D* 38
≡ Information Tiers-Monde *F* 163
≡ of Kurdish Associations in Europe *DK* 82
≡ Office for the Vietnamese in the Diaspora *IT* 124
Coordination Région Europe D 201
Coordination Suisse Asile *CH* 152
Corby Irish Centre *UK* 48
Córdoba Acoge *E* 151
Cork Action for Bosnia-Hercegovina *IR* 23
Cork Diocesan Emigration Service *IR* 141
Correio Associativo F 98
Corriere d'Italia D 74
Corriere degli Italiani CH 76
Corrispondenza Italia IT 144
Couleur locale *F* 163
Council for the Advancement of Arab-British Understanding *UK* 11
≡ of African & Afro-Caribbean Churches *UK* 21
≡ of British Pakistanis *UK* 93
≡ of Christians & Jews *UK* 178
≡ of Churches for Britain & Ireland *UK* 222
≡ for the Defence of Human Rights & Freedoms *SR* 212
≡ for Education in World Citizenship *UK* 222, *NI* 229
Council of Europe BE 190, *F* 197, 235
≡ Minority Youth Committee *DK* 132, *D* 200, *NL* 208, *UK* 154
Council of European Jamaats *UK* 57
≡ National Youth Committees *BE* 190
Council for International Educational Exchanges *UK* 222

Council of Irish Associations; County Associations *UK* 48
Council for Islamic Affairs *UK* 57
≡ of Jews from Germany *UK* 80
≡ of Lithuanian Youth Organisations *LH* 207
≡ of Mosques; of Mosques & Islamic Organisations in Sheffield; of Mosques UK & Éire *UK* 57
≡ for the Preservation of the Holy Places of Islam *UK* 57
≡ for Racial Justice *UK* 178
≡ for Social Responsibility *UK* 222
≡ of Voluntary Agencies Working in Germany *D* 200
Counter Information *UK* 244
The Countrywoman UK 176
Coup de Pilon *F* 3
Court of Justice of the EU *LX* 207
Coventry Anti-Harassment & Attacks Network *UK* 178
≡ Black Mental Health Association *UK* 21
≡ Income & Legal Rights Service *UK* 222
≡ Inter Faith Group *UK* 178
≡ Law Centre *UK* 222
≡ Racial Equality Council *UK* 178
≡ West Indian Community Assoc. *UK* 125
Cradley Heath Mosque & Muslim Association *UK* 57
Craigavon Asian Women's Centre *NI* 16
≡ Travellers Support Committee *NI* 118
Craobh Naomh Fiachra *LX* 46
Crawley Council for Community Relations *UK* 184
Crawley Islamic Centre & Mosque *UK* 57
CRD News NI 247
Creative Support Ltd *UK* 222
Crewe Central Community Group *UK* 178
Cricklefield Refugee Project *UK* 154
Critiques et Perspectives BE 231
Croce Rossa Italiana *IT* 205
La Croix Bleu des Arméniens *F* 11
Croix Rouge de Belgique *BE* 190
≡ Française *F* 197
≡ Luxembourgeoise *LX* 207
≡ Suisse *CH* 217, 219
Cross-Cultural Association *GR* 168
Croydon Racial Equality Council *UK* 178
Crucible UK 220
Cruz Roja Española *E* 151, 214-5
CSC Vormingswerk—De Wereld van Anne Frank *BE* 160
Cuadernos Africa-América Latina E 216
Cuba Sí IR UK 31
Cuba Solidarity Campaign *UK* 31
Cuba Support Group *IR* 31
Cultur Cooperation *D* 166
Cultura Africana *E* 4
Cultura e Solidarietà IT 169
Cultural Iranian Union Club Roubek Khoudy-Barbaroudy *DK* 45
≡ & Islamic Society of Harrow *UK* 57
Cultural Trends UK 246
Cultural Unity Working Group *UK* 154
Culture et Liberté, Association nationale pour le développement culturel du monde du travail *F* 197
Culture et Politique en Méditerranée *F* 234
Culturele Vereniging Adrar *NL* 90
Cultures et Santé *BE* 232
Cultureword Publishers & Identity Writing Group *UK* 21
Cultúrlann Eireannach *F* 46
Cumann Lúthcleas Gael *LX* 46, *UK* 48
CVJM-Gesamtverband *D* 200
Cypriot Advisory Service; Community Centre; Women's League *UK* 31
Czechoslovak Jewish Aid Trust *UK* 80

Dachverband der Ausländischer-kulturvereine in Bremen *D* 166
≡ der Minderheitenjugendlichen in West-Europa *D* 200
Daily Awaz International UK 101
Daily Jang UK 123
Daiwa Anglo-Japanese Foundation *UK* 78
Dal Khalsa *UK* 106
Dalston Mosque *UK* 57
Danchurchaid, Inter-Church Aid & World Service *DK* 194
Danish Action for Romania *DK* 102
≡ Assoc. for International Co-operation; Centre for Human Rights *DK* 194
≡ Committee for Aid to Afghan Refugees *DK* 1
≡ Helsinki Committee *DK* 194
≡ -Irish Society *DK* 46
≡ National Institute of Social Research *DK* 233
≡ Red Cross *DK* 194
≡ Refugee Council *DK* 132

Danish Save the Children *DK* 195
≡ United Nations Association *DK* 194
Danmarks Lærerhøjskole *DK* 232
Danmarksposten; Danmarks Radio—
Indvandrerredaktionen *DK* 132
Dansk-Brasiliansk Selskab *DK* 23
≡ -Bulgarsk Selskab *DK* 24
≡ Canadisk Selskab *DK* 25
≡ Filippinsk Kvindegruppe *DK* 35
≡ Flygtningehjælp *DK* 132
≡ Hollandsk Selskab *DK* 32
≡ International Venskabsorganisation
DK 161
≡ -Islandsk Samfund *DK* 43
≡ -Japansk Selskab *DK* 78
≡ Kontaktkreds for Bangladesh
International Action Group *DK* 16
≡ -Kubansk Forening *DK* 31
≡ -Kurdisk Kultur- og Solidaritets-forening;
-Kurdisk Kulturcenter *DK* 82
≡ Latin Amerikansk Kvindeforening *DK* 83
≡ nationalkomité for World University
Service *DK* 195
≡ -Polsk Forening i Aalborg *DK* 96
≡ Røde Kors *DK* 194
≡ -Rumansk Forening *DK* 102
≡ -Tamilsk Forening i Aalborg; -Tamilsk
Venskabsforening; -Thai Forening *DK* 115
Dansk-Tyrkisk Arbejder Forening; Forening
i Herning; Ungdomsforening *DK* 119
Dansk Ungdoms Fællesråd; Unicef Komite
DK 194
Danske Center for Menneskerettigheder;
Kvinders Nationalråd *DK* 194
Dar al Amal, Association Coopérative de
Femmes Immigrées *BE* 88
Dar Al-Dawa; Dar al Da'wa al Islamiya
UK 57
Dar Al-Ifta *UK* 58
Dar al Maghrib, Association de
l'Immigration Marocaine *BE* 88
Dar Al-Taqwa; Dar ul Aloom Siddiqia
Mosque *UK* 57
Dar-ul-Aman Housing Association *UK* 93
Dar-ul-Ehsan Publications *UK* 57
Dar-ul-Uloom *UK* 62
≡ Ahl-e-Sunnat *UK* 59
≡ Islamia Education & Cultural Society;
Islamia & Mosque; Jamia Chashtiah *UK* 57
Dar-Uloom Qadiria Jilania *UK* 57
Dar-us-Salam Mosque *UK* 57
Darek Nyuma *E* 4
Darlaston Bangladeshi Muslim Organisation
UK 18
Dartford Racial Equality Council *UK* 178
Darul Ahsan *UK* 57
Darul-Amaan Association *UK* 55
Darul Aman Trust *UK* 57
Darul Ifta UK *UK* 58
Darul Ifta UK & Europe *UK* 63
Darul Muslimat *UK* 58
Darul Uloom; Al Arabiya Al Islamiya;
Islamic High School *UK* 58
Darwen Mosque *UK* 58
Dashmesh Darbar Sikh Temple; Singh
Sabha Bhatra Gurdwara *UK* 106
Daubhill Muslim Society; Dawat Ul Islam
Mosque *UK* 58
Dawatul Islam; Central Co-ordinating
Committee; Coventry Cross Mosque &
Islamic Centre; Youth Group *UK* 58
Dawoodi Bohra Welfare Society *UK* 58
Day-Mer *UK* 83
De Poort-Beraber Begeleidingheid *BE* 131
Dearne Muslim Society *UK* 58
Defence for Children International *NL* 208,
CH 217
Défense des droits des français musulmans
de Romans et ses environs *F* 53
Defipresse *BE* 189
Delegación Diocesana de Migraciones *E* 151
Délégation Catholique pour la Coopération
F 197
≡ des Missions Catholiques Italiennes *F* 74
Delegazione Immigrati Extracomunitari
Toscana *IT* 144
≡ Missioni Cattoliche Italiani *NL* 76
Délégués Diocesains de la Pastorale des
Migrants *F* 138
Demesh Sikh Temple *UK* 106
Democracy Now *UK* 48
Democratic Youth League of Finland *SF* 195
Démocratie et progrès pour le Bénin *F* 19
Demokratik Isçi Dernekleri Federasyonu
D 120, *NL* 121
≡ Sosyal Dernekler Federasyoni *NL* 121
≡ Yurtseverler Birligi Federasyonu *D* 120
Demos Dokumentationsgruppen *DK* 161
Departament de Migració de Caritas
Diocesana de Barcelona *E* 151
Departamento para os Assuntos Europeus
e Relações Externas *PR* 211

Departamento Confederal de Inmigración;
de Inmigrantes *E* 151
≡ de Relações Internacionais e Convenções
de Segurança Social *PR* 211
Departement Sociologie en Sociale Beleid
BE 231
Department of Arabic & Islamic Studies; of
Comparative Religion *UK* 244
≡ of East Asian Studies *UK* 14
≡ of Education *IR* 204
≡ for Education & Employment *UK* 226
≡ of Finance & Personnel *NI* 229
≡ of Geography *UK* 245
≡ of Islamic Languages & Culture *NL* 54
≡ of Justice *IR* 204
≡ of Social Anthropology *NI* 247
≡ of Social Sciences *D* 237
≡ of Social Security *UK* 220
≡ of Social Studies *UK* 232
≡ for World Service *CH* 218
Deptford Vietnamese Community Project
UK 125
Derby Anti-Fascist Action; Campaign
Against Racism & Fascism *UK* 178
≡ Irish Association *UK* 48
≡ Open Centre Multi-Faith Group *UK* 178
≡ Pakistan Community Centre *UK* 93
≡ Racial Equality Council *UK* 178
≡ West Indian Community Assoc. *UK* 125
Derde Wereld Informatiehuis *NL* 171
Derry Emigration Bureau *NI* 158
Des Pardes; *Des Vides* *UK* 101
Deserteursberatung *AT* 129
Desh Barta Newsweekly *UK* 19
Detached Asian Girls Project *UK* 14
Detention Advice Service *UK* 154
Deutsch-Französisches Jugendwerk *D* 36
≡ -iberoamerikanischer Kulturkreis *D* 83
≡ -Irische Gesellschaft *D* 46
Deutsch Lernen *D* 140
Deutsch-Vietnamesische Freundschafts-
kreis Reistrommel *D* 124
Deutsche Flüchtlingshilfe Bonn *D* 138
≡ Friedensgesellschaft—Kriegsdienstver-
weigerer; Gewerkschaftsbundjugend;
Rechtsberaterkonferenz *D* 200
≡ Schule Brussel *BE* 37
≡ Stiftung für UNO-Flüchtlingshilfe *D* 139
Deutscher Akademischer Austauschdienst;
Bundesjugendring *D* 200
≡ Caritasverband *D* 201
≡ Gewerkschaftsbund Bundesvorstand
Ausländische Arbeitnehmer *D* 139
≡ Paritätischer Wohlfahrtsverband *D* 201
≡ Volkshochschul-Verband *D* 166
Deutsches Institut für internationale
pädagogische Forschung *D* 236
≡ Jugendinstitut *D* 201
≡ Komitee der Jugendkampagne des
Europarates *D* 166
≡ Kontakt Informationszentrum *GR* 37
≡ Rotes Kreuz *D* 201
Deutschsprachige Evangelische Gemeinde
E 37
Development Aid from People to People
NR 210
≡ Education Association *UK* 178
Development Review *IR* 168
Dewsbury Irish National League Club *UK* 48
≡ Muslim Association *UK* 55
Dhar ul Ehsan Centre *UK* 58
Diaconal Office of the Reformed Churches
in the Netherlands *NL* 208
Diakonia *S* 216
Diakonisches Werk Duisburg; der
Evangelische-Lutherische Kirche in
Thüringen; der Evangelischen Kirche in
Deutschland; in der Pommerschen
Evangelische Kirche *D* 201
Dialog *DK* 194
Diálogo do Emigrante *D* 99
Dialogue for European Alternatives
Network *BE* 129
Didsbury Mosque & Islamic Centre *UK* 58
Dienst der Gastarbeiders ABVV; voor
migrerende arbeiders en vluchtelingen
ACV *BE* 132
≡ Vreemdelingenzaken *BE* 192
Différences *F* 164
Différents *F* 163
Dimensione Lavoro *IT* 144
Dinh Huong *F* 124
Dion *UK* 48
Dipartimento per l'informazione e l'editoria
Sportello immigrati *IT* 205
Dirección General de Extranjería y Asilo
E 214
≡ de Migraciones *E* 215
≡ de la Policía *E* 214
≡ de Relaciones con la Diáspora *E* 151
Directie voor de Emigratie; Vluchtelingen,
Minderheden en Asielzokers *NL* 208

Directie Vreemdelingenzaken *NL* 208
Direction générale de la Sécurité sociale
BE 190
≡ de la Population et des Migrations *F* 197
Directorate of Human Rights *F* 197
Directory of Internationalism *NL* 173
Direktoratet for Social Sikring og Bistand;
Udlændinge *DK* 194
Direzione Generale per l'Impiego *IT* 206
Disabled Asian Women's Network *UK* 14
Discriminatie Meldpunt Tegelen *NL* 171
Displaced Persons Centre Information
Service *NL* 240
Diwa Asian Women's Network *UK* 14
Doan ket *F* 124
Doc-Lap-Zentrum *D* 110
Documentation réfugiés *F* 234
Dokumentation om Indvandrere *DK* 233
Dokumentations- und Informationszentrum
Menschenrechte in Lateinamerika *D* 83
≡ und Kulturzentrum Deutscher Sinti und
Roma *D* 103
≡ og Rådgivningcenteret om
Racediskrimination *DK* 161
Dokumentationsarchiv *CH* 243
≡ den Österreichischen Widerstandes
AT 231
Dokumentationsstelle Migration Inter-
kulturelle Erziehung Hochschule *D* 236
Dom Polski *UK* 96
Dominica Overseas Nationals Association;
UK Association *UK* 32
Dominot *BE* 119
Doncaster Council for Racial Equality
UK 178
Doncaster Mosque Trust *UK* 58
Donegal Association *UK* 48
Dortmund Türkischer Volksverein *D* 120
Dossier Europa Migrazione *IT* 239
Dossier Nicaragua *BE* 91
Dostiyo Asian Women & Girls Organisation
UK 14
Terry Downing Centre *UK* 48
Dritte Welt Haus Bielefeld *D* 166
Droits de l'Homme et Solidarité *F* 197
Droits et Libertés *F* 164
The Drum *UK* 178
Drummond Street Four Campaign *UK* 14
Drustvo za prostovoljno delo MOST—SCI
Slovenia *SV* 212
Dublin Anti-Fascist Action *IR* 168
≡ Association *UK* 48
≡ Committee for Travelling People *IR* 117
≡ Islamic Society *IR* 54
Dublin Travellers Education & Development
Group; Inter-Cultural Project *IR* 117
Dudley Mosque *UK* 58
Dudley Racial Equality Council *UK* 178
Duemilastagioni *IT* 144
DUHA, Kancelar pro Cechy *CS* 161
Carl-Duisberg-Gesellschaft *D* 139
Duisburger Institut für Sprach- und
Sozialforschung *D* 236
Durham Council for Racial Equality; County
Racial Equality Council *UK* 178
Dutch Association of Greece *GR* 32
≡ Interchurch Aid *NL* 210
≡ Pot Project *UK* 154
≡ Red Cross *NL* 210
≡ Refugee Council *NL* 147
Dwars-Antifa—groenlinkse jongeren-
organisatie *NL* 171

Ealing Borough Council Housing
Department *UK* 154
≡ Borough Law Centre *UK* 222
≡ Racial Equality Council *UK* 178
≡ Travellers Bashley Road Project *UK* 117
Earls Court Advice Centre *UK* 222
East African Association; Association of
North London; Muslim Association; Sunni
Muslim Jama'at *UK* 32
East European Advice Centre *UK* 33
East London Black Women's Organisation
UK 21
≡ Chinese Assoc. Tower Hamlets *UK* 29
≡ Mosque Trust *UK* 58
≡ Sanctuary Association *UK* 154
East Staffordshire Racial Equality Council
UK 178
≡ Sussex County Council Bilingual
Support Service *UK* 154
≡ Sussex Islamic Association *UK* 58
≡ Timor Ireland Solidarity Campaign *IR* 116
≡ Timor Solidarity Campaign *UK* 116
≡ West Community Project *UK* 154
Eastbourne Islamic Project; Islamic Society;
Mosque *UK* 58
≡ Racial Equality Council *UK* 178
Eastern Digest *UK* 14
Eastern European Aid *NI* 33

Eastern Eye UK 14
Eastleigh & District Irish Society UK 48
Easton Masjid UK 58
Eastwards Trust UK 14
Friedrich-Ebert-Stiftung D 236
Ebony Sistren Housing Association UK 21
Eccles & Salford Islamic Society UK 58
Echange et Promotion; Echanges Culturels
   en Méditerranée F 163
Echanges et Méditerranée F 164
Echec à l'Echec BE 189
Echo de l'Immigration—Ensemble LX 145
Echos de Tunisie F 118
Ecole d'Alphabétisation Mons-Borinage
   BE 190
   ≡ de formateurs et d'animateurs en
     milieux migrants F 136
   ≡ française de Rome IT 36
   ≡ Ouvrière Grècque BE 38
Economic & Social Commitee BE 190
   ≡ Research Council UK 244
   ≡ Research Institute IR 238
Ecos do Sur E 174
Ecotec UK 220
Ecowas Womens Group UK 178
Edara Talimul Islam UK 58
Edelweiss-Piraten D 166
Edhi International Foundation UK UK 58
Edinburgh Anti-Fascist Action UK 178
   ≡ Direct Aid to Bosnia & Croatia UK 23
   ≡ District Council UK 222
   ≡ Ethnic Enterprise Centre UK 154
   ≡ Ethnic Minorities Employment Access
     UK 154
   ≡ Latin America Solidarity Campaign
     UK 84
Edition Parabolis D 236
Editions Arcantiere F 234
Education for Democracy in South Africa
   UK 109
Educational Grants Advisory Service
   UK 222
Educational Research UK 246
Eenheid en Samenwerking BE 119
Eesti Inimôiguste Institut;
   Noorsoouhenduste Kogu EE 195
Eglise Arménienne Apostolique BE 11
Eglise Orthodoxe Grècque des Archanges
   St-Michel et St-Gabriel; de St-Jean
   Baptiste BE 38
Eglise Orthodoxe Russe de la Résurrection;
   St-André; St-Job; St-Nicolas; St-Panta-
   leimon et St-Nicolas; Ste-Anne BE 103
Egyptian Community in Greece GR 33
Eine Welt für alle D 166
Einwanderer-Treff D 139
Ekaya Housing Association; Ektha Housing
   Association UK 154
El Fac-isard F 8
El Kalima BE 10
El Kantra BE 132
El Nahdha UK 119
El Salvador Committee for Human Rights;
   Solidarity Campaign UK 104
Elahi Mosque & Islamic Cultural Centre
   UK 58
Elcahuih E 28
Elderly Asian Development Group UK 14
Elevorganisationen i Sverige S 216
Elland Mosque Association UK 93
Elleniko Instituto Allilengyis ke Synergasias
   me tis Anaptyssomenes Chores GR 203
O Elo BE 97, NL 101
Emancipatieraad NL 209
Emek BE 119
Emerald Social Club UK 48
Emigrant Advice; Centre; Service IR 141
Emigrant Advice Unit NI 158
O Emigrante F 98, PR 148
Emigration Advisory Bureau; Research &
   Action Group IR 141
Emigrazione IT 144
Emigrazione/Immigrazione Centro Studi
   IT 239
Emigrazione Notizie IT 144
Emigrazione Oggi D 74
Emmanuel Pentecostal Church UK 222
Employment Conditions Abroad UK 154
Empreinte F 196
Encontro BE 97
Encontro Português F 98
Encuentro BE 73
Enfance Espoir; et Partage F 197
Enfants Déplacés BE 131
   ≡ du Mékong F 124
   ≡ du Monde F 197
   ≡ réfugiés du monde F 136
Enfield Racial Equality Council UK 178
   ≡ Refugee Consortium UK 154
   ≡ Saheli Asian Women's Centre UK 14
Enfoprensa BE 27
The Enlightenment UK 9

Ente Milanese Assistenza Solidarietà
   Integrazione IT 144
   ≡ Nazionale ACLI Istruzione Professionale
     D 74, IT 144, UK 77
   ≡ Pro Italia D 74
Enterprise Europe UK 33
L'Entraide BE 88
Entraide franco-vietnamienne F 124
   ≡ Lao-Hmong F 83
   ≡ Protestante Suisse CH 217
   ≡ et Solidarité Protestante BE 131
Entre autres F 233
Entreprendre Ensemble F 163
Entrepueblos E 174
Entwicklungspolitischer Dokumentation-
   und Pressedienst CH 243
Eötvös Lóránd University H 238
Epitheorisi Koinonikon Erevnon GR 238
Epsom & District Irish Society UK 48
Equal Access Project; Opportunities
   Commission UK 222
Equal Opportunities Review UK 245
Equal Opportunities Units UK 182
Equality at Work; Works Consultancy &
   Training UK 178
EquiLibre F 136
Equip de Treball Africa Negra a
   l'Ensenyament E 4
Equipe de recherches Migrations internatio-
   nales du travail et sociétés d'origine F 234
   ≡ Technique Interventions Interculturelles
     F 163
Equipes Pastorales des Migrants F 138
ERASMUS Agence francophone BE 190
Erasmus Universiteit NL 240
Eretrianske Forening i Danmark DK 34
Eritrean Community in Haringey;
   Community in the United Kingdom UK 34
   ≡ People's Liberation Front IT 34
   ≡ Relief Association DK UK 34
Eritreanske Hjælpeorganisation DK 34
Eritreische Vereinigung zur Gegenseitigen
   Unterstützung D 34
Escola de Formació en Mitjans Didàctics
   E 242
Escuela de Estudios Arabes E 11
Escuela de Formación Específica en
   Materias de Inmigración E 242
Esercito della Salvezza IT 36
Esha'atul Islam Mosque UK 58
Espace F 164
Espace Cambodge F 25
   ≡ Culturelle Caraïbéen F 26
   ≡ Interculturel Méditérranéen F 163
   ≡ Pluriel Amitiés sans frontières F 164
Espagnols de Reims F 112
España Africans' Social Unity E 4
Esperance gens du voyage Arras F 117
Esperance maghrébine monsoise F 86
Espoir Togo-Bénin Organisation Amitié
   F 116
Essex County Council Social Services
   Department—Refugee Services UK 154
   ≡ Islamic Education Trust UK 58
   ≡ Racial Equality Council UK 178
Estadística de Empleo E 215
Ethiopia Information IT 34
Ethiopian Community in GB UK 34
   ≡ Evangelical Christian Fellowship GR 34
   ≡ World Federation UK 102
Ethnic Alcohol Counselling in Hounslow
   UK 154
   ≡ Community Service UK 18
   ≡ Health Unit UK 246
Ethnic Minorities Advice Centre; Advice
   Service; Law Centre; Representative
   Council UK 154
Ethnic & Minority Studies Programme
   H 238
   ≡ Minority Training & Employment Project;
     Network UK 154
   ≡ Research UK 244
   ≡ Studies Network NI 247
   ≡ Study Group UK 244
   ≡ Switchboard UK 154
Ethnicity Research Group UK 244
Ethnikon Kentron Koinonikon Erevnon
   GR 238
   ≡ Symboulion Organoseon Neon Ellados
     GR 203
*Etnie: scienza politica e cultura dei popoli
   minoritari* IT 239
Etniske Mindretals Sammenslutning DK 132
Etoile maghrébine F 86
Les Etudes Tsiganes F 40
EURES Office communautaire BE 190
Euro African Foundation IT 3
Euro Citizen Action Service BE 190
Eurocultura IT 169
Eurologement F 197
Europa-Bro (Büro?) D 166
Europa Centrum NL 171

Europa van Morgen NL 209
Europa de les Nacions E 150
Europäische Bewegung Deutschland D 201
   ≡ Föderation Freier Radios F 163
   ≡ Forum für Migrationstudien D 236
   ≡ Kommission D 201
Europäisches Bürgerforum AT 159, D 166
   ≡ Migrationsmuseum; Migrationszentrum
     D 237
   ≡ Zentrum AT 231
Europarat F 197
Europavertretung der Nationalen
   Befreiungsfront Kurdistans D 82
Europe at School D 166
European Anti-Poverty Network BE 190,
   IR 204
   ≡ Association for Transcultural Group
     Analysis F 164
European Bureau for Conscientious
   Objection BE 190
   ≡ Lesser-Used Languages IR 204
European Centre AT 231
European Centre for the Advanced Training
   of Travellers IR 117
   ≡ Global Interdependence & Solidarity
     PR 211
   ≡ Travellers IR 117
   ≡ Work & Society NL 146, 171, 240, E 242
European Churches' Working Group on
   Asylum & Refugees CH 152
   ≡ Citizens' Association F 196
   ≡ Civic Forum AT 159, D 166, CH 175
European Commission of Human Rights;
   against Racism & Intolerance F 197
European Committee for the Defence of
   Refugees & Immigrants F 163, CH 175
   ≡ Committee on Migrations F 197
   ≡ Community Action Scheme for the
     Mobility of University Students;
     Community Organisation of Socialist
     Youth BE 190
   ≡ Confederation of Youth Clubs DK 194
   ≡ Conference of Binational-Bicultural
     Relationships F 164
   ≡ Contact Group on Urban Industrial
     Mission UK 222
   ≡ Coordination Bureau BE 190
   ≡ Co-ordination on the Right to Family Life
     for Migrants F 136, UK 155
   ≡ Council of Jewish Communities UK 80
   ≡ Council on Refugees & Exiles UK 244
   ≡ Counter Network UK 223
   ≡ Court of Human Rights F 197
   ≡ Cultural Foundation NL 209
   ≡ Cultural Fund F 197
   ≡ Documentation Centre & Observatory
     on Migration & Ethnic Relations NL 240
   ≡ Ecumenical Commission for Church &
     Society; Educational Exchanges—Youth
     for Understanding; Employment Services
     Network BE 190
European Federation for Intercultural
   Learning BE 160
   ≡ of Overseas Cypriots CY 132
   ≡ of Youth Service Organisations F 197
European Forum for Migration Studies
   D 236
   ≡ Foundation Centre BE 190
   ≡ Foundation for the Improvement of
     Living & Working Conditions IR 238
   ≡ Group for the Study of Deviance &
     Social Control UK 244
   ≡ Human Rights Foundation BE 190
European Journal of Intercultural Studies
   NL 240
European Legal Network on Asylum
   AT 129, BE 131, DK 132, F 137, D 200, GR
   140, IR 141, IT 143, 238, LX 145, NL NR 147,
   PR 211, SV 212, E 150, S 152, UK 154
   ≡ Local Authorities Information Network
     on Ethnic Minority Policies NL 171
   ≡ Migration Centre; Migration Museum
     D 237
   ≡ Movement—UK UK 223
European Network Against Nationalism,
   Racism & Fascism & in support of
   migrants & refugees NL 173
   ≡ of Guidance Resource Centres BE 192
European Network of Women BE 190
   ≡ Peace Research Association D 201
European Race Audit UK 245
European Research Centre UK 244
   ≡ on Migration & Ethnic Relations NL 240
European Science Foundation F 235
   ≡ Social Fund BE 190
   ≡ Solidarity Towards Equal Participation of
     Peoples UK 223
   ≡ Support Centre for Migrants & Refugees
     NL 240
   ≡ Student Information Bureau AT 187
European Trade Union Confederation;
   Youth BE 190

European Trade Union Institute *BE* 232
≡ Union of Arabic & Islamic Scholars
   AT 10
≡ Union of Jewish Students *BE* 78
≡ Union Youth Exchange Bureau *BE* 190
≡ Young Homelessness Network *UK* 223
≡ Youth Campaign against Racism,
   Xenophobia, Antisemitism & Intolerance
   CS 161, *F* 197
European Youth Exchange *D* 166
≡ Foundation; Information & Counselling
   Agency *F* 197
Europees Steunpunt Migranten en
   Vluchtelingen *NL* 240
Europese Commissie; Culturele Stichting
   NL 209
EUROSOCIAL *AT* 231
Euskal Herriko Unibersitatea *E* 242
Eusko Jaurlitza *E* 151
Evangelho e Vida *F* 137
Evangelical Christians for Racial Justice
   UK 179
Evangelisch Hulp- en Ontwikkelings-
   organisatie *BE* 190
Evangelisch-Lutherische Kirche *IR* 37
Evangelische Arbeitsgemeinschaft für
   Entwicklungszusammenarbeit *AT* 187
≡ Missionsgesellschaft in Basel *CH* 217
≡ Studentengemeinde *D* 201
Evangelischer Arbeitskreis für Weltmission
   in Österreich *AT* 187
Evangelisches Missionszentrum *D* 201
Evington Muslim Centre *UK* 58
Evrou Thrakis—Griekse Cultuur en
   Dansvereniging *BE* 38
Exeter Anti-Fascist Action *UK* 179
Exil *DK* 132
Exil: Centre médico-psychosocial pour
   réfugiés *BE* 131
Exil—Kulturkoordination *D* 139
Exile *UK* 157
EXIS Centrum voor Internationale
   Jongeren-activiteiten *NL* 209
Exit Visa *UK* 80
De Expeditie—Centrum voor geweldloze
   verandering *NL* 209
Experiment in Europe *BE* 160
Expo *S* 175
Expression immigré(e)s-français(es) *F* 136
Expressions Maghrébines au Féminin *F* 86
Extravoce *IT* 144

Fachhochschule im Verwaltung und
   Rechtspflege Berlin *D* 237
Faculté de Nice adhérente de SOS Racisme
   F 165
Fællesinitiativet mod Racisme *DK* 161
Fællesklubben for Indvandrere og Danskere
   DK 132
Fagbladet *DK* 195
Fagforeninger mod racisme *DK* 161
Faim et Développement *F* 136
Fair Trials International *UK* 154
Fairplay 91 *DK* 161
Faith Asylum Refuge *UK* 155
Faiz-ul-Quran Madrassa *UK* 58
Fakultät für Sozialwissenschaften *D* 237
Falkland Islands Association *UK* 35
Family Immigration Rights *UK* 155
Family Welfare Association *UK* 223
Farbe Bekennen—Eine grün-offene
   Initiative in NRW *D* 166
Farnworth Cultural Centre *UK* 155
Fascisme Onderzoeks Kollektief *NL* 171
Fatih Moskee Turks Islamitisch Centrum
   NL 121
Federação das Associações de Cabo Verde
   PR 26
≡ das Comunidades Portuguêses *NL* 101
≡ de Mulheres para a Paz Mundial *PR* 211
Federació Catalana d'ONG pel
   Desenvolupment *E* 242
≡ de Col.lectivus d'Inmigrants *E* 151
Federación de Amigos y Comerciantes
   Marroquies *E* 90
Federación de Asociaciones y Centros de
   Integración y Ayuda a Marginados *E* 151
≡ Culturales de Españoles Emigrados en
   Francia *F* 112
≡ de Emigrantes Españoles *NL UK* 113
≡ Juveniles y de Alumnos *D* 112
≡ de Padres de Alumnos Españoles *NL* 113
≡ de Padres de Familias y Alumnos *D* 112
≡ Pro-Inmigrantes Extranjeros *E* 151
Federación de Centros de Acogida de In-
   migrantes Extranjeros en Andalucía *E* 151
≡ Española de Universidades Populares
   E 242
≡ de Iglesias Evangélicas de España *E* 215
≡ de Organizaciones para Refugiados y
   Asilados *E* 151

Federación de Universitarios Solidarios
   E 174
Federal Office for Statistics *CH* 243
Federatie van autonome centra voor
   maatschappelijk werk *BE* 190
≡ Demokratische Verenigingen Arbeiders
   uit Turkije *NL* 121
≡ van Griekse Verenigingen *NL* 39
≡ Joegoslavische Verenigingen *NL* 126
Federatie Nederlandse Vakbewegingen
   Jongeren *NL* 209
≡ Secretariaat voor Etnische Minderheden
   NL 146
Federatie van Turkse Islamitische Kulturele
   Verenigingen in Belgie *BE* 119
≡ Vluchtelingen-Organisaties *NL* 146
Fédération des Associations Africaines
   d'Echanges et de Développement *F* 3
≡ Culturelles Espagnoles Emigrantes *F* 112
≡ Démocratiques Espagnoles *LX* 113
≡ Démocratiques Marocaines *BE* 88
≡ Espagnoles des Emigrés à Luxembourg;
   Espagnoles au Luxembourg *LX* 113
≡ d'Expression Portugaise de Lorraine *F* 98
≡ islamiques d'Afrique, des Comores et
   Antilles *F* 53
≡ de Parents d'Elèves Espagnols *BE* 110
Fédération des Associations Portugaises de
   l'air consulaire de Marseille; de l'air
   consulaire de Nantes; en France; du Nord;
   de Toulouse; des Vosges *F* 98
Fédération des associations de solidarité
   avec les travailleurs immigrés *F* 136
≡ de Travailleurs et Commerçants
   Marocains en France *F* 89
≡ de Travailleurs Turcs de Belgique *BE* 119
Federation of Bangladeshi Associations;
   Bangladeshi Women's Associations;
   Bangladeshi Youth Organisations *UK* 18
≡ Black Housing Organisations *UK* 21
Fédération des Centres Sociaux et Socio-
   culturels de France *F* 197
≡ Communautés Helléniques *BE* 38
Federation of Cypriot Organisations *GR* 31
≡ of Danish Tamil Organisations *DK* 115
≡ for a Democratic China *F* 28, *NL UK* 29
≡ of Educational Societies of Greek
   Cypriots *UK* 31
Fédération des Exilés en Europe *F* 137
≡ des Familles de France *F* 197
≡ Française des Clubs UNESCO *F* 164
Federation of Hungarian Jews in GB *UK* 43
≡ Independent Advice Centres *UK* 223
≡ Indian Organisations *UK* 44
Fédération des Institutions Socio-
   Culturelles *BE* 86
Fédération Internationale des Droits de
   l'Homme *F* 197, *IT* 205
≡ de la Résistance *AT* 159
≡ des Résistants *H* 168
≡ des Sociétés de la Croix Rouge et du
   Croissant Rouge *CH* 218
≡ Terre des Hommes *CH* 217
Federation of Irish Societies *UK* 48
≡ Italian Centres *UK* 77
Fédération Italienne Travailleurs Emigrés et
   Familles *BE* 73
≡ Mondiale des Cités Unies et Villes
   Jumelées *F* 198
Federation of Mosques; Muslim
   Organisations of Leicestershire *UK* 58
Fédération Nationale des Associations de
   Réception et de Réadaptation Sociale
   F 137
≡ Léo Lagrange *F* 198
≡ des Marocains de France *F* 89
≡ des Musulmans de France *F* 53
Federation of Pakistani Organisations *UK* 93
≡ Pathidar Associations *UK* 14
Fédération régionale des associations
   musulmanes du Sud-est de France *F* 53
Federation of Sikh Gurdwaras &
   Organizations *UK* 106
≡ Spanish Centres & Associations *UK* 113
≡ Student Islamic Societies *UK* 58
Fédération des Travailleurs de l'Afrique
   Noire; d'Afrique Noire Immigrés *F* 3
Fédération pour l'Unité des Réfugiés *F* 137
≡ des Victimes du Nazisme Enrolées de
   Force *LX* 169
Federation of Western Thrace Turks'
   Associations in Germany *D* 120
Federazione di Associazioni e Comitati
   Scuola-Famiglia *UK* 77
≡ Italiane Emigrati in Germania *D* 74
≡ Italiani Emigrati; Scuola-Famiglia *UK* 77
Federazione delle Chiese Evangeliche in
   Italia—Servizio Rifugiati e Migranti *IT* 144
≡ Internazionale dei Diritti dell'Uomo
   IT 205
≡ Italiana Lavoratori Emigrati e Famiglie
   BE 73, *D* 74, *IT* 144, *LX NL* 76, *UK* 77

Federazione delle Organizzazioni delle
   Comunità Straniere in Italia *IT* 144
≡ Organizzazioni Cristiane per il Servizio
   Internazionale Volontario *IT* 205
≡ di Studenti Grecchi *IT* 38
Feed the Children *UK* 223
Fel et Yasmine—Association des jeunes
   tunisiens à Grenoble *F* 118
Female Prisoners Welfare Project Hibiscus
   UK 223
Femmes d'ici et d'ailleurs *F* 137
Femmes inter associations *F* 137
≡ sans frontières *F* 164
≡ sous lois musulmanes *F* 53
≡ Traits d'Union *BE* 88
Fermento *BE* 73
Fethard & Killusty Society *UK* 48
La Feuille du Baobab *F* 135
Fiches juridiques et pratiques *F* 137
Fife Racial Equality Council *UK* 179
Filipijnengroep Nederland *NL* 35
Filipino Association *NI* 36
≡ Chaplaincy *UK* 36
≡ Christian Fellowship *GR* 35
≡ Irish Group *IR* 35
≡ Seamen's Organization *GR* 35
≡ Trade Union Society *IR* 35
≡ Women's Association Manchester *UK* 36
Finland Futures Research Centre *SF* 233
Finlands Studenten Förbund *SF* 195
Finnchurchaid *SF* 195
Finnish Church Guild; Institute *UK* 36
≡ Red Cross *SF* 195
≡ Refugee Council *SF* 133
≡ Youth Co-operation Alliance *SF* 195
Flash *BE* 188
Flash Contacts Echanges *LX* 239
Flüchtlingsbeauftragte Graz *AT* 129
Flüchtlingsberatung/Flüchtlingsbetreuung
   der Evangelische Kirche *AT* 129
Flüchtlingsforum *D* 201
Flüchtlingsinformation *CH* 243
Flüchtlingsrat; NordRhein-Westfalen *D* 139
Fluchtseiten *CH* 152
Flughafendienst *AT* 187
Flughafensozialdienst Berlin-Schönefeld;
   Frankfurt; München II *D* 201
Flygtningenævnet *DK* 194
Flygtningenyt *DK* 132
Flygtningesekretariatet *DK* 194
Flyktinggruppernas och Asylrådens
   Riksförbund *S* 152
FN-Forbundet *DK* 194
Focus *F* 74
Focus on Ireland & the Wider World *IR* 168
Föderation der Arbeitervereine aus
   Kurdistan in Deutschland *D* 82
Föderation der Demokratischen Arbeiter-
   vereine *D* 120
≡ Arbeitervereine Kurdistans *D* 82
≡ Patriotenbunde *D* 120
Föderation der Immigrantenvereine aus der
   Türkei *D* 121
≡ der Kurdisch Türkischen Arbeitervereine
   D 82
≡ Progressiver Volksvereine in Europa
   D 120
≡ der Volksvereine Türkischer Sozial-
   demokraten *D* 120
Foleshill Asian Group *UK* 14
Folgen der Arbeitsmigration für Bildung und
   Erziehung *D* 237
Folha Informativa *D* 99-100
Folinha Portuguêsa *UK* 101
Folkebevægelsen mod Fremmedhad *DK* 194
Folkekirkens Nødhjælp *DK* 194
Fondation Arche de la Fraternité *F* 196
≡ pour la Cohabitation des Communautés
   et la Coopération Internationale *F* 164
≡ Européenne de la Science *F* 235
≡ Calouste Gulbenkian *F* 98
≡ du Japon *F* 78
≡ libanaise pour la paix civile *F* 85
≡ Danielle Mitterrand *F* 198
≡ Nationale des Sciences Politiques *F* 234
≡ Roi Baudouin *BE* 190
≡ René Seydoux pour le Monde
   Méditerranéen *F* 235
≡ Soros *F* 198
≡ Tolstoï *BE* 32, *F* 33
≡ pour la Vie Associatif *F* 198
Fondazione Giovanni Agnelli *IT* 205
≡ Lelio Basso *IT* 206
≡ Leone Caetani—Accademia Nazionale
   dei Lincei; Cariplo *IT* 239
≡ Italiana per il Volontariato *IT* 206
≡ Migrantes *IT* 144
≡ Tolstoi *IT* 33
≡ Franco Verga *IT* 144
Fonds d'Action Sociale pour les
   Travailleurs Immigrés; pour l'installation
   locale des réfugiés *F* 198

Fonds zur Integration von Flüchtlingen
AT 129
≡ National de la Recherche Scientifique
BE 232
≡ Social Juif Unifié F 79
≡ Soziokultur D 201
≡ Vredesprojekten NL 209
Food & Agricultural Research Management
UK 5
Foodfirst Information & Action Network
BE 190
Football Supporters Association UK 179
Foras Aisenna Saothair IR 204
Foras Éireannach Gnóthaí Eorpacha BE 46
Forbundet af Arbejdere fra Tyrkiet DK 119
≡ Jøder fra Polen; Polske Jøder DK 78
Foreign & Commonwealth Office UK 223
Foreningen af Arbejdere fra Kurdistan
DK 82
≡ Arbejdere fra Tyrkiet DK 119
≡ Demokrater fra Kurdistan DK 82
Foreningen Demos DK 161
≡ af Guinea i Danmark DK 39
≡ af Indvandrerarbejdere i Taastrup DK 132
≡ for Indvandrere og Danskere DK 161
≡ af Marokkanske Arbejdere DK 89
≡ af Tyrkiske Arbejdere; af Tyrkiske
Demokratiske Arbejdere DK 119
≡ af Vietnamesiske Flygtninge DK 124
≡ af Zanzibarier i Skandinavien DK 115
Formation Insertion Jeunes BE 190
≡ Recherce, Animation auprès des
Travailleurs Etrangers F 137
≡ et Travail en Quartier Populaire—Atelier
BE 160
Foro Africano E 4
Foro de Inmigrantes E 215
FORSA, landelijk steunpunt Antillianen en
Arubanen NL 9
Forschungsinstitut Ausländerforschung und
Ausländerpolitik D 237
Forschungsstelle Arbeitsmigration Flücht-
lingsbewegung und Migrationspolitik;
Ausländischer Arbeiterkinder D 237
Forum Buntes Deutschland D 166
≡ Civique Européen AT 159, F 163, D 166,
CH 175
≡ Comunità Brasiliana IT 23
≡ delle Comunità Straniere IT 144
≡ contre le racisme; Ecole pour un seul
monde CH 175
FORUM—Instituut voor Multiculturele
Ontwikkeling NL 146
Forum des Migrants de l'Union Européenne
BE 131
≡ gegen Rassismus; Schule für eine Welt
CH 175
Forward Project UK 21
Le *Foulard—Solidarité* BE 161
Foundation for African Arts UK 5
≡ for Black Bereaved Families UK 21
≡ Housing Association UK 7
Foundation for Human Rights S 216
≡ the Improvement of the Status of
Gypsies CS 40
≡ International Understanding DK 232
≡ Mediterranean Studies GR 238
Foyer Culturel de Seraing BE 160
≡ Espagnol F 112
≡ d'Etudiants Asiatiques F 12
≡ libanais F 85
≡ Notre Dame F 46
≡ St-Fridolin F 98
≡ Sportif F 112
France Algérie F 9
≡ Libertés F 198
≡ Louisiane F 123
≡ plus F 164
≡ Terre d'Asile F 137
Franco-British Association F 24
≡ Council; Society UK 36
Franco-Scottish Society UK 36
Frankfurter Rechtshilfekomitee für
Ausländer D 139
Fraternità Italo-Polacca IT 96
Fraternité Algérienne en France F 9
Frauen in der Einen Welt D 166
Frauenaktion Scheherazade D 139
Fraueninformationszentrum 3. Welt CH 153
Frederikssund Fremmedarbejderklub DK 161
Fredligt Arbete till Insikt Medmänsklighet
Ansvar Unionen S 175
Fredsfonden DK 194
Free Ethiopia IT 34
Free Church Council of Sweden S 216
≡ Iraqi Council UK 46
≡ Kuwait Campaign UK 83
≡ Legal Advice Centres IR 204
≡ Representation Unit UK 223
Freie Universität Berlin D 237
Freiheitlich Türkisch-Deutscher
Freundschaftsvereine D 120

Fremden-Info D 139
French Red Cross F 197
≡ Society for Irish Studies F 46
Frente Anti-Racista PR 173
≡ Patriótico Manuel Rodríguez LX 28
Frères des Hommes F 164
Freudenberg-Stiftung D 237
Freundschaftskreis der Marokkanischen
Arbeiter D 89
Friedensbrugg—Friedensförderung Projekte
in Kontliktgebiete CH 217
Friedenszentrum Martin-Niemöller-Haus
D 166
Friedrich-Ebert-Stiftung D 237
Friends of Bangladesh UK 18
≡ of Birzeit University UK 95
≡ Community Relations Committee UK 179
≡ of India Society UK 44
≡ of Iran Campaign for Democracy &
Human Rights UK 45
≡ of People BG 193
≡ World Committee for Consultation
CH 218
Frivilligorganisationernas Fond för
Mankliga Rattigheten S 216
Front anti-fasciste BE 160
≡ de l'Indépendance BE 160
≡ islamique du salut BE 8, D UK 9
Fronte Popolare di Liberazione della Eritrea
IT 34
Frontline UK 21
Frysk Anty-Fassisme Komitee NL 171
Független Szövetsége H 140
Fulbright Commission UK 123
Fulham Irish Society UK 48
Fundação Aga-Khan e da Comunidade
Ismaelita PR 54
≡ Calouste Gulbenkian PR 241
≡ Lar do Emigrante Português no Mundo
PR 148
Fundació per la Pau E 215
≡ Servei Girona de Pedagogía Social E 242
Fundación para el Desarollo del
Cooperativismo y la Economía Social E 84
≡ Española para la Cooperación E 215
≡ Internacional Olof Palme E 174
≡ Liberal José Martí E 31
≡ San Juan de Tremanes E 101
≡ Santa Lucía E 41
≡ Paulino Torras E 242
≡ Solidaridad Democrática E 216
Fundashon pa Organisashonnan Regional y
Sentral Antiano y Arubano NL 9

Gabinete Emigração e Desenvolvimento
PR 241
≡ de Estudios sobre la Emigración E 242
Gabungan Jajasan Maluku NL 88
Gaelic Athletic Association LX 46, UK 48
Gagile Theatre Company UK 48
Galaxie F 164
O Galo NL 101
Galway Association UK 48
Gambia Association of Great Britain UK 37
Gambianske Forening i Danmark DK 37
Gamkol Sharif Mosque UK 58
Gandhi School H 40
Gao Lacho Drom E 41
Gap Activity Projects UK 179
Garavi Gujrat UK 40
Gardarem Lou Larzac F 164
Alcide de Gasperi Foundation for Peace &
International Co-operation IT 206
Gastvrij Antwerpen BE 131
Gateshead Law Centre UK 223
Gathering of Muslim Parents UK 58
Geeta Bhavan UK 42
Gemeentelijk Allochtonen Overleg NL 209
≡ Discriminatie Meldpunt Leeuwarden
NL 171
Gemeinschaft der Vereine Jugoslawischer
Bürger D 126
General Diaconal Council of the Dutch
Reformed Church NL 209
General Secretariat for Equal Rights; Youth
GR 203
General Union of Eritrean Workers IT 34
≡ Jordanian Students IT 81
≡ Lebanese Students & Workers IT 85
≡ Palestinian Doctors & Pharmacists IT 95
≡ Palestinian Workers NL 95
≡ Palestinian Students GR IR IT UK 95
Génération Beur F 19
Génération 2001 F 164
Génération E BE 110
Génération Intégration F 163
Génériques F 164
Genus IT 239
German Academic Exchange Service UK 37
≡ Dhammaduta Society D 113
≡ Lutheran Church UK 37

German Red Cross Society D 201
German Welfare Council UK 37
Germanwatch D 166
Germany Alert NL 171
Gesellschaft für bedrohte Völker AT 159,
D 166, LX 169
Gesellschaft zur Förderung Ausländischer
Jugendlichen D 139
≡ Behinderte Türkische Kinder D 121
Gesellschaft der Freunde des Sahrauischen
Volkes D 104
≡ Minderheiten in der Schweiz CH 153
≡ Österreich-Vietnam AT 123
≡ Türkischer Mediziner D 120
Ghamkol Mosque UK 58
Ghana Community München D 38
≡ Human Rights Committee; Kwambo
Refugees & Migrants Community Action
Group; Muslim Union; Refugee Welfare
Group UK 38
≡ Union DK 37, UK 38
Ghanesiske Forening DK 37
Ghazal & Beat UK 101
Ghosia Mosque UK 58
Ghousia Jamia Masjid; Mosque UK 58
Ghousia Mosque UK 58, 68
≡ & Community Centre UK 58
Ghousia Mosque Trust; Qasmia Mosque &
Darul Uloom; Razvia Jamiah Mosque &
Islamic Centre UK 59
≡ Razvia Mosque UK 65
Gilani Noor Mosque UK 59
Gillingham Mosque UK 63
Il Giornale dei Lavoratori D 74
Girlington Muslim Welfare Assoc. UK 59
Gita Bhavan; Hindu Temple UK 42
Glasgow Central Mosque & Islamic Centre
UK 59
≡ Irish Society UK 48
≡ Sharing of Faiths Group UK 179
The Gleaner UK 78
Glenamaddy Society; Glenbeigh & District
Society UK 48
Globaal NL 208
Global Computer Network for Environment,
Peace & Human Rights UK 223
Le Globe F 164
Glodwick Bangladesh Mosque Committee
UK 18
Glór an Deorí UK 48
Gloucester Chinese Community Group
UK 29
≡ Council for Racial Equality UK 179
≡ & District Irish Club UK 48
≡ Islamic Trust UK 59
≡ Law Centre UK 223
Gloucestershire County Council; Race
Advice Service; Race Equality Council
UK 179
Gneeveguilla Society UK 48
Goan Welfare Association UK 38
Gobernación Civil de Madrid E 215
Le Goeland, Centre d'Expression et de
Créativité BE 160
Goethe-Institut D 201, IR UK 37
Golden Mosque UK 59
Gosford Asian Group UK 14
Græske Forening i Danmark DK 38
Graffiti BE 160
Graiguenamanagh & District Society UK 48
Grampian Racial Equality Council UK 179
Granada Acoge E 151
Granby Advice & Information Project
UK 223
Gravesend Citizens Advice Bureau UK 223
≡ & Dartford Muslim Association UK 59
Grays Anti-Fascist Action UK 179
Great Britain-China Centre UK 29
Greater London Action for Racial Equality
UK 179
≡ Bangladeshi Catering Association UK 18
Greater Manchester Anti-Racist Alliance
UK 179
≡ Bangladeshi Association UK 18
≡ Immigration Aid Unit UK 155
≡ Sikh Community UK 106
GRECO 13 F 235
Greek Anti-Poverty Network; Committee
for International Democratic Solidarity
GR 203
≡ Cypriot Association UK 31
≡ -Filipino Friendship Association GR 35
≡ Irish Society GR 46
Greek Orthodox Church TR UK 39
≡ Church of the Holy Transfiguration;
Community Church UK 39
Greek Red Cross GR 203
≡ Refugee Council H 140
≡ -Turkish Solidarity Union GR 121
Green Ink Writers' Co-operative UK 48
Green Party Anti-Racist & Anti-Fascist
Network UK 179

Greenwich Asian Women's Refuge; Asian Women's Resource Centre *UK* 14
≡ Campaign Against Racial Attacks *UK* 179
≡ Chinese Association; Chinese Community School *UK* 29
≡ Community Law Centre *UK* 223
≡ Council for Racial Equality *UK* 179
≡ Gujarati Samaj *UK* 40
≡ Mind Networks *UK* 6
≡ Mosque & Islamic Centre *UK* 59
≡ Pakistan Muslim Welfare Assoc. *UK* 93
≡ Refugee Association *UK* 155
≡ Travellers Support Group *UK* 117
Le Grès, Groupe Animation Quartier *BE* 191
Grey Wolves *UK* 122
Il Grido di Guerra *IT* 205
Griechische Gemeinde; Düsseldorf; Hannover; München; Stuttgart *D* 38
Grieks Cultureel Centrum Hellas *BE* 38
Griekse Federatie voor Gemeenschappen *NL* 39
≡ Gemeenschap Genk *BE* 38
≡ Gemeenschap Gorinchem Archemidis; Ortodoxe Kerk; Vereniging Anagennisi *NL* 39
Groen Links *NL* 209
Group for Ethnic Minority Studies *UK* 246
Groupe d'Animation et de Formation des Femmes Immigrées *BE* 131
≡ Chants et Danses du Maghreb *F* 86
≡ Contact Sensibilisation *BE* 160
Groupe Culturel et Artistique Nova Makedonija *F* 86
≡ et récréatif des Portugais *F* 98
Groupe Développement *F* 198
≡ Espagnol d'Action Culturelle *BE* 110
≡ d'Etude des Migrations et des Relations Interethniques *BE* 232
≡ folklorique portugais de Bourgoin-Jallieu 'Les Etoiles Dorées' *F* 98
≡ folklorique Souvenir du Portugal *F* 99
≡ des Immigrés de Tubize *BE* 131
≡ d'Information et de Soutien aux Travailleurs Immigrés *F* 137
≡ Italien d'Action Socioculturelle *BE* 74
≡ Orsay *F* 137
Groupe de recherche et d'analyse des Migrations Internationales; sur le Développement Rural *F* 235
≡ sur l'Histoire de l'Immigration *BE* 232
≡ sur l'Immigration du Sud-Est Asiatique *F* 110
≡ et d'Etudes sur le Proche Orient *F* 235
Groupe Santé Josaphat *BE* 131
Groupe typique et folklorique portugais de Meudon-la-Forêt *F* 99
Groupement pour les Droits des Minorités *F* 164
≡ d'Etude et de Recherche des Méthodes Actives d'Education *F* 235
≡ des français musulmans pour la jeunesse et l'entraide *F* 53
Groupement de Recherches Coordonnées sur les Migrations Internationales; d'Echanges et de Communication *F* 235
Grüne-Alternative-Jugendinitiative *AT* 187
Grup de recerca Immigració i minories ètniques *E* 242
Grupo Desportivo Assomada *PR* 9
≡ de Estudo e Acção sobre a Emigração Temporária *PR* 241
≡ Recreativo Unidos das Ilhas *PR* 148
≡ de Solidariedade com America Latina *PR* 84
≡ de Trabajo Emigración Europea *E* 214
Gruppo Africano Cultura e Sport *IT* 4
≡ Boliviani *IT* 23
≡ Camerunesi *IT* 25
≡ Italiano de Molenbeek *BE* 74
≡ Latino-Americano *IT* 84
≡ di Volontariato Civile *IT* 169
Grups de Recerca i Actuació sobre Minories Culturals i Treballadors Estrangers *E* 242
Guardia di Finanza *IT* 206
Guatemala Committee for Human Rights *UK* 39
Gujarat Muslim Association; Society *UK* 40
Gujarat Samachar *UK* 15, 40
Gujarat Sunni Muslim Community Centre; Gujarati Muslim Al-Madina; Gujarati Sunni Muslim Society; Gujerati Cultural Association *UK* 40
Gulistan *NL* 1
Gurbuz Yabas *NL* 121
Gurdwara Ajit Darbar; Amrit Parchar Dharmak Diwan; Grays; Guru Granth; Guru Har Rai Sahib; Guru Nanak Parkash; Khalsa Mero Roop Hai Khas *UK* 106
≡ Namdhari Sangat *UK* 107
≡ Nanak Darbar; Nanaksar *UK* 106

Gurdwara Parbhandak Committee *UK* 107
≡ & Sikh Community Centre; Sikh Sangat; Singh Sabha; Sri Guru Singh Sabha *UK* 106
Gurkha Welfare Trusts *UK* 91
Guru Arjan Dev Gurdwara; Gobind Singh Gurdwara; Kaldighar Gurdwara; Nanak Darbar Gurdwara *UK* 106
Guru Nanak Devji Gurdwara *UK* 108
≡ Foundation UK *UK* 107
≡ Gurdwara; Nishkam Sewak Jatha; Parkash Sikh Temple; Sat Sang Gurdwara *UK* 106
Guru Ravidas Gurdwara; Teg Bahadur Gurdwara *UK* 107
Gurutze Gorria *E* 215
Guyana Berbice Assoc.; Friends Assoc.; United Sad'r Islamic Anjuman *UK* 40
Gwent Bangladeshi Association *UK* 18
≡ Racial Equality Council *UK* 179
Gypsy Council for Education, Culture, Welfare & Civil Rights *UK* 41

Haags Initiatief tegen Fascisme en Discriminatie; Meld- en Registratiepunt Discriminatie Zaken *NL* 171
Haagse Morokkaanse Vereniging *NL* 90
Haarlem Release *NL* 171
Hackett House *UK* 49
Hackney Afro-Caribbean Mental Health Programme *UK* 7
≡ Chinese Community Services *UK* 29
≡ Citizens Rights Group *UK* 223
≡ Community Defence Association *UK* 179
≡ Cypriot Association *UK* 32
≡ English Language Scheme *UK* 155
≡ Irish Association *UK* 48
≡ Law Centre *UK* 223
≡ Muslim Council; Muslim Women's Council *UK* 59
≡ Pakistan Women's Welfare Centre *UK* 93
≡ Race Equality Unit; Racial Equality Council *UK* 179
Haiti Support Campaign; Group *UK* 41
Halifax Anti-Fascist Action *UK* 179
Halkci *D* 120
Halkevi Turkish Community Centre *UK* 122
Les Halles de Schaerbeek *BE* 160
Halt *BE* 160
Hamdard Day Centre *UK* 93
Hammersmith & Fulham Community Law Centre *UK* 223
≡ Irish Centre *UK* 50
≡ Racial Equality Council *UK* 179
Hand in Hand voor Demokratie en Verdraagzamheid *BE* 131
Hand in Hand Trust *UK* 223
Handicap International *BE* 191, *F* 198
Handsworth Law Centre *UK* 223
≡ Mosque; Mosque/Islamic Centre *UK* 59
Hanfi Sunni Muslim Association *UK* 59
≡ Circle *UK* 65, 70
Hanifa Masjid *UK* 59
Hansib Publishing *UK* 13, 27, 125
Harambee Centre for Environmental & Development Education *UK* 244
≡ Housing Association *UK* 21
Hare Krishna movement *UK* 42
Harehills & Chapeltown Law Centre *UK* 223
Haringey Advice & Information Service *UK* 48
Haringey Chinese Centre; Community School *UK* 29
Haringey Irish Association; Community Care Centre; Cultural & Community Centre *UK* 48
Haringey Racial Equality Council; Harassment Monitoring Project *UK* 179
Haringey Refugee Consortium *UK* 155
≡ Travellers Support Group *UK* 117
Harlesden Advice Centre *UK* 223
Harlow Community Relations Council *UK* 179
Harlow Irish Association *UK* 48
Harmony *IR* 168
Haroonia Islamic Centre *UK* 59
Harrow Inter-Faith Council *UK* 179
≡ Muslim Education Society *UK* 59
≡ Racial Equality Council *UK* 179
Hartlepool Muslim Welfare Assoc. *UK* 59
Hastings Voluntary Action *UK* 243
Hathanuri Islamic Book Centre *UK* 59
Haus der Kulturen der Welt *D* 166
Das Haus—La Maison—The House *IR* 168
Haut Commissariat des Nations Unies pour les Réfugiés *BE* 191, *F* 198, *LX* 207
Havan Project *UK* 14
El Hawakati Le Conteur *F* 10
Hayes Citizens Advice Bureau *UK* 223
Hazrat Dewan Hazoori Centre *UK* 59
hCa Balkan Project *NL* 23

Health Advocacy Services for Turkish & Kurdish Speaking Communities *UK* 122
Health Unlimited *UK* 223
Heaton Mosque *UK* 59
Hebrew Immigrant Aid Society *IT* 79
HEGOA, Centro de Documentación e Investigaciones sobre Paises en Desarrollo *E* 242
Heilig-Kreuz-Gemeinde *D* 201
Hellenic Centre *UK* 39
Helliniki Koinonia *GR* 238
Helping Hands—Koordinationsbüro für Flüchtlingshilfe *AT* 129
Helsingforskomitee *NR* 211
Helsinki Citizen's Assembly Projekten *NL* 209
Helsinki Committee *CT CS* 193, *NR* 211
Hemel Hempstead Irish Society *UK* 48
Hendon Islamic Centre & Mosque *UK* 59
Her Majesty's Immigration Service *UK* 224
Heraa Islamic Centre *UK* 59
Hertfordshire Anti-Fascist Action *UK* 179
Hibiscus Caribbean Elderly Group *UK* 27
Hidayatul Muslim Society *UK* 59
Terrence Higgins Trust *UK* 223
High Wycombe Irish Association *UK* 48
Highfields & Belgrave Community Law Centre *UK* 223
Highfields Workshops *UK* 6
Hijaz *UK* 72
Hijra Mosque; School *UK* 59
Hilfswerk der Evangelischen Kirchen *CH* 217
Hillfields Mosque & Muslim Assoc. *UK* 59
Hillingdon Borough Irish Association *UK* 48
≡ Legal Resource Centre *UK* 223
≡ Race Equality Project *UK* 179
Hinckley Muslim Association *UK* 59
Hind Samachar *UK* 41
Hindi International Development Instigator *UK* 41
Hindu Association of Leamington Spa; Centre; College; Community Centre; Cultural Centre; Cultural Society of Slough; Religious & Cultural Society; Swayam Sevada Sang; Temple *UK* 42
Hindu Vishwa *UK* 43
Hindu Women's Group *UK* 42
Histoire des identités nationales, du racisme et des migrations en Europe *F* 235
Hit Racism for Six Campaign *UK* 179
Hitchin Mosque *UK* 59
Hitslink Advice Agency *UK* 155
Hitt Husid *IS* 203
Hizb ul Ulama; ut-Tahrir *UK* 59
Hjælp *DK* 194
Hjalparstofnun Kirkjunnar *IS* 203
Hjemstavnsforeningen for Vietnamesere i Aalborg *DK* 124
HMD International *UK* 223
Hnutí Obcanské Solidarity a Tolerance *CS* 161
Hochschule für Wirtschaft und Politik *D* 237
Hogar Español *LX* 113
≡ Altas Torres de Waterschei *BE* 110
Hoge Commissaris van de Verenigde Naties voor Vluchtelingen/voor Vluchtelingen van de Verenigde Naties *BE* 191, *NL* 209
Hoher Flüchtlingskommissar der Vereinten Nationen *D* 201
Hoja del CESSAR *E* 213
Holborn Islamic & Welfare Centre *UK* 59
Holocaust Educational Trust; Survivors Centre *UK* 80
Holstenbroegnens Indvandrerforening *DK* 132
Holy Party *UK* 59
A Hombros de Trabajadores *E* 215
Home Office *UK* 223-4
≡ Immigration & Nationality Department *UK* 220, 226
Hommes et Migrations *F* 233
Honduras Committee for Human Rights *UK* 43
Hoppets Stjarna *S* 216
Hopscotch Asian Women's Centre *UK* 18
Horizons 2000 *BE* 130
Horn of Africa Community Group *UK* 5
El Hornero *UK* 123
Hospitalisation Bretagne sans frontières *F* 198
Hosting for Overseas Students *UK* 155
Hounslow Afro-Caribbean Association *UK* 6
≡ Asian Women's Community Centre *UK* 14
≡ Chinese Community Centre *UK* 29
≡ Council Housing Services Dept *UK* 223
≡ Jamia Masjid & Islamic Centre *UK* 59
≡ Law Centre *UK* 223
≡ Monitoring Project; Racial Equality Council; Voluntary Action *UK* 179

Hove Hindu Community; Group *UK* 42
Hove Somali Community *UK* 108
Hove Urdu Speaking Group *UK* 123
Huddersfield Caribbean Association *UK* 7
≡ Citizens Advice Bureau *UK* 224
≡ Council of Islamic Affairs *UK* 59
≡ Irish Society *UK* 49
≡ Muslim Burial Council *UK* 59
Huelva Acoge *E* 151
Huis van Migranten *NL* 146
Hull & District Racial Equality Council
UK 180
≡ Irish Society *UK* 49
≡ Mosque & Islamic Centre *UK* 59
Hulpverlening aan ontheemden *BE* 131
Human Concern International *S* 54
≡ Rights Association of Turkey *TR* 219
Human Rights Bulletin *UK* 27
Human Rights Centre *UK* 245
≡ Documentation Centre *F* 235
≡ Foundation of Turkey *TR* 219
≡ Information Centre *F* 235
≡ Information & Documentation System
International *CH* 243
≡ Law Centre *UK* 245
Human Rights Monitor *CH* 218
Human Rights Watch *BE* 191, *UK* 224
Humanist; Humanist Association *NR* 173
Humanistisch Overleg Mensenrechten
NL 209
Humanistische Jongeren *BE* 191
Humanistische Union *D* 201
Humanitarian Aid Medical Development
UK 223
Humanitas Rotterdam *NL* 90
Humberside Law Centre *UK* 224
Alexander von Humboldt Stiftung *D* 237
Hungarian Catholic Chaplaincy *UK* 43
≡ Democratic Union of Romania *RO* 43
≡ Federation of Resisters & Antifascists
H 168
≡ Peace Association *H* 203
≡ Society *UK* 43
Hürriyet *UK* 122
Hussaini/Hussania Islamic Mission *UK* 59
Hyde Bangladesh Welfare Assoc. *UK* 18
Hyndburn Council of Mosques *UK* 59
Hyndburn & Rossendale Racial Equality
Council *UK* 180
Hyson Green Law Centre *UK* 226

Iatriko Kentro Apokatiastasis Thymaton
Vassanistirion *GR* 140
Ibadur Rahman Trust *UK* 69
≡ & Jamia Mosque *UK* 93
Iberia Cultura *F* 112
Iberian Switchboard Committee *UK* 113
Ibis *DK* 195
Ibn Sina *BE* 88
Icelandic Red Cross *IS* 203
ID-Archiv *NL* 240
Idara Isha'at al Islam; Minhaj ul Quran
UK 59
Ideal Turks Werknemersvereniging *NL* 121
Ideen für antirassistische und
antifaschistische Arbeit *D* 166
Les idées en mouvement *F* 235
Idra-il-Jaaferiya Mosque *UK* 59
Idrima Marangopoulou gia ta Dikeomata
tou Anthropou *GR* 203
≡ Meteon Hersonesou tou Aimou *GR* 238
Ierse Vriendenkring *BE* 46
Stichting Ifoudar *NL* 90
Iglesia Británica de San Jorge *E* 24
≡ Ortodoxa Griega *E* 39
≡ Ortodoxa Rumana *E* 102
Igreja dos Católicos da lingua Alemã;
Evangélica Alemã *PR* 37
≡ Italiana do Loreto *PR* 76
≡ de S. António dos Portuguêses *IT* 100
Ihmisoikeudet; Ihmisoikeuksien ja
Kansalaisvapauksien Puolesta *SF* 195
Ilford Hindu Centre *UK* 42
≡ Islamic Centre & Mosque; Muslim
Society *UK* 59
Iligh *BE* 88
Ilm-o-Adab Mission *UK* 59
Images Nord-Sud *F* 163
Images Spectacles et Musiques du Monde
F 164
Imamia Mission; Imams & Mosques
Council *UK* 59
Imanbarra Mosque *UK* 60
Imani Ujima Centre *UK* 6
Immigranten Politisches Forum *D* 139
Immigrantengemeinschaft der Türkei;
Immigrantenverband der Türkei in
Oldenburg Umgebung; Immigrantenverein
aus der Türkei Nürnberg Umgebung *D* 121
Immigranternas Riksförbund *S* 152
Immigrants Aid Trust *UK* 155

Immigrants Welfare Association *UK* 155
Immigratie en Naturalisatiedienst *NL* 209
Immigration Advisory Service *UK* 155
≡ Appellate Authority *UK* 224
≡ & Asylum Administration *LH* 207
≡ Law Practitioners Association *UK* 155
≡ & Nationality Department *UK* 224
≡ Office *IR* 204, *UK* 224, *NI* 229
≡ Service *UK* 224
Immunity Legal Centre *UK* 224
Incontro e solidarietà *IT* 144
Indenrigsministeriet *DK* 195
Independent Immigration Support Agency
UK 155
≡ Living Alternatives *UK* 224
Index on Censorship *UK* 245
Indiamail; India Society; *India Weekly*
UK 44
Indian American Society *NI* 123
≡ Arts Council in the UK; Association;
Association of Manchester; Business
Forum; Centre *UK* 44
≡ Chamber of Commerce in Northern
Ireland; Community Centre *UK* 44
≡ Community Centre; Community Centre
Association *UK* 44
≡ Cultural Association *DK* 43
≡ Cultural & Educational Forum; Ladies
Club; Muslim Association; Muslim
Federation; Muslim Professionals Group;
Muslim Welfare Society; Muslims Relief
Committee; Overseas Congress; Overseas
Youth Congress UK; Parents' Association;
Senior Citizens' Centre *UK* 44
≡ Teacher Training & Ethnic Minorities
Recruitment & Retention Project *UK* 245
≡ Volunteers for Community Service
UK 44
≡ Welfare Association in Denmark *DK* 43
≡ Welfare Society; Women's Assoc. *UK* 44
Indian Workers' Association; Great Britain;
Shaheed Udahan Singh; Southall *UK* 44
Indonesisch Documentatie en Informatie
Centrum *NL* 45
Industrial Relations Services *UK* 245
Indvandraverket *S* 216
Indvandrer Kvindecentret; Kvindeprojektet i
Hvidovre Kommune *DK* 132
Indvandrercentret; Indvandrerforeningen i
Horsens; Indvandrerforeningernes
Sammenslutning i Danmark *DK* 132
Indvandrerklubben Ishøj; Indvandrerkvinde-
Klub i Hillerød; Indvandrerkvinde-
foreningen Soldue *DK* 133
Indvandrernes Fællesklub i Brøndby
Strand; Fællesråd i Danmark; Kultur og
Solidaritetsforening; Kulturforening i
Lyngby; Velfærds- og Kulturkomite *DK* 133
Indvandrerrådet; Indvandrerrådgivning;
Indvandrersolidaritet *DK* 133
Info-Diffusion Immigrés *BE* 232
Info-Migrações *PR* 241
Info-Türk *BE* 119
Infoblatt *D* 201
Infobüro Nicaragua *D* 91
Infordoc *F* 197
Informanaga *IT* 144
Informatie-Actiecentrum Assata *NL* 171
Information—Foi—Développement *F* 164
Information on Ireland *UK* 49
Informationen *D* 202
Informations, Dokumentation und
Aktionszentrum für eine multikulturelle
Zukunft *D* 166
Informationscenter for studie- og
udviklingsrejser *DK* 194
Informationsdienst zur Ausländerarbeit
D 236
Informationskontoret for Udlændinge
DK 133
Informationsstelle Lateinamerika *D* 83
Informationszentrum Dritte Welt; für
Fremdsprachenforschung *D* 237
Informatiu *E* 215
Informer pour Agir *BE* 129
Infosud *CH* 243
Infowinkel Phoenix *NL* 240
Ingiltere Türkiyeli Kibrisli Kadinla Birligi
UK 122
Iniciativa Gitana *E* 41
Initiative Antirassistische Politik *D* 166
≡ gegen Ausländerfeindlichkeit, Rassismus
und Antisemitismus *AT* 159
≡ 'Human Rights in Kurdistan' *D* 82
≡ für Menschenrechte *D* 139
≡ für Menschenrechte in Indonesien *D* 44
≡ Schwarze Deutsche *D* 19
Inkworks Project *UK* 21
Inmigrante *E* 149
Innisfree Housing Association *UK* 49
Inquest—United Campaign for Justice
UK 224

Inquilab Housing Association *UK* 22
Insertions *F* 233
Insight *UK* 27
Inspraakorgaan Marokkaanen en Tunisiers
NL 87
≡ Turken in Nederland *NL* 121
≡ Welzijn Molukkers *NL* 88
Institiúid Teangeolaíochta na hÉireann
IR 204
Institut für angewandte Sozialforschung;
Arbeitsmarkt- und Berufsforschung *D* 237
≡ Aus- und Weiterbildung im Mittelstand
und in kleineren Unternehmen *BE* 191
Institut Autrichien *F* 16
≡ Britannique de Paris *F* 24
≡ Català d'Estudis Mediterranis *E* 242
≡ de Drets Humans de Catalunya *E* 215
≡ des Droits de l'Homme de Lyon *F* 198
≡ für Erwachsenenbildung des DVV *D* 237
≡ d'Etudes Néohelléniques de Paris *F* 38
≡ d'Etudes et de Recherches Interethniques et Interculturelles *F* 235
≡ de Formation et de Coopération
Décentralisée *F* 198
≡ franco-maghrébin pour la jeunesse *F* 86
≡ Franco-Portugais de Lisbonne *PR* 36
≡ für Hohere Studien *AT* 231
≡ für interkulturelle Erziehung *D* 237
≡ für interkulturelle Zusammenarbeit
AT 159
Institut international de la démocratie *F* 198
≡ des Droits de l'Homme; de Recherche et
de Formation sur Education, Cultures et
Développement *F* 235
Institut für Kulturelle Weiterbildung *D* 166
≡ Kurde de Bruxelles *BE* 82
≡ Kurde de Paris *F* 82
Institut für Migrations- und Rassismusforschung; Migrationsforschung,
Ausländerpädagogik und Zweitsprachendidaktik; Migrationsforschung und
interkulturelle Studien *D* 237
Institut du Monde Arabe *F* 10
Institut National Conféderal d'Assistance et
de Défense des Travailleurs Italiens *F* 74
≡ d'Etudes Démographiques *F* 235
≡ de la Jeunesse et de l'Education
populaire *F* 198
Institut Néerlandais *F* 32
≡ du Pacifique *F* 92
≡ für Politikwissenschaft *D* 237
≡ pour la Promotion des Travailleurs
Etrangers *F* 137
≡ de recherche sur l'environnement
construit *CH* 243
Institut de Recherches et d'Etudes sur le
Monde Arabe et Musulman; sur le Monde
Arabe Contemporain; sur les sociétés
contemporaines *F* 235
Institut for Samfunds- og Erhvervsudvikling
DK 232
≡ de Sociologie *BE* 232
≡ für Sozialarbeit und Sozialpädagogik
D 236
≡ für Soziologie *D* 237
≡ UCJFP *F* 79
Institute for African Alternatives *UK* 5
≡ of Black Economic Empowerment *NL* 19
≡ of Commonwealth Studies *UK* 16, 245
≡ of Community Studies *UK* 245
≡ of Cultural Affairs *BE* 191
≡ of Development Studies *UK* 245
≡ of Education *UK* 177
≡ for German Studies *UK* 37
≡ of Indian Arts & Cultures *UK* 43
≡ for Intercultural Relations—Simply
Human *S* 175
≡ of International Law & International
Relations *AT* 188
≡ for International Migration Issues *NL* 240
Institute of Irish Studies *UK* 49
≡ Islamic Education; Islamic Studies;
Ismaili Studies *UK* 60
≡ Jewish Affairs; Jewish Studies *UK* 80
≡ Latin American Studies *UK* 84
Institute of Manpower Studies *UK* 245
≡ for Migration & Ethnic Studies *NL* 240
≡ of Muslim Minority Affairs *UK* 60
≡ of Political Science *DK* 233
≡ for Public Policy Research; of Race
Relations *UK* 245
≡ of Social Studies *NL* 240
≡ of Transcultural Health Care; for War &
Peace Reporting *UK* 245
≡ for Yiddish Studies *UK* 80
Instituto Alemão *PR* 37
≡ de Apoio á Emigração e Comunidades
Portuguêsas *PR* 211
≡ Británico em Portugal *PR* 24
≡ Cervantes *IR* 112, *PR UK* 113
≡ de Ciências Sociais *PR* 241
≡ de Cooperación Iberoamericana *E* 84

Instituto de Cooperación con el Mundo
Arabe *E* 11
≡ das Cooperadoras da Família *IT* 100
≡ Español de Emigración *E* 151
≡ de Estudios Islámicos *E* 54
≡ de Estudios Políticos para América
Latina y Africa *E* 242
≡ de Estudos para o Desenvolvimento
Internacional *PR* 242
≡ Hispánico de Estudios Gitanos *E* 41
≡ Hispano-Arabe de Cultura *E* 11
≡ Hispano-Italiano de Cultura *E* 76
≡ Indo-Português *PR* 43
≡ de Investigação Científico Tropical
PR 241
≡ Italiano de Cultura em Portugal *PR* 76
≡ de la Juventud; Nacional de Empleo
E 215
Instituto Nacional de Estadística *E* 242
≡ de Servicios Sociales *E* 213, 215
Instituto Português da Juventude *PR* 211
≡ de Relaciones Europeo-Latinoamericanos
E 84
≡ Romano de Servicios Sociales y
Culturales *E* 151
≡ Secular de Cooperadoras da Família
E 101
≡ Superior das Ciências do Trabalho e da
Empresa *PR* 241
Institutt for Menneskerettigheter *NR* 210
Instituut voor Migratie- en Etnische Studies
NL 240
≡ Multiculturele Ontwikkeling *NL* 146
≡ Sociale Geografie; Sociologisch-
Economisch Onderzoek; Toegepaste
Sociale Wetenschappen *NL* 240
Integral *E* 215
Integratiecentrum Mozaïk Onthaal voor
Gastarbeiders *BE* 131
Inter-Active *CH* 217
Inter-Church Aid *GR* 140
Inter-Cultureel Instituut *NL* 240
Interfaith Action *UK* 180
Interfaith Education Centre *UK* 245
Inter-Faith Matters; Inter Faith Network
UK 180
Interfaith News UK 185
Inter Faith Panel *UK* 184
Inter migrants information *F* 137
Inter Service Migrants *F* 137
Interacção França-Portugal *F* 99, *PR* 36
Interaction France-Portugal *F* 99
Interafricaine de Goussainville *F* 3
Interassociations pour l'Insertion des
Immigrés et Réfugiés en Moselle *F* 137
Intercapa—Solidarité Etudiants Etranger
F 137
Interculture-Charleroi *BE* 160
Interdepartmental Committee on
Emigration *IR* 141
Interessengemeinschaft der mit Ausländern
Verheirateten Frauen *D* 139
Interface migrants *F* 235
Interférences Culturelles *F* 164
Intergovernmental Committee on Evacuees
F 136
≡ for Migrations *AT* 188, *BE* 192, *GR* 203
Interights *UK* 224
Interim Cheshire Racial Equality Council
UK 180
Interkerkelijk Vredesberaad *NL* 209
Interkerkelijke Organisatie voor
Ontwikkelingssamenwerking *NL* 209
≡ Werkgroep—Kerk en Asielzoekers
NL 146
Interkulturelles Projekt Babylon *D* 166
Interkulturelles Zentrum *AT* 159
Intermon *E* 174
Intermundo *CH* 217
Internationaal Hulpbetoon van Caritas
Catholica *BE* 192
≡ Netwerk van lokale initiatieven voor
asielzoekers *NL* 146
≡ Vrouwen Centrum Antillianen *NL* 10
International Affairs UK 246
International Alert *UK* 224
International Alliance of Women *GR* 203
International Association for Cross-Cultural
Psychology *NL* 240
≡ for the Exchange of Students for
Technical Experience *NL* 209
≡ of Former Prisoners of Concentration
Camps *RS* 174
≡ of Immigrant Women *S* 152
≡ for Intercultural Education *NL* 240
≡ for Religious Freedom *D* 201, *UK* 224
≡ for the Study of Racism *NL* 240
≡ of Democratic Lawyers *BE* 189
International Auschwitz Committee
BE 160, *PL* 173
≡ Catholic Migration Commission *GR* 203,
CH 217, *TR* 219

International Centre on Conflict Resolution
& Ethnicity *NI* 247
≡ Centre for Islamic Studies *UK* 60
≡ Centre for Multicultural Education
UK 180
≡ Christian Youth Exchange *BE* 191, *D* 166
≡ Coalition for Development Action *BE* 191
≡ Commission of Jurists *CH* 217
≡ Committee for Human Rights in Taiwan
NL 29
≡ Committee of the Red Cross *CH* 218
≡ Communication Project *D* 166
≡ Community Service *UK* 224
≡ Concentration Camp Committee *AT* 231
≡ Confederation of Free Trade Unions
BE 191
International Council of Christians & Jews
D 201
≡ on Social Welfare *AT* 188
≡ of Voluntary Agencies *CH* 217
International Court of Justice *NL* 209
≡ Cultural Centre *AL* 187
≡ Development Centre *UK* 246
≡ Development Rights & Peace
Documentation Centre *F* 233
≡ Development Studies *DK* 233
≡ Documentation & Communication
Centre *IT* 239
≡ Falcon Movement *BE* 191
International Federation of Catholic
Parochial Youth Communities *CH* 217
≡ for Human Rights *F* 197, *IT* 205
≡ of Liberal & Radical Youth *BE* 191
≡ of Red Cross & Red Crescent Societies
CH 218
≡ of Resistance Movements *AT* 159
International Fellowship of Reconciliation
AT 188, *NL* 171
≡ Friendship League *SF* 162
≡ Futures Library *AT* 231
≡ Health Exchange *UK* 224
≡ Human Relations *BE* 232
≡ Humanist & Ethical Union *NL* 209
International Institute for Democracy *F* 198
≡ for Human Rights *F* 235
≡ of Humanitarian Law *IT* 239
≡ for Migration Issues; of Social History
NL 240
International Islamic Mission *UK* 60
International Journal of Refugee Law
UK 245
International Labour Office *F* 196
≡ Labour Organization *CH* 218
≡ League for Human Rights *D* 201
≡ League for the Rights & Freedom of
Peoples *CH* 175
≡ Legal Centre for the Protection of
Human Rights *UK* 224
International Migration CH 218
International Migration Project *UK* 245
International Migration Review IT 239
International Movement Against All Forms
of Discrimination & Racism *CH* 175
≡ of Rights & Humanity *CH* 153
International Muslim Organisation *UK* 62
≡ Network for Ireland *IR* 141
≡ Organisation for the Elimination of All
Forms of Racial Discrimination *CH* 175
≡ Organisation for Human Rights in Iraq
S 46
≡ Organization for Migration *AT* 188,
BE 192, *F* 199, *D* 201, *GR* 203, *IT* 206,
NL 209, *PR* 212, *E* 215, *CH* 218, *UK* 224
≡ Panjabi Literary Society *UK* 101
≡ Peace Bureau *CH* 218
≡ Peace Centre *BH* 193
≡ Pentecostal City Mission Church *UK* 7,
224
≡ Political Science Association *IR* 238
≡ Progress Organisation *AT* 188
≡ Red Cross & Red Crescent Movement
CH 218
≡ Registry of World Citizens *F* 164
≡ Rehabilitation Council for Torture
Victims *DK* 133
≡ Rescue Committee *F* 198, *D* 201, *IT* 206,
E 214, *CH* 218
≡ Research Programme on Root Causes of
Human Rights Violations *NL* 241
≡ Romany Union *UK* 103
≡ Sachsenhausen Committee *F* 163
≡ Save the Children Alliance; Service for
Human Rights *CH* 218
≡ Sikh Youth Federation *UK* 107
≡ Social Service *D* 201, *GR* 203, *IT* 206,
NL 209, *E* 216, *CH* 218-9, *UK* 224
International Society UK 180
≡ of African Lawyers *UK* 5
≡ for Human Rights *D* 201, *UK* 224
≡ for Krishna Consciousness *IR* 41, *UK* 42
International Sociological Association
IT 239

International Solidarity Tower Hamlets
UK 180
≡ Student House *UK* 155
≡ Supreme Council of Sikhs *UK* 107
≡ Tamil Foundation *UK* 115
≡ Task Force for the Rural Poor *UK* 44
≡ Union for the Scientific Study of
Population *BE* 232
≡ Union of Socialist Youth *AT* 188
≡ Union of Students *CS* 193
≡ Venskabsklub Blåkildegard;
Venskabsklub i Taastrup *DK* 161
≡ Voluntary Service *NI* 229
≡ Working Group for Indigenous Affairs
DK 161
≡ Young Catholic Students *BE* 191
≡ Youth & Student Movement for the
United Nations *CH* 218
Internationale Begegnung in
Gemeinschaftsdiensten *D* 167
≡ Christelijke Vredes Dienst *NL* 209
≡ Gesellschaft für Menschenrechte *D* 201
L'Internationale de l'Imaginaire F 164
Internationale Initiative Hochfeld *D* 167
≡ Kulturforum; Kvindeforening *DK* 161
≡ Liberale Solidariteit *BE* 192
≡ Liga für Menschenrechte *D* 201
≡ Organisatie voor Migratie *NL* 209
≡ Roma-Union *D* 103
≡ Solidaritätsfonds von Bündnis 90/Die
Grünen *D* 167
≡ Vrouwenwerking Flora *BE* 160
Internationaler Arbeitskreis Migration und
Psychische Gesundheit *D* 237
≡ Arbeitskreis Sonnenberg *D* 167
≡ Bund für Sozialarbeit und Jugend-
sozialwerk; Kulturaustausch *D* 237
≡ Kulturkreis Moers *D* 167
≡ Sozialdienst *D* 201
≡ Versohnungsbund *AT* 188
Internationales Begegnungszentrum
Friedenshaus; Bildungs- und
Begegungswerk *D* 167
Internationalt Forum *DK* 161
Internationella Arbetslag *S* 152
Internationella Kulturutbyte *S* 175
Interracial Solidarity *UK* 180
Inxauseta *F* 19
Ipswich Caribbean Association *UK* 27
≡ & District Irish Society *UK* 49
≡ & Suffolk Council for Racial Equality
UK 180
IQRA Trust *UK* 60
Iraaks Culturele Vereniging; Democratisch
Centrum *NL* 45
Iraanse Studenten Associatie;
Vluchtelingen-Zelforganisatie *NL* 45
Iran Yearbook UK 45
Iranian Association; Community Centre;
Counselling & Advice Society; Welfare
Association *UK* 45
Iraniani Democratici *IT* 45
Iransk-Danske Kulturel og Social Forening;
Kulturforening; Solidaritetsforening *DK* 45
Iranske Forening i Danmark *DK* 45
Iraqi Community Association; National
Congress *UK* 46
Iraqiske-Turkmenske Forening *DK* 45
Ireland-Chile Solidarity Group *IR* 28
≡ Cuba Solidarity Campaigan *IR* 31
≡ Funds *IR* 204
≡ India Cultural Society *IR* 43
≡ Portugal Society *IR* 100
≡ South Africa Association *IR* 109
Ireland & the Wider World IR 168
IRIE! Dance Theatre *UK* 22
Irische Pfarrkommission *D* 46
Irish Anti-Apartheid Movement *IR* 109
≡ Anti-Extradition Committee *IR* 141
≡ Arab Society *IR* 10
≡ Artists in Britain *UK* 49
≡ Association for Migration Studies *IR* 238
Irish in Britain History Centre;
Representation Group *UK* 49
Irish in Britain Directory UK 47
Irish Centre; Birmingham *UK* 49
≡ Drama Group *UK* 50
≡ Hostels; Housing *UK* 49
≡ for the Study of Human Rights *IR* 238
Irish Chaplaincy in Britain *UK* 49-51
≡ Chaplains in Europe *BE DK F D IT LX NL
PR* 46
≡ Chinese Cultural Society *IR* 28
≡ Club *UK* 49
≡ Club of Belgium *BE* 46
≡ College—Irish Cultural Centre *F* 46
≡ Colombian Support Group *IR* 30
≡ Commission on Culture & Education
UK 49
≡ Commission for Justice & Peace *IR* 204
≡ Commission for Prisoners Overseas
IR 141, *UK* 49

Irish Community Alcohol Service; Care
UK 49
≡ Care Merseyside UK 50
Irish Council for Civil Liberties IR 204
≡ for Overseas Students IR 141
Irish Democrat UK 48
Irish Democratic League Club;
Development Centre; Drama & Dance
Company UK 49
Irish Echo UK 49
Irish El Salvador Support Committee IR 104
Irish Emigrant IR 141
Irish & English Catholic Community PR 46
≡ Episcopal Commission for Emigrants
IR 141
≡ Finnish Society IR 36
≡ Freedom Movement; Gay Helpline; Gay
Men's Network; in Greenwich Project;
Heritage UK 49
Irish Heritage UK 51
Irish Hispanic Society E 47
≡ Housing Forum UK 49
≡ Indian Cultural Society IR 43
≡ Institute for European Affairs BE 46
≡ in Islington Project; Legion UK 49
≡ Lesbian Network UK 51
≡ Mental Health Group UK 49
≡ Methodist World Development Fund
NI 229
≡ Mozambique Solidarity IR 91
≡ National Council UK 49
≡ Nicaragua Support Group IR 91
≡ -Norwegian Society IR 104
≡ Peace Council IR 204
≡ Peace Initiative UK 49
Irish Post UK 50
Irish Red Cross Society IR 204
≡ Refugee Council IR 141
≡ Refugee Trust IR 168
≡ Romanian Adoptive Parents Group
IR 102
≡ Scandinavian Club IR 104
≡ in Scotland Forum; Society of Harrow;
Student Network UK 50
Irish Studies in Britain; Irish Studies
Centre; *Irish Studies Review* UK 50
Irish Support & Advice Service UK 50
≡ -Swedish Society IR 104
≡ Traveller Movement IR 117
≡ Welfare Bureau UK 47, 50
Irish Women Artists Group; in Greenwich;
in Islington; in Wandsworth UK 50
Irish Women's Abortion Support Group
UK 50
≡ Housing Action Group; Video Production
Group; Writing Group UK 51
Irish World UK 50
Irish World Heritage Centre UK 50
Irland Verein D 46
Ishøj Indvandrerforening DK 133
IS in Brief D 201
Isis International IT 206
Islam et jeunesse F 53
Islam-Rat für die BRD D 53
Islami Darasagh UK 60
Islamia Girls' High School; Girls' School;
Ibadat Khan Association; Madrassa;
Primary School; Schools Trust UK 60
Islamic Academy; of Manchester UK 60
Islamic Alliance of Afghan Mujahideen UK 1
≡ Arts Centre; Association; Association of
Aberdeen; Association of East Ham;
Association of South Humberside UK 60
≡ Book Centre UK 55, 60, 65, 69, 72
≡ Book House UK 71
≡ Book Service UK 56, 58
≡ Brotherhood UK 60
Islamic Centre UK 55, 60, 62-63, 70
≡ of Brent; Edgware UK 60
≡ Heathrow UK 66
≡ South Wales; of West Bromwich UK 60
Islamic Circle Organisation UK 60
≡ College UK 60, 66
≡ Community Centre; Community Centre
& Mosque Bina Mahal; Computing Centre;
Council of Europe UK 60
≡ Council on Palestine UK 95
≡ Council of Scotland; Cultural
Association UK 60
≡ Cultural Centre RS 54, UK 60-61, 70
≡ Cultural & Educational Centre; Cultural
Foundation; Cultural Society; Dawah
Academy; Defence Council UK 61
Islamic Education Centre UK 61, 67
≡ & Cultural Society; Society; & Training
Centre; Trust UK 61
Islamic Educational Centre & Mosque
Trust; & Cultural Centre; Institute UK 61
≡ Welfare Association UK 56
Islamic Environmental Research Centre;
Fhikka Propieshtan Mosque; Forum of
Europe; Foundation UK 61

Islamic Foundation of Ireland IR 54
≡ Guidance Society; Information Bureau;
Information Centre; Information Services;
Information Trust; International Front;
Lending & Reference Library UK 61
≡ Library UK 63
≡ Marriages Introductory Service &
Counselling UK 61
≡ Mission Society; Missionary Society
UK 63
≡ Outreach UK 61
≡ Pakistani Community Centre UK 93
≡ Party of Britain UK 61
≡ Propagation Centre UK 57, 61
Islamic Quarterly UK 61
Islamic Relief UK 61
≡ Relief Agency IR 54
≡ Religious Centre & Mosque; Resource
Centre UK 61
≡ Rights Movement UK 67
≡ School Ahl-e-Hadith UK 62
≡ Shariah Council UK 61
≡ Socialist Movement UK 57
Islamic Society UK 61, 70
≡ of Britain UK 61, 72
≡ of Darlington; of the Faithful; of Gwent
UK 61
≡ for the Promotion of Religious Tolerance
UK 62
≡ of Worthing UK 72
Islamic Study Centre UK 60
≡ Teaching Centre UK 64
≡ Teaching & Community Centre; Texts
Society UK 62
The Islamic Times UK 70
Islamic Trust & Jamia Mosque;
Maidenhead; Youth Section UK 62
Islamic Union UK 60
≡ Universal Association; Video & Audio
Services Centre UK 62
≡ Vision UK 61
≡ Voluntary Service Newham; Welfare
Association; Welfare Circle UK 62
≡ Youth Movement UK 62, 65, 69, 72
Islamische Vereinigung der neuen
Weltsicht in Europa D 120
Isle of Man Irish Society IM 52
Isle of Wight Irish Society UK 50
Islington African Project UK 5
≡ Anti-Racist & Anti-Fascist Action UK 180
≡ Chinese Association UK 29
≡ Council Race Equality Unit UK 180
≡ Health & Race Group UK 155
≡ Muslim Association UK 62
≡ Refugee Working Party UK 155
≡ Somali Community UK 108
≡ Travellers Support Group UK 117
≡ Turkish Cypriot & Turkish Elderly Group;
Turkish Women's Group UK 122
≡ Women's Counselling Centre UK 224
Ismaili Centre; Community; Cultural Centre
& Mosque; Muslim Group UK 62
Ismalia Moslem Group UK 62
Istanbul Klub DK 119
Istituto di Cooperazione Economica
Internazionale IT 169
≡ di Diffusione dalla Cultura Araba,
Siciliana e Mediterranea; di Diritto Publico;
Internazionale di Diritto Umanitario IT 239
≡ per l'istruzione professionale e
assistenza emigrati BE 74, IT 144
≡ Italiano di Cultura LX NL 76
≡ Italo-Africano IT 4
≡ Italo Cinese IT 28
≡ Nazionale di Assistenza Sociale IT 144,
UK 77
≡ Nazionale Confederale di Assistenza
F 74, IT 206, LX 76, UK 77
≡ per l'Oriente C.A. Nallino; per Relazioni
Italia, Africa, America Latina, Medio
Oriente; di Ricerche sulla Economia
Mediterranea IT 239
≡ Ricerche Economiche e Sociali IT 205
≡ di Ricerche sulla Popolazione IT 239
≡ Salesiano dello Sacro Cuore IT 206
≡ Fernando Santi F D 74, IT 144, UK 77
≡ per lo Studio della Multietnicità IT 239
≡ di Tutela e di Assistenza ai Lavoratori
IT 206, LX 76, UK 77
Italia Libera LX 76
Italia Razzismo IT 169
Italiaanse Federatie NL 76
Italian Assoc. of Leamington Spa UK 77
≡ Association of Northern Ireland NI 77
≡ Catholic Mission UK 77
≡ Cultural Institute IR 75
≡ Red Cross IT 205
≡ Society for Protection of Emigrants &
their Families UK 76
Italiani nel Mondo; Italiani in Scozia UK 77
Italienische Vereinigung für Kulturelles
Wesen und Sozialrecht D 74

Italiensk Center; Dansk Forening Århus
DK 74
Ithaad ul Muslimin UK 62
Itinera Anales E 242
Ittehad-ul-Muslemeen Sandwell UK 70
Iuventus E 174
Ivorian Refugee/Relief Action Group UK 78
Iwerliewen fir Bedreete Volleker LX 169
Stichting Izouran NL 90

J Projekt, Marokkaanse Contact
Functionarissen NL 90
*Jaarwerk Statistiek van de Buitenlandse
Migratie* NL 240
Jaén Acoge E 151
Jagaran News UK 13
Jagonari Asian Women's Educational
Resource Centre UK 14
Jagoran UK 19
*Jahrbuch für Vergleichende
Sozialforschung* D 236
Jain Community; *Jain Quarterly*; Jain
Samaj Europe UK 78
Jakilea F 18
Jalalabad Association; Mosque UK 18
≡ Mosque & Islamic Centre UK 62
≡ Overseas Organization UK 18
Jalalia Mosque UK 62
Jalaram Prathna Mandal UK 42
Jama Masjid; Mosque UK 62
Jama'a al-Islamiya UK 85
Jama'at e Ahl-i Hadith UK 62
Jamaica Caribbean Society; Community
Services Group; Society UK 78
Jamatia Mosque & Islamic Centre UK 62
Jame Masjid Ghousia UK 70
≡ Gulshane Baghdad; e-Noor; Trust UK 62
Jamea Masjid Islamic Cultural Centre UK 62
Jamia Al-Karam; Hanfia-Taleem-ul-Islam
UK 62
Jamia Islamia UK 64
≡ & Islamic Study Centre; Mosque UK 62
Jamia Masjid UK 56, 59, 60, 62-63, 67, 70
≡ e-Farooq-e-Azam UK 62
≡ e Raza UK 59
≡ Hanifa UK 61
≡ Islamic Centre UK 62
≡ Sultania; Tajdare UK 63
Jamia Mosque UK 60, 63, 68, 94
≡ Mosque Trust; Naqshbandia Nawabia
UK 63
Jamiah Mosque UK 63
Jamiat Ahl-e-Hadith UK 63, 67
≡ Ahle-Hadith; Ahle Hadith Mosque UK 63
≡ al Da'wa CH 54
≡ al-Ulama Britain; e Judullah; Ihyaa
Minhaj Al Sunnah; Islah-ul-Muslimeen;
Tabligh-ul-Islam; ul Muslemeen; ul-
Muslimin; Ulama Markazi UK 63
Jamiate-Nizam-e-Islam UK 55
Jamiyat e-Tabligh-e-Islam; el-Hadith
Mosque; Tabligh-ul-Islam; Tabligh-ul-Islam
Mission UK 63
Jamme Masjid UK 63
Jammu & Kashmir Council for Human
Rights; Kashmir Liberation Front UK 81
Janomot Newsweekly UK 19
Japan Information & Cultural Centre;
Society UK 78
Japanese Community Centre UK 78
≡ Labour Camp Survivors' Association
UK 180
≡ Women in Foreign Countries GR 78
Japanske Kvinders Kultur Sammenslutning
DK 78
Jeman Association UK 155
Jersey Chinese Association CI 30
Jersey Irish Society CI 52
Jersey Rights Association CI 158
Jerusalem & Peace Service Consultancy
Office UK 95
Jesuit Refugee Service IT 144, UK 155
Jeugd voor Europa BE 191
Jeugdatelier Gastarbeiders BE 131
Jeugdhuis Oke BE 119
Jeugdhuis Rzoezie BE 191
Jeugdvoorlichting 1940-1945 NL 171
Jeugdzorg Eisden BE 119
Jeunes Arabes de Lyon et Banlieue F 10
Jeunes Juristes Béninois pour un Etat de
Droit F 19
Jeunes pour le Monde GR 203
Jeunesse pour l'Action Démocratique en
Europe F 198
≡ pour l'Europe BE 191
≡ Maghrébine BE 86, F 86
Jeunesse Ouvrière Chretienne BE 191
≡ Espagnole en France F 112
Jeunesse sportive culturelle algérienne et
de loisirs de Givors F 9
Jewish Agency for Israel UK 81

Jewish Care; *Jewish Chronicle* UK 80
Jewish Community Action; Council for
  Community Relations; Council of Racial
  Equality; Feminist Group UK 80
Jewish Gazette; *Jewish Herald* UK 80
Jewish Memorial Council UK 80
≡ Organisation of Prisoners of Fascist
  Concentration Camps RS 79
Jewish People UK 80
Jewish Refugees Committee UK 80
≡ Representative Council IR 79, UK 80
≡ Social Aid Agency NL 79
≡ Socialist Group UK 80
Jewish Telegraph UK 80
Jewish Welfare Board; Women's Network
  UK 80
Jinnah Community Development Service
  UK 63
Joegoslavisch Komitee NL 126
Joint Committee for Palestine UK 95
Joint Council for Anglo-Caribbean
  Churches UK 9
≡ for the Welfare of Immigrants UK 155
Joint Israel Appeal UK 73
Claudia Jones Organization UK 22
Jonge Democraten NL 209
Jonge Europese Federalisten NL 209
Jongeren Tegen Racisme BE 160, NL 171
≡ in Europa NL 171
Jongerenbond NL 171
Joods Historisch Museum NL 79
Joodse Sociale Dienst BE 78
≡ Studenten en Jongeren Vereniging NL 79
Jossour F 89
Le Journal de l'Alpha BE 191
Journal of Islamic Studies UK 63, 69
Journal des Juristes Démocrates BE 189
Journal of Refugee Studies UK 245
Journal für Sozialforschung AT 231
Jovems sem Fronteiras PR 149
Jóvenes contra la Intolerancia E 174
Jóvenes Españoles Organizados en
  Hamburgo D 112
JP Bulletin NL 208
Judicial Studies Board UK 245
Jugend für Europa BE 191, D 201
Jugend gegen Rassismus in Europa D 167
Jugoslaviske Forening; i Danmark; Dzemal
  Bijedic DK 125
≡ Edward Kardelj; Liria DK 126
≡ Makedonija DK 85
≡ Prespa DK 126
Jugoslaviske Klub Besa; Branko Copic;
  Djerdap; Ivo Lolo Ribar; Kadinjaca DK 126
≡ Makedonia DK 86
≡ Timok; Veljko Vlahovic DK 126
Jugoslaviske Kvindeklub Nada Dimic
  DK 126
Juma Masjid UK 63
June 4 China Support Group UK 30
Jungdemokraten—Junge Linke D 201
Junge Europäischer Föderalisten AT 187,
  D 167
Jungsozialisten Schweiz CH 218
Just News NI 229
Justice UK 225
Justice Alliance Campaign UK 22
Justice Nigeria UK 92
Justícia i Pau; Justicia y Paz E 215
Justitia et Pax D 201
Justitsministeriet DK 194
Juventud Obrera D 112
Juventud Obrera Cristiana F D 112
Jyllands Tyrkiske Ungdoms Indvandrer-
  forening DK 119

Kaamyabi UK 155
Kaapverdianse Arbeidersvereniging NL 26
Kababayan NL 35
Kabisag IT 35
Kairos Europa D 202
Kairos Youth Co-ordination BE 191
Kaisahan at Samahan ng Mangagawan
  Pilipino; Samahan ng Migranteng Pilipino
  sa Gresya GR 35
≡ Nan Mga Mangagawan Pilipino IT 35
Kala Sangam Academy of South Asian
  Performing Arts UK 14
Kalayaan—Justice for Overseas Domestic
  Workers UK 36
Kalgi Dhar Gurdwara Sahib Ji UK 107
Kali Theatre Company UK 14
Kalyi Jag H 140
Kampagnekomitee Österreich, Jugend-
  kampagne des Europarates AT 159
Kansainvälinen Vapaaehtoistyö SF 195
Kanz-ul-Iman Muslim Welfare Assoc. UK 63
Karman Centre Association; Karmand
  Community Centre UK 93
Karuna Trust UK 44
Kashif-ul-Uloom Mosque UK 63

Kashmir Book Centre; Centre; Muslim
  Community Centre; Muslim Welfare
  Association UK 81
≡ Society in Denmark DK 81
≡ Workers' Association UK 81
Kashmiri Youth Project UK 81
Kassel University D 237
Katholieke Universiteit Brabant NL 241
≡ te Leuven BE 232
≡ te Nijmegen NL 239, 240
Katholisch-Akademischer Austauschdienst
  D 202
Katholische Aktion-Platform gegen
  Ausländerfeindlichkeit AT 159
≡ Gemeinde Deutscher Sprache PR 37
≡ Zentralstelle für Entwicklungshilfe D 202
Katholisches Sozialinstitut D 237
Kathoulesch Manneractioun LX 207
Katolsk Informationscenter DK 133
Kemet UK 22
Kensington & Chelsea Racial Equality
  Council UK 180
≡ Citizens Advice Bureau UK 225
≡ Mosque UK 63
Kent Anti-Fascist Action Committee UK 180
Kent Muslim Welfare Association UK 63
Kentron Erevnistis Hellinikis Koinonias;
  Erevnon gia tis Gynaikes tis Mesogeiou
  GR 238
Kerk v.d. Aartsengelen Michaël en Gabriël;
  v.d. Heilige Drievuldigheid en SS Cosmos
  en Damiaan BE 38
Kerken en Multi-Culturele Samenleving
  NL 171
Kerry Association UK 50
Kerry Emigrant Support Group IR 141
Khalistan News UK 101
Khaniqahi-Ni'matullahi UK 63
Khatme Nubuwwat Centre UK 72
Khawateen Association of Asian Muslim
  Ladies UK 64
Khilari Group UK 93
Khizra Mosque UK 64
Khoei Foundation UK 55
Khoja Shia Ithna Ash'ari Muslim
  Community UK 72
≡ Ithna 'Ashari Muslim Jamaat; Ithna
  Asheri Mosque & Muslim Community of
  Leeds; Muslim Community of Gloucester
  UK 64
Khuddam-al-Ahmadiyya Youth Association;
  Khuddam-ul-Ahmadiyya Association;
  Khuddan-ul-Ahmadiyya UK 64
The Khyber UK 123
Kilburn Irish Pensioners Group; Young
  Women's Group; Youth Action Group;
  Youth Project UK 50
Kildare Association; Kilkenny Association;
  Kilrush Society; Kiltane Society; Kilteely &
  Dromkeen Society UK 50
Kinara Asian Women's Refuge UK 14
Kinderhaus der deutschen Kinderschutz-
  bundes D 202
King Fahd Academy UK 64
King Faisal Mosque UK 63
King George of Podiebrady Foundation for
  European Co-operation CS 193
Martin Luther King Organization H 168
Kings College London UK 244-5
Kings Cross Chinese Women's Group
  UK 30
≡ Mosque & Islamic Centre UK 64
Kings Heath Afro-Caribbean Club UK 7
Kings Heath Mosque UK 64
Kingston Group for Racial Understanding
  UK 180
≡ Mosque; Muslim Association; Muslim
  Women's Association UK 64
≡ Racial Equality Council UK 180
Kinsale Society UK 50
Kiran Asian Women's' Aid UK 14
Kirkens Korshærs Sociale Indvandrer-
  rådgivning DK 133
Kirklees Asian Women's Welfare
  Association UK 14
≡ Black Workers' Group UK 22
≡ & Calderdale Inter-Faith Fellowship
  UK 180
≡ Community Law Centre UK 225
≡ Metropolitan Council Equal
  Opportunities Unit; Racial Equality
  Council; Steering Committee for
  Community Relations UK 180
Kirklich Beauftrager für Ausländerarbeit
  D 139
Kirkon Ulkomaanapu SF 195
*KLD-Brief Ausländische Flüchtlinge und
  Aussiedler* D 201
Kleintje Muurkrant NL 170
Klub 70 Jugoslaviske Klub DK 126
Klubben af Danmarks Jiddishister DK 78
≡ for Indvandrerarbejdere i Ishøj DK 133

Knightsbridge Mosque UK 64
*Knipselkrant Minderheden, Discriminatie en
  Racisme* NL 240
Kφbenhavns Finske Forening DK 36
≡ Kommunes Indvandrerrådgivning DK 133
≡ Retshjælp DK 194
Koerdische Arbeidersunie; Arbeiders-
  vereniging Nederland NL 83
Kokani Muslims UK 64
Kokni Muslim Association; Cultural &
  Youth Organisation UK 64
≡ Welfare Society UK 66
Kolletief Anti Fascistisch/Kapitalistisch
  Archief NL 240
Kollektief voor het Onthaal van Chileense
  Vluchtelingen BE 28
Kölner Appell D 40
Koloriek BE 160
Kom Over Magazine NL 146
Komitee für eine Welt D 167
≡ für Grundrechte und Demokratie D 202
≡ Marokkaanse Arbeiders in NL NL 90
≡ für medizinische und soziale Hilfe für
  Palästinenser AT 95
≡ Schluss mit dem Schnüffelstaat CH 218
≡ Utrecht tegen Racisme en Fascisme
  NL 171
≡ Zelfstandig Verblijfsrechten voor
  Migranten-vrouwen NL 146
≡ Zuidelijk Afrika NL 110
Komiteen for Udlændinges Retssikkerhed
  DK 133
*Konfrontatie—Onafhankelijk Links
  Maandblad* NL 240
Koninklijk Commissariaat voor het
  Migrantenbeleid BE 191
Kontakt International Magdeburg D 167
Kontakt der Kontinenten NL 171
Kontaktorgaan Internationale Solidariteit
  BE 160
Kontrola Kontrolpean E 215
Koordinierungsstelle der österreichischen
  Bischofskonferenz für internationale
  Entwicklung und Mission AT 188
Krishna Temple NI 43
Krishna Yoga Mandir UK 42
Kristelig Studenter-Settlements Rådgivning
  for Indvandrere DK 133
Ksisli Jamaat Hyderi Islamic Centre UK 64
Kulturen in Beweging BE 160
Kulturkomitee für Ausländische
  Arbeitnehmer D 139
Kultur-Künstlerische Gesellschaft/Kulturno-
  Umetnicko Drustvo Boro i Ramiz D 126
Kunsill Nazzjonali Taz-Zghazagh M 208
Kurdische Gemeinde in Deutschland D 82
Kurdish Centres; Cultural Centre;
  Information Centre; Relief Assoc.; Society
  of Manchester; Workers Assoc. UK 83
Kurdiske Forening i Aalborg; Kulturcenter i
  Danmark DK 82
Kurdistan Committee GR 82
Kurdistan Human Rights Bulletin UK 83
Kurdistan Human Rights Project;
  Information Centre UK 83
Kurdistan-Komitee D 82
Kurdistan Report D 82, UK 83
Kurdistan Solidarity Committee; Workers'
  Association UK 83
Kush Housing Association UK 225
Kyrwicks Lane Mosque UK 64

La Gaitana Housing Co-op UK 84
La Ralha, Amicale des Sahariens F 104
Laboratoire d'anthropologie et de
  préhistoire des pays de la Méditerrannée
  Occidentale; d'anthropologie urbaine;
  Population/Environnement; de Recherches
  Economiques et Sociales; des sociétés
  pluriethniques et pluriculturelles F 235
Labour Asylum Rights Campaign UK 155
≡ Committee on Ireland UK 50
≡ International UK 155
≡ Middle East Council UK 88
≡ Party Black Section UK 22
≡ Party Irish Society; Women for Ireland
  UK 50
Labourmovements International Forum
  DK 194
Lacio Drom IT 40
Lajana Ama-u-Lah UK 64
Lalkar UK 44
Lalla Rookh NL 114
Lambeth Chinese Community Assoc. UK 30
≡ Irish Women's Group UK 50
≡ Welfare Rights Unit UK 225
Lanarkshire Campaign Against Racism &
  Fascism UK 164
Lanarkshire Muslim Society UK 64
Lancashire Council of Mosques; Islamic
  Society UK 64

Lancaster University *UK* 244
Landelijk Aanmeldingspunt *NL* 145
≡ Bureau Racismebestrijding *NL* 171
≡ India Werkgroep *NL* 43
≡ Inspraakorgaan Zuideuropeanen *NL* 34
≡ Kontakt Groep Verzetsgepensioneerden *NL* 171
≡ Platform Woonwagenbewoners en Zigeuners *NL* 40
≡ Steunpunt Buitenlandse Vrouwencentra *NL* 146
≡ Werkgroep Consumentenrecht *NL* 209
Landelijke Advies- en Overlegstructuur Minderhedenbeleid *NL* 146
≡ Federatie voor Surinamers; Federatie Surinaamse Vrouwenzaken; Federatie van Welzijnsorganisaties voor Surinamers *NL* 114
≡ Inspraakorgaan Antillianen en Arubanen *NL* 10
≡ Organisatie Surinaamse Vrouwen *NL* 114
≡ Samenwerking van Organisaties van Buitenlandse Arbeiders *NL* 146
≡ Sinti Organisatie *NL* 40
≡ Vereniging van Alleenstaande Arabische Vrouwen *NL* 10
≡ vereniging van Anti-Discriminatie Bureaus en meldpunten *NL* 172
Landesarbeitsgemeinschaft ausländische Flüchtlinge in Nordrhein-Westfalen *D* 139
Landesinstitut für Schule- und Weiterbildung *D* 237
Landesverband der Spanischen Eltervereine in der BRD *D* 112
Landsforeningen af Danske Flygtningevenner *DK* 133
Landsorganisationen Red Barnet *DK* 195
Landsrådet for Norske Ungdoms-organisasjoner *NR* 210
≡ för Sveriges Ungdomsorganisationer *S* 216
Langley Irish Society *UK* 50
Language Line *UK* 155
Laois Association *UK* 50
Shiji Lapite Memorial Committee *UK* 180
Lárionad Taighde agus Doicmédúcháin *NI* 247
Las Palmas Acoge *E* 151
Latin America Bureau *UK* 85
≡ Groups in Norway *NR* 84
≡ Newsletters *UK* 85
≡ Solidarity Committee *IR* 84
Latin American Advisory Committee; Arts Association; Association; Centre; Community Health Group; Co-operative Development Project; Cultural Centre; Disabled Group; Refugee Organisations against the Asylum Bill; Research & Socio-Cultural Studies Centre *UK* 85
≡ Welfare Group *UK* 84
≡ Women's Aid; Women's Rights Service *UK* 85
Latinamerikansk Kulturcenter *DK* 83
Latinamerikanske Børneværksteder *DK* 83
Latvian Welfare Fund *UK* 85
Lavoro Italiano nel Mondo *IT* 206
Law Centre—NI *NI* 229
Law Centres; Federation *UK* 225
Lawyers for Palestinian Human Rights *UK* 95
Le Cana, Centre de Formation et de Préparation à l'Emploi *F* 137
Lea Bridge Mosque *UK* 64
League of British Muslims *UK* 64
League for Human & Youth Rights *CS* 193
League of Sudeten German Expellees *D* 37
Leamington Irish Club *UK* 50
Leargás Exchange Bureau *IR* 204
Leeds Alliance against Racism & Fascism; Anti-Fascist Action *UK* 180
≡ Black Health Forum *UK* 21-22
≡ Citizens Advice Bureau *UK* 225
≡ Concord Inter-Faith Fellowship *UK* 180
≡ Council for Overseas Student Affairs *UK* 155
≡ Divided Families Campaign; Fans United Against Racism *UK* 180
≡ Jewish Representative Council *UK* 80
≡ Muslim Council *UK* 55
≡ Racial Equality Council *UK* 180
≡ Vietnamese Community Assoc. *UK* 124
Leeward Islands People's Association *UK* 6
Lega Artisti Scrittori Giornalisti Iracheni in Italia *IT* 45
≡ Bulgara per i Diritti dell'Uomo *IT* 24
≡ per la Difesa dei Diritti in Iran; per i Diritti dei Lavoratori Iraniani; Internazionale per la Difesa dei Diritti Civile e Democratici in Iran *IT* 45
≡ Internazionale per i Diritti e la Liberazione dei Popoli *IT* 169
≡ Italo-Filippina di Emigrati *IT* 35

Legal Action Group; Defence & Monitoring Group *UK* 225
Leicester Anti-Fascist Action; Anti-Fascist Alliance; City Council Race Relations Unit; Council of Faiths *UK* 180
≡ Irish Society *UK* 50
≡ Islamic Centre *UK* 64
≡ Muslim Society *UK* 65
≡ Racial Equality Council; Racism Awareness Consortium *UK* 180
≡ Rights Centre *UK* 225
Leicestershire Steering Group for Racial Justice *UK* 180
Leids Instituut voor Sociaal Wetenschappelijk Onderzoek *NL* 240
Leigos para o Desenvolvimento *PR* 173
Leitrim Association *UK* 50
Lesbian & Gay Black Group *UK* 22
≡ Coalition Against Racism *UK* 180
Lettera ai soci *IT* 142, 238
Lettere di Collegamento *IT* 95
Lettre de Abdelkrim *E* 87
Lettre d'Action Familiale *F* 197
La lettre de la citoyenneté; La lettre du Coup de Soleil *F* 162
Lettre de Tiddukla *F* 118
Lëtzebuerger Fluchtlingsrôt *LX* 145
Lëtzebuerger Scouten *LX* 208
Leuven/Louvain *BE* 46
Levante *IT* 10
Lewisham Action on Policing *UK* 180
≡ Council Housing Race Equality Unit *UK* 225
≡ Irish Centre; Irish Community Centre *UK* 50
≡ & Kent Islamic Centre *UK* 64
≡ Racial Equality Council *UK* 181
Lewsey Muslim Cultural Society; Leytonstone Islamic Association *UK* 64
Liberal International Human Rights Committee *DK* 194
Liberation *UK* 181
≡ Tigers of Tamil Eelam *D* 115
Liberian Assoc.; Assoc. of Manchester; Women Assoc. of Manchester *UK* 85
Liberté *CH* 217
Libertés sans frontières *F* 198
Liberty *UK* 225
Libre Pensamiento *E* 214
Life & Light *UK* 41
Lifeline *UK* 126
Liga Africana de Defensa de los Derechos Humanos *E* 4
≡ dos Africanos e Amigos de Africa *PR* 4
≡ dos Angolanos e Amigos de Angola *PR* 9
≡ de Imigrantes Africanos de Expressão Portuguêsa *PR* 4
≡ voor mensenrechten *BE* 191
≡ de Mutilados e Invalidos de la Guerra de España *F* 112
≡ voor de Rechten van de Mens *NL* 209
Ligue Anti-impérialiste; belge pour la défense des droits de l'homme *BE* 191
≡ des Droits de l'Homme *BE* 191, *F* 198
≡ des Familles *BE* 191
≡ Française de l'Enseignement et de l'Education Permanente *F* 235
≡ internationale contre le racisme et l'antisémitisme *F* 164, *CH* 175
≡ internationale pour les droits et la libération des peuples *IT* 169, *CH* 175
≡ Suisse des Droits de l'Homme *CH* 218
Le Ligueur *BE* 191
Ligurian Association of Great Britain *UK* 76
Limburgse Immigratie Stichting *NL* 146
Linguistics Institute of Ireland *IR* 204
Link Africa *UK* 6
Lire et Ecrire *BE* 191
Lithuanian Youth Association in Great Britain *UK* 85
Liverpool Anti-Fascist Action; Anti-Racist Community Arts Association *UK* 181
≡ 8 Law Centre *UK* 225
≡ Irish Centre *UK* 50
≡ Muslim Society *UK* 55, 64
≡ Somali Community *UK* 108
Livres sans frontières *F* 25
Lobster *UK* 245
Local Authorities Race Relations Information Exchange *UK* 245
≡ Economic Consortium *UK* 155
≡ Government International Bureau *UK* 225
Logement et Promotion Sociale *F* 198
Lohana Community North London *UK* 14
Lokamaya Press *UK* 155
London Advice Services Alliance *UK* 225
≡ Alliance Against Racism & Fascism; Anti-Fascist Action *UK* 181
≡ Black Women Health Action Project *UK* 22
≡ Borough of Greenwich *UK* 177
≡ Borough of Waltham Forest *UK* 181

London Camogie Board *UK* 50
≡ Central Mosque Trust *UK* 61
≡ Chinese Health Resource Centre *UK* 30
≡ Conference on Overseas Students *UK* 155
≡ Equal Opportunities Federation *UK* 181
≡ Federation of Chinese Women *UK* 30
≡ Gypsy Traveller Unit *UK* 227
≡ Interpreting Project *UK* 155
London Irish Centre; Network *UK* 50
London Irish News *UK* 50
London Irish Pensioners Action Group; Rugby Football Club; Women's Centre; Youth Forum *UK* 51
London Islamic Cultural Society *UK* 64
≡ Islamic Turkish Association *UK* 122
≡ Jame Masjid Trust *UK* 64
≡ Ladies' Football Board *UK* 51
≡ Mosque *UK* 55
≡ Research Centre *UK* 245
≡ Society of Jews & Christians *UK* 181
≡ Sufi Centre for Holistic Studies *UK* 71
≡ Tamil Sangam *UK* 115
≡ Travellers Forum *UK* 117
≡ Turkish Radio *UK* 122
≡ Voluntary Service Council *UK* 6, 225
Londonskiy Kurier *UK* 103
Longford Association *UK* 51
Longsight and Levenshulme Anti-Racist Group *UK* 181
≡ Moss Side Community Project *UK* 225
≡ Moss Side Community Women's Project *UK* 15
Lothian Black Forum *UK* 22
Lothian Racial Equality Council *UK* 181
Loughborough Irish Association *UK* 51
Loughborough University *UK* 244
Louisburg & District Society *UK* 51
Louvain Development Trust *IR* 141
L'Ouverture Theatre Trust *UK* 155
Lower Saxony Refugee Council *D* 139
Lungiana *UK* 76
Lupe e.V. *D* 237
Lusitano *PR* 148
Lutheran Church in Ireland *IR* 37
Lutheran World Federation *CH* 218
Luton Community Relations Council *UK* 181
≡ & Dunstable Irish Care & Advice Association; Irish Advice Bureau *UK* 51
≡ Law Centre *UK* 225
≡ Mosque *UK* 61
≡ Women's Aid Asian Refuge *UK* 15
Luxembourg Red Cross *LX* 207
Luxembourg Scottish Country Club *LX* 24
Lycée Français de Belgique Jean Monnet *BE* 36
Lycée italien Dante Alighieri *F* 74

Maboko Na Maboko *IT* 4
Macca Mosque & Muslim Community Centre *UK* 64
Machitún Theatre *UK* 85
Macondo *BE* 30
Madina House *UK* 69
≡ Islamic Cultural Studies Centre; Kashif-ul-Aloom; Masjid *UK* 64
≡ Mosque *UK* 64, 70
≡ Mosque Trust *UK* 64
Madni Islamic Community Assoc. *UK* 64
≡ Jamia Masjid *UK* 60, 94
≡ Masjid; Muslim Girls' High School *UK* 64
Madras House *UK* 64
Madrasa al-Arabia al-Islamia; al-Tawhid *UK* 65
≡ Salfia *UK* 63
≡ Taleem-ul-Islam *UK* 65
Madrasah e Islamiah *UK* 65
≡ Salfia *UK* 63
Madrassa 58, 72
≡ Arabia Taleemul Qur'an *UK* 65
≡ e-Hizful Qur'an *UK* 62
≡ Islamia; Jila-ul-Quloob; Karimia *UK* 65
≡ Noor ul Islam *UK* 40, 65
≡ Taleem-ul-Qur'an *UK* 65
≡ Talim-ul-Islam *UK* 59, 68
≡ Zia-ul-Qur'an *UK* 65
Madrassah Qasim Ul-Uloom *UK* 72
Madresa-e-Talimuddin *UK* 66
Madresa Islamic Talemuddin *UK* 65
Madressa *UK* 58, 73
≡ Bhinat; e Anjuman-e-Ghousia Ashrafia *UK* 65
≡ e Ramiyah *UK* 71
≡ Ghosia Tabligh-ul-Islam & Mosque; Islam Talimuddin & Mosque *UK* 65
≡ Islamia Talimuddin *UK* 64
≡ Islamiya; Majlis Itihad e Islam; Talim ul Islam *UK* 65
Madressah Talim-ul-Islam *UK* 65
Magenta *NL* 172
Maghreb contemporain *F* 235

Maghreb-Machrek F 233
Magyarországi Ifjúsági Szervezetek
   Országos Tanácsa H 203
Maha Bodhi Society of Sri Lanka UK 113
Maharashtra Mandal London UK 42
Mahnwache Deutzer Brücke D 167
Maisha—Centro di Cultura Africana IT 4
Maison Arabe de Culture Ouvrière BE 10
   ≡ de la culture arménienne F 11
   ≡ des Cultures du Monde F 164
   ≡ d'Espagne F 111
   ≡ de l'Etranger F 137
   ≡ des Femmes du Hédas; de la Promotion
      Sociale F 198
   ≡ de la Réunion F 102
   ≡ des Sciences de l'Homme F 235
   ≡ de Tous les Couleurs F 164
Majlis Ansarullah; e-Iqbal Islamic Education
   Society; e-Muhammadi UK 65
Makedonija DK 86
Makki Masjid UK 63
Makki Mosque UK 65
Málaga Acoge E 151
Malaysia Hall IR 87
Malaysian Centre; Islamic Study Group
   UK 87
   ≡ Students' Centre NI 87
Malcolm X Centre UK 22
Malkoktail F 86
Mama Cash NL 146
Mañana DK 161
Manchester Action Committee on Health
   Care for Ethnic Minorities UK 155
   ≡ Against Immigration Controls UK 181
   ≡ Alliance for a Democratic China UK 30
   ≡ Anti-Fascist Action UK 181
   ≡ Bangladeshi Women's Project UK 18
Manchester Black Environment Network;
   Lesbian Support Group; Lesbian Writing
   Group; Resource Centre UK 22
Manchester Celtic Cultural Society UK 51
Manchester Chinese Christian Church;
   Elderly People's Group; Youth Group
   UK 30
Manchester Citizens Advice Bureau UK 225
   ≡ Council for Community Relations UK 181
   ≡ Council of Mosques UK 65
   ≡ Council for Racial Equality UK 181
   ≡ Federation of Chinese Associations
      UK 30
   ≡ Hindu Cultural Society UK 42
   ≡ Inter-Faith Group UK 181
   ≡ Irish Education Group UK 51
   ≡ Jewish Community Council; Jewish
      Socialists UK 80
   ≡ Muslim Welfare Association UK 65
   ≡ Pakistani Welfare & Information Centre
      UK 93
   ≡ Polish Club UK 96
   ≡ Ukrainian Association UK 123
Manchester Vietnamese Community
   Association; Housing Project; Interpreters
   Group UK 124
Manchester Wai Yin Chinese Women
   Centre UK 30
Mandela Centre UK 181
Mangrove First Base UK 6
Mani Tese '76 IT 206
Le Manifeste—contre le FN et le
   Nationalisme F 164
Manor Park Islamic Cultural Centre UK 65
Manos Unidas E 174
Manushi Project UK 14
Marangoulos Foundation for Human
   Rights GR 203
Mare Pral, Association d'entraide des gens
   du voyage de l'Indre F 117
Markazi Jamia Ghousia Masjid; Jamia
   Masjid; Jamia Mosque UK 65
   ≡ Jamiat-e Ahlehadith & Community
      Centre; Mosque UK 65
Markfield Dawah Centre UK 61
Marlborough Road Mosque UK 65
Marokkaans WAO Komitee NL 90
Marokkaanse Culturele Vereniging BE 89
   ≡ Jongeren Vereniging Dordrecht-
      Zwijndrecht; Vrouwenvereniging NL 90
Marokkanischer Arbeiterverband D 89
Marokkanske Forening i Danmark DK 89
Maroof-e-Islam UK 65
Más E 215
Masjeed-e-Quba UK 65
Masjid Adam UK 63
   ≡ Al-Aqsa UK 72
   ≡ Al Falah UK 61
   ≡ Al Furqan UK 65
   ≡ al Haque UK 58
   ≡ Al-Islam UK 65
   ≡ al-Rahman UK 58
   ≡-e-al-Ameen ≡ UK 65
   ≡ e Aneesul Islam UK 59
   ≡-e-Aqsa UK 70

Masjid-e-Bilal & East London Islamic
   Centre; & Islamic Centre; & Muslim
   Community Centre UK 65
Masjid -e-Falah UK 65
   ≡-e-Farooq-e-Azam UK 63
   ≡-e-Hidaya UK 65
   ≡-e-Hidayah UK 59
   ≡ e Ilahi UK 64
   ≡-e-Noor UK 40, 65
   ≡-e-Noor-ul-Islam UK 65
   ≡-e-Nur-ul-Islam UK 61
   ≡-e-Omar UK 68
   ≡-e-Raza UK 65
   ≡-e-Rizwan UK 64
   ≡-e-Sajideen UK 65
   ≡-e-Tauheed-ul-Islam UK 66
   ≡-e-Umar UK 66-67
   ≡-i-Khizra UK 66
   ≡ Shah Jalal UK 18
   ≡ Tabuk UK 58
   ≡-ul-Imam-il-Bukhari UK 66
   ≡-ul-Momineen UK 65
Masjide-e Jamia Al Madina UK 66
Masjidun-Nur UK 65
MaterialDienst Asyl D 139
Maternity Links UK 225
Mauritian International UK 87
Mauritian Muslim Welfare Association;
   Mauritius Association of GB; Mauritius
   Community; *Mauritius News* UK 87
Mauthausen Fellowship NL 173
Mayday D 166
Mayo Association; Youth Assoc. UK 51
Maziar DK 32
Mbaaku Black Roof Women's Group UK 22
MDN Ltd UK 6
MED TV UK 83
Medair CH 218
Médecins du Monde F 198
   ≡ sans Frontières BE 191, F 198, LX
      NL 208, CH 218, UK 225
   ≡ du Secours Populaire Français F 199
Media Workers Against the Nazis UK 181
Mediazione—Cooperativa Sociale IT 4
Medical Aid for Palestinians UK 95
   ≡ Aid for Poland Fund UK 96
   ≡ Emergency Relief International UK 225
   ≡ Foundation for the Care of Victims of
      Torture UK 225
   ≡ Rehabilitation Centre for Torture Victims
      GR 140
   ≡ & Scientific Aid for Vietnam, Laos &
      Cambodia UK 110
Medico International D 202
Médicos del Mundo E 151
Médicos Sin Fronteras E 215
Medicus Mundi E 215
Medien gegen Rassismus D 167
Medina Islamic Mission UK 66
   ≡ Masjid & Islamic Centre UK 69
   ≡ Mosque UK 40, 60
Mediterranean Women GR 238
Medway & Gillingham Racial Equality
   Council; Inter-Faith Group UK 181
   ≡ Towns Gurdwara UK 107
Mehr-ul-Millat Islamic Centre & Mosque
   UK 66
Meldpunt Discriminatie Apeldoorn; Leiden;
   Vlaardingen; Zaanstreek; Zwolle NL 172
Meldpunt Rassendiscriminatie Delft;
   Utrecht tegen Discriminatie NL 172
Mellemfolkeligt Samvirke DK 194
Mémoire Fertile F 164
Memon Association; Jamatt UK 66
Le Ménilmuche F 162
O Mensagem LX 100
Mensen Rechten Magazine NL 241
Sir Robert Menzies Centre for Australian
   Studies UK 16
Mercator E 150
Merger NL 240
Merhaba die Neue Brücke D 138
Merseyside Action Against Racial
   Terrorism; Anti-Fascist Action UK 181
   ≡ Chinese Community Services UK 30
   ≡ Immigration Advice Unit UK 156
   ≡ Interfaith Group; Racial Equality Council
      UK 181
   ≡ Somali Association UK 108
Merton African Caribbean Organisation
   UK 6
   ≡ Chinese Community Association UK 30
   ≡ Council Translation Services Project
      UK 225
   ≡ Racial Equality Council UK 181
Mesa de Entidades—Colectivo de Organiz-
   aciones no Gobernamentales E 215
Mesopotamien Assyrischer Verein D 16
Mesquita de Lisboa PR 54
Message International UK 72
Message of Islam Movement UK 66
Messages F 198

Messaggero UK 76
Il Messaggero del Islam IT 54
Methodist Church Division of Social
   Responsibility UK 225
Methodist International House UK 156
Mexico Support Group UK 88
Mezquita E 54
Middle East Broadcasting Centre UK 11
Middle East Economic Digest UK 88
Middlesbrough Law Centre UK 225
Middleton Road Mosque UK 66
Midlands Asian Sports Forum UK 15
   ≡ Chinese Association UK 30
   ≡ Refugee Council UK 156
   ≡ Vietnamese Community Assoc. UK 124
Midleton Society UK 51
Migraciones E 151
Migrações PR 148, 211
Migrance F 164
Migrant Advisory Service; Helpline UK 156
   ≡ Media UK 245
   ≡ & Refugee Communities Forum; Rights
      Action Network UK 156
   ≡ Services Unit UK 225
   ≡ Support Unit; Training Company UK 156
Migrant Women GR 35
Migranten Kultureel en Sociaal Trefpunt
   BE 131
Migranten Nieuwsblad NL 241
Migranten-werkwinkel Amsterdam voor
   mediterranen NL 146
   ≡ voor Surinamers en Antillianen NL 114
Migranten-werkwinkel Den Haag NL 146
Migrantenoverleg Mechelen BE 232
Migrantenvoorlichting NL 146
Migrantenwerking Waasland BE 131
Migranti-press IT 144
Migrants Associations' Information
   Network in Europe NL 146
Migrants Formation F 234
Migrants Forum of the European Union
   BE 131
Migrants Nouvelles F 234
Migrants' Resource Centre UK 156
Migration and Ethnic Relations Group for
   European Research NL 240
   ≡ Ethnicity Research Centre UK 245
Migration Newssheet BE 232
Migration Research Unit UK 245
Migration Today CH 219
Migration & Visa Department UK 223
Migrations V 158
Migrations et Développement F 164
Migrations Etudes F 233
Migrations et Pastorale F 137
Migrations Santé F 136
Migrations Santé—Languedoc F 137
Migrations Société F 234
Migreurope BE 131
Milap UK 123
Millen Advice Point UK 225
Millerntor Roar! Antifaschistische Fußball-
   Fans D 167
Millham Street Mosque UK 65
Milliyet UK 122
Milton Keynes Irish Society UK 51
   ≡ Racial Equality Council UK 181
Minaret House UK 66
Minceir Misli IR 117
Minderheden-werkwinkel Breda NL 146
Minhaj-ul-Qur'an Movement UK 93
Ministère des Affaires Etrangères BE 191,
   F 198, LX 208
   ≡ de la Communauté Française BE 192
   ≡ de l'Emploi et du Travail BE 189
   ≡ de la Famille LX 207-8
   ≡ de l'Intérieur; de la Jeunesse et des
      Sports F 198
   ≡ de la Justice BE 192, LX 208
   ≡ de la Solidarité F 196
   ≡ du Travail LX 207
   ≡ de l'Emploi et de la Formation F 195
Ministerie van Binnenlandse Zaken NL 209
   ≡ Buitenlandse Betrekkingen BE 191
   ≡ Buitenlandse Zaken NL 209
   ≡ Justitie BE 192, NL 208-9
   ≡ Sociale Zaken en Werkgelegenheid
      NL 208-210
   ≡ Tewerkstelling en Arbeid BE 189
   ≡ de Vlaamse Gemeenschap BE 192
   ≡ Welzijn, Volksgezondheid en Cultuur
      NL 208
Ministério da Administração Interna PR 211
Ministerio de Asuntos Exteriores; Asuntos
   Sociales E 215
   ≡ Educación y Ciencia E 216
Ministério de Emprêgo e Segurança Social
   PR 211
Ministerio del Interior E 214
Ministério da Justiça PR 211
Ministerio de Trabajo y Seguridad Social
   E 151, 215, 242

Ministerium der Deutschsprachigen
   Gemeinschaft *BE* 192
Ministero degli Affari Esteri; dell'Interno;
   del Lavora e della Previdenza Sociale
   IT 206
Ministry of Foreign Affairs *GR* 203
≡ Housing, Culture & Immigration *S* 216
≡ Labour *GR* 203
≡ Public Order *GR* 202-3
≡ for Social Affairs & Health *SF* 195
Minoriteternas Intressegrupp *S* 152
Minorities Resource Centre *UK* 245
Minority Arts Advisory Service *UK* 245
≡ Group Support Service *UK* 156
≡ Rights Group *F* 164, *UK* 225
≡ Studies *DK* 233
Minzhuzhongguo Zhen Xian *F* 28
Misereor—Aktion gegen Hunger und
   Krankheit *D* 202
Misión Católica Portuguesa *E* 101
Missão Católica Portuguêsa *BE* 97, *F* 99,
   D 99, 100, *LX* 100, *NL E* 101
Mission Catholique Espagnole *F* 112, *LX* 113
≡ Italienne *LX* 76
≡ Polonaise *LX* 96
≡ Portugaise *BE* 97, *F* 99, *LX* 100
≡ Slave et Hongroise *LX* 108
Mission pour le Développement des
   Echanges Méditerranéens *F* 164
≡ de liaison interministérielle pour la lutte
   contre les trafics de main d'oeuvre *F* 198
Mission et service parmi les migrants *F* 137
Missione Cattolica Italiana *BE DK D F* 74,
   LX 76, *UK* 77
Missione—Migrazione BE 74
Missions to Seamen *UK* 156
Mitalee Women's Employment & Training
   UK 18
Mitcham Citizens Advice Bureau *UK* 225
John Mitchel's 32-County Social Club;
   Mitchelstown & District Society *UK* 51
MitMenschen; *Mitteilungen AT* 188
MiZaMir *NL* 209
Mødestedet for Indvandrere og Danskere
   DK 133
Mødregruppen for Jugoslaviske Kvinder
   DK 126
Mohajir Qoumi Movement *UK* 93
Molinos de Viento *NL* 113
Le Monde Juif F 79
Eduardo Mondlane Stichting *NL* 110
Mondo Unico *IT* 169
Monitor NR 173
Montserrat Overseas People's Progressive
   Alliance *UK* 88
Moorgate Mosque Society *UK* 63
Morgengrauen D 167
Moroccan Information & Advice Centre
   Association; Islamic Association *UK* 90
≡ Workers' Association *GI* 89
Mosaisk Troessamfund *DK* 78
Moscow Magazine RS 149
Mosaic *UK* 181
Moskee Al-Kabir *NL* 54
Moskee van Brussel *BE* 52
Mosque UK 17-18, 56, 59-62, 64-72, 81, 93-4
≡ Anwar-e-Madina *UK* 93
≡ & Community Centre; & Islamic Centre;
   & Islamic Community Centre; & Madrassa
   Zia-ul-Quran; & Madressa Talimuddin; &
   Muslim Community Centre *UK* 67
Mosquée de Bruxelles *BE* 52
Mosquée de Paris *F* 53
Moss Side Afro-Caribbean Luncheon Club
   UK 7
≡ & Hulme Black Women One Parent
   Family Group *UK* 22
≡ & Hulme Forum *UK* 226
≡ Netball & Gospel Women's Group *UK* 22
≡ People's Centre *UK* 156
Motamar al-Alam al-Islami *CH* 54
Mount Pleasant Islamic Trust *UK* 64
Mouvement d'Action Judiciaire *F* 198
≡ Chrétien pour la Paix *BE* 192, *F* 199
≡ contre le Racisme et pour l'Amitié entre
   les Peuples *F* 164
≡ contre le racisme, l'antisémitisme et la
   xénophobie *BE* 160
≡ pour la défense des droits de la femme
   noire *F* 137
≡ pour l'Egalité et contre le Racisme *F* 164
≡ des Etudiants Socialistes Sénégalais
   F 105
≡ international Aide à Toute Détresse
   F 164
≡ Kanaky-Solidarité *F* 37
≡ de Solidarité pour les Iles du Cap-Vert
   F 25
Mouvements F 199
Movement for Colonial Freedom *UK* 181
Movement for Islamic Resurgence *UK* 67
Movimento Anziani Italiani, England *UK* 77

Movimento Cristão para a Paz *PR* 212
≡ Cristiano Lavoratori *UK* 76
≡ Filippine *IT* 35
≡ Português Contra o Apartheid *PR* 109
≡ Studentesco per l'Organizzazione
   Internazionale *IT* 206
Movimiento de Hermandad de
   Trabajadores; por la Paz, el Desarme y la
   Libertad *E* 215
Mozambique Angola Committee;
   Information Service *UK* 91
MS Indvandrerdokumentation *DK* 233
Muhajiroun *UK* 67
Muhul Islam Saddiqia Mosque *UK* 67
Multi-Agency Racial Harrassment Project
   UK 181
Multicultural Resource Centre *NI* 247
≡ Support Service; Resource Unit *UK* 181
Multicultural Teaching UK 245
Multi-Faith Centre *UK* 246
Multi-Lingual Community Rights Shop
   UK 156
Multi-Racial Project *UK* 181
Mundo Juvenil D 112
Mundo Negro *E* 5
Mundri Relief & Development Assoc. *E* 114
Murcia Acoge *E* 151
Muridin al Haq *UK* 67
Musée National de la Résistance *BE* 160
Muslim Action Group *UK* 67
≡ Advice Centre *UK* 67, 93
≡ Advisory & Community Welfare Council;
   Aid *UK* 67
Muslim Association UK 63, 67
≡ of Barking & Dagenham; of Bradford; of
   Croydon; of Manchester *UK* 67
Muslim Bazar Kallayan Somity *UK* 67
≡ Book Service *UK* 58
≡ Booksellers *UK* 69
≡ Brothers Association; Butchers
   Association; Centre; College *UK* 67
Muslim Community Bookshop *UK* 65
≡ Centre *UK* 57, 63-64, 67, 69-70
≡ Education Centre; & Education Centre;
   House; Studies Institute; & Welfare
   Centre *UK* 67
Muslim Council *UK* 67
Muslim Cultural Association *UK* 67
≡ Centre *UK* 60
≡ Society; & Welfare Association *UK* 67
Muslim Culture & Promotional Group;
   Defence Council; Doctors & Dentists
   Association *UK* 67
Muslim Education Centre *UK* 64, 66
≡ Co-ordinating Council; & Family Welfare
   Society; & Literary Service *UK* 67
Muslim Education Quarterly UK 60
Muslim Education Trust *UK* 67
≡ Educational Trust; Funeral Association;
   Funeral Society *UK* 68
Muslim Girls Community School; High
   School; School; Secondary School; &
   Young Women's Association *UK* 68
Muslim Health Clinic; House; Information
   Service; Institute; Institute for Research &
   Planning; Kumbar Women's Group *UK* 68
≡ Ladies Circle *UK* 71
≡ League *UK* 68
≡ Liaison Committee *UK* 56
≡ Mother Tongue Association *UK* 68
Muslim News UK 68
Muslim Parents Assoc.; Parents Assoc.
   Madressa; Parliament of GB; Prayer House
   Community Centre; Rights International;
   Schools Trust; Shia Ithna Asheri Jamaat
   of Essex; Society & Mosque; Solidarity
   Committee; Study Group; Teachers
   Association; Unity Organization *UK* 68
Muslim Welfare Association; Association
   Plaistow; Centre; & Community Centre;
   House *UK* 68
≡ Society *UK* 68, 70
≡ Society, Madrassa & Mosque; Society &
   Parents Association; Trust *UK* 68
The Muslim Woman UK 69
Muslim Women's Assoc. *UK* 57, 61, 69
≡ Association of Croydon; Centre;
   Counselling Service; Group; Helpline;
   Welfare Association *UK* 69
Muslim Youth Association in the UK;
   Centre; Cultural Society; Foundation;
   Movement *UK* 69
≡ Movement of Malaysia *UK* 87
≡ Organisation *UK* 69
Muslimet UK; *MuslimWise UK* 69
Il Musulmano IT 54
Mutual Community Care Assoc. *UK* 226

═══════════════════════════

Nacionalni Savez Mladezi Hrvatske *CT* 193
Nadace Tolerance *CS* 161
Nadim F 162

NAFSIYAT Intercultural Therapy Centre
   UK 156
Nagina Mosque & Urdu School *UK* 69
Nailah—Black Women's Writing
   Performance Group *UK* 22
Namdhari Sikh Sangat UK *UK* 107
Nanak Sar Thakht *UK* 107
Nanaksar Gurdwara Gursikh Temple; Ishar
   Darbar; Sikh Temple *UK* 107
Naqshbandi Order; Naqshbandia Aslamiyya
   Spiritual Centre *UK* 69
Narodniy Dim Oekraiens Cultureel Centrum
   BE 122
Narodny Trudovniy Soyuz *F* 103
Narool Islam Turkish Mosque *UK* 122
Nas Dom *BE* 108
Nationaal Comité 4 en 5 mei *NL* 172
≡ Kommitee voor Onthaal *BE* 130
≡ Oorlogs- en Verzetsmuseum *NL* 241
National Anti-Racist Movement in
   Education *UK* 181
≡ Asian Marriage Guidance Council *UK* 12
≡ Assembly against Racism *UK* 181
National Association of Asian Youth *UK* 15
≡ of Citizens Advice Bureaux *UK* 226
≡ of Development Education Centres
   UK 181
≡ of Ghanaian Communities *D* 38
≡ for Multiracial Education *UK* 181
≡ of Muslim Youth *UK* 69
≡ of Racial Equality Councils *UK* 181
≡ of Teachers of Travellers *UK* 117
≡ of Vanik Associations *UK* 42
National Black Alliance; Business
   Association; Caucus *UK* 22
National Campaign for the Homeless *IR* 204
≡ Coalition of Anti-Deportation Campaigns
   UK 156
≡ Coalition for Black Volunteering;
   Convention of Black Mental Health;
   Convention of Black Teachers *UK* 22
National Council of Bangladeshi
   Organizations in the UK *UK* 18
≡ for Civil Liberties *UK* 225
≡ of Hindu Temples *UK* 42
≡ for Panjabi Teaching *UK* 101
≡ of Swedish Youth Organisations *S* 216
≡ for Travelling People *IR* 117
≡ for Voluntary Organisations *UK* 226
≡ for the Welfare of Prisoners Abroad
   UK 157
National Democratic Front of the
   Philippines *NL* 35
≡ Economic & Social Council *IR* 238
National Federation of Cypriots in GB *UK* 32
≡ of Far East Prisoners of War *UK* 181
≡ of Self-Help Organisations *UK* 156
National Foundation for Educational
   Research *UK* 246
≡ Gypsy Council; Gypsy Education
   Council *UK* 41
≡ Health Service Ethnic Health Unit
   UK 246
≡ Hindu Student Forum *UK* 42
National Institute of Economic & Social
   Research *UK* 246
≡ for Social Work Race Equality Unit
   UK 181
National Liaison Committee of Diocesan
   Justice & Peace Groups *UK* 226
≡ Muslim Education Council *UK* 71
≡ Network against Detentions &
   Deportations *UK* 177
≡ Peace Council *NR* 210
≡ Salvation Front *UK* 85
≡ Security Service *GR* 203
≡ Spiritual Assembly of the Baha'is *IR* 16
≡ Training & Employment Authority *IR* 204
National Union of Eritrean Women; Eritrean
   Workers *IT* 34
≡ Refugee Organisations *UK* 156
National Union of Students *UK* 226
≡ Unions of Students in Europe *AT* 187
≡ Welfare Organisation *GR* 203
≡ Yad Vashem Educational Trust *UK* 247
≡ Youth Council *IR* 204
Nationale Koordinationsstelle EURES *D* 200
≡ Mahn- und Gedenkstätte Buchenwald
   D 167
Nationality Division *UK* 226
≡ & Treaty Department *UK* 223
Friedrich-Naumann-Stiftung *D* 202
Navin Weekly UK 41
Nayoua—Association des Femmes
   Ivoriennes en France *F* 77
Naz Project *UK* 156
Nederland bekent Kleur—Comité 21 maart
   NL 172
Nederlands Auschwitz Comité *NL* 172
≡ Centrum Buitenlanders; Expertise-
   centrum over de Multiculturele
   Samenleving *NL* 146

Nederlands Instituut voor Zorg en Welzijn; Interuniversitair Demografisch Instituut *NL* 241
≡ Juristen Comité voor de Mensenrechten; Migratie Instituut *NL* 210
≡ Vereniging van Journalisten *NL* 173
Nederlandse Moslimraad *NL* 54
≡ Rode Kruis *NL* 210
Neeli Masjid & Islamic Centre *UK* 69
Neesa Well Women Drop-in Project *UK* 15
Nepal Kingdom Foundation; Nepalwatch *UK* 91
Nero e non Solo! *IT* 169
Netherlands Committee for Multilateral Youth Work *NL* 210
≡ Institute of Human Rights *NL* 241
≡ Irish Society *NL* 46
Netherlands Quarterly of Human Rights NL 241
Netwerk Onderwijs en Werkgelegenheid Molukkers *NL* 88
Network of National Minorities Youth in Western Europe *D* 139
Netzwerk Friedenskooperative *D* 202
≡ gegen Gewalt und Rassismus *D* 167
≡ Menschenrechte *D* 202
New African; *New African Yearbook UK* 6
New Britain UK 40
New Community NL 240
New Consensus *UK* 51
New Ethnicities Unit *UK* 246
New Internationalist UK 182
New Jewel Movement Group *UK* 39
New Life UK 15, 40
New Life Women's Group *UK* 124
New Moon UK 80
New Muslim Project *UK* 69
New Testament Church of God *UK* 7, 226
New Voice UK 15
New Zealand News UK UK 91
Newcastle Black Youth Movement *UK* 21
≡ Central Mosque *UK* 94
≡ Law Centre *UK* 226
Newham Advice Service *UK* 12
≡ African, Caribbean & Asian Advocacy Project *UK* 22
≡ African Caribbean Centre *UK* 6
≡ Asian Women's Project *UK* 15
≡ Association of Faiths *UK* 182
≡ Bengali Community Trust *UK* 18
≡ Chinese Association *UK* 30
≡ Churches Immigration Support Group *UK* 156
≡ Citizens Advice Bureau *UK* 226
≡ Community Renewal Programme; Council for Racial Equality; Council Social Services Department Race Equality Section *UK* 182
≡ & District Friends of Ireland *UK* 47
≡ Irish Society *UK* 51
≡ Monitoring Project *UK* 182
≡ Muslim Citizens Association; Muslim Council; Muslim Women's Association; North Islamic Association *UK* 69
≡ Racial Equality Council *UK* 182
≡ Refugees Centre *UK* 156
≡ Rights Centre; Rights Law Centre *UK* 226
≡ Somali Association *UK* 108
≡ Tamil Welfare Association *UK* 115
Newmarket Society; Newport & Burrishroole Society *UK* 51
Newry Emigration Advice Unit *NI* 158
Newsletter for Irish Prisoners Overseas IR 141
Newtown Cultural Project *UK* 178
Ng Yip Chinese Association *UK* 30
Nia Centre *UK* 22
Nicandros BE 38
Nicaragua Gesellschaft *D* 91
Nicaragua Health Fund *UK* 92
Nicaragua-Komiteen *DK* 91
Nicaragua Solidarity Campaign *UK* 92
Nigeria Now UK 92
Nigeria Welfare & Monitoring Council *UK* 92
Nigerian Citizens' Association; Community Trust in the UK; Elderly Group *UK* 92
≡ Irish Friendship Association *IR* 92
≡ Muslim Association; National Union; National Union Women's Group *UK* 92
≡ Students Union *IT* 92
≡ Youth Group *UK* 92
Nippon Club *UK* 78
Noas Ark NR 147
Nφd DK 194
Nomads V 158
Nomen Nescio NL 241
Nomos Verlagsgesellschaft *D* 237
No-one is Illegal UK 155
Noor ul Aslam Jamia al-Masjid *UK* 62
Noor-ul-Islam Mosque *UK* 69
Noor-ul-Quran *UK* 93

Noor-Ul-Uloom Mosque *UK* 69
Nordic Council *S* 216
≡ Council of Ministers *DK* 194
≡ Youth Committee *DK* 194
Nordiska Zigenarrådet *S* 41
Norges Rode Kors; Norsk Folkehjelp *NR* 210
Norsk Organisasjon for Asylsφkere *NR* 147
Norske Afghanistanhjelpen *NR* 1
≡ Flyktningeråd *NR* 148
≡ Menneskerettighetsfond; Menneskerettighetshuset *NR* 211
North American Catholic Church *E* 123
North British Muslim Trust *UK* 69
North East Black Housing Development Project *UK* 22
≡ Coalition for Asylum Rights *UK* 156
≡ Lancashire Community Relations Council *UK* 177
≡ London Advocacy *UK* 226
North East Refugee Service; North of England Refugee Service *UK* 156
North Hertfordshire Irish Association *UK* 51
≡ Islington Law Centre; Kensington Law Centre *UK* 226
≡ Lambeth Bangladesh Welfare Association *UK* 18
≡ Lambeth Law Centre; Lewisham Law Centre *UK* 226
North London Central Mosque *UK* 67
≡ Mosque *UK* 69
≡ Zoroastrian Association *UK* 45
North Manchester Black Health Forum *UK* 22
≡ Law Centre *UK* 226
≡ Mosque *UK* 69
≡ Pakistan Community Association *UK* 93
North-South Centre *PR* 211
≡ Staffordshire Racial Equality Council *UK* 182
≡ West Chinese Sunday School *UK* 30
≡ West Monitoring Group; Yorkshire Racial Equality Council *UK* 182
Northampton Irish Centre *UK* 51
≡ Racial Equality Council *UK* 182
Northern Cyprus Group *UK* 32
Northern Ireland African Centre *NI* 6
≡ Association of Citizens Advice Bureaux; Centre in Europe *NI* 229
≡ Community Relations Council; Council for Ethnic Equality *NI* 185
≡ Council for Ethnic Minorities *NI* 158
≡ Council for Travelling People *NI* 118
≡ Council for Voluntary Action *NI* 229
Northern Ireland Research Briefing NI 247
Northern Ireland Voluntary Trust *NI* 229
Northern Refugee Centre *UK* 156
Northern Tamil Association *UK* 115
Norwegian Club *UK* 92
≡ Human Rights Centre *NR* 211
≡ Institute of Human Rights; Red Cross *NR* 210
≡ Refugee Council *NR* 148
Norwich Anti-Fascist Action *UK* 182
≡ Ihsan Mosque *UK* 69
≡ & Norfolk Racial Equality Council *UK* 182
Notizie Evangeliche IT 144
Notizie dall'Italia IT 205
Notizie fatto Problemi dell'Emigrazione IT 142
Notting Hill Housing Group *UK* 226
Nottingham Anti-Fascist Alliance *UK* 182
≡ Area Council for Overseas Student Affairs *UK* 156
≡ Bangladeshis' Association *UK* 18
≡ Black Initiative *UK* 22
≡ City Council Race & Housing Project *UK* 182
≡ & District Citizens Advice Bureau *UK* 226
≡ & District Racial Equality Council *UK* 182
≡ & E. Midlands Irish Social Centre *UK* 51
≡ Inter-Faith Group *UK* 182
≡ Law Centre *UK* 226
Nottinghamshire Anti-Fascist Alliance *UK* 182
Le Nouvel Espoir *BE* 160
Nouv'elles F 196
Nouvelles de Liban F 165
Núcleo Apoio a Timorenses *PR* 116
Nucleus Legal Advice Centre *UK* 156
Le Nuove Libertà IT 205
Nusrat-ul-Islam Mosque *UK* 69
Nutan Din UK 13
Nyhedsbrev DK 161
Nyhedsbrev om Indvandrere DK 233
Nyt fra Danmark DK 133

Obaid ul Rahman Islamic Society *UK* 69
Objectif immigrés BE 130
Objectif Tolérance *F* 164
Objectif 479.917—Non au Racisme et Fascisme; Objektief 479.917 *BE* 161

Obra do Apostolado do Mar; Católica Portuguêsa de Migrações *PR* 148
≡ Nacional de Pastoral e Promoção dos Ciganos *PR* 40
Observatoire des Migrations Internationales dans la Region Nord-Pas-de-Calais *F* 235
Observatorio de la Inmigración *E* 242
Ockenden Venture *UK* 156
Odense Flygtningevenner *DK* 133
Oecumenische vluchtelingendienst *BE* 130
Oeuvres Hospitalières Françaises de l'Ordre de Malte *F* 198
Oeuvres sociales d'outre-mer *F* 199
Off Limits *D* 237
Office Départemental pour l'Insertion des Communautés Etrangères *F* 199
≡ des Etrangers *BE* 192
≡ Fédéral des Réfugiés *CH* 218
≡ français de protection des réfugiés et apatrides; des migrations internationales *F* 199
≡ of Tibet *UK* 116
Oficina de Asesoramiento para Trabajadores Extranjeros y Emigrantes Retornados *E* 151
≡ de Asilo y Refugio *E* 214
≡ de Derechos Humanos *E* 215
≡ de Inmigración *E* 151
≡ Internacional de Rescate *E* 214
Ogoni Community Association *UK* 92
Ohne Rüstung leben—Ökumenische Aktion für Frieden und Gerechtigkeit *D* 202
Oikos PR 173
Oksforder Yidish Press *UK* 80
Ökumenischer Vorbereitundausschuß zur Woche der ausländische Mitburger *D* 139
Ökumenisches Studienwerk *D* 202
Okumeniske Fællesråd i Danmark *DK* 194
Old Trafford Muslim Society; Oldbury Mosque & Muslim Welfare Assoc. *UK* 69
Oldham Action Against Racism; Council for Racial Equality *UK* 182
≡ Law Centre *UK* 226
≡ Muslim Housing Association *UK* 69
≡ Racial Equality Council *UK* 182
Olive Branch *IR* 204
Oloçum/Genèse F 120
Oltreconfine D 74
Omar Mosque & Islamic Society *UK* 69
Ombudsman for Aliens *SF* 195
On Board UK 80
On the Move V 158
One Love Training Centre *UK* 6
One Nation Forum *UK* 15
One World IR 168
One World Action *UK* 226
≡ Centre *NI* 247
≡ Group of Broadcasters *UK* 182
Onthaalcentrum Gastarbeiders Boom; voor Gastarbeiders Brussel; Molenbeek *BE* 131
Open Eye *UK* 182
Open Grenzen *BE* 131
Open Society Fund *AL* 187, *BH BG CT* 193, *EE* 195, *LH* 207
Opera Nomadi, Associazione de Promozione della Cultura Nomade *IT* 40
Opération Villages Roumains-France *F* 102
Oratorium St Jan v.h. Evangelie—Griekse Orthodoxe; Oratoire St-Jean-l'Evangeliste Orthodoxe Grècque *BE* 38
Organisasjonen Mot Offentlig Discriminering *NR* 173
Organisatie van Mensenrechten in Irak *NL* 45
Organisation for Black Arts Advancement & Learning Activities *UK* 22
≡ of Blind African Caribbeans *UK* 6
≡ pour la Coopération et le Développement Economiques *F* 199
≡ Development Unit *UK* 22
≡ franco-tunisienne d'action sociale *F* 118
≡ of Human Rights in Iraq *UK* 46
≡ Internationale pour les Migrations *BE* 192 *F* 199, *CH* 218
≡ Mondiale contre la Torture *CH* 218
≡ of Muslim Women *UK* 63
≡ Pan Africaine de Lutte contre le Sida *F* 3
≡ for Rehabilitation through Training *IT* 79
≡ for Sickle Cell Anaemia Research *UK* 22
≡ Suisse d'Aide aux Réfugiés *CH* 153
≡ des travailleurs maliens du Cercle de Diema en France *F* 87
Organising Bureau of European School Student Unions *NL* 210
≡ Office of the World Islamic League *F* 53
Organização Internacional para as Migrações *PR* 212
≡ pela Libertação de Palestina *PR* 95
≡ dos Médicos Caboverdianos *PR* 26
≡ das Mulheres Caboverdeanas em Firenze; das Mulheres Caboverdeanas na Itália *IT* 26

Organização de Quadros Técnicos Caboverdianos *PR* 26
Organización Internacional para la Migración *E* 215, *CH* 218
≡ de Técnicos y Profesionales Guineanos *E* 33
Organization for Economic Co-operation & Development *F* 199
Organizzazione delle Donne Capoverdiane a Firenze; delle Donne Capoverdiane in Italia *IT* 26
≡ di Studenti Africani a Genova *IT* 4
Oriental Institute *UK* 246
Oriente moderno *IT* 239
ORSTOM/Démographie *F* 236
Oshwal Association of the UK *UK* 78
Osprey International Students Advice Centre *UK* 156
Osservatorio sull'immigrazione *IT* 206
≡ Nazionale sulla Xenofobia *IT* 169
Østafrikanske Forening *DK* 32
Österreichische Gesellschaft Rettet das Kind; Jungarbeiterbewegung; Rotes Kreuz *AT* 188
Österreichischer Bundesjugendring; Informationsdienst für Entwicklungs-politik *AT* 188
Österreichisches Hilfskomitee für Afghanistan *AT* 1
≡ Institut für Menschenrechte; Komitee gegen die Folter *AT* 188
≡ Kuratorium für Fluchtlingshilfe *AT* 187
≡ Nord-Sud Institut für Entwicklungs-zusammenarbeit *AT* 188
The Outrigger *UK* 92
Outsider *UK* 225
Ouvertures *F* 197
Overlegcentrum voor integratie van vluchtelingen *BE* 131
Overlegorgaan van Joden en Christenen *NL* 172
Overseas Chinese Association *UK* 30
≡ Doctors Association *UK* 156
≡ Fellowship of Nigerian Christian Women *UK* 92
Overseas Indian *UK* 44
Overseas Labour Service *UK* 226
≡ Paphos Association in England *UK* 32
≡ Placing Unit *UK* 226
≡ Students Trust; Teachers Social Circle *UK* 156
Oxfam *BE* 192, *UK* 226
Oxford Arab Group *UK* 11
≡ Centre for Islamic Studies *UK* 69
≡ House *UK* 109
≡ Islamic Centre *UK* 69
≡ L'Chaim Society *UK* 80
≡ Mosque Society; Muslim Welfare House *UK* 69
≡ Round Table of Religions *UK* 182
Oxfordshire Chinese Community & Advice Centre *UK* 30
≡ Immigration & Nationality Project *UK* 156
≡ Racial Equality Council *UK* 182

Pa Flykt Bakgrunn; Pa Flykt Nyheter NR 148
På Let Dansk *DK* 233
Pacific Islands Society *UK* 92
Pädagogik der Gastarbeiter Kinder *LX* 169
Pädagoginnen und Pädagogen für den Frieden *D* 202
Pädagogische Arbeitstelle *D* 237
Paddington Law Centre *UK* 226
Paikaar *UK* 94
Du Pain sur la Planche *BE* 131
Pak-Pakhtoon Association; Pakistan Association of Edinburgh *UK* 93
Pakistan Association of Italy *IT* 93
≡ British Social Association *UK* 93
≡ Chhachhi Association; Christian Women's Association *UK* 94
≡ Community Centre *UK* 93-94
≡ Cultural Institute; Enterprise Centre; Ex-Servicemen's Association *UK* 94
≡ Forum *UK* 93
≡ Institute; Islamic Centre; Kashmir Death Committee; Longsight United Association; Moslem Centre *UK* 94
Pakistan Muslim Association; Assoc. of Barking & Ilford; Community Assoc.; Welfare Assoc.; Welfare Society *UK* 94
Pakistan Overseas Euro Association *UK* 94
≡ Pashtun & Baluch Society *DK* 92
≡ Pathans Assoc.; Peoples Party *UK* 94
≡ Peoples Society *DK* 92
≡ Social Institute; Society; Sports & Welfare Association; Women's Association; Women's Welfare Association; Workers' Association; Writers' Assoc.; Youth Forum; Youth League *UK* 94

Pakistani Business Executives Club; Community Centre; Cultural Centre; Muslim Community Centre; Muslim Welfare Association; Social & Cultural Society *UK* 94
≡ Social Welfare Committee *DK* 92
≡ Social & Welfare Society; Welfare Association; Workers Association *UK* 94
Pakistansk Forening; Forening i Ishøj; Indvandrerforening i Taastrup *DK* 92
≡ Kulturforening *DK* 133
≡ Ungdomsforening *DK* 93
Pakistanske Forening; Studiekreds *DK* 93
Pakolainen; Pakolais Neuvonta; Pakolaistiedote *SF* 133
Pal Platform *UK* 156
Palæstinensiske Arbejderes Forbund; Forening i Aalborg *DK* 95
Palestine Information Office *IR* 95
Palestine Liberation Organization *PR UK* 95
Palestine Post; Palestine Solidarity *UK* 95
Palestine Solidarity Campaign; Palestinian Lebanon Relief Fund *UK* 95
Olof Palmes Internationella Centrum; Minnesfond för internationella Förståelse *S* 216
Pan African Legal Advisory Services *UK* 6
≡ News Agency *F* 236
≡ Organization; Refugee Housing Co-op *UK* 6
Pan-Islamic Cultural Organization *UK* 69
Panah *UK* 22
Panjab Research Group *UK* 102
Panjabi Darpan *UK* 102
Panjabi Parents' Association of East London; Progressive Writers' Association; Writers' Association, Southall *UK* 102
Panther *UK* 22
O Papagaio de Nordhorn *D* 100
Par SIPAR Là *F* 110
Para a Frente *BE* 97
Paraguay Committee for Human Rights *UK* 95
Pargham-e-Islam Trust *UK* 69
Parikiaki *UK* 39
Paritätischer Wohlfahrtsverband *D* 202
James Parkes Library *UK* 246
Parkside Health Equal Access Project *UK* 226
Parliamentary Black Caucus *UK* 22
Parrochia degli Italiani *E* 76
Parroquia y Capilla de Nuestra Señora de la Merced *E* 24
≡ San Luis de los Franceses *E* 36
≡ San Nicolás de Bari *E* 76
Partages *F* 199
Partei des Demokratisches Sozialismus—Arbeitsgemeinschaft Antirassismus *D* 167
Partenaire *BE* 188
Partito Democratico della Sinistra *UK* 77
Partnership against Racial Harassment in Somerset *UK* 182
Passages *F* 134
Passerelles *F* 233
PATH Ltd *UK* 156
Patriotic Union of Kurdistan *DK* 82
Patronato INCA-CGIL *LX* 76
Patterns of Prejudice *UK* 80
Pax Christi *BE* 192, *D* 202, *IR* 204, *NL* 210
Paz y Cooperación *E* 174
A paz é possível en Timor Leste *PR* 116
Pazifik-Informationsstelle *D* 92
Peace Brigades International *UK* 226
Peace Groups Information Centre *CS* 193
Peace & Justice Issues *IR* 204
Peace Union of Bohemia & Moravia *CS* 193
Peacemaker *IR* 168
Peckham Black Women's Centre *UK* 22
Peckham Mosque; Pendle Council of Mosques *UK* 69
Penfield Mosque *UK* 71
Pentecostal Mission Aid for Developing Countries *S* 216
People Active Through Community Help *IR* 141
People's National Party *UK* 78
≡ Progressive Party *UK* 40
≡ Trust *UK* 156
Pepper Pot Club *UK* 7
Perdesan *UK* 102
Periodic Review *NL* 240
Peru Support Group *UK* 96
Peshkar *UK* 15
Pestalozzi Children's Village Foundation *CH* 219
Peterborough Inter-Faith Council; Racial Equality Council *UK* 182
VPA PETRA *BE* 193
PETRA National Co-ordination Unit *IR* 204
PETRA Youth Bureau *BE* 192
Peuples méditérranéens *F* 235
Peuples solidaires *F* 164

Pfarre Schwechat *AT* 188
Phare Democracy Programme *BE* 192
Pharmaciens sans frontières *F* 199
Philippine British Residents League; Centre *UK* 36
≡ International Center for Human Rights *BE* 35
≡ Women's Network in Europe Babaylan *D* 35
Philippines Resource Centre *UK* 36
Phillips-Universität *D* 237
Physicians for Human Rights *UK* 226
Piccadilly Advice Centre *UK* 226
Piccolo Pianta *IT* 205
Wilhelm-Pieck-Universität Rostock *D* 237
Pieds noirs, Pieds blancs *F* 164
Le Piment Collectif Pédagogique *BE* 232
Pingst Missionens U-Landshjalp *S* 216
Pissara *E* 216
Pitsmoor Citizens Advice Bureau *UK* 226
Pitt Street Settlement *UK* 157
Plataforma Jóvenes contra la Intolerancia *E* 174
Plataforma ONED *PR* 148
Plataforma di Organisaschonnan Antiano e Arubano *NL* 10
Plate-Forme de Vigilance pour les Réfugiés *BE* 131
Platform Anti-Racisme Eindhoven *NL* 172
≡ Fortress Europe *S* 175, *UK* 157
≡ Illegale Vluchtelingen *NL* 146
≡ Marokkaanse Jongeren *NL* 90
≡ Migrantenorganisaties Vlaanderen *BE* 131
≡ des Organisations Démocratiques des Immigrés en Europe *NL* 146
Plattform gegen Ausläderfeindlichkeit und Rassismus *AT* 159
Plumstead Community Law Centre *UK* 227
Pluri'elles *BE* 189
Plymouth Racial Equality Council *UK* 182
Poale Zion *UK* 80
Pogrom *D* 166
Point de Rencontre Culturelle et Social des Migrants *BE* 131
Points critiques *BE* 78
Polícia de Estrangeiros *PR* 212
Policy Group on Anti-Racism Awareness *NL* 172
Policy Studies Institute *UK* 246
Polish Air Force Association *UK* 96
≡ Anti-Nazi League *PL* 173
≡ Association in Slough; Catholic Assoc.; Catholic Centre; Catholic Church; Catholic Club *UK* 96
≡ Citizens' Committee for Refugees; Club; Ex-Servicemen's Club *UK* 97
≡ Jewish Ex-Servicemen's Assoc.; Jewish Refugee Fund *UK* 80
≡ Naval Association *UK* 96
≡ Parish Club; Parish Social Club; Social Club *UK* 97
≡ Social & Cultural Association *IR* 96
Politica Internazionale *IT* 239
Politiek Info Centrum De Invalshoek *NL* 170
Politis *F* 165
Polonez Laan op Vurten *BE* 96
Polonia Polish Club *UK* 97
Polska Rada Mlodziezy *PL* 211
Polske Forening Ognisko *DK* 96
Poltava—Oekrainse Volksdansgroep *BE* 122
A Ponte *D* 99
Pontifica Commissio Justitia et Pax *V* 230
≡ de Spirituali Migratorum atque Itinerantium *V* 158
Pontifical Commission for Justice & Peace *V* 230
≡ for the Pastoral Care of Migrants & Itinerant People *V* 158
Pools Schoolcomité *BE* 96
Pop against Racism *NL* 172
Popda Muslim Welfare Association *UK* 18
Popular Movement for the Liberation of Armenia *UK* 12
Population et Sociétés *F* 235
O Portal *D* 100
Portsmouth Irish Society *UK* 51
Portsmouth Muslim Society *UK* 70
Portugal FM *LX* 100
Portugees Centrum *NL* 101
Portugiesisch Pfarrkommission *D* 99
Portugiesische Verein; von Remscheid *D* 99
Portugiesischer Elternverein *D* 100
Portugiesisches Kulturzentrum *D* 99
Portugiesisches Zentrum; Marburg; Mittenburg; Osnabrück *D* 99
Portugisiske Forening og Klub *UK* 97
Portuguese Club of Jersey *CI* 101
Portuguese Community Centre *UK* 101
Portuguêses Unidos de Beaufort *LX* 100
Positively Irish Action on AIDS *UK* 51
Posten LX 32

Pottery Lane Advice Centre UK 227
Pragati Asian Women's Association UK 15
Prague Post CS 24
Praxis UK 157
Presbyterian Church Women's Group
  PR 212
Presença Portuguêsa F 137
Présence Africaine F 236
Présence Croix Rouge F 197
Presencia Gitana E 41
Preston Gujarati Muslim Society UK 40
 ≡ Hanfi Sunni Muslim Society; Muslim
   Cultural Centre; Muslim Society; & West
   Lancashire Council of Mosques UK 70
 ≡ & Western Lancashire Racial Equality
   Council UK 182
Pride UK 23
Princes Street Advice Centre UK 227
Le Printemps de l'antiracisme CH 175
Prismes F 137
Prisoners Abroad UK 157
Pro Asyl—Bundesweite
  Arbeitsgemeinschaft für Flüchtlinge D 139
Probashi Samachar UK 19
Stichting Probrasa NL 147
PrODUct for Action UK 22
Profil F 233
Progetto Domani—Cultura e Sviluppo
  IT 169
Progetto Inserimento per le Persone di
  Lingua Straniera IT 144
Programa de Apoyo a Extranjeros E 152
Programma Interdisciplinair Onderzoek Oor-
  zaken Mensenrechten Schendingen NL 241
Programme for Human Rights Studies;
  Programmet for Menneskeretighetsstudier
  NR 241
Progress Report NL 241
Progressive Volkseinheit der Türkei D 121
Project Aisa NL 147
 ≡ Anti Racistische Evaluatie Leermiddelen
   NL 241
 ≡ AQUA D 139
 ≡ Fullemploy UK 157
 ≡ Integratie Nieuwkomers NL 147
 ≡ Kiu Wah UK 30
 ≡ Pehchan UK 15
Projectgroep Evaluatie Welzijn 0-18 jarige
  Allochtonen NL 241
Projekt Multikulturelle Feministische
  Bildungsarbeit D 167
Promoción de Colectivos Marginados E 152
Promotion Sociale des Travailleurs
  Immigrés F 137
Promozione Tecnologie Esperienze
  Organizzazione IT 239
Prosalus E 215
Prospettive Nord-Sud IT 169
Protestants sociaal centrum—
  Oecumenische vluchtelingendienst
  BE 130-1
Protoporos BE 38
Provincie Limburg, Dienst Onthaal van
  Gastarbeiders BE 192
Psychologischer Dienst für Italiener und
  Spanier; Psychosoziale Hilfen für Politisch
  Verfolgte; Psychosoziales Zentrum für
  ausländische Flüchtlingen; Psychosoziales
  Zentrum Dietrich Koch D 139
PTA Research & Welfare Association UK 51
Public Broadcasting for a Multicultural
  Europe NL 172
Publikationsverzeichnis D 237
Puerto Rico Support Group UK 101
Puglia nel Mondo IT 143
Punjab Human Rights Organization; Punjab
  Mail; Punjab Times; Punjab Welfare
  Association; Punjabi Cultural Society;
  Punjabi Group; Punjabi Guardian; Punjabi
  Language Development Board UK 102
Pwyllgor Cyslltiadau Cymdeithas de
  Morgannwg UK 182

Q News UK 70
Qalb Centre UK 15
Qing Hua Chinese School UK 30
QPS Reporter UK 227
Quaderni Federasti IT 238
Quaker Committee on Government
  Openness UK 227
 ≡ Community Relations Committee UK 179
 ≡ Council for European Affairs BE 192
 ≡ Peace & Service UK 227
 ≡ United Nations Office CH 218
Quakers & Race UK 179
4 L Tiers Monde F 24
Quba Culra Mosque UK 70
Queen Mary College UK 246
Queen's University Belfast NI 247
Questura, Ufficio Stranieri IT 206

Quetzal—Associazione Culturale Italo-
  Guatemalteca IT 39
Quo Vadis F 233
Quwat-ul-Islam Mosque; Quwatul Islam
  Masjid; Quwwat-ul-Islam Mosque &
  Islamic Society UK 70
Quwwatul Islam Markazi Jamia Mosque
  Mehria Ghosia; Mosque UK 70

Raad van Kerken NL 210
Rådgivningsbyrån för asylsökande och
  flyktingar S 152
Rådgivningskontor for Indvandrer DK 133
Rabaz D 167
Race & Class UK 245
Race Equality Consultative Forum; Units
  UK 182
Race & Immigration UK 246
Race for Opportunity Campaign UK 182
 ≡ & Public Policy Research Unit UK 246
 ≡ Relations Employment Advisory Service
   UK 227
 ≡ Relations Research Unit; Today
   Collective UK 246
Racial Attacks Monitoring Project;
  Discrimination Legal Defence Fund;
  Equality Councils UK 182
Racial Justice UK 179
RAD—Genossenschaft der Landstrasse
  CH 218
Rada Mládeze Cech, Moravy a Slezska
  CS 193
Stichting RADAR NL 172
Rädda Barnen S 216
Radha Krishna Temple UK 42, NI 43
Radical Anti-Fascist Action PL 173
Radio Amitié F 165
 ≡ Beur F 19
 ≡ Club de Esch LX 101
 ≡ Communauté Judaïque F 79
 ≡ Gazelle—Assoc. Rencontre Amitié F 165
 ≡ Norte Emissora Portuguêsa LX 101
 ≡ Paris Lisboa SA PR 148
 ≡ Pays—Le contact avec les pays F 236
 ≡ Venceremos F 104
Radlett Irish Society UK 51
Rafiki UK 22
The Rainbow UK 178
Raj Yoga Centre UK 42
Ramgarhia Circle; Community Centre Hall;
  Gurdwara; Sports Club UK 107
Raphaelswerk—Dienst am Menschen
  Unterwegs D 139
Rapporteurs sans Frontières F 236
Rappresentanti Indiani IT 43
Rassegna di studi etiopici IT 239
Rassemblement des Camerounais
  Résidents à Barcelone E 25
 ≡ Etudiants Algériens en Europe F 9
 ≡ Etudiants Maghrébins en Savoie F 86
 ≡ femmes pour la Paix BE 192
 ≡ Tunisiens en France F 118
Rasta Living; Rastafarian Advisory Service
  UK 102
Rauoi Kross Islands IS 203
Ravensbruck Fellowship F 162
Ravi UK 123
Raza Academy; Jamiah Mosque & Islamic
  Centre; Mosque UK 70
Reading Campaign Against Racism &
  Fascism UK 183
 ≡ & District Irish Association UK 51
Reading Federation of Muslim
  Organisations UK 70
 ≡ of the Pakistani Community UK 94
Reading Inter-Faith Group UK 183
 ≡ International Support Centre UK 227
 ≡ Islamic Centre; Muslim Women's
   Association UK 70
 ≡ Racial Equality Council UK 183
Réalisation d'Etudes Projets Originaux et
  Nouveaux Services F 236
Réalités familiales F 199
Rebel DK 161
Recherches et Etudes sur les Migrations et
  les Pathologies; et Formations F 236
Der Rechte Rand D 237
Rechtsberatung für Asylsuchende CH 153
Rechtshulp, Maandblad voor de sociale
  praktijk NL 241
Recursos d'Animació internacional E 242
Red Barnet Danmark DK 195
Red Cross—Red Crescent CH 218
Red Intercultural de Innovación Social
  E 174
Redbridge Council of Faiths; Racial Equality
  Council UK 183
 ≡ Refugee Forum UK 157
Redditch Community Relations Council
  UK 183
Redress Trust UK 157

Referat Flüchtlings und Aussiedlerhilfe
  D 201
Referendum Doppelte Staatsbürgerschaft
  D 167
Reflexes F 163
Refugee Abstracts CH 219
Refugee Action UK 125, 157
 ≡ Agency IR 141
 ≡ Arrivals Project UK 157
 ≡ Assessment & Guidance Project UK 246
Refugee Community News UK 157
Refugee Council UK 157
 ≡ Education & Training Advisory Service
   UK 229
 ≡ Home IR 204
 ≡ Housing UK 157
Refugee Issues UK 246
Refugee Legal Advisory Services IR 141
 ≡ Legal Centre UK 157
 ≡ Primary Education Project IR 204
 ≡ Reception Centre GR 140
 ≡ Resettlement Committee IR 141
 ≡ Studies Programme UK 246
 ≡ Support Centre; Training & Employment
   Centre UK 157
 ≡ Trust IR 168
 ≡ Women's Association UK 157
 ≡ Year Trust IR 168
Refugees CH 152, 219
Refugees International UK 157
Refugiados E 150, 213
Réfugiés d'aujourd'hui/Réfugiés d'hier
  BE 129
Refugio D 139
Regards F 137
Regent's College UK 244
Região das Equipas de Língua Portuguêsa
  no Estrangeiro PR 148
Regionaal Centrum Buitenlanders NL 147
 ≡ Integratiecentrum Migranten Oost-
   Vlaanderen BE 131
Regionale Arbeitsstelle für Ausländerfragen
  D 139
 ≡ zur Förderung Ausländischer Kinder
   D 202
Regroupement des Travailleurs Maliens en
  France F 87
Rehabilitation & Research Centre for
  Torture Victims; Rehabiliterings- og
  Forskningcentret for Torturofre DK 133
Reintegration Centre for Return Migration
  GR 140
Reisweg NL 209
Le Relais BE 131
Relief Society of Tigray D UK 116
Religious Advice Centre UK 183
Religious Society of Friends UK 227
REMISIS: revue bibliographique F 236
Rencontre F 163
Rencontre Internationale des Femmes
  Noires F 19
Rencontre plurielle F 165
Rencontre Portugais F 98
Reperes F 137
Répertoire Méditerranéen F 235
Répertoire sur le monde arabe F 10
Research Committee on Migration IT 239
Research Unit on European-Latin American
  Relations UK 85
 ≡ Racism & Migration UK 246
Réseau Accompagnement Actions
  Médiations Interculturels Saônois F 137
 ≡ d'Etude des Migrations et des Relations
   Euro-méditerranéennes F 236
Réseau d'information pour les Associations
  d'Immigrés en Europe NL 146
 ≡ sur les Migrations Internationales; Tiers
   Monde des Centres de Documentation
   pour le Développement F 236
Réseau juridique européen pour l'asile
  F 137
Resettlement Fund F 197
Resource Unit to Promote Black
  Volunteering UK 22
Respontar de Angola PR 9
RETURN Group UK 95
Returned Volunteer Action UK 183
Review of African Political Economy UK 6
Review of Population Reviews F 234
Revista de Ciências Sociais PR 241
Revista del Volontariato IT 206
Revue du Droit des Etrangers BE 130
Revue Europeenne des Migrations
  Internationales F 234
Revue de la Jeunesse LX 207
Revue du Monde Musulman et de la
  Méditerranée F 233
Rheinisch Westfälische Auslands-
  gesellschaft und Auslånds Institut D 167
Aled Richards Trust Black Communities
  Project UK 20
Richerche e Proposte IT 239

Richmond & District Irish Society *UK* 51
Richmond Inter-Faith Group *UK* 183
Rights & Justice; Office; Shop *UK* 227
Rijksuniversiteit Leiden *NL* 29, 240-1
Riksförbundet Stoppa Rasismen *S* 175
Ringsted Gæstearbejderklub *DK* 133
La Rioja Acoge *E* 152
Risorse *IT* 168
RNB Enterprises *UK* 123
Robert Jungk Foundation *AT* 231
Rochdale Campaign Against Racism &
   Fascism; Employment Advice Project;
   Interfaith Action *UK* 183
≡ Law Centre; Metropolitan Borough
   Council Equal Opportunities Unit *UK* 227
≡ Muslim Society *UK* 70
≡ Racial Equality Council *UK* 183
Rode Jeugd—Jongerenorganisatie van de
   PvdA *BE* 192
Rode Kruis van België *BE* 190
Rode Kruis Koerier *NL* 210
Roehampton Institute London *UK* 246
Roinn Oideachais *IR* 204
Rojo y Negro *E* 214
Rom e.V. *D* 103
Roma- und Cinti-Union; National Congress
   D 103
≡ Parliament in Hungary *H* 103
≡ Union *D* 103
Romale *EE* 133
Romani Center for Social Intervention &
   Studies *RO* 242
≡ National Party *SK* 103
≡ Union *F* 103
Romanian Group for Intercultural Action
   RO 174
Romanian Orphanage Trust *UK* 102
Romano Centro *AT* 129
Romano Jekhetanipe *D* 103
Romano Lil *IT* 40
Roof Group *UK* 16
Rookery Road West Indian Youth Club
   UK 125
Roots; Roots of Culture Foundation *UK* 7
Roscommon Association *UK* 51
Rose des Vents *F* 163
Roshni Asian Women's Resource Centre;
   Nottingham Asian Women's Aid *UK* 15
Roskilde Kommunes Indvandrerklub *DK* 133
Roskilde Universitetscenter *DK* 233
Rote Falken Österreich *AT* 159
Rotherham Racial Equality Council *UK* 183
Rotterdams Informatie Centrum *NL* 210
Rotterdamse anti-discriminatie actieraad
   NL 172
Rowley Regis Muslim Welfare Association
   UK 70
Joseph Rowntree Charitable Trust *UK* 246
Royal African Society *UK* 6
≡ Asiatic Society *UK* 246
≡ College of Nursing Immigration Advisory
   Service *UK* 227
≡ Institute of International Affairs; Over-
   Seas League *UK* 246
Rugby Irish Association *UK* 51
≡ Mosque Committee *UK* 70
≡ Racial Equality Council *UK* 183
Ruhr-Universität *D* 237
Runnymede Trust *UK* 246
Bertrand Russell Peace Foundation *UK* 227
Russian Charitable Antifascist Fund *RS* 174
≡ & East European Research Centre
   UK 246
≡ Union of Former Prisoners of Fascist
   Concentration Camps *RS* 174
Russische Orthodoxe Kerk van St-Andreas;
   St Anna; St Job; St Niklaas; SS Panta-
   leimon en Niklaas; de Verrijzenis *BE* 103
Rwanda-Burundi Action Group *UK* 104
Rwanda Development Trust *UK* 104

Sabha Ramgarhia Sikh Temple *UK* 107
SADAA Housing Association *UK* 22
Saddam Hussein Mosque *UK* 70
Safax Vereniging voor Tamazight Cultuur
   NL 90
Safestart Foundation *UK* 51
Sagar *UK* 19
Sahara Asian Women's Project *UK* 15
Saheli *UK* 15, *UK* 22
Sai Baba Centre *UK* 42
St Albans Irish Association *UK* 51
St Andrew's Church of Scotland *BE* 24
St Brendan's; Irish Centre *UK* 51
St Catherine Street Mosque Committee
   UK 70
St Finbarr's Social Club *UK* 51
St Kieran's School for Traveller Children
   IR 117
St Kitts, Nevis & Anguilla Assoc. *UK* 82
St Louise Project *UK* 49

St Patrick's Club *UK* 51
St Patrick's College *IR* 238
St Pauls Advice Centre *UK* 157
St Vincent & the Grenadines Association
   UK 125
Sajad *UK* 14
Salesian Institute of the Sacred Heart
   IT 206
Salford Law Centre *UK* 227
Salford Mosque *UK* 70
Salongo Afrikan & Caribbean Dance &
   Music Resource Project *UK* 23
Saltley Action Centre *UK* 227
Salvation Army *IT* 205
Samachar *NL* 17
Samarbetsorganet för Invandrar-
   organisationer i Sverige *S* 175
Samenwerking Verzet 1940-1945 *NL* 172
≡ Verzetzdeelnemers 1940-1945 *BE* 161
Samenwerkingsverband Marokkaanen en
   Tunisiers *NL* 87
Saminourra *S* 216
Sammenslutning af Tyrkiske Arbejder-
   foreninger i Danmark *DK* 119
Samora *NR* 173
Samspil *DK* 233
Samye Ling Tibetan Centre *UK* 116
Sanatan Temple & Community Centre
   UK 107
Sandiwan *E* 35
Sandwell African Caribbean Development
   Agency *UK* 6
≡ Asian Mental Health Service *UK* 15
≡ Central Mosque Trust *UK* 70
≡ Confederation of Bangladeshi Muslim
   Organisations *UK* 18
≡ Muslim Education Association *UK* 95
≡ Muslims Organisation *UK* 69
≡ Pakistan Muslim Womens Association;
   Pakistani Muslim Welfare Assoc. *UK* 95
≡ Racial Equality Council *UK* 183
Sangam Assoc. of Asian Women *UK* 15
Sangat Bhadra Sikh Temple *UK* 108
Sangat Singh Sabha Gurdwara *UK* 107
Sanglap *UK* 19
Sant Nirankari Mandal *UK* 107
Santé et Communication *F* 137
Santé Sud *F* 199
Saoirse *UK* 50
Sarajevo Centre for Peace *BH* 193
Sardegna Africa *IT* 4
SATHI Project *UK* 15
Satya Sai Baba Satsang *UK* 42
Saudi Arabian Educational Office *UK* 104
Save the Children *AT* 188, *S* 216, *UK* 227
Savile Town Muslim Jamaat *UK* 70
Savoirs et Formation *F* 135
Saz Rock *D* 121
Scandinavian Center for Monitoring Human
   Rights in Transylvania *DK* 116
≡ Institute of African Studies *S* 5
Scarborough Irish Society *UK* 51
School for Advanced Urban Studies *UK* 246
≡ of East Asian Studies *UK* 15, 78, 82
≡ of Oriental & African Studies *UK* 29, 246
≡ of Slavonic & East European Studies
   UK 246
≡ Zonder Racisme *BE* 160, *NL* 172
Schulstelle 3. Welt *CH* 243
Schwarzer Faden *D* 167
Schweizerische Arbeitsgemeinschaft der
   Jugendverbände *CH* 218
≡ Flüchtlingshilfe *CH* 153
Schweizerisches Arbeiterhilfswerk—
   Flüchtlingsdienst *CH* 153
≡ Komitee für UNICEF *CH* 218
≡ Rotes Kreuz *CH* 217, 219
Scottish Action Against Racism & Fascism
   in Europe; Anti-Racist Alliance; Anti-
   Racist Teacher Education Network *UK* 183
≡ Asian Action Committee *UK* 15
Scottish Asian Voice *UK* 15
Scottish Catholic International Aid Fund
   UK 227
≡ Centre for Japanese Studies *UK* 78
≡ Council for Civil Liberties *UK* 227
≡ Council for Racial Equality *UK* 183
≡ Cuba Defence Campaign *UK* 31
≡ Education & Action for Development
   UK 183
≡ Ethnic Minorities Research Unit *UK* 246
≡ European Aid *UK* 227
≡ Refugee Council *UK* 157
Scunthorpe & District Community
   Relations Council *UK* 183
≡ Irish Society *UK* 51
≡ & South Humberside Racial Equality
   Council *UK* 183
Scuola per Extra Comunitari *IT* 144
Scuola Portoghese in Roma *IT* 100
SEA Housing Co-operative *UK* 227
Searchlight *UK* 183, 224

Secours Catholique *F* 199
≡ International de Caritas Catholica *BE* 192
≡ populaire *F* 199
Secretaria de Estado da Emigração e
   Comunidades Portuguêsas *PR* 212
Secretaría de Relaciones Culturales *E* 215
Secretariado Arquidiocesano de Migração
   PR 148
≡ Coordenador das Associações para a
   Legalização *PR* 26
≡ Diocesano de Migração *PR* 148
≡ Europeo Oscar Romero de Solidaridad
   con los Pueblos Centroamericanos *CH* 27
Secrétariat d'Etat chargée des immigrés
   F 197
≡ Socio-Pastoral de l'Immigration *LX* 145
Secretário Diocesano de Migração *PR* 148-9
Sectie Interculturele Pedagogiek *NL* 241
Las Segovias *E* 27
Segretaria per gli Esteri, Diocesi di Milano
   IT 145
Selbstandige Imigrantinnen *D* 139
Selby Centre *UK* 227
Self-Help News *UK* 156
Selly Oak Colleges *UK* 57, 80, 244
Une semaine en Haïti *F* 41
Séminaire polonaise à Paris *F* 96
Seminário Scalabriniano *PR* 149
Sénégalais du pays de Montbéliard *F* 105
Sennacieca Asocio Tutmundo *F* 165
Serbian National Organisation; National
   Welfare Centre; Orthodox Church;
   Orthodox Church of St Lazar *UK* 105
Servas International *DK* 195
Servei d'Acol.liment d'Infants i Famílies els
   Quatre Vents *E* 152
Service d'Acceuil et d'Aide à la Main-
   d'Oeuvre Immigrée *BE* 131
≡ des Etrangers *LX* 145
≡ et de Formation pour Immigrés et
   Réfugiés; des Immigrés *BE* 131
≡ et d'Information Juridique *LX* 145
Service Civil International *AT* 188, *BE* 192,
   F 199, *D* 202, *CH* 219
≡ d'Education Permanente des Adultes
   BE 189
≡ emploi chargé des réfugiés *F* 199
≡ des Etrangers *LX* 208
≡ euro-centroaméricain pour la
   coopération démocratique *BE* 27
≡ de l'Immigration *LX* 208
≡ d'Immigration et d'Acceuil de la
   Province de Liège *BE* 192
≡ des immigrés; Interdiocésain des
   Travailleurs Immigrés *F* 137
≡ International pour les Droits de l'Homme
   CH 218
≡ Justice et Développement *F* 196
≡ Migrants *F* 136
≡ National de la Pastorale des Migrants
   F 137-8
≡ for Overseas Cypriots *CY* 193
Service Provincial d'Immigration et
   d'Acceuil de Limbourg; du Hainaut *BE* 192
Service to Refugees, World Council of
   Churches *GR* 140
≡ réfugiés-migrants *F* 197
Service Social d'Aide aux Emigrants *F* 138
≡ des Etrangers *BE* 130-1
≡ familial nord africain *F* 92
≡ pour les Immigrés Portugais *LX* 101
≡ International *CH* 219
≡ Juif *BE* 78
Service Socio-Pastoral Inter-
   communautaire *LX* 145
Service des Travailleurs Migrants de la
   FGTB; et Réfugiés de la CSC *BE* 132
Servicio Exterior de la Iglesia Evangélica
   E 216
≡ de Refugiados y Extranjeros *E* 151
≡ de Refugiados y Migrantes *E* 150
≡ Social Internacional *E* 216
Servicios Centrales *E* 213
Serviço de Apoio a Refugiados *PR* 211
≡ Católico dos Portuguêses *F* 99
≡ Diocesano de Migração *PR* 149
≡ de Estrangeiros *PR* 212
≡ de Fronteiras e Imigração *PR* 212
Servizio Civile Internazionale *IT* 206
≡ Emigrazione-Immigrazione; Immigrazione
   IT 144
≡ Immigrazione-Cooperazione Umbria
   IT 206
≡ Informazione América Latina *IT* 84
Servizio Migranti *IT* 144
Servizio Orientamento Esteri di Milano
   IT 145
≡ per i problemi dei lavoratori extra-
   comunitari; Sociale Internazionale *IT* 206
Sevilla Acoge--Centro de Acogida de
   Inmigrantes Extranjeros *E* 152
SFI-Nyt *DK* 233

Shafaq *UK* 123
Shah Jalal Mosque *UK* 65, 70
Shah Jalal Mosque & Madrassa *UK* 17
Shah Jehan Mosque *UK* 72
Shahjalal Mosque *UK* 17
Shair-E-Rabbani Islamic Centre *UK* 70
Shakti—South Asian Lesbian & Gay
   Network *UK* 15
Shakti Women's Aid *UK* 157
Shalom Immigration & Legal Advisory
   Service *UK* 157
Shalom Mental Health Centre *UK* 80
Shanti Asian Women's Refuge *UK* 15
SHAP Working Party on World Religions in
   Education *UK* 246
Shariat Council *UK* 63
Sharing of Faiths *UK* 179
Sharrow Action Committee Against Racism
   & Fascism *UK* 183
Sheffield African Caribbean Mental Health
   Association *UK* 6
   ≡ Against Racism & Fascism *UK* 183
   ≡ & District Afro Caribbean Community
   Association *UK* 6
   ≡ Irish Social Centre *UK* 51
   ≡ Islamic Centre *UK* 70
   ≡ Law Centre *UK* 227
   ≡ Racial Equality Council *UK* 183
   ≡ Rotherham & District Council of
   Muslims *UK* 70
Shepherd's Bush Mosque; Committee
   UK 70
Shi'a Islamic Centre *UK* 70
Shia Ithna-Asheri Jama'at Mosque;
   Mosque *UK* 70
Shiloh Youth Development Project *UK* 227
Shiromani Akali Dal UK *UK* 107
Shobana Jeyasingh Dance Company *UK* 44
Shqiperia e Re AL 159
Shree Ganapathy Temple; Gita Bhavan
   Mandir *UK* 42
Shree Hindu Community Centre; Gujarati
   Samaj; Mandir; Samaj Mandal; Temple
   Geeta Bhawan; Temple Society *UK* 42
Shree Kadwa Patidas Samaj UK; Kalyan
   Mandal; Krishna Mandir; Ram Krishna
   Centre *UK* 42
Shree Sanatan Deevya Mandal; Dharma
   Mandal; Mandir; Seva Samaj *UK* 42
Shree Swaminarayan Hindu Temple *UK* 42
Shri Dashmesh Sikh Temple *UK* 107
   ≡ Krishna Mandir Sabha; Narthi Sanatan
   Hindu Mandir; Swaminarayan Sanatan
   Hindu Mandir *UK* 42
SI Education Society *UK* 70
Si Yu Chinese Times NL 29
Sia—National Development Agency for the
   Black & Minority Ethnic Voluntary Sector
   UK 157
Sickle Cell Society *UK* 7
Sicurrezza Sociale Oggi IT 144
Sierra Leone Association; Community;
   Friendship Assoc. of Manchester *UK* 105
   ≡ National Union *E* 105
Sikh Association; Bhatra Temple *UK* 107
Sikh Bulletin; Sikh Committee for Interfaith
   Relations; Sikh Community *UK* 107
Sikh Community Centre *UK* 107-8
Sikh Courier International *UK* 107
Sikh Cultural Society of Coventry; Cultural
   Society of GB; Doctors' Association UK;
   Educational Council *UK* 107
   ≡ Foundation Denmark *DK* 106
   ≡ Gurdwara; Gurdwara South London;
   Human Rights Group; Human Rights
   Internet *UK* 107
Sikh Messenger UK 107
Sikh Missionary Resources Centre;
   Missionary Society; Parents' Society
   UK 107
Sikh Parivaar UK 106
Sikh Sewak; Sikh Study Forum *UK* 107
Sikh Temple *UK* 107, 108
Sikh Temple Association *UK* 106
   ≡ Temple Sewakjatha Sangat Bhadra
   Manchester; Union of Manchester;
   Welfare Mission *UK* 108
Sikh Youth International; Sikh Youth
   Service *UK* 108
Silesian People's Association *D* 37
Silkeborg Indvandrersamvirke;
   Indvandrersolidaritet *DK* 133
Sin Detenerse E 149
Sin Fronteras E 150
Sinai Centrum *NL* 241
Sindacato dei Collaboratori Familiari *IT* 206
Sindicat de Treballadors de l'Ensenyment
   E 216
Sinfin Together Project *UK* 183
Sing Tao UK 30
Singh Sabha; Bhatra Gurdwara; Gurdwara
   UK 108

Single Parent Action Network *UK* 227
Sinologisch Instituut *NL* 29
St Jan-Baptistkerk—Griekse Orthodoxe
   BE 38
St Pasar Amsterdam *NL* 147
Skibbereen & District Society *UK* 51
Skill IT 144
Skinheads Against Racial Prejudice *NI* 185
Slough Irish Society Club *UK* 51
   ≡ Islamic Trust *UK* 70
   ≡ Race Equality Council *UK* 183
Slovenski Raziskovalni Institut *IT* 108
Small Heath Mosque *UK* 70
Smethwick Bangladeshi Muslim Welfare
   Association *UK* 18
   ≡ Mosque; Pakistani Muslims Association
   UK 70
Michael Sobell Centre *UK* 80
Sociaal en Cultureel Planbureau;
   Economische Raad; Wetenschappelijke
   Afdeling *NL* 210
Social Action Forum *UK* 157
   ≡ Community of Ghanaians in Lombardy
   IT 38
   ≡ & Economic Research Institute *NL* 240
   ≡ & Pastoral Action *UK* 227
   ≡ Work Foundation *GR* 140
Sociale Dienst Scheepvaart *NL* 147
   ≡ voor Vreemdelingen *BE* 131
Socialforskiningsinstituttet *DK* 233
Socialist Affairs UK 227
Socialist Educational International *BE* 191
Socialist International *UK* 227
Socialistisch Jeugdverbond; Socialistische
   Solidariteit—Sociale dienst *BE* 192
Sociedad Hispano-Belga de Ayuda Mutua
   BE 111
Società Mutuo Soccorso tra Senegalesi a
   Bergamo *IT* 105
Société Africaine de Culture *F* 236
   ≡-Bureau Organisation Ligue Islamique
   Mondiale *F* 53
   ≡ Dante Alighieri *F* 74
   ≡ pour l'Education, la Formation et le
   Recherche Interculturelles *F* 236
   ≡ Française d'Etudes Irlandaises *F* 46
   ≡ Nationale de Construction de Logements
   pour les Travailleurs *F* 199
   ≡ pour les Peuples Menacés *LX* 169
   ≡ de St-Vincent de Paul *F* 199
Society of Afghan Residents *UK* 1
   ≡ for Anglo-Chinese Understanding *UK* 30
   ≡ of Asian Lawyers *UK* 15
   ≡ of Black Lawyers *UK* 23
   ≡ for Intercultural Education, Training &
   Research *UK* 241
   ≡ for International Development *IT* 239
   ≡ for Latin American Studies *UK* 85
   ≡ for Threatened Peoples *AT* 159, *D* 166,
   LX 169
Sociologisches Institut *CH* 243
Sociology Centre *NL* 241
SOH Berichten NL 210
Sojourners House *UK* 7
Sol-Peru *UK* 96
O Sol do Portugal F 98
Sólás Anois *UK* 51
Sole d'Italia BE 74, *LX* 75
Solidaire *BE* 161
Solidaridad Democrática; para el Desarrollo
   y la Paz *E* 216
   ≡ 2000 *E* 174
   ≡ Educación y Desarrollo *E* 216
   ≡ Internacional *E* 215
Solidarietà internazionale IT 168
Solidarietà Nomade *IT* 169
Solidaritätsvereine Bremerhaven *D* 121
Solidarité BE 189
Solidarité Arabe *BE* 89
   ≡ Développement Pair International *F* 165
   ≡ et Développement Tchad-France *F* 27
   ≡ Etudiants Etrangers *BE* 132
   ≡ Femmes-Algérie *F* 9
   ≡ aux Femmes d'ici et d'ailleurs *F* 165
   ≡ français migrants *F* 138
   ≡ franco arménienne *F* 11
   ≡ immigrés Epône-Mezieres *F* 138
   ≡ libérale internationale *BE* 192
   ≡ Migrants *F* 138
   ≡ mondiale *BE* 193
   ≡ des réfugiés israélites *F* 79
   ≡ socialiste—Service social *BE* 192
Solidarités Jeunesses *F* 199
Solidariteitsfonds X min Y *NL* 147
Solidariteitsvereniging Marokkaanse
   Werknemers *BE* 89
Solidaritets- og Kulturforening i Ringsted
   DK 161
Solidarity *UK* 221
Solidarity with Latin America *UK* 85
Solidarnosc *IT* 96
Solinger Appell *D* 167

Somali Anglo British Association; Assoc. of
   Greater Manchester *UK* 109
Somali Community Association; Central
   London; & Cultural Association;
   Manchester *UK* 109
Somali Danish Friendship Assoc. *DK* 108
   ≡ Education Project; Health Advocacy
   Project; Islamic Circle Organisation;
   Mental Health Project; Progressive
   Association; South London Community;
   Women's Cultural & Care Group;
   Women's Group *UK* 109
Somalia Community *DK* 108
Somalia Relief Association *UK* 109
Soros Foundation *BH BG CT* 193, *EE* 195,
   F 198, *LT LH* 207, *RO* 212
SOS-Arbeitskreis *AT* 129
SOS Arrazakera *E* 174
SOS Ça Bouge *F* 165
SOS Mitmensch *AT* 129
SOS Mitmenschschüler/innen *AT* 188
SOS-Racisme *BE DK* 161, *F* 165, *LX* 169,
   NL 172, *E* 174, *CH* 175
SOS Racismo *PR* 173, *E* 174
SOS Rasisme Norway *NR* 173
SOS Rassismus *D* 166-7
SOS Ratsismos *GR* 168
SOS Razzismo *IT* 169
SOS Refoulement *F* 138
SOS Solidarité *F* 199
SOS-Torture *CH* 218
South African Research Group *UK* 109
   ≡ Asia Bureau *D* 12
   ≡ Asia Solidarity Group *UK* 15
   ≡ East Islamic Society *UK* 70
   ≡ East London Irish Society *UK* 52
   ≡ East London Muslim Association *UK* 70
   ≡ Glamorgan Race Equality Council *UK* 182
   ≡ Indian Muslim Association *UK* 44
   ≡ Islington Law Centre *UK* 227
   ≡ Kirklees Community Relations Council
   UK 180
South London Irish Association; Irish
   Welfare Association *UK* 52
   ≡ Islamic Centre; Muslim Assoc. *UK* 70
   ≡ Tamil Welfare Group *UK* 115
   ≡ Manchester Jamia Mosque *UK* 72
   ≡ Manchester Law Centre *UK* 227
   ≡ Newham Action on Policing *UK* 183
   ≡ Side Monitoring Group *UK* 183
   ≡ Tyneside Bangladesh Muslim Cultural
   Association *UK* 18
South Wales Anti-Fascist Action *UK* 177
   ≡ Divided Families Campaign *UK* 183
   ≡ Vietnamese Community *UK* 125
South West London Anti-Fascist
   Association *UK* 183
Southall Black Sisters; Black Women's
   Centre *UK* 23
   ≡ Community Law Centre *UK* 222
   ≡ Monitoring Group *UK* 183
Southall Review UK 183
Southall Rights Legal Advice Centre *UK* 157
Southampton Citizens Advice Bureau
   UK 228
   ≡ Racial Equality Council *UK* 183
Southend Irish Association *UK* 52
   ≡ Islamic Trust; Muslim Assoc. *UK* 71
Southern Africa Economic Research Unit
   UK 110
   ≡ Sudanese Welfare Association *UK* 114
Southwark African Organisation *UK* 6
   ≡ Asian Women's Refuge Group *UK* 15
   ≡ Black Elderly Group *UK* 20
   ≡ Black Workers Group *UK* 23
   ≡ Council for Racial Equality; Council
   Racial Equality Unit *UK* 183
   ≡ Cypriot Community Group *UK* 32
   ≡ Law Centre; Law Project *UK* 228
   ≡ Muslim Association; Muslim Women's
   Association *UK* 71
   ≡ Refugee Project *UK* 158
   ≡ Victim Support Scheme *UK* 228
   ≡ Vietnamese/Chinese Refugee
   Community *UK* 125
Soutien Dignité Aide Travailleurs Africains
   F 3
   ≡ à l'Initiative Privée pour l'Aide à la
   Reconstruction du Sud-Est Asiatique *F* 110
Sozialdienst für Ausländer Theresa-von-
   Avila-Haus *D* 140
   ≡ Griechen *D* 38
   ≡ Italiener *D* 74
   ≡ Koreaner *D* 82
   ≡ Mitbürger aus dem ehemaligen
   Jugoslawien *D* 126
   ≡ Philippinos *D* 35
   ≡ Portugiesen *D* 100
Sozialinstitute der Katholische
   Arbeitnehmer-Bewegung *D* 237
Sozialistische Jugend Österreichs *AT* 188
Sozialkritischer Arbeitskreis *D* 238

Spanische Christliche Arbeiterjugend;
Jugendinitiative Hamburg *D* 112
Spanischer Jugendverein *D* 112
Spanisches Gemeindezentrum; Zentrum
D 112
Spanish Club *UK* 113
≡ Cultural Institute *IR* 112
≡ Pensioners' Day Centre *UK* 113
≡ Red Cross *E* 151
≡ Society Dublin *IR* 112
Spanske Forening *DK* 111
Sparkbrook Islamic Centre *UK* 71
Specialarbejderforbundet i Danmark *DK* 195
Specifieke Migranten Initiativen Foyer
BE 132
Spinnrad *AT* 188
Spiro Institute for the Study of Jewish
History & Culture *UK* 81
Sprachverband Deutsch für ausländische
Arbeitnehmer *D* 140
Sprogpædagogisk Center *DK* 161
Sri Guru Gobind Singh Gurdwara; Nanak
Gurdwara; Nanak Singh Gurdwara;
Ravidas Sabha; Singh Gurdwara; Singh
Sabha; Singh Sabha Gurdwara; Teg
Bahadur Sikh Temple *UK* 108
Sri Lanka Association for Peace &
Democracy; Islamic UK Assoc. *UK* 113
Sri Lanka Monitor *UK* 114
Sri Lanka Resource Centre *NR* 113
≡-UK Friendship Association *UK* 114
Sri Lankans *UK* 114
SRM Materiali *IT* 144
Stafford Irish Society *UK* 52
Stafford Racial Equality Council *UK* 184
Standing Advisory Commission on Human
Rights *NI* 229
Standing Committee of Experts on
International Immigration, Refugee &
Criminal Law *NL* 241
Standing Conference of African & Asian
Organisations *UK* 156
≡ for the Co-ordination & Co-operation of
the Romani Associations in Europe *D* 103
≡ on Inter-Faith Dialogue in Education; of
Jews, Christians & Muslims in Europe
UK 184
≡ for Racial Equality in Europe *IT* 169,
UK 184
Standing International Forum on Ethnic
Conflict *UK* 224
Star of Hope International *S* 216
Statens Indvandrerkonsulenter *DK* 195
Statewatch *UK* 246
Stedelijke Raad van Marokkaanse
Gemeenschap in Amsterdam *NL* 90
Stella Maris *PR* 148
Stepney Mosque *UK* 71
Steunfonds Allochtone Startende Onder-
nemers; Vluchtelingen Organisaties *NL* 147
Steunpunt Anti-Rassen Discriminatie
NL 172
Stevenage & District Irish Assoc. *UK* 52
Stichting... if not listed here, see next
significant word in title
Stichting 1940-1945 *NL* 172
≡ Auschwitz *BE* 161
≡ Balans; ter Bestrijding van het Anti-
semitisme; Burgerschapskunde *NL* 172
≡ Displaced Persons Centre *NL* 240
≡ Doen *NL* 147
≡ Nederlandse Moslimvrouwen Al-Nisa
NL 54
≡ Oecumenische Hulp *NL* 210
≡ Omroep Allochtonen; Optie; Pharos—
Steunpunt Gezondheidszorg Vluchtelingen
NL 147
≡ Promotie door Turkse en Arabische
Vrouwen *NL* 54
≡ Provinciaal Platform Antiracisme *NL* 172
≡ de Schoof *NL* 170
≡ Triodos-Doen *NL* 147
≡ Uitwisseling *NL* 172
≡ Vluchteling; voor Vluchteling-Studenten
NL 147
≡ Voorlichting Gezondheidszorg
Buitenlanders *NL* 241
Stiftelsen för Internationelt Ungdomsutbyte
S 216
Stiftung Entwicklung und Frieden *D* 202
≡ gegen Rassismus und Antisemitismus
CH 175
≡ Kinder in Afrika *D* 3
≡ Kinderdorf Pestalozzi *CH* 219
≡ Mitarbeit *D* 140
≡ Umverteilen *D* 167
Die Stimme *D* 166
Stimulering Internationale Uitwisseling
Horeca *NL* 210
Stipendienfonds des Landeskirchen; der
Universitäten *D* 202
Stirling Islamic Centre *UK* 71

Stockholms Universitet *S* 243
Stockton & Hartlepool Law Centre;
Stockwell & Clapham Law Centre *UK* 228
Stodforening till Relief Society of Tigray i
Sverige *S* 116
Stoke-on-Trent Citizens Advice Bureau
UK 228
Stonebridge Asian Elders Social Group
UK 15
Stonewall Immigration Group *UK* 158
Stoneyholme Jamia Masjid & Islamic
Centre *UK* 71
Stop the Detentions Action Group *UK* 158
Stop-Racisme *F* 165
Stop Rassismus *D* 167
Marie Stopes International *UK* 225
Stoppt Nazi-Zeitungen *D* 167
Stottekomiteen for Ghassan Kanafanis
Kultur Fond *DK* 85
Stratford Irish Community Association;
Society *UK* 52
Strathclyde Community Relations Council;
Student Assembly Against Racism *UK* 184
Student Islamic Society *UK* 71
Studenti Insieme *IT* 3
Studie- en Informatiecentrum
Mensenrechten *NL* 241
Study Centre for Christian-Jewish
Relations *UK* 81
Subah; Subco Elders Day Centre *UK* 15
Subdirección de Cooperación Internacional
E 216
Subsidiefonds Plaatselijke Aktiviteiten
NL 172
Sudan Human Rights Organisation; *Sudan
Monitor*; Sudan Musicians Assoc.; Sudan
Relief & Rehabilitation Assoc.; *Sudan
Update* *UK* 114
Sudanese Association of Sussex; Coptic
Association; Victims of Torture Group;
Women's Association *UK* 114
Südostasien-Informationsstelle *D* 110
Südosteuropa Gesellschaft *D* 110
Sufi Order of the Chisti; Order Inter-
national; Order of the West; Way *UK* 71
Sughra Mosque *UK* 71
Suman *UK* 15
Suncokret—Centre for Grassroots
Voluntary Work *CT* 193
Sunderland Mosque *UK* 71
Sunni Islamic Cultural Society of
Repatriated French Muslims *F* 53
≡ Mosque; Muslim Association; Muslim
Jamat *UK* 71
Suomen Ammattiliittojen
Solidaarisuuskeskus *SF* 162
≡ Nuorisoyhteistyö Allianssi *SF* 195
≡ Pakolaisapu *SF* 133
≡ Punainen Risti ; Ylioppilaskuntien Liga
SF 195
Support Project for Asian Women &
Families with a Child with a Disability
UK 15
Supreme Council of British Muslims *UK* 71
≡ for the Islamic Resistance in Iraq *UK* 46
Surati Muslim Khalifa Society *UK* 71
Surbiton Irish Society *UK* 52
Surinaams Inspraakorgaan; Surinaamse
Arbeiders en Werkers Organisatie;
Surinaamse Stichting; Surinameisische
Grundung *UK* 114
Surma Community Centre; *Surma
Newsweekly* *UK* 19
Surti Khalifa Sunatwal Society *UK* 71
Survival International *F* 165, *UK* 228
SUSI Interkulturelles Frauenzentrum *D* 167
Sussex Bangladeshi Association *UK* 18
≡ Hindu Union *UK* 41
≡ Muslim Society *UK* 71
≡ Racial Equality Council *UK* 184
≡ Turkish Community *UK* 122
Sutton Islamic Centre *UK* 71
Sutton Racial Equality Council *UK* 184
Svalorna i Sverige Latin Amerika Sectionen
S 84
Svensk Filippinska Foreningen *S* 35
Svenska Afghanistankommitten *S* 1
≡ Flyktingrådet *S* 152
≡ FN-Förbundet; Kyrkans Mission *S* 216
≡ Muslimska Ungdomsförbund *S* 54
≡ Röda Korsets Ungdomsförbund *S* 216
Sveriges Frikyrkosamråd; Social-
demokratiska Ungdomsförbund *S* 216
Swaminarayan Hindu Mission *UK* 43
Swedish Committee for the Human Rights
of Kurdish People *S* 83
≡ Filipino Association *S* 35
≡ Iran Committee *S* 45
≡ National Red Cross Society *S* 216
≡ Refugee Council *S* 152
≡ United Nations Association *S* 216
Swiatowy Zwiacek Miast Pokuje *PL* 211

Swindon Ismaili Community *UK* 71
Swinford Society *UK* 52
Swiss Benevolent Society *UK* 114
≡ Committee for UNICEF *CH* 218
≡ Red Cross *CH* 217, 219
≡ Study Group for Ethnic Research *CH* 243
Sybidi papers; *Sybidi périodique* *BE* 232
Sydjysk Universitetscenter *DK* 232
Syndicat des Avocats; de la Magistrature
F 199
Syrian Arab Association *UK* 115
Système Bibliographique et Documentaire
relatif à l'Immigration *BE* 232

Ta Ha Publishers *UK* 71
Ta Nea *UK* 39
Tabligh *F* 53
Tabligi Markaz *UK* 70
Taca Eisimirceach Chiarraí *IR* 141
Tacis Democracy Programme *BE* 192
Tahanan—Centro de Filipinos *E* 35
Taiba Mosque *UK* 61
Taiyabah Mosque & Community Centre;
Taiyyibah Mosque & Madressa *UK* 71
Talawa Theatre Company *UK* 23
Taleem ul Islam Trust; Talim-ul-Qur'an
UK 71
Tameer-e-Pakistan Tanzeem *UK* 95
Tameside Racial Equality Council *UK* 184
Tamil Action Committee *UK* 115
≡-Danish Friendship Association *DK* 115
≡ Dutch Solidarity Association *NL* 115
≡ Information Centre; Refugee Action
Group; Refugee Centre; Refugee Housing
Assoc.; Rehabilitation Organisation *UK* 115
≡ World Cultural Association *F* 115
Tamilmul Quran Mosque & Madressa *UK* 71
Tamilsk Dansk Venskabsforening; Forening
i Vejle *DK* 115
Tam-Tam *IT* 169
TAPOL, Indonesia Human Rights Campaign
UK 45
Tauheed-ul-Islam Girls' High School *UK* 66
Tawakkulia Islamic Society & Mosque
UK 71
Tayside Community Relations Council
UK 184
An Teach Irish Housing Association *UK* 47
Tear Fund *BE* 190, *UK* 228
Technical University of Berlin *D* 237
Tehrik-i-Nizam-i-Qurran e Sunnah *UK* 71
Telephone Legal Advice Service for
Travellers *UK* 117
Telford Central America Group *UK* 27
Telford West Indian Association *UK* 125
Telugu Talli *UK* 44
Témoignage ACO *F* 195
Témoignage Chrétien *F* 199
Temple Buddhapaeipa *UK* 115
Templemore Society *UK* 52
Tendance nationale union islamique en
France, Section Bourgoin-Jallieu *F* 53
Terre des Femmes—Menschenrechte für
die Frau *D* 202
Terre des Hommes *F* 138, *D* 202, *NL* 210
Territorio *IT* 168
Terzo Mondo *IT* 239
Testemunho *F* 99, 195
Texture *F* 165
Thailandsk Kulturcenter *DK* 115
Thames Valley Irish Society *UK* 52
Thamesdown Community Law Centre
UK 228
≡ Islamic Association *UK* 71
≡ Racial Equality Council *UK* 184
Theatro Technis *UK* 32
Thing Tin *F* 124
Third World Centre *UK* 184
≡ First *UK* 228
≡ Voice *UK* 233
Three Boroughs Race Equality Project
UK 184
Three Sisters Press *UK* 80
Thuislozenzorg Vlaanderen *BE* 192
Thurgauer Beratungsstelle für
Asylsuchende *CH* 153
Thüringer Antifa Nachrichten *D* 167
Thurles, Moycarkey & Borris Society;
Thurrock & Tilbury Irish Assoc. *UK* 52
Tibet Foundation; Information Network
UK 116
Tibet News Review *UK* 116
Tibet Society & Tibet Relief Fund *UK* 116
Tibet Support Group *IR* 115, *NL* 116
Tibetan Community in Britain; Refugee
Charitable Trust *UK* 116
Tiddukla *F* 118
Tiempo de Paz *E* 215
Tigray Development Association; Tigrayan
People's Liberation Front *UK* 116
Tijdschrift voor Vreemdelingenrecht *BE* 232

Time to Go *UK* 50
Timor Oriental *PR* 116
Tipton Muslim Trust Association *UK* 71
Tipton & Tividale Islamic Centre; Muslim
   Welfare Association *UK* 71
Tolstoy Foundation *BE* 32, *F D GR IT* 33,
   D 140
Tolstoy Hilfs- und Kulturwerk *D* 140
Wolfe Tone Society *UK* 52
Tools for Self Reliance *UK* 184
Tooting Irish Society *UK* 52
Torbay Islamic Centre *UK* 71
Tottenham Irish Women's Group *UK* 52
≡ Mosque *UK* 58
≡ Legal Advice Centre; Neighbourhood
   Law Centre *UK* 228
Tour d'horizon *F* 137
Tower Hamlets Anti-Racist Committee;
   Association for Racial Equality *UK* 184
≡ Council Social Services Directorate
   Equalities Unit; East Citizens Advice
   Bureau; Law Centre *UK* 228
≡ Racial Equality Council *UK* 184
Trade Union Aid for Palestine *UK* 95
≡ China Campaign *UK* 30
≡ Friends of Palestine *UK* 95
≡ International Research & Education
   Group *UK* 184
Trades Union Congress *UK* 228
Trafford Community Relations Committee
   UK 184
Training & Development Consortium *UK* 18
Training & Employment Agency *NI* 229
Trait d'Union *F* 165
Tralee Society *UK* 52
Trans-cultures *F* 165
Trans-European Mobility Scheme for
   University Studies *BE* 192
Trans-National Institute *NL* 241
Transcultura *DK* 161
Transcultural Psychiatry Society *UK* 184
≡ Unit *UK* 246
Transithuis *BE* 132
Transmission *IR* 203
Trasna *UK* 50
Travail *F* 199
Traveller Research Unit *UK* 117
Travellers Community Social Workers;
   Resource Centre; Rights Organization
   UK 117
Travelling High School *NR* 210
≡ Mission to the Travelling People *UK* 117
Tribune *F* 198
Tribune Immigrée *BE* 232
Trinidad & Tobago Association *UK* 118
Trocaire *IR* 168
Troops Out Movement *UK* 52
Trust Fund for Disabled Refugees *CH* 153
Truth & Justice for Mark Harris Campaign
   UK 184
Tufnde Endam—Solidarités villageoises
   F 105
Tunesische Vereinigung *D* 119
Tung Sing Housing Association *UK* 30
Türk-Danis—Centre Turc d'information,
   d'animation culturelle et d'aide sociale
   BE 119
Türk Halkevi; Iscileri Dernegi *D* 121
≡ Kultur Dengi *BE* 119
Türkei-Informationsbüro; Zentrum *D* 121
Turkey Today *UK* 122
Türkische Beratungstelle der Arbeiter-
   wohlfahrt; Islamische Union *D* 121
Türkischer Arbeiter- und Studentenverein;
   Arbeiterverein; Arbeitnehmerverein in
   München; Arbeitsverein; Frauenverein
   Kassel *D* 121
≡ Gemeinde zu Berlin *D* 120
≡ Verein für Wissenschaft und Kultur;
   Volksverein *D* 121
Türkisches Wissenschafts- und
   Technologie-Zentrum *D* 120
Turkish Cypriot Community Association;
   Cypriot Research Group *UK* 32
≡ Democrats Union *GR* 121
≡ Education Group *UK* 122
≡ Islamic Cultural Federation *NL* 122
≡ & Kurdish Women's Group; Mosque
   UK 122
≡ Red Crescent Society *TR* 219
Türkiye Göçmenler Birligi; Türkiyeli
   Göçmen Dernekleri Federasyonu *D* 121
Turks Jongerenkomitee Voorst; Komitee
   Beverwijk *NL* 122
Turkse Arbeidersvereniging Nederland
   NL 122
≡ Culturele Vereniging Waterschei;
   Culturele Vereniging Winterslag;
   Democratische Culturele Volksvereining;
   Eenheid van Beringen; Rangers
   Waterschei *BE* 119
≡ Vereniging; Vrouwenvereniging *NL* 122

Turnhoutse Buurt- en Wijkwerking *BE* 132
Turnpike Lane Advice Bureau *UK* 228
TV Asia *UK* 15
TV Guia *F* 98
Tweede Generatie—Provinciaal Overleg
   Migranten Jeugdwellzijnswerk *BE* 132
Tyne & Wear Anti-Fascist Association;
   Community Relations Council; Racial
   Equality Council *UK* 184
Tyneside Irish Centre *UK* 52
Tyrkisk-Dansk Forening; Dansk
   Venskabsforening i Ikast; Klub *DK* 119
≡ Kultur- og Undervisningscenter;
   Kulturforening; Arbejderes
   Solidaritetsforening *DK* 120
Tyrkiske Forældreforening; Forening i
   Farum; Uzbek Tyrkeres Familieforening
   DK 120
Tyrone Association *UK* 52
Tzigane International *F* 40

Udenrigsministeriet *DK* 195
Udlændinges Aktionsforening *DK* 133
Udumuz Çocuklar ou Les enfants de
   l'espoir *F* 120
Ufficio Accoglienza *IT* 142
≡ Accoglienza Studenti Esteri *IT* 145
≡ Centrale per l'Emigrazione Italiana *IT* 144
≡ Centrale Studenti Esteri in Italia *IT* 145
≡ Confederale Migrazione *IT* 143
≡ Documentazione e Pastorale, Missione
   Cattoliche Italiane in Germania *D* 75
≡ Emigrazione-Immigrazione delle Regioni
   IT 206-7
Ufficio Lavoratori Immigrati; Stranieri *IT* 143
Ufficio Rifugiati *IT* 207
Ufficio Stranieri e Nomadi *IT* 145
Uganda AIDS Action Fund; Asylum
   Seekers Association; Community Relief
   Assoc.; Welfare Action Group *UK* 122
Ugandas Forening for Forældre og
   Rehabilitering *DK* 122
Ujamaa Arts Project *UK* 247
Ujima Housing Association *UK* 158
Ukaidi Advice Centre *UK* 158
UKCOSA: Council for International
   Education *UK* 158
Ukrainian Association of GB; Association &
   Social Club; Religious Society of St
   Sophia; Social Club *UK* 123
Ukrajinska Parochia *E* 122
Ulama Board UK *UK* 62
Umanità Europea *IT* 142
Umbri nel Mondo *LX* 76
Umoja wa Wazanzibari Skandinavia *DK* 115
Under Paraplyen *DK* 194
Undervisningsministeriet *DK* 195
Ung Vänster *S* 216
Ungdomsriksdag '94—För vår
   gemensamma framtid *S* 217
União Centro Cooperativo *LX* 101
≡ das Cidades Capitais Luso-Afro-
   Américo-Asiáticas *PR* 173
≡ das Instituções de Solidariedade Social
   PR 212
Unidad Hispano Latina *E* 84
Unie der Joodse Oud-Weerstanders *BE* 78
Union Africaine pour le Service, la
   Solidarité et l'Entraide *F* 3
≡ Amicale des Portugais d'Echternach
   LX 101
≡ des amicales marocaines en France *F* 89
Union des Associations Immigrées de
   Rennes *F* 138
≡ Clubs et Associations Yougoslaves
   F 126
≡ Communautés Africaine et Malgache *F* 3
Unión de Cubanos de Tenerife *E* 31
Union Culturelle Française des Arméniens
   en France *F* 11
≡ des travailleurs de Turquie *F* 120
Union der Demokraten Kurdistans *D* 82
≡ départementale des clubs RE.PER.ES
   F 163
≡ of Eritreans *GR* 34
≡ des Etudiants Algériens de Nantes *F* 9
≡ des Etudiants Juifs de France *F* 79
≡ Européenne des Fédéralistes *LX* 169
≡ Familiale Cap-Verdienne *LX* 26
≡ des familles turques de Grigny *F* 120
≡ des femmes immigrés originaires de la
   Guinée-Bissau *F* 39
Unión General de Trabajadores *NL LX* 113,
   E 149-151
≡ Sección Juventud *E* 216
≡ Secretaría de Emigración *E* 152
Union Générale des Associations gestion-
   naires de foyers de travailleurs *F* 199
≡ Travailleurs Sénégalais en France *F* 105
≡ Vietnamiens de France; Vietnamiens du
   Rhône *F* 124

Union of Greeks in the Netherlands *NL* 39
≡ of Hungarian Youth Organizations of
   Romania *RO* 43
≡ des Immigrés de l'Eure *F* 138
Unión de Inmigrantes Dominicanos *E* 32
Union Inter Service Migrants *F* 137
Union Internationale pour l'Etude
   Scientifique de la Population *BE* 232
≡ des organismes familiaux *F* 199
Union of the Iranian Community in Leeds
   UK 45
≡ islamique d'enseignement et de
   recherche; Islamique des Etudiants *F* 53
≡ des jeunes tunisiens d'Orléans *F* 118
≡ de la Jeunesse Ivorienne—Casa dello
   Studente *IT* 77
≡ of Jewish Students *UK* 81
Union des juifs du Maroc; pour la
   résistance et l'entraide *F* 79
Unión Liberal Cubana *E* 31
Union of Liberal & Progressive Synagogues
   UK 81
≡ des Marocains à l'Etranger *BE* 89
≡ des Mosquées Marocaines *NL* 90
Union of Muslim Families *UK* 67
≡ Families in GB; Organisations *UK* 71
Union of Muslims in Hackney *UK* 59
Union Mutuelle des Communautés Issues
   de l'Immigration *F* 138
Union Nationale d'Associations pour
   l'Acceuil de l'Enfant Réfugié *F* 138
≡ des associations familiales *F* 199
≡ des Associations Gestionnaires de
   Foyers de Travailleurs Migrants; des
   déportés de Rawa Ruska *F* 138
≡ des Etudiant(e)s du Luxembourg *LX* 208
Union néerlandaise en France *F* 32
≡ portugaise de Lens et environs *F* 99
≡ des Progressistes Juifs *BE* 78
Unión Proxima *E* 31
Union des Rapatriés Musulmans *F* 53
≡ ressortissants d'Afrique Central et
   d'Angola *F* 27
≡ ressortisants sénégalais de l'Eure *F* 105
Union of Shop, Distributive & Allied
   Workers *UK* 184
Unión Sindical Obrera *E* 151
Union des Travailleurs Africains en France;
   d'Afrique Noire de l'Oise *F* 3
≡ et Commerçants Marocains *F* 89
≡ immigrés de Sevran *F* 138
≡ Immigrés Tunisiens *F* 118
≡ ivoriens en France *F* 77
≡ Mauritaniens en France *F* 87
≡ Sénégalais en France—Action
   Revendicative *F* 105
≡ Turcs en Belgique *BE* 119
Union of Turkish Progressives in Britain;
   Workers *UK* 122
Unione Artisti Iraniani in Italia *IT* 45
≡ delle Comunità ed Organizzazioni
   Islamiche in Italia *IT* 54
≡ Cristiana degli Enti tra e per gli Emigrati
   Italiani *IT* 144
≡ Donne Italiane nel Lussemburgo *LX* 76
Unione Generale Lavoratori Eritrei *IT* 34
≡ dei Medici e Farmacisti Palestinesi *IT* 95
≡ Studenti Giordani *IT* 81
≡ degli Studenti e Lavoratori Libanesi *IT* 85
≡ Studenti Palestini *IT* 95
Unione dei Giovani Socialisti Congolesi
   IT 31
≡ Immigrati Nordafricani *IT* 92
≡ Italiana degli Immigrati *IT* 145
≡ Italiana del Lavoro *IT* 145, 207
≡ Lavoratori Emigrati Veneti *IT* 145
≡ Marocchini El Massira *IT* 90
Unione Nazionale delle Associazioni degli
   Immigrati ed Emigrati *IT* 145, *UK* 77
≡ Associazioni Italiane Emigrati *D* 75, *LX* 76
≡ Donne Eritree; Lavoratori Eritrei *IT* 34
≡ Studenti Siriani *IT* 115
Unione Pugliesi Emigrati e Famiglie *LX* 76
Unione Studenti Musulmani; in Italia *IT* 54
Unitè de recherche Anthropologique des
   populations contemporaines et
   préhistoriques *F* 236
United Anglo-Caribbean Society *UK* 9
≡ Asian Organization *UK* 15
≡ Asian Workers' Association *IT* 12
≡ Campaign Against Racism *UK* 184
≡ Caribbean Association *UK* 27
United Colours of Football *UK* 179
United Democratic Youth Organisation
   CY 193
≡ Evangelical Project Legal Centre *UK* 228
≡ Hebrew Immigration Aid Service *GR IT*
   CH 79
United for Intercultural Action *NL* 173
United Kingdom Action Committee *UK* 71
≡ Asian Women's Association; Asian
   Women's Conference *UK* 15

United Kingdom Committee for UNICEF UK 228
≡ Council for Overseas Student Affairs UK 158
≡ Cuba Friendship Society UK 31
≡ Hindi Samiti UK 41
≡ Ireland Trans-Frontier Committee UK 52
≡ Islamic Academy UK 71
≡ Islamic Mission UK 56, 59-60, 62-65, 67, 69, 71-72
≡ Islamic Trust UK 72
≡ Jewish Aid & International Development UK 81
≡ Muslim Women Association UK 72
≡ Pakistani Welfare Society UK 95
≡ Standing Council on Central & East European Jewry UK 81
United Kingdom Turkish Islamic Assoc.; Centre; Cultural Centre UK 122
United Moslem Organization; Muslim Committee UK 72
United Nations Association UK 228
≡ Centre for Human Rights CH 219
≡ Centre for Social Development & Humanitarian Affairs AT 188
≡ Children's Fund; Commission on Human Rights CH 219
≡ Documentation Centre E 242
≡ Educational, Scientific & Cultural Organisation F 199
≡ High Commissioner for Refugees AL 187, AT 188, BE 191, BH BG CT CY CS 193, F 198, D 201, GR H 203, IT 204, LX 207, NL 209, PL PR 211, RO RS SK SV SR E 212, S 217, CH TR 219, UK 228
≡ Non-Governmental Liaison Service CH 219
≡ Relief & Works Agency for Palestine Refugees in the Near East AT 188
≡ University NI 247
≡ Voluntary Fund for Victims of Torture CH 219
≡ of Youth NL 173, UK 184
United Towns Organisation F 198
Uniting Britain—for a just society UK 184
Unity of Afro-Caribbean People UK 7
≡ Centre of South London UK 23
≡ Hall Committee UK 62
≡ Helpline; Housing Association UK 158
Universidad Autónoma de Barcelona E 242
≡ Obrera BE 110
≡ Pontifica de Comillas; Popular de Cartagena E 242
Universidade Aberta de Lisboa; de Lisboa PR 241
≡ Nova de Lisboa PR 242
Università degli Studi di Urbino IT 239
Universität Bonn D 121
≡ Essen; Hamburg D 237
≡ Kiel D 238
≡ Köln D 237
≡ Konstanz; Osnabrück D 238
≡ Zürich CH 243
Université de Bordeaux F 3
≡ Catholique de Louvain BE 232
≡ de Haut-Bretagne-Rennes 2 F 234
≡ Libre de Bruxelles BE 83, 232
≡ de Liège au Sart-Tilman BE 231
≡ de Lyon 2 F 236
≡ de Nancy II F 234
≡ Ouvrière BE 110
≡ de Paix BE 232
≡ de Paris V F 236
≡ de Paris VIII F 233
≡ de Poitiers F 234
≡ de Provence F 233-5
≡ Stendhal F 74
≡ Paul Valéry Montpellier 3 F 235
Universiteit van Amsterdam NL 240-1
≡ Antwerpen BE 231
≡ Utrecht NL 54, 240
Universiteris pel Tercer Mon E 174
Universitet Århus DK 232-3
University Assistance Fund NL 147
≡ of Birmingham UK 37
≡ of Bologna IT 239
≡ of Bradford UK 16, 85, 126, 246
≡ of Bristol UK 246
≡ of Cambridge UK 84, 244
≡ College Galway IR 238
≡ of Copenhagen DK 233
≡ of Dundee UK 245
≡ of East London UK 246
≡ of Essex UK 221, 245
≡ of Exeter UK 11, 244
≡ of Glasgow UK 84, 246
≡ of Hull UK 43
≡ of Leeds UK 14, 244, 246
≡ of Leicester UK 244
≡ of Liverpool UK 49, 84, 113
≡ of London UK 16, 29, 84, 177, 243, 245-7
≡ of Manchester UK 244

University of North London UK 50, 246
≡ of Nottingham UK 245
≡ of Oxford UK 85, 245-6
≡ of Sheffield UK 15, 78, 82, 245
≡ of Southampton UK 246
≡ of Stirling UK 78
≡ of Sussex UK 244-5
≡ of Ulster NI 247
≡ of Wales NI 117
≡ of Warwick UK 244
≡ of Wolverhampton UK 246
Unregelmassige Info-Blatter D 121
Unrepresented Nations & Peoples Organisation NL 147
Unterkommission des Pastoral-kommission—Seelsorge am Menschen unterwegs D 140
Unterstützungskomitee für politisch verfolgte Ausländer/innen AT 188
Upton Park Islamic Centre UK 62
Urafriki Tanzania F 115
Urban Trust UK 157
Urdu Society Mosque UK 123
Urgence F 165
USDAW Race Relations Committee UK 184
UWAIS Foundation UK 72

Vakgroep Taal en Minderheden NL 241
Valencia Acoge E 152
Bernard Van Leer Foundation NL 210
Vänskapsförbundet Sverige-Nicaragua S 91
Vauxhall Law Centre UK 228
Vedic Society UK 43
Veneto Emigrazione IT 145
Venskabs- og Kulturforeningen i Ringsted DK 161
Venskabsforening Danmark-Kina DK 28
Venskabsforeningen for Danskere og Indvandrere; Flygtninge-, Indvandrer- og Danske Kvinder DK 161
Vent du Nord/Vent du Sud BE 161
Verband Armenischer Vereinigungen D 11
≡ für Ausländerhilfe in Kärnten und Osttirol AT 129
≡ bi-nationaler Familien und Partnerschaften D 140
≡ der Freien Rumanen und Deutschen aus Rumanien D 102
≡ der Initiativgruppen in der Ausländerarbeit D 140
≡ der Islamischen Kulturzentren D 53
≡ der Koreaner in Deutschland D 82
≡ Schweizerischer Jüdischer Fürsorgen CH 79
Verdrukt NL 208
Verein für Afghanische Flüchtlingshilfe D 1
≡ Arbeiter und Studenten aus Türkei; von Arbeiter aus Türkei D 121
≡ der Arbeitnehmer Kurdistans in Köln D 82
Verein zur Förderung des Deutsch-Türkischen Sportjugendaustausches D 121
≡ Ethnischer Minderheiten; und Integration von Ausländische Juendlicher D 140
Verein für Gegenseitigkeit D 238
≡ Griechischen Bürger in Europa D 38
≡ der Indochina-Flüchtlinge, Chinesischer Abstammung D 110
≡ Iranischer Flüchtlinge D 45
≡ ISOP—Flüchtlingsbetreuung AT 129
≡ der Jugoslawische Bürger D 126
≡ Menschen in der Stadt D 167
≡ Mutter-Kind Stube D 140
≡ für Psychische Gesundheit von Migranten D 140
≡ Rom D 103
≡ der Sozialberater für Türken in NRW; der Türkischen Arbeitnehmer D 121
≡ der Vietnamesischen Flüchtlinge D 124
≡ Zebra AT 129
Vereinigung der Marokkanischen Emigranten in der BRD D 89
≡ Tunesier in Deutschland D 119
≡ Verfolgten des Naziregimes/Bund der Antifaschisten D 167
Verenigd Verzet 1940-1945 NL 173
Vereniging van Iraanse Vluchtelingen NL 45
≡ Kinderen van Verzetsdeelnemers 1940-45 NL 173
≡ Lau Mazirel NL 147
≡ van Marokkaanse Jongeren BE 88
≡ voor Rechtshulp NL 210
≡ voor Solidariteit BE 161
≡ voor Technische Samenwerking BE 192
≡ der Vlaamse Onthaaltehuizen BE 132
≡ VluchtelingenWerk Nederland NL 147
Vervolgingsslachtoffers NVT NL 173
Verzeichnis Forschung und Lehre D 237
Verzetsmuseum Amsterdam NL 241
Vétérinaires sans frontières F 199
VIA-Magazin; Viaticus D 140

Vicaria Solidaritet-Støttegruppe DK 132
Victoria Park Mosque UK 72
Vie Féminine BE 129
Vienna Malayalee Association AT 87
Viet Nam AT 123
Vietnam Refugee National Council UK 125
Vietnamese Assistance Service; Catholic Association; Cultural Association; Elderly People's Club UK 125
≡ Irish Association IR 124
≡ Refugee Children & Young People's Project UK 227
Vietnamesisk Ungdomsforening i København; Vietnamsiske Buddhistiske Forening i Århus DK 124
Village Aid UK 6
Virages BE 231
Vishwa Hindu Parishad DK 41, UK 43
≡ Temple UK 43
Vishwadharma UK 40
Vision Mondiale Internationale CH 219
Visva Adhyatmik Sansthan UK 43
Vivre Ensemble CH 175
Vlaams Centrum voor Integratie van Migranten; Overlegcomité Migratie BE 132
≡ Platform voor International Jongerenwerk BE 192
Vlaamse Dienst voor Arbeidsbemiddeling en Beroepsopleiding; Kommissie Rechtvaadig-heid en Vrede BE 192
≡ Werkgroep Indianen Zuid-Amerika BE 83
VluchtelingenWerk; Nieuwegein Stichting; Rijnmond; Stichting; Zeist Stichting NL 147
Voce degli Afro-Italiani IT 4
La Voce degli Italiani UK 76
The Voice UK 6
Voice of the Arab World UK 11
Voice of the Emigrant UK 48
La Voix des Femmes BE 161
Volcano Press UK 67
Volkshaus D 121
Volkswagen-Stiftung D 202
Volontari per lo Sviluppo IT 143
Volonteurope UK 222
Voluntari e Terzo Mondo IT 205
Voluntariado de Madres Dominicanas E 32
Voluntary Service International IR 204
≡ Overseas UK 228
Voluntary Voice UK 225
De Vonk NL 173
Voorlichtingscentrum Vluchtelingen en Vreemdelingen BE 131
Vous et Nous F 138
Voz da Missão D 100
Voz da Queiriga PR 149
Voz Viva D 100
Vreemdelingendienst NL 208, 210
Vrienden van El Kantra BE 132
Vrienden van Kerwin NL 173
Vriendenkring Dachau BE 161
Vriendenkring Mauthausen NL 173
Vrijwillge Internationale Aktie NL 210
Vrouwenvereniging voor Vrede BE 192

Wai Yin Centre; Chinese Women Society UK 30
Wales Anti-Racist Alliance UK 184
Raoul Wallenberg Institutet for Manslika Rattigheter och Humanitar Ratt S 243
Walsall Interfaith Group; Racial Equality Council UK 184
Waltham Forest Afro-Caribbean Senior Citizens Club UK 7
≡ All Faiths Group UK 184
≡ Anti-Deportation Campaign UK 158
≡ Asian Centre UK 15
≡ Immigration Aid Centre UK 158
≡ Irish Association; Irish Project UK 52
≡ Muslim Welfare Society UK 72
≡ Pakistan Muslim Welfare Assoc. UK 95
≡ Racial Equality Council UK 184
≡ Refugee Project UK 158
≡ Social Justice Unit UK 228
≡ Young People's Housing Project UK 12, 23
Walthamstow Citizens Advice Bureau UK 228
Wandsworth Council; Interpreting Service; Law Centre UK 228
≡ Racial Equality Group UK 184
Wangar UK 106
WarReport UK 245
War Resisters International; on Want UK 228
Wara Wara—Association des Aymaras F 23
Warrington Law Centre UK 228
Warwick District Racial Equality Council UK 185
Washwood Heath Muslim Centre UK 72
Waterford Association UK 52

Watford Citizens Advice Bureau; Council Corporate Equality Advice Team *UK* 229
≡ Irish Association; Irish Centre *UK* 52
≡ Racial Equality Council *UK* 185
≡ School of Arabic & Islamic Studies *UK* 247
Wednesbury Bangladesh Muslim Welfare Association *UK* 18
Weekly Journal UK 23
Weekly News CH 218
Welcome—Centro Sociale per Famiglie Immigrate *IT* 145
Welfare Centre *UK* 158
Welfare Rights Unit *NI* 229
Wellingborough Anti-Fascist Alliance *UK* 185
≡ Irish Association *UK* 52
≡ Multi-Faith Group; Racial Equality Council *UK* 185
Welsh Refugee Council *UK* 158
Weltfriedensdienst *D* 202
Welzijnszorg *BE* 193
Wembley & Harrow Indian Assoc. *UK* 44
Wembley Mosque & Islamic Centre *UK* 72
Wen Wei Po UK 30
Wereldfederalisten Beweging *NL* 210
Wereldsolidariteit *BE* 193
Werkgroep Integratie Vluchtelingen *BE* 132
≡ Migranten in Media *NL* 173
≡ Rechtsbijstand Vreemdelingenzaken *NL* 147
≡ tegen Fascisme en Racisme; tegen Racisme *NL* 173
Werking met Kansarme Jeugd *BE* 119
Werklozen-Jongerenwerking *BE* 132
Werkstett 3 *D* 167
Werneth Mosque & Urdu School *UK* 72
Wesleyan Holiness Church *UK* 229
Wessex Shi'a Ithna 'Asheri Jamat *UK* 72
West African Senior Citizens Centre; Welfare Association *UK* 125
West Belfast Travellers Project *NI* 118
≡ Bowling Community Advice & Training Centre *UK* 158
≡ Bromwich Afro-Caribbean Resource Centre *UK* 7
≡ End Mosque *UK* 72
≡ German Federation of Expellees *D* 37
West Glamorgan Community Relations Council; Race Equality Council *UK* 185
West Hertfordshire NHS Trust *UK* 229
West Indian Centre *UK* 18
≡ Community Centre *UK* 125
≡ Cultural Centre *UK* 6
West Indian Digest UK 125
West Indian Ex-Servicemen's & Women's Association; Family Counselling Service; Family & Educational Council *UK* 125
≡ Federation *UK* 7
≡ Leadership Council *UK* 6
≡ League *UK* 125
≡ Organisation Co-ordinating Committee; Progressive Association; Sports Club & Community Centre; Sports & Social Club; Standing Conference *UK* 125
West London Asian Health Agency *UK* 15
≡ Irish Society *UK* 52
≡ Islamic Centre *UK* 72
West Lothian Mosque & Community Centre *UK* 72
West Midlands Anti-Deportation Campaign *UK* 158
≡ Caribbean Parents & Friends Association *UK* 27
≡ Consortium Project on Indian Teacher Training *UK* 245
≡ Practice Development Centre *UK* 247
West Scotland Central America Network *UK* 27
≡ Sussex Arabic Community *UK* 11
≡ Sussex Bangladeshi Association *UK* 18
≡ Yorkshire Racial Equality Council *UK* 176
Western Buddhist Order Padmaloka Madhyamaloka *UK* 24
Westminster Race Equality Council *UK* 185
Wexford Association *UK* 52
Whalley Range Afro Care Group *UK* 7
Whitechapel Mosque *UK* 58
WIR e.V.—Forum für ein Besseres Verstandnis zwischen Deutschen und Ausländern *D* 167
Wiener Institut für Entwicklungsfragen und Zusammenarbeit *AT* 188
Wiener Integrationsfonds *AT* 159
Wiener Library *UK* 81
Simon Wiesenthal Center *F* 165
Wilberforce Council *UK* 229
Wiltshire Racial Equality Council *UK* 185
Wimbledon Mosque *UK* 72

Windsor Fellowship *UK* 158
Winterthurer Beratungsstelle für Asylsuchende *CH* 153
Wissenschaftszentrum Berlin für Sozialforschung *D* 238
Witham & District Irish Association *UK* 52
Woking Community Relations Forum *UK* 185
≡ & District Irish Society *UK* 52
≡ Muslim Association *UK* 72
Wolverhampton Afro-Caribbean Development Agency *UK* 7
≡ Black Community Action Group *UK* 23
≡ Borough Council Race Relations Office; Inter-Faith Group; Racial Equality Council *UK* 185
Women in Development, Europe *IR* 204
Women & Ireland Network *UK* 52
Women's Aid to Former Yugoslavia *UK* 126
≡ Association of Tigray in Europe *IT* 116
≡ Campaign for Soviet Jewry *UK* 81
≡ International League for Peace & Freedom *CH* 175, *UK* 229
≡ Racism Awareness Group *NI* 185
≡ Roof *UK* 16
≡ World Summit Foundation *CH* 219
Worcester Racial Equality Council *UK* 185
Wordt Vervolgd NL 208
Work Permits Section *NI* 229
Workers' Autonomous Federation of China *UK* 30
Workgroup Black Feminist *NL* 19
Working Group Against Racism in Children's Resources *UK* 185
≡ Asylum in Churches *D* 140
≡ Indigenous Peoples *NL* 210
≡ on Legal Aid for Refugees *NL* 147
Working Peoples Alliance *UK* 40
World Ahl Ul-Bayt (A.S.) Islamic League; League *UK* 72
World Alliance of Young Men's Christian Associations *CH* 219
≡ Assembly of Muslim Youth *UK* 72
≡ Assembly of Youth *DK* 195
≡ Association for the School as an Instrument of Peace *CH* 175
≡ Congress of Faiths *UK* 185
≡ Council of Churches *IT* 207, *CH* 219
≡ Council of Hindus *UK* 43
≡ Council of Muslim Youth *UK* 72
≡ Development Movement *UK* 229
World Faiths Insight UK 185
World Federation of Democratic Youth *H* 203
≡ Khoja Shia Ithna Ash'ari Muslim Communities *UK* 72
≡ Overseas Cypriots *CY* 132
≡ United Nations Associations *CH* 219
World Islamic Call Society *CH* 54
≡ Council *UK* 72
≡ Forum *DK* 53, *UK* 72
≡ Mission *UK* 72
≡ Mission Centre *UK* 63
World Jewish Alliance *F* 79
≡ Jewish Congress *F CH* 79
≡ Kashmir Freedom Movement *UK* 81
≡ Muslim Congress *CH* 54
≡ Muslim League *CH* 54, *UK* 72
≡ Organisation of Young Esperantists *NL* 173
World Organization against Torture *CH* 218
≡ of Former Czechoslovak Jews *UK* 81
World Peace Council *SF* 195
World Poverty Review IR 204
World Romany Congress *UK* 103
World Student Christian Federation *CH* 219
The World Today UK 246
World University Service *D* 202, *IR* 141, *CH* 219, *UK* 229
≡ Vision International *CH* 219
≡ of Women *D* 202
≡ Young Women's Christian Association *CH* 219
≡ Zionist Organization *UK* 81
Worlds End Neighbourhood Advice Centre *UK* 229
Worthing Islamic Social & Welfare Society *UK* 62
Worthing Muslim Society *UK* 72
Wycombe & District Race Equality Steering Committee; Racial Equality Council *UK* 185
Wycombe Islamic Mission *UK* 63
Wythenshawe Irish Society *UK* 52
Wythenshawe Law Centre *UK* 229

XYZ Women's Group *UK* 16

Yaa Asantewaa Arts Centre *UK* 6
Yad Vashem Charitable Trust *UK* 247
Yakeen Asian Women's Counselling Project *UK* 14
Yemeni Community Association; Workers' Association *UK* 125
Yes to a Colourful Community *NR* 173
York Anti-Fascist Action *UK* 185
York & District Council for Community Relations *UK* 182
York Muslim Association; Yorkshire Muslim Association *UK* 73
Young European Federalists *BE* 193
≡ Generation Society of Romania *RO* 212
≡ Hindu Progressive Mandal *UK* 43
≡ Indian Forward Block *UK* 44
≡ Irish Men's Group *UK* 50
≡ Men's Christian Association *F* 196, *IT* 207
≡ Muslim Association *UK* 73
≡ Muslim Organisation *UK* 57, 71, 73
≡ Muslim Women's Group *UK* 73
Young Muslims *UK* 73
≡ Girls Group *UK* 68
≡ Girls Section; Loughborough *UK* 73
≡ Organisation *UK* 63, 73
≡ Sheffield *UK* 68
≡ Walsall *UK* 67
≡ Wolverhampton *UK* 72
Young Women's Christian Association— Progetto Donne Migranti e Rifugiate *IT* 145
Youth against Racism in Europe *D* 167, *NL* 171, *UK* 185
≡ Against Racism & Facism *UK* 185
≡ Assoc. for European Friendship *RO* 173
≡ Committee of the Coalition of Left & Progress *GR* 203
≡ Council of Latvia *LT* 207
≡ Council of the Swedish Immigrant Organisations *S* 152
≡ for Democratic Action in Europe *F* 198
≡ for Development & Co-operation *NL* 210
≡ Exchange Centre *UK* 221
≡ for Europe *BE* 191, *GR* 203, *IR IT* 204, *NL* 209, *E* 215, *UK* 221
≡ for a Europe Without Borders *NL* 173
≡ for Exchange & Understanding *D* 167
≡ Forum of the European Union *BE* 193
≡ for the World *GR* 203
Yugoslav Royal Draza Mihailovic Assoc.; Studies Research Group *UK* 126

Zabavno Rekreatiuni Club Beograd *F* 105
ZAG Redaktion *D* 165
Zahra Trust UK *UK* 73
Zainab Languages School *UK* 93
Zaire Digest BE 126
Zairean Community Association *UK* 127
Zakaria Mosque *UK* 70, 73
Zakariya Muslim Girls' High School *UK* 73
ZAP D 167
Zar Aktuell D 237
Zara Elderly Asian Group *UK* 16
Zawiya Centre *UK* 16
≡ Islamic Centre; Mosque *UK* 73
Zebra Zentrum zur sozial-medizinischen, rechtlichen und kulturellen Betreuung von Ausländer/innen in Österreich *AT* 129
Zeitschrift Gemeinsam D 202
Zeitschrift für Turkeistudien D 121
Zells Info- en Adviescentrum *BE* 132
Zena UK 34
Zentrale Dokumentationsstelle der Freien Wohlfahrtspflege für Flüchtlinge *D* 238
Zentrale Wohlfahrtspflege/Wohlfahrtsstelle der Juden in Deutschland *D* 79
Zentralrat deutscher Sinti und Roma *D* 103
Zentralrat der Juden in Deutschland *D* 79
Zentralstelle für Arbeitsvermittlung *D* 202
≡ für Asylanten- und Flüchtlingsbetreuung *AT* 129
≡ Pastoral Deutschen Bischofskonferenz— Referat Auslanderseelsorge *D* 140
Zentralverband der Assyrischen Vereinigungen in Deutschland *D* 16
≡ Griechischen Gemeinden *D* 38
≡ Ukrainischer Emigration *D* 122
Zentrum der Jugoslawen in München *D* 126
Zentrum für Migranten und interkulturelle Studien *D* 238
≡ Türkeistudien; Türkische Studien *D* 121
Zghazagh Hbieb in-Natura *M* 208
Zig-Zag DK 195
Zimbabwe Society *UK* 127
Stichting ZOA Vluchtelingenzorg *NL* 147
Zoroastrian Community *UK* 45
Zundbrief CH 153

ACRONYMS

3BREP UK 184
3W1 UK 228

A SEED NL 208
A3W D 165
AA E 149
AAA F 12, 134, CH 152
AAB D CH 109
AABN NL 109
AAC GR 202, UK 12
AAE F 8
AAEN PR 148
AAFK F 81
AAFTE F 134
AAHIMAFE E 4
AAHTMF F 134
AAM UK 110
AAMA PR 9
AAMIS F 137
AAP IT 3
AAPGE E 33
AAR; AART UK 175
AATERR; AATM F 134
AAVAA UK 243
AAWA UK 12
A&BCLC UK 220
ABIDOZ D 165
ABP D 166
ABPO UK 20
ABS UK 19
ABVV BE 132
ABVV-J BE 189
AACA UK 12
ACAC E 213
ACADOME F 86
ACCE F IT 3
ACAFOM F 134
ACAI IT 25
ACAM E 91
ACAP IT 168
ACAP-77 F 97
ACAS F 8
ACASEA F 110
ACAT F 195, D 200, LX 207
ACATPL F 118
ACB NL 145
ACBA UK 6
ACC F 162
ACCDU UK 6
ACCIR F 2
ACCIS UK 5
ACDA BE 96
ACDUC F 134
ACE UK 243
ACEF-AITEF LX 75
ACEI IT 34
ACERT UK 41
ACFF UK 6
ACFM F 86
ACIC E 84
ACIEAM F 2
ACIM IT 87
ACIMA PR 9
ACIS UK 243
ACIU DK 193
ACJ D 112
ACK E 83
ACL IT 28
ACLA; ACLAV IT 84
ACLB BE 73
ACLC UK 6
ACLI BE 73, F D 74, IT 141, 204-5, LX 75, UK 76

ACMC F 86
ACMHA UK 7
ACMS F 86
ACNA F 92, UK 6
ACNUR IT 204, PR 211, E 212
ACO F 195
ACORD UK 5
ACPFM F 134
ACPS F 97
ACRA PR 9
ACSAB IT 3
ACSAR E 149
ACSE IT 142
ACSI IT 141
ACT F 31, E 212, NI 118
ACTSA UK 110
ACTTF F 120
ACUGE E 33
ACV BE 132
ACVFP IT 25
ACVS PR 26
ACW BE 160
ADAESER IT 141
ADASER IT 10
ADATMI F 134
ADB NL 170
ADCFA F 86
ADDE BE 130
ADDHA F 2
ADF F 118
ADFE F 134, IT LX 36
ADFI F 134
ADHMA F 10
ADIA IT 3
ADIAP LX 100
ADISL F 113
ADiTi UK 12
ADM F 134
ADO NL 208
ADRD NL 170
ADRI F 233
AEAPA E 10
AEC F 196, IT 31, UK 91
AECI E 212
AECLA F 10
AEEEIF F 53
AEFTI F 134-5
AEGEE NL 208
AEGM UK 12
AEI E 242
AEIG E 41
AELAS E 84
AEMACC E 10
AEME E 90
AER F 138
AES F 134
AESI IS 203
AET UK 5
AETE F 10
AEVAM F 124
AFA F 110, D 165, H IR 168, NL 170, E 149, UK 175-182, 185
AFASPA F 2
AFATE F 111
AFCL F 31
AFEC F 111
AFEZIECA F 126
AFF-FAF BE 160
AFFOR UK 175
AFIC F 2
AFIF F 134
AFJD F 196
AFLF F 83

AFM F 86
AFMAC E 4
AFMDR F 86
AFO NL 170
AFPA F 97
AfPiC UK 220
AFR F 135
AFRAM F 2
AFRANE F 1
AFRICA F 8
AFS NL 169-170, S 175
AFSE E 174
AFSIU S 175
AFT F 115
AFTAM F 134
AFVP F 2
AFZE D 165
AGAH D 138
AGEAM F 8
AGECOOP F 195
AGEFALE F 8
Agenor F 129
AGG D 200
AGIN IT 38
AGISRA D 166
AGIY UK 47
AGKE F 81
AGO UK 41
AGSAL LX 75
AHAEP IT 33
AHMI F 135
AI AT 187, DK 193, D 200, IT 204, LX 207, NL 208, NR 210, UK 220, NI 229
AICF F 195
AICOS IT 205
AIDDA F 233
AIEB IT 142
AIECM IT 238
AIEP IT 33
AIF DK 161, E 35
AIJD BE 189
AINAI IT 92
AIPI F 162
AIRCM F 86, 233
AIRE UK 220
AIRKF F 77
AISOHAF F 41
AITEF IT 142, UK 76
AITEF-CALE D 74
AJDC IT 79
AJEX UK 80
AJF F 134
AJM BE 88, F 86
AJMF F 135
AJMK F 82
AJPEG F 111
AJR UK 80
AKARSU D 138
AKS CH 152
AKTIF D 82
AL S 216
ALC E 101
ALCE F 111
ALCA; ALFA F 8
Allianssi SF 195
ALTIC; ALTIF F 135
AMA UK 220
AMAT F 116
AMAV IT 87
AMC F 86
AMDE E 32
AMEL F 8

AMEZAFI IT 126
AMF F 89
AMGT D 120
AMI F 162, PR 211
AMIC E 149
AMIM E 90
AMKA D 165
AMLI F 135
AMMU NL 90
AMPAE E 4
AMR; AMTIP F 135
ANAFE F 135
ANAREF F 134
ANC DK F IT NL E UK 109
ANED IT 168
ANEOM F 86
ANERM PR 91
ANF PL 173
ANFE BE 73, IT 142, LX 75, UK 76
ANGI F 162
ANJV NL 208
ANL IR 168, UK 176
ANOLF IT 142
ANPE F 195
APAD F 196
APAJI BE 130
APART UK 35
APB F 97
APCLAI IT 84
APCS F 98
APCV F 162
APD BE 129
APDA UK 13
APDH; APDHE E 213
APE F 134
APEC F 98
APFEEF F 111
APFS F 196
APGE E 33
API-COLF IT 205
APIA E 149
APIAC F 97
APICA F 8
APIFOMEJ F 86
APL IT 96
APM F 98, GR 11
APMAR F 134
APNA UK 13
APOYAR E 149
APPAM F 86
APPELAF F 10
APS F 2, IT 205, NL 239
APSCR F 98
APSSI PR 211
APTE RO 173
ApTibeT UK 116
ARA F 165, UK 176
ARAC F 162
ARACOVA E 149
ARAFA UK 180
ARAFK NL 170
ARAP F 98
ARBA LX 24
ARC UK 13
ARCA F 27
ARCOTERRE F 196
ARE PR 148
AREL LX 124
AREMF LX 75
ARENA F 196
ARETE; ARFEM F 135
ARFI IT 142

ARG NL 170
ARGF F 87
ARHAG UK 5
ARIC D 165, NL 170
ARIS CH 175
ARLHM F 83
ARM UK 5
ARMBF F 87
ARPAFC F 28
ARPEI IT 34
ARPEL LX 75
ARRF UK 16
ARSM F 105
ARULEF LX 75
ASAAR F 135
ASADH F 10
ASAF F 2
ASAFP IT 3
ASAL F 162
ASAMLA F 135
ASAR IT 3
ASAUK UK 5
ASCA BE 9
ASCAO F 2
ASCEJ F 79
ASCTT F 120
ASDEALE F 8
ASECA F 162
ASECB F 25
ASEF F 162
ASEN UK 243
ASF F 196, D 165
ASFC F 25
ASFIR F 162
ASGI IT 238
ASI F 135, UK 220
ASIAN UK 12
ASIFAH F 2
ASKV NL 145
ASL IT 104-5
ASLIR RO 173
ASPAL F 83
ASPE IT 238
ASPER IT 142
ASPIC F 162
ASPP IT 105
ASRA UK 13
ASRIM IT 104
ASRO UK 243
ASSEAS F 2
ASSEFTA F 134
ASSETIMA F 8
ASSFAM F 135
ASSIA IT 11
ASSIR IT 77
ASSOFAC F 162
ASSORIM IT 77
ASSOTRAF F 2
ASSRA IT 105
ASTA F 8
ASTI F 135, LX 145, E 149
ASTM F 135
ASW D 165
ATAMS F 10
ATAS IT 142
ATCM F 89
ATD F 164
ATE E 151
ATF F 118
ATFA F 8
ATFAL LX 75
ATIDG NL 121
ATIME E 90
ATLIK F 3
ATM F 163
ATMF F 89

ATNRT F 19
ATT F 120
AUC DK 232
AUCV PR 26
AUGB UK 123
AVA-BASTA F 163
AUJF F 79
AVAI F 135
AVID UK 153
AWA; AWAAZ UK 13
AWR AT 231
AWWG UK 5
AZAT; AZI IT 126

BA-PO BE 130
BAAF UK 221
BAASO UK 153
BACEE UK 33
BACS; BAG UK 25
BAGB UK 16
BAGIV D 138
BAI IT 17
BAIS UK 47
BARC UK 5
BARG UK 176
BAWSO UK 20
BBB UK 6
BBFS UK 24
BBVS UK 21
BCA UK 243
BCC UK 222
BCET UK 116
BCHV BE 130
BCLC UK 220-1
BCRC UK 31
BCYP UK 29
BD BE 189
BdA D 166
BDR AT 187
BEI UK 20
BEJ-JEF AT 187
BEST UK 221
BETB D 120
BF D 200
BfA CH 217
BGS D 200
BHAF; BHAN; BHASEL UK 20
BHT HALC UK 220
BIA F 1, UK 43
BIAS UK 47
BIFF D 166
BIHR UK 244
BIM AT 187
BIMHG UK 47
BIPS UK 45
BIT F 196, CH 218
BIVS D 236
BiZa NL 209
BKA UK 81
BLVRM BE 189
BMS UK 87
BODS CH 175
BPSC NL 11
BRAMU UK 176
BRC UK 157
BREC UK 176
BRPF UK 227
BSR UK 220
BSV D 138
BTBTM D 120
BTC UK 21, 122
BTEDG NI 118
BTEG UK 21
BTIDF BE 119
BTSE D 120
BTSP NI 118

BUKO *D* 200
BYC *UK* 221
BYM *UK* 21
BZFO *D* 138

CAABU *UK* 11
CAAL *BE* 10
CAAR *F* 136
CAB *UK* 225
CACIS *IT* 142
CADE *E* 87
CADEF *F* 3
CADIM *F* 89
CAE *IT* 142
CAEPF *D* 112
CAF *F* 3
CAFE *UK* 177
CAFLI *LX* 76
CAGE *D* 38
CAHAN *UK* 178
CAHRC *UK* 27
CAIA *UK* 12
CAIAB *UK* 177
CAIAD *UK* 153
CAIBS *BE* 73
CAIE *F* 136, *CH* 152
CAIF; CAIR *F* 136
CAJ *D* 112, *Nl* 229
CAMAF *F* 86
CAND *UK* 5
CAPA *UK* 178
CAPL *LX* 100
Cara *UK* 47
CARARD *F* 135
CARE *PR* 148, *UK* 177
CARF *UK* 177-8, 180, 183
CARJ; CARL *UK* 177
CARP *PR* 148
CAS *F* 3
CASA *F* 98, *LX* 100
CASAS *F* 135
CAST *IT* 105, 142
CATI *BE* 130
CAUM *E* 174
CAV *IT* 142
CBA *NL* 208
CBAR *BE* 130
CBF *UK* 80
CBH *IT* 23
CBMEC *BE* 86
CBP *UK* 93
CBS *NL* 240
CBW *BE* 130
CCA *IT* 10
CCAE *BE* 2, *F IT* 3
CCBI *UK* 222
CCCC *UK* 29
CCDF *F* 25
CCDH *LX* 39
CCE *LX* 46, *UK* 48
CCEE *E* 150
CCFD *F* 136
CCIVS *F* 197
CCJ *UK* 178
CCL *LX* 27
CCME *BE* 130, *UK* 154
CCOO *LX* 113, *E* 149-150, 214
CCP *LX* 100
CCPF *F* 98
CCRE *F* 111
CCRIAG *LX* 75
CCRJ *UK* 177
CCRU *NI* 229
CDAIC *LX* 239
CDDHPB *F* 18
CDDI *IT* 143
CDG *D* 139
CDHG *E* 39
CDLR *UK* 104
CDPI *LX* 169
CDPM *LX* 145
CDR *CH* 243
CDS *IT* 168

CDSALA *E* 242
CE *F* 197
CEAEE *D* 112
CEAIN; CEAR *E* 150
CEBAG *BE* 130
CEC *CH* 152
CECDH *F* 196
CEDAM *F* 89
CEDEAL *E* 84
CEDEP *F* 98
CEDETIM *F* 233
CEDIA *E* 150
CEDIDELP *F* 233
CEDIRED *F* 163
CEDISS *E* 242
Cedom *D* 74
CEDOR *IT* 84
CEDORECK *F* 82
CEDRI *F* 163, *E* 45, *CH* 175
CEDU *IT* 238
CEFA-UO *BE* 110
CEFEM *PR* 241
CEFISEM *F* 135, 234
CEFRA *F* 12
CEHMC *F* 233
CEIAL *IT* 84
CELF *F* 163
CELSI; CeLSI-CGIL; CELSTRA *IT* 143
CEM *BE* 130, *F* 197, *IT* 238, *E* 150
CEME *BE* 130
CEMRI *PR* 241
CEMRIC *F* 233
CEMYC *DK* 132, *D* 200, *NL* 208, *UK* 154
CENSIS *IT* 239
CENYC *BE* 190
CEOC *F* 233
CERAG *UK* 155
CERAM *F* 118
CERCIC *F* 74
CERD *CH* 175
CERF; CERI; CERIEM *F* 234
CERISE *F* 233
CERM; CEROAC *F* 234
CES *PR* 241
CESAM *F* 196
CESES *IT* 238
CeSIL *IT* 143
CESSAR *E* 213
CESVITEM *IT* 168
CETF *F* 118
CETIM *CH* 175
CEU *UK* 33
CEWC *UK* 222, *NI* 229
CFA *F* 12
CFD *CH* 152
CFDT *F* 196
CFEP *BE* 189
CFMW *IT NL* 35, *UK* 36
CGH *UK* 222
CGI-UGT *E* 150
CGIL *IT* 143, 205
CGJL *LX* 207
CGT *F* 196, *E* 214
CGTP-IN *PR* 148
CHCF *BE* 38
CHEAM *F* 234
CHF *F* 41, 111
CIAC *UK* 29
CIBEDO *D* 166
CIC *BE* 130, *IT* 168
CICRED *F* 234
CICS *IT* 205
CICV *IT* 26
CID *F* 163
CIDAA *F* 109
CIDAC *PR* 241
CIDAF *E* 4

CIDEAL *E* 84
CIDF *F* 196
CIDI *NL* 73
CIDOB *E* 242
CIDSE *BE* 190
CIDSI *IT* 142
CIEE *BE* 130, *UK* 222
CIEHPK *F* 25
CIEMEN *E* 150
CIEMI *F* 234
CIEP *BE* 130
CIES *IT* 168
CIFE *IT* 238
CIGRI *IT* 205
CIIC *E* 4
CIIR *UK* 221
CIMADE *F* 136
CIMEA *IT* 205
CIMERSS *F* 234
CIMO *SF* 233
CIO *UK* 44
CIPA *BE* 231
CIPIE *E* 84
CIR *IT* 205, *E* 214
CIRE *BE* 130
CIRES *E* 242
CIS *F* 163, *E* 242
CISCAI *IT* 143
CISIA *F* 9
CISM *IT* 144
CISO-Zuid *BE* 232
CISP *IT* 239
CISPI *IT* 168-9
CISV *IT* 143, *UK* 221
CIT *UK* 244
CITAA *IT* 54
CITE *E* 149-150
CITM *F* 163
CITMI *LX* 169, *E* 150
CIVIL *BE* 124
CJE *E* 214
CJEF *BE* 190
CLACA *E* 84
CLAE *LX* 145
CLAP *F* 136
CLAT *NL* 84
CLB *F* 98
CLCG *LX* 46, *UK* 48
CLISMA *F* 137
CLP *F* 136
CLSRI *IT* 45
CMA *BE* 88
CMAL *PR* 4
CME *UK* 177
CMJ *F CH* 79
CMP *BE* 189
CMSI *IR* 203
CMSSM *F* 136
CNA *BE* 130
CNAJEP *F* 196
CNDP *F* 234
CNE *F* 110
CNFP *IT* 92
CNGS *SM* 212
CNIDFF; CNIPI *F* 196
CNJC *E* 214
CNRS *F* 234
CNT *E* 214
CNV *NL* 146, 208
CNVA *F* 196
COA *NL* 145
COACUM *E* 174
COASIT *F* 74
COBEFF *BE* 131
CoCAIS *UK* 77
COCIS *IT* 205
COEMIT *IR* 75, *LX* 76
COFACE *BE* 189
COFRIMI *F* 234
COI *UK* 244
COJASOR *F* 79
COLARCH *BE* 28
COM.IT.AS *LX* 76
COMEDE *F* 136
COMETT *BE* 189,

192, *DK* 195
ComItEs *LX* 76
Comeurim *BE* 130
COMRADE *E* 150
COMSET *IT* 105
COMT *NL* 240
COOP-DES *IT* 143
COOPI *IT* 169
CORAS *UK* 30
COREZAG *UK* 127
COS *F* 135
COS/VWW *NL* 170
COSPE *IT* 169
COTRAMI *F* 136
COV *NL* 145
CP *F* 3
CPDHC *E* 30
CPMT *LX* 145
CPR *PR* 211
CRARDDA *F* 136
CRATE *IT* 143, *UK* 76
CRC *NI* 185
CRD *NI* 247
CRDI *F* 234
CRE *UK* 222
CRE-SAE *E* 151
CREC *UK* 177-8
CREDOC *F* 234
CRER *UK* 244
CRESAB; CRESM *F* 234
CRF; CRI *F* 197
CRICF *F* 31
CRIDA *F* 163
CRIDI *F* 234
CRIF *F* 79, 234
CRIJ *BE* 189
CRISS *RO* 242
CRS *CH* 217, 219
CSA *DK* 26
CSAJ *CH* 218
CSC *BE* 132, *UK* 31, *NI* 247
CSCIN *BE* 130
CSDA *F* 136
CSDDA *CH* 152
CSDHA *AT* 188
CSDI *IT* 205
CSER *IT* 239, *UK* 76
CSIC *UK* 57
CSIL *IT* 143
CSP *CH* 217
CSPO *UK* 244
CSSTM *F* 196
CSTM *IT* 239
CSV *UK* 222
CTA *F* 9, *UK* 27
CTM *BE* 88, *IT* 168-9, 239
CTP; CTPL *BE* 97
CTSC *NI* 118
CUAMM *IT* 239
CUCO *D* 166
CUFA *GR* 35
CUM *IT* 239
CUWG *UK* 154
CVJM *D* 200
CWIAC *UK* 154
CWRG *UK* 29

DAAD *D* 200, *UK* 37
DAB *D* 166
DBMO *UK* 18
DACAAR *DK* 1
DAMID *D* 236
DAPP *NR* 210
DAWN *UK* 14
DBJR *D* 200
DCA; DCHR *DK* 194
DCI *NL* 208, *CH* 217
DCI-USO *E* 151
DCTP *IR* 117
DDM *E* 151
DEA *UK* 178

DEE *UK* 226
DEFIS *BE* 189
DFG-KV *D* 200
DFHB *D* 138
DFJW *D* 36
DGB *D* 139, 200
DHKD *BE* 119
DHS *F* 197
DIAL *F* 83
DIB *BE* 192
DICCC *UK* 58
DIDF *D* 120, *NL* 121
DIK-AOF *DK* 161
DIML *D* 83
DIPF; DISS *D* 236
DITIB *D* 121
DLK *DK* 83
DNF *NR* 148
DOF *DK* 194
DOK-WI-CH *CH* 243
DONA *UK* 32
DÖW *AT* 231
DPM *F* 197
DPWV *D* 201
DR *F* 234
DRC *DK* 132, 161
DRICSS *PR* 211
DRK *D* 200
DSDF *NL* 121
DTEDG *IR* 117
DTU *DK* 119
DUF *DK* 194
DVV; DWH *D* 166
DWICA *UK* 125
DYBF *D* 120

EACH *UK* 154
EAF *IT* 3
EAFORD *CH* 175
EAPN *BE* 190, *IR* 204
EASU *E* 4
EAWM *AT* 187
EBCO; ECA; ECAS *BE* 190
ECB *F* 164
ECF *NL* 209
ECG *GR* 33, *UK* 222
ECOSY *BE* 190
ECRE *UK* 244
ECRJ *UK* 179
ECS *NL* 209, *UK* 18
ECUK *UK* 34
ECUME *F* 163
ECWGAR *CH* 152
ECWS *NL* 146, 171, 240, *E* 242
ECYC *DK* 194
EDCOMER *NL* 240
EDGE *UK* 154
EDON *CY* 193
EEDDA *GR* 203
EEE-YFU *BE* 190
EEMEA *UK* 154
EFAM *F* 136
EFC *BE* 190
EFEMI *E* 242
EFIL *BE* 160
EFYSO *F* 197
EHRF *BE* 190
EICM *F* 163
EIE *BE* 160
EIP *CH* 175
EK *GR* 82
EKD *D* 201
EKKE *GR* 238
ELAINE *NL* 171
ELENA *AT* 129, *BE* 131, *F* 137, *D* 200, *GR* 140, *IR* 141, *IT* 143, 238, *LX* 145, *NL NR* 147, *PR* 211, *SV* 212, *E* 150, *S* 152, *UK* 154
ELSSOC *UK* 104
EMAF *F* 86

EMASI *IT* 144
EMDA *UK* 176
EMG *CH* 217
EMIM *IT* 239
EMRC *UK* 154
ENAIP *D* 74, *IT* 144, *UK* 77
ENK *EE* 195
EOC *UK* 222
EPER *CH* 217
EPI *D* 74
EPLF *IT* 34
ERA *DK UK* 34
ERAG *IR* 141
ERASMUS *BE* 190, 192, *DK* 195, *D* 200
ERC *UK* 154, 244
ERCOMER *NL* 240
EREC *UK* 178
ERM *F* 136
ERYICA *F* 197
ESD *BE* 131
ESF *BE* 190
ESG *D* 201
ESHA *UK* 21
ESIB *AT* 187
ESMV *NL* 240
ESN *NI* 247
ESONE *GR* 203
ESOP *BE* 131
ESPAS *F* 164
ESRC *UK* 244
ESRI *IR* 238
ETANE *E* 4
ETM *BE* 189
ETNICS *F* 163
ETUC *BE* 190
ETUI *BE* 232
EUJS *BE* 78
EuPRA *D* 201
EURES *BE* 190, 192, *DK* 194, *F* 195, *IR* 204
EuroStep *UK* 223
EUYEB *BE* 190
EYE *D* 166
EYF *F* 197
EYHN *UK* 223

F3CI *F* 164
FABER *D* 237
FACEEF *D* 112
FACIAM *E* 151
FADEL *LX* 113
FADM *BE* 88
FAEEH *NL* 113
FAEEL; FAEL *LX* 113
FAEPL *F* 98
FAF *F* 9
FAFK *NL* 171
FAIACA *F* 53
FAIE *UK* 77
FAIEG *D* 74
FAIN *E* 151
FAIR *UK* 155
FAJA *D* 112
FAPEB *BE* 110
FAPV *F* 98
FARM *UK* 5
FARR *S* 152
FAS *F* 198, *IR* 204
FASFA *UK* 77
FASTI *F* 136
FAT *DK* 119
FATCMF *F* 89
FATIMA *S* 175
FATTB *BE* 119
FBHO *UK* 21
FCCB *IT* 35
FCE *LX* 239
FCEI-SRM *IT* 144
FCF *GR* 35
FCO *UK* 223
FCPH *NL* 101
FCSF *F* 197
FEDER-COLF *IT* 206

FEDORA E 151
FEE F 137
FETAF F 3
FETRANI F 3
FFCU F 164
FGTB BE 132
FHA UK 7
FI BE 160
FIA-ISM F 137
FIAC UK 223
FIAN BE 190
FIDH F 197, IT 205
FIJD D 166
FILEF BE 73, D 74, IT 144, LX NL 76, UK 77
FILOR F 198
FIMCAP CH 217
FIOP E 174
FIR AT 159, DK 161, H 168
FIS BE 8, D 9, UK 9, 48
FISC BE 86
FISOG CS 40
FITDH CH 217
FIVOL IT 206
FIZ CH 153
FLAC IR 204
FMCV F 198
FMF DK 194
FMS GR 238
FNARS F 137
FNF DK 194
FNMF F 53, 89
FNRS BE 232
FNSP F 234
FNST D 202
FNV NL 146, 209
FO-INTER E 149
FOCSI IT 144
FOCSIV IT 205
FOK NL 171
FONDA F 198
FORUM NL 114, 146
FOSIS UK 58
FPLE IT 34
FPWP UK 223
FRATE F 137
FRU UK 223
FSJU F 79
FTDA F 137
FUNDESCOOP E 84

GAA LX 46, UK 48
GAFFI BE 131
GAIP UK 223
GAO IT 169, NL 209
GAP UK 179
GbV D 166
GCARA UK 179
GCS BE 160
GDF D 121
GDM F 164
GEMITO IT 143
GERMAE F 235
GfbV AT 159
GFD DK 38
GFSV D 104
GISTI F 137
GLARE; GLOSREC UK 179
GMBA UK 18
GMIAU UK 155
GMS CH 153
GPARAFN UK 179
GRA CH 175
GRAI RO 174
GRAMC E 242
GRAMI; GRDR; GREC; GRECO F 235
GreenNet UK 223
GREM BE 232
GREPO F 235
GRISEA F 110

GSAL PR 84
GUEW IT 34
GUDI PR 148
GuiDanAss DK 39
GVC IT 169

HAC UK 223
HACA UK 6
HACMHP UK 7
HBCLC UK 223
hCa NL 23
HDB D 121
HDF D 120
HEGOA E 242
HEKS CH 217
HELINAS GR 203
HFRAF H 168
HIAS GR IT CH 79
HICCC UK 48
HIFD NL 171
HINARME F 235
HJ BE 191
HLRC UK 223
HOM NL 209
HOST CS 161, UK 155
HRDC F 235
HREC UK 179
HTB D 120
HTIB; HTKB; HTOB NL 122
HU D 201
HUR-TURK D 120
HURIDOCS CH 243

IAAM IR 109
IABS NL 208
IAC PL 173
IADL BE 189
IAECP PR 211
IAESTE NL 209
IAF D 139-140
IAIE NL 240
IAL S 152
IAS UK 155
IASR NL 240
IAT UK 155
IBB; IBG D 167
IBRG UK 49
IBSJ D 237
IBZ D 167
ICA BE 191, DK 43, UK 27, 29, 46
ICAS IT 142, UK 45
ICCC AT 231
ICCJ D 201
ICCL IR 204
ICCO NL 209
ICDA BE 191
ICEL IT 169
ICEM E 242
ICFTU BE 191
ICH UK 49
ICI NL 240
ICIS UK 60
ICJ NL 209, CH 217
ICJP IR 204
ICM AT 188, BE 192, GR 203
ICMA E 11
ICMC GR 203, CH 217, TR 219
ICOS IR 141
ICPO IR 141, UK 49
ICRC CH 218
ICREC UK 180
ICSW AT 188
ICU DK 194
ICVA CH 217
ICVD NL 209
ICYE BE 191, D 166
ID-Archiv NL 240
IDA D 166
IDERIC F 235
IDOC IT 239

IDS UK 245
IECE IR 141
IEDI PR 242
IEE E 151
IEPALA E 242
IESC IR 104
IFCOD F 198
IFD DK 133, F 164
IFL SF 162
IFLRY; IFM-SEI BE 191
IFOR AT 188, NL 171
IFP F 99
IFRCS CH 218
IFS D 237, IT 144
IGARA AT 159
IGFM D 201
IHE UK 224
IHEU NL 209
IIA IT 4
IID F 198
IIDH F 235
IIH D 167
IIHL IT 239
IIMI NL 240
IISA UK 155
IJA UK 80
IJAR NL 79
IKA D 237
IKM D 167
IKSF DK 133
IKU S 175
IKV NL 209
ILA D 83, UK 224
ILAS UK 84
ILO F 196, CH 218
ILPA UK 155
IMA F 10
IMDAR CH 175
IMES NL 240
IMMA UK 60
IMWS UK 44
IMXA GR 238
INAS-CISL IT 144, UK 77
INC UK 46
INCA F 74, IT 206, LX 76, UK 77
INCORE NI 247
IND-sam DK 132
INDOC NL 45
INE E 242
INED F 235
INEM E 215
INFODOC UK 244
INLIA NL 146
INSERSO E 213, 215
INTAF UK 44
IOM AT 188, BE 192, F 199, D 201, GR 203, IT 206, NL 209, PR 212, E 215, CH 218, UK 224
IOT NL 121
IPA UK 44
IPALMO IT 239
IPB CH 218
IPCI UK 61
IPF D 139
IPO AT 188
IPPR UK 245
IPSA IR 238
IPTR F 137
IQRA UK 60
IRC F 198, IT 206, E 214
IRCT DK 133
IREM IT 239
IREMAM F 235
IRES IT 205
IRESCO F 234-5
IRFED F 235
IRP IT 239
IRR UK 245
IRWC F 164

IS DK 133, D 201
ISA IT 239
ISAA IR 109
ISCA CH 218
ISD D 19
ISEO NL 240
ISHR D 201, UK 224
ISKCON IR 41, UK 42, NI 43
ISM F 137
ISMM F 164
ISMU IT 239
ISM-U F 137
ISMUN CH 218
ISOP AT 129
ISS D 201, GR 203, IT 206, NL 209, 240, E 216, CH 218-9, UK 224
ISRA IR 54
ISYF UK 107
ITAL IT 206, LX 76, UK 77
ITCH UK 245
ITE IR 204
ITM IR 117
ITS NL 240
ITT UK 245
IUS CS 193
IUSSP BE 232
IUSY; IVB AT 188
IVCS UK 44
IVS NI 229
IVVdN D 167
IVZO NL 45
IWA; IWA-GB; IWA-S UK 44
IWASG UK 50
IWCC UK 224
IWGIA DK 161
IWM NL 88
IWPR UK 245
IYCS-IMCS BE 191
iz3w D 237

JADE F 198
JALB F 10
JCA; JCCR UK 80
JCEF F 31
JCI E 174
JCWI UK 155
JD NL 209
JD-JL D 201
JEF BE 193, D 167, NL 209
JICC UK 78
JINT vzw BE 191
JJBED F 19
JOC BE 191, F D 112
JRA CI 158
JRCT UK 246
JRE D 167
JRS IT 144
JTR NL 171
JTR-SZR BE 160
JTRE NL 171
Juso CH 218

KAAD D 202
KAB D 237
KAFKA NL 240
KAIROS BE 191
KAMPI IT 35
Kasapi GR 35
KAWTAL F 2
KCC UK 83
KDK UK 171
KEGME GR 238
KESG IR 141
KHRP UK 83
KINNAT UK 155
KIS BE 160
KIYAG UK 50
KKDK D 82
KKKH NL 83

KMA LX 207
KMAN; KMAR NL 90
KMWA UK 63
KNZM M 208
KolOCh BE 28
KOMKAR DK F D 82
KOO AT 188
KREC UK 180
KRV BE 192
KSPM GR 140
KSSE IT 82
KUD D 126
KURF NL 171
KVAN NL 90
KVAVN NL 26
KVT SF 195
KWA UK 83
KZA NL 110
KZVR NL 146

LAA UK 85
LAARF UK 181
LAB UK 85
LABORES F 235
LADOSEI IT 34
LAF D 139
LAG UK 225
LAMP NL 145
LAO NL 146
LAP UK 180
LAPMO F 235
LARRIE UK 245
LAWA UK 85
LBDH BE 191
LBHF UK 22
LBR NL 171
LBWHAP UK 22
LCCA; LCHRC UK 30
LCOS UK 155
LD PR 173
LDH BE 191, F 198
LDMG UK 225
LFCW UK 30
LFEEP F 235
LFSV NL 114
LIA NL 10
LIAEP; LIAFRICA PR 4
LIANGOLA PR 9
LICRA F 164, CH 175
LIDLIP IT 169, CH 175
LIFE IT 35
LiJOT LH 207
LINGUA DK 195, D 139, IR 204, UK 221
LIP UK 155
LISWO NL 240
LIYF UK 51
LIZE NL 34
LJP LT 207
LKG NL 171
LMIGE F 112
LNU NR 210
LOSV NL 114
Lot-AL F 83
LPE F 235
LPWZ NL 40
LRC UK 245
LREC UK 180-1
LSBV; LSOBA NL 146
LSU S 216
LV NL 172
LVAAV NL 10
LVSC UK 6, 225

MAARTG UK 181
MAC UK 91
MACHEM UK 155
MACWC UK 67
MAGIC UK 181
MAIE UK 77
MAINE NL 146
Maisha IT 4
MAP UK 95
MAV D 89
MBC UK 11

MBS UK 113
MCCA UK 226
MCCR UK 181
MCI DK 74
MCL UK 76
MCP BE 192, LX 100, PR 212
MCRE UK 181
MCV BE 89
M&D F 164
MD Asyl D 139
MDEM F 164
MDM F 198
MDM-CASSIM E 151
MEED UK 88
MER F 164
MERGER NL 240
MERLIN; MFCVT UK 225
MFHR GR 203
MHT E 215
MIACA UK 90
MIAU UK 156
MIG S 152
MIGRINTER F 234
MIKST BE 131
MISSERM F 137
MISZOT H 203
MISZSZ RO 43
MLKO H 168
MNM IT 4
MODEFEN F 137
MOM BE 232
Mon-3 E 174
MOST SV 212
MPDL E 215
MQM UK 93
MRAP F 164
MRASH F 137
MRAX BE 160
MRDA E 114
MREC UK 181
MRG UK 225
MRM NL 241
MS DK 194
MSF BE 191, F 198, LX NL 208, E 215, CH 218, UK 225
MSOI IT 206
MTC UK 156
MUTD NL 172
MVCA UK 124
MVVN NL 90
MWAN UK 181
MWAOK NL 90

NACAAP UK 22
NACAB UK 226
NACOSA UK 156
NADA SF 195
NADEC UK 181
NAFIF F 77
NAFSIYAT UK 156
NAGA IT 144
NAGG D 38
NAME UK 181
NAMY UK 69
NARIC IT 205
NAWP UK 15
NBI UK 22
NBK NL 172
NCB NL 146
NCBV UK 22
NCCL UK 225
NCPT UK 101
NCRE; NCRP UK 182
NCTP IR 117
NCVO UK 226
NDREC UK 182
NEBHDP UK 22
NEMS NL 146
NERS UK 156
NFER UK 246
NFSHO UK 156
NHF UK 92

NICEE *NI* 185
NICEM *NI* 158
NICRC *NI* 185
NICVA *NI* 229
NIDI *NL* 241
NIFA *IR* 92
NILSA *IT* 92
NIVON *NL* 210
NIVT *NI* 229
NIZW *NL* 241
NJCM *NL* 210
NKLC *UK* 226
NMI *NL* 210
NMP *UK* 182
NMR *NL* 54
NN *NL* 241
NNU *UK* 92
NOAS *NR* 147
NRC *UK* 226
NREC *UK* 182
NSC *UK* 92
NUEW *IT* 34
NURO *UK* 156
NUS *UK* 226
NVJ *NL* 173
NYIAN *IT* 144

Obaala *UK* 22
OBAC *UK* 6
OBESSU *NL* 210
ÖBJR *AT* 188
OBS *D* 236
OCCAC *UK* 30
OCDE *F* 199
OCGB; OCIV *BE* 131
OCMT *CH* 218
OCPM *PR* 148
ODICE *F* 199
ODU *UK* 22
OECD *F* 199
OEK *D* 38
OFPRA *F* 199
OFTAS *F* 118
OHFOM *F* 198
ÖIE *AT* 188
OIKOS *PR* 173
OIM *BE* 192, *F* 199, *PR* 212, *E* 215, *CH* 218
OIR *E* 214
ÖJAB *AT* 188
OJEC *NL* 172
OLP *PR* 95
OMCV *IT* 26
OMHA *UK* 69
OMI *F* 199
OMINOR *F* 235
OMOD *NR* 173
OMRI *NL* 45
ONPPC *PR* 40
ONX *IT* 169
OPALS *F* 3
OREC *UK* 182
ORFAN *UK* 102
ORL *D* 202
ORSTOM *F* 236
OSAG *IT* 4
OSAR *CH* 153
OSCAR *UK* 22
OSF-SF *BH BG CT* 193, *EE* 195, *LH* 207
OTEPGE *E* 33
OTMCDF *F* 87
OTOA *F* 116
OWWA *E* 35

PAEX *E* 152
PAF *DK* 95
PARE *NL* 172
PAREL *NL* 241
PAS-DVV *D* 237
PATCH *IR* 141

PBI *UK* 226
PBME *NL* 172
PCWA *UK* 94
PCYF *BE* 192
PDS *D* 167, *UK* 77
PETRA *BE* 191-3, *D* 139-140, 202, *IR* 204, *LX* 207
PFE *S* 175
PHARE *BE* 192
PIAA *UK* 51
PICHR *BE* 35
PIME *IT* 205
PIN *NL* 147
PIOOM *NL* 241
PIV *NL* 146
PJCI *E* 174
PLO *PR UK* 95
PMU *S* 216
PNP *UK* 78
POA *NL* 10
POMAK *CY* 132
POSK *IR* 96
PPF *D* 202
PPP *UK* 40, 94
PRG *UK* 102
PRM *PL* 211
PROCOMAR *E* 152
ProDoCS *IT* 169
PROTEO *IT* 239
PSC *UK* 95
PSF *F* 199
PSI *UK* 246
PSO *F* 164
PSTI *F* 137
PSZ *D* 139
PUK *DK* 82
PWA *UK* 94
PYC *E* 174
PYF *UK* 94

QMC *UK* 246
QPS *UK* 227
QUNO *CH* 218

RAA *D* 202
RAAF *PL* 173
RADAR *NL* 172
RAI *E* 242
RAMP *UK* 182
RAP *UK* 157
RAPP *UK* 246
RARCAMERS *E* 25
RCJ *F* 79
RCT *DK* 133
RCU *D* 103
RDLDF *UK* 182
REALE *F* 9
REAP *UK* 183
REC *UK* 182
RELPE *PR* 148
REMISIS *F* 236
REMS *F* 86
Reperes *F* 137
RE.PER.ES *F* 163
REPONSE *F* 236
REST *D S UK* 116
RETAS *UK* 229
REU *UK* 181
RIC *NL* 210
RIC-CERDIC *F* 236
RIFEN *F* 19
RIFFI *S* 152
RIIA *UK* 246
RITMO *F* 236
RLC *UK* 157
RMCMS *CS* 193
RNC *D* 103
ROAPE *UK* 6
ROOF *RS* 79
RREAS *UK* 227
RSC *UK* 157

RSF *F* 236
RTEC *UK* 157
RTF *F* 118
RTMF *F* 87
RUBV *UK* 22
RUC *DK* 233
RVA *UK* 183
RWA *UK* 157
RWI *S* 243

SAC *UK* 227
SACDA *UK* 6
SACHR *NI* 229
SACMHA *UK* 6
SACU *UK* 30
SADAA *UK* 22
SADACCA *UK* 6
SAF *F* 199
Safia *F* 165
SAH *CH* 153
SAI *E* 152
SAJV *CH* 218
SAK *S* 1
SAO *UK* 6
SAPA *UK* 32
SAR *UK* 1
SASK *SF* 162
SAT *F* 165
SAUS *UK* 246
SAWO *NL* 114
SBK *NL* 172
SCAL *PR* 26
SCCL; SCDC; SCF *UK* 227
SCI *AT* 188, *BE* 192, *F* 199, *D* 202, *IT* 206, *CH* 219
SCIAF *UK* 227
SCIFDE *UK* 184
SCIRI *UK* 46
SCOGIL *IT* 38
SCOMBO *UK* 18
SCORE *IT* 169, *UK* 184
SCP *NL* 210
SCRC *UK* 184
SD *E* 216
SDNL *SF* 195
SEA *UK* 227
SEAD *UK* 183
SEC *NL* 171
SED *E* 216
SEE *BE* 132
SEF *D* 202
SEMRU *UK* 246
SER *NL* 210
SER.GI *E* 242
SESOPI *LX* 207
Seucode *BE* 27
SF *LT* 207
SFF *S* 35
SFH *CH* 153
SFI *DK* 233
SGB *UK* 42
SGREC *UK* 182
SGI/UvA *NL* 240
SHAP *UK* 246
SHARP *NI* 185
SHRO *UK* 114
SI *DK* 133, *E* 215, *UK* 227
SIAL *IT* 84
SICC *BE* 192
SID *DK* 195, *IT* 239
SIETAR *F* 236, *NL* 241
SIH *NL* 210
SIM *NL* 241
SIO *NL* 114
SIOS *S* 152
SIPAR *F* 110
SITI *F* 137
SIU *S* 216

SJ-MCP *F* 199
SJÖ *AT* 188
SJV *BE* 192
SKF *DK* 161
SKIP *CH* 219
SKM *S* 216
SLAS *UK* 85
SLFWS *NL* 114
SLORI *IT* 108
SM *F* 199
SMG *UK* 183
SMO *UK* 69
SMR *NL* 90
SMT *NL* 87
SNAP *UK* 183
SNPM *F* 137-8
SOAS *UK* 246
SODEPAZ *E* 216
SOEM *IT* 145
SOFA *F* 9
SOH *NL* 210
Solida'Mis *F* 138
SONACOTRA *F* 199
SOS *F* 152
SOS Racism *and similar names: see main index*
SOS REPERES; SOSRE *F* 199
SOUNDIATA *F* 3
SoZaWe *NL* 209
SPA *NL* 172
SPAN *UK* 227
SPPAR *NL* 172
SPR/FRK *SF* 195
SRC *S* 152, *UK* 157
SREC *UK* 183-4
SRK *UK* 217, 219
SRP *UK* 158
SRRA *UK* 114
SSAE *F* 138
SSE *BE* 131
SSI *IT* 206, *E* 216, *CH* 219
SSU *S* 216
STAD *DK* 119
STARD *NL* 172
STASON *NL* 147
STEI *E* 216
STGR *RO* 212
STIBA *NL* 172
STOA *NL* 147
SU *NL* 172
SV; SVO *NL* 147
SWF *GR* 140
SYBIDI *BE* 232
SYL *SF* 195
SZMP *PL* 211

TACIS *BE* 192
TADCO *UK* 18
TAPOL *UK* 45
TASV *D* 121
TdH *NL* 210
TDV *DK* 115
TEJO *NL* 173
TEMPUS *BE* 192, *DK* 195
TFC *UK* 52
TFSR *UK* 184
TGB *D* 120-1
THREC *UK* 184
TIKF *BE* 119
TLAST *UK* 117
TOM *UK* 52
TPLF *UK* 116
TREC *UK* 184
TREF Charlois *NL* 172
TRO *UK* 115
TU-DER *DK* 119
TÜBIKS *D* 121
TUC *UK* 228

TUDID *DK* 119
TUFP *UK* 95
TUIREG; TWAFA *UK* 184

UAAF *UK* 122
UAF *NL* 147
UAIR *F* 138
UAMF *F* 89
UCA *UK* 27
UCAM *F* 3
UCAR *UK* 184
UCCLA *PR* 173
UCEI; UCEMI *IT* 144
UCFAF *F* 11
UCJFP *F* 79
UCJG *F* 79
UCOII *IT* 54
UCSEI *IT* 145
UDEP *D* 75
UDI *LX* 76
UEJF *F* 79
UGLE *IT* 34
UGSC *IT* 31
UGT *LX NL* 113, *E* 149-152, 216
UGTSF *F* 105
UGVF *F* 124
UICL *UK* 45
UIDE *E* 32
UIL *IT* 145, 207
UINA *IT* 92
UIOF *F* 199
UJI *IT* 77
UJIDU *IT* 77
UJS *UK* 81
UKCOSA *UK* 158
UKJAID *UK* 81
ULEV *IT* 145
ULPS *UK* 81
UMCII *F* 138
UMMON *NL* 90
UMO *UK* 71
UN-NGLS *CH* 219
UNA-UK *UK* 228
UNAF *F* 199
UNAFO *F* 138
UNAIE *D* 75, *IT* 145, *LX* 76, *UK* 77
UNASSE *F* 3
UNEL *LX* 208
UNESCO *F* 199
UNHCR *AL* 187, *AT* 188, *BE* 191, *BG CT CY CS* 193, *F* 198, *D* 201, *GR H* 203, *IT* 204, *LX* 207, *NL* 209, *PL PR* 211, *RO RS SR SK SV E* 212, *S* 217, *CH TR* 219, *UK* 228
UNICEF *CH* 219, *UK* 228
UNITED *NL* 173
UNITI *IT* 145
UNOY *NL* 173
UNPO *NL* 147
UNRWA *AT* 188
UNVFVT *CH* 219
UOHI *IT* 145
UPE *LX* 76
UPJB *BE* 78
USDAW *UK* 184
USMI *IT* 54
USO *E* 151
UTAF *F* 3
UTANO *F* 3
UTIS *F* 138
UTIT *F* 118
UTMF *F* 87
UTO *F* 198
UTSF/AR *F* 105

UWAIS *UK* 72

VAVBD *D* 11
VCIM *BE* 132
VDAB *BE* 192
VHP *DK* 41, *UK* 43
VIA *D* 140, *NL* 210
VIFB *D* 45
VIKZ *D* 53
VIVN *NL* 45
VMS *D* 167
VOCOM *BE* 132
VOMADO *E* 32
VON *NL* 146
VPIJ *BE* 192
VSBT-NRW *D* 121
VSF *F* 199
VSI *IR* 204
VSJF *CH* 79
VSO *UK* 228
VVA *BE* 161
VVN *NL* 147
VVN-BdA *D* 167
VVO *BE* 132
VWR *NL* 147

WACDA *UK* 7
WAFC *UK* 30
WATE *IT* 116
WAY *DK* 195
WBO *UK* 24
WCC *GR* 140, *IT* 207, *CH* 219
WCF *UK* 185
WDK *D* 82
WDM *UK* 229
WFBN *NL* 210
WFD *D* 202
WFDY *H* 203
WFYPHP *UK* 23
WGARCR *UK* 185
WHIA *UK* 44
WIDE *IR* 204
WILPF *CH* 175, *UK* 229
WIR e.V. *D* 167
WISC *UK* 125
WIZA *BE* 83
WJC *F CH* 79
WLAHA *UK* 15
WMADC *UK* 158
WoW *UK* 228
WPC *SF* 195
WRAG *NI* 185
WREC *UK* 185
WRI *UK* 228
WS *BE* 193
WTFR *NL* 173
WUS *D* 202, *IR* 141, *CH* 219, *UK* 229
WVI; WYWCA *CH* 219
WZO *UK* 81

XminY *NL* 147

YDC *NL* 210
YEK-KOM *D* 82
YEU *D* 167
YEWB *NL* 173
YF *BE* 193
YRE *UK* 185
YWCA *IT* 145, 207

ZACA; ZAIRAG *UK* 127
ZAVD *D* 16
ZDWF *D* 238
ZFT *D* 121
ZHIN *M* 208
ZIS *D* 238
ZOA *NL* 147

AMENDMENTS AND NEW ENTRIES

Joint Council for the Welfare of Immigrants
115 Old Street, London EC1V 9JR, United Kingdom
fax [+44] (0171) 251 5110
e-mail jcwi@mcr1.poptel.org.uk, or ciaran@mcr1.poptel.org.uk

Please complete and return this form to ensure that your organisation is listed correctly in the next edition of the Directory, and on the disk-based and on-line electronic versions. Forms may be photocopied and posted or faxed, or the details sent in a letter, postcard or e-mail message (do not telephone). Please type or write clearly and keep the descriptions short; you need not answer all the questions, and should not give any information which you do not want to be published. We may edit the descriptions but will base listings on the information provided. We prefer to have the information from an officer of the body concerned, but please let us know about any organisation which you think should be included. Please mark envelopes or postcards "European Directory", or give "European Directory" as the subject or first line in your fax or e-mail message.

NAME OF
ORGANISATION _____ ACRONYM (or abbreviation) _____

CONTACT
PERSON _____ TITLE (e.g. Secretary, Chair, President) _____

POSTAL ADDRESS _____

_____ POSTAL CODE _____ COUNTRY _____

Office address (if different from postal address) _____

TELEPHONE (area code _____) _____ FAX _____

E-MAIL ADDRESS (Internet format, e.g. jcwi@poptel.org.uk) _____

BRIEF DESCRIPTION (structure, history, activities, publications; continue overleaf if necessary):

For example, is this an international, national, regional or local body? An agency of national or local government, a voluntary-sector body, a community organisation, an educational, research or academic centre, a private-sector or media body? Does it represent or serve people of just one ethnic group, or one category, such as refugees? Is it a federation or umbrella group—if so, how many affiliated organisations? Does it have individual members—how many? Is it a local branch or section of a larger organisation (give details) or does it have has local branches or sections— how many? Do the activities include advice, welfare work, information, publishing, lobbying, legal services, community representation, cultural or religious or educational activities, research, library/archive/documentation, campaigns, events or exhibitions?

Information provided by _____
Status (e.g. Secretary) _____
Telephone number (if different from that above) _____
Date _____